FIFTH EDITION Out of Many

VOLUME TWO

Out of Many

FIFTH EDITION

A HISTORY OF THE AMERICAN PEOPLE

John Mack Faragher
YALE UNIVERSITY

Mari Jo Buhle
BROWN UNIVERSITY

Daniel Czitrom
MOUNT HOLYOKE COLLEGE

Susan H. Armitage
WASHINGTON STATE UNIVERSITY

PEARSON

Prentice
Hall

Upper Saddle River, NJ 07458

Library of Congress Cataloging-in-Publication Data
Out of many: a history of the American people / John Mack Faragher . . . [et al].—5th ed.
   p.   cm.
Includes bibliographical references and index.
ISBN 0-13-194461-4 (v.1) — ISBN 0-13-194466-5 (v.2)
   1. United States–History.   I. Faragher, John Mack, 1945–
E178.1.O935 2005d
973–dc22   2005047575

TO OUR STUDENTS,
OUR SISTERS,
AND OUR BROTHERS

VP, Editorial Director: Charlyce Jones Owen
Editorial Assistant: Maureen Diana
Editor-in-Chief, Development: Rochelle Diogenes
Senior Development Editor: Roberta Meyer
Associate Editor: Emsal Hasan
Senior Media Editor: Deborah O'Connell
VP, Director of Production and Manufacturing: Barbara Kittle
Managing Editor: Joanne Riker
Production Liaison: Randy Pettit
Prepress and Manufacturing Manager: Nick Sklitsis
Prepress and Manufacturing Buyer: Benjamin Smith
Director of Marketing: Heather Shelstad
Marketing Assistant: Jennifer Lang
Creative Design Director: Leslie Osher

Cover and Interior Design: Kathryn Foot
Director, Image Resource Center: Melinda Reo
Manager, Visual Research: Beth Brenzel
Manager, Rights and Permissions: Zina Arabia
Manager, Cover Visual Research and Permissions: Karen Sanatar
Image Permission Coordinator: Carolyn Gaunt
Pearson Imaging Center: Joe Conti, Cory Skidds, Greg Harrison, Rob Uibelhoer, Ron Walko
Photo Researcher: Teri Stratford
Project Management/Composition: Lorenza Compagnone, Preparé, Inc.
Printer/Binder: Courier Companies, Inc.
Cover Printer: Phoenix Color Corporation
Cover Art: A recently arrived family of European immigrants at Ellis Island, c. 1900. The Granger Collection.

Credits and acknowledgments borrowed from other sources and reproduced, with permission, in this textbook appear on appropiate page within text or on page C-1.

Pearson Education Ltd., London
Pearson Education Australia Pty, Limited, Sydney
Pearson Education Singapore, Pte., Ltd.
Pearson Education North Asia Ltd., Hong Kong

Pearson Education, Canada, Ltd, Toronto
Pearson Educación de Mexico, S.A. de C.V.
Pearson Education–Japan, Tokyo
Pearson Education Malaysia, Pte., Ltd.

10 9 8 7 6 5 4 3 2 1
ISBN 0-13-194466-5

BRIEF CONTENTS

CONTENTS

4

SLAVERY AND EMPIRE,
1441–1770   80

5 THE CULTURES OF COLONIAL NORTH AMERICA, *1700–1780*   II4

6 FROM EMPIRE TO INDEPENDENCE, *1750–1776*   I44

7

THE AMERICAN REVOLUTION,
1776–1786   176

8

THE NEW NATION,
1786–1800   206

INDUSTRY AND THE NORTH,
1790s–1840s 326

13

COMING TO TERMS WITH THE NEW AGE, *1820s–1850s*
356

18 CONQUEST AND SURVIVAL:
The Trans–Mississipi West, 1860–1900   514

19 THE INCORPORATION OF AMERICA, 1865–1900 548

22

WORLD WAR I,
1914–1920   640

24 THE GREAT DEPRESSION AND THE NEW DEAL, 1929–1940   708

25

WORLD WAR II,
1941–1945   742

28 THE CIVIL RIGHTS MOVEMENT, *1945–1966* 844

30

THE CONSERVATIVE ASCENDANCY, *1974–1991*　　　　　　　　920

31 TOWARD A TRANSNATIONAL AMERICA, *since 1988*   956

CHAPTER OPENING ILLUSTRATIONS

Chapter 1: Painting of Cahokia Mounds, Collinsville, Illinois by Michael Hampshire.
Cahokia Mounds State Historic Site—painting by Michael Hampshire.

Chapter 2: Christopher Columbus surveys the New World from the deck of his ship. Sailors stand or kneel around Columbus. Engraving by W. Wellstood from a painting by G. Harvey.
Library of Congress.

Chapter 3: Dutch governor Peter Stuyvesant oversees the arrival of mail from a galleon before anxious colonists and surly sea dogs in New Amsterdam, circa 1647.
Public Buildings Administration, Section of Fine Arts.

Chapter 4: The slave deck of the bark "Wildfire." Here, slaves were brought into Key West on April 30, 1800 in this print from a nineteenth-century newspaper.
Courtesy of the Library of Congress.

Chapter 5: This painting portrays George Whitefield as he preaches an outdoor sermon to a crowd of eagerly penitent worshippers.
Mark Sexton. The Granger Collection.

Chapter 6: Patrick Henry delivers an impassioned speech to the enthusiastic approbation of the Virginia House of Burgesses.
Courtesy of the Library of Congress.

Chapter 7: Christina Henrietta Caroline Ackland (1750–1815) travels down the Hudson to American General Gates' camp for a pass to cross the lines to nurse her husband, British Major Ackland, wounded in the second Battle of Saratoga, 7th October 1777. From the original by Alonzo Chappel.
Getty Images Inc. Hulton Archive Photos.

Chapter 8: Congress Voting Independence, by Savage/Pine.
Courtesy of The Historical Society of Pennsylvania Collection, Atwater Kent Museum of Philadeplphia.

Chapter 9: American General Andrew Jackson interviews Creek warrior William Weatherford (Red Eagle) in a tent in this undated engraving.
Getty Images Inc. Hulton Archive Photos.

Chapter 10: African-American slaves/farm workers carry sacks of cotton on their heads while leaving a South Carolina plantation field. Stereograph, ca. 1860 by G.N. Barnard, *Returning from the Cotton Fields in South Carolina*.
Returning from the Cotton Fields in South Carolina, ca. 1860, stereograph by Barbard, negative number 47843. © Collection of The New York Historical Society.

Chapter 11: The Attempted Assassination of the President of the United States, Jan. 30, 1835. As the funeral procession of the Hon. Warren R. Davis was moving from the Capitol of the United States, Richard Lawrence, a supposed maniac, rushed from the crowd and snapped two heavily loaded pistols immediately at the body of President Jackson, both of which providentially missed fire. Lawrence was instantly arrested by persons present, examined by Judge Cranch, and committed for trial. Drawn from a sketch by an eyewitness.
Library of Congress.

Chapter 12: Dutton St. boarding houses in Lowell, Massachusetts were constructed in a community setting around textile mills. The building with the cupola is a mill. The two buildings that look like individual residences were housing for the young women who worked in the mills and were built pre-1845. Buildings with dormers also were worker housing built in 1845.
Dutton St. Boarding Houses, Lowell, MA., 1845. Museum of American Textiles History.

Chapter 13: Female students at work while sitting on benches along wooden tables in an 1840 pencil and watercolor illustration titled *Girls Evening School* by an unidentified artist.
Unidentified artist (American, about 1840), *Girl's Evening School*, about 1840, U.S. Graphite pencil and watercolor on paper, Sheet: 34.3 x 45.9 cm (13 1/2 x 18 1/16 in.) Museum of Fine Arts, Boston. The M. and M. Karolik Collection of American Watercolors, Drawings, and Prints, 1800-1875, 53.2431 Photograph ©2006 Museum of Fine Arts, Boston.

Chapter 14: General Zachary Taylor at the Battle of Buena Vista, Mexico, 22-23 February 1847.
The Granger Collection.

Chapter 15: Abraham Lincoln delivers a speech in a debate with Senator Stephen Douglas during the 1858 senatorial campaign in Illinois. Lincoln, Douglas, and numerous dignitaries congregate on a platform before a crowd of spectators in this illustration by Robert Marshall.
Illinois State Historical Library.

Chapter 16: A Union officer and members of Company C, 1st Conn. Artillery stand behind a large cannon at Fort Brady. Photograph by Mathew Brady, 1864.
Corbis/Bettmann.

Chapter 17: J. W. Watts, Reading the Emancipation Proclamation.
Courtesy of the Library of Congress.

Chapter 18: General William Tecumseh Sherman (1820–1891) and the Peace Commission meet with Cheyenne and Arapaho Indians at Fort Laramie in Wyoming to try to end Red Cloud's War. The resulting treaty secured the removal of U.S. troops from several Powder River forts, as well as promised the Powder River Valley as a Sioux hunting ground.
Getty Images Inc. Hulton Archive Photos.

Chapter 19: Workers pose beside a huge ladle at a steel mill in Pittsburgh, Pennsylvania ca. 1900.
Courtesy of the Library of Congress.

Chapter 20: Dynamic American orator William Jennings Bryan stands on a platform above a crowd during a campaign.
Brown Brothers.

Chapter 21: Suffragettes Holding Victory Jubilee, 1920. Elated women wave American flags and blow noisemakers on a car on a street on August 31, 1920.
Corbis/Bettmann.

Chapter 22: A crowd of people stand on the shore watching the luxury ocean liner Lusitania leave from New York on May 1, 1915.
Corbis/Bettmann.

Chapter 23: A line of young men and women in various poses doing the Charleston as they compete in a dance contest in downtown St. Louis in 1925.
Missouri Historical Society, St. Louis.

Chapter 24: Two boys sit next to disparaging signs at a Hooverville shanty town in Washington, DC in 1932.
Getty Images Inc. Hulton Archive Photos.

Chapter 25: African American soldiers man a field cannon while digging an earth embankment below a camouflage net on a World War II battlefield.
Corbis/Bettmann.

Chapter 26: Actor Robert Taylor testifies before the House Un-American Activities Committee.
AP Wide World Photos.

Chapter 27: President Kennedy gives his inaugural address at the Capitol. Listening in the front row, from left: Vice President Lyndon B. Johnson; Richard Nixon, Kennedy's campaign opponent; Senator John Sparkmano of Alabama; and former president Harry Truman.
AP Wide World Photos.

Chapter 28: An African-American man drinking at a segregated drinking fountain in Oklahoma City, Oklahoma.
Russell Lee. Getty Images Inc. Hulton Archive Photos.

Chapter 29: A peace demonstrator taunts military police during this confrontation in front of the Pentagon during an anti-Vietnam War protest.
UPI Corbis/Bettmann.

Chapter 30: A Volkswagen "Beetle" sits at a gas station during the gasoline shortage and energy crisis of the 1970s. The sign states the limit of fuel per customer.
Owen Franken/Corbis/Bettmann

Chapter 31: Rescue workers stand near the rubble of the fallen World Trade Center towers in New York on September 13, 2001.
REUTERS/Pool/Beth Kaiser. Corbis/Bettmann.

Maps

Denotes Interactive Map Exploration

CHARTS, GRAPHS & TABLES

OVERVIEW TABLES

OUT OF MANY VOICES

PREFACE

Out of Many: A History of the American People, fifth edition, offers a distinctive and timely approach to American history, highlighting the experiences of diverse communities of Americans in the unfolding story of our country. The stories of these communities offer a way of examining the complex historical forces shaping people's lives at various moments in our past. The debates and conflicts surrounding the most momentous issues in our national life—independence, emerging democracy, slavery, westward settlement, imperial expansion, economic depression, war, technological change—were largely worked out in the context of local communities. Through communities we focus on the persistent tensions between everyday life and those larger decisions and events that continually reshape the circumstances of local life. Each chapter opens with a description of a representative community. Some of these portraits feature American communities struggling with one another: African slaves and English masters on the rice plantations of colonial Georgia, or *Tejanos* and Americans during the Texas war of independence. Other chapters feature portraits of communities facing social change: the feminists of Seneca Falls, New York, in 1848, or the African Americans of Montgomery, Alabama, in 1955. As the story unfolds we find communities growing to include ever larger groups of Americans: the soldiers from every colony who forged the Continental Army into a patriotic national force at Valley Forge during the American Revolution, or the moviegoers who aspired to a collective dream of material prosperity and upward mobility during the 1920s.

Out of Many is also the only American history text with a truly continental perspective. With community vignettes from New England to the South, the Midwest to the far West, we encourage students to appreciate the great expanse of our nation. For example, a vignette of seventeenth-century Sante Fé, New Mexico, illustrates the founding of the first European settlements in the New World. We present territorial expansion into the American West from the viewpoint of the Mandan villagers of the upper Missouri River of North Dakota. We introduce the policies of the Reconstruction era through the experience of African Americans in Hale County, Alabama. A continental perspective drives home to students that American history has never been the preserve of any particular region.

Out of Many includes extensive coverage of our diverse heritage. Our country is appropriately known as "a nation of immigrants," and the history of immigration to America, from the seventeenth to the twenty-first centuries, is fully integrated into the text. There is sustained and close attention to our place in the world, with special emphasis on our relations with the nations of the Western Hemisphere, especially our near neighbors, Canada and Mexico. The statistical data in the final chapter has been completely updated with the results of the 2000 census.

In these ways *Out of Many* breaks new ground, but without compromising its coverage of the traditional turning points that we believe are critically important to an understanding of the American past. Among these watershed events are the Revolution and the struggle over the Constitution, the Civil War and Reconstruction, and the Great Depression and World War II. In *Out of Many*, however, we seek to integrate the narrative of national history with the story of the nation's many diverse communities. The Revolutionary and Constitutional period tested the ability of local communities to forge a new unity, and success depended on their ability to build a nation without compromising local identity. The Civil War and Reconstruction formed a second great test of the balance between the national ideas of the Revolution and the power of local and sectional communities. The Depression and the New Deal demonstrated the importance of local communities and the growing power of national institutions during the greatest economic challenge in our history. *Out of Many* also looks back in a new and comprehensive way—from the vantage point of the beginning of a new century and the end of the cold war—at the salient events of the last fifty years and their impact on American communities. The community focus of *Out of Many* weaves the stories of the people and the nation into a single compelling narrative.

Out of Many, fifth edition, is completely updated with the most recent scholarship on the history of America and the United States. All the chapters have been extensively revised and rewritten. The final chapter details the tumultuous events of the new century, including a completely new section on the "War on Terror," and concluding with the national election of 2004. Throughout the book the text and graphics are presented in a stunning new design. Moreover, this edition incorporates two important new features. Each chapter includes two short excerpts from letters, personal diaries, or first person accounts called "Out of Many Voices," giving students the opportunity to read the perspectives of both well-known and ordinary Americans on the course of historic events. Moreover, selected chapters include a two-page feature we call "Whose History Is It?" using text and graphics to focus on notable public controversies that have taken place over the meaning of historical events. Americans have frequently come to blows over different ways of interpreting the past, and this feature helps students see that arguments over the meaning of the past have never been confined to the classroom.

SPECIAL FEATURES

With each edition of *Out of Many* we have sought to strengthen its unique integration of the best of traditional American history with its innovative community-based focus and strong continental perspective. This new version is no exception. A wealth of special features and pedagogical aids reinforces our narrative and helps students grasp key issues.

■ **Community and Diversity.** *Out of Many*, fifth edition, opens with an introduction titled "Communitiy and Diversity" that acquaints students with the major themes of the book, providing them with a framework for understanding American History.

■ **Whose History Is It? NEW** to the fifth edition, this special illustrated feature located at the end of chapters 1, 4, 9, 14, 17, 25, 27, 29 uses text and graphics to focus on notable public controversies that have taken place over the meaning of historical events.

■ **Out of Many Voices. NEW** to the fifth edition are short excerpts from letters, personal diaries, or first person accounts that give the perspectives of both well-known and ordinary Americans on the course of historic events.

■ **Map Explorations.** Selected maps in each chapter are provided in an interactive format on the new *ONEKEY* website available with the text. They provide interactive exploration of key geographical, chronological, and thematic concepts to reinforce the content contained in the maps and the text. Students can access each map individually using the url provided with the map or find them within chapters when exploring the website.

■ **Overview tables.** Overview tables provide students with a summary of complex issues.

■ **Graphs, charts, and tables.** Every chapter includes one or more graphs, charts, or tables that help students understand important events and trends.

■ **Photos and Illustrations.** The abundant illustrations in *Out of Many* include many that have never before been used in an American history text. Extensive captions treat the images as visual primary source documents from the American past, describing their source and explaining their significance. In addition, each chapter opens with a stunning visual that relates to the chapter content and introduces students to the importance of visual documents in the study of history.

■ **Chronologies.** A chronology at the end of each chapter helps students build a framework of key events.

■ **Review Questions.** Review questions at the end of chapters help students review, reinforce, and retain the material in each chapter and encourage them to relate the material to broader issues in American history.

■ **Recommended Readings.** The works in the short, annotated Recommended Reading list at the end of each chapter have been selected with the interested introductory student in mind.

PRINT SUPPLEMENTS

Instructor's Resource Manual

A time-saver in developing and preparing lecture presentations, the *Instructor's Resource Manual* contains chapter outlines, detailed chapter overviews, lecture topics, discussion questions, readings, and information about audio-visual resources.

Test Item File

The *Test Item File* contains more than 1,500 multiple-choice, identification, matching, true-false, and essay test questions and 10–15 questions per chapter on the maps found in each chapter. The guide includes a collection of blank maps that can be photocopied and used for map testing purposes or for other class exercises.

Prentice Hall Test Generator

This commercial-quality computerized test management program, available for Windows and Macintosh environments, allows instructors to select items from the *Test Item File* and design their own exams.

Transparency Package

Includes full-color transparency acetates of all the maps, charts, and graphs in the text for use in the classroom.

History Notes, Volumes I and II

History Notes is a new type of study aid that provides tests for each chapter that students can use to assess their level of understanding of chapter material. It includes identification terms, multiple-choice questions, short essay questions, and map questions. *History Notes* is available free when packaged with *Out of Many*.

Documents Set, Volumes I and II

This collection of more than 300 primary source documents directly relates to the themes and content of the text. Each document is approximately two pages long and includes a brief introduction and study questions intended to encourage students to analyze the document critically and relate it to the content of the text. The *Documents Set* is available at a substantial discount when packaged with *Out of Many*.

Retrieving the American Past

Written and developed by leading historians and educators, this reader is an on-demand history database that offers 300 primary source documents on key topics in American History. Each module includes an introduction, several primary documents and secondary sources, follow-up questions, and recommendations for further reading. By deciding which modules to include and the order in which they will appear, instructors can compile a custom reader to fit their needs. Contact your local Prentice Hall representative for more information about this exciting custom publishing option.

Many Lives, Many Stories: Biographies in American History

This two-volume collection of sixty-two biographies in American history was written specifically to match the chapter sequence and themes of *Out of Many*. Introductions, pre-reading questions, suggested readings, and a special prologue about the role of biography in the study of American history enrich this important new supplement. Available free when packaged with *Out of Many*.

Prentice Hall's *OneSearch* with *Research Navigator TM*

 This brief guide introduces students to tools for finding, evaluating, and using resources on the internet. It includes a section avoiding plagiarism and using sources effectively, tips for finding information related to history on the internet and for documenting electronic sources, and an access code to the *Research Navigator TM* website. *OneSearch* is available for free when packaged with *Out of Many*. Contact your local Prentice Hall representative for details.

Prentice Hall and Penguin Bundle Program

 Prentice Hall and Penguin are pleased to provide adopters of *Out of Many* with an opportunity to receive significant discounts when orders for *Out of Many* are bundled together with Penguin titles in American history. Please contact your local Prentice Hall representative for details.

MULTIMEDIA SUPPLEMENTS

U.S. History Documents CD-ROM

Bound into every copy of *Out of Many* and organized according to the main periods in American History, this document CD-ROM contains over 300 primary source documents in an easily-navigated PDF file. Each document is accompanied by essay questions that can be answered via the CD-ROM or via a dedicated website.

OneKey

 A unique online resource, *OneKey* lets you and your students access the many teaching and learning resources for *Out of Many* all in one place. For students, it means access to documents, quizzes, map explorations, interactive learning activities, video, audio, e-book portions of the text, and other pedagogical material organized by major sections within chapters to reinforce and apply what they are learning in class and from the text. For instructors, it means access to the student's resources, *and* all of the instructional material available to use in teaching with the text, including instructor's manual material, test questions from the test item file, additional documents for assignment, images, maps, charts, and graphs from the text, video and audio clips, and Powerpoint ^{TM} presentations and questions for use with CRS technology in the classroom. Access to this unique website is free to students when packaged with the text. For more information about this exciting new resource, contact your local Prentice Hall representative for a tour.

Companion Website™

www.prenhall.com/faragher

With the *Out of Many Companion Website*™ students can take full advantage of the Web in tandem with the text to enrich their study of American history. The *Companion Website*™ features chapter review tests, learning objectives, and study questions that students can use to assess their comprehension of chapter content.

Instructor's Resource Center on CD-ROM

 This CD-ROM, like the *OneKey* website, includes all of the instuctor supplements, multimedia resources, and images and art from *Out of Many*.

Research Navigator™

This unique resource helps your students make the most of their research time. From finding the right articles and journals, to citing sources, drafting and writing effective papers, and completing research assignments, **Research Navigator™** simplifies and streamlines the entire process. Access to **Research Navigator™** is available with every copy of the *OneSearch* guide and with the *OneKey* website. For more information, contact your local Prentice Hall representative.

ACKNOWLEDGMENTS

In the years it has taken to bring *Out of Many* from idea to reality and to improve it in successive editions, we have often been reminded that although writing history sometimes feels like isolated work, it actually involves a collective effort. We want to thank the dozens of people whose efforts have made the publication of this book possible.

We wish to thank our many friends at Prentice Hall for their efforts in creating the fifth edition of *Out of Many*: Yolanda de Rooy, President; Charlyce Jones Owen, Editorial Director; Carolyn Viola John, Development Editor; Leslie Osher, Creative Design Director; Randy Pettit, Production Liaison; Kathryn Foot, Interior and Cover Designer; Lorenza Compagnone, Prepare, Inc., Production Editor; and Janet Masterson, Copy Editor.

Historians around the country greatly assisted us by reading and commenting on chapters for this and previous editions. We want to thank each of them for the commitment of their valuable time:
Margaret Spratt, *University of Southern Maine*
Elizabeth Hayes Turner, *University of North Texas*
James A. Hijiya, *University of Massachusetts*
Dartmouth Kathryn Abbott, *Western Kentucky University*
Ericka Verba, *Santa Monica College*
Kirsten Fermaglich, *Michigan State University*
Edward E. Baptist, *Cornell University*
Kevin Kern, *University of Akron Charlotte Brooks, SUNY, Albany*.

Although we share joint responsibility for the entire book, the chapters were individually authored: John Mack Faraher wrote chapters 1–8; Susan Armitage wrote chapters 9–16; Mari Jo Buhle wrote chapters 18–20, 25–26, 29; and Daniel Czitrom wrote chapters 17, 21–24, 27–28. (For this edition, Professors Buhle and Czitrom co-authored Chapters 30–31.)

Each of us depended on a great deal of support and assistance with the research and writing that went into this book. We want to thank: Kathryn Abbott, Nan Boyd, Krista Comer, Jennifer Cote, Crista DeLuzio, Keith Edgerton, Carol Frost, Jesse Hoffnung Garskof, Pailin Gaither, Jane Gerhard, Todd Gernes, Mark Krasovic, Melani McAlister, Cristi, Rebecca McKenna, and Mitchell, Ani Mukherji, J. C. Mutchler, Keith Peterson, Alan Pinkham, Tricia Rose, Gina Rourke, Jessica Shubow, Gordon P. Utz, Jr., and Maura Young.

Our families and close friends have been supportive and ever so patient over the many years we have devoted to this project. But we want especially to thank Paul Buhle, Meryl Fingrutd, Bob Greene, and Michele Hoffnung.

About the Authors

Chris Freitag

John Mack Faragher

John Mack Faragher is Arthur Unobskey Professor of American History, chair of the Program in American Studies, and director of the Howard R. Lamar Center for the Study of Frontiers and Borders at Yale University. Born in Arizona and raised in southern California, he received his B.A. at the University of California, Riverside, and his Ph.D. at Yale University. He is the author of *Women and Men on the Overland Trail* (1979), *Sugar Creek: Life on the Illinois Prairie* (1986), *Daniel Boone: The Life and Legend of an American Pioneer* (1992), *The American West: A New Interpretive History* (2000), and *A Great and Noble Scheme: The Tragic Story of the Expulsion of the French Acadians from their American Homeland* (2005).

Mari Jo Buhle

Mari Jo Buhle is William R. Kenan Jr. University Professor and Professor of American Civilization and History at Brown University, specializing in American women's history. She received her B.A. from the University of Illinois, Urbana–Champaign, and her Ph.D. from the University of Wisconsin, Madison. She is the author of *Women and American Socialism, 1870–1920* (1981) and *Feminism and Its Discontents: A Century of Struggle with Psychoanalysis* (1998). She is also coeditor of *Encyclopedia of the American Left,* second edition (1998). Professor Buhle held a fellowship (1991–1996) from the John D. and Catherine T. MacArthur Foundation.

Daniel Czitrom

Daniel Czitrom is Professor of History at Mount Holyoke College. Born and raised in New York City, he received his B.A. from the State University of New York at Binghamton and his M.A. and Ph.D. from the University of Wisconsin, Madison. He is the author of *Media and the American Mind: From Morse to McLuhan* (1982), which won the First Books Award of the American Historical Association and has been translated into Spanish and Chinese. He has served as a historical consultant and a featured on-camera commentator for several documentary film projects, including two recent PBS series, *New York: A Documentary Film* and *American Photography: A Century of Images.* He is co-author of the forthcoming book, *Rediscovering Jacob Riis,* and currently serves on the Executive Board of the Organization of American Historians.

Susan H. Armitage

Susan H. Armitage is Claudius O. and Mary R. Johnson Distinguished Professor of History at Washington State University. She earned her Ph.D. from the London School of Economics and Political Science. Among her many publications on western women's history are three coedited books, *The Women's West* (1987), *So Much To Be Done: Women on the Mining and Ranching Frontier* (1991), and *Writing the Range: Race, Class, and Culture in the Women's West* (1997). She currently serves as an editor of a series of books on women and American history for the University of Illinois Press. She is the editor of *Frontiers: A Journal of Women's Studies.*

COMMUNITY & DIVERSITY

One of the most characteristic features of our country has always been its astounding variety. The American people include the descendants of native Indians, colonial Europeans, Africans, and migrants from virtually every country and continent. Indeed, as we enter a new century the United States is absorbing a flood of immigrants from Latin America and Asia that rivals the great tide of people from eastern and southern Europe one hundred years ago. What's more, our country is one of the world's most spacious, incorporating more than 3.6 million square miles of territory. The struggle to meld a single nation out of our many far-flung communities is what

much of American history is all about. That is the story told in this book.

Every human society is made up of communities. A community is a set of relationships linking men, women, and their families to a coherent social whole that is more than the sum of its parts. In a community people develop the capacity for unified action. In a community people learn, often through trial and error, how to transform and adapt to their environment. The sentiment that binds the members of a community together is the mother of group identity and ethnic pride. In the making of history, communities are far more important than even the greatest of leaders, for the community is the

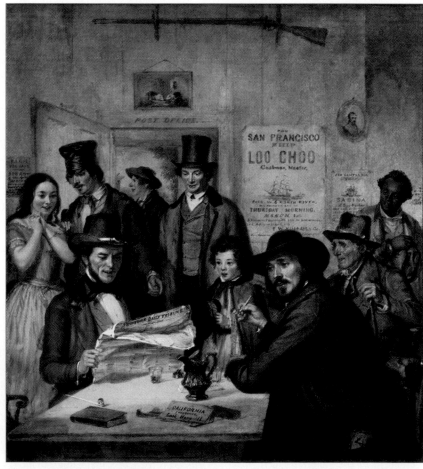

William Sidney Mount (1807–1868) *California News* 1850. Oil on canvas. The Long Island Museum of American Art, History and Carriages.

Gift of Mr. and Mrs. Ward Melville, 1955.

Harvey Dinnerstein, *Underground, Together* 1996, oil on canvas, 90" × 107".

Photograph courtesy of Gerold Wunderlich & Co., New York, NY.

institution most capable of passing a distinctive histori-cal tradition to future generations.

Communities bind people together in multiple ways. They can be as small as local neighborhoods, in which people maintain face-to-face relations, or as large as the nation itself. This book examines American history from the perspective of community life—an ever-widening frame that has included larger and larger groups of Americans.

Networks of kinship and friendship, and connec-tions across generations and among families, establish the bonds essential to community life. Shared feelings about values and history establish the basis for com-mon identity. In communities, people find the power to act collectively in their own interest. But American communities frequently took shape as a result of seri-ous conflicts among groups, and within communities there has often been significant fighting among com-peting groups or classes. Thus the term *community*, as we use it here, includes tension and discord as well as harmony and agreement.

For years there have been persistent laments about the "loss of community" in modern America. But com-munity has not disappeared—it is continually being reinvented. Until the late eighteenth century, commu-nity was defined primarily by space and local geogra-phy. But in the nineteenth century communities began to be reshaped by new and powerful historical forces such as the marketplace, industrialization, the corpora-tion, mass immigration, mass media, and the growth of the nation-state. In the twentieth century, Americans have struggled to balance commitments to several communities simultaneously. These were defined not simply by local spatial arrangements, but by categories as varied as racial and ethnic groups, occupations, political affiliations, and consumer preferences.

The "American Communities" vignettes that open each chapter reflect this shift. Most of the vignettes in the pre–Civil War chapters focus on geographically defined communities, such as the ancient Indian city at Cahokia, or the experiment in industrial urban planning in early nineteenth-century Lowell, Massachusetts. In the post–Civil War chapters different and more modern kinds of communities make their appearance. In the 1920s, movies and radio offered a new kind of community—a community of identification with dreams of freedom, material success, upward mobility, youth and beauty. In the 1950s, rock 'n' roll music helped germinate a new national community of teenagers, with profound effects on the culture of the entire country in the second half of the twentieth century. In the late 1970s, fear of nuclear accidents like the one at Three Mile Island brought concerned citizens together in communities around the country and produced a national movement opposing nuclear power.

The title for our book was suggested by the Latin phrase selected by John Adams, Benjamin Franklin, and Thomas Jefferson for the Great Seal of the United States: *E Pluribus Unum*—"Out of Many Comes Unity." These men understood that unity could not be imposed by a powerful central authority but had to develop out of mutual respect among Americans of different backgrounds. The revolutionary leadership expressed the hope that such respect could grow on the basis of a remarkable proposition: "We hold these truths to be self-evident, that all men are created equal; that they

are endowed by their Creator with certain unalienable rights; that among these are life, liberty, and the pursuit of happiness." The national government of the United States would preserve local and state authority but would guarantee individual rights. The nation would be strengthened by guarantees of difference.

"Out of Many"—that is the promise of America, and the premise of this book. The underlying dialectic of American history, we believe, is that as a people we need to locate our national unity in the celebration of the differences that exist among us; these differences can be our strength, as long as we affirm the promise of the Declaration. Protecting the "right to be different," in other words, is absolutely fundamental to the continued existence of democracy, and that right is best protected by the existence of strong and vital communities. We are bound together as a nation by the ideal of local and cultural differences protected by our common commitment to the values of our Revolution.

Today those values are endangered by terrorists using the tactics of mass terror. In the wake of the September 11, 2001, attack on the United States, and with the continuing threat of biological, chemical, or even nuclear assaults, Americans can not afford to lose

Thomas Satterwhite Noble, *Last Sale of Slaves on the Courthouse Steps*, 1860, oil on canvas, Missouri Historical Society.

faith in our historic vision. The United States is a multicultural and transnational society. The thousands of victims buried in the smoking ruins of the World Trade Center included people from dozens of different ethnic and national groups. We must fight to protect and defend the promise of our diverse nation

Our history shows that the promise of American unity has always been problematic. Centrifugal forces have been powerful in the American past, and at times the country has seemed about to fracture into its component parts. Our transformation from a collection of groups and regions into a nation has been marked by painful and often violent struggles. Our past is filled with conflicts between Indians and colonists, masters and slaves, Patriots and Loyalists, Northerners and Southerners, Easterners and Westerners, capitalists and workers, and sometimes the government and the people. War can bring out our best, but it can also bring out our worst. During World War II thousands of Japanese American citizens were deprived of their rights and locked up in isolated detention centers simply because of their ethnic background. Americans often appear to be little more than a contentious collection of peoples with conflicting interests, divided by region and background, race and class.

Our most influential leaders have also sometimes suffered a crisis of faith in the American project of "liberty and justice for all." Thomas Jefferson not only believed in the inferiority of African Americans, but he feared that immigrants from outside the Anglo-American tradition might "warp and bias" the development of the nation "and render it a heterogeneous, incoherent, distracted mass." We have not always lived up to the American promise, and there is a dark side to our history. It took the bloodiest war in American history to secure the human rights of African Americans, and the struggle for full equality for all our citizens has yet to be won. During the great influx of immigrants in the early twentieth century, fears much like Jefferson's led to movements to Americanize the foreign born by forcing them, in the words of one leader, "to give up the languages, customs, and methods of life which they have brought with them across the ocean, and adopt instead the language, habits, and customs of this country, and the general standards and ways of American living." Similar thinking motivated Congress at various times to bar the immigration of Africans, Asians, and other ethnic groups and people of color into the country, and to force assimilation on American Indians by denying them the freedom to practice their religion or even to speak their own language. Such calls for restrictive unity still resound in our own day.

But other Americans have argued for a more fulsome version of Americanization. "What is the American, this new man?" asked the French immigrant Michel Crévecoeur in 1782. "A strange mixture of blood which you will find in no other country." In America, he wrote, "individuals of all nations are melted into a new race of men." A century later Crévecoeur was echoed by historian Frederick Jackson Turner, who believed that "in the crucible of the frontier, the immigrants were Americanized, liberated, and fused into a mixed race, English in neither nationality nor characteristics. The process has gone on from the early days to our own."

The process by which diverse communities have come to share a set of common American values is one of the most fundamental aspects of our history. It did not occur, however, because of compulsory Americanization programs, but because of free public education, popular participation in democratic politics, and the impact of popular culture. Contemporary America does have a common culture: We share a commitment to freedom of thought and expression, we join in the aspirations to own our own homes and send our children to college, we laugh at the same television programs.

To a degree that too few Americans appreciate, this common culture resulted from a complicated process of mutual discovery that took place when different ethnic and regional groups encountered one another. Consider just one small and unique aspect of our culture: the barbecue. Americans have been barbecuing since before the beginning of written history. Early settlers adopted this technique of cooking from the Indians—the word itself comes from a native term for a framework of sticks over a fire on which meat was slowly cooked. Colonists typically barbecued pork, fed on Indian corn. African slaves lent their own touch by introducing the use of hot sauces. The ritual that is a part of nearly every American family's Fourth of July silently celebrates the heritage of diversity that went into making our common culture.

The American educator John Dewey recognized this diversity early in the last century. "The genuine American, the typical American, is himself a hyphenated character," he declared, "international and interracial in his make-up." The point about our "hyphenated character," Dewey believed, "is to see to it that the hyphen connects instead of separates." We, the authors of Out of Many, share Dewey's perspective on American history. "Creation comes from the impact of diversity," wrote the American philosopher Horace Kallen. We also endorse Kallen's vision of the American promise: "A democracy of nationalities, cooperating voluntarily and autonomously through common institutions, . . . a multiplicity in a unity, an orchestration of mankind." And now, let the music begin.

Reconstruction

1863–1877

CHAPTER OUTLINE

Hale County, Alabama: From Slavery to Freedom in a Black Belt Community

On a bright Saturday morning in May 1867, 4,000 former slaves eagerly streamed into the town of Greensboro, bustling seat of Hale County in west-central Alabama. They came to hear speeches from two delegates to a recent freedmen's convention in Mobile and to find out about the political status of black people under the Reconstruction Act just passed by Congress. Tensions mounted in the days following this unprecedented gathering, as military authorities began supervising voter registration for elections to the upcoming constitutional convention that would rewrite the laws of Alabama. On June 13, John Orrick, a local white, confronted Alex Webb, a politically active freedman, on the streets of Greensboro. Webb had recently been appointed a voter registrar for the district. Orrick swore he would never be registered by a black man, and shot Webb dead. Hundreds of armed and angry freedmen formed a posse to search for Orrick, but failed to find him. Galvanized by Webb's murder, 500 local freedmen formed a chapter of the Union League, the Republican Party's organizational arm in the South. The chapter functioned as both a militia company and a forum to agitate for political rights.

Violent political encounters between black people and white people were common in Southern communities in the wake of the Civil War. Communities throughout the South struggled over the meaning of freedom in ways that reflected their particular circumstances. The 4 million freed people constituted roughly one-third of the total Southern population, but the black–white ratio in individual communities varied enormously. In some places, the Union army had been a strong presence during the war, hastening the collapse of the slave system and encouraging experiments in free labor. Other areas had remained relatively untouched by the fighting. In some areas, small farms prevailed; in others, including Hale County, large plantations dominated economic and political life.

West-central Alabama had emerged as a fertile center of cotton production just two decades before the Civil War. There, African Americans, as throughout the South's black belt, constituted more than three-quarters of the population. With the arrival of federal troops in the spring of 1865, African Americans in Hale County, like their counterparts elsewhere, began to challenge the traditional organization of plantation labor.

One owner, Henry Watson, found that his entire workforce had deserted him at the end of 1865. "I am in the midst of a large and fertile cotton growing country," Watson wrote to a partner. "Many plantations are entirely without labor, many plantations have insufficient labor, and upon none are the laborers doing their former accustomed work." Black women refused to work in the fields, preferring to stay home with their children and tend garden plots. Nor would male field hands do any work, such as caring for hogs, that did not directly increase their share of the cotton crop.

Above all, freed people wanted more autonomy. Overseers and owners thus grudgingly allowed them to work the land "in families," letting them choose their own supervisors and find their own provisions. The result was a shift from the gang labor characteristic of the antebellum period,

Greensboro

in which large groups of slaves worked under the harsh and constant supervision of white overseers, to the sharecropping system, in which African American families worked small plots of land in exchange for a small share of the crop. This shift represented less of a victory for newly freed African Americans than a defeat for plantation owners, who resented even the limited economic independence it forced them to concede to their black workforce.

Only a small fraction—perhaps 15 percent—of African American families were fortunate enough to be able to buy land. The majority settled for some version of sharecropping, while others managed to rent land from owners, becoming tenant farmers. Still, planters throughout Hale County had to change the old routines of plantation labor. Local African Americans also organized politically. In 1866, Congress had passed the Civil Rights Act and sent the Fourteenth Amendment to the Constitution to the states for ratification; both promised full citizenship rights to former slaves. Hale County freedmen joined the Republican Party and local Union League chapters. They used their new political power to press for better labor contracts, demand greater autonomy for the black workforce, and agitate for the more radical goal of land confiscation and redistribution. "The colored people are very anxious to get land of their own to live upon independently; and they want money to buy stock to make crops," reported one black Union League organizer. "The only way to get these necessaries is to give our votes to the [Republican] party." Two Hale County former slaves, Brister Reese and James K. Green, won election to the Alabama state legislature in 1869.

It was not long before these economic and political gains prompted a white counterattack. In the spring of 1868, the Ku Klux Klan—a secret organization devoted to terrorizing and intimidating African Americans and their white Republican allies—came to Hale County. Disguised in white sheets, armed with guns and whips, and making nighttime raids on horseback, Klansmen flogged, beat, and murdered freed people. They intimidated voters and silenced political activists. Planters used Klan terror to dissuade former slaves from leaving plantations or organizing for higher wages.

With the passage of the Ku Klux Klan Act in 1871, the federal government cracked down on the Klan, breaking its power temporarily in parts of the former Confederacy. But no serious effort was made to stop Klan terror in the west Alabama black belt, and planters there succeeded in reestablishing much of their social and political control.

The events in Hale County illustrate the struggles that beset communities throughout the South during the Reconstruction era after the Civil War. The destruction of slavery and the Confederacy forced African Americans and white people to renegotiate their old economic and political roles. These community battles both shaped and were shaped by the victorious and newly expansive federal government in Washington. In the end, Reconstruction was only partially successful. Not until the "Second Reconstruction" of the twentieth-century civil rights movement would the descendants of Hale County's African Americans begin to enjoy the full fruits of freedom—and even then not without challenge.

KEY TOPICS

- Competing political plans for reconstructing the defeated Confederacy
- Difficult transition from slavery to freedom for African Americans
- The political and social legacy of Reconstruction in the Southern states
- Post–Civil War transformations in the economic and political life of the North

THE POLITICS OF RECONSTRUCTION

When General Robert E. Lee's men stacked their guns at Appomattox, the bloodiest war in American history ended. More than 600,000 soldiers had died during the four years of fighting, 360,000 Union and 260,000 Confederate. Another 275,000 Union and 190,000 Confederate troops had been wounded. Although President Abraham Lincoln insisted early on that the purpose of the war was to preserve the Union, by 1863, it had evolved as well into a struggle for African American liberation. Indeed, the political, economic, and moral issues posed by slavery were the root cause of the Civil War, and the war ultimately destroyed slavery, although not racism, once and for all.

The Civil War also settled the Constitutional crisis provoked by the secession of the Confederacy and its justification in appeals to states' rights. The name "United States" would from now on be understood as a singular rather than a plural noun, signaling an important change in the meaning of American nationality. The old notion of the United States as a voluntary union of sovereign states gave way to the new reality of a single nation, in which the federal government took precedence over the individual states. The key historical developments of the Reconstruction era revolved around precisely how the newly strengthened national government would define its relationship with the defeated Confederate states and the 4 million newly freed slaves.

The Defeated South

The white South paid an extremely high price for secession, war, and defeat. In addition to the battlefield casualties, the Confederate states sustained deep material and psychological wounds. Much of the best agricultural land lay waste, including the rich fields of northern Virginia, the Shenandoah Valley, and large sections of Tennessee, Mississippi, Georgia, and South Carolina. Many towns and cities—including Richmond, Atlanta, and Columbia, South Carolina—were in ruins. By 1865, the South's most precious commodities, cotton and African American slaves, no longer were measures of wealth and prestige. Retreating Confederates destroyed most of the South's cotton to prevent its capture by federal troops. What remained was confiscated by Union agents as contraband of war. The former slaves, many of whom had fled to Union lines during the latter stages of the war, were determined to chart their own course in the reconstructed South as free men and women.

It would take the South's economy a generation to overcome the severe blows dealt by the war. In 1860, the South held roughly 25 percent of the nation's wealth; a decade later it controlled only 12 percent. Many white Southerners resented their conquered status, and white notions of race, class, and "honor" died hard. A white North Carolinian, for example, who had lost almost everything dear to him in the war— his sons, home, and slaves—recalled in 1865 that in spite of all his tragedy he still retained one thing. "They've left me one inestimable privilege— to hate 'em. I git up at half-past four in the morning, and sit up till twelve at night, to hate 'em."

Emancipation proved the most bitter pill for white Southerners to swallow, especially the planter elite. Conquered and degraded, and in their view robbed of their slave property, white people responded by regarding African Americans more than ever as inferior to themselves. In the antebellum South, white skin had defined a social bond

Decorating the Graves of Rebel Soldiers, *Harper's Weekly*, August 17, 1867. After the Civil War, both Southerners and Northerners created public mourning ceremonies honoring fallen soldiers. Women led the memorial movement in the South which, by establishing cemeteries and erecting monuments, offered the first cultural expression of the Confederate tradition. This engraving depicts citizens of Richmond, Virginia, decorating thousands of Confederate graves with flowers at the Hollywood Memorial Cemetery on the James River. A local women's group raised enough funds to transfer over 16,000 Confederate dead from Northern cemeteries for reburial in Richmond.

SOURCE: The Granger Collection, New York.

that transcended economic class. It gave even the lowliest poor white a badge of superiority over even the most skilled slave or prosperous free African American. Emancipation, however, forced white people to redefine their world. The specter of political power and social equality for African Americans made racial order the consuming passion of most white Southerners during the Reconstruction years. In fact, racism can be seen as one of the major forces driving Reconstruction and, ultimately, undermining it.

Abraham Lincoln's Plan

By late 1863, Union military victories had convinced President Lincoln of the need to fashion a plan for the reconstruction of the South (see Chapter 16). Lincoln based his reconstruction program on bringing the seceded states back into the Union as quickly as possible. He was determined to respect private property (except in the case of slave property), and he opposed imposing harsh punishments for rebellion. His Proclamation of Amnesty and Reconstruction of December 1863 offered "full pardon" and the restoration of property, not including slaves, to white Southerners willing to swear an oath of allegiance to the United States and its laws, including the Emancipation Proclamation. Prominent Confederate military and civil leaders were excluded from Lincoln's offer, though he indicated that he would freely pardon them.

The president also proposed that when the number of any Confederate state's voters who took the oath of allegiance reached 10 percent of the number who had voted in the election of 1860, this group could establish a state government that Lincoln would recognize as legitimate. Fundamental to this Ten Percent Plan was acceptance by the reconstructed governments of the abolition of slavery. Lincoln's plan was designed less as a blueprint for Reconstruction than as a way to shorten the war and gain white people's support for emancipation. It angered those Republicans—known as Radical Republicans—who advocated not only equal rights for the freedmen but a tougher stance toward the white South.

In July 1864, Senator Benjamin F. Wade of Ohio and Congressman Henry W. Davis of Maryland, both Radicals, proposed a harsher alternative to the Ten Percent Plan. The Wade-Davis bill required 50 percent of a seceding state's white male citizens to take a loyalty oath before elections could be held for a convention to rewrite the state's constitution. The bill also guaranteed equality before the law (although not suffrage) for former slaves. Unlike the president, the Radical Republicans saw Reconstruction as a chance to effect a fundamental transformation of Southern society. They thus wanted to delay the process until war's end and to limit participation to a small number of Southern Unionists. Lincoln viewed Reconstruction as part of the larger effort to win the war and abolish slavery. He wanted to weaken the Confederacy by creating new state governments that could win broad support from Southern white people. The Wade-Davis bill threatened his efforts to build political consensus within the Southern states, and Lincoln therefore pocket-vetoed it, by refusing to sign it within ten days of the adjournment of Congress.

Redistribution of Southern land among former slaves posed another thorny issue for Lincoln, Congress, and federal military officers. As Union armies occupied parts of the South, commanders had improvised a variety of arrangements involving confiscated plantations and the African American labor force. For example, in 1862, General Benjamin F. Butler began a policy of transforming slaves on Louisiana sugar plantations into wage laborers under the close supervision of occupying federal troops. Butler's policy required slaves to remain on the estates of loyal planters, where they would receive wages according to a fixed schedule, as well as food and medical care for the aged and sick. Abandoned plantations would be leased to Northern investors. By 1864, some 50,000 African American laborers on nearly 1,500 Louisiana estates worked either directly for the government or for individual planters under contracts supervised by the army.

In January 1865, General William T. Sherman issued Special Field Order 15, setting aside the Sea Islands off the Georgia coast and a portion of the South Carolina low-country rice fields for the exclusive settlement of freed people. Each family would receive forty acres of land and the loan of mules from the army—the origin, perhaps, of the famous call for "forty acres and a mule" that would soon capture the imagination of African Americans throughout the South. Sherman's intent was not to revolutionize Southern society, but to relieve the demands placed on his army by the thousands of impoverished African Americans who followed his march to the sea. By the summer of 1865, some 40,000 freed people, eager to take advantage of the general's order, had been settled on 400,000 acres of "Sherman land."

Conflicts within the Republican Party prevented the development of a systematic land distribution program. Still, Lincoln and the Republican Congress supported other measures to aid the emancipated slaves. In March 1865, Congress established the Freedmen's Bureau. Along with providing food, clothing, and fuel to destitute former slaves, the bureau was charged with supervising and managing "all the abandoned lands in the South and the control of all subjects relating to refugees and freedmen." The act that established the bureau also stated that forty acres of abandoned or confiscated land could be leased to freed slaves or white Unionists, who would have an option to purchase after three years and "such title thereto as the United States can convey."

At the time of Lincoln's assassination, his Reconstruction policy remained unsettled and incomplete. In its broad outlines, the president's plans had seemed to favor a speedy restoration of the Southern states to the

Photography pioneer Timothy O'Sullivan took this portrait of a multigenerational African American family on the J.J. Smith plantation in Beaufort, South Carolina, 1862. Many white plantation owners in the area had fled, allowing slaves like these to begin an early transition to freedom before the end of the Civil War.

SOURCE: Corbis/Bettmann.

Union and a minimum of federal intervention in their affairs. But with his death, the specifics of postwar Reconstruction had to be hammered out by a new president, Andrew Johnson of Tennessee, a man whose personality, political background, and racist leanings put him at odds with the Republican-controlled Congress.

Andrew Johnson and Presidential Reconstruction

Andrew Johnson, a Democrat and former slaveholder, was a most unlikely successor to the martyred Lincoln. By trade a tailor, educated by his wife, Johnson overcame his impoverished background and served as state legislator, governor, and U.S. senator. Throughout his career, Johnson had championed yeoman farmers and viewed the South's plantation aristocrats with contempt. He was the only Southern member of the U.S. Senate to remain loyal to the Union, and he held the planter elite responsible for secession and defeat. In 1862, Lincoln appointed Johnson to the difficult post of military governor of Tennessee. There he successfully began wartime Reconstruction and cultivated Unionist support in the mountainous eastern districts of that state.

In 1864, the Republicans, in an appeal to Northern and border state "War Democrats," nominated Johnson for vice president. But despite Johnson's success in Ten-

nessee and in the 1864 campaign, many Radical Republicans distrusted him, and the hardscrabble Tennessean remained a political outsider in Republican circles. In the immediate aftermath of Lincoln's murder, however, Johnson appeared to side with those Radical Republicans who sought to treat the South as a conquered province. The new president hinted at indicting prominent Confederate officials for treason, disfranchising them, and confiscating their property. Such tough talk appealed to Radical Republicans. But support for Johnson quickly faded as the new president's policies unfolded. Johnson defined Reconstruction as the province of the executive, not the legislative branch, and he planned to restore the Union as quickly as possible. He blamed individual Southerners—the planter elite—rather than entire states for leading the South down the disastrous road to secession. In line with this philosophy, Johnson outlined mild terms for reentry to the Union.

In the spring of 1865, Johnson granted amnesty and pardon, including restoration of property rights except slaves, to all Confederates who pledged loyalty to the Union and support for emancipation. Fourteen classes of Southerners, mostly major Confederate officials and wealthy landowners, were excluded. But these men could apply individually for presidential pardons. During his tenure Johnson pardoned roughly 90 percent of those who applied. Significantly, Johnson instituted this plan while Congress was not in session.

By the fall of 1865, ten of the eleven Confederate states claimed to have met Johnson's requirements to reenter the Union. On December 6, 1865, in his first annual message to Congress, the president declared the "restoration" of the Union virtually complete. But a serious division within the federal government was taking shape, for the Congress was not about to allow the president free rein in determining the conditions of Southern readmission.

Andrew Johnson used the term "restoration" rather than "reconstruction." A lifelong Democrat with ambitions to be elected president on his own in 1868, Johnson hoped to build a new political coalition composed of Northern Democrats, conservative Republicans, and Southern Unionists. Firmly committed to white supremacy, he opposed political rights for the freedmen. Johnson's open sympathy for his fellow white Southerners, his antiblack bias, and his determination to control the course of Reconstruction placed him on a collision course with the powerful Radical wing of the Republican Party.

The Radical Republican Vision

Most Radicals were men whose careers had been shaped by the slavery controversy. At the core of their thinking lay a deep belief in equal political rights and equal economic opportunity, both guaranteed by a powerful national government. They argued that once free labor, universal education, and equal rights were implanted in the South, that region would be able to share in the North's material wealth, progress, and fluid social mobility. Representative George W. Julian of Indiana typified the Radical vision for the South. He called for elimination of the region's "large estates, widely scattered settlements, wasteful agriculture, popular ignorance, social degradation, the decline of manufactures, contempt for honest labor, and a pampered oligarchy." This process would allow Republicans to develop "small farms, thrifty tillage, free schools, social independence, flourishing manufactures and the arts, respect for honest labor, and equality of political rights."

In the Radicals' view, the power of the federal government would be central to the remaking of Southern society, especially in guaranteeing civil rights and suffrage for freedmen. In the most far-reaching proposal, Representative Thaddeus Stevens of Pennsylvania called for the confiscation of 400 million acres belonging to the wealthiest 10 percent of Southerners, to be redistributed to black and white yeomen and Northern land buyers. "The whole fabric of Southern society must be changed," Stevens told Pennsylvania Republicans in September 1865, "and never can it be done if this opportunity is lost. How can republican institutions, free schools, free churches, free social intercourse exist in a mingled community of nabobs and serfs?"

Northern Republicans were especially outraged by the stringent "black codes" passed by South Carolina, Mississippi, Louisiana, and other states. These were designed to restrict the freedom of the black labor force and keep freed people as close to slave status as possible. Laborers who left their jobs before contracts expired would forfeit wages already earned and be subject to arrest by any white citizen. Vagrancy, very broadly defined, was punishable by fines and involuntary plantation labor. Apprenticeship clauses obliged black children to work without pay for employers. Some states attempted to bar African Americans from land ownership. Other laws specifically denied African Americans equality with white people in civil rights, excluding them from juries and prohibiting interracial marriages.

The black codes underscored the unwillingness of white Southerners to accept the full meaning of freedom for African Americans. The Radicals, although not a majority of their party, were joined by moderate Republicans, as growing numbers of Northerners grew suspicious of white Southern intransigence and the denial of political rights to freedmen. When the Thirty-ninth Congress convened in December 1865, the large Republican majority prevented the seating of the white Southerners elected to Congress under President Johnson's provisional state governments. Republicans also established the Joint Committee on Reconstruction. After hearing extensive testimony from a broad range of witnesses, it concluded that not only were old Confederates back in power in the South but that black codes and racial violence required increased protection for African Americans.

As a result, in the spring of 1866, Congress passed two important bills designed to aid African Americans. The landmark Civil Rights bill, which bestowed full citizenship on African Americans, overturned the 1857 *Dred Scott* decision and the black codes. It defined all persons born in the United States (except Indian peoples) as national citizens, and it enumerated various rights, including the rights to make and enforce contracts, to sue, to give evidence, and to buy and sell property. Under this bill, African Americans acquired "full and equal benefit of all

Office of the Freedmen's Bureau, Memphis, Tennessee, *Harper's Weekly*, June 2, 1866. Established by Congress in 1865, the Freedmen's Bureau provided economic, educational, and legal assistance to former slaves in the post–Civil War years. Bureau agents were often called upon to settle disputes between black and white Southerners over wages, labor contracts, political rights, and violence. While most Southern whites only grudgingly acknowledged the Bureau's legitimacy, freed people gained important legal and psychological support through testimony at public hearings like this one.

SOURCE: Library of Congress.

laws and proceedings for the security of person and property as is enjoyed by white citizens."

Congress also voted to enlarge the scope of the Freedmen's Bureau, empowering it to build schools and pay teachers, and also to establish courts to prosecute those charged with depriving African Americans of their civil rights. The bureau achieved important, if limited, success in aiding African Americans. Bureau-run schools helped lay the foundation for Southern public education. The bureau's network of courts allowed freed people to bring suits against white people in disputes involving violence, nonpayment of wages, or unfair division of crops. The very existence of courts hearing public testimony by African Americans provided an important psychological challenge to traditional notions of white racial domination.

But an angry President Johnson vetoed both of these bills. In opposing the Civil Rights bill, Johnson denounced the assertion of national power to protect African American civil rights, claiming it was a "stride toward centralization, and the concentration of all legislative powers in the national Government." But Johnson's intemperate attacks on the Radicals—he damned them as traitors unwilling to restore the Union—united moderate and Radical Republicans and they succeeded in overriding the vetoes. Congressional Republicans, led by the Radical faction, were now unified in challenging the president's power to direct Reconstruction and in using national authority to define and protect the rights of citizens.

In June 1866, fearful that the Civil Rights Act might be declared unconstitutional, and eager to settle the basis for the seating of Southern representatives, Congress passed the Fourteenth Amendment. The amendment defined national citizenship to include former slaves ("all persons born or naturalized in the United States") and prohibited the states from violating the privileges of citizens without due process of law. It also empowered Congress to reduce the representation of any state that denied the suffrage to males over twenty-one. Republicans adopted the Fourteenth Amendment as their platform for the 1866 congressional elections and suggested that Southern states would have to ratify it as a condition of readmission. President Johnson, meanwhile, took to the stump in August to support conservative Democratic and Republican candidates. His unrestrained speeches often degenerated into harangues, alienating many voters and aiding the Republican cause.

For their part, the Republicans skillfully portrayed Johnson and Northern Democrats as disloyal and white Southerners as unregenerate. Republicans began an effective campaign tradition known as "waving the bloody shirt"—reminding Northern voters of the hundreds of thousands of Yankee soldiers left dead or maimed by the war. In the November 1866 elections, the Republicans increased their majority in both the House and the Senate and gained control of all the Northern states. The stage was now set for a battle between the president and Congress. Was it to be Johnson's "restoration" or Congressional Reconstruction?

Congressional Reconstruction and the Impeachment Crisis

United against Johnson, Radical and moderate Republicans took control of Reconstruction early in 1867. In March, Congress passed the First Reconstruction Act over Johnson's veto. This act divided the South into five military districts subject to martial law. To achieve restoration, Southern states were first required to call new constitutional conventions, elected by universal manhood suffrage. Once these states had drafted new constitutions, guaranteed African American voting rights, and ratified the Fourteenth Amendment, they were eligible for readmission to the Union. Supplementary legislation, also passed over the president's veto, invalidated the provisional governments established by Johnson, empowered the military to administer voter registration, and required an oath of loyalty to the United States (see Map 17.1).

Congress also passed several laws aimed at limiting Johnson's power. One of these, the Tenure of Office Act, stipulated that any officeholder appointed by the president with the Senate's advice and consent could not be removed until the Senate had approved a successor. In this way, congressional leaders could protect Republicans, such as Secretary of War Edwin M. Stanton, entrusted with implementing Congressional Reconstruction. In August 1867, with Congress adjourned, Johnson suspended Stanton and appointed General Ulysses S. Grant interim secretary of war. This move enabled the president to remove generals in the field that he judged to be too radical and replace them with men who were sympathetic to his own views. It also served as a challenge to the Tenure of Office Act. In January 1868, when the Senate overruled Stanton's suspension, Grant broke openly with Johnson and vacated the office. Stanton resumed his position and barricaded himself in his office when Johnson attempted to remove him once again.

Outraged by Johnson's relentless obstructionism, and seizing upon his violation of the Tenure of Office Act as a pretext, Radical and moderate Republicans in the House of Representatives again joined forces and voted to impeach the president by a vote of 126 to 47 on February 24, 1868, charging him with eleven counts of high crimes and misdemeanors. To ensure the support of moderate Republicans, the articles of impeachment focused on violations of the Tenure of Office Act. The case against Johnson would have to be made on the basis of willful violation of the law. Left unstated were the Republicans' real reasons for wanting the president removed: Johnson's political views and his opposition to the Reconstruction Acts.

MAP EXPLORATION

To explore an interactive version of this map,
go to **www.prenhall.com/faragher5/map17.1**

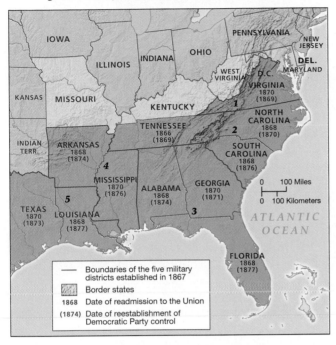

MAP 17.1 Reconstruction of the South, 1866–77 Dates
for the readmission of former Confederate states to the Union
and the return of Democrats to power varied according
to the specific political situations in those states.

An influential group of moderate Senate Republicans feared the damage a conviction might do to the constitutional separation of powers. They also worried about the political and economic policies that might be pursued by Benjamin Wade, the president pro tem of the Senate and a leader of the Radical Republicans, who, because there was no vice president, would succeed to the presidency if Johnson were removed from office. Behind the scenes during his Senate trial, Johnson agreed to abide by the Reconstruction Acts. In May, the Senate voted 35 for conviction, 19 for acquittal—one vote shy of the two-thirds necessary for removal from office. Johnson's narrow acquittal established the precedent that only criminal actions by a president—not political disagreements—warranted removal from office.

The Election of 1868

By the summer of 1868, seven former Confederate states (Alabama, Arkansas, Florida, Louisiana, North Carolina, South Carolina, and Tennessee) had ratified the revised constitutions, elected Republican governments, and ratified the Fourteenth Amendment. They had thereby earned read-

mission to the Union. Though Georgia, Mississippi, Texas, and Virginia still awaited readmission, the presidential election of 1868 offered some hope that the Civil War's legacy of sectional hate and racial tension might finally ease.

Republicans nominated Ulysses S. Grant, the North's foremost military hero. An Ohio native, Grant had graduated from West Point in 1843, served in the Mexican War, and resigned from the army in 1854. Unhappy in civilian life, Grant received a second chance during the Civil War. He rose quickly to become commander in the western theater, and he later destroyed Lee's army in Virginia. Although his armies suffered terrible losses, Grant enjoyed tremendous popularity after the war, especially when he broke with Johnson. Totally lacking in political experience, Grant admitted, after receiving the nomination, that he had been forced into it in spite of himself.

Significantly, at the very moment that the South was being forced to enfranchise former slaves as a prerequisite for readmission to the Union, the Republicans rejected a campaign plank endorsing black suffrage in the North. Their platform left "the question of suffrage in all the loyal States . . . to the people of those States." State referendums calling for black suffrage failed in eight Northern states between 1865 and 1868, succeeding only in Iowa and Minnesota. The Democrats, determined to reverse Congressional Reconstruction, nominated Horatio Seymour, former governor of New York and a long-time foe of emancipation and supporter of states' rights.

The Ku Klux Klan, founded as a Tennessee social club in 1866, emerged as a potent instrument of terror (see the opening of this chapter). In Louisiana, Arkansas, Georgia, and South Carolina the Klan threatened, whipped, and murdered black and white Republicans to prevent them from voting. This terrorism enabled the Democrats to carry Georgia and Louisiana, but it ultimately cost the Democrats votes in the North. In the final tally, Grant carried twenty-six of the thirty-four states for an electoral college victory of 214 to 80. But he received a popular majority of less than 53 percent, beating Seymour by only 306,000 votes. Significantly, more than 500,000 African American voters cast their ballots for Grant, demonstrating their overwhelming support for the Republican Party. The Republicans also retained large majorities in both houses of Congress.

In February 1869, Congress passed the Fifteenth Amendment, providing that "the right of citizens of the United States to vote shall be not denied or abridged on account of race, color, or previous condition of servitude." To enhance the chances of ratification, Congress required the three remaining unreconstructed states—Mississippi, Texas, and Virginia—to ratify both the Fourteenth and Fifteenth Amendments before readmission. They did so, and rejoined the Union in early 1870. The Fifteenth Amendment was ratified in February 1870. In the

The Fifteenth Amendment, 1870. The Fifteenth Amendment, ratified in 1870, stipulated that the right to vote could not be denied "on account of race, color, or previous condition of servitude." This illustration expressed the optimism and hopes of African Americans generated by this Consitutional landmark aimed at protecting black political rights. Note the various political figures (Abraham Lincoln, John Brown, Frederick Douglass) and movements (abolitionism, black education) invoked here, providing a sense of how the amendement culminated a long historical struggle.

SOURCE: Courtesy of the Library of Congress.

narrow sense of simply readmitting the former Confederate states to the Union, Reconstruction was complete.

Woman Suffrage and Reconstruction

The battles over the political status of African Americans proved an important turning point for women as well. The Fourteenth and Fifteenth Amendments, which granted citizenship and the vote to freedmen, both inspired and frustrated women's rights activists. Many of these women had long been active in the abolitionist movement. During the war, they had actively supported the Union cause through their work in the National Woman's Loyal League and the United States Sanitary Commission. Elizabeth Cady Stanton and Susan

B. Anthony, two leaders with long involvement in both the antislavery and feminist movements, objected to the inclusion of the word "male" in the Fourteenth Amendment. "If that word 'male' be inserted," Stanton predicted in 1866, "it will take us a century at least to get it out."

Insisting that the causes of the African American vote and the women's vote were linked, Stanton, Anthony, and Lucy Stone founded the American Equal Rights Association in 1866. The group launched a series of lobbying and petition campaigns to remove racial and sexual restrictions on voting from state constitutions. Throughout the nation, the old abolitionist organizations and the Republican Party emphasized passage of the Fourteenth and Fifteenth Amendments and withdrew funds and support from the cause of woman suffrage. Disagreements over these amendments divided suffragists for decades.

OVERVIEW

RECONSTRUCTION AMENDMENTS TO THE CONSTITUTION, 1865–1870

Amendment and Date Passed by Congress	Main Provisions	Ratification Process (3/4 of all states including ex- Confederate states required)
13 (January 1865)	• Prohibited slavery in the United States	December 1865 (27 states, including 8 Southern states)
14 (June 1866)	• Conferred national citizenship on all persons born or naturalized in the United States • Reduced state representation in Congress proportionally for any state disfranchising male citizens • Denied former Confederates the right to hold state or national office • Repudiated Confederate debt	July 1868 (after Congress made ratification a prerequisite for readmission of ex-Confederate states to the Union)
15 (February 1869)	• Prohibited denial of suffrage because of race, color, or previous condition of servitude	March 1870 (ratification required for readmission of Virginia, Texas, Mississippi, and Georgia)

The radical wing, led by Stanton and Anthony, opposed the Fifteenth Amendment, arguing that ratification would establish an "aristocracy of sex," enfranchising all men while leaving women without political privileges. In arguing for a Sixteenth Amendment that would secure the vote for women, they used racist and elitist appeals. They urged "American women of wealth, education, virtue, and refinement" to support the vote for women and oppose the Fifteenth Amendment "if you do not wish the lower orders of Chinese, Africans, Germans, and Irish, with their low ideas of womanhood to make laws for you and your daughters." Other women's rights activists, including Lucy Stone and Frederick Douglass, asserted that "this hour belongs to the Negro." They feared a debate over woman suffrage at the national level would jeopardize passage of the two amendments.

By 1869, woman suffragists had split into two competing organizations. The moderate American Woman Suffrage Association (AWSA), led by Lucy Stone, Julia Ward Howe, and Henry Blackwell, focused on achieving woman suffrage at the state level. It maintained close ties with the Republican Party and the old abolitionist networks, worked for the Fifteenth Amendment, and actively sought the support of men. The more radical wing founded the all-female National Woman Suffrage Association (NWSA). For the NWSA, the vote represented only one part of a broad spectrum of goals inherited from the Declaration of Sentiments manifesto adopted at the first women's rights convention held in 1848 at Seneca Falls, New York (see Chapter 13).

Women did not win the vote in this period, but they did establish an independent suffrage movement that eventually drew millions of women into political life. The NWSA in particular demonstrated that self-government and democratic participation in the public sphere were crucial for women's emancipation. The failure of woman suffrage after the Civil War was less a result of factional fighting than of the larger defeat of Radical Reconstruction and the ideal of expanded citizenship.

THE MEANING OF FREEDOM

For 4 million slaves, freedom arrived in various ways in different parts of the South. In many areas, slavery had collapsed long before Lee's surrender at Appomattox. In regions far removed from the presence of federal troops, African Americans did not learn of slavery's end until the spring of 1865. There were thousands of sharply contrasting stories, many of which revealed the need for freed slaves to confront their owners. One Virginia slave, hired out to another family during the war, had been working in the fields when a friend told her she was now free. "Is dat so?" she exclaimed. Dropping her hoe, she ran the seven miles to her old place, confronted her former mistress, and shouted, "I'se free! Yes, I'se free! Ain't got to work fo' you no mo'." But regardless of specific regional circumstances,

Susan B. Anthony (1820–1906) and Elizabeth Cady Stanton (1815–1902), the two most influential leaders of the woman suffrage movement, ca. 1892. Anthony and Stanton broke with their longtime abolitionist allies after the Civil War, when they opposed the Fifteenth Amendment. They argued that the doctrine of universal manhood suffrage it embodied would give consitutional authority to the claim that men were the social and political superiors of women. As founders of the militant National Woman Suffrage Association, Stanton and Anthony established an independent woman suffrage movement with a broader spectrum of goals for women's rights, and drew millions of women into public life during the late nineteenth century.

SOURCE: Courtesy of the Susan B. Anthony House, Rochester, NY www.susanbanthonyhouse.org.

the meaning of "freedom" would be contested for years to come. The deep desire for independence from white control formed the underlying aspiration of newly freed slaves. For their part, most Southern white people sought to restrict the boundaries of that independence. As individuals and as members of communities transformed by emancipation, former slaves struggled to establish economic, political, and cultural autonomy. They built on the twin pillars of slave culture—the family and the church—to consolidate and expand African American institutions and thereby laid the foundation for the modern African American community.

Emancipation greatly expanded the choices available to African Americans. It helped build confidence in their ability to effect change without deferring to white people. Freedom also meant greater uncertainty and risk. But the vast majority of African Americans were more than willing to take their chances.

Moving About

The first impulse of many emancipated slaves was to test their freedom. The simplest, most obvious way to do this involved leaving home. Throughout the summer and fall of 1865, observers in the South noted enormous numbers of freed people on the move. One former slave squatting in an abandoned tent outside Selma, Alabama, explained his feeling to a Northern journalist: "I's want to be free man, cum when I please, and nobody say nuffin to me, nor order me roun'." When urged to stay on with the South Carolina family she had served for years as a cook, a slave woman replied firmly: "No, Miss, I must go. If I stay here I'll never know I am free."

Yet many who left their old neighborhoods returned soon afterward to seek work in the general vicinity, or even on the plantation they had left. Many wanted to separate themselves from former owners, but not from familial ties and friendships. Others moved away altogether, seeking jobs in nearby towns and cities. Many former slaves left predominantly white counties, where they felt more vulnerable and isolated, for new lives in the relative comfort of predominantly black communities. In most Southern states, there was a significant population shift toward black belt plantation counties and towns after the war. Many African Americans, attracted by schools, churches, and fraternal societies as well as the army, preferred the city. Between 1865 and 1870, the African American population of the South's ten largest cities doubled, while the white population increased by only 10 percent.

Disgruntled planters had difficulty accepting African American independence. During slavery, they had expected obedience, submission, and loyalty from African Americans. Now many could not understand why so many former slaves wanted to leave, despite urgent pleas to continue working at the old place. The deference and humility white people expected from African Americans could no longer be taken for granted. Indeed, many freed people went out of their way to reject the old subservience. Moving about freely was one way of doing this, as was refusing to tip one's hat to white people, ignoring former masters or mistresses in the streets, and refusing to step aside on sidewalks. When freed people staged parades, dances, and picnics to celebrate their new freedom, as they did, for example, when commemorating the Emancipation Proclamation, white people invariably condemned them angrily for "insolence," "outrageous spectacles," or "putting on airs."

The African American Family

Emancipation allowed freed people to strengthen family ties. For many former slaves, freedom meant the opportunity to reunite with long-lost family members. To track down relatives, freed people trekked to faraway places, put ads in newspapers, sought the help of Freedmen's Bureau agents, and questioned anyone who might have information about loved ones. Many thousands of family reunions, each with its own story, took place after the war. One North Carolina slave, who had seen his parents separated by sale, recalled many years later what for him had been the most significant aspect of freedom. "I has got thirteen great-gran' chilluns an' I know whar dey ever'one am. In slavery times dey'd have been on de block long time ago. "Thousands of African American couples who had lived together under slavery streamed to military and civilian authorities and demanded to be legally married. By 1870, the two-parent household was the norm for a large majority of African Americans. For many freed people, the attempt to find lost relatives dragged on for years. Searches often proved frustrating, exhausting, and ultimately disappointing. Some "reunions" ended painfully with the discovery that spouses had found new partners and started new families.

Emancipation brought changes to gender roles within the African American family as well. By serving in the Union army, African American men played a more direct role than women in the fight for freedom. In the political sphere, black men could now serve on juries, vote, and hold office; black women, like their white counterparts, could not. Freedmen's Bureau agents designated the husband as household head and established lower wage scales for women laborers. African American editors, preachers, and politicians regularly quoted the biblical injunction that wives submit to their husbands.

African American men asserted their male authority, denied under slavery, by insisting their wives work at home instead of in the fields. African American women generally wanted to devote more time than they had under slavery to caring for their children and to performing such domestic chores as cooking, sewing, gardening, and laundering. Yet African American women continued to work outside the home, engaging in seasonal field labor for wages or working a family's rented plot. Most rural black families barely eked out a living, and thus the labor of every family member was essential to survival. The key difference from slave times was that African American families themselves, not white masters and overseers, decided when and where women and children worked.

African American Churches and Schools

The creation of separate African American churches proved the most lasting and important element of the energetic institution building that went on in post-emancipation years. Before the Civil War, Southern Protestant churches had relegated slaves and free African Americans to second-class membership. Black worshipers were required to sit in the back during services, they were denied any role in church governance, and they were excluded from Sunday schools. Even in larger cities, where all-black congregations sometimes built their own churches, the law required white pastors. In rural areas, slaves preferred their own preachers to the sermons of local white ministers, who quoted Scripture to justify slavery and white supremacy. "That old white preachin' wasn't nothin'," former slave Nancy Williams recalled. "Old white preachers used to talk with their tongues without sayin' nothin', but Jesus told us slaves to talk with our hearts."

In communities around the South, African Americans now pooled their resources to buy land and build their own churches. Before these structures were completed, they might hold services in a railroad boxcar, where Atlanta's First Baptist Church began, or in an outdoor arbor, the original site of the First Baptist Church of Memphis. By late 1866, Charleston's African American community could boast of eleven churches in the city—five Methodist, two Presbyterian, two Episcopalian, one Baptist, and one Congregational. In rural areas, different denominations frequently shared the same church building. Churches became the center not only for religious life, but for many other activities that defined the African American community: schools, picnics, festivals, and political meetings.

The church became the first social institution fully controlled by African Americans. In nearly every community, ministers, respected for their speaking and organizational skills, were among the most influential leaders. By 1877, the great majority of black Southerners had withdrawn from white-dominated churches. In South Carolina, for example, only a few hundred black Methodists attended biracial churches, down from over 40,000 in 1865. Black Baptist churches, with their decentralized and democratic structure and more emotional services, attracted the greatest number of freed people. By the end of Reconstruction, the vast majority of African American Christians belonged to black Baptist or Methodist churches.

The rapid spread of schools reflected African Americans' thirst for self-improvement. Southern states had prohibited education for slaves. But many free black people managed to attend school, and a few slaves had been able to educate themselves. Still, over 90 percent of the South's adult African American population was illiterate in 1860. Access to education thus became a central part of the meaning of freedom. Freedmen's Bureau agents repeatedly expressed amazement at the number of makeshift classrooms organized by African Americans in rural areas. A bureau officer described these "wayside schools": "A negro riding on a loaded wagon, or sitting on a hack waiting for a train, or by the cabin door, is often seen, book in hand delving after the rudiments of knowledge. A group on the platform of a depot,

An overflow congregation crowds into Richmond's First African Baptist Church in 1874. Despite their poverty, freed people struggled to save, buy land, and erect new buildings as they organized hundreds of new black churches during Reconstruction. As the most important African American institution outside the family, the black church, in addition to tending to spiritual needs, played a key role in the educational and political life of the community.

SOURCE: The Granger Collection.

after carefully conning an old spelling book, resolves itself into a class."

African American communities received important educational aid from outside organizations. By 1869, the Freedmen's Bureau was supervising nearly 3,000 schools serving over 150,000 students throughout the South. Over half the roughly 3,300 teachers in these schools were African Americans, many of whom had been free before the Civil War. Other teachers included dedicated Northern white women, volunteers sponsored by the American Missionary Association (AMA). The bureau and the AMA also assisted in the founding of several black colleges, including Tougaloo, Hampton, and Fisk, designed to train black teachers. Black self-help proved crucial to the education effort. Throughout the South in 1865 and 1866, African Americans raised money to build schoolhouses, buy supplies, and pay teachers. Black artisans donated labor for construction, and black families offered room and board to teachers.

Land and Labor After Slavery

Most newly emancipated African Americans aspired to quit the plantations and to make new lives for themselves. Leaving the plantation was not as simple as walking off. Some freed people did find jobs in railroad building, mining, ranching, or construction work. Others raised subsistence crops and tended vegetable gardens as squatters. White planters, however, tried to retain African Americans as permanent agricultural laborers. Restricting the employment of former slaves was an important goal of the black codes. For example, South Carolina legislation in 1865 provided that "no person of color shall pursue or practice the art, trade, or business of an artisan, mechanic, or shopkeeper, or any other

trade employment, or business, besides that of husbandry, or that of a servant under contract for service or labor" without a special and costly permit.

The majority of African Americans hoped to become self-sufficient farmers. Many former slaves believed they were entitled to the land they had worked throughout their lives. General Oliver O. Howard, chief commissioner of the Freedmen's Bureau, observed that many "supposed that the Government [would] divide among them the lands of the conquered owners, and furnish them with all that might be necessary to begin life as an independent farmer." This perception was not merely a wishful fantasy. Frequent reference in the Congress and the press to the question of land distribution made the idea of "forty acres and a mule" not just a pipe dream but a matter of serious public debate.

Above all, African Americans sought economic autonomy, and ownership of land promised the most independence. "Give us our own land and we take care of ourselves," was how one former slave saw it. "But widout land, de ole massas can hire us or starve us, as dey please." At the Colored Convention in Montgomery, Alabama, in May 1867, delegates argued that the property now owned by planters had been "nearly all earned by the sweat of our brows, not theirs. It has been forfeited to the government by the treason of its owners, and is liable to be confiscated whenever the Republican Party demands it." But by 1866, the federal government had already pulled back from the various wartime experiments involving the breaking up of large plantations and the leasing of small plots to individual families. President Johnson directed General Howard of the Freedmen's Bureau to evict tens of thousands of freed people settled on confiscated and abandoned land in southeastern Virginia, southern Louisiana, and the Georgia and South Carolina low country. These evictions created a deep sense of betrayal among African Americans. A former Mississippi slave, Merrimon Howard, bitterly noted that African Americans had been left with "no land, no house, not so much as a place to lay our head. . . . We were friends on the march, brothers on the battlefield, but in the peaceful pursuits of life it seems that we are strangers." (See Map 17.2.)

By the late 1860s, sharecropping had emerged as the dominant form of working the land. Sharecropping represented a compromise between planters and former slaves. Under sharecropping arrangements that were usually very detailed, individual families contracted with landowners to be responsible for a specific plot. Large plantations were thus broken into family-sized farms. Gen-

erally, sharecropper families received one-third of the year's crop if the owner furnished implements, seed, and draft animals, or one-half if they provided their own supplies. African Americans preferred sharecropping to gang labor, as it allowed families to set their own hours and tasks and offered freedom from white supervision and control. For planters, the system stabilized the workforce by requiring sharecroppers to remain until the harvest and to employ all family members. It also offered a way around the chronic shortage of cash and credit that plagued the postwar South. (See Out of Many Voices: "Sharecropping Contract.")

Freed people did not aspire to sharecropping. Owning land outright or tenant farming (renting land) were both more desirable. But though black sharecroppers clearly enjoyed more autonomy than in the past, the vast

MAP 17.2 The Barrow Plantation, Oglethorpe County, Georgia, 1860 and 1881 (approx. 2,000 acres) These two maps, based on drawings from *Scribner's Monthly*, April 1881, show some of the changes brought by emancipation. In 1860, the plantation's entire black population lived in the communal slave quarters, right next to the white master's house. In 1881, black sharecropper and tenant families lived on individual plots, spread out across the land. The former slaves had also built their own school and church.

OUT OF MANY VOICES

SHARECROPPING CONTRACT BETWEEN REUBEN GOULDIN AND D. KUNKLE, AUGUSTA COUNTY VIRGINIA, JANUARY 1, 1867

Among the most important and controversial activities of the Freedmen's Bureau was the effort to regulate labor relations in the post-Emancipation South. Planters and former slaves improvised a variety of sharecropping arrangements, and work contracts were often overseen by local Freedmen's Bureau agents. The following agreement was placed on file at the Freedmen's Bureau in Augusta County, Virginia, in early 1867. Note the highly detailed account of mutual obligations established for both the sharecropper and the land owner.

MEMO OF CONTRACT FOR CROPPING ON THE shares this year entered into this 1st day of January 1867 between D. Kunkle and Reuben Gouldin as follows. Gouldin is to work himself and furnish the necessary labour to put in at least say twenty-five acres each corn, wheat and oats, and cultivate the same in such fields on the place upon which he resides as Kunkle may designate and Gouldin is to take good care of and feed all the stock on the premises, to haul and chop ready for use the firewood for Kunkle, work his garden and one additional acre, in cane and potatoes or a part of each and to mend up and renew the fences in such way as Kunkle may direct, so as to secure the crops, and is to use energy and industry in carrying on the business—and Gouldin is to have one

eighth (1/8) of all the field crops raised—namely of the corn, wheat and oats, to have his house rent, garden and firewood free of charge and after the 1st of April the use of one milk cow and for any other work pertaining to the crop, done by Gouldin or his family for Kunkle or his family—Gouldin is to have a fair remuneration—to be settled up at least once each month, and it is understood they are to do all such work when called upon—Gouldin is to have one eighth of the wheat crop now in the ground and is to sow [and put in] as much and leave it should he remain but one year and he is to prepare all the crops raised for mill or market. It is further understood that should Kunkle become dissatisfied with Gouldin's way of doing business, he may at any time cancel this contract by giving Gouldin thirty days notice and paying him at the rate of twelve dollars per month for his services—in lieu of any part of the crop, provided however that should Kunkle not give such notice before the 1st day of August Gouldin shall remain the year out and receive a part of the crop as herein before provided, Kunkle to furnish the horse, seed, and all the tools necessary for carrying on the business. ■

SOURCE: Edward L. Ayers, comp., *The Valley of the Shadow: Two Communities in the American Civil War*, http://valley.vcdh.virginia.edu/, © 1993–2004.

majority never achieved economic independence or land ownership. They remained a largely subordinate agricultural labor force.

Sharecropping came to dominate the Southern agricultural economy and African American life in particular. By 1880, about 80 percent of the land in the black belt states—Mississippi, Alabama, and Georgia—had been divided into family-sized farms. Nearly three-quarters of black Southerners were sharecroppers. Often several families worked adjoining parcels of land in common, pooling their labor in order to get by. Men usually oversaw crop production. Women went to the fields seasonally during planting or harvesting, but they mainly tended to household chores and child care. In addition, women frequently held jobs that might bring in cash, such as raising chickens or taking in laundry. The cotton har-

vest engaged all members of the community, from the oldest to the youngest.

The Origins of African American Politics

Inclusion, rather than separation, was the objective of early African American political activity. The greatest political activity by African Americans occurred in areas occupied by Union forces during the war. In 1865 and 1866, African Americans throughout the South organized scores of mass meetings, parades, and petitions that demanded civil equality and the right to vote. In the cities, the growing web of churches and fraternal societies helped bolster early efforts at political organization. (See Out Many Voices: "An Address to the Loyal Citizens and Congress of the United States")

Hundreds of African American delegates, selected by local meetings or churches, attended statewide political conventions held throughout the South in 1865 and 1866. Previously free African Americans, as well as black ministers, artisans, and veterans of the Union army, tended to dominate these proceedings, setting a pattern that would hold throughout Reconstruction. Convention debates sometimes reflected the tensions within African American communities, such as friction between poorer former slaves and better-off free black people, or between lighter- and darker-skinned African Americans. But most of these state gatherings concentrated on passing resolutions on issues that united all African Americans. The central concerns were suffrage and equality before the law. As the delegates to an Alabama convention asserted in 1867: "We claim exactly the same rights, privileges and immunities as are enjoyed by white men—we ask nothing more and will be content with nothing less. . . . The law no longer knows white nor black, but simply men, and consequently we are entitled to ride in public conveyances, hold office, sit on juries and do everything else which we have in the past been prevented from doing solely on the ground of color."

The passage of the First Reconstruction Act in 1867 encouraged even more political activity among African Americans. The military started registering the South's electorate, ultimately enrolling approximately 735,000 black and 635,000 white voters in the ten unreconstructed states. Five states—Alabama, Florida, Louisiana, Mississippi, and South Carolina—had black electoral majorities. Fewer than half the registered white voters

OUT OF MANY VOICES

AN ADDRESS TO THE LOYAL CITIZENS AND CONGRESS OF THE UNITED STATES, CONVENTION OF COLORED CITIZENS, ALEXANDRIA, VIRGINIA, AUGUST 2–5, 1865

After the Civil War, thousands of recently freed slaves and free blacks took part in grassroots political meetings all over the South. The resolution excerpted below illustrates the deep concerns expressed by delegates over the lenient Reconstruction policies pursued by President Johnson. In particular, they feared the quick return to power of defeated Confederate forces, and worried that African American political rights would be quickly crushed without a Federal military presence.

WE, THE UNDERSIGNED MEMBERS OF A CONVENTION of colored citizens of the State of Virginia, would respectfully represent that, although we have been held as slaves, and denied all recognition as a constituent of your nationality for almost the entire period of the duration of your Government, and that by your permission we have been denied either home or country, and deprived of the dearest rights of human nature: yet when you and our immediate oppressors met in deadly conflict upon the field of battle—the one to destroy and the other to save your Government and nationality, we, with scarce an exception, in our inmost souls espoused your cause, and watched, and prayed, and waited, and labored for your success.

Well, the war is over, the rebellion is "put down," and we are declared free! Four fifths of our enemies are paroled or amnestied, and the other fifth are being pardoned, and the President has, in his efforts at the reconstruction of the civil government of the States, late in rebellion, left us entirely at the mercy of these subjugated but unconverted rebels, in everything save the privilege of bringing us, our wives and little ones, to the auction block.

We warn you in time that our only safety is in keeping them under Governors of the military persuasion until you have so amended the Federal Constitution that it will prohibit the States from making any distinction between citizens on account of race or color. In one word, the only salvation for us besides the power of the Government, is in the possession of the ballot. Give us this, and we will protect ourselves. We are "sheep in the midst of wolves," and nothing but the military arm of the Government prevents us and all the truly loyal white men from being driven from the land of our birth. Do not then, we beseech you, give to one of these "wayward sisters" the rights they abandoned and forfeited when they rebelled until you have secured our rights by the aforementioned amendment to the Constitution. ■

SOURCE: Paul Halsall, comp., *Internet Modern History Sourcebook*, http://www.fordham.edu/halsall/mod/modsbook27.html (halsall@fordham.edu, 1997, rev. 2001).

W. L. Sheppard, "Electioneering at the South," *Harper's Weekly*, July 25, 1868. Throughout the Reconstruction-era South, newly freed slaves took a keen interest in both local and national political affairs. The presence of women and children at these campaign gatherings illustrates the importance of contemporary political issues to the entire African American community.

SOURCE: Library of Congress.

participated in the elections for state constitutional conventions in 1867 and 1868. In contrast, four-fifths of the registered black voters cast ballots in these elections. Much of this new African American political activism was channeled through local Union League chapters throughout the South. However, as the fate of Alex Webb in Hale County, Alabama, again makes clear, few whites welcomed this activism.

Begun during the war as a Northern, largely white middle-class patriotic club, the Union League now became the political voice of the former slaves. Union League chapters brought together local African Americans, soldiers, and Freedmen's Bureau agents to demand the vote and an end to legal discrimination against African Americans. It brought out African American voters, instructed freedmen in the rights and duties of citizenship, and promoted Republican candidates. Not surprisingly, newly enfranchised freedmen voted Republican and formed the core of the Republican Party in the South. For most ordinary African Americans, politics was inseparable from economic issues, especially the land question. Grass-roots political organizations frequently intervened in local disputes with planters over the terms of labor contracts. African American political groups closely followed the congressional debates over Reconstruction policy and agitated for land confiscation and distribution. Perhaps most important, politics was the only arena where black and white Southerners might engage each other on an equal basis.

SOUTHERN POLITICS AND SOCIETY

By the summer of 1868, when the South had returned to the Union, the majority of Republicans believed the task of Reconstruction to be finished. Ultimately, they put their faith in a political solution to the problems facing the vanquished South. That meant nurturing a viable two-party system in the Southern states, where no Republican Party had ever existed. If that could be accomplished, Republicans and Democrats would compete for votes, offices, and influence, just as they did in Northern states. Most Republican congressmen were moderates, conceiving Reconstruction in limited terms. They rejected radical calls for confiscation and redistribution of land, as well as permanent military rule of the South. The Reconstruction Acts of 1867 and 1868 laid out the requirements for the readmission of Southern states, along with the procedures for forming and electing new governments.

Yet over the next decade, the political structure created in the Southern states proved too restricted and fragile to sustain itself. To most Southern whites, the active participation of African Americans in politics seemed extremely dangerous. Federal troops were needed to protect Republican governments and their supporters from violent opposition. Congressional action to monitor Southern elections and protect black voting rights became routine. Despite initial successes, Southern Republicanism proved an unstable coalition of often conflicting elements, unable to sustain effective power for very long. By 1877, Democrats had regained political control of all the former Confederate states.

Southern Republicans

Three major groups composed the fledgling Republican coalition in the postwar South. African American voters made up a large majority of Southern Republicans throughout the Reconstruction era. Yet African Americans outnumbered whites in only three Southern states; thus, Republicans would have to attract white support to win elections and sustain power.

A second group consisted of white Northerners, derisively called "carpetbaggers" by native white Southerners. Most carpetbaggers combined a desire for personal gain with a commitment to reform the "unprogressive" South by developing its material resources and introducing Yankee institutions, such as free labor and free public schools. Most were veterans of the Union army who stayed in the South after the war. Others included Freedmen's Bureau agents and businessmen who had invested capital in cotton plantations and other enterprises.

Carpetbaggers tended to be well educated and from the middle class. Albert Morgan, for example, was an army veteran from Ohio who settled in Mississippi after the war.

When he and his brother failed at running a cotton plantation and sawmill, Morgan became active in Republican politics as a way to earn a living. He won election to the state constitutional convention, became a power in the state legislature, and risked his life to keep the Republican organization alive in the Mississippi Delta region. Although they made up a tiny percentage of the population, carpetbaggers played a disproportionately large role in Southern politics. They won a large share of Reconstruction offices, particularly in Florida, South Carolina, and Louisiana and in areas with large African American constituencies.

The third major group of Southern Republicans were the native whites pejoratively termed "scalawags." They had even more diverse backgrounds and motives than the Northern-born Republicans. Some were prominent prewar Whigs who saw the Republican Party as their best chance to regain political influence. Others viewed the party as an agent of modernization and economic expansion. "Yankees and Yankee notions are just what we want in this country," argued Thomas Settle of North Carolina. "We want their capital to build factories and workshops. We want their intelligence, their energy and enterprise." Loyalists during the war and traditional enemies of the planter elite (most were small farmers), these white Southerners looked to the Republican Party for help in settling old scores and relief from debt and wartime devastation.

Yet few white Southerners identified with the political and economic aspirations of African Americans. Moderate elements more concerned with maintaining white control of the party, and encouraging economic investment in the region, outnumbered and defeated "confiscation radicals" who focused on obtaining land for African Americans.

Reconstructing the States: A Mixed Record

With the old Confederate leaders barred from political participation, and with carpetbaggers and newly enfranchised African Americans representing many of the plantation districts, Republicans managed to dominate the ten Southern constitutional conventions of 1867–69.

Most of the conventions produced constitutions that expanded democracy and the public role of the state. The new documents guaranteed the political and civil rights of African Americans, and they abolished property qualifications for officeholding and jury service, as well as imprisonment for debt. They created the first state-funded systems of education in the South, to be administered by state commissioners. The new constitutions also mandated establishment of orphanages, penitentiaries, and homes for the insane. The changes wrought in the South's political landscape seemed quite radical to many. In 1868, only three years after the end of the war, Republicans came to power in most of the Southern states. By 1869, new constitutions had been ratified in all the old Confederate states. "These constitutions and governments," one South Carolina

Democratic newspaper vowed bitterly, "will last just as long as the bayonets which ushered them into being, shall keep them in existence, and not one day longer."

Republican governments in the South faced a continual crisis of legitimacy that limited their ability to legislate change. They had to balance reform against the need to gain acceptance, especially by white Southerners. Their achievements were thus mixed. In the realm of race relations there was a clear thrust toward equal rights and against discrimination. Republican legislatures followed up the federal Civil Rights Act of 1866 with various antidiscrimination clauses in new constitutions and laws prescribing harsh penalties for civil rights violations. While most African Americans supported autonomous African American churches, fraternal societies, and schools, they insisted that the state be "color-blind." African Americans could now be employed in police forces and fire departments, serve on juries, school boards, and city councils, and they could hold public office at all levels of government.

Segregation, though, became the norm in public school systems. African American leaders often accepted segregation because they feared that insistence on integrated education would jeopardize funding for the new school systems. They generally agreed with Frederick Douglass that separate schools were "infinitely superior" to no schools at all. So while they opposed constitutional language requiring racial segregation in schools, most African Americans were less interested in the abstract ideal of integrated education than in ensuring educational opportunities for their children and employment for African American teachers.

Demands by African Americans to prohibit segregation in railroad cars, steamboats, theaters, and other public spaces revealed and heightened the divisions within the Republican Party. Moderate white Republicans feared such laws would only further alienate potential white supporters. But by the early 1870s, as black influence and assertiveness grew, laws guaranteeing equal access to transportation and public accommodation were passed in many states. By and large, though, such civil rights laws were difficult to enforce in local communities.

In economic matters, Republican governments failed to fulfill African Americans' hopes of obtaining land. Few former slaves possessed the cash to buy land in the open market, and they looked to the state for help. Republicans tried to weaken the plantation system and promote black ownership by raising taxes on land. Yet, even when state governments seized land for nonpayment of taxes, the property was never used to help create black homesteads. In Mississippi, for example, 6 million acres, or about 20 percent of the land, had been forfeited by 1875. Yet virtually all of it found its way back to the original owners after they paid minimal penalties.

Republican leaders envisioned promoting Northern-style capitalist development—factories, large towns, and diversified agriculture—through state aid. Much Republican state lawmaking was devoted to encouraging railroad construction. This government backing gave railroad companies credibility and helped them raise capital. In exchange, states received liens on railroads as security against defaults on payments to bondholders.

Between 1868 and 1872, the Southern railroad system was rebuilt and over 3,000 new miles of track added, an increase of almost 40 percent. But in spite of all the new laws, it proved impossible to attract significant amounts of Northern and European investment capital. The obsession with railroads withdrew resources from education and other programs. As in the North, it also opened the doors to widespread corruption and bribery of public officials. Railroad failures eroded public confidence in the Republicans' ability to govern. The "gospel of prosperity" ultimately failed to modernize the economy or solidify the Republican Party in the South.

White Resistance and "Redemption"

The emergence of a Republican Party in the reconstructed South brought two parties, but not a two-party system, to the region. The opponents of Reconstruction, the Democrats, refused to acknowledge Republicans' right to participate in Southern political life. In their view, the Republican Party, supported primarily by the votes of former slaves, was the partisan instrument of the Northern Congress. Since Republicans controlled state governments, this denial of legitimacy meant, in effect, a rejection of state authority itself. In each state, Republicans were split between those who urged conciliation in an effort to gain white acceptance and those who emphasized consolidating the party under the protection of the military.

From 1870 to 1872, the Ku Klux Klan fought an ongoing terrorist campaign against Reconstruction governments and local leaders. Although not centrally organized, the Klan was a powerful presence in nearly every Southern state. It acted as a kind of guerrilla military force in the service of the Democratic Party, the planter class, and all those who sought the restoration of white supremacy. Planters sometimes employed Klansmen to enforce labor discipline by driving African Americans off plantations to deprive them of their harvest share.

In October 1870, after Republicans carried Laurens County in South Carolina, bands of white people drove 150 African Americans from their homes and murdered 13 black and white Republican activists. In March 1871, three African Americans were arrested in Meridian, Mississippi, for giving "incendiary" speeches. At their court hearing, Klansmen killed two of the defendants and the Republican judge, and thirty more African Americans were murdered in a day of rioting. The single bloodiest episode of Reconstruction era violence took place in Colfax, Louisiana, on Easter Sunday 1873. Nearly 100 African Americans were murdered after they failed to hold a besieged courthouse during a contested election.

Southern Republicans looked to Washington for help. In 1870 and 1871, Congress passed three Enforcement Acts designed to counter racial terrorism. These declared that interference with voting was a federal offense. The acts provided for federal supervision of voting, and authorized the president to send the army and to suspend the writ of habeas corpus in districts declared to be in a state of insurrection. The most sweeping measure was the Ku Klux Klan Act of April 1871, which made the violent infringement of civil and political rights a federal crime punishable by the national government. Attorney General Amos T. Akerman prosecuted hundreds of Klansmen in North Carolina and Mississippi. In October 1871, President Grant sent federal troops to occupy nine South Carolina counties; they rounded up thousands of Klan members. By the election of 1872, the federal government's intervention had helped break the Klan and restore a semblance of law and order.

The Civil Rights Act of 1875 outlawed racial discrimination in theaters, hotels, railroads, and other public places. But the law proved more an assertion of principle than a direct federal intervention in Southern affairs. Enforcement required African Americans to take their cases to the federal courts, a costly and time-consuming procedure.

As wartime idealism faded, Northern Republicans became less inclined toward direct intervention in Southern affairs. They had enough trouble retaining political control in the North. In 1874, the Democrats gained a majority in the House of Representatives for the first time since 1856. Key Northern states also began to fall to the Democrats. Northern Republicans slowly abandoned the freedmen and their white allies in the South. Southern Democrats were also able to exploit a deepening fiscal crisis by blaming Republicans for excessive extension of public credit and the sharp increase in tax rates. Republican governments had indeed spent public money for new state school systems, orphanages, roads, and other internal improvements.

Gradually, conservative Democrats "redeemed" one state after another. Virginia and Tennessee led the way in 1869, North Carolina in 1870, Georgia in 1871, Texas in 1873, and Alabama and Arkansas in 1874. In Mississippi, white conservatives employed violence and intimidation to wrest control in 1875 and "redeemed" the state the following year. Republican infighting in Louisiana in 1873 and 1874 led to a series of contested election results, including bloody clashes between black militia and armed whites, and finally to "redemption" by the Democrats in 1877. Once these states returned to Democratic rule, African Americans faced obstacles to voting, more stringent controls on plantation labor, and deep cuts in social services.

Several Supreme Court rulings involving the Fourteenth and Fifteenth Amendments effectively constrained federal protection of African American civil rights. In the

The Ku Klux Klan emerged as a potent political and social force during Reconstruction, terrorizing freed people and their white allies. An 1868 Klan warning threatens Louisiana governor Henry C. Warmoth with death. Warmoth, an Illinois-born "carpetbagger," was the state's first Republican governor. Two Alabama Klansmen, photographed in 1868, wear white hoods to hide their identities.

SOURCE: (a) From The Henry Clay Warmoth Papers # 752, Southern Historical Collection, Wilson Library, University of North Carolina at Chapel Hill; (b) Rutherford B. Hayes Presidential Center.

so-called Slaughterhouse cases of 1873, the Court issued its first ruling on the Fourteenth Amendment. The cases involved a Louisiana charter that gave a New Orleans meat-packing company a monopoly over the city's butchering business on the grounds of protecting public health. A rival group of butchers had sued, claiming the law violated the Fourteenth Amendment, which prohibited states from depriving any person of life, liberty, or property without due process of law. The Court held that the Fourteenth Amendment protected only the former slaves, not butchers, and that it protected only national citizenship rights, not the regulatory powers of states. The ruling in effect denied the original intent of the Fourteenth Amendment— to protect against state infringement of national citizenship rights as spelled out in the Bill of Rights.

Three other decisions curtailed federal protection of black civil rights. In *United States* v. *Reese* (1876) and *United*

States v. *Cruikshank* (1876), the Court restricted congressional power to enforce the Ku Klux Klan Act. Future prosecution would depend on the states, rather than on federal authorities. In these rulings, the Court held that the Fourteenth Amendment extended the federal power to protect civil rights only in cases involving discrimination by states; discrimination by individuals or groups was not covered. The Court also ruled that the Fifteenth Amendment did not guarantee a citizen's right to vote; it only barred certain specific grounds for denying suffrage— "race, color, or previous condition of servitude." This interpretation opened the door for Southern states to disfranchise African Americans for allegedly nonracial reasons. States back under Democratic control began to limit African American voting by passing laws restricting voter eligibility through poll taxes and property requirements.

Finally, in the 1883 Civil Rights Cases decision, the Court declared the Civil Rights Act of 1875 unconstitutional, holding that the Fourteenth Amendment gave Congress the power to outlaw discrimination by states, but not by private individuals. The majority opinion held that black people must no longer "be the special favorite of the laws." Together, these Supreme Court decisions marked the end of federal attempts to protect African American rights until well into the next century.

White Yeomen, White Merchants, and "King Cotton"

The Republicans' vision of a "New South" remade along the lines of the Northern economy failed to materialize. Instead, the South declined into the country's poorest agricultural region. Unlike Midwestern and Western farm towns burgeoning from trade in wheat, corn, and live-stock, Southern communities found themselves almost entirely dependent on the price of one commodity. In the post–Civil War years, "King Cotton" expanded its realm, as greater numbers of small white farmers found themselves forced to switch from subsistence crops to growing cotton for the market (see Map 17.3).

A chronic shortage of capital and banking institutions made local merchants and planters the sole source of credit. They advanced loans and supplies to small owners, tenant farmers, and sharecroppers in exchange for a lien, or claim, on the year's cotton crop. They often charged usurious interest rates on advances, while marking up the prices of the goods sold in their stores. Taking advantage of the high illiteracy rates among poor Southerners, landlords and merchants easily altered their books to inflate the figures. At the end of the year, share-croppers and tenants found themselves deep in debt to stores for seed, supplies, and clothing. Despite hard work and even bountiful harvests, few small farmers could escape from heavy debt.

MAP EXPLORATION

To explore an interactive version of this map, go to **www.prenhall.com/faragher/map17.3**

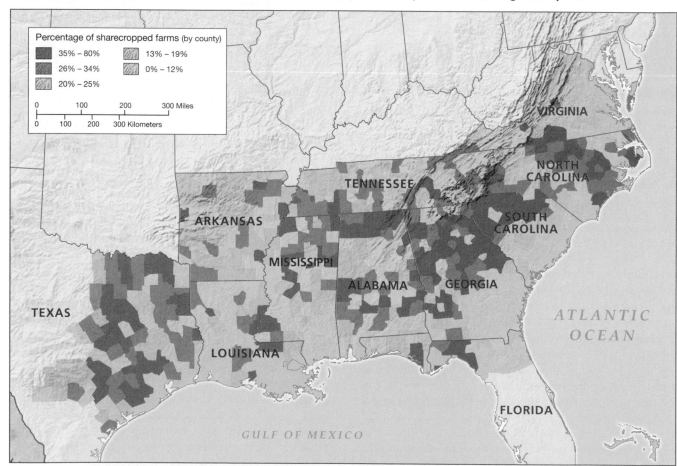

MAP 17.3 Southern Sharecropping and the Cotton Belt, 1880 The economic depression of the 1870s forced increasing numbers of Southern farmers, both white and black, into sharecropping arrangements. Sharecropping was most pervasive in the cotton belt regions of South Carolina, Georgia, Alabama, Mississippi, and east Texas.

The spread of the "crop lien" system as the South's main form of agricultural credit forced more and more farmers into cotton growing. The transition to cotton dependency developed unevenly, at different speeds in different parts of the South. Penetration by railroads, the availability of commercial fertilizers, and the opening up of new lands to cultivation were key factors in transforming communities from diversified, locally oriented farming to the market-oriented production of cotton.

The pent-up demand for cotton following the war brought high prices (as much as 43 cents per pound) through the late 1860s. But as the "crop lien" system spread, and as more and more farmers turned to cotton growing as the only way to obtain credit, expanding production depressed prices. Competition from new cotton centers in the world market, such as Egypt and India, accelerated the downward spiral. As cotton prices declined alarmingly, to roughly 11 cents per pound in 1875 to 5 cents by the early 1890s, per capita wealth in the South fell steadily, equaling only one-third that of the East, Midwest, or West by the 1890s. Small farmers caught up in a vicious cycle of low cotton prices, debt, and dwindling food crops found their old ideal of independence sacrificed to the cruel logic of the cotton market.

By 1880, nearly 40 percent of all Southern farms were operated by tenants and sharecroppers. About one-third of the white farmers and nearly three-quarters of the African American farmers in the cotton states were sharecroppers or tenants. To obtain precious credit, most found themselves forced to produce cotton for market, and thus became enmeshed in the debt-ridden crop lien system. In traditional cotton producing areas, especially the black belt, landless farmers growing cotton had replaced slaves growing cotton. In the upcountry and newer areas of cultivation, cotton-dominated commercial agriculture, with landless tenants and sharecroppers as the main workforce, had replaced the more diversified subsistence economy of the antebellum era.

One class of white Southerners benefiting from these arrangements were local merchants. As hundreds of new villages (communities of less than 2,500 people) sprang up in every corner of the South, especially in the new upcountry and Piedmont settlements, local merchants provided both goods and credit for local farmers. With their power based on control of credit and marketing, merchants emerged as a new economic elite unconnected to the antebellum planters whose power had rested on the ownership of land and slaves. But within both the new towns and the old planter elite, white families increasingly defined their social position by celebrating a certain type of ideal household. Women found meaning in their role as upholders of domestic virtue by creating a comfortable home environment and tending to the needs of children and husbands. Men were to be of strong moral fiber and to provide material support

for the family. These elite ideals, articulated in magazines, schools, sermons, and other public discourse, rested on a belief that one's ability to reach the standards of womanhood and manhood rested solely upon moral character and individual choice.

RECONSTRUCTING THE NORTH

Abraham Lincoln liked to cite his own rise as proof of the superiority of the Northern system of "free labor" over slavery. "There is no permanent class of hired laborers amongst us," Lincoln asserted. "Twenty-five years ago, I was a hired laborer. The hired laborer of yesterday, labors on his own account today; and will hire others to labor for him tomorrow. Advancement—improvement in condition— is the order of things in a society of equals." But the triumph of the North brought with it fundamental changes in the economy, labor relations, and politics that brought Lincoln's ideal vision into question. The spread of the factory system, the growth of large and powerful corporations, and the rapid expansion of capitalist enterprise all hastened the development of a large unskilled and routinized workforce. Rather than becoming independent producers, more and more workers found themselves consigned permanently to wage labor.

The old Republican ideal of a society bound by a harmony of interests had become overshadowed by a grimmer reality of class conflict. A violent national railroad strike in 1877 was broken only with the direct intervention of federal troops. That conflict struck many Americans as a turning point. Northern society, like the society of the South, appeared more hierarchical than equal. That same year, the last federal troops withdrew from their Southern posts, marking the end of the Reconstruction Era. By then, the North had undergone its own "reconstruction" as well.

The Age of Capital

In the decade following Appomattox, the North's economy continued the industrial boom begun during the Civil War. By 1873, America's industrial production had grown 75 percent over the 1865 level. By that time, too, the number of nonagricultural workers in the North had surpassed the number of farmers. Between 1860 and 1880, the number of wage earners in manufacturing and construction more than doubled, from 2 million to over 4 million. Only Great Britain boasted a larger manufacturing economy than the United States. During the same period, nearly 3 million immigrants arrived in America, almost all of whom settled in the North and West.

The railroad business both symbolized and advanced the new industrial order. Shortly before the Civil War, enthusiasm mounted for a transcontinental line. Private companies took on the huge and expensive job of construction, but the federal government funded the project, providing the largest subsidy in American history. The Pacific Railway Act of 1862 granted the Union Pacific and the Central Pacific rights to a broad swath of land extending from Omaha, Nebraska, to Sacramento, California. An 1864 act bestowed a subsidy of $15,000 per mile of track laid over smooth plains country and varying larger amounts up to $48,000 per mile in the foothills and mountains of the Far West. The Union Pacific employed gangs of Irish American and African American workers to lay track heading west from Omaha.

Meanwhile the Central Pacific, pushing east from California, had a tougher time finding workers, and began recruiting thousands of men from China. In 1868, the Senate ratified the Burlingame Treaty, giving Chinese the right to emigrate to the U.S., while specifiying that "nothing contained herein shall be held to confer naturalization." The right to work in America, in other words, did not bestow any right to citizenship. Some 12,000 Chinese laborers (about 90 percent of the workforce) bore the brunt of the difficult conditions in the Sierra Nevada mountains, where blizzards, landslides, and steep rock faces took an awful toll. Chinese workers earned a reputation for toughness and efficiency. "If we found we were in a hurry for a job of work," wrote one of the Central Pacific's superintendents, "it was better to put on Chinese at once". Working in baskets suspended by ropes, Chinese laborers chipped away at solid granite walls and became expert in the use of nitroglycerin for blasting through the mountains. But after completion of the transcontinental line threw thousands of Chinese railroad workers onto the California labor market, the open door immigration pledge in the Burlingame Treaty would soon be eclipsed by a virulent tide of anti-Chinese agitation among Western politicians and labor unions. In 1882, Congress passed the Chinese Exclusion Act, suspending any further Chinese immigration for ten years.

On May 10, 1869, Leland Stanford, the former governor of California and president of the Central Pacific Railroad, traveled to Promontory Point in Utah Territory to hammer a ceremonial golden spike, marking the finish of the first transcontinental line. Other railroads went up with less fanfare. The Southern Pacific, chartered by the state of California, stretched from San Francisco to Los Angeles, and on through Arizona and New Mexico to connections with New Orleans. The Atchison, Topeka, and Santa Fe reached the Pacific in 1887 by way of a southerly route across the Rocky Mountains. The Great Northern, one of the few lines financed by private capital, extended west from St. Paul, Minnesota, to Washington's Puget Sound.

Railroad corporations became America's first big businesses. Railroads required huge outlays of investment capital, and their growth increased the economic power of banks and investment houses centered in Wall Street. Bankers often gained seats on the boards of directors of these railroad companies, and their access to capital sometimes gave them the real control of railways. By the early 1870s the Pennsylvania Railroad stood as the nation's largest single company, with more than 20,000 employees. A new breed of aggressive entrepreneur sought to ease cutthroat competition by absorbing smaller companies and forming "pools" that set rates and divided the market. A small group of railroad executives, including Cornelius Vanderbilt, Jay Gould, Collis P. Huntington, and James J. Hill, amassed unheard-of fortunes. When he died in 1877, Vanderbilt

Chinese immigrants, like these section gang workers, provided labor and skills critical to the successful completion of the first transcontinental railroad. This photo was taken in Promontory, Utah Territory, in 1869.

SOURCE: The Denver Public Library, Western History Collection.

left his son $100 million. By comparison, a decent annual wage for working a six-day week was around $350.

Railroad promoters, lawyers, and lobbyists became ubiquitous figures in Washington and state capitals, wielding enormous influence among lawmakers. "The galleries and lobbies of every legislature," one Republican leader noted, "are thronged with men seeking . . . an advantage." Railroads benefited enormously from government subsidies. Between 1862 and 1872, Congress alone awarded more than 100 million acres of public lands to railroad companies and provided them over $64 million in loans and tax incentives.

Some of the nation's most prominent politicians routinely accepted railroad largesse. Republican senator William M. Stewart of Nevada, a member of the Committee on Pacific Railroads, received a gift of 50,000 acres of land from the Central Pacific for his services. The worst scandal of the Grant administration grew out of corruption involving railroad promotion. As a way of diverting funds for the building of the Union Pacific Railroad, an inner circle of Union Pacific stockholders created the dummy Crédit Mobilier construction company. In return for political favors, a group of prominent Republicans received stock in the company. When the scandal broke in 1872, it politically ruined Vice President Schuyler Colfax and led to the censure of two congressmen.

Other industries also boomed in this period, especially those engaged in extracting minerals and processing natural resources. Railroad growth stimulated expansion in the production of coal, iron, stone, and lumber, and these also received significant government aid. For example, under the National Mineral Act of 1866, mining companies received millions of acres of free public land. Oil refining enjoyed a huge expansion in the 1860s and 1870s. As with railroads, an early period of fierce competition soon gave way to concentration. By the late 1870s, John D. Rockefeller's Standard Oil Company controlled almost 90 percent of the nation's oil-refining capacity.

Liberal Republicans and the Election of 1872

With the rapid growth of large-scale, capital-intensive enterprises, Republicans increasingly identified with the interests of business rather than the rights of freedmen or the antebellum ideology of "free labor." The old Civil War–era Radical Republicans had declined in influence. State Republican parties now organized themselves around the spoils of federal patronage rather than grand causes such as preserving the Union or ending slavery. Despite the Crédit Mobilier affair, Republicans had no monopoly on political scandal. In 1871, New York City newspapers reported the shocking story of how Democratic Party boss William M. Tweed and his friends had systematically stolen tens of millions from the city treasury. The "Tweed Ring" had received enormous bribes and kickbacks from city

contractors and businessmen. Grotesquely caricatured by Thomas Nast's cartoons in *Harper's Weekly*, Tweed emerged as the preeminent national symbol of increasingly degraded and dishonest urban politics. But to many, the scandal represented only the most extreme case of the routine corruption that now plagued American political life.

By the end of President Grant's first term, a large number of disaffected Republicans sought an alternative. The Liberal Republicans, as they called themselves, shared several core values. First, they emphasized the doctrines of classical economics, stressing the law of supply and demand, free trade, defense of property rights, and individualism. They called for a return to limited government, arguing that bribery, scandal, and high taxes all flowed from excessive state interference in the economy.

Liberal Republicans were also suspicious of expanding democracy. "Universal suffrage," Charles Francis Adams Jr. wrote in 1869, "can only mean in plain English the government of ignorance and vice—it means a European, and especially Celtic, proletariat on the Atlantic coast, an African proletariat on the shores of the Gulf, and a Chinese proletariat on the Pacific." Liberal Republicans believed that politics ought to be the province of "the best men"—educated and well-to-do men like themselves, devoted to the "science of government." They proposed civil service reform as the best way to break the hold of party machines on patronage.

Although most Liberal Republicans had enthusiastically supported abolition, the Union cause, and equal rights for freedmen, they now opposed continued federal intervention in the South. The national government had done all it could for the former slaves; they must now take care of themselves. "Root, Hog, or Die" was the harsh advice offered by Horace Greeley, editor of the *New York Tribune*. In the spring of 1872, a diverse collection of Liberal Republicans nominated Greeley to run for president. A longtime foe of the Democratic Party, Greeley nonetheless won that party's presidential nomination as well. He made a new policy for the South the center of his campaign against Grant. The "best men" of both sections, he argued, should support a more generous Reconstruction policy based on "universal amnesty and impartial suffrage." All Americans, Greeley urged, must put the Civil War behind them and "clasp hands across the bloody chasm."

Grant easily defeated Greeley, carrying every state in the North and winning 56 percent of the popular vote. Most Republicans were not willing to abandon the regular party organization, and "waving the bloody shirt" was still a potent vote-getter. But the 1872 election accelerated the trend toward federal abandonment of African American citizenship rights. The Liberal Republicans quickly faded as an organized political force. But their ideas helped define a growing conservative consciousness among the Northern public. For the rest of the century, their political and economic views attracted a growing number of middle-class professionals and businessmen. This agenda included retreat from the ideal of racial justice, hostility toward trade unions, suspicion of working-class and immigrant political power, celebration of competitive individualism, and opposition to government intervention in economic affairs.

The Depression of 1873

In the fall of 1873, the postwar boom came to an abrupt halt as a severe financial panic triggered a deep economic depression. The collapse resulted from commercial overexpansion, especially, speculative investing in the nation's railroad system. The investment banking house of Jay Cooke and Company failed in September 1873, when it found itself unable to market millions of dollars in Northern Pacific Railroad bonds. Soon, other banks and brokerage houses, especially those dealing in railroad securities, caved in as well, and the New York Stock Exchange suspended operations. By 1876, half the nation's railroads had defaulted on their bonds. Over the next two years, more than 100 banks folded and 18,000 businesses shut their doors. The depression that began in 1873 lasted sixty-five months—the longest economic contraction in the nation's history until then.

The human toll of the depression was enormous. As factories began to close across the nation, the unemployment rate soared to about 15 percent. In many cities, the jobless rate was much higher; roughly one-quarter of New York City workers were unemployed in 1874. Many thousands of men took to the road in search of work, and the "tramp" emerged as a new and menacing figure on the social landscape. The Pennsylvania Bureau of Labor Statistics noted that never before had "so many of the working classes, skilled and unskilled . . . been moving from place to place seeking employment that was not to be had." Farmers were also hard hit by the depression. Agricultural output continued to grow, but prices and land values fell sharply.

Mass meetings of workers in New York and other cities issued calls to government officials to create jobs through public works. But these appeals were rejected. Indeed, many business leaders and political figures denounced even meager efforts at charity. E. L. Godkin wrote in the Christmas 1875 issue of *The Nation* that "free soup must be prohibited, and all classes must learn that soup of any kind, beef or turtle, can be had only by being paid for." Men such as Godkin saw the depression as a natural, if painful, part of the business cycle, one that would allow only the strongest enterprises (and workers) to survive. They dismissed any attempts at government interference, in the form of either job creation or relief for the poor.

The depression of the 1870s prompted many workers and farmers to question the old free-labor ideology that celebrated a harmony of interests in Northern society. More people voiced anger at and distrust of large corporations that exercised great economic power from outside their communities. Businessmen and merchants, meanwhile, especially in large cities, became more conscious of their own class interests. New political organizations, such as Chicago's Citizens' Association, united businessmen in campaigns for fiscal conservatism and defense of property rights. In national politics, the persistent depression made the Republican Party, North and South, more vulnerable than ever.

"The Tramp," *Harper's Weekly*, September 2, 1876. The depression that began in 1873 forced many thousands of unemployed workers to go "on the tramp" in search of jobs. Men wandered from town to town, walking or riding railroad cars, desperate for a chance to work for wages or simply for room and board. The "tramp" became a powerful symbol of the misery caused by industrial depression and, as in this drawing, an image that evoked fear and nervousness among the nation's middle class.

SOURCE: The Picture Bank, Frank & Marie-Therese Wood Print Collection.

The Electoral Crisis of 1876

With the economy mired in depression, Democrats looked forward to capturing the White House in 1876.

New scandals plaguing the Grant administration also weakened the Republican Party. In 1875, a conspiracy surfaced between distillers and U.S. revenue agents to cheat the government out of millions in tax revenues. The government secured indictments against more than 200 members of this "Whiskey Ring," including Orville E. Babcock, Grant's private secretary. Though acquitted, thanks to Grant's intervention, Babcock resigned in disgrace. In 1876, Secretary of War William W. Belknap was impeached for receiving bribes for the sale of trading posts in Indian Territory, and he resigned to avoid conviction (see Map 17.4).

Democrats hammered away at the Grant administration's low standard of honesty in government, and for president, they nominated Governor Samuel J. Tilden of New York, who brought impeccable reform credentials to his candidacy. In 1871, he had helped expose and prosecute the "Tweed Ring" in New York City. As governor, he had toppled the "Canal Ring," a graft-ridden scheme involving inflated contracts for repairs on the Erie Canal. In their platform, the Democrats linked the issue of corruption to an attack on Reconstruction policies. They blamed the Republicans for instituting "a corrupt centralism" that subjected Southern states to "the rapacity of carpetbag tyrannies," riddled the national government "with incapacity, waste, and fraud," and "locked fast the prosperity of an industrious people in the paralysis of hard times."

Republican nominee Rutherford B. Hayes, governor of Ohio, also sought the high ground. As a lawyer in Cincinnati, he had defended runaway slaves. Later, he had distinguished himself as a general in the Union army. Republicans charged Tilden with disloyalty during the war, income tax evasion, and close relations with powerful railroad interests. Hayes promised, if elected, to support an efficient civil service system, to vigorously prosecute officials who betrayed the public trust, and to introduce a system of free universal education.

On an election day marred by widespread vote fraud and violent intimidation, Tilden received 250,000 more popular votes than Hayes. But Republicans refused to concede victory, challenging the vote totals in the electoral college. Tilden garnered 184 uncontested electoral votes, one shy of the majority required to win, while Hayes received 165. The problem centered in 20 disputed votes from Florida, Louisiana, South Carolina, and Oregon. In each of the three Southern states two sets of electoral votes were returned. In Oregon, which Hayes had unquestionably carried, the Democratic governor nevertheless replaced a disputed Republican elector with a Democrat.

The crisis was unprecedented. In January 1877, Congress moved to settle the deadlock, establishing an Electoral Commission composed of five senators, five representatives, and five Supreme Court justices; eight were Republicans and seven were Democrats. The commission voted along strict partisan lines to award all the contested electoral votes to Hayes. Outraged by this

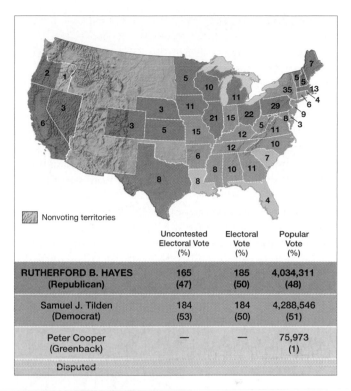

	Uncontested Electoral Vote (%)	Electoral Vote (%)	Popular Vote (%)
RUTHERFORD B. HAYES (Republican)	165 (47)	185 (50)	4,034,311 (48)
Samuel J. Tilden (Democrat)	184 (53)	184 (50)	4,288,546 (51)
Peter Cooper (Greenback)	—	—	75,973 (1)
Disputed			

Nonvoting territories

MAP 17.4 The Election of 1876 The presidential election of 1876 left the nation without a clear-cut winner.

decision, Democratic congressmen threatened a filibuster to block Hayes's inauguration. Violence and stalemate were avoided when Democrats and Republicans struck a compromise in February. In return for Hayes's ascendance to the presidency, the Republicans promised to appropriate more money for Southern internal improvements, to appoint a Southerner to Hayes's cabinet, and to pursue a policy of noninterference ("home rule") in Southern affairs.

Shortly after assuming office, Hayes ordered removal of the remaining federal troops in Louisiana and South Carolina. Without this military presence to sustain them, the Republican governors of those two states quickly lost power to Democrats. "Home rule" meant Republican abandonment of freed people, Radicals, carpetbaggers, and scalawags. It also effectively nullified the Fourteenth and Fifteenth Amendments and the Civil Rights Act of 1866. The "Compromise of 1877" completed repudiation of the idea, born during the Civil War and pursued during Congressional Reconstruction, of a powerful federal government protecting the rights of all American citizens. As one black Louisianan lamented, "The whole South—every state in the South—had got into the hands of the very men that held us slaves." Other voices hailed this turning point in policy. "The negro," declared *The Nation*, "will disappear from the field of national politics. Henceforth, the nation, as a nation, will have nothing more to do with him."

CONCLUSION

Reconstruction succeeded in the limited political sense of reuniting a nation torn apart by the Civil War. The Radical Republican vision, emphasizing racial justice, equal civil and political rights guaranteed by the Fourteenth and Fifteenth Amendments, and a new Southern economy organized around independent small farmers, never enjoyed the support of the majority of its party or the Northern public. By 1877, the political force of these ideals was spent, and the national retreat from them nearly complete.

The end of Reconstruction left the way open for the return of white domination in the South. The freed people's political and civil equality proved only temporary. It would take a "Second Reconstruction," the civil rights movement of the next century, to establish full black citizenship rights once and for all.

The federal government's failure to pursue land reform left former slaves without the economic independence needed for full emancipation. Yet the newly autonomous black family, along with black-controlled churches, schools, and other social institutions, provided the foundations for the modern African American community. If the federal government was not yet fully committed to protecting equal rights in local communities, the Reconstruction Era at least pointed to how that goal might be achieved. Even as the federal government retreated from the defense of equal rights for black people, it took a more aggressive stance as the protector of business interests. The Hayes administration responded decisively to one of the worst outbreaks of class violence in American history by dispatching federal troops to several Northern cities to break the Great Railroad Strike of 1877. In the aftermath of Reconstruction, the struggle

CHRONOLOGY

1865	Freedmen's Bureau established
	Abraham Lincoln assassinated
	Andrew Johnson begins Presidential Reconstruction
	Black codes begin to be enacted in Southern states
	Thirteenth Amendment ratified
1866	Civil Rights Act passed
	Congress approves Fourteenth Amendment
	Ku Klux Klan founded
1867	Reconstruction Acts, passed over President Johnson's veto, begin Congressional Reconstruction
	Tenure of Office Act
	Southern states call constitutional conventions
1868	President Johnson impeached by the House, but acquitted in Senate trial
	Fourteenth Amendment ratified
	Most Southern states readmitted to the Union
	Ulysses S. Grant elected president
1869	Congress approves Fifteenth Amendment
	Union Pacific and Central Pacific tracks meet at Promontory Point in Utah Territory
	Suffragists split into National Woman Suffrage Association and American Woman Suffrage Association
1870	Fifteenth Amendment ratified
1871	Ku Klux Klan Act passed
	"Tweed Ring" in New York City exposed
1872	Liberal Republicans break with Grant and Radicals, nominate Horace Greeley for president
	Crédit Mobilier scandal
	Grant reelected president
1873	Financial panic and beginning of economic depression
	Slaughterhouse cases
1874	Democrats gain control of House for first time since 1856
1875	Civil Rights Act
1876	Disputed election between Samuel Tilden and Rutherford B. Hayes
1877	Electoral Commission elects Hayes president
	President Hayes dispatches federal troops to break Great Railroad Strike and withdraws last remaining federal troops from the South

between capital and labor had clearly replaced "the Southern question" as the number one political issue of the day. "The overwhelming labor question has dwarfed all other questions into nothing," wrote an Ohio Republican. "We have home questions enough to occupy attention now."

REVIEW QUESTIONS

1. How did various visions of a "reconstructed" South differ? How did these visions reflect the old political and social divisions that had led to the Civil War?
2. What key changes did emancipation make in the political and economic status of African Americans? Discuss the expansion of citizenship rights in the post–Civil War years. To what extent did women share in the gains made by African Americans?
3. What role did such institutions as the family, the church, the schools, and the political parties play in the African American transition to freedom?
4. How did white Southerners attempt to limit the freedom of former slaves? How did these efforts succeed, and how did they fail?
5. Evaluate the achievements and failures of Reconstruction governments in the Southern states.
6. What were the crucial economic changes occurring in the North and South during the Reconstruction era?

RECOMMENDED READING

David W. Blight, *Race and Reunion: The Civil War in American Memory* (2001). An elegantly written and deeply researched inquiry into how Americans "remembered" the Civil War in the half century after Appomattox, arguing that sectional reconciliation came at the cost of racial division.

Paul A. Cimbala and Randall M. Miller, eds., *The Freedmen's Bureau and Reconstruction* (1999). A wide ranging collection of the latest scholarship, with special attention to recapturing the historical voices of freed people.

Jane Dailey, *Before Jim Crow: The Politics of Race in Postemancipation Virginia* (2000). A fine study that focuses on the tension between the drive to establish white supremacy and the struggle for biracial coalitions in post–Civil War Virginia politics.

Laura F. Edwards, *Gendered Strife & Confusion: The Political Culture of Reconstruction* (1997). An ambitious analysis of how gender ideologies played a key role in shaping the party politics and social relations of the Reconstruction-Era South.

Michael W. Fitzgerald, *The Union League Movement in the Deep South* (1989). Uses the Union League as a lens through which to examine race relations and the close connections between politics and economic change in the post–Civil War South.

Eric Foner, *Reconstruction: America's Unfinished Revolution, 1863–1877* (1988). The most comprehensive and thoroughly researched overview of the Reconstruction Era.

Jacqueline Jones, *Labor of Love, Labor of Sorrow* (1985). Includes excellent material on the work and family lives of African American women in slavery and freedom.

Leon Litwack, *Been in the Storm So Long: The Aftermath of Slavery* (1979). A richly detailed analysis of the transition from slavery to freedom; excellent use of African American sources.

Elizabeth Regosin, *Freedom's Promise: Ex-Slave Families and Citizenship in the Age of Emancipation* (2002). A thoughtful analysis of how freedmen and freedwomen asserted familial relationships as a means to claiming citizenship rights after emancipation, based on research into federal pension applications made by dependent survivors of Civil War soldiers.

Scott Reynolds Nelson, *Iron Confederacies: Southern Railways, Klan Violence, and Reconstruction* (1999). Pathbreaking analysis of how conservative Southern and Northern business interests rebuilt the South's railroad system and also achieved enormous political power within individual states.

 For additional study resources for this chapter, go to the *Companion Website*, http://www.prenhall.com/faragher.

WHOSE HISTORY IS IT?

FLYING THE STARS AND BARS:
THE CONTESTED MEANING OF THE CONFEDERATE FLAG

In March 2000, thousands of demonstrators rallied outside the Capitol in Montgomery, Alabama, calling on state officials to once again fly the Confederate flag over the building. This rally was organized by the League of the South, a group dedicated to celebrating white Southern history and culture. But are displays of the Confederate flag reflections of the fierce pride many white Southerners have for the "Lost Cause" or a reaction to the progress African-Americans have made since the Civil Rights movement of the 1950s and 1960s? The flag is the same design as the battle flag carried in the field by Confederate troops during the Civil War. Throughout the South, the revived use of the Confederate flag began as part of the white backlash against the campaign to end legal segregation. In 1963 Alabama Gov. George C. Wallace ordered the Confederate battle flag to fly on top of the Montgomery state capitol to protest a visit by Attorney General Robert F. Kennedy, who had come to town to discuss desegregation of the state's schools.

Since that time, many Americans around the country have adopted it as an all-purpose symbol of rebellion and resistance to authority, displayed on posters, clothing, bumper stickers, and featured in music videos. But for most African-Americans the Confederate flag meant something quite different. In the summer of 1988 fourteen black Alabama state legislators were arrested for trespassing on state property when they attempted to scale a chain-link fence and remove the flag. Rep. Alvin Holmes, one of those arrested, said, "When I walk up the Capitol steps, instead of seeing the American flag, the flag that

This 1871 painting by Richard Norris Brooke depicts Confederate soldiers at the end of the Civil War, furling the rebel battle flag for the last time. In the postwar Reconstruction years, the Ku Klux Klan adapted it as a symbol of white supremacy and resistance to Federal authority.
AP Wide World Photos.

I served under when I was in the United States Army, I see a flag that represents treason, sedition, slavery, and oppression toward my people."

Many whites insisted the old flag was about regional identity and pride, not race, a "symbol of heritage" somehow divorced from the historical brutality of slavery. John Napier, a retired Air Force colonel and leader of the Sons of Confederate veterans argued, "We celebrate our civil rights history. There are those of us who feel the earlier struggle should be commemorated historically, too. While we're running around naming streets for Rosa Parks, which I have no problem with, you're getting into removing all the symbols of the Confederacy." African-Americans, for whom the flag symbolized slavery, racism, segregation, and violence, tried to distinguish between private and public displays. "I see nothing wrong with someone flying the Confederate flag even on their front lawn or putting it on their bumper stickers,"said Earl Shinhoster, an official of the NAACP. "I do, however, see something wrong when the state promotes something that many people find offensive." In a 2001 referendum, Mississippi, voters overwhelmingly approved retaining the Confederate symbol as part of the state flag. In South Carolina, the NAACP led an effective economic boycott against the state to protest continued flying of the Stars and Bars over the capitol. A compromise solution removed the flag from the capitol, but kept it flying nearby. As long as private and public displays of the Confederate flag persist, so will the highly charged debates over the historical meanings it embodies.

Although the University of Mississippi officially disassociated itself from the Confederate flag in 1981, it continued to fly among fans at this 1995 Ole Miss football game in Oxford. ▶

AP Wide World Photos.

Demonstrators from the Harriet Tubman Freedom House burn the Confederate flag in this 2000 protest against the Stars and Bars flying over the state capitol in Columbia, South Carolina.

AP Wide World Photos.

Two years after Mississippi voters decided to keep the Confederate battle emblem as part of the state flag, the issue remained politically charged. This yard sign from the 2003 governor's race expresses support for Republican candidate Haley Barbour, who attacked Democratic Governor Ronnie Musgrove for insisting on giving voters a chance to decide the state flag's design. ▼

AP Wide World Photos.

Confederate flags are frequently used as all purpose symbols of cultural rebellion. This one appears on a stock car at the North Florida Speedway in Wewahitchka, 2002. ▶

Richard Bickel, CORBIS-NY.

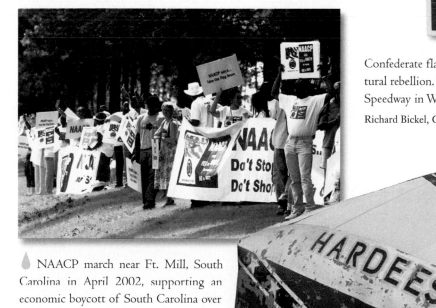

NAACP march near Ft. Mill, South Carolina in April 2002, supporting an economic boycott of South Carolina over the continued presence of the Confederate flag at the state house in Columbia.

AP Wide World Photos.

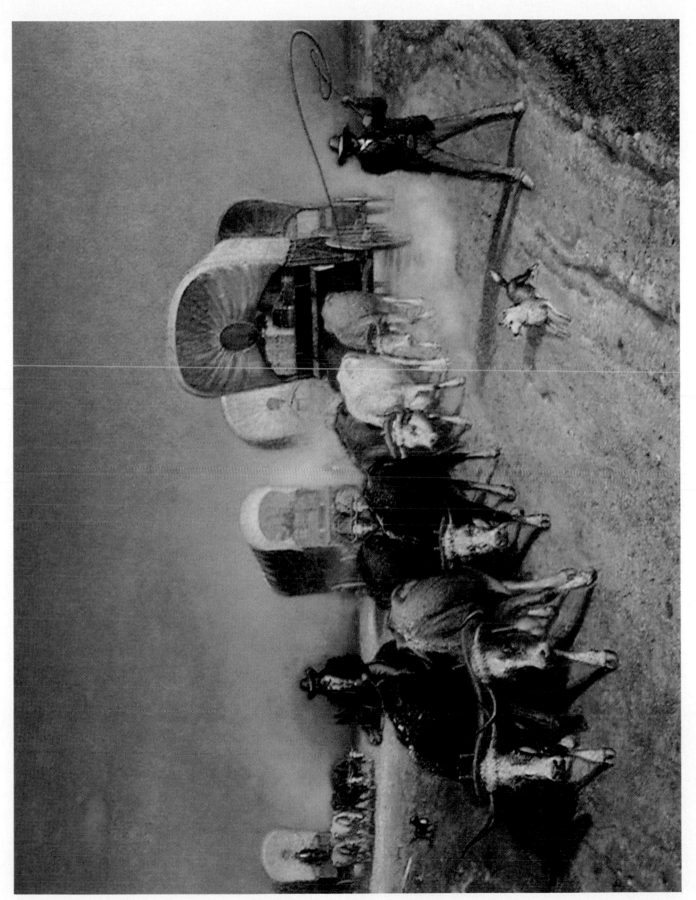

Painting by Samuel Colman (1832–1920, American), *Ships of the Plains*.
PictureQuest.

CHAPTER

18

Conquest and Survival:
The Trans–Mississippi West

1860–1900

CHAPTER OUTLINE

The Oklahoma Land Rush

Decades after the event, cowboy Evan G. Barnard vividly recalled the preparations made by settlers when Oklahoma territorial officials announced the opening of No Man's Land to the biggest "land rush" in American history. "Thousands of people gathered along the border. . . . As the day for the race drew near, the settlers practiced running their horses and driving carts." Finally, the morning of April 22, 1889, arrived. "At ten o'clock people lined up . . . ready for the great race of their lives." Like many others, Barnard displayed his guns prominently on his hips, determined to discourage competitors from claiming the 160 acres of prime land that he intended to grab for himself.

Evan Barnard's story was one strand in the larger tale of the destruction and creation of communities in the trans–Mississippi West. In the 1830s, the federal government designated what was to become the state of Oklahoma as Indian Territory, reserved for the Five Civilized Tribes (Cherokees, Chickasaws, Choctaws, Creeks, and Seminoles) who had been forcibly removed from their eastern lands. All five tribes had reestablished themselves as sovereign republics in Indian Territory. The Cherokees and Chocktaws became prosperous cotton growers. The Creeks managed large herds of hogs and cattle, and the Chickasaws grazed not only cattle but also sheep and goats on their open fields. The Five Tribes also ran sawmills, gristmills, and cotton gins. Indian merchants were soon dealing with other tribespeople as well as licensed white traders and even contracting with the federal government.

The Civil War, however, took a heavy toll on their success. Some tribes, slaveholders themselves, sided with the Confederacy; others with the Union. When the war ended, more than 10,000 people—nearly one-fifth of the population of Indian Territory—had died. To make matters worse, new treaties required the Five Civilized Tribes to cede the entire western half of the territory, including the former northern Indian territory of Nebraska and Kansas, for the resettlement of tribes from other regions.

Western Oklahoma thereby became home to thousands of newly displaced peoples, including the Pawnees, Peorias, Ottawas, Wyandots, and Miamis. Many small tribes readily took to farming and rebuilt their communities. But the nomadic, buffalo-hunting Kiowas, Cheyennes, Comanches, and Arapahoes did not settle so peacefully. They continued to traverse the plains until the U.S. Army finally forced them onto reservations. Eventually, more than 80,000 tribespeople were living on twenty-one separate reservations in western Oklahoma, all governed by agents appointed by the federal government.

The opening of the unassigned far western district of Oklahoma known as No Man's Land to non-Indian homesteading, however, signaled the impending end of Indian sovereignty. Many non-Indians saw this almost 2-million-acre strip as a Promised Land, perfect for dividing into thousands of small farms. African Americans, many of whom were former slaves of Indian planters, appealed to the federal government for the right to stake claims there. Another group of would-be homesteaders, known as "Boomers," quickly tired of petitioning and invaded the district in 1880, only to be booted out by the Tenth Cavalry. Meanwhile, the railroads, seeing the potential for lucrative commerce, put constant

Indian Territory
(Oklahoma)

pressure on the federal government to open No Man's Land for settlement. In 1889, the U.S. Congress finally gave in.

Cowboy Barnard was just one of thousands to pour into No Man's Land on April 22, 1889. Many home-steaders simply crossed the border from Kansas. South-erners, dispossessed by warfare and economic ruin in their own region, were also well represented. Market-minded set-tlers claimed the land nearest the railroads, and by nightfall of April 22, they had set up tent cities along the tracks. In a little over two months, after 6,000 homestead claims had been filed, the first sod houses appeared, sheltering grow-ing communities of non-Indian farmers, ranchers, and other entrepreneurs. Some Indian leaders petitioned the federal government for the right to resettle on new land distant from white settlers, but nothing came from their efforts.

Dramatic as it was, the land rush of 1889 was only one in a series of events that soon dispossessed Okla-homa's Indians of their remaining lands. First, the fed-eral government broke up the estates held collectively by various tribes in western Oklahoma, assigning to indi-viduals the standard 160-acre allotment and allowing non-Indian homesteaders to claim the rest. Then, in 1898, Congress passed the Curtis Act, which formally ended Indian communal land ownership and thereby legally dis-solved Indian Territory. Members of the former Indian nations were directed to dismantle their governments, abandon their estates, and join the ranks of other home-steaders. The flood of whites into Oklahoma left the Indi-ans outnumbered ten to one in lands once wholly theirs (see Map 18.1).

When Oklahoma was granted statehood in 1907, a commentator in the *Daily Oklahoman* said, "The uniting of Indian Territory with Oklahoma Territory in statehood removes the last particle of that vast domain, which in the early part of the last century was set aside by Congress as an eternal home for the red man." Later generations of Oklahomans often cele-brated the origin of their state as Indian territory. Even the name of their state—Oklahoma—means "the land of the red man." At the formal ceremony marking state-hood, just before the newly elected governor took the oath of office, a mock wedding ceremony conveyed the new relationship: a tough and virile cowboy, repre-senting white people, took as his submissive wife a demure Indian maiden.

By 1907, nearly one-quarter of the entire popu-lation of the United States lived west of the Missis-sippi River. Hundreds of new communities, supported primarily by cattle ranching, agriculture, mining, or other industries, had not only grown with the emerg-ing national economy but helped to shape it in the process. The newcomers had also brought poverty, warfare, and death, destroying ways of life that had formed centuries earlier; and they drastically trans-formed the physical landscape. Through their activi-ties and the support of Easterners, the United States realized an ambition that John L. O'Sullivan had described in 1845 as the nation's "manifest destiny to overspread the continent" and remake it in a new image. But in this onward march of empire, the native Amer-ican world was swept away.

KEY TOPICS

- The impact of western expansion on Indian societies
- The West as an "internal empire" and the development of new technologies and new industries
- The creation of new communities and the displacement of old communities
- The West as myth and legend

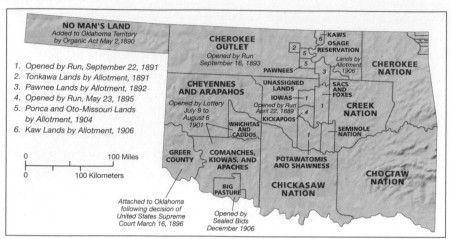

MAP 18.1 Oklahoma Territory Land openings to settlers came at different times, making new land available through various means.

SOURCE: From *Historical Atlas of Oklahoma*, 3rd edition, by John W. Morris, Charles R. Goins and Edwin C. McReynolds. Copyright © 1965, 1976, 1986 by the University of Oklahoma Press, Norman. Reprinted by permission of the publisher. All rights reserved.

INDIAN PEOPLES UNDER SIEGE

The Indians living west of the Mississippi River keenly felt the pressure of the gradual incorporation of the West into the American nation. California became a state in 1850, Oregon in 1859. Congress consolidated the national domain in the next decades by granting territorial status to Utah, New Mexico, Washington, Dakota, Colorado, Nevada, Arizona, Idaho, Montana, and Wyoming. The purchase of Alaska in 1867 added an area twice the size of Texas and extended the nation beyond its contiguous borders so that it reached almost to Russia and the North Pole. The federal government made itself the custodian of all these thinly settled regions, with appointed white governors supervising the transition from territorial status to statehood.

A series of events brought large numbers of white settlers into these new states and territories: the discovery of gold in California in 1848, the opening of western lands to homesteaders in 1862, and the completion of the transcontinental railroad in 1869. With competition for the land and its resources escalating into violent skirmishes and small wars, federal officials became determined to end tribal rule and bring Indians into the American mainstream.

On the Eve of Conquest

Before the European colonists reached the New World, various Indian tribes had occupied Western lands for more than 20,000 years. Hundreds of tribes, totaling perhaps a million members, had adapted to such extreme climates as the desert aridity of present-day Utah and Nevada, the bitter cold of the northern Great Plains, and the seasonally heavy rain of the Pacific Northwest. Many cultivated maize (corn), foraged for wild plants, fished, or hunted game. Several tribes built cities with several thousand inhabitants and traded across thousands of miles of western territory.

Invasion by the English, Spanish, and other Europeans brought disease, religious conversion, and new patterns of commerce. But geographic isolation still gave many tribes a margin of survival unknown in the East. At the close of the Civil War, approximately 360,000 Indian people still lived in the trans-Mississippi West, the majority of them in the Great Plains (see Map 18.2).

The surviving tribes adapted to changing conditions. The Plains Indians learned to ride the horses and shoot the guns introduced by Spanish and British traders. The Pawnees migrated farther westward to evade encroaching non-Indian settlers, while the Sioux and the Comanches fought neighboring tribes to gain control of large stretches of the Great Plains. The Southwestern Hopis and Zunis, conquered earlier by the Spanish, continued to trade extensively with the Mexicans who lived near them. Some tribes took dramatic steps toward accommodation with white ways. Even before they were uprooted and moved across the Mississippi River, the Cherokees had learned English, converted to Christianity, established a constitutional republic, and become a nation of farmers.

Legally, the federal government had long regarded Indian tribes as autonomous nations residing within American boundaries and had negotiated numerous treaties with them over land rights and commerce. But pressured by land-hungry whites, several states had violated these federal treaties so often that the U.S. Congress passed the Indian Removal Act of 1830 (see Chapter 10), which provided funds to relocate all Eastern tribes by force if necessary. The Cherokees challenged this legislation, and the Supreme Court ruled in their favor in *Cherokee Nation v. Georgia* (1831). Ignoring the Court's decision, President Andrew Jackson, known as a hardened Indian fighter, forced many tribes to cede their land and remove to Indian Territory. There, it was believed, they might live undisturbed by whites and gradually adjust to "civilized" ways. But soon, the onslaught of white settlers, railroad entrepreneurs, and prospectors rushing for gold pressured tribes to cede millions of their acres to the United States. In 1854, to open the Kansas and Nebraska Territories for white settlement, the federal government simply abolished the northern half of Indian

MAP EXPLORATION

To explore an interactive version of this map, go to **www.prenhall.com/faragher5/map18.2**

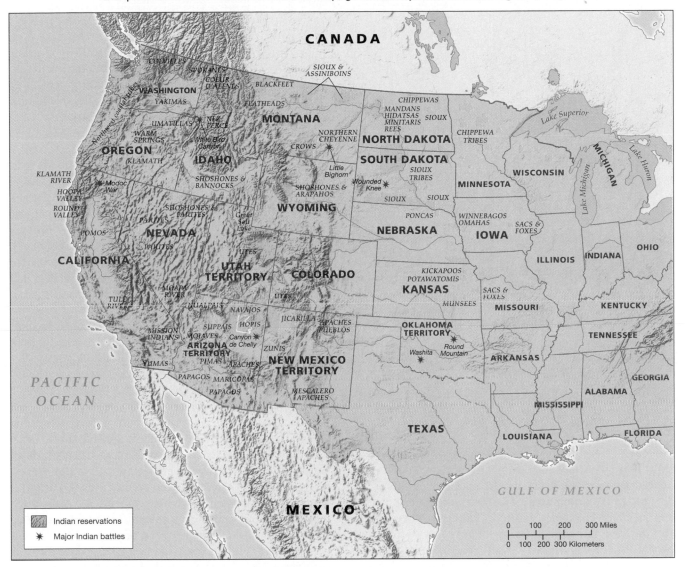

MAP 18.2 Major Indian Battles and Indian Reservations, 1860–1900 As commercial routes and white populations passed through and occupied Indian lands, warfare inevitably erupted. The displacement of Indians to reservations opened access by farmers, ranchers, and investors to natural resources and to markets.

Territory. As demand for resources and land accelerated, the entire plan for a permanent Indian Territory fell apart.

Reservations and the Slaughter of the Buffalo

As early as the 1840s, highly placed officials had outlined a plan to subdue the intensifying rivalry over natural resources and land. Under the terms of their proposal, individual tribes would agree to live within clearly defined zones—reservations—and, in exchange, the Bureau of Indian Affairs would provide guidance, while U.S. military forces ensured protection. This reservation policy also reflected the vision of many "Friends of the Indian," educators and Protestant missionaries who aspired to "civilize the savages." By the end of the 1850s, eight Western reservations had been established where Indian peoples were induced to speak English, take up farming, and convert to Christianity.

The Oglala Sioux spiritual leader, Chief Red Cloud in an 1868 photograph. Here, he is seen with (l. to r.) Red Dog, Little Wound, interpreter John Bridgeman (standing), (Red Cloud), American Horse, and Red Shirt. He ventured to Washington with this delegation to discuss with President Ulysses S. Grant the various provisions of the peace treaty, just signed, to end the violent conflict over the Bozeman Trail.

SOURCE: National Anthropological Archives.

Several tribes did sign treaties, although often under duress. High-handed officials, such as governor Isaac Stevens of Washington Territory, made no attempt at legitimate negotiations, choosing instead to intimidate or deceive the tribal chiefs. After their leaders were coerced into signing away 45,000 square miles of tribal land, state officials moved the Indians onto three reservations. The Suquamish leader Seattle admitted defeat but warned the governor: "Your time of decay may be distant, but it will surely come."

The federal government repeatedly reduced the size of land allotments, forcing tribes to compete with each other for increasingly scarce resources and making subsistence farming on the reservation virtually impossible. The Medicine Lodge Treaty of 1867 assigned reservations in existing Indian Territory to Comanches, Plains (Kiowa) Apaches, Kiowas, Cheyennes, and Arapahoes, bringing these tribes together with Sioux, Shoshones, and Bannocks. All told, more than 100,000 people found themselves competing intensely for survival. Over the next decade, a group of Quakers appointed by President Ulysses S. Grant attempted to mediate differences among the tribes and to supply the starving peoples with food and seed. At the same time, white prospectors and miners continued to flood the Dakota Territory.

"They crowded in," Iron Teeth, a Cheyenne woman, recalled bitterly, "so we had to move out." Moreover, corrupt officials of the Bureau of Indian Affairs routinely diverted funds for their own use and reduced food supplies, a policy promoting malnutrition, demoralization, and desperation.

The nomadic tribes that hunted and gathered over large territories saw their freedom sharply curtailed. The Lakotas, or Western Sioux, a loose confederation of bands scattered across the northern Great Plains, were one of the largest and most adaptive of all Indian nations. Seizing buffalo-hunting territory from their rivals, the Pawnees and the Crows, the Sioux had learned to follow the herds on horseback. Buffalo meat and hides fed and clothed the Sioux and satisfied many of their other needs as well. Images of buffalo appeared in their religious symbols and ceremonial dress.

The mass slaughter of the buffalo brought this crisis to a peak. In earlier eras, vast herds of buffalo had literally darkened the western horizon. As gunpowder and the railroad moved west, the number of buffalo fell rapidly. Non-Indian traders avidly sought fur for coats, hide for leather, bones for fertilizer, and heads for trophies. New rifles, like the .50 caliber Sharps, could kill at 600 feet; one sharpshooter bragged of killing 3,000 buffalo. Army commanders encouraged the slaughter, accurately predicting that starvation would break tribal resistance to the reservation system. With their food sources practically destroyed, diseases such as smallpox and cholera (brought by fur traders) sweeping through their villages, and their way of life undermined, many Great Plains tribes, including many Sioux, concluded that they could only fight or die.

The Indian Wars

In 1864, large-scale war erupted. Having decided to terminate all treaties with tribes in eastern Colorado, territorial governor John Evans encouraged a group of white civilians, the Colorado Volunteers, to stage raids through Cheyenne campgrounds. Seeking protection, Chief Black Kettle brought a band of 800 Cheyennes to a U.S. fort and received orders to set up camp at Sand Creek. Feeling secure in this arrangement, Black Kettle sent out most of his young warriors to hunt. Several weeks later, on November 29, 1864, the Colorado Volunteers and soldiers attacked. While Black Kettle held up a U.S. flag and a white truce banner, a disorderly group of 700 men, many of them drunk, slaughtered 105 Cheyenne women and children and 28 men. They mutilated the corpses and took scalps back to Denver to exhibit as trophies. Iron Teeth, who survived, remembered seeing a woman "crawling along on the ground, shot, scalped, crazy, but not yet dead." Months after the Sand Creek Massacre, bands of Cheyennes, Sioux, and Arapahoes were still retaliating, burning civilian outposts and sometimes killing whole families.

The Sioux played the most dramatic roles in the Indian Wars. In 1851, believing the U.S. government would recognize their own rights of conquest over other Indian tribes, the Sioux relinquished large tracts of land as a demonstration of good faith. But within a decade, a mass invasion of miners and the construction of military forts along the Bozeman Trail in Wyoming, the Sioux's principal buffalo range, threw the tribe's future into doubt. During the Great Sioux War of 1865–67, the Oglala Sioux warrior Red Cloud fought the U.S. Army to a stalemate and forced the government to abandon its forts, which the Sioux then burned to the ground. The Treaty of Fort Laramie, signed in 1868, restored only a temporary peace to the region.

The Treaty of Fort Laramie granted the Sioux the right to occupy the Black Hills, or Paha Sapa, their sacred land, "as long as the grass shall grow," but the discovery of gold soon undermined this guarantee. White prospectors hurriedly invaded the territory. Directed to quash rumors of fabulous deposits of the precious metal, Lieutenant Colonel George Armstrong Custer organized a surveying expedition to the Black Hills during the summer of 1874, but, contrary to plan, the Civil War hero described rich veins of ore that could be cheaply extracted. The U.S. Congress then pushed to purchase the territory for Americans. To protect their land, thousands of Sioux, Cheyenne, and Arapaho warriors moved into war camps during the summer of 1876 and prepared for battle.

After several months of skirmishes between the U.S. Army and Indian warriors, Lieutenant Colonel Custer decided to rush ahead to a site in Montana that was known to white soldiers as Little Bighorn and to Lakotas as Greasy Grass. This foolhardy move offered the allied Cheyenne and Sioux warriors a perfect opportunity to cut off Custer's logistical and military support. On June 25, 1876, Custer and his troops were wiped out by one of the largest Indian contingents ever assembled, an estimated 2,000 to 4,000 warriors.

"Custer's Last Stand" gave Indian-haters the emotional ammunition to whip up public excitement. After Custer's defeat, Sitting Bull reportedly said, "Now they will never let us rest." The U.S. Army tracked down the disbanded Indian contingents one by one and forced them to surrender. In February, 1877, Sioux leadership in the Indian Wars ended.

Among the last to hold out against the reservation system were the Apaches in the Southwest. Most Apache bands had abided by the Medicine Lodge Treaty of 1867, but in 1874, some of the Apache bands, unable to tolerate the harsh conditions on the reservation, returned to their old ways of seizing territory and stealing cattle.

Pursued by the U.S. Army, the Apaches earned a reputation as intrepid warriors. Brilliant strategists like Geronimo and skilled horse-riding braves became legendary for lightning-swift raids against the white outposts in the rugged Arizona terrain. In 1874–75, the Kiowas and the Comanches, both powerful tribes, joined the Apaches in one of the bloodiest conflicts of the era, the Red River

Kiowa Preparing for a War Expedition, ca. 1887. This sketch on paper was made by an Indian artist, Silverhorn, who had himself taken part in the final revolt of the Kiowas in 1874. He later became a medicine man, and then served as a private in the U.S. Cavalry at Fort Sill, Oklahoma Territory.

SOURCE: Silverhorn (Native American), *Kiowa Preparing for a War Expedition.* From *Sketchbook,* 1887. Graphite, ink and crayon on paper. Collection of the McNay Art Museum, Gift of Mrs. Terrell Bartlett.

War. The U.S. Army ultimately prevailed, although less by military might than by denying Indians access to food. Small-scale warfare sputtered on until September 1886, when Geronimo, his band reduced to only thirty people, finally surrendered, thereby ending the Indian Wars.

The Nez Percé

The Nez Percé (meaning "pierced nose") had been given their name by French-speaking fur trappers, who thought they had seen members of the tribe wearing decorative shells in their septums. For generations, the Nez Percé had regarded themselves as good friends to white traders and settlers. Living in the plateau where Idaho, Washington, and Oregon now meet, they had saved the Lewis and Clark expedition from starvation in 1803. The Nez Percé had occasionally assisted American armies against hostile tribes, and many of them were converts to Christianity.

But the discovery of gold on Nez Percé territory in 1860 changed their relations with whites for the worse. In 1863, pressed by prospectors and mining companies, government officials demanded that the Nez Percé cede 6 million acres, nine-tenths of their land, at less than ten cents per acre. Some of the Nez Percé leaders agreed to the terms of the treaty, which had been fraudulently signed on behalf of the entire tribe, but others refused. At first, federal officials listened to Nez Percé complaints against the treaty and decided to allow them to remain on their land. But, in response to pressure from settlers and politicians, they almost immediately reversed their decision, ordering the Nez Percé, including Chief Joseph and his followers, to sell their land and to move onto a reservation.

Intending to comply, Chief Joseph's band set out from the Wallowa Valley with their livestock and all the possessions they could carry. Along the way, some young members of another Indian band traveling with them rode away from camp to avenge the death of one of their own by killing several white settlers. Hoping to explain the situation, a Nez Percé truce team approached U.S. troops. The troops opened fire, and the Indian riders fired back, killing one-third of the soldiers. Brilliantly outmaneuvering vengeful U.S. troops sent to intercept them, the 750 Nez Percé—including women, children, and the elderly—retreated for some 1,400 miles into Montana and Wyoming through mountains and prairies, and across the Bitterroot Range. Over the three-and-a-half months of their journey, Nez Percé braves fought 2,000 regular U.S. troops and eighteen Indian auxiliary detachments in eighteen separate engagements and two major battles. U.S. troops finally trapped the Nez Percé in the Bear Paw Mountains of northern Montana, just 30 miles from the Canadian border. Suffering from hunger and cold, they surrendered.

Promised they would be returned to Oregon, the Nez Percé were sent instead to disease-ridden bottom-land near Fort Leavenworth in Kansas, and then to Oklahoma. Arguing for the right of his people to return to their Oregon reservation, Joseph spoke eloquently through an interpreter, to Congress in 1879. "Treat all men alike. Give them all the same law. Give them all an even chance to live and grow. All men were made by the same Great Spirit Chief," Joseph pleaded. The last remnant of Joseph's band were deported under guard to a non-Nez Percé reservation in Washington, where Chief Joseph died in 1904 "of a broken heart," and where his descendants continue to live in exile to this day.

THE INTERNAL EMPIRE

Since the time of Christopher Columbus, the Americas had inspired in Europeans visions of a land of incredible wealth, free for the taking. In the nineteenth century, the North American continent, stretching across sparsely populated territories toward the Pacific Ocean, revived this fantasy, especially as early reports conjured dreams of mountains of gold and silver. Determined to make their fortunes, be it from copper in Arizona, wheat in Montana, or oranges in California, numerous adventurers traveled west. As a group, they carried out the largest migration and greatest commercial expansion in American history.

But the settlers themselves also became the subjects of a huge "internal empire" whose financial, political, and industrial centers of power remained in the East. A vast system of international markets also shaped the development of mines, farms, and new communities, even as Americans romantically imagined the West to be the last frontier of individual freedom and wide open spaces. Only a small number of settlers actually struck it rich in the great extractive industries—mining, lumbering, ranching, and farming—that ruled the Western economy. Meanwhile, older populations—Indian peoples, Hispanic peoples, and more recently settled communities like the Mormons—struggled to create places for themselves in this new expansionist order.

Mining Towns

The discovery of gold in California in 1848 roused fortune seekers from across the United States, Europe, and as far away as Chile and China; just ten years later, approximately 35,000 Chinese men were working in Western mines. Meanwhile, prospecting parties searching for the mother lode overran the territories, setting a pattern for intermittent rushes for gold, silver, and copper that extended from the Colorado mountains to the Arizona deserts, from California to Oregon and Washington, and from Alaska to the Black Hills of South Dakota. Mining camps and boomtowns

MAP EXPLORATION

To explore an interactive version of this map, go to **www.prenhall.com/faragher5/map18.3**

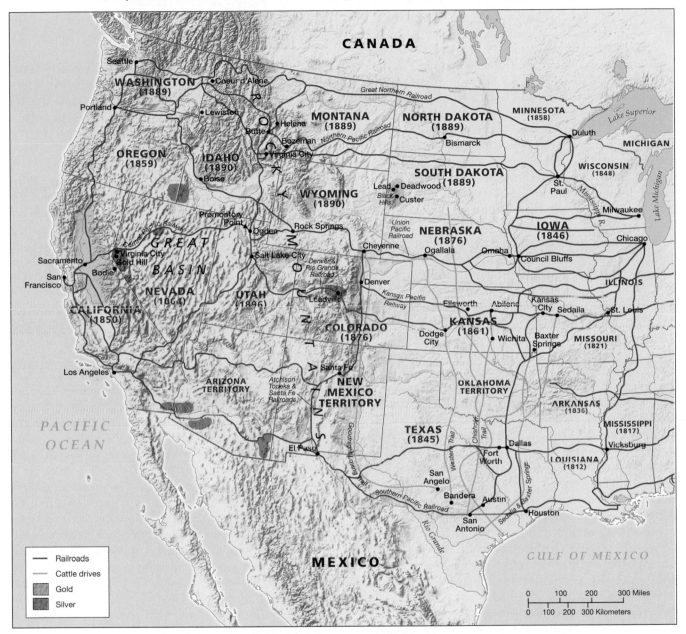

MAP 18.3 Railroad Routes, Cattle Trails, Gold and Silvers Rushes, 1860–1900
By the end of the nineteenth century, the vast region of the West was crosscut by hundreds of lines
of transportation and communication. The trade in precious metals and in cattle helped build
a population almost constantly on the move, following the rushes for gold or the herds of cattle.

SOURCE: *Encyclopedia of American Social History.*

soon dotted what had once been thinly settled regions and speeded the urban development of the West. The population of California alone jumped from 14,000 in 1848 to 223,856 just four years later. Mining soon brought the West into a vast global market for capital, commodities, and labor (see Map 18.3).

The mining industry quickly grew from its treasure-hunt origins into a grand corporate enterprise. The Comstock Lode of silver, discovered by Henry Comstock along the Carson River in Nevada in 1859, sent about 10,000 miners across the Sierra Nevada from California, but few individuals came out wealthy. Comstock himself eventually sold his claims for a mere $11,000 and two mules. Those reaping the huge profits were the entrepreneurs who could afford to invest in the heavy—and expensive—equipment necessary to drill more than 3,000 feet deep and to hire engineers with the technical knowledge to manage the operations.

The most successful mineowners bought out the smaller claims and built an entire industry around their stakes. They found investors to finance their expansion and used the borrowed capital to purchase the latest in extractive technology, such as new explosives, compressed-air or diamond-headed rotary drills, and wire cable. They gained access to timber to fortify their underground structures and water to feed the hydraulic pumps that washed down mountains. They built smelters to refine the crude ore into ingots and often financed railroads to transport the product to distant markets. By the end of the century, the Anaconda Copper Mining Company, which had mining interests throughout the West, had expanded into hydroelectricity to become one of the most powerful corporations in the nation.

The mining corporations laid the basis for a new economy as well as an interim government and established many of the region's first white settlements. Before the advent of railroads, ore had to be brought out of, and supplies brought into, mining areas by boats, wagons, and mules traveling hundreds of miles over rough territory. The railroad made transportation of supplies and products easier and faster. The shipping trade meanwhile grew into an important industry of its own, employing thousands of merchants, peddlers, and sailors. Gold Hill and nearby Virginia City, Nevada, began as a cluster of small mining camps and by the early 1860s became a thriving urban community of nearly 6,000 people. A decade later, the population had quadrupled, but it subsequently fell sharply as the mines gave out. Occasionally, ore veins lasted long enough—as in Butte, Montana, center of the copper-mining district—to create permanent cities.

The many boomtowns, known as "Helldorados," flourished, if only temporarily, as ethnically diverse communities. Men outnumbered women by as much as ten to one, and very few lived with families or stayed very long. They often bunked with male kin and worked alongside friends or acquaintances from their hometown or with fellow immigrants. The Chinese men, the sojourners who hoped to find riches in the "Gold Mountain" of America before returning home, clustered together and created their own institutions such as social clubs, temples, and fraternal societies known as tongs. Some miners lived unusually well, feasting on oysters trucked in at great expense. Amateur sporting events, public lectures, and large numbers of magazines and books filled many of their leisure hours. But the town center was usually the saloon, where, as one observer complained, men "without the restraint of law, indifferent to public opinion, and unburdened by families, drink whenever they feel like it, whenever they have the money to pay for it, and whenever there is nothing else to do."

The Western labor movement began in these camps, partly as a response to dangerous working conditions. In the hardrock mines of the 1870s, one of every thirty workers was disabled, one of eighty killed. Balladeers back in Ireland sang of Butte as the town "where the streets were paved with Irish bones," and departing emigrants promised their mothers that they would never go underground in Montana. Miners began to organize in the 1860s, demanding good pay for dangerous and life-shortening work. In 1892, miners in the Coeur d'Alene region of Idaho, in the aftermath of a bitter and violent strike, formed the Western Federation of Miners, which became, by the end of the century, one of the strongest unions in the nation.

When mineowners' private armies "arrested" strikers or fought their unions with rifle fire, miners burned down the campsites, seized trains loaded with ore, and sabotaged company property. The miners' unions also helped to secure legislation mandating a maximum eight-hour day for certain jobs and workmen's compensation for injuries. Such laws were enacted in Idaho, Arizona, and New Mexico by the 1910s, long before similar laws in most Eastern states.

The unions fought hard, but they did so exclusively for the benefit of white workers. The native-born and the Irish and Cornish immigrants (from Cornwall, England) far outnumbered other groups before the turn of the century, when Italians, Slavs, and Greeks began to replace them. Labor unions eventually admitted these new immigrants, but refused Chinese, Mexican, Indian, and African American workers. (See Out of Many Voices: Reminiscences of a Chinese Immigrant.)

When prices and ore production fell sharply, not even unions could stop the owners from shutting down the mines and leaving ghost towns in their wake. Often they also left behind an environmental disaster.

In 1890, Nicholas Creede discovered a rich vein of high-grade silver on a tributary of the Rio Grande River in Colorado. His small camp quickly grew into a boom town of more than 10,000.
This photograph, taken during the years of the silver rush, shows crowds flocking to the saloons, shops, and dance halls that lined Main Street. "It's day all day in the day time," the editor of the local newspaper commented, "And there is no night in Creede."

SOURCE: From the collections of Henry Ford Museum & Greenfield Village.

Hydraulic mining, which used water cannons to blast hillsides and expose gold deposits, drove tons of rock and earth into the rivers and canyons. By the late 1860s, southern California's rivers were clogged, producing floods that wiped out towns and farms. In 1893, Congress finally passed the Caminetti Act, giving the state the power to regulate the mines. (The act also created the Sacramento River Commission, which began to replace free-flowing rivers with canals and dams.) Underground mining continued unregulated, using up whole forests for timbers and filling the air with dangerous, sulfurous smoke.

Mormon Settlements

While western expansion fostered the growth of new commercial cities such as the numerous if unstable mining towns, it simultaneously placed new restrictions on established communities. The Mormons (members of the Church of Jesus Christ of Latter-Day Saints) had fled western New York in the 1830s for Illinois and Missouri, only to face greater persecution in the Midwest. When their founder, Joseph Smith, was murdered after announcing that an angel had told him that it is "the will of Heaven that a man have more than one wife," the community sought refuge in the West. Led by their new prophet, Brigham Young, the Mormons migrated in 1846–47 to the Great Salt Lake Basin to form an independent theocratic state called Deseret and to affirm the sanctity of plural marriage, or polygamy.

By 1870, more than 87,000 Mormons lived in Utah Territory, creating relatively stable communities that were unique in the West for their religious and ethnic homogeneity. Contrary to federal law, church officials forbade the selling of land. Mormons instead held property in common. They created sizable settlements complemented by satellite villages joined to communal

OUT OF MANY VOICES

REMINISCENCES OF A CHINESE IMMIGRANT

Born in a village in the province of Canton, the young boy Lee Chew heard stories of the "Gold Mountain" of the United States. At age twenty, shortly before the passage of the Chinese Exclusion Act, he convinced his parents to pay the $50 steerage fare for the ocean voyage to San Francisco. In 1903, now in middle-age, he recounts this chapter of his life in the reform magazine The Independent.

THE CHINESE LAUNDRYMAN DOES NOT LEARN HIS trade in China; there are no laundries in China. ... All the Chinese laundrymen here were taught in the first place by American women just as I was taught.

When I went to work for that American family I could not speak a word of English, and I did not know anything about house work. The family consisted of husband, wife and two children. They were very good to me and paid me $3.50 a week, of which I could save $3. ...

When I first opened a laundry it was in company with a partner, who had been in the business for some years. We went to a town about 500 miles inland, where a railroad was building. We got a board shanty and worked for the men employed by the railroads. ...

We were three years with the railroad, and then went to the mines, where we made plenty of money in gold dust, but had a hard time, for many of the miners were wild men who carried revolvers and after drinking would come into our place to shoot and steal shirts, for which we had to pay. ... One of these men hit his head hard against a flat iron and all the miners came and broke our laundry, chasing us out of town. They were going to hang us. We lost all our property and $365 in money, which a member of the mob must have found.

Luckily most of our money was in the hands of Chinese bankers in San Francisco. I drew $500 and went East to Chicago, where I had a laundry for three years, during which I increased my capital to $2,500. After that I was four years in Detroit. I went home to China in 1897, but returned in 1898, and began a laundry business in Buffalo. ...

Americans are not all bad ... Still, they have their faults, and their treatment of us is outrageous. ... ■

SOURCE: Lee Chew, "Life of a Chinese Immigrant," The Independent, 54 (February 19, 1903), pp. 417–23.

farmlands and a common pasture. Relying on agricultural techniques learned from local Indian tribes, the Mormons built dams for irrigation and harvested a variety of crops from desert soil. Eventually, nearly 500 Mormon communities spread from Oregon to Idaho to northern Mexico (see Map 18.4).

However, as territorial rule tightened, the Mormons saw their unique way of life once again threatened. The newspapers and the courts repeatedly assailed the Mormons for the supposed sexual excesses of their system of plural marriage, condemning them as heathens and savages. Preceded by prohibitory federal laws enacted in 1862 and 1874, the Supreme Court finally ruled against polygamy in the 1879 case of United States v. Reynolds, which granted the freedom of belief but not the freedom of practice. In 1882, Congress passed the Edmunds Act, which effectively disfranchised those who believed in or practiced polygamy and threatened them with fines and imprisonment. Equally devastating was the Edmunds-Tucker Act, passed five years later, which destroyed the temporal power of the Mormon Church by confiscating all assets over $50,000 and establishing a federal commission to oversee all elections in the territory. By the early 1890s, Mormon leaders officially renounced the practice of plural marriage.

Although Brigham Young wed twenty-seven women and fathered fifty-six children, no more than 15 to 20 percent of Mormon families practiced polygamy and even then, two wives was the norm. Still, the "celestial" law of plural marriage had been central to the Mormons' messianic mission. Forced to give up the right to the practice, they gave up many other aspects of their distinctive communal life, including the common ownership of land. By the time Utah became a state in 1896, Mormon communities resem-

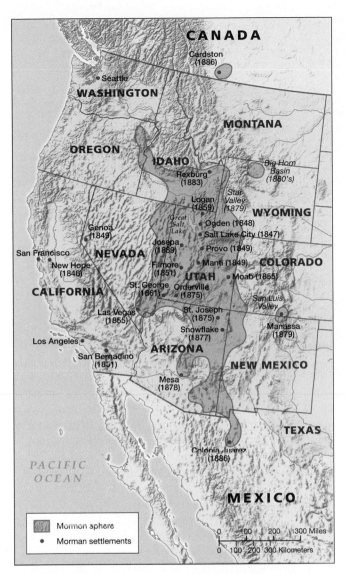

MAP 18.4 Mormon Cultural Diffusion, ca. 1883 Mormon settlements permeated many sparsely populated sections of Idaho, Nevada, Arizona, Wyoming, Colorado, and New Mexico. Built with church backing and the strong commitment of community members, they survived and even prospered in adverse climates.

SOURCE: *Mormon Cultural Diffusion, ca. 1883*, Donald W. Meinig, "The Geography of the American West, 1847-1964" from The Annals of the Association of American Geographers 55, no. 2, June 1965.

bled in some ways the society that the original settlers had sought to escape. Nevertheless, they combined their religious cohesion with leadership in the expanding regional economy to become a major political force in the West.

Mexican Borderland Communities

The Mexican-American War ended in 1848 with the United States taking fully half of all Mexican territory—the future states of Arizona, California, Nevada, and Utah, most of New Mexico, and parts of Wyoming, and Colorado. The Gadsden Purchase of 1853 rounded off this prize, giving the United States a strip of land, rich in copper deposits, that stretched from El Paso west to the Colorado River—in short, all the land north of the Rio Grande River. Reflecting upon the new continental empire in North America, a British writer summed up the significance of the recent acquisitions. The United States had become, he wrote, "a power of the first class, a nation which it is very dangerous to offend and almost impossible to attack."

The Treaty of Guadalupe Hidalgo allowed the Hispanic people north of the Rio Grande to choose between immigrating to Mexico or staying in what was now the United States. But the new Mexican-American border, one of the longest unguarded boundaries in the world, could not successfully sever communities that had been connected for centuries. What gradually emerged, was an economically and socially interdependent zone, the Anglo-Hispanic borderlands linking the United States and Mexico.

Although under the treaty all Hispanics were formally guaranteed citizenship and the "free enjoyment of their liberty and property," local "Anglos" (as the Mexicans called white Americans) often violated these provisions and, through fraud or coercion, took control of the land. The Sante Fe Ring, a group of lawyers, politicians, and land speculators, stole millions of acres from the public domain and grabbed over 80 percent of the Mexicano landholdings in New Mexico alone. More often, Anglos used new federal laws to their own benefit.

For a time, Arizona and New Mexico seemed to hold out hope for a mutually beneficial interaction between Mexicanos and Anglos. A prosperous class of Hispanic landowners, with long-standing ties to Anglos through marriage, had established itself in cities like Albuquerque and Tucson, old Spanish towns that had been founded in the seventeenth and eighteenth centuries. Estevan Ochoa, merchant, philanthropist, and the only Mexican to serve as mayor of Tucson following the Gadsden Purchase, managed to build one of the largest business empires in the West. In Las Cruces, New Mexico, an exceptional family such as the wealthy Amadors could shop by mail from Bloomingdales, travel to the World's Fair in Chicago, and send their children to English-language Catholic schools. Even the small and struggling Mexicano middle class could afford such modern conveniences as kitchen stoves and sewing machines. These Mexican elites, well integrated into the emerging national economy, continued to wield political power as ranchers, landlords, and real estate developers until the end of the century. They secured passage of bills for education in their regions and often served as superintendents of local schools. Several prominent merchants became territorial delegates to Congress.

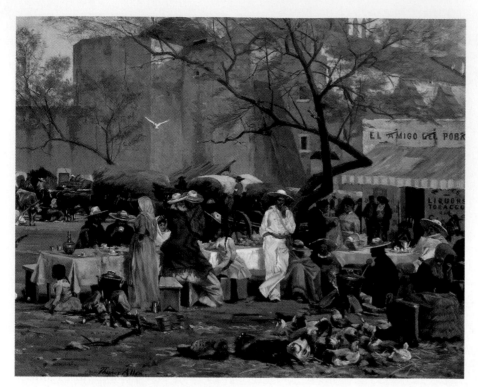

Mexican Americans in San Antonio continued to conduct their traditional market bazaar well after the incorporation of this region into the United States. Forced off the land and excluded from the better-paying jobs in the emerging regional economy, many Mexicanos, and especially women, sought to sell the products of their own handiwork for cash or for bartered food and clothing.

SOURCE: Thomas Allen, *Market Plaza*, 1878–1879. Oil on canvas, 26″ × 39½″. Witte Museum, San Antonio, Texas.

dresses. Formerly at the center of a communal society, Mexicanas found themselves with fewer options in the cash economy. What wages they could now earn fell below even the low sums paid to their husbands, and women lost status within both the family and community.

Occasionally, Mexicanos organized to reverse these trends or at least to limit the damage done to their communities. In the border town of Brownsville, Texas, in 1859, Juan Nepomuceno Cortina, known as the Red Robber of the Rio Grande, and sixty of his followers pillaged white-owned stores and killed four Anglos who had gone unpunished for murdering several Mexicans. "Cortina's War" marked the first of several sporadic rebellions. As late as the 1880s, Las Gorras Blancas, a band of agrarian rebels in New Mexico, were destroying railroad ties and farm machinery and posting demands for justice on fences of the new Anglo farms and ranches. In 1890, Las Gorras turned from social banditry to political organization, forming *El Partido del Pueblo Unido* (The People's Party). Organized along similar lines, *El Alianzo Hispano-Americano* (The Hispanic-American Alliance) was formed "to protect and fight for the rights of Spanish Americans" through political action. *Mutualistes* (mutual aid societies) provided sickness and death benefits to Mexican families.

But the majority of Mexicans who had lived in the mountains and deserts of the Southwest for well over two centuries were less prepared for these changes. Most had worked outside the commercial economy, farming and herding sheep for their own subsistence. Before 1848, they had few contacts with the outside world. With the Anglos came land closures as well as commercial expansion, prompted by railroad, mining, and timber industries. Many poor families found themselves crowded onto plots too small for subsistence farming. Many turned to seasonal labor on the new Anglo-owned commercial farms, where they became the first of many generations of poorly paid migratory workers. Other Mexicanos adapted by taking jobs on the railroad or in the mines. Meanwhile, their wives and daughters moved to the new towns and cities in such numbers that by the end of the century, Mexicanos had become a predominantly urban population, dependent on wages for survival.

Women were quickly drawn into the expanding network of market and wage relations. They tried to make ends meet by selling produce from their backyard gardens; more often they worked as seamstresses or laun-

Despite many pressures, Mexicanos preserved much of their cultural heritage. Many persisted in older ways simply because they had few choices. In addition, the influx of new immigrants from Mexico helped to reinforce traditional cultural norms. Beginning in the late 1870s, the modernizing policies of Porfirio Diaz, the president of Mexico from 1876 to 1911, brought deteriorating living conditions to the masses of poor people, and prompted a migration northward that accelerated through the first decades of the twentieth century. These newcomers revitalized old customs and rituals associated with family and religion. The Roman Catholic Church retained its influence in the community, and most Mexicans continued to turn to the church to baptize infants, to celebrate the feast days of their patron saints, to marry, and to bury the dead. Special saints like the Virgin of Guadalupe and distinctive holy days like the Day of the Dead survived, along with fiestas celebrating the change of seasons. Many communities continued to commemorate Mexican national holidays, such as *Cinco de Mayo* (the Fifth of May), marking the Mexican victory over French invaders in the battle of Puebla in 1862. Spanish language and Spanish place names continued to distinguish the Southwest.

THE OPEN RANGE

The slaughter of the buffalo made way for the cattle industry, one of the most profitable businesses in the West. Texas longhorns, introduced by the Spanish, numbered over 5 million at the close of the Civil War and represented a potentially plentiful supply of beef for Eastern consumers. In the spring of 1866, entrepreneurs such as Joseph G. McCoy began to build a spectacular cattle market in the eastern part of Kansas, where the Kansas Pacific Railroad provided crucial transportation links to slaughtering and packing houses and commercial distributors in Kansas City, St. Louis, and Chicago.

In 1867, only 35,000 head of cattle reached McCoy's new stockyards in Abilene, but 1868 proved the first of many banner years. Drovers pushed herd after herd north from Texas through Oklahoma on the trail marked out by part-Cherokee trader Jesse Chisholm. Great profits were made on Texas steers bought for $7–$9 a head and sold in Kansas for upward of $30. In 1880, nearly 2 million cattle were slaughtered in Chicago alone. For two decades, cattle represented the West's bonanza industry.

The Long Drives

The great cattle drives depended on the cowboy, a seasonal or migrant worker. After the Civil War, cowboys—one for every 300–500 head of cattle on the trail—rounded up herds of Texas cattle and drove them as much as 1,500 miles north to grazing ranches or to the stockyards where they were readied for shipping by rail to Eastern markets. The boss supplied the horses, the cowboy his own bedroll, saddle, and spurs. The workday lasted from sunup to sundown, with short night shifts for guarding the cattle. Scurvy, a widespread ailment, could be traced to the basic chuckwagon menu of sowbelly, beans, and coffee, a diet bereft of fruits and vegetables. The cowboy worked without protection from rain or hail, and severe dust storms could cause temporary blindness. As late as 1920, veterans of the range complained that no company would sell life insurance to a cowboy.

In return for his labor, the cowboy received at the best of times about $30 per month. Wages were usually paid in one lump sum at the end of a drive, a policy that encouraged cowboys to spend their money quickly and recklessly in the booming cattle towns of Dodge City, Kansas, or Cheyenne, Wyoming. In the 1880s, when wages began to fall along with the price of beef, cowboys fought back by stealing cattle or by forming unions. In 1883, many Texas cowboys struck for higher wages; nearly all Wyoming cowboys struck in 1886. Aided by the legendary camaraderie fostered in the otherwise desolate conditions of the long drive, cowboys, along with miners, were among the first Western workers to organize against employers.

Like other parts of the West, the cattle range was ethnically diverse. Between one-fifth and one-third of all workers were Indian, Mexican, or African American. Indian cowboys worked mainly on the northern plains and in Indian Territory; the *vaqueros*, who had previously worked on the Mexican cattle *haciendas*, or huge estates, predominated in South Texas and California. African American cowboys worked primarily in Texas, where the range cattle industry was founded.

Like the vaqueros, African American cowboys were highly skilled managers of cattle. Some were sons of former slaves who had been captured from the African territory of Gambia, where cattle raising was an age-old art. Unlike Mexicans, they earned wages comparable to those paid to Anglos and, especially during the early years, worked in integrated drover parties. By the 1880s, as the center of the cattle industry shifted to the more settled regions around the northern ranches, African Americans were forced out, and they turned to other kinds of work.

Very few women participated in the long drives. Sally Redus, wife of an early Texas cattleman, once accompanied her husband on the trip from Texas to Kansas. Carrying her baby on her lap, she most likely rode the enormous distance "sidesaddle," with both legs on one side of the horse. Most women stayed back at the ranch. Occasionally, a husband and wife worked as partners, sharing even the labor of wrangling cattle, and following her husband's death, a woman might take over altogether. Elizabeth Collins, for example, turned her husband's large ranch into an extraordinarily prosperous business, earning for herself the title "Cattle Queen of Montana." The majority of wives attended to domestic chores, caring for children and maintaining the household. Their daughters, however, often tagged along after their fathers and learned to love outdoor work. They were soon riding astride, "clothespin style," roping calves, branding cattle or cutting their ears to mark them, and castrating bulls. But not until 1901 did a woman dare to enter an official rodeo contest.

The Sporting Life

In cattle towns as well as mining camps, saloons, gambling establishments, and dance halls were regular features on the horizon. The hurdy-gurdy, a form of hand organ, supplied raucous music for cowboys eager to spend their money and blow off steam after the long drive. Here they found dancing partners, often called

Curly Wolves Howled on Saturday Night, a commercial woodcut from the 1870s. The artist, recording this scene at a tavern near Billings, Montana, captured what he called a "Dude and a Waitress" dancing the "Bull Calves' Medley on the Grand Piano." Illustrations depicting a wild and lively West appeared prominently in magazines like *Harper's Weekly,* which circulated mainly among readers east of the Mississippi.

SOURCE: Courtesy of the Library of Congress.

making or domestic service, they found few alternatives to prostitution in the cattle towns, where the cost of food and lodging was notoriously high. Still, earnings in prostitution were slim, except during the cattle-shipping season when young men outnumbered women by as much as three to one. In the best of times, a fully employed Wichita prostitute might earn $30 per week, nearly two-thirds of which would go for room and board. Injury or even death from violent clients, addiction to narcotics such as cocaine or morphine, and venereal disease were workaday dangers.

Community and Conflict

The combination of prostitution, gambling, and drinking discouraged the formation of stable communities. According to a Kansas proverb, "There's no Sunday west of Junction City and no god west of Salina." Personal violence was notoriously commonplace on the streets and in the barrooms of cattle towns and mining camps populated mainly by young, single men. Many Western towns such as Wichita outlawed the carrying of handguns, but enforcement usually lagged. Local specialty shops and mail-order catalogues continued to sell weapons with little regulation. But contrary to popular belief, gunfights were relatively rare. Local police officers, such as Wyatt Earp and James "Wild Bill" Hickok, worked mainly to keep order among drunken cowboys.

hurdy-girls or hurdies. If they wanted to do more than dance, the cowboy and his partner could retreat to one of the small rooms for rent, which were often located at the rear of the building.

During the first cattle drive to Abilene in 1867, only a few women worked as prostitutes; but by the following spring, McCoy's assistant recalled, "they came in swarms, & as the weather was warm 4 or 5 girls could huddle together in a tent very comfortably." Although some women worked in trailside "hoghouses," the best-paid prostitutes congregated in the brothel districts. Most cattle towns boasted at least one bawdy house. Dodge City had two: one with white prostitutes for white patrons; another with black prostitutes for both white and black men. Although prostitution was illegal in most towns, the laws were rarely enforced until the end of the century, when reformers led campaigns to shut down the red-light districts. Until then, prostitution supplied these women with the largest source of employment outside the home.

Perhaps 50,000 women engaged in prostitution west of the Mississippi during the second half of the nineteenth century. Like the cowboys who bought their services, most prostitutes were unmarried and in their teens or twenties. Often fed up with underpaid jobs in dress-

ulated mainly by young, single men. Many Western towns such as Wichita outlawed the carrying of handguns, but enforcement usually lagged. Local specialty shops and mail-order catalogues continued to sell weapons with little regulation. But contrary to popular belief, gunfights were relatively rare. Local police officers, such as Wyatt Earp and James "Wild Bill" Hickok, worked mainly to keep order among drunken cowboys.

After the Civil War, violent crime, assault, and robbery rose sharply throughout the United States. In the West, the most prevalent crimes were horse theft and cattle rustling, which peaked during the height of the open range period and then fell back by the 1890s. Death by legal hanging or illegal lynching—at "necktie parties" in which the victims were "jerked to Jesus"—was the usual sentence. In the last half of the century, vigilantes acting outside the law mobilized more than 200 times, claiming altogether more than 500 victims.

The "range wars" of the 1870s produced violent conflicts. By this time, both farmers and sheep herders were encroaching on the fields where cattle had once grazed freely. Sheep chew grass down to its roots, making it practically impossible to raise cattle on land they have grazed. Farmers meanwhile set about building fences to protect their domestic livestock and property. Great cattle barons fought back against farmers by ordering cowboys to cut the new barbed-wire fences. Rivalry among the owners of livestock was even more vicious, particularly in the Southwest and Pacific Northwest. In those areas, Mexicano shepherds and Anglo cattlemen often fought each other for land. In Lincoln County, New Mexico, the feuds grew so intense in 1878 that one faction hired gunman Billy the Kid to protect its interests. President Rutherford B. Hayes finally sent troops to halt the bloodshed. As one historian has written, violence was "not a mere sideshow" but "an intrinsic part of western society."

The cattle barons helped to bring about their own demise, but they did not go down quietly. Ranchers eager for greater profits, and often backed by foreign capital, overstocked their herds, and eventually the cattle began to deplete the limited supply of grass. Finally, during 1885–87, a combination of summer drought and winter blizzards killed 90 percent of the cattle in the northern Plains. By the time of the "big die-up," returns on investments were already declining, and many ranchers fell into bankruptcy. The era of the long drive that inspired so much Western lore proved to be a relatively short-lived phenomenon.

FARMING COMMUNITIES ON THE PLAINS

The vision of a huge fertile garden extending from the Appalachians to the Pacific Ocean had inspired Americans since the early days of the republic. But the first explorers who actually traveled through the Great Plains quashed this dream. "The Great Desert" was the name they gave to the region stretching west from Kansas and Nebraska, north to Montana and the Dakotas, and south again to Oklahoma and Texas. Few trees fended off the blazing sun of summer or promised a supply of lumber for homes and fences. The occasional river or stream flowed with "muddy gruel" rather than pure, sweet water. Economically, the entire region appeared as hopelessly barren as it was vast. It took massive improvements in both transportation and farm technology—as well as unrelenting advertising and promotional campaigns—to open the Great Plains to widescale agriculture.

The Homestead Act

The Homestead Act of 1862 offered the first incentive to prospective white farmers. This act granted a quarter section (160 acres) of the public domain free to any settler who lived on the land for at least five years and improved it; or a settler could buy the land for $1.25 per acre after only six months' residence. Restricting its

provisions to unmarried women, the Homestead Act encouraged adventurous and hard-working women to file between 5 and 15 percent of the claims, which allowed approximately 400,000 households to build farms for themselves.

Homesteaders achieved their greatest success in the central and upper Midwest, where the soil was rich and weather relatively moderate. But those settlers lured to the Great Plains by descriptions of land "carpeted with soft grass—a sylvan paradise" found themselves locked in a fierce struggle with the harsh climate and arid soil. Nearly half of all homesteaders failed to improve the land and therefore lost their claims.

The dream of a homestead nevertheless died hard. Five years after the passage of the Homestead Act, *New York Tribune* editor Horace Greeley still advised his readers to strike off "into the broad, free West" and "make yourself a farm from Uncle Sam's generous domain, you will crowd nobody, starve nobody, and . . . neither you nor your children need evermore beg for Something to Do." He was wrong. Although the Homestead Act did spark the largest migration in American history, only 10 percent of all farmers got their start under its terms.

Most settlers acquired their land outright. State governments and land companies usually held the most valuable land near transportation and markets, and the majority of farmers were willing to pay a hefty price for those benefits. The big-time land speculators did even better, plucking choice locations at bargain prices and selling high. And the railroads, which received land grants from the federal government, did best, selling off the holdings near their routes at top dollar.

Populating the Plains

The rapid settlement of the West could not have taken place without the railroad. Although the Homestead Act offered prospective farmers free land, it was the railroad that promoted settlement, brought people to their new homes, and carried crops and cattle to Eastern markets. The railroads therefore wielded tremendous economic and political power throughout the West. Their agents—reputed to know every cow in the district—made major decisions regarding territorial welfare. In designing routes and locating depots, railroad companies put whole communities "on the map," or left them behind.

Along with providing transportation links between the East and the West and potential markets as distant as China, the Western railroads directly encouraged settlement. Unlike the railroads built before the Civil War, which followed the path of villages and towns, the Western lines preceded settlement. Bringing people west became their top priority, and the railroad companies conducted aggressive promotional and marketing campaigns. Agents enticed Easterners and Europeans alike

In 1887, Lizzie Chrisman filed the first homestead claim on Lieban Creek in Custer County, Nebraska. Joined by her three sisters, she is shown here standing in front of her sod cabin. "Soddies," as these small houses were called, were constructed of stacked layers of cut prairie turf, which were eventually fortified by a thick network of roots. The roofs, often supported by timber, were usually covered with more sod, straw, and small branches.

SOURCE: Nebraska State Historical Society, Solomon D. Butcher Collection.

with long-term loans and free transportation by rail to distant points in the West. For example, the Santa Fe Railroad sent agent C. B. Schmidt to Germany, where he managed to entice nearly 60,000 Germans to settle along the rail line. The railroads also sponsored land companies to sell parcels of their own huge allotments from the federal government. The National Land Company, founded in Chicago in 1869, alone organized sixteen colonies of mainly European immigrants in parts of Kansas and Colorado.

More than 2 million Europeans, many recruited by professional promoters, settled the Great Plains between 1870 and 1900. Some districts in Minnesota seemed to be virtual colonies of Sweden; others housed the largest number of Finns in the New World. Nebraska, whose population as early as 1870 was 25 percent foreign-born, concentrated Germans, Swedes, Danes, and Czechs. But Germans outnumbered all other immigrants by far. A smaller portion of European immigrants reached Kansas, still fewer the territories to the south where Indian and Hispanic peoples and African Americans remained the major ethnic populations.

Many immigrants found life on the Great Plains difficult but endurable. "Living in Nebraska," the locals joked, "is a lot like being hanged; the initial shock is a bit abrupt, but once you hang there for awhile you sort of get used to it." The German-speaking Russians who settled the Dakotas discovered soil similar to that of their homeland but weather that was even more severe. Having earlier fled religious persecution in Germany for Russia, they brought with them heavy coats and the technique of using sun-dried bricks to build houses in areas where lumber was scarce. These immigrants often provided examples for other settlers less familiar with such harsh terrain.

Having traveled the huge distance with kin or members of their Old World villages, immigrants tended to form tight-knit communities on the Great Plains. Many married only within their own group. For example, only 3 percent of Norwegian men married women of a different ethnic background. Like many Mexicanos in the Southwest, several immigrant groups retained their languages well into the twentieth century, usually by sponsoring parochial school systems and publishing their own newspapers. A few groups closed their communities to outsiders. The Poles who migrated to central Nebraska in the 1880s, for example, formed an exclusive settlement; and the German Hutterites, who disavowed private property, lived in seclusion as much as possible, in the Bon Homme colony of South Dakota, established in 1874.

Among the native-born settlers of the Great Plains, the largest number had migrated from states bordering the Mississippi River. Settling as individual families rather than as whole communities, they faced an exceptionally solitary life on the Great Plains. To stave off isolation, homesteaders sometimes built their homes on the adjoining corners of their homestead plots. Still, the prospect of doing better, which brought most homesteaders to the Great Plains in the first place, caused many families to keep seeking greener pastures. Mobility was so high that between one-third and one-half of all households pulled up stakes within a decade.

Communities eventually flourished in prosperous towns like Grand Island, Nebraska; Coffeyville, Kansas; and Fargo, North Dakota, that served the larger agricultural region. Built alongside the railroad, they grew into commercial centers, home to banking, medical, legal, and retail services. Town life fostered a special intimacy; even in the county graveyard, it was said, a town resident remained among neighbors. But closeness did not necessarily promote social equality or even friendship.

OUT OF MANY VOICES

MEMORIES OF CAVALRY LIFE

Mrs. Orsemus Boyd published this memoir in part as a tribute to her husband, who died while in active service to his country. She describes her arrival at Camp Halleck, Nevada, where she joined her husband a few months after they married in October, 1867.

WHEN COURAGE TO LOOK AROUND HAD AT LAST been mustered, I found that my new home was formed of two wall tents pitched together so the inner one could be used as a sleeping and the outer one as a sitting room. A calico curtain divided them, and a carpet made of barley sacks covered the floor. In my weary state of mind and body the effect produced was far from pleasant. The wall tents were only eight feet square, and when windowless and doorless except for the one entrance, as were those, they seemed from the inside much like a prison.

As I lay in bed that night, feeling decidedly homesick, familiar airs, played upon a very good piano, suddenly sounded in my ears. It seemed impossible that there could be a fine musical instrument such a distance from civilization, particularly when I remembered the roads over which we had come, and the cluster of tents that alone represented human habitation. The piano, which I soon learned belonged to our captain's wife, added greatly to her happiness, and also the pleasure of us all, though its first strains only intensified my homesick longings.

This lady and myself were the only women at the post, which also included, besides our respective husbands, the doctor and an unmarried first lieutenant. The latter, as quartermaster and commissary, controlled all supplies, could make us either comfortable or the reverse, as he chose. . . .

My housekeeping was simplified by absolute lack of materials. I had, as a basis of supplies, during the succeeding two years, nothing but soldiers' rations, which consisted entirely of bacon, flour, beans, coffee, tea, rice, sugar, soap, and condiments. Our only luxury was dried apples, and with these I experimented in every imaginable way until toward the last my efforts to disguise them utterly failed, and we returned to our simple rations. ◼

SOURCE: Mrs. Orsemus Boyd, *Calvary Life in Tent and Field* (New York: J. Selwin Tait & Son), 1994; as reprinted in Christiane Fischer, ed., *Let Them Speak for Themselves: Women in the American West, 1849–1900* (New York: E.P. Dutton, 1978), pp. 11–12, 116.

A social hierarchy based on education (for the handful of doctors and lawyers) and, more important, investment property (held mainly by railroad agents and bankers) governed relationships between individuals and families. Reinforced by family ties and religious and ethnic differences, this hierachy often persisted across generations. (See Out of many Voices: Memories of Cavalry Life.)

Work, Dawn to Dusk

By the 1870s, the Great Plains, once the home of buffalo and Indian hunters, was becoming a vast farming region populated mainly by immigrants from Europe and white Americans from east of the Mississippi. In place of the first one-room shanties, sod houses, and log cabins stood substantial frame farmhouses, along with a variety of other buildings like barns, smokehouses, and stables. But the built environment took nothing away from the predominating vista—the expansive fields of grain. "You have no idea, Beulah," wrote a Dakota farmer to his wife, "of what [the wheat farms] are like until you see them. For mile after mile there is not a sign of a tree or stone and just as level as the floor of your house. . . . Wheat never looked better and it is nothing but wheat, wheat, wheat."

Most farm families survived, and prospered if they could, through hard work, often from dawn to dusk. Men's activities in the fields tended to be seasonal, with heavy work during planting and harvest; at other times, their labor centered on construction or repair of buildings and on taking care of livestock. Women's activities were usually far more routine, week in and week out: cooking and canning of seasonal fruit and vegetables, washing, ironing, churning cream for butter, and keeping chickens for their eggs. Women tended to the young children, and they might occasionally take in boarders, usually young men working temporarily in railroad construction. Many women complained about the ceaseless drudgery, especially when they watched their husbands invest in farm equipment rather than in domestic appliances. Others relished the challenge.

Milking the cows, hauling water, and running errands to neighboring farms could be done by the children, once they had reached the age of nine or so. The "one-room school," where all grades learned together, taught the basics of literacy and arithmetic that a future farmer or commercial employee would require. Older sons and daughters might move to the nearest town to earn money to contribute to the family coffer.

The harsh climate and unyielding soil nevertheless forced all but the most reclusive families to seek out friends and neighbors. Many hands were needed to clear the land for cultivation or for roadbeds, to raise houses and barns, or to bring in a harvest before a threatening storm. Neighbors might agree to work together haying, harvesting, and threshing grain. A well-to-do farmer might "rent" his threshing machine in exchange for a small cash fee and, for instance, three days' labor. His wife might barter her garden produce for her neighbor's bread and milk or for help during childbirth or disability. Women often combined work and leisure in quilting bees and sewing circles, where they made friends while sharing scraps of material and technical information. Whole communities turned out for special events, such as the seasonal husking bees and apple bees, which were organized mainly by women.

Much of this informal barter, however, resulted from lack of cash rather than from a lasting desire to cooperate. When annual harvests were bountiful, even the farm woman's practice of bartering goods with neighbors and local merchants—butter and eggs in return for yard goods or seed—diminished sharply, replaced by cash transactions. Still, wheat production proved unsteady in the last half of the nineteenth century, and few farm families could remain reliant wholly on themselves.

For many farmers, the soil simply would not yield a livelihood, and they often owed more money than they took in. Start-up costs, including the purchase of land and equipment, put many farmers deep in debt to local creditors. Some lost their land altogether. By the turn of the century, more than one-third of all farmers in the United States were tenants on someone else's land.

The Garden of Eden was not to be found on the prairies or on the plains, no matter how hard the average farm family worked. Again and again, foreclosures wiped out the small landowner through dips in commodity prices, bad decisions, natural disasters, or illness. In one especially bad year, 1881, a group of farmers in western Iowa chose to burn off, rather than harvest, their wheat because the yield promised to be so small. The swift growth of rural population soon ended. Although writers and orators alike continued to celebrate the family farm as the source of virtue and economic well-being, the hard reality of big money and political power told a far different story.

THE WORLD'S BREADBASKET

During the second half of the nineteenth century commercial farms employed the most intensive and extensive methods of agricultural production in the world. Hard-working farmers brought huge numbers of acres under cultivation, while new technologies allowed them to achieve unprecedented levels of efficiency in the planting and harvesting of crops. As a result, farming became increasingly tied to international trade, and mod-

This "thirty-three horse team harvester" was photographed at the turn of the century in Walla Walla, Washington. Binding the grain into sheaves before it could hit the ground, the "harvester" cut, threshed, and sacked wheat in one single motion.

SOURCE: Library of Congress.

ern capitalism soon ruled Western agriculture, as it did the mining and cattle industries.

New Production Technologies

Only after the trees had been cleared and grasslands cut free of roots could the soil be prepared for planting. But as farmers on the Great Plains knew so well, the sod west of the Mississippi did not yield readily to cultivation and often broke the cast-iron plows typically used by Eastern farmers. Farther west, some farmers resorted to drills to plant seeds for crops such as wheat and oats. Even in the best locations, where loamy, fertile ground had built up over centuries into eight or more inches of decayed vegetation, the preliminary breaking, or "busting," of the sod required hard labor. One man would guide a team of five or six oxen pulling a plow through the soil, while another regulated the depth of the cut, or furrow. But, as a North Dakota settler wrote to his wife back in Michigan, after the first crop, the soil became as "soft as can be, any team [of men and animals] can work it."

Agricultural productivity depended as much on new technology as on the farmers' hard labor. In 1837, John Deere had designed his famous "singing plow" that easily turned prairie grasses under and turned up even highly compacted soils. Around the same time, Cyrus McCormick's reaper began to be used for cutting grain; by the 1850s, his factories were turning out reapers in mass quantities. The harvester, invented in the 1870s, drew the cut stalks upward to a platform where two men could bind them into sheaves; by the 1880s, an automatic knotter tied them together. Drastically reducing the number of people traditionally required for this work, the harvester increased the pace many times over. The introduction of mechanized corn planters and mowing or raking machines for hay all but completed the technological arsenal (see Table 18.1).

In the 1890s, the U.S. commissioner of labor measured the impact of technology on farm productivity. Before the introduction of the wire binder in 1875, he reported, a farmer could not plant more than 8 acres of wheat if he were to harvest it successfully without help; by 1890, the same farmer could rely on his new machine to handle 135 acres with relative ease and without risk of spoilage. The improvements in the last half of the century allowed an average farmer to produce up to ten times more than was possible with the old implements.

Scientific study of soil, grain, and climatic conditions was another factor in the record output. Beginning in the mid-nineteenth century, federal and state governments added inducements to the growing body of expertise, scientific information, and hands-on advice. Through the Morrill Act of 1862, "land-grant" colleges acquired space for campuses in return for promising to institute agricultural programs. The Department of Agriculture, which attained cabinet-level status in 1889, and the Weather Bureau (transferred from the War Department in 1891) also made considerable contributions to farmers' knowledge. The federal Hatch Act of 1887, which created a series of state experimental stations, provided for basic agricultural research, especially in the areas of soil minerals and plant growth. Many states added their own agricultural stations, usually connected with state colleges and universities.

Nature nevertheless often reigned over technological innovation and seemed in places to take revenge against these early successes. West of the 98th meridian—a north-south line extending through western Oklahoma, central Kansas and Nebraska, and eastern Dakota—perennial dryness due to an annual rainfall of less than 20 inches constantly threatened to turn soil into dust and to break plows on the hardened ground. Summer heat burned out crops and ignited grass fires. Mountains of winter snows turned rivers into spring torrents that flooded fields; heavy fall rains washed crops away. Even good weather invited worms and flying insects to infest the crops. During the 1870s, grasshoppers in clouds a mile long ate everything organic, including tree bark and clothes.

Producing for the Global Market

Farming changed in important ways during the last third of the nineteenth century. Although the family remained the primary source of labor, farmers tended to put more emphasis on production for exchange rather than for home use. They continued to plant vegetable gardens and often kept fowl or livestock for the family's consumption, but farmers raised crops mainly for a market that stretched across the world.

Wheat farmers in particular prospered. With the world population increasing at a rapid rate, the international demand for wheat was enormous, and American farmers made huge profits from the sale of this crop. Wheat production ultimately served as a barometer of the

TABLE 18.1	HAND v. MACHINE LABOR ON THE FARM, ca. 1880			
	Time Worked		Labor Cost	
Crop	Hand	Machine	Hand	Machine
Wheat	61 hours	3 hours	$3.55	$0.66
Corn	39 hours	15 hours	3.62	1.51
Oats	66 hours	7 hours	3.73	1.07
Loose Hay	21 hours	4 hours	1.75	0.42
Baled Hay	35 hours	12 hours	3.06	1.29

This painting by the British-born artist Thomas Hill (1829–1908) depicts workers tending strawberry fields in the great agricultural valley of Northern California. Chinese field hands, such as the two men shown here, supplied not only cheap labor but invaluable knowledge of specialized fruit and vegetable crops.

SOURCE: Thomas Hill, *Irrigating at Strawberry Farm, Santa Clara*, 1888. Courtesy of The Bancroft Library, University of California, Berkeley

seven leading grain-growing states increased from 64.4 acres to more than 100 acres.

California Agribusiness

The trend toward bonanza farming reached an apex in California, where farming as a business surpassed farming as a way of life. Bankers, railroad magnates, and other Anglos made rich by the Gold Rush took possession of the best farming land in the state. They introduced the latest technologies, built dams and canals, and invested huge amounts of capital, setting the pattern for the state's prosperous agribusiness. Farms of nearly 500 acres dominated the California landscape in 1870; by the turn of the century, two-thirds of the state's arable land was in 1,000-acre farms. As land reformer and social commentator Henry George noted, California was "not a country of farms but a country of plantations and estates."

agricultural economy in the West. Farmers in all corners of the region, from Nebraska to California, expanded or contracted their holdings and planned their crops according to the price of wheat.

The new machines and expanding market did not necessarily guarantee success. Land, draft animals, and equipment remained very expensive, and start-up costs could keep a family in debt for decades. A year of good returns often preceded a year of financial disaster. Weather conditions, international markets, and railroad and steamship shipping prices all proved equally unpredictable and heartless.

The new technology and scientific expertise favored the large, well-capitalized farmer over the small one. Such is the story of the large-scale wheat operations in the great Red River Valley of North Dakota. Here, a shrewd worker such as Oliver Dalrymple could take advantage of a spectacular bonanza. When Dalrymple started out in 1875, he managed a farm owned by two officials of the Northern Pacific Railroad. He cleared their land, planted wheat, and yielded a sizable harvest the first year. He did much better the second year and began to invest in his own farm. A decade later, his operations included 32,000 acres in wheat and 2,000 in oats. Dalrymple now had the financial resources to use the latest technology to harvest these crops and to employ up to 1,000 seasonal laborers at a time. The majority of farmers with fewer resources expanded at more modest rates. Between 1880 and 1900, average farm size in the

This scale of production made California the national leader in wheat production by the mid-1880s. But it also succeeded dramatically with fruit and vegetables. Large- and medium-sized growers, shrewdly combined in cooperative marketing associations during the 1870s and 1880s, used the new refrigerator cars to ship their produce in large quantities to the East and on to Europe. By 1890, cherries, apricots, and oranges, packed with mountains of ice, made their way into homes across the United States.

California growers learned quickly that they could satisfy consumer appetites and even create new ones. Orange producers packed their products individually in tissue paper, a technique designed to convince Eastern consumers that they were about to eat a luxury fruit. By the turn of the century, advertisers for the California Citrus Growers' Association described oranges as a necessity for good health, inventing the trademark "Sunkist" to be stamped on each orange. Meanwhile California's grape growing grew into a big business. Long considered inferior to French wines, California wines found a ready market at lower prices. Other grape growers made their fortunes in raisins. One company trademarked its raisins as "Sun Maid" and packaged them for schoolchildren in the famous "nickel" box.

By 1900, California had become the model for American agribusiness, not the home of self-sufficient homesteaders but the showcase of heavily capitalized farm factories that employed a huge tenant and migrant workforce, including many Chinese. After the mines gave out and work on the transcontinental railroad ended, thousands of Chinese helped to bring new lands under cultivation. Renting their land, Chinese tenant farmers specialized in labor-intensive crops such as vegetables and fruits, and peddled their crops door-to-door or sold them in roadside stands. Others worked in packing and preserving in all the major agricultural regions of the state. However, the Chinese, like the majority of field hands, rarely rose to the ranks of agricultural entrepreneurs. By the turn of the century, amid intense legislative battles over land and irrigation rights, it was clear that the rich and powerful dominated California agribusiness.

The Toll on the Land

Viewing the land as a resource to command, the new inhabitants often looked past the existing flora and fauna toward a landscape remade strictly for commercial purposes. The changes they produced in some areas were nearly as cataclysmic as those that occurred during the Ice Age.

Banishing many existing species, farmers "improved" the land by introducing exotic plants and animals— that is, biological colonies indigenous to other regions and continents. Farmers also unintentionally introduced new varieties of weeds, insect pests, and rats. Surviving portions of older grasslands and meadows eventually could be found only alongside railroad tracks, in graveyards, or inside national parks.

Numerous species disappeared altogether or suffered drastic reduction. The grizzly bear, for example, an animal exclusive to the West, could once be found in large numbers from the Great Plains to California and throughout much of Alaska; by the early decades of the twentieth century, one nature writer estimated that only 800 survived, mostly in Yellowstone National Park. At the same time, the number of wolves declined from perhaps as many as 2 million to just 200,000. By the mid-1880s, no more than 5,000 buffalo survived in the entire United States, and little remained of the once vast herds but great heaps of bones sold for $7.50 per ton.

The slaughter of the buffalo had a dramatic impact, not only on the fate of the species, but also on the grasslands of the Great Plains. Overall, the biological diversity of the region had been drastically reduced. Having killed off the giant herds, ranchers and farmers quickly shifted to cattle and sheep production. Unlike the roaming buffalo, these livestock did not range widely and soon devoured the native grasses down to their roots. With the ground cover destroyed, the soil eroded and became barren. By the end of the century, huge dust storms swept across the plains.

In 1873, the U.S. Congress passed the Timber Culture Act, which allotted homesteaders an additional 160 acres of land in return for planting and cultivating forty acres of trees. Because residence was not required, and because tree planting could not be assessed for at least thirteen years, speculators filed for several claims at once, then turned around and sold the land without having planted a single tree. Although some forests were restored, neither the weather nor the soil improved.

Large-scale commercial agriculture also took a heavy toll on inland waters. Before white settlement, rainfall had drained naturally into lakes and underground aquifers, and watering spots were abundant throughout the Great Plains. Farmers mechanically rerouted and dammed water to irrigate their crops, causing many bodies of water to disappear and the water table to drop significantly. In the 1870s, successful ranchers in California pressed for ever greater supplies of water and contracted Chinese work gangs to build the largest irrigation canal in the West. In 1887, the state of California formed irrigation districts, securing bond issues for the construction of canals, and other Western states followed. But by the 1890s, irrigation had seemed to reach its limit without federal support. The Newlands or National Reclamation Act of 1902 added 1 million acres of irrigated land, and state irrigation districts added more than 10 million acres. Expensive to taxpayers, and ultimately benefiting corporate farmers rather than small landowners, these projects further diverted water and totally transformed the landscape.

Although Western state politicians and federal officials debated water rights for decades, they rarely considered the impact of water policies on the environment. Lake Tulare in California's Central Valley, for example, had occupied up to 760 square miles. After farmers began to irrigate their land by tapping the rivers that fed Tulare, the lake shrank dramatically, covering a mere 36 square miles by the early twentieth century. Finally the lake, which had supported rich aquatic and avian life for thousands of years, disappeared entirely. The land left behind, now wholly dependent on irrigation, grew so alkaline in spots that it could no longer be used for agricultural purposes.

The need to maintain the water supply indirectly led to the creation of national forests and the Forest Service. Western farmers supported the General Land Revision Act of 1891, which gave the president the power to establish forest reserves to protect watersheds against the threats posed by lumbering, overgrazing, and forest fires. In the years that followed, President Benjamin Harrison established fifteen forest reserves exceeding 16 million acres, and President Grover Cleveland added more than 21 million acres. But only in 1897 did the secretary of the interior finally gain the authority to regulate the use of these reserves.

The Forest Management Act of 1897 and the National Reclamation Act of 1902 set the federal government on the path of large-scale regulatory activities. The Forest Service was established in 1905, and in 1907, forest reserves were transferred from the Department of the Interior to the Department of Agriculture.

The federal government would now play an even larger role in economic development of the West, dealing mainly with corporate farmers and ranchers eager for improvements.

THE WESTERN LANDSCAPE

Throughout the nineteenth century, many Americans viewed western expansion as the nation's "manifest destiny," and just as many marveled at the region's natural and cultural wonders. The public east of the Mississippi craved stories about the West and visual images of its sweeping vistas. Artists and photographers built their reputations on what they saw and imagined. Scholars, from geologists and botanists to historians and anthropologists, toured the trans-Mississippi West in pursuit of new data. The region and its peoples came to represent what was both unique and magnificent about the American landscape (see Map 18.5).

Nature's Majesty

By the end of the century, scores of writers had described spectacular, breathtaking natural sites like the Grand Tetons and High Sierras, vast meadows of waving grasses and beautiful flowers, expansive canyons and rushing white rivers, and exquisite deserts covered with sagebrush or dotted with flowering cactus, stark yet enticing.

Moved by such evidence, the federal government began to set aside huge tracts of land as nature reserves. In 1864, Congress passed the Yosemite Act, which placed the spectacular cliffs and giant sequoias under the management of the state of California. Meanwhile, explorers returned to the East awestruck by the varied terrain of the Rocky Mountains, the largest mountain chain in North America, and described huge sky-high lakes, boiling mud, and spectacular waterfalls. In 1872, Congress named Yellowstone the first national park. Yosemite and Sequoia in California, Crater Lake in Oregon, Mount Ranier

MAP 18.5 The Establishment of National Parks and Forests The setting aside of land for national parks saved large districts of the West from early commercial development and industrial degradation, setting a precedent for the later establishment of additional parks in economically marginal, but scenic, territory. The West, home to the vast majority of park space, became a principal site of tourism by the end of the nineteenth century.

Albert Bierstadt became one of the first artists to capture on enormous canvases the vastness and rugged terrain of Western mountains and wilderness. Many other artists joined Bierstadt to form the Rocky Mountain School. In time, the camera largely replaced the paintbrush, and most Americans formed an image of these majestic peaks from postcards and magazine illustrations.

SOURCE: Albert Bierstadt (1830-1902), *Merced River, Yosemite Valley*, 1866. Oil on canvas, H. 36 in, W. 50 in. (91.4 × 127 cm). Signed and dated (lower right) Abierstadt/1866. The Metropolitan Museum of Art, Gift of the sons of William Paton, 1909 (09.214.1) Photograph ©1988 The Metropolitan Museum of Art

in Washington, and Glacier in Montana all became national parks between 1890 and 1910.

Landscape painters, particularly the group that became known as the Rocky Mountain School, also piqued the public's interest in Western scenery. In the 1860s, German-born Albert Bierstadt, equipped with a camera, traveled the Oregon Trail. Using his photographs as inspiration, Bierstadt painted mountains so wondrous that they seemed nearly surreal, projecting a divine aura behind the majesty of nature. His "earthscapes"—huge canvases with exacting details of animals and plants—thrilled viewers and sold for tens of thousands of dollars.

The Legendary Wild West

By the end of the century, many Americans, rich and poor alike, imagined the West as a land of promise and opportunity and, above all, of excitement and adventure. Future president Theodore Roosevelt helped to promote this view. Soon after his election to the New York State Assembly in 1882, Roosevelt was horrified to see himself lampooned in the newspapers as a dandy and a weakling. A year later, after buying a ranch in South Dakota, he began to reconstruct his public

image. He wrote three books recounting his adventures in the West, claiming that they had instilled in him not only personal bravery and "hardihood," but self-reliance. The West, Roosevelt insisted, meant "vigorous manhood."

The first "westerns," the "dime novels" that sold in the 1860s in editions of 50,000 or more, reflected these myths. Competing against stories about pirates, wars, crime, and sea adventures, westerns outsold the others. Edward Zane Carroll Judson's *Buffalo Bill, the King of the Border Men*, first published in 1869, spawned hundreds of other novels, thousands of stories, and an entire magazine devoted to Buffalo Bill. Real-life African American cowboy Nat Love lived on in the imaginations of many generations as Edward L. Wheeler's dime novel hero "Deadwood Dick," who rode the range as a white cowboy in black clothes in over thirty stories. His girlfriend "Calamity Jane"—"the most reckless buchario in ther Hills"—also took on mythic qualities.

Railroad promoters and herd owners actively promoted these romantic and heroic images. Cowman Joseph McCoy staged Wild West shows in St. Louis and Chicago, where Texas cowboys entertained prospective buyers by roping calves and breaking horses. Many cowboys played up this imaginary role, dressing and talking to match the stories told about them. The first professional photographers often made their living touring the West, setting up studios where cowboys and prostitutes posed in elaborate costumes.

The former Pony Express rider, army scout, and famed buffalo hunter William F. Cody hit upon the idea of an extravaganza that would bring the legendary West to those who could never experience it in person. "Buffalo Bill" Cody made sharpshooter Annie Oakley a star performer. Entrancing crowds with her stunning accuracy with pistol or rifle, Oakley shot dimes in midair and cigarettes from her husband's mouth. Cody also hired Sioux Indians and hundreds of cowboys to perform in mock stagecoach robberies and battles. With far less fanfare, many veteran cowboys enlisted themselves on "dude ranches" for tourists or performed as rope twirlers or yodeling singers in theaters across the United States.

Buffalo Bill's "Wild West Show" poster from 1899. William Cody's theatrical company toured the United States and Europe for decades, reenacting various battles, and occasionally switching to football (cowboys versus Indians). Cody's style set the pace for both rodeos and Western silent films.

SOURCE: Library of Congress.

The "American Primitive"

New technologies of graphic reproduction encouraged painters and photographers to provide new images of the West, authentic as well as fabricated. A young German American artist, Charles Schreyvogel, saw Buffalo Bill's tent show in Buffalo and decided to make the West his life's work. His canvases depicted Indian warriors and U.S. cavalry fighting furiously but without blood and gore. Charles Russell, a genuine cowboy, painted the life he knew, but also indulged in imaginary scenarios, producing paintings of buffalo hunts and first encounters between Indian peoples and white explorers.

Frederic Remington, the most famous of all the Western artists, left Yale Art School to visit Montana in 1881, became a Kansas sheepherder and tavern owner, and then returned to painting. Inspired by newspaper stories of the army's campaign against the Apaches, he made himself into a war correspondent and captured vivid scenes of battle in his sketches. Painstakingly accurate in physical details, especially of horses, his paintings celebrated the "winning of the West" from the Indian peoples. By the turn of the century, Remington was the chief magazine illustrator of Western history.

Remington joined hundreds of other painters and engravers in reproducing the most popular historic event: Custer's Last Stand. Totally fictionalized by white artists to show a heroic General Custer personally holding off advancing Indian warriors, these renditions dramatized the romance and tragedy of conquest. Indian artists recorded Custer's defeat in far less noble fashion.

Photographers often produced highly nuanced portraits of Indian peoples. Dozens of early photographers from the Bureau of American Ethnology captured the gaze of noble tribespeople or showed them hard at work digging clams or grinding corn. President Theodore Roosevelt praised Edward Sheriff Curtis for vividly conveying tribal virtue. Generations later, in the 1960s and 1970s, Curtis's photographs again captured the imagination of Western enthusiasts, who were unaware or unconcerned that this sympathetic artist had often posed his subjects or retouched his photos to blur out any artifacts of white society.

Painters and photographers led the way for scholarly research on the various Indian societies. The early ethnographer and pioneer of fieldwork in anthropology Lewis Henry Morgan, devoted his life to the study of Indian family or kinship patterns, mostly of Eastern tribes such as the Iroquois, who adopted him into their Hawk Clan. In 1851, he published *League of the Ho-de-no-sau-nee, or Iroquois,* considered the first scientific account of an Indian tribe. A decade later, Morgan ventured into Cheyenne country to examine the naming patterns of this tribe. In his major work, *Ancient Society,* published in 1877, he posited a universal process of social evolution leading from savagery to barbarism to civilization.

One of the most influential interpreters of the cultures of living tribespeople was the pioneering ethnographer Alice Cunningham Fletcher. In 1879, Fletcher met Susette (Bright Eyes) La Flesche of the Omaha tribe, who was on a speaking tour to gain support for her people, primarily to prevent their removal from tribal lands. Fletcher, then forty-two years old, accompanied La Flesche to Nebraska, telling the Omahas that she had come "to learn, if you will let me, something about your tribal organization, social customs, tribal rites, traditions and songs. Also to see if I can help you in any way." After transcribing hundreds of songs, Fletcher became well known as an expert on Omaha music. She also promoted assimilation through the allotment of individual claims to 160-acre homesteads, eked out of tribal lands, and helped to draft the model legislation that was enacted by Congress as the Omaha Act of 1882. In 1885, Fletcher produced for the U.S. Senate a report titled *Indian Education and*

OVERVIEW

MAJOR INDIAN TREATIES AND LEGISLATION OF THE LATE NINETEENTH CENTURY

1863	Nez Percé Treaty	Signed illegally on behalf of the entire tribe, in which the Nez Percé abandoned 6 million acres of land in return for a small reservation in northeastern Oregon. Led to Nez Percé wars, which ended in 1877 with the surrender of Chief Joseph.
1867	Medicine Lodge Treaty	Assigned reservations in existing Indian Territory to Comanches, Plains (Kiowa), Apaches, Kiowas, Cheyennes, and Arapahoes, bringing these tribes together with Sioux, Shoshones, Bannocks, and Navajos.
1868	Treaty of Fort Laramie	Successfully ended Red Cloud's war by evacuating federal troops from Sioux Territory along the Bozeman Trail; additionally granted Sioux ownership of the western half of South Dakota and rights to use Powder River country in Wyoming and Montana.
1871		Congress declares end to treaty system.
1887	Dawes Severalty Act	Divided communal tribal land, granting the right to petition for citizenship to those Indians who accepted the individual land allotment of 160 acres. Successfully undermined sovereignty.

Civilization, one of the first general statements on the status of Indian peoples. As a founder of the American Anthropological Society and president of the American Folklore Society, she encouraged further study of Indian societies.

While white settlers and the federal government continued to threaten the survival of tribal life, Indian lore became a major pursuit of scholars and amateurs alike. Adults and children delighted in turning up arrowheads. Fraternal organizations such as the Elks and Eagles borrowed tribal terminology. The Boy Scouts and Girl Scouts, the nation's premier youth organizations, used tribal lore to instill strength of character. And the U.S. Treasury stamped images of tribal chiefs and buffalo on the nation's most frequently used coins.

THE TRANSFORMATION OF INDIAN SOCIETIES

In 1871, the U.S. government formally ended the treaty system, eclipsing without completely abolishing the sovereignty of Indian nations. Still, the tribes persisted. Using a mixture of survival strategies from farming and trade to the leasing of reservation lands, they both adapted to changing conditions and maintained old traditions.

Reform Policy and Politics

By 1880, many Indian tribes had been forcibly resettled on reservations, but very few had adapted to white ways. For decades, reformers, mainly from the Protestant churches, had lobbied Congress for a program of salvation through assimilation, and they looked to the Board of Indian Commissioners, created in 1869, to carry out this mission. The board often succeeded in mediating conflicts among the various tribes crowded onto reservations, but made far less headway in converting them to Christianity or transforming them into prosperous farming communities. The majority of Indian peoples lived in poverty and misery, deprived of their traditional means of survival and more often than not, subjected to fraud by corrupt government officials and private suppliers. Reformers who observed these conditions firsthand nevertheless remained unshaken in their belief that tribespeople must be raised out of the darkness of ignorance into the light of civilization. Some conceded, however, that the reservation system might not be the best means to this end.

Unlike most Americans, who saw the conquest of the West as a means to national glory, some reformers were genuinely outraged by the government's continuous violation of treaty obligations and the military enforcement of the reservation policy. One of the most influential was Helen Hunt Jackson, a noted poet and author of children's stories. In 1879, Jackson had attended a lecture in Hartford, Connecticut, by a chief of the Ponca tribe whose destitute people had been forced from their Dakota homeland. Heartstruck, Jackson lobbied former abolitionists such as Wendell Phillips to work for Indians' rights and herself began to write against government policy. Her book-length exposé, *A Century of Dishonor,* published in 1881, detailed the plight of Indian peoples.

Jackson threw herself into the Indian Rights Association, an offshoot of the Women's National Indian Association (WNIA), which had been formed in 1874 to rally public support for a program of assimilation. The two organizations helped to place Protestant missionaries in the West to work to eradicate tribal customs as well as to convert Indian peoples to Christianity. According to the reformers' plans, men would now farm as well as hunt, while women would leave the fields to take care of home and children. Likewise, all communal practices would be abandoned in favor of individually owned homesteads, where families could develop in the "American" manner and even celebrate proper holidays such as the Fourth of July. Children, hair trimmed short, would be placed in boarding schools where, removed from their parents' influence, they would shed traditional values and cultural practices. By 1882, the WNIA had gathered 100,000 signatures on petitions urging Congress to phase out the reservation system, to establish universal education for Indian children, and to award title to 160 acres to any Indian individual willing to work the land.

The Dawes Severalty Act, passed by Congress in 1887, incorporated many of these measures and established federal Indian policy for decades to come. The act allowed the president to distribute land, not to tribes, but to individuals legally "severed" from their tribes. The commissioner of Indian affairs rendered the popular interpretation that "tribal relations should be broken up, socialism destroyed and the family and autonomy of the individual substituted. The allotment of land in severalty, the establishment of local courts and police, the development of a personal sense of independence and the universal adoption of the English language are means to this end."

Those individuals who accepted the land allotment of 160 acres and agreed to allow the government to sell unallotted tribal lands (with some funds set aside for education) could petition to become citizens of the United States. A little over a decade after its enactment, many reformers believed that the Dawes Act had resolved the basis of the "Indian problem." Hollow Horn Bear, a Sioux chief, offered a different opinion, judging the Dawes Act to be "only another trick of the whites."

The Dawes Act successfully undermined tribal sovereignty but offered little compensation. Indian religions and sacred ceremonies were banned, the telling of legends and myths forbidden, and shaman and medicine men imprisoned or exiled for continuing their traditional practices. "Indian schools" forbade Indian languages, clothing styles, and even hair fashions in order to "kill the Indian . . . and save the man," as one schoolmaster put it.

These and other measures did little to integrate Indians into white society. Treated as savages, Indian children fled most white schools. Nor did adults receive much encouragement to become property holders. Government agencies allotted them inferior farmland, inadequate tools, and little training for agricultural self-sufficiency. Seeing scant advantage in assimilating, only a minority of adults dropped their tribal religion for Christianity or their communal ways for the accumulation of private property. Within the next forty years, the Indian peoples lost 60 percent of the reservation land remaining in 1887 and 66 percent of the land allotted to them as homesteaders. The tenets of the Dawes Act were not reversed until 1934. In that year, Congress passed the Indian Reorganization Act, which affirmed the integrity of Indian cultural institutions and returned some land to tribal ownership (see Chapter 24).

The Ghost Dance

After the passage of the Dawes Severalty Act, one more cycle of rebellion remained for the Sioux. In 1888, the Paiute prophet Wovoka, ill with scarlet fever, had a vision during a total eclipse of the sun. In his vision, the Creator told him that if the Indian peoples learned to love each other, they would be granted a special place in the afterlife. The Creator also gave him the Ghost Dance, which the prophet performed for others and soon spread throughout the tribe. The Sioux came to believe that when the day of judgment came, all Indian peoples who had ever lived would return to their lost world and white peoples would vanish from the earth. The chant sounded:

> *The whole world is coming.*
> *A nation is coming, a nation is coming.*
> *The Eagle has brought the message to the tribe.*
> *The father says so, the father says so.*
> *Over the whole earth they are coming.*
> *The buffalo are coming, the buffalo are coming.*
> *The Crow has brought the message to the tribe,*
> *The Father says so, the Father says so.*

Many white settlers and federal officials feared the Ghost Dancers, even though belief in a sudden divine judgment was common among Christians and Jews. Before the Civil War, Protestant groups such as the Millerites, who had renounced personal property and prepared themselves for the millennium, were tolerated by other Americans. But after decades of Indian warfare, white Americans took the Ghost Dance as a warning of tribal retribution rather than a religious ceremony. As thousands of Sioux danced to exhaustion, local whites intolerantly demanded the practice be stopped. The U.S. Seventh Cavalry, led in part by survivors of the Battle of Little Bighorn, rushed to the Pine Ridge Reservation, and a group of the Sioux led by Big Foot, now fearing mass murder, moved into hiding in the Bad Lands of South Dakota. After a skirmish, the great leader Sitting Bull and his young son lay dead.

The Seventh Calvary pursued the Sioux Ghost Dancers and 300 undernourished Sioux, freezing and without horses, to Wounded Knee Creek on the Pine Ridge Reservation. There, on December 29, 1890, while the peace-seeking Big Foot, who had personally raised a white flag of surrender, lay dying of pneumonia, they were surrounded by soldiers armed with automatic guns. The U.S. troops expected the Sioux to surrender their few remaining weapons, but an accidental gunshot from one deaf brave who misunderstood the command caused panic on both sides.

Within minutes, 200 Sioux had been cut down and dozens of soldiers wounded, mostly by their own cross fire. For two hours soldiers continued to shoot at anything that moved—mostly women and children straggling away. Many of the injured froze to death in the snow; others were transported in open wagons and finally laid out on beds of hay under Christmas decorations at the Pine Ridge Episcopal church. The massacre, which took place almost exactly 400 years after Columbus "discovered" the New World for Christian civilization, seemed to mark the final conquest of the continent's indigenous peoples.

Black Elk later recalled, "I can see that something else died there in the bloody mud, and was buried in the blizzard. A people's dream died there. It was a beautiful dream. . . . The nation's hoop is broken and scattered. There is no center any longer, and the sacred tree is dead."

Endurance and Rejuvenation

The most tenacious tribes were those occupying land rejected by white settlers or those distant from their new communities. Still, not even an insular, peaceful agricultural existence on semiarid, treeless terrain necessarily provided protection. Nor did a total willingness to peacefully accept white offers prevent attack.

The Pimas of Arizona, for instance, had a well-developed agricultural system adapted to a scarce supply of water, and they rarely warred with other tribes. After the arrival of white settlers, they integrated Christian symbolism into their religion, learned to speak English, and even fought with the U.S. cavalry against the Apaches. Still, the Pimas saw their lands stolen, their precious waterways diverted, and their families impoverished.

The similarly peaceful Yana tribes of California, hunters and gatherers rather than farmers, were even less fortunate. Suffering enslavement, prostitution, and multiple new diseases from white settlers, they faced near extinction within a generation. One Yana tribe, the Yahi, chose simply to disappear. For more than a decade, they lived in caves and avoided all contact with white settlers.

Many tribes found it difficult to survive in the proximity of white settlers. The Flatheads, for example, seemed to Indian commissioners in the Bitterroot region of Montana to be destined for quick assimilation. They had refused to join the Ghost Dance and had agreed to sell their rich tribal land and move to a new reservation. But while waiting to be moved, the dispossessed Flatheads nearly starved. When they finally reached the new reservation in October 1891, the remaining 250 Flatheads put on their finest war paint and whooped and galloped their horses, firing guns in the air in celebration. But disappointment and tragedy lay ahead. The federal government drastically reduced the size of the reservation, using a large part of it to provide a national reserve for buffalo. Only handfuls of Flatheads, mostly elderly, continued to live together in pockets of rural poverty.

In 1890, the celebrated artist Frederic Remington (1861–1909) produced this color sketch, shown here in black and white, of Oglala Sioux at the Pine Ridge Indian Reservation in South Dakota. By this time, Remington had established himself as a leading illustrator of western themes, including the Indian Wars. He had traveled extensively in the West, gathering information, making sketches, and taking photographs, which he later used at his studio in New Rochelle, New York. Remington sold his illustrations to major magazines, including *Harper's Weekly*. The ghost dance of 1890, pictured here, provided artists like Remington with vivid imagery. The dancers wore brightly patterned robes and shirts, some decorated with stars symbolizing the coming of a new age for the Indians.

SOURCE: The Image Works.

A majority of tribes, especially smaller ones, sooner or later reached numbers too low to maintain their collective existence. Intermarriage, although widely condemned by the white community, drew many young people outside their Indian communities. Some tribal leaders also deliberately chose a path toward assimilation. The Quapaws, for example, formally disbanded in the aftermath of the Dawes Severalty Act. The minority that managed to prosper in white society as tradespeople or farmers abandoned their language, religious customs, and traditional ways of life. Later generations petitioned the federal government and regained tribal status, established ceremonial grounds and cultural centers (or bingo halls), and built up one of the most durable powwows in the state. Even so, much of the tribal lore that had underpinned distinct identity had simply vanished.

For those tribes who remained on reservations, the aggressively assimilationist policies of the Office of Indian Affairs (OIA) challenged their traditional ways. The Southern Ute, for example, at one time hunted, fished, and gathered throughout a huge region spanning the Rocky Mountains and the Great Basin. In 1848, they began to sign a series of treaties in accord with the reservation policy of the U.S. government. Twenty years later their territory had been reduced to approximately one-quarter of Colorado Territory, and in 1873, they had further relinquished about one-quarter of this land. After the passage of the Dawes Act, the U. S. government, pressured by white settlers, gave the tribe two choices: they could break up their communal land holdings and accept the 160 acres granted to the male heads of families, or they could maintain their tribal status and move to a reservation in Utah. The Utes divided over the issue, but a considerable number chose to live on reservations under the administration of the OIA.

Under the terms of the Dawes Act, Southern Ute men and women endured continuous challenges to their egalitarian practices. The OIA assumed, for example, that Ute men would represent the tribe in all official matters, a policy that forced Ute women to petition the U.S. government to recognize their rights and concerns. Similarly, Ute women struggled to hold on to their roles as producers within the subsistence family economy against the efforts of the OIA agents to train them for homemaking alone. In the 1880s, the OIA established a matrons program to teach Ute women to create a "civilizing" home, which included new lessons about sanitation, home furnishings, and health care. But even fifty years later, some Ute preferred to live at least part of the year in a teepee in a multigenerational family, rather than in a private residence designed for a single married couple and their children.

A small minority of tribes, grown skillful in adapting to dramatically changing circumstances, managed to persist and even grow. Never numbering more than a few thousand people, during the late eighteenth century the Cheyennes had found themselves caught geographically between aggressive tribes in the Great Lakes region and had migrated into the Missouri area, where they split into small village-sized communities. By the mid-nineteenth century, they had become expert horse traders on the Great Plains, well prepared to meet the massive influx of white settlers by shifting their location frequently. They avoided the worst of the pestilence that spread from the diseases white people carried, and likewise survived widespread intermarriage with the Sioux in the 1860s and 1870s. Instructed to settle, many Cheyenne took up elements of the Christian religion and became farmers, also without losing their tribal identity. Punished by revenge-hungry soldiers after the battle of Little Bighorn, their lands repeatedly taken away, they still held on. The Cheyennes were survivors.

The Navajos experienced an extraordinary renewal, largely because they built a life in territory considered worthless by whites. Having migrated to the Southwest from the northwestern part of the continent perhaps 700 years ago, the Diné ("the People"), as they called themselves, had already survived earlier invasions by the Spanish. In 1863, they had been conquered again through the cooperation of hostile tribes led by the famous Colonel Kit Carson. Their crops burned, their fruit trees destroyed, 8,000 Navajo were forced in the 300-mile "Long Walk" to the desolate Bosque Redondo reservation, where they nearly starved. Four years later, the Indian Bureau allowed the severely reduced tribe to return to a fraction of its former lands.

By 1880, the Navajos' population had returned to nearly what it had been before their conquest by white Americans. Quickly depleting the deer and antelope on their hemmed-in reservation, they had to rely on sheep alone as a food reserve during years of bad crops. With their wool rugs and blankets much in demand in the East, the Navajos increasingly turned to crafts, eventually including silver jewelry as well as weaving, to survive. Although living on the economic margin, they persevered to become the largest Indian nation in the United States.

The nearby Hopis, like the Navajos, survived by stubbornly clinging to lands unwanted by white settlers, and by adapting to drastically changing conditions. A famous tribe of "desert people," the Hopis had lived for centuries in their cliff cities. Their highly developed theological beliefs, peaceful social system, sand paintings, and kachina dolls interested many educated and influential whites. The resulting publicity helped them gather the public supporters and financial resources needed to fend off further threats to their reservations.

Fortunate Northwestern tribes remained relatively isolated from white settlers until the early twentieth cen-

CHRONOLOGY

1848	Treaty of Guadalupe Hidalgo		*1872*	Yellowstone National Park created
1849–60s	California Gold Rush		*1873*	Timber Culture Act
				Red River War
1853	Gadsden Purchase		*1874–75*	Sioux battles in Black Hills of Dakotas
1858	Comstock Lode discovered		*1876*	Custer's Last Stand
1859	Cortina's War in South Texas		*1877*	Defeat of the Nez Percé
1862	Homestead Act makes free land available		*1881*	Helen Hunt Jackson, *A Century of Dishonor*
	Morrill Act authorizes "land-grant" colleges		*1882*	Edmunds Act outlaws polygamy
1865–67	Great Sioux War		*1885–87*	Droughts and severe winters cause the collapse of the cattle boom
1866	Texas cattle drives begin		*1887*	Dawes Severalty Act
	Medicine Lodge Treaty established reservation system		*1890*	Sioux Ghost Dance movement
	Alaska purchased			Massacre of Lakota Sioux at Wounded Knee
1869	Board of Indian Commissioners created			Census Bureau announces the end of the frontier line
	Buffalo Bill, the King of the Border Men, sets off "Wild West" publishing craze		*1897*	Forest Management Act gives the federal government authority over forest reserves
1870s	Grasshopper attacks on the Great Plains			

tury, although they had begun trading with white visitors centuries earlier. Northwestern peoples relied largely on salmon and other resources of the region's rivers and bays. In potlatch ceremonies, leaders redistributed tribal wealth and maintained their personal status and the status of their tribe by giving lavish gifts to invited guests. Northwest peoples also made intricate wood carvings, including commemorative "totem" poles, that recorded their history and identified their regional status. Northwestern peoples maintained their cultural integrity in part through connections with kin in Canada, as did Southern tribes with kin in Mexico. In Canada and Mexico, native populations suffered less pressure from new populations and retained more tribal authority than in the United States.

Indian nations approached their nadir as the nineteenth century came to a close. The descendants of the great pre-Columbian civilizations had been conquered by foreigners, their population reduced to fewer than 250,000. Under the pressure of assimilation, the remaining tribespeople became known to non-Indians as "the vanishing Americans." It would take several generations before Indian sovereignty experienced a resurgence.

CONCLUSION

The transformation of the trans-Mississippi West pointed up the larger meaning of expansion. Almost overnight, mines opened, cities grew, and farms and cattle ranches spread out across the vast countryside. New communities formed rapidly and often displaced old ones. In 1890, the director of the U.S. Census announced that the nation's "unsettled area has been so broken into by isolated bodies of settlement that there can hardly be said to be a frontier line."

The development of the West met the nation's demands for mineral resources for its expanding industries and agricultural products for the people of the growing cities. Envisioning the West as a cornucopia whose boundless treasures would offer themselves to the willing pioneer, most of the new residents failed to calculate the odds against their making a prosperous livelihood as miners, farmers, or petty merchants. Nor could they appreciate the long-term consequences of the violence they brought with them from the battlefields of the Civil War to the far reaches of the West.

Americans had brought in commercial capitalism and their political and legal systems, as well as many of their social and cultural institutions. Ironically though, even after statehood, white settlers would still be only distant representatives of an empire whose financial, political, and industrial centers remained in the Northeast. In return for raw produce or ore drawn out of soil or rock, they received washtubs, clothes, and whiskey; model legal statutes; and doctors, lawyers, and teachers. But they were often frustrated by their continued isolation, and they were enraged at the federal regulations that governed them, and at the Eastern investors and lawyers who seemed poised on all sides to rob them of the fruits of their labor. Embittered Westerners, along with Southerners, would form the core of a nationwide discontent that would soon threaten to uproot the American political system.

REVIEW QUESTIONS

1. Discuss the role of federal legislation in accelerating and shaping the course of westward expansion.

2. How did the incorporation of Western territories into the United States affect Indian nations such as the Sioux or the Nez Percé? Discuss the causes and consequences of the Indian Wars. Discuss the significance of reservation policy and the Dawes Severalty Act for tribal life.

3. What were some of the major technological advances in mining and in agriculture that promoted the development of the Western economy?

4. Describe the unique features of Mexicano communities in the Southwest before and after the mass immigration of Anglos. How did changes in the economy affect the patterns of labor and the status of women in these communities?

5. What role did the Homestead Act play in western expansion? How did farm families on the Great Plains divide chores among their members? What factors determined the likelihood of economic success or failure?

6. Describe the responses of artists, naturalists, and conservationists to the Western landscape. How did their photographs, paintings, and stories shape perceptions of the West in the East?

RECOMMENDED READING

Jon Gjerde, *The Minds of the West: Ethnocultural Evolution in the Rural Middle West, 1830–1917* (1997). A combination cultural and economic history that weighs the importance of ethnicity in the shaping of American identities in the farming regions of the Middle West. Gjerde pays close attention to the religious institutions and systems of belief of European immigrants as the basis of community formation.

Robert V. Hine and John Mack Faragher, *The American West: A New Interpretive History* (2000). A sweeping, amply illustrated survey of Western history with reference to recent scholarship. The authors emphasize Native Americans and include rich material on ethnicity, the environment, and the role of women.

John C. Hudson, *Making the Corn Belt: A Geographical History of Middle-Western Agriculture* (1994). An ecologically oriented study of corn growing that traces its development from Indians to Southerners moving westward.

David Igler, *Industrial Cowboys: Miller & Lux and the Transformation of the Far West, 1850–1920* (2001). A novel blend of business, labor, ethnic, and environmental history: a study of one of the nation's largest industrial enterprises by the turn of the century, the sprawling cattle ranch owned by the entrepreneurs, Miller & Lux. Igler's study of the San Joaquin Valley situates California's agribusiness squarely within the history of industrial capitalism.

Andrew C. Isenberg, *The Destruction of the Bison: An Environmental History, 1750–1920* (2000). A rich study of the forces behind the near-extinction of the bison, with special attention to the interplay among Indians, Euroamericans, and the environment of the Great Plains. Isenberg constructs a narrative that is as much cultural as economic in framing the problem.

Karl Jacoby, *Crimes Against Nature: Squatters, Poachers, Thieves, and the Hidden History of American Conservation* (2001). A complex analysis of the origins of national parks in the Adirondacks, Yellowstone, and the Grand Canyon. Rather than focusing on the individuals and groups that led the conservation of vast public lands, Jacoby switches perspective to focus on those who were dispossessed by the process.

Elizabeth Jameson and Susan Armitage, eds., *Writing the Range* (1997). A collection of essays on women in the West that presents an inclusive historical narrative based on the experiences of women of differing backgrounds, races, and ethnic groups.

Katherine M. B. Osburn, *Southern Ute Women: Autonomy and Assimilation on the Reservation, 1887–1934* (1998). Presents a careful analysis of the impact of the Dawes Act on the role and status of women among the Southern Ute. Osburn acknowledges the changes brought by the Office of Indian Affairs programs on the reservations, but emphasizes the resistance of the Ute and the retention of old ways.

Glenda Riley, *Building and Breaking Families in the American West* (1996). Essays covering the variety of cultures in the American West, organized topically to highlight courtship, marriage and intermarriage, and separation and divorce.

Martha A. Sandweiss, *Print the Legend: Photography and the American West* (2002). Richly illustrated exploration of the tenuous relationship between history and memory. Sandweiss persuasively argues that highly stylized photographs have figured prominently in shaping our understanding of the West.

Thomas E. Sheridan, *Los Tucsonenses: The Mexican Community in Tucson, 1854–1941* (1986). A highly readable account of Mexican-American communities in the Southwest. Sheridan shows how a midcentury accommodation of Anglos and Mexicanos faded with the absorption of the region into the national economy, and with the steady displacement of the Mexicano community from its agricultural landholdings.

Liping Zhu, *A Chinaman's Chance: The Chinese on the Rocky Mountain Mining Frontier* (1997). Studies the mining communities of Chinese in the Boise Basin of Idaho. Zhu emphasizes the success the Chinese enjoyed not only as miners but as merchants in the face of discriminatory practices and laws.

For additional study resources for this chapter, go to the *Companion Website*, **http://www.prenhall.com/faragher**.

CHAPTER 19

The Incorporation of America

1865–1900

CHAPTER OUTLINE

Packingtown, Chicago, Illinois

Approaching Packingtown, the neighborhood adjoining the Union Stockyards, the center of Chicago's great meatpacking industry, one noticed first the pungent odor, a mixture of smoke, fertilizer, and putrid flesh, blood, and hair from the slaughtered animals. A little closer, the stench of the uncovered garbage dump blended in. Finally, one crossed "Bubbly Creek," a lifeless offshoot of the Chicago River, aptly named for the effect of the carbolic acid gas that formed from the decaying refuse poured in by the meatpacking plants. Railroads crisscrossed the entire area, bringing in thousands of animals each day and carrying out meat for sale in markets across the country.

Packingtown occupied about one square mile of land bounded by stockyards, packing plants, and freight yards. With a population of 30,000 to 40,000 at the end of the nineteenth century, it was a rapidly growing community of old and new immigrants who depended on the meatpacking industry for their livelihood. An average household included six or seven people—parents, two or three children, and two or three boarders. Typically, they lived in wooden houses divided into four or more flats. Although Irish, Germans, Bohemians, Poles, Lithuanians, and Slovaks were squeezed together in this solidly working-class neighborhood, strong ethnic identities persisted. Few households included residents of more than one nationality, and interethnic marriages were rare. Nearly everyone professed the Roman Catholic faith, yet each ethnic group maintained its own church and often its own parochial school, where children were taught in their parents' language. Political organizations, fraternal societies, and even gymnastic clubs and drama groups reflected these ethnic divisions.

The one local institution that bridged the different groups was the saloon. Located on virtually every street corner, saloons offered important services to the community, hosting weddings and dances, providing meeting places for trade unions and fraternal societies, and cashing paychecks. During the frequent seasons of unemployment, Packingtown workers spent a lot of time in saloons. Here, they often made friends across ethnic divisions, an extension of their common work experience in the nearby stockyard and packinghouses.

Most of the meatpacking industry's first "knife men"—the skilled workers in the "killing gangs" that managed the actual slaughtering and cutting operations—were German and Irish. Many had learned their butcher's craft in the Old Country. Below them were the common laborers, mainly recent immigrants from eastern Europe. Having no previous experience in meatpacking, these workers found themselves in the lowest paid jobs, such as the by-product manufacturing of glue and oleo. A sizable portion had never before earned wages. They soon discovered, as one Lithuanian laborer put it, that "money was everything and a man without money must die." But the money available—a daily wage of $2 (or less)—was often not enough. The death rate from tuberculosis in Packingtown was thought to be the highest in Chicago and among the highest in the nation.

The Packingtown community, small and insular as it seemed to the residents, was bound into an elaborate

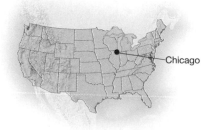

Chicago

economic network that reached distant parts of the United States, transforming the ways farmers raised livestock and grains, railroads operated, and consumers ate their meals. These workers helped make Chicago a gateway city, a destination point for raw materials coming in from the West as well as a point of export for products of all kinds.

Chicago meatpackers, led by the "big five" of Armour, Cudahy, Morris, Schwarzschild and Sulzberger, and Swift, expanded more than 900 percent between 1870 and 1890, dominating the national market for meat and establishing a standard for monopoly capitalism in the late nineteenth century. In the process, they also became the city's largest manufacturing employer. They built huge, specialized factories during the 1860s and 1870s that speeded the killing process and—thanks to mountains of ice brought by rail from ponds and lakes—operated year round. The introduction of an efficiently refrigerated railroad car in the 1880s made it possible to ship meat nationwide. Consumers had long believed that only meat butchered locally was safe to eat, but now cheap Chicago-packed beef and pork began to appear on every meateater's table. Local packinghouses throughout the Midwest succumbed to the ruthless competition from Chicago.

Chicago's control of the mass market for meat affected all aspects of the industry. Midwestern farmers practically abandoned raising calves on open pastures. Instead, they bought two-year-old steers from the West and fattened them on homegrown corn in feedlots, making sure that bulk went into edible parts rather than muscle and bone. The feedlot—a kind of rural factory—replaced pasture, just as pasture had earlier supplanted prairie grasslands.

Few of the workers in Chicago's stockyards had seen a farm since they left their homelands. But as the working hands of what poet Carl Sandburg would later call the "Hog butcher for the world, . . . City of the big shoulders," they played their part, along with the farmer, the grain dealer, the ironworker, the teamster, and many others in bringing together the neighboring countryside and the city to create a regional center for the production of meat and its distribution nationwide.

By the final decades of the nineteenth century, the nation's eyes were fixed on Chicago. The city had become home to several of the most technologically advanced industries in the world, and huge profits had created a population of extraordinarily wealthy individuals. At the same time, the city also gave rise to an exceptionally militant labor movement. In 1886, workers from several of the city's major industries, including meatpacking, led a nation-wide campaign for shorter hours. In early May, a huge demonstration protesting police violence against strikers ended in tragedy when a bomb exploded and killed several people in the city's Haymarket Square. In its aftermath, a wave of fear swept over the nation. Chicago, many Americans believed, was leading the way—but to what?

KEY TOPICS

- The rise of big business and the formation of the national labor movement
- The transformation of Southern society
- The growth of cities
- The Gilded Age
- Changes in education
- Commercial amusements and organized sports

THE RISE OF INDUSTRY, THE TRIUMPH OF BUSINESS

At the time of the Civil War, the typical American business firm was a small enterprise, owned and managed by a single family, and producing goods for a local or regional market. By the turn of the century, businesses depending on large-scale investments had organized as corporations and grown to unforeseen size. These mammoth firms could afford to mass-produce goods for national and even international markets. At the helm stood unimaginably wealthy men, such as Andrew Carnegie, Philip Danforth Armour, Jay Gould, and John D. Rockefeller, all powerful leaders of a new national business community.

Revolutions in Technology and Transportation

The Centennial Exposition of 1876, held in Philadelphia, celebrated not so much the American Revolution 100 years earlier as the industrial and technological promise of the century to come. The visiting emperor of Brazil spoke into an unfamiliar device on display and gasped, "My God, it talks!" The telephone, patented that year by Alexander Graham Bell, signaled the rise of the United States to world leadership in industrial technology (see Map 19.1).

The year 1876 also marked the opening of Thomas Alva Edison's laboratory in Menlo Park, New Jersey, one of the first devoted to industrial research. Three years later, his research team hit upon its most marketable

MAP EXPLORATION

To explore an interactive version of this map, go to
www.prenhall.com/faragher5/map19.1

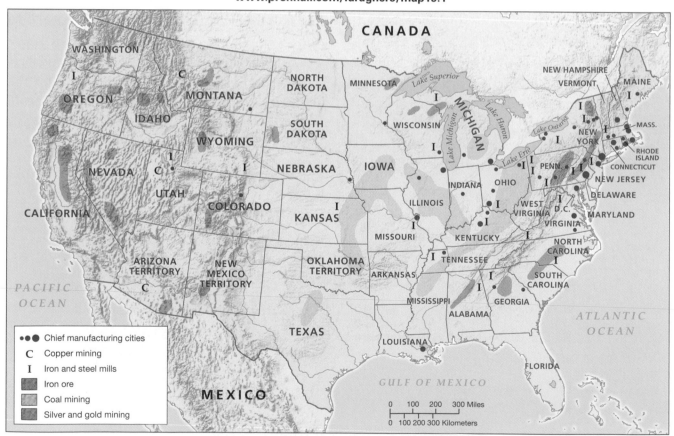

MAP 19.1 Patterns of Industry, 1900 Industrial manufacturing concentrated in the Northeast and Midwest, while the raw materials for production came mostly from other parts of the nation.

In 1887, Thomas Alva Edison (1847–1931) moved his laboratory from Menlo Park to West Orange, New Jersey. This photograph, taken in 1901, shows him in what many historians consider the first industrial research facility. Here, he invented the alkaline storage battery, the phonograph, and the kinetoscope, the first machine to allow one person at a time to view motion pictures.

SOURCE: Corbis/Bettman

invention, an incandescent lamp that burned for more than thirteen hours. By 1882, the Edison Electric Light Company had launched its service in New York City's financial district. A wondrous source of light, electricity revolutionized both urban life and industry, soon replacing steam as the major source of power.

By this time, American inventors, who had filed nearly half a million patents since the close of the Civil War, were previewing the marvels of the next century. Henry Ford, working for the Detroit Edison Company, was already experimenting with the gasoline-burning internal combustion engine and designing his own automobile. By 1900, American companies had produced more than 4,000 automobiles. The prospect of commercial aviation emerged in 1903, when Wilbur and Orville Wright staged the first airplane flight near Kitty Hawk, North Carolina.

A major force behind economic growth was the vast transcontinental railroad, completed in 1869. The addition of three more major rail lines (the Southern Pacific; the Northern Pacific; and the Atchison, Topeka, and Santa Fe) in the early 1880s, and the Great Northern, a decade later, completed the most extensive transportation network in the world. As the nation's first big business and recipient of generous government subsidies, railroads linked cities in every state and served as a nationwide distributor of goods. Freight trains carried the bountiful natural resources, such as iron, coal, and minerals that supplied the raw materials for industry, as well as food and other commodities for the growing urban populations.

The monumental advances in transportation and communication facilitated the progressively westward relocation of industry. The geographic center of manufacturing (as computed by the gross value of products) was near the middle of Pennsylvania in 1850, in western Pennsylvania by 1880, and near Mansfield, Ohio, in 1900.

Industry grew at a pace that was not only unprecedented but previously unimaginable. In 1865, the annual production of goods was estimated at $2 billion; by 1900, it stood at $13 billion, transforming the United States from fourth to first in the world in terms of productivity. By the early twentieth century, American industry manufactured one-third of the world's goods.

Mechanization Takes Command

This second industrial revolution depended on many factors, but none was more important than the application of new technologies to increase the productivity of labor and the volume of goods. Machines, factory managers, and workers together created a system of continuous production by which more could be made, and faster, than anywhere else on earth. Higher productivity depended not only on machinery and technology but on economies of scale and speed, reorganization of factory labor and business management, and the unparalleled growth of a market for goods of all kinds.

All these changes depended in turn on anthracite coal, a new source of fuel, which was widely used after 1850. Reliable and inexpensive sources of energy made possible dramatic changes in the industrial uses of light, heat, and motion. Equally important, coal fueled the great open-hearth furnaces and mills of the iron and steel industries. By the end of the century, the U.S. steel industry was the world's largest, churning out rails to carry trains and parts to make more machines to produce yet more goods.

New systems of mass production replaced wasteful and often chaotic practices and speeded up the delivery of finished goods. In the 1860s, meatpackers set up one of the earliest production lines. The process of converting livestock into meat began with a live animal. A chain around the hind leg whirled the body to an overhead rail, which carried it to slaughter—all in barely half a minute's time. Then hair and bristles were removed by a scraping machine, the carcass shifted to a conveyer belt where the chest was split and the organs removed, and the body placed in a cooler. This "disassembly line" displaced patterns of hand labor that were centuries old.

The production line became standard in most areas of manufacturing.

Sometimes the invention of a single machine could instantly transform production, mechanizing every stage from processing the raw material to packaging the product. The cigarette-making machine, patented in 1881, shaped the tobacco, encased it in an endless paper tube, and snipped off the tube at cigarette-length intervals. This machine could produce more than 7,000 cigarettes per hour, replacing the worker who at best made 3,000 per day. After a few more improvements, fifteen machines could meet the total demand for American cigarettes. Within a generation, continuous production became standard in most areas of manufacturing, revolutionizing the making of furniture, cloth, grain products, soap, and canned goods; the refining, distilling, and processing of animal and vegetable fats; and eventually, the manufacture of automobiles.

Expanding the Market for Goods

To distribute the growing volume of goods and to create a dependable market, businesses demanded new techniques of merchandising on a national and, in some cases, international scale. For generations, legions of sellers, or "drummers," had worked their routes, pushing goods, especially hardware and patent medicines, to individual buyers and local retail stores. By the end of the nineteenth century, the manufacturers of mass-produced goods had launched massive advertising campaigns to induce consumers to buy their brands over local or home-made items. Procter and Gamble, for example, eventually convinced the American housewife that its solid vegetable shortening, created in its laboratory from the surplus of cottonseed oil used to make its popular soaps, was a better choice for baking and frying than the familiar animal fats and lard, and distributors soon could not keep up with the consumer demand for Crisco.

In 1869, Francis Wayland Ayer founded an agency that would handle some of the most successful advertising campaigns of the era. Ayer's managed the accounts of such up-and-coming companies as Montgomery Ward and the National Biscuit Company, which sold millions of packaged biscuits under the trademarked name of "Uneeda." With the help of this new sales tool, gross revenues of retailers raced upward from $8 million in 1860 to $102 million in 1900.

Mail-order houses helped to get these new products fo consumers. Accompanying the consolidation of the railroad lines, the postal system expanded. Rates were lowered for shipping freight and postage alike. By 1896, rural free delivery had reached distant communities.

Growing directly out of these services, the successful Chicago-based mail-order houses drew rural and urban consumers into a common marketplace. Sears, Roebuck and Company and Montgomery Ward offered an enormous variety of goods, from shoes to buggies to gasoline stoves and cream separators. The mail-order catalogue also returned to rural folks the fruits of their own labor, now processed and packaged for easy use. The Sears catalogue offered Armour's summer sausage as well as Aunt Jemima's Pancake Flour and Queen Mary Scotch Oatmeal, both made of grains that came from the agricultural heartland. In turn, the purchases made by farm families through the Sears catalogue sent cash flowing into Chicago.

The chain store achieved similar economies of scale. By 1900, a half-dozen grocery chains had sprung up. The largest was A&P, originally named the Great Atlantic and Pacific Tea Company to celebrate the completion of the transcontinental railroad. Frank and Charles Woolworth offered inexpensive variety goods in five-and-ten-cent stores. Other chains selling drugs, costume jewelry, shoes, cigars, and furniture soon appeared, offering a greater selection of goods and lower prices than the small, independent stores.

Opening shortly after the Civil War, department stores began to take up much of the business formerly enjoyed by specialty shops, offering a spectrum of services that included restaurants, rest rooms, ticket agencies, nurseries, reading rooms, and post offices. Elegantly appointed with imported carpets, sweeping marble staircases, and crystal chandeliers, the department store raised retailing to new heights. By the close of the century, the names of Marshall Field of Chicago, Filene's of Boston, The Emporium of San Francisco, Wanamaker's of Philadelphia, and Macy's of New York had come to represent the splendors of those great cities as well as the apex of mass retailing.

Integration, Combination, and Merger

The business community aspired to exercise greater control of the economy and to enlarge the commercial empire. From the source of raw materials to the organization of production, from the conditions of labor to the climate of public opinion, business leaders acted shrewdly. Economic cycles alternating between rapid growth and sharp decline also promoted the rise of big business. Major economic setbacks in 1873 and 1893 wiped out weaker competitors, allowing the strongest firms to rebound swiftly and to expand their sales and scale of operation during the recovery period.

Businesses grew in two distinct, if overlapping, ways. Through *vertical integration* a firm gained control of production at every step of the way—from raw materials through processing to the transporting and merchandising of the finished items. In 1899, the United Fruit Company began to build a network of wholesale houses in the United States, and within two years it had opened distribution centers in twenty-one major cities. Eventually, it controlled an elaborate system of Central American plantations and temperature-controlled shipping and storage facilities for its highly perishable bananas. The firm became one of the nation's largest corporations.

The second means of growth, *horizontal combination,* entailed gaining control of the market for a single product. The most famous case was the Standard Oil Company, founded by John D. Rockefeller in 1870. Operating out of Cleveland in a highly competitive but lucrative field, Rockefeller first secured preferential rates from railroads eager to ensure a steady supply of oil. He then convinced or coerced other local oil operators to sell their stock to him. The Standard Oil Trust, established in 1882, controlled over 90 percent of the nation's oil-refining industry.

In 1890, Congress passed the Sherman Antitrust Act to restore competition by encouraging small business and outlawing "every . . . combination . . . in restraint of trade or commerce." Ironically, the courts interpreted the law in ways that inhibited the organization of trade unions (on the ground that they restricted the free flow of labor), and actually helped the consolidation of business. More than 2,600 firms vanished between 1898 and 1902 alone. By

1910, the industrial giants that would dominate the American economy until the last half of the twentieth century—U.S. Rubber, Goodyear, American Smelting and Refining, Anaconda Copper, General Electric, Westinghouse, Nabisco, Swift and Company, Armour, International Harvester, Eastman Kodak, and American Can—had already incorporated as the nation's biggest businesses.

The Gospel of Wealth

Ninety percent of the nation's business leaders were Protestant, and the majority attended church services regularly. They attributed their personal achievement to hard work and perseverance and made these the principal tenets of a new faith that imbued the pursuit of wealth with old-time religious zeal.

One version of this "gospel of wealth" justified the ruthless behavior of the so-called "robber barons," who accumulated unprecedented wealth and power through shady deals and conspiracies. Speculator Jay Gould, known in the popular press as the "Worst Man in the World," wrung his fortune, it was widely believed, from the labor of others. He rose quickly from his modest origins through a series of unsavory financial maneuvers.

Speculation in railroads proved to be Gould's forte. He took over the Erie Railroad, paying off New York legislators to get the state to finance its expansion, and he acquired the U.S. Express Company by pressuring and tricking its stockholders. When threatened with arrest, Gould sold off his shares for $9 million and moved on to the Union Pacific, where he cut wages, precipitated strikes, and manipulated elections in the Western and Plains states. Tired of being caricatured in the press as a great swindler, he bought the leading newspapers. At his death, one obituary described Jay Gould as "an incarnation of cupidity and sordidness," whose life symbolized "idolatrous homage [to] the golden calf."

Andrew Carnegie—the "Richest Man in the World"—offered a strikingly different model. He represented the "captain of industry," who had risen from the ranks through diligence, and who refused to worship wealth for its own sake. Late in his life, he outlined his personal philosophy in a popular essay, *The Gospel of Wealth* (1889),

John D. Rockefeller, who formed the Standard Oil Company in 1870, sought to control all aspects of the industry, from the transportation of crude oil to the marketing and distribution of the final products. By the end of the decade, after making shrewd deals with the railroads and underselling his rivals, he managed to control 90 percent of the oil-refining industry. To further consolidate his interests, in 1882 Rockefeller created the Standard Oil Trust, which, by integrating both vertically and horizontally, became a model for other corporations and an inspiration for critical commentary and antitrust legislation. This cartoon, published in *Puck* in 1904, shows the stranglehold Standard Oil had on government and industry alike. In 1911, in response to an antitrust suit, the Supreme Court ordered the company to break up.

SOURCE: Courtesy of the Library of Congress.

This engraving of steel manufacturing at Andrew Carnegie's plant in 1886 features a Bessemer Converter, which converts molten pig iron into steel. The process was named after Sir Henry Bessemer of Sheffield, England, who first patented the process in 1855.

SOURCE: The Granger Collection, New York (0009141/4E452.14).

stepped into the superintendent's job. While improving passenger train service, he invested brilliantly to build funds for his next venture.

Carnegie built an empire in steel. A genius at vertical integration, he undercut his competitors by using the latest technology and designing his own system of cost analysis. By 1900, Carnegie managed the most efficient steel mills in the world, which accounted for one-third of the nation's output. When he sold out to J. P. Morgan's new United States Steel Corporation in 1901, his personal share of the proceeds came to $225 million.

Carnegie was well known as a civic leader. From one point of view, he was a factory despot who underpaid his employees and ruthlessly managed their working conditions. But to the patrons of the public libraries, art museums, concert halls, colleges, and universities that he funded, Carnegie appeared to be the single greatest philanthropist of the age. By the time he died, he had given away his massive personal fortune.

Whether following the rough road of Gould or the smooth path of Carnegie, the business community worked together to fashion the new conservative ideology of Social Darwinism, which purportedly explained, and justified, why some Americans grew rich while others remained poor. Derived from the famed British naturalist Charles Darwin's scientific theories of evolution presented in *On the Origin of Species* (1859), social Darwinism superimposed the brutal struggle for existence that supposedly dominated nature onto modern society, and underscored the principle of "survival of the fittest." The Yale professor William Graham Sumner gave this idea an economic spin. In an essay published in 1883 entitled *What Social Classes Owe to Each Other*, he argued that only a few individuals were capable of putting aside selfish pleasures to produce the capital needed to drive the emerging industrial economy and, moreover, they were fully deserving of their great fortunes. In contrast, the vast majority, too

explaining that "there is no genuine, praiseworthy success in life if you are not honest, truthful, and fair-dealing."

A poor immigrant from Scotland, Carnegie spent his boyhood studying bookkeeping at night while working days in a textile mill. In 1852, he became the personal secretary of the superintendent of the Pennsylvania Railroad's Western division. He learned quickly and soon lazy or profligate to rise above poverty, deserved their own miserable fates. To tamper with this "natural" order by establishing welfare programs to help the poor or redistributing wealth in any way would be hazardous to society. Meanwhile, the popular writer Horatio Alger produced a more temperate version of this credo. Publishing more than 100 rags-to-riches novels, he created heroes who manage to rise out of poverty by both hard work and luck and ultimately acquire, if not vast wealth, middle-class respectability and comfort.

LABOR IN THE AGE OF BIG BUSINESS

Like the gospel of wealth, the "gospel of work" affirmed the dignity of hard work, the virtue of thrift, and the importance of individual initiative. But unlike business leaders, the philosophers of American working people did not believe in riches as the proof of work well done, or in the lust for power as the driving force of progress. On the contrary, they contended that honesty and competence should become the cornerstones of a society "so improved that labor shall become a blessing instead of a curse."

This faith inspired a slender minority, less than 3 percent of the workforce, to form unions in various trades and industries. Despite its small size, the labor movement represented the most significant and lasting response of workers to the rise of big business and the consolidation of corporate power.

The Wage System

The accelerating growth of industry, especially the steady mechanization of production, dramatically changed employer-employee relations and created new categories of workers. Both in turn fostered competition among workers and created conditions often hazardous to health.

For most craft workers, the new system destroyed long-standing practices, chipped away at their customary autonomy, and placed them in competition with other, mainly unskilled workers. Frederick Winslow Taylor, the pioneer of scientific management, explained that managers must "take all the important decisions . . . out of the hands of workmen." Teams of ironworkers, for example, had previously set the rules of production as well as their wages, while the company supplied equipment and raw materials. Once steel replaced iron, most companies gradually introduced a new system. Managers now constantly supervised workers, set the pace of production and rate of payment, and introduced new, faster machinery that made many skills obsolete. In the woodworking trades, highly skilled cabinetmakers, who for generations had brought their own tools to the factory, were largely replaced with "green hands"—immigrants, including many women—who with only minimal training and close supervision could operate new woodworking machines at cheaper rates of pay.

Not all trades conformed to this pattern. The garment industry, for example, grew at a very fast pace in New York, Boston, Chicago, Philadelphia, Cleveland, and St. Louis, but retained older systems of labor along with the new. The highly mechanized factories employed hundreds of thousands of young immigrant women, while the outwork system, established well before the Civil War, contracted ever-larger numbers of families to work in their homes on sewing machines or by hand. However, companies relied on a "sweating" system that fostered extreme competition between these two groups of workers by continually increasing daily production quotas. Paid by the piece—a seam stitched, a collar turned, a button attached—workers labored faster and longer at home or in the factory to forestall a dip in wages.

The new system of production required a vast number of people. Lured by the promise of a paying job in industry, many young men and women fled the family farm for the factory. A smaller number escaped the peonage system of agricultural labor in the South. By far, the largest proportion came from Europe or Asia. In many occupations—meat processing, clothing and textile manufacturing, cigar making, and mining, for example—immigrants predominated by the end of the century.

Industrial expansion also offered new opportunities for women to work outside the home. African American and immigrant women found employment in trades least affected by technological advances, such as domestic service. In contrast, English-speaking white women moved into the better-paying clerical and sales positions in the rapidly expanding business sector. After the typewriter and telephone came into widespread use in the 1890s, the number of women employed in office work rose even faster. At the turn of the century, 8.6 million women worked outside their homes—nearly triple the number in 1870.

By contrast, African American men found themselves excluded from many fields. In Cleveland, for example, the number of black carpenters declined after 1870, just as the volume of construction was rapidly increasing. African American men were also systematically driven from restaurant service and barred from newer trades such as boilermaking, plumbing, electrical work, and paperhanging, which European immigrants secured for themselves.

Discriminatory or exclusionary practices fell hardest on workers recruited earlier from China to work in the mines, in the construction of railroads, and in market gardening. By the 1870s, white workers and proprietors of small businesses had formed a potent and racist anti-Chinese movement to protest "cheap Chinese labor" and to demand a halt to Chinese immigration. Calling for deportation measures, white rioters razed Chinese neighborhoods. In 1882, Congress responded to the violence by passing the Chinese Exclusion Act, which suspended Chinese immigration for ten years, limited the civil rights of resident Chinese, and forbade their naturalization.

For even the best-placed wage earners, the new workplace could be unhealthy, even dangerous. Meat-packing produced its own hazards—the dampness of the pickling room, the sharp blade of the slaughtering knife, and the noxious odors of the fertilizer department. Factory owners often failed to mark high-voltage wires, locked fire doors, and allowed the emission of toxic

fumes. Extractive workers, such as coal and copper miners, labored in mineshafts where the air could suddenly turn poisonous, and where cave-ins were possible and deadly. Moreover, machines ran faster in American factories than anywhere else in the world, and workers who could not keep up or suffered serious injury found themselves without a job.

Even under less hazardous conditions, workers complained about the tedium of performing repetitive tasks for many hours each day. Although federal employees had been granted the eight-hour day in 1868, most workers still toiled upward of ten or twelve hours. "Life in a factory," one textile operative grumbled, "is perhaps, with the exception of prison life, the most monotonous life a human being can live." Nor could glamour be found in the work of saleswomen in the elegant department stores. Clerks could not sit down, despite workdays as long as sixteen hours in the busy season, or hold "unnecessary conversations" with customers or other clerks. Despite these disadvantages, most women preferred sales and manufacturing jobs to domestic service, which required live-in servants to be on call seven days a week, enjoying at best an occasional afternoon off.

Moreover, steady employment was rare. Between 1866 and 1897, fourteen years of prosperity stood against seventeen of hard times. The major depressions of 1873–79 and 1893–97 were the worst in the nation's history up to that time. Three "minor" recessions (1866–67, 1883–85, and 1890–91) did not seem insignificant to the millions who lost their jobs during those periods.

The Knights of Labor

The Noble and Holy Order of the Knights of Labor, founded by a group of Philadelphia garment cutters in 1869, grew to become the largest labor organization in the nineteenth century. Led by Grand Master Workman Terence V. Powderly, the order sought to bring together wage earners, regardless of skill. Only by organizing widely, Powderly insisted, would workers be able to achieve their "emancipation" from wage slavery.

The Knights endorsed a variety of reform measures—the restriction of child labor, a graduated income tax, more land set aside for homsteading, the abolition of contract labor, and monetary reform—to offset the power of the industrialists. They believed that the "producing classes," once freed from the grip of corporate monopoly and the curses of ignorance and alcohol, would transform the United States into a genuinely democratic society.

As an alternative to the wage system, the Knights promoted producers' cooperatives. In these factories, workers collectively made all decisions on prices and wages and shared all the profits. Local assemblies launched thousands of small co-ops, such as the Our

Thomas Nast (1840–1902), the most famous political cartoonist of the 1860s and 1870s, used his art to comment on pressing political issues, such as the plight of former slaves during Reconstruction, the evils of machine politics, and the rivalry between the national political parties. His drawings were made into wood engravings that were then printed in newspapers or popular magazines such as *Harper's Weekly.* In this cartoon published in 1871, Nast depicts Columbia protecting a Chinese immigrant from a racist mob.

SOURCE: Stock Montage, Inc./Historical Pictures Collection.

OUT OF MANY VOICES

WORKING IN A GLOVE FACTORY

Born in 1880, Agnes Nestor published this description of her experiences making gloves in a Chicago factory in 1898, the year she led a walkout to protest the piecework system and the fees the employers charged to rent their machines. The glove workers won their strike, and Nestor went on to become a union representative and prominent trade unionist in the city.

THE WHISTLE BLOWS AT 7 A.M. BUT THE PIECE workers have until 7:30 to come in to work. The penalty for coming late (after 7:30 A.M.) is the loss of a half day as the girls cannot then report to work until noon. . . .

When we begin our day's work we never know what our day's pay will be. We have to figure to make up for time we lose. Although it is not our fault it is at our expense. For instance: a dozen gloves may be cut from very heavy leather and very difficult to sew; or perhaps when we go to the desk for work we may have to stand waiting in line ten to twenty minutes; or the belt of our machine may break and we may have to walk around the factory two or three times before we find the

belt boy who, perhaps, is hidden under a table fixing a belt, and then we have to wait our turn; or we go to another desk to get our supplies such as needles, thread, welt, etc. But what we dread most of all is the machine breaking down as we do not know how long it will take to repair it. . . .

When I started in the trade and saw girls working at that dreadful pace every minute, I wondered how they could keep up the speed. But it is not until you become one of them that you can understand. . . .

At half-past nine the whistle blows again and we have five minutes for a light lunch. This time we have to make up so we work until 5:35 P.M. At noon we have only half an hour, which means that the girls have to bring cold lunches. . . . While half an hour seems a short time for lunch still a great many girls take ten or fifteen minutes of this to trim their gloves or whatever work they can do while the power is shut down. The girls all eat at their places, two or three grouping together. . . . ■

SOURCE: Agnes Nestor, "A Day's Work Making Gloves" (1898), in Agnes Nestor, *Woman's Labor Leader* (Rockford, Ill.: Bellevue Books Publishing Co, 1954), pp. 37–41.

Girls Co-operative Manufacturing Company, which was established by Chicago seamstresses in the 1880s. The Knights also ran small cooperative cigar shops and grocery stores, often housed in their own assembly buildings. Successful for a time, most cooperatives could not compete against the heavily capitalized enterprises and ultimately failed.

The Knights reached their peak during the great campaign for a shorter workday. The Eight-Hour League, led by Ira Steward, advocated a "natural" rhythm of eight hours for work, eight hours for sleep, and eight hours for leisure. After staging petition campaigns, marches, and a massive strike in New York City, the movement collapsed during the economic recession of the 1870s. The Knights helped revive it in the next decade, and this time, the campaign aroused widespread support from sympathetic consumers, who boycotted brands of beer, bread, and other products made in longer-hour shops.

Membership grew from a few thousand in 1880 to nearly three-quarters of a million six years later. The

organization was already committed to securing "for both sexes equal pay for equal work," but Leonora Barry, who was now appointed to organize women, helped to increase their share of membership to 10 percent. The Knights also organized African American workers—20,000 to 30,000 nationally—mainly in separate assemblies within the organization. However, the organization's open-handedness did not extend to Chinese workers, who were systematically excluded from membership.

During the first weeks of May 1886, more than a third-of-a-million workers demonstrated for the eight-hour day by walking off their jobs. Approximately 200,000 of them won shorter hours, including Packing-town's workers, who joined the Knights of Labor en masse. To celebrate, the Chicago community staged a huge parade of twelve marching bands and twenty-eight decorated wagons. Despite such a promising beginning, the shorter-hours campaign ended in tragedy.

On May 4, 1886, following a series of confrontations between strikers and authorities, a protest against police

At the 1886 General Assembly of the Knights of Labor, which met in Richmond, Virginia, sixteen women attended as delegates. Elizabeth Rodgers, the first woman in Chicago to join the Knights and the first woman to serve as a master workman in a district assembly, attended with her two-week old daughter. The convention established a Department of Women's Work and appointed Leonora M. Barry, a hosiery worker, as general investigator.

SOURCE: © Bettmann/CORBIS.

simple unionism," the AFL sought recognition of its union status to bargain with employers for better working conditions, higher wages, and shorter hours. In return, it offered compliant firms the benefit of amenable day-to-day relations with the most highly skilled wage earners. Only if companies refused to bargain in good faith would union members resort to strikes.

The new federation, with twelve national unions and 140,000 affiliated members in 1886, rapidly pushed ahead of the rival Knights by organizing craft workers. AFL president Samuel Gompers disregarded unskilled workers, racial minorities, and immigrants, believing they were impossible to organize and even unworthy of membership. He also believed in the "family wage," which was to be earned by men. Women, Gompers insisted, belonged in the home and not in the factory where they would serve only to lower wages. Under his leadership, the AFL advanced the interests of the "aristocrat of labor," the best-paid worker in the world.

violence at Chicago's Haymarket Square seemed to be ending quietly until someone threw a bomb that killed one policeman and left seven others fatally wounded. Police responded by firing wildly into the crowd, killing an equal number. After Chicago authorities arrested a group of anarchists, a sensational trial ended in death sentences, although no evidence linked the accused to the bombing. Four of the convicted were hanged, one committed suicide, and three other "Haymarket Martyrs," as they were called, remained jailed until pardoned in 1893, by Illinois governor John Peter Altgeld.

The Knights of Labor were crushed. Employers' associations successfully pooled funds to rid their factories of troublesome agitators, and announced that companies would no longer bargain with unions. In Packingtown, the Big Five firms drew up a blacklist to get rid of labor organizers, and quickly reinstituted the ten-hour day. The wage system had triumphed.

The American Federation of Labor

The events of 1886 also signaled the rise of a very different kind of organization, the American Federation of Labor (AFL). Unlike the Knights, the AFL accepted the wage system. Following a strategy of "pure and

Unlike the national leadership, local AFL members recuperated some of the best qualities of the Knights of Labor and established a firm basis for a new labor movement. They provided support to strikers, gathered votes for prolabor political candidates, sponsored social activities, and often published their own weekly newspapers.

Chicago's Central Labor Federation embodied the new spirit of the AFL. After the Haymarket tragedy, trade unionists worked more closely with urban reformers. Finding allies among women's clubs and church groups, within the state legislature, and even among some socially minded members of the business community, they cultivated an atmosphere of civic responsibility. The Illinois Factory Investigation Act of 1893 offered evidence of their hard work and patience, securing funds from the state legislature to monitor working conditions and particularly, to improve the woeful situation of the many women and children who worked in sweatshops.

Although the AFL represented only a small minority of working Americans—about 10 percent at the end of the century—local unions often played important roles in their communities. They may not have been able to slow the steady advance of mass production, which diminished the craft worker's autonomy and eliminated some of the most desirable jobs, but AFL members managed to make their presence felt. Local politicians courted their votes, and Labor Day, first celebrated in the 1880s, became a national holiday in 1894.

THE NEW SOUTH

"Fifteen years have gone over" since the Civil War, journalist Whitelaw Reid complained, yet the South "still sits crushed, wretched, busy displaying and bemoaning her wounds." Physically and financially devastated by the war, the South had little investment capital and relatively few banks to manage it. The area was economically stagnant, its per capita wealth only 27 percent of that of the Northeastern states. The South's countryside receded into greater isolation and poverty, while its few urban regions moved very slowly into the era of modern industry and technology. The Southern economy was held back by dependence on Northern finance capital, continued reliance on cotton production, and the legacy of slavery.

An Internal Colony

In the 1870s, a vocal and powerful new group of Southerners headed by Henry Woodfin Grady, editor of the *Atlanta Constitution,* insisted that the region enjoyed a great potential in its abundant natural resources of coal, iron, turpentine, tobacco, and lumber. Grady and his peers envisioned a "New South" where modern textile mills operated efficiently and profitably, close to the sources of raw goods, the expansive fields of cotton, and a plentiful and cheap supply of labor, unrestricted by unions or by legal limitations on the employment of children. Arguing against those planters who aspired to rejuvenate the agricultural economy based on the cultivation of a few staple crops, this group forcefully promoted industrial development and welcomed Northern investors.

Northern investors secured huge concessions from Southern state legislatures, including land, forest, and mineral rights and large tax exemptions. Exploiting the incentives, railroad companies laid more than 22,000 miles of new track, connecting the region to national markets and creating new cities. By 1890, a score of large railroad companies, centered mainly in New York, held more than half of all the track in the South.

Northerners also employed various means to protect their investments from Southern competition. By the late 1870s, Southern merchants, with help from foreign investors, had begun to run iron factories around Birmingham, Alabama. Southern iron production was soon encroaching on the Northeastern market. To stave off this competition, Andrew Carnegie ordered the railroads to charge higher freight fees to Birmingham's iron producers. New York bankers later succeeded in expatriating Birmingham's profits through stock ownership in Southern firms. After the turn of the century, U.S. Steel simply bought out the local merchants and took over much of Birmingham's production.

The production of cotton textiles followed a similar course. Powerful merchants and large landowners, realizing that they could make high profits by controlling the cotton crop from field to factory, promoted the vertical integration of the cotton industry. The number of mills in the South grew from 161 in 1880 to 400 in 1900. Southern investors supplied large amounts of the capital for the industrial expansion and technological improvements. The latest machines ran the new mills, and the South boasted the first factory fully equipped with electricity. Production in the four leading cotton-manufacturing states—North Carolina, South Carolina, Georgia, and Alabama—skyrocketed, far outpacing the New England mills.

Recognizing the potential for great profit, Northern manufacturers, including many New England mill owners, shifted their investments to the South. By the 1920s, Northern investors held much of the South's wealth, including the major textile mills, but returned through employment or social services only a small share of the profits to the region's people.

Beyond iron or steel and textiles, Southern industry remained largely extractive and, like the South itself, rural. Turpentine and lumbering businesses pushed ever further into diminishing pine forests, the sawmills and distilleries moving with them. Toward the end of the century, fruit canning and sugar refining flourished. For the most part, Southern enterprises mainly produced raw materials for consumption or use in the North, thereby perpetuating the economic imbalance between the sections.

The governing role of capital investments from outside the region reinforced long-standing relationships. Even rapid industrialization—in iron, railroads, and textiles—did not carry the same consequences achieved in the North. The rise of the New South reinforced, rather than diminished, the region's status as the nation's internal colony.

Southern Labor

The advance of Southern industry did little to improve the working lives of most African Americans, who made up more than one-third of region's population. Although the majority continued to work in agriculture, large numbers found jobs in industries such as the railroad. In booming cities like Atlanta, they even gained skilled positions as bricklayers, carpenters, and painters. For the most part, however, African Americans were limited to unskilled, low-paying jobs. In the textile mills and cigarette factories, which employed both black and white workers, the workforce was rigidly segregated. African Americans were assigned mainly to janitorial jobs and rarely worked alongside the white workers who tended the machines. Nearly all African American women who earned wages

The processing of raw tobacco employed thousands of African American women, who sorted, stripped, stemmed, and hung tobacco leaves as part of the redrying process. After mechanization was introduced, white women took jobs as cigarette rollers, but black women kept the worst, most monotonous jobs in the tobacco factories. The women shown in this photograph are stemming tobacco in a Virginia factory while their white male supervisor oversees their labor.

SOURCE: Valentine Richmond History Center.

did so as household workers; girls as young as ten worked as domestics or as nurses for white children.

Most trade unions refused membership to black workers. Locals of the all-white carpenters' union, for example, maintained a segregation policy so absolute that if too few members were available for a job, the union would send for out-of-town white workers rather than employ local members of the black carpenters' union. In an Atlanta mill in 1897, 1,400 white women operatives went on strike when the company proposed to hire two black spinners.

Only at rare moments did Southern workers unite across racial lines. In the 1880s, the Knights of Labor briefly organized both black and white workers. At its high point, the Knights enrolled two-thirds of Rich-

mond's 5,000 tobacco operatives and made significant inroads among quarry workers, coopers, typographers, iron molders, and builders. But when white politicians and local newspapers began to raise the specter of black domination, the Knights were forced to retreat.

Wages throughout the South were low for both black and white workers. Southern textile workers' wages were barely half those of New Englanders. In the 1880s, when investors enjoyed profits ranging from 30 percent to 75 percent, Southern mill workers earned as little as 12 cents per hour. Black men earned at or below the poverty line of $300 per year, while black women rarely earned more than $120, and white women about $220 annually. The poorest paid workers were children, the mainstay of Southern mill labor.

As industry expanded throughout the nation, so too did the child labor force. This was especially so in the South. In 1896, only one in twenty Massachusetts mill workers was younger than sixteen, but one in four North Carolina cotton mill operatives was that age or younger. Traditions rooted in the agricultural economy reinforced the practice of using the labor of all family members, even the very young. Seasonal labor, such as picking crops or grinding sugarcane, put families on the move, making formal education all but impossible. Not until well into the twentieth century did compulsory school attendance laws effectively restrict child labor in the South.

A system of convict labor also thrived in the South. Bituminous coal mines and public work projects of all kinds, especially in remote areas, employed disciplinary methods and created living and working conditions reminiscent of slavery. African Americans constituted up to 90 percent of the convict workforce. Transported and housed like animals—chained together by day and confined in portable cages at night—these workers suffered high mortality rates. White politicians expressed pride in what they called the "good roads movement"— the chief use of convict labor—as proof of regional progress.

The Transformation of Piedmont Communities

The impact of the New South was nowhere greater than in the Piedmont, the region extending from southern Virginia and the central Carolinas into northern Alabama and Georgia. After 1870, long-established farms and plantations gave way to railroad tracks, textile factories, numerous mill villages, and a few sizable cities. By the turn of the century, five Piedmont towns had populations over 10,000. Even more dramatic was the swelling number of small towns with populations between 1,000 and 5,000— from fourteen in 1870 to fifty-two in 1900. Once the

South's backcountry, the Piedmont now surpassed New England in the production of yarn and cloth, to stand first in the world.

Rural poverty and the appeal of a new life encouraged many farm families to strike out for a mill town. Those with the least access to land and credit—mainly widows and their children and single women—were the first to go into the mills. Then families sent their children. Some families worked in the mills on a seasonal basis, between planting and harvesting. But as the agricultural crisis deepened, more and more people abandoned the countryside entirely for what they called "public work."

A typical mill community—a company town, owned "lock, stock, and barrel" by the manufacturers—comprised rows of single-family houses, a small school, several churches, a company-owned store, and the home of the superintendent, who governed everyone's affairs. The manager of the King Cotton Mill in Burlington, North Carolina, not only kept the company's accounts in order, purchased raw material, and sold the finished yarn, but even bought Christmas presents for the workers' children. It was not unknown for a superintendent to prowl the neighborhood to see which families burned their lanterns past nine o'clock at night and, finding a violator, to knock on the door and tell the offenders to go to bed. Millworkers frequently complained that they had no private life at all. A federal report published shortly after the turn of the century concluded that "all the affairs of the village and the conditions of living of all the people are regulated entirely by the mill company. Practically speaking, the company owns everything and controls everything, and to a large extent controls everybody in the mill village."

Mill superintendents also relied on schoolteachers and clergy to set the tone of community life. They hired and paid the salaries of Baptist and Methodist ministers to preach a faith encouraging workers to be thrifty, orderly, temperate, and hardworking. The schools, similarly subsidized by the company, reinforced the lesson of moral and social discipline required of industrial life, and encouraged students to follow their parents into the mill. But it was mainly young children between six and eight years old who attended school. When more hands were needed in the mill, superintendents plucked out those youngsters and sent them to join their older brothers and sisters who were already at work.

Piedmont mill villages like Greenville, South Carolina, and Burlington, Charlotte, and Franklinville, North Carolina, nevertheless developed a cohesive character typical of isolated rural communities. The new residents maintained many aspects of their agricultural pasts, tilling small gardens and keeping chickens, pigs, and cows in their yards. Factory owners rarely paved roads or sidewalks or provided adequate sanitation. Mud, flies, and diseases such as typhoid fever flourished. Millworkers endured poverty and health hazards by strengthening community ties through intermarriage. Within a few generations, most of the village residents had, according to one study, "some connection to each other, however distant, by marriage," blood, or both. Even the men and women without families boarded in households where privacy was scarce and collective meals created a familylike atmosphere. Historians have called this complex of intimate economic, family, and community ties the customs of incorporation.

THE INDUSTRIAL CITY

Before the Civil War, manufacturing had centered in the countryside, in new factory towns such as Lowell, Massachusetts, and Troy, New York. By the end of the nineteenth century, 90 percent of all manufacturing took place in big cities. The metropolis stood at the center of the growing industrial economy, a magnet drawing raw material, capital, and labor, and a key distribution point for manufactured goods. The industrial city inspired both great hope and great trepidation. Civic leaders often bragged about its size and rate of growth; immigrants wrote to their countryfolk of its pace, both exciting and exhausting.

Populating the City

The population of cities grew at double the rate of the nation's population as a whole. In 1860, only sixteen cities had more than 50,000 residents. By 1890, one-third of all Americans were city dwellers. Eleven cities claimed more than 250,000 people.

The nation's largest cities—New York, Chicago, Philadelphia, St. Louis, Boston, and Baltimore—achieved international fame for the size and diversity of their populations. Many of their new residents had migrated from rural communities within the United States. Between 1870 and 1910, an average of nearly 7,000 African Americans moved north each year, hoping to escape the poverty and oppression prevailing in the South and to find better-paying jobs. By the end of the century, nearly 80 percent of African Americans in the North lived in urban areas. Whereas many young white men sought their fortunes in the West, their sisters more often migrated to cities in search of work in manufacturing or domestic service. By the end of the century, young women outnumbered young men in most east coast cities.

Immigrants and their children were the major source of urban population growth in the late nineteenth century. Most of those in the first wave of immigration, before the Civil War, had settled in the countryside. In contrast, in the last half of the nineteenth century, it was the industrial

MAP EXPLORATION

To explore an interactive version of this map, go to **www.prenhall.com/faragher5/map19.2**

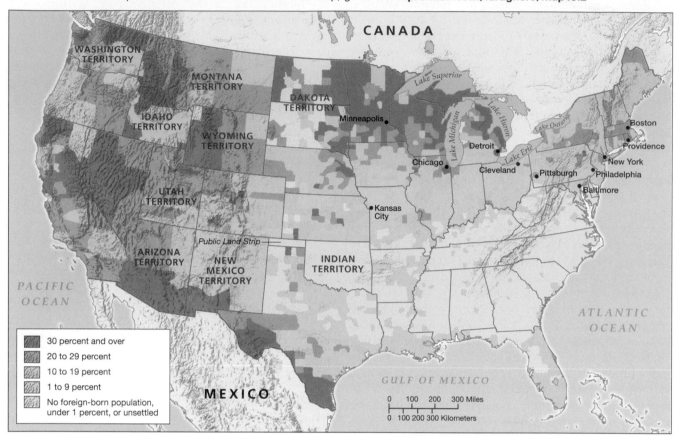

Legend:
- 30 percent and over
- 20 to 29 percent
- 10 to 19 percent
- 1 to 9 percent
- No foreign-born population, under 1 percent, or unsettled

MAP 19.2 Population of Foreign Birth by Region, 1880 European immigrants after the Civil War settled primarily in the industrial districts of the northern Midwest and parts of the Northeast. French Canadians continued to settle in Maine, Cubans in Florida, and Mexicans in the Southwest, where earlier immigrants had established thriving communities.

SOURCE: Clifford L. Lord and Elizabeth H. Lord, *Lord & Lord Historical Atlas of the United States* (New York: Holt, 1953).

city that drew the so-called new immigrants, who came primarily from eastern and southern Europe. In 1880, San Francisco claimed the highest proportion of foreign born (45 percent), although not the largest number. By the turn of the century, Chicago had more Germans than all but a few German cities and more Poles than most Polish cities; New York had more Italians than a handful of the largest Italian cities, and Boston had nearly as many Irish as Dublin. In almost every group except the Irish, men outnumbered women (see Map 19.2).

Like rural migrants, immigrants came to the American city to take advantage of the expanding opportunities for employment. While many hoped to build a new home in the land of plenty, many others intended to work hard, save money, and return to their families in the Old Country. In the 1880s, for example, nearly half of all Italian, Greek, and Serbian men returned to their native lands. Others could not return to their homelands or did not wish to. Jews, for instance, had emigrated to escape persecution in Russia and Russian-dominated Polish and Romanian lands. A Yiddish writer later called this generation the "Jews without Jewish memories. . . . They shook them off in the boat when they came across the seas. They emptied out their memories."

Of all groups, Jews had the most experience with urban life. Forbidden to own land in most parts of Europe and boxed into *shtetls* (villages), Jews had also formed thriving urban communities in Vilna, Berlin, London, and Vienna. Many had worked in garment manufacturing, in London's East End, for example, and followed a path to American cities like New York, Rochester, Philadelphia, or Chicago where the needle trades flourished.

Other groups, the majority coming from rural parts of Europe, sought out their kinfolk in American cities, where they could most easily find housing and employment. Bohemians settled largely in Chicago, Pittsburgh, and Cleveland. French Canadians, a relatively small group of a few hundred thousand, emigrated from Quebec and settled almost exclusively in New England and upper New York State. Finding work mainly in textile mills, they transformed smaller industrial cities like Woonsocket, Rhode Island, into French-speaking communities. Cubans, themselves often first- or second-generation immigrants from Spain, moved to Ybor City, a section of Tampa, Florida, to work in cigar factories. Still other groups tended toward cities dominated by fishing, shoemaking, or even glassblowing, a craft carried directly from the Old Country. Italians, the most numerous among the new immigrants, settled mainly in Northeastern cities, laying railroad track, excavating subways, and erecting buildings.

Resettlement in an American city did not necessarily mark the end of the immigrants' travels. Newcomers, both native-born and immigrant, moved frequently from one neighborhood to another and from one city to another. As manufacturing advanced outward from the city center, working populations followed. American cities experienced a total population turnover three or four times during each decade of the last half of the century.

The Urban Landscape

Faced with a population explosion and an unprecedented building boom, the cities encouraged the creation of many beautiful and useful structures, including commercial offices, sumptuous homes, and efficient public services. At the same time, cities did little to improve the conditions of the majority of the population, who worked in dingy factories and lived in crowded tenements. Open space decreased as American cities grew.

OUT OF MANY VOICES

AN ITALIAN IMMIGRANT'S FIRST IMPRESSIONS

In 1898, Leonard Covello left his small village in Italy, with his mother and brothers, to join his father in New York City. After twenty days of travel at sea, they at first relished the sights of their new country. Their mood changed, however, after they arrived at their tenement apartment, and Mrs. Covello cried for the comforts she had left behind in Italy. Her eleven-year-old son adjusted quickly, finding simple pleasures in a trip to the candy store. As an adult, Leonard Covello taught school in East Harlem.

AND WHEN FINALLY WE SAW THE TOWERING buildings and rode the screeching elevated train and saw the long, unending streets of the metropolis that could easily swallow a thousand Aviglianese towns, she [his mother] accepted it with the mute resignation as *la volonta di dio* [the will of God], while her heart longed for the familiar scenes and faces of loved ones and the security of a life she had forever left behind....

The sunlight and fresh air of our mountain home . . . were replaced by four walls and people over and under and on all sides of us. Silence and sunshine, things of the past, now replaced by a new urban montage. The cobbled streets. The endless monotonous rows of tenement buildings that shut out the sky. The traffic of wagons and carts and carriages, and the clopping of horses' hooves which struck sparks at night. . . . The clanging of bells and the screeching of sirens as a fire broke out somewhere in the neighborhood. Dank hallways. Long flights of wooden stairs and the toilet in the hall. . . .

There was a counter covered with glass and all manner and kinds of sweets such as we had never seen. Candy, my father told us, grinning. This is what we call candy in America. We were even allowed to select the kind we wanted. I selected some little round cream-filled chocolates which tasted like nothing I had ever eaten before. The only candy I knew was confetti, which we had on feast days or from the pocket of my uncle, the priest, on some special occasion. ■

SOURCE: Leonard Covello, *The Heart Is the Teacher* (New York: McGraw-Hill, 1958), p. 19, 21.

In his watercolor *The Bowery at Night*, painted in 1885, W. Louis Sonntag Jr. shows a New York City scene transformed by electric light. Electricity transformed the city in other ways as well, as seen in the electric streetcars and elevated railroad.

SOURCE: *The Bowery at Night*, 1885. Watercolor. Museum of the City of New York.

the city's magnificent public architecture: its stately public library, fine arts and science museums, and orchestra hall. Back Bay opened onto the Fenway Park system designed by the nation's premier landscape architect, Frederick Law Olmsted.

The industrial city established a new style of commerical and civic architecture. Using fireproof materials, expanded foundations, and internal metal construction, the era's talented architects focused on the factory and office building. Concentrating as many offices as possible in the downtown areas, they fashioned hundreds of buildings from steel, sometimes decorating them with elaborate wrought-iron facades. The office building could rise seven, ten, even twenty stories high.

Architects played a key role in the late nineteenth-century City Beautiful movement. Influenced by American wealth and its enhanced role in the global economy, they turned to the monumental or imperial style, laying grand concrete boulevards at enormous public cost. New sports amphitheaters spread pride in the city's accomplishments. New schools, courthouses, capitols, hospitals, museums, and huge new art galleries, museums, and concert halls promoted urban excitement as well as cultural uplift. The imperial style also increased congestion and noise, making the city a more desirable place to visit than to live.

The city also inspired other architectural marvels. Opened in 1883, the Brooklyn Bridge won wide acclaim from engineers, journalists, and poets as the most original American construction. Designed by John Roebling, who died from an accident early in its construction, and by his son Washington Roebling, who became an invalid during its construction, the bridge was considered an aesthetic and practical wonder. Its soaring piers, elegant arches, and intricate steel cables convey an image of strength and elasticity, inspiring a belief among artists and writers in the potential of technology to unite function and beauty. The Brooklyn Bridge also helped to speed the transformation of rural townships into suburban communities.

American streets customarily followed a simple grid-iron pattern. Builders leveled hills, filled ponds, and pulled down any farms or houses in the way. City officials usually lacked any master plan, save the idea of endless expansion. Factories often occupied the best sites, typically near waterways, where goods could be easily transported and chemical wastes dumped.

Built by the thousands after the Civil War, the tenement was designed to maximize the use of space. A typical tenement sat on a lot 25 by 100 feet and rose to five stories. There were four families on each floor, each with three rooms. By 1890, New York's Lower East Side packed more than 700 people per acre into back-to-back buildings, producing one of the highest population densities in the world.

At the other end of the urban social scale, New York's Fifth Avenue, St. Paul's Summit Avenue, Chicago's Michigan Avenue, and San Francisco's Nob Hill fairly gleamed with new mansions and town houses. Commonwealth Avenue marked Boston's fashionable Back Bay district, built on a filled-in 450-acre tidal flat. State engineers planned this community, with its magnificent boulevard, uniform five-story brownstones, and back alleys designed for deliveries. Like wealthy neighborhoods in other cities, Back Bay also provided space for

Like the railroad, but on a smaller scale, streetcars and elevated railroads changed business dramatically, because they moved traffic of many different kinds—

information, people, and goods—faster and farther than before. Although San Francisco introduced the first mechanically driven cable car in 1873, within a decade, Chicago would claim the most extensive cable car system in the world. The first electrified street railway was tested in Richmond, Virginia in 1888, and by 1895, more than 800 communities operated systems of electrically powered cars or trolleys on track totaling 10,000 miles. In 1902, New York opened its subway system, which would grow to become the largest in the nation.

The City and the Environment

By making it possible for a great number of workers to live in communities distant from their place of employment, mass transportation allowed the metropolitan region to grow dramatically. By the end of the nineteenth century, suburban trains were bringing nearly 100,000 riders daily into the city of Chicago. Suburbs sprang up outside the major cities, offering many professional workers quiet residential retreats from the city's busy and increasingly polluted downtown.

Electric trolleys eliminated the tons of waste from horsecars that had for decades fouled city streets. But the new rail systems also increased congestion and created new safety hazards for pedestrians. During the 1890s, 600 people were killed each year by Chicago's trains. Elevated trains, designed to avoid these problems, placed entire communities under the shadow of noisy and rickety wooden platforms. Despite many technological advances, the quality of life in the nation's cities did not necessarily improve.

Modern water and sewer systems now constituted a hidden city of pipes and wires, mirroring the growth of the visible city above ground. These advances, which brought indoor plumbing to most homes, did not, however, eradicate serious environmental or health problems. Most cities continued to dump sewage into nearby bodies of water. Moreover, most municipal governments established separate clean-water systems through the use of resevoirs, rather than outlawing upriver dumping by factories. Downriver communities began to complain about unendurable stench from the polluted rivers and streams.

The unrestricted burning of coal to fuel the railroads and to heat factories and homes after 1880 greatly intensified urban air pollution. Noise levels continued to rise in the most compacted living and industrial areas. Overcrowded conditions and inadequate sanitary facilities bred tuberculosis, smallpox, and scarlet fever, among other contagious diseases. Children's diseases like whooping cough and measles spread rapidly through poor neighborhoods such as Packingtown. By the 1890s, many urban school systems employed doctors and nurses to screen children for common contagious diseases. But only after the turn of the century, amid an intensive campaign against municipal corruption, did laws and administrative practices address the serious problems of public health (see Chapter 21).

Meanwhile, the distance between the city and the countryside narrowed. Naturalists had hoped for large open spaces—a buffer zone—to preserve farmland and wild areas, protect future water supplies, and diminish regional air pollution. But soon, the industrial landscape invaded the countryside. Nearby rural lands not destined for private housing or commercial development became sites for water treatment and sewage plants, garbage dumps, and graveyards—services essential to the city's growing population.

THE RISE OF CONSUMER SOCIETY

The growth of industry and the spread of cities had a profound impact on all regions of the United States. During the final third of the nineteenth century, the standard of living climbed, although unevenly and erratically. Real wages (pay in relation to the cost of living) rose, fostering improvements in nutrition, clothing, and housing. More and cheaper products were within the reach of all but the very poor. Food from the farms became more abundant and varied—grains for bread or beer; poultry, pork, and beef; fresh fruits and vegetables from California. Although many Americans continued to acknowledge the moral value of hard work, thrift, and self-sacrifice, the explosion of consumer goods and services promoted sweeping changes in behavior and beliefs. Leisure, play, and consumption became part of a new ideal and measure of success. Nearly everyone felt the impact of the transformation from a producer to a consumer society, although in vastly and increasingly different ways.

"Conspicuous Consumption"

Labeled the "Gilded Age" by humorist and social critic Mark Twain, the era following the Civil War favored the growth of a new class united in its pursuit of money and leisure. The well-to-do enjoyed great status throughout the nineteenth century, but only after the war did financiers and industrialists form national networks to establish their upper-class identity and to consolidate their power. Business leaders built diverse stock portfolios and often served simultaneously on the boards of several corporations. Similarly, they intertwined their interests by joining the same religious, charitable, athletic, and professional societies. Their wives and children vacationed together in the sumptuous new seashore and mountain resorts, while they themselves made deals in the exclusive social clubs and on the golf links of suburban country clubs. Just as Dun and Bradstreet ranked the leading corporations, the Social Register identified the 500 families that controlled most of the nation's wealth.

According to economist and social critic Thorstein Veblen, the rich had created a new style of "conspicuous consumption." The Chicago mansion of real estate tycoon Potter Palmer, for example, was constructed without exterior doorknobs. Not only could no one enter uninvited, but a visitor's calling card supposedly passed through the hands of twenty-seven servants before admittance was allowed. A vice president of the Chicago & Northwestern Railroad, Perry H. Smith, built his marble palace in the style of the Greek Renaissance. Its ebony staircase was trimmed in gold, its butler's pantry equipped with faucets not only for hot and cold water, but for iced champagne. The women who oversaw these elaborate households served as measures of their husbands' status, according to Veblen, by adorning themselves in jewels, furs, and dresses of the latest Paris design.

Conspicuous consumption reached toward new heights of extravagance. In New York, wealthy families hosted dinner parties for their dogs or pet monkeys, dressing the animals in fancy outfits for the occasion. Railroad magnate "Diamond Jim" Brady commonly enjoyed after-theater snacks at the city's "lobster palaces," where he consumed vast quantities of food—oysters for an appetizer, two soups, fish, a main dinner of beef and vegetables, punches and sherbet on the side, dessert, coffee, and quarts of orange juice.

Perhaps no display of wealth matched the ostentation of the "cottages" of Newport, Rhode Island, where the upper class created a summer community that displayed its power of consumption in grand style. Architect H. H. Richardson and his protégés built enormous manor houses more magnificent than the English homes they mimicked. Here, young men and women engaged in new amateur sports such as polo, rowing, and lawn tennis. Young and old alike joined in yachting and golf tournaments.

Toward the end of the century, the wealthy added a dramatic public dimension to the "high life." New York's Waldorf-Astoria hotel, which opened in 1897, incorporated the grandeur of European royalty, but with an important difference. Because rich Americans wanted to be watched, the elegantly appointed corridors and restaurants were visible to the public through huge windows. The New York rich also established a unique custom to welcome the New Year: they opened wide the curtains of their Fifth Avenue mansions so that passersby could marvel at the elegant decor.

The wealthy also became the leading patrons of the arts as well as the chief procurers of art treasures from Europe and Asia. They provided the bulk of funds for the new symphonies, operas, and ballet companies, which soon rivaled those of Continental Europe. Nearly all major museums and art galleries, including the Boston Museum of Fine Arts, the Philadelphia Museum of Art, the Art Institute of Chicago, and the Metropolitan Museum of Art in New York, were founded during the last decades of the nineteenth century.

Self-Improvement and the Middle Class

A new middle class, very different from its predecessor, formed during the last half of the century. The older middle class comprised the owners or superintendents of small businesses, doctors, lawyers, teachers, and ministers and their families. The new middle class included these professionals but also the growing number of salaried employees—the managers, technicians, clerks, and engineers who worked in the complex web of corporations and government. Long hours of labor earned their families a modest status and sufficient income to live securely in style and comfort and, equally important, to separate work and home.

By the end of the century, many middle-class families were nestled in suburban retreats from the noise, filth, and dangers of the city. This peaceful domestic setting, with its manicured lawns and well-placed shrubs, afforded both privacy and rejuvenation as well as the separation of business from leisure and the breadwinner from his family for most of the day. Assisted by modern transportation systems, men often traveled one to two hours each day, five or six days a week, to their city offices and back again. Women and children stayed behind.

Middle-class women devoted a large part of their day to care of the home. They frequently employed one or two servants but relied increasingly on the many new appliances to get their work done. Improvements in the kitchen stove, such as the conversion from wood fuel to gas, saved a lot of time. Yet, simultaneously, with the widespread circulation of cookbooks and recipes in newspapers and magazines, as well as the availability of new foods, the preparation of meals became more complex and time-consuming. New devices such as the eggbeater speeded some familiar tasks, but the era's fancy culinary practices offset any gains in saving time. Similarly, the new carpet sweepers surpassed the broom in efficiency, but the fashionable high-napped carpeting demanded more care. Thus, rather than diminishing with technological innovation, household work expanded to fill the time available.

By the end of the century, though, middle-class women were spending the greatest part of their time on consumption. They took charge of the household budget and purchased an ever expanding range of machine-made goods, packaged foods, manufactured clothing, and personal luxuries. With the rise of department stores, which catered specifically to them, shopping combined work and pleasure and became a major pastime for women.

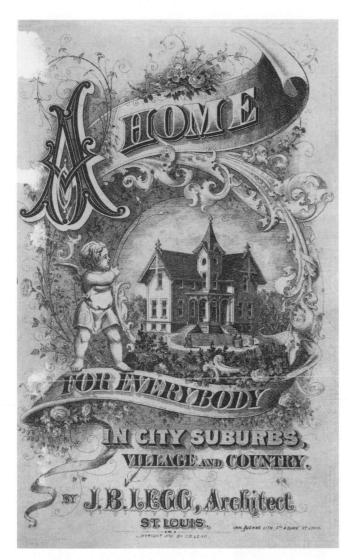

Taken from J. B. Legg's architecture book, this page illustrates the ideal suburban home. His book, published in 1876, was aimed at the prospering middle class.

SOURCE: Courtesy of the Library of Congress.

Almost exclusively white, Anglo-Saxon, and Protestant, the new middle class embraced "culture" not for purposes of conspicuous consumption but as a means of self-improvement. Whole families visited the new museums and art galleries. One of the most cherished institutions, the annual season of lectures at the Chautauqua campgrounds in upstate New York, brought thousands of families together in pursuit of knowledge of literature and the fine arts. The middle class also provided the bulk of patrons for the new public libraries.

Middle-class families applied the same standards to their leisure activities. What one sporting-goods entrepreneur rightly called the "gospel of EXERCISE" involved men and women in calisthenics and outdoor activities, not so much for pleasure as for physical and mental discipline. Hiking was a favorite among both men and women and required entirely new outfits: for women, loose upper garments and skirts short enough to prevent dragging; for men, rugged outer wear and jaunty hats. Soon, men and women began camping out, with almost enough amenities to re-create a middle-class home in the woods. Roller-skating and ice-skating, which became crazes shortly after the Civil War, took place in specially designed rinks in almost every major town. By the 1890s, the "safety" bicycle had also been marketed. It replaced the large-wheel variety, which was difficult to keep upright. A good-quality "bike" cost $100 and, like the piano, was a symbol of middle-class status. In 1895, Chicago hosted thirty-three cycle clubs comprising nearly 10,000 members.

Leisure became the special province of middle-class childhood. Removed from factories and shops and freed from many domestic chores, children enjoyed creative play and physical activity. Summer camps, offering several weeks of sports and handicrafts, attracted many children to New England during this period. The toy market boomed, and lower printing prices helped children's literature flourish. Children's magazines such as *St. Nicholas* and *Youth's Companion* were filled with stories, poems, and pictures. Slightly older children read westerns, sports novels of many kinds, and such perennial and uplifting classics as *Little Women* and *Black Beauty*.

Life in the Streets

Immigrants often weighed the material abundance they found in the United States against their memories of the Old Country. One could "live better" here, but only by working much harder. In letters home, immigrants described the riches of the new country but warned friends and relatives not to send weaklings, who would surely die of stress and strain amid the alien and intense commercialism of American society. In many immigrant communities, alcoholism and suicide rates soared. Embittered German immigrants called their new land *Malhuerica*, "misfortune"; Jews called it *Ama Reka*, Hebrew for "without soul"; and Slavs referred to it as *Dollerica*.

Many newcomers, having little choice about their place of residence, concentrated in districts marked off by racial or ethnic lines. In San Francisco, city ordinances prevented Chinese from operating laundries in most of the city's neighborhoods, and the city's schools excluded their children. In the 1880s, Chinese San Franciscans, representing 10 percent of the city's population, crowded into a dozen blocks of restaurants, shops, and small factories known as Chinatown. In Los Angeles and San Antonio, Mexicans lived in distinctive barrios. In most cities, African American families were similarly compelled to remain in the dingiest, most crime-ridden, and dangerous sections of town.

Young people new to the city often found lodging in small residential hotels or boardinghouses. The Young Men's Christian Association (YMCA), established in the 1850s, and the Young Women's Christian Association (YWCA), organized a decade later, provided temporary residences mainly to native-born, white, self-supporting men and women. The most successful "women adrift," such as clerical workers and retail clerks, lived in the new furnished-room districts bordering the city's business center. The least prosperous landed on "skid row," where homeless people spent time in the rough taverns, eating free lunches in return for purchased beer, waiting for casual labor, and sometimes trading sexual favors for money.

The working-class home did not necessarily ensure privacy or offer protection from the dangers of the outside world. In the tenements, families often shared their rooms with other families or paying boarders. During the summer heat, adults, children, and boarders alike competed for a sleeping place on the fire escape or roof, and all year round, noise resounded through paper-thin walls. But so complex and varied were income levels and social customs that no single pattern emerged. Packingtown's Slovaks, Lithuanians, and Poles, for example, frequently took in boarders, yet Bohemians rarely did. Neither did the skilled iron rollers who worked at the Carnegie Steel Company in Homestead, Pennsylvania. These well-paid craft workers often owned their own homes, boasting parlors and even imported Belgian carpets. At the other extreme, Italian immigrants, who considered themselves fortunate to get work with a shovel, usually lived in overcrowded rented apartments, just a paycheck away from eviction.

Whether it was a small cottage or a tenement flat, the working-class home involved women and children in routines of household labor without the aid of new mechanical devices. In addition to cooking and cleaning, women used their cramped domestic space for work that provided a small income. They gathered their children—and their husbands after a hard day's labor—to sew garments, wrap cigars, string beads, or paint vases for a contractor who paid them by the piece. And they cooked and cleaned for the boarders whose rent supplemented the family income.

Despite working people's slim resources, their combined buying power created new and important markets for consumer goods. Often they bought shoddy replicas of products sold to the middle class: cheaper canned goods, inferior cuts of meat, and partially spoiled fruit. Several leading clothing manufacturers specialized in inexpensive ready-to-wear items, usually copied from patterns designed for wealthier consumers, but constructed hastily from flimsy materials. Patent medicines for ailments caused by working long periods in cramped conditions sold well in working-class communities, where money for doctors was scarce. Their high alcohol content might lift a person's spirits, if only temporarily.

The close quarters of the urban neighborhood allowed immigrants to preserve many Old World customs. In immigrant communities such as Chicago's Packingtown, Pittsburgh's Poletown, New York's Lower East Side, or San Francisco's Chinatown, people usually spoke their native language while visiting their friends and relatives. The men might play cards while women and children gathered in the stairwell or on the front stoop to trade stories. In good weather, they walked and talked, an inexpensive pastime common in European cities. No organization was as important as the fraternal society, which sponsored social clubs and provided insurance benefits. Social organi-

The intersection of Orchard and Hester Streets on New York's Lower East Side, photographed ca. 1905. Unlike the middle classes, who worked and played hidden away in offices and private homes, the Jewish lower-class immigrants who lived and worked in this neighborhood spent the greater part of their lives on the streets.

SOURCE: The Granger Collection.

zations, known as *huiguan*, were especially important in preserving clan and dialect among the largely male unmarried population of Chinese San Francisco. Immigrants also re-created Old World religious institutions such as the temple, church, or synagogue, or secular institutions such as German family-style taverns or Russian Jewish tearooms. Chinese theaters, in inexpensive daily and nightly performances, presented dramas depicting historical events or explicating moral teachings, and thereby preserved much of Chinese native culture. Immigrants also replicated their native cuisine (as much as available foods allowed) and sang their own songs, accompanied by the polka, mazurka, or tamburitza, according to tradition. They married, baptized children, and buried their dead according to Old World customs.

In the cosmopolitan cities, immigrants, by being innovative entrepreneurs as well as the best customers, helped to shape the emerging popular culture. German immigrants, for example, created Tin Pan Alley, the center of the popular music industry. They also became the first promoters of ragtime, which found its way north from Storyville, the red-light district of New Orleans. Created by African American and creole bands, ragtime captivated those teenage offspring of immigrants who rushed to the new dance halls.

When developers realized that "wholesome fun" for the masses could pay better than upper-class leisure or lower-class vice, they decided to transform Coney Island into a magnificent seaside park filled with ingenious amusements such as water slides, mechanized horse races, carousels, roller coasters, and fun houses. On the rides or at the nearby beach, young men and women could easily meet apart from their parents, cast off their inhibitions, and enjoy a hug or kiss. Or they could simply stroll through the grounds, looking at exotic performers, enjoying make-believe trips to the Far East or even the moon, entranced by fantastic towers, columns, minarets, and lagoons lit up at night to resemble dreams rather than reality. At Coney Island or at Riverview, Chicago's oldest amusement park, located on the city's North Side, millions of working-class people enjoyed cheap thrills that offset the hardships of their working lives.

CULTURES IN CONFLICT, CULTURE IN COMMON

The new commercial entertainments gave Americans from various backgrounds more in common than they would otherwise have had. On New York's Lower East Side, for instance, theater blossomed with dramas that Broadway would adopt years later, while children dreamed of going "uptown" where the popular songs they heard on the streets were transcribed onto sheet music and sold in stores throughout the city. Even so, nothing could smooth the tensions caused by conflicting claims to the same resources, such as public schools and urban parks.

Education

As industries grew and cities expanded, so did the nation's public school system. Business and civic leaders realized that the welfare of society now depended on an educated population, one possessing the skills and knowledge required to keep both industry and government running. In the last three decades of the nineteenth century, the idea of universal free schooling, at least for white children, took hold. Kindergartens in particular flourished. St. Louis, Missouri, opened the first public school kindergarten in 1873, and by the turn of the century, more than 4,000 similar programs throughout the country enrolled children between the ages of three and seven.

Public high schools, which were rare before the Civil War, also increased in number, from 160 in 1870 to 6,000 by the end of the century. In Chicago alone, average daily attendance multiplied sixfold. Despite this spectacular growth, which was concentrated in urban industrial areas, as late as 1890 only 4 percent of children between the ages of fourteen and seventeen were enrolled in school, the majority of them girls planning to become teachers or office workers. Most high schools continued to serve mainly the middle class. In 1893, the National Education Association reaffirmed the major purpose of the nation's high schools as preparation for college, rather than for work in trades or industry, and endorsed a curriculum of rigorous training in the classics, such as Latin, Greek, and ancient history. The expected benefits of this kind of education rarely outweighed the immediate needs of families who depended on their children's wages. At the end of the century, 50 percent of the children in Chicago between the ages of ten and twelve were working for wages.

Higher education also expanded along several lines. Agricultural colleges formed earlier in the century developed into institutes of technology and took their places alongside the prestigious liberal arts colleges. To extend learning to the "industrial classes," Representative Justin Morrill of Vermont sponsored the Morrill Federal Land Grant Act of 1862, which funded a system of state colleges and universities for teaching agriculture and mechanics "without excluding other scientific and classic studies." Meanwhile, established private institutions like Harvard, Yale, Princeton, and Columbia grew, with the help of huge endowments from business leaders such as Rockefeller and Carnegie. By 1900, sixty-three Catholic colleges were serving mainly the children of immigrants from Ireland and eastern and southern Europe. Still, as the overall number of colleges and universities grew from 563 in 1870 to nearly 1,000 by 1910, only 3 percent of the college-age population took advantage of these new opportunities.

One of the most important developments occurred in the area of professional training. Although medical and law schools dated from the mid-eighteenth century, their numbers grew rapidly after the Civil War. Younger professions, such as engineering, pharmacy, and journalism, also established specialized training institutions. In 1876, the Johns Hopkins University pioneered a program of research and graduate studies, and by the end of the century, several American universities, including Stanford University and the University of Chicago, offered advanced degrees in the arts and sciences.

This expansion benefited women, who previously had had little access to higher education. After the Civil War, a number of women's colleges were founded, beginning in 1865 with Vassar, which set the academic standard for the remainder of the century. Smith and Wellesley followed in 1875, Bryn Mawr in 1885. By the end of the century, 125 women's colleges offered a first-rate education comparable to that given to men at Harvard, Yale, or Princeton. Meanwhile, coeducation grew at an even faster rate; by 1890, 47 percent of the nation's colleges and universities admitted women. The proportion of women college students changed dramatically. Women constituted 21 percent of undergraduate enrollments in 1870, 32 percent in 1880, and 40 percent in 1910. Despite these gains, many professions remained closed to women.

An even greater number of women enrolled in vocational courses. Normal schools, which offered one- or two-year programs for women who planned to become elementary school teachers, developed a collegiate character after the Civil War and had become accredited state teachers' colleges by the end of the century. Normal schools enrolled many women from rural areas, particularly from poor families. Upon graduation, these women filled the personnel ranks of the rapidly expanding system of public education. Other institutions, many founded by middle-class philanthropists, also prepared women for vocations. For example, the first training school for nurses opened in Boston in 1873, followed in 1879 by a diet kitchen that taught women to become cooks in the city's hospitals. Founded in 1877, the Women's Educational and Industrial Union offered a multitude of classes to Boston's wage-earning women, ranging from elementary French and German to drawing, watercoloring, and oil and china painting: to dressmaking and millinery, stenography and typing: as well as crafts less familiar to women, such as upholstering, cabinetmaking, and carpentry. In the early 1890s, when the entering class at a large women's college like Vassar still averaged under 100, the Boston Women's Educational and Industrial Union reported that its staff of 83 served an estimated 1,500 clients per day. By that time, one of its most well-funded programs was a training school for domestic servants.

George Washington Carver (1864–1943), who had been born in slavery, had been invited by Booker T. Washington to direct agricultural research at the Tuskegee Institute in Alabama. A leader in development of agriculture in the New South, Carver promoted crop diversification to rejuvenate soil that was depleted by the continuous planting of cotton and encouraged the cultivation of alternative, high-protein crops such as peanuts and soybeans. He designed his programs in sustainable agriculture mainly for African American farmers and sharecroppers rather than for commercial purposes.

SOURCE: The Granger Collection, New York.

The leaders of the business community had also begun to promote manual training for working-class and immigrant boys. One leading San Francisco merchant described the philosophy behind this movement as a desire to train boys "to earn a living with little study and plenty of work." Craft unionists in several cities actively opposed this development, preferring their own methods of apprenticeship to training programs they could not control. But local associations of merchants and manufacturers lobbied hard for "industrial education" and raised funds to supplement the public school budget. In 1884, the Chicago Manual Training School opened, teaching "shop work" along with a few academic subjects, and by 1895, all elementary and high schools in the city offered courses that trained working-class boys for future jobs in industry and business.

The expansion of education did not benefit all Americans or benefit them all in the same way. Because African Americans were often excluded from colleges attended by white students, special colleges were founded shortly after the Civil War. All-black Atlanta and Fisk universities both soon offered rigorous curricula in the liberal arts. Other institutions, such as Hampton, founded in 1868, specialized in vocational training, mainly in manual trades. Educator Booker T. Washington encouraged African Americans to resist "the craze for Greek and Latin learning" and to strive for practical instruction. In 1881, he founded the Tuskegee Institute in Alabama to provide industrial education and moral uplift. By the turn of the century, Tuskegee enrolled 1,400 men and women in more than thirty different vocational courses, including special cooking classes for homemakers and domestic servants. Black colleges, including Tuskegee, trained so many teachers, that by the century's end the majority of black schools were staffed by African Americans.

The nation's educational system was becoming more inclusive and yet more differentiated. The majority of children attended school for several years or more. At the same time, students were tracked—by race, gender, and class—to fill particular roles in an industrial society.

Leisure and Public Space

Most large cities set aside open land for leisure-time use by residents. New York's Central Park opened for ice-skating in 1858, providing a model for urban park systems across the United States. In 1869, planners in Chicago secured funds to create a citywide system comprising six interconnected large parks, and within a few years, Lincoln Park, on the city's north side, was attracting crowds of nearly 30,000 on Sundays. These parks were rolling expanses, cut across by streams and pathways and footbridges and set off by groves of trees, ornamental shrubs, and neat flower gardens. According to the designers' vision, the urban middle class might find here a respite from the stresses of modern life. To ensure this possibility, posted regulations forbade many activities, ranging from walking on the grass to gambling, picnicking, or ball playing without permission, to speeding in carriages.

The working classes had their own ideas about the use of parks and open land. Trapped in overcrowded tenements or congested neighborhoods, they wanted space for sports, picnics, and lovers' trysts. Young people openly defied ordinances that prohibited play on the grassy knolls, while their elders routinely voted against municipal bonds that did not include funds for more recreational space in their communities. Immigrant ward representatives on the Pittsburgh City Council, for instance, argued that band shells for classical music meant little to their constituents, while spaces suitable for sports meant much.

Eventually, most park administrators set aside some sections for playgrounds and athletic fields and others for public gardens and band shells. Yet intermittent conflicts erupted. The Worcester, Massachusetts, park system, for example, allowed sports leagues to schedule events but prohibited pickup games. This policy gave city officials more control over the use of the park for outdoor recreation, but at the same time forced many ball-playing boys into the streets. When working-class parents protested, city officials responded by instituting programs of supervised play, to the further dismay of the children.

Public drinking of alcoholic beverages, especially on Sunday, provoked similar disputes. Pittsburgh's "blue laws," forbidding businesses to open on Sunday, were rigidly enforced when it came to neighborhood taverns, while large firms like the railroads enjoyed exemptions. Although the Carnegie Institute hoped to discourage Sunday drinking by sponsoring alternative events, such as free organ recitals and other concerts, many working people, especially beer-loving German immigrants, continued to treat Sunday as their one day of relaxation. In Chicago, when not riding the streetcars to the many beer gardens and taverns that thrived on the outskirts, Germans gathered in large numbers for picnics in the city's parks.

Toward the end of the century, many park administrators relaxed the rules and expanded the range of permitted activities. By this time, large numbers of the middle class had become sports enthusiasts and pressured municipal governments to turn meadowlands into tennis courts and golfing greens. In the 1890s, bicycling brought many women into the parks. Still, not all city residents enjoyed these facilities. Officials in St. Louis, for example, barred African Americans from the city's grand Forest Park and set aside the smaller Tandy Park for their use. After challenging this policy in court, African Americans won a few concessions, such as the right to picnic at any time in Forest Park and to use the golf course on Monday mornings.

National Pastimes

Toward the end of the century, the younger members of the urban middle class had begun to find common ground in lower-class pastimes, especially ragtime music. Introduced to many Northerners by the African American composer Scott Joplin at the Chicago World's Fair of 1893, "rag" quickly became the staple of entertainment in the new cabarets and nightclubs. Middle-class urban dwellers began to seek out ragtime bands, and congregated in nightclubs and even on the rooftops of posh hotels to listen and dance and even to drink.

Vaudeville, the most popular form of commercial entertainment since the 1880s, also bridged middle- and working-class tastes. Drawing on a variety-show tradition of singers, dancers, comedians, jugglers, and acrobats, who had entertained Americans since colonial days, "vaude" became a big business that made ethnic and racial stereotypes and the daily frustrations of city life into major topics of amusement. Vaudeville palaces—ten in New York, six in Philadelphia, five in Chicago, and at least one in every other large city—attracted huge, "respectable" crowds that sampled between twenty and thirty dramatic, musical, and comedy acts averaging fifteen minutes each. One study estimated that before vaudeville gave way to movie theaters in the 1920s, between 14 and 16 percent of all city dwellers attended shows at least once a week. Sunday matinees were especially popular with women and children.

Sports, however, outdistanced all other commercial entertainments in appealing to all kinds of fans and managing to create a sense of national identity. No doubt the most popular parks in the United States were the expanses of green surrounded by grandstands and marked by their unique diamond shape—the baseball fields. During the last quarter of the nineteenth century, the amateur sport of gentlemen and Union soldiers suddenly became the "national pastime." Both American and English children had for years been playing a form of baseball, known mainly as "rounders," when a group of young men in Manhattan formed the Knickerbocker Base Ball Club in 1845 and proceeded to set down the

game's rules in writing. Baseball clubs soon formed in many cities, and shortly after the Civil War, traveling teams with regular schedules made baseball a professional sport. The formation of the National League in 1876 encouraged other spectator sports, but for generations, baseball remained the most popular.

Rowdy behavior gave the game a working-class ambience. Well-loved players known for their saloon brawls occasionally disappeared for a few days on "benders." Team owners, themselves often proprietors of local breweries, counted heavily on beer sales in the parks. Having to contend with hundreds of drunken fans, officials maintained order only with great difficulty. Outfielders occasionally leaped into the grandstand to punch spectators who had heckled them. To attract more subdued middle-class fans, the National League raised admission prices, banned the sale of alcohol, and observed Sunday blue laws. Catering to a working-class audience, the American Association kept the price of admission low, sold liquor, and played ball on Sunday.

Baseball, like many other sports, soon became incorporated into the larger business economy. In Chicago, for example, the first baseball clubs organized in the 1850s. After the Civil War, local merchants, such as Marshall Field, began to support teams, and by the end of the decade there were more than fifty company-sponsored teams, playing in the local leagues. By 1870, a Chicago Board of Trade team emerged as the city's first professional club, the White Stockings. Capitalized as a joint stock company, the White Stockings soon succeeded in recruiting a star pitcher from the Boston Red Stockings, Albert Spalding, who eventually became manager and then president of the team. Spalding also came to see baseball as a source of multiple profits. He procured the exclusive rights to manufacture the official ball and the rule book, while producing large varieties of other sporting equipment. Meanwhile, he built impressive baseball parks in Chicago, with seating for 10,000 and special private boxes above the grandstands for the wealthy. He easily became the foremost figure in the National League.

Spalding also succeeded in tightening the rules of participation in the sport. In 1879, he dictated the "reserve clause," which prevented players from negotiating a better deal and leaving the team that originally signed them. He

One of the finest American painters of the period, known for realistic depictions of physical exertion in amateur athletics, Thomas Eakins here turned his attention to the commercial baseball park. The batter and catcher appear as well-poised athletes, dignified in their dress and manner—everything that the baseball player of the late nineteenth century was not very likely to be.

SOURCE: Thomas Eakins, *Baseball Players*, 1875. Watercolor. The Rhode Island School of Design Museum of Art.

encouraged his player-manager "Cap" Anson to forbid the White Stockings from playing against any team with an African American member. The firing of Moses "Fleet" Walker, an African-American, from the Cincinnati team in 1884 marked the first time the color line had been drawn in a major professional sport. Effectively excluded, African Americans organized their own traveling teams. In the 1920s, they formed the Negro Leagues, which produced some of the nation's finest ballplayers.

Players occasionally organized to regain control over their sport. They frequently complained about low wages and arbitrary rules, and like factory workers in the 1880s, they formed their own league, the Brother-hood of Professional Base Ball Players, with profits divided between participants and investors. This effort failed, partly because fans would not desert the estab-lished leagues, but mostly because successful baseball franchises demanded large quantities of capital. Ameri-can sports had become big business.

As attendance continued to grow, the enthusiasm for baseball straddled major social divisions, bringing together Americans of many backgrounds, if only on a limited basis. By the end of the century, no section of the daily newspaper drew more readers than the sports pages. Although it interested relatively few women, sports news riveted the attention of men from all social classes. Loy-alty to the "home team" helped to create an urban iden-tity, while individual players became national heroes.

CONCLUSION

By the end of the nineteenth century, industry and the growing cities had opened a new world for Americans. Fresh from Europe or from the native countryside, ordi-nary urban dwellers struggled to form communities of fel-low newcomers through work and leisure, in the factory, the neighborhood, the ballpark, and the public school. Meanwhile, their "betters," the wealthy and the new middle class, made and executed the decisions of indus-try and marketing, established the era's grand civic insti-tutions, and set the tone for high fashion and art.

Rich and poor alike shared many aspects of the new order. Yet, inequality persisted and increased, as much a part of the new order as the Brooklyn Bridge or advertising. During the mostly prosperous 1880s, optimists believed that unfair treatment based on region, on class, and per-haps even on race and gender might ease in time. By the depressed 1890s, however, these hopes had worn thin, and the lure of overseas empire appeared as one of the few goals that held together a suffering and divided nation.

C H R O N O L O G Y

1862	Morrill Act authorizes "land-grant" colleges	*1883*	William Graham Sumner published the social Darwinist classic *What Social Classes Owe to Each Other*
1869	Knights of Labor founded		
1870	Standard Oil founded	*1886*	Campaigns for eight-hour workday peak
1873	Financial panic brings severe depression		Haymarket riot and massacre discredit the Knights of Labor
1876	Baseball's National League founded		American Federation of Labor founded
	Alexander Graham Bell patents the telephone	*1890*	Sherman Antitrust Act passed
1879	Thomas Edison invents the incandescent bulb	*1893*	Stock market panic precipitates severe depression
	Depression ends	*1895*	Coney Island opens
1881	Tuskegee Institute founded	*1896*	Rural free delivery begins
1882	Peak of immigration to the United States (1.2 million) in the nineteenth century	*1900*	Andrew Carnegie's *Gospel of Wealth* recommends honesty and fair dealing
	Chinese Exclusion Act passed	*1901*	U.S. Steel Corporation formed
	Standard Oil Trust founded		

REVIEW QUESTIONS

1. Discuss the sources of economic growth in the decades after the Civil War. Historians often refer to this period as the era of the "second industrial revolution." Do you agree with this description?

2. Describe the impact of new technologies and new forms of production on the routines of industrial workers. How did these changes affect African American and women workers in particular? What role did trade unions play in this process?

3. Choose one major city, such as Boston, New York, Chicago, Birmingham, or San Francisco, and discuss changes in its economy, population, and urban space in the decades after the Civil War.

4. Discuss the role of Northern capital in the development of the New South. How did the rise of industry affect the lives of rural Southerners?

Analyze these changes from the point of view of African Americans.

5. How did urban life change during the Gilded Age? How did economic development affect residential patterns? How did the middle class aspire to live during the Gilded Age? How did their lifestyles compare with those of working-class urbanites?

6. How did the American educational system change to prepare children for their adult roles in the new industrial economy?

7. How did the rise of organized sports and commercial amusements reflect and shape social divisions at the end of the century? Which groups were affected most (or least) by new leisure activities?

RECOMMENDED READING

Cindy S. Aron, *Working at Play: A History of Vacations in the United States* (1999). Covers the expansion of vacations from wealthy families to the middle class in the nineteenth century. Aron examines several types of settings, ranging from the grand summer hotels and posh resorts to camping vacations in the new national parks.

James R. Barrett, *Work and Community in the Jungle* (1987). A very close study of the Packingtown district of Chicago, Illinois, at the turn of the century. Barrett describes the transformation of animals to meat in great stockyards and processing plants. He also provides rich documentation of neighborhood life.

Sven Beckert, *The Monied Metropolis: New York City and the Consolidation of the American Bourgeoisie, 1850–1896* (2001). A highly informative study of the rise of the industrial elite, their business strategies, political advances, and engagements with consumer culture. This book examines the formation of a distinct social

class and assesses the power they amassed during the Gilded Age.

William Cronon, *Nature's Metropolis: Chicago and the Great West* (1991). Analyzes the changing economic and political relationship between the city of Chicago and the surrounding countryside. Cronon demonstrates, through a variety of evidence, the tight interdependence of urban and rural regions.

Sarah Deutsch, *Women and the City: Gender, Space, and Power in Boston, 1870–1940* (2000). A close study of women's struggle to define the shape of the modern city, and to ease the oppressive quality of spacial divisions along lines of gender, race, and class. Deutsch illustrates the efforts of women to exert their own principles of "moral geography" in shaping Boston's urban landscape.

Tera W. Hunter, *To 'Joy My Freedom: Southern Black Women's Lives and Labors after the Civil War* (1997). A careful study of African American working women in the New South city of Atlanta. Hunter covers their various occupations in the modern urban economy without sacrificing attention to their pursuits of pleasure in the emerging world of mass entertainments and leisure.

David F. Noble, *America by Design: Science, Technology and the Rise of Corporate Capitalism* (1977). A view of scientific advancement and its connections with the expanding economy. Noble shows how scientific breakthroughs were often created for, but especially adapted to, corporate purposes.

Dave Roediger and Franklin Rosemont, eds., *Haymarket Scrapbook* (1986). A large, beautifully illustrated book about the events and consequences of the Haymarket tragedy.

Roy Rosenzweig and Elizabeth Blackmar, *The Park and the People: A History of Central Park* (1992). A multifaceted history of a major institution in New York City. The authors analyze the history of Central Park as both a designed natural landscape and as a common space shaped by those who use it.

William G. Roy, *Socializing Capital: The Rise of the Large Industrial Corporation in America* (1997). A sociologist, Roy examines key years in business history, 1898 to 1904, when companies shifted from private ownership by families, to groups of investors and stockholders. He examines the rise of the corporation in relation to improvements in both technology and efficiency in production.

Susan Strasser, *Satisfaction Guaranteed: The Making of the American Mass Market* (1989). A clear and concise explanation of marketing and distribution during the rise of consumer society. Illustrated with examples of early advertising.

Alan Trachtenberg, *The Incorporation of America: Culture and Society in the Gilded Age* (1982). One of the best and most readable overviews of the post–Civil War era. Trachtenberg devotes great care to describing the rise of the corporation to the defining institution of national life, and the reorientation of culture to reflect the new middle classes employed by the corporation.

For additional study resources for this chapter, go to the *Companion Website*, http://www.prenhall.com/faragher.

Commonwealth and Empire

1870–1900

The Cooperative Commonwealth

Edward Bellamy's *Looking Backward* (1888), the century's best-selling novel after Harriet Beecher Stowe's *Uncle Tom's Cabin,* tells the story of a young man who awakens in the year 2000, after a sleep lasting more than 100 years. He is surprised to learn that Americans have solved their major problems. Poverty, crime, war, taxes, air pollution—even housework—no longer exist. Nor are there politicians, capitalists, bankers, or lawyers. Most amazing, gone is the great social division between the powerful rich and the suffering poor. In the year 2000, everyone lives in material comfort, happily and harmoniously. No wonder Bellamy's hero shudders at the thought of returning to the late nineteenth century, a time of "worldwide bloodshed, greed and tyranny."

Community and cooperation are the key concepts in Bellamy's utopian tale. The nation's businesses, including farms and factories, have been given over to the collective ownership of the people. Elected officials now plan the production and distribution of goods for the common well-being. With great efficiency, they even manage huge department stores and warehouses full of marvelous manufactured goods and oversee majestic apartment complexes with modern facilities for cooking, dining, and laundering. To get the necessary work done, an industrial army enlists all adult men and women, but automated machinery has eliminated most menial tasks. The workday is only four hours; vacations extend to six months of each year. At forty-five, everyone retires to pursue hobbies, sports, and culture.

Bellamy envisioned his technological utopia as promoting the "highest possible physical, as well as mental, development for everyone." There was nothing fantastic in this plan, the author insisted. It simply required Americans to share equally the abundant resources of their land. If the nation's citizens actually lived up to their democratic ideals, Bellamy declared, the United States would become a "cooperative commonwealth," that is, a nation governed by the people for their common welfare.

Bellamy, a journalist and writer of historical fiction from Chicopee Falls, Massachusetts, moved thousands of his readers to action. His most ardent fans endorsed his program for a "new nation" and formed the Nationalist movement, which by the early 1890s reached an apex of 165 clubs. Terence V. Powderly of the Knights of Labor declared himself a Nationalist. Many leaders of the woman suffrage movement also threw in their support. They endorsed *Looking Backward*'s depiction of marriage as a union of "perfect equals" and admired Bellamy's sequel, *Equality* (1897), which showed how women might become "absolutely free agents" by ending their financial dependence on men.

During the 1890s, Bellamy's disciples actually attempted to create new communities along the lines set forth in *Looking Backward*. The best-known and longest-lasting of these settlements was established in Point Loma, California, in 1897. Situated on 330 acres, with avenues winding through gardens and orchards newly planted with groves of eucalyptus trees, Point Loma was known for its physical beauty. Many young married couples chose to live in small bungalows, which were scattered throughout the colony's grounds; others opted for private rooms in a large communal building. Either way, they all met twice daily to share meals and usually spent their leisure hours together. On the ocean's edge, the residents constructed an outdoor amphitheater and staged plays and concerts.

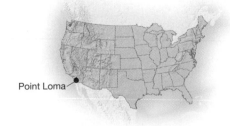

Point Loma

The colony's founder, Katherine Tingley, described Point Loma as "a practical illustration of the possibility of developing a higher type of humanity." No one earned wages, but all 500 residents lived comfortably. They dressed simply in clothes manufactured by the community's women. The majority of the men worked in agriculture. They conducted horticultural experiments that yielded new types of avocados and tropical fruits, and eventually produced over half of the community's food supply. Children, who slept in a special dormitory from the time they reached school age, enjoyed an outstanding education. They excelled in the fine arts, including music and drama, and often demonstrated their talents to audiences in nearby San Diego.

The Point Loma community never met all of its expenses, but with the help of donations from admirers across the country, it remained solvent for decades. Baseball entrepreneur Albert Spalding, who lived there during his retirement, helped make up the financial deficit. As late as the 1950s, the community still had some seventy-five members living on about 100 acres of land.

Even relatively successful cooperative communities such as Point Loma, however, could not bring about the changes that Bellamy hoped to see, and he knew it. Only a mobilization of citizens nationwide could overturn the existing hierarchies and usher in the egalitarian order depicted in *Looking Backward*. Without such a rigorous challenge, the economic and political leadership that had been emerging since the Civil War would continue to consolidate its power and become even further removed from popular control.

The last quarter of the nineteenth century saw just such a challenge, producing what one historian calls "a moment of democratic promise." Ordinary citizens sought to renew the older values of community through farm and labor organizations and created a massive political movement known as populism. At the same time, middle-class men and women were inspired to action by a rising religious movement known as the Social Gospel. They sponsored numerous philanthropic and charitable societies to address the growing number of problems caused by poverty. But, despite their good will, they could not clearly see that their desire to usher in a cooperative commonwealth did little to alleviate some of most immediate and pressing problems, such as worsening racial tensions throughout the nation and the rise of Jim Crow in the South. Equally important, they could not see that the fate of the nation depended increasingly on events beyond its territorial boundaries.

Those opposed to Bellamy's plans for a cooperative commonwealth, including most business leaders and politicians, nurtured their own, alternative vision of the future: an American empire extending to far distant lands. Hoping to expand their possibilities for profit, they looked overseas. Especially in the 1890s, when a severe economic depression spread across the nation, many business and political leaders reasoned that new foreign markets for the goods that most Americans could no long afford to buy would not only end the financial crisis but ease social tensions at home. "American factories are making more than the American people can use; American soil is producing more than they can consume. Fate has written our policy for us; the trade of the world must and shall be ours," declared Senator Albert Beveridge of Indiana in 1897. By the end of the century, the United States had engaged in a major war—the Spanish-American War—that produced the nation's first overseas empire.

KEY TOPICS

- The growth of federal and state governments and the consolidation of the modern two-party system
- The development of mass protest movements
- Economic and political crisis in the 1890s
- The United States as a world power
- The Spanish-American War

TOWARD A NATIONAL GOVERNING CLASS

The basic structure of government changed dramatically in the last quarter of the nineteenth century. Mirroring the fast-growing economy, public administration expanded at all levels—municipal, county, state, and federal—and took on greater responsibility for regulating society, especially market and property relations.

This expansion offered ample opportunities for politicians who were eager to compete against one another for control of the new mechanisms of power. Political campaigns, especially those staged for the presidential elections, became mass spectacles, and votes became precious commodities. The most farsighted politicians attempted to rein in the growing corruption and to promote both efficiency and professionalism in the expanding structures of government.

The Growth of Government

Before the Civil War, local governments attended mainly to the promotion and regulation of trade, and relied on private enterprise to supply vital services such as fire protection and water supply. As cities became more responsible for their residents' well-being, they introduced professional police and firefighting forces and began to finance school systems, public libraries, and parks. This expansion demanded huge increases in local taxation.

At the national level, mobilization for the Civil War and Reconstruction had demanded an unprecedented degree of coordination, and the federal government continued to expand under the weight of new tasks and responsibilities. Federal revenues also skyrocketed, from $257 million in 1878 to $567 million in 1900. The administrative bureaucracy grew dramatically, as well, from 50,000 employees in 1871 to 100,000 only a decade later.

The modern apparatus of departments, bureaus, and cabinets took shape amid this upswing. The Department of Agriculture was established in 1862 to provide information to farmers and to consumers of farm products. The Department of the Interior, which had been created in 1849, grew into the largest and most important federal department other than the Post Office. It came to comprise more than twenty agencies, including the Bureau of Indian Affairs, the U.S. Geological Survey, and the Bureau of Territorial and International Affairs. The Department of the Treasury, responsible for collecting federal taxes and customs as well as printing money and stamps, grew from 4,000 employees in 1873 to nearly 25,000 in 1900.

The nation's first independent regulatory agency took charge of the nation's most important industry. The Interstate Commerce Commission (ICC) was created in 1887 to bring order to the growing patchwork of state laws concerning railroads. The five-member commission appointed by the president approved freight and passenger rates set by the railroads. The ICC could take public testimony on possible violations, examine company records, and generally oversee enforcement of the law. This set a precedent for future regulation of trade as well as for positive government—that is, for the intervention of the government into the affairs of private enterprise. It also marked a shift in the balance of power from the states to the federal government.

The Machinery of Politics

Only gradually did Republicans and Democrats adapt to the demands of governmental expansion. The Republican Party continued to run on its Civil War record, pointing to its achievements in reuniting the nation and in passing new reform legislation. Democrats, by contrast, sought to reduce the influence of the federal government, slash expenditures, repeal legislation, and protect states' rights. While Republicans held on to their long-time constituencies, Democrats gathered support from Southern white voters and immigrants newly naturalized in the North. But neither party commanded a clear majority of votes until the century drew to a close.

Presidents in the last quarter of the century—Rutherford B. Hayes (1877–81), James A. Garfield (1881), Chester A. Arthur (1881–85), Grover Cleveland (1885–89), Benjamin Harrison (1889–93), and Cleveland again (1893–97)—lacked luster. They willingly yielded power to Congress and the state legislatures. Only 1 percent of the popular vote separated the presidential candidates in three of five elections between 1876 and 1892. Congressional races were equally tight, less than 2 percentage points separating total votes for Democratic and Republican candidates in all but one election in the decade before 1888. Democrats usually held a majority in the House and Republicans a majority in the Senate. With neither party sufficiently strong to govern effectively, Congress passed little legislation before 1890.

One major political issue that separated the two parties was the tariff. First instituted in 1789 to raise revenue for the young republic, the tariff imposed a fee on imported goods, especially manufactured commodities. Soon, its major purpose became the protection of the nation's "infant industries" from foreign competition. Manufacturing regions, especially the Northeast, favored a protective policy, while the Southern and Western agricultural regions opposed high tariffs as unfair to farmers and ranchers who had to pay the steep fees on imported necessities. Democrats, with a stronghold among Southern voters, argued for sharp reductions in the tariff as a way to save the rural economy and to give a boost to workers. Republicans, who represented mainly business interests, raised tariffs to new levels on a wide array of goods during the Civil War, and retained high tariffs as long as they held power.

In 1888, Grover Cleveland, with his running mate, Allen G. Thurman, led a spirited campaign for reelection to the presidency. Although he played up his strong record on civil service reform and tariff reduction, Cleveland, an incumbent, lost the election to his Republican challenger, Benjamin Harrison. Cleveland tallied the greatest number of popular votes, but Harrison easily won in the Electoral College by a margin of 233 to 168. In this lithograph campaign poster, the Democratic ticket invokes the legacy of Thomas Jefferson and the patriotism of Uncle Sam.

SOURCE: The Granger Collection, New York.

Although their platforms encompassed broad national issues, none more important than the tariff, both parties operated essentially as state or local organizations and, as such, waged spectacular political campaigns in their communities. "We work through one campaign," quipped one candidate, "take a bath and start in on the next." Election paraphernalia—leaflets or pamphlets, banners, hats, flags, buttons, inscribed playing cards, or clay pipes featuring a likeness of a candidate's face or the party symbol—became a major expense for both parties. Partisans embraced the Democratic donkey or the Republican elephant as symbols of party fidelity. And voters did turn out. During the last quarter of the century, participation in presidential elections peaked at nearly 80 percent of those eligible to vote. Thousands, in fact, voted several times on any given election day; voters who had died, or had never lived, also miraculously cast ballots.

The rising costs of maintaining local organizations and orchestrating mammoth campaigns drove party leaders to seek ever-larger sources of revenue. Winners often seized and added to the "spoils" of office through an elaborate system of payoffs. Legislators who supported government subsidies for railroad corporations, for instance, commonly received stock in return and sometimes cash bribes. At the time, few politicians or business leaders regarded these practices as unethical.

At the local level, powerful bosses and political machines dominated both parties. Democrats William

Marcy Tweed of New York's powerful political organization, Tammany Hall, and Michael "Hinky Dink" Kenna of Chicago, specialized in giving municipal jobs to loyal voters and holiday food baskets to their families. Hundreds of smaller political machines ruled cities and rural courthouses through a combination of "boodle" (bribe money) and personal favors.

A large number of federal jobs, meanwhile, changed hands each time the presidency passed from one party to another. More than 50 percent of all federal jobs were patronage positions—nearly 56,000 in 1881—jobs that could be awarded to loyal supporters as part of the "spoils" of the winner. Observers estimated that decisions about congressional patronage filled one-third of all legislators' time. No wonder Bellamy's utopian community operated without politicians and political parties.

The Spoils System and Civil Service Reform

As early as 1865, Republican representative Thomas A. Jenckes of Rhode Island proposed a bill for civil service reform, but the majority in Congress, fearing that such a measure would hamper candidates in their relentless pursuit of votes, refused to pass reform legislation. Finally, a group comprising mainly professors, newspaper editors, lawyers, and ministers organized the Civil Service Reform Association and enlisted Democratic senator George H. Pendleton to sponsor reform legislation.

In January 1883, a bipartisan congressional majority passed the Pendleton Civil Service Reform Act. This measure allowed the president to create, with Senate approval, a three-person commission to draw up a set of guidelines for executive and legislative appointments. The commission established a system of standards for various federal jobs and instituted "open, competitive examinations for testing the fitness of applicants for public service." The Pendleton Act also barred political candidates from funding their campaigns by assessing a "tax" on the salaries of holders of party-sponsored government jobs.

Although patronage did not disappear entirely, many departments of the federal government took on a professional character similar to that which doctors, lawyers, and scholars were imposing on their fields through regulatory societies such as the American Medical Association and the American Historical Association. At the same time, the federal judiciary began to act more aggressively to establish the parameters of government. With the Circuit Courts of Appeals Act of 1891, Congress granted the U.S. Supreme Court the right to review all cases at will.

Despite these reforms, many observers still viewed government as a reign of self-interest and corruption. Edward Bellamy agreed. He advised Americans to organize their communities for the specific purpose of wresting control of government from the hands of politicians.

FARMERS AND WORKERS ORGANIZE THEIR COMMUNITIES

Farmers and workers began to organize in the late 1860s and succeeded in building powerful national organizations to oppose, as a Nebraska newspaper put it, "the wealthy and powerful classes who want the control of government to plunder the people." As the nation's most important industry, the railroad played a large part in generating this unrest. By the end of the century, the communities whose livelihoods depended directly or indirectly on the railroads presented the most significant challenge to the two-party system since the Civil War—the populist movement.

The Grange

In 1867, white farmers in the Midwest formed the Patrons of Husbandry for their own "social, intellectual, and moral improvement." Led by Oliver H. Kelley, this fraternal society resembled the secretive Masonic order. Whole families staffed a complex array of offices and engaged in mysterious rituals involving passwords, flags, songs, and costumes. In many farming communities, the headquarters of the local chapter, known as the Grange (a word for "farm"), became the main social center, the site of summer dinners and winter dances.

The Granger movement spread rapidly, especially in areas where farmers were experiencing their greatest hardships. Great Plains farmers barely survived the blizzards, grasshopper infestations, and droughts of the early 1870s. Meanwhile, farmers throughout the trans-Mississippi West and the South watched the prices for grains and cotton fall year by year in the face of growing competition from producers in Canada, Australia, Argentina, Russia, and India. In the hope of improving their condition through collective action, many farmers joined their local Grange. The Patrons of Husbandry soon swelled to more than 1.5 million members.

Grangers blamed hard times on a band of "thieves in the night"—especially railroads and banks—that charged exorbitant fees for service. They fumed at American manufacturers, such as Cyrus McCormick, who sold farm equipment more cheaply in Europe than in the United States. They raged at the banks that charged high interest rates for the money farmers had to borrow to pay the steep prices for equipment and raw materials.

Grangers mounted their greatest assault on the railroad corporations. By bribing state legislators, railroads enjoyed a highly discriminatory rate policy, commonly charging farmers more to ship their crops short distances than over long hauls. In 1874, several Midwestern states responded to pressure and passed a series of so-called Granger laws establishing maximum shipping rates. Grangers also complained

The symbols chosen by Grange artists represented their faith that all social value could be traced to honest labor and most of all to the work of the entire farm family. The hardworking American required only the enlightenment offered by the Grange to build a better community.

SOURCE: Library of Congress.

trol one-third of the grain elevators and warehouses in the state. In other states, Grangers ran banks as well as fraternal life and fire insurance companies.

The deepening depression of the late 1870s wiped out most of these cooperative programs. By 1880, Grange membership had fallen to 100,000. Meanwhile, the Supreme Court overturned most of the key legislation regulating railroads. Despite these setbacks, the Patrons of Husbandry had nonetheless promoted a model of collective action and cooperation that would remain at the heart of agrarian protest movements until the end of the century.

The Farmers' Alliance

Agrarian unrest did not end with the downward turn of the Grange but instead moved south. In the 1880s, farmers organized in communities where both poverty and the crop-lien system prevailed (see Chapter 17). New South newspaper writers and politicians advised farmers to trim expenditures and to diversify out of cotton into other crops. But with household budgets falling from $50 to as low as $10 a year, Southern farmers had no leeway to cut expenses. And the cost of shipping perishable crops made diversification untenable despite the falling price of cotton. In response to these conditions, Texas farmers—proclaiming "Equal Rights to All, Special Privileges to None"—began to organize. Establishing more than 500 chapters in Texas alone, and cooperative stores, complemented by the cooperative merchandising of crops, the Southern Farmers' Alliance became a viable alternative to the capitalist marketplace—for white farmers.

Excluded from the Southern Alliance, the Colored Farmers' Alliance organized on its own and grew from its beginnings in Texas and Arkansas in 1886, to claim more than a million members across the South. Although racially distinct, the two alliances occasionally cooperated and convened their major meetings at the same time. But their already strained relationship became increasingly so when black cotton pickers began to oganize to demand higher wages from white farmers. When fifteen cotton pickers

to their lawmakers about the price-fixing policies of grain wholesalers and operators of grain elevators. In 1873, the Illinois legislature passed a Warehouse Act establishing maximum rates for storing grains. Chicago firms challenged the legality of this measure, but in *Munn* v. *Illinois* (1877), the Supreme Court upheld the law, ruling that states had the power to regulate privately owned businesses like the railroads in the public interest.

Determined to buy less and produce more, Grangers created a vast array of cooperative enterprises for both the purchase of supplies and the marketing of crops. They established local grain elevators, set up retail stores, and even manufactured some of their own farm machinery. As early as 1872, the Iowa Grange claimed to con-were killed during a brutal strike, the white Farmers' Alliance, choosing to distance itself from the strikers, kept silent.

The Northern Farmers' Alliance took shape in the Great Plains states, drawing upon larger organizations in Minnesota, Nebraska, Iowa, Kansas, and the Dakota Territory. During 1886 and 1887, summer drought followed winter blizzards and ice storms, reducing wheat harvests by one-third on the plains. Locusts and cinch bugs ate much of the rest. As if this were not enough, prices on the world market fell sharply for what little remained. Skilled agitators played upon these hardships—especially the overpowering influence of railroads over the farmers' lives—, and by 1890, the Kansas Alliance alone claimed 130,000 members.

Grangers had pushed legislation that would limit the salaries of public officials, provide public school students with books at little or no cost, establish a program of teacher certification, and widen the admissions policies of the new state colleges. But only rarely did they put up candidates for office. In comparison, the Farmers' Alliance had few reservations about taking political stands or entering electoral races. At the end of the 1880s, regional alliances drafted campaign platforms demanding state ownership of the railroads, a graduated income tax, lower tariffs, restriction of land ownership to citizens, and easier access to money through "the free and unlimited coinage of silver." In several states, alliance candidates for local and state office won elections. By 1890, the alliances had gained control of the Nebraska legislature and held the balance of power in Minnesota and South Dakota.

Workers Search for Power

The railroad became the focus of protests by workers as well as farmers. Within the few months after the Panic of 1873 (see Chapter 17), which produced 25 percent unemployment in many cities, workers struck so many times that the *New York Railroad Gazette* complained, "Strikes are . . . as much a disease of the body politic as the measles or indigestion are of our physical organization." Although most of these strikes ended in failure, they revealed the readiness of workers to spell out their grievances in a direct and dramatic manner. They also suggested how strongly many townspeople, including merchants who depended on workers' wages, would support local strikes and turn them into community uprisings (see Map 20.1).

Despite these warnings, the railroad corporations were unprepared for the Great Uprising of 1877, the first nationwide strike. The strike began in Martinsburg, West Virginia, where workers protesting a 10 percent wage cut uncoupled all engines. No trains would run, they promised, until wages were restored. Within a few days, the strike had spread along the railroad routes to New York, Buffalo, Pittsburgh, Chicago, Kansas City, and San Francisco. In all these cities, workers in various industries and masses of the unemployed formed angry crowds, defying armed militia ordered to disperse them

MAP EXPLORATION

To explore an interactive version of this map, go to
www.prenhall.com/faragher5/map20.1

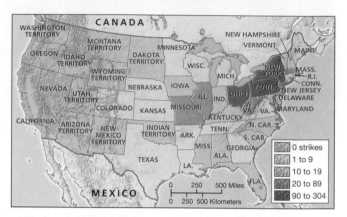

MAP 20.1 Strikes by State, 1880 Most strikes after the Uprising of 1877 could be traced to organized trades, concentrated in the manufacturing districts of the Northeast and Midwest.

SOURCE: *Carville Earle, Geographical Inquiry and American Historical Problems* (Stanford, CA: Stanford University Press, 1992).

by any means. The crowds halted train traffic, sometimes pulling up entire rails and seizing carloads of food for hungry families. Energized by the activity, workers in St. Louis even took over the city's administration.

The rioting persisted for nearly a week, spurring business leaders to call for the deportation, arrest, or execution of strike leaders. Fearing a "national insurrection," President Hayes set a precedent by calling in the U.S. Army to suppress the strike. In Pittsburgh, federal troops fired into a crowd and killed more than twenty people. By the time the strike finally ended, more than 100 people were dead.

Memories of the Uprising of 1877 haunted business and government officials for decades, prompting the creation of the National Guard and the construction of armories in working-class neighborhoods. Workers also drew lessons from the events. Before the end of the century, more than 6 million workers would strike in industries ranging from New England textiles to Southern tobacco factories to Western mines. While the Farmers' Alliance put up candidates in the South and Plains states, workers launched labor parties in dozens of industrial towns and cities.

In New York City, popular economist and land reformer Henry George, with the ardent support of the city's Central Labor Council and the Knights of Labor, put himself forward in 1886 as candidate for mayor on the United Labor Party ticket. His best-selling book *Progress and Poverty* (1879), advocated a sweeping tax on all property to generate enough revenue to allow all Americans to live in comfort. George called upon "all honest citizens" to join in independent political action as "the only hope

The Great Uprising of 1877, which began as a strike of railroad workers, spread rapidly to communities along the railroad routes. Angry crowds defied the armed militia and the vigilantes hired to disperse them. In Philadelphia, for example, strikers set fire to the downtown, destroying many buildings before federal troops were brought in to stop them. More than a hundred people died before the strike ended, and the railroad corporations suffered about a $10 million loss in property.

SOURCE: The Granger Collection, New York.

of exposing and breaking up the extortion and speculation by which a standing army of professional politicians corrupt the people whom they plunder."

Tammany Hall delivered many thousands of the ballots cast for George straight into the Hudson River. Nevertheless, George managed to finish a respectable second with 31 percent of the vote, running ahead of young patrician Theodore Roosevelt. Although his campaign ended in defeat, George had issued a stern warning to the entrenched politicians. Equally important, his impressive showing encouraged labor groups in other cities to form their own parties.

In the late 1880s, labor parties won seats on many city councils and state legislatures. The Milwaukee People's Party elected the mayor, a state senator, six assemblymen, and one member of Congress. In smaller industrial towns where workers outnumbered the middle classes, labor parties did especially well. In Rochester, New Hampshire, with a population of only 7,000, workers, mainly shoemakers, elected a majority slate, from city council to mayor.

Women Build Alliances

Women helped build both the labor and agrarian protest movements, while campaigning for their own rights as citizens. Like woman suffrage leader Elizabeth Cady Stanton, many women believed that "government based on caste and class privilege cannot stand." In its place,

as Bellamy predicted in *Equality*, would arise a new cooperative order, in which women would be "absolutely free agents in the disposition of themselves."

Women in the Knights of Labor lobbied for the creation of a special department within the organization "to investigate the abuses to which our sex is subjected by unscrupulous employers, to agitate the principles which our Order teaches of equal pay for equal work and the abolition of child labor." Delegates to the 1886 convention approved the plan with little dissent and appointed knit-goods worker Leonora M. Barry general investigator. With perhaps 65,000 women members at its peak, the Knights ran day-care centers for the children of wage-earning mothers, and occasionally even set up cooperative kitchens to reduce the drudgery of cooking.

The Grangers issued a charter to a local chapter only when women were well represented on its rolls, and in the 1870s, delegates to its conventions routinely gave speeches endorsing woman suffrage and even dress reform. In both the Northern and Southern Alliances, women made up perhaps one-quarter of the membership, and several advanced through the ranks to become leading speakers and organizers. Mary E. Lease achieved lasting fame for advising farmers to raise less corn and more hell.

Women in both the Knights of Labor and the Farmers' Alliance found their greatest leader in Frances E. Willard, the most famous woman of the nineteenth century. Willard assumed that women, who guarded their families' physical and spiritual welfare, would, if granted the right to vote, extend their influence throughout the whole society. From 1878 until her death in 1897, Willard presided over the Woman's Christian Temperance Union (WCTU), at the time the largest organization of women in the world, and encouraged her numerous followers to "do everything." WCTU members preached total abstinence from the consumption of alcohol, but they also worked to reform the prison system, eradicate prostitution, and eliminate the wage system. Willard went so far as to draw up plans for a new system of government whereby all offices, right up to the presidency, would be shared jointly by men and women. By the end of the century, she had mobilized nearly 1 million women to, in her words, "make the whole world HOMELIKE."

Frances E. Willard (1839-1898) became a full-time activist
for the National Woman's Christian Temperance Union in 1874.
From 1879 until her death, she served as president, pushing
the organization to expand its interests beyond temperance under
the rubric of her "do-everything" policy. Under her leadership,
the WCTU established 39 departments promoting a wide array
of reform causes ranging from the establishment of free
kindergartens to the prohibition of the manufacure of cigarettes.

SOURCE: Library of Congress.

Willard also advocated temperance work among
African American women. In the 1880s, the WCTU
served as one of the few Southern organizations to experiment in "interracial cooperation," the phrase used by
activists for work across racial lines. In North Carolina, for
example, although the state WCTU gathered members
into separate black and white chapters, local temperance
women occasionally sponsored common campaigns.
Although the number of affiliated African American
women remained small, the Southern branches of WCTU
served as an important and relatively safe arena for not
only temperance agitation but other forms of "racial uplift."

Under Willard's leadership, the WCTU grew into the
major force for woman suffrage, far surpassing the American Woman Suffrage Association and the National
Woman Suffrage Association. By 1890, when the two rival
suffrage associations merged to form the National American Woman Suffrage Association, the WCTU had already
pushed the heart of the suffrage campaign into the Great
Plains states and the West. In these regions, agitation for
the right to vote provided a political bridge among women

organized in the WCTU, Farmers' Alliance, Knights of
Labor, and various local suffrage societies.

Although women lecturers such as Mary E. Lease
were outstanding crowd pleasers, women failed to gain
much support for woman suffrage. Only in Colorado
did local third-party candidates support the 1893 campaign that secured women's right to vote in that state. In
the South, the majority of women themselves opposed
their enfranchisement, and the campaign for woman suffrage stalled until well after the turn of the century.

Populism and the People's Party

In December 1890, the Farmers' Alliance called a meeting
at Ocala, Florida, to press for a national third-party movement. This was a risky proposition because the Southern
Alliance hoped to capture control of the Democratic Party,
whereas many farmers in the Plains states voted Republican. In some areas, however, the Farmers' Alliance established its own parties, put up full slates of candidates for
local elections, won majorities in state legislatures, and even
sent a representative to Congress. Reviewing these successes, delegates at Ocala decided to push ahead and form
a national party, and they appealed to other farm, labor, and
reform organizations to join them. Edward Bellamy considered this development "the largest opportunity yet presented," and enthusiastically endorsed the third-party effort.

In February 1892, 1,300 representatives from the
Farmers' Alliance, the Knights of Labor, and the Colored
Farmers' Alliance, among others, met in St. Louis under
a broad banner that read: "We do not ask for sympathy
or pity. We ask for justice." The new People's Party called
for government ownership of railroads, banks, and telegraph lines, prohibition of large landholding companies,
a graduated income tax, an eight-hour workday, and
restriction of immigration. The most ambitious plan called
for the national government to build local warehouses
—"subtreasuries"— where farmers could store their crops
until prices reached acceptable levels. While waiting out
a poor market, farmers could maintain solvency by borrowing as much as 80 percent against the current value
of their produce and pay only a very small interest rate.

The Populists, as supporters of the People's Party
styled themselves, quickly became a major factor in American politics. In some Southern states, Populists cooperated with local Republicans in sponsoring "pepper and
salt" state and local tickets that put black and white candidates on a single slate. To hold their voters, some
Democrats adopted the Populist platform wholesale; others resorted to massive voter fraud and intimidation. In
the West, Democrats threw their weight behind the Populist ticket mainly to defeat the ruling Republicans.

In 1892, Populists scored a string of local victories. In
Idaho, Nevada, Colorado, Kansas, and North Dakota, they
won 50 percent or more of the vote. Nationwide, they
elected three governors, ten representatives to Congress,

OUT OF MANY VOICES

A POPULIST WOMAN ON WOMEN'S RIGHTS

ettie Gay was an active member of the Farmers' Alliance in Columbus, Texas. In this excerpt from an article entitled "The Influence of Women in the Alliance," she writes about women's participation in local chapters of the Alliance and responsibilities in the field of social betterment.

THE MEETINGS [OF THE FARMERS' ALLIANCE] GIVE recreation to the mind, and the physical being is for a time relieved from incessant toil. The entire being is invigorated, and the mind is prepared for the reception of such truths as fit her to be companion, mother, and citizen. . . . [W]oman has not been considered a factor in the great movement, until of late years, but she comes prominently to the front in the Alliance, and demands that she be allowed to render service in the great battle for human rights, better conditions, happier homes, and a higher civilization generally. In fact, she has come to the conclusion that she has some grievances for which remedies should be found, and that she owes it as a duty to herself and society to help work out the social and political salvation of the people.

I believe that there are remedies for most of the evils which afflict society; that poverty and want are the chief causes of crime; and the reason why so many people are found occupying unnatural conditions, is because of the violation of the principles of justice and right, by the government allowing the few to monopolize the land, money, and transportation, which deprives a large portion of the people of their natural right to apply their labor to the gifts of nature. Under such conditions, the people become dependent, hopeless slaves, —a condition which drives the last spark of manhood and womanhood from their bosoms,— and they become outcasts and criminals, and fill our jails and penitentiaries and other places of shame. . . .

If I understand the object of the Alliance, it is organized not only to better the financial condition of the people, but to elevate them socially, and in every other way, and make them happier and better, and to make this world a fit habitation for man, by giving to the people equal opportunities. Every woman who has at heart the welfare of the race should attach herself to some reform organization, and lend her help toward the removal of the causes which have filled the world with crime and sorrow, and made outcasts of so many of her sex.   ■

SOURCE: Mrs. Bettie Gay, "The Influence of Women in the Alliance," in N.A. Dunning, ed., *The Farmers' Alliance History and Agricultural Digest* (Washington, DC: The Alliance Publishing Co., 1891). pp. 310–11.

---

and five senators. The national ticket, headed by Iowan James B. Weaver and James G. Field, a former Confederate solider, lost to Democrats Grover Cleveland and Adlai E. Stevenson, but received more than 1 million votes (8.5 percent of the total) and 22 electoral college votes—the only time since the Civil War that a third party had received any electoral votes. Despite poor showings among urban workers east of the Mississippi, Populists looked forward to the next round of state elections in 1894. But the great test would come with the presidential election in 1896.

THE CRISIS OF THE 1890s

Populist Ignatius Donnelly wrote in the preface to his pessimistic novel *Caesar's Column* (1891) that industrial society appears to be a "wretched failure" to "the great mass of mankind." On the road to disaster rather than to the egalitarian community that Bellamy had envisioned, "the rich, as a rule, hate the poor; and the poor are coming to hate the rich . . . society divides itself into two hostile camps. . . . They wait only for the drum beat and the trumpet to summon them to armed conflict."

A series of events in the 1890s shook the confidence of many citizens in the reigning political system. But nothing was more unsettling than the severe economic depression that consumed the nation and lasted for five years. Many feared—while others hoped—that the entire political system would topple.

The Depression of 1893

The railroads, the major force behind economic growth, now helped to usher in a great depression. Overextended, especially in construction, the major rail lines went bankrupt in 1893. The business boom of nearly two decades ended, and the entire economy ground to a halt. The depression that followed made the hard times of the 1870s appear a mere rehearsal for worse misery to come.

The collapse of the Philadelphia and Reading Railroad, followed by the downfall of the National Cordage Company, precipitated a crash in the stock market and

Jacob Coxey's "Commonwealth of Christ Army," April 1894. Attracting the sympathetic attention of working people and the hostility of most of the wealthier classes, "Industrial Armies" marched through U.S. cities enroute to the nation's capital.

SOURCE: Library of Congress.

Populist Jacob Sechler Coxey decided to gather the masses of unemployed into a huge army and then to march to Washington, DC, to demand from Congress a public works program. On Easter Sunday, 1894, Coxey left Massillon, Ohio, with several hundred followers. Meanwhile, brigades from across the country joined his "petition in boots." Although the marchers received a warm welcome from most communities along the way, U.S. Attorney General Richard C. Olney, a former lawyer for the railroad companies, conspired with local officials to halt them. Only 600 men and women reached the nation's capital, where the police first clubbed and then arrested the leaders for trespassing on the grass. "Coxey's Army" quickly disbanded, but not before voicing the public's growing impatience with government apathy toward the unemployed.

Strikes: Coeur d'Alene, Homestead, and Pullman

Meanwhile, in several locations, the conflict between labor and capital had escalated to the brink of civil war. Wage cuts in the silver and lead mines of northern Idaho led to one of the bitterest conflicts of the decade. To put a brake on organized labor, mineowners had formed a "protective association," and in March 1892, they announced a wage cut throughout the Coeur d'Alene district. After the miners' union rejected the lowered wage scale, the owners locked out all union members and brought in strikebreakers by the trainload. Unionists tried peaceful methods of protest. But after three months of stalemate, they loaded a railcar with explosives and blew up a mine. Strikebreakers fled, while mineowners appealed to the Idaho governor for assistance. More than 300 union members were herded into bullpens, where they were kept for several weeks before their trial. Ore production meanwhile resumed with "scab" labor, and by November, when the troops were withdrawn, the mineowners declared a victory. But the miners' union survived, and most members eventually regained their jobs.

Coeur d'Alene strikers had been buoyed by the news that steelworkers at Homestead, Pennsylvania, had likewise taken guns in hand to defend their union. Members of the Amalgamated Iron, Steel and Tin Workers, the most powerful union of the AFL, had carved out an admirable position for themselves in the Carnegie Steel Company. Well paid, proud of their skills, the unionists

sent waves of panic splashing over banks across the country. In a few months, more than 150 banks went into receivership, and hundreds more closed; nearly 200 railroads and more than 15,000 businesses also slipped into bankruptcy. Agricultural prices meanwhile continued to plummet until they reached new lows. The economy slowly began to pick up again in 1897, but the new century arrived before prosperity returned.

In many cities, unemployment rates reached 25 percent; Samuel Gompers, head of the American Federation of Labor (AFL), estimated nationwide unemployment at 3 million. Few people starved, but millions suffered. Inadequate diets prompted a rise in communicable diseases, such as tuberculosis and pellagra. Unable to buy food, clothes, or household items, families learned to survive with the barest minimum.

Tens of thousands "rode the rails" or went "on the tramp" to look for work, hoping that their luck might change in a new city or town. Some panhandled for the nickel that could buy a mug of beer and a free lunch at a saloon. By night they slept in parks. Vagrancy laws (enacted during the 1870s) forced many into prison. In New York City alone, with more than 20,000 homeless people, thousands ended up in jail. Newspapers warned against this "menace" and blamed the growing crime rates on the "dangerous classes."

In 1894, to protest a cut in wages, the workers of the Pullman Palace Car Company struck. Eugene V. Debs, president of the American Railway Union, ordered a nationwide boycott against the Pullman Company. The United States Cavalry was brought in to escort the trains run by "scab" laborers.

SOURCE: Library of Congress.

dramatized the importance of the railroad as well as the extent of collusion between the government and corporations to crush the labor movement.

Pullman, Illinois, just south of Chicago, had been constructed as a model industrial community. Its creator and proprietor, George M. Pullman, had manufactured luxurious "sleeping cars" for railroads since 1881. He built his company as a self-contained community, with the factory at the center, surrounded by modern cottages, a library, churches, parks, an independent water supply, even its own cemetery, but no saloons. The Pullman Palace Car Company deducted rent, library fees, and grocery bills from each worker's weekly wages. In good times, workers enjoyed a decent livelihood, although many resented Pullman's autocratic control of their daily affairs.

When times grew hard, the company cut wages by as much as one-half, in some cases down to less than $1 a day. Charges for food and rent remained unchanged. Furthermore, factory supervisors sought to make up for declining profits by driving workers to produce more. In May 1894, after Pullman fired members of a committee that had drawn up a list of grievances, workers voted to strike.

Pullman workers found their champion in Eugene V. Debs, who had recently formed the American Railway Union (ARU) in order to bring railroad workers across the vast continent into one organization. Debs, the architect of the ARU's victory over the Great Northern rail line just one month earlier, advised caution, but delegates to an ARU convention voted to support a nationwide boycott of all Pullman cars. This action soon turned into a sympathy strike by railroad workers across the country.

Compared to the Uprising of 1877, the orderly Pullman strike at first produced little violence. ARU officials urged strikers to ignore all police provocations and hold their ground peacefully. But Attorney General Richard C. Olney, claiming that the ARU was disrupting mail shipments (actually Debs had banned such interference), issued a blanket injunction against the strike. On July 4, President Cleveland sent federal troops to Chicago, over Illinois governor John Peter Altgeld's objections. After a bitter confrontation that left thirteen people dead and more than fifty wounded, the army dispersed the strikers. For the next week, railroad workers in twenty-six other states resisted federal troops, and a dozen more people were killed. On July 17, the strike

customarily directed their unskilled helpers without undue influence of company supervisors. But, determined to gain control over every stage of production, Carnegie and his chairman, Henry C. Frick, decided not only to lower wages but to break the union.

In 1892, when the Amalgamated's contract expired, Frick announced a drastic wage cut. He also ordered a wooden stockade built around the factory, with grooves for rifles and barbed wire on top. When Homestead's city government refused to assign police to disperse the strikers, Frick dispatched a barge carrying a private army armed to the teeth. Gunfire broke out and continued throughout the day. After the governor sent the Pennsylvania National Guard to restore order, Carnegie's factory reopened, with strikebreakers doing the work.

After four months, the union was forced to concede a crushing defeat, not only for itself but, in effect, for all steelworkers. The Carnegie company reduced its workforce by 25 percent, lengthened the workday, and cut wages 25 percent for those who remained on the job. If the Amalgamated Iron, Steel and Tin Workers, known throughout the industry as the "aristocrats of labor," could be brought down, less-skilled workers could expect little from the corporate giants. Within a decade, every major steel company operated without union interference.

Just two years after the strikes at Coeur d'Alene and Homestead, the greatest railway strike since 1877 again finally ended when federal marshals arrested Debs and other leaders.

Assailing the arrogance of class privilege that encouraged the government to use brute force against its citizens, Debs concluded that the labor movement could not regain its dignity under the present system. An avid fan of Bellamy's *Looking Backward*, he came out of jail committed to the ideals of socialism, and in 1898 helped to form a political party dedicated to its principles.

Tens of thousands of people supported Debs. Declining nomination on the Populist ticket in 1896, he ran for president as a socialist in 1900 and in four subsequent elections. The odds against him grew with the scale of the booming economy, but Debs made his point on moral grounds. His friend James Whitcomb Riley, the nation's most admired sentimental poet, wrote in rural dialect that Debs had "the kindest heart that ever beat/betwixt here and the jedgment [judgment] seat."

The Social Gospel

Like Edward Bellamy, a growing number of Protestant and Catholic clergy and lay theologians noted a discrepancy between the ideals of Christianity and prevailing attitudes toward the poor. Like Bellamy, they could no longer sanction an economic system that allowed so many to toil long hours under unhealthy conditions and for subsistence wages. They demanded that the church lead the way to a new cooperative order.

Ministers called for civil service reform and the end of child labor. Supporting labor's right to organize and, if necessary, to strike, they petitioned government officials to regulate corporations and place a limit on profits. Washington Gladden, a Congregationalist minister, warned that if churches continued to ignore pressing social problems, they would devolve into institutions whose sole purpose was to preserve obscure rituals and superstitions. In the wake of the Great Uprising of 1877, he had called upon his congregation in Columbus, Ohio, to take an active part in the fight against social injustice. Gladden's *Applied Christianity* (1886) appealed to the nation's business leaders to return to Christ's teachings.

Catholics, doctrinally more inclined than Protestants to accept poverty as a natural condition, joined the social gospel movement in smaller numbers. In the early 1880s, Polish Americans broke away from the Roman Catholic Church to form the Polish National Church, which was committed to the concerns of working people. Irish Americans, especially prominent in the Knights of Labor, encouraged priests to ally themselves with the labor movement. Pope Leo XIII's encyclical *Rerum Novarum* (1891) endorsed the right of workers to form trade unions.

The depression of the 1890s produced an outpouring of social gospel treatises. The very popular *If Christ Came to Chicago* (1894), by British journalist W. T. Stead, forced readers to confront the "ugly sight" of a city with 200 millionaires and 200,000 unemployed men. It inspired Edward Everett Hale's *If Jesus Came to Boston* (1894), which similarly questioned social inequalities. The most famous tract, *In His Steps* (1896), by Methodist minister Charles M. Sheldon of Topeka, Kansas, urged middle-class readers to rethink their actions in the light of the simple question "What would Jesus do?"

Women guided the social gospel movement in their communities. The WCTU trained hundreds and thousands of Protestant women in social uplift. By the mid-1880s, in nearly every city, groups of white women affiliated with various evangelical Protestant sects were raising funds to establish small, inexpensive residential hotels for working women, whose low wages rarely covered the price of safe, comfortable shelter. At the forefront of this movement, was the Young Women's Christian Association (YWCA), which by 1900 had more than 600 local chapters. The "Y" sponsored a range of services for needy Christian women, ranging from homes for the elderly and for unmarried mothers to elaborate programs of vocational instruction and physical fitness. The Girls' Friendly Societies, an organization of young women affiliated with Episcopal churches, sponsored similar programs. Meanwhile, Catholic lay women and nuns served the poor women of their faith, operating numerous schools, hospitals, and orphanages.

To a greater degree than white women, African American women embraced the social gospel. Affiliated principally with the Baptist Church, they sponsored similar programs and, in addition, emphasized the importance of education to racial uplift. Excluded by the whites-only policy of the YWCA in many localities, African American women organized their own chapters, and branched out to form nurseries, orphanages, hospitals, and nursing homes. In Chicago, for example, African American women organized to provide temporary lodging to young African American women who were new to the city and searching for work. Their main project, the Phyllis Wheatley Home, opened in 1908 to provide a "Christian influence," in the words of the founders, and to procure respectable employment for its boarders. Meanwhile, in Washington, DC, more than 300,000 African American women were sponsoring almost fifty similar societies to assist the self-supporting women of their race. Fannie Barrier Williams, a leader in racial uplift, acknowledged the importance of the churches as "the great preparatory schools in which the primary lessons of social order, mutual trustfulness and united effort have been taught."

The Election of 1896

With the economy still in ruins and social unrest mounting, Republicans, Democrats, and Populists alike sought a solution in currency reform. A desperate President Grover Cleveland demanded the repeal of the Sherman Silver Purchase Act of 1890, which had restored government support for silver mining. He insisted that only the gold

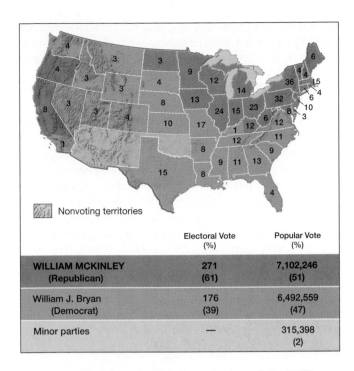

	Electoral Vote (%)	Popular Vote (%)
WILLIAM MCKINLEY (Republican)	**271** **(61)**	**7,102,246** **(51)**
William J. Bryan (Democrat)	176 (39)	6,492,559 (47)
Minor parties	—	315,398 (2)

Nonvoting territories

MAP 20.2 Election of 1896 Democratic candidate William Jennings Bryan carried most of rural America but could not overcome Republican William McKinley's stronghold in the populous industrial states.

standard, an inflexible anchor for the real value of currency, could pull the nation out of depression. Cleveland succeeded but in the process destroyed his own support in Congress, and the midterm elections of 1894 brought the largest shift in congressional power in American history: the Republicans gained 117 seats, while the Democrats lost 113. The "Silver Democrats" of Cleveland's own party began to look to the Populists, mainly Westerners and farmers who favored "free silver"—that is, the unlimited coinage of silver, considered a lever for inflated currency, easier repayment of debts, and rapid growth of the economy. Meanwhile, Republicans confidently began to prepare for the presidential election of 1896, warming to what they called the "battle of the standards" (see Map 20.2).

Populists had been buoyed by the 1894 elections, which delivered to their candidates nearly 1.5 million votes—a gain of 42 percent over their 1892 totals. They made impressive inroads into several Southern states. West of the Mississippi, political excitement steadily increased. David Waite, the Populist governor of Colorado, talked of a coming revolution and declared, "It is better, infinitely better, that blood should flow [up] to the horses' bridles rather than our national liberties should be destroyed." Still, even in the Midwest, where Populists doubled their vote, they managed to win less than 7 percent of the total.

As Populists prepared for the 1896 presidential campaign, they found themselves at a crossroad: what were

they to do with the growing popularity of the Democratic candidate, William Jennings Bryan? Bryan, a Nebraska lawyer, had won a congressional seat in 1890. After seizing the Populist slogan "Equal Rights to All, Special Privilege to None," he now became a major contender for president of the United States, wooing potential voters in a two-year national speaking tour. Pouring new life into his divided party, he pushed Silver Democrats to the forefront.

At the 1896 party convention, the thirty-six-year-old spellbinding orator thrilled delegates with his evocation of agrarian ideals. "Burn down your cities and leave our farms," Bryan preached, "and your cities will spring up again as if by magic; but destroy our farms and the grass will grow in the streets of every city in the country." What became one of the most famous speeches in American political history, closed on a yet more dramatic note.

This Republican campaign poster of 1896 depicts William McKinley standing on sound money and promising a revival of prosperity. The depression of the 1890s shifted the electorate into the Republican column.

SOURCE: The Granger Collection, New York.

Spreading his arms to suggest the crucified Christ figure, Bryan pledged to answer all demands for a gold standard by saying, "You shall not press down upon the brow of labor this crown of thorns, you shall not crucify mankind upon a cross of gold." The next day, he carried the Democratic presidential nomination with thunderous applause.

Populists swiftly realized that by nominating Bryan, the Democrats had stolen their thunder. Many feared rightly that the growing emphasis on currency would overshadow their more important planks, such as government ownership of the nation's railroads and the subtreasury plan. But they also recognized that Bryan had emerged as the major opponent of corporate power. "If we fuse [with the Democratic presidential ticket]," one Populist explained, "we are sunk; if we don't fuse, all the silver men we have will leave us for the more powerful Democrats." In the end, Populists nominated Bryan for president and one of their own, Georgian Tom Watson, as the vice presidential candidate. Most of the state Democratic Party organizations, however, rejected the "fusion" ticket and stuck to Bryan and his Democratic running mate, Arthur Sewall.

The Republican campaign for Civil War veteran William McKinley outdid all previous American politics in money and expertise. Raising up to $7 million from business interests, it outspent Bryan more than ten to one. Delivering a hard-hitting negative campaign, Republicans consistently cast Bryan as a dangerous radical, willing to risk the nation's well-being and cost voters their jobs—or worse.

McKinley triumphed in the most important presidential election since Reconstruction. Bryan managed to win 46 percent of the popular vote but failed to carry the Midwest, West Coast, or Upper South, urban voters, or Catholics. The Populist following, disappointed and disillusioned, dwindled away. Apathy set in among voters at large, and participation spiraled downward from the 1896 peak when nearly 80 percent of the electorate turned out.

Once in office, McKinley enlivened the executive branch and actively promoted a mixture of probusiness and expansionist measures. He supported the Dingley Tariff of 1897, which raised import duties to an all-time high. In 1897, he also encouraged Congress to create the United States Industrial Commission, which would plan business regulation; in 1898, he promoted a bankruptcy act that eased the financial situation of small businesses; and he proposed the Erdman Act of the same year, which established a system of arbitration to avoid rail strikes. The Supreme Court ruled in concert with the president, finding eighteen railways in violation of antitrust laws, and granting states the right to regulate hours of labor under certain circumstances. In 1900, he settled the currency issue by overseeing the passage of the Gold Standard Act.

McKinley's triumph ended the popular challenge to the nation's governing system. With prosperity returning by 1898, the president encouraged Americans to go for "a full dinner pail," the winning Republican slogan of the 1900 presidential campaign. With news of his second triumph, stock prices on Wall Street skyrocketed.

THE AGE OF SEGREGATION

Campaign rhetoric aside, McKinley and Bryan had differed only slightly on the major problems facing the nation in the 1890s. Neither Bryan, the reformer, nor McKinley, the prophet of prosperity, addressed the escalation of racism and nativism (antiimmigrant feeling) throughout the nation. After the election, McKinley made white supremacy a major tenet of his foreign policy; Bryan, twice more a presidential contender, championed the white race and deemed "social equality" impossible. However, the election of 1896 clearly revealed the power of the conservative ascendancy and the consolidation of white supremacy as a means to control politics and delimit citizenship. For African Americans, this period became known as the "nadir," an era of widespread repression and violence.

Nativism and Jim Crow

Toward the end of the century, many political observers noted, the nation's patriotic fervor took on a strongly nationalistic and antiforeign tone. For several decades, striking workers and their employers alike tended to blame "foreigners" for the hard times. AFL leader Samuel Gompers had spoken out against "Asiatic Coolieism" in support of the Chinese Exclusion Act of 1882, the first in the nation's history to restrict a group of immigrants on the basis of their race or nationality. Gompers, himself a Jewish immigrant from Europe, now lobbied Congress to restrict immigration from eastern and southern Europe. Even the sons and daughters of earlier immigrants attacked the newcomers as unfit for democracy. Imagining a Catholic conspiracy directed by the pope, semisecret organizations such as the American Protective Association sprang up to defend American institutions. Fourth of July orators continued to celebrate freedom and liberty but more often boasted about the might and power of their nation (see Figure 20.1).

With the decline of Populism, white supremacy tightened its grip on the South to become the foundation of politics in the region. Local and state governments codified racist ideology by passing discriminatory and segregationist legislation, which became known as Jim Crow laws. The phrase, dating from the early decades of the nineteenth century, was made popular by a white minstrel in black face who used the name "Jim Crow" to characterize all African Americans. Before the Civil War, abolitionists described segregated railroad cars as "Jim Crow." By the end of the century, "Jim Crow" referred to the customs of segregation that were becoming codified by law and practice throughout the South. With nine of every ten black Americans living in this region, the significance of this development was sweeping.

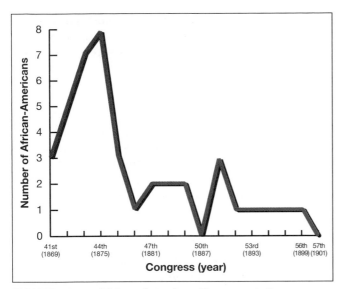

FIGURE 20.1 **African American Representation in Congress, 1867–1900** Black men served in the U.S. Congress from 1870 until 1900. All were Republicans.

"The supremacy of the white race of the South," New South promoter Henry W. Grady declared in 1887, "must be maintained forever . . . because the white race is the superior race." To secure their privileges, Grady and other white Southerners acted directly to impose firm standards of segregation and domination and to forestall any appearance of social equality. State after state in the South enacted new legislation to cover facilities such as restaurants, public transportation, and even drinking fountains. Signs "White Only" and "Colored" appeared over theaters, parks, rooming houses, and toilets. In banks, post offices, and stores, blacks were required to wait until all whites had been served, and special rules prohibited such common practices as trying on shoes or hats before purchasing them.

The United States Supreme Court upheld the new discriminatory legislation. Its decisions in the *Civil Rights Cases* (1883) overturned the Civil Rights Act of 1875; in *Plessy* v. *Ferguson* (1896), the Court upheld a Louisiana state law formally segregating railroad passenger cars on the basis of the "separate but equal" doctrine, and thereby established a precedent for segregation, North as well as South. In *Cumming* v. *Richmond County Board of Education* (1899), the Court allowed separate schools for blacks and whites, even where facilities for African American children did not exist.

The new restrictions struck especially hard at the voting rights of African Americans. Southern states enacted new literacy tests and property qualifications for voting, demanding proof of $300 to $500 in property and the ability to read and write. Loopholes permitted poor whites to vote even under these conditions, except where they threatened the Democratic Party's rule. "Grandfather clauses," invented in Louisiana, exempted from all restrictions those who had been entitled to vote on January 1, 1867, together

with their sons and grandsons, a measure that effectively enfranchised whites while barring African Americans. In 1898, the Supreme Court ruled that poll taxes and literacy requirements enacted in order to prevent blacks (and some poor whites) from voting were a proper means of restricting the ballot to "qualified" voters. By this time, only 5 percent of the Southern black electorate voted, and African Americans were barred from public office and jury service. Supreme Court Justice John Marshall Harlan, the lone dissenter in *Plessy* v. *Ferguson*, lamented that the Court's majority rulings gave power to the states "to place in a condition of legal inferiority a large body of American citizens." Depriving African Americans of equal rights and protection under the law, Jim Crow legislation encouraged states outside the South to pass similar measures.

Mob Violence and Lynching

Racial violence in turn escalated. Race riots, in which dozens of African Americans were killed, broke out in small towns like Phoenix, South Carolina, and in large cities like New Orleans. In November 1898, in Wilmington, North Carolina, where a dozen African Americans had ridden out the last waves of the Populist insurgency to win appointments to minor political office, a group of white opponents organized White Government Leagues to root them out. A young black newspaper writer, Alex Manly, struck back, writing an editorial that challenged a cornerstone of white supremacist ideology: the purity of white Southern womanhood. Manly accused white men of being lax in protecting the virtue of their women and suggested, moreover, that some white women actually chose to have sexual liaisons with black men. Outraged by these claims, a mob that included the leaders of the white business community burned down Manly's newspaper office. Then, shots were fired into a crowd of black bystanders, and twelve were shot down in what came to be known as the Wilmington massacre. Hoping to ease tensions, African Americans resigned their positions on the city council. Nearly 1,500 African Americans, many prominent leaders of their community, decided to pull up stakes altogether and fled. "It come so," a black woman explained, "that we in this town is afraid of a white face."

Not only murderous race riots but thousands of lynchings took place. Between 1882 and the turn of the century, the number of lynchings usually exceeded 100 each year; 1892 produced a record 230 deaths (161 black, 69 white). Mobs often burned or dismembered victims in order to drag out their agony and entertain the crowd of onlookers. Announced in local newspapers, lynchings in the 1890s became public spectacles of extraordinary sadism as well as entertainment for entire white families. The railroads sometimes offered special excursion rates for travel to these events, and merchants printed graphic postcards as souvenirs.

Antilynching became the one-woman crusade of Ida B. Wells, young editor of a black newspaper in Memphis.

After three local black businessmen were lynched in 1892, Wells vigorously denounced the outrage, blaming the white business competitors of the victims. Her stand fanned the tempers of local whites, who destroyed her press and forced the outspoken editor to leave Tennessee.

Wells set out to investigate lynching in a systematic fashion. She paid special attention to the common white defense of lynching—that it was a necessary response to attempts by black men to rape white women. Her 1895 pamphlet *A Red Record* showed that the vast majority of black lynching victims had not even been accused of sexual transgression. Wells argued that lynching was primarily a brutal device to eliminate African Americans who had become too prosperous or powerful.

Wells launched an international movement against lynching, lecturing across the country and in Europe, demanding an end to the silence about this barbaric crime. Her work also inspired the growth of a black women's club movement. The National Association of Colored Women, founded in 1896, provided a home for black women activists who had been excluded from white women's clubs. United by a growing sense of racial pride, black women's clubs took up the antilynching cause, and also fought to protect black women from exploitation by white men and from charges of sexual depravity.

Tom Watson

Few white reformers rallied to defend African Americans. At its 1899 convention, the National American Woman Suffrage Association appeased new Southern white members by voting down a resolution condemning racial segregation in public facilities. A far greater tragedy was a racist turn in the Populist movement, whose leaders, even in the South, had at times challenged white supremacy. The story of Thomas E. Watson, briefly a champion of interracial unity, illustrates the rise and fall of hopes for an egalitarian South.

Son of a prosperous cotton farmer who had been driven into bankruptcy during the depression of the 1870s, Tom Watson had once campaigned to restore the civil rights of Southern African Americans. "Why is not the colored tenant [farmer] open to the conviction that he is in the same boat as the white tenant; the colored laborer with the white laborer?" he asked. Watson planned to overturn Democratic rule by capturing and building up the black vote for the People's Party.

Although Watson himself distinguished between the "equal rights," which he supported, and the "social equality," which he opposed, his followers in Georgia were jailed, shot at, denied the protection of the courts, and driven from their churches. Tens of thousands regarded him as a savior. Flowers decorated the bridges along his speaking routes, crowds standing in pouring rain begged him to continue speaking, and wagons of loyalists carried Winchester rifles to defend him from armed attack. Preaching government ownership of railroads and banks and political equality for both races, Watson stirred the only truly grass-roots interracial movement the South had yet seen.

By early 1896, however, Watson perceived that the increasing ardor for free silver and the move toward cooperation with Democrats would doom the Populist movement. He nevertheless accepted the nomination for vice president on the "fusion" ticket and campaigned in several states. After McKinley's triumph, Watson withdrew from politics, returning to his Georgia farm to write popular histories of the United States and to plot his future.

Watson returned to public life after the turn of the century but with a totally different approach to race relations. He still bitterly attacked the wealthy classes but now blamed black citizens for conspiring against poor whites. Political salvation now hinged, he concluded, on white supremacy. Watson expressed a Southern variation of the new national creed that prepared Americans to view the luckless inhabitants of distant lands as ripe for colonization by the United States.

"IMPERIALISM OF RIGHTEOUSNESS"

Many Americans attributed the crisis of 1893–97 not simply to the collapse of the railroads and the stock market, but to basic structural problems: an overbuilt economy and an insufficient market for goods. Profits from total sales of manufactured and agricultural products had grown substantially over the level achieved in the 1880s, but output increased even more rapidly. While the number of millionaires shot up from 500 in 1860 to more than 4,000 in 1892, the majority of working people lacked enough income to buy back a significant portion of what they produced. As Republican Senator Albert J. Beveridge of Indiana put it, "We are raising more than we can consume. . . . making more than we can use. Therefore, we must find new markets for our produce, new occupation for our capital, new work for our labor."

The White Man's Burden

The Columbian Exposition, which commemorated the four hundredth anniversary of Columbus's landing, opened in Chicago less than two months after the nation's economy had collapsed. On May Day 1893, crowds began to flock to the fair, a complex of more than 400 buildings, newly constructed in beaux arts design. Such expositions, President McKinley proclaimed, served as "timekeepers of progress."

Agriculture Hall showcased the production of corn, wheat, and other crops and featured a gigantic globe encircled by samples of American-manufactured farm machinery. The symbolism was evident: all eyes were on worldwide markets for American products. Another building housed a model of a canal cut across Nicaragua, suggesting the ease with which American traders might reach

Asian markets if transport ships could travel directly from the Caribbean to the Pacific. One of the most popular exhibits, attracting 20,000 people a day, featured a mock ocean liner built to scale by the International Navigation Company, where fair goers could imagine themselves as "tourists," sailing in luxury to distant parts of the world.

The World's Fair also "displayed" representatives of the people who populated foreign lands. The Midway Plaisance, a strip nearly a mile long and more than 600 feet wide, was an enormous sideshow of recreated Turkish bazaars and South Sea island huts. There were Javanese carpenters, Dahomean drummers, Egyptian swordsmen, and Hungarian Gypsies, as well as Eskimos, Syrians, Samoans, and Chinese. Very popular was the World Congress of Beauty, parading "40 Ladies from 40 Nations" dressed in native costume. Another favorite attraction was "Little Egypt," who performed at the Persian Palace of Eros; her *danse du ventre* became better known as the hootchy-kootchy. According to the guidebook, all these peoples had come "from the nightsome North and the splendid South, from the wasty West and the effete East, bringing their manners, customs, dress, religions, legends, amusements, that we might know them better." One of the exposition's directors, Frederick Ward Putnam, head of Harvard's Peabody Museum of American Archeology and Ethnology, explained more fully that the gathering gave fair goers "a grand opportunity to see . . . the material advantages which civilization brings to mankind."

By celebrating the brilliance of American industry and simultaneously presenting the rest of the world's people as a source of exotic entertainment, the planners of the fair delivered a powerful message. Former abolitionist Frederick Douglass, who attended the fair on "Colored People's Day," recognized it immediately. He noted that the physical layout of the fair, by carefully grouping exhibits, sharply divided the United States and Europe from the rest of the world, namely from the nations of Africa, Asia, and the Middle East. Douglass objected to the stark contrast setting off Anglo-Saxons from people of color, an opposition between "civilization" and "savagery." Although Ida B. Wells boycotted the fair, Douglass attended, using the occasion to deliver a speech upbraiding those white Americans for their racism.

The Chicago World's Fair gave material shape to prevalent ideas about the superiority of American civilization and its racial order. At the same time, by showcasing American industries, it made a strong case for commercial expansion abroad. Social gospeler Josiah Strong, a Congregational minister who had begun his career trying to convert Indians to Christianity, provided a timely synthesis. Linking economic and spiritual expansion, he advocated an "imperialism of righteousness" conducted by white Americans, who, with "their genius for colonizing," were best suited to "Christianizing" and "civilizing" the people of Africa and the Pacific and beyond. It was the white American, Strong argued, who had been "divinely commissioned to be, in a peculiar sense, his brother's keeper." Many newspaper reporters and editorialists agreed that it would be morally wrong for Americans to shirk what the British poet Rudyard Kipling called the "White Man's Burden."

Foreign Missions

The push for overseas expansion coincided with a major wave of religious evangelism and foreign missions. Early in the nineteenth century, Protestant missionaries, hoping to fulfill what they believed to be a divine command to carry God's message to all peoples and to win converts for their church, had focused on North America. Many disciples, like Josiah Strong himself, headed west and stationed themselves on Indian reservations. Others worked among the immigrant populations of the nation's growing cities. As early as the 1820s, however, a few missionaries had traveled to the Sandwich Islands (Hawai'i) in an effort to supplant the indigenous religion with Christianity. After the Civil War, following the formation of the Women's Union Missionary Society of Americans for Heathen Lands, the major evangelical Protestant denominations all sponsored missions directed at foreign lands.

By the 1890s, college campuses blazed with missionary excitement, and the intercollegiate Student Volunteers for Foreign Missions spread rapidly under the slogan "The Evangelicization of the World in This Generation." Magazines bristled with essays such as "The Anglo-Saxon and the World's Redemption." Young Protestant women rushed to join foreign missionary societies. In 1863, there had been only 94 Methodist women missionaries in China; by 1902 the number had jumped to 783. In all, some twenty-three American Protestant churches had established missions in China by the turn of the century, the majority staffed by women. By 1915, more than 3 million women had enrolled in forty denominational missionary societies, surpassing in size all other women's organizations in the United States. Their foreign missions ranged from India and Africa to Syria, the Pacific Islands, and nearby Latin America.

By 1898, Protestants claimed to have made Christians of more than 80,000 Chinese, a tiny portion of the population, but a significant stronghold for American interests in their nation. The missionaries did more than spread the gospel. They taught school, provided rudimentary medical care, offered vocational training programs, and sometimes encouraged young men and women to pursue a college education in preparation for careers in their homelands. Such work depended on, and in turn inspired, enthusiastic church members in the United States.

Outside the churches proper, the YMCA and YWCA, which had set up nondenominational missions for the working poor in many American cities, also embarked on a worldwide crusade to reach non-Christians. By the turn of the century, the YWCA had foreign branches in Ceylon (present-day Sri Lanka) and China. After foreign branches multiplied in the next decade, a close observer ironically

By the end of the nineteenth century, women represented 60 percent of the American missionary force in foreign lands. This photograph shows two Methodist women using "back chairs," a traditional form of transportation, at Mount Omei in Szechwan, China.

SOURCE: Courtesy of the Divinity School, Yale University.

Since the American Revolution, many Americans had regarded all nearby nations as falling naturally within their own territorial realm, destined to be acquired when opportunity allowed. Seward advanced these imperialist principles in 1867 by negotiating the purchase of Alaska (known at the time as Seward's Icebox) from Russia for $7.2 million, and he hoped someday to see the American flag flying over Canada and Mexico. Meanwhile, with European nations launched on their own imperialist missions in Asia and Africa, the United States increasingly viewed the Caribbean as an "American lake" and all of Latin America as a vast potential market for U.S. goods. The crisis of the 1890s transformed this long-standing desire into a perceived economic necessity. Large-scale conquest, however, appeared to American leaders more expensive and less appealing than economic domination and selective colonization. Unlike European imperialists, powerful Americans dreamed of empire without large-scale permanent military occupation and costly colonial administration.

suggested that the United States had three great occupying forces: the army, the navy, and the "Y." He was not far wrong.

Missionaries played an important role both in generating public interest in foreign lands and in preparing the way for American economic expansion. As Josiah Strong aptly put it, "Commerce follows the missionary."

An Overseas Empire

Not only missionaries, but business and political leaders, had set their sights on distant lands, which, in turn, meant new markets. In the 1860s, Secretary of State William Henry Seward, under Abraham Lincoln and then under Andrew Johnson, encouraged Americans to defer to "a political law—and when I say political law, I mean higher law, a law of Providence—that empire has [had], for the last three thousand years." Seward correctly predicted that foreign trade would play an increasingly important part in the American economy. Between 1870 and 1900, exports more than tripled, from about $400 million to over $1.5 billion, with textiles and agricultural products leading the way. But as European markets for American goods began to contract, business and political leaders, of necessity, looked more eagerly to Asia as well as to lands closer by.

Americans focused their expansionist plans on the Western Hemisphere, determined to dislodge the dominant power, Great Britain. In 1867, when Canada became a self-governing dominion, American diplomats hoped to annex their northern neighbor, believing that Great Britain would gladly accede in order to concentrate its imperial interests in Asia. But Great Britain refused to give up Canada, and the United States backed away. Central and South America proved more accommodating to American designs (see Map 20.3).

Republican stalwart James G. Blaine, secretary of state under presidents Garfield and Harrison, determined to work out a Good Neighbor policy (a phrase coined by Henry Clay in 1820). "What we want," he explained, "are the markets of these neighbors of ours that lie to the south of us. We want the $400,000,000 annually which to-day go to England, France, Germany and other countries. With these markets secured new life would be given to our manufactures, the product of the Western farmer would be in demand, the reasons for and inducements to strikers, with all their attendant evils, would cease." Bilateral treaties with Mexico, Colombia, the British West Indies, El Salvador, and the Dominican Republic allowed American business to

MAP EXPLORATION

To explore an interactive version of this map, go to **www.prenhall.com/faragher5/map20.3**

MAP 20.3 The American Domain, ca. 1900 The United States claimed numerous islands in the South Pacific and intervened repeatedly in Latin America to secure its economic interests.

dominate local economies, importing their raw materials at low prices and flooding their local markets with goods manufactured in the United States. Often, American investors simply took over the principal industries of these small nations, undercutting national business classes. The first Pan-American Conference, held in 1889–90, marked a turning point in hemispheric relations.

The Good Neighbor policy depended, Blaine knew, on peace and order in the Latin American states. As early as 1875, when revolt shook Venezuela, the Department of State warned European powers not to meddle. If popular uprisings proved too much for local officials, the U.S. Navy would intervene and return American allies to power.

In 1883, wishing to enforce treaties and protect overseas investments, Congress appropriated funds to build

up American seapower. Beginning with ninety small ships, over one-third of them wooden, the navy grew quickly to include modern steel fighting ships. The hulls of these ships were painted a gleaming white, and the armada was known as the Great White Fleet. One of the most popular exhibits at the Chicago World's Fair featured full-sized models of the new armor-plated steel battleships. Congress also established the Naval War College in Newport, Rhode Island, in 1884, to train the officer corps. One of its first presidents, Captain Alfred Thayer Mahan, prescribed an imperialist strategy based on command of the seas. His book, *The Influence of Sea Power upon American History, 1660–1873* (1890), helped to define American foreign policy at the time. Mahan insisted that international strength rested not only on open markets, but on the

Brought to power with the assistance of American businessmen, Queen Liliuokalani sought to limit outsider influence. American Marines, Christian missionaries, and sugar planters joined in 1893 to drive her from her throne. A century later, the U.S. government apologized to native Hawai'ians for this illegal act.

SOURCE: Library of Congress.

control of colonies. He advocated the annexation of bases in the Caribbean and the Pacific to enhance the navy's ability to threaten or wage warfare.

The annexation of Hawai'i on July 7, 1898, followed nearly a century of economic penetration and diplomatic maneuver. American missionaries, who had arrived in the 1820s to convert Hawai'ians to Christianity, began to buy up huge parcels of land and to subvert the existing feudal system of landholding. They also encouraged American businesses to buy into sugar plantations, and by 1875, U.S. corporations dominated the sugar trade. They tripled the number of plantations by 1880, and sent Hawai'ian sugar duty-free to the United States. By this time, Hawai'i appeared, in Blaine's opinion, to be "an outlying district of the state of California," and he began to push for annexation. In 1887, a new treaty allowed the United States to build a naval base at Pearl Harbor on the island of Oahu.

The next year, American planters took a step further, arranging the overthrow of the weak King Kalakaua and securing a new government allied to their economic interests. In 1891, the new ruler, Queen Liliuokalani, struck back by issuing a constitution granting her more discretionary power. The U.S. minister, prompted by the pineapple magnate Sanford B. Dole, responded by calling for military assistance. On January 16, 1893, U.S. sailors landed on Hawai'i to protect American property. Liliuokalani was deposed, a new provisional government was installed, and Hawai'i was proclaimed an American protectorate (a territory protected and partly controlled by the United States). The American diplomat John L. Stevens, stationed in Hawai'i, eagerly wired Washington that the "Hawai'ian pear is now fully ripe, and this is the golden hour for the United States to pluck it." President Cleveland refused to consider annexation, but five years later McKinley affirmed a joint congressional resolution under which Hawai'i would become an American territory in 1900. The residents of Hawai'i were not consulted about this momentous change in their national identity.

Hawai'i was often viewed as a steppingstone to the vast Asian markets. A U.S. admiral envisioned the happy future: "The Pacific is the ocean bride of America—China, Japan and Korea—and their innumerable islands, hanging like necklaces about them, are the bridesmaids . . . Let us as Americans . . . determine while yet in our power, that no commercial rival or hostile flag can float with impunity over the long swell of the Pacific sea."

To accelerate railroad investment and trade, a consortium of New York bankers created the American China Development Company in 1896. They feared, however, that the tottering Manchu dynasty would fall to European, Russian, and Japanese colonial powers, which would then prohibit trade with the United States. Secretary of State John Hay responded in 1899 by proclaiming the Open Door policy. According to this doctrine, outlined in notes to six major powers, the United States enjoyed the right to advance its commercial interests anywhere in the world, at least on terms equal to those of the other imperialist nations. The Chinese marketplace was too important to lose.

Chinese nationalist rebellion, however, threatened to overwhelm all the outsiders' plans for China. An antiforeign secret society known as the Harmonious Righteous Fists (dubbed "Boxers" by the Western press) rioted repeatedly in 1898 and 1899, actually occupying the capital city of Peking (present day Beijing) and surrounding the foreign embassies. Shocked by the deaths of thousands, including many Chinese converts to Christianity, and determined to maintain American economic interests, President McKinley, not bothering to request congressional approval, contributed 5,000 U.S. troops to an international army that put down the Boxer uprising. The Boxer Rebellion dramatized the Manchu regime's inability to control its own subjects, and strengthened John Hay's determination to preserve the economic status quo. A second series of Open Door notes by the secretary of state restated the intention of the United States to trade in China and laid the basis for twentieth-century foreign policy.

THE SPANISH–AMERICAN WAR

During his 1896 campaign, William McKinley firmly committed himself to the principle of economic expansion. It was for him the proper alternative to Edward Bellamy's program for a cooperative commonwealth. Indeed, he once described his "greatest ambition" as achieving American supremacy in world markets. As president, McKinley not only reached out for markets, but took his nation into war, while proclaiming its humanitarian and democratic goals (see Map 20.4).

The Spanish-American War was the most popular war since the American war for independence from Great Britain. It was short, lasting only sixteen weeks. It claimed relatively few lives—about 2,500 men died from diseases, mainly yellow fever, typhoid, or malaria—ten times the number killed in combat. And the war cost the government only $250 million. When it ended, the United States waged another war and annexed the Philippines. By the end of the century, the nation had joined Europe and Japan in the quest for empire, and had become a formidable world power with territories spread out across the Caribbean Sea and Pacific Ocean.

A "Splendid Little War" in Cuba

"I have ever looked on Cuba," Thomas Jefferson wrote, "as the most interesting addition which could ever be made to our system of States." Before the Civil War,

MAP EXPLORATION

To explore an interactive version of this map, go to **www.prenhall.com/faragher5/map20.4**

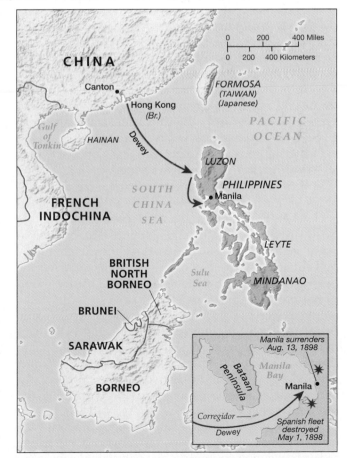

MAP 20.4 The Spanish-American War In two theaters of action, the United States used its naval power adeptly against a weak foe.

Southerners hoped to acquire Cuba, still owned by Spain, for the expansion of slavery in its sugar mills, tobacco plantations, and mines. After attempting several times to buy the island outright, the United States settled for the continuation of the status quo, reaffirming Jefferson's conclusion that preserving Cuba's "independence against all the world, *except* Spain . . . would be nearly as valuable to us as if it were our own." Throughout the nineteenth century, the United States resolved to protect Spain's sovereignty over Cuba against the encroachment of other powers, including Cuba itself.

In Cuba, a movement for independence began in the mid-1860s when Spain, its empire in ruins, began to impose stiff taxes on the island. After defeat during the Ten Years War of 1868–78 and yet another series of setbacks, the insurgents rallied under the nationalist leadership of José Martí. In May 1895, Spanish troops ambushed and killed Martí, turning him into a martyr and fanning the flames of rebellion. By July, the rebels declared Cuba a republic and established a rudimentary government. Meanwhile, the war for independence moved closer to Havana, the island's seat of power.

Many Americans, invoking the legacy of their own war for independence, supported the movement for *Cuba Libre*. Grisly stories of Spain's treatment of captured insurrectionists circulated in American newspapers and aroused popular sympathy for the Cuban cause. In 1896, both the Democratic and Republican parties adopted planks supporting Cuba's freedom. President Cleveland refused to back the Cuban revolutionaries and instead urged Spain to grant the island a limited autonomy. Even when Congress passed a resolution in 1896 welcoming the future independence of Cuba, Cleveland and his advisers demurred.

After he took over the office, President McKinley also drew back. In his Inaugural Address, he declared, "We want no wars of conquest; we must avoid the temptation of territorial aggression." The tide turned, however, when Spain appeared unable to maintain order. In early 1898, public indignation, whipped up by tabloid press headlines and sensational stories, turned into frenzy on February 15, when an explosion ripped through the battleship USS *Maine*, stationed in Havana harbor, ostensibly to rescue American citizens.

McKinley, suspecting war was close, had already begun to prepare for intervention. Newspapers ran banner headlines charging a Spanish conspiracy, although there was no proof. The impatient public meanwhile demanded revenge for the death of 266 American sailors. Within days, a new slogan appeared: "Remember the Maine! To Hell with Spain!"

Finally, on April 11, McKinley asked Congress for a declaration of war against Spain. Yet Congress barely passed the war resolution on April 25, and only with the inclusion of an amendment by Senator Henry Teller of Colorado that disclaimed "any disposition or intention to exercise sover-

eignty, jurisdiction or control over said island, except for the pacification thereof." McKinley called for 125,000 volunteers, and men seeking to enlist nearly overwhelmed the administration. For the first time, former Confederates served in the higher ranks of the U.S. Army, symbolically uniting North and South in this patriotic endeavor. African Americans volunteered in great numbers, in a display of patriotism and also in sympathy with Cubans who were, like themselves, a generation or less away from slavery. By the end of April, the fighting had begun.

An outpouring of patriotic joy inspired massive parades, topical songs, and an overpowering enthusiasm. "Populists, Democrats, and Republicans are we," went one jingle, "But we are all Americans to make Cuba free." Just as the Civil War inspired masses of women to form relief societies so, too, did the Spanish–American war. The Women's Relief Corps and women's clubs across the country raised money and sent food and medical supplies to U.S. military camps.

Ten weeks later, the war was all but over. On land, Lieutenant Colonel Theodore Roosevelt—who boasted of killing Spaniards "like jackrabbits"—led his Rough Riders to victory. On July 3, the main Spanish fleet near Santiago Bay was destroyed; two weeks later Santiago itself surrendered, and the war drew to a close. Although fewer than 400 Americans died in battle, disease and the inept treatment of the wounded created a medical disaster, spreading sickness and disease to more than 20,000 in the regiments. Roosevelt nevertheless felt invigorated by the conflict, agreeing with John Hay that it had been a "splendid little war."

On August 12, at a small ceremony in McKinley's office marking Spain's surrender, the United States secured Cuba's independence from Spain but not its own sovereignty. One member of Congress thus announced the unanticipated outcome of the war from Cuba's point of view: "What greater liberty, freedom, and independence can be obtained than that enjoyed under the protection of our flag?" On January 1, 1899, ceremonies in Havana marked the end of four hundred years of Spanish rule and the passage of sovereignty over the island to the United States. The Cubans who waged the struggle for independence for nearly forty years sat on the sidelines, the words of José Martí—"Cuba must be free from Spain and the United States"—receding into the distant past.

American businesses proceeded to tighten their hold on Cuban sugar plantations, while U.S. military forces oversaw the formation of a constitutional convention that made Cuba a protectorate of the United States. Under the Platt Amendment, sponsored by Republican senator Orville H. Platt of Connecticut in 1901, Cuba was required to provide land for American bases; to devote national revenues to pay back debts to the United States; to sign no treaty that would be detrimental to American interests; and to acknowledge the right of the United States to intervene at any time to protect its interests in Cuba. During the occupation, which lasted

DESTRUCTION OF THE U.S. BATTLESHIP MAINE
IN HAVANA HARBOR FEB'Y 15TH 1898.

This illustration from the popular press depicts the explosion of the battleship *Maine* in the Havana harbor on February 15, 1898. War-mongering newspaper editors and journalists immediately charged the Spaniards with mining the harbor or torpedoing the ship. A U.S. commission created to investigate the explosion agreed, thereby paving the way to war with Spain, which Congress declared on April 25, 1898. In 1976, another team of experts investigated the explosion and concluded that it resulted not from an attack but from a coal bunker fire within the battleship. SOURCE: Chicago Historical Society.

until 1902, there were more U.S. troops in Cuba than during the war. After the U.S. withdrawal, the terms of the Platt amendment were incorporated into the Cuban-American Treaty of 1903. This treaty, which remained in place until 1934, paved the way for American domination of the island's sugar industry and contributed to anti-American sentiment among Cuban nationalists.

War in the Philippines

The Philippines, another of Spain's colonies, seemed an especially attractive prospect, its 7,000 islands a natural way station to the markets of mainland Asia. In 1897, Assistant Secretary of the Navy Theodore Roosevelt and President McKinley had discussed the merits of taking the Pacific colony in the event of war with Spain. At the first opportunity, McKinley acted to bring these islands into the U.S. strategic orbit. Shortly after Congress declared war on Spain,

on May 4, the president dispatched 5,000 troops to occupy the Philippines. George Dewey, a Civil War veteran who commanded the American Asiatic Squadron, was ordered to "start offensive action." During the first week of the conflict, he demolished the Spanish fleet in Manila Bay through seven hours of unimpeded target practice. Once the war ended, McKinley refused to sign the armistice unless Spain relinquished all claims to its Pacific islands. When Spain conceded, McKinley quickly drew up plans for colonial administration. He pledged "to educate the Filipinos, and to uplift and civilize and Christianize them." But after centuries of Spanish rule, the majority of islanders—already Christians—were eager to create their own nation.

The Filipino rebels, like the Cubans, at first welcomed American troops and fought with them against Spain. But when the Spanish-American War ended and they perceived that American troops were not preparing to leave, the rebels, led by Emilio Aguinaldo, turned against their former allies and attacked the American base of operations in Manila in February 1899. Predicting a brief skirmish, American commanders seriously underestimated the population's capacity to endure great suffering for the sake of independence.

U.S. troops had provoked this conflict in various ways. Military leaders, the majority veterans of the Indian Wars, commonly described the natives as "gugus," and reported themselves, as one said, as "just itching to get at the niggers." While awaiting action, American soldiers repeatedly insulted or physically abused civilians, raped Filipino women, and otherwise whipped up resentment.

The resulting conflict took the form of modern guerrilla warfare, with brutalities on both sides. By the time the fighting slowed down in 1902, 4,300 American lives had been lost, and one of every five Filipinos had died in battle or from starvation or disease. On some of the Philippine islands, intermittent fighting lasted until 1935.

The United States nevertheless refused to pull out. In 1901, William Howard Taft headed a commission that established a special apparatus to rule in the Philippines; after 1905, the president appointed a Filipino governor general to maintain the provincial government. Meanwhile, Americans bought up the best land and invested heavily in the island's sugar economy.

The conquest of the Philippines, which remained a U.S. territory until 1946, evoked for its defenders the vision of empire. At the very least, the Philippines joined Hawai'i as yet another stepping stone for U.S. merchants en route to China. At the end of the Spanish-American War, the United States advanced its interests in the Caribbean to include Puerto Rico, ceded by Spain, and eventually the Virgin Islands of St. Thomas, St. John, and St. Croix, purchased from Denmark in 1917. The acquisition of Pacific territories, including Guam, marked the emergence of the United States as a global colonial power.

Once again, Josiah Strong proclaimed judgment over an era. His famous treatise *Expansion* (1900) roundly defended American overseas involvements by carefully distinguishing between freedom and independence. People could achieve freedom, he argued, only under the rule of law. And because white Americans had proven themselves

OUT OF MANY VOICES

SOLDIERS' LETTERS FROM THE PHILIPPINE–U.S. WAR

These letters from soldiers who were fighting the U.S. war in the Philippines were written to friends and family but were often published in local newspapers or magazines. The Anti-Imperialist League, responding to government censorship of news reports of the war, made these and many other similar letters available to Americans at home "as a valuable source of information as to the real situation."

ARTHUR MINKLER, OF THE KANSAS REGIMENT:

"We advanced four miles and we fought every inch of the way; . . . saw twenty-five dead insurgents in one place and twenty-seven in another, besides a whole lot of them scattered along that I did not count. . . . It was like hunting rabbits; an insurgent would jump out of a hole or the brush and run; he would not get very far. . . . I suppose you are not interested in the way we do the job. We take no prisoners. At least the Twentieth Kansas do not."

Leonard F. Adams, of Ozark, in the Washington Regiment:

"I don't know how many men, women, and children the Tennessee boys did kill. They would not take prisoners. One company of the Tennessee boys was sent to headquarters with thirty prisoners, and got there with about a hundred chickens and no prisoners."

F.A. Blake, of California, in charge of the Red Cross:

"I never saw such execution in my life, and hope never to see such sights as met me on all sides as our little corps passed over the field, dressing wounded. Legs and arms nearly demolished; total decapitation; horrible wounds in chest and abdomens, showing the determination of our soldiers to kill every man in sight. The Filipinos did stand their ground heroically, contesting every inch, but proved themselves unable to stand the deadly fire of our well-trained and eager boys in blue. I counted seventy-nine dead natives in one small field, and learned that on the other side of the river their bodies were stacked up for breastworks."

A private from Miami County Kansas Regiment:

"I suppose the people back home did not expect us to have any fighting, but we have already had the greatest land fight of the war, and it may take a great deal more to finish it yet, for we may have to kill all the black rascals before they are conquered. . . ." ■

SOURCE: Jim Zwick, ed., "Anti-Imperialism in the United States, 1898–1935." http://www.boondocksnet.com\

superior in the realm of government, they could best bring "freedom" to nonwhite peoples by setting aside the ideal of national independence for a period of enforced guidance. Many began to wonder, however, whether the United States could become an empire without sacrificing its democratic spirit, and to ask whether the subjugated people were really so fortunate under the rule of the United States.

Critics of Empire

No mass movement formed to forestall U.S. expansion, but distinguished figures like Mark Twain, Andrew Carnegie, William Jennings Bryan, and Harvard philosopher William James voiced their opposition strongly. Dissent followed two broad lines of argument. In 1870, when President Grant urged the annexation of Santo Domingo, the nation-state occupying half of the island of Hispaniola (Haiti occupying the other half), opponents countered by insisting that the United States stood unequivocally for the right of national self-determination and the consent of the governed. Others opposed annexation on the ground that dark-skinned and "ignorant" Santo Domingans were unworthy of American citizenship. These two contrary arguments, democratic and racist, were sounded repeatedly as the United States joined other nations in the armed struggle for empire.

Organized protest to military action, especially against the widely reported atrocities in the Philippines, owed much to the Anti-Imperialist League, which was founded by a small group of prominent Bostonians. In historic Faneuil Hall, which had witnessed the birth of both the American Revolution and the antislavery movement, a mass meeting was convened in June 1898 to protest the "insane and wicked ambition which is driving the nation to ruin." Within a few months, the league reported 25,000 members. Most supported American economic expansion, but advocated free trade rather than political domination as the means to reach this goal. All strongly opposed the annexation of new territories. The league drew followers from every walk of life, including such famous writers as Charles Francis Adams and Mark Twain, *Nation* editor E. L. Godkin, African American scholar W. E. B. Du Bois, and Civil War veteran Thomas Wentworth Higginson.

The Anti-Imperialist League brought together like-minded societies from across the country, encouraged mass meetings, and published pamphlets, poems, and broadsides. The *National Labor Standard* expressed the common hope that all those "who believe in the Republic against Empire should join." By 1899, the league claimed a half-million members. A few outspoken antiimperialists, such as former Illinois governor John Peter Altgeld, openly toasted Filipino rebels as heroes. Morrison Swift, leader of the Coxey's Army contingent from Massachusetts, formed a Filipino Liberation Society and sent antiwar materials to American troops. Others, such as Samuel Gompers, a league vice president, felt no sympathy for conquered peoples,

"Uncle Sam Teaches the Art of Self-Government," editorial cartoon, 1898. Expressing a popular sentiment of the time, a newspaper cartoonist shows the rebels as raucous children who constantly fight among themselves and need to be brought into line by Uncle Sam. The Filipino leader, Emilio Aguinaldo, appears as a dunce for failing to learn properly from the teacher. The two major islands where no uprising took place, Puerto Rico and Hawai'i, appear as passive but exotically dressed women, ready to learn their lessons. SOURCE: Library of Congress.

describing Filipinos as "perhaps nearer the condition of savages and barbarians than any island possessed by any other civilized nation on earth." Gompers simply wanted to prevent colonized nonwhites from immigrating into the United States and "inundating" American labor.

Military leaders and staunch imperialists did not distinguish between racist and nonracist antiimperialists. They called all dissenters "unhung traitors" and demanded their arrest. Newspaper editors accused universities of harboring antiwar professors, although college students as a group were enthusiastic supporters of the war.

Within the press, which overwhelmingly supported the Spanish-American War, the voices of opposition appeared primarily in African American and labor papers. The *Indianapolis Recorder* asked rhetorically in 1899, "Are the tender-hearted expansionists in the United States Congress really actuated by the desire to save the Filipinos from self-destruction or is it the worldly greed for gain?" The *Railroad Telegrapher* similarly commented, "The wonder of it all is that the working people are willing to lose blood and treasure in fighting another man's battle."

CHRONOLOGY

1867	Grange founded
	Secretary of State Seward negotiates the purchase of Alaska
1874	Granger laws begin to regulate railroad shipping rates
1877	Rutherford B. Hayes elected president
	Great Uprising of 1877
1879	Henry George publishes *Progress and Poverty*
1881	President James A. Garfield assassinated; Chester A. Arthur becomes president
1882	Chinese Exclusion Act
1883	Pendleton Act passed
1884	Grover Cleveland elected president
1887	Interstate Commerce Act creates the Interstate Commerce Commission
1888	Edward Bellamy publishes *Looking Backward*
	Colored Farmers' Alliance formed
	Benjamin Harrison elected president
1889	National Farmers' Alliance formed
1890	Sherman Silver Purchase Act
	McKinley tariff enacted
	National American Woman Suffrage Association formed
1891	Populist (People's) Party formed

1892	Coeur d'Alene miners' strike
	Homestead strike
	Ida B. Wells begins crusade against lynching
1893	Western Federation of Miners formed
	Financial panic and depression
	World's Columbian Exhibition opens in Chicago
1894	"Coxey's Army" marches on Washington, DC
	Pullman strike and boycott
1896	*Plessy* v. *Ferguson* upholds segregation
	William McKinley defeats William Jennings Bryan for president
1897	Dingley tariff again raises import duties to an all-time high
1898	Eugene V. Debs helps found Social Democratic Party
	Hawai'i is annexed
	Spanish–American War begins
	Anti-Imperialist League formed
	Wilmington, NC, massacre
1899	*Cumming* v. *Richmond County Board of Education* sanctions segregated education
	Secretary of State John Hay announces Open Door policy
	Guerrilla war begins in the Philippines
1900	Gold Standard Act
	Josiah Strong publishes *Expansion*

Most Americans put aside their doubts and welcomed the new era of imperialism. Untouched by the private tragedies of dead or wounded American soldiers and the mass destruction of civilian society in the Philippines, the vast majority could approve Theodore Roosevelt's defense of armed conflict: "No triumph of peace is quite so great as the supreme triumphs of war."

CONCLUSION

The conflicts marking the last quarter of the nineteenth century that pitted farmers, workers, and the proprietors of small businesses against powerful outside interests had offered Americans an important moment of democratic promise. By the end of the century, however, the rural and working-class campaigns to retain a large degree of self-government in their communities had been defeated, their organizations destroyed, their autonomy eroded. The rise of a national governing class and its counterpart, the large bureaucratic state, established new rules of behavior, new sources of prestige, and new rewards for the most successful citizens.

But the nation would pay a steep price in the next era, for the failure of democratic reform. Regional antagonisms, nativist movements against the foreignborn, and above all deepening racial tensions blighted American society. As the new century opened, progressive reformers moved to correct flaws in government while accepting the framework of a corporate society and its overseas empire. But they found the widening divisions in American society difficult—if not impossible—to overcome.

REVIEW QUESTIONS

1. Discuss some of the problems accompanying the expansion of government during the late nineteenth century. What role did political parties play in this process? Explain how a prominent reformer such as James Garfield might become a leading "machine" politician?

2. What were the major causes and consequences of the Populist movement of the 1880s and 1890s? Why did the election of 1896 prove so important to the future of American politics?

3. Discuss the role of women in both the Grange and the People's Party. What were their specific goals?

4. Discuss the causes and consequences of the financial crisis of the 1890s. How did various reformers and politicians respond to the event? What kinds of programs did they offer to restore the economy or reduce poverty?

5. How did the exclusion of African Americans affect the outcome of populism? Explain the rise of Jim Crow legislation in the South, and discuss its impact on the status of African Americans.

6. Describe American foreign policy during the 1890s. Why did the United States intervene in Cuba and the Philippines? What were some of the leading arguments for and against overseas expansion?

RECOMMENDED READING

Steven Hahn, *A Nation Under Our Feet: Black Political Struggles in the Rural South from Slavery to the Great Migration* (2003). A sweeping history of African American politics with an eye on their influence in shaping the South and the nation in the last half of the nineteenth century. Hahn emphasizes the emergence of political communities and highlights the 1880s as a period of exceptional assertiveness on the part of Southern African Americans.

Evelyn Brooks Higginbotham, *Righteous Discontent: The Women's Movement in the Black Baptist Church, 1880–1920* (1993). Documents the central role of women in shaping the theology and racial uplift programs of the National Baptist Convention, the largest denomination of African Americans at the end of the nineteenth century.

Matthew Frye Jacobson, *Barbarian Virtues: The United States Encounters Foreign Peoples at Home and Abroad, 1876–1917* (2000). Links the histories of immigration and empire-building to examine public discussions about foreign people, especially their "fitness" for self-government. Jacobson casts the search for markets as backdrop for cultural history.

Amy Kaplan, *The Anarchy of Empire in the Making of U.S. Culture* (2002). A set of essays connecting continental expansionism and overseas imperialism to domestic politics, including predominant notions of gender. Kaplan examines both participants in this project and their critics.

Michael Kazin, *The Populist Persuasion: An American History* (1995, rev. ed., 1998). A fresh interpretation of Populist-style movements through the nineteenth and twentieth centuries that suggests such movements can be either "right" or "left," depending upon circumstances.

Walter LaFeber, *The New Empire: An Interpretation of American Expansion, 1860–1898* (1963, 1998). The best overview of U.S. imperial involvement in the late nineteenth century. LaFeber shows how overseas commitments grew out of the economic expansionist assumptions of American leaders and expanded continuously, if often chaotically, with the opportunities presented by the crises experienced by the older imperial powers.

Leon F. Litwack, *Trouble in Mind: Black Southerners in the Age of Jim Crow* (1998). An expansive social history of the first generation of African Americans born in freedom and surviving a period of extraordinary violent and repressive race relations in the South. Litwack examines the retrenchment of their political and civil rights, but emphasizes their resourcefulness and resistance.

David O. Stowell, *Streets, Railroads, and the Great Strike of 1877* (1999). Examines in close detail the uprising of 1877 in Buffalo, Albany, and Syracuse, New York, casting the strike simultaneously as a struggle between workers and the railroad corporations, and an attempt by the community to protest against usurpation of streets by the trains. Stowell emphasizes the importance of the urban setting of this strike and provides ample data on the physical injuries inflicted by trains on local residents.

William Appleman Williams, *Empire as a Way of Life: An Essay on the Causes and Character of America's Present Predicament* (1982). A lucid general exploration of American views of empire. Williams shows that Americans allowed the idea of empire and, more generally, economic expansion, to dominate their concept of democracy, especially in the last half of the nineteenth century.

 For additional study resources for this chapter, go to the *Companion Website*, **http://www.prenhall.com/faragher**.

Urban America and the Progressive Era

1900—1917

The Henry Street Settlement House: Women Settlement House Workers Create a Community of Reform

A shy and frightened young girl appeared in the doorway of a weekly home-nursing class for women on Manhattan's Lower East Side. The teacher beckoned her to come forward. Tugging on the teacher's skirt, the girl pleaded in broken English for the teacher to come home with her. "Mother," "baby," "blood," she kept repeating. The teacher gathered up the sheets that were part of the interrupted lesson in bed making. The two hurried through narrow, garbage-strewn, foul-smelling streets, then groped their way up a pitch-dark, rickety staircase. They reached a cramped, two-room apartment, home to an immigrant family of seven and several boarders. There, in a vermin-infested bed, encrusted with dried blood, lay a mother and her newborn baby. The mother had been abandoned by a doctor because she could not afford his fee.

The teacher, Lillian Wald, was a twenty-five-year-old nurse at New York Hospital. Years later, she recalled this scene as her baptism by fire and the turning point in her life. Born in 1867, Wald had enjoyed a comfortable upbringing in a middle-class German Jewish family in Rochester. Despite her parents' objections, she had moved to New York City to become a professional nurse. Resentful of the disdainful treatment nurses received

from doctors, and horrified by the inhumane conditions at a juvenile asylum she worked in, Wald determined to find a way of caring for the sick in their neighborhoods and homes. With nursing school classmate Mary Brewster, Wald rented a fifth-floor walk-up apartment on the Lower East Side and established a visiting nurse service. The two provided professional care in the home to hundreds of families for a nominal fee of 10 to 25 cents. They also offered each family they visited information on basic health care, sanitation, and disease prevention. In 1895, philanthropist Jacob Schiff generously donated a red brick Georgian house on Henry Street as a new base of operation.

The Henry Street Settlement stood in the center of perhaps the most overcrowded neighborhood in the world, New York's Lower East Side. Roughly 500,000 people were packed into an area only as large as a mid-sized Kansas farm. Population density was about 500 per acre, roughly four times the figure for the rest of New York City, and far more concentrated than even the worst slums of London or Calcutta. A single city block might have as many as 3,000 residents. Home for most Lower East Siders was a small tenement apartment that might include paying boarders squeezed in alongside the immediate family. Residents were mostly recent immigrants from southern and eastern Europe: Jews, Italians, Germans, Greeks, Hungarians, Slavs. Men, women, and children toiled in the garment shops, small factories, retail stores, breweries, and warehouses to be found on nearly every street.

The Henry Street Settlement became a model for a new kind of reform community composed essentially of college-educated women who encouraged and supported one another in a wide variety of humanitarian, civic, political, and cultural activities. Settlement house living arrangements closely resembled those in the dormitories of such new

New York City

women's colleges as Smith, Wellesley, and Vassar. Like these colleges, the settlement house was an "experiment," but one designed, in settlement house pioneer Jane Addams's words, "to aid in the solution of the social and industrial problems which are engendered by the modern conditions of urban life." Unlike earlier moral reformers, who tried to impose their ideas from outside, settlement house residents lived in poor communities and worked for immediate improvements in the health and welfare of those communities. Yet, as Addams and others repeatedly stressed, the college-educated women were beneficiaries as well. The settlement house allowed them to preserve a collegial spirit, satisfy the desire for service, and apply their academic training.

With its combined moral and social appeal, the settlement house movement attracted many educated young women and grew rapidly. There were six settlement houses in the United States in 1891, some 74 in 1897, more than 200 by 1900, and more than 400 by 1910. Few women made settlement work a career, but those who did, typically chose not to marry, and most lived together with female companions. As the movement flourished, settlement house residents called attention to the plight of the poor, and fostered respect for different cultural heritages in countless articles and lectures. Leaders of the movement, including Jane Addams, Lillian Wald, and Florence Kelley, emerged as influential political figures during the progressive era.

Wald attracted a dedicated group of nurses, educators, and reformers to live at the Henry Street Settlement. By 1909, Henry Street had more than forty residents, supported by the donations of well-to-do New Yorkers. Wald and her allies convinced the New York Board of Health to assign a nurse to every public school in the city. They lobbied the Board of Education to create the first school lunch programs. They persuaded the city to set up municipal milk stations to ensure the purity of milk. Henry Street also pioneered tuberculosis treatment and prevention. Its leaders became powerful advocates for playground construction, improved street cleaning, and tougher housing inspection. The settlement's Neighborhood Playhouse became an internationally acclaimed center for innovative theater, music, and dance.

Lillian Wald became a national figure—an outspoken advocate of child labor legislation and woman suffrage, and a vigorous opponent of American involvement in World War I. She offered Henry Street as a meeting place to the National Negro Conference in 1909, out of which emerged the National Association for the Advancement of Colored People. It was no cliché for Wald to say, as she did on many occasions, "The whole world is my neighborhood."

During the first two decades of the twentieth century, millions of Americans identified themeselves as "progressives" and most, like Lillian Wald, were first drawn to causes and campaigns rooted in their local communities. But many soon saw that confronting the grim realities of an urban and industrial society required national and even global strategies for pursuing reform. These included cleaning up the political process, harnessing the power of the state to regulate the excesses of capitalism, responding to the influx of new immigrants, and creating innovative forms of journalism to publicize wretched social conditions. By the time America entered World War I in 1917, progressivism had reshaped the political and social landscape of the entire nation.

KEY TOPICS

- The political, social, and intellectual roots of progressive reform
- Tensions between social justice and social control
- The urban scene and the impact of new immigration
- Political activism by the working class, women, and African Americans
- Progressivism in national politics

THE CURRENTS OF PROGRESSIVISM

Between the 1890s and World War I, a large and diverse number of Americans claimed the political label "progressive." Progressives could be found in all classes, regions, and races. They shared a fundamental ethos, or belief, that America needed a new social consciousness to cope with the problems brought on by the enormous rush of economic and social change in the post–Civil War decades. Yet progressivism was no unified movement with a single set of principles. It is best understood as a varied collection of reform communities, often fleeting, uniting citizens in a host of political, professional, and religious organizations, some of which were national in scope.

As a political movement, progressivism flowered in the soil of several key issues: ending political corruption, bringing more businesslike methods to governing, and offering a more compassionate legislative response to the excesses of industrialism. As a national movement, progressivism reached its peak in 1912, when the four major presidential candidates all ran on some version of a progressive platform. This last development was an important measure of the extent to which local reform movements, like the Henry Street Settlement, and new intellectual currents, had captured the political imagination of the nation.

Some progressives focused on expanding state and federal regulation of private interests for the public welfare. Others viewed the rapid influx of new immigrants and the explosive growth of large cities as requiring more stringent social controls. Another variant emphasized eliminating corruption in the political system as the key to righting society's wrongs. In the South, progressivism was for white people only. Progressives could be forward looking in their vision or nostalgic for a nineteenth-century world rapidly disappearing. Self-styled progressives often found themselves facing each other from opposite sides of an issue.

Unifying Themes

Three basic attitudes underlay the various crusades and movements that emerged in response to the fears gnawing at large segments of the population. The first was anger over the excesses of industrial capitalism and urban growth. At the same time, progressives shared an essential optimism about the ability of citizens to improve social and economic conditions. They were reformers, not revolutionaries. Second, progressives emphasized social cohesion and common bonds as a way of understanding how modern society and economics actually worked. They largely rejected the ideal of individualism that had informed nineteenth-century economic and political theory. For progressives, poverty and success hinged on more than simply individual character; the economy was more than merely a sum of individual calculations. Progressives thus opposed social Darwinism, with its claim that any effort to improve social conditions would prove fruitless because society is like a jungle, in which only the "fittest" survive. Third, progressives believed in the need for citizens to intervene actively, both politically and morally, to improve social conditions. They pushed for a stronger government role in regulating the economy and solving the nation's social problems.

Progressive rhetoric and methods drew on two distinct sources of inspiration. One was evangelical Protestantism, particularly the late nineteenth-century social gospel movement. Social gospelers rejected the idea of original sin as the cause of human suffering. They emphasized both the capacity and the duty of Christians to purge the world of poverty, inequality, and economic greed. A second strain of progressive thought looked to natural and social scientists to develop rational measures for improving the human condition, believing that experts trained in statistical analysis and engineering could make government and industry more efficient. Progressivism thus offered an uneasy combination of social justice and social control, a tension that would characterize American reform for the rest of the twentieth century.

The Female Dominion

In the 1890s, the settlement house movement had begun to provide an alternative to traditional concepts of private charity and humanitarian reform. Settlement workers found they could not transform their neighborhoods without confronting a host of broad social questions: chronic poverty, overcrowded tenement houses, child labor, industrial accidents, public health. As on Henry Street, college-educated, middle-class women constituted a key vanguard in the crusade for social justice. As reform communities, settlement houses soon discovered the need to engage the political and cultural life of the larger communities that surrounded them.

Jane Addams founded one of the first settlement houses, Hull House, in Chicago in 1889, after years of struggling to find work and a social identity equal to her talents. A member of one of the first generations of American women to attend college, Addams was a graduate of Rockford College. Many educated women were dissatisfied with the life choices conventionally available to them: early marriage or the traditional female professions of teaching, nursing, and library work. Settlement work provided these women with an attractive alternative. Hull House was located in a run-down slum area of Chicago. It had a day nursery, a dispensary for medicines and

OVERVIEW

CURRENTS OF PROGRESSIVISM

	Key Figures	Issues
Local Communities	Jane Addams, Lillian Wald, Florence Kelley, Frederic C. Howe, Samuel Jones	• Improving health, education, welfare in urban immigrant neighborhoods • Child labor, eight-hour day • Celebrating immigrant cultures • Reforming urban politics • Municipal ownership/regulation of utilities
State	Robert M. LaFollette, Hiram Johnson, Al Smith	• Limiting power of railroads, other corporations • Improving civil service • Direct democracy • Applying academic scholarship to human needs
National	James K. Vardaman, Hoke Smith, Theodore Roosevelt, Woodrow Wilson	• Disfranchisement of African Americans • Trustbusting • Conservation and Western development • National regulation of corporate and financial excesses • Reform of national banking
Intellectual/Cultural	Jacob Riis, Lincoln Steffens, Ida Tarbell, Upton Sinclair, S. S. McClure	• Muckraking
	John Dewey	• Education reform
	Louis Brandeis	• Sociological jurisprudence
	Edwin A. Ross	• Empowering "ethical elite"

medical advice, a boardinghouse, an art gallery, and a music school. Addams often spoke of the "subjective necessity" of settlement houses. By this she meant that they gave young, educated women a way to satisfy their powerful desire to connect with the real world. "There is nothing after disease, indigence and guilt," she wrote, "so fatal to life itself as the want of a proper outlet for active faculties."

Social reformer Florence Kelley helped direct the support of the settlement house movement behind groundbreaking state and federal labor legislation. Arriving at Hull House in 1891, Kelley found what she

described as a "colony of efficient and intelligent women." In 1893, she wrote a report detailing the dismal conditions in sweatshops, and the effects of long hours on the women and children who worked in them. This report became the basis for landmark legislation in Illinois that limited women to an eight-hour workday, barred children under fourteen from working, and abolished tenement labor. Illinois governor John Peter Altgeld appointed Kelley as chief inspector for the new law. In 1895, Kelley published *Hull House Maps and Papers*, the first scientific study of urban poverty in America.

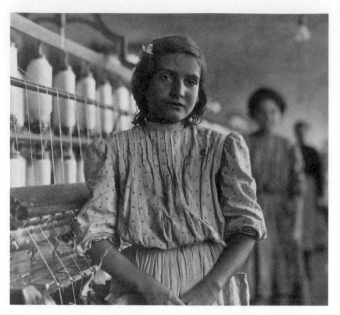

Photographer Lewis Hine, one of the pioneers of social documentary photography, made this evocative 1908 portrait of "Mamie," a typical young spinner working at a cotton mill in Lancaster, South Carolina. The National Child Labor Committee hired Hine to help document, publicize, and curb the widespread employment of children in industrial occupations. "These pictures," Hine wrote, "speak for thmselves and prove that the law is being violated."

SOURCE: Lewis Hine (American, 1874–1940), *A Carolina Spinner*, 1908. Gelatin silver print, 4 3/4 × 7 in. Milwaukee Art Museum, Gift of the Sheldon M. Barnett Family. M1973.83.

A portrait of the young Jane Addams, probably taken around the time she founded Hull House in Chicago, in 1889.

SOURCE: Wallace Kirkland/Time Life Pictures. Getty Images/Time Life Pictures.

Moving to Henry Street Settlement in 1898, Kelley served as general secretary of the new National Consumers' League. With Lillian Wald, she established the New York Child Labor Committee and pushed for the creation of the U.S. Children's Bureau, established in 1912. Its director, the first woman to head a federal bureau, was Julia Lathrop, another alumna of Hull House.

New female-dominated occupations, such as social work, public health nursing, and home economics, allowed women to combine professional aspirations with the older traditions of female moral reform, especially those centered on child welfare. The new professionalism, in turn, sustained reform commitments and a female dominion that simultaneously expanded the social welfare function of the state, and increased women's public authority and influence.

Kelley, Addams, Wald, Lathrop and their circle consciously used their power as women to reshape politics in the progressive era. Electoral politics and the state were historically male preserves, but female social progressives turned their gender into an advantage. Activists like Kelley used their influence in civil society to create new state powers in the service of social justice. ""Women's place is Home," wrote reformer Rheta Childe Dorr, "but Home is not contained within the four walls of an individual home. Home is the community."

The Urban Machine

By the turn of the century, Democratic Party machines, usually dominated by first- and second-generation Irish, controlled the political life of most large American cities. The keys to machine strength were disciplined organization and the delivery of essential services to both immigrant communities and business elites. The successful machine politician viewed his work as a business, and he accumulated his capital by serving people who needed assistance. For most urban dwellers, the city was a place of economic and social insecurity. Recent immigrants in particular faced frequent unemployment, sickness, and discrimination. In exchange for votes, machine politicians offered their constituents a variety of services. These included municipal jobs in the police and fire departments, work at city construction sites, intervention with legal problems, and food and coal during hard times.

For those who did business with the city—construction companies, road builders, realtors—staying on the machine's good side was simply another business expense. In exchange for valuable franchises and city contracts, businessmen routinely bribed machine politicians and contributed liberally to their campaign funds. George Washington Plunkitt, a stalwart of

New York's Tammany Hall machine, good-naturedly defended what he called "honest graft": making money from inside information on public improvements. "It's just like lookin' ahead in Wall Street or in the coffee or cotton market. . . . I seen my opportunities and I took 'em."

The machines usually had close ties to organized prostitution and gambling, as well as more legitimate commercial entertainments.Many machine figures began as saloonkeepers, and liquor dealers and beer brewers provided important financial support for "the organization." Vaudeville and burlesque theater, boxing, horse racing, and professional baseball were other urban enterprises with economic and political links to machines. Entertainment and spectacle made up a central element in the machine political style as well. Constituents looked forward to the colorful torchlight parades, free summer picnics, and riverboat excursions regularly sponsored by the machines.

On New York City's Lower East Side, where the Henry Street Settlement was located, Timothy D. "Big Tim" Sullivan embodied the popular machine style. Big Tim, who had risen from desperate poverty, remained enormously popular with his constituents until his death in 1913. Critics charged that Sullivan controlled the city's gambling and made money from prostitution. But his real fortune came through his investments in vaudeville and the early movie business. Sullivan, whose district included the largest number of immigrants and transients in the city, provided shoe giveaways and free Christmas dinners to thousands every winter. To help pay for these and other charitable activities, he informally taxed the saloons, theaters, and restaurants in the district.

In the early twentieth century, to expand their base of support, political machines in the Northeast began concentrating more on passing welfare legislation beneficial to working-class and immigrant constituencies. In this way, machine politicians often allied themselves with progressive reformers in state legislatures. In New York, for example, Tammany Hall figures such as Robert Wagner, Al Smith, and Big Tim Sullivan worked with middle-class progressive groups to pass child labor laws, factory safety regulations, worker compensation plans, and other efforts to make government more responsive to social needs. As Jewish and Catholic immigrants expanded in number and proportion in the city population, urban machines also began to champion cultural pluralism, opposing prohibition and immigration restrictions and defending the contributions made by new ethnic groups in the cities.

Political Progressives and Urban Reform

Political progressivism originated in the cities. It was both a challenge to the power of machine politics and a response to deteriorating urban conditions. City governments, especially in the Northeast and industrial Midwest, seemed hardly capable of providing the basic services needed to sustain large populations. For example, an impure water supply left Pittsburgh with one of the world's highest rates of death from typhoid, dysentery, and cholera. Most New York City neighborhoods rarely enjoyed street cleaning, and playgrounds were nonexistent. "The challenge of the city," Cleveland progressive Frederic C. Howe said in 1906, "has become one of decent human existence."

Reformers placed much of the blame for urban ills on the machines, and looked for ways to restructure city government. The "good government" movement, led by the National Municipal League, fought to make city management a nonpartisan, even nonpolitical, process by bringing the administrative techniques of large corporations to cities. Reformers revised city charters in favor of stronger mayoral power and expanded use of appointed administrators and career civil servants. They drew up blueprints for model charters, ordinances, and zoning plans designed by experts trained in public administration.

Business and professional elites became the biggest boosters of structural reforms in urban government. In the summer of 1900, a hurricane in the Gulf of Mexico unleashed a tidal wave on Galveston, Texas. To cope with this disaster, leading businessmen convinced the state legislature to replace the mayor-council government with a small board of commissioners. Each commissioner was elected at large, and each was responsible for a different city department. Under this plan, voters could more easily identify and hold accountable those responsible for city services. The city commission, enjoying both policymaking and administrative powers, proved very effective in rebuilding Galveston. By 1917, nearly 500 cities, including Houston, Oakland, Kansas City, Denver, and Buffalo, had adopted the commission form of government. Another approach, the city manager plan, gained popularity in small and midsized cities. In this system, a city council appointed a professional, nonpartisan city manager to handle the day-to-day operations of the community.

Progressive politicians who focused on the human problems of the industrial city championed a different kind of reform, one based on changing policies rather than the political structure. In Cleveland, for example, wealthy businessman Thomas L. Johnson, served as mayor from 1901 to 1909. He emphasized both efficiency and social welfare. His popular program included lower streetcar fares, public baths, milk and meat inspection, and an expanded park and playground system.

Progressivism in the Statehouse: West and South

Their motives and achievements were mixed, but progressive politicians became a powerful force in many state capitals. In Wisconsin, Republican dissident Robert

M. La Follette forged a coalition of angry farmers, small businessmen, and workers with his fiery attacks on railroads and other large corporations. Leader of the progressive faction of the state Republicans, "Fighting Bob" won three terms as governor (1900–06), then served as a U.S. senator until his death in 1925. As governor, he pushed through tougher corporate tax rates, a direct primary, an improved civil service code, and a railroad commission designed to regulate freight charges. La Follette used faculty experts at the University of Wisconsin to help research and write his bills. Other states began copying the "Wisconsin Idea"—the application of academic scholarship and theory to the needs of the people.

In practice, LaFollette's railroad commission accomplished far less than progressive rhetoric claimed. It essentially represented special interests—commercial farmers and businessmen seeking reduced shipping rates. Ordinary consumers did not see lower passenger fares or reduced food prices. And as commissioners began to realize, the national reach of the railroads limited the effectiveness of state regulation.

Western progressives displayed the greatest enthusiasm for institutional political reform. In the early 1900s, Oregon voters approved a series of constitutional amendments designed to strengthen direct democracy. The two most important were the *initiative*, which allowed a direct vote on specific measures put on the state ballot by petition, and the *referendum*, which allowed voters to decide on bills referred to them by the legislature. Other reforms included the direct *primary*, which allowed voters to cross party lines, and the *recall*, which gave voters the right to remove elected officials by popular vote. Widely copied throughout the West, all these measures intentionally weakened political parties.

Western progressives also targeted railroads, mining and timber companies, and public utilities for reform. Large corporations such as Pacific Gas and Electric and the Southern Pacific Railroad had amassed enormous wealth and political influence. They were able to corrupt state legislatures and charge consumers exorbitant rates. An alliance between middle-class progressives and working-class voters reflected growing disillusionment with the ideology of individualism that had helped pave the way for the rise of the big corporation. In California, attorney Hiram Johnson won a 1910 progressive campaign for governor on the slogan "Kick the Southern Pacific Railroad Out of Politics." In addition to winning political reforms, Johnson also put through laws regulating utilities and child labor, mandating an eight-hour day for working women, and providing a state-worker compensation plan.

In the South, the populist tradition of the 1880s and 1890s had been based in part on a biracial politics of protest. But Southern progressivism was for white people only. Indeed, Southern progressives believed that the disfranchisement of black voters and the creation of a legally segregated public sphere were necessary preconditions for political and social reform. With African Americans removed from political life, white Southern progressives argued, the direct primary system of nominating candidates would give white voters more influence. Between 1890 and 1910, Southern states passed a welter of statutes specifying poll taxes, literacy tests, and property qualifications, with the explicit goal of preventing voting by blacks. This systematic disfranchisement of African American voters stripped black communities of any political power. To prevent the disfranchisement of poor white voters under these laws, states established so-called understanding and grandfather clauses. Election officials had discretionary power to decide whether an illiterate person could understand and reasonably interpret the Constitution when read to him. Unqualified white men were also registered if they could show that their grandfathers had voted.

Southern progressives also supported the push toward a fully segregated public sphere. Between 1900 and 1910, Southern states strengthened "Jim Crow" laws requiring separation of races in restaurants, streetcars, beaches, and theaters. Schools were separate, but hardly equal. A 1916 Bureau of Education study found that per capita expenditures for education in Southern states averaged $10.32 a year for white children and $2.89 for black children. And African American teachers received far lower salaries than their white counterparts. Black taxpayers, in effect, subsidized improved schools for whites, even as they saw their own children's educational opportunities deteriorate. The legacy of Southern progressivism was thus closely linked to the strengthening of the legal and institutional guarantees of white supremacy.

Based mostly in New South towns and cities, and with growing strength among educated professionals, small businessmen, and women's benevolent societies, Southern progressives organized to control both greedy corporations and "unruly" citizens. Citizens groups, city boards of trade, and newspapers pressed reluctant legislators to use state power to regulate big business. Between 1905 and 1909, nearly every Southern state moved to regulate railroads by mandating lower passenger and freight rates. Prohibition enjoyed wide appeal in the South, as progressives active in the Anti-Saloon League argued that banning the alcohol trade would protect the family structure and victimized women, as well as reduce crime among African Americans. Employing aggressive lobbying, petitions, and massive parades, prohibition forces succeeded in pushing six Southern states to ban the manufacture and sale of alcoholic beverages by 1909. Southern progressives also directed their energies at the related problems of child labor and educational reform. In 1900, at least one-quarter of all Southern cotton mill workers were between the ages of ten and sixteen, many of whom worked over sixty hours per week. Led by reform minded ministers Edgar Gardner Murphy and Alexander McKelway, and drawing upon the activism of white club women, reformers attacked child labor by focusing on the welfare of children and their mothers and emphasizing the degradation of "Anglo Saxons." In 1903, Alabama and North Carolina enacted the first state child labor laws, setting twelve as a minimum age for employment. But the laws were weakened by many exemptions and no provisions for enforcement, as lawmakers also heard the loud complaints from parents and mill owners who resented the efforts of reformers to limit their choices.

New Journalism: Muckraking

Changes in journalism helped fuel a new reform consciousness by drawing the attention of millions to urban poverty, political corruption, the plight of industrial workers, and immoral business practices. As early as 1890, journalist Jacob Riis had shocked the nation with his landmark book *How the Other Half Lives*, a portrait of New York City's poor. Riis's book included a remarkable series of photographs he had taken in tenements, lodging houses, sweatshops, and saloons. These striking pictures, combined with Riis's analysis of slum housing patterns, had a powerful impact on a whole generation of urban reformers.

Within a few years, magazine journalists had turned to uncovering the seamier side of American life. The key innovator was S. S. McClure, a young Midwestern editor who in 1893, started America's first large-circulation magazine, *McClure's*. Charging only a dime for his monthly, McClure effectively combined popular fiction with articles on science, technology, travel, and recent history. He attracted a new readership among the urban middle class through aggressive subscription and promotional campaigns, as well as newsstand sales. By the turn of the century, *McClure's* and several imitators— *Munsey's, Cosmopolitan, Collier's, Everybody's,* and the *Saturday Evening Post*—had circulations in the hundreds of thousands. Making extensive use of photographs and illustrations, these cheap upstarts soon far surpassed older, more staid and expensive magazines such as the *Atlantic Monthly* and *Harper's* in circulation.

In 1902, McClure began hiring talented reporters to write detailed accounts of the nation's social problems. Lincoln Steffens's series *The Shame of the Cities* (1902) revealed the widespread graft at the center of American urban politics. He showed how big-city bosses routinely worked hand in glove with businessmen seeking lucrative municipal contracts for gas, water, electricity, and mass transit. Ida Tarbell, in her *History of the Standard Oil Company* (1904), thoroughly documented how John D. Rockefeller ruthlessly squeezed out competitors with unfair business practices. Ray Stannard Baker wrote detailed portraits of life and labor in Pennsylvania coal towns.

McClure's and other magazines discovered that "exposure journalism" paid off handsomely in terms of increased circulation. The middle-class public responded to this new combination of factual reporting and moral exhortation. A series such as Steffens's fueled reform campaigns that swept individual communities. Between 1902 and 1908, magazines were full of articles exposing insurance scandals, patent medicine frauds, and stock market swindles. Upton Sinclair's 1906 novel *The Jungle*, a socialist tract set among Chicago packinghouse workers, exposed the filthy sanitation and abysmal working conditions in the stockyards and the meatpacking industry. In an effort to boost sales, Sinclair's publisher devoted an entire issue of a monthly magazine it owned, *World's Work,* to articles and photographs that substantiated Sinclair's devastating portrait.

In 1906, David Graham Phillips, in a series for *Cosmopolitan* called "The Treason of the Senate," argued that many conservative U.S. senators were no more than mouthpieces for big business. President Theodore Roosevelt, upset by Phillips's attack on several of his friends and supporters, coined a new term when he angrily denounced Phillips and his colleagues as "muckrakers" who "raked the mud of society and never looked up."

This picture of Bohemian immigrant cigar makers at work in a New York City tenement first appeared in Jacob Riis's *How the Other Half Lives* (1890), a pathbreaking work of "exposure journalism." Apartments like these, owned and rented out by cigar manufacturers, served as both living quarters and workshops, leading to filthy and unhealthy conditions. Note how the entire family works together to roll as many cigars as possible.

SOURCE: *Bohemian Cigar Makers at Work in Their Tenement,* ca. 1890. Museum of the City of New York, The Jacob A. Riis Collection, #147.90.13.1.150.

Partly due to Roosevelt's outburst, the muckraking vogue began to wane. But muckraking had demonstrated the powerful potential for mobilizing public opinion on a national scale. Reform campaigns need not be limited to the local community. Ultimately, they could engage a national community of informed citizens.

Intellectual Trends Promoting Reform

On a deeper level than muckraking, a host of early twentieth-century thinkers challenged several of the core ideas in American intellectual life. Their new theories of education, law, economics, and society provided effective tools for reformers. The emergent fields of the social sciences—sociology, psychology, anthropology, and economics—emphasized empirical observation of how people actually lived and behaved in their communities. Progressive reformers linked the systematic analysis of society and the individual characteristic of these new fields of inquiry to the project of improving the material conditions of American society.

Sociologist Lester Frank Ward, in his pioneering work *Dynamic Sociology* (1883), offered an important critique of social Darwinism, the then orthodox theory that attributed social inequality to natural selection and the "survival of the fittest." Ward argued that the conservative social theorists responsible for social Darwinism, such as Herbert Spencer and William Graham Sumner, had wrongly applied evolutionary theory to human affairs. They had confused organic evolution with social evolution. Nature's method was genetic: unplanned, involuntary, automatic, and mechanical. By contrast, civilization had been built on successful human intervention in the natural processes of organic evolution. "Every implement or utensil," Ward argued, "every mechanical device, every object of design, skill, and labor, every artificial thing that serves a human purpose, is a triumph of mind over the physical forces of nature in ceaseless and aimless competition."

Philosopher John Dewey criticized the excessively rigid and formal approach to education found in most American schools. In books such as *The School and Society* (1899) and *Democracy and Education* (1916), Dewey advocated developing what he called "creative intelligence" in students, which could then be put to use in improving society. Schools ought to be "embryonic communities," miniatures of society, where children were encouraged to participate actively in different types of experiences. By cultivating imagination and openness to new experiences, schools could develop creativity and the habits required for systematic inquiry. Dewey's belief that education was the "fundamental method of social progress and reform" inspired generations of progressive educators.

At the University of Wisconsin, John R. Commons founded the new field of industrial relations and organized a state industrial commission that became a model for other states. Working closely with Governor Robert M. La Follette, Commons and his students helped draft pioneering laws in worker compensation and public utility regulation. Another Wisconsin faculty member, economist Richard Ely, argued that the state was "an educational and ethical agency whose positive aim is an indispensable condition of human progress." Ely believed the state must directly intervene to help solve public problems. He rejected the doctrine of laissez faire as merely "a tool in the hands of the greedy." Like Commons, Ely worked with Wisconsin lawmakers, applying his expertise in economics to reforming the state's labor laws.

Progressive legal theorists began challenging the conservative view of constitutional law that had dominated American courts. Since the 1870s, the Supreme Court had interpreted the Fourteenth Amendment (1868) as a guarantee of broad rights for corporations. That amendment, which prevented states from depriving "any person of life, liberty, or property, without due process of law," had been designed to protect the civil rights of African Americans against violations by the states. But the Court, led by Justice Stephen J. Field, used the due process clause to strike down state laws regulating business and labor conditions. The Supreme Court and state courts had thus made the Fourteenth Amendment a bulwark for big business and a foe of social welfare measures.

The most important dissenter from this view was Oliver Wendell Holmes Jr. A scholar and Massachusetts judge, Holmes believed the law had to take into account changing social conditions. And courts should take care not to invalidate social legislation enacted democratically. After his appointment to the Supreme Court in 1902, Holmes authored a number of notable dissents to conservative court decisions overturning progressive legislation. Criticizing the majority opinion in *Lochner* v. *New York* (1905), in which the Court struck down a state law setting a ten-hour day for bakers, Holmes insisted that the Constitution "is not intended to embody a particular theory."

Holmes's pragmatic views of the law seldom convinced a majority of the Supreme Court before the late 1930s. But his views influenced a generation of lawyers who began practicing what came to be called sociological jurisprudence. In *Muller* v. *Oregon* (1908), the Court upheld an Oregon law limiting the maximum hours for working women, finding that the liberty of contract "is not absolute." Noting that "woman's physical structure and the performance of maternal functions place her at a disadvantage," the Court found that "the physical well-being of woman becomes an object of public interest and care." Louis Brandeis, the state's attorney, amassed statistical, sociological, and economic data, rather than traditional legal arguments, to support his arguments. The "Brandeis Brief" became a common strategy for lawyers defending the constitutionality of progressive legislation.

SOCIAL CONTROL AND ITS LIMITS

Many middle- and upper-class Protestant progressives feared that immigrants and large cities threatened the stability of American democracy. They worried that alien cultural practices were disrupting what they viewed as traditional American morality. Edward A. Ross's landmark work *Social Control* (1901), a book whose title became a key phrase in progressive thought, argued that society needed an "ethical elite" of citizens "who have at heart the general welfare and know what kinds of conduct will promote this welfare." Progressives often believed they had a mission to frame laws and regulations for the social control of immigrants, industrial workers, and African Americans. This was the moralistic and frequently xenophobic side of progressivism, and it provided a powerful source of support for the regulation of drinking, prostitution, leisure activities, and schooling. Organizations devoted to social control constituted other versions of reform communities. But these attempts at moral reform met with mixed success amid the extraordinary cultural and ethnic diversity of America's cities.

The Prohibition Movement

During the last two decades of the nineteenth century, the Woman's Christian Temperance Union had grown into a powerful mass organization. The WCTU appealed especially to women angered by men who used alcohol and then abused their wives and children. It directed most of its work toward ending the production, sale, and consumption of alcohol. But local WCTU chapters put their energy into nontemperance activities as well, including homeless shelters, Sunday schools, prison reform, child nurseries, and woman suffrage. The WCTU thus provided women with a political forum in which they could fuse their traditional moral posture as guardians of the home with broader public concerns. By 1911, the WCTU, with a quarter million members, was the largest women's organization in American history.

Other temperance groups had a narrower focus. The Anti-Saloon League, founded in 1893, began by organizing local-option campaigns in which rural counties and small towns banned liquor within their geographical limits. It drew much of its financial support from local businessmen, who saw a link between closing a community's saloons and increasing the productivity of workers. The league was a one-issue pressure group that played effectively on antiurban and antiimmigrant prejudice. League lobbyists hammered away at the close connections among saloon culture, liquor dealers, brewers, and big-city political machines.

The battle to ban alcohol revealed deep ethnic and cultural divides within America's urban communities. Opponents of alcohol were generally "pietists," who viewed the world from a position of moral absolutism. These included native-born, middle-class Protestants associated with evangelical churches, along with some old-stock Protestant immigrant denominations. Opponents of prohibition were generally "ritualists" with less arbitrary notions of personal morality. These were largely new-stock, working-class Catholic and Jewish immigrants, along with some Protestants, such as German Lutherans.

The Social Evil

Many of the same reformers who battled the saloon and drinking also engaged in efforts to eradicate prostitution. Crusades against "the social evil" had appeared at intervals throughout the nineteenth century. But they reached a new level of intensity between 1895 and 1920. In part, this new sense of urgency stemmed from the sheer growth of cities and the greater visibility of prostitution in red-light districts and neighborhoods. Antiprostitution campaigns epitomized the diverse makeup and mixed motives of so much progressive reform. Male business and civic leaders joined forces with feminists, social workers, and clergy to eradicate "commercialized vice."

Between 1908 and 1914, exposés of the "white slave traffic" became a national sensation. Dozens of books, articles, and motion pictures alleged an international conspiracy to seduce and sell girls into prostitution. Most of these materials exaggerated the practices they attacked. They also made foreigners, especially Jews and southern Europeans, scapegoats for the sexual anxieties of native-born whites. In 1910, Congress passed legislation that permitted the deportation of foreign-born prostitutes or any foreigner convicted of procuring or employing them. That same year, the Mann Act made it a federal offense to transport women across state lines for "immoral purposes."

Reformers had trouble believing that any woman would freely choose to be a prostitute; such a choice was antithetical to conventional notions of female purity and sexuality. But for wage-earning women, prostitution was a rational choice in a world of limited opportunities. Maimie Pinzer, a prostitute, summed up her feelings in a letter to a wealthy female reformer: "I don't propose to get up at 6:30 to be at work at 8 and work in a close, stuffy room with people I despise, until dark, for $6 or $7 a week! When I could, just by phoning, spend an afternoon with some congenial person and in the end have more than a week's work could pay me." The antivice crusades succeeded in closing down many urban red-light districts and larger brothels, but these were replaced by the streetwalker and call girl, who were more vulnerable to harassment and control by policemen and pimps. Rather than eliminating prostitution, reform efforts transformed the organization of the sex trade.

The Redemption of Leisure

Progressives faced a thorny issue in the growing popularity of commercial entertainment. For large numbers of working-class adults and children, leisure meant time and money spent at vaudeville and burlesque theaters, amusement parks, dance halls, and motion picture houses. These competed with municipal parks, libraries, museums, YMCAs, and school recreation centers. For many cultural traditionalists, the flood of new urban commercial amusements posed a grave threat. As with prostitution, urban progressives sponsored a host of recreation and amusement surveys detailing the situation in their individual cities. "Commercialized leisure," warned Frederic C. Howe in 1914, "must be controlled by the community, if it is to become an agency of civilization rather than the reverse."

By 1908, movies had become the most popular form of cheap entertainment in America. One survey estimated

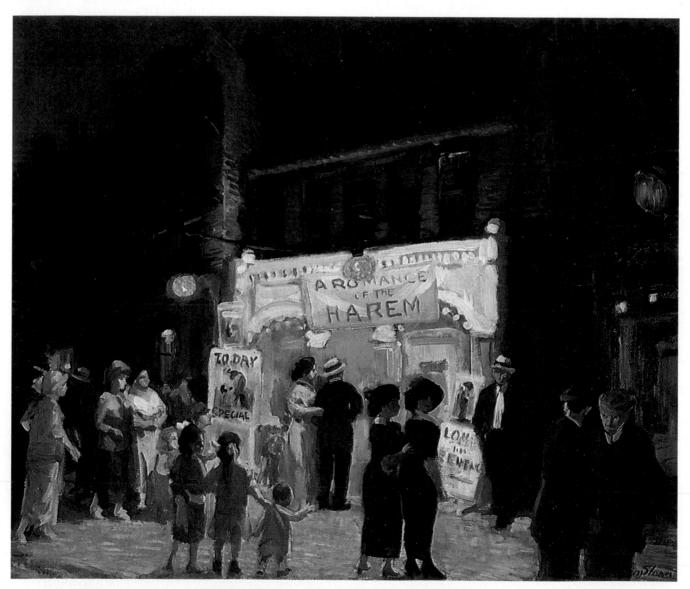

Movies, by John Sloan, 1913, the most talented artist among the so-called Ashcan realist school of painting. Active in socialist and bohemian circles, Sloan served as art editor for *The Masses* magazine for several years. His work celebrated the vitality and diversity of urban working-class life and leisure, including the new commercial culture represented by the motion picture.

SOURCE: John Sloan, *Movies,* 1913. Oil painting. The Toledo Museum of Art.

that 11,500 movie theaters attracted 5 million patrons each day. For 5 or 10 cents, "nickelodeon" theaters offered programs that might include a slapstick comedy, a Western, a travelogue, and a melodrama. Early movies were most popular in the tenement and immigrant districts of big cities, and with children. As the films themselves became more sophisticated and as "movie palaces" began to replace cheap storefront theaters, the new medium attracted a large middle-class clientele as well.

Progressive reformers seized the chance to help regulate the new medium as a way of improving the commercial recreation of the urban poor. Movies held out the promise of an alternative to the older entertainment traditions, such as concert saloons and burlesque theater, that had been closely allied with machine politics and the vice economy. In 1909, New York City movie producers and exhibitors joined with the reform-minded People's Institute to establish the voluntary National Board of Censorship (NBC). Movie entrepreneurs, most of whom were themselves immigrants, sought to shed the stigma of the slums, attract more middle-class patronage, and increase profits. A revolving group of civic activists reviewed new movies, passing them, suggesting changes, or condemning them. Local censoring committees all over the nation subscribed to the board's weekly bulletin. They aimed at achieving what John Collier of the NBC called "the redemption of leisure." By 1914, the NBC was reviewing 95 percent of the nation's film output.

Standardizing Education

Along with reading, writing, and mathematics, schools inculcated patriotism, piety, and respect for authority. Progressive educators looked to the public school primarily as an agent of "Americanization." Elwood Cubberley, a leading educational reformer, expressed the view that schools could be the vehicle by which immigrant children could break free of the parochial ethnic neighborhood. "Our task," he argued in *Changing Conceptions of Education* (1909), "is to break up these groups or settlements, to assimilate and amalgamate these people as a part of our American race, and to implant in their children, so far as can be done, the Anglo-Saxon conception of righteousness, law and order, and popular government."

The most important educational trends in these years were the expansion and bureaucratization of the nation's public school systems. In most cities, centralization served to consolidate the power of older urban elites who felt threatened by the large influx of immigrants. Children began school earlier and stayed there longer. Kindergartens spread rapidly in large cities. They presented, as one writer put it in 1903, "the earliest opportunity to catch the little Russian, the little Italian, the little German, Pole, Syrian,

and the rest and begin to make good American citizens of them." By 1918, every state had some form of compulsory school attendance. High schools also multiplied, extending the school's influence beyond the traditional grammar school curriculum. In 1890, only 4 percent of the nation's youth between fourteen and seventeen were enrolled in school; by 1930, the figure was 47 percent.

High schools reflected a growing belief that schools should be comprehensive, multifunctional institutions. In 1918, the National Education Association offered a report defining Cardinal Principles of Secondary Education. These included instruction in health, family life, citizenship, and ethical character. Academic programs prepared a small number of students for college. Vocational programs trained boys and girls for a niche in the new industrial order. Boys took shop courses in metal trades, carpentry, and machine tools. Girls learned typing, bookkeeping, sewing, cooking, and home economics. The Smith-Hughes Act of 1917 provided federal grants to support these programs and set up a Federal Board for Vocational Education.

WORKING-CLASS COMMUNITIES AND PROTEST

The Industrial Revolution, which had begun transforming American life and labor in the nineteenth century, reached maturity in the early twentieth. In 1900, out of a total labor force of 28.5 million, 16 million people worked at industrial occupations and 11 million on farms. By 1920, in a labor force of nearly 42 million, almost 29 million were in industry, but farm labor had declined to 10.4 million. The world of the industrial worker included large manufacturing towns in New England; barren mining settlements in the West; primitive lumber and turpentine camps in the South; steelmaking and coal-mining cities in Pennsylvania and Ohio; and densely packed immigrant ghettos from New York to San Francisco, where workers toiled in garment-trade sweatshops.

All these industrial workers shared the need to sell their labor for wages in order to survive. At the same time, differences in skill, ethnicity, and race proved powerful barriers to efforts at organizing trade unions that could bargain for improved wages and working conditions. So, too, did the economic and political power of the large corporations that dominated much of American industry. Yet there were also small, closely knit groups of skilled workers, such as printers and brewers, who exercised real control over their lives and labors. And these years saw many labor struggles that created effective trade unions or laid the groundwork for others.

Industrial workers also became a force in local and national politics, adding a chorus of insistent voices to the calls for social justice.

New Immigrants from Two Hemispheres

On the eve of World War I, close to 60 percent of the industrial labor force was foreign-born. Most of these workers were among the roughly 9 million new immigrants from southern and eastern Europe who arrived in the United States between 1900 and 1914. In the nineteenth century, much of the overseas migration had come from the industrial districts of northern and western Europe. English, Welsh, and German artisans had brought with them skills critical for emerging industries such as steelmaking and coal mining. Unlike their predecessors, nearly all the new Italian, Polish, Hungarian, Jewish, and Greek immigrants lacked industrial skills. They thus entered the bottom ranks of factories, mines, mills, and sweatshops.

These new immigrants had been driven from their European farms and towns by several forces, including the undermining of subsistence farming by commercial agriculture; a falling death rate that brought a shortage of land; and religious and political persecution. American corporations also sent agents to recruit cheap labor. Except for Jewish immigrants, a majority of whom fled virulent anti-Semitism in Russia and Russian Poland, most newcomers planned on earning a stake and then returning home. Hard times in America forced many back to Europe. In the depression year of 1908, for example, more Austro-Hungarians and Italians left than entered the United States (see Map 21.1).

The decision to migrate usually occurred through social networks—people linked by kinship, personal acquaintance, and work experience. These "chains," extending from places of origin to specific destinations in the United States, helped migrants cope with the considerable risks entailed by the long and difficult journey. A study conducted by the U.S. Immigration Commission in 1909, found that about 60 percent of the new immigrants had their passage arranged by immigrants already in America.

Immigrant communities used ethnicity as a collective resource for gaining employment in factories, mills, and mines. One Polish steelworker recalled how the process operated in the Pittsburgh mills: "Now if a Russian got his job in a shear department, he's looking for a buddy, a Russian buddy. He's not going to look for a Croatian buddy. And if he sees the boss looking for a man he says, 'Look, I have a good man,' and he's picking out his friends. A Ukrainian department, a Russian department, a Polish

MAP 21.1 Immigration to the United States, 1901–20

Newly landed European immigrant families on the dock at Ellis Island in New York harbor, 1900. Originally a black and white photograph, this image was later color tinted for reproduction as a postcard or book illustration.
SOURCE: The Granger Collection, New York.

department. And it was a beautiful thing in a way." Such specialization of work by ethnic origin was quite common throughout America's industrial communities.

The low-paid, backbreaking work in basic industry became nearly the exclusive preserve of the new immigrants. In 1907, of the 14,359 common laborers employed at Pittsburgh's U.S. Steel mills, 11,694 were eastern Europeans. For twelve-hour days and seven-day weeks, two-thirds of these workers made less than $12.50 a week, one-third less than $10.00. This was far less than the $15.00 that the Pittsburgh Associated Charities had estimated as the minimum for providing necessities for a family of five. Small wonder that the new immigration was disproportionately male. One-third of the immigrant steelworkers were single, and among married men who had been in the country less than five years, about two-thirds reported that their wives were still in Europe. Workers with families generally supplemented their incomes by taking in single men as boarders.

Not all of the new immigrants came from Europe, as hemispheric migration increased sharply as well. Over 300,000 French Canadians arrived in the United States between 1900 and 1930, settling mostly in New England.

But the maturing continental railroad system had widened the choice of destinations to communities in upstate New York and Detroit, which had the largest number of French Canadian migrants outside of New England. The pull of jobs in New England's textile industry, along with its physical proximity, attracted male farmers and laborers unable to make a living in the rural districts of Quebec. Roughly one-third of female migrants were domestic servants looking for the higher pay and greater independence associated with factory labor. The significant French Canadian presence in communities such as Lowell, Holyoke, Manchester, Nashua, and Waterville often made them the largest single ethnic group. By 1918, for example, one-quarter of the Fall River, Massachusetts, population of 28,000 was French Canadian. French language churches, newspapers, private schools, and mutual benefit societies reinforced the distinctive cultural milieu, and the presence of kin or fellow villagers facilitated the arrival of largely rural migrants into these new, highly industrialized, and urbanized settings.

Mexican immigration also grew in these years, providing a critical source of labor for the West's farms, railroads, and mines. Between 1900 and 1914, the number of people of Mexican descent living and working in the United

States tripled, from roughly 100,000 to 300,000. Economic and political crises spurred tens of thousands of Mexico's rural and urban poor to emigrate north. Large numbers of seasonal agricultural workers regularly came up from Mexico to work in the expanding sugar beet industry, and then returned. But a number of substantial resident Mexican communities also emerged in the early twentieth century.

Throughout Texas, California, New Mexico, Arizona, and Colorado, Western cities developed *barrios*, distinct communities of Mexicans. Mexican immigrants attracted by jobs in the smelting industry made El Paso the most thoroughly Mexican city in the United States. In San Antonio, Mexicans worked at shelling pecans, becoming perhaps the most underpaid and exploited group of workers in the country. By 1910, San Antonio contained the largest number of Mexican immigrants of any city. In southern California, labor agents for railroads recruited Mexicans to work on building new interurban lines around Los Angeles.

Between 1898 and 1907, more than 80,000 Japanese entered the United States. The vast majority were young men working as contract laborers in the West, mainly in California. American law prevented Japanese immigrants (the *Issei*) from obtaining American citizenship, because they were not white. This legal discrimination, along with informal exclusion from many occupations, forced the Japanese to create niches for themselves within local economies. Most Japanese settled near Los Angeles, where they established small communities centered around fishing, truck farming, and the flower and nursery business. In 1920, Japanese farmers produced 10 percent of the dollar volume of California agriculture on 1 percent of the farm acreage. By 1930, over 35,000 Issei and their children (the *Nisei*) lived in Los Angeles.

Urban Ghettos

In large cities, new immigrant communities took the form of densely packed ghettos. By 1920, immigrants and their children constituted almost 60 percent of the population of cities over 100,000. They were an even larger percentage in major industrial centers such as Chicago, Pittsburgh, Philadelphia, and New York. The sheer size and dynamism of these cities made the immigrant experience more complex there than in smaller cities and more isolated communities. Workers in the urban garment trades toiled for low wages and suffered layoffs, unemployment, and poor health. But conditions in the small, labor-intensive shops of the clothing industry differed significantly from those in the large-scale, capital-intensive industries like steel.

New York City had become the center of both Jewish immigration and America's huge ready-to-wear clothing industry. The city's Jewish population was 1.4 million in 1915, almost 30 percent of its inhabitants. In small factories, lofts, and tenement apartments some 200,000 people, most of them Jews, some of them Italians, worked in the

clothing trades. Most of the industry operated on the grueling piece-rate, or task, system, in which manufacturers and subcontractors paid individuals or teams of workers to complete a certain quota of labor within a specific time.

The garment industry was highly seasonal. A typical work week was sixty hours, with seventy common during busy season. But there were long stretches of unemployment in slack times. Often forced to work in cramped, dirty, and badly lit rooms, garment workers strained under a system in which time equaled money. Morris Rosenfeld, a presser of men's clothing who wrote Yiddish poetry, captured the feeling:

> The tick of the clock is the boss in his anger
> The face of the clock has the eye of a foe
> The clock—I shudder—Dost hear how it draws me?
> It calls me "Machine" and it cries to me "Sew!"

In November 1909, two New York garment manufacturers responded to strikes by unskilled women workers by hiring thugs and prostitutes to beat up pickets. The strikers won the support of the Women's Trade Union League, a group of sympathetic female reformers that included Lillian Wald, Mary Dreier, and prominent society figures. The Uprising of the 20,000, as it became known, swept through the city's garment district. The strikers demanded union recognition, better wages, and

New York City police set up this makeshift morgue to help identify victims of the disastrous Triangle Shirtwaist Company fire, March 25, 1911. Unable to open the locked doors of the sweatshop and desperate to escape from smoke and flames, many of the 146 who died had leaped eight stories to their death.

SOURCE: UPI Corbis/Bettmann.

safer and more sanitary conditions. They drew support from thousands of suffragists, trade unionists, and sympathetic middle-class women as well. Hundreds of strikers were arrested, and many were beaten by police. After three cold months on the picket line, the strikers returned to work without union recognition. But the International Ladies Garment Workers Union (ILGWU), founded in 1900, did gain strength and negotiated contracts with some of the city's shirtwaist makers. The strike was an important breakthrough in the drive to organize unskilled workers into industrial unions. It opened the doors to women's involvement in the labor movement and created new leaders, such as Clara Lemlich, Pauline Newman, and Rose Schneiderman.

On March 25, 1911, the issues raised by the strike took on new urgency when a fire raced through three floors of the Triangle Shirtwaist Company. As the flames spread, workers found themselves trapped by exit doors that had been locked from the outside. Fire escapes were nonexistent. Within half an hour, 146 people, mostly young Jewish women, had been killed by smoke or had leaped to their death. In the bitter aftermath, women progressives led by Florence Kelley and Frances Perkins of the National Consumers' League joined with Tammany Hall leaders Al Smith, Robert Wagner, and Big Tim Sullivan to create a New York State Factory Investigation Commission. Under Perkins's vigorous leadership, the commission conducted an unprecedented round of public hearings and on-site inspections, leading to a series of state laws that dramatically improved safety conditions and limited the hours for working women and children. (See Out of Many Voices: "We have Found You Wanting".)

OUT OF MANY VOICES

ROSE SCHNEIDERMAN, "WE HAVE FOUND YOU WANTING," APRIL 2, 1911

In the aftermath of the disastrous Triangle Fire, thousands of New Yorkers participated in protests and memorial meetings around the city. Rose Schneiderman, a Polish-born hat worker who had once worked at the Triangle Company, became an organizer of the International Ladies Garment Workers Union. Her moving speech reflected the tensions between newly class-conscious and increasingly radical workers, and middle- and upper-class reformers looking for more moderate legislative solutions for improving factory safety and sweatshop conditions.

I WOULD BE A TRAITOR TO THOSE POOR BURNED bodies, if I were to come here to talk good fellowship. We have tried you good people of the public—and we have found you wanting.

The old Inquisition had its rack and its thumbscrews and its instruments of torture with iron teeth. We know what these things are today: the iron teeth are our necessities, the thumbscrews are the high-powered and swift machinery close to which we must work, and the rack is here in the firetrap structures that will destroy us the minute they catch fire.

This is not the first time girls have been burned alive in this city. Every week I must learn of the untimely death of one of my sister workers. Every year thousands of us are maimed. The life of men and women is so cheap and property is so sacred! There are so many of us for one job, it matters little if 140-odd are burned to death.

We have tried you, citizens! We are trying you now and you have a couple of dollars for the sorrowing mothers and brothers and sisters by way of a charity gift. But every time the workers come out in the only way they know to protest against conditions which are unbearable, the strong hand of the law is allowed to press down heavily upon us.

Public officials have only words of warning for us—warning that we must be intensely orderly and must be intensely peaceable, and they have the workhouse just back of all their warnings. The strong hand of the law beats us back when we rise—back into the conditions that make life unbearable.

I can't talk fellowship to you who are gathered here. Too much blood has been spilled. I know from experience it is up to the working people to save themselves. And the only way is through a strong working-class movement. ■

SOURCE: Leon Stein, *The Triangle Fire* (New York: Carroll & Graf, 1962), 144–45.

Company Towns

Immigrant industrial workers and their families often established their communities in a company town, where a single large corporation was dominant. Cities such as Lawrence, Massachusetts; Gary, Indiana; and Butte, Montana, revolved around the industrial enterprises of Pacific Woolen, U.S. Steel, and Anaconda Copper. Workers had little or no influence over the economic and political institutions of these cities. In the more isolated company towns, residents often had no alternative but to buy their food, clothing, and supplies at company stores, usually for exorbitantly high prices. But they did maintain some community control in other ways. Family and kin networks, ethnic lodges, saloons, benefit societies, churches and synagogues, and musical groups affirmed traditional forms of community in a setting governed by individualism and private capital.

On the job, modern machinery and industrial discipline meant high rates of injury and death. In Gary, non-English speaking immigrant steelworkers suffered twice the accident rate of English-speaking employees, who could better understand safety instructions and warnings. A 1910 study of work accidents revealed that nearly a fourth of all new steelworkers were killed or injured each year. Mutual aid associations, organized around ethnic groups, offered some protection through cheap insurance and death benefits.

In steel and coal towns, women not only maintained the household and raised the children, they also boosted the family income by taking in boarders, sewing, and laundry. Many women also tended gardens and raised chickens, rabbits, and goats. Their produce and income helped reduce dependence on the company store. Working-class women felt the burdens of housework more heavily than their middle-class sisters. Pump water, indoor plumbing, and sewage disposal were often available only on a pay-as-you-go basis. The daily drudgery endured by working-class women far outlasted the "man-killing" shift worked by the husband. Many women struggled with the effects of their husbands' excessive drinking and faced early widowhood.

The adjustment for immigrant workers was not so much a process of assimilation as adaptation and resistance. Work habits and Old World cultural traditions did not always mesh with factory discipline or Taylor's "scientific management." A Polish wedding celebration might last three or four days. A drinking bout following a Sunday funeral might cause workers to celebrate "St. Monday" and not show up for work. Employers made much of the few Slavs allowed to work their way up into the ranks of skilled workers and foremen. But most immigrants were far more concerned with job security than with upward mobility. As new immigrants became less transient and more permanently settled in company towns, they increased their involvement in local politics and union activity.

The power of large corporations in the life of company towns was most evident among the mining communities of the West, as was violent labor conflict. The Colorado Fuel and Iron Company (CFI) employed roughly half of the 8,000 coal miners who labored in that state's mines. In mining towns such as Ludlow and Trinidad, the CFI thoroughly dominated the lives of miners and their families. "The miner," one union official observed, "is in this land owned by the corporation that owns the homes, that owns the boarding houses, that owns every single thing there is there . . . not only the mines, but all the grounds, all the buildings, all the places of recreation, as well as the school and church buildings." By the early twentieth century, new immigrants, such as Italians, Greeks, Slavs, and Mexicans, composed a majority of the population in these Western mining communities.

In September 1913, the United Mine Workers led a strike in the Colorado coalfields, calling for improved safety, higher wages, and recognition of the union. Thousands of miners' families moved out of company housing and into makeshift tent colonies provided by the union. In October, Governor Elias Ammons ordered the Colorado National Guard into the tense strike region to keep order. The troops, supposedly neutral, proceeded to ally themselves with the mine operators. By spring, the strike had bankrupted the state, forcing the governor to remove most of the troops. The coal companies then brought in large numbers of private mine guards who were extremely hostile toward the strikers. On April 20, 1914, a combination of guardsmen and private guards surrounded the largest of the tent colonies at Ludlow, where more than a thousand mine families lived. A shot rang out (each side accused the other of firing), and a pitched battle ensued that lasted until the poorly armed miners ran out of ammunition. At dusk, the troops burned the tent village to the ground, routing the families and killing fourteen, eleven of them children. Enraged strikers attacked mines throughout southern Colorado in an armed rebellion that lasted ten days, until President Woodrow Wilson ordered the U.S. Army into the region. News of the Ludlow Massacre shocked millions, and aroused widespread protests and demonstrations against the policies of Colorado Fuel and Iron and its owner, John D. Rockefeller Jr.

The AFL: "Unions, Pure and Simple"

Following the depression of the 1890s, the American Federation of Labor (AFL) emerged as the strongest and most stable organization of workers. Samuel Gompers's strategy of recruiting skilled labor into unions organized by craft had paid off. Union membership climbed from under 500,000 in 1897 to 1.7 million by 1904. Most of this growth took place in AFL affiliates in coal mining, the building trades, transportation, and machine shops. The national unions—the United Mine Workers of America, the Brotherhood of Carpenters and Joiners, the International Association of Machinists—represented workers of specific occupations in collective bargaining. Trade autonomy and exclusive jurisdiction were the ruling principles within the AFL.

But the strength of craft organization also gave rise to weakness. In 1905, Gompers told a union gathering in Minneapolis that "caucasians" would not "let their standard of living be destroyed by negroes, Chinamen, Japs, or any others." Those "others" included the new immigrants from eastern and southern Europe, men and women, who labored in the steel mills and garment trades. Each trade looked mainly to the welfare of its own. Many explicitly barred women and African Americans from membership. There were some important exceptions. The United Mine Workers of America (UMWA) followed a more inclusive policy, recruiting both skilled underground pitmen and the unskilled aboveground workers. The UMWA even tried to recruit strikebreakers brought in by coal operators. With 260,000 members in 1904, the UMWA became the largest AFL affiliate.

AFL unions had a difficult time holding on to their gains. Economic slumps, technological changes, and aggressive counterattacks by employer organizations could be devastating. Trade associations using management-controlled efficiency drives fought union efforts to regulate output and shop practices. The National Association of Manufacturers (NAM), a group of smaller industrialists founded in 1903, launched an "open shop" campaign to eradicate unions altogether. "Open shop" was simply a new name for a workplace where unions were not allowed. Unfriendly judicial decisions also hurt organizing efforts.

In 1906, a federal judge issued a permanent injunction against an iron molders strike at the Allis Chalmers Company of Milwaukee. In the so-called Danbury Hatters' Case (*Loewe* v. *Lawler*, 1908), a federal court ruled that secondary boycotts, aimed by strikers at other companies doing business with their employer, such as suppliers of materials, were illegal under the Sherman Antitrust Act. Long an effective labor tactic, secondary boycotts were now declared a conspiracy in restraint of trade. Not until the 1930s would unions be able to count on legal support for collective bargaining and the right to strike.

The IWW: "One Big Union"

Some workers developed more radical visions of labor organizing. In the harsh and isolated company towns of Idaho, Montana, and Colorado, miners suffered from low wages, poor food, and primitive sanitation, as well as injuries and death from frequent cave-ins and explosions. The Western Federation of Miners (WFM) had gained strength in the metal mining regions of the West by leading several strikes marred by violence. In 1899, during a strike in the silver mining district of Coeur d'Alene, Idaho, the Bunker Hill and Sullivan Mining Company had enraged the miners by hiring armed detectives and firing all union members. Desperate miners retaliated

by destroying a company mill with dynamite. Idaho's governor declared martial law and obtained federal troops to enforce it. In a pattern that would become familiar in Western labor relations, the soldiers served as strikebreakers, rounding up hundreds of miners and imprisoning them for months in makeshift bullpens.

In response to the brutal realities of labor organizing in the West, most WFM leaders embraced socialism and industrial unionism. In 1905, leaders of the WFM, the Socialist Party, and various radical groups gathered in Chicago to found the Industrial Workers of the World (IWW). The IWW charter proclaimed bluntly, "The working class and the employing class have nothing in common. . . . Between these two classes a struggle must go on until the workers of the world unite as a class, take possession of the earth and the machinery of production, and abolish the wage system."

William D. "Big Bill" Haywood, an imposing, one-eyed, hard-rock miner, emerged as the most influential and flamboyant spokesman for the IWW, or Wobblies, as they were called. Haywood, a charismatic speaker and effective organizer, regularly denounced the AFL for its conservative emphasis on organizing skilled workers by trade. He insisted that the IWW would exclude no one from its ranks. The Wobblies concentrated their efforts on miners, lumberjacks, sailors, "harvest stiffs," and other casual laborers.

The IWW briefly became a force among Eastern industrial workers, tapping the rage and growing militance of the immigrants and unskilled. In 1909, an IWW–led steel strike at McKees Rocks, Pennsylvania, challenged the power of U.S. Steel. In the 1912 "Bread and Roses" strike in Lawrence, Massachusetts, IWW organizers turned a spontaneous walkout of textile workers into a successful struggle for union recognition. Wobbly leaders such as Haywood, Elizabeth Gurley Flynn, and Joseph Ettor used class-conscious rhetoric and multilingual appeals to forge unity among the ethnically diverse Lawrence workforce of 25,000.

The IWW failed to establish permanent organizations in the Eastern cities, but it remained a force in the lumber camps, mines, and wheat fields of the West. In spite of its militant rhetoric, the IWW concerned itself with practical gains. "The final aim is revolution," said one Wobbly organizer, "but for the present let's see if we can get a bed to sleep in, water enough to take a bath in and decent food to eat." But when the United States entered World War I, the Justice Department used the IWW's anticapitalist rhetoric and antiwar stance to crush it.

Rebels in Bohemia

During the 1910s, a small but influential community of painters, journalists, poets, social workers, lawyers, and political activists coalesced in the New York City neighborhood of Greenwich Village. These cultural radicals, nearly all of middle-class background and hailing from

Publicity poster for the 1913 pageant, organized by John Reed and other Greenwich Village radicals, supporting the cause of striking silk workers in Paterson, New Jersey. This poster drew on aesthetic styles associated with the Industrial Workers of the World, typically including a heroic, larger-than-life image of a factory laborer.

SOURCE: The original Paterson Pageant Program, on which this drawing appeared, is part of the collection of the American Labor Museum/Botto House National Landmark. The poster is a copy of the program cover.

provincial American towns, shared a deep sympathy toward the struggles of labor, a passion for modern art, and an openness to socialism and anarchism. "Village bohemians," especially the women among them, challenged the double standard of Victorian sexual morality, rejected traditional marriage and sex roles, advocated birth control, and experimented with homosexual relations. They became a powerful national symbol for rebellion and the merger of political and cultural radicalism.

The term "bohemian" referred to anyone who had artistic or intellectual aspirations and who lived with disregard for conventional rules of behavior. Other American cities, notably Chicago at the turn of the cen-

tury, had supported bohemian communities. But the Village scene was unique, if fleeting. The neighborhood offered cheap rents, studio space, and good ethnic restaurants, and it was close to the exciting political and labor activism of Manhattan's Lower East Side. The worldview of the Village's bohemian community found expression in *The Masses*, a monthly magazine founded in 1911 by socialist critic Max Eastman, who was also its editor. "The broad purpose of *The Masses*," wrote John Reed, one of its leading writers, "is a social one—to everlastingly attack old systems, old morals, old prejudices—the whole weight of outworn thought that dead men have saddled upon us." Regular contributors included radical labor journalist Mary Heaton Vorse, artists John Sloan and George Bellows, and writers Floyd Dell and Sherwood Anderson.

For some, Greenwich Village offered a chance to experiment with sexual relationships or work arrangements. For others, it was an escape from small-town conformity, or a haven for like-minded artists and activists. Yet the Village bohemians were united in their search for a new sense of community. Intellectuals and artists, as well as workers, feeling alienated from the rest of society, sought shelter in the collective life and close-knit social relations of the Village community.

The Paterson, New Jersey, silk workers' strike of 1913 provided the most memorable fusion of bohemian sensibility and radical activism. After hearing Haywood speak about the strike at Mabel Dodge's apartment, John Reed offered to organize a pageant on the strikers' behalf at Madison Square Garden. The idea was to publicize the strike to the world and also raise money. The Villagers helped write a script, designed sets and scenery, and took care of publicity. A huge crowd watched more than a thousand workers reenact the silk workers' strike, complete with picket line songs, a funeral, and speeches by IWW organizers. The spectacular production was an artistic triumph but a financial disaster. The Village bohemia lasted only a few years, a flame snuffed out by the chill political winds accompanying America's entry into World War I. Yet for decades, Greenwich Village remained a mecca for young men and women searching for alternatives to conventional ways of living.

WOMEN'S MOVEMENTS AND BLACK AWAKENING

Progressive era women were at the forefront of several reform campaigns, such as the settlement house movement, prohibition, suffrage, and birth control. Millions of others took an active role in new women's associations that combined self-help and social mission. These organizations gave women a place in public life, increased their influence in civic affairs, and nurtured a new generation of female leaders.

In fighting racial discrimination, African Americans had a more difficult task. As racism gained ground in the political and cultural spheres, black progressives fought defensively to prevent the rights they had secured during Reconstruction from being further undermined. Still, they managed to produce leaders, ideas, and organizations that would have a long-range impact on American race relations.

The New Woman

The settlement house movement discussed in the opening of this chapter was just one of the new avenues of opportunity that opened to progressive-era women. A steady proliferation of women's organizations attracted growing numbers of educated, middle-class women in the early twentieth century. With more men working in offices, more children attending school, and family size declining, the middle-class home was emptier. At the same time, more middle-class women were graduating from high school and college. In 1870, only 1 percent of college-age Americans had attended college, about 20 percent of them women; by 1910, about 5 percent of college-age Americans attended college, but the proportion of women among them had doubled to 40 percent.

Single-sex clubs brought middle-class women into the public sphere by celebrating the distinctive strengths associated with women's culture: cooperation, uplift, service. The formation of the General Federation of Women's Clubs in 1890, brought together 200 local clubs representing 20,000 women. By 1900, the federation boasted 150,000 members, and by World War I, it claimed to represent over a million women. The women's club movement combined an earlier focus on self-improvement and intellectual pursuits with newer benevolent efforts on behalf of working women and children. The Buffalo Union, for example, sponsored art lectures for housewives, and classes in typing, stenography, and bookkeeping for young working women. It also maintained a library, set up a "noon rest" downtown where women could eat lunch, and ran a school for training domestics.

For many middle-class women, the club movement provided a new kind of female-centered community. Club activity often led members to participate in other civic ventures, particularly "child-saving" reforms, such as child labor laws and mothers' pensions. Some took up the cause of working-class women, fighting for protective legislation and offering aid to trade unions. As

wives and daughters of influential and well-off men in their communities, clubwomen had access to funds and could generate support for projects they undertook.

Other women's associations made even more explicit efforts to bridge class lines between middle-class homemakers and working-class women. The National Consumers' League (NCL), started in 1898 by Maud Nathan and Josephine Lowell, sponsored a "white label" campaign in which manufacturers who met safety and sanitary standards could put NCL labels on their food and clothing. Under the dynamic leadership of Florence Kelley, the NCL took an even more aggressive stance, by publicizing labor abuses in department stores and lobbying for maximum-hour and minimum-wage laws in state legislatures. In its efforts to protect home and housewife, worker and consumer, the NCL embodied the ideal of "social housekeeping."

Birth Control

The phrase "birth control," coined by Margaret Sanger around 1913, described her campaign to provide contraceptive information and devices for women. Sanger had seen her own mother die at age forty-nine after bearing eleven children. In 1910, Sanger was a thirty-year-old nurse and housewife living with her husband and three children in a New York City suburb. Excited by a socialist lecture she had attended, she convinced her husband to move to the city, where she threw herself into the bohemian milieu. She became an organizer for the IWW, and in 1912, she wrote a series of articles on female sexuality for a socialist newspaper.

A supportive crowd surrounds birth control pioneer Margaret Sanger and her sister, Ethel Byrne, as they leave the Court of Special Services in New York City in 1917. Police had recently closed Sanger's first birth control clinic in the immigrant neighborhood of Brownsville, New York and Sanger herself had spent a month in jail.
SOURCE: CORBIS-NY.

When postal officials confiscated the paper for violating obscenity laws, Sanger left for Europe to learn more about contraception. She returned to New York determined to challenge the obscenity statutes with her own magazine, the *Woman Rebel*. Sanger's journal celebrated female autonomy, including the right to sexual expression and control over one's body. When she distributed her pamphlet *Family Limitation*, postal inspectors confiscated copies and she found herself facing forty-five years in prison. In October 1914, she fled to Europe again. In her absence, anarchist agitator Emma Goldman and many women in the Socialist Party took up the cause.

An older generation of feminists had advocated "voluntary motherhood," or the right to say no to a husband's sexual demands. The new birth control advocates embraced contraception as a way of advancing sexual freedom for middle-class women, as well as responding to the misery of those working-class women who bore numerous children while living in poverty. Sanger returned to the United States in October 1915. After the government dropped the obscenity charges, she embarked on a national speaking tour. In 1916, she again defied the law by opening a birth control clinic in a working-class neighborhood in Brooklyn and offering birth control information without a physician present. Arrested and jailed, she gained more publicity for her crusade. Within a few years, birth control leagues and clinics could be found in every major city and most large towns in the country. (See Out of Many Voices "How Can One Control the Size of a Family?".)

OUT OF MANY VOICES

"HOW CAN ONE CONTROL THE SIZE OF A FAMILY?": LETTER TO MARGARET SANGER

As the leading advocate for birth control, Margaret Sanger received some 250,000 letters from American women anxious for her advice and help. Many of these letters included detailed descriptions of their family lives, health problems, and economic circumstances. Sanger later published a selection from this correspondence to help publicize the need for accessible and affordable birth control.

WHEN I WAS A GIRL MY MOTHER BEGGED ME NOT to marry, for she thought my freedom was the most precious thing in the world and she told me that after I was married I would have no holidays nor pastimes nor anything, only just baby after baby, and that when I didn't have one I would be worried to death expecting to become pregnant any time. But I was twenty-four years old; I had no special talent; and was not, I think, especially adapted to the work I was doing and I did not care to follow in the steps of other so-called "old maids" in our office; moreover I was in love and I have never regretted the step I took and the loss of my "freedom." My first baby was born eleven months after marriage. When my first baby was sixteen months old the second was born and died. He was a little "blue baby" and lived just three weeks and I believe that his heart was probably affected.

About three months after he was born I became pregnant again and I expect my third baby to be born in a few months and I have been married but a little more than three years. So far, I think I have no organic disease but ever since I became pregnant the second time I have been so lifeless with absolutely no pep or ambition and sometimes I am so weak that I can't lift my little son on to my lap to dress him. Besides this weakness I have no interest for anything. I can't concentrate my thoughts long enough to think of something that would be nice for supper tonight and I am always just this way. Then too, I have another great worry. I know my husband loves me but he likes recreation. Sometimes I think he is unusually restless and pleasure-loving. We used to visit other young couples and have them in for supper and cards and go to a show occasionally even up to the time for me to be confined, but this last year he never asks me to go with him anywhere and he goes out with some of the men almost every night. Besides I never feel like entertaining or dressing to go and I am always tired enough for bed by 9 o'clock. Of course, his pleasures are absolutely harmless now but I'm so afraid they will become more dangerous unless I can arouse myself and become more of a companion after the baby is born. And what chance have I? ∎

SOURCE: Margaret Sanger, *Motherhood in Bondage* (New York: Brentano's, 1928), 221–237.

Racism and Accommodation

At the turn of the century, four-fifths of the nation's 10 million African Americans still lived in the South, where most eked out a living working in agriculture. In the cities, most blacks were relegated to menial jobs, but a small African American middle class of entrepreneurs and professionals gained a foothold by selling services and products to the black community. They all confronted a racism that was growing in both intensity and influence in American politics and culture. White racism came in many variants and had evolved significantly since slavery days. The more virulent strains, influenced by Darwin's evolutionary theory, held that blacks were a "degenerate" race, genetically predisposed to vice, crime, and disease and destined to lose the struggle for existence with whites. By portraying blacks as incapable of improvement, racial Darwinism justified a policy of repression and neglect toward African Americans.

African Americans also endured a deeply racist popular culture that made hateful stereotypes of black people a normal feature of political debate and everyday life. Benjamin Tillman, a U.S. senator from South Carolina, denounced the African American as "a fiend, a wild beast, seeking whom he may devour." Thomas Dixon's popular novel *The Clansman* (1905) described the typical African American as "half child, half animal, the sport of impulse, whim, and conceit . . . a being who, left to his will, roams at night and sleeps in the day, whose speech knows no word of love, whose passions, once aroused, are as the fury of a tiger." In Northern cities "coon songs," based on gross caricatures of black life, were extremely popular in theaters and as sheet music. As in the antebellum minstrel shows, these songs reduced African Americans to creatures of pure appetite—for food, sex, alcohol, and violence.

Southern progressives articulated a more moderate racial philosophy. They also assumed the innate inferiority of blacks, but they believed that black progress was necessary to achieve the economic and political progress associated with a vision of the New South. Their solution to the "race problem" stressed paternalist uplift. Edgar Gardner Murphy, an Episcopal clergyman and leading Alabama progressive, held that African Americans need not be terrorized. The black man, Murphy asserted, "will accept in the white man's country the place assigned him by the white man, will do his work, not by stress of rivalry, but by genial cooperation with the white man's interests."

Amid this political and cultural climate, Booker T. Washington won recognition as the most influential black leader of the day. Born a slave in 1856, Washington was educated at Hampton Institute in Virginia, one of the first freedmen's schools devoted to industrial education. In 1881, he founded Tuskegee Institute, a black school in Alabama devoted to industrial and moral education. He became the leading spokesman for racial accommodation, urging blacks to focus on economic improvement and self-reliance, as opposed to political and civil rights. In an 1895 speech delivered at the Cotton States Exposition in Atlanta, Washington outlined the key themes of accommodationist philosophy. "Cast down your buckets where you are," Washington told black people, meaning they should focus on improving their vocational skills as industrial workers and farmers. "In all things that are purely social," he told attentive whites, "we can be as separate as the fingers, yet one as the hand in all things essential to mutual progress."

Washington's message won him the financial backing of leading white philanthropists and the respect of progressive whites. His widely read autobiography, *Up from Slavery* (1901), stands as a classic narrative of an American self-made man. Written with a shrewd eye toward cementing his support among white Americans, it stressed the importance of learning values such as frugality, cleanliness, and personal morality. But Washington also gained a large following among African Americans, especially those who aspired to business success. With the help of Andrew Carnegie, he founded the National Negro Business League to preach the virtue of black business development in black communities.

Washington also had a decisive influence on the flow of private funds to black schools in the South. Publicly he insisted that "agitation of questions of social equality is the extremest folly." But privately, Washington also spent money and worked behind the scenes trying to halt disfranchisement and segregation. He offered secret financial support, for example, for court cases that challenged Louisiana's grandfather clause, the exclusion of blacks from Alabama juries, and railroad segregation in Tennessee and Georgia.

Racial Justice, the NAACP, Black Women's Activism

Washington's focus on economic self-help remained deeply influential in African American communities long after his death in 1915. But alternative black voices challenged his racial philosophy while he lived. In the early 1900s, scholar and activist W. E. B. Du Bois created a significant alternative to Washington's leadership. A product of the black middle class, Du Bois had been educated at Fisk University and Harvard, where in 1895, he became the first African American to receive a Ph.D. His book *The Philadelphia Negro* (1899) was a pioneering work of social science that refuted racist stereotypes by, for example, discussing black contributions to that city's political life and describing the wide range of black business activity. In *The Souls of Black Folk* (1903), Du Bois declared prophetically that "the problem of the twentieth century is the problem of the color line." Through essays on black history,

In July 1905, a group of African American leaders met in Niagara Falls, Ontario, to protest legal segregation and the denial of civil rights to the nation's black population. This portrait was taken against a studio backdrop of the falls. In 1909, the leader of the Niagara movement, W. E. B. Du Bois (second from right, middle row) founded and edited *The Crisis,* the influential monthly journal of the National Association for the Advancement of Colored People.

SOURCE: Photographs and Print Division, Schomburg Center for Research in Black Culture, The New York Public Library, Astor, Lenox and Tilden Foundations.

culture, education, and politics, Du Bois explored the concept of "double consciousness." Black people, he argued, would always feel the tension between an African heritage and their desire to assimilate as Americans. *Souls* represented the first effort to embrace African American culture as a source of collective black strength and something worth preserving.

Du Bois criticized Booker T. Washington's philosophy for its acceptance of "the alleged inferiority of the Negro." The black community, he argued, must fight for the right to vote, for civic equality, and for higher education for the "talented tenth" of their youth. In 1905, Du Bois and editor William Monroe Trotter brought together a group of educated black men to oppose Washington's conciliatory views. Discrimination they encountered in Buffalo, New York, prompted the men to move

their meeting to Niagara Falls, Ontario. "Any discrimination based simply on race or color is barbarous," they declared. "Persistent manly agitation is the way to liberty." The Niagara movement protested legal segregation, the exclusion of blacks from labor unions, and the curtailment of voting and other civil rights.

The Niagara movement failed to generate much change. But in 1909, many of its members, led by Du Bois, attended a National Negro Conference held at the Henry Street Settlement in New York. The group included a number of white progressives sympathetic to the idea of challenging Washington's philosophy. A new, interracial organization emerged from this conference, the National Association for the Advancement of Colored People. Du Bois, the only black officer of the original NAACP, founded and edited the *Crisis,* the influential NAACP monthly journal. For the next several decades, the NAACP would lead struggles to overturn legal and economic barriers to equal opportunity.

The disfranchisement of black voters in the South severely curtailed African American political influence. In response, African American women created new strategies to challenge white supremacy and improve life in their communities. As Sallie Mial, a North Carolina Baptist home missionary told her male brethren, "We have a peculiar work to do. We can go where you cannot afford to go." Founded in 1900, the Women's Convention of the National Baptist Convention, the largest black denomination in the United States, offered African American women a new public space to pursue reform work and "racial uplift." They organized settlement houses and built playgrounds; they created day-care facilities and kindergartens; they campaigned for women's suffrage, temperance, and advances in public health. In effect, they transformed church missionary societies into quasi social service agencies. Using the motto "Lifting as We Climb," the National Association of Colored Women Clubs by 1914 boasted 50,000 members in 1,000 clubs nationwide.

NATIONAL PROGRESSIVISM

The progressive impulse had begun at local levels and percolated up. Progressive forces in both major political parties pushed older, entrenched elements to take a more aggressive stance on the reform issues of the day. Both Republican Theodore Roosevelt and Democrat Woodrow Wilson laid claim to the progressive mantle during their presidencies—a good example of how on the national level, progressivism animated many perspectives. In their pursuit of reform agendas, both significantly reshaped the office of the president. As progressivism moved to Washington, nationally organized interest groups and public opinion began to rival the influence of the old political parties in shaping the political landscape.

Theodore Roosevelt and Presidential Activism

The assassination of William McKinley in 1901 made forty-two-year-old Theodore Roosevelt the youngest man to ever hold the office of president. Born to a wealthy New York family in 1858, Roosevelt overcame a sickly childhood through strenuous physical exercise and rugged outdoor living. After graduating from Harvard, he immediately threw himself into a career in the rough and tumble of New York politics. He won election to the state assembly, ran an unsuccessful campaign for mayor of New York, served as president of the New York City Board of Police Commissioners, and went to Washington as assistant secretary of the navy. During the Spanish-American War, he won national fame as leader of the Rough Rider regiment in Cuba. Upon his return, he was elected governor of New York, and then in 1900, vice president. Roosevelt viewed the presidency as a "bully pulpit"—a platform from which he could exhort Americans to reform their society—and he aimed to make the most of it.

Roosevelt was a uniquely colorful figure, a shrewd publicist, and a creative politician. His three-year stint as a rancher in the Dakota Territory; his fondness for hunting and nature study; his passion for scholarship, which resulted in ten books before he became president—all these set "T. R." apart from most of his upper-class peers. Roosevelt preached the virtues of "the strenuous life," and he believed that educated and wealthy Americans had a special responsibility to serve, guide, and inspire those less fortunate.

In style, Roosevelt made key contributions to national progressivism. He knew how to inspire and guide public opinion. He stimulated discussion and aroused curiosity like no one before him. In 1902, Roosevelt demonstrated his unique style of activism when he personally intervened in a bitter strike by anthracite coal miners. Using public calls for conciliation, a series of White House bargaining sessions, and private pressure on the mine owners, Roosevelt secured a settlement that won better pay and working conditions for the miners, but without recognition of their union. Roosevelt also pushed for efficient government as the solution to social problems. Unlike most nineteenth-century Republicans, who had largely ignored economic and social inequalities, Roosevelt frankly acknowledged them. Administrative agencies run by experts, he believed, could find rational solutions that could satisfy everyone.

Trustbusting and Regulation

One of the first issues Roosevelt faced was growing public concern with the rapid business consolidations taking place in the American economy. In 1902, he directed the Justice Department to begin a series of prosecutions under the Sherman Antitrust Act. The first target was the Northern Securities Company, a huge merger of transcontinental railroads brought about by financier J. P. Morgan. The deal would have created a giant holding company controlling nearly all the long-distance rail lines from Chicago to California. The Justice Department fought the case all the way through a hearing before the Supreme Court. In *Northern Securities* v. *United States* (1904), the Court held that the stock transactions constituted an illegal combination in restraint of interstate commerce.

This case established Roosevelt's reputation as a "trust-buster." During his two terms, the Justice Department filed forty-three cases under the Sherman Antitrust Act to restrain or dissolve business monopolies. These included actions against the so-called tobacco and beef trusts and the Standard Oil Company. Roosevelt viewed these suits as necessary to publicize the issue and assert the federal government's ultimate authority over big business. But he did not really believe in the need to break up large corporations. Unlike many progressives, who were nostalgic for smaller companies and freer competition, Roosevelt accepted centralization as a fact of modern economic life and considered government regulation the best way to deal with big business.

After easily defeating Democrat Alton B. Parker in the 1904 election, Roosevelt felt more secure in pushing

This 1909 cartoon by Clifton Berryman depicts President Theodore Roosevelt slaying those trusts he considered "bad" for the public interest while restraining those whose business practices he considered "good" for the economy. The image also plays on TR's well-publicized fondness for big game hunting.

SOURCE: The Granger Collection, New York.

for regulatory legislation. In 1906, Roosevelt responded to public pressure for greater government intervention and, overcoming objections from a conservative Congress, signed three important measures into law. The Hepburn Act strengthened the Interstate Commerce Commission (ICC), established in 1887 as the first independent regulatory agency, by authorizing it to set maximum railroad rates and inspect financial records.

Two other laws passed in 1906 also expanded the regulatory power of the federal government. The battles surrounding these reforms demonstrate how progressive measures often attracted supporters with competing motives. The Pure Food and Drug Act established the Food and Drug Administration (FDA), which tested and approved drugs before they went on the market. The Meat Inspection Act (passed with help from the shocking publicity surrounding Upton Sinclair's muckraking novel, *The Jungle*) empowered the Department of Agriculture to inspect and label meat products. In both cases, supporters hailed the new laws as providing consumer protection against adulterated or fraudulently labeled food and drugs.

But regulatory legislation found advocates among American big business as well. Large meatpackers such as Swift and Armour strongly supported stricter federal regulation as a way to drive out smaller companies that could not meet tougher standards. The new laws also helped American packers compete more profitably in the European export market by giving their meat the official seal of federal inspectors. Large pharmaceutical manufacturers similarly supported new regulations that would eliminate competitors and patent medicine suppliers. Thus these reforms won support from large corporate interests that viewed stronger federal regulation as a strategy for consolidating their economic power. Progressive-era expansion of the nation-state had its champions among—and benefits for—big business as well as American consumers.

Conservation, Preservation, and the Environment

As a naturalist and outdoorsman, Theodore Roosevelt also believed in the need for government regulation of the natural environment. He worried about the destruction of forests, prairies, streams, and the wilderness. The conservation of forest and water resources, he argued, was a national problem of vital import. In 1905, he created the U.S. Forest Service and named conservationist Gifford Pinchot to head it. Pinchot recruited a force of forest rangers to manage the reserves. By 1909, total timber and forest reserves had increased from 45 to 195 million acres, and more than 80 million acres of mineral lands had been withdrawn from public sale.

On the broad issue of managing America's natural resources, the Roosevelt administration took the middle ground between preservation and unrestricted commercial development. "Wilderness is waste," Pinchot was fond of saying, reflecting an essentially utilitarian vision that balanced the demands of business with wilderness conservation. But other voices championed a more radical vision of conservation, emphasizing the preservation of wilderness lands against the encroachment of commercial exploitation. The most influential and committed of these was John Muir, an essayist and founder of the modern environmentalist movement. Muir made a passionate and spiritual defense of the inherent value of the American wilderness. Wild country, he argued, had a mystical power to inspire and refresh. "Climb the mountains and get their good tidings," he advised. "Nature's peace will flow into you as the sunshine into the trees. The winds will blow their freshness into you, and the storms their energy, while cares will drop off like autumn leaves." Muir served as first president of the Sierra Club, founded in 1892 to preserve and protect the mountain regions of the west coast as well as Yellowstone National Park in Wyoming, Montana, and Idaho.

William Robinson Leigh painted this landscape, *Grand Canyon 1911*, one of many Western scenes he created. Like many contemporaries, Leigh expressed his frustration with trying to capture the sublime in nature: "It challenges man's utmost skill; it mocks and defies his puny efforts to grasp and perpetuate, through art, its inimitable grandeur."

SOURCE: Leigh, William Robinson (1866-1955), *Grand Canyon*, 1911. Oil on canvas, 66" × 99". Collection of The Newark Museum, Newark, New Jersey, Gift of Henry Wallington Wack, 1930. Inv.: 30.203. © The Newark Museum / Art Resource, New York.

A bitter, drawn-out struggle over new water sources for San Francisco revealed the deep conflicts between conservationists, represented by Pinchot, and preservationists, represented by Muir. After a devastating earthquake in 1906, San Francisco sought federal approval to dam and flood the spectacular Hetch Hetchy Valley, located 150 miles from the city in Yosemite National Park. The project promised to ease the city's chronic freshwater shortage and to generate hydroelectric power. Conservationists and their urban progressive allies argued that developing Hetch Hetchy would be a victory for the public good over greedy private developers, since the plan called for municipal control of the water supply. To John Muir and the Sierra Club, Hetch Hetchy was a "temple" threatened with destruction by the "devotees of ravaging commercialism." Both sides lobbied furiously in Congress and wrote scores of articles in newspapers and magazines. Congress finally approved the reservoir plan in 1913; utility and public development triumphed over the preservation of nature. Although they lost the battle for Hetch Hetchy, the preservationists gained much ground in the larger campaign of alerting the nation to the dangers of a vanishing wilderness. They began to use their own utilitarian rationales, arguing that national parks would encourage economic growth through tourism and provide Americans with a healthy escape from urban and industrial areas. In 1916, the preservationists obtained their own bureaucracy in Washington with the creation of the National Park Service.

The Newlands Reclamation Act of 1902 represented another important victory for the conservation strategy of Roosevelt and Pinchot. With the goal of turning arid land into productive family farms through irrigation, the act established the Reclamation Bureau within the Department of the Interior and provided federal funding for dam and canal projects. But in practice, the bureau did more to encourage the growth of large-scale agribusiness and Western cities than small farming. The Roosevelt Dam on Arizona's Salt River, along with the forty-mile Arizona Canal, helped develop the Phoenix area. The Imperial Dam on the Colorado River diverted water to California's Imperial and Coachella Valleys. The Newlands Act thus established a growing federal presence in managing water resources, the critical issue in twentieth-century Western development.

Republican Split

By the end of his second term, Roosevelt had moved beyond the idea of regulation, to push for the most far-reaching federal economic and social programs ever proposed. He saw the central problem as "how to exercise . . . responsible control over the business use of vast wealth." To that end, he proposed restrictions on the use of court injunctions against labor strikes, as well as an eight-hour day for federal employees, a worker compensation law, and federal income and inheritance taxes.

In 1908, Roosevelt kept his promise to retire after a second term. He chose Secretary of War William Howard Taft as his successor. Taft easily defeated Democrat William Jennings Bryan in the 1908 election. During Taft's presidency, the gulf between "insurgent" progressives and the "stand pat" wing split the Republican Party wide open. To some degree, the battles were as much over style as substance. Compared with Roosevelt, the reflective and judicious Taft brought a much more restrained concept of the presidency to the White House. He supported some progressive measures, including the constitutional amendment legalizing a graduated income tax (ratified in 1913), safety codes for mines and railroads, and the creation of a federal Children's Bureau (1912). But in a series of bitter political fights involving tariff, antitrust, and conservation policies, Taft alienated Roosevelt and many other progressives.

After returning from an African safari and a triumphant European tour in 1910, Roosevelt threw himself back into national politics. He directly challenged Taft for the Republican Party leadership. In a dozen bitter state presidential primaries (the first ever held), Taft and Roosevelt fought for the nomination. Although Roosevelt won most of these contests, the old guard still controlled the national convention, and renominated Taft in June 1912. Roosevelt's supporters stormed out, and in August, the new Progressive Party nominated Roosevelt and Hiram Johnson of California as its presidential ticket. Roosevelt's "New Nationalism" presented a vision of a strong federal government, led by an activist president, regulating and protecting the various interests in American society. The platform called for woman suffrage, the eight-hour day, prohibition of child labor, minimum-wage standards for working women, and stricter regulation of large corporations.

The Election of 1912: A Four-Way Race

With the Republicans so badly divided, the Democrats sensed a chance for their first presidential victory in twenty years. They chose Governor Woodrow Wilson of New Jersey as their candidate. Although not nearly as well known nationally as Taft and Roosevelt, Wilson had built a strong reputation as a reformer. The son of a Virginia Presbyterian minister, Wilson spent most of his early career in academia. He studied law at the University of Virginia and then earned a Ph.D. in political science from Johns Hopkins. After teaching history and political science at several schools, he became president of Princeton University in 1902. In 1910, he won election as New Jersey's governor, running against the state Democratic machine. He won the Democratic nomination for president with the support of many of the party's progressives, including William Jennings Bryan (see Map 21.2).

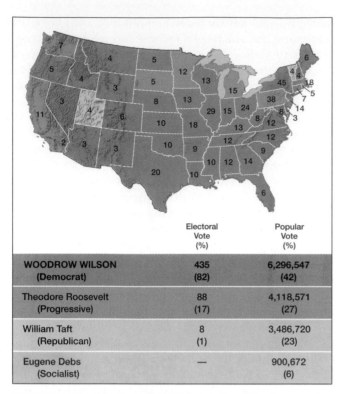

	Electoral Vote (%)	Popular Vote (%)
WOODROW WILSON (Democrat)	435 (82)	6,296,547 (42)
Theodore Roosevelt (Progressive)	88 (17)	4,118,571 (27)
William Taft (Republican)	8 (1)	3,486,720 (23)
Eugene Debs (Socialist)	—	900,672 (6)

MAP 21.2 The Election of 1912 The split within the Republican Party allowed Woodrow Wilson to become only the second Democrat since the Civil War to be elected president. Eugene Debs's vote was the highest ever polled by a Socialist candidate.

Wilson declared himself and the Democratic Party to be the true progressives. Viewing Roosevelt rather than Taft as his main rival, Wilson contrasted his New Freedom campaign with Roosevelt's New Nationalism. Crafted largely by progressive lawyer Louis Brandeis, Wilson's platform was far more ambiguous than Roosevelt's. The New Freedom emphasized restoring conditions of free competition and equality of economic opportunity. Wilson did favor a variety of progressive reforms for workers, farmers, and consumers. But in sounding older, nineteenth-century Democratic themes of states' rights and small government, Wilson argued against allowing the federal government to become as large and paternalistic as Roosevelt advocated. "What this country needs above everything else," Wilson argued, "is a body of laws which will look after the men who are on the make rather than the men who are already made."

Socialist party nominee Eugene V. Debs offered the fourth and most radical choice to voters. The Socialists had more than doubled their membership since 1908, to more than 100,000. On election days, Socialist strength was far greater than that, as the party's candidates attracted increasing numbers of voters. By 1912, more than a thousand Socialists held elective office in thirty-three states and

160 cities. Geographically, Socialist strength had shifted to the trans-Mississippi South and West.

An inspiring orator who drew large and sympathetic crowds wherever he spoke, Debs proved especially popular in areas with strong labor movements and populist traditions. He wrapped his socialist message in an apocalyptic vision. Socialists would "abolish this monstrous system and the misery and crime which flow from it." Debs and the Socialists also took credit for pushing both Roosevelt and Wilson farther toward the left. Both the Democratic and Progressive Party platforms contained proposals that had been considered extremely radical only ten years earlier.

In the end, the divisions in the Republican Party gave the election to Wilson. He won easily, polling 6.3 million votes to Roosevelt's 4.1 million. Taft came in third with 3.5 million. Eugene Debs won 900,000 votes, 6 percent of

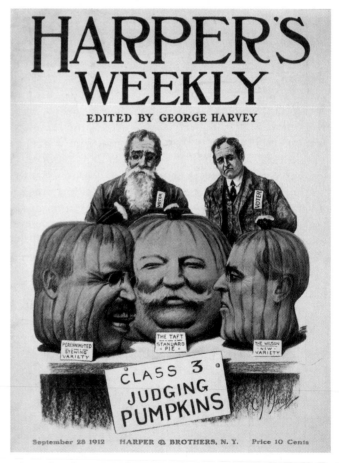

This political cartoon, drawn by Charles Jay Budd, appeared on the cover of *Harper's Weekly*, September 28, 1912. It employed the imagery of autumn county fairs to depict voters as unhappy with their three choices for president. Note that the artist did not include the fourth candidate, Socialist Eugene V. Debs, who was often ignored by more conservative publications such as *Harper's*.

SOURCE: Theodore Roosevelt Collection, Harvard College Library.

the total, for the strongest Socialist showing in American history. Even though he won with only 42 percent of the popular vote, Wilson swept the electoral college with 435 votes to Roosevelt's 88 and Taft's 8, giving him the largest electoral majority up to that time. In several respects, the election of 1912 was the first "modern" presidential race. It featured the first direct primaries, challenges to traditional party loyalties, an issue-oriented campaign, and a high degree of interest-group activity.

Woodrow Wilson's First Term

As president, Wilson followed Roosevelt's lead in expanding the activist dimensions of the office. He became more responsive to pressure for a greater federal role in regulating business and the economy. This increase in direct lobbying—from hundreds of local and national reform groups, Washington-based organizations, and the new Progressive Party—was itself a new and defining feature of the era's political life. With the help of a Democratic-controlled Congress, Wilson pushed through a significant battery of reform proposals.

The Underwood-Simmons Act of 1913 substantially reduced tariff duties on a variety of raw materials and manufactured goods, including wool, sugar, agricultural machinery, shoes, iron, and steel. Taking advantage of the newly ratified Sixteenth Amendment, which gave Congress the power to levy taxes on income, it also imposed the first graduated tax (up to 6 percent) on personal incomes. The Federal Reserve Act that same year restructured the nation's banking and currency system. It created twelve Federal Reserve Banks, regulated by a central board in Washington. Member banks were required to keep a portion of their cash reserves in the Federal Reserve Bank of their district. By raising or lowering the percentage of reserves required, "the Fed" could either discourage or encourage credit expansion by member banks. Varying the interest rate charged on loans and advances by Federal Reserve Banks to member banks also helped regulate both the quantity and cost of money circulating in the national economy. By giving central direction to banking and monetary policy, the Federal Reserve Board diminished the power of large private banks.

Wilson also supported the Clayton Antitrust Act of 1914, which replaced the old Sherman Act of 1890 as the nation's basic antitrust law. The Clayton Act reflected the growing political clout of the American Federation of Labor. It exempted unions from being construed as illegal combinations in restraint of trade, and it forbade federal courts from issuing injunctions against strikers. But Wilson adopted the view that permanent federal regulation was necessary for checking the abuses of big business. The Federal Trade Commission (FTC), established in 1914, sought to give the federal government the same sort of regulatory control over corporations that the ICC had over railroads. Wil-

son believed a permanent federal body like the FTC would provide a method for corporate oversight superior to the erratic and time-consuming process of legal trustbusting. Wilson's hope that the FTC would usher in an era of harmony between government and business recalled the aims of Roosevelt and his big business backers in 1912.

On social issues, Wilson proved more cautious in his first two years. His initial failure to support federal child labor legislation and rural credits to farmers angered many progressives. A Southerner, Wilson also sanctioned the spread of racial segregation in federal offices. As the reelection campaign of 1916 approached, Wilson worried about defections from the labor and social justice wings of his party. He proceeded to support a rural credits act providing government capital to federal farm banks, as well as federal aid to agricultural extension programs in schools. He also came out in favor of a worker compensation bill for federal employees, and he signed the landmark Keating-Owen Act, which banned children under fourteen from working in enterprises engaged in interstate commerce. Although it covered less than 10 percent of the nation's 2 million working children, the new law established a minimum standard of protection, and put the power of federal authority behind the principle of regulating child labor. But by 1916, the dark cloud of war in Europe had already begun to cast its long shadow over progressive reform.

CONCLUSION

The American political and social landscape was significantly altered by progressivism, but these shifts reflected the tensions and ambiguities of progressivism itself. A review of changes in election laws offers a good perspective on the inconsistencies that characterized progressivism. Nearly every new election law had the effect of excluding some people from voting, while including others. For African Americans, progressivism largely meant disfranchisement from voting altogether. Direct primary laws eliminated some of the most blatant abuses of big-city machines, but in cities and states dominated by one party, the majority party's primary effectively decided the general election. Stricter election laws made it more difficult for third parties to get on the ballot, another instance in which progressive reform had the effect of reducing political options available to voters. Voting itself steadily declined in these years.

Overall, party voting became a less important form of political participation. Interest-group activity, congressional and statehouse lobbying, and direct appeals to public opinion gained currency as ways of influencing government. Business groups and individual trade associations were among the most active groups pressing their demands on government. Political action often shifted from legislatures to the new administrative agencies and commissions created

CHRONOLOGY

1889	Jane Addams founds Hull House in Chicago
1890	Jacob Riis publishes *How the Other Half Lives*
1895	Booker T. Washington addresses Cotton States Exposition in Atlanta, emphasizing an accommodationist philosophy
	Lillian Wald establishes Henry Street Settlement in New York
1898	Florence Kelley becomes general secretary of the new National Consumers' League
1900	Robert M. La Follette elected governor of Wisconsin
1901	Theodore Roosevelt succeeds the assassinated William McKinley as president
1904	Lincoln Steffens publishes *The Shame of the Cities*
1905	President Roosevelt creates U.S. Forest Service and names Gifford Pinchot head
	Industrial Workers of the World is founded in Chicago
1906	Upton Sinclair's *The Jungle* exposes conditions in the meatpacking industry
	Congress passes Pure Food and Drug Act and Meat Inspection Act and establishes Food and Drug Administration
1908	In *Muller* v. *Oregon* the Supreme Court upholds a state law limiting maximum hours for working women

1909	Uprising of 20,000 garment workers in New York City's garment industries helps organize unskilled workers into unions
	National Association for the Advancement of Colored People (NAACP) is founded
1911	Triangle Shirtwaist Company fire kills 146 garment workers in New York City
	Socialist critic Max Eastman begins publishing *The Masses*
1912	Democrat Woodrow Wilson wins presidency, defeating Republican William H. Taft, Progressive Theodore Roosevelt, and Socialist Eugene V. Debs
	Bread and Roses strike involves 25,000 textile workers in Lawrence, Massachusetts
	Margaret Sanger begins writing and speaking in support of birth control for women
1913	Sixteenth Amendment, legalizing a graduated income tax, is ratified
1914	Clayton Antitrust Act exempts unions from being construed as illegal combinations in restraint of trade
	Federal Trade Commission is established
	Ludlow Massacre occurs
1916	National Park Service is established

to deal with social and economic problems. Popular magazines and journals grew significantly in both number and circulation, becoming more influential in shaping and appealing to national public opinion.

Social progressives and their allies could point to significant improvements in the everyday lives of ordinary Americans. On the state level, real advances had been made through a range of social legislation covering working conditions, child labor, minimum wages, and worker compensation. Social progressives, too, had discovered the power of organizing into extraparty lobbying groups, such as the National Consumers' League and the National American Woman Suffrage Association. Yet the tensions between fighting for social justice and the

urge toward social control remained unresolved. The emphasis on efficiency, uplift, and rational administration often collided with humane impulses to aid the poor, the immigrant, the slum dweller. The large majority of African Americans, blue-collar workers, and urban poor remained untouched by federal assistance programs.

Progressives had tried to confront the new realities of urban and industrial society. What had begun as a discrete collection of local and state struggles, had by 1912 come to reshape state and national politics. Politics itself had been transformed by the calls for social justice. Federal and state power would now play a more decisive role than ever in shaping work, play, and social life in local communities.

REVIEW QUESTIONS

1. Discuss the tensions within progressivism between the ideals of social justice and the urge for social control. What concrete achievements are associated with each wing of the movement? What were the driving forces behind them?

2. Describe the different manifestations of progressivism at the local, state, and national levels. To what extent did progressives redefine the role of the state in American politics?

3. What gains were made by working-class communities in the progressive era? What barriers did they face?

4. How did the era's new immigration reshape America's cities and workplaces? What connections can you draw between the new immigrant experience and progressive era politics?

5. Analyze the progressive era from the perspective of African Americans. What political and social developments were most crucial, and what legacies did they leave?

6. Evaluate the lasting impact of progressive reform. How do the goals, methods, and language of progressives still find voice in contemporary America?

RECOMMENDED READING

James Chace, *1912: Wilson, Roosevelt, Taft & Debs—The Election that Changed the Country* (2004). Narrative account of this pivotal presidential election that revolved around competing visions of progressivism.

Alan Dawley, *Struggles for Justice: Social Responsibility and the Liberal State* (1991). Offers an important interpretation of progressivism that focuses on how the working class and women pushed the state toward a more activist role in confronting social problems.

Maureen Flanagan, *Seeing With Their Hearts: Chicago Women and the Vision of the Good City, 1871–1933* (2002). Examines how Progressive-era activist women drew upon traditions of maternalism, motherhood, and social housekeeping to create alternative models for both the modern city and a more equitable society.

Morton Keller, *Regulating a New Society: Public Policy and Social Change in America, 1900–1930* (1994). A comprehensive study of public policymaking on local and national levels in early twentieth-century America.

Arthur Link and Richard L. McCormick, *Progressivism* (1983). The best overview of progressivism and electoral politics.

Michael McGerr, *A Fierce Discontent: The Rise and Fall of the Progressive Movement in America, 1870–1920* (2003). A new synthesis arguing that the heart of Progressivism lay in the efforts of the urban middle class to reshape the behavior of both the poor and the wealthy.

Michael Perman, *Struggle for Mastery: Disfranchisement in the South, 1888–1908* (2001). A comprehensive, state-by-state overview of the campaigns to remove African Americans from the electoral process.

Daniel T. Rodgers, *Atlantic Crossings: Social Politics in a Progressive Age* (1998). A magisterial work of comparative history focusing on the transnational conversations that deeply influenced American progressive thinkers and reformers.

Elizabeth Sanders, *Roots of Reform: Farmers, Workers, and the American State, 1877–1917* (1999). Arguing for the centrality of agrarian movements in shaping progressive era reform, Sanders explores the irony of how these efforts led to an increasingly bureaucratic state.

Christine Stansell, *American Moderns: Bohemian New York and the Creation of a New Century* (2000). Vividly written account that places radical politics and "New Women" at the center of the shaping of modernism.

For additional study resources for this chapter, go to the *Companion Website*, **http://www.prenhall.com/faragher**.

World War I

1914–1920

Vigilante Justice in Bisbee, Arizona

Early in the morning of July 12, 1917, 2,000 armed vigilantes swept through Bisbee, Arizona, acting on behalf of the Phelps-Dodge mining company and Bisbee's leading businessmen to break a bitter strike that had crippled Bisbee's booming copper industry. The vigilantes seized miners in their homes, on the street, and in restaurants and stores. Any miner who wasn't working or willing to work was herded into Bisbee's downtown plaza, where two machine guns commanded the scene. From the Plaza, more than 2,000 were marched to the local baseball park. There, mine managers gave them a last chance to return to work. Hundreds accepted and were released. The remaining 1,400 were forced at gunpoint onto a freight train, which took them 173 miles east to Columbus, New Mexico, where they were dumped in the desert.

The Bisbee deportation occurred against a complex backdrop. America had just entered World War I, corporations were seeking higher profits, and labor militancy was on the rise. Bisbee was only one of many American communities to suffer vigilantism during the war. Any number of offenses—not displaying a flag, failing to buy war bonds, criticizing the draft, alleged spying, any apparently "disloyal" behavior—could trigger vigilante action. In Western communities like Bisbee, vigilantes used the superpatriotic mood to settle scores with labor organizers and radicals.

Arizona was the leading producer of copper in the United States. With a population of 8,000, Bisbee lay in the heart of the state's richest mining district. The giant Phelps-Dodge Company dominated Bisbee's political and social life. It owned the town's hospital, department store, newspaper, library, and largest hotel. With the introduction of new technology and open pit mining after 1900, unskilled laborers—most of them Slavic, Italian, Czech, and Mexican immigrants—had increasingly replaced skilled American and English-born miners in Bisbee's workforce.

America's entry into the war pushed the price of copper to an all-time high, prompting Phelps-Dodge to increase production. Miners viewed the increased demand for labor as an opportunity to flex their own muscle and improve wages and working conditions. Two rival union locals, one affiliated with the American Federation of Labor (AFL), the other with the more radical Industrial Workers of the World (IWW), or "Wobblies," sought to organize Bisbee's workers. On June 26, 1917, Bisbee's Wobblies went on strike. They demanded better mine safety, an end to discrimination against union workers, and a substantial pay increase. The IWW, making special efforts to attract lower-paid, foreign-born workers to their cause, even hired two Mexican organizers. Although the IWW had only 300 or 400 members in Bisbee, more than half the town's 4,700 miners supported the strike.

The walkout was peaceful, but Walter Douglas, district manager for Phelps-Dodge, was unmoved. "There will be no compromise," he declared, "because you cannot compromise with a rattlesnake." Douglas, Cochise County Sheriff Harry Wheeler, and Bisbee's leading businessmen met secretly to plan the July 12 deportation. The approximately 2,000 men they deputized to carry it out were members of Bisbee's Citizens' Protective League and the Workers Loyalty League. These vigilantes included company officials, small businessmen, professionals, and antiunion workers. Local telephone and telegraph offices

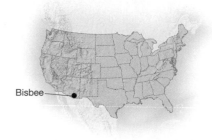

Bisbee

agreed to isolate Bisbee by censoring outgoing messages. The El Paso and Southwestern Railroad, a subsidiary of Phelps-Dodge, provided the waiting boxcars.

The participants in this illegal conspiracy defended themselves by exaggerating the threat of organized labor. They also appealed to patriotism and played on racial fears. The IWW opposed American involvement in the war, making it vulnerable to charges of disloyalty. A proclamation, posted in Bisbee the day of the deportation, claimed, "There is no labor trouble—we are sure of that—but a direct attempt to embarrass and injure the government of the United States." Sheriff Wheeler told a visiting journalist he worried that Mexicans "would take advantage of the disturbed conditions of the strike and start an uprising, destroying the mines and murdering American women and children."

An army census of the deportees, who had found temporary refuge at an army camp in Columbus, New Mexico, offered quite a different picture. Of the 1,400 men, 520 owned property in Bisbee. Nearly 500 had already registered for the draft, and more than 200 had purchased Liberty Bonds. More than 400 were married with children; only 400 were members of the IWW. Eighty percent were immigrants, including nearly 400 Mexicans. A presidential mediation committee concluded that "conditions in Bisbee were in fact peaceful and free from manifestations of disorder or violence." The deported miners nonetheless found it difficult to shake the accusations that their strike was anti-American and foreign inspired.

At their camp, the miners organized their own police force and elected an executive committee to seek relief. The presidential mediation committee criticized the mine companies and declared the deportation illegal. But it also denied that the federal government had any juris-diction in the matter. Arizona's attorney general refused to offer protection for a return to Bisbee.

In September, the men began gradually to drift away from Columbus. Only a few ever returned to Bisbee. The events convinced President Wilson that the IWW was a subversive organization and a threat to national security. The Justice Department began planning an all-out legal assault that would soon cripple the Wobblies. But Wilson could not ignore protests against the Bisbee outrage from such prominent and patriotic Americans as Samuel Gompers, head of the American Federation of Labor. To demonstrate his administration's commitment to harmonious industrial relations, the president appointed a special commission to investigate and mediate wartime labor conflicts. But Arizona's mines would remain union free until the New Deal era of the 1930s.

The labor struggle in Bisbee, Arizona reflected the new tensions of a nation at war. Labor shortages brought on by wartime production proved a boon for organized labor. But wartime patriotism also provided cover for business and conservative groups to aggressively attack labor and radical groups in the courts and in the streets. Most Progressive activists would turn their attention away from reform projects and toward the task of mobilizing a society for battle, as the federal government expanded its influence enormously. Yet some longtime Progressive causes, like Prohibition and woman suffrage, were finally enacted into law under the banner of wartime necessity. A booming economy attracted millions of rural African American migrants to the cities, where their new presence triggered a wave of racist repression. Although the United States spent only about a year and a half in the fighting, the upheavals brought on by the Great War would be felt for decades to come.

KEY TOPICS

- America's expanding international role
- From neutrality to participation in the Great War
- Mobilizing the society and the economy for war
- Dissent and its repression
- Woodrow Wilson's failure to win the peace

BECOMING A WORLD POWER

In the first years of the new century, the United States pursued a more vigorous and aggressive foreign policy than it had in the past. Presidents Theodore Roosevelt, William Howard Taft, and Woodrow Wilson all contributed to "progressive diplomacy," in which commercial expansion was backed by a growing military presence in the Caribbean, Asia, and Mexico. This policy reflected a view of world affairs that stressed moralism, order, and a special, even God-given, role for the United States. By 1917, when the United States entered the Great War, this policy had already secured the country a place as a new world power.

Roosevelt: The Big Stick

Theodore Roosevelt left a strong imprint on the nation's foreign policy. Like many of his class and background, "T.R." took for granted the superiority of Protestant Anglo-American culture and the goal of spreading its values and influence. He believed that to maintain and increase its economic and political stature, America must be militarily strong. In 1900, Roosevelt summarized his activist views, declaring, "I have always been fond of the West African proverb, 'Speak softly and carry a big stick, you will go far.'"

Roosevelt brought the "big stick" approach to several disputes in the Caribbean region. Since the 1880s, several British, French, and American companies had pursued various plans for building a canal across the Isthmus of Panama, thereby connecting the Atlantic and Pacific Oceans. The canal was a top priority for Roosevelt, and he tried to negotiate a leasing agreement with Colombia, of which Panama was a province. But when the Colombian Senate rejected a final American offer in the fall of 1903, Roosevelt invented a new strategy. A combination of native forces and foreign promoters associated with the canal project plotted a revolt against Colombia. Roosevelt kept in touch with at least

THE WORLD'S CONSTABLE.

This 1905 cartoon portraying President Theodore Roosevelt, "The World's Constable," appeared in *Judge* magazine. In depicting the president as a strong but benevolent policeman bringing order in a contentious world, the artist Louis Dalrymple drew on familiar imagery from Roosevelt's earlier days as a New York City police commissioner.

SOURCE: The Granger Collection.

one leader of the revolt, Philippe Bunau-Varilla, an engineer and agent for the New Panama Canal Company, and the president let him know that U.S. warships were steaming toward Panama.

On November 3, 1903, just as the USS *Nashville* arrived in Colón harbor, the province of Panama declared itself independent of Colombia. The United States immediately recognized the new Republic of Panama. Less than two weeks later, Bunau-Varilla, serving as a minister from Panama, signed a treaty granting the United States full sovereignty in perpetuity over a ten-mile-wide canal zone. America guaranteed Panama's independence and agreed to pay it $10 million initially and an additional $250,000 a year for the canal zone. Years after the canal was completed, the U.S. Senate voted another $25 million to Colombia as compensation.

The Panama Canal was a triumph of modern engineering and gave the United States a tremendous strategic and commercial advantage in the Western Hemisphere. It took eight years to build and cost hundreds of poorly paid manual workers their lives. Several earlier attempts to build a canal in the region had failed. But with better equipment and a vigorous campaign against disease, the United States succeeded. In 1914, after $720 million in construction costs, the first merchant ships sailed through the canal.

"The inevitable effect of our building the Canal," wrote Secretary of State Elihu Root in 1905, "must be to require us to police the surrounding premises." Roosevelt agreed. He was especially concerned that European powers might step in if America did not. In 1903, Great Britain, Germany, and Italy had imposed a blockade on Venezuela in a dispute over debt payments owed to private investors. To prevent armed intervention by the Europeans, Roosevelt in 1904, proclaimed what became known as the Roosevelt Corollary to the Monroe Doctrine. "Chronic wrongdoing, or an impotence which results in a general loosening of the ties of civilized society," the statement read, justified "the exercise of an international police power" anywhere in the hemisphere. Roosevelt invoked the corollary to justify U.S. intervention in the region, beginning with the Dominican Republic in 1905. To counter the protests of European creditors (and the implied threat of armed intervention), Washington assumed management of the Dominican debt and customs services. Roosevelt and later presidents cited the corollary to justify armed intervention in the internal affairs of Cuba, Haiti, Nicaragua, and Mexico.

With the outbreak of the Russo-Japanese War in 1904, Roosevelt worried about the future of the Open Door policy in Asia. In 1899, in a series of diplomatic notes, Secretary of State John Hay had won approval for the so-called Open Door approach, giving all nations equal access to trading and development rights in China. A total victory by Russia or Japan could upset the balance of power in East Asia and threaten American business enterprises there. He became especially concerned after the Japanese scored a series of military victories over Russia and began to loom as a dominant power in East Asia.

Roosevelt mediated a settlement of the Russo-Japanese War at Portsmouth, New Hampshire, in 1905 (for which he was awarded the 1906 Nobel Peace Prize). In this settlement, Japan won recognition of its dominant position in Korea and consolidated its economic control over Manchuria. Yet repeated incidents of anti-Japanese racism in California kept American-Japanese relations strained. In 1906, for example, the San Francisco school board, responding to nativist fears of a "yellow peril," ordered the segregation of Japanese, Chinese, and Korean students. Japan angrily protested. In 1907, in the so-called gentlemen's agreement, Japan agreed not to issue passports to Japanese male laborers looking to emigrate to the United States, and Roosevelt promised to fight anti-Japanese discrimination. He then persuaded the San Francisco school board to exempt Japanese students from the segregation ordinance.

But Roosevelt did not want these conciliatory moves to be interpreted as weakness. He thus built up American naval strength in the Pacific, and in 1908, he sent battleships to visit Japan in a muscle-flexing display of sea power. In that same year, the two burgeoning Pacific powers reached a reconciliation. The Root-Takahira Agreement affirmed the "existing status quo" in Asia, mutual respect for territorial possessions in the Pacific, and the Open Door trade policy in China. From the Japanese perspective, the agreement recognized Japan's colonial dominance in Korea and southern Manchuria.

Taft: Dollar Diplomacy

Roosevelt's successor, William Howard Taft, believed he could replace the militarism of the big stick with the more subtle and effective weapon of business investment. Taft and his secretary of state, corporate lawyer Philander C. Knox, followed a strategy (called "dollar diplomacy" by critics) in which they assumed that political influence would follow increased U.S. trade and investment. As Taft explained in 1910, he advocated "active intervention to secure for our merchandise and our capitalists opportunity for profitable investment."

Overall American investment in Central America grew rapidly, from $41 million in 1908 to $93 million by 1914. Most of this money went into railroad construction, mining, and plantations. The United Fruit Company alone owned about 160,000 acres of land in the Caribbean by 1913. But dollar diplomacy ended up requiring military support. The Taft administration sent the navy and the marines to intervene in political disputes in Honduras and Nicaragua, propping up factions pledged to protect American business interests. A contingent of

U.S. Marines remained in Nicaragua until 1933. The economic and political structures of Honduras and Nicaragua were controlled by both the dollar and the bullet (see Map 22.1).

In China, Taft and Knox pressed for a greater share of the pie for U.S. investors. They gained a place for U.S. bankers in the European consortium, building the massive new Hu-kuang Railway in southern and central China. But Knox blundered by attempting to "neutralize" the existing railroads in China. He tried to secure a huge international loan for the Chinese government that would allow it to buy up all the foreign railways and develop new ones. Both Russia and Japan, which had fought wars over their railroad interests in Manchuria, resisted this plan as a threat to the arrangements hammered out at Portsmouth with the help of Theodore

MAP EXPLORATION

To explore an interactive version of this map, go to **www.prenhall.com/faragher5/map22.1**

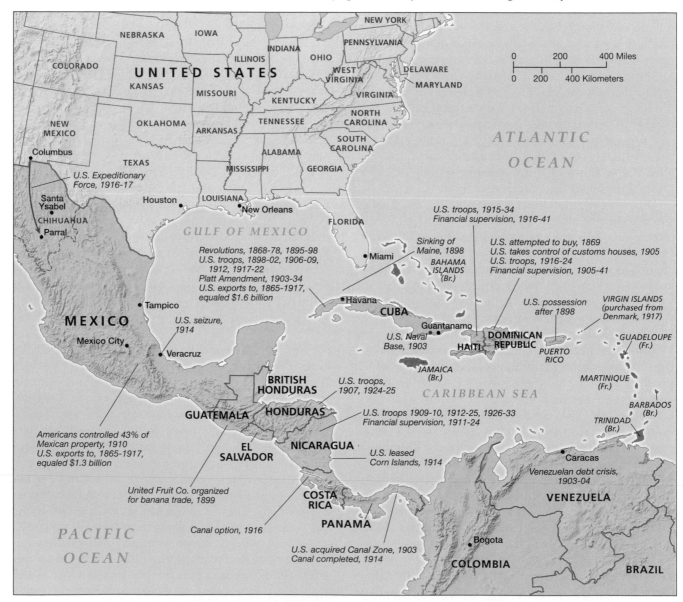

MAP 22.1 The United States in the Caribbean, 1865–1933 An overview of U.S. economic and military involvement in the Caribbean during the late nineteenth and early twentieth centuries. Victory in the Spanish-American War, the Panama Canal project, and rapid economic investment in Mexico and Cuba all contributed to a permanent and growing U.S. military presence in the region.

Roosevelt. Knox's "neutralization" scheme, combined with U.S. support for the Chinese Nationalists in their 1911 revolt against the ruling Manchu dynasty, prompted Japan to sign a new friendship treaty with Russia. The Open Door to China was now effectively closed, and American relations with Japan began a slow deterioration that ended in war thirty years later.

Wilson: Moralism and Realism in Mexico

Right after he took office in 1913, President Woodrow Wilson observed that "it would be the irony of fate if my administration had to deal chiefly with foreign affairs." His political life up to then had centered on achieving progressive reforms in the domestic arena. As it turned out, Wilson had to face international crises from his first day in office. These were of a scope and complexity unprecedented in U.S. history. Wilson had no experience in diplomacy, but he brought to foreign affairs a set of fundamental principles that combined a moralist's faith in American democracy with a realist's understanding of the power of international commerce. He believed that American economic expansion, accompanied by democratic principles and Christianity, was a civilizing force in the world.

Wilson, like most corporate and political leaders of the day, emphasized foreign investments and industrial exports as the keys to the nation's prosperity. He believed that the United States, with its superior industrial efficiency, could achieve supremacy in world commerce if artificial barriers to free trade were removed. He championed and extended the Open Door principles of John Hay, advocating strong diplomatic and military measures "for making ourselves supreme in the world from an economic point of view." Wilson often couched his vision of a dynamic, expansive American capitalism in terms of a moral crusade. As he put it in a speech to a congress of salesmen, "[Since] you are Americans and are meant to carry liberty and justice and the principles of humanity wherever you go, go out and sell goods that will make the world more comfortable and more happy, and convert them to the principles of America." Yet he quickly found that the complex realities of power politics could interfere with moral vision.

Wilson's policies toward Mexico, which foreshadowed the problems he would encounter in World War I, best illustrate his difficulties. The 1911 Mexican Revolution had overthrown the brutally corrupt dictatorship of Porfirio Díaz, and popular leader Francisco Madero had won wide support by promising democracy and economic reform for millions of landless peasants. But the U.S. business community was nervous about the future of its investments which, in the previous generation, had come to dominate the Mexican economy. By 1910, American companies owned over one-quarter—130 million acres—of Mexico's land, including over half of its coastlines and

This 1914 political cartoon comments approvingly on the interventionist role adopted by the United States in Latin American countries. By depicting President Woodrow Wilson as a schoolteacher giving lessons to children, the image captures the paternalistic views that American policy makers held toward nations like Mexico, Venezuela, and Nicaragua.

SOURCE: The Granger Collection, New York.

border areas. A handful of American mining companies had led the way in exploiting Mexican natural resources, using high capitalization, advanced technology, and sophisticated marketing networks to win control of roughly four-fifths of the gold, silver, and copper extracted from Mexican mines. Similar patterns developed in the timber and petroleum sectors, and Mexican capitalists owned very little of the nation's export industries. Meanwhile, in Mexican industrial communities such as Tampico—transformed into an overcrowded and badly polluted boomtown by the expanding oil industry— virtually all Mexican workers were relegated to unskilled and badly paying jobs.

Wilson at first gave his blessing to the revolutionary movement, expressed regret over the Mexican-American War of 1846–48, and disavowed any interest in another war. But right before he took office, Wilson was stunned by the ousting and murder of Madero by his chief lieutenant, General Victoriano Huerta. Other nations, including Great Britain and Japan, recognized the Huerta regime, but Wilson refused. He announced that the United States would support only governments that rested on the rule of law. An armed faction opposed to Huerta, known as the Constitutionalists and led by Venustiano Carranza, emerged in northern Mexico. Both sides rejected an effort by Wilson to broker a compromise between them. Carranza, an ardent nationalist, pressed for the right to buy U.S. arms, which he won in 1914. Wilson also isolated Huerta diplomatically by persuading the British to withdraw their support in exchange for American guarantees of English property interests in Mexico.

But Huerta stubbornly remained in power. In April 1914, Wilson used a minor insult to U.S. sailors in Tampico as an excuse to invade. American naval forces bombarded and then occupied Veracruz, the main port through which Huerta received arms shipments. Nineteen Americans and 126 Mexicans died in the battle, which brought the United States and Mexico close to war, and provoked anti-American demonstrations in Mexico and throughout Latin America. Wilson accepted the offer of the ABC Powers—Argentina, Brazil, and Chile—to mediate the dispute. Huerta rejected a plan for him to step aside in favor of a provisional government. But then in August, Carranza managed to overthrow Huerta. Playing to nationalist sentiment, Carranza too denounced Wilson for his intervention.

As war loomed in Europe, Mexico's revolutionary politics continued to frustrate Wilson. For a brief period, Wilson threw his support behind Francisco "Pancho" Villa, Carranza's former ally, who now led a rebel army of his own in northern Mexico. But Carranza's forces dealt Villa a major setback in April 1915. In October, its attention focused on the war in Europe, the Wilson administration recognized Carranza as Mexico's de facto president. Meanwhile, Pancho Villa, feeling betrayed, turned on the United States and tried to provoke a crisis that might draw Washington into war with Mexico. In 1916, Villa led several raids in Mexico and across the border into the United States that killed a few dozen Americans. The man once viewed by Wilson as a fighter for democracy was now dismissed as a dangerous bandit.

In March 1916, enraged by Villa's defiance, Wilson dispatched General John J. Pershing and an army that eventually numbered 15,000 to capture him. For a year, Pershing's troops chased Villa in vain, penetrating 300 miles into Mexico. The invasion made Villa a symbol of national resistance in Mexico, and his army grew from 500 men to 10,000 by the end of 1916. Villa's effective hit-and-run guerrilla tactics kept the U.S. forces at bay. A frustrated General Pershing complained that he felt "just a little bit like a man looking for a needle in a haystack." He urged the U.S. government to occupy the northern Mexican state of Chihuahua and later called for the occupation of the entire country.

Skirmishes between American forces and Carranza's army brought the two nations to the brink of war again in June 1916. Wilson prepared a message to Congress asking permission for American troops to occupy all of northern Mexico. But he never delivered it. There was fierce opposition to war with Mexico throughout the country. Perhaps more important, mounting tensions with Germany caused Wilson to hesitate. He told an aide that "Germany is anxious to have us at war with Mexico, so that our minds and our energies will be taken off the great war across the sea." Wilson thus accepted negotiations by a face-saving international commission.

Wilson's attempt to guide the course of Mexico's revolution and protect U.S. interests left a bitter legacy of suspicion and distrust in Mexico. It also suggested the limits of a foreign policy tied to a moral vision rooted in the idea of American exceptionalism. Militarism and imperialism, Wilson had believed, were hallmarks of the old European way. American liberal values—rooted in capitalist development, democracy, and free trade—were the wave of the future. Wilson believed the United States could lead the world in establishing a new international system based on peaceful commerce and political stability. In both the 1914 invasion and the 1916 punitive expedition, Wilson declared that he had no desire to interfere with Mexican sovereignty. But in both cases, that is exactly what he did. The United States, he argued, must actively use its enormous moral and material power to create the new order. That principle would soon engage America in Europe's bloodiest war and its most momentous revolution.

THE GREAT WAR

World War I, or the Great War, as it was originally called, took an enormous human toll on an entire generation of Europeans. The unprecedented slaughter on the battlefields of Verdun, Ypres, Gallipoli, and scores of other places appalled the combatant nations. At the war's start in August 1914, both sides had confidently predicted a quick victory. Instead, the killing dragged on for more than four years, and in the end, transformed the old power relations and political map of Europe. The United States entered the war reluctantly, and American forces played a supportive, rather than a central, role in the military outcome. Yet the wartime experience left a sharp imprint on the nation's economy, politics, and cultural life—one that would last into the next decades.

The Guns of August

Only a complex and fragile system of alliances had kept the European powers at peace with each other since 1871. Two great competing camps had evolved by 1907: the Triple Alliance (also known as the Central Powers), which included Germany, Austria-Hungary, and Italy; and the Triple Entente (also known as the Allies), which included Great Britain, France, and Russia. At the heart of this division was the competition between Great Britain, long the world's dominant colonial and commercial power, and Germany, which had powerful aspirations for an empire of its own.

The alliance system managed to keep small conflicts from escalating into larger ones for most of the late nineteenth and early twentieth centuries. But its inclusiveness was also its weakness: the alliance system threatened to entangle many nations in any war that did erupt. On June 28, 1914, Archduke Franz Ferdinand, heir to the throne of the unstable Austro-Hungarian Empire, was assassinated in Sarajevo, Bosnia. The archduke's killer was a Serbian nationalist who believed the Austro-Hungarian province of Bosnia ought to be annexed to neighboring Serbia. Germany pushed Austria-Hungary to retaliate against Serbia, and the Serbians in turn asked Russia for help.

By early August, both sides had exchanged declarations of war and begun mobilizing their forces. Germany invaded Belgium and prepared to move across the French border. But after the German armies were stopped at the River Marne in September, the war settled into a long, bloody stalemate. New and grimly efficient weapons, such as the machine gun and the tank, and the horrors of trench warfare, meant unprecedented casualties for all involved. Centered in northern France, the fighting killed 5 million people over the next two and a half years.

American Neutrality

The outbreak of war in Europe shocked Americans. President Wilson issued a formal proclamation of neutrality and urged citizens to be "impartial in thought as well as in action." In practice, powerful cultural, political, and economic factors made the impartiality advocated by Wilson impossible. The U.S. population included many ethnic groups with close emotional ties to the Old World. Out of a total population of 92 million in 1914, about one-third were "hyphenated" Americans, either foreign-born or having one or both parents who were immigrants. Strong support for the Central Powers could be found among the 8 million German-Americans, as well as the 4 million Irish-Americans, who shared their ancestral homeland's historical hatred of English rule. On the other side, many Americans were at least mildly pro-Allies due to cultural and language bonds with Great Britain and the tradition of Franco-American friendship.

Both sides bombarded the United States with vigorous propaganda campaigns. The British effectively exploited their bonds of language and heritage with Americans. Reports of looting, raping, and the killing of innocent civilians by German troops circulated widely in the press. Many of these atrocity stories were exaggerated, but verified German actions—the invasion of neutral Belgium, submarine attacks on merchant ships, and the razing of towns—lent them credibility. German propagandists blamed the war on Russian expansionism and France's desire to avenge its

defeat by Germany in 1870–71. It is difficult to measure the impact of war propaganda on American public opinion. As a whole, though, it highlighted the terrible human costs of the war, and thus strengthened the conviction that America should stay out of it.

Economic ties between the United States and the Allies were perhaps the greatest barrier to true neutrality. Early in the war, Britain imposed a blockade on all shipping to Germany. The United States, as a neutral country, might have insisted on the right of nonbelligerents to trade with both sides, as required by international law. But in practice, although Wilson protested the blockade, he wanted to avoid antagonizing Britain and disrupting trade between the United States and the Allies. Trade with Germany all but ended while trade with the Allies increased dramatically. As war orders poured in from Britain and France, the value of American trade with the Allies shot up from $824 million in 1914 to $3.2 billion in 1916. By 1917, loans to the Allies exceeded $2.5 billion compared to loans to the Central Powers of only $27 million. As America's annual export trade jumped from $2 billion in 1913 to nearly $6 billion in 1916, the nation enjoyed a great economic boom—transforming the economy in places like Bisbee, Arizona—and the United States became neutral in name only.

Preparedness and Peace

In February 1915, Germany declared the waters around the British Isles to be a war zone, a policy that it would enforce with unrestricted submarine warfare. All enemy shipping, despite the requirements of international law to the contrary, would be subject to surprise submarine attack. Neutral powers were warned that the problems of identification at sea put their ships at risk. The United States issued a sharp protest to this policy, calling it "an indefensible violation of neutral rights," and threatened to hold Germany accountable.

On May 7, 1915, a German U-boat sank the British liner *Lusitania* off the coast of Ireland. Among the 1,198 people who died, were 128 American citizens. The *Lusitania* was in fact, secretly carrying war materials, and passengers had been warned about a possible attack. Wilson nevertheless denounced the sinking as illegal and inhuman, and the American press loudly condemned the act as barbaric. An angry exchange of diplomatic notes led Secretary of State William Jennings Bryan to resign in protest against a policy he thought too warlike.

Tensions heated up again in March 1916 when a German U-boat torpedoed the *Sussex*, an unarmed French passenger ship, injuring four Americans. President Wilson threatened to break off diplomatic relations with Germany unless it abandoned its methods of submarine warfare. He won a temporary diplomatic victory when Germany promised that all vessels would be visited prior to attack. But the crisis also prompted Wilson to begin preparing for war. The National Security League, active

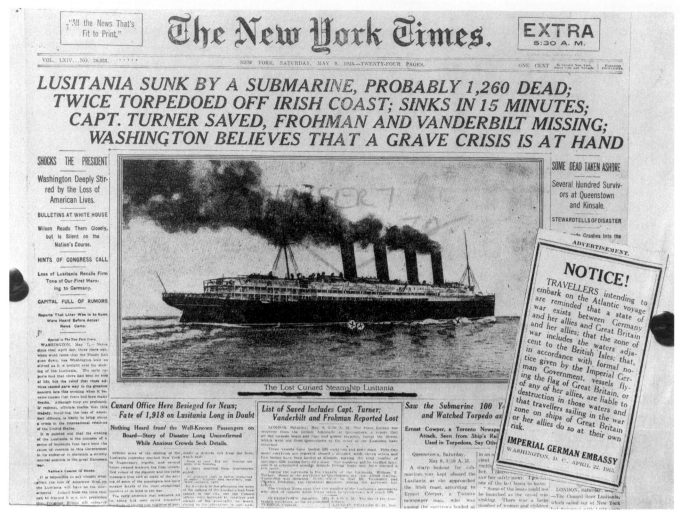

The New York Times printed a special Extra edition announcing that a German submarine had torpedoed the British passenger liner *Lusitania* on May 7, 1915, off the Irish coast. The ship's manifest later revealed that the *Lusitania* carried a shipment of arms along with its passengers. The 1,198 lives lost included 128 Americans and the incident helped push the United States toward "preparedness" for war.

SOURCE: © Bettmann/CORBIS.

in large Eastern cities and bankrolled by conservative banking and commercial interests, helped push for a bigger army and navy and, most important, a system of universal military training. In June 1916, Congress passed the National Defense Act, which more than doubled the size of the regular army to 220,000 and integrated the state National Guards under federal control. In August, Congress passed a bill that dramatically increased spending for new battleships, cruisers, and destroyers.

Not all Americans supported these preparations for battle, and opposition to military buildup found expression in scores of American communities. As early as August 29, 1914, 1,500 women clad in black had marched down New York's Fifth Avenue in the Woman's Peace Parade. Out of this gathering evolved the American Union against

Militarism, which lobbied against the preparedness campaign and against intervention in Mexico. Antiwar feeling was especially strong in the South and Midwest.

A group of thirty to fifty House Democrats, led by majority leader Claude Kitchin of North Carolina, stubbornly opposed Wilson's military buildup. Jane Addams, Lillian D. Wald, and many other prominent progressive reformers spoke out for peace. A large reservoir of popular antiwar sentiment flowed through the culture in various ways. Movie director Thomas Ince won a huge audience for his 1916 film *Civilization*, which depicted Christ returning to reveal the horrors of war to world leaders. Two of the most popular songs of 1915 were "Don't Take My Darling Boy Away" and "I Didn't Raise My Boy to Be a Soldier."

Wilson acknowledged the active opposition to involvement in the war by adopting the winning slogan "He Kept Us Out of War" in the 1916 presidential campaign. He made a point of appealing to progressives of all kinds, stressing his support for the eight-hour day and his administration's efforts on behalf of farmers. The war-induced prosperity no doubt helped him to defeat conservative Republican Charles Evans Hughes in a very close election. But Wilson knew that the peace was as fragile as his victory.

Safe for Democracy

By the end of January 1917, Germany's leaders had decided against a negotiated peace settlement, placing their hopes instead in a final decisive offensive against the Allies. On February 1, 1917, with the aim of breaking the British blockade, Germany declared unlimited submarine warfare, with no warnings, against all neutral and belligerent shipping. This strategy went far beyond the earlier, more limited use of the U-boat. The decision was made with full knowledge that it might bring America into the conflict. In effect, German leaders were gambling that they could destroy the ability of the Allies to fight, before the United States would be able to effectively mobilize manpower and resources.

Wilson was indignant and disappointed. He still hoped for peace, but Germany had made it impossible for him to preserve his twin goals of U.S. neutrality and freedom of the seas. Reluctantly, Wilson broke off diplomatic relations with Germany and called on Congress to approve the arming of U.S. merchant ships. On March 1, the White House shocked the country when it made public a recently intercepted coded message, sent by German foreign secretary Arthur Zimmermann to the German ambassador in Mexico. The Zimmermann note proposed that an alliance be made between Germany and Mexico if the United States entered the war. Zimmermann suggested that Mexico take up arms against the United States and receive in return the "lost territory in New Mexico, Texas, and Arizona." The note caused a sensation, and became a very effective propaganda tool for those who favored U.S. entry into the war. The specter of a German-Mexican alliance helped turn the tide of public opinion in the Southwest, where opposition to U.S. involvement in the war had been strong.

Revelation of the Zimmermann note stiffened Wilson's resolve. He issued an executive order in mid-March, authorizing the arming of all merchant ships and allowing them to shoot at submarines. In that month, German U-boats sank seven U.S. merchant ships, leaving a heavy death toll. Anti-German feeling increased, and thousands took part in prowar demonstrations in New York, Boston, Philadelphia, and other cities. Wilson finally called a special session of Congress to ask for a declaration of war.

On April 2, on a rainy night, before a packed and very quiet assembly, Wilson made his case. He reviewed the escalation of submarine warfare, which he called "warfare against mankind," and said that neutrality was no longer feasible or desirable. But the conflict was not merely about U.S. shipping rights, Wilson argued. He employed highly idealistic language to make the case for war, reflecting his deeply held belief that America had a special mission as mankind's most enlightened and advanced nation:

> It is a fearful thing to lead this great peaceful people into war, into the most terrible and disastrous of all wars, civilization itself seeming to be in the balance. But the right is more precious than peace, and we shall fight for the things which we have always carried nearest to our hearts—for democracy, for the right of those

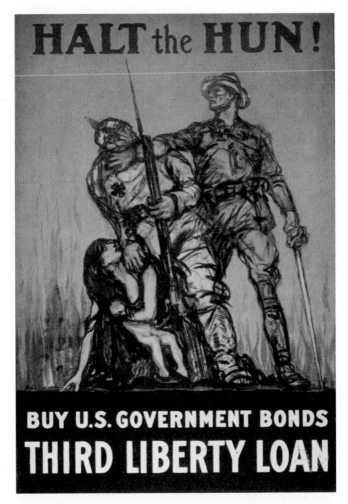

Halt the Hun! This 1918 Liberty Loan poster used anti-German sentiment to encourage the purchase of war bonds. Its depiction of an American soldier as the protector of an innocent mother and child implied that the Germans were guilty of unspeakable war crimes.

SOURCE: The Granger Collection.

who submit to authority to have a voice in their own governments, for the rights and liberties of small nations, for a universal dominion of right by such a concert of free peoples as shall bring peace and safety to all nations and make the world itself at last free.

Wilson's eloquent speech won over the Congress, most of the press, and even his bitterest political critics, such as Theodore Roosevelt. The Senate adopted the war resolution 82 to 6, the House 373 to 50. On April 6, President Wilson signed the declaration of war. All that remained was to win over the American public.

AMERICAN MOBILIZATION

The overall public response to Wilson's war message was enthusiastic. Most newspapers, religious leaders, state legislatures, and prominent public figures endorsed the call to arms. But the Wilson administration was less certain about the feelings of ordinary Americans and their willingness to fight in Europe. It therefore took immediate steps to win over public support for the war effort, to place a legal muzzle on antiwar dissenters, and to establish a universal military draft. War mobilization was above all, a campaign to unify the country.

Selling the War

Just a week after signing the war declaration, Wilson created the Committee on Public Information (CPI) to organize public opinion. It was dominated by its civilian chairman, the journalist and reformer George Creel. He had become a personal friend of Wilson's while handling publicity for the 1916 Democratic campaign. Creel quickly transformed the CPI from its original function as coordinator of government news, into a sophisticated and aggressive agency for promoting the war. To sell the war, Creel raised the art of public relations to new heights. He enlisted more than 150,000 people to work on a score of CPI committees. They produced more than 100 million pieces of literature— pamphlets, articles, books—that explained the causes and meaning of the war. The CPI also created posters, slides, newspaper advertising, and films to promote the war. It called upon movie stars such as Charlie Chaplin, Mary Pickford, and Douglas Fairbanks to help sell war bonds at huge rallies. Famous journalists like the muckraker Ida Tarbell and well-known artists like Charles Dana Gibson were recruited. Across the nation, a volunteer army of 75,000 "Four Minute Men" gave brief patriotic speeches before stage and movie shows.

The CPI led an aggressively negative campaign against all things German. Posters and advertisements depicted the Germans as Huns, bestial monsters outside the civilized world. German music and literature, indeed the German language itself, were suspect, and were ban-

ished from the concert halls, schools, and libraries of many communities. The CPI also urged ethnic Americans to abandon their Old World ties, to become "unhyphenated Americans." The CPI's push for conformity would soon encourage thousands of local, sometimes violent, campaigns of harassment against German-Americans, radicals, and peace activists.

Fading Opposition to War

By defining the call to war as a great moral crusade, President Wilson was able to win over many Americans who had been reluctant to go to war. In particular, many liberals and progressives were attracted to the possibilities of war as a positive force for social change. Many progressives identified with President Wilson's definition of the war as an idealistic crusade to defend democracy, spread liberal principles, and redeem European decadence and militarism. John Dewey, the influential philosopher, believed the war offered great "social pos-

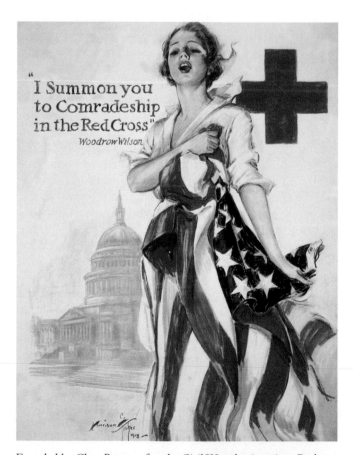

Founded by Clara Barton after the Civil War, the American Red Cross grew in both size and importance during World War I. Female volunteers, responding to humanitarian and patriotic appeals combined in posters like this one, provided most of the health and sanitary services to military and civilian casualties of the war.

SOURCE: Library of Congress.

sibilities" for developing the public good through science and greater efficiency.

The writer and cultural critic Randolph Bourne was an important, if lonely, voice of dissent among intellectuals. A former student of Dewey's at Columbia University, Bourne wrote a series of antiwar essays warning of the disastrous consequences for reform movements of all kinds. He was particularly critical of "war intellectuals" such as Dewey, who were so eager to shift their energies to serving the war effort. "War is essentially the health of the State," Bourne wrote, and he accurately predicted sharp infringements on political and intellectual freedoms.

The Woman's Peace Party, founded in 1915 by feminists opposed to the preparedness campaign, dissolved. Most of its leading lights—Florence Kelley, Lillian D. Wald, and Carrie Chapman Catt—threw themselves into volunteer war work. Catt, leader of the huge National American Woman Suffrage Association (NAWSA), believed that supporting the war might help women win the right to vote. She joined the Women's Committee of the Council of National Defense and encouraged suffragists to mobilize women for war service of various kinds. A few lonely feminist voices, such as Jane Addams, continued steadfastly to oppose the war effort. But war work proved very popular among activist middle-class women. It gave them a leading role in their communities—selling bonds, coordinating food conservation drives, and working for hospitals and the Red Cross.

"You're in the Army Now"

The central military issue facing the administration was how to raise and deploy U.S. armed forces. When war was declared, there were only about 200,000 men in the

Troops of the American Expeditionary Force in Southampton, England, embarking for the front in France, 1917. By November 1918, when the Great War ended, more than 2 million American soldiers were in Europe.

SOURCE: Thomas Derrick (20th CE), *American Troops in Southhampton Embarking for France*, 1917. Imperial War Museum, London. Snark/Art Resource, NY.

army. Traditionally, the United States had relied on volunteer forces organized at the state level. But volunteer rates after April 6 were less than they had been for the Civil War or the Spanish-American War, reflecting the softness of prowar sentiment. The administration thus introduced the Selective Service Act, which provided for the registration and classification for military service of all men between ages twenty-one and thirty-five. To prevent the widespread opposition to the draft that had occurred during the Civil War, the new draft had no unpopular provision allowing draftees to buy their way out of service by paying for a substitute.

On June 5, 1917, nearly 10 million men registered for the draft. There was scattered organized resistance, but overall, registration records offered evidence of national support. A supplemental registration in August 1918 extended the age limits to eighteen and forty-five. By the end of the war, some 24 million men had registered. Of the 2.8 million men eventually called up for service, about 340,000, or 12 percent, failed to show up. Another 2 million Americans volunteered for the various armed services.

The vast, polyglot army posed unprecedented challenges of organization and control. But progressive elements within the administration also saw opportunities for pressing reform measures involving education, alcohol, and sex. Army psychologists gave the new Stanford-Binet intelligence test to all recruits, and were shocked to find illiteracy rates as high as 25 percent. The low test scores among recent immigrants and rural African Americans undoubtedly reflected the cultural biases embedded in the tests and a lack of proficiency in English for many test takers. After the war, intelligence testing became a standard feature of America's educational system.

Ideally, the army provided a field for social reform and education, especially for the one-fifth of U.S. soldiers born in another country. "The military tent where they all sleep side by side," Theodore Roosevelt predicted, "will rank next to the public schools among the great agents of democratization." The recruits themselves took a more lighthearted view, while singing the army's praises:

> Oh, the army, the army, the democratic army,
> They clothe you and feed you because the army needs you
> Hash for breakfast, beans for dinner, stew for suppertime,
> Thirty dollars every month, deducting twenty-nine.
> Oh, the army, the army, the democratic army,
> The Jews, the Wops, and the Dutch and Irish Cops,
> They're all in the army now!

Racism in the Military

But African Americans who served found severe limitations in the U.S. military. They were organized into totally segregated units, barred entirely from the marines and the Coast Guard, and largely relegated to working as cooks, laundrymen, stevedores, and the like in the army and navy. Thousands of black soldiers endured humiliating, sometimes violent treatment, particularly from Southern white officers.

African American soldiers of the 369th Infantry Regiment fighting in the trenches on the Western front, 1918. Nearly 400,000 black man served in World War I, but due to the racist beliefs held by most military and political leaders, only 42,000 went into combat. "Many of the white field officers," wrote black Lieutenant Howard H. Long, "seemed far more concerned with reminding their Negro subordinates that they were Negroes than they were in having an effective unit that would perform well in combat."

SOURCE: The Granger Collection, New York.

African American servicemen faced hostility from white civilians as well, North and South, often being denied service in restaurants and admission to theaters near training camps. The ugliest incident occurred in Houston, Texas, in August 1917. Black infantrymen, incensed over continual insults and harassment by local whites, seized weapons from an armory and killed seventeen civilians. The army executed thirty black soldiers and imprisoned forty-one others for life, denying any of them a chance for appeal.

More than 200,000 African Americans eventually served in France, but only about one in five saw combat, as opposed to two out of three white soldiers. Black combat units served with distinction in various divisions of the French army. The French government awarded the Croix de Guerre to the all-black 369th U.S. Infantry regiment, and 171 officers and enlisted men were cited individually for exceptional bravery in action. African American soldiers by and large enjoyed a friendly reception from French civilians as well. The contrast with their treatment at home would remain a sore point with these troops upon their return to the United States.

Americans in Battle

President Wilson appointed General John J. Pershing, recently returned from pursuing Pancho Villa in Mexico, as commander of the American Expeditionary Force (AEF). Pershing insisted that the AEF maintain its own identity, distinct from that of the French and British armies. He was also reluctant to send American troops into battle before they had received at least six months' training. The AEF's combat role would be brief but intense: not until early 1918 did AEF units reach the front in large numbers; eight months later, the war was over (see Map 22.2).

Like Ulysses S. Grant, Pershing believed the object of war to be total destruction of the enemy's military power. He expressed contempt for the essentially defensive tactics of trench warfare pursued by both sides. But the brutal power of modern military

MAP 22.2 The Western Front, 1918 American units saw their first substantial action in late May, helping to stop the German offensive at the Battle of Cantigny. By September, more than 1 million American troops were fighting in a counteroffensive campaign at St. Mihiel, the largest single American engagement of the war.

technology had made trench warfare inevitable from 1914 to 1917. The awesome firepower of the machine gun and long-range artillery made the massed frontal confrontations of the Civil War era obsolete. The grim reality of life in the trenches—cold, wet, lice-ridden, with long periods of boredom and sleeplessness—also made a mockery of older romantic notions about the glory of combat.

In the early spring of 1918, the Germans launched a major offensive that brought them within fifty miles of Paris. In early June, about 70,000 AEF soldiers helped the French stop the Germans in the battles of Château-Thierry and Belleau Wood. In July, Allied forces led by Marshal Ferdinand Foch of France, began a counteroffensive designed to defeat Germany once and for all. American reinforcements began flooding the ports of Liverpool in England and Brest and Saint-Nazaire in France. The "doughboys" (a nickname for soldiers dating back to Civil War–era recruits who joined the army for the money) streamed in at a rate of over 250,000 a month. By September, General Pershing had more than a million Americans in his army. (See Out of Many Voices: "Trench Warfare".)

In late September 1918, the AEF took over the southern part of a 200-mile front in the Meuse-Argonne offensive. In seven weeks of fighting, most through terrible mud and rain, U.S. soldiers used more ammunition than the entire Union army had in the four years of the Civil War. The Germans, exhausted and badly outnumbered, began to fall back and look for a cease-fire. On November 11, 1918, the war ended with the signing of an armistice.

The massive influx of American troops and supplies no doubt hastened the end of the war. About two-thirds of the U.S. soldiers saw at least some fighting, but even they managed to avoid the horrors of the sustained trench warfare that had marked the earlier years of the war. For most Americans at the front, the war experience was a mixture of fear, exhaustion, and fatigue. Their

OUT OF MANY VOICES

"TRENCH WARFARE," LETTER FROM PRIVATE SAM ROSS, 42ND DIVISION, AMERICAN EXPEDITONARY FORCE, 1917

The brutal trench warfare of the First World War was nothing like the romantic stories of battle that American boys had grown up with. Most American soldiers were unprepared for the combination of fear, sleep deprivation, bad weather, tedium, and moments of instant death. This letter from an American private serving in France in the summer of 1917 conveys a sense of the utter strangeness of trench warfare.

OUR (FIRST) TRENCH WAS AN OLD ONE AND pretty well shot to pieces. The first night I was in it, it was very quiet; no artillery at all. The only thing that broke the silence was once in awhile a sniper would shoot at something, and the rats running around sounded like someone chasing after you. . . . Standing post at night is something—you see there is thirty feet of wire in front of our trench and the posts are put in very irregular. It is almost impossible to find a place where you could see clear through the wire, even in daylight, and at night, every post or broken tree looks like a man and if you look long enough the object seems to move.

The first night I stood post I imagined the trees were men and at times I saw them stoop down and climb over the wire, but after that I was used to it and learned how to tell a man from a tree. If you give a false alarm it means that the fellows who are sleeping in dugouts are wakened and have to come up and "stand to." At the best, the fellows get very little sleep, and if there are any alarms, they get none at all; so the wise Hun has all kinds of ways to coax an alarm, cats are used; and they have whistles that make moaning noises. You hear a cat on the wire and one of these whistles are blown, and you look out and think there is a man cutting the wire, and let her go. . . . It rained only once while we were in and it was bad enough in dry weather, but when you have to stand in mud, it must be hell.

We were troubled quite a little by snipers, stick your head over and zip—they use a high power air gun and there is no flash, so they are very hard to locate. ■

SOURCE: The Doughboy Center, Great War Society, http://www.worldwar1.com/tgws/pres.htm.

time in France would remain a decisive moment in their lives. In all, more than 52,000 Americans died in battle. Another 60,000 died from influenza and pneumonia, half of these while still in training camp. More than 200,000 Americans were wounded in the war. These figures, awful as they were, paled against the estimated casualties (killed and wounded) suffered by the European nations: 9 million for Russia, more than 6 million for Germany, nearly 5 million for France, and over 2 million each for Great Britain and Italy.

OVER HERE

In one sense, World War I can be understood as the ultimate progressive crusade, a reform movement of its own. Nearly all the reform energy of the previous two decades was turned toward the central goal of winning the war. The federal government would play a larger role than ever in managing and regulating the wartime economy. Planning, efficiency, scientific analysis, and cooperation were key principles for government agencies and large volunteer organizations. Although much of the regulatory spirit was temporary, the war experience started some important and lasting organizational trends in American life.

Organizing the Economy

In the summer of 1917, President Wilson established the War Industries Board (WIB) as a clearinghouse for industrial mobilization to support the war effort. Led by the successful Wall Street speculator Bernard M. Baruch, the WIB proved a major innovation in expanding the regulatory power of the federal government. Given broad authority over the conversion of industrial plants to wartime needs and the manufacture of war materials, the WIB had to balance price controls against war profits. Only by ensuring a fair rate of return on investment, could it encourage stepped-up production.

The WIB eventually handled 3,000 contracts worth $14.5 billion with various businesses. Standardization of goods brought large savings and streamlined production. Baruch continually negotiated with business leaders, describing the system as "voluntary cooperation with the big stick in the cupboard." At first Elbert Gary of U.S. Steel refused to accept the government's price for steel, and Henry Ford balked at limiting private car production. But when Baruch warned that he would instruct the military to take over their plants, both industrialists backed down.

In August 1917, Congress passed the Food and Fuel Act, authorizing the president to regulate the production and distribution of the food and fuel necessary for the war effort. To lead the Food Administration (FA), Wilson appointed Herbert Hoover, a millionaire engineer who had already won fame for directing a program of war relief for Belgium. He became one of the best-known figures of the war administration. Hoover imposed price controls on certain agricultural commodities, such as sugar, pork, and wheat. These were purchased by the government and then sold to the public through licensed dealers. The FA also raised the purchase price of grain, so that farmers would increase production. But Hoover stopped short of imposing mandatory food rationing, preferring to rely on persuasion, high prices, and voluntary controls.

Hoover's success, like George Creel's at the CPI, depended on motivating hundreds of thousands of volunteers in thousands of American communities. The FA coordinated the work of local committees that distributed posters and leaflets urging people to save food, recycle scraps, and substitute for scarce produce. The FA directed patriotic appeals for "Wheatless Mondays, Meatless Tuesdays, and Porkless Thursdays." Hoover exhorted Americans to "go back to simple food, simple clothes, simple pleasures." He urged them to grow their own vegetables. These efforts resulted in a sharp cutback in the consumption of sugar and wheat as well as a boost in the supply of livestock. The resultant increase in food exports helped sustain the Allied war effort.

The enormous cost of fighting the war, about $33 billion, required unprecedentedly large expenditures for the federal government. The tax structure shifted dramatically as a result. Taxes on incomes and profits replaced excise and customs levies as the major source of revenue. The minimum income subject to the graduated federal income tax, in effect only since 1913, was lowered to $1,000 from $3,000, increasing the number of Americans who paid income tax from 437,000 in 1916 to 4,425,000 in 1918. Tax rates were as steep as 70 percent in the highest brackets.

The bulk of war financing came from government borrowing, especially in the form of the popular Liberty Bonds sold to the American public. Bond drives became highly organized patriotic campaigns that ultimately raised a total of $23 billion for the war effort. The administration also used the new Federal Reserve Banks to expand the money supply, making borrowing easier. The federal debt jumped from $1 billion in 1915 to $20 billion in 1920.

The Business of War

Overall, the war meant expansion and high profits for American business. Between 1916 and 1918, Ford Motor Company increased its workforce from 32,000 to 48,000, General Motors from 10,000 to 50,000. Total capital expenditure in U.S. manufacturing jumped from $600 million in 1915 to $2.5 billion in 1918. Corporate profits as a whole nearly tripled between 1914 and 1919, and many large businesses did much better than that. Annual prewar profits for United States Steel, for example, had averaged $76 million; in 1917, they were $478 million. The total value of farm produce rose from $9.8 billion in 1914 to $21.3 billion by 1918. Expanded farm acreage and increased investment in farm machinery led to a jump of 20–30 percent in overall farm production.

The most important and long-lasting economic legacy of the war was the organizational shift toward corporatism in American business. The wartime need for efficient management, manufacturing, and distribution could be met only by a greater reliance on the productive and marketing power of large corporations. Never before had business and the federal government cooperated so closely. Under war administrators like Baruch and Hoover, entire industries (such as radio manufacturing) and economic sectors (such as agriculture and energy) were organized, regulated, and subsidized. War agencies used both public and private power—legal authority and voluntarism—to hammer out and enforce agreements. Here was the genesis of the modern bureaucratic state.

Some Americans worried about the wartime trend toward a greater federal presence in their lives. As *The Saturday Evening Post* noted, "All this government activity will be called to account and re-examined in due time." Although many aspects of the government–business partnership proved temporary, some institutions and practices grew stronger in the postwar years. Among these were the Federal Reserve Board, the income tax system, the Chamber of Commerce, the Farm Bureau, and the growing horde of lobbying groups that pressed Washington for special interest legislation.

Labor and the War

Organized labor's power and prestige, though by no means equal to those of business or government, clearly grew during the war. The expansion of the economy, combined with army mobilization and a decline in immigration from Europe, caused a growing wartime labor shortage. As the demand for workers intensified, the federal government was forced to recognize that labor, like any other resource or commodity, would have to be more carefully tended to than in peacetime. For the war's duration, working people generally enjoyed higher wages and a better standard of living. Trade unions, especially those affiliated with the American Federation of Labor (AFL), experienced a sharp rise in membership. In effect, the government took in labor as a junior partner in the mobilization of the economy.

Samuel Gompers, president of the AFL, emerged as the leading spokesman for the nation's trade union movement. An English immigrant and cigar maker by trade, Gompers had rejected the socialism of his youth for a philosophy of "business unionism." By stressing the concrete gains that workers could win through collective bargaining with employers, the AFL had reached a total membership of about 2 million in 1914. Virtually all its members were skilled white males, organized in highly selective crafts in the building trades, railroads, and coal mines.

Gompers pledged the AFL's patriotic support for the war effort, and in April 1918, President Wilson appointed him to the National War Labor Board (NWLB). During 1917, the nation had seen thousands of strikes involving more than a million workers. Wages were usually at issue, reflecting workers' concerns with spiraling inflation and higher prices. The NWLB, cochaired by labor attorney Frank Walsh and former president William H. Taft, acted as a kind of supreme court for labor, arbitrating disputes and working to prevent disruptions in production. The great majority of these interventions resulted in improved wages and reduced hours of work.

Most important, the NWLB supported the right of workers to organize unions, and furthered the acceptance of the eight-hour day for war workers—central aims of the labor movement. It also backed time-and-a-half pay for overtime, as well as the principle of equal pay for women workers. AFL unions gained more than a million new members during the war, and overall union membership rose from 2.7 million in 1914 to more than 5 million by 1920.

Wartime conditions often meant severe disruptions and discomfort for America's workers. Overcrowding, rapid workforce turnover, and high inflation rates were typical in war-boom communities. In Bridgeport, Connecticut, a center for small-arms manufacturing, the population grew by 50,000 in less than a year. In 1917, the number of families grew by 12,000, but available housing stock increased by only 6,000 units.

In the Southwest, the demand for wartime labor temporarily eased restrictions against the movement of Mexicans into the United States. The Immigration Act of 1917, requiring a literacy test and an $8 head tax, had cut Mexican immigration nearly in half, down to about 25,000 per year. But employers complained of severe shortages of workers. Farmers in Arizona's Salt River Valley and southern California needed hands to harvest grain, alfalfa, cotton, and fruit. El Paso's mining and smelting industries, Texas's border ranches, and southern Arizona's railroads and copper mines insisted they depended on unskilled Mexican labor as well.

Responding to these protests, in June 1917, the Department of Labor suspended the immigration law for the duration of the war, and negotiated an agreement with the Mexican government permitting some 35,000 Mexican contract laborers to enter the United States. Mexicans let in through this program had to demonstrate they had a job waiting before they could cross the border. They received identification cards and transportation to their place of work from American labor contractors. Pressure from Southwestern employers kept the exemptions in force until 1921, well after the end of the war, demonstrating the growing importance of cheap Mexican labor to the region's economy.

If the war boosted the fortunes of the AFL, it also spelled the end for more radical elements of the U.S.

labor movement. The Industrial Workers of the World (IWW), unlike the AFL, had concentrated on organizing unskilled workers into all-inclusive industrial unions. The Wobblies denounced capitalism as an unreformable system based on exploitation, and they opposed U.S. entry into the war. IWW leaders advised their members to refuse induction for "the capitalists' war."

The IWW had grown in 1916 and 1917. It gained strength among workers in several areas crucial to the war effort: copper mining, lumbering, and wheat harvesting. In September 1917, just after the vigilante attack in Bisbee and the IWW's efforts to expose it, the Wilson administration responded to appeals from Western business leaders for a crackdown on the Wobblies. Justice Department agents, acting under the broad authority of the recently passed Espionage Act, swooped down on IWW offices in more than sixty towns and cities, arresting more than 300 people and confiscating files. The mass trials and convictions that followed, broke the back of America's radical labor movement and marked the beginning of a powerful wave of political repression.

Women workers at the Midvale Steel and Ordnance Company in Pennsylvania, 1918. Wartime labor shortages created new opportunities for over one million women to take high-wage manufacturing jobs like these. The opening proved temporary, however, and with the war's end, nearly all of these women lost their jobs. By 1920, the number of women employed in manufacturing was lower than it had been in 1910.

SOURCE: National Archives and Records Administration.

Women at Work

For many of the 8 million women already in the labor force, the war meant a chance to switch from low-paying jobs, such as domestic service, to higher-paying industrial employment. About a million women workers joined the labor force for the first time. Of the estimated 9.4 million workers directly engaged in war work, some 2.25 million were women. Of these, 1.25 million worked in manufacturing. Female munitions plant workers, train engineers, drill press operators, streetcar conductors, and mail carriers became a common sight around the country. World War I also marked the first time that women were mobilized directly into the armed forces. Over 16,000 women served overseas with the AEF in France, where most worked as nurses, clerical workers, telephone operators, and canteen operators. Another 12,000 women served stateside in the navy and U.S. Marine Corps, and tens of thousands of civilian women were employed in army offices and hospitals. But the war's impact on women was greatest in the broader civilian economy.

In response to the widened range of female employment, the Labor Department created the Women in Industry Service (WIS). Directed by Mary Van Kleeck, the service advised employers on using female labor and formulated general standards for the treatment of women workers. The WIS represented the first attempt by the federal government to take a practical stand on improving working conditions for women. Its standards included the eight-hour day, equal pay for equal work, a minimum wage, the prohibition of night work, and the provision of rest periods, meal breaks, and restroom facilities. These standards had no legal force, however, and WIS inspectors found that employers often flouted them. They were accepted nonetheless as goals, by nearly every group concerned with improving the conditions of working women.

At war's end, women lost nearly all their defense-related jobs. Wartime women railroad workers, for example, were replaced by returning servicemen, through the application of laws meant to protect women from hazardous conditions. But the war accelerated female employment in fields already dominated by women. By 1920, more

MAP EXPLORATION

To explore this interactive map, go to **www.prenhall.com/faragher5/map22.3**

MAP 22.3 Woman Suffrage by State, 1869–1919 Dates for the enactment of woman suffrage in the individual states. Years before ratification of the Nineteenth Amendment in 1920, a number of Western states had legislated full or partial voting rights for women. In 1917, Montana suffragist Jeannette Rankin became the first woman elected to Congress.

SOURCE: Barbara G. Shortridge, *Atlas of American Women* (New York: Macmillan, 1987).

women who worked outside the home did so in white-collar occupations—as telephone operators, secretaries, and clerks, for example—than in manufacturing or domestic service. The new awareness of women's work led Congress to create the Women's Bureau in the Labor Department, which continued the WIS wartime program of education and investigation through the postwar years.

Woman Suffrage

The presence of so many new women wageworkers, combined with the highly visible volunteer work of millions of middle-class women, helped finally to secure the vote for women. Volunteer war work—selling bonds, saving food, organizing benefits—was very popular among housewives and clubwomen. These women played a key

role in the success of the Food Administration, and the Women's Committee of the Council of National Defense included a variety of women's organizations.

Until World War I, the fight for woman suffrage had been waged largely within individual states. Western states and territories had led the way. Various forms of woman suffrage had become law in Wyoming in 1869, followed by Utah (1870), Colorado (1893), Idaho (1896). Rocky Mountain and Pacific coast states did not have the sharp ethno-cultural divisions between Catholics and Protestants that hindered suffrage efforts in the East. For example, the close identification in the East between the suffrage and prohibition movements, led many Catholic immigrants and German Lutherans to oppose the vote for women, because they feared it would lead to prohibition (see Map 22.3).

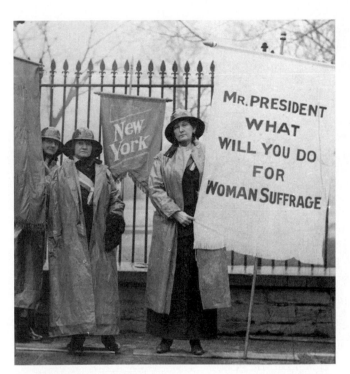

Members of the National Woman's Party picketed President Wilson at the White House in 1917. Their militant action in the midst of the war crisis aroused both anger and sympathy. The NWP campaign helped push the president and the Congress to accept woman suffrage as a "war measure."

SOURCE: Library of Congress.

The U.S. entry into the war provided a unique opportunity for suffrage groups to shift their strategy to a national campaign for a constitutional amendment granting the vote to women. The most important of these groups was the National American Woman Suffrage Association. Before 1917, most American suffragists had opposed the war. Under the leadership of Carrie Chapman Catt, the NAWSA threw its support behind the war effort and doubled its membership to 2 million. Catt gambled that a strong show of patriotism would help clinch the century-old fight to win the vote for women. The NAWSA pursued a moderate policy of lobbying Congress for a constitutional amendment and calling for state referendums on woman suffrage.

At the same time, more militant suffragists led by the young Quaker activist Alice Paul, injected new energy and more radical tactics into the movement. Dissatisfied with the NAWSA's conservative strategy of quiet lobbying and orderly demonstrations, Paul left the organization in 1916. She joined forces with Western women voters to form the National Woman's Party. Borrowing from English suffragists, this party pursued

a more aggressive and dramatic strategy of agitation. Paul and her supporters picketed the White House, publicly burned President Wilson's speeches, and condemned the president and the Democrats for failing to produce an amendment. In one demonstration, they chained themselves to the White House fence, and after their arrest, went on a hunger strike in jail. The militants generated a great deal of publicity and sympathy.

Although some in the NAWSA objected to these tactics, Paul's radical approach helped make the NAWSA position more acceptable to Wilson. Carrie Chapman Catt used the president's war rhetoric as an argument for granting the vote to women. The fight for democracy, she argued, must begin at home, and she urged passage of the woman suffrage amendment as a "war measure." She won Wilson's support, and in 1917, the president urged Congress to pass a woman suffrage amendment as "vital to the winning of the war." The House did so in January 1918 and a more reluctant Senate approved it in June 1919. Another year of hard work was spent convincing the state legislatures. In August 1920, Tennessee gave the final vote needed to ratify the Nineteenth Amendment to the Constitution, finally making woman suffrage legal nationwide.

Prohibition

Another reform effort closely associated with women's groups triumphed at the same time. The movement to eliminate alcohol from American life had attracted many Americans, especially women, since before the Civil War. Temperance advocates saw drinking as the source of many of the worst problems faced by the working class, including family violence, unemployment, and poverty. By the early twentieth century, the Woman's Christian Temperance Union, with a quarter-million members, had become the single largest women's organization in American history.

The moral fervor that accompanied America's entry into the war provided a crucial boost to the cause. With so many breweries bearing German names, the movement benefited as well from the strong anti-German feeling of the war years. Outlawing beer and whiskey would also help to conserve precious grain, prohibitionists argued.

In 1917, a coalition of progressives and rural fundamentalists in Congress pushed through a constitutional amendment providing for a national ban on alcoholic drinks. The Eighteenth Amendment was ratified by the states in January 1919, and became the law of the land one year later. Although Prohibition would create a host of problems in the postwar years, especially as a stimulus for the growth of organized crime, many Americans, particularly native Protestants, considered it a worthy moral reform.

Seattle policemen wearing protective gauze face masks during the influenza epidemic of 1918. The pandemic killed over half a million Americans and some twenty million people worldwide.

SOURCE: Time Life Pictures/National Archives. Getty Images/Time Life Pictures.

Public Health

Wartime mobilization brought deeper government involvement with public health issues, especially in the realm of sex hygiene, child welfare, and disease prevention. The rate of venereal disease among draftees was as high as 6 percent in some states, presenting a potential manpower problem for the army. In April 1917, the War Department mounted a vigorous campaign against venereal disease, which attracted the energies of progressive-era sex reformers—social hygienists and antivice crusaders. Under the direction of Raymond Fosdick and the Commission on Training Camp Activities, the military educated troops on the dangers of contracting syphilis and gonorrhea and distributed condoms to soldiers. "A Soldier who gets a dose," warned a typical poster, "is a Traitor."

The scientific discussions of sex, to which recruits were subjected in lectures, pamphlets, and films were surely a first for the vast majority of them. Venereal disease rates for soldiers declined by more than 300 percent during the war. The Division of Venereal Diseases, created in the summer of 1918 as a branch of the U.S. Public Health Service, established clinics offering free medical treatment to infected persons.

The wartime boost to government health work continued into the postwar years. The Children's Bureau, created in 1912 as a part of the Labor Department, undertook a series of reports on special problems growing out of the war: the increase in employment of married women, the finding of day care for children of working mothers, and the growth of both child labor and delinquency. In 1918, Julia C. Lathrop,

chief of the bureau, organized a "Children's Year" campaign designed to promote public protection of expectant mothers and infants, and to enforce child labor laws. In 1917, Lathrop, who had come to the Children's Bureau from the settlement house movement, proposed a plan to institutionalize federal aid to the states for protection of mothers and children. Congress finally passed the Maternity and Infancy Act in 1921, appropriating over $1 million a year to be administered to the states by the Children's Bureau. In the postwar years, clinics for prenatal and obstetrical care grew out of these efforts, and greatly reduced the rate of infant and maternal mortality and disease.

The disastrous influenza epidemic of 1918–19 offered the most serious challenge to national public health during the war years. Part of a worldwide pandemic that claimed as many as 20 million lives, few Americans paid attention to the disease until it swept through military camps and Eastern cities in September 1918. A lethal combination of the "flu" and respiratory complications (mainly pneumonia) killed roughly 550,000 Americans in ten months. Most victims were young adults between the ages of twenty and forty. Professional groups such as the American Medical Association, called for massive government appropriations to search for a cure. Congress did appropriate a million dollars to the Public Health Service to combat and suppress the epidemic, but it offered no money for research. The Public Health Service found itself overwhelmed by calls for doctors, nurses, and treatment facilities. Much of the care for the sick and dying came from Red Cross nurses and volunteers working in local communities across the nation. With a war on, and the nation focused on reports from the battlefront, even a public health crisis of this magnitude went relatively unnoticed.

REPRESSION AND REACTION

World War I exposed and intensified many of the deepest social tensions in American life. On the local level, as exemplified by the Bisbee deportations, vigilantes increasingly took the law into their own hands to punish those suspected of disloyalty. The push for national unity led the federal government to crack down on a wide spectrum of dissenters from its war policies. The war inflamed racial hatred, and the worst race riots in the nation's history exploded in several cities. At war's end, a newly militant labor movement briefly asserted itself in mass strikes around the nation. Over all these developments loomed the 1917 Bolshevik Revolution in Russia. Radicals around the world had drawn inspiration from what looked like the first successful revolution against a capitalist state. Many conservatives worried that similar revolutions were imminent. From 1918 through 1920, the federal government directed a repressive antiradical campaign that had crucial implications for the nation's future.

Muzzling Dissent: The Espionage and Sedition Acts

The Espionage Act of June 1917 became the government's key tool for the suppression of antiwar sentiment. It set severe penalties (up to twenty years' imprisonment and a $10,000 fine) for anyone found guilty of aiding the enemy, obstructing recruitment, or causing insubordination in the armed forces. The act also empowered the postmaster general to exclude from the mails any newspapers or magazines he thought treasonous. Within a year, the mailing rights of forty-five newpapers had been revoked. These included several anti-British and pro-Irish publications, as well as such leading journals of American socialism as the Kansas-based *Appeal to Reason*, which had enjoyed a prewar circulation of half a million, and *The Masses*.

To enforce the Espionage Act, the government had to increase its overall police and surveillance machinery. Civilian intelligence was coordinated by the newly created Bureau of Investigation in the Justice Department. This agency was reorganized after the war as the Federal Bureau of Investigation (FBI). In May 1918, the Sedition Act, an amendment to the Espionage Act, outlawed "any disloyal, profane, scurrilous, or abusive language intended to cause contempt, scorn, contumely, or disrepute" to the government, Constitution, or flag.

These acts became a convenient vehicle for striking out at socialists, pacifists, radical labor activists, and others who resisted the patriotic tide. The most cele-

brated prosecution came in June 1918, when federal agents arrested Eugene V. Debs in Canton, Ohio, after he gave a speech defending antiwar protesters. Sentenced to ten years in prison, Debs defiantly told the court: "I have been accused of having obstructed the war. I admit it. Gentlemen, I abhor war. I would oppose the war if I stood alone." Debs served thirty-two months in federal prison before being pardoned by President Warren G. Harding on Christmas Day 1921.

The Supreme Court upheld the constitutionality of the acts in several 1919 decisions. In *Schenck* v. *United States*, the Court unanimously agreed with Justice Oliver Wendell Holmes's claim that Congress could restrict speech if the words "are used in such circumstances and are of such a nature as to create a clear and present danger." The decision upheld the conviction of Charles Schenck for having mailed pamphlets urging potential army inductees to resist conscription. In *Debs* v. *United States*, the Court affirmed the guilt of Eugene V. Debs for his antiwar speech in Canton, even though he had not explicitly urged violation of the draft laws. Finally, in *Abrams* v. *United States*, the Court upheld Sedition Act convictions of four Russian immigrants who had printed pamphlets denouncing American military intervention in the Russian Revolution. The nation's highest court thus endorsed the severe wartime restrictions on free speech.

The deportation of striking miners in Bisbee offered an extreme case of vigilante activity. Thousands of other instances took place as government repression and local vigilantes reinforced each other. The American Protective League, founded with the blessing of the Justice Department, mobilized 250,000 self-appointed "operatives" in more than 600 towns and cities. Members of the league, mostly businessmen, bankers, and former policemen, spied on their neighbors and staged a series of well-publicized "slacker" raids on antiwar protesters and draft evaders. Many communities, inspired by Committee on Public Information campaigns, sought to ban the teaching of the German language in their schools or the performance of German music in concert halls.

The Great Migration and Racial Tensions

Economic opportunity brought on by war prosperity triggered a massive migration of rural black Southerners to Northern cities. From 1914 to 1920, somewhere between 300,000 and 500,000 African Americans left the rural South for the North. Chicago's black population increased by 65,000, or 150 percent; Detroit's by 35,000, or 600 percent. Acute labor shortages led Northern factory managers to recruit black migrants to the expanding industrial centers. The Pennsylvania Railroad alone drew 10,000 black workers from Florida and south Georgia. Black workers eagerly left low-paying jobs as field hands and domestic servants for the chance at relatively high-paying work in

This Southern African American family is shown arriving in Chicago around 1910. Black migrants to Northern cities often faced overcrowding, inferior housing, and a high death rate from disease. But the chance to earn daily wages of $6 to $8 (the equivalent of a week's wages in much of the South), as well as the desire to escape persistent racial violence, kept the migrants coming.

SOURCE: © Stock Montage, Inc./Historical Pictures Collection.

TABLE 22.1

THE GREAT MIGRATION: BLACK POPULATION GROWTH IN SELECTED NORTHERN CITIES, 1910–20

City	1910		1920		
	No.	Percent	No.	Percent	Percent Increase
New York	91,709	1.9%	152,467	2.7%	66.3%
Chicago	44,103	2.0	109,458	4.1	148.2
Philadelphia	84,459	5.5	134,229	7.4	58.9
Detroit	5,741	1.2	40,838	4.1	611.3
St. Louis	43,960	6.4	69,854	9.0	58.9
Cleveland	8,448	1.5	34,451	4.3	307.8
Pittsburgh	25,623	4.8	37,725	6.4	47.2
Cincinnati	19,739	5.4	30,079	7.5	53.2

SOURCE: U.S. Department of Commerce.

meatpacking plants, shipyards, and steel mills (see Table 22.1).

Kinship and community networks were crucial in shaping what came to be called the Great Migration. They spread news about job openings, urban residential districts, and boardinghouses in Northern cities. Black clubs, churches, and fraternal lodges in Southern communities frequently sponsored the migration of their members, as well as return trips to the South. Single African American women often made the trip first, because they could more easily obtain steady work as maids, cooks, and laundresses. Relatively few African American men actually secured high-paying skilled jobs in industry or manufacturing. Most had to settle for such low-paying occupations as construction laborers, teamsters, janitors or porters. (See Out of Many Voices: "Letters From the Great Migration, 1917".)

The persistence of lynching and other racial violence in the South no doubt contributed to the Great Migration. But racial violence was not limited to the South. Two of the worst race riots in American history occurred as a result of tensions brought on by wartime migration. On July 2, 1917, in East St. Louis, Illinois, a ferocious mob of whites attacked African Americans, killing at least 200. Before this riot, some of the city's manufacturers had been steadily recruiting black labor as a way to keep local union demands down. Unions had refused to allow black workers as members, and politicians had cynically exploited white racism in appealing for votes. In Chicago, on July 27, 1919, antiblack rioting broke out on a Lake Michigan beach. For two weeks, white gangs hunted African Americans in the streets and burned hundreds out of their homes. Twenty-three African Americans and fifteen whites died, and more than 500 were injured. Yet in both East St. Louis and Chicago, local

OUT OF MANY VOICES

LETTERS FROM THE GREAT MIGRATION, 1917

Between 1914 and 1920, some 300–500,000 African Americans moved from the rural South to the urban North and West, creating one of the largest internal migrations in U.S. history. The Chicago Defender, the nation's most influential African American newspaper, actively encouraged Southern blacks to migrate North, and it regularly published letters detailing the motives for this journey and the obstacles to making it.

LUTCHER, LA., MAY 13, 1917

Dear Sir: I have been reading the Chicago defender and seeing so many advertisements about the work in the north I thought to write you concerning my condition. I am working hard in the south and can hardly earn a living. I have a wife and one child and can hardly feed them. I thought to write and ask you for some information concerning how to get a pass for myself and family. I dont want to leave my family behind as I cant hardly make a living for them right here with them and I know they would fare hard if I would leave them. If there are any agents in the south there havent been any of them to Lutcher if they would come here they would get at least fifty men. Please sir let me hear from you as quick as possible. Now this is all. Please dont publish my letter, I was out in town today talking to some of the men and they say if they could get passes that 30 or 40 of them would come. But they havent got the money and they dont know how to come. But they are good strong and able working men. If you will instruct me I will instruct the other men how to come as they all want to work. Please dont publish this because we have to whisper this around among our selves because the white folks are angry now because the negroes are going north.

PORT ARTHUR, TEXAS, 5/5th/17

Dear Sir: I am a reader of the Chicago Defender I think it is one of the Most Wonderful Papers of our race printed. Sirs I am writeing to see if You all will please get me a job. And Sir I can wash dishes, wash iron nursing work in groceries and dry good stores. Just any of these I can do. Sir, who so ever you get the job from please tell them to send me a ticket and I will pay them. When I get their as I have not got enough money to pay my way. I am a girl of 17 years old and in the 8 grade at Knox Academy School. But on account of not having money enough I had to stop school. Sir I will thank you all with all my heart. May God Bless you all. Please answer in return mail. ■

SOURCE: *Journal of Negro History*, Vol. IV, 1919, pp. 417, 317.

---

authorities held African Americans responsible for the violence. President Wilson refused requests for federal intervention or investigation.

In terms of service in the armed forces, compliance with the draft, and involvement in volunteer work, African Americans had supported the war effort as faithfully as any group. In 1917, despite a segregated army and discrimination in defense industries, most African Americans thought the war might improve their lot. But black disillusionment about the war grew quickly, as did a newly militant spirit. A heightened sense of race consciousness and activism was evident among black veterans and the growing black communities of Northern cities. Taking the lead in the fight against bigotry and injustice, the NAACP held a national conference in 1919 on lynching. It pledged to defend persecuted African Americans, publicize the horrors of lynch law, and seek federal legislation against "Judge Lynch." By 1919, membership in the NAACP had reached 60,000 and the circulation of its journal exceeded half a million.

Labor Strife

The relative labor peace of 1917 and 1918 dissolved after the armistice. More than 4 million American workers were involved in some 3,600 strikes in 1919 alone. This unprecedented strike wave had several causes. Most of the modest wartime wage gains were wiped out by spiraling inflation and high prices for food, fuel, and housing. With the end of government controls on industry, many employers withdrew their recognition of unions. Difficult working conditions, such as the twelve-hour day in steel mills, were still routine in some industries.

Several of the postwar strikes received widespread national attention. They seemed to be more than simple economic conflicts, and they provoked deep fears about the larger social order. In February 1919, a strike in the shipyards of Seattle, Washington, over wages escalated into a general citywide strike involving 60,000 workers. The local press and Mayor Ole Hanson denounced the strikers as revolutionaries. Hanson effectively ended the strike by requesting federal troops to occupy the city. In September, Boston policemen went out on strike when the police commissioner rejected a citizens' commission study that recommended a pay raise. Massachusetts governor Calvin Coolidge called in the National Guard to restore order, and won a national reputation by crushing the strike. The entire police force was fired.

The biggest strike took place in the steel industry, and involved some 350,000 steelworkers. Centered in several Midwestern cities, this epic struggle lasted from September 1919 to January 1920. The AFL had hoped to build on wartime gains in an industry that had successfully resisted unionization before the war. The major demands were union recognition, the eight-hour day, and wage increases. The steel companies used black strikebreakers and armed guards to keep the mills running. Elbert Gary, president of U.S. Steel, directed a sophisticated propaganda campaign that branded the strikers as revolutionaries. Public opinion turned against the strike and condoned the use of state and federal troops to break it. The failed steel strike proved to be the era's most bitter and devastating defeat for organized labor.

AN UNEASY PEACE

The armistice of November 1918 ended the fighting on the battlefield, but the war continued at the peace conference. In the old royal palace of Versailles near Paris, delegates from twenty-seven countries spent five months hammering out a settlement. Yet neither Germany nor Russia was represented. The proceedings were dominated by leaders of the "Big Four": David Lloyd George (Great Britain), Georges Clemenceau (France), Vittorio Orlando (Italy), and Woodrow Wilson (United States). President Wilson saw the peace conference as a historic opportunity to project his domestic liberalism onto the world stage. But the stubborn realities of power politics would frustrate Wilson at Versailles and lead to his most crushing defeat at home.

The Fourteen Points

Wilson arrived in Paris with the United States delegation in January 1919. He believed the Great War revealed the bankruptcy of diplomacy based on alliances and the "balance of power." Peacemaking, he thought, meant an opportunity for America to lead the rest of the world toward a new vision of international relations. He brought with him a plan for peace that he had outlined

a year earlier in a speech to Congress on U.S. war aims. The Fourteen Points, as they were called, had originally served wartime purposes: to appeal to antiwar factions in Austria-Hungary and Germany, to convince Russia to stay in the war, and to help sustain Allied morale. As a blueprint for peace, they contained three main elements. First, Wilson offered a series of specific proposals for setting postwar boundaries in Europe and creating new countries out of the collapsed Austro-Hungarian and Ottoman empires. The key idea here was the right of all peoples to "national self-determination." Second, Wilson listed general principles for governing international conduct, including freedom of the seas, free trade, open covenants instead of secret treaties, reduced armaments, and mediation for competing colonial claims. Third, and most important, Wilson called for a League of Nations to help implement these principles and resolve future disputes.

The Fourteen Points offered a plan for world order deeply rooted in the liberal progressivism long associated with Wilson. The plan reflected a faith in efficient government and the rule of law as means for solving international problems. It advocated a dynamic democratic capitalism as a middle ground between Old World autocracy and revolutionary socialism.

The most controversial element, both at home and abroad, would prove to be the League of Nations. The heart of the League covenant, Article X, called for collective security as the ultimate method of keeping the peace: "The members of the League undertake to respect and preserve as against external aggression the territorial integrity and existing political independence of all Members." In the United States, Wilson's critics would focus on this provision as an unacceptable surrender of the nation's sovereignty and independence in foreign affairs.

Wilson in Paris

Despite Wilson's devotion to "open covenants," much of the negotiating at Versailles was in fact done in secret among the Big Four. The ideal of self-determination found limited expression. The independent states of Austria, Hungary, Poland, Yugoslavia, and Czechoslovakia were carved out of the homelands of the beaten Central Powers. But the Allies resisted Wilson's call for independence for the colonies of the defeated nations. A compromise mandate system of protectorates gave the French and British control of parts of the old German and Turkish empires in Africa and West Asia. Japan won control of former German colonies in China. Among those trying, but failing, to influence the treaty negotiations were the sixty-odd delegates to the first Pan African Congress, held in Paris at the same time as the peace talks. The group included Americans W. E. B. Du Bois and William Monroe Trotter as well as representatives from Africa and the West Indies. All were

Woodrow Wilson, Georges Clemenceau, and David Lloyd George are among the central figures depicted in John Christen Johansen's *Signing of the Treaty of Versailles*. But all the gathered statesmen appear dwarfed by their surroundings.

SOURCE: John Christen Johansen, *Signing of the Treaty of Versailles*, 1919, National Portrait Gallery, Smithsonian Institution, Washington D.C./Art Resource, New York.

disappointed with the failure of the peace conference to grant self-determination to thousands of Africans living in former German colonies.

Another disappointment for Wilson came with the issue of war guilt. He had strongly opposed the extraction of harsh economic reparations from the Central Powers. But the French and British, with their awful war losses fresh in mind, insisted on making Germany pay. The final treaty contained a clause attributing the war to "the aggression of Germany," and a commission later set German war reparations at $33 billion. Bitter resentment in Germany over the punitive treaty helped sow the seeds for the Nazi rise to power in the 1930s.

The final treaty was signed on June 28, 1919, in the Hall of Mirrors at the Versailles palace. The Germans had no choice but to accept its harsh terms. President Wilson had been disappointed by the secret deals and the endless compromising of his ideals, no doubt underestimating the stubborn reality of power politics in the wake of Europe's most devastating war. He had nonetheless won a commitment to the League of Nations, the centerpiece of his plan, and he was confident that the

American people would accept the treaty. The tougher fight would be with the Senate, where a two-thirds vote was needed for ratification.

The Treaty Fight

Preoccupied with peace conference politics in Paris, Wilson had neglected politics at home. His troubles had actually started earlier. Republicans had captured both the House and the Senate in the 1918 elections. Wilson had then made a tactical error by including no prominent Republicans in the U.S. peace delegation. He therefore faced a variety of tough opponents to the treaty he brought home.

Wilson's most extreme enemies in the Senate were a group of about sixteen "irreconcilables," opposed to a treaty in any form. Some were isolationist progressives, such as Republicans Robert M. La Follette of Wisconsin and William Borah of Idaho, who opposed the League of Nations as steadfastly as they opposed American entry into the war. Others were racist xenophobes like Democrat James Reed of Missouri. He objected, he said, to submitting questions to a tribunal "on which a nigger from Liberia, a nigger from Honduras, a nigger from India, and an unlettered gentleman from Siam, each have votes equal to the great United States of America."

The less dogmatic, but more influential, opponents were led by Republican Henry Cabot Lodge of Massachusetts, powerful majority leader of the Senate. They had strong reservations about the League of Nations, especially the provisions for collective security in the event of a member nation's being attacked. Lodge argued that this provision impinged on congressional authority to declare war, and placed unacceptable restraints on the nation's ability to pursue an independent foreign policy. Lodge proposed a series of amendments that would have weakened the League. But Wilson refused to compromise, motivated in part by the long-standing hatred he and Lodge felt toward each other.

In September, Wilson set out on a speaking tour across the country to drum up support for the League and the treaty. The crowds were large and responsive, but they did not change any votes in the Senate. The strain took its toll. On September 25, after speaking in Pueblo, Colorado, the sixty-three-year-old Wilson collapsed from exhaustion. His doctor canceled the rest of the trip. A week later, back in Washington, the president suffered a stroke that left him partially paralyzed. In November, Lodge brought the treaty out of committee for a vote, having appended to it fourteen reservations— that is, recommended changes. A bedridden Wilson stubbornly refused to compromise, and instructed Democrats to vote against the Lodge version of the treaty. On November 19, Democrats joined with the "irreconcilables" to defeat the amended treaty, 39 to 55.

Wilson refused to budge. In January, he urged Democrats to either stand by the original treaty or vote it down. The 1920 election, he warned, would be "a great and solemn referendum" on the whole issue. In the final vote, on March 19, 1920, twenty-one Democrats broke with the president and voted for the Lodge version, giving it a majority of 49 to 35. But this was seven votes short of the two-thirds needed for ratification. As a result, the United States never signed the Versailles Treaty, nor did it join the League of Nations. The absence of the United States weakened the League and made it more difficult for the organization to realize Wilson's dream of a peaceful community of nations.

The Russian Revolution and America's Response

Since early 1917, the turmoil of the Russian Revolution had changed the climate of both foreign affairs and domestic politics. The repressive and corrupt regime of Czar Nicholas II had been overthrown in March 1917 by a coalition of forces demanding change. The new provisional government, headed by Alexander Kerensky, vowed to keep Russia in the fight against Germany. But the war had taken a terrible toll on Russian soldiers and civilians, and had become very unpopular. The radical Bolsheviks, led by V. I. Lenin, gained a large following by promising "peace, land, and bread," and they began plotting to seize power. The Bolsheviks followed the teachings of German revolutionary Karl Marx, emphasizing the inevitability of class struggle and the replacement of capitalism by communism.

In November 1917, the Bolsheviks took control of the Russian government. In March 1918, to the dismay of the Allies, the new Bolshevik government negotiated a separate peace with Germany, the Treaty of Brest-Litovsk. Russia was now lost as a military ally, and her defection made possible a massive shift of German troops to the Western Front. As civil war raged within Russia, British and French leaders wanted to help counterrevolutionary forces overthrow the new Bolshevik regime, as well as reclaim military supplies originally sent for use against the Germans.

Although sympathetic to the March revolution overthrowing the czar, President Wilson refused to recognize the authority of the Bolshevik regime. Bolshevism represented a threat to the liberal-capitalist values that Wilson believed to be the foundation of America's moral and material power, and that provided the basis for the Fourteen Points. At the same time, however, Wilson at first resisted British and French pressure to intervene in Russia, citing his commitment to national self-determination and noninterference in other countries' internal affairs.

By August 1918, as the Russian political and military situation became increasingly chaotic, Wilson agreed to British and French plans for sending troops to Siberia and northern Russia. Meanwhile, Japan poured troops into Siberia and northern Manchuria in a bid to control the commercially important Chinese Eastern and Trans-Siberian railways. After the Wilson administration negotiated an agreement that placed these strategic railways under international control, the restoration and protection of the railways became the primary concern of American military forces in Russia.

Wilson's idealistic support for self-determination had succumbed to the demands of international power politics. Eventually, some 15,000 American troops served in northern and eastern Russia, with some remaining until 1920. They stayed for two reasons: to counter Japanese influence, and to avoid alienating the British and French, who opposed withdrawal. The Allied armed intervention widened the gulf between Russia and the West. In March 1919, Russian Communists established the Third International, or Comintern. Their call for a worldwide revolution deepened Allied mistrust, and the Paris Peace Conference essentially ignored the new political reality posed by the Russian Revolution.

The Red Scare

The revolutionary changes taking place in Russia became an important backdrop for domestic politics. In the United States, it became common to blame socialism, the IWW, trade unionism in general, and even racial disturbances on foreign radicals and alien ideologies. The accusation of Bolshevism became a powerful weapon for turning public opinion against strikers and political dissenters of all kinds. In truth, by 1919, the American radicals were already weakened and badly split. The Socialist Party had around 40,000 members. Two small Communist Parties, made up largely of immigrants, had a total of perhaps 70,000. In the spring of 1919, a few extremists mailed bombs to prominent business and political leaders. That June, simultaneous bombings in eight cities killed two people and damaged the residence of Attorney General A. Mitchell Palmer. With public alarm growing, state and federal officials began a coordinated campaign to root out subversives and their alleged Russian connections.

Palmer used the broad authority of the 1918 Alien Act, which enabled the government to deport any immigrant found to be a member of a revolutionary organization prior to or after coming to the United States. In a series of raids in late 1919, Justice Department agents in eleven cities arrested and roughed up several hundred members of the IWW and the Union of Russian Workers. Little evidence of revolutionary intent was found, but 249 people were deported, including prominent anarchists Emma Goldman and

CHRONOLOGY

1903	U.S. obtains Panama Canal rights
1905	President Theodore Roosevelt mediates peace treaty between Japan and Russia at Portsmouth Conference
1908	Root-Takahira Agreement with Japan affirms status quo in Asia and Open Door policy in China
1911	Mexican Revolution begins
1914	U.S. forces invade Mexico
	Panama Canal opens
	World War I begins in Europe
	President Woodrow Wilson issues proclamation of neutrality
1915	Germany declares war zone around Great Britain
	German U-boat sinks *Lusitania*
1916	Pancho Villa raids New Mexico, is pursued by General Pershing
	Wilson is reelected
	National Defense Act establishes preparedness program
1917	February: Germany resumes unrestricted submarine warfare

	March: Zimmermann Note, suggesting a German-Mexican alliance, shocks Americans
	April: United States declares war on the Central Powers
	May: Selective Service Act is passed
	June: Espionage Act is passed
	November: Bolshevik Revolution begins in Russia
1918	January: Wilson unveils Fourteen Points
	May: Sedition Act is passed
	June: U.S. troops begin to see action in France
	November: Armistice ends war
1919	January: Eighteenth Amendment (Prohibition) is ratified
	Wilson serves as Chief U.S. negotiator at Paris Peace Conference
	June: Versailles Treaty is signed in Paris
	July: Race riot breaks out in Chicago
	Steel strike begins in several Midwestern cities
	November: Palmer raids begin
1920	March: Senate finally votes down Versailles Treaty and League of Nations
	August: Nineteenth Amendment (woman suffrage) is ratified
	November: Warren G. Harding is elected president

Alexander Berkman. In early 1920, some 6,000 people in thirty-three cities, including many U.S. citizens and noncommunists, were arrested and herded into prisons and bullpens. Again, no evidence of a grand plot was found, but another 600 aliens were deported. The Palmer raids had a ripple effect around the nation, encouraging other repressive measures against radicals. In New York, the state assembly refused to seat five duly elected Socialist Party members.

A report prepared by a group of distinguished lawyers questioned the legality of the attorney general's tactics. Palmer's popularity had waned by the spring of 1920, when it became clear that his predictions of revolutionary uprisings were wildly exaggerated. But the Red Scare left an ugly legacy: wholesale violations of constitutional rights, deportations of hundreds of innocent people, fuel for the fires of nativism and intolerance. Business groups, such as the National Association of Manufacturers, found "Red-baiting" to be an effective tool in postwar efforts to keep unions out of their factories. Indeed, the government-sanctioned Red Scare reemerged later in the century as a powerful political force.

The Red Scare took its toll on the women's movement as well. Before the war, many suffragists and feminists had maintained ties and shared platforms with socialist and labor groups. The suffrage movement in particular had brought together women from very different class backgrounds and political perspectives. But the calls for "100 percent Americanism" during and after the war, destroyed the fragile alliances that had made a group such as the National American Woman Suffrage Association so powerful. Hostility to radicalism marked the political climate of the 1920s, and this atmosphere narrowed the political spectrum for women activists.

The Election of 1920

Woodrow Wilson had wanted the 1920 election to be a "solemn referendum" on the League of Nations and his conduct of the war. Ill and exhausted, Wilson did not run for reelection. A badly divided Democratic Party compromised on Governor James M. Cox of Ohio as its candidate. A proven vote-getter, Cox distanced himself from Wilson's policies, which had come under withering attack from many quarters.

The Republicans nominated Senator Warren G. Harding of Ohio. A political hack, the handsome and genial Harding had virtually no qualifications to be president, except that he looked like one. Harding's campaign was vague and ambiguous about the Versailles Treaty and almost everything else. He struck a chord with the electorate in calling for a retreat from Wilsonian idealism. "America's present need," he said, "is not heroics but healing; not nostrums but normalcy; not revolution but restoration."

The notion of a "return to normalcy" proved very attractive to voters exhausted by the war, inflation, big government, and social dislocation. Harding won the greatest landslide in history to that date, carrying every state outside the South and taking the popular vote by 16 million to 9 million. Republicans retained their majorities in the House and Senate as well. Socialist Eugene V. Debs, still a powerful symbol of the dream of radical

social change, managed to poll 900,000 votes from jail. But the overall vote repudiated Wilson and the progressive movement. Americans seemed eager to pull back from moralism in public and international controversies. Yet many of the economic, social, and cultural changes wrought by the war would accelerate during the 1920s. In truth, there could never be a "return to normalcy."

CONCLUSION

Compared to the casualties and social upheavals endured by the European powers, the Great War's impact on American life might appear slight. Yet the war created economic, social, and political dislocations that helped reshape American life long after Armistice Day. Republican administrations invoked the wartime partnership between government and industry to justify an aggressive peacetime policy fostering cooperation between the state and business. Wartime production needs contributed to what economists later called "the second industrial revolution." Patriotic fervor and the exaggerated specter of Bolshevism were used to repress radicalism, organized labor, feminism, and the entire legacy of progressive reform.

The wartime measure of national prohibition evolved into perhaps the most contentious social issue of peacetime. Sophisticated use of sales techniques, psychology, and propaganda during the war helped define the newly powerful advertising and public relations industries of the 1920s. The growing visibility of immigrants and African Americans, especially in the nation's cities, provoked a xenophobic and racist backlash in the politics of the 1920s. More than anything else, the desire for "normalcy" reflected the deep anxieties evoked by America's wartime experience.

REVIEW QUESTIONS

1. What central issues drew the United States deeper into international politics in the early years of the century? How did American presidents justify a more expansive role? What diplomatic and military policies did they exploit for these ends?

2. Compare the arguments for and against American participation in the Great War. Which Americans were most likely to support entry? Which were more likely to oppose it?

3. How did mobilizing for war change the economy and its relationship to government? Which of these changes, if any, spilled over to the postwar years?

4. How did the war affect political life in the United States? What techniques were used to stifle dissent? What was the war's political legacy?

5. To what extent was the war an extension of progressivism?

6. Analyze the impact of the war on American workers. How did the conflict affect the lives of African Americans and women?

7. What principles guided Woodrow Wilson's Fourteen Points? How would you explain the United States' failure to ratify the Treaty of Versailles?

RECOMMENDED READING

Marc Allen Eisner, *From Warfare State to Welfare State: World War I, Compensatory State Building, and the Limits of the Modern Order* (2000). Demonstrates how, to compensate for the limited capacities of the state to wage total war, policymakers incorporated business organizations and structures into the network of committees coordinating the war effort.

Robert Hannigan, *The New World Power: American Foreign Policy, 1898–1917* (2002). An ambitious analysis of how the American policy-making elite sought to impose political and economic order around the globe.

Jennifer D. Keene, *Doughboys, the Great War, and the Remaking of America* (2001). Examines the persistent conflicts between citizen-soldiers and army authorities, as well as the long-range political impact of mass military service throughout the twentieth century.

Kathleen Kennedy, *Disloyal Mothers and Scurrilous Citizens: Women and Subversion During World War I* (1999). Analyzes the Federal government's campaign against antiwar women activists and their refusal to adhere to accepted notions of "patriotic motherhood."

Thomas J. Knock, *To End All Wars: Woodrow Wilson and the Quest for a New World Order* (1992). A persuasive analysis of Wilson's internationalism, its links to his domestic policies, and his design for the League of Nations.

Paul L. Murphy, *World War I and the Origin of Civil Liberties* (1979). A good overview of the various civil liberties issues raised by the war, and government efforts to suppress dissent.

Ronald Schaffer, *America in the Great War: The Rise of the War Welfare State* (1991). Excellent material on how the war transformed the relationship between business and government and spurred improved conditions for industrial workers.

Joe William Trotter Jr., ed., *The Great Migration in Historical Perspective* (1991). An excellent collection of essays examining the Great Migration, with special attention to issues of class and gender within the African American community.

Susan Zeiger, *In Uncle Sam's Service: Women Workers With the American Expeditionary Force, 1917–1919* (1999). The first in-depth study of American women's experiences with the armed forces overseas.

Robert H. Zieger, *America's Great War: World War I and the American Experience* (2000). The best new one-volume synthesis on how the war transformed the United States and its role in the world.

 For additional study resources for this chapter, go to the *Companion Website*, http://www.prenhall.com/faragher.

The Twenties

1920–1929

CHAPTER OUTLINE

The Movie Audience and Hollywood:
Mass Culture Creates a New National Community

I nside midtown Manhattan's magnificent new Roxy Theater, a sellout crowd eagerly settled in for opening night. Outside, thousands of fans cheered wildly at the arrival of movie stars such as Charlie Chaplin, Gloria Swanson, and Harold Lloyd. A squadron of smartly uniformed ushers guided patrons under a five-story-tall rotunda to some 6,200 velvet-covered seats. The audience marveled at the huge gold and rose-colored murals, classical statuary, plush carpeting, and Gothic-style windows. It was easy to believe newspaper reports that the theater had cost $10 million to build. Suddenly, light flooded the orchestra pit and 110 musicians began playing "The Star Spangled Banner." A troupe of 100 performers took the stage, dancing ballet numbers and singing old Southern melodies such as "My Old Kentucky Home" and "Swanee River." Congratulatory telegrams from President Calvin Coolidge and other dignitaries flashed on the screen. Finally, the evening's feature presentation, *The Love of Sunya*, starring Gloria Swanson, began. Samuel L. "Roxy" Rothapfel, the theater's designer, had realized his grand dream—to build "the cathedral of the motion picture."

When Roxy's opened in March 1927, nearly 60 million Americans "worshiped" each week at movie theaters across the nation. The "movie palaces" of the 1920s were designed to transport patrons to exotic places and different times. As film pioneer Marcus Loew put it, "We sell tickets to theaters, not movies." Every large community boasted at least one opulent movie theater. Houston's Majestic was built to represent an ancient Italian garden; it had a ceiling made to look like an open sky, complete with stars and cloud formations. The Tivoli in Chicago featured opulent French Renaissance decor; Grauman's Egyptian in Los Angeles recreated the look of a pharaoh's tomb; and Albuquerque's Kimo drew inspiration from Navajo art and religion.

The remarkable popularity of motion pictures, and later radio, forged a new kind of community. A huge national audience regularly went to the movies, and the same entertainment could be enjoyed virtually anywhere in the country by just about everyone. Movies emerged as the most popular form in the new mass culture, with an appeal that extended far beyond the films themselves, or even the theaters. Americans embraced the cult of celebrity, voraciously consuming fan magazines, gossip columns, and news of the stars. By the 1920s, the production center for this dream world was Hollywood, California, a suburb of Los Angeles that had barely existed in 1890.

Motion picture companies found Hollywood an alluring alternative to the east coast cities where they had been born. Its reliably sunny and dry climate was ideal for year-round filming. Its unique surroundings offered a perfect variety of scenic locations—mountains, desert, ocean—and downtown Los Angeles was only an hour away. Land was cheap and plentiful. And because Los Angeles was the leading nonunion, open-shop city in the country, so was labor. By the early 1920s, Hollywood produced more than 80 percent of the nation's motion pictures and was assuming mythical status. The isolation of the town, its great distance from the Eastern cities, its lack of traditional sources of culture and learning—all contributed to movie folk looking at life in a self-consciously "Hollywood" way.

With its feel of a modern frontier boomtown, Hollywood was a new kind of American community. It lured

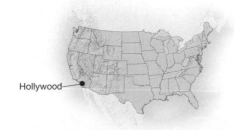

Hollywood

the young and cosmopolitan with the promise of upward mobility and a new way of life. Most of the top studio executives were Jewish immigrants from eastern and central Europe. In contrast to most Americans, who hailed from rural areas or small towns, more than half of Hollywood's writers, directors, editors, and actors were born in cities of over 100,000. Two-thirds of its performers were under thirty-five, and three-fourths of its actresses were under twenty-five. More than 90 percent of its writers (women made up one-third to one-half of this key group) had attended college or worked in journalism. The movies this untypical community created evoked the pleasures of leisure, consumption, and personal freedom, redefining the nation's cultural values in the 1920s.

Movie stars dominated Hollywood. Charlie Chaplin, Mary Pickford, Rudolph Valentino, Gloria Swanson, and Douglas Fairbanks became popular idols as much for their highly publicized private lives as for their roles on screen. Many accumulated great wealth, becoming the nation's experts on how to live well. Movie folk built luxurious mansions in a variety of architectural styles, and outfitted them with swimming pools, tennis courts, golf courses, and lavish gardens.

Visitors often noted that Hollywood had no museums, art galleries, live theater, or other traditional institutions of high culture. How would the town's wealthy movie elite spend their time and money? By 1916, Charlie Chaplin, a working-class immigrant from the London slums, was earning $10,000 a week for the comedies that made his the most famous face in the world. He recalled trying to figure out what to do with his new wealth. "The money I earned was legendary, a symbol in figures, for I had never actually seen it. I therefore had to do something to prove I had it. So I procured a secretary, a valet, a car, a chauffeur."

Ordinary Americans found it easy to identify with movie stars despite their wealth and status. Unlike industrialists or politicians, stars had no social authority over large groups of employees or voters. They, too, had to answer to a boss, and most had risen from humble beginnings. But above all, Hollywood, like the movies it churned out, represented for millions of Americans new possibilities: freedom, material success, upward mobility, and the chance to remake one's very identity. By the end of the decade, the Hollywood "dream factory" had helped forge a national community whose collective aspirations and desires were increasingly defined by those possibilities, even if relatively few Americans realized them during the 1920s.

Although it became a preeminent symbol around the globe for America's growing cultural and economic influence, Hollywood was by no means a typical 1920s community. Nor did Hollywood films offer anything near an accurate reflection of the complexities of American society. American life would increasingly be defined by an urban-based mass media that claimed the entire nation for its audience. Yet resentment toward and resistance against the new popular culture was widespread. Movies celebrated prosperity, new technologies, and expanded consumerism, but these were by no means shared equally among Americans in the decade following World War I. And while Hollywood films touted the promise of the modern, and the potential for anyone to remake themselves, tenacious belief in the old-fashioned verities of prewar America fueled some of strongest political and cultural currents of the decade.

KEY TOPICS

- A second industrial revolution that transforms the economy
- The promise and limits of prosperity in the 1920s
- New mass media and the culture of consumption
- Republican Party dominance
- Political and cultural opposition to modern trends

POSTWAR PROSPERITY AND ITS PRICE

Republican Warren G. Harding won the presidency in 1920, largely thanks to his nostalgic call for a "return to normalcy." But in the decade following the end of World War I, the American economy underwent profound structural changes that guaranteed life would never be "normal" again. The 1920s saw an enormous increase in the efficiency of production, a steady climb in real wages, a decline in the length of the average employee's work week, and a boom in consumer-goods industries. Americans shared unevenly in the postwar prosperity, and by the end of the decade, certain basic weaknesses in the economy helped to bring on the worst depression in American history. Yet overall, the nation experienced crucial transformations in how it organized its business, earned its living, and enjoyed its leisure time.

The Second Industrial Revolution

The prosperity of the 1920s rested on what historians have called the "second industrial revolution" in American manufacturing, in which technological innovations made it possible to increase industrial output without expanding the labor force. Electricity replaced steam as the main power source for industry in these years, making possible the replacement of older machinery with more efficient and flexible electric machinery. In 1914, only 30 percent of the nation's factories were electrified; by 1929, 70 percent relied on the electric motor rather than the steam engine.

Much of the newer, automatic machinery could be operated by unskilled and semiskilled workers, and it boosted the overall efficiency of American industry. Thus in 1929, the average worker in manufacturing produced roughly three-quarters more per hour than he or she had in 1919. The machine industry itself, particularly the manufacture of electrical machinery, led in productivity gains, enjoying one of the fastest rates of expansion. It employed more workers than any other manufacturing sector—some 1.1 million in 1929—supplying not only a growing home market, but 35 percent of the world market as well.

During the late nineteenth century, heavy industries such as machine tools, railroads, iron, and steel had pioneered mass-production techniques. These industries manufactured what economists call producer-durable goods. In the 1920s, modern mass-production techniques were increasingly applied as well to newer consumer-durable goods—automobiles, radios, washing machines, and telephones—permitting firms to make large profits while keeping prices affordable. Other consumer-based industries, such as canning, chemicals, synthetics, and plastics, began to change the everyday lives

of millions of Americans. With more efficient management, greater mechanization, intensive product research, and ingenious sales and advertising methods, the consumer-based industries helped to nearly double industrial production in the 1920s.

America experienced a building boom during the 1920s, and its construction industry played a large role in the new prosperity. Expenditures for residential housing, nonresidential building, and public construction projects all showed steady growth after 1921. The demand for new housing was unprecedented, particularly with the backlog created during World War I, when little new construction took place. The growth in automobile ownership, as well as improvements in public mass transit, made suburban living more attractive to families and suburban construction more profitable for developers.

The Modern Corporation

In the late nineteenth century, individual entrepreneurs such as John D. Rockefeller in oil and Andrew Carnegie in steel had provided a model for success. They maintained both corporate control (ownership) and business leadership (management) in their enterprises. In the 1920s, a managerial revolution increasingly divorced ownership of corporate stock from the everyday control of businesses (see Figure 23.1). The new corporate

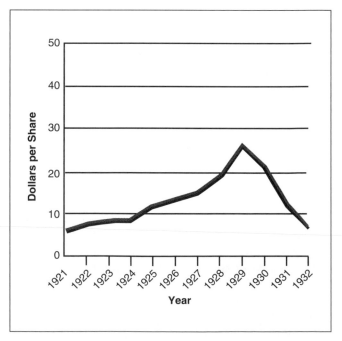

FIGURE 23.1   Stock Market Prices, 1921–32 Common stock prices rose steeply during the 1920s. Although only about 4 million Americans owned stocks during the period, "stock watching" became something of a national sport.

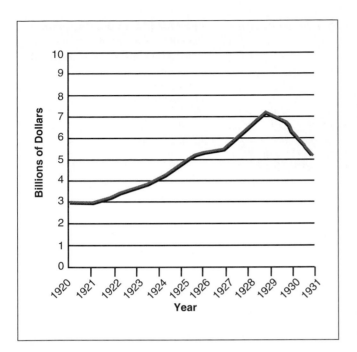

FIGURE 23.2 Consumer Debt, 1920–31 The expansion of consumer borrowing was a key component of the era's prosperity. These figures do not include mortgages or money borrowed to purchase stocks. They reveal the great increase in "installment buying" for such consumer durable goods as automobiles and household appliances.

ideal was to be found in men such as Alfred P. Sloan of General Motors and Owen D. Young of the Radio Corporation of America. A growing class of salaried executives, plant managers, and engineers formed a new elite, who made corporate policy without themselves having a controlling interest in the companies they worked for. They stressed scientific management and the latest theories of behavioral psychology in their effort to make their workplaces more productive, stable, and profitable (see Figure 23.2).

During the 1920s, the most successful corporations were those that led in three key areas: the integration of production and distribution, product diversification, and the expansion of industrial research. Until the end of World War I, for example, the chemical manufacturer Du Pont, had specialized in explosives such as gunpowder. After the war, Du Pont moved aggressively into the consumer market with a diverse array of products. The company created separate but integrated divisions that produced and distributed new fabrics (such as rayon), paints, dyes, and celluloid products (such as artificial sponges). The great electrical manufacturers—General Electric and Westinghouse—similarly transformed themselves after the war. Previously concentrating on lighting and power equipment, they now diversified into household appli-

ances like radios, washing machines, and refrigerators. The chemical and electrical industries also led the way in industrial research, hiring personnel to develop new products and test their commercial viability.

By 1929, the 200 largest corporations owned nearly half the nation's corporate wealth—that is, physical plant, stock, and property. Half the total industrial income—revenue from sales of goods—was concentrated in 100 corporations. Oligopoly—the control of a market by a few large producers—became the norm. Four companies packed almost three-quarters of all American meat. Another four rolled nine out of every ten cigarettes. National chain grocery stores, clothing shops, and pharmacies began squeezing out local neighborhood businesses. One grocery chain alone, the Great Atlantic and Pacific Tea Company (A&P), accounted for 10 percent of all retail food sales in America. Its 15,000 stores sold a greater volume of goods than Ford Motor Company at its peak. These changes meant that Americans were increasingly members of national consumer communities, buying the same brands all over the country, as opposed to locally produced goods.

Welfare Capitalism

The wartime gains made by organized labor, and the active sympathy shown to trade unions by government agencies such as the National War Labor Board troubled most corporate leaders. To challenge the power and appeal of trade unions and collective bargaining, large employers aggressively promoted a variety of new programs designed to improve worker well-being and morale. These schemes, collectively known as welfare capitalism, became a key part of corporate strategy in the 1920s.

One approach was to encourage workers to acquire property through stock-purchase plans or, less frequently, home-ownership plans. By 1927, 800,000 employees had more than $1 billion invested in more than 300 companies. Other programs offered workers insurance policies covering accidents, illness, old age, and death. By 1928, some 6 million workers had group insurance coverage valued at $7.5 billion. Many plant managers and personnel departments consciously worked to improve safety conditions, provide medical services, and establish sports and recreation programs for workers. Employers hoped such measures would encourage workers to identify personally with the company and discourage complaints on the job. To some extent they succeeded. But welfare capitalism could not solve the most chronic problems faced by industrial workers: seasonal unemployment, low wages, long hours, and unhealthy factory conditions.

Large corporations also mounted an effective antiunion campaign in the early 1920s called "the American plan," a name meant to associate unionism with foreign

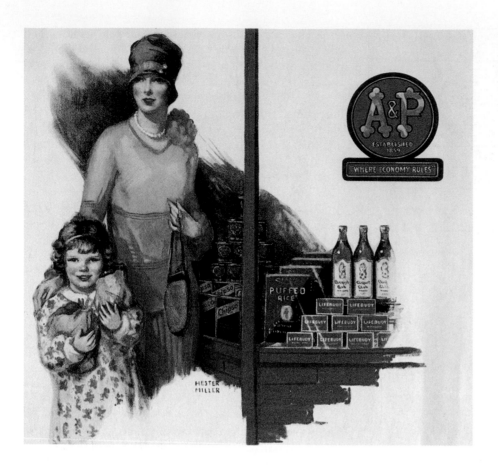

The A&P grocery chain expanded from 400 stores in 1912 to more than 15,000 by the end of the 1920s, making it a familiar sight in communities across America. A&P advertisements, like this one from 1927, emphasized cleanliness, order, and the availability of name-brand goods at discount prices.

SOURCE: A&P Food Stores LTD.

and un-American ideas. Backed by powerful business lobbies such as the National Association of Manufacturers and the Chamber of Commerce, campaign leaders called for the open shop, in which no employee would be compelled to join a union. If a union existed, nonmembers would still get whatever wages and rights the union had won—a policy that put organizers at a disadvantage in signing up new members.

The open shop undercut the gains won in a union shop, where new employees had to join an existing union, or a closed shop, where employers agreed to hire only union members. As alternatives, large employers such as U.S. Steel and International Harvester began setting up company unions. Their intent was to substitute largely symbolic employee representation in management conferences for the more confrontational process of collective bargaining. These management strategies contributed to a sharp decline in the ranks of organized labor. Total union membership dropped from about 5 million in 1920 to 3.5 million in 1926. A large proportion of the remaining union members were concentrated in the skilled crafts of the building and printing trades. A conservative and timid union leadership was also responsible for the trend. William Green, who became president of the American Federation of Labor after the death of Samuel Gompers in 1924, showed no

real interest in getting unorganized workers, such as those in the growing mass-production industries of automobiles, steel, and electrical goods, into unions. The federal government, which had provided limited wartime support for unions, now reverted to a more probusiness posture. The Supreme Court in particular, was unsympathetic toward unions, consistently upholding the use of injunctions to prevent strikes, picketing, and other union activities.

The Auto Age

In their classic community study *Middletown* (1929), sociologists Robert and Helen Lynd noted the dramatic impact of the car on the social life of Muncie, Indiana. "Why on earth do you need to study what's changing this country?" asked one lifelong Muncie resident in 1924. "I can tell you what's happening in just four letters: A-U-T-O!" This remark hardly seems much of an exaggeration today. No other single development could match the impact of the postwar automobile explosion on the way Americans worked, lived, and played. The auto industry offered the clearest example of the rise to prominence of consumer durables. During the 1920s, America made approximately 85 percent of all the world's passenger cars. By 1929, the motor vehicle

Finished automobiles roll off the moving assembly line at the Ford Motor Company, Highland Park, Michigan, ca. 1920. During the 1920s, Henry Ford achieved the status of folk hero, as his name became synonymous with the techniques of mass production. Ford cultivated a public image of himself as the heroic genius of the auto industry, greatly exaggerating his personal achievements.

SOURCE: Brown Brothers.

industry was the most productive in the United States in terms of value. In that year, the industry added 4.8 million new cars to the more than 26 million—roughly one for every five people—already on American roads.

This extraordinary new industry had mushroomed in less than a generation. Its great pioneer, Henry Ford, had shown how the use of a continuous assembly line could drastically reduce the number of worker hours required to produce a single vehicle. Ford revolutionized the factory shop floor with new, custom-built machinery, such as the engine-boring drill press and the pneumatic wrench, and a more efficient layout. "Every piece of work in the shop moves," Ford boasted. "It may move on hooks or overhead chains, going to assembly in the exact order in which the parts are required; it may travel on a moving platform, or it may go by gravity,

but the point is that there is no lifting or trucking of anything other than materials." In 1913, it took thirteen hours to produce one automobile. In 1914, at his sprawling new Highland Park assembly plant just outside Detroit, Ford's system finished one car every ninety minutes. By 1925, cars were rolling off his assembly line at the rate of one every ten seconds.

In 1914, Ford startled American industry by inaugurating a new wage scale: $5 for an eight-hour day. This was roughly double the going pay rate for industrial labor, along with a shorter workday as well. But in defying the conventional economic wisdom of the day, Ford acted less out of benevolence than out of shrewdness. He understood that workers were consumers as well as producers, and the new wage scale helped boost sales of Ford cars. It also reduced the high turnover rate in his labor force and increased worker efficiency. Roughly two-thirds of the labor force at Ford consisted of immigrants from southern and eastern Europe. By the early 1920s Ford also employed about 5,000 African Americans, more than any other large American corporation. Ford's mass-production system and economies of scale permitted him to progressively reduce the price of his cars, bringing them within the reach of millions of Americans. The famous Model T, thoroughly standardized and available only in black, cost just under $300 in 1924—about three months' wages for the best-paid factory workers.

By 1927, Ford had produced 15 million Model Ts. But by then, the company faced stiff competition from General Motors, which had developed an effective new marketing strategy. Under the guidance of Alfred P. Sloan, GM organized into separate divisions, each of which appealed to a different market segment. Cadillac, for example, produced GM's most expensive car, which was targeted at the wealthy buyer; Chevrolet produced its least expensive model, which was targeted at working-class and lower-middle-class buyers. The GM business structure, along with its attempts to match production with demand through sophisticated market research and sales forecasting, became a widely copied model for other large American corporations.

The auto industry provided a large market for makers of steel, rubber, glass, and petroleum products. It stimulated public spending for good roads, and extended the housing boom to new suburbs. Showrooms, repair shops, and gas stations appeared in thousands of communities. New small enterprises, from motels to billboard advertising to roadside diners, sprang up as motorists took to the highway. Automobiles widened the experience of millions of Americans. They made the exploration of the world outside the local community easier and more attractive. For some, the car merely reinforced old social patterns, making it easier for them to get to church on Sunday, for example, or visit neighbors. Others used their cars to go to new places, shop in nearby cities, or take vacations. The automobile made leisure, in the sense of getting away from the routines of work and school, a more regular part of everyday life. It undoubtedly also changed the courtship practices of America's youth. Young people took advantage of the car to gain privacy and distance from their parents. "What on earth do you want me to do?" complained one "Middletown" high school girl to her anxious father. "Just sit around home all evening?" Many had their first sexual experiences in cars.

Cancel distance & conquer weather

The woman who drives her own Ford Closed Car is completely independent of road and weather conditions in any season.

It enables her to carry on all those activities of the winter months that necessitate travel to and fro—in or out of town. Her time and energy are conserved; her health is protected, no matter how bitterly cold the day, or how wet and slushy it is underfoot.

A Ford Sedan is always comfortable—warm and snug in winter, and in summer with ventilator and windows open wide, as cool and airy as an open car.

This seasonal comfort is combined with fine looks and Ford dependability; no wonder there is for this car so wide and ever-growing a demand.

FORD MOTOR COMPANY, DETROIT, MICHIGAN

TUDOR SEDAN, $580   ·.·   FORDOR SEDAN, $660
COUPE, $520   ·.·   ALL PRICES F. O. B. DETROIT

Ford
CLOSED CARS

Until 1924, Henry Ford had disdained national advertising for his cars. But as General Motors gained a competitive edge by making yearly changes in style and technology, Ford was forced to pay more attention to advertising. This ad was directed at "Mrs. Consumer," combining appeals to female independence and motherly duties.

SOURCE: Ford Motor Company.

Cities and Suburbs

Cars also promoted urban and suburban growth. The federal census for 1920 was the first in American history in which the proportion of the population that lived in urban places (those with 2,500 or more people) exceeded the proportion of the population living in rural areas. More revealing of urban growth was the steady increase in the number of big cities. In 1910, there were sixty cities with more than 100,000 inhabitants; in 1920, there were sixty-eight; and by 1930, there were ninety-two. During the 1920s, New York grew by 20 percent, to nearly 7 million, whereas Detroit, home of the auto industry, doubled its population, to nearly 2 million.

Cities promised business opportunity, good jobs, cultural richness, and personal freedom. They attracted millions of Americans, white and black, from small towns and farms, as well as immigrants from abroad. Immigrants were drawn to cities by the presence there of family and people of like background, in already established ethnic communities. In a continuation of the Great Migration that began during World War I, roughly 1.5 million African Americans from the rural South migrated to cities in search of economic opportunities during the 1920s, doubling the black populations of New York, Chicago, Detroit, and Houston.

Houston offers a good example of how the automobile shaped an urban community. In 1910, it was a sleepy railroad town with a population of about 75,000 that served the Texas Gulf coast and interior. The enormous demand for gasoline and other petroleum products helped transform the city into a busy center for oil refining. Its population soared to 300,000 by the end of the 1920s. Abundant cheap land and the absence of zoning ordinances, combined with the availability of the automobile, pushed Houston to expand horizontally rather than vertically. It became the archetypal decentralized, low-density city, sprawling miles in each direction from downtown, and thoroughly dependent upon automobiles and roads for its sense of community. Other Sunbelt cities, such as Los Angeles, Miami, and San Diego, experienced similar land-use patterns and sharp population growth during the decade.

Suburban communities grew at twice the rate of their core cities, also thanks largely to the automobile boom. Undeveloped land on the fringes of cities became valuable real estate. Grosse Pointe, near Detroit, and Elmwood Park, near Chicago, grew more than 700 percent in ten years. Long Island's Nassau County, just east of New York City, tripled in population. All the new "automobile suburbs" differed in important ways from earlier suburbs built along mass transit lines. The car allowed for a larger average lot size, and in turn, lower residential density.

Exceptions: Agriculture, Ailing Industries

Amid prosperity and progress, there were large pockets of the country that lagged behind. Advances in real income and improvements in the standard of living for workers and farmers were uneven at best. During the 1920s, one-quarter of all American workers were employed in agriculture, yet the farm sector failed to share in the general prosperity. The years 1914–19 had been a kind of golden age for the nation's farmers. Increased wartime demand, along with the devastation of much of European agriculture, had led to record-high prices for many crops. In addition, the wartime Food Administration had encouraged a great increase in agricultural production. But with the war's end, American farmers began to suffer from a chronic worldwide surplus of such farm staples as cotton, hogs, and corn.

Prices began to drop sharply in 1920. Cotton, which sold at 37 cents a pound in mid-1920, fell to 14 cents by year's end. Hog and cattle prices declined nearly 50 percent. By 1921, net farm income was down more than half from the year before. Land values also dropped, wiping out billions in capital investment. Behind these aggregate statistics were hundreds of thousands of individual human tragedies on the nation's 6 million farms. A 1928 song, "Eleven Cent Cotton," expressed the farmer's lament:

> 'Leven cent cotton, forty cent meat,
> How in the world can a poor man eat?
> Pray for the sunshine, 'cause it will rain,
> Things gettin' worse, drivin' us insane.

In the South, farmers' dependency on "King Cotton" deepened, as the region lagged farther behind the rest of the nation in both agricultural diversity and standard of living. Cotton acreage expanded, as large and heavily mechanized farms opened up new land in Okla-homa, west Texas, and the Mississippi-Yazoo delta. But in most of the South, from North Carolina to east Texas, small one- and two-mule cotton farms, most under 50 acres, still dominated the countryside. While editors, state officials, and reformers preached the need for greater variety of crops, Southern farmers actually raised less corn and livestock by the end of the decade. With few large urban centers and inadequate transportation, even those Southern farmers who had access to capital found it extremely difficult to find reliable markets for vegetables, fruit, poultry, or dairy products. The average Southern farm had land and buildings worth $3,525; for Northern farms, the figure was $11,029. The number of white tenant farmers increased by 200,000 during the 1920s, while black tenantry declined slightly as a result of the Great Migration. Some 700,000 Southern farmers, roughly half white and half black, still labored as sharecroppers. Modern conveniences such as electricity, indoor plumbing, automobiles, and phonographs remained far beyond the reach of the great majority of Southern farmers. Widespread rural poverty, poor diet, little access to capital—the world of Southern agriculture had changed very little since the days of Populist revolt in the 1890s.

The most important initiatives for federal farm relief were the McNary-Haugen bills, a series of complicated measures designed to prop up and stabilize farm prices. The basic idea, borrowed from the old Populist proposals of the 1890s, was for the government to purchase farm surpluses and either store them until prices rose or sell them on the world market. The result was supposed to be higher domestic prices for farm products. But President Calvin Coolidge viewed these measures as unwarranted federal interference in the economy, and vetoed the McNary-Haugen Farm Relief bill of 1927 when it finally passed Congress. Hard-pressed farmers would not benefit from government relief until the New Deal programs implemented in response to the Great Depression in the 1930s.

To be sure, some farmers thrived. Improved transportation and chain supermarkets allowed for a wider and more regular distribution of such foods as oranges, lemons, and fresh green vegetables. Citrus, dairy, and truck farmers in particular, profited from the growing importance of national markets. Wheat production jumped more than 300 percent during the 1920s. Across the plains of Kansas, Nebraska, Colorado, Oklahoma, and Texas, wheat farmers brought the methods of industrial capitalism to the land. They hitched disc plows and combined harvester-threshers to gasoline-powered tractors, tearing up millions of acres of grassland to create a vast wheat factory. With prices averaging above $1 per bushel over the decade, mechanized farming created a new class of large-scale wheat entrepreneurs on the plains. Ida Watkins, "the Wheat Queen" of Haskell

County, Kansas, made a profit of $75,000 from her 2,000 acres in 1926. Hickman Price needed twenty-five combines to harvest the wheat on his Plainview, Texas, farm—34,500 acres stretching over fifty-four square miles. When the disastrous dust storms of the 1930s rolled across the grassless plains, the long-range ecological impact of destroying so much native vegetation became evident.

But overall, per capita farm income remained well below what it had been in 1919, and the gap between farm and nonfarm income widened. By 1929, the average income per person on farms was $223, compared with $870 for nonfarm workers. By the end of the decade, hundreds of thousands had quit farming altogether for jobs in mills and factories. And fewer farmers owned their land. In 1930, 42 percent of all farmers were tenants, compared with 37 percent in 1919.

Large sectors of American industry also failed to share in the decade's general prosperity. As oil and natural gas gained in importance, America's coal mines became a less important source of energy. A combination of shrinking demand, new mining technology, and a series of losing strikes reduced the coal labor force by one-quarter. The United Mine Workers, perhaps the strongest AFL union in 1920, with 500,000 members, had shrunk to 75,000 by 1928. Economic hardship was widespread in many mining communities dependent on coal, particularly Appalachia and the southern Midwest. And those miners who did work, earned lower hourly wages.

The number of miles of railroad track actually decreased after 1920, as automobiles and trucks began to displace trains. In textiles, shrinking demand and overcapacity (too many factories) were chronic problems. The women's fashions of the 1920s generally required less material than had earlier fashions, and competition from synthetic fibers such as rayon depressed demand for cotton textiles. To improve profit margins, textile manufacturers in New England and other parts of the Northeast began a long-range shift of operations to the South, where nonunion shops and substandard wages became the rule. Between 1923 and 1933, 40 percent of New England's textile factories closed, and nearly 100,000 of the 190,000 workers employed there lost their jobs. Older New England manufacturing centers such as Lawrence, Lowell, Nashua, Manchester, and Fall River were hard hit by this shift.

The center of the American textile industry shifted permanently to the Piedmont region of North and South Carolina. Southern mills increased their work force from 220,000 to 257,000 between 1923 and 1933. By 1933, they employed nearly 70 percent of the workers in the industry. One of the biggest new textile communities was Gastonia, North Carolina, which proudly called itself the "South's City of Spindles." As the dominant employers and overall economic powers in Southern textile communities, manufacturers aggressively tried to improve productivity and cut costs. Southern mills generally operated night and day, used the newest labor-saving machinery, and cut back on the wage gains of the World War I years.

THE NEW MASS CULTURE

New communications media reshaped American culture in the 1920s. The phrase "Roaring Twenties" captures the explosion of image- and sound-making machinery that came to dominate so much of American life. Movies, radio, new kinds of journalism, the recording industry, and a more sophisticated advertising industry were deeply connected with the new culture of consumption. They also encouraged the parallel emergence of celebrity as a defining element in modern life. As technologies of mass impression, the media established national standards and norms for much of our culture—habit, dress, language, sounds, social behavior. For millions of Americans, the new media radically altered the rhythms of everyday life, and redefined what it meant to be "normal." To be sure, most working-class families had only limited access to the world of mass consumption—and many had only limited interest in it. But the new mass culture helped redefine the ideal of "the good life" and made the images, if not the substance, of it available to a national community.

Movie-Made America

The early movie industry, centered in New York and a few other big cities, had made moviegoing a regular habit for millions of Americans, especially immigrants and the working class. They flocked to cheap, storefront theaters, called nickelodeons, to watch short Westerns, slapstick comedies, melodramas, and travelogues. By 1914, there were about 18,000 "movie houses" showing motion pictures, with more than 7 million daily admissions and $300 million in annual receipts. With the shift of the industry westward to Hollywood, movies entered a new phase of business expansion.

Large studios such as Paramount, Fox, Metro-Goldwyn-Mayer (MGM), Universal, and Warner Brothers dominated the business with longer and more expensively produced movies—feature films. These companies were founded and controlled by immigrants from Europe, all of whom had a talent for discovering and exploiting changes in popular tastes. Adolph Zukor, the Hungarian-born head of Paramount, had been a furrier in New York City. Warsaw-born Samuel Goldwyn, a founder of MGM, had been a glove salesman. William Fox, of Fox Pictures, began as a garment cutter in Brooklyn. Most of the immigrant moguls had started in the

Thomas Hart Benton's 1930 painting *City Activities with Dance Hall* depicts the excitement and pleasures associated with commercialized leisure in the Prohibition era, reflecting urban America's dominance in defining the nation's popular culture.

SOURCE: Thomas Hart Benton, *City Activities with Dance Hall* from *America Today*, 1930. Distemper and egg tempera on gessoed linen with oil glaze 92 × 134 1/2 inches. Collection, AXA Financial, Inc., through its subsidiary, The Equitable Life Assurance Society of the U.S. ©AXA Financial, Inc.

business by buying or managing small movie theaters before beginning to produce films.

Each studio combined the three functions of production, distribution, and exhibition, and each controlled hundreds of movie theaters around the country. The era of silent films ended when Warner Brothers scored a huge hit in 1927 with *The Jazz Singer*, starring Al Jolson, which successfully introduced sound. New genres—musicals, gangster films, and screwball comedies—soon became popular. The higher costs associated with "talkies" also increased the studios' reliance on Wall Street investors and banks for working capital.

At the heart of Hollywood's success was the star system and the accompanying cult of celebrity. Stars became vital to the fantasy lives of millions of fans. For many in the audience, there was only a vague line separating the on-screen and off-screen adventures of the stars. Studio publicity, fan magazines, and gossip columns reinforced this ambiguity. Film idols, with their mansions, cars, parties, and private escapades, became the national experts on leisure and consumption. Their movies generally emphasized sexual themes and celebrated youth, athleticism, and the liberating power of consumer goods. Young Americans in particular looked to movies to learn how to dress, wear their hair, talk, or kiss. One researcher looking into the impact of moviegoing on young people, asked several to keep "motion picture diaries." "Upon going to my first dance I asked the hairdresser to fix my hair like Greta Garbo's," wrote one eighteen-year-old college student. "In speaking on graduation day I did my best to finish with the swaying-like curtsy which Pola Negri taught me from the screen. "(See Out of Many Voices: "Kissing Rudy Valentino" on page 684.)

But many Americans, particularly in rural areas and small towns, worried about Hollywood's impact on traditional sexual morality. They attacked the permissiveness associated with Hollywood life, and many states created censorship boards to screen movies before allowing them to be shown in theaters. To counter growing calls for government censorship, Hollywood's studios came up with a plan to censor themselves. In 1922, they hired Will Hays to head the Motion Picture Producers and Distributors of America. Hays was just what the immigrant moguls needed. An Indiana Republican, elder in the Presbyterian Church, and former postmaster general under President Harding, he personified Midwestern Protestant respectability. As the movie industry's czar, Hays lobbied against censorship laws, wrote pamphlets defending the movie business, and began setting guidelines for what could and could not be depicted on the screen. He insisted that movies be treated like any other industrial enterprise, for he understood the relationship between Hollywood's success and the growth of the nation's consumer culture.

Radio Broadcasting

In the fall of 1920, Westinghouse executive Harry P. Davis noticed that amateur broadcasts from the garage of an employee had attracted attention in the local Pittsburgh press. A department store advertised radio sets

OUT OF MANY VOICES

"KISSING RUDY VALENTINO": A HIGH SCHOOL STUDENT AT THE MOVIES IN THE 1920S

As movie going became the most popular form of the new mass culture, traditionalists worried about the new medium's impact on the morals and social lives of young people. The Payne Fund sponsored a series of research studies on the movies' influence, some of which were based on movie "autobiographies" written by high school students. One anonymous female student from Detroit revealed the growing power of the movies and celebrity culture on her and her friends.

I NEARLY ALWAYS HAVE GONE AND YET GO TO THE theater with someone. I hate to go alone as it is more enjoyable to have someone to discuss the picture with. Now I go with a bunch of girls or on a date with girls and boys or with one fellow.

The day-dreams instigated by the movies consist of clothes, ideas on furnishings, and manners. I don't day-dream much. I am more concerned with materialistic things and realisms. Nevertheless it is hard for any girl not to imagine herself cuddled up in some voluptuous ermine wrap, etc.

Goodness knows, you learn plenty about love from the movies. That's their long run; you learn more from actual experience,

though! You do see how the gold-digger systematically gets the poor fish in tow. You see how the sleek-haired, long-earringed, languid-eyed siren lands the men. You meet the flapper, the good girl, 'n' all the feminine types and their little tricks of the trade. We pick up their snappy comebacks which are most handy when dispensing with an unwanted suitor, a too ardent one, too backward one, etc. And believe me, they observe and remember, too.

I can remember when we all nudged one another and giggled at the last close-up in a movie. I recall when during the same sort of close-up when the boy friend squeezes your arm and looks soulfully at you. Oh, it's lotsa fun! No, I never fell in love with my movie idol. When I don't know a person really, when I know I'll never have a chance with 'em, I don't bother pining away over them and writing them idiotic letters as some girls I've known do. I have imagined playing with a movie hero many times though that is while I'm watching the picture. I forget about it when I'm outside the theater. Buddy Rogers and Rudy Valentino have kissed me oodles of times, but they don't know it. God bless 'em! ■

SOURCE: Herbert Blumer, *Movies and Conduct* (New York: Arno Press and the New York Times, 1970), 217–218, 220–223.

---

capable of picking up these "wireless concerts." Davis converted this amateur station to a stronger one at the Westinghouse main plant. Beginning with the presidential election returns that November, station KDKA offered regular nightly broadcasts that were probably heard by only a few hundred people. Radio broadcasting, begun as a service for selling cheap radio sets left over from World War I, would soon sweep the nation.

Before KDKA, wireless technology had been of interest only to the military, the telephone industry, and a few thousand "ham" (amateur) operators who enjoyed communicating with each other. The "radio mania" of the early 1920s was a response to the new possibilities offered by broadcasting. By 1923, nearly 600 stations had been licensed by the Department of Commerce, and about 600,000 Americans had bought radios. Early programs included live popular music, the playing of phono-

graph records, talks by college professors, church services, and news and weather reports. For millions of Americans, especially in rural areas and small towns, radio provided a new and exciting link to the larger national community of consumption.

Who would pay for radio programs? In the early 1920s, owners and operators of radio stations included radio equipment manufacturers, newspapers, department stores, state universities, cities, ethnic societies, labor unions, and churches. But by the end of the decade, commercial (or "toll") broadcasting emerged as the answer. The dominant corporations in the industry—General Electric, Westinghouse, Radio Corporation of America (RCA), and American Telephone and Telegraph (AT&T)—settled on the idea that advertisers would foot the bill for radio. Millions of listeners might be the consumers of radio shows, but sponsors were to be the customers. Only the sponsors and their advertising agencies enjoyed a direct relationship with broadcasters. Sponsors advertised directly or indirectly to the mass audience through such shows as the *Eveready Hour,* the *Ipana Troubadours,* and the *Taystee Loafers.* AT&T leased its nationwide system of telephone wires to allow the linking of many stations into powerful radio networks, such as the National Broadcasting Company (1926) and the Columbia Broadcasting System (1928).

NBC and CBS led the way in creating popular radio programs that relied heavily on older cultural forms. The variety show, hosted by vaudeville comedians, became network radio's first important format. Radio's first truly national hit, The *Amos 'n' Andy Show* (1928), was a direct descendant of nineteenth-century "blackface" minstrel entertainment. Radio did more than any previous medium to publicize and commercialize previously isolated forms of American music such as country-and-western, blues, and jazz. Broadcasts of baseball and college football games proved especially popular. In 1930, some 600 stations were broadcasting to more than 12 million homes with radios, or roughly 40 percent of American families. By that time, all the elements that characterize the present American system of broadcasting—regular daily programming paid for and produced by commercial advertisers, national networks carrying shows across the nation, and mass ownership of receiver sets in American homes—were in place.

Radio broadcasting created a national community of listeners, just as motion pictures created one of viewers. But since it transcended national boundaries, broadcasting had a powerful hemispheric impact as well. In both Canada and Mexico, governments established national broadcasting systems to bolster cultural and political nationalism. Yet American shows—and advertising—continued to dominate Canadian airwaves. Large private Mexican radio stations were often started in partnership with American corporations such as RCA, as a way to create demand for receiving sets. Language barriers limited the direct impact of U.S. broadcasts, but American advertisers became the backbone of commercial radio in Mexico. Radio broadcasting thus significantly amplified the influence of American commercialism throughout the hemisphere.

New Forms of Journalism

A new kind of newspaper, the tabloid, became popular in the postwar years. The *New York Daily News,* founded in 1919 by Joseph M. Patterson, was the first to develop the tabloid style. Its folded-in-half page size made it convenient to read on buses or subways. The *Daily News* devoted much of its space to photographs and other illustrations. With a terse, lively reporting style that emphasized sex, scandal, and sports, *Daily News* circulation reached 400,000 in 1922, and 1.3 million by 1929.

This success spawned a host of imitators in New York and elsewhere. New papers like the *Chicago Times* and the *Los Angeles Daily News* brought the tabloid style to cities across America, while some older papers, such as the *Denver Rocky Mountain News,* adopted the new format. The circulation of existing dailies was little affected. Tabloids had instead discovered an audience of millions who had never read newspapers before. Most of these new readers were poorly educated working-class city dwellers, many of whom were immigrants or children of immigrants.

The tabloid's most popular new feature was the gossip column, invented by Walter Winchell, an obscure former vaudevillian who began writing his column "Your Broadway and Mine" for the *New York Daily Graphic* in 1924. Winchell described the secret lives of public figures with a distinctive, rapid-fire, slangy style that made the reader feel like an insider. He chronicled the connections among high society, show business stars, powerful politicians, and the underworld. By the end of the decade, scores of newspapers "syndicated" Winchell's column, making him the most widely read—and imitated—journalist in America.

Journalism followed the larger economic trend toward consolidation and merger. Newspaper chains like Hearst, Gannett, and Scripps-Howard flourished during the 1920s. There was a sizable increase in the number of these chains and in the percentage of total daily circulation that was chain-owned. By the early 1930s, the Hearst organization alone controlled twenty-six dailies in eighteen cities, accounting for 14 percent of the nation's newspaper circulation. One of every four Sunday papers sold in America was owned by the Hearst group. One journalist lamented this standardization in 1930: "When one travels through the country on a Sunday on a fast train and buys Sunday papers, one finds the same 'comics,' the same Sunday magazines, the same special 'features' in almost all of them and, of course, in most of them precisely the same Associated Press news." New forms of journalism, like radio and the movies, contributed to the growth of a national consumer community.

Advertising Modernity

A thriving advertising industry both reflected and encouraged the growing importance of consumer goods in American life. Previously, advertising had been confined mostly to staid newspapers and magazines and offered little more than basic product information. The most creative advertising was usually for dubious products, such as patent medicines. The successful efforts of the government's Committee on Public Information, set up to "sell" World War I to Americans, suggested that new techniques using modern communication media could convince people to

This 1920 magazine advertisement touts the wonders of a new model vacuum cleaner. Much of the advertising boom in the post World War I years centered on the increasing number of consumer durable goods, such as household appliances, newly available to typical American families.

SOURCE: The Granger Collection, New York.

buy a wide range of goods and services. As a profession, advertising reached a higher level of respectability, sophistication, and economic power in American life during the 1920s.

The larger ad agencies moved toward a more scientific approach, by sponsoring market research and welcoming the language of psychology to their profession. Advertisers began focusing on the needs, desires, and anxieties of the consumer, rather than on the qualities of the product. "There are certain things that most people believe," noted one ad agency executive in 1927. "The moment your copy is linked to one of those beliefs, more than half your battle is won." Ad agencies and their clients invested extraordinary amounts of time, energy, and money trying to discover and, to some extent, shape those beliefs. Leading agencies such as Lord and Thomas in Chicago and J. Walter Thompson in New York, combined knowledge gained from market research and con-

sumer surveys with carefully prepared ad copy and graphics to sell their clients' wares.

High-powered ad campaigns made new products like Fleischmann's Yeast, Kleenex, and Listerine household words across the country. Above all, advertising celebrated consumption itself as a positive good. In this sense, the new advertising ethic was a therapeutic one, promising that products would contribute to the buyer's physical, psychic, or emotional well-being. Certain strategies, such as appeals to nature, medical authority, or personal freedom, were used with great success. Many of these themes and techniques are still familiar today. Well-financed ad campaigns were especially crucial for marketing newer consumer goods such as cars, electrical appliances, and personal hygiene products.

The Phonograph and the Recording Industry

Like radio and movies, the phonograph came into its own in the 1920s as a popular entertainment medium. Originally marketed in the 1890s, early phonographs used wax cylinders that could both record and replay. But the sound quality was poor, and the cylinders were difficult to handle. The convenient permanently grooved disc recordings introduced around World War I, were eagerly snapped up by the public, even though the discs could not be used to make recordings at home. The success of records transformed the popular music business, displacing both cylinders and sheet music as the major source of music in the home.

Dance crazes such as the fox trot, tango, and grizzly bear, done to complex ragtime and Latin rhythms, boosted the record business tremendously. Dixieland jazz, which recorded well, also captured the public's fancy in the early 1920s, and records provided the music for new popular dances like the Charleston and the black bottom. In 1921, more than 200 companies produced some 2 million records, and annual record sales exceeded 100 million.

Record sales declined toward the end of the decade, due to competition from radio. But in a broader cultural sense, records continued to transform American popular culture. Record companies discovered lucrative regional and ethnic markets for country music, which appealed primarily to white Southerners, and blues and jazz, which appealed primarily to African Americans. Country musicians like the Carter Family and Jimmie Rodgers, and blues singers like Blind Lemon Jefferson and Ma Rainey and Bessie Smith, had their performances put on records for the first time. Their records sold mainly in specialized "hillbilly" and "race" markets. Yet they were also played over the radio, and millions of

The Pittsburgh Crawfords, one of the most popular and successful baseball teams in the Negro National League, organized in 1920. Excluded from major league baseball by a "whites only" policy, black ballplayers played to enthusiastic crowds of African Americans from the 1920s through the 1940s. The "Negro leagues" declined after major league baseball finally integrated in 1947.

SOURCE: National Baseball Hall of Fame Library, Cooperstown, N.Y.

Americans began to hear musical styles and performers who had previously been isolated from the general population. The combination of records and radio started an extraordinary cross-fertilization of American musical styles that continues to this day.

Sports and Celebrity

During the 1920s, spectator sports enjoyed an unprecedented growth in popularity and profitability. As radio, newspapers, magazines, and newsreels exhaustively documented their exploits, athletes took their place alongside movie stars in defining a new culture of celebrity. Big-time sports, like the movies, entered a new corporate phase. Yet it was the athletes themselves, performing extraordinary feats on the field and transcending their often humble origins, who attracted millions of new fans. The image of the modern athlete—rich, famous, glamorous, and often a rebel against social convention—came into its own during the decade.

Major league baseball had more fans than any other sport, and its greatest star, George Herman "Babe" Ruth, embodied the new celebrity athlete. In 1920, the game had suffered a serious public relations disaster with the unfolding of the "Black Sox" scandal. The previous year, eight members of the poorly paid Chicago White Sox had become involved in a scheme to "throw" the World Series in exchange for large sums of money from gamblers. Although they were acquitted in the courts, baseball commissioner Judge Kenesaw Mountain Landis, looking to remove any taint of gambling from the sport, banned the accused players for life. Landis's actions won universal acclaim, but doubts about the integrity of the "national pastime" lingered.

Ruth was a larger-than-life character off the field as well as on. In New York, media capital of the nation, newspapers and magazines chronicled his enormous appetites—for food, whiskey, expensive cars, and big-city nightlife. He hobnobbed with politicians, movie stars, and gangsters, and he regularly visited sick children in hospitals. Ruth became the first athlete avidly sought after by manufacturers for celebrity endorsement of their products. As one of the most photographed individuals of the era, Ruth's round, beaming face became a familiar image around the world. In 1930, at the onset of the Great Depression, when a reporter told him that his $80,000 salary was more than President Herbert Hoover's, the Babe replied good naturedly, "Well, I had a better year than he did."

Baseball attendance exploded during the 1920s, reaching a one-year total of 10 million in 1929. The attendance boom prompted urban newspapers to increase their baseball coverage, and the larger dailies featured separate sports sections. The best sportswriters, such as Grantland Rice, Heywood Broun, and Ring Lardner, brought a poetic sensibility to descriptions of the games and their stars. William K. Wrigley, owner of the Chicago Cubs, discovered that by letting local radio stations broadcast his team's games, the club could win new fans, especially among housewives.

Among those excluded from major league baseball were African Americans, who had been banned from the game by an 1890s "gentleman's agreement" among owners. During the 1920s, black baseball players and entrepreneurs developed a world of their own, with several professional and semiprofessional leagues catering to expanding African American communities in cities. The largest of these was the Negro National League, organized in 1920 by Andrew "Rube" Foster. Black ballclubs also played exhibitions against, and frequently defeated, teams of white major leaguers. African Americans had their own baseball heroes, such as Josh Gibson and Satchel Paige, who no doubt would have been stars in the major leagues if not for racial exclusion.

The new media configuration of the 1920s created heroes in other sports as well. Radio broadcasts and increased journalistic coverage made college football a big-time sport, as millions followed the exploits of star players such as Illinois's Harold E. "Red" Grange and Stanford's Ernie Nevers. Teams like Notre Dame, located in sleepy South Bend, Indiana, but coached by the colorful Knute Rockne, could gain a wide national following. The center of college football shifted from the old elite schools

This 1925 *Judge* cartoon, "Sheik with Sheba," drawn by John Held Jr., offered one view of contemporary culture. The flashy new automobile, the hip flask with illegal liquor, the cigarettes, and the stylish "new woman" were all part of the "Roaring Twenties" image.

SOURCE: The Granger Collection.

of the Ivy League to the big universities of the Midwest and Pacific coast, where most of the players were now second-generation Irish, Italians, and Slavs. Athletes like boxers Jack Dempsey and Gene Tunney, tennis players Bill Tilden and Helen Wills, and swimmers Gertrude Ederle and Johnny Weissmuller became household names who brought legions of new fans to their sports.

A New Morality?

Movie stars, radio personalities, sports heroes, and popular musicians became the elite figures in a new culture of celebrity defined by the mass media. They were the model for achievement in the new age. Great events and abstract issues were made real through movie close-ups, radio interviews, and tabloid photos. The new media relentlessly created and disseminated images that are still familiar today: Babe Ruth trotting around the bases after hitting a home run; the wild celebrations that greeted Charles Lindbergh after he completed the first solo transatlantic airplane flight in 1927; the smiling gangster Al Capone, bantering with reporters who transformed his criminal exploits into important news events.

But images do not tell the whole story. Consider one of the most enduring images of the "Roaring Twenties," the flapper. She was usually portrayed on screen, in novels, and in the press as a young, sexually aggressive woman with bobbed hair, rouged cheeks, and short skirt. She loved to dance to jazz music, enjoyed smoking cigarettes, and drank bootleg liquor in cabarets and dance halls. She could also be competitive, assertive, and a good pal. As writer Zelda Fitzgerald put it in 1924: "I think a woman gets more happiness out of being gay, light-hearted, unconventional, mistress of her own fate. . . . I want [my daughter] to be a flapper, because flappers are brave and gay and beautiful." (See Out of Many Voices: "To Bob or Not to Bob.")

Was the flapper a genuine representative of the 1920s? Did she embody the "new morality" that was so widely discussed and chronicled in the media of the day? The flapper certainly did exist, but she was neither as new nor as widespread a phenomenon as the image would suggest. The delight in sensuality, personal pleasure, and rhythmically complex dance and music had long been key elements of subcultures on the fringes of middle-class society: bohemian enclaves, communities of political radicals, African American ghettos, working-class dance halls. In the 1920s, these activities became normative for a growing number of white middle-class Americans, including women. Jazz, sexual experimentation, heavy makeup, and cigarette smoking spread to college campuses.

The emergence of homosexual subcultures also reflected the newly permissive atmosphere of the

OUT OF MANY VOICES

TO BOB OR NOT TO BOB: CHANGING FASHION AND THE "NEW WOMAN" OF THE 1920S

One of the more striking and controversial markers of a "new woman" was the short, sculpted "bob" hairdo, a rejection of the old-fashioned, upswept, carefully layered hair styling of the prewar years. Here, the singer Mary Garden explains her reasons for "bobbing," and what it symbolizes for her.

WHY DID I BOB MY HAIR? FOR SEVERAL REASONS. I did it because I wanted to, for one thing; because I found it easier to take care of; because I thought it more becoming; and because I felt freer without long, entangling tresses. But above and beyond these and several other reasons I had my hair cut short because, to me, it typified a progressive step, in keeping with the inner spirit that animates my whole existence.

In one way, whether I wear my hair short or not is of little importance. But viewed in another way, bobbed hair is not just a trivial, independent act of hair-dressing separate and apart from my life itself. It is part and parcel of life—one of the myriad things which by themselves may apparently mean nothing, but which in the aggregate help to form that particular complexity of expression which is myself.

Bobbed hair is a state of mind and not merely a new manner of dressing my head. It typifies growth, alertness, up-to-dateness, and is part of the expression of the *élan vital!* [spirit] It is not just a fad of the moment, either like mah jong or cross-word puzzles. At least I don't think it is. I consider getting rid of our long hair one of the many little shackles that women have cast aside in their passage to freedom. Whatever helps their emancipation, however small it may seem, is well worth while.

When I consider the achievements of women in the past few years in the field of athletics I find it impossible to do so without taking into account the tremendous freedom-giving changes in fashion that have accompanied them. And enjoying the blessings of short hair is a necessary part of those fashion changes. To my way of thinking, long hair belongs to the age of general feminine helplessness. Bobbed hair belongs to the age of freedom, frankness, and progressiveness. ■

SOURCE: Mary Garden, "Why I Bobbed My Hair," *Pictorial Review*, April 1927, 8ff.

---

postwar years. Although such subcultures had been a part of big city life since at least the 1890s, they had been largely confined to working-class saloons associated with the urban underworld. By the 1920s, the word "homosexual" had gained currency as a scientific term for describing romantic love between women or between men, and middle-class enclaves of self-identified homosexuals took root in cities like New York, Chicago, and San Francisco. Often organized around speakeasies, private clubs, tea rooms, and masquerade balls, this more-public homosexual world thrived in bohemian neighborhoods such as New York's Greenwich Village and in the interracial nightclubs of Harlem. These venues also attracted heterosexual tourists and those looking to experiment with their sexuality, as well as homosexuals, for whom they served as important social centers. But if these enclaves provided some sense of community and safety for homosexuals, the repressive shadow of the larger culture was never far away. In 1927, the actress and playwright (and future movie star) Mae West, presented her original play "The Drag" on Broadway, featuring male drag queens playing themselves. But a firestorm of protest from the press, politicians, and mainstream Broadway producers quickly forced authorities to padlock the theater.

Several sources, most of them rooted in earlier years, can be found for the increased sexual openness of the 1920s. Troops in the armed forces during World War I had been exposed to government-sponsored sex education. New psychological and social theories like those of Havelock Ellis, Ellen Key, and Sigmund Freud stressed the central role of sexuality in human experience, maintaining that sex is a positive, healthy impulse that, if repressed, could damage mental and emotional health. The pioneering efforts of Margaret Sanger in educating women about birth control had begun before World War I (see Chapter 21). In the 1920s, Sanger campaigned vigorously—through her journal *Birth Control Review*, in books, on speaking tours—to make contraception freely available to all women.

Sociological surveys also suggested that genuine changes in sexual behavior began in the prewar years among both married and single women. Katherine Bement Davis's pioneering study of 2,200 middle-class women, carried out in 1918 and published in 1929, revealed that most used contraceptives and described sexual relations in positive terms. A 1938 survey of 777 middle-class females found that among those born between 1890 and 1900, 74 percent were virgins before marriage; for those born after 1910, the figure dropped to 32 percent. Women born after the turn of the century were twice as likely to have had premarital sex as those born before 1900. The critical change took place in the generation that came of age in the late teens and early twenties. By the 1920s, male and female "morals" were becoming more alike.

RESISTANCE TO MODERNITY

One measure of the profound cultural changes of the 1920s was the hostility and opposition expressed toward them by large sectors of the American public. Deep and persistent tensions, with ethnic, racial, and geographical overtones, characterized much of the decade's politics. The postwar Red Scare had given strength to the forces of antiradicalism in politics and traditionalism in culture. Resentments over the growing power of urban culture were very strong in rural and small-town America. The big city, in this view, stood for all that was alien, corrupt, and immoral in the country's life. Several trends and mass movements reflected this anger and the longing for a less-complicated past.

Prohibition

The Eighteenth Amendment, banning the manufacture, sale, and transportation of alcoholic beverages, took effect in January 1920. Prohibition was the culmination of a long campaign that associated drinking with the degradation of working-class family life and the worst evils of urban politics. Supporters, a coalition of women's temperance groups, middle-class progressives, and rural Protestants, hailed the new law as "a noble experiment." But it became clear rather quickly that enforcing the new law would be extremely difficult. The Volstead Act of 1919 established a federal

Prohibition Bureau to enforce the Eighteenth Amendment. Yet the bureau was severely understaffed, with only about 1,500 agents to police the entire country.

The public demand for alcohol, especially in the big cities, led to widespread lawbreaking. Drinking was such a routine part of life for so many Americans, that bootlegging quickly became a big business. Illegal stills and breweries, as well as liquor smuggled in from Canada, supplied the needs of those Americans who continued to drink. Nearly every town and city had at least one "speakeasy," where people could drink and enjoy music and other entertainment. Local law enforcement personnel, especially in the cities, were easily bribed to overlook these illegal establishments. By the early 1920s, many Eastern states no longer made even a token effort at enforcing the law.

But because liquor continued to be illegal, Prohibition gave an enormous boost to violent organized crime. The profits to be made in the illegal liquor trade dwarfed the traditional sources of criminal income—gambling, prostitution, and robbery. The pattern of organized crime in the 1920s, closely resembled the larger trends in American business: smaller operations gave way to larger and more-complex combinations. Successful organized crime figures, like Chicago's Al "Scarface" Capone, became celebrities in their own right and received heavy coverage in the mass media. Capone himself shrewdly used the rhetoric of the Republican new era to defend himself: "Everybody calls me a racketeer. I call myself a businessman. When I sell liquor it's bootlegging. When my patrons serve it on a silver tray on Lake Shore Drive, it's hospitality."

Organized crime, based on its huge profits from liquor, also made significant inroads into legitimate businesses, labor unions, and city government. By the time Congress and the states ratified the Twenty-first Amendment in 1933, repealing Prohibition, organized crime was a permanent feature of American life. Prohibition did, in fact, significantly reduce per capita consumption of alcohol. In 1910, annual per capita consumption stood at 2.6 gallons; in 1934, the figure was less than a gallon. Yet among young people, especially college students, the excitement associated with speakeasies and lawbreaking contributed to increase drinking during Prohibition.

Immigration Restriction

Sentiment for restricting immigration, growing since the late nineteenth century, reached its peak immediately after World War I. Antiimmigrant feeling reflected the growing preponderance after 1890 of "new immigrants"—those from southern and eastern Europe—over the immigrants from northern and western Europe, who had predominated before 1890. Between 1891 and 1920, roughly 10.5 million immigrants arrived from southern and eastern Europe. This was nearly twice as

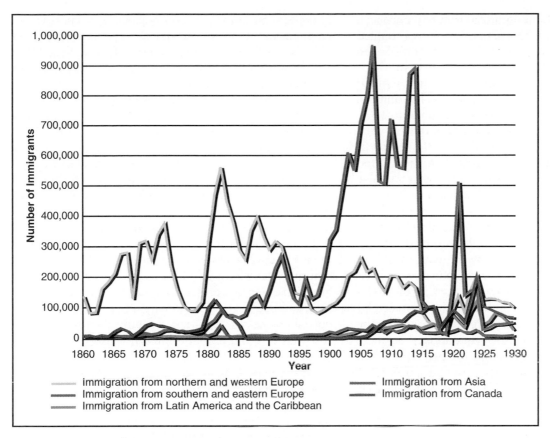

FIGURE 23.3   Annual Immigration to United States, 1860–1930

many as arrived during the same years from northern and western Europe.

The "new immigrants" were mostly Catholic and Jewish, and they were darker-skinned than the "old immigrants." To many Americans, they seemed more exotic, more foreign, and less willing and able to assimilate the nation's political and cultural values. They were also relatively poorer, more physically isolated in the nation's cities, and less politically strong than earlier immigrants. In the 1890s, the anti-Catholic American Protective Association called for a curb on immigration, and by exploiting the economic depression of that decade, it reached a membership of 2.5 million. In 1894, a group of prominent Harvard graduates, including Henry Cabot Lodge and John Fiske, founded the Immigration Restriction League, providing an influential forum for the fears of the nation's elite. The league used newer scientific arguments, based on a flawed application of Darwinian evolutionary theory and genetics, to support its call for immigration restriction.

Theories of scientific racism, which had become more popular in the early 1900s, reinforced antiimmigrant bias. The most influential statement of racial hierarchy was Madison Grant's *The Passing of the Great Race* (1916), which distorted genetic theory to argue that America was com-

mitting "race suicide." According to Grant, inferior Alpine, Mediterranean, and Jewish stock threatened to extinguish the superior Nordic race that had made America great. Eugenicists, who enjoyed considerable vogue in those years, held that heredity determined almost all of a person's capacities, and that genetic inferiority predisposed people to crime and poverty. Such pseudoscientific thinking sought to explain historical and social development solely as a function of "racial" differences.

Against this background, the war and its aftermath provided the final push for immigration restriction. The "100 percent American" fervor of the war years fueled nativist passions. So did the Red Scare of 1919–20, which linked foreigners with Bolshevism and radicalism of all kinds in the popular mind. The postwar depression coincided with the resumption of massive immigration, bringing much hostile comment on the relationship between rising unemployment and the new influx of foreigners. The American Federation of Labor proposed stopping all immigration for two years. Sensational press coverage of organized crime figures, many of them Italian or Jewish, also played a part.

In 1921, Congress passed the Immigration Act, setting a maximum of 357,000 new immigrants each year.

Quotas limited annual immigration from any European country to 3 percent of the number of its natives counted in the 1910 U.S. census. But restrictionists complained that the new law still allowed too many southern and eastern Europeans in, especially since the northern and western Europeans did not fill their quotas. The Johnson-Reed Immigration Act of 1924 revised the quotas to 2 percent of the number of foreign-born counted for each nationality in the census for 1890, when far fewer southern or eastern Europeans were present in the United States. The maximum total allowed each year was also cut, to 164,000. The quota laws did not apply to Canada, Mexico, or any other nation in the western hemisphere.

The 1924 Immigration Act also included a clause prohibiting the entry of "aliens ineligible to citizenship," thereby excluding immigrants from the nations of East and South Asia. Since nearly all Asians had already been barred from legal immigration, either by the Chinese Exclusion Act of 1882 or the "barred Asiatic zone" created by Congress in 1917, the 1924 clause was in fact, aimed at the exclusion of Japanese immigrants. An outraged Japanese government retaliated by imposing a 100 percent tariff on goods imported from America. This new restriction dovetailed with two recent Supreme Court decisions, *Ozawa* v. *U.S.* (1922) and *U.S.* v. *Thind* (1923), in which the Court held that Japanese and Asian Indians were unassimilable aliens and racially ineligible for U.S. citizenship. By the 1920s, American law had thus created the peculiar new racial category of "Asian," and codified the principle of racial exclusion in immigration and naturalization law.

The Ku Klux Klan

If immigration restriction was resurgent nativism's most significant legislative expression, a revived Ku Klux Klan was its most effective mass movement. The original Klan had been formed in the Reconstruction South as an instrument of white racial terror against newly freed slaves (see Chapter 17). It had died out in the 1870s. The new Klan, born in Stone Mountain, Georgia, in 1915, was inspired by D. W. Griffith's racist spectacle *The Birth of a Nation*, a film released in that year depicting the original KKK as a heroic organization. The new Klan patterned itself on the secret rituals and antiblack hostility of its predecessor, and until 1920, it was limited to a few local chapters in Georgia and Alabama.

When Hiram W. Evans, a dentist from Dallas, became imperial wizard of the Klan in 1922, he transformed the organization. Evans hired professional fundraisers and publicists and directed an effective recruiting scheme that paid a commission to sponsors of new members. The Klan advocated "100 percent Americanism" and "the faithful maintenance of White Supremacy." It staunchly supported the enforcement of Prohibition, and it attacked birth control and Darwinism. The new Klan made a special target of the Roman Catholic Church, labeling it a hostile and dangerous alien power. In a 1926 magazine piece titled "The Klan's Fight for Americanism," Evans alleged that the Church's "theocratic autocracy and its claim to full authority in temporal as well as spiritual matters, all make it impossible for it as a church, or for its members if they obey it, to cooperate in a free democracy in which Church and State have been separated."

The new Klan presented itself as the righteous defender of the embattled traditional values of small-town Protestant America. But ironically, to build its membership rolls, it relied heavily on the publicity, public relations, and business techniques associated with modern urban culture. By 1924, the new Klan counted more than 3 million members across the country. President Harding had joined in a special White House ceremony. Its slogan, "Native, White, Protestant Supremacy," proved especially attractive in the Midwest and South, including many cities. Klansmen boycotted businesses, threatened families, and sometimes resorted to violence—public whippings, arson, and lynching—against their chosen enemies. The Klan's targets sometimes included white Protestants accused of sexual promiscuity, blasphemy, or drunkenness, but most victims were African Americans, Catholics, and Jews. Support for Prohibition enforcement probably united Klansmen more than any single issue.

On another level, the Klan was a popular social movement. Many members were more attracted by the Klan's spectacular social events and its efforts to reinvigorate community life than by its attacks on those considered outsiders. Perhaps a half million women joined the Women of the Ku Klux Klan, and women constituted nearly half of the Klan membership in some states. Klanswomen drew on family and community traditions, such as church suppers, kin reunions, and gossip campaigns, to defend themselves and their families against what they saw as corruption and immorality. One northern Indiana Klanswoman recalled, "Store owners, teachers, farmers . . . the good people, all belonged to the Klan. They were going to clean up the government, and they were going to improve the school books that were loaded with Catholicism." The Klan's power was strong in many communities precisely because it fit so comfortably into the everyday life of white Protestants.

At its height, the Klan also became a powerful force in Democratic Party politics, and it had a strong presence among delegates to the 1924 Democratic National Convention. The Klan began to fade in 1925, when its Indiana leader, Grand Dragon David C. Stephenson, became involved in a sordid personal affair. Stephenson had picked up a young secretary at a party, got her drunk on bootleg liquor, and then assaulted her on a train. After the woman took poison and died, Stephenson was

Women members of the Ku Klux Klan in New Castle, Indiana, August 1, 1923. The revived Klan was
a powerful presence in scores of American communities during the early 1920s, especially among
native-born white Protestants, who feared cultural and political change. In addition to preaching "100
percent Americanism," local Klan chapters also served a social function for members and their families.

SOURCE: Ball State University Libraries, Archives & Special Collections, W.A. Swift Photo Collection.

convicted of manslaughter. With one of its most famous leaders disgraced and in jail, the new Klan began to lose members and influence.

Religious Fundamentalism

Paralleling political nativism in the 1920s, was the growth of religious fundamentalism. In many Protestant churches, congregations focused less on religious practice and worship than on social and reform activities in the larger community. By the early 1920s, a fundamentalist revival had developed in reaction to these tendencies. The fundamentalists emphasized a literal reading of the Bible, and they rejected the tenets of modern science as inconsistent with the revealed word of God. Fundamentalist publications and Bible colleges flourished, particularly among Southern Baptists.

One special target of the fundamentalists was the theory of evolution, first set forth by Charles Darwin in his landmark work *The Origin of Species* (1859). Using fossil evidence, evolutionary theory suggested that over time, many species had become extinct, and that new ones had emerged through the process of natural selection. These ideas directly contradicted the account of one, fixed creation in the Book of Genesis. Although most Protestant clergymen had long since found ways of blending the scientific theory with their theology, fundamentalists launched an attack on the teaching of Darwinism in schools and universities. By 1925, five Southern state legislatures had passed laws restricting the teaching of evolution.

A young biology teacher, John T. Scopes, deliberately broke the Tennessee law prohibiting the teaching of Darwinism in 1925, in order to challenge it in court. The resulting trial that summer in Dayton, a small town near Chattanooga, drew international attention to the controversy. Scopes's defense team included attorneys from the American Civil Liberties Union and Clarence Darrow, the most famous trial lawyer in America. The prosecution was led by William Jennings Bryan, the old Democratic standard-bearer who had thrown himself into the fundamentalist and antievolutionist cause. Held in a circus atmosphere in sweltering heat, the trial attracted thousands of reporters and partisans to Dayton, and was broadcast across the nation by the radio.

The 1925 Scopes trial attracted an enormous amount of media attention, as well as many anti-evolution crusaders. This group set up shop near the Dayton, Tennessee courthouse.
SOURCE: Corbis/Bettmann.

The Scopes "monkey trial"—so called because fundamentalists trivialized Darwin's theory into a claim that humans were descended from monkeys—became one of the most publicized and definitive moments of the decade. The real drama was the confrontation between Darrow and Bryan. Darrow, denied by the judge the right to call scientists to testify for the defense, put the "Great Commoner," Bryan, himself, on the stand as an expert witness on the Bible. Bryan delighted his supporters with a staunch defense of biblical literalism. But he also drew scorn from many of the assembled journalists, including cosmopolitan types such as H. L. Mencken of the *Baltimore Sun*, who ridiculed Bryan's simplistic faith. Scopes's guilt was never in question. The jury convicted him quickly, although the verdict was later thrown out on a technicality. Bryan died a week after the trial; his epitaph read simply, "He kept the Faith." The struggle over the teaching of evolution continued in an uneasy stale-mate; state statutes were not repealed, but prosecutions for teaching evolution ceased. Fundamentalism, a religious creed and a cultural defense against the uncertainties of modern life, continued to have a strong appeal for millions of Americans.

THE STATE, THE ECONOMY, AND BUSINESS

Throughout the 1920s, a confident Republican Party dominated national politics, certain that it had ushered in a "new era" in American life. A new and closer relationship between the federal government and American business became the hallmark of Republican policy in both domestic and foreign affairs during the administrations of three successive Republican presidents: Warren Harding (1921–23), Calvin Coolidge (1923–29), and Herbert Hoover (1929–33). And Republicans never tired of claiming that the business-government partnership their policies promoted was responsible for the nation's economic prosperity.

Harding and Coolidge

Handsome, genial, and well-spoken, Warren Harding may have looked the part of a president—but acting like one was another matter. Harding was a product of small-town Marion, Ohio, and the machine politics in his native state. Republican Party officials had made a point of keeping Senator Harding, a compromise choice, as removed from the public eye as possible in the 1920 election. They correctly saw that active campaigning could only hurt their candidate by exposing his shallowness and intellectual weakness. Harding understood his own limitations. He sadly told one visitor to the White House shortly after taking office, "I knew that this job would be too much for me."

Harding surrounded himself with a close circle of friends, the "Ohio gang," delegating to them a great deal of administrative power. The president often conducted business as if he were in the relaxed, convivial, and masculine confines of a small-town saloon. In the summer of 1923, Harding began to get wind of the scandals for which his administration is best remembered. He wearily told his friend, Kansas journalist William Allen White: "This is a hell of a job! I have no trouble with my enemies. . . . But my damned friends, . . . White, they're the ones that keep me walking the floor nights."

Soon after Harding's death from a heart attack in 1923, a series of congressional investigations soon revealed a deep pattern of corruption. Attorney General Harry M. Daugherty had received bribes from violators of the Prohibition statutes. He had also failed to investigate graft in the Veterans Bureau, where Charles R. Forbes had pocketed a large chunk of the $250 million spent on hospitals and supplies. The worst affair was the Teapot Dome scandal involving Interior Secretary Albert Fall. Fall received hundreds of thousands of dollars in payoffs when he secretly leased navy oil reserves in Teapot Dome, Wyoming, and Elk Hills, California, to two private oil developers. He eventually became the first cabinet officer ever to go to jail.

But the Harding administration's legacy was not all scandal. Andrew Mellon, an influential Pittsburgh banker, served as secretary of the treasury under all three Republican presidents of the 1920s. One of the richest men in America, and a leading investor in the Aluminum Corporation of America and Gulf Oil, Mellon believed government ought to be run on the same conservative principles as a corporation. He was a leading voice for trimming the federal budget and cutting taxes on incomes, corporate profits, and inheritances. These cuts,

Calvin Coolidge combined a spare, laconic political style with a flair for publicity. He frequently posed in the dress of a cowboy, farmer, or Indian chief.

SOURCE: Corbis/Bettmann.

he argued, would free up capital for new investment, and thus promote general economic growth. Mellon's program sharply cut taxes for both higher-income brackets and for businesses. By 1926, a person with an income of a million a year paid less than a third of the income tax he or she had paid in 1921. Overall, Mellon's policies succeeded in rolling back much of the progressive taxation associated with Woodrow Wilson.

When Calvin Coolidge succeeded to the presidency, he seemed to most people the temperamental opposite of Harding. Born and raised in rural Vermont, elected governor of Massachusetts, and coming to national prominence only through the 1919 Boston police strike (see Chapter 22), "Silent Cal" was the quintessential New England Yankee. Taciturn, genteel, and completely honest, Coolidge believed in the least amount of government possible. He spent only four hours a day at the office. His famous aphorism, "The business of America is business," perfectly captured the core philosophy of the Republican new era. He was in awe of wealthy men such as Andrew Mellon, and he thought them best suited to make society's key decisions.

Coolidge easily won election on his own in 1924. He benefited from the general prosperity and the contrast he provided with the disgraced Harding. Coolidge defeated little-known Democrat John W. Davis, the compromise choice of a party badly divided between its rural and urban wings. Also running was Progressive Party candidate Robert M. La Follette of Wisconsin, who mounted a reform campaign that attacked economic monopolies and called for government ownership of utilities. In his full term, Coolidge showed most interest in reducing federal spending, lowering taxes, and blocking congressional initiatives. He saw his primary function as clearing the way for American businessmen. They, after all, were the agents of the era's unprecedented prosperity.

Herbert Hoover and the "Associative State"

The most influential figure of the Republican new era was Herbert Hoover, who as secretary of commerce, dominated the cabinets of Harding and Coolidge before becoming president himself in 1929. A successful engineer, administrator, and politician, Hoover effectively embodied the belief that enlightened business, encouraged and informed by the government, would act in the public interest. In the modern industrial age, Hoover believed, the government needed only to advise private citizens' groups about what national or international polices to pursue. "Reactionaries and radicals," he wrote in *American Individualism* (1922), "would assume that all reform and human advance must come through government. They have forgotten that progress must come from the steady lift of the individual and that the measure of national idealism and progress is the quality of idealism in the individual."

Hoover thus fused a faith in old-fashioned individualism with a strong commitment to the progressive possibilities offered by efficiency and rationality. Unlike an earlier generation of Republicans, Hoover wanted not just to create a favorable climate for business, but to actively assist the business community. He spoke of creating an "associative state," in which the government would encourage voluntary cooperation among corporations, consumers, workers, farmers, and small businessmen. This became the central occupation of the Department of Commerce under Hoover's leadership. Under Hoover, the Bureau of Standards became one of the nation's leading research centers, setting engineering standards for key American industries such as machine tools and automobiles. The bureau also helped standardize the styles, sizes, and designs of many consumer products, such as canned goods and refrigerators.

Hoover actively encouraged the creation and expansion of national trade associations. By 1929, there were about 2,000 of them. At industrial conferences called by the Commerce Department, government officials explained the advantages of mutual cooperation in figuring prices and costs and then publishing the information. The idea was to improve efficiency by reducing competition. To some, this practice violated the spirit of antitrust laws, but in the 1920s, the Justice Department's Antitrust Division took a very lax view of its responsibility. In addition, the Supreme Court consistently upheld the legality of trade associations. The government thus provided an ideal climate for the concentration of corporate wealth and power. The trend toward large corporate trusts and holding companies had been well under way since the late nineteenth century, but it accelerated in the 1920s. By 1929, the 200 largest American corporations owned almost half the total corporate wealth and about a fifth of the total national wealth. Concentration was particularly strong in manufacturing, retailing, mining, banking, and utilities. The number of vertical combinations—large, integrated firms that controlled the raw materials, manufacturing processes, and distribution networks for their products—also increased. Vertical integration became common not only in older industries, but also in the automobile, electrical, radio, motion picture, and other new industries as well.

War Debts, Reparations, Keeping the Peace

The United States emerged from World War I the strongest economic power in the world. The war transformed it from the world's leading debtor nation to its most important creditor. European governments owed the U.S. government about $10 billion in 1919. In the private sector, the war ushered in an era of expanding American investment abroad. As late as 1914, foreign investments in the United States were about $3 billion more than the total of American capital invested abroad. By 1919, that situation was reversed: America had $3 billion more invested abroad than foreigners had invested in the United States. By 1929, the surplus was $8 billion. New York replaced London as the center of international finance and capital markets.

During the 1920s, war debts and reparations were the single most divisive issue in international economics. In France and Great Britain, which both owed the United States large amounts in war loans, many concluded that the Uncle Sam who had offered assistance during wartime, was really a loan shark in disguise. In turn, many Americans viewed Europeans as ungrateful debtors. As President Coolidge acidly remarked, "They hired the money, didn't they?" In 1922, the U.S. Foreign Debt Commission negotiated an agreement with the debtor nations that called for them to repay $11.5 billion over a sixty-two-year period. But by the late 1920s, the European financial situation had become so desperate, that the United States agreed to cancel a large part of these debts. Continued insistence by the United States that the Europeans pay at least a portion of the debt, fed anti-American feeling in Europe and isolationism at home.

The Germans believed that war reparations, set at $33 billion by the Treaty of Versailles, not only unfairly punished the losers of the conflict but, by saddling their civilian economies with such massive debt, also deprived them of the very means to repay. In 1924, Herbert Hoover and Chicago banker Charles Dawes worked out a plan to aid the recovery of the German economy. The Dawes Plan reduced Germany's debt, stretched out the repayment period, and arranged for American bankers to lend funds to Germany. These measures helped stabilize Germany's currency and allowed it to make reparations payments to France and Great Britain. The Allies, in turn, were better able to pay their war debts to the United States.

The United States never joined the League of Nations, but it maintained an active, if selective, involvement in world affairs. In addition to the Dawes Plan and the American role in naval disarmament, the United States joined the league-sponsored World Court in 1926, and was represented at numerous league conferences. In 1928, with great fanfare, the United States and sixty-two other nations signed the Pact of Paris (better known as the Kellogg-Briand Pact, for the U.S. Secretary of State Frank B. Kellogg and French Foreign Minister Aristide Briand who initiated it), which grandly and naively renounced war in principle. Peace groups, such as the Woman's Peace Party and the Quaker-based Fellowship of Reconciliation, hailed the pact for formally outlawing war. But critics charged that the Kellogg-Briand Pact was essentially meaningless, since it lacked powers of enforcement and relied solely on the moral force of world opinion. Within weeks of its ratification, the U.S. Congress had appropriated $250 million for new battleships.

Commerce and Foreign Policy

Throughout the 1920s, Secretary of State Charles Evans Hughes and other Republican leaders pursued policies designed to expand American economic activity abroad. They understood that capitalist economies must be dynamic; they must expand their markets if they were to thrive. The focus must be on friendly nations, and investments that would help foreign citizens to buy American goods. Toward this end, Republican leaders urged close cooperation between bankers and the government as a strategy for expanding American investment and economic influence abroad. They insisted that invest-

ment capital not be spent on U.S. enemies, such as the new Soviet Union, or on nonproductive enterprises such as munitions and weapons. Throughout the 1920s, investment bankers routinely submitted loan projects to Hughes and Secretary of Commerce Hoover for informal approval, thus reinforcing the close ties between business investment and foreign policy.

American oil, autos, farm machinery, and electrical equipment supplied a growing world market. Much of this expansion took place through the establishment of branch plants overseas by American companies. America's overall direct investment abroad increased from $3.8 billion in 1919 to $7.5 billion in 1929. Leading the American domination of the world market were General Electric, Ford, and Monsanto Chemical. American oil companies, with the support of the State Department, also challenged Great Britain's dominance in the oil fields of the Middle East and Latin America, forming powerful cartels with English firms.

The strategy of maximum freedom for private enterprise, backed by limited government advice and assistance, significantly boosted the power and profits of American overseas investors. But in Central and Latin America, in particular, aggressive U.S. investment also fostered chronically underdeveloped economies, dependent on a few staple crops (sugar, coffee, cocoa, bananas) grown for export. American investments in Latin America more than doubled between 1924 and 1929, from $1.5 billion to over $3.5 billion. A large part of this money went to taking over vital mineral resources, such as Chile's copper and Venezuela's oil. The growing wealth and power of U.S. companies made it more difficult for these nations to grow their own food or diversify their economies. U.S. economic dominance in the hemisphere also hampered the growth of democratic politics by favoring autocratic, military regimes that could be counted on to protect U.S. investments.

PROMISES POSTPONED

The prosperity of the 1920s was unevenly distributed and enjoyed across America. Older, progressive reform movements that had pointed out inequities, faltered in the conservative political climate. But the Republican new era did inspire a range of critics deeply troubled by unfulfilled promises in American life. Feminists sought to redefine their movement in the wake of the suffrage victory. Mexican immigration to the United States shot up, and in the burgeoning Mexican American communities of the Southwest and Midwest, economic and social conditions were very difficult. African Americans, bitterly disappointed by their treatment during and after the Great War, turned to new political and cultural strategies. Many American intellectuals found themselves deeply alienated from the temper and direction of modern American society.

Feminism in Transition

The achievement of the suffrage removed the central issue that had given cohesion to the disparate forces of female reform activism. In addition, female activists of all persuasions found themselves swimming against a national tide of hostility to political idealism. During the 1920s, the women's movement split into two main wings over a fundamental disagreement about female identity. Should activists stress women's differences from men—their vulnerability and the double burden of work and family—and continue to press for protective legislation, such as laws that limited the length of the work week for women? Or should they emphasize the ways that women were like men—sharing similar aspirations—and push for full legal and civil equality?

In 1920, the National American Woman Suffrage Association reorganized itself as the League of Women Voters. The league represented the historical mainstream of the suffrage movement, those who believed that the vote for women would bring a nurturing sensibility and a reform vision to American politics. This view was rooted in politicized domesticity, the notion that women had a special role to play in bettering society: improving conditions for working women, abolishing child labor, humanizing prisons and mental hospitals, and serving the urban poor. Most league members continued working in a variety of reform organizations, and the league itself concentrated on educating the new female electorate, encouraging women to run for office, and supporting laws for the protection of women and children.

A newer, smaller, and more militant group was the National Woman's Party (NWP), founded in 1916 by militant suffragist Alice Paul. The NWP downplayed the significance of suffrage and argued that women were still subordinate to men in every facet of life. The NWP opposed protective legislation for women, claiming that such laws reinforced sex stereotyping and prevented women from competing with men in many fields. Largely representing the interests of professional and business women, the NWP focused on passage of a brief Equal Rights Amendment (ERA) to the Constitution, introduced in Congress in 1923: "Men and women shall have equal rights throughout the United States and every place subject to its jurisdiction."

Many of the older generation of women reformers opposed the ERA as elitist, arguing that far more women benefited from protective laws than were injured by them. Mary Anderson, director of the Women's Bureau in the Department of Labor, argued

that "women who are wage earners, with one job in the factory and another in the home, have little time and energy left to carry on the fight to better their economic status. They need the help of other women and they need labor laws." ERA supporters countered that maximum-hours laws or laws prohibiting women from night work prevented women from getting many lucrative jobs. M. Carey Thomas, president of Bryn Mawr College, defended the ERA with language reminiscent of laissez faire: "How much better by one blow to do away with discriminating against women in work, salaries, promotion and opportunities to compete with men in a fair field with no favour on either side!"

But most women's groups did not think there was a "fair field." Positions solidified. The League of Women Voters, the National Consumers' League, and the Women's Trade Union League opposed the ERA. ERA supporters generally stressed individualism, competition, and the abstract language of "equality" and "rights." ERA opponents emphasized the grim reality of industrial exploitation and the concentration of women workers in low-paying jobs in which they did not compete directly with men. ERA advocates dreamed of a labor market that might be, one in which women might have the widest opportunity. Anti-ERA forces looked at the labor market as it was, insisting it was more important to protect women from existing exploitation. The NWP campaign failed to get the ERA passed by Congress, but the debates it sparked would be echoed during the feminist movement of the 1970s, when the ERA became a central political goal of a resurgent feminism.

A small number of professional women made real gains in the fields of real estate, banking, and journalism. The press regularly announced new "firsts" for women, such as Amelia Earhart's 1928 airplane flight across the Atlantic. Anne O'Hare McCormick won recognition as the "first lady of American journalism" for her reporting and editorial columns in the *New York Times*. In 1900, less than 18 percent of employed women worked in clerical, managerial, sales, and professional areas. By 1930, the number was 44 percent. But studies showed that most of these women were clustered in the low-paying areas of typing, stenography, bookkeeping, cashiering, and sales clerking. Men still dominated in the higher-paid and managerial white-collar occupations.

The most significant, if limited, victory for feminist reformers was the 1921 Sheppard-Towner Act, which established the first federally funded health-care program, providing matching funds for states to set up prenatal and child health care centers. These centers also provided public health nurses for house calls. Although hailed as a genuine reform breakthrough, especially for women in rural and isolated communities, the act aroused much opposition. The NWP disliked it for its assumption that all women were mothers. Birth control advocates such as Margaret Sanger complained that contraception was not part of the program. The American Medical Association (AMA) objected to government-sponsored health care and to nurses who functioned outside the supervision of physicians. By 1929, largely as a result of intense AMA lobbying, Congress cut off funds for the program.

Mexican Immigration

While immigration restriction sharply cut the flow of new arrivals from Europe, the 1920s also brought a dramatic influx of Mexicans to the United States. Mexican immigration, which was not included in the immigration laws of 1921 and 1924, had picked up substantially after the outbreak of the Mexican Revolution in 1911, when political instability and economic hardships provided incentives to cross the border to *El Norte.* According to the U.S. Immigration Service, an estimated 459,000 Mexicans entered the United States between 1921 and 1930, more than double the number for the previous decade. The official count no doubt underrepresented the true numbers of immigrants from Mexico. Many Mexicans shunned the main border crossings at El Paso, Texas; Nogales, Arizona; and Calexico, California, and thus avoided paying the $8 head tax and $10 visa fee (see Figure 23.4).

The primary pull was the tremendous agricultural expansion occurring in the American Southwest. Irrigation and large-scale agribusiness had begun transforming California's Imperial and San Joaquin Valleys from arid desert into lucrative fruit and vegetable fields. Cotton pickers were needed in the vast plantations of Lower Rio Grande Valley in Texas and the Salt River Valley in Arizona. The sugar beet fields of Michigan, Minnesota, and Colorado also attracted many Mexican farm workers. American industry had also begun recruiting Mexican workers, first to fill wartime needs and later to fill the gap left by the decline in European immigration.

The new Mexican immigration appeared more permanent than previous waves—that is, more and more newcomers stayed—and, like other immigrants, settled in cities. This was partly the unintended consequence of new policies designed to make immigration more difficult. As the Border Patrol (established in 1924) made border crossing more difficult (through head taxes, visa fees, literacy tests, and document checks), what had once been a two-way process for many Mexicans became a one-way migration. Permanent communities of Mexicans in the United States grew rapidly. By 1930, San Antonio's Mexican community accounted for roughly 80,000 people out of a total population of a quarter million. Around 100,000 Mexicans lived in central and east Los Angeles, including 55,000 who attended city schools. Substantial

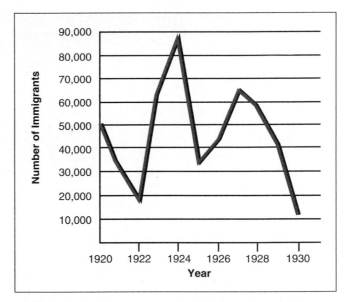

FIGURE 23.4   Mexican Immigration to the United States in the 1920s Many Mexican migrants avoided official border crossing stations so they would not have to pay visa fees. Thus these official figures probably underestimated the true size of the decade's Mexican migration. As the economy contracted with the onset of the Great Depression, immigration from Mexico dropped off sharply.

Mexican communities also flourished in Midwestern cities such as Chicago, Detroit, Kansas City, and Gary. Many of the immigrants alternated between agricultural and factory jobs, depending on the seasonal availability of work. Mexican women often worked in the fields alongside their husbands. They also had jobs as domestics and seamstresses, or took in laundry and boarders.

Racism and local patterns of residential segregation confined most Mexicans to barrios. Housing conditions were generally poor, particularly for recent arrivals, who were forced to live in rude shacks without running water or electricity. Disease and infant mortality rates were much higher than average, and most Mexicans worked at low-paying, unskilled jobs and received inadequate health care. Legal restrictions passed by states and cities made it difficult for Mexicans to enter teaching, legal, and other professions. Mexicans were routinely banned from local public works projects as well. Many felt a deep ambivalence about applying for American citizenship. Loyalty to the Old Country was strong, and many cherished dreams of returning to live out their days in Mexico.

Nativist efforts to limit Mexican immigration were thwarted by the lobbying of powerful agribusiness interests. The Los Angeles Chamber of Commerce typically employed racist stereotyping in arguing to keep the borders open. Mexicans, it claimed, were naturally suited for

ALAMO CITY EMPLOYMENT AGENCY
OFICINA DE ENGANCHES DE BRACEROS MEXICANOS.
W. J. LEWIS. PROP   SALIDAS PARA TODAS PARTES DE ESTADOS UNIDOS.   Cr. 8622. Tr. 3854.

...WIS, OF THE ALAMO CITY EMPLOYMENT AGENCY, DISTRIBUTING BREAD THREE TIMES A DAY TO MEXICANS WHO ARE IN DISTRESS WAITING TO BE

Mexican workers gathered outside a San Antonio labor bureau in 1924. These employment agencies contracted Mexicans to work for Texas farmers, railroads, and construction companies. Note the three Anglo men in front (wearing suits and ties), who probably owned and operated this agency. During the 1920s, San Antonio's Mexican population doubled from roughly 40,000 to over 80,000, making it the second largest *colonia* in *El Norte* after Los Angeles.

SOURCE: Goldbeck Collection, Harry Ransom Humanities Research Center, University of Texas at Austin. Photo by Summerville (46ND).

agriculture, "due to their crouching and bending habits, . . . while the white is physically unable to adapt himself to them."

Mutual aid societies—*mutualistas*—became key social and political institutions in the Mexican communities of the Southwest and Midwest. They provided death benefits and widows' pensions for members and also served as centers of resistance to civil rights violations and discrimination. In 1928, the Federation of Mexican Workers Unions formed in response to a large farm labor strike in the Imperial Valley of California. A group of middle-class Mexican professionals in Texas organized the League of United Latin American Citizens (LULAC) in 1929. The founding of these organizations marked only the beginnings of a long struggle to bring economic, social, and racial equality to Mexican Americans.

The "New Negro"

The Great Migration spurred by World War I showed no signs of letting up during the 1920s, and African American communities in Northern cities grew

rapidly. By far the largest and most influential of these communities was New York City's Harlem. Previously a residential suburb, Harlem began attracting middle-class African Americans in the prewar years. After the war, heavy black migration from the South and the Caribbean encouraged real estate speculators and landlords to remake Harlem as an exclusively black neighborhood. Between 1920 and 1930, some 120,000 new black arrivals settled in Harlem, giving it a black population of roughly 200,000 (see Map 23.1).

Harlem emerged as the demographic and cultural capital of black America, but its appeal transcended national borders, as mass migration from the Caribbean helped reshape the community. Between 1900 and 1930, some 300,000 West Indians emigrated to the United States, roughly half of whom settled in New York City. By the late 1920s, about one-quarter of Harlem's population had been born in Jamaica, Barbados, Trinidad, the Bahamas, and other parts of the Caribbean. Some of the leading cultural, business, and political figures of the era—poet Claude McKay, newspaper publisher P. M. H. Savory, labor organizer Hubert Harrison, black nationalist Marcus Garvey—had roots in the West

MAP EXPLORATION

To explore an interactive version of this map, go to **www.prenhall.com/faragher5/map23.1**

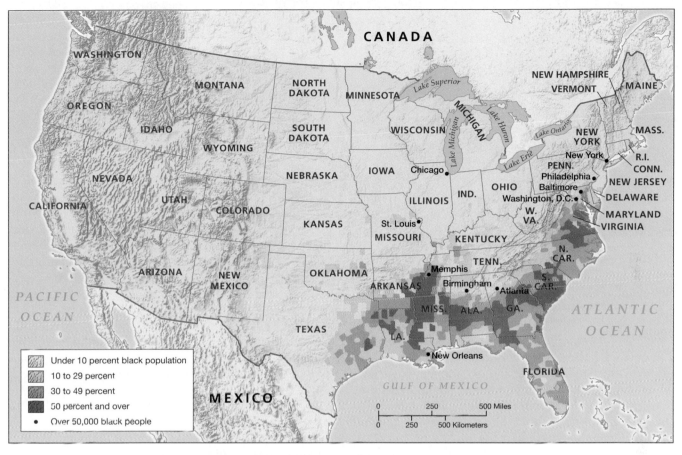

MAP 23.1 Black Population, 1920 Although the Great Migration had drawn hundreds of thousands of African Americans to the urban North, the Southern states of the former Confederacy still remained the center of the African American population in 1920.

Indies. Most black Caribbean migrants came from societies where class differences mattered more than racial ones, and many refused to accept racial bigotry without protest. A large number also carried with them entrepreneurial experience that contributed to their success in running small businesses. Intraracial tensions and resentment between American-born blacks and an increasingly visible West Indian population was one reflection of Harlem's transformation into a hemispheric center for black people.

The demand for housing in this restricted geographical area led to skyrocketing rents, but most Harlemites held low-wage jobs. This combination produced extremely overcrowded apartments, unsanitary conditions, and the rapid deterioration of housing stock. Disease and death rates were abnormally high. Harlem was well on its way to becoming a slum. Yet Harlem also

boasted a large middle-class population and supported a wide array of churches, theaters, newspapers and journals, and black-owned businesses. It became a mecca, as poet and essayist James Weldon Johnson wrote, for "the curious, the adventurous, the enterprising, the ambitious, and the talented of the entire Negro world. "Poet Langston Hughes expressed the excitement of arriving in the community in 1921: "I can never put on paper the thrill of the underground ride to Harlem. I went up the steps and out into the bright September sunlight. Harlem! I stood there, dropped my bags, took a deep breath and felt happy again."

Harlem became the political and intellectual center for what writer Alain Locke called the "New Negro." Locke was referring to a new spirit in the work of black writers and intellectuals, an optimistic faith that encouraged African Americans to develop

The critic and photographer Carl Van Vechten took this portrait of Harlem Renaissance poet Langston Hughes in 1932. The print next to Hughes reflects the influence of African art, an important source of inspiration for Harlem Renaissance artists and writers.

SOURCE: Carl Van Vechten (1880-1964), *Langston Hughes*, 1932. Photograph, gelatin silver print, 14.1 × 21.4 cm. Gift of Prentiss Taylor. National Portrait Gallery, Smithsonian Institution, Washington, DC/Art Resource, NY.

and celebrate their distinctive culture, firmly rooted in the history, folk culture, and experiences of African American people. This faith was the common denominator uniting the disparate figures associated with the Harlem Renaissance. The assertion of cultural independence resonated in the poetry of Langston Hughes and Claude McKay, the novels of Zora Neale Hurston and Jessie Fauset, the essays of Countee Cullen and James Weldon Johnson, the acting of Paul Robeson, and the blues singing of Bessie Smith. Most would agree with Johnson when he wrote in 1927 that "nothing can go farther to destroy race prejudice than the recognition of the Negro as a creator and contributor to American civilization."

There was a political side to the "New Negro" as well. The newly militant spirit that black veterans had brought home from World War I matured and found a variety of expressions in the Harlem of the 1920s. New leaders and movements began to appear alongside established organizations like the National Association for the Advancement of Colored People. A. Philip Randolph began a long career as a labor leader, socialist, and civil rights activist in these years, editing the *Messenger* and organizing the Brotherhood of Sleeping Car Porters. Harlem was also headquarters to Marcus Garvey's Universal Negro Improvement Association. An ambitious Jamaican immigrant who had moved to Harlem in 1916, Garvey created a mass movement that

stressed black economic self-determination and unity among the black communities of the United States, the Caribbean, and Africa. His newspaper, *Negro World*, spoke to black communities around the world, urging black businesses to trade among themselves. With colorful parades and rallies and a central message affirming pride in black identity, Garvey attracted as many as a million members worldwide.

Garvey's best-publicized project was the Black Star Line, a black-owned and -operated fleet of ships that would link people of African descent around the world. But insufficient capital and serious financial mismanagement resulted in the spectacular failure of the enterprise. In 1923, Garvey was found guilty of mail fraud in his fundraising efforts; he later went to jail and was subsequently deported to England. Despite the disgrace, Harlem's largest newspaper, the *Amsterdam News*, explained Garvey's continuing appeal to African Americans: "In a world where black is despised, he taught them that black is beautiful. He taught them to admire and praise black things and black people."

Through the new mass media of radio and phonograph records, millions of Americans now listened and danced to a distinctively African American music, as jazz began to enter the cultural mainstream. The best jazz bands of the day, led by artists such as Duke Ellington, Fletcher Henderson, Cab Calloway, and Louis Armstrong, often had their performances broadcast live from such Harlem venues as the Cotton Club and Small's Paradise. Yet these clubs themselves were rigidly segregated. Black dancers, singers, and musicians provided the entertainment, but no African Americans were allowed in the audience. Chronicled in novels and newspapers, Harlem became a potent symbol to white America of the ultimate good time. Yet the average Harlemite never saw the inside of a nightclub. For the vast majority of Harlem residents, working menial jobs for low wages and forced to pay high rents, the day-to-day reality was depressingly different.

Intellectuals and Alienation

War, Prohibition, growing corporate power, and the deep currents of cultural intolerance troubled many intellectuals in the 1920s. Some felt so alienated from the United States, that they left to live abroad. In the early 1920s, Gertrude Stein, an American expatriate writer living in Paris, told the young novelist Ernest Hemingway: "All of you young people who served in the war, you are a lost generation." The phrase "a lost generation" was widely adopted as a label for American writers, artists, and intellectuals of the postwar era. Yet it is difficult to generalize about so diverse a community. For one thing, living abroad attracted only a handful of American writers. Alienation and disillusion with American life were prominent subjects in the literature and thought of the 1920s, but artists and thinkers developed these themes in very different ways.

The mass slaughter of World War I provoked revulsion and a deep cynicism about the heroic and moralistic portrayal of war so popular in the nineteenth century. Novelists Hemingway and John Dos Passos, who both served at the front as ambulance drivers, depicted the war and its aftermath in world-weary and unsentimental tones. The search for personal moral codes that would allow one to endure life with dignity and authenticity was at the center of Hemingway's fiction. In the taut, spare language of *The Sun Also Rises* (1926) and *A Farewell to Arms* (1929), he questioned idealism, abstractions, and large meanings. As Jake Barnes, the wounded war hero of *The Sun Also Rises* explained, "I did not care what it was all about. All I wanted to know was how to live it."

Hemingway and F. Scott Fitzgerald were the most influential novelists of the era. Fitzgerald joined the army during World War I but did not serve overseas. His work celebrated the youthful vitality of the "Jazz Age" (a phrase he coined), but was also deeply distrustful of the promises of American prosperity and politics. His first novel, *This Side of Paradise* (1920), won a wide readership around the country with its exuberant portrait of a "new generation," "dedicated more than the last to the fear of poverty and the worship of success; grown up to find all Gods dead, all wars fought, all faiths in man shaken." Fitzgerald's finest work, *The Great Gatsby* (1925), written in the south of France, depicted the glamorous parties of the wealthy, while evoking the tragic limits of material success.

At home, many American writers engaged in sharp attacks on small-town America and what they viewed as its provincial values. Essayist H. L. Mencken, caustic editor of the *American Mercury*, heaped scorn on fundamentalists, Prohibition, and nativists, while ridiculing what he called the "American booboisie." Mencken understood the power of the small town and despaired of reforming politics. "Our laws," he wrote, "are invented, in the main, by frauds and fanatics, and put upon the statute books by poltroons and scoundrels." Fiction writers also skewered small-town America, achieving commercial and critical success in the process. Sherwood Anderson's *Winesburg, Ohio* (1919) offered a spare, laconic, pessimistic, yet compassionate, view of middle America. He had a lasting influence on younger novelists of the 1920s.

The most popular and acclaimed writer of the time was novelist Sinclair Lewis. In a series of novels satirizing small-town life, such as *Main Street* (1920) and especially *Babbitt* (1922), Lewis affectionately mocked his characters. His treatment of the central character in Babbitt—George Babbitt of Zenith—also had a strong element of self-mockery, for Lewis could offer no alternative set of values to Babbitt's crass self-promotion, hunger for success, and craving for social acceptance. In 1930, Lewis became the first American author to win the Nobel Prize for literature.

In the aftermath of the postwar Red Scare, American radicalism found itself on the defensive throughout the 1920s. But one *cause célèbre* did attract a great deal of support from intellectuals. In 1921, two Italian American immigrants, Nicola Sacco and Bartolomeo Vanzetti, were tried and convicted for murder in the course of robbing a shoe factory in South Braintree, Massachusetts. Neither Sacco, a shoemaker, nor Vanzetti, a fish peddler, had criminal records, but both had long been active in militant anarchist circles, labor organizing, and antiwar agitation. Their trial took place amidst an intense atmosphere of nativist and antiradical feeling, and both the judge and prosecuting attorney engaged in clearly prejudicial conduct toward the defendants. A six-year struggle to save Sacco and Vanzetti following the trial failed, despite attracting support from a broad range of liberal intellectuals, including Harvard law professor and future Supreme Court justice Felix Frankfurter. The two men were finally executed in 1927, and for many years, their case would remain a powerful symbol of how the criminal justice system could be tainted by political bias and antiimmigrant fervor. Another side of intellectual alienation was expressed by writers critical of industrial progress and the new mass culture. The most important of these were a group of poets and scholars centered in Vanderbilt University in Nashville, Tennessee, collectively known as the Fugitives. They included Allen Tate, John Crowe Ransom, Donald Davidson, and Robert Penn Warren, all of whom invoked traditional authority, respect for the past, and older agrarian ways as ideals to live by. The Fugitives attacked industrialism and materialism as modern-day ills. Self-conscious Southerners, they looked to the antebellum

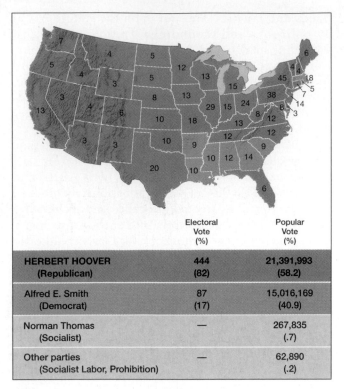

	Electoral Vote (%)	Popular Vote (%)
HERBERT HOOVER (Republican)	444 (82)	21,391,993 (58.2)
Alfred E. Smith (Democrat)	87 (17)	15,016,169 (40.9)
Norman Thomas (Socialist)	—	267,835 (.7)
Other parties (Socialist Labor, Prohibition)	—	62,890 (.2)

MAP 23.2 The Election of 1928 Although Al Smith managed to carry the nation's twelve largest cities, Herbert Hoover's victory in 1928 was one of the largest popular and electoral landslides in the nation's history.

plantation-based society as a model for a community based on benevolence toward dependents (such as black people and women) and respect for the land. Their book of essays, *I'll Take My Stand* (1930), was a collective manifesto of their ideas.

Not all intellectuals, of course, were critics of modern trends. Some, like the philosopher John Dewey, retained much of the prewar optimism and belief in progress. But many others, such as Walter Lippmann and Joseph Wood Krutch, articulated a profound uneasiness with the limits of material growth. In his 1929 book *A Preface to Morals*, the urbane and sophisticated Lippmann expressed doubts about the moral health of the nation. Modern science and technological advances could not address more cosmic questions of belief. The erosion of old religious faiths and moral standards, along with the triumph of the new mass culture, had left many people with nothing to believe in.

The Election of 1928

The presidential election of 1928 served as a kind of national referendum on the Republican new era. It also revealed just how important ethnic and cultural dif-

ferences had become in defining American politics. The contest reflected many of the deepest tensions and conflicts in American society in the 1920s: native-born versus immigrant; Protestant versus Catholic; Prohibition versus legal drinking; small-town life versus the cosmopolitan city; fundamentalism versus modernism; traditional sources of culture versus the new mass media (see Map 23.2).

The 1928 campaign featured two politicians who represented profoundly different sides of American life. Al Smith, the Democratic nominee for president, was a pure product of New York City's Lower East Side. Smith came from a background that included Irish, German, and Italian ancestry, and he was raised as a Roman Catholic. He rose through the political ranks of New York's Tammany Hall machine. A personable man with a deep sympathy for poor and working-class people, Smith served four terms as governor of New York, pushing through an array of laws reforming factory conditions, housing, and welfare programs. Two of his closest advisers were the progressives Frances Perkins and Belle Moskowitz. Smith thus fused older-style machine politics with the newer reform emphasis on state intervention to solve social problems.

Herbert Hoover easily won the Republican nomination after Calvin Coolidge announced he would not run for reelection. Hoover epitomized the successful and forward-looking American. An engineer and self-made millionaire, he offered a unique combination of experience in humanitarian war relief, administrative efficiency, and probusiness policies. Above all, Hoover stood for a commitment to voluntarism and individualism as the best method for advancing the public welfare. He was one of the best-known men in America and promised to continue the Republican control of national politics.

Smith himself quickly became the central issue of the campaign. His sharp New York accent, jarring to many Americans who heard it over the radio, marked him clearly as a man of the city. So did his brown derby and fashionable suits, as well as his promise to work for the repeal of Prohibition. As the first Roman Catholic nominee of a major party, Smith also drew a torrent of anti-Catholic bigotry, especially in the South and Midwest. Nativists and Ku Klux Klanners shamelessly exploited old anti-Catholic prejudices and intimidated participants in Democratic election rallies. But Smith was also attacked from more respectable quarters. Bishop James Cannon, head of the Southern Methodist Episcopal Church, insisted that "no subject of the Pope" should be permitted to occupy the White House. For his part, Smith ran a largely conservative race. He appointed John Raskob, a Republican vice president of General Motors, to manage his campaign, and tried to outdo

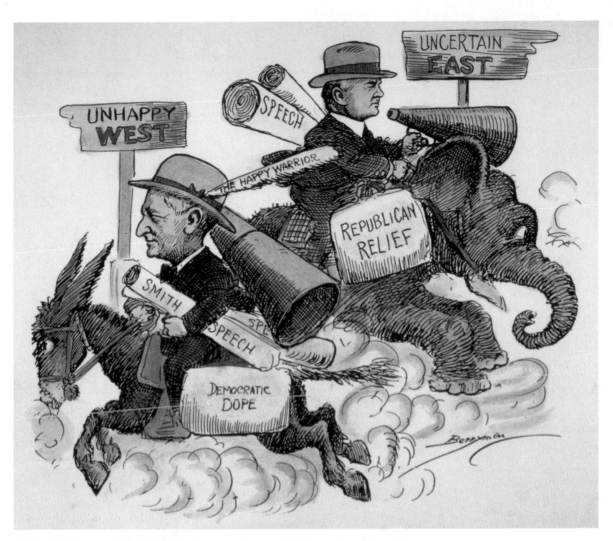

Clifford K. Berryman's 1928 political cartoon interpreted that year's presidential contest along sectional lines. It depicted the two major presidential contenders as each setting off to campaign in the regions where their support was weakest. For Democrat Al Smith, that meant the West, and for Republican Herbert Hoover, the East.

SOURCE: Copyright, 1928, *Lost Angeles Times*. Reprinted by permission.

Hoover in his praise for business. He avoided economic issues such as the unevenness of the prosperity, the plight of farmers, or the growing unemployment. Democrats remained regionally divided over Prohibition, Smith's religion, and the widening split between rural and urban values. Hoover did not have to do much, other than take credit for the continued prosperity.

Hoover polled 21 million votes to Smith's 15 million, and swept the electoral college 444 to 87, including New York State. Even the Solid South, reliably Democratic since the Civil War, gave five states to Hoover— a clear reflection of the ethnocultural split in the party. Yet the election offered important clues to the future of the Democrats. Smith ran better in the big cities of the North and East than any Democrat in modern times. He outpolled Hoover in the aggregate vote of the nation's twelve largest cities and carried six of them, thus pointing the way to the Democrats' future dominance with urban, Northeastern, and ethnic voters.

CONCLUSION

America's big cities, if not dominant politically, now defined the nation's cultural and economic life as never before. The mass media of motion pictures, broadcasting, and chain newspapers brought cosmopolitan entertainments

CHRONOLOGY

1920 Prohibition takes effect

Warren G. Harding is elected president

Station KDKA in Pittsburgh goes on the air

Census reports that urban population is greater than rural population for the first time

1921 First immigration quotas are established by Congress

Sheppard-Towner Act establishes first federally funded health-care program

1922 Washington conference produces Five-Power Treaty, scaling down navies

1923 Equal Rights Amendment is first introduced in Congress

Harding dies in office; Calvin Coolidge becomes president

1924 Ku Klux Klan is at height of its influence

Dawes Plan for war reparations stabilizes European economies

Johnson-Reed Immigration Act tightens quotas established in 1921

1925 Scopes trial pits religious fundamentalism against modernity

F. Scott Fitzgerald publishes *The Great Gatsby*

1926 National Broadcasting Company establishes first national radio network

1927 McNary-Haugen Farm Relief bill finally passed by Congress, but is vetoed by President Coolidge as unwarranted federal interference in the economy

Warner Brothers produces *The Jazz Singer*, the first feature-length motion picture with sound

Charles Lindbergh makes first solo flight across the Atlantic Ocean

1928 Kellogg-Briand Pact renounces war

Herbert Hoover defeats Al Smith for the presidency

1929 Robert and Helen Lynd publish their classic community study, *Middletown*

and values to the remotest small communities. The culture of celebrity knew no geographic boundaries. New consumer durable goods associated with mass-production techniques—automobiles, radios, telephones, household appliances—were manufactured largely in cities. The advertising and public relations companies that sang their praises were also distinctly urban enterprises. Even with the curtailing of European immigration, big cities attracted a kaleidoscopic variety of migrants: white people from small towns and farms, African Americans from the rural South, Mexicans from across the border, intellectuals and professionals looking to make their mark.

Many Americans, of course, remained deeply suspicious of postwar cultural and economic trends. Yet the partisans of Prohibition, members of the Ku Klux Klan, and religious fundamentalists usually found themselves on the defensive against what they viewed as alien cultural and economic forces centered in the metropolis. Large sectors of the population did not share in the era's prosperity. But the large numbers who did—or at least had a taste of good times—ensured Republican political dominance throughout the decade. Thus, America in the 1920s balanced dizzying change in the cultural and economic realms with conservative politics. The reform crusades that attracted millions during the progressive era were a distant memory. Political activism was no match for the new pleasures promised by technology and prosperity.

REVIEW QUESTIONS

1. Describe the impact of the "second industrial revolution" on American business, workers, and consumers. Which technological and economic changes had the biggest impact on American society?

2. Analyze the uneven distribution of the 1920s' economic prosperity. Which Americans gained the most, and which were largely left out?

3. How did an expanding mass culture change the contours of everyday life in the decade following World War I? What role did new technologies of mass communication play in shaping these changes? What connections can you draw between the "culture of consumption" then, and today?

4. What were the key policies and goals articulated by Republican political leaders of the 1920s? How did they apply these to both domestic and foreign affairs?

5. How did some Americans resist the rapid changes taking place in the post–World War I world? What cultural and political strategies did they employ?

6. Discuss the 1928 election as a mirror of the divisions in American society.

RECOMMENDED READING

Roger Daniels, *Guarding the Golden Door: American Immigration Policy and Immigrants Since 1882* (2002). A comprehensive overview by a pioneering scholar in the field, with special emphasis on how racism and ehtnocentrism have shaped American immigration policy.

Lynn Dumenil, *The Modern Temper: America in the 1920s* (1995). An excellent synthesis of recent scholarship, which emphasizes the ambivalence that many Americans felt toward the emergence of modern society.

David J. Goldberg, *Discontented America: The United States in the 1920s* (1999). Focuses on Americans' continuing discomfort with racial, ethnic, religious, and class difference during the decade.

Desmond King, *Making Americans: Immigration, Race, and the Origins of Diverse Democracy* (2000). Fine analysis of the shift of U.S. immigration policies in the 1920s, with special attention to the influence of eugenics, and the long-term consequences of the new restrictive legislation.

Nancy Maclean, *Behind the Mask of Chivalry: The Making of the Second Ku Klux Klan* (1994). An excellent case study of the KKK in Athens, Georgia, with important insights on the Klan's relationship to issues involving gender and class difference.

Charles L. Ponce de Leon, *Self Exposure: Human Interest Journalism and the Emergence of Celebrity in America, 1890–1940* (2002). A thoughtful cultural history that explores the intersection of new mass media, journalism, and the American fascination with celebrity.

Susan Smulyan, *Selling Radio: The Commercialization of American Broadcasting, 1920–1934* (1994). The best analysis of the rise of commercial radio broadcasting in the 1920s.

 For additional study resources for this chapter, go to the *Companion Website*, http://www.prenhall.com/faragher.

The Great Depression and the New Deal

1929–1940

Sit-Down Strike at Flint:
Automobile Workers Organize a New Union

I n the gloomy evening of February 11, 1937, 400 tired, unshaven, but very happy strikers marched out of the sprawling automobile factory known as Fisher Body Number 1 in Flint, Michigan. Most carried American flags and small bundles of clothing. A makeshift banner on top of the plant announced "Victory Is Ours." A wildly cheering parade line of a thousand supporters greeted the strikers at the gates. Shouting with joy, honking horns, and singing songs, the celebrants marched to two other factories to greet other emerging strikers. After forty-four days, the great Flint sit-down strike was over.

Flint was the heart of production for General Motors, the largest corporation in the world. In 1936, GM's net profits had reached $285 million, and its total assets were $1.5 billion. Originally a center for lumbering and then carriage making, Flint had boomed with the auto industry during the 1920s. Thousands of migrants streamed into the city, attracted by assembly line jobs averaging about $30 a week. By 1930, Flint's population had grown to about 150,000 people, 80 percent of whom depended on work at General Motors. A severe housing shortage made living conditions difficult. Parts of the city resembled a mining camp, with workers living in tar-paper shacks, tents, and even railroad cars.

The Great Depression hit Flint very hard. Employment at GM fell from a 1929 high of 56,000 to fewer than 17,000 in 1932. As late as 1938, close to half the city's families were receiving some kind of emergency relief. By that time, as in thousands of other American communities, Flint's private and county relief agencies had been overwhelmed by the needs of the unemployed and their families. Two new national agencies based in Washington, DC, the Federal Emergency Relief Administration and the Works Progress Administration, had replaced local sources of aid during the economic crisis. These New Deal programs embodied a new federal approach to providing relief and employment to American communities unable to cope with the enormity of mass unemployment.

The New Deal also encouraged labor organizing by legally assuring the right to union membership for the first time in American history. The United Automobile Workers (UAW) came to Flint in 1936, seeking to organize GM workers into one industrial union. The previous year, Congress had passed the National Labor Relations Act (also known as the Wagner Act), which made union organizing easier by guaranteeing the right of workers to join unions and bargain collectively. The act established the National Labor Relations Board to oversee union elections and prohibit illegal anti-union activities by employers. But the obstacles to labor organizing were still enormous.

Unemployment was high, and GM had maintained a vigorous anti-union policy for years. By the fall of

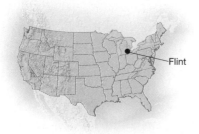
Flint

1936, the UAW had signed up only a thousand members. The key moment came with the seizure of two Flint GM plants by a few hundred auto workers on December 30, 1936. The idea was to stay in the factories until strikers could achieve a collective bargaining agreement with General Motors. "We don't aim to keep the plants or try to run them," explained one sit-downer to a reporter, "but we want to see that nobody takes our jobs. We don't think we're breaking the law, or at least we don't think we're doing anything really bad."

A new and daring tactic—the sit-down strike—gained popularity among American industrial workers during the 1930s. In 1936, there were 48 sit-downs involving nearly 90,000 workers, and in 1937 some 400,000 workers participated in 477 sit-down strikes. Sit-downs expressed the militant exuberance of the rank and file. As one union song of the day put it:

> When they tie the can to a union man,
> Sit down! Sit down!
> When they give him the sack they'll take him back,
> Sit down! Sit down!
> When the speed up comes, just twiddle your thumbs,
> Sit down! Sit down!
> When the boss won't talk don't take a walk,
> Sit down! Sit down!

The Flint strikers carefully organized themselves into what one historian called "the sit down community." Each plant elected a strike committee and appointed its own police chief and sanitary engineer. No alcohol was allowed, and strikers were careful not to destroy company property. Committees were organized for food preparation, recreation, sanitation, education, and contact with the outside. A Women's Emergency Brigade—the strikers' wives, mothers, and daughters—provided crucial support preparing food and maintaining militant picket lines.

As the strike continued through January, support in Flint and around the nation grew. Overall production in the GM empire dropped from 53,000 vehicles per week to 1,500. Reporters and union supporters flocked to the plants. On January 11, in the so-called Battle of Running Bulls, strikers and their supporters clashed violently with Flint police and private GM guards. Michigan governor Frank Murphy, sympathetic to the strikers, brought in the National Guard to protect them. He refused to enforce an injunction obtained by GM to evict the strikers.

In the face of determined unity by the sit-downers, GM gave in, and recognized the UAW as the exclusive bargaining agent in all sixty of its factories. The strike was perhaps the most important in American labor history, sparking a huge growth in union membership in the automobile and other mass-production industries. Rose Pesotta, a textile union organizer, described the wild victory celebration in Flint's overflowing Pengelly Building: "People sang and joked and laughed and cried, deliriously joyful. Victory meant a freedom they had never known before. No longer would they be afraid to join unions."

Out of the tight-knit, temporary community of the sit-down strike, emerged a looser yet more permanent kind of community: a powerful, nationwide trade union of automobile workers. The UAW struggled successfully to win recognition and collective bargaining rights from other carmakers, such as Chrysler and Ford. The national UAW, like other new unions in the mass-production industries, was composed of locals around the country. The permanent community of unionized auto workers won significant improvements in wages, working conditions, and benefits. Locals also became influential in the political and social lives of their larger communities—industrial cities such as Flint, Detroit, and Toledo. Nationally, organized labor provided crucial political support for many of the social welfare initiatives associated with the New Deal: federal relief, a Social Security system, new standards regulating minimum wages and maximum hours, and Washington-based efforts to improve the nation's housing. By the late 1930s, conservative resistance would limit the scope of New Deal reforms. But organized labor would remain a crucial component of the New Deal political coalition, and a key power broker in the Democratic Party, for decades to come.

KEY TOPICS

- Causes and consequences of the Great Depression
- The politics of hard times
- Franklin D. Roosevelt and the two New Deals
- The expanding federal sphere in the South and West
- American cultural life during the 1930s
- Legacies and limits of New Deal reform

HARD TIMES

No event of the twentieth century had a more profound impact on American life than the Great Depression of the 1930s. Statistics can document a slumping economy, mass unemployment, and swelling relief rolls—but these numbers tell only part of the story. The emotional and psychological toll of these years, what one writer called "the invisible scar," must also be considered in understanding the worst economic crisis in American history. Even today, depression-era experiences retain a central, even mythical, place in the lives and memories of millions of American families.

The Bull Market

Stock trading in the late 1920s captured the imagination of the broad American public. The stock market resembled a sporting arena, millions following stock prices as they did the exploits of Babe Ruth or Jack Dempsey. Many business leaders and economists as much as told Americans that it was their duty to buy stocks. John J. Raskob, chairman of the board of General Motors, wrote an article for the *Ladies' Home Journal* titled "Everybody Ought to Be Rich." A person who saved $15 each month and invested it in good common stocks would, he claimed, have $80,000 within twenty years.

During the bull market of the 1920s, stock prices increased at roughly twice the rate of industrial production. Paper value far outran real value. By the end of the decade, stocks that had been bought mainly on the basis of their earning power, which was passed on to stockholders in the form of dividends, now came to be purchased only for the resale value after their prices rose. Anyone reading the financial pages of a newspaper would be amazed at the upward climb. In 1928 alone, for example, the price of Radio Corporation of America stock shot up from 85 points to 420; Chrysler stock more than doubled, from 63 to 132.

Yet only about 4 million Americans owned any stocks at all, out of a total population of 120 million. Many of these stock buyers had been lured into the market through easy-credit, margin accounts. Margin accounts allowed investors to purchase stocks by making a small down payment (as low as 10 percent), borrowing the rest from a broker, and using the shares as collateral, or security, on the loan. Just as installment plans had stimulated the automobile and other industries, "buying on the margin" brought new customers to the stock market. Investment trusts, similar to today's mutual funds, attracted many new investors with promises of high returns based on their managers' expert knowledge of the market. Corporations with excess capital found that lending money to stockbrokers was more profitable than plowing it back into their own plants to develop new technologies. All these new approaches to buying stock contributed to an expansive and optimistic atmosphere on Wall Street.

The Crash

Although often portrayed as a one- or two-day catastrophe, the Wall Street crash of 1929 was in reality a steep slide. The bull market peaked in early September, and prices drifted downward. On October 23, the Dow Jones industrials lost 21 points in one hour, and many large investors concluded the boom was over. The boom itself rested on expectations of continually rising prices; once those expectations began to melt, the market had to decline. On Monday, October 28, the Dow lost 38 points, or 13 percent of its value. On October 29, "Black Tuesday," the bottom seemed to fall out. Over 16 million shares, more than double the previous record, were traded as panic selling took hold. For many stocks, no buyers were available at any price.

The situation worsened. The market's fragile foundation of credit, based on the margin debt, quickly crumbled. Many investors with margin accounts had no

Stockbrokers, their customers, and employees of the New York Stock Exchange gather nervously on Wall Street during the stock market crash of 1929. October 29 was the worst single day in the 112-year history of the exchange, as panic selling caused many stocks to lose half their value.

SOURCE: Brown Brothers.

choice but to sell when stock values fell. Since the shares themselves represented the security for their loans, more money had to be put up to cover the loans when prices declined. By mid-November, about $30 billion in the market price of stocks had been wiped out. Half the value of the stocks listed in *The New York Times* index was lost in ten weeks.

The nation's political and economic leaders downplayed the impact of Wall Street's woes. Secretary of the Treasury Andrew Mellon spoke for many in the financial world when he described the benefits of the slump: "It will purge the rottenness out of the system. High costs of living and high living will come down. People will work harder, live a more moral life. Values will be adjusted, and enterprising people will pick up

the wrecks from less competent people." At the end of 1929, hardly anyone was predicting that a depression would follow the stock market crash.

Underlying Weaknesses

It would be oversimple to say that the stock market crash "caused" the Great Depression. But like a person who catches a chill, the economy after the crash became less resistant to existing sources of infection. The resulting sickness revealed underlying economic weaknesses left over from the previous decade. First, workers and consumers by and large received too small a share of the enormous increases in labor productivity. Between 1923 and 1929, manufacturing output per worker-hour increased by 32 percent. But wages during the same period rose only 8 percent, or one-quarter the rise in productivity. Moreover, the rise in productivity itself had encouraged overproduction in many industries. The farm sector had never been able to regain its prosperity of the World War I years. Farmers suffered under a triple burden of declining prices for their crops, a drop in exports, and large debts incurred by wartime expansion (see Chapter 23).

The most important weakness in the economy was the extremely unequal distribution of income and wealth. In 1929, the top 0.1 percent of American families (24,000 families) had an aggregate income equal to that of the bottom 42 percent (11.5 million families). The top 5 percent of American families received 30 percent of the nation's income; the bottom 60 percent got only 26 percent. About 71 percent of American families had annual incomes below $2,500. Nearly 80 percent of the nation's families (21.5 million households) had no savings; the top 0.1 percent held 34 percent of all savings. The top 0.5 percent of Americans owned 32.4 percent of the net wealth of the entire population—the greatest such concentration of wealth in the nation's history (see Table 24.1).

The stock market crash undermined the confidence, investment, and spending of businesses and the well-to-do. Manufacturers decreased their production and began laying off workers, and layoffs brought further declines in consumer spending, and another round of production cutbacks. A spurt of consumer spending might have checked this downward spiral, but consumers had less to spend as industries laid off workers and reduced work hours. With a shrinking market for products, businesses were hesitant to expand. A large proportion of the nation's banking funds were tied to the speculative bubble of Wall Street stock buying. Many banks began to fail as anxious depositors withdrew their funds, which were uninsured. Thousands of families lost their savings to these failures. An 86 percent plunge in agricultural prices between 1929 and 1933, compared to a decline in agricultural production of only 6 percent, brought suffering to America's farmers.

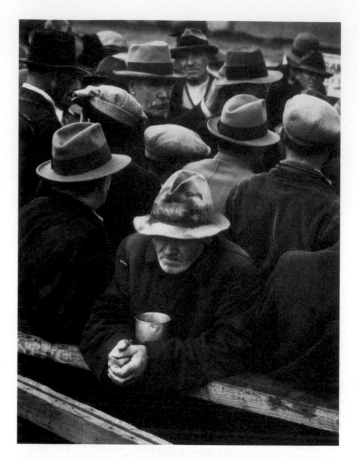

Dorothea Lange captured the lonely despair of unemployment in *White Angel Bread Line, San Francisco, 1933.* During the 1920s, Lange had specialized in taking portraits of wealthy families, but by 1932, she could no longer stand the contradiction between her portrait business and "what was going on in the street." She said of this photograph: "There are moments such as these when time stands still and all you can do is hold your breath and hope it will wait for you."

SOURCE: Dorothea Lange, *White Angel Breadline, San Francisco, 1933.* Copyright the Dorothea Lange Collection, The Oakland Museum of California, City of Oakland. Gift of Paul S. Taylor.

TABLE 24.1	DISTRIBUTION OF TOTAL FAMILY INCOME AMONG VARIOUS SEGMENTS OF THE POPULATION, 1929–44 (IN PERCENTAGES)					
Year	Poorest Fifth	Second Poorest Fifth	Middle Fifth	Second Wealthiest Fifth	Wealthiest Fifth	Wealthiest 5 Percent
1929		12.5	13.8	19.3	54.4	30.0
1935–1936	4.1	9.2	14.1	20.9	51.7	26.5
1941	4.1	9.5	15.3	22.3	48.8	24.0
1944	4.9	10.9	16.2	22.2	45.8	20.7

SOURCE: Adapted from U.S. Bureau of the Census, *Historical Statistics of the United States, Colonial Times to 1970*, Bicentennial Edition (Washington, DC: U.S. Government Printing Office, 1975), p. 301.

Mass Unemployment

At a time when unemployment insurance did not exist and public relief was completely inadequate, the loss of a job could mean economic catastrophe for workers and their families. Massive unemployment across America became the most powerful sign of a deepening depression. In 1930, the Department of Labor estimated that 4.2 million workers, or roughly 9 percent of the labor force, were out of work. These figures nearly doubled in 1931, and by 1933, 12.6 million workers—over one-quarter of the labor force—were without jobs. Other sources put the figure that year above 16 million, or nearly one out of every three workers. None of these statistics tells us how long people were unemployed or how many Americans found only part-time work.

What did it mean to be unemployed and without hope in the early 1930s? Figures give us only an outline of the grim reality. Many Americans, raised believing that they were responsible for their own fate, blamed themselves for their failure to find work. Contemporary journalists and social workers noted the common feelings of shame and guilt expressed by the unemployed. Even those who did not blame themselves struggled with feelings of inadequacy, uselessness, and despair. One unemployed Houston woman told a relief caseworker, "I'm just no good, I guess. I've given up ever amounting to anything. It's no use." "Drives a man crazy, or drives him to drink, hangin' around," said an out-of-work Connecticut knife maker. A West Virginia man wrote his senator to complain, "My children have not got no shoes and clothing to go to school with, and we haven't got enough bed clothes to keep us warm." For the most desperate, contemplating suicide was not unusual. "Can you be so kind as to advise me as to which would be the most human way to dispose of my self and family, as this is about the only thing that I see left to do," one despondent Pennsylvania man inquired of a state relief agency.

Joblessness proved especially difficult for men between the ages of thirty-five and fifty-five, the period in their lives when family responsibilities were heaviest. Nathan Ackerman, a psychiatrist who went to Pennsylvania to observe the impact of prolonged unemployment on coal miners, found an enormous sense of "internal distress":

> They hung around street corners and in groups. They gave each other solace. They were loath to go home because they were indicted, as if it were their fault for being unemployed. A jobless man was a lazy good-for-nothing. The women punished the men for not bringing home the bacon, by withholding themselves sexually. . . . These men suffered from depression. They felt despised, they were ashamed of themselves. They cringed, they comforted one another. They avoided home.

Unemployment upset the psychological balance in many families by undermining the traditional authority of the male breadwinner. Women, because their labor was cheaper than men's, found it easier to hold onto jobs. Female clerks, secretaries, maids, and waitresses earned much less than male factory workers, but their jobs were more likely to survive hard times. Pressures on those lucky enough to have a job increased as well. Anna Novak, a Chicago meat packer, recalled the degrading harassment at the hands of foremen: "You could get along swell if you let the boss slap you on the behind and feel you up. God, I hate that stuff, you don't know!" Men responded in a variety of ways to unemployment. Some withdrew emotionally; others became angry or took to drinking.

Isaac Soyer's *Employment Agency*, a 1937 oil painting, offered one of the decade's most sensitive efforts at depicting the anxiety and sense of isolation felt by millions of depression-era job hunters.

SOURCE: Isaac Soyer, *Employment Agency*, 1937. Oil on canvas, 34½″ × 45″. Whitney Museum of American Art.

A few committed suicide. One Chicago social worker, writing about unemployment in 1934, summed up the strains she found in families: "Fathers feel they have lost their prestige in the home; there is much nagging, mothers nag at the fathers, parents nag at the children. Children of working age who earn meager salaries find it hard to turn over all their earnings and deny themselves even the greatest necessities and as a result leave home." Fear of unemployment and a deep desire for security marked the depression generation.

Hoover's Failure

The enormity of the Great Depression overwhelmed traditional—and meager—sources of relief. In most communities across America, these sources were a patchwork of private agencies and local government units, such as towns, cities, or counties. They simply lacked the money, resources, and staff to deal with the worsening situation. In large urban centers like Detroit and Chicago, unemployment approached 50 percent by 1932. Smaller communities could not cope either. One West Virginia coal-mining county with 1,500 unemployed miners, had only $9,000 to meet relief needs for that year. Unemployed transients, attracted by warm weather, posed a special problem for communities in California and Florida. By the end of 1931, Los Angeles had 70,000 nonresident jobless and homeless men; new arrivals numbered about 1,200 a day.

There was great irony, even tragedy, in President Hoover's failure to respond to human suffering. He had administered large-scale humanitarian efforts during World War I with great efficiency, yet he failed to face the facts of the depression. He ignored all the mounting evidence to the contrary when he claimed in his 1931 State of the Union Address, "Our people are providing against distress from unemployment in true American fashion by magnificent response to public appeal and by action of the local governments."

Hoover resisted the growing calls from Congress and local communities for a greater federal role in relief efforts or public works projects. He worried, as he told Congress after vetoing one measure, about injuring "the initiative and enterprise of the American people." The President's Emergency Committee for Unemployment, established in 1930, and its successor, the President's Organization for Unemployment Relief (POUR), created in 1931, did little more than encourage local groups to raise money to help the unemployed. Hoover's plan for recovery centered on restoring business confidence. His administration's most important institutional response to the depression was the Reconstruction Finance Corporation (RFC), established in early 1932 and based on the War Finance Corporation of the World War I years. The RFC was designed to make government credit available to ailing banks, railroads, insurance companies, and other businesses, thereby stimulating economic activity. The key assumption here was that the credit problem was one of supply (for businesses) rather than demand (from consumers). But given the public's low purchasing power, most businesses were not interested in obtaining loans for expansion.

The RFC managed to save numerous banks and other businesses from going under, but its approach did not hasten recovery. And Hoover was loath to use the RFC to make direct grants to states, cities, or individuals. In July 1932, congressional Democrats pushed through the Emergency Relief Act, which authorized the RFC to lend $300 million to states that had exhausted their own relief funds. Hoover grudgingly signed the bill, but less than $30 million had actually been given out by the end of 1933.

Protest and the Election of 1932

By 1932, the desperate mood of many Americans was finding expression in direct, sometimes violent, protests that were widely covered in the press. On March 7, communist organizers led a march of several thousand Detroit auto workers and unemployed to the Ford River Rouge factory in nearby Dearborn. When the demonstrators refused orders to turn back, Ford-controlled police fired tear gas and bullets, killing four and seriously wounding fifty others. Some 40,000 people attended a tense funeral service a few days later. Desperate farmers in Iowa organized the Farmers' Holiday Association, aimed at raising prices by refusing to sell produce. In August, some 1,500 farmers turned back cargo trucks outside Sioux City, Iowa, and made a point by dumping milk and other perishables into ditches (see Map 24.1).

The spring of 1932 also saw the "Bonus Army" begin descending on Washington, DC. This protest took its name from a 1924 act of Congress that had promised a $1,000 bonus—in the form of a bond that would not mature until 1945—to every veteran of World War I. The veterans who were gathering in Washington demanded immediate payment of the bonus in cash. By summer, they and their families numbered around 20,000, and were camped out all over the capital city. Their lobbying convinced the House to pass a bill for immediate payment, but the Senate rejected the bill, and most of the veterans left. At the end of July, U.S. Army troops led by Chief of Staff General Douglas MacArthur, forcibly evicted the remaining 2,000 veterans from their encampment. MacArthur exaggerated the menace of the peaceful demonstrators, insisting they were driven by "the essence of revolution." The spectacle of these unarmed and unemployed men, the heroes of 1918,

MAP EXPLORATION

To explore an interactive version of this map,
go to **www.prenhall.com/faragher5/map24.1**

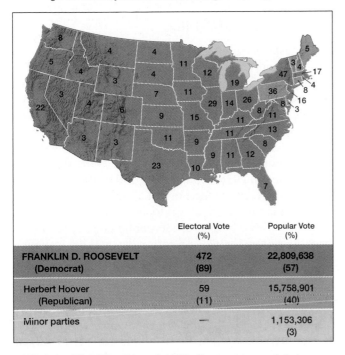

	Electoral Vote (%)	Popular Vote (%)
FRANKLIN D. ROOSEVELT (Democrat)	472 (89)	22,809,638 (57)
Herbert Hoover (Republican)	59 (11)	15,758,901 (40)
Minor parties	—	1,153,306 (3)

MAP 24.1 The Election of 1932 Democrats owed their overwhelming victory in 1932 to the popular identification of the depression with the Hoover administration. Roosevelt's popular vote was about the same as Hoover's in 1928, and FDR's Electoral College margin was even greater.

driven off by bayonets and bullets, provided the most disturbing evidence yet of the failure of Hoover's administration.

In 1932, Democrats nominated Franklin D. Roosevelt, governor of New York, as their candidate. Roosevelt's acceptance speech stressed the need for reconstructing the nation's economy. "I pledge you, I pledge myself," he said, "to a new deal for the American people." Roosevelt's plans for recovery were vague at best. He frequently attacked Hoover for reckless and extravagant spending and accused him of trying to center too much power in Washington. He also spoke of the need for government to meet "the problem of underconsumption" and to help in "distributing wealth and products more equitably." Hoover bitterly condemned Roosevelt's ideas as a "radical departure" from the American way of life. But with the depression growing worse every day, probably any Democrat would have defeated Hoover. The Democratic victory was overwhelming. Roosevelt carried forty-two states, taking the electoral

college 472 to 59 and the popular vote by about 23 million to 16 million. Democrats won big majorities in both the House and the Senate. The stage was set for FDR's "new deal."

FDR AND THE FIRST NEW DEAL

No president of this century had a greater impact on American life and politics than Franklin Delano Roosevelt. To a large degree, the New Deal was a product of his astute political skills and the sheer force of his personality. The only president ever elected to four terms, FDR would loom as the dominant personality in American political life through depression and war. Roosevelt's leadership also inaugurated a forty-year-long period during which the Democrats would be the nation's majority party.

FDR the Man

Franklin Delano Roosevelt was born in 1882 in Dutchess County, New York, where he grew up an only child, secure and confident, on his family's vast estate. Franklin's father, James, had made a fortune through railroad investments, but he was already in his fifties when Franklin was born, and it was his mother, Sara Delano, who was the dominant figure in his childhood. Roosevelt's education at Groton, Harvard, and Columbia Law School reinforced the aristocratic values of his family: a strong sense of civic duty, the importance of competitive athletics, and a commitment to public service.

In 1905, Franklin married his distant cousin, Anna Eleanor Roosevelt, niece of President Theodore Roosevelt. Eleanor would later emerge as an influential adviser and political force on her own. Franklin turned to politics as a career early on. He was elected as a Democrat to the New York State Senate in 1910, served as assistant navy secretary from 1913 to 1920, and was nominated for vice president by the Democrats in the losing 1920 campaign.

In the summer of 1921, Roosevelt was stricken with polio at his summer home. He was never to walk again without support. The disease strengthened his relationship with Eleanor, who encouraged him not only to fight his handicap, but to continue his political career. The disease and FDR's response to it proved a turning point. His patience and determination in fighting the illness transformed him. The wealthy aristocrat, for whom everything had come relatively easily, now personally understood the meaning of struggle and hardship. "Once I spent two years lying in bed trying to move my big toe," he recalled. "After that anything else seems easy."

Elected governor of New York in 1928, Roosevelt served two terms and won a national reputation for

This *New Yorker* magazine cover depicted an ebullient Franklin D. Roosevelt riding to his 1933 inauguration in the company of a glum Herbert Hoover. This drawing typified many mass-media images of the day, contrasting the different moods and temperaments of the new President and the defeated incumbent.

SOURCE: Franklin D. Roosevelt Library.

reform. As governor, his achievements included instituting unemployment insurance, strengthening child labor laws, providing tax relief for farmers, and providing pensions for the old. As the depression hit the state, he slowly increased public works and set up a Temporary Emergency Relief Administration. With his eye on the White House, he began assembling a group of key advisers, the "brains trust," who would follow him to Washington. The central figures were Columbia Law School professor and progressive Raymond Moley; two economists, Rexford G. Tugwell and Adolf A. Berle; and attorneys Samuel Rosenman, Basil O'Connor, and Felix Frankfurter. The "brain trusters" shared a faith in the power of experts to set the economy right, and a basic belief in government-business cooperation. They rejected the old progressive dream of recreating an ideal society of small producers. Structural economic reform, they argued, must accept the modern reality of large corporate enterprise based on mass-production and distribution.

Restoring Confidence

In the first days of his administration, Roosevelt conveyed a sense of optimism and activism that helped restore the badly shaken confidence of the nation. "First of all," he told Americans in his Inaugural Address on March 4, 1933, "let me assert my firm belief that the only thing we have to fear is fear itself." The very next day, he issued an executive order calling for a four-day "bank holiday" to shore up the country's ailing financial system. More than 1,300 banks failed in 1930, more than 2,000 in 1931. Contemporary investigations had revealed a disquieting pattern of stock manipulation, illegal loans to bank officials, and tax evasion that helped erode public confidence in the banking system. Between election day and the inauguration, the banking system had come alarmingly close to shutting down altogether, due to widespread bank failures and the hoarding of currency.

Roosevelt therefore called for a special session of Congress to deal with the banking crisis as well as with unemployment aid and farm relief. On March 12, he broadcast his first "fireside chat" to explain the steps he had taken to meet the financial emergency. These radio broadcasts became a standard part of Roosevelt's political technique, and they proved enormously successful. They gave courage to ordinary Americans and communicated a genuine sense of compassion from the White House.

Congress immediately passed the Emergency Banking Act, which gave the president broad discretionary powers over all banking transactions and foreign exchange. It authorized healthy banks to reopen only under licenses from the Treasury Department, and provided for greater federal authority in managing the affairs of failed banks. By the middle of March, about half the country's banks, holding about 90 percent of the nation's deposits, were open for business again. Banks began to attract new deposits from people who had been holding back their money. The bank crisis had passed.

The Hundred Days

From March to June of 1933—"the Hundred Days"— FDR pushed through Congress an extraordinary number of acts designed to combat various aspects of the depression. What came to be called the New Deal was no unified program to end the depression, but rather an improvised series of reform and relief measures, some of which seemed to contradict each other.

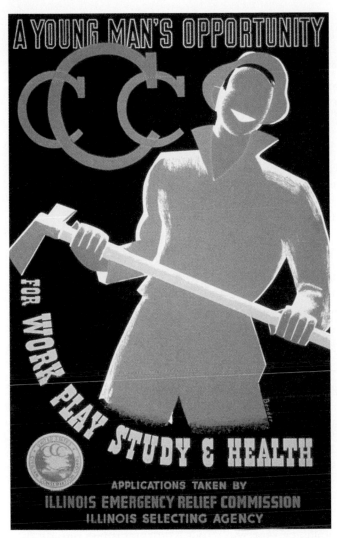

A recruitment poster represents the Civilian Conservation Corps as much more than simply an emergency relief measure, stressing character building and the opportunity for self-improvement. By the time the CCC expired in 1942, it had become one of the most popular of all the New Deal programs.

SOURCE: © CORBIS.

Roosevelt responded to pressures from Congress, from business, and from organized labor, but he also used his own considerable influence over public opinion to get his way.

Five measures were particularly important and innovative. The Civilian Conservation Corps (CCC), established in March as an unemployment relief effort, provided work for jobless young men in protecting and conserving the nation's natural resources. Road construction, reforestation, flood control, and national park improvements were some of the major projects performed

in work camps across the country. CCC workers received room and board and $30 each month, up to $25 of which had to be sent home to dependents. By the time the program was phased out in 1942, more than 2.5 million youths had worked in some 1,500 CCC camps.

In May, Congress authorized $500 million for the Federal Emergency Relief Administration (FERA). Half the money went as direct relief to the states; the rest was distributed on the basis of a dollar of federal aid for every three dollars of state and local funds spent for relief. This system of outright federal grants differed significantly from Hoover's approach, which provided only for loans. Establishment of work relief projects, however, was left to state and local governments. To direct this massive undertaking FDR tapped Harry Hopkins, a streetwise former New York City social worker driven by a deep moral passion to help the less fortunate and an impatience with bureaucracy. Hopkins would emerge as the key figure administering New Deal relief programs.

The Agricultural Adjustment Administration (AAA) was set up to provide immediate relief to the nation's farmers. The AAA established a new federal role in agricultural planning and price setting. It established parity prices for basic farm commodities, including corn, wheat, hogs, cotton, rice, and dairy products. The concept of parity pricing was based on the purchasing power that farmers had enjoyed during the prosperous years of 1909 to 1914. That period now became the benchmark for setting the prices of farm commodities. The AAA also incorporated the principle of subsidy, whereby farmers received benefit payments in return for reducing acreage or otherwise cutting production where surpluses existed. The funds for these payments were to be raised from new taxes on food processing.

The AAA raised total farm income and was especially successful in pushing up the prices of wheat, cotton, and corn. But it had some troubling side effects as well. Landlords often failed to share their AAA payments with tenant farmers, and they frequently used benefits to buy tractors and other equipment that displaced sharecroppers. Many Americans were disturbed, too, by the sight of surplus crops, livestock, and milk being destroyed while millions went hungry.

The Tennessee Valley Authority (TVA) proved to be one of the most unique and controversial projects of the New Deal era. The TVA, an independent public corporation, built dams and power plants, produced cheap fertilizer for farmers, and, most significantly, brought cheap electricity for the first time to thousands of people in six Southern states. Denounced by some as a dangerous step toward socialism, the TVA stood for decades as a model of how careful government planning could

OVERVIEW

KEY LEGISLATION OF THE FIRST NEW DEAL ("HUNDRED DAYS," MARCH 9–JUNE 16, 1933)

Legislation	Purpose
Emergency Banking Relief Act	Enlarged federal authority over private banks Government loans to private banks
Civilian Conservation Corps	Unemployment relief Conservation of natural resources
Federal Emergency Relief Administration	Direct federal money for relief, funneled through state and local governments
Agricultural Adjustment Administration	Federal farm aid based on parity pricing and subsidy
Tennessee Valley Authority	Economic development and cheap electricity for Tennessee Valley
National Industrial Recovery Act	Self-regulating industrial codes to revive economic activity
Public Works Administration	Federal public works projects to increase employment and consumer spending

dramatically improve the social and economic welfare of an underdeveloped region.

On the very last of the Hundred Days, Congress passed the National Industrial Recovery Act, the closest attempt yet at a systematic plan for economic recovery. In theory, each industry would be self-governed by a code hammered out by representatives of business, labor, and the consuming public. Once approved by the National Recovery Administration (NRA) in Washington, led by General Hugh Johnson and symbolized by the distinctive Blue Eagle stamp, the codes would have the force of law. In practice, almost all the National Recover Administration (NRA) codes were written by the largest firms in any given industry; labor and consumers got short shrift. The sheer administrative complexities involved with code writing and compliance made a great many people unhappy with the NRA's operation. Finally, the Public Works Administration (PWA), led by Secretary of the Interior Harold Ickes, authorized $3.3 billion for the construction of roads, public buildings, and other projects. The idea was to provide jobs, and thus stimulate the economy through increased consumer spending. A favorite image for this kind of spending was "priming the pump." Just as a farmer had to prime a pump with water before it could draw more water from the well, the government had to prime the economy with jobs for the unemployed. Eventually the PWA spent over $4.2 billion building roads, schools, post offices, bridges, courthouses, and other public buildings around the country. In thousands of communities today, these structures remain the most tangible reminders of the New Deal era.

LEFT TURN AND THE SECOND NEW DEAL

The Hundred Days legislative package tried to offer something for everybody. Certainly the active, can-do spirit in Washington brought reassurance that the nation was back on track. Yet the depression remained a stark reality for many millions. From the beginning, the New Deal had loud and powerful critics who complained bitterly that FDR had overstepped the traditional boundaries of government action. Others were angry that Roosevelt had not done nearly enough. These varied voices of protest helped shape the political debates of FDR's first term. Ultimately, they would push the New Deal in more radical directions.

Roosevelt's Critics

Criticism of the New Deal came from the right and the left. On the right, pro-Republican newspapers and the American Liberty League, a group of conservative businessmen organized in 1934, denounced Roosevelt and his advisers. They held the administration responsible for what they considered an attack on property rights, the growing welfare state, and the decline of personal liberty. Dominated by wealthy executives of DuPont and General Motors, the league attracted support from a group of conservative Democrats, including Al Smith, the former presidential candidate, who declared the New Deal's laws "socialistic." The league supported anti-New Dealers for Congress, but in the 1934 election, Democrats built up their majorities from 310 to 319 in the House and from 60 to 69 in the Senate—an unusually strong showing for the incumbent party in a midterm election.

Some of Roosevelt's staunchest early supporters turned critical. Father Charles E. Coughlin, a Catholic priest in suburban Detroit, attracted a huge national radio audience of 40 million listeners with passionate sermons attacking Wall Street, international bankers, and "plutocratic capitalism." Coughlin at first supported Roosevelt and the New Deal, and he tried to build a close personal relationship with the president. But by 1934, the ambitious Coughlin, frustrated by his limited influence on the administration, began attacking FDR. Roosevelt was a tool of special interests, he charged, who wanted dictatorial powers. New Deal policies were part of a communist conspiracy, threatening community autonomy with centralized federal power. Coughlin finally broke with FDR and founded the National Union for Social Justice. More troublesome for Roosevelt and his allies were the vocal and popular movements on the left. These found the New Deal too timid in its measures. In California, well-known novelist and socialist Upton Sinclair entered the 1934 Democratic primary for governor by running on a program he called EPIC, for End Poverty in California. He proposed a $50 a month pension for all poor people over age sixty. His campaign also emphasized a government-run system of "production for use" (rather than profit) workshops for the unemployed. Sinclair shocked local and national Democrats by winning the primary easily. He lost a close general election only because the Republican candidate received heavy financial and tactical support from wealthy Hollywood studio executives and frightened regular Democrats.

Another Californian, Francis E. Townsend, a retired doctor, created a large following among senior citizens with his Old Age Revolving Pension plan. He called for payments of $200 per month to all people over sixty, provided the money was spent within thirty days. The pensions would be financed by a national 2 percent tax on all commercial transactions. This plan managed to attract a nationwide following of more than 3 million by 1936. But Townsend's plan was essentially regressive, since it proposed to tax all Americans equally, regardless of their income.

Huey Long, Louisiana's flamboyant backcountry orator, posed the greatest potential threat to Roosevelt's leadership. Long had captured Louisiana's governorship in 1928, by attacking the state's entrenched oil industry and calling for a radical redistribution of wealth. In office, he significantly improved public education, roads, medical care, and other public services, winning the loyalty of the state's poor farmers and industrial workers. Elected to the U.S. Senate in 1930, Long came to Washington with national ambitions. He at first supported Roosevelt, but in 1934, his own presidential ambitions and his impatience with the pace of New Deal measures led to a break with Roosevelt.

Long organized the Share Our Wealth Society. Its purpose, he thundered, "was to break up the swollen fortunes of America and to spread the wealth among all our people." Limiting the size of large fortunes, Long promised, would mean a homestead worth $5,000 and a $2,500 annual income for everyone. Although Long's economics were fuzzy at best, he undoubtedly touched a deep nerve with his "Every Man a King" slogan. A secret poll in the summer of 1935 stunned the Democratic National Committee by showing that Long might attract 3 or 4 million votes. Only his assassination that September by a disgruntled political enemy, prevented Long's third-party candidacy, which might have proved disastrous for FDR.

In the nation's workplaces and streets, a rejuvenated and newly militant labor movement also loomed as a force to be reckoned with. Unemployed Councils, organized largely by the Communist Party in industrial cities, held marches and rallies demanding public works projects and relief payments. Section 7a of the National Industrial Recovery Act required that workers be allowed to bargain collectively with employers, through representatives of their own choosing. Though this provision of the NIRA was not enforced, it did help raise expectations and spark union organizing. Almost 1.5 million workers took part in some 1,800 strikes in 1934.

But employers resisted unionization nearly everywhere, often with violence and the help of local and state police. In Minneapolis that year, a local of the International Brotherhood of Teamsters won a bloody strike against the combined opposition of the union's own national officials, vehemently anti-union employers, and a brutal city police force. Also in 1934, a San Francisco general strike in support of striking members of the International Longshoremen's Association (ILA) effectively shut down the city. Employer use of strikebreakers and violent intimidation prompted an outpouring of support for the ILA from the city's working class, as well as from many shopkeepers and middle-class professionals.

The Second Hundred Days

The popularity of leaders like Sinclair, Townsend, and Long suggested Roosevelt might be losing electoral support among workers, farmers, the aged, and the unemployed. In early 1935, Roosevelt and his closest advisers responded by turning left and concentrating on a new program of social reform. They had three major goals: strengthening the national commitment to creating jobs; providing security against old age, unemployment, and illness; and improving housing conditions and cleaning slums. What came to be called "the Second Hundred Days," marked the high point of progressive lawmaking in the New Deal.

In April, the administration pushed through the Emergency Relief Appropriation Act, which allocated $5 billion for large-scale public works programs for the jobless. New Deal economists, following the theories of Britain's John Maynard Keynes, argued that each government dollar spent had a multiplier effect, pumping two or three dollars into the depressed gross national product. Over the next seven years, the WPA, under Harry Hopkins' leadership, oversaw the employment of more than 8 million Americans on a vast array of construction projects: roads, bridges, dams, airports, and sewers. Among the most innovative WPA programs, were community service projects that employed thousands of jobless artists, musicians, actors, and writers.

The landmark Social Security Act of 1935 provided for old-age pensions and unemployment insurance. A payroll tax on workers and their employers created a fund from which retirees received monthly pensions after age sixty-five. Payment size depended upon how much employees and their employers had contributed over the years. The unemployment compensation plan established a minimum weekly payment and a minimum number of weeks during which those who lost jobs could collect. The Social Security Board administered this complex system of federal-state cooperation. The original law failed to cover domestics and farm workers, many of whom were Latinos and African Americans. It also made no provisions for casual laborers or public employees. The old-age pensions were quite small at first, as little as $10 a month. And to collect unemployment, one had to have first lost a job. But the law, which has since been amended many times, established the crucial principle of federal responsibility for America's most vulnerable citizens.

In July 1935, Congress passed the National Labor Relations Act, often called the Wagner Act for its chief sponsor, Democratic senator Robert F. Wagner of New York. For the first time, the federal government guaranteed the right of American workers to join, or form, independent labor unions, and bargain collectively for improved wages, benefits, and working conditions. The National Labor Relations Board would conduct secret-ballot elections in shops and factories to determine which union, if any, workers desired as their sole bargaining agent. The law also defined and prohibited unfair labor practices by employers, including firing workers for union activity. The Wagner Act, described as "the Magna Carta for labor," quickly proved a boon to union growth, especially in previously unorganized industries such as automobiles, steel, and textiles. It set the stage for the sit-down strike in Flint and for General Motors' eventual acceptance of union labor in its factories.

Finally, the Resettlement Administration (RA) produced one of the most utopian New Deal programs, one designed to create new kinds of model communities. Established by executive order, and led by key brain truster Rexford G. Tugwell, the RA helped destitute farm families relocate to more productive areas. It granted loans for purchasing land and equipment, and it directed reforestation and soil erosion projects, particularly in the hard-hit Southwest. Due to lack of funds and poor administration, however, only about 1 percent of the projected 500,000 families were actually moved. Tugwell, one of the New Deal's most ardent believers in planning, was more successful in his efforts at creating model greenbelt communities, combining the best of urban and rural environments. Though his vision was only partially fulfilled, several of these communities, such as Greenhills, near Cincinnati, and Greendale, near Milwaukee, still thrive.

OVERVIEW

KEY LEGISLATION OF THE SECOND NEW DEAL (1935–38)

Legislation	Purpose
Emergency Relief Appropriations Act (1935)	Large-scale public works program for the jobless (includes Works Progress Administration)
Social Security Act (1935)	Federal old-age pensions and unemployment insurance
National Labor Relations Act (1935)	Federal guarantee of right to organize trade unions and collective bargaining
Resettlement Administration (1935)	Relocation of poor rural families Reforestation and soil erosion projects
National Housing Act (1937)	Federal funding for public housing and slum clearance
Fair Labor Standards Act (1938)	Federal minimum wage and maximum hours

Labor's Upsurge: Rise of the CIO

In 1932, the American labor movement was nearly dead. Only 2.8 million workers were union members, a half-million fewer than in 1929 and more than 2 million fewer than in 1920. Yet by 1942, unions claimed more than 10.5 million members, nearly a third of the total nonagricultural work force. This remarkable turnaround was one of the key events of the depression era. The growth in the size and power of the labor movement permanently changed the work lives and economic status of millions, as well as the national and local political landscapes.

At the core of this growth, was a series of dramatic successes in the organization of workers in large-scale, mass-production industries such as automobiles, steel, rubber, electrical goods, and textiles. Workers in these fields had largely been ignored by the conservative, craft-conscious unions that dominated the American Federation of Labor. At the 1935 AFL convention, a group of more militant union officials led by John L. Lewis (of the United Mine Workers) and Sidney Hillman (of the Amalgamated Clothing Workers) formed the Committee for Industrial Organization (CIO). Their goal was to organize mass-production workers by industry rather than by craft. They emphasized the need for opening the new unions to all, regardless of a worker's level of skill. And they differed from nearly all old-line AFL unions by calling for the inclusion of black and women workers. (See Out of Many Voices: "I Was Able to Make My Voice Really Ring Out".)

The gruff son of a Welsh miner, Lewis was articulate, ruthless, and very ambitious. He saw the new legal protection given by the Wagner Act as a historic opportunity. But despite the Act—whose constitutionality was unclear until 1937—Lewis knew that establishing permanent unions in the mass-production industries would

OUT OF MANY VOICES

"I WAS ABLE TO MAKE MY VOICE REALLY RING OUT"

During the landmark sit-down strike of 1936, the Women's Emergency Brigade provided crucial support to the male auto workers who stayed inside the Flint, Michigan, General Motors plant. Brigade women picketed, demonstrated, and brought in food and supplies. Here Genora Johnson recounts how she found her own voice in appealing for women's support during the famous "Battle of the Running Bulls," when police tried to regain control of the GM plant by force.

SO ANYWAY, THE SOUND CAR WAS DOWN THERE, and we had Victor Reuther as the primary speaker. And then he would pull up other men, making their appeals, and this went on and on. It never dawned on me, you know, to speak. In the first place, this was primarily a man's operation, and I'm down there helping out, although I never thought too much about men and women when we were right in the heart of a battle, come to think about it. But it never dawned on me I'd never made any kind of a public speech over a microphone, and it—until he came back and told us. He said, "Well, we may have lost the battle. The war is not lost, but we may have lost this battle." And he gave us the idea that we had to prepare people for, you know, this little defeat. And I said to him then, I said, "Well, Victor, why don't I speak over the—why don't I talk to them over the loudspeaker, if the battery is going down." And he says, "Well, we've got nothing to lose." ... So that's when I got up to take the mike. And, again, there, you lose yourself. You go beyond yourself and think of the cause. And I was able to make my voice really ring out on that one because I knew that battery was going down. We only had a few moments left. And so, that's when I appealed to the women of Flint. I bypassed everybody else then and went right to the women and told them what was happening. So that's when I said, "There are women down here, mothers of children, and I beg of you to come down here and stand with your husband, your loved ones," you know, "your brothers, and even your sweethearts," because we had a lot of couples going together, and I'd get their girlfriends.

But I saw a first woman struggling, and I noticed that she had started to come down, and a cop grabbed her by the coat and she went right out of that coat. And she just kept right on coming. And as soon as that happened, other women broke through, and again we had that situation where cops didn't want to fire into backs of women. And once they did that, the men came, naturally, and that was the end of the battle. ■

SOURCE: http://www.historicalvoices.org/flint Oral history courtesy of Sherna Gluck, *Feminist History Project.*

be a bruising battle. He committed the substantial resources of the United Mine Workers to a series of organizing drives, focusing first on the steel and auto industries. Many CIO organizers were communists or radicals of other persuasions, and their dedication, commitment, and willingness to work within disciplined organizations proved invaluable in the often dangerous task of creating industrial unions. Militant rank-and-file unionists were often ahead of Lewis and other CIO leaders. The sit-down strike—refusing to work but staying in the factory to prevent "scab" workers from taking over—emerged as a popular tactic among rubber and auto workers. After the dramatic breakthrough in the Flint sit-down strike at General Motors, membership in CIO unions grew rapidly. In eight months, membership in the United Automobile Workers alone soared from 88,000 to 400,000. CIO victories in the steel, rubber, and electrical industries followed, but often at a very high cost. One bloody example of the perils of union organizing was the 1937 Memorial Day Massacre in Chicago. In a field near the struck Republic Steel Mill in South Chicago, police fired into a crowd of union supporters, killing ten workers and wounding scores more.

Philip Evergood, *American Tragedy* (1937). A classic example of the social realism characteristic of much depression-era art, this painting depicts the police violence against strikers at the Republic Steel Mill. Evergood was one of many artists who found work in the Federal Art Project, painting murals in public buildings.

SOURCE: Philip Evergood, *American Tragedy*, 1937, oil on canvas, $29\frac{1}{2}'' \times 39\frac{1}{2}''$. Private Collection, Terry Dintenfass Gallery.

In 1938, CIO unions, now boasting nearly 4 million members, withdrew from the AFL and reorganized themselves as the Congress of Industrial Organizations. For the first time ever, the labor movement had gained a permanent place in the nation's mass-production industries. Organized labor took its place as a key power broker in Roosevelt's New Deal and the national Democratic Party. Frances Perkins, FDR's secretary of labor and the nation's first woman cabinet member, captured the close relationship between the new unionism and the New Deal: "Programs long thought of as merely labor welfare, such as shorter hours, higher wages, and a voice in the terms of conditions of work, are really essential economic factors for recovery."

The New Deal Coalition at High Tide

Did the American public support Roosevelt and his New Deal policies? Both major political parties looked forward to the 1936 elections as a national referendum, and the campaign itself was an exciting and hard-fought contest. Very few political observers predicted its lopsided result. Republicans nominated Governor Alfred M. Landon of Kansas, who had gained attention by surviving the Democratic landslide of 1934. An easygoing, colorless man with little personal magnetism, Landon emphasized a nostalgic appeal to traditional American values. His campaign served as a lightning rod for all those, including many conservative Democrats, who were dissatisfied with Roosevelt and the direction he had taken.

Roosevelt attacked the "economic royalists" who denied that government "could do anything to protect the citizen in his right to work and his right to live." At the same time, FDR was careful to distance himself from radicalism. "It was this administration," he declared, "which saved the system of private profit and free enterprise after it had been dragged to the brink of ruin." As Roosevelt's campaign crossed the country, his advisers were heartened by huge and enthusiastic crowds, especially in large cities like Chicago and Pittsburgh. Still, the vast majority of the nation's newspapers endorsed Landon. And a widely touted "scientific" poll by the *Literary Digest* forecast a Republican victory in November.

Election day erased all doubts. Roosevelt carried every state but Maine and Vermont, polling 61 percent of the popular vote. Democrats increased their substantial majorities in the House and Senate as well. The *Literary Digest*, it turned out, had drawn the sample for its poll from people whose addresses were listed in telephone directories and car registration records, thus omitting the poorer Americans who had no telephones or cars—and who supported Roosevelt. In 1936, the Democrats drew millions of new voters into the political process, and at the same time, forged a new coalition of voters that would dominate national politics for two generations.

This "New Deal coalition," as it came to be known, included traditional-minded white Southern Democrats, big-city political machines, industrial workers of all races, trade unionists, and many depression-hit farmers. Black voters in the North and West, long affiliated with the Republicans as the party of Abraham Lincoln, went Democratic in record numbers. The Great Depression was by no means over. But the New Deal's active response to the nation's misery, particularly the bold initiatives taken in 1935, had obviously struck a powerful chord with the American electorate.

Roosevelt was especially popular among first- and second-generation immigrants of Catholic and Jewish descent, and the New Deal drew enthusiastic support from millions who had never bothered with politics. As one Slovak worker in Chicago's stockyards put it, "Our people did not know anything about the government until the depression years. In my neighborhood, I don't remember anyone voting." The severity of the Great Depression had overwhelmed the ethnically based support networks—mutual benefit societies, immigrant banks, and religious charities—that had traditionally helped so many to survive hard times. Popular federal programs like Social Security, the WPA, and Home Owners Loan Corporation mortgages changed the consciousness of a generation of the ethnic working class. In exchange for their votes, they now looked to the state—especially the federal government—for relief, protection, and help in achieving the American dream.

THE NEW DEAL IN THE SOUTH AND WEST

In regional terms, the New Deal had its most profound impact in the South and the West. Federal farm programs moved Southern agriculture away from its longtime dependence upon sharecropping and tenant farming and helped reorganize it around new patterns of wage labor and agribusiness. New Deal dam building and power projects introduced electricity to millions of rural Southerners and thereby transformed their lives. Western citizens received more from the federal government in per capita payments for welfare, work relief, and loans than the people of any other section. New Deal programs, based on a philosophy of rational planning of resource use, reshaped Western agriculture, water and energy sources, and Indian policy. From Great Plains farming communities in Kansas and Oklahoma, to Pacific Coast cities such as Los Angeles and Seattle, federal subsidy and management became an integral part of Western life. In the process, the New Deal helped propel both the South and the West into the modern era and laid the groundwork for the postwar boom in the "Sunbelt."

Southern Farming and Landholding

In 1930, less than half of all Southern farmers owned their own land; over three-quarters of the region's African American farmers and nearly half of its white farmers toiled as sharecroppers or tenants. Few of these earned any cash income at all, and those that did, averaged only about $100 annually. The continued dominance of cotton and a few other crops, such as tobacco, had only intensified the Depression by glutting the market and keeping crop prices at rock bottom. The Agricultural Adjustment Administration succeeded in boosting prices by paying farmers to "plow under"—take their land out of production. But particularly in the South, these federal subsidies went overwhelmingly to large landowners, who controlled local county committees charged with administering AAA programs.

Most planters did not share these payments with sharecroppers and tenants, and individual protest was usually futile. One Louisiana tenant farmer who dared ask his landlord if his AAA payment had arrived, was told, "I had better move before he killed me. And he gave me 24 hours to be gone off the farm." The Southern Tenant Farmers Union (STFU), founded in 1934, emerged as an important voice of collective protest against AAA policies. Active in six Southern states and composed of about thirty thousand tenant farmers (over half of whom were black), the STFU protested evictions, called strikes to raise farm labor wages, and challenged landlords to give tenants their fair share of subsidy payments. The STFU succeeded in drawing national attention to the plight of sharecroppers and tenant farmers, but it failed to influence national farm policy.

Many landowners also used the new cash infusion to buy labor-saving machinery, such as tractors and mechanical harvesters. The reduction of cultivated land, along with a growing reliance on mechanized farming, resulted in lower demand for labor and an increase in evictions. Uprooted tenants, sharecroppers, and day laborers found themselves on the road in search of work, and many thousands migrated to cities and towns. New Deal policies helped destroy the old sharecropping and tenant system, but they did so largely by helping landowners prosper while providing little relief for the landless. Those farmers who had access to government funds were able to diversify their crops, consolidate holdings, and work their land more efficiently. But for between one and two million tenants, sharecroppers, and day laborers, the future would lay in industrial centers like Memphis, Birmingham, Chicago, and Detroit.

Rural Electrification and Public Works

Perhaps no New Deal initiative had more impact on Southern communities than electrification. Only about 3 percent of rural Southerners had access to electric power in the early 1930s, and farmhouses generally lacked such amenities as electric lighting, indoor plumbing, refrigerators, and washing machines. The Tennessee Valley Authority and the Rural Electrification Administration helped millions of Southern households move into the modern era by making electricity available for the first time. The TVA became a powerful symbol of how public investment and government planning could significantly improve the lives of ordinary Americans. It built sixteen dams across some 800 miles of the Tennessee River, bringing flood control and electric power to hundreds of thousands of families in seven Southern states. It also significantly reduced consumer electric rates in many cities and towns by providing a cheaper alternative to private utilities. Pursuing a regional planning approach that cut across state lines, the TVA also created landscaped parks, rural libraries, and better school systems. By 1944, the TVA was the largest power producer in the United States. If rural life was still harsh, electrification allowed farm families to enjoy radio, electric lights, and other conveniences that other Americans had long taken for granted. (See Out of Many Voices: "What REA Service Means to Our Farm Home.")

OUT OF MANY VOICES

"WHAT REA SERVICE MEANS TO OUR FARM HOME"

The Rural Electrification Administration was one of several New Deal agencies that brought electricity to millions of rural, mostly Southern, households. In 1939, Rose Dudley Scearce of Shelby, Kentucky, described how electricity helped transform the daily lives of rural Americans, especially women, bringing them into the modern era.

THE FIRST BENEFIT WE RECEIVED FROM THE REA service was lights, and aren't lights grand? My little boy expressed my sentiments when he said, "Mother, I didn't realize how dark our house was until we got electric lights." Recently I read in the *Rural Electrification NEWS* that the radio was the most popular appliance that had been bought. So, like the rest of the people, we changed our storage-battery radio into an electric radio. This was our next benefit.

Next we bought an electric refrigerator. Of course, next after a refrigerator comes making ice cream in the trays. We changed our washing machine from a machine driven by gasoline to one driven by the electric current as our next improvement. The machine was all right with gasoline, but, my, the noise it made! It is such a blessed relief to do the laundry in peace and quiet. We changed our pump for the pressure tank in our bathroom and water system from a hand pump to an electric pump. I did not buy an electric iron at first, as I do not do my own ironing. I was impressed, when I did, at how much improved irons were since I moved to the country. I can turn my dial on the iron to any fabric I may be ironing and the iron will stay the temperature needed for the fabric until I move the dial.

The next benefit we received from the current was our electric stove. We were so anxious for the current that we wired our house many months before the current was turned on, and we wired our kitchen for an electric range. Before the current was turned on, when anyone asked me what appliance I wanted most I always said that I wanted a vacuum cleaner. Now with the vacuum cleaner, I can even dust the furniture before I clean the carpet, the carpet gets clean, and I stay in a good humor.

So you see I am thoroughly enjoying the many things that electricity had made possible, and I am enjoying life more because I have more time to spend visiting my friends, studying and reading, and doing the things that make life richer and fuller. ■

SOURCE: New Deal Network, http://newdeal.feri.org/default.cfm
Originally published in *Rural Electrification News*, March 1939.

The Dust Bowl

An ecological and economic disaster of unprecedented proportions struck the Southern Great Plains in the mid-1930s. The region had suffered several drought years in the early 1930s. Such dry spells occurred regularly, in roughly twenty-year cycles. But this time, the parched earth became swept up in violent dust storms, the likes of which had never been seen before. The dust storms were largely the consequence of years of stripping the landscape of its natural vegetation. During World War I, wheat brought record-high prices on the world market, and for the next twenty years, Great Plains farmers turned the region into a vast wheat factory (see Map 24.2).

The wide flatlands of the Great Plains were especially suited to mechanized farming, and gasoline-powered tractors, disc plows, and harvester-thresher combines increased productivity enormously. Back in 1830, it had taken some fifty-eight hours of labor to bring an acre of wheat to the granary; in much of the Great Plains a hundred years later, it required less than three hours. As wheat prices fell in the 1920s, farmers broke still more land to make up the difference with increased production. Great Plains farmers had created an ecological time bomb that exploded when drought returned in the early 1930s. With native grasses destroyed for the sake of wheat growing, there was nothing left to prevent soil erosion. Dust storms blew away tens of millions of acres of rich topsoil, and thousands of farm families left the region. Those who stayed, suffered deep economic and psychological losses from the calamity. The hardest-hit regions were western Kansas, eastern Colorado, western Oklahoma, the Texas Panhandle, and eastern New Mexico. It was the calamity in this southern part of the Plains that prompted a Denver journalist to coin the phrase "Dust Bowl."

Black blizzards of dust a mile and a half high rolled across the landscape, darkening the sky and whipping the earth into great drifts that settled over hundreds of miles. Dust storms made it difficult for humans and livestock to breathe, and destroyed crops and trees over vast areas. Dust storms turned day into night, terrifying those caught in them. "Dust pneumonia" and other respiratory infections afflicted thousands, and many travelers found themselves stranded in automobiles and trains unable to move. The worst storms occurred in the early spring of 1935. A Garden City, Kansas, woman gave an account of her experience for the *Kansas City Times*:

> All we could do about it was just sit in our dusty chairs, gaze at each other through the fog that filled the room and watch that fog settle slowly and silently, covering everything—including ourselves—in a thick, brownish gray blanket. When we opened the door swirling whirlwinds of soil beat against us unmercifully. The door and windows were all shut tightly, yet those tiny particles seemed to seep through the very walls. It got into cupboards and clothes closets; our faces were as dirty as if we had rolled in the dirt; our hair was gray and stiff and we ground dirt between our teeth.

Several federal agencies intervened directly to relieve the distress. Many thousands of Great Plains farm families were given direct emergency relief by the Resettlement Administration. Other federal assistance included crop and seed loans, moratoriums on loan payments, and temporary jobs with the Works Progress Administration. In most Great Plains counties, from one-fifth to one-third of the families applied for relief; in the hardest-hit communities, as many as 90 percent of the families received direct government aid. The Agricultural Adjustment Administration paid

MAP EXPLORATION

To explore an interactive version of this map, go to **www.prenhall.com/faragher5/map24.2**

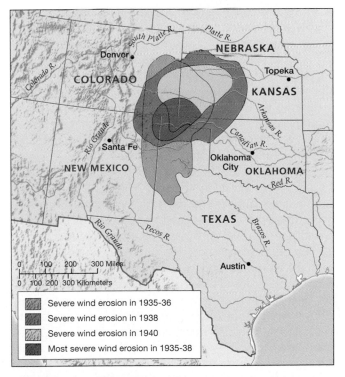

MAP 24.2 The Dust Bowl, 1935–40 This map shows the extent of the Dust Bowl in the Southern Great Plains. Federal programs designed to improve soil conservation, water management, and farming practices could not prevent a mass exodus of hundreds of thousands out of the Great Plains.

Years of Dust. This 1936 poster by the artist and photographer Ben Shahn, served to publicize the work of the Resettlement Administration, which offered aid to destitute farm families hit hard by the Dust Bowl. Shahn's stark imagery here was typical of the documentary aesthetic associated with Depression-era art and photography.

SOURCE: The Granger Collection / © Estate Of Ben Shahn / Liscensed By Vaga, New York, NY.

wheat farmers millions of dollars not to grow what they could not sell and encouraged the diversion of acreage from soil-depleting crops like wheat to soil-enriching crops such as sorghum.

The federal government also pursued longer-range policies designed to alter land-use patterns, reverse soil erosion, and nourish the return of grasslands. The Department of Agriculture, under Secretary Henry A. Wallace, sought to change farming practices. The spearhead for this effort was the Soil Conservation Service (SCS), which conducted research into controlling wind and water erosion, set up demonstration projects, and offered technical assistance, supplies, and equipment to farmers engaged in conservation work on farms and ranches. The SCS pumped additional federal funds into the Great Plains and created a new rural organization, the soil conservation district, which administered conservation regulations locally.

By 1940, the acreage subject to blowing in the Dust Bowl area of the Southern plains had been reduced from roughly 50 million acres to less than 4 million acres. In the face of the Dust Bowl disaster, New Deal farm policies had restricted market forces in agriculture. But the return of regular rainfall and the outbreak of World War II led many farmers to abandon the techniques that the SCS had taught them to accept. Wheat farming expanded and farms grew, as farmers once again pursued commercial agriculture with little concern for its long-term effects on the land.

While large landowners and ranchers reaped sizable benefits from AAA subsidies and other New Deal programs in the Southern plains, tenant farmers and sharecroppers received very little. In the cotton lands of Texas, Oklahoma, Missouri, and Arkansas, thousands of tenant and sharecropper families were forced off the land. They became part of a stream of roughly 300,000 people, disparagingly called "Okies," who migrated to California in the 1930s. California migrants included victims of the Dust Bowl, but the majority were blue-collar workers and small businessmen looking to improve their economic lot. California suffered from the depression along with the rest of the nation, but it still offered more jobs, higher wages, and higher relief payments than the states of the Southern plains. Most Okies could find work only as poorly paid agricultural laborers in the fertile San Joaquin and Imperial Valley districts. There they faced discrimination and scorn as "poor white trash" while they struggled to create communities amid the squalor of migrant labor camps. Only with the outbreak of World War II and the pressing demand for labor, were migrants able to significantly improve their situation.

Mexican farm laborers faced stiff competition from Dust Bowl refugees. By the mid-1930s, they no longer dominated California's agricultural workforce. In 1936, an estimated 85 to 90 percent of the state's migratory workers were white Americans, as compared to less than 20 percent before the depression. Mexican farm worker families who managed to stay employed in California, Texas, and Colorado saw their wages plummet.

Southwestern communities, responding to racial hostility from unemployed whites and looking for ways to reduce their welfare burden, campaigned to deport Mexicans and Mexican Americans. Employers, private charities, and the Immigration and Naturalization Service joined in this effort. Authorities made little effort to distinguish citizens from aliens; most of the children they deported had been born in the United States and were citizens. Los Angeles County had the most aggressive campaign, using boxcars to ship out more than 13,000 Mexicans between 1931 and 1934. The hostile climate convinced thousands more to leave voluntarily. Approximately one-third of Los Angeles's 150,000 Mexican and Mexican American residents left the city in the early 1930s. Overall, nearly one-half million left the United States during the decade. Some Mexican deportees crossed the border with a melancholy song on their lips:

> And so I take my leave,
> may you be happy.
> Here the song ends,
> but the depression goes on forever.

Water Policy

The New Deal ushered in the era of large-scale water projects, designed to provide irrigation and cheap power and to prevent floods. The long-range impact of these undertakings on Western life was enormous. The key government agency in this realm was the Bureau of Reclamation of the Department of the Interior, established under the National Reclamation Act of 1902. The bureau's original responsibility had been to construct dams and irrigation works and thereby encourage the growth of small farms throughout the arid regions of the West. Until the late 1920s, the bureau's efforts had been of little consequence, providing irrigation for only a very small portion of land. But its fortunes changed when its focus shifted to building huge multipurpose dams, designed to control entire river systems (see Map 24.3).

The first of these projects was the Boulder Dam (later renamed the Hoover Dam). The dam, actually begun during the Hoover administration, was designed to harness the Colorado River, wildest and most isolated of the major Western rivers. Its planned benefits included flood prevention, the irrigation of California's Imperial Valley, the supplying of domestic water for southern California, and the generation of cheap electricity for Los Angeles and southern Arizona. Hoover, however, had opposed the public power aspect of the project, arguing that the government ought not to compete with private utility companies. This position was contrary to that of most Westerners, who believed cheap public power was critical for development. Roosevelt's support for government-sponsored power projects was a significant factor in his winning the political backing of the West in 1932 and subsequent election years.

Boulder Dam was completed in 1935, with the help of funds from the Public Works Administration. Its total cost was $114 million, which was to be offset by the sale of the hydroelectric power it generated. Los Angeles and neighboring cities built a 259-mile aqueduct, costing $220 million, to channel water to their growing populations. Lake Mead, created by construction of the dam, became the world's largest artificial lake, extending 115 miles up the canyon and providing a popular new recreation area. The dam's irrigation water helped make the Imperial Valley, covering over 500,000 acres, one of the most productive agricultural districts in the world.

The success of Boulder Dam transformed the Bureau of Reclamation into a major federal agency with huge resources at its disposal. In 1938, it completed the All-American Canal—an 80-mile channel connecting the Colorado River to the Imperial Valley, with a 130-mile branch to the Coachella Valley. The canal cost $24 million to build and carried a flow of water equal to that of the Potomac River. More than a million acres of desert land were opened up to the cultivation of citrus fruits, melons, vegetables, and cotton. Irrigation districts receiving water promised to repay, without interest, the cost of the canal over a forty-year period. This interest-free loan was in effect, a huge government subsidy to the private growers who benefited from the canal.

In 1935, the bureau began the giant Central Valley Project (CVP). The Central Valley, stretching through the California interior, is a 500-mile oblong watershed with an average width of 125 miles. The idea was to bring water from the Sacramento River in the North down to the arid lands of the larger San Joaquin Valley in the South. Completed in 1947, the project eventually cost $2.3 billion. The CVP stored water and transferred it to the drier southern regions of the state. It also provided electricity, flood control, and municipal water. The federal government, local municipalities, and buyers of electric power paid most of the cost, and the project proved a boon to large-scale farmers in the Sacramento and San Joaquin River Valleys.

The largest power and irrigation project of all was the Grand Coulee Dam, northwest of Spokane, Washington. Completed in 1941, it was designed to convert the power of the Columbia River into cheap electricity, and to irrigate previously uncultivated land, thereby stimulating the economic development of the Pacific Northwest. The construction of Grand Coulee employed tens of thousands of workers and pumped millions of dollars into the region's badly depressed economy. Between 1933 and 1940, Washington State ranked first in per capita federal expenditures. In the longer run, Grand Coulee provided the cheapest electricity in the United States, and helped attract new manufacturing to a region previously dependent on the export of raw materials, such as lumber and metals.

These technological marvels and the new economic development they stimulated were not without an environmental and human cost. The Grand Coulee and smaller dams nearby reduced the Columbia River, long a potent symbol of the Western wilderness, to a string of lakes. Spawning salmon could no longer run the river above the dam. In California, the federal guarantee of river water made a relative handful of large farmers fabulously wealthy. But tens of thousands of farm workers, mostly of Mexican descent, labored in the newly fertile fields for very low wages, and their health suffered from

MAP EXPLORATION

To explore an interactive version of this map, go to **www.prenhall.com/faragher5/map24.3**

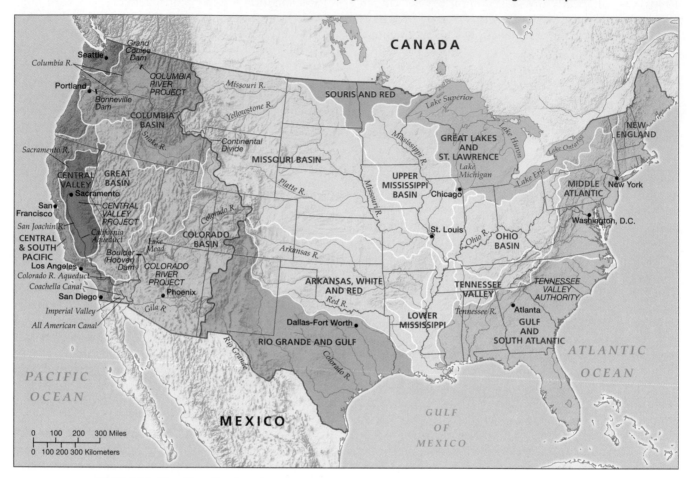

MAP 24.3 The New Deal and Water This map illustrates U. S. drainage areas and the major large-scale water projects begun or completed by federal agencies in them during the New Deal. By providing irrigation, cheap power, flood control, and recreation areas, these public works had a historically unprecedented impact on America's Western communities.

contact with pesticides. The Colorado River, no longer emptying into the Pacific, began to build up salt deposits, making its water increasingly unfit for drinking or irrigation. Water pollution in the form of high salinity continues to plague the 2,000-mile river to this day.

A New Deal for Indians

The New Deal brought important changes and some limited improvements to the lives of Indians. In 1933, some 320,000 Indian people, belonging to about 200 tribes, lived on reservations. Most were in Oklahoma, Arizona, New Mexico, and South Dakota. Indian peo-

ple suffered from the worst poverty of any group in the nation, and an infant mortality rate twice that of the white population. The incidence of alcoholism and other diseases, such as tuberculosis and measles, was much higher on the reservation than off. Half of all those on reservations were landless, forced to rent or live with relatives. The Bureau of Indian Affairs (BIA), oldest of the federal bureaucracies in the West, had a long history of corruption and mismanagement. The BIA had for years, tried to assimilate Indians through education, and had routinely interfered with Indian religious affairs and tribal customs. In 1928, the Merriam Report, prepared by the Institute for Government Research, had offered a scathing and widely publicized critique of BIA misman-agement. But the Hoover administration made no effort to reform the agency.

In 1933, President Roosevelt appointed John Col-lier to bring change to the BIA. Collier had deep roots in progressive-era social work and community organizing in Eastern big-city slums. During the 1920s, he had become passionately interested in Indian affairs after spending time in Taos, New Mexico. He became involved with the struggle of the Pueblo Indians to hold onto their tribal lands, and he had served as executive secretary of the American Indian Defense Association. As the new BIA head, Collier pledged to "stop wronging the Indi-ans and to rewrite the cruel and stupid laws that rob them and crush their family lives." Collier became the driving force behind the Indian Reorganization Act (IRA) of 1934. The IRA reversed the allotment provisions of the Dawes Severalty Act of 1887, which had weakened tribal sovereignty by shifting the distribution of land from tribes to individuals (see Chapter18). The new legislation per-mitted the restoration of surplus reservation lands to tribal ownership, and allocated funds for the purchase of addi-tional lands and for economic development. At its heart, the IRA sought to restore tribal structures by making the tribes instruments of the federal government. Any tribe that ratified the IRA could then elect a tribal council that would enjoy federal recognition as the legal tribal gov-ernment. Collier fought first to get the legislation through a reluctant Congress, which, uneasy with reversing the long-standing policy of Indian assimilation, insisted on many changes to Collier's original plan.

The more difficult battle involved winning approval by Indian peoples. Collier's efforts to win acceptance of the IRA met with mixed results on the reservations. Lin-guistic barriers made it nearly impossible for some tribes to fully assess the plan. The Papagos of southern Arizona, for example, had no words for "budget" and "representa-tive." Their language made no distinction among the terms "law," "rule," "charter," and "constitution," and they used the same word for "president," "reservation agent," "king," and "Indian commissioner." In all, 181 tribes organized gov-ernments under the IRA, while 77 tribes rejected it.

The Navajos, the nation's largest tribe, with over 40,000 members, rejected the IRA, illustrating some of the contradictions embedded in federal policy. The Navajo refusal came as a protest against the BIA's forced reduction of their livestock, part of a soil conservation program. The government blamed Navajo sheep for the gullying and erosion that threatened to fill in Lake Mead and make Boulder Dam inoperable. But the Navajos believed the erosion stemmed not from overgrazing, but from lack of sufficient water and inadequate acreage on the reservation. Facing loss of half their sheep, Navajos took their anger out on Collier, rejecting the reorgani-zation plan.

Under Collier's tenure, the BIA became much more sensitive to Indian cultural and religious freedom. The number of Indian people employed by the BIA itself increased from a few hundred in 1933, to more than 4,600 in 1940. Collier trumpeted the principle of Indian political autonomy, a radical idea for the day. But in practice, both the BIA and Congress regularly interfered with reservation governments, especially in money mat-ters. Collier often dictated economic programs for tribes, which Congress usually underfunded. For the long run, Collier's most important legacy was the reassertion of the status of Indian tribes as semisovereign nations. In 1934, a Department of the Interior lawyer, Nathan Mar-gold, wrote a legal opinion that tribal governments retained all their original powers—their "internal sov-ereignty"—except when these were specifically limited by acts of Congress. In later years, U.S. courts would uphold the Margold Opinion, leading to a significant restoration of tribal rights and land to Indian peoples of the West.

DEPRESSION-ERA CULTURE

American culture in the 1930s, like all other aspects of national life, was profoundly shaped by the Great Depression. The themes and images in various cultural forms frequently reflected depression-related problems. Yet contradictory messages coexisted, sometimes within the same novel or movie. With American capitalism fac-ing its worst crisis, radical expressions of protest and revolution were more common than ever. But there were also strong celebrations of individualism, nostalgia for a simpler, rural past, and searches for core American virtues. The 1930s also saw important shifts in the organ-ization and production of culture. For a brief but signif-icant moment, the federal government offered substantial and unprecedented support to artists and writers. In the realm of popular culture, Hollywood movies, network radio broadcasting, and big-band jazz achieved a central place in the everyday lives of Americans.

A New Deal for the Arts

The depression hit America's writers, artists, and teach-ers just as hard as blue-collar workers. In 1935, the WPA allocated $300 million for the unemployed in these fields. Over the next four years, Federal Project No. 1, an umbrella agency covering writing, theater, music, and the visual arts, proved to be one of the most innovative and successful New Deal programs. "Fed-eral One," as it was called, offered work to desperate artists and intellectuals, enriched the cultural lives of millions, and left a substantial legacy of artistic and cultural production. Nearly all these works were informed by the spirit of the documentary impulse, a

Fletcher Martin painted *Mine Rescue* (1939) in the Kellogg, Idaho, post office. The work was part of a Treasury Department program that employed unemployed artists to beautify government buildings. The mural was eventually removed under pressure from local citizens who worried that it might upset those who had lost loved ones in mine accidents.

SOURCE: Fletcher Martin (1904–79), *Mine Rescue*, 1939. Copyright Smithsonian American Art Museum, Washington, DC/Art Resource, NY.

deep desire to record and communicate the experiences of ordinary Americans.

At its height, the Federal Writers Project employed 5,000 writers on a variety of programs. Most notably, it produced a popular series of state and city guidebooks, each combining history, folklore, and tourism. The 150-volume "Life in America" series included valuable oral histories of former slaves, studies of ethnic and Indian cultures, and pioneering collections of American songs and folk tales. Work on the Writers Project helped many American writers to survive, hone their craft, and go on to great achievement and prominence. These included Ralph Ellison, Richard Wright, Margaret Walker, John Cheever, Saul Bellow, and Zora Neale Hurston. Novelist Anzia Yezierska recalled a strong spirit of camaraderie among the writers: "Each morning I walked to the Project as light hearted as if I were going to a party." The Federal Theater Project (FTP), under the direction of the dynamic Hallie Flanagan of Vassar College, reached as many as 30 million Americans with its productions. The FTP sought to expand the audience for theater beyond the regular patrons of the commercial stage. Tickets for its productions were cheap, and it made variety of dramatic forms available. Among its most successful productions were the "Living Newspaper" plays, based on contemporary controversies and current events. Other FTP productions brought classics as well as new

plays to communities. Among the most successful productions were T. S. Eliot's *Murder in the Cathedral*, Maxwell Anderson's *Valley Forge*, and Orson Welles's version of *Macbeth*, set in Haiti with an all-black cast. The FTP supported scores of community-based theatrical units around the country, giving work and experience to actors, playwrights, directors, and set designers. It brought vital and exciting theater to millions who had never attended before.

The Federal Music Project, under Nikolai Sokoloff of the Cleveland Symphony Orchestra, employed 15,000 musicians, and financed hundreds of thousands of low-priced public concerts by touring orchestras. The Composers' Forum Laboratory supported new works by American composers such as Aaron Copland and William Schuman.

Among the painters who received government assistance through the Federal Art Project were Willem de Kooning, Jackson Pollock, and Louise Nevelson. The FAP also employed painters and sculptors to teach studio skills and art history in schools, churches, and settlement houses. It also commissioned artists to paint hundreds of murals on the walls of post offices, meeting halls, courthouses, and other government buildings. All these projects, declared Holger Cahill, director of the FAP, were aimed at "raising a generation sensitive to their visual environment and capable of helping to improve it."

The Documentary Impulse

"You can right a lot of wrongs with 'pitiless publicity,'" Franklin Roosevelt once declared. Social change, he argued, "is a difficult thing in our civilization unless you have sentiment." During the 1930s, an enormous number of artists, novelists, journalists, photographers, and filmmakers tried to document the devastation wrought by the depression in American communities. They also depicted people's struggles to cope with, and reverse, hard times. Mainstream mass media, such as the photo essays found in *Life* magazine or "March of Time" newsreels, also adapted this stance.

The "documentary impulse" became a prominent style in 1930s cultural expression. The most direct and influential expression of the documentary style was the photograph. In 1935, Roy Stryker, chief of the Historical Section of the Resettlement Administration (later part of the Farm Security Administration), gathered a remarkable group of photographers to help document the work of the agency. Stryker encouraged them to photograph whatever caught their interest, even if the pictures had no direct connection with RA projects. These photographers, including Dorothea Lange, Walker Evans, Arthur Rothstein, Russell Lee, Ben Shahn, and Marion Post Wolcott, left us the single most significant visual record of the Great Depression. The photographers traveled through rural areas, small towns, and migrant labor camps, often not stopping even long enough to learn the names of their subjects. They produced powerful images of despair and resignation as well as hope and resilience. Stryker believed that the faces of the subjects were most memorable. "You could look at the people," he wrote, "and see fear and sadness and desperation. But you saw something else, too. A determination that not even the depression could kill. The photographers saw it—documented it."

That double vision, combining a frank portrayal of pain and suffering with a faith in the possibility of overcoming disaster, could be found in many other cultural works of the period. John Steinbeck's *Grapes of Wrath* (1939) sympathetically portrayed the hardships of Oklahoma Dust Bowl migrants on their way to California. "We ain't gonna die out," Ma Joad asserts near the end of the book. "People is goin' on—changin' a little, maybe, but goin' right on." A similar, if more personal, ending could be found in Margaret Mitchell's 1936 bestseller *Gone with the Wind*. Although this romantic novel was set in the Civil War–era South, many Americans identified with Scarlett O'Hara's determination to overcome the disaster of war. Many writers interrupted their work to travel around the country and discover the thoughts and feelings of ordinary people. "With real events looming larger than any imagined happenings,"

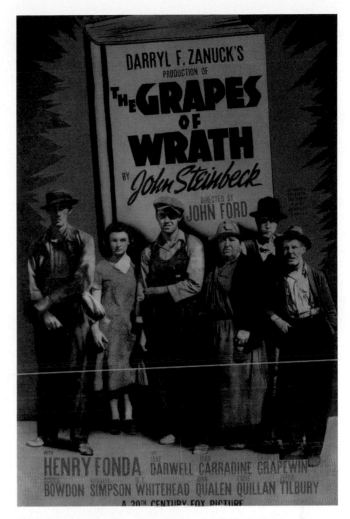

Publicity poster for the movie *The Grapes of Wrath* (1940), which depicted the journey of the Joad family from the Dust Bowl of Oklahoma to the promised land of California. Director John Ford's adaptation of John Steinbeck's best selling novel reflected the influence of the "documentary impulse" in Hollywood films and other forms of Depression-era popular culture.

SOURCE: The Advertising Archives.

novelist Elizabeth Noble wrote, "documentary films and still photographs, reportage and the like have taken the place once held by the grand invention." Writers also found a remarkable absence of bitterness and a great deal of faith. James Rorty, in *Where Life Is Better* (1936), was actually encouraged by his cross-country trip. "I had rediscovered for myself a most beautiful land, and a most vital, creative, and spiritually unsubdued people."

Waiting for Lefty

For some, the capitalist system itself, with its enormous disparities of private wealth amid desperate poverty, was the culprit responsible for the Great Depression.

Relatively few Americans became communists or socialists in the 1930s (at its height, the Communist Party of the United States had perhaps 100,000 members), and many of these remained active for only a brief time. Yet Marxist analysis, with its emphasis on class conflict and the failures of capitalism, had a wide influence on the era's thought and writing.

Some writers joined the Communist Party, believing it to be the best hope for political revolution. They saw in the Soviet Union, an alternative to an American system that appeared mired in exploitation, racial inequality, and human misery. Communist writers, like the novelist Michael Gold and the poet Meridel LeSueur, sought to radicalize art and literature, and they celebrated collective struggle over individual achievement. Granville Hicks, an editor of the radical magazine the *New Masses*, flatly declared: "If there is any other working interpretation of the apparent chaos than that which presents itself in terms of the class struggle, it has not been revealed."

A more common pattern for intellectuals, especially when they were young, was brief flirtation with communism. Many African American writers, attracted by the Communist Party's militant opposition to lynching, job discrimination, and segregation, briefly joined the party, or found their first supportive audiences there. These included Richard Wright, Ralph Ellison, and Langston Hughes. Many playwrights and actors associated with New York's influential Group Theater were part of the Communist Party orbit in those years. One production of the group, Clifford Odets's *Waiting for Lefty* (1935), depicted a union organizing drive among taxi drivers. At the play's climax, the audience was invited to join the actors in shouting "Strike!" A commercial and political success, it offered perhaps the most celebrated example of radical, politically engaged art.

Left-wing influence reached its height after 1935 during the "Popular Front" period. Alarmed by the rise of fascism in Europe, communists around the world followed the Soviet line of uniting with liberals and all other antifascists. The American Communist Party adopted the slogan "Communism is Twentieth-Century Americanism." Communists became strong supporters of Roosevelt's New Deal, and their influence was especially strong within the various WPA arts projects. Some 3,000 Americans volunteered for the Communist Party–organized Abraham Lincoln Brigade, which fought in the Spanish Civil War on the republican side, against the fascists led by Francisco Franco. The Lincolns' sense of commitment and sacrifice appealed to millions of Americans sympathetic to the republican cause. Communists and other radicals, known for their dedication and effectiveness, also played a leading role in the difficult CIO unionizing drives in the auto, steel, and electrical industries.

Film and Radio in the 1930s

Despite the depression, the mass-culture industry expanded enormously during the 1930s. If mass culture offered little in the way of direct responses to the economic and social problems of the day, it nonetheless played a more integral role than ever in shaping the rhythms and desires of the nation's everyday life. The coming of "talking pictures" toward the end of the 1920s, helped make movies the most popular entertainment form of the day. More than 60 percent of Americans attended one of the nation's 20,000 movie houses each week. Through fan magazines and gossip columns, they followed the lives and careers of movie stars more avidly than ever. With so many movies being churned out by Hollywood studios for so many fans, it is difficult to generalize about the cultural impact of individual films. Moviegoing itself, usually enjoyed with friends, family, or a date, was perhaps the most significant development of all.

Several film genres proved enormously popular during the 1930s. Gangster films did very well in the early depression years. *Little Caesar* (1930), starring Edward G. Robinson, and *Public Enemy* (1931), with James Cagney, set the standard. They all depicted violent criminals brought to justice by society—but along the way, they gave audiences a vicarious exposure to the pleasures of wealth, power, and lawbreaking. Social disorder could also be treated comically, as in such Marx Brothers films as *Duck Soup* (1933) and *A Night at the Opera* (1935). Mae West's popular comedies, such as *She Done Him Wrong* (1933) and *I'm No Angel* (1933), made people laugh by subverting expectations about sex roles. West was an independent woman, not afraid of pleasure. When Cary Grant asked her, "Haven't you ever met a man who could make you happy?" she replied, "Sure, lots of times."

Movie musicals offered audiences extravagant song-and-dance spectacles, as in Busby Berkeley's *Gold Diggers of 1933*, and *42nd Street* (1933). "Screwball comedies" featured sophisticated, fast-paced humor and usually paired popular male and female stars: Clark Gable and Claudette Colbert in *It Happened One Night* (1934), Katharine Hepburn and Cary Grant in *Bringing Up Baby* (1938). A few movies, notably from the Warner Brothers studio, tried to offer a more "socially conscious" view of depression-era life. These included *I Am a Fugitive from a Chain Gang* (1932), *Wild Boys of the Road* (1933), and *Black Legion* (1936). By and large, however, Hollywood avoided confronting controversial social or political issues.

Some 1930s filmmakers expressed highly personal visions of core American values. Two who succeeded in capturing both popular and critical acclaim were Walt Disney and Frank Capra. By the mid-1930s, Disney's animated cartoons had become moral tales that stressed keeping order and following the rules. The Mickey

Reginald Marsh, *Twenty Cent Movie*, 1936. Marsh documented the urban landscape of the 1930s with great empathy, capturing the city's contradictory mix of commercialism, optimism, energy, and degradation. The popularity of Hollywood films and their stars reached new heights during the Great Depression.

SOURCE: Reginald Marsh, *Twenty Cent Movie*, 1936. Egg tempera on composition board. 40″ × 40″. Whitney Museum of American Art.

Mouse cartoons and the full-length features, such as *Snow White and the Seven Dwarfs* (1937), pulled back from the fantastic stretching of time and space in earlier cartoons. Capra's comedies, such as *Mr. Deeds Goes to Town* (1936) and *You Can't Take It with You* (1938), idealized a small-town America, with close families and comfortable homes. Although Capra's films dealt with contemporary problems more than most,—he seemed to suggest that most of the country's ills could be solved if only its leaders learned the old-fashioned values of "common people"—kindness, loyalty, charity.

Radio broadcasting emerged as the most powerful medium of communication in the home, profoundly changing the rhythms and routines of everyday life. In 1930, roughly 12 million American homes, 40 percent of the total, had radio sets. By the end of the decade, radios

could be found in 90 percent of the nation's homes. Advertisers dominated the structure and content of American radio, forming a powerful alliance with the two large networks, the National Broadcasting Company (NBC) and the Columbia Broadcasting System (CBS). The Federal Communications Commission, established in 1934, continued long-standing policies that favored commercial broadcasting over other arrangements, such as municipal or university programming.

The depression actually helped radio expand. An influx of talent arrived from the weakened worlds of vaudeville, ethnic theater, and the recording industry. The well-financed networks offered an attractive outlet to advertisers seeking a national audience. Radio programming achieved a regularity and professionalism absent in the 1920s, making it much easier for a listener to identify a show with its sponsor. Much of network radio was based on older cultural forms. The variety show, hosted by comedians and singers, and based on the old vaudeville format, was the first important style. It featured stars like Eddie Cantor, Ed Wynn, Kate Smith, and Al Jolson, who constantly plugged the sponsor's product. The use of a studio audience recreated the human interaction so necessary in vaudeville. The popular comedy show *Amos 'n' Andy*, adapted the minstrel "blackface" tradition to the new medium. White comedians Freeman Gosden and Charles Correll used only their two voices to invent a world of stereotyped African Americans for their millions of listeners.

The spectacular growth of the daytime serial, or soap opera, dominated radio drama. Aimed mainly at women working in the home, these serials alone constituted 60 percent of all daytime shows by 1940. Soaps such as *Ma Perkins*, *Helen Trent*, and *Clara Lou and Em* revolved around strong, warm female characters who provided advice and strength to weak, indecisive friends and relatives. Action counted very little; the development of character and relationships was all-important. Thrillers such as *Inner Sanctum* and *The Shadow*, which emphasized crime and suspense, made great use of music and sound effects to sharpen their impact.

Finally, radio news arrived in the 1930s, showing the medium's potential for direct and immediate coverage of events. Network news and commentary shows multiplied rapidly over the decade. Complex political and economic issues and the impending European crisis fueled a news hunger among Americans. A 1939 survey found that 70 percent of Americans relied on the radio as their prime source of news. Yet commercial broadcasting, dominated by big sponsors and large radio manufacturers, failed to cover politically controversial events, such as labor struggles.

The Swing Era

One measure of radio's cultural impact was its role in popularizing jazz. Before the 1930s, jazz was heard largely among African Americans and a small coterie of white fans and musicians. Regular broadcasts of live performances began to expose a broader public to the music. So did radio disc jockeys who played jazz records on their shows. Bands led by black artists such as Duke Ellington, Count Basie, and Benny Moten began to enjoy reputations outside of traditional jazz centers like Chicago, Kansas City, and New York.

Benny Goodman became the key figure in the "swing era," largely through radio exposure. Goodman, a white, classically trained clarinetist, had been inspired by African American bandleaders Fletcher Henderson and Don Redman. These men created arrangements for big bands that combined harmonic call-and-response patterns with breaks for improvised solos. Goodman purchased a series of arrangements from Henderson, smoothing out the sound, but keeping the strong dance beat. His band's late-Saturday-night broadcasts began to attract attention.

In 1935, at the Palomar Ballroom in Los Angeles, Goodman made the breakthrough that established his enormous popularity. When the band started playing the Henderson arrangements, the young crowd, primed by the radio broadcasts, roared its approval and began to dance wildly. Goodman's music was perfect for doing the jitterbug or lindy hop, dances borrowed from African American culture. As "the King of Swing," Goodman helped make big-band jazz a hit with millions of teenagers and young adults from all backgrounds. In the late 1930s, big-band music by the likes of Goodman, Basie, Jimmie Lunceford, and Artie Shaw accounted for the majority of million-selling records.

Jacob Lawrence, *Many Whites Come to Harlem to Watch the Negroes Dance* (1943) was part of the artist's series called "Harlem Paintings." The image celebrates the energy and creativity of black ballroom dancers while commenting upon the tradition of white visitors "slumming" in Harlem.

SOURCE: Jacob Lawrence (1917–2000), *Many Whites Come to Harlem to Watch the Negroes Dance*, from the "Harlem Paintings," 1943. Gouache on paper, 14 × 21". Private Collection © Photograph Courtesy of Gwendolyn Knight Lawrence/Art Resource, NY/© Artists Rights Society.

THE LIMITS OF REFORM

In his second Inaugural Address, Roosevelt emphasized that much remained to be done to remedy the effects of the depression. Tens of millions of Americans were still denied the necessities for a decent life. "I see one third of a nation ill-housed, ill-clad, ill-nourished," the president said. With his stunning electoral victory, the future for further social reform seemed bright. Yet by 1937, the New Deal was in retreat. A rapid political turnaround over the next two years put continuing social reform efforts on the defensive.

Court Packing

In May 1935, in *Schecter* v. *United States*, the Supreme Court found the National Recovery Administration unconstitutional in its entirety. In early 1936, ruling in *Butler* v. *United States*, the Court invalidated the Agricultural Adjustment Administration, declaring it an unconstitutional attempt at regulating agriculture. The Court was composed mostly of Republican appointees, six of whom were over seventy. Roosevelt looked for a way to get more friendly judges on the high court.

In February 1937, a frustrated FDR asked Congress for legislation that would expand the Supreme Court from nine to a maximum of fifteen justices. The president would be empowered to make a new appointment whenever an incumbent judge failed to retire upon reaching age seventy. Roosevelt argued that age prevented justices from keeping up with their workload, but few people believed this logic. Newspapers almost unanimously denounced FDR's "court-packing bill."

Even more damaging was the determined opposition from a coalition of conservatives and outraged New Dealers in the Congress, such as Democratic senator Burton K. Wheeler of Montana. The president gamely fought on, maintaining that his purpose was simply to restore the balance of power among the three branches of the federal government. As the battle dragged on through the spring and summer, FDR's claims weakened. Conservative justice Willis Van Devanter announced plans to retire, giving Roosevelt the chance to make his first Court appointment.

More important, the Court upheld the constitutionality of some key laws from the second New Deal, including the Social Security Act and the National Labor Relations Act. At the end of August, FDR backed off from his plan and accepted a compromise bill that reformed lower court procedures, but left the Supreme Court untouched. FDR lost the battle for his judiciary proposal, but he may have won the war for a more responsive Court. Still, the political price was very high. The Court fight badly weakened Roosevelt's relations with Congress. Many more conservative Democrats now felt free to oppose further New Deal measures.

The Women's Network

The Great Depression and the New Deal brought some significant changes for women in American economics and politics. Most women continued to perform unpaid domestic labor within their homes, work that was not covered by the Social Security Act. A growing minority, however, also worked for wages and salaries outside the home. By 1940, 25.1 percent of the workforce was female. There was also an increase in married working women as a result of hard times. But sexual stereotyping still routinely forced women into low-paying and low-status jobs.

The New Deal brought a measurable, if temporary, increase in women's political influence. For those women associated with social reform, the New Deal opened up possibilities to effect change. A "women's network," linked by personal friendships and professional connections, made its presence felt in national politics and government. Most of the women in this network had long been active in movements promoting suffrage, labor law reform, and welfare programs.

Eleanor Roosevelt became a powerful political figure in her own right, actively using her prominence as First Lady to fight for the liberal causes she believed in. She revolutionized the role of the political wife, by taking a position involving no institutional duties and turning it into a base for independent action. Privately, she enjoyed great influence with her husband, and her support for a cause could give it instant credibility. She worked behind the scenes with a wide network of women professionals and reformers whom she had come to know in the 1920s. She was a strong supporter of protective labor legislation for women, and her overall outlook owed much to the social reform tradition of the women's movement. One of Eleanor Roosevelt's first public acts as First Lady was to convene a White House Conference on the Emergency Needs of Women, in November 1933. She helped Ellen Woodward, head of women's projects in the Federal Emergency Relief Administration, find jobs for 100,000 women, ranging from nursery school teaching to sewing. Roosevelt worked vigorously for antilynching legislation, compulsory health insurance, and child labor reform, and fought racial discrimination in New Deal relief programs. She saw herself as the guardian of "human values" within the administration, a buffer between depression victims and government bureaucracy. She frequently testified before legislative committees, lobbied her husband privately and the Congress publicly, and wrote a widely syndicated newspaper column.

Eleanor Roosevelt's closest political ally was Molly Dewson. A long-time social worker and suffragist, Dewson wielded a good deal of political clout as director of the Women's Division of the national Democratic Party. Under her leadership, women for the first time played a central role in shaping the party platform and running election campaigns. Dewson proved a tireless organizer, traveling to cities and towns around the country and educating women about Democratic policies and candidates. Her success impressed the president, and he relied on her judgment in recommending political appointments. Dewson placed more than a hundred women in New Deal positions.

Perhaps Dewson's most important success came in persuading FDR to appoint Frances Perkins secretary of labor—the first woman cabinet member in U.S. history. A graduate of Mount Holyoke College and a veteran activist for social welfare and reform, Perkins had served as FDR's industrial commissioner in New York before coming to Washington. As labor secretary, Perkins embodied the gains made by women in appointive offices. Her department was responsible for creating the Social Security Act and the Fair Labor Standards Act of 1938, both of which incorporated protective measures long advocated by women reformers. Perkins defined feminism as "the movement of women to participate in service to society." New Deal agencies opened up spaces for scores of women in the federal bureaucracy. These women were concentrated in Perkins's Labor Department, the FERA and WPA, and the Social Security Board. In addition, the social work profession, which remained roughly two-thirds female in the 1930s, grew enormously in response to the massive relief and welfare programs. In sum, although the 1930s saw no radical challenges to existing male and female roles, working-class women and professional women held their own and managed to make some gains.

A New Deal for Minorities?

"The Negro was born in Depression," recalled Clifford Burke. "It only became official when it hit the white man." Long near the bottom of the American economic ladder, African Americans suffered disproportionately through the difficult days of the 1930s. The old saying among black workers that they were "last hired, first fired" was never more true than during times of high unemployment. With jobs made scarce by the depression, even traditional "Negro occupations"—domestic service, cooking, janitorial work, elevator operating—were coveted. One white clerk in Florida expressed a widely held view among white Southerners when he defended a lynch mob attack on a store with black employees: "A nigger hasn't got no right to have a job when there are white men who can do the work and are out of work."

Overall, the Roosevelt administration made little overt effort to combat the racism and segregation entrenched in American life. FDR was especially worried about offending the powerful Southern Democratic congressmen who were a key element in his political coalition. And local administration of many federal programs meant that most early New Deal programs routinely accepted discrimination. The CCC established separate camps for African Americans. The NRA labor codes tolerated lower wages for black workers doing the same jobs as white workers. African Americans could not get jobs with the TVA. When local AAA committees in the South reduced acreage and production to boost prices, thousands of black sharecroppers and farm laborers were forced off the land. Racism was also embedded in the entitlement provisions of the Social Security Act. The act excluded domestics and casual laborers—workers whose ranks were disproportionately African Americans—from old-age insurance.

Yet some limited gains were made. President Roosevelt issued an executive order in 1935 banning discrimination in WPA projects. In the cities, the WPA, paying minimum wages of $12 a week, enabled thousands of African Americans to survive. Between 15 and 20 percent of all

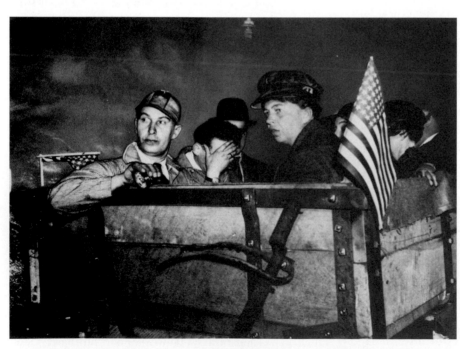

First Lady Eleanor Roosevelt rides with miners in a flag-decorated car during a visit to the mining town of Bellaire, Ohio in 1935. Mrs. Roosevelt was more outspoken than the President in championing the rights of labor and African Americans, and she actively used her prestige as First Lady in support of social justice causes.

SOURCE: AP Wide World Photos.

WPA employees were black people, although African Americans made up less than 10 percent of the nation's population. The Public Works Administration, under Harold Ickes, constructed a number of integrated housing complexes and employed more than its fair share of black workers in construction.

FDR appointed several African Americans to second-level positions in his administration. This group became known as "the Black Cabinet." Mary McLeod Bethune, an educator who rose from a sharecropping background to found Bethune-Cookman College, proved a superb leader of the Office of Minority Affairs in the National Youth Administration. Her most successful programs substantially reduced black illiteracy. Harvard-trained Robert Weaver advised the president on economic affairs, and in 1966, became the first black cabinet member when he was appointed secretary of housing and urban development. Hard times were especially trying for Mexican Americans as well. As the Great Depression drastically reduced the demand for their labor, they faced massive layoffs, deepening poverty, and deportation. During the 1930s, over 400,000 Mexican nationals and their children returned to Mexico, often coerced by local officials unwilling to provide them with relief, but happy to offer train fare to border towns. Many native-born Americans argued that deporting Mexicans could reduce unemployment for U.S. citizens. But these claims reflected deep racial prejudice, inflamed by the economic crisis. In Detroit, deportations reduced the size of that city's thriving Mexican *colonia* from 15,000 to 3,000 by 1933. In Los Angeles, where 100,000 Mexicans constituted the largest *colonia* in the Unites States, fully one-third became *repatriados*. For those who stayed, the New Deal programs did little to help. The AAA benefited large growers, not stoop laborers. Neither the National Labor Relations Act nor the Social Security Act made any provisions for farm laborers. The Federal Emergency Relief Administration and the Works Progress Administration did, at first, provide relief and jobs to the needy, irrespective of citizenship status. But after 1937, the WPA eliminated aliens from eligibility, causing great hardship for thousands of Mexican families. By World War II, *colonias* would increasingly be dominated by the American-born second generation, rather than those born in Mexico. And since only citizens or aliens who had begun the process of naturalization were eligible for public works jobs, these programs motivated more Mexican immigrants to become U.S. citizens.

The New Deal record for minorities was mixed at best. African Americans, especially in the cities, benefited from New Deal relief and work programs, though this assistance was not color-blind. Black industrial workers made inroads into labor unions affiliated with the CIO. The New Deal made no explicit attempt to attack the deeply rooted patterns of racism and discrimination in American life. The deteriorating economic and political conditions faced by Mexicans and Mexican Americans resulted in a mass reverse exodus. Yet by 1936, for the first time ever, a majority of black voters had switched their political allegiance to the Democrats—concrete evidence that they supported the directions taken by FDR's New Deal.

The Roosevelt Recession

The nation's economy had improved significantly by 1937. Unemployment had declined to "only" 14 percent (9 million people), farm prices had improved to 1930 levels, and industrial production was slightly higher than the 1929 mark. Economic traditionalists, led by Secretary of the Treasury Henry Morgenthau, called for reducing the federal deficit, which had grown to more than $4 billion in fiscal year 1936. Roosevelt, always uneasy about the growing national debt, called for large reductions in federal spending, particularly in WPA and farm programs. Federal Reserve System officials, worried about inflation, tightened credit policies.

Rather than stimulating business, the retrenchment brought about a steep recession. The stock market collapsed in August 1937, and industrial output and farm prices plummeted. Most alarming was the big increase in unemployment. By March 1938, the jobless rate hovered around 20 percent, with more than 13 million people looking for work. As conditions worsened, Roosevelt began to blame the "new depression" on a "strike of capital," claiming businessmen had refused to invest because they wanted to hurt his prestige. In truth, the administration's own severe spending cutbacks were more responsible for the decline.

The blunt reality was that even after five years, the New Deal had not brought about economic recovery. Throughout 1937 and 1938, the administration drifted. Roosevelt received conflicting advice on the economy. Some advisers, suspicious of the reluctance of business to make new investments, urged a massive antitrust campaign against monopolies. Others urged a return to the strategy of "priming the economic pump" with more federal spending. Emergency spending bills in the spring of 1938 pumped new life into the WPA and the PWA. But Republican gains in the 1938 congressional elections made it harder than ever to get new reform measures through.

There were a couple of important exceptions. The 1938 Fair Labor Standards Act established the first federal minimum wage (twenty-five cents an hour) and set a maximum work week of forty-four hours for all employees engaged in interstate commerce. The National Housing Act of 1937, also known as the Wagner-Steagall Act, funded public housing construction and slum clearance and provided rent subsidies for low-income families. But by and large, by 1938, the reform whirlwind of the New Deal was over.

CHRONOLOGY

1929	Stock market crash
1930	Democrats regain control of the House of Representatives
1932	Reconstruction Finance Corporation established to make government credit available
	Bonus Army marches on Washington
	Franklin D. Roosevelt elected president
1933	Roughly 13 million workers unemployed
	The "hundred days" legislation of the First New Deal
	Twenty-first Amendment repeals Prohibition (Eighteenth Amendment)
1934	Indian Reorganization Act repeals Dawes Severalty Act and reasserts the status of Indian tribes as semisovereign nations
	Growing popularity of Father Charles E. Coughlin and Huey Long, critics of Roosevelt
1935	Second New Deal
	Committee for Industrial Organization (CIO) established

	Dust storms turn the Southern Great Plains into the Dust Bowl
	Boulder Dam completed
1936	Roosevelt defeats Alfred M. Landon in reelection landslide
	Sit-down strike begins at General Motors plants in Flint, Michigan
1937	General Motors recognizes United Automobile Workers
	Roosevelt's "Court-packing" plan causes controversy
	Memorial Day Massacre in Chicago demonstrates the perils of union organizing
	"Roosevelt recession" begins
1938	CIO unions withdraw from the American Federation of Labor to form the Congress of Industrial Organizations
	Fair Labor Standards Act establishes the first federal minimum wage

CONCLUSION

Far from being the radical program its conservative critics charged, the New Deal did little to alter fundamental property relations or the distribution of wealth. Indeed, most of its programs largely failed to help the most powerless groups in America—migrant workers, tenant farmers and sharecroppers, African Americans, and other minorities. But the New Deal profoundly changed many areas of American life. Overall, it radically increased the role of the federal government in American lives and communities. Western and Southern communities in particular were transformed through federal intervention in water, power, and agricultural policies. Relief programs and the Social Security system established at least the framework for a welfare state. For the first time in American history, the national government took responsibility for assisting its needy citizens. And also for the first time, the federal government guaranteed the rights of workers to join trade unions, and it set standards for minimum wages and maximum hours. In politics, the New Deal established the Democrats as the majority party. Some version of the Roosevelt New Deal coalition would dominate the nation's political life for another three decades.

The New Deal's efforts to end racial and gender discrimination were modest at best. Some of the more ambitious programs, such as subsidizing the arts or building model communities, enjoyed only brief success. Other reform proposals, such as national health insurance, never got off the ground. Conservative counterpressures, especially after 1937, limited what could be changed. Still, the New Deal did more than strengthen the presence of the national government in people's lives. It also fed expectations that the federal presence would intensify. Washington became a much greater center of economic regulation and political power, and the federal bureaucracy grew in size and influence. With the coming of World War II, the direct role of national government in shaping American communities would expand beyond the dreams of even the most ardent New Dealer.

REVIEW QUESTIONS

1. What were the underlying causes of the Great Depression? What consequences did it have for ordinary Americans, and how did the Hoover administration attempt to deal with the crisis?

2. Analyze the key elements of Franklin D. Roosevelt's first New Deal program. To what degree did these succeed in getting the economy back on track, and in providing relief to suffering Americans?

3. How did the so-called Second New Deal differ from the first? What political pressures did Roosevelt face that contributed to the new policies?

4. How did the New Deal reshape Western communities and politics? What specific programs had the greatest impact in the region? How are these changes still visible today?

5. Evaluate the impact of the labor movement and radicalism on the 1930s. How did they influence American political and cultural life?

6. To what extent were the grim realities of depression reflected in popular culture? To what degree were they absent?

7. Discuss the long- and short-range effects of the New Deal on American political and economic life. What were its key successes and failures? What legacies of New Deal-era policies and political struggles can you find in contemporary America?

RECOMMENDED READING

Anthony J. Badger, *The New Deal: The Depression Years, 1933–1940* (1989). Very useful overview that emphasizes the limited nature of New Deal reforms.

Alan Brinkley, *The End of Reform: New Deal Liberalism in Recession and War* (1995). A sophisticated analysis of the political and economic limits faced by New Deal reformers from 1937 through World War II.

Lizabeth Cohen, *Making a New Deal: Industrial Workers in Chicago, 1919–1939* (1990). A brilliant study that demonstrates the transformation of immigrant and African American workers into key actors in the creation of the CIO, and in New Deal politics, and illuminates the complex relationship between ethnic cultures and mass culture.

Michael Denning, *The Cultural Front: The Laboring of American Culture in the Twentieth Century* (1997). A provocative reinterpretation of 1930s culture, emphasizing the impact of the Popular Front and its lasting influence on American modernism and mass culture.

Ronald Edsforth, *The New Deal: America's Response to the Great Depression* (2000). A concise political history of the 1930s, offering an excellent synthesis of the massive secondary literature.

David M. Kennedy, *Freedom From Fear: The American People in Depression and War* (1999). An absorbing narrative account of the U.S. experience in depression and war.

Richard Lowitt, *The New Deal and the West* (1984). A comprehensive study of the New Deal's impact in the West, with special attention to water policy and agriculture.

Robert S. McElvaine, *The Great Depression: America, 1929–1941* (1984). The best one-volume overview of the Great Depression. It is especially strong on the origins and early years of the worst economic calamity in American history.

Lois Scharf, *To Work and to Wed* (1980). Examines female employment and feminism during the Great Depression.

Harvard Sitkoff, *A New Deal for Blacks* (1978). Focuses on the narrow gains made by African Americans from New Deal measures, as well as the racism that pervaded most government programs.

 For additional study resources for this chapter, go to the *Companion Website*, http://www.prenhall.com/faragher.

CHAPTER

25

World War II

1941–1945

Los Alamos, New Mexico

On Monday, July 16, 1945, at 5:29:45 AM, Mountain War Time, the first atomic bomb exploded in a brilliant flash visible in three states. Within just seven minutes, a huge, multicolored, bell-shaped cloud soared 38,000 feet into the atmosphere and threw back a blanket of smoke and soot to the earth below. The heat generated by the blast was four times the temperature at the center of the sun, and the light produced rivaled that of nearly twenty suns. Even ten miles away people felt a strong surge of heat. The giant fireball ripped a crater a half-mile wide in the ground, fusing the desert sand into glass. The shock wave blew out windows in houses more than 200 miles away. The blast killed every living creature—squirrels, rabbits, snakes, plants, and insects—within a mile and the smells of death lingered for nearly a month.

Very early that morning, Ruby Wilkening had driven to a nearby mountain ridge, where she joined several other women waiting for the blast. Wilkening worried about her husband, a physicist, who was already at the test site. No one knew exactly what to expect, not even the scientists who developed the bomb.

The Wilkenings were part of a unique community of scientists who had been marshaled for war. President Franklin D. Roosevelt, convinced by Albert Einstein and other physicists that the Nazis might successfully develop an atomic bomb, had inaugurated a small nuclear research program in 1939. Soon after the United States entered World War II, the president released resources to create the Manhattan Project and placed it under the direction of the Army Corps of Engineers. By December 1942 a team headed by Italian-born Nobel Prize–winner Enrico Fermi had produced the first chain reaction in uranium under the University of Chicago's football stadium. Now the mission was to build a new, formidable weapon of war, the atomic bomb.

In March 1943, the government moved the key researchers and their families to Los Alamos, New Mexico, a remote and sparsely populated region of soaring peaks, ancient Indian ruins, modern Pueblos, and villages occupied by the descendants of the earliest Spanish settlers. Some families occupied a former boys' preparatory school until new houses could be built; others doubled up in rugged log cabins or nearby ranches. Construction of new quarters proceeded slowly, causing nasty disputes between the "long-hairs" (scientists) and the "plumbers" (army engineers) in charge of the grounds. Despite the chaos, outstanding American and European scientists eagerly signed up. Most were young, with an average age of twenty-seven, and quite a few were recently married. Many couples began their families at Los Alamos, producing a total of nearly a thousand babies between 1943 and 1949.

The scientists and their families formed an exceptionally close-knit community, united by the need for secrecy and their shared antagonism toward their army guardians. The military atmosphere was oppressive. Homes and laboratories were cordoned off by barbed wire and guarded by military police. Everything, from linens to food packages, was stamped "Government Issue." The scientists were followed by security personnel whenever they left Los Alamos. Several scientists were reprimanded for discussing their work at home, although many of their wives worked forty-eight hours a week in the Technical Area. All outgoing mail was censored. Well-known scientists commonly

Los Alamos

worked under aliases—Fermi became "Eugene Farmer"—and code names were used for such terms as atom, bomb, and uranium fission. Los Alamos children were registered without surnames at nearby public schools. Even automobile accidents, weddings, and deaths went unreported. Only a group thoroughly committed to the war effort could accept such restrictions on personal liberty.

A profound urgency motivated the research team, which included refugees from Nazi Germany and Fascist Italy and a large proportion of Jews. The director of the project, California physicist J. Robert Oppenheimer, promoted a scientific élan that offset the military style of commanding general Leslie Groves. Just thirty-eight, slightly built, and deeply emotional, "Oppie" personified the idealism that helped the community of scientists overcome whatever moral reservations they held about placing such a potentially ominous weapon in the hands of the government.

In the Technical Area of Los Alamos, Oppenheimer directed research. At seven o'clock each workday morning, the siren dubbed "Oppie's Whistle" called the other scientists to their laboratories to wrestle with the theoretical and practical problems of building an atomic device. From May to November 1944, after the bomb had been designed, the key issue was testing it. Many scientists feared a test might fail, scattering the precious plutonium at the bomb's core and discrediting the entire project. Finally, with plutonium production increasing, the Los Alamos team agreed to test "the gadget" at a site 160 miles away.

The unprecedented scientific mobilization at Los Alamos mirrored changes occurring throughout American society as the nation rallied behind the war effort. Six-teen million men and women left home for military service and nearly as many moved to take advantage of wartime jobs. In becoming what President Franklin Roosevelt called "a great arsenal of democracy," the American economy quickly and fully recovered from the Great Depression. Several states in the South and Southwest experienced huge surges in population. California alone grew by 2 million people, a large proportion from Mexico. Many broad social changes with roots in earlier times—the economic expansion of the West, the erosion of farm tenancy among black people in the South and white people in Appalachia, and the increasing employment of married women—accelerated during the war. The events of the war eroded old communities, created new ones like Los Alamos, and transformed nearly all aspects of American society.

The transition to wartime was, however, far from smooth. Suspecting Japanese Americans of disloyalty, President Roosevelt ordered the forced relocation of more than 112,000 men, women, and children to internment camps. Although African Americans won a promise of job equity in defense and government employment, hundreds of race riots broke out in the nation's cities. In Los Angeles, Mexican American youth, flaunting a new style of dress, provoked the ire of white sailors who proceeded to assault them, almost at random. And families of all kinds found themselves strained by wartime dislocations.

The United States nevertheless emerged from World War II far stronger than its European allies, who bore the brunt of the fighting. Indeed, the nation was now strong enough to claim a new role as the world's leading superpower.

KEY TOPICS

- The events leading to Pearl Harbor and the declaration of war
- The marshaling of national resources for war
- American society during wartime
- The mobilization of Americans into the armed forces
- The war in Europe and Asia
- Diplomacy and the atomic bomb

THE COMING OF WORLD WAR II

The worldwide Great Depression further undermined a political order that had been shaky since World War I. Production declined by nearly 40 percent, international trade dropped by as much as two-thirds, unemployment rose, and political unrest spread across Europe and Asia. Demagogues played upon nationalist hatreds, fueled by old resentments and current despair, and offered solutions in the form of territorial expansion by military conquest.

Preoccupied with restoring the domestic economy, President Franklin D. Roosevelt had no specific plan to deal with growing conflict elsewhere in the world. Moreover, the majority of Americans strongly opposed foreign entanglements. But as debate over diplomatic policy heated up, terrifying events overseas pulled the nation steadily toward war.

The Shadows of War

War spread first across Asia. With imperialist ambitions of its own, yet reliant on other nations for natural resources like oil, Japan turned its sights on China and seized the province of Manchuria in 1931. When reprimanded by the League of Nations, Japan simply withdrew from the organization. Continuing its expansionist drive, Japan launched a full-scale invasion of China in 1937. While taking over the capital city of Nanking, Japan's army murdered as many as 300,000 Chinese men, women, and children and destroyed much of the city. Within a year, Japan controlled all but China's western interior and threatened all Asia and the Pacific.

Meanwhile, the rise of authoritarian nationalism in Italy and Germany cast a dark shadow over Europe. The economic hardships brought on by the Great Depression— and, in Germany, resentment over the harsh terms of the Treaty of Versailles, which ended World War I—fueled the rise of demagogic mass movements. Glorifying war as a test of national virility, the Italian Fascist dictator Benito Mussolini seized power in 1922 and declared, "We have buried the putrid corpse of liberty." In Germany, the National Socialists (Nazis), led by Adolf Hitler, combined militaristic rhetoric with a racist doctrine of Aryan (Nordic) supremacy that claimed biological superiority for the blond-haired and blue-eyed peoples of northern Europe and classified nonwhites, including Jews, as "degenerate races."

Hitler, who became chancellor of Germany in January 1933 with the backing of major industrialists and about a third of the electorate, prepared for war. With his brown-shirted storm troopers ruling the streets, he quickly destroyed opposition parties and effectively made himself dictator of the strongest nation in central Europe. Renouncing the disarmament provisions of the Versailles treaty, he began to rebuild Germany's armed forces.

The prospect of war grew as both Mussolini and Hitler began to act on their imperial visions. In 1935 Italy invaded Ethiopia and formally claimed the impoverished African kingdom as a colony. In 1936 Hitler sent 35,000 troops to occupy the Rhineland, a region demilitarized by the Versailles treaty. When the Spanish Civil War broke out later that year, Italy and Germany both supported the fascist insurrection of General Francisco Franco and then, in November, drew up a formal alliance to become the Rome–Berlin Axis. Hitler was now nearly ready to put into operation his plan to secure *Lebensraum*—living space for Germany's growing population—through further territorial expansion.

After annexing his native Austria, Hitler turned his attention to Czechoslovakia, a country which both Britain and France were pledged by treaty to assist. War seemed imminent. But Britain and France surprised Hitler by agreeing, at a conference in Munich the last week of September 1938, to allow Germany to annex the Sudetenland, a part of Czechoslovakia bordering Germany. In return, Hitler pledged to stop his territorial advance. Less than six months later, in March 1939, Hitler seized the rest of Czechoslovakia.

By this time, much of the world was aware of the horror of Hitler's regime, especially its virulent racist doctrines. After 1935, when Hitler published the notorious Nuremberg Laws denying civil rights to Jews, the campaign against them became steadily more vicious. On the night of November 9, 1938, Nazi storm troopers rounded up Jews, beating them mercilessly and murdering an untold number. They smashed windows in Jewish shops, hospitals, and orphanages and burned synagogues to the ground. This attack came to be known as *Kristallnacht*, "the Night of Broken Glass." The Nazi government soon expropriated Jewish property and excluded Jews from all but the most menial forms of employment. Pressured by Hitler, Hungary and Italy also enacted laws against Jews.

Isolationism

World War I had left a legacy of strong isolationist sentiment in the United States. Senseless slaughter might be a centuries-old way of life in Europe, many Americans reasoned, but not for the United States, which, as Thomas Jefferson had advised, should stay clear of "entangling alliances." College students, seeing themselves as future cannon fodder, began to demonstrate against war. As late as 1937, nearly 70 percent of Americans responding to a Gallup poll stated that U.S. involvement in World War I had been a mistake (see Figure 25.1).

This sentiment won strong support in Congress. In 1934, a special committee headed by Republican senator Gerald P. Nye of North Dakota had charged weapons manufacturers with driving the United States into World War I in the hopes of windfall profits, which, in fact,

FIGURE 25.1 Gallup Polls: European War and World War I, 1938–1940 These three polls conducted by the American Insitute of Public Opinion indicate the persistence of isolationist sentiment and popular criticism of U.S. involvement in World War I. Many respondents believed the United States, despite its commitments to European allies, should stay out of war. After 1940, in the aftermath of Nazi military victories in Europe, many Americans reconsidered their opposition, fearing a threat to democracy in their own nation.

OCTOBER 2, 1938
EUROPEAN WAR

If England and France go to war against Germany do you think the United States can stay out?

Yes	57%	
No	43	

By Region

	Yes	No
New England	46%	54%
Middle Atlantic	61	39
East Central	60	40
West Central	57	43
South	60	40
West	51	49

Interviewing Date 9/15–20/1938, Survey #132, Question #4

FEBRUARY 21, 1940
EUROPEAN WAR

If it appears that Germany is defeating England and France, should the United States declare war on Germany and send our army and navy to Europe to fight?

Yes	23%
No	77

7 percent expressed no opinion.

Interviewing Date 2/2–7/1940, Survey #183-K, Question #6

DECEMBER 16, 1940
EUROPEAN WAR

Do you think it was a mistake for the United States to enter the last World War?

Yes	39%
No	42
No opinion	19

By Political Affiliation
Democrats

Yes	33%
No	46
No opinion	21

Republicans

Yes	46%
No	38
No opinion	16

Interviewing Date 11/21–30/1940, Survey #244-K, Question #6

many realized. In 1935, Congress passed the first of five Neutrality Acts to deter future entanglements, requiring the president to declare an embargo on the sale and shipment of munitions to all belligerent nations.

Isolationism spanned the political spectrum. In 1938 socialist Norman Thomas gathered leading liberals and trade unionists into the Keep America Out of War Congress; the communist-influenced American League against War and Fascism claimed more than 1 million members. In 1940 the arch-conservative Committee to Defend America First was formed to oppose U.S. intervention. Some America Firsters championed the Nazis while others simply advocated American neutrality. Chaired by top Sears executive Robert E. Wood, the America First Committee quickly gained attention because its members included such well-known personalities as movie stars Robert Young and Lillian Gish, automobile manufacturer Henry Ford, and Charles A. Lindbergh, famous for his 1927 solo flight across the Atlantic. Within a year, America First had launched more than 450 chapters and claimed more than 850,000 members.

Roosevelt Readies for War

While Americans looked on anxiously, the twists and turns of world events prompted President Franklin D. Roosevelt to ready the nation for war. In October 1937 he had called for international cooperation to "quarantine the aggressors." But a poll of Congress revealed that a two-thirds majority opposed economic sanctions, calling any such plan a "back door to war." Forced to draw back, Roosevelt nevertheless won from Congress $1 billion in appropriations to enlarge the navy.

Everything changed on September 1, 1939, when Hitler invaded Poland. Committed by treaty to defend Poland against unprovoked attack, Great Britain and France issued a joint declaration of war against Germany two days later. After the fall of Warsaw at the end of the month, the fighting slowed to a near halt. Even along their border, French and German troops did not exchange fire. From the east, however, the invasion continued. Just two weeks before Hitler overran Poland, the Soviet Union had stunned the world by signing a nonaggression pact with its former enemy. The Red Army now entered Poland, and the two great powers proceeded to split the hapless nation between them. Soviet forces then headed north, invading Finland on November 30. The European war had begun.

Calculating that the United States would stay out of the war, Hitler began a crushing offensive against western Europe in April 1940. Using the technique of *blitzkrieg* (lightning war)—massed, fast-moving columns of tanks supported by air power—that had overwhelmed Poland, Nazi troops moved first against Germany's northern neighbors. After taking Denmark and Norway, the Nazi armored divisions swept over Holland, Belgium, and Luxembourg and sent more than 338,000 British troops into retreat across the English Channel from Dunkirk. Hitler's army,

joined by the Italians, easily conquered France in June 1940. Hitler now turned toward England. In the Battle of Britain, Nazi bombers pounded population and industrial centers while U-boats cut off incoming supplies.

Even with Great Britain under attack, opinion polls indicated Americans' determination to stay out of the war. But most Americans, like Roosevelt himself, believed that the security of the United States depended on both a strong defense and the defeat of Germany. Invoking the Neutrality Act of 1939, which permitted the sale of arms to Britain, France, and China, the president clarified his position: "all aid to the Allies short of war." In May 1940 he began to

Japanese attack planes devastated the U.S. fleet stationed on the Hawai'ian island of Oahu. Before December 7, 1941, few Americans had heard of Pearl Harbor, but the "sneak" attack became a symbol of Japanese treachery and the necessity for U.S. revenge.

SOURCE: National Archives and Records Administration.

transfer surplus U.S. planes and equipment to the Allies. In September the president secured the first peacetime military draft in American history, the Selective Service Act of 1940, which sent 1.4 million men to army training camps by July 1941.

President Roosevelt could not yet admit the inevitability of U.S. involvement —especially during an election year. His popularity had dropped with the "Roosevelt recession" that began in 1937, raising doubts that he could win what would be an unprecedented third term. In his campaign he promised voters not to "send your boys to any foreign wars." Roosevelt and his vice presidential candidate Henry Wallace won by a margin of 5 million popular votes over the Republican darkhorse candidate, Wendell L. Willkie of Indiana.

Roosevelt now moved more aggressively to aid the Allies in their struggle with the Axis powers. In his annual message to Congress, he proposed a bill that would allow the president to sell, exchange, or lease arms to any country whose defense appeared vital to U.S. security. Passed by Congress in March, 1941, the Lend-Lease Act made Great Britain the first beneficiary of massive aid. After Congress authorized the merchant marine to sail fully armed while conveying lend-lease supplies directly to Britain, a formal declaration of war was only a matter of time.

In August 1941 Roosevelt met secretly at sea off Newfoundland with British prime minister Winston Churchill to map military strategy and declare common goals for the postwar world. Known as the Atlantic Charter, their proclamation specified the right of all peoples to live in freedom from fear, want, and tyranny. The Atlantic Charter also called for free trade among all nations, disarmament, and an end to territorial seizures.

By this time the European war had moved to a new stage. Having conquered the Balkans, Hitler set aside the expedient Nazi-Soviet Pact to resume his quest for the entire European continent. In June 1941 Hitler invaded the Soviet Union, promising its rich agricultural land to German farmers. Observing this dramatic escalation, the United States moved closer to intervention.

Pearl Harbor

Throughout 1940 and much of 1941 the United States focused on events in Europe, but the war in Asia went on. Roosevelt, anticipating danger to American interests in the Pacific, had directed the transfer of the Pacific Fleet from bases in California to Pearl Harbor, on the island of Oahu, Hawai'i, in May 1940. Less than five months later, on September 27, Japan formally joined Germany and Italy as the Asian partner of the Axis alliance.

The United States and Japan each played for time. Roosevelt wanted to save his resources to fight against Germany and, moreover, wanted to avoid the possibility of fighting a two-front war; Japan's leaders gambled that America's preoccupation with Europe might allow them to conquer all of Southeast Asia, including the French colonies in Indochina (Vietnam, Cambodia, and Laos) and the British possessions of Burma and India. When Japan occupied Indochina in July 1941, however, Roosevelt responded by freezing Japanese assets in the United States and cutting off its oil supplies.

Confrontation with Japan now looked likely. U.S. intelligence had broken the Japanese secret diplomatic code, and the president knew that Japan was preparing to attack somewhere in the Pacific. By the end of November, he had placed all American forces on high alert.

On the day after the attack on Pearl Harbor, President Franklin D. Roosevelt addressed a joint session of Congress and asked for an immediate declaration of war against Japan. The resolution passed with one dissenting vote, and the United States entered World War II.

SOURCE: AP Wide World Photos.

Early Sunday morning, December 7, 1941, Japanese carriers launched an attack on the Pacific fleet at Pearl Harbor that caught American forces completely by surprise. Within two hours, Japanese pilots had destroyed nearly 200 American planes and badly damaged the fleet; more than 2,400 Americans were killed and nearly 1,200 wounded. On the same day, Japan struck U.S. bases on the Philippines, Guam, and Wake Island.

The next day, President Roosevelt addressed Congress, "Yesterday," he announced, "December 7, 1941— a date which will live in infamy—the United States of America was suddenly and deliberately attacked by the naval and air forces of the Empire of Japan." With only one dissenting vote—by pacifist Jeannette Rankin of Montana, who had voted against U.S. entry into World War I in 1917—Congress approved the president's request for a declaration of war. Three days later, Japan's European Allies, Germany and Italy, declared war on the United States.

ARSENAL OF DEMOCRACY

By the time the United States entered World War II, the U.S. economy had already been regeared for military purposes. Late in 1940, President Roosevelt had called upon all Americans to make the nation a "great arsenal of democracy." Once the United States entered World War II, the federal government began to pour an unprecedented amount of energy and money into wartime production and assigned a huge army of experts to manage it. This vast marshaling of resources was neither simple nor speedy, but it ultimately brought a concentration of power in the federal government that exceeded anything planned by the New Deal. It also brought an end to the Great Depression.

Mobilizing for War

A few days after the United States declared war on Germany, Congress passed the War Powers Act, which established a precedent for executive authority that would endure long after the war's end. The president gained the power to reorganize the federal government and create new agencies; to establish programs censoring all news and information and abridging civil liberties; to seize property owned by foreigners; and even to award government contracts without competitive bidding.

Roosevelt promptly created special wartime agencies. At the top of his agenda was a massive reorientation and management of the economy, and an alphabet soup of new agencies arose to fill any gaps. The Supply Priorities and Allocation Board (SPAB) oversaw the use of scarce materials and resources vital to the war, adjusting domestic consumption (even ending it for some products such as automobiles) to military needs. The Office of Price Administration (OPA) checked the threat of

inflation by imposing price controls. The National War Labor Board (NWLB) mediated disputes between labor and management. The War Manpower Commission (WMC) directed the mobilization of military and civilian services. And the Office of War Mobilization (OWM) coordinated operations among all these agencies.

Several new agencies focused on domestic propaganda. The attack on Pearl Harbor evoked an outpouring of rage against Japan and effectively quashed much opposition to U.S. intervention. Nevertheless the government stepped in to fan the fires of patriotism and to shape public opinion. In June 1942 the president created the Office of War Information (OWI) to engage the press, radio, and film industry in an informational campaign— in short, to sell the war to the American people.

The OWI gathered data and controlled the release of news, emphasizing the need to make reports on the war both dramatic and encouraging. Like the Committee on Public Information during World War I, during the first twenty-one months of the war the new agency banned the publication of advertisements, photographs, and newsreels showing American dead, fearing that such images would demoralize the public. In 1943, worrying that Americans had become overconfident, officials changed their policy. A May issue of *Newsweek* featured graphic photographs of Americans wounded in battle, explaining that "to harden home-front morale, the military services have adopted a new policy of letting civilians see photographically what warfare does to men who fight." The OWI also published leaflets and booklets for the armed services and flooded enemy ranks with subversive propaganda.

Propaganda also fueled the selling of war bonds. Secretary of the Treasury Henry Morgenthau, Jr. not only encouraged Americans to buy government bonds to finance the war but planned a campaign "to use bonds to sell the war, rather than vice versa." Buying bonds would "mean bullets in the bellies of Hitler's hordes!" Discovering through research that Americans felt more antagonism to Japan than Germany, Morgenthau directed his staff to use more negative stereotypes of the Japanese in their advertising copy. Polls showed, however, that most Depression-stung Americans bought war bonds—$185.7 billion by war's end—mainly to invest safely, to counter inflation, and to save for postwar purchases.

The federal government also sponsored various measures to prevent subversion of the war effort. The Federal Bureau of Investigation (FBI) was kept busy, its appropriation rising from $6 million to $16 million in just two years. The attorney general authorized wiretapping in cases of espionage or sabotage, but the FBI used it extensively—and illegally—in domestic surveillance. The Joint Chiefs of Staff created the Office of Strategic Services (OSS) to assess the enemy's military strength, to gather intelligence information, and to oversee espionage activities. Its head, Colonel William Donovan, envisioned the OSS as an "adjunct to military strategy" and engaged leading social scientists to plot psychological warfare against the enemy.

One important outcome of these activities was to increase the size of the government many times over its New Deal level. It cost about $250 million a day to fight the war, and the federal government spent twice as much during the war as it had during its entire prior history. The number of federal employees nearly quadrupled, from a little over 1 million in 1940 to nearly 4 million by the war's end.

The exception to this pattern of expansion was the New Deal itself. As President Roosevelt announced in 1942, "Dr. New Deal" had been replaced by "Dr. Win the War." No longer carrying the heavy responsibility of bringing the nation out of the Great Depression, his administration directed all its resources toward securing the planes, ships, guns, and food required for victory. Moreover, the 1942 elections weakened the New Deal coalition by unseating many liberal Democrats. The Republicans gained forty-six new members in the House of Representatives, nine in the Senate. Republicans now had greater opportunity to quash proposals to extend the social programs instituted during the 1930s. One by one, New Deal agencies vanished.

Organizing the Economy

The decisive factor for victory, even more than military prowess and superior strategy, would be, many observers agreed, the ability of the United States to outproduce its enemies. The country enjoyed many advantages to meet this challenge: a large industrial base, abundant natural resources (largely free from interference by the war), and a civilian population large enough to permit it to increase both its labor force and its armed forces. Defense spending would lift the United States out of the Great Depression and create the biggest economic boom in the history of any nation. But first the entire civilian economy had to be both expanded and transformed for the production of arms and other military supplies.

By the summer of 1941 the federal government was pouring vast amounts into defense production. Six months after the attack on Pearl Harbor, allocations topped $100 billion for equipment and supplies, which exceeded what American firms had produced in any previous wars. Facing war orders too large to fill, American industries were now primed for all-out production. Factories operated around-the-clock, seven days a week. In January 1943 Roosevelt formed the War Production Board to "exercise general responsibility" for all this activity.

With better equipment and more motivation, American workers proved twice as productive as the Germans, five times as productive as the Japanese. No wonder the actual volume of industrial output expanded at the fastest rate in American history. Military production alone grew

from 2 percent of the 1939 total gross national product to 40 percent of the 1943 total. "Something is happening," announced *Time* magazine, "that Adolf Hitler does not understand . . . it is the miracle of production."

Businesses scored huge profits from military contracts. The government provided low-interest loans and even direct subsidies for the expansion of facilities, with generous tax write-offs for retooling. The 100 largest corporations, which manufactured 30 percent of all goods in 1940, garnered 70 percent of all war and civilian contracts and the bulk of the war profits. On the other hand, many small businesses closed, a half-million between 1941 and 1943 alone.

Defense production transformed entire regions. The impact was strongest in the West—the major staging area for the war in the Pacific—where the federal government spent nearly $40 billion for military and industrial expansion. California secured 10 percent of all federal funds, and by 1944 Los Angeles had become the nation's second largest manufacturing center, only slightly behind Detroit. The South also benefited from 60 of the army's 100 new camps. Its textile factories hummed: the army alone required nearly 520 million pairs of socks and 230 million pairs of pants. The economic boom lifted entire populations out of sharecropping and tenancy into well-paid industrial jobs in the cities and pumped unprecedented profits into southern business. Across the country the rural population decreased by almost 20 percent.

Despite a "Food for Freedom" program, American farmers could not keep up with the rising international demand or even the domestic market for milk, potatoes, fruits, and sugar. The Department of Agriculture reached its goals only in areas such as livestock production, thanks to skyrocketing wholesale prices for meat. The war also speeded the development of large-scale, mechanized production of crops, including the first widespread use of chemical fertilizers and pesticides. By 1945 farm income had doubled, but thousands of small farms had disappeared, never to return.

New Workers

The wartime economy brought an unprecedented number of new workers into the labor force. The *bracero* (from *brazo*, Spanish for "arms") program, negotiated by United States and Mexico in 1942, brought more than 200,000 Mexicans into the United States for short-term employment mainly as farm workers. Wartime production also opened trades that had been previously closed to Mexican Americans, such as shipbuilding. Sioux and Navajos were hired in large numbers to build ordnance depots and military training centers. African Americans secured in just four years a greater variety of jobs than in the seven decades since the outbreak of the Civil War. The number of black workers rose from 2,900,000 to 3,800,000.

Facing a shortage of workers and increased production demands, the War Manpower Commission and the Office of War Information conducted a campaign to recruit women into the labor force. Women were encouraged to "take a job for your husband/son/brother" and to "keep the world safe for your children." Higher wages also enticed many women to take jobs in factories producing aircraft, ships, and ordnance. This photograph, taken in 1942, shows a woman working in a munitions factory.

SOURCE: The Granger Collection, New York.

The war most dramatically altered the wage-earning patterns of women. The female labor force grew by over 50 percent, reaching 19.5 million in 1945. The rate of growth proved especially high for white women over the age of thirty-five, and for the first time married women became the majority of female wage earners. The employment rate changed comparatively little for African American women; fully 90 percent had been in the labor force in 1940. However, many black women left domestic service for higher-paying jobs in industry. (See Out of Many Voices: Working in Defense Plants.)

Neither government nor industry rushed to recruit women. Well into the summer of 1942 the Department of War advised businesses to hold back from hiring women "until all available male labor in the area had first been employed." Likewise, neither government nor industry expected women to stay in their jobs when the war ended. "Rosie the Riveter" appeared in posters and advertisements as the model female citizen, but only "for the duration." In Washington DC, women bus drivers were given badges to wear on their uniforms that read: "I am taking the place of a man who went to war."

For the most part, advertisers used conventional gender stereotypes to make wartime jobs appealing to women. Recruitment posters and informational films depicted women's new industrial jobs as simple variations of domestic tasks. Where once housewives sewed curtains for their kitchens, they now produced silk parachutes. Their skill with a vacuum cleaner easily translated into riveting on huge ships. "Instead of cutting a cake," one newsreel explained, "this woman [factory worker] cuts the pattern of aircraft parts. Instead of baking a cake, this woman is cooking gears to reduce the tension in the gears after use."

Compared to the Great Depression, when married women were barred from many jobs, World War II opened up new fields. The number of women automobile workers, for example, jumped from 29,000 to

TABLE 25.1	STRIKES AND LOCKOUTS IN THE UNITED STATES, 1940–45			
Year	Number of Strikes	Number of Workers Involved	Number of Man-Days Idle	Percent of Total Employed
1940	2,508	576,988	6,700,872	2.3
1941	4,288	2,362,620	23,047,556	8.4
1942	2,968	839,961	4,182,557	2.8
1943	3,752	1,981,279	13,500,529	6.9
1944	4,956	2,115,637	8,721,079	7.0
1945	4,750	3,467,000	38,025,000	12.2

Despite "no-strike" pledges, workers staged wildcat strikes in the war years. Union leaders negotiated shorter hours, higher wages, and seniority rules and helped to build union membership to a new height. When the war ended, nearly 30 percent of all nonagricultural workers were union members.

SOURCE: "Work Stoppages Caused by Labor-Management Disputes in 1945," *Monthly Labor Review*, May 1946, p. 720; and Martin Glaberman, *War Time Strikes* (Detroit: Bewick, 1980), p. 36.

200,000, that of women electrical workers from 100,000 to 374,000. Polled near the end of the war, the overwhelming majority—75 percent—of women workers expressed a desire to keep working, preferably at the same jobs.

Although 17 million new jobs were created during the war, the economic gains were not evenly distributed. Wages increased by as much as 50 percent but never as fast as profits or prices. This widely reported disparity produced one of the most turbulent periods in American labor history (see Table 25.1). More workers went on strike in 1941, before the United States entered the war, than in any previous year except 1919. A militant union drive at Ford Motor Company's enormous River Rouge plant made the United Auto Workers (UAW) one of the most powerful labor organizations in the world. Total union membership increased from 10.5 million to 14.7 million, with the women's share alone rising from 11 to 23 percent. Unions also enrolled 1,250,000 African Americans, twice the prewar number.

Once the United States entered the war, the major unions dutifully agreed to no-strike pledges for its duration. Nevertheless, rank-and-file union members sporadically staged illegal "wildcat" strikes during the war. The most dramatic, a walkout of more than a half-million coal miners in 1943 led by the rambunctious John L. Lewis, withstood the attacks of the government and the press. Roosevelt repeatedly ordered the mines seized, only to find, as Lewis retorted, that coal could not be mined with bayonets. The Democratic majority in Congress passed the first federal antistrike bill, giving the president power to penalize strikers, even to draft them. And yet the strikes grew in size and number, reaching a level greater than in any other four-year period in American history.

OUT OF MANY VOICES

WORKING IN DEFENSE PLANTS

Born in Mexico, Margarita Salazar McSweyn moved with her family to Los Angeles when she was still an infant and grew up in the tightly knit Mexican community of Boyle Heights. When World War II began, she was working in a beauty shop in her neighborhood. In this excerpt from her oral history made when she was sixty-five, she recalls the appeal of employment in the defense plants, where she took a job drilling the wings of airplanes.

. . . I COULD SEE THAT I WASN'T GOING TO MAKE that much money working as an [beauty] operator and the money was in defense. Everybody would talk about the overtime and how much more money it was. And it was exciting. Being involved in that era you figured you were doing something for your country—and at the same time making money.

There was ads all over. I thought I would give it a try and see if I could do it. There was so much talk about it being such hard work, and I had never done hard work. The ads, they'd talk about the riveting and running some sort of machine—dimpling, I think they called it. It wasn't for the glamour. You weren't going to meet all these guys; you would be working primarily with women. . . .

They checked you out, your American citizenship and stuff like that. They told you what to wear: pants and a hair net, always.

Makeup, they didn't care, as long as you wore your pants and wore sensible shoes and kept your hair out of the way.

That first day, when I went, I was startled. That building is pretty large and each floor had something different. . . . I used to get lost going from one department to another, till finally I got to know the other girls and I'd go in and out with them. . . .

I started complaining about my legs, but you didn't change jobs just because you had a whim. You really had to have a reason, especially if you were a good, steady employee that they could depend on to work overtime. I had gone to the doctor and gotten shots for my legs, for veins, so I actually had a good reason. . . .

I wanted to work sitting down . . . They figured that the toolshed would be the best, because I wouldn't have to walk so much. I'd help the man that was in charge. . . .

. . . I think in a way the job at Lockheed did have an impact because I got to know about tools, which I never did before. I could clean something or go back there in cracks and drill a hole. Not that I'm mechanically inclined, but I was able to do it. ■

SOURCE: Sherna B. Gluck, *Rosie the Riveter Revisited: Women, the War, and Social Change* (Boston: Twayne Publishers, 1987), pp. 85–90.

THE HOME FRONT

Most Americans thoroughly appreciated the burst of prosperity brought on by wartime production, but they also experienced food rationing, long workdays, and separation from loved ones. Alongside national unity ran deep conflicts on the home front. Racial and ethnic hostilities flared repeatedly and on several occasions erupted in violence.

Families in Wartime

Despite the uncertainties of wartime, or perhaps because of them, men and women rushed into marriage. The surge in personal income caused by the wartime economic boom meant that many young couples could afford to set up their own households—something their counterparts in the 1930s had not been able to do. As one social scientist remarked at the time, "Economic conditions were ripe for a rush to the altar." For other couples, the prospect of separation provided the incentive. The U.S. Census Bureau estimated that between 1940 and 1943 at least a million more people married than would have been expected had there been no war. The marriage rate skyrocketed, peaking in 1946, but by 1946 the number of divorces also set records.

Housing shortages were acute, and rents were high. So scarce were apartments that taxi drivers became, for an extra fee, up-to-the-minute guides to vacancies. Able to set their own terms, landlords frequently discriminated against families with children and even more so against racial minorities.

Supplying a household was scarcely less difficult. Although retailers extended their store hours into the evenings and weekends, shopping had to be squeezed in between long hours on the job. Extra planning was necessary for purchasing government-rationed staples such as meat, cheese, sugar, milk, coffee, gasoline, and even shoes. To free up commercially grown produce for the troops overseas, many families grew their own fruits and vegetables. In 1943, the peak year of Victory Gardens, three-fifths of the population were "growing their own," which amounted to a staggering 8 million tons of food that year.

Although the Office of Price Administration tried to prevent inflation and ensure an equitable distribution of

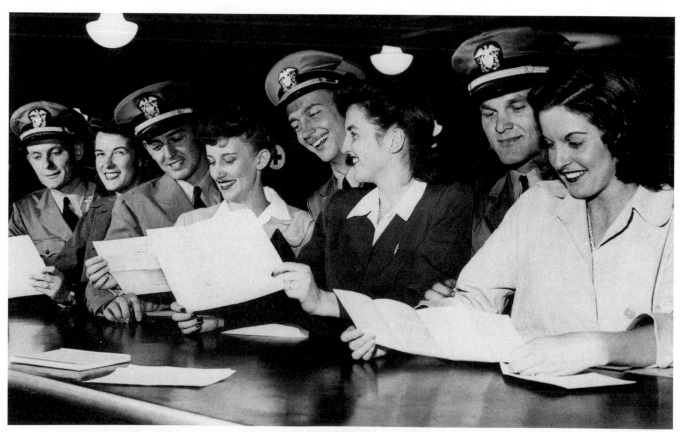

Students at Officers' Training School at Northwestern University, who were not allowed to marry until they were commissioned as ensigns, apply for marriage licenses in Chicago, August 20, 1943, shortly before graduation. These young couples helped the marriage rate skyrocket during World War II.

SOURCE: © Bettmann/CORBIS.

foodstuffs, many women found it nearly impossible to manage both a demanding job and a household. This dual responsibility contributed to high turnover and absentee rates in factories.

The care of small children became a major problem. Wartime employment or military service often separated husbands and wives, leaving children in the hands of only one parent. But even when families stayed together, both adults often worked long hours, sometimes on different shifts. Although the War Manpower Commission estimated that as many as 2 million children needed some form of child care, federally funded day-care centers served less than 10 percent of defense workers' children. In most communities, the limited facilities sponsored by industry or municipal governments could not keep up with the growing number of "latchkey" children.

Juvenile delinquency rose during the war. With employers often relaxing minimum age requirements for employment, many teenagers quit school for the high wages of factory jobs. Runaways drifted from city to city, finding temporary work at wartime plants or at military installations. Gangs formed in major urban areas, leading to brawling, prostitution, or automobile thefts for joy rides. Overall, however, with so many young men either employed or serving in the armed forces, crime by juvenile as well as adult males declined. In contrast, complaints against girls, mainly for sexual offenses or for running away from home, increased significantly. In response, local officials created various youth agencies and charged them with developing more recreational and welfare programs. Meanwhile, local school boards appealed to employers to hire only older workers, and toward the end of the war the student dropout rate began to decline.

Public health improved greatly during the war. Forced to cut back on expenditures for medical care during the Great Depression, many Americans now spent large portions of their wartime paychecks on doctors, dentists, and prescription drugs. But even more important were the medical benefits provided to the more than 16 million men inducted into the armed forces and their dependents. Nationally, incidences of such communicable diseases as typhoid fever, tuberculosis, and diphtheria dropped considerably, the infant death rate fell by more than a third, and life expectancy increased by three years. The death rate in 1942, excluding battle deaths, was the lowest in the nation's history. In the South and Southwest, however, racism and widespread poverty combined to halt or even reverse these trends. These regions continued to have the highest infant and maternal mortality rates in the nation.

The Internment of Japanese Americans

After the attack on Pearl Harbor, many Americans feared an invasion of the mainland and suspected Japanese Americans of secret loyalty to an enemy government. On December 8, 1941, the federal government froze the financial assets of those born in Japan, known as Issei, who had been barred from U.S. citizenship. Meanwhile, in the name of national defense, a coalition of politicians, patriotic organizations, business groups, and military officials called for the removal of all Americans of Japanese descent from Pacific coastal areas. Although a State Department intelligence report certified their loyalty, Japanese Americans—two-thirds of whom were American-born citizens—became the only ethnic group singled out for legal sanctions.

More than 110,000 Japanese Americans were interned during World War II, some for up to four years. This photograph, taken by Dorothea Lange (1895–1965), the famed photographer of Depression Era migrant families, shows the Mochida family in May 1942 waiting for a bus that will take them to a relocation camp.

SOURCE: Photri-Microstock, Inc.

Charges of sedition masked long-standing racial prejudices. The press began to use the word "Jap" in headlines, while political cartoonists employed blatant racial stereotypes. Popular songs appeared with titles like "You're a Sap, Mister Jap, to Make a Yankee Cranky." "The very fact that no sabotage has taken place to date," an army report suggested, with twisted logic, "is a disturbing and confirming indication that action will be taken."

On February 19, 1942, President Roosevelt signed Executive Order 9066, which in effect authorized the exclusion of more than 112,000 Japanese American men, women, and children from designated military areas, mainly in California, but also in Oregon, Washington, and southern Arizona. The army prepared for forced evacuation, rounding up and removing Japanese Americans from the communities where they had lived and worked, sometimes for generations.

During the spring of 1942, Japanese American families received one week's notice to close up their businesses and homes. Told to bring only what they could carry, they were then transported to one of the ten internment camps managed by the War Relocation Authority. The guarded camps were located as far away as Arkansas, although the majority had been set up in the remote desert areas of Utah, Colorado, Idaho, Arizona, Wyoming, and California. Karl G. Yoneda described his quarters at Manzanar in northern California:

> There were no lights, stoves, or window panes. My two cousins and I, together with seven others, were crowded into a 25 × 30 foot room. We slept on army cots with our clothes on. The next morning we discovered that there were no toilets or washrooms. . . . We saw GIs manning machine guns in the watchtowers. The barbed wire fence which surrounded the camp was visible against the background of the snow-covered Sierra mountain range. "So this is the American-style concentration camp," someone remarked.

By August, virtually every West Coast resident who had at least one Japanese grandparent had been interned. (See Out of Many Voices: Memories of Japanese Internment.)

The Japanese American Citizens League charged that "racial animosity" rather than military necessity had dictated the internment policy. Despite the protest of the American Civil Liberties Union and several church groups against the abridgment of the civil rights of Japanese Americans, the Supreme Court in Korematsu v. United States (1944) upheld the constitutionality of relocation on grounds of national security. By this time a program of gradual release was in place, although the last center, at Tule Lake, California, did not close until March 1946. In protest, nearly 6,000 Japanese Americans renounced their U.S. citizenship. Japanese Americans had lost homes and businesses valued at $500 million in what many historians judge as being the worst violation of American civil liberties during the war. Not until 1988 did the U.S. Congress vote reparations of $20,000 and a public apology to each of the 60,000 surviving victims.

"Double V": Victory at Home and Abroad

Throughout the war, African American activists conducted a "Double V" campaign, mobilizing not only for Allied victory but for their own rights as citizens. "The army is about to take me to fight for democracy," one Detroit resident said, "but I would as leave fight for democracy right here." Black militants demanded, at a minimum, fair housing and equal employment opportunities.

Even before the United States entered the war, A. Philip Randolph, president of both the Brotherhood of Sleeping Car Porters and the National Negro Congress, had begun to mobilize against discrimination. At a planning meeting in Chicago a black woman proposed sending African Americans to Washington DC, "from all over the country, in jalopies, in trains, and any way they can get there until we get some action from the White House." African Americans across the country began to prepare for a "great rally" of no less than 100,000 people to be held at the Lincoln Memorial on the Fourth of July.

Eager to stop the March on Washington movement, President Roosevelt met with Randolph, who proposed an executive order "making it mandatory that Negroes be permitted to work in [defense] plants." Randolph reviewed several drafts before approving the text that became, on June 25, 1941, Executive Order 8802, banning discrimination in defense industries and government. The president later appointed a Fair Employment Practices Committee to hear complaints and to redress grievances. Randolph called off the march but remained determined to "shake up white America."

Other civil rights organizations formed during wartime to fight both discrimination and Jim Crow practices, including segregation in the U.S. armed forces. The interracial Congress of Racial Equality (CORE), formed by pacifists in 1942, staged sit-ins at Chicago, Detroit, and Denver restaurants that refused to serve African Americans. In several cities, CORE used nonviolent means to challenge racial segregation in public facilities. Meanwhile, membership in the National Association for the Advancement of Colored People (NAACP), which took a strong stand against discrimination in defense plants and in the military, grew from 50,000 in 1940 to 450,000 in 1946.

The toughest struggles against discrimination took place, however, in local communities. Approximately 1.2 million African Americans had left the rural South

OUT OF MANY VOICES

MEMORIES OF JAPANESE INTERNMENT DURING WORLD WAR II

Born in California and just seven years old in 1942, Jeanne Wakatsuki was interned with her family during World II. Prior to the war, she lived in Long Beach, where her father and brothers caught fish to support the family. In her memoir published in 1973, she recalls her arrival in Manzanar, an internment camp located in the desert of Southern California, where she and ten thousand other Japanese Americans spent the duration of the war.

THE NAME MANZANAR MEANT NOTHING TO US when we left Boyle Heights [a neighborhood in Los Angeles]. We didn't know where it was or what it was. We went because the government ordered us to. . . .

I had never been outside Los Angeles County, never traveled more than ten miles from the coast, had never even ridden on a bus. I was full of excitement, the way any kid would be, and wanted to look out the window. But for the first few hours the shades were drawn. . . .

We rode all day. By the time we reached our destination, the shades were up. It was late afternoon. The first thing I saw was a yellow swirl across a blurred, reddish setting sun. The bus was being pelted by what sounded like splattering rain. It wasn't rain. This was my first look at something I would soon know very well, a billowing flurry of dust and sand churned up by the wind through Owens Valley.

We drove past a barbed-wire fence, through a gate, and into an open space where trunks and sacks and packages had been dumped from the baggage trucks that drove out ahead of us. I could see a few tents set up, the first rows of black barracks, and beyond, blurred by sand, rows of barracks that seemed to spread for miles across this plain. . . .

After dinner we were taken to Block 16, a cluster of fifteen barracks that had just been finished a day or so earlier—although finished was hardly the word for it. The shacks were built of one thickness of pine planking covered with tarpaper. They sat on concrete footings, with about two feet of open space between the floorboards and the ground. . . .

Each barracks was divided into six units, sixteen by twenty feet, about the size of a living room, with one bare bulb hanging from the ceiling and an oil stove for heat. We were assigned two of these for the twelve people in our family group. . . . We were issued steel army cots, two brown army blankets each, and some mattress covers, which my brothers stuffed with straw. ■

SOURCE: Jeanne Wakatsuki Houston and James D. Houston, *Farewell to Manzanar* (1973).

to take jobs in wartime industries, and they faced not only serious housing shortages but whites intent on keeping them out of the best jobs and neighborhoods. For example, "hate strikes" broke out in defense plants across the country when African Americans were hired or upgraded to positions customarily held by white workers. In 1942, 20,000 white workers at the Packard Motor Car Company in Detroit walked out to protest the promotion of three black workers. One year later, at a nearby U.S. Rubber Company factory, more than half the white workers walked out when African American women began to operate the machinery.

Detroit was also the site of bloody race riots. In February 1942, when twenty black families attempted to move into new federally funded apartments adjacent to a Polish American community, a mob of 700 armed white protesters halted the moving vans and burned a cross on the project's grounds. Two months later, 1,750 city police and state troopers supervised the move of these families into the Sojourner Truth Housing Project, named after the famous abolitionist and former slave. The following summer, racial violence reached its wartime peak. Twenty-five blacks and nine whites were killed and more than 700 were injured. By the time the 6,000 federal troops restored order, property losses topped $2 million. One writer reported: "I thought that I had witnessed an experience peculiar to the Deep South. On the streets of Detroit I saw again the same horrible exhibition of uninhibited hate as they fought and killed one another—white against black—in a frenzy of homicidal mania, without rhyme or reason."

This painting is by Horace Pippin, a self-taught African American artist who began painting as therapy for an injury suffered while serving with the U.S. Army's 369th Colored Infantry Regiment during World War I. It is one of a series drawn during World War II illustrating the contradiction between the principles of liberty and justice, for which Americans were fighting abroad, and the reality of race prejudice at home.

SOURCE: Horace Pippin (1888–1946), *Mr. Prejudice,* 1943. Oil on canvas, 18 × 14 inches. Philadelphia Museum of Art, Gift of Dr. and Mrs. Matthew T. Moore. Photo by Graydon Wood (1984–108–1).

During the summer of 1943 more than 270 racial conflicts occurred in nearly fifty cities. The poet Langston Hughes, who supported U.S. involvement in the war, wrote:

> *Looky here, America*
> *What you done done—*
> *Let things drift*
> *Until the riots come*
>
> *Yet you say we're fighting*
> *For democracy.*
> *Then why don't democracy*
> *Include me?*
>
> *I ask you this question*
> *Cause I want to know*
> *How long I got to fight*
> *BOTH HITLER—AND JIM CROW.*

Zoot-Suit Riots

On the night of June 4, 1943, sailors poured into nearly 200 cars and taxis to drive through the streets of East Los Angeles in search of Mexican Americans dressed in zoot suits. The sailors assaulted their victims at random, even chasing one youth into a movie theater and stripping him of his clothes while the audience cheered. Riots broke out and continued for five days.

Two communities had collided, with tragic results. The sailors had only recently been uprooted from their hometowns and regrouped under the strict discipline of boot camp. Now stationed in southern California while awaiting departure overseas, they came face-to-face with Mexican American teenagers wearing long-draped coats, pegged pants, pocket watches with oversized chains, and big floppy hats. To the sailors, the zoot suit was not just a flamboyant fashion. Unlike the uniform the young sailors wore, the zoot suit signaled defiance and a lack of patriotism.

The zoot-suiters, however, represented less than 10 percent of their community's youth. More than 300,000 Mexican Americans were serving in the armed forces (a number representing a greater proportion of their draft-age population than other Americans), and they served in the most hazardous branches, the paratrooper and marine corps. Many others were employed in war industries in Los Angeles, which had become home to the largest community of Mexican Americans in the nation. For the first time Mexican Americans were finding well-paying jobs, and, like African Americans, they expected their government to protect them from discrimination.

Military and civilian authorities eventually contained the zoot-suit riots by ruling several sections of Los Angeles off-limits to military personnel, and the city council passed legislation making the wearing of a zoot suit in public a criminal offense. Many Mexican Americans expressed concern about their personal safety; some feared that, after the government rounded up the Japanese, they would be the next group sent to internment camps.

Popular Culture and "The Good War"

Global events shaped the lives of American civilians but appeared to touch them only indirectly in their everyday activities. Food shortages, long hours in the factories, and even fears for loved ones abroad did not take away all the pleasures of full employment and prosperity. With money in their pockets, Americans spent freely at vacation resorts, country clubs, racetracks, nightclubs, dance halls, and movie theaters. Sales of books skyrocketed, and spectator sports attracted huge audiences.

Popular music seemed to bridge the growing racial divisions of the neighborhood and the work place. Transplanted southern musicians, black and white, brought their regional styles to northern cities. Played on jukeboxes in bars, bus stations, and cafes, "country" and "rhythm & blues" not only won over new audiences but also inspired musicians themselves to crisscross old boundaries. Musicians of the war years "made them steel guitars cry and whine," Ray Charles recalled. They also paved the way musically for the emergence of rock and roll a decade later.

Many popular songs featured war themes. Personal sentiment meshed with government directive to depict a "good war," justifying massive sacrifice. The war was to be seen as a worthy and even noble cause. The plaintive "A Rainbow at Midnight" by country singer Ernest Tubb expressed the hope of a common "dogface" soldier looking beyond the misery and horror to the promise of a brighter tomorrow. "Till Then," recorded by the Mills Brothers, a harmonious black quartet, offered the prospect of a romantic reunion when "the world will be free." The era's best-known tune, Irving Berlin's "White Christmas," evoked a lyrical nostalgia of past celebrations with family and friends close by. On the lighter side, novelty artist Spike Jones made his name with the "razz" or "Bronx cheer," in "We're Going to Ffft in the Fuehrer's Face."

Hollywood artists meanwhile threw themselves into a perpetual round of fundraising and morale-boosting public events. Movie stars called on fans to buy war bonds and to support the troops. Combat films such as *Action in the North Atlantic* made heroes of ordinary Americans under fire, depicting GIs of different races and ethnicities discovering their common humanity. Movies with antifascist themes, such as *Tender Comrade*, promoted friendship among Russians and Americans, while films like *Since You Went Away* portrayed the loyalty and resilience of families with servicemen stationed overseas.

The wartime spirit also infected the juvenile world of comics. The climbing sales of nickel "books" spawned a proliferation of patriotic superheroes such as the Green Lantern and Captain Marvel. Even Bugs Bunny put on a uniform and fought sinister-looking enemies.

Fashion designers did their part. Padded shoulders and straight lines became popular for both men and women. Patriotic Americans, such as civil defense volunteers and Red Cross workers, fancied uniforms, and women employed in defense plants wore pants, often for the first time. Restrictions on materials also influenced fashion. Production of nylon stockings was halted because the material was needed for parachutes; women's skirts were shortened, while the War Production Board encouraged cuffless "Victory Suits" for men. Executive Order M-217 restricted the colors of shoes manufactured during the war to "black, white, navy blue, and three shades of brown."

Never to see a single battle, safeguarded by two oceans, many Americans nevertheless experienced the war years as the most intense of their entire lives. Popular music, Hollywood movies, radio programs, and advertisements—all screened by the Office of War Information—encouraged a sense of personal involvement in a collective effort to preserve democracy at home and to save the world from fascism. No one was excluded, no action considered insignificant. Even casual conversation came under the purview of the government, which warned that "Loose Lips Sink Ships."

MEN AND WOMEN IN UNIFORM

During World War I, American soldiers served for a relatively brief period and in small numbers. A quarter-century later, World War II mobilized 16.4 million Americans into the armed forces. Although only 34 percent of men who served in the army saw combat—the majority during the final year of the war—the experience had a powerful impact on nearly everyone. Whether working in the steno pool at Great Lakes Naval Training Center in northern Illinois or slogging through mud with rifle in hand in the Philippines, many men and women saw their lives reshaped in unpredictable ways. For those who survived, the war often proved to be the defining experience of their lives.

Creating the Armed Forces

Before the European war broke out in 1939, the majority of the 200,000 men in the U.S. armed forces were employed as military police, engaged in such tasks as patrolling the Mexican border or occupying colonial possessions, such as the Philippines. Neither the army nor the navy was prepared for the scale of combat World War II entailed. Only the U.S. Marine Corps, which had been planning since the 1920s to wrest control of the western Pacific from Japan, was poised to fight.

On October 16, 1940, National Registration Day, all men between the ages of twenty-one and thirty-six were legally obligated to register for military service. After the United States entered the war, the draft age was lowered to eighteen, and local boards were instructed to choose first from the youngest.

One-third of the men examined by the Selective Service were rejected. Surprising numbers were refused induction because they were physically unfit for military service. For the first time, men were screened for "neuropsychiatric disorders or emotional problems," and approximately 1.6 million were rejected on this reason. At a time when only one American in four graduated from high school, induction centers turned away many conscripts because they were functionally illiterate. But those who passed the screening tests joined the best-educated army in history: nearly half of white draftees had graduated from high school and 10 percent had attended college.

The officer corps, whose top-ranking members were from the Command and General Staff School at Fort Leavenworth, tended to be highly professional, politically conservative, and personally autocratic. General Douglas MacArthur, supreme commander in the Pacific theater, was said to admire the discipline of the German army and to disparage political democracy. General Dwight D. Eisenhower, however, supreme commander of the Allied forces in Europe, projected a new and contrasting spirit. Distrusted by MacArthur and many of the older brass, Eisenhower appeared to his troops a model of leadership.

The democratic rhetoric of the war and the sudden massive expansion of the armed forces contributed to this transformation of the officer corps. A shortage of officers during World War I had prompted a huge expansion of the Reserve Officer Training Corps, but it still could not meet the demand for trained officers. Racing to make up for the deficiency, Army Chief of Staff George Marshall opened schools for officer candidates. In 1942, in seventeen-week training periods, these schools produced more than 54,000 platoon leaders. Closer in sensibility to the civilian population, these new officers were the kind of leaders Eisenhower sought.

Most GIs (short for "government issue"), who were the vast majority of draftees, had limited contact with officers at the higher levels and instead forged bonds with their company commanders and men within their own combat units. "Everyone wants someone to look up to when he's scared," one GI explained. Most of all, soldiers depended on the solidarity of the group and the loyalty of their buddies to pull them through the war. Proud to serve in "the best-dressed, best-fed, best-equipped army in the world," the majority of these citizen-soldiers wanted foremost "to get the task done" and return soon to their families and communities.

Women Enter the Military

With the approach of World War II, Massachusetts Republican congresswoman Edith Nourse Rogers proposed legislation for the formation of a women's corps. The army instead drafted its own bill, which both Rogers and Eleanor Roosevelt supported, creating in May 1942 the Women's Army Auxiliary Corps (WAAC), later changed to Women's Army Corps (WAC). In 1942–43 other bills established a women's division of the navy (WAVES), the Women's Airforce Service Pilots, and the Marine Corps Women's Reserve.

Overall, more than 350,000 women served in World War II, two-thirds of them in the WACS and WAVES. As a group, they were better educated and more skilled—although paid less—than the average soldier. However, military policy prohibited women from supervising male workers, even in offices.

Although barred from combat, women were not necessarily protected from danger. Nurses accompanied the troops into combat in Africa, Italy, and France, treated men under fire, and dug and lived in their own foxholes. More than 1,000 women flew planes, although not in combat missions. Others worked as photographers and cryptoanalysts. The vast majority remained far from battlefronts, however, stationed mainly within the United States, where they served in administration, communications, clerical, or health-care facilities.

The WACS and WAVES were both subject to hostile commentary and bad publicity. The overwhelming majority of soldiers believed that most WACS were prostitutes, and the War Department itself, fearing "immorality" among women in the armed forces, closely monitored

New recruits to the Women's Army Corps (WAC) pick up their clothing "issue" (allotment). These volunteers served in many capacities, from nursing men in combat to performing clerical and communication duties "stateside" (within the United States). Approximately 140,000 women served in the WACS during World War II.

SOURCE: National Archives and Records Administration.

their conduct and established much stricter rules for women than for men. The U.S. Marine Corps even used intelligence officers to ferret out suspected lesbians or women who showed "homosexual tendencies" (as opposed to homosexual acts), both causes for dishonorable discharge.

Old Practices and New Horizons

The Selective Service Act, in response to the demands of African American leaders, specified that "there shall be no discrimination against any person on account of race or color." The draft brought hundreds of thousands of young black men into the army, and African Americans enlisted at a rate 60 percent above their proportion of the general population. By 1944 black soliders represented 10 percent of the army's troops, and overall approximately 1 million African Americans served in the armed forces during World War II. The army, however, channeled black recruits into segregated, poorly equipped units, which were commanded by white officers. Secretary of War Henry Stimson refused to challenge this policy, saying that the army could not operate effectively as "a sociological laboratory." The majority served in the Signal, Engineer, and Quartermaster Corps, mainly in construction or stevedore work. Only toward the end of the war, when the shortage of infantry neared a crisis, were African Americans permitted to rise to combat status. The all-black 761st Tank Battalion, the first African American unit in combat, won a Medal of Honor after 183 days in action. And despite the very small number of African Americans admitted to the Air Force, the 99th Pursuit Squadron earned high marks in action against the feared German air force, the Luftwaffe. Even the Marine Corps and the Coast Guard agreed to end their historic exclusion of African Americans, although they recruited and promoted only a small number.

The ordinary black soldier, sailor, or marine experienced few benefits from the late-in-the-war gains of a few. They encountered discrimination everywhere, from the army canteen to the religious chapels. Even the blood banks kept blood segregated by race (although a black physician, Dr. Charles Drew, had invented the process for storing plasma). The year 1943 marked the peak of unrest, with violent confrontations between blacks and whites breaking out at military installations, especially in the South where the majority of African American soldiers were stationed. Toward the end of the war, to improve morale among black servicemen, the army relaxed its policy of segregation, mainly in recreational facilities. Although enforcement was uneven and haphazard, the new policy paved the way for integration within a decade of the war's end.

The army also grouped Japanese Americans into segregated units, sending most to fight far from the Pacific theater. Better educated than the average soldier, many Nisei soldiers who knew Japanese served stateside as interpreters and translators. When the army decided to create a Nisei regiment, more than 10,000 volunteers stepped forward, only one in five of whom was accepted. The Nisei 442nd fought heroically in Italy and France and became the most decorated regiment in the war.

Despite segregation, the armed forces ultimately pulled Americans of all varieties out of their communities. Many Jews and other second-generation European immigrants, for example, described their stint in the military as an "Americanizing" experience. Many Indian peoples left reservations for the first time, approximately 25,000 serving in the armed forces. Many Navajo "code talkers," for example, who used a special code based on their native language to transmit information among military units, learned English in special classes established by the marines. For many African Americans, military service provided a bridge to postwar civil rights agitation. Amzie Moore, who later helped to organize the Mississippi Freedom Democratic Party, traced his understanding that "people are just people" to his experiences in the armed forces during World War II.

Many homosexuals also discovered a wider world. Despite a policy barring them from military service, most slipped through mass screening at induction centers. Moreover, the emotional pressures of wartime, especially the fear of death, encouraged close friendships, and homosexuals in the military often found more room than in civilian life to express their sexual orientation openly. In army canteens, for example, men often danced with one another, whereas in civilian settings they would have been subject to ridicule or even arrest for such activity. "The war is a tragedy to my mind and soul," one gay soldier confided, "but to my physical being, it's a memorable experience." Lesbian WACS and WAVES had similar tales.

Most soldiers looked back at the war, with all its dangers and discomforts, as the greatest experience they would ever know. As the *New Republic* predicted in 1943, they met fellow Americans from every part of the country and recognized for the first time in their lives "the bigness and wholeness of the United States." "Hughie was a Georgia cracker, so he knew something about moonshine," remembered one soldier. Another fondly recalled "this fellow from Wisconsin we called 'Moose.'" The army itself promoted these expectations of new experience. *Twenty-Seven Soldiers* (1944), a government-produced film for the troops, showed Allied soldiers of several nationalities all working together in harmony.

The Medical Corps

The chance of being killed in combat was surprisingly small, estimated at less than 1 in 50, but the risk of injury was much higher. By the time the war ended, the army reported 949,000 casualties, including 175,000 who had been killed in action. Although the European Theater produced the greatest number of casualities, the Pacific held grave dangers in addition to artillery fire. For the soldiers fighting in hot, humid jungles, malaria, typhus, diarrhea, or dengue fever posed the most common threat to their lives. For the 25th Infantry Division, which landed in Guadalcanal in 1943, the malaria-carrying mosquito proved a more formidable enemy than Japanese forces.

The prolonged stress of combat also took a toll in the form of "battle fatigue." Despite the rigorous screening of recruits, more than 1 million soldiers suffered at one time or another from debilitating psychiatric symptoms, and the number of men discharged for neuropsychiatric reasons was 2.5 times greater than in previous wars. The cause, psychiatrists concluded, was not individual weakness but long stints in the front lines. In France, for example, where soldiers spent up to 200 days in the field without a break from fighting, thousands cracked, occasionally inflicting wounds on themselves in order to be sent home. One who simply fled the battlefront, Private Eddie Slovik, was tried and executed for desertion—the first such execution since the Civil War. In 1944 the army concluded that eight months in combat was the maximum and instituted, when replacements were available, a rotation system to relieve exhausted soldiers.

To care for sick and wounded soldiers, the army depended on a variety of medical personnel. Soldiers received first aid training as part of basic training, and they went into battle equipped with bandages to treat minor wounds. For the most part, however, they relied on the talents of trained physicians and medics. The Army Medical Corps sent doctors to the front lines. Working in makeshift tent hospitals, these physicians advanced surgical techniques and, with the use of new "wonder" drugs such as penicillin, saved the lives of many wounded soldiers. Of the soldiers who underwent emergency surgery on the field, more than 85 percent survived. Overall, less than 4 percent of all soldiers who received medical care died as a result of their injuries. Much of the success in treatment came from the use of blood plasma, which reduced the often lethal effect of shock from severe bleeding. By 1945, the American Red Cross Blood Bank, which was formed four years earlier, had collected more than 13 million units of blood from volunteers, converted most of it into dried plasma, and made it readily available throughout the European Theater.

Grateful for the care of skilled surgeons, many soldiers nevertheless named medics the true heroes of the battlefront. Between thirty to forty medics were attached to each infantry battalion, and they were responsible for emergency first aid and for transporting the wounded to the aid station and if necessary on to the field hospital. Many medics were recruited from the approximately 35,000 conscientious objectors, who were defined by the Selective Service as a person "who, by reason of religious training and belief, is conscientiously opposed to participation in war in any form."

In the military hospitals, American nurses supplied the bulk of care to recovering soldiers. Before World War II, the Army Nurse Corps, created in 1901, was scarcely a military organization, with recruits earning neither military pay nor rank. To overcome the short supply of nurses, Congress extended military rank to nurses in 1944, although only for the duration and for six months after the war ended. In 1945 Congress came close to passing a bill to draft nurses. Like medics, army nurses went first to training centers in the United States, learning how to dig foxholes and dodge bullets before being sent overseas. By 1945, approximately 56,000 women, including 500 African American women, were on active duty in the Army Nurse Corps, staffing medical facilities in every theater of the war.

Prisoners of War

Approximately 120,000 Americans became prisoners of war (POWs). Those captured by the Germans were taken back to camps—*Olfags* for officers or *Stalags* for enlisted men—where they sat out the remainder of the war, mainly fighting boredom. Registered by the Swiss Red Cross, they could receive packages of supplies and occasionally join work brigades. By contrast, Russian POWs were starved and occasionally murdered in German camps.

Conditions for POWs in the Pacific were, however, worse than abysmal. Of the 20,000 Americans captured in the Philippines early in the war, only 40 percent survived to return home in 1945. At least 6,000 American and Filipino prisoners, beaten and denied food and water, died on the notorious eighty-mile "Death March" through the jungles on the Bataan Peninsula in 1942. After the survivors reached the former U.S. airbase Camp O'Donnell, hundreds died weekly in a cesspool of disease and squalor.

The Japanese army felt only contempt for POWs; its own soldiers evaded capture by killing themselves. The Imperial Army assigned its most brutal troops to guard prisoners and imposed strict and brutal discipline in the camps. In a postwar survey, 90 percent of former POWs from the Pacific reported that they had been beaten. A desire for retribution, as well as racist attitudes, prompted GIs to treat Japanese prisoners far more brutally than enemy soldiers captured in Europe or Africa.

A painting by Sidney Simon of American POWs freed from Japanese captors at Bilibid prison,
in Manila, 1945, after the U.S. reconquest of the Philippines. The battle of the Philippine Sea
and the battle of Leyte Gulf during the previous year had nearly broken Japanese resistance in the area,
but the clean-up process revealed the awful price that Americans and their Filippino allies had paid.
As prisoners of war, they had suffered terribly from malnutrition and improperly attended wounds
and from an unsparing and inhumane Japanese military code of behavior.

SOURCE: Sidney Simon, *P.O.W.s at Bilibid Prison*, 1945. Oil on canvas, 25 × 30 inches. Center of Military History,
U.S. Army.

THE WORLD AT WAR

During the first year of declared war, the Allies remained
on the defensive. Hitler's forces held the European Continent and pounded England with aerial bombardments while
driving deep into Russia and across northern Africa to take
the Suez Canal. The situation in the Pacific was scarcely better. Just two hours after the attack on Pearl Harbor, Japanese planes struck the main U.S. base in the Philippines and
demolished half the air force commanded by General
Douglas MacArthur. Within a short time, MacArthur was
forced to withdraw his troops to the Bataan Peninsula,
admitting that Japan had practically seized the Pacific. Roosevelt called the news "all bad," and his military advisers
predicted a long fight to victory (see Map 25.1).

But the Allies enjoyed several important advantages:
vast natural resources and a skilled workforce with sufficient reserves to accelerate the production of weapons

MAP EXPLORATION

To explore an interactive version of this map, go to **www.prenhall.com/faragher5/map25.1**

	Axis powers before World War II
	Extent of Axis control early Nov. 1942
	Allies
	Neutral nations
↖	Allied Troop movements
✹	Major battles/ Allied victories

MAP 25.1 The War in Europe The Allies remained on the defensive during the first years of the war, but by 1943 the British and Americans, with an almost endless supply of resources, had turned the tide.

and ammunitions; the determination of millions of antifascists throughout Europe and Asia; and the capacity of the Soviet Union to endure immense losses. Slowly at first, but then with quickening speed, these advantages made themselves felt.

Soviets Halt Nazi Drive

The weapons and tactics of World War II were radically different from those of World War I. Unlike World War I, which was fought by immobile armies kept in trenches by bursts of machine-gun fire, World War II was a war of offensive maneuvers punctuated by surprise attacks. Its chief weapons were tanks and airplanes, combining mobility and concentrated firepower. Also of major importance were artillery and explosives, which according to some estimates accounted for over 30 percent of the casualties. Major improvements in communication systems, mainly two-way radio transmission and radiotelephony that permitted commanders to stay in contact with division leaders, also played a decisive role from the beginning of the war.

Early on, Hitler had used these methods to seize the advantage, purposefully creating terror among the stricken populations of western Europe as he routed their armies. The Royal Air Force, however, fought the Luftwaffe to a standstill in the Battle of Britain, frustrating Hitler's hopes of invading England. In the summer of 1941, he turned his attention to the east, hoping to invade and conquer the Soviet Union before the United States entered the war. But he had to delay the invasion in order to support Mussolini, whose weak army had been pushed back in North Africa and Greece. The attack on Russia did not come until June 22, six weeks later than planned and too late to achieve its goals before the brutal Russian winter began.

The burden of the war now fell on the Soviet Union. From June to September, Hitler's forces overran the Red Army, killing or capturing nearly 3 million soldiers and leaving thousands to die from exposure or starvation. But Nazi commanders did not count on civilian resistance. The Soviets rallied, cutting German supply lines and sending every available resource to Soviet troops concentrated just outside Moscow. After furious fighting and the onset of severe winter weather, the Red Army launched a massive counterattack, catching the freezing German troops off guard. For the first time, the Nazi war machine suffered a major setback.

Turning strategically away from Moscow, during the summer of 1942 German troops headed toward Crimea and the rich oil fields of the Caucasus. Still set on conquering the Soviet Union and turning its vast resources to his own use, Hitler decided to attack Stalingrad, a major industrial city on the Volga River. The Soviets suffered more casualties during the following battles than Americans did during the entire war. But intense house-to-house and street fighting and a massive Soviet counteroffensive took an even greater toll on the Nazi fighting machine. By February 1943, the German Sixth Army had met defeat, overpowered by Soviet troops and weapons. More than 100,000 German soldiers surrendered.

Already in retreat but plotting one last desperate attempt to halt the Red Army, the Germans threw most of their remaining armored vehicles into action at Kursk, in the Ukraine, in July 1943. The clash quickly developed into the greatest land battle in history. More than 2 million troops and 6,000 tanks went into action. After another stunning defeat, the Germans had decisively lost the initiative. Their only option was to delay the advance of the Red Army against their homeland.

Meanwhile, the Soviet Union had begun to recover from its early losses, even as tens of millions of its own people remained homeless and near starvation. Assisted by the U.S. Lend-Lease program, by 1942 the Soviets were outproducing Germany in many types of weapons and other supplies. Nazi officers and German civilians alike began to doubt that Hitler could win the war. The Soviet victories had turned the tide of the war.

The Allied Offensive

In the spring of 1942, Germany, Italy, and Japan commanded a territory extending from France to the Pacific Ocean. They controlled central Europe and a large section of the Soviet Union as well as considerable parts of China and the southwestern Pacific. But their momentum was flagging. American shipbuilding outpaced the punishment Nazi submarines inflicted on Allied shipping, and sub-sinking destroyers greatly reduced the submarines' threat. The United States far outstripped Germany in the production of landing craft and amphibious vehicles, two of the most important innovations of the war. Also outnumbered by the Allies, the German air force was limited to defensive action. On land, the United States and Great Britain had the trucks and jeeps to field fully mobile armies, while German troops marched in and out of Russia with packhorses.

Still, German forces represented a mighty opponent on the European Continent. Fighting the Nazis almost alone, the Soviets repeatedly appealed for the creation of a Second Front, an Allied offensive against Germany from the west. The Allies focused instead on securing North Africa and then on an invasion of Italy, hoping to move from there into central Europe.

On the night of October 23–24, 1942, near El Alamein in the desert of western Egypt, the British Eighth Army halted a major offensive by the German Afrika Korps, headed by General Erwin Rommel, the famed "Desert Fox." Although suffering heavy losses—approximately 13,000 men and more than 500 tanks—British forces destroyed the Italian North African Army and much of Germany's Afrika Korps. Americans entered the war in Europe as part of Operation Torch, the landing of British and

American troops on the coast of Morocco and Algeria in November 1942, the largest amphibious military landing to that date. The Allies then fought their way along the coast, entering Tunis in triumph six months later. With the surrender of a quarter-million Germans and Italians in Tunisia in May 1943, the Allies controlled North Africa and had a secure position in the Mediterranean. During the North African campaign, the Allies announced that they would accept nothing less than the unconditional surrender of their enemies. In January 1943, Roosevelt and Churchill had met in Casablanca in Morocco and ruled out any possibility of negotiation with the Axis powers. Roosevelt's supporters hailed the policy as a clear statement of goals, a promise to the world that the scourge of fascism would be completely banished. Stalin, who did not attend the meeting, criticized the policy, fearing that it would only increase the enemy's determination to fight to the end. Other critics similarly charged that the demand for total capitulation would serve to prolong the war and lengthen the casualty list.

Allied aerial bombing further increased pressure on Germany. Many U.S. leaders believed that in the B-17 Flying Fortress, the air force possessed the ultimate weapon, "the mightiest bomber ever built." The U.S. Army Air Corps described this bomber as a "humane" weapon, capable of hitting specific military targets and sparing the lives of civilians. But when weather or darkness required pilots to depend on radar for sightings, they couldn't distinguish clearly between factories and schools or between military barracks and private homes, and bombs might fall within a range of nearly two miles from the intended target. American pilots preferred to bomb during daylight hours, while the British bombed during the night. Bombing missions over the Rhineland and the Ruhr successfully took out many German factories. But the Germans responded by relocating their plants, often dispersing light industry to the countryside.

Determined to break German resistance, the Royal Air Force redirected its main attack away from military sites to cities, including fuel dumps and public transportation. Hamburg was practically leveled. Between 60,000 and 100,000 people were killed, and 300,000 buildings were destroyed. Sixty other cities were hit hard, leaving 20 percent of Germany's total residential area in ruins. The very worst air raid of the war—650,000 incendiary bombs dropped on the city of Dresden, destroying 8 square miles and killing 135,000 civilians—had no military value.

The Allied strategic air offensive weakened the German economy and undermined civilian morale. Moreover, in trying to defend German cities and factories, the Luftwaffe sacrificed many of its fighter planes. When the Allies finally invaded western Europe in the summer and fall of 1944, they would enjoy superiority in the air.

The Allied Invasion of Europe

During the summer of 1943, the Allies began to advance on southern Italy. On July 10, British and American troops stormed Sicily from two directions and conquered the island in mid-August. King Vittorio Emmanuel dismissed Mussolini, calling him "the most despised man in Italy," and Italians, by now disgusted with the Fascist government, celebrated in the streets. Italy surrendered to the Allies on September 8, and Allied troops landed on the southern Italian peninsula. But Hitler sent new divisions into Italy, occupied the northern peninsula, and effectively stalled the Allied campaign. When the European war ended, the German and Allied armies were still battling on Italy's rugged terrain.

Elsewhere in occupied Europe, armed uprisings against the Nazis spread. The brutalized inhabitants

As part of the air war on Germany, Allied bombers launched a devastating attack on Dresden, a major economic center, in February 1945. Of the civilians who died, most from burns or smoke inhalation during the firestorm, a large number were women and children, refugees from the Eastern Front. The city was left in ruins.

SOURCE: Fred Ramage. Getty Images Inc. - Hulton Archive Photos.

of Warsaw's Jewish ghetto repeatedly rose up against their tormentors during the winter and spring of 1943. Realizing that they could not hope to defeat superior forces, they finally sealed off their quarter, executed collaborators, and fought invaders, street by street and house by house. Scattered revolts followed in the Nazi labor camps, where military prisoners of war and civilians were being worked to death on starvation rations.

Partisans were active in many sections of Europe, from Norway to Greece and from Poland to France. Untrained and unarmed by any military standard, organized groups of men, women, and children risked their lives to distribute antifascist propaganda, taking action against rich and powerful Nazi collaborators. They smuggled food and weapons to clandestine resistance groups and prepared the way for Allied offensives. As Axis forces grew weaker and partially withdrew, the partisans worked more and more openly, arming citizens to fight for their own freedom.

Meanwhile, Stalin continued to push for a second front. Stalled in Italy, the Allies prepared in early 1944 for Operation Overlord, a campaign to retake the Continent with a decisive counterattack through France. American and British forces began by filling the southern half of England with military camps. All leaves were canceled. New weapons, such as amphibious armored vehicles, were carefully camouflaged. Fortunately, Hitler had few planes or ships left, so the Germans could defend the coast only with fixed bunkers whose location the Allies ascertained. Operation Overlord began with a preinvasion air assault that dropped 76,000 tons of bombs on Nazi targets.

The Allied invasion finally began on "D-Day," June 6, 1944. Under steady German fire the Allied fleet brought to the shores of Normandy more than 175,000 troops and more than 20,000 vehicles—an accomplishment unimaginable in any previous war. Although the Germans had responded slowly, anticipating an Allied strike at Calais instead of Normandy, at Omaha Beach they had prepared their defense almost perfectly. Wave after wave of Allied landings met machine-gun and mortar fire, and the tides filled with corpses and those pretending to be dead. Some 2,500 troops died, many before they could fire a shot. Nevertheless, in the next six weeks,

D-Day landing, June 6, 1944, marked the greatest amphibious maneuver in military history. Troop ships ferried Allied soldiers from England to Normandy beaches. Within a month, nearly 1 million men had assembled in France, ready to retake western and central Europe from German forces.

SOURCE: © Bettmann/Corbis.

nearly 1 million more Allied soldiers came ashore, broke out of Normandy, and prepared to march inland.

As the fighting continued, all eyes turned to Paris, the premier city of Europe. Allied bombers pounded factories producing German munitions on the outskirts of the French capital. As dispirited German soldiers retreated, many now hoping only to survive, the French Resistance unfurled the French flag at impromptu demonstrations on Bastille Day, July 14. On August 10, railway workers staged one of the first successful strikes against Nazi occupiers, and three days later the Paris police defected to the Resistance, which proclaimed in leaflets that "the hour of liberation has come." General Charles de Gaulle, accompanied by Allied troops, arrived in Paris on August 25 to become president of the reestablished French Republic.

One occupied European nation after another now swiftly fell to the Allied armies. But the Allied troops had only reached a resting place between bloody battles.

The High Cost of European Victory

In September 1944 Allied commanders searched for a strategy to end the war quickly. Missing a spectacular chance to move through largely undefended territory and on to Berlin, they turned north instead, intending to open the Netherlands for Allied armies on their way to Germany's industrial heartland. Faulty intelligence reports overlooked a well-armed German division at Arnhem, Holland, waiting to cut Allied paratroopers to pieces. By the end of the battle, the Germans had captured 6,000 Americans.

In a final, desperate effort to reverse the Allied momentum, Hitler directed his last reserves, a quarter-million men, at Allied lines in the Belgian forest of the Ardennes. In what is known as the Battle of the Bulge, the Germans took the Allies by surprise, driving them back 50 miles before they were stopped. This last effort—the bloodiest single campaign Americans had been involved in since the battle of Gettysburg—exhausted the German capacity for counterattack. After Christmas Day 1944, the Germans fell back, retreating into their own territory.

The end was now in sight. In March 1945 the Allies rolled across the Rhine and took the Ruhr Valley with its precious industrial resources. The defense of Germany, now hopeless, had fallen into the hands of young teenagers and elderly men. By the time of the German surrender, May 8, Hitler had committed suicide in a Berlin bunker and high Nazi officials were planning their escape routes. The casualties of the Allied European campaign had been enormous, if still small compared to those of the Eastern Front: more than 200,000 killed and almost 800,000 wounded, missing, or dead in non-battle accidents and unrelated illness.

The War in Asia and the Pacific

The war that had begun with Pearl Harbor rapidly escalated into scattered fighting across a region of the world far larger than all of Europe, stretching from Southeast Asia to the Aleutian Islands. Japan followed up its early advantage by cutting the supply routes between Burma and China, crushing the British navy, and seizing the Philippines, Hong Kong, Wake Island, British Malaya, and Thailand. Although China offically joined the Allies on December 9, 1941, and General Stillwell arrived in March as commander of the China-Burma-India theater, the military mission there remained on the defensive. Meanwhile, after tenacious fighting on the Bataan Peninsula and on the island of Corregidor, the U.S. troops not captured or killed retreated to Australia (see Map 25.2).

At first, nationalist and anticolonial sentiment played into Japanese hands. Japan succeeded with only 200,000 men because so few inhabitants of the imperial colonies of Britain and France would fight to defend them. Japan installed puppet "independent" governments in Burma and the Philippines. But the new Japanese empire proved terrifyingly cruel. A panicky exodus of refugees precipitated a famine in Bengal, India, which took nearly 3,500,000 lives in 1943. Nationalists from Indochina to the Philippines turned against the Japanese, establishing guerrilla armies that cut Japanese supply lines and prepared the way for Allied victory.

Six months after the disaster at Pearl Harbor, the United States began to regain naval superiority in the central Pacific and halt Japanese expansion. In an aircraft carrier duel with spectacular aerial battles during the Battle of the Coral Sea on May 7 and 8, the United States blocked a Japanese threat to Australia. A month later, the Japanese fleet converged on Midway Island, which was strategically vital to American communications and the defense of Hawai'i. American strategists, however, thanks to specialists who had broken Japanese codes, knew when and where the Japanese planned to attack. The two carrier fleets, separated by hundreds of miles, clashed at the Battle of Midway on June 4. American planes sank four of Japan's vital aircraft carriers and destroyed hundreds of planes, ending Japan's offensive threat to Hawai'i and the west coast of the United States.

But the war for the Pacific was far from over. By pulling back their offensive perimeter, the Japanese concentrated their remaining forces. Their commanders calculated that bitter fighting, with high casualties on both sides, would wear down the American troops. The U.S. command, divided between General Douglas MacArthur in the southwest Pacific and Admiral Chester Nimitz in the central Pacific, needed to develop a counterstrategy to strangle the Japanese import-based economy and to retake strategic islands closer to the homeland.

The Allies launched their counteroffensive campaign on the Solomon Islands and Papua, near New Guinea. American and Australian ground forces fought together through the jungles of Papua, while the marines prepared to attack the Japanese stronghold of Guadalcanal. American forces ran low on food and ammunition during the fierce six-month struggle on Guadalcanal, while the Japanese were reduced to eating roots and berries. American logistics were not always well planned: a week before Christmas in the subtropical climate, a shipment of winter coats arrived! But with strong supply lines secured in a series of costly naval battles, the Americans were finally victorious in February 1943, proving that they could defeat Japanese forces in brutal jungle combat.

For the next two years, the U.S. Navy and Marine Corps, in a strategy known as "island hopping," pushed to capture a series of important atolls from their well-armed Japanese defenders and open a path to Japan. The first of these assaults, which cost more than 1,000 marines their lives, was on Tarawa, in November 1943, in the Gilbert Islands. In subsequent battles in 1944, American forces occupied Guam, Saipan, and Tinian in the Marianas Islands, within air range of the Japanese home islands. In another decisive naval engagement, the Battle of the Philippine Sea, fought in June 1944, the Japanese fleet suffered a crippling loss.

In October 1944, General MacArthur led a force of 250,000 to retake the Philippines. In a bid to defend the islands, practically all that remained of the Japanese navy threw itself at the American invaders in the Battle of Leyte Gulf, the largest naval battle in history. The Japanese lost eighteen ships, leaving the United States in control of the

Pacific. While MacArthur continued to advance toward Luzon, the marines waged a successful battle on the small but important island of Iwo Jima. The death toll, however, was high, with casualties estimated at nearly 27,000. The ground fighting in the Philippines, meanwhile, cost 100,000 Filipino civilians their lives and left Manila devastated.

The struggle for the island of Okinawa, 350 miles southwest of the home islands of Japan and the site of vital airbases, proved even more bloody. The invasion of the island, which began on Easter Sunday, April 1, 1945, was the largest amphibious operation mounted by Americans in the Pacific war. It was met by waves of Japanese

kamikaze ("divine wind") pilots flying suicide missions in planes with a 500-pound bomb and only enough fuel for a one-way flight. On the ground, U.S. troops used flame-throwers, each with three hundred gallons of napalm, against the dug-in Japanese. More Americans died or were wounded here than at Normandy. By the end of June, the Japanese had lost 140,000, including 42,000 civilians.

With the war over in Europe, the Allies concentrated on Japan, and their air and sea attacks on mainland Japan began to take their toll. U.S. submarines drastically reduced the ability of ships to reach Japan with supplies. Since the taking of Guam, American

MAP EXPLORATION

To explore an interactive version of this map, go to **www.prenhall.com/faragher5/map25.2**

MAP 25.2 War in the Pacific Across an ocean battlefield utterly unlike the European theater, Allies battled Japanese troops near their homeland.

bombers had been able to reach Tokyo and other Japanese cities, with devastating results. Massive fire bombings burned thousands of civilians alive in their mostly wood or bamboo homes and apartments and left hundreds of thousands homeless.

Japan could not hold out forever. Without a navy or air force, the government could not transport the oil, tin, rubber, and grain needed to maintain its soldiers. Great Britain and particularly the United States, however, pressed for quick unconditional surrender. They had special reasons to hurry. Earlier they had sought a commitment from the Soviet Union to invade Japan, but now they looked beyond the war, determined to prevent the Red Army from taking any territories held by the Japanese. These calculations and the anticipation that an invasion would be extremely bloody set the stage for the use of a secret weapon that American scientists had been preparing: the atomic bomb.

THE LAST STAGES OF WAR

From the attack on Pearl Harbor until mid-1943, President Roosevelt and his advisers had focused on military strategy rather than on plans for peace. But once the defeat of Nazi Germany appeared in sight, high government officials began to reconsider their diplomatic objectives. Roosevelt wanted both to crush the Axis powers and to establish a system of collective security to prevent another world war. He knew he could not succeed without the cooperation of the other key leaders, Stalin and Churchill.

During 1944 and 1945, the "Big Three" met to hammer out the shape of the postwar world. Although none of these nations expected to reach a final agreement, neither did they anticipate how quickly they would be confronted with momentous global events. It soon became clear that the only thing holding the Allies together was the mission of destroying the Axis.

The Holocaust

Not until the last stages of the war did Americans learn the extent of Hitler's atrocities. As part of his "final solution to the Jewish question," Hitler had ordered the systematic extermination of not only Jews, but Gypsies, other "inferior races,"

homosexuals, and anyone deemed an enemy of the Reich. Beginning in 1933, and accelerating after 1941, the Nazis murdered as many as 6 million Jews, 250,000 Gypsies, and 60,000 homosexuals, among others.

During the war the U.S. government released little information on what came to be known as the Holocaust. Although liberal magazines such as the *Nation* and small committees of intellectuals tried to call attention to what was happening in German concentration camps, major news media like the *New York Times* and *Time* magazine treated reports of Nazi genocide as minor news items. The experience of World War I, during which the press had published stories of German atrocities that proved in most cases to have been fabricated by the British, had bred a skeptical attitude in the American public. As late as 1943, only 43 percent of Americans polled believed that Hitler was systematically murdering European Jews.

Leaders of the American Jewish community, however, were better informed than the general population, and since the mid-1930s had been petitioning the government to suspend the immigration quotas to allow German Jews to take refuge in the United States. Both Roosevelt and Congress denied their requests. Even after the United States entered the war, the president maintained that the liberation of European Jews depended primarily on a speedy and total Allied victory. In December 1942 he brushed off a delegation

Belsen Camp: The Compound for Women, painted by American artist Leslie Cole, depicts Belsen as the Allied troops found it when they invaded Germany in 1945.

SOURCE: Leslie Cole, *Belsen Camp: The Compound for Women.* Imperial War Museum, London.

that presented him with solid evidence of Nazi genocide. Not until January 1944 did Roosevelt agree to change government policy. At that time, Secretary of the Treasury Henry Morgenthau, a Jew himself, gave the president a report on "one of the greatest crimes in history, the slaughter of the Jewish people in Europe," and suggested that it was anti-Semitism in the State Department that had stalled the development of an aggressive plan of action. Within a week, in part to avoid scandal, Roosevelt issued an executive order creating the War Refugee Board.

American Jews also pleaded with the president for a military strike against the rail lines leading to the notorious extermination camp in Auschwitz, Poland. Roosevelt again did not respond. The War Department, however, affirmed that Allied armed forces would not be employed "for the purpose of rescuing victims of enemy oppression unless such rescues are the direct result of military operations conducted with the objective of defeating the armed forces of the enemy." In short, the government viewed civilian rescue as a diversion from decisive military operations.

The extent of Nazi depravity was finally revealed to Americans when Allied troops invaded Germany and liberated the death camps. Touring the Ohrdruf concentration camp in April 1945, General Eisenhower found barracks crowded with corpses and crematories still reeking of burned flesh. "I want every American unit not actually in the front lines to see this place," Eisenhower declared. "We are told that the American soldier does not know what he is fighting for. Now, at least, he will know what he is fighting against."

The Yalta Conference

In preparing for the end of the war, Allied leaders began to reassess their goals. The Atlantic Charter, drawn up before the United States had entered the war, stated noble objectives for the world after the defeat of fascism: national self-determination, no territorial aggrandizement, equal access of all peoples to raw materials and collaboration for the improvement of economic opportunities, freedom of the seas, disarmament, and "freedom from fear and want." Now, four years later, Roosevelt—ill and exhausted—realized that neither Great Britain nor the Soviet Union intended to abide by any code of conduct that compromised its national security or conflicted with its economic interests in other nations or in colonial territories. Stalin and Churchill soon reached a new agreement, one that projected their respective "spheres of influence" over the future of central Europe.

In early February 1945, Roosevelt held his last meeting with Churchill and Stalin at Yalta, a Crimean resort on the Black Sea. Seeking their cooperation, the pres-

ident recognized that prospects for postwar peace also depended on compromise. Although diplomats avoided the touchy phrase "spheres of influence"—the principle according to which the great powers of the nineteenth century had described their claims to dominance over other nations—it was clear that this principle guided all negotiations. Neither the United States nor Great Britain did more than object to the Soviet Union's plan to retain the Baltic states and part of Poland as a buffer zone to protect it against any future German aggression. In return, Britain planned to reclaim its empire in Asia, and the United States hoped to hold several Pacific islands in order to monitor any military resurgence in Japan. The delegates also negotiated the terms of membership in the United Nations, which had been outlined at a meeting several months earlier.

The biggest and most controversial item on the agenda at Yalta was the Soviet entry into the Pacific war, which Roosevelt believed necessary for a timely Allied victory. After driving a hard bargain involving rights to territory in China, Stalin agreed to declare war against Japan within two or three months of Germany's surrender.

Roosevelt announced to Congress that the Yalta meeting had been a "great success," proof that the wartime alliance remained intact. Privately, however, the president concluded that the outcome of the conference revealed that the Atlantic Charter had been nothing more than "a beautiful idea."

The death of Franklin Roosevelt of a stroke on April 12, 1945, cast a dark shadow over all hopes for long-term, peaceful solutions to global problems. Stung by a Republican congressional comeback in 1942, Roosevelt had rebounded in 1944 to win an unprecedented fourth term as president. In an overwhelming electoral college victory (432 to 99), he had defeated Republican New York governor Thomas E. Dewey. Loyal Democrats continued to link their hopes for peace to Roosevelt's leadership, but the president did not live to witness the surrender of Germany on May 8, 1945. And now, as new and still greater challenges were appearing, the nation's great pragmatic idealist was gone.

The Atomic Bomb

Roosevelt's death made cooperation among the Allied nations much more difficult. His successor, Harry Truman, who had been a Kansas City machine politician, a Missouri judge, and a U.S. senator, lacked diplomatic experience as well as Roosevelt's personal finesse. As a result, negotiations at the Potsdam Conference, held just outside Berlin from July 17 to August 2, 1945, lacked the spirited cooperation characteristic of the wartime meetings of Allied leaders that Roosevelt had attended. The American, British, and Soviet delegations

CHRONOLOGY

1931 September: Japan occupies Manchuria

1933 March: Adolf Hitler seizes power

May: Japan quits League of Nations

1935 October: Italy invades Ethiopia

1935– Neutrality Acts authorize the president to block
1937 the sale of munitions to belligerent nations

1937 August: Japan invades China

October: Franklin D. Roosevelt calls for international cooperation against aggression

1938 March: Germany annexes Austria

September: Munich Agreement lets Germany annex Sudetenland of Czechoslovakia

November: *Kristallnacht*, Nazis attack Jews and destroy Jewish property

1939 March: Germany annexes remainder of Czechoslovakia

August: Germany and the Soviet Union sign nonaggression pact

September: Germany invades Poland; World War II begins

November: Soviet Union invades Finland

1940 April–June: Germany's *Bliztkrieg* sweeps over Western Europe

September: Germany, Italy, and Japan—the Axis powers—conclude a military alliance

First peacetime military draft in American history

November: Roosevelt is elected to an unprecedented third term

1941 March: Lend-Lease Act extends aid to Great Britain

May: German troops secure the Balkans

A. Philip Randolph plans March on Washington movement for July

June: Germany invades Soviet Union

Fair Employment Practices Committee formed

August: The United States and Great Britain agree to the Atlantic Charter

December: Japanese attack Pearl Harbor; United States enters the war

1942 January: War mobilization begins

February: Executive order mandates internment of Japanese Americans

May–June: Battles of Coral Sea and Midway give the United States naval superiority in the Pacific

August: Manhattan Project begins

November: United States stages amphibious landing in North Africa; Operation Torch begins

1943 January: Casablanca Conference announces unconditional surrender policy

February: Soviet victory over Germans at Stalingrad

April–May: Coal miners strike

May: German Afrika Korps troops surrender in Tunis

July: Allied invasion of Italy

Summer: Race riots break out in nearly fifty cities

1944 June–August: Operation Overlord and liberation of Paris

November: Roosevelt elected to fourth term

1945 February: Yalta Conference renews American-Soviet alliance

February–June: United States captures Iwo Jima and Okinawa in Pacific

April: Roosevelt dies in office; Harry Truman becomes president

May: Germany surrenders

July–August: Potsdam Conference

August: United States drops atomic bombs on Hiroshima and Nagasaki; Japan surrenders had a huge agenda, including reparations, the future of Germany, and the status of other Axis powers such as Italy. Although they divided sharply over most issues, they held fast to the demand of Japan's unconditional surrender.

It was during the Potsdam meetings that Truman first learned about the successful testing of an atomic bomb in New Mexico. Until this time, the United States had been pushing the Soviet Union to enter the Pacific war as a means to avoid a costly U.S. land invasion, and at Potsdam Truman secured Stalin's promise to be in the war against Japan by August 15. But after Secretary of War Stimson received a cable reading "Babies satisfactorily born," U.S. diplomats concluded that Soviet assistance was no longer needed to bring the war to an end.

On August 3, 1945, Japan wired its refusal to surrender. Three days later, the Army Air Force B-29 bomber *Enola Gay* dropped the bomb that destroyed the Japanese city of Hiroshima. As estimated 40,000 people died instantly; in the following weeks 100,000 more died from radiation poisoning or burns; by 1950 the death toll reached 200,000.

An editorialist wrote in the Japanese *Nippon Times*, "This is not war, this is not even murder; this is pure nihilism . . . a crime against God which strikes at the very basis of moral existence." In the United States, several leading religious publications echoed this view. The *Christian Century* interpreted the use of the bomb as a "moral earthquake" that made the long-denounced use of poison gas by Germany in World War I utterly insignificant by comparison. Albert Einstein, whose theories about the atom provided the foundation for Manhattan Project, observed, that the atomic bomb had changed everything except the nature of man.

Most Americans learned about the atomic bomb for the first time on August 7, when the news media reported the destruction and death it had wrought in Hiroshima. But concerns about the implications of this new weapon were soon overwhelmed by an outpouring of relief when Japan surrendered on August 14 after a second bomb destroyed Nagasaki, killing another 70,000 people.

The Allied insistence on unconditional surrender and the decision to use the atomic bomb against Japan remain two of the most controversial aspects of the war. Although Truman stated in his memoirs, written much later, that he gave the order with the expectation of saving "a half a million American lives" in

ground combat, no such official estimate exists. An intelligence document of April 30, 1946, states, "The dropping of the bomb was the pretext seized upon by all leaders as the reason for ending the war, but ¨ [even if the bomb had not been used] the Japanese would have capitulated upon the entry of Russia into the war." There is no question, however, that the use of nuclear force did strengthen the U.S. diplomatic mission. It certainly intimidated the Soviet Union, which would soon regain its status as a major enemy of the United States. Truman and his advisers in the State Department knew that their atomic monopoly could not last, but they hoped that in the meantime the United States could play the leading role in building the postwar world.

CONCLUSION

The new tactics and weapons of the Second World War, such as massive air raids and the atomic bomb, made warfare incomparably more deadly than before to both military and civilian populations. Between 40 and 50 million people died in World War II—four times the number in World War I—and half the casualties were women and children. More than 405,000 Americans died, and more than 670,000 were wounded. Although slight compared to the casualties suffered by other Allied nations—more than 20 million Soviets died during the war—the human cost of World War II for Americans was second only to that of the Civil War.

Coming at the end of two decades of resolutions to avoid military entanglements, the war pushed the nation's leaders to the center of global politics and into risky military and political alliances that would not outlive the war. The United States emerged the strongest nation in the world, but in a world where the prospects for lasting peace appeared increasingly remote. If World War II raised the nation's international commitments to a new height, its impact on ordinary Americans was not so easy to gauge. Many new communities formed as Americans migrated in mass numbers to new regions that were booming as a result of the wartime economy. Enjoying a rare moment of full employment, many workers new to well-paying industrial jobs anticipated further advances against discrimination. Exuberant at the Allies' victory over fascism and the return of the troops, the majority were optimistic as they looked ahead.

REVIEW QUESTIONS

1. Describe the response of Americans to the rise of nationalism in Japan, Italy, and Germany during the 1930s. How did President Franklin D. Roosevelt ready the nation for war?
2. What role did the federal government play in gearing up the economy for wartime production?
3. How did the war affect the lives of American women?
4. Discuss the causes and consequences of the Japanese American internment program.
5. Describe the role of popular culture in promoting the war effort at home.
6. How did military service affect the lives of those who served in World War II?
7. What were the main points of Allied military strategy in both Europe and Asia?
8. How successful were diplomatic efforts in ending the war and in establishing the terms of peace?

RECOMMENDED READING

Philip D. Beidler, *The Good War's Greatest Hits: World War II and American Remembering* (1998). Examines the popular culture produced about World War II, such as movies, photographs, cartoons, and books, to show how these sources created a lasting image of World War II as the "good war."

Allan Berube, *Coming Out under Fire: The History of Gay Men and Women in World War Two* (1990). A study of government policy toward homosexuals during the war and the formation of a gay community. Berube offers many insights into the new opportunities offered homosexuals through travel and varied companionship and the effects of sanctions against them.

Kenneth S. Davis, *FDR, the War Presdient, 1940–1943* (2000). The fifth volume in Davis's biography of Franklin D. Roosevelt, this massive text examines the president's frenetic efforts to create a coherent policy for American involvement in World War II.

Laura Hein and Mark Selden, eds., *Living With the Bomb: American and Japanese Cultural Conflict in the Nuclear Age* (1997). Essays dealing with the ambiguous legacy of the atomic bomb in both the United States and Japan. Reviews the "official story" of the bomb as the symbol of U.S. triumph in the "Good War" in light of the growing number of dissenting voices and the impact of both views on memorials and museum exhibits.

John W. Jeffries, *Wartime America: The World War II Homefront* (1996). Provides a useful synthesis of scholarship and assesses the major differences in the interpretations of leading historians.

David M. Kennedy, *The American People in World War II* (1999). The second volume in Kennedy's Pulitzer Prize-winning *Freedom from Fear*, this book examines U.S. strategy to win the war from the perspective of the nation's leader as well as its citizens. The narrative interweaves overseas military events and homefront experiences.

Gerald F. Linderman, *The World within War: America's Combat Experience in World War II* (1997). Emphasizes the less glamorous aspects of war, mainly the strains placed on the combat soldiers on the front lines. Linderman examines in especially close detail the grim experiences of army infantrymen and the marine riflemen who fought in the Pacific campaign and provides a nuanced analysis of their complex responses to the horror of war.

Katrina R. Mason, *Children of Los Alamos: An Oral History of the Town Where the Atomic Age Began* (1995). Recollections of those who spent their childhood in Los Alamos. They describe their affection for the geographical setting as well as sense of safety growing up in a community so well protected. They also comment on the ethnic diversity of those who populated the town and on the pride they took in their parents' contribution to building the bomb and ending the war.

Neil R. McMillen, ed., *Remaking Dixie: The Impact of World War II on the American South* (1997). A collection of essays on the impact of World War II on the South that pay special attention to the experiences of African Americans and women. Several authors question the degree to which Southern society was transformed by wartime mobilization.

J. Robert Moskin, *Mr. Truman's War: The Final Victories of World War II and the Birth of the Postwar World* (1996). A lively history of the final stages of World War II, including the surrender of Germany and the emergence of postwar foreign policy. Moskin provides an assessment of the impact of the war on social and economic conditions in the United States.

Eduardo Obregón Pagán, *Murder at the Sleepy Lagoon: Zoot Suits, Race, and Riot in Wartime L.A.* (2003).

Examines the 1942 murder trial of seventeen young Chicanos for an alleged gang slaying and the zoot suit riots that followed just several months later. Pagán provides a rich portrait of urban culture as well as race relations as setting for the murder and court trial.

Ronald Takaki, *Double Victory: A Multicultural History of America in World War II* (2000). A history of the war years told from the perspective of ethnically diverse Americans. Takaki examines the tension between the "good war" and the treatment of people of color and the response to the Holocaust.

Kenneth William Townsend, *World War II and the American Indian* (2000). A close study of the policies developed by the Bureau of Indian Affairs to bring American Indians into the war effort.

Emily Yellin, *Our Mothers' War: American Women at Home and at the Front During World War II* (2004). Makes a convincing case, based on a wealth of primary courses, that the war greatly changed the expectations for many American women.

For additional study resources for this chapter, go to the *Companion Website*, http://www.prenhall.com/faragher.

WHOSE HISTORY IS IT?

EXHIBITING THE ENOLA GAY

On Aug 6, 1945, at 2:45 A.M. local time, the Enola Gay, a B-29 bomber took off from the U.S. air base on Tinian Island in the western Pacific. Six and a half hours later, at 8:15 A.M. Japan time, Little Boy, an atomic bomb weighing 8000 lbs and containing destructive power equal to 12.5 kilotons of TNT was dropped and exploded a minute later over central Hiroshima. Most people exposed to thermal rays within a half-mile radius of ground zero died. Tile and glass melted; all combustible materials were consumed. Concrete buildings near ground zero had ceilings crushed and windows and doors blown off.

Specialists worked for nearly a decade to restore the components of the Enola Gay, making the B-29 bomber the museum's largest restoration project. This photograph shows the forward fuselage with bomb bay and the propellers. If fully assembled, the Enola Gay is too big and too heavy to fit in the museum.

National Air and Space Museum/Smithsonian Institution.

The scientists at Los Alamos, New Mexico took pride in the successful detonation of the atomic bomb and, like other Americans, welcomed the prospect of Japan's surrender and the end of the devastating conflict. J. Robert Oppenheimer, chief scientist of the Manhattan Project, nevertheless expressed a sentiment equally common at the time, reporting that he was a "little scared of what I have made."

More than a half-century later, Americans were no more certain about the meaning of this event. At the center of the controversy were two nagging questions: was the atomic bomb necessary to end the war quickly and to save the lives of hundreds of thousands of Americans? Was the decision to deploy the bomb morally unambiguous given the death toll of 200,000 Japanese civilians at Hiroshima and over 70,000 at Nagasaki, and the number of people who sought treatment as a result of the bombing and radiation (over 350,000 as of 1990)?

In 1994, these issues formed the backdrop of a major controversy as the curatorial staff of the Smithsonian Institution's

National Air and Space Museum (NASM) circulated their plans for an exhibition on the Enola Gay. Many veterans who had served in the Pacific, objected strongly to raising such questions—they had no doubt that Truman had made the right decision to drop the bomb to save American lives and shorten the war. Critics charged that the museum staff had crafted a lop-sided, anti-American message. A writer in Time magazine accused the curators of portraying the Japanese as "more or less innocent victims of American beastliness and lust for revenge." The nation's largest veteran organization, the American Legion, issued a public letter to President Clinton calling for the cancellation of the exhibit as planned. Eventually, the U.S. Senate passed a nonbinding resolution reminding the NASM staff of its "obligation to portray history in the proper context of the time."

On June 28, 1995 the exhibit finally opened, in greatly reduced form. The original plans for photographs of "ground zero" in Hiroshima were scrapped, and what remained were several restored components of the B-29 aircraft, such as its fuselage, propellers, and cockpit, and minimal textual explanation. "The aircraft speaks for itself in this exhibit," Smithsonian director I. Michael Heyman remarked, "and, 50 years after its mission, it continues to evoke strong emotions, in those who look at it."

A 1999 survey of public opinion showed that Americans continued to consider the atomic bombing of Japan "The Story of the Century." Likewise, most readily acknowledged the scientific importance of the Manhattan Project. Nevertheless, the larger meaning of this chapter in U.S. history remains highly controversial.

The so-called mushroom cloud has become a familiar, iconic image of the power released with the explosion of atomic bombs. Here, a photograph of the mushroom cloud from the atomic bomb Little Boy that was dropped on Hiroshima is paired with American Pop artist Andy Warhol's silk-screen on canvas, Atomic Bombs, which was produced in the 1960s. National Archives and Records Administration.

This photograph shows the Genbaku Dome, the exterior of one of the buildings in central Hiroshima to survive the bombing. After the atomic bomb fell, fires thoughout the central city combined to make a huge fire storm. A "black rain" of radioactive debris caused by the blast fell for more than a hour, covering an even wider area. More than a quarter of the city's population died immediately following the explosion, and few buildings within a radius of three miles were left standing.

Bettmann/Corbis.

Atomic age adventures were popular themes in comic books during the 1950s. *Atomic War*, which appeared at the height of the Korean War, featured atomic weapons used against Communist nations. This genre continued to be produced well into the 1960s.

The Authentic History Center

Peace activists around the world commemorate August 6th as "Hiroshima Day," whereas most Americans celebrate "Victory Over Japan Day," or V-J Day." This photograph shows demonstrators gathering at the United Nations in New York City on the fifteenth anniversary of the dropping of the atomic bomb over Japan.

AP Wide World Photos.

The Hiroshima Peace memorial Museum and Park, which is located at the city center, opened in 1955. The Genbaku Dome appears in the background of this photograph. Every year, on August 6th, people gather to offer prayers for those who died in the bombing and to express their hope for peace.

John Van Hasselt. Corbis/Sygma.

The Cold War

1945–1952

CHAPTER OUTLINE

AMERICAN COMMUNITIES

University of Washington, Seattle: Students and Faculty Face the Cold War

In May 1948, a philosophy professor at the University of Washington in Seattle answered a knock on his office door. Two state legislators, members of the state's Committee on Un-American Activities, entered. "Our information," they charged, "puts you in the center of a Communist conspiracy."

The accused professor, Melvin Rader, had never been a Communist. A self-described liberal, Rader drew fire because he had joined several organizations supported by Communists. During the 1930s, in response to the rise of Nazism and fascism, Rader had become a prominent political activist in his community. At one point he served as president of the University of Washington Teacher's Union, which had formed during the upsurge of labor organizing during the New Deal. When invited to join the Communist Party, Rader bluntly refused. "The experience of teaching social philosophy had clarified my concepts of freedom and democracy," he later explained. "I was an American in search of a way—but it was not the Communist way."

Despite this disavowal, Rader was caught up in a Red Scare that curtailed free speech and political activity on campuses throughout the United States. At some universities, such as Yale, the Federal Bureau of Investigation (FBI) set up camp with the consent of the college administration, spying on students and faculty, screening the credentials of job or scholarship applicants, and seeking to entice students to report on their friends or roommates. The University of Washington administration turned down the recommendation of the Physics Department to hire J. Robert Oppenheimer because the famed atomic scientist, and former director of Los Alamos Scientific Laboratory, had become a vocal opponent of the arms race and the proliferation of nuclear weapons.

Although one state legislator claimed that "not less than 150 members" of the University of Washington faculty were subversives, the state's Committee on Un-American Activities turned up just six members of the Communist Party. These six were brought up before the university's Faculty Committee on Tenure and Academic Freedom, charged with violations ranging from neglect of duty to failing to inform the university administration of their party membership. Three were ultimately dismissed, while the other three were placed on probation.

What had provoked this paranoia? Instead of peace in the wake of World War II, a pattern of cold war—icy relations—prevailed between the United States and the Soviet Union. Uneasy allies during World War II, the two superpowers now viewed each other as archenemies, and nearly all other nations lined up with one or the other of them. Within the United States, the cold war demanded pledges of absolute loyalty from citizens in every institution, from the university to trade unions and from the mass media and Hollywood to government itself. If not for the outbreak of the cold war, this era would have marked one of the most fruitful in the history of higher education. The Servicemen's Readjustment Act, popularly known as the G.I. Bill of Rights, passed by Congress in 1944, offered stipends covering tuition and living expenses to veterans attending vocational schools or college. By the 1947–48 academic year, the federal government was subsidizing nearly half

Seattle

780

of all male college students. Between 1945 and 1950, 2.3 million students benefited from the G.I. Bill, at a cost of more than $10 billion.

At the University of Washington the student population in 1946 had grown by 50 percent over its prewar peak of 10,000, and veterans represented fully two-thirds of the student body. A quickly expanded faculty taught into the evening to use classroom space efficiently. Meanwhile, the state legislature pumped in funds for the construction of new buildings, including dormitories and prefabricated units for married students. These war-weary undergraduates had high expectations for their new lives during peacetime.

The cold war put a damper on many such activities. FBI director J. Edgar Hoover testified that the college campuses were centers of "red propaganda," full of teachers "tearing down respect for agencies of government, belittling tradition and moral custom and . . . creating doubts in the validity of the American way of life." Due to Communistic teachers and "Communist-line textbooks," a senator lamented, thousands of parents sent "their sons and daughters to college as good Americans," only to see them return home "four years later as wild-eyed radicals."

Although these extravagant charges were never substantiated, several states, including Washington, enacted or revived loyalty-security programs, obligating all state employees to swear in writing their loyalty to the United States and to disclaim membership in any subversive organization. Nationwide, approximately 200 faculty members were dismissed outright and many others were denied tenure. Thousands of students simply left school, dropped out of organizations, or changed friends after "visits" from FBI agents or interviews with administrators. The main effect on campus was the restraint of free speech generally and fear of criticizing U.S. racial, military, or diplomatic policies in particular.

This gloomy mood reversed the wave of optimism that had swept through America only a few years earlier. V-J Day, marking victory over Japan, had erupted into a two-day national holiday of wild celebrations, complete with ticker-tape parades, spontaneous dancing, and kisses for returned G.I.s. Americans, living in the richest and most powerful nation in the world, finally seemed to have gained the peace they had fought and sacrificed to win. But peace proved fragile and elusive.

KEY TOPICS

- Prospects for world peace at end of World War II
- Diplomatic policy during the cold war
- The Truman presidency
- Anticommunism and McCarthyism
- Cold war culture and society
- The Korean War

GLOBAL INSECURITIES AT WAR'S END

The war that had engulfed the world from 1939 to 1945 created an international interdependence that no country could ignore. The legendary African American folk singer Leadbelly (Huddie Ledbetter) added a fresh lyric to an old spiritual melody: "We're in the same boat, brother. . . . And if you shake one end you're going to rock the other." Never before, not even at the end of World War I, had hopes been so strong for a genuine "community of nations." But, as a 1945 opinion poll indicated, most Americans believed that prospects for a durable peace rested to a large degree on harmony between the Soviet Union and the United States.

Financing the Future

In 1941 Henry Luce, publisher of *Time, Life,* and *Fortune* magazines, had forecast the dawn of "the American Century." Americans must, he wrote, "accept whole-heartedly our duty and our opportunity as the most powerful and vital nation in the world and in consequence to assert upon the world the full impact of our influence, for such means as we see fit." Indeed, immediately after the bombing of Hiroshima, President Truman pronounced the United States "the most powerful nation in the world—the most powerful nation, perhaps, in all history." The president and his advisors declared a definitive end to the era of isolation.

Americans had good reason to be confident about their prospects for setting the terms of reconstruction. Unlike Great Britain and France, the United States had not only escaped the ravages of the war but had actually prospered. By June 1945, the capital assets of manufacturing had increased 65 percent over prewar levels and were equal in value to approximately half the entire world's goods and services.

Yet many Americans recognized that it was the massive government spending to pay for the war— more than $340 billion— rather than New Deal programs, that had ended the nightmare of the 1930s. A great question loomed: What would happen when wartime production slowed and millions of troops returned home?

"We need markets—big markets—in which to buy and sell," answered Assistant Secretary of State for Economic Affairs Will Clayton. Just to maintain the current level of growth, the United States needed an estimated $14 billion in exports—an unprecedented amount. Many business leaders even looked to the Soviet Union as a potential trading partner. With this prospect vanishing, Eastern European markets threatened, and large chunks of former colonial territories closed off, U.S. business and government leaders became determined to integrate Western Europe and Asia into a liberal international economy open to American trade and investment.

During the final stages of the war, President Roosevelt's advisers laid plans to establish U.S. primacy in the postwar global economy. In July 1944 representatives from forty-four Allied nations met at Bretton Woods, New Hampshire, and established the International Monetary Fund (IMF) and the International Bank for Reconstruction and Development (World Bank) to help rebuild war-torn Europe and to assist development in other nations. By stabilizing exchange rates to permit the expansion of international trade, the IMF would deter currency conflicts and trade wars—two maladies of the 1930s that were largely responsible for the political instability and national rivalries leading to World War II. As the principal supplier of funds for the IMF and the World Bank—more than $7 billion to each—the United States had the greatest influence over policy, including the allocation of loans.

The Soviet Union participated in the Bretton Woods conference but refused to ratify the agreements that, in essence, allowed the United States to rebuild the world economy along capitalist lines. By spurning both the World Bank and the IMF, the Soviet Union cut off the possibility of aid to its own people as well as to its Eastern European client states and, equally important, isolated itself economically.

The Division of Europe

The Atlantic Charter of 1941 committed the Allies to recognize the right of all nations to self-determination and to renounce all claims to new territories as the spoils of war. The Allied leaders themselves, however, violated the charter's main points before the war had ended by dividing occupied Europe into spheres of influence (see Chapter 25) (see Map 26.1).

So long as Franklin Roosevelt remained alive, this strategy had seemed reconcilable with world peace. The president had balanced his own international idealism with his belief that the United States was entitled to extraordinary influence in Latin America and the Philippines and that other great powers might have similar privileges or responsibilities elsewhere. Roosevelt also recognized the diplomatic consequences of the brutal ground war that had been fought largely on Soviet territory: the Soviet Union's unnegotiable demand for territorial security along its European border.

From the early days of the war, the USSR was intent on reestablishing its 1941 borders, and by the time of the Potsdam Conference in July 1945 the Soviets had not only regained but extended their territory. Much of eastern Europe, including a large portion of Poland and the little Baltic nations, was now under its control as client states. But the question remained: Did the USSR aim to bring all of Europe into the Communist domain?

When the Allies turned to plan the future of Germany, this question loomed over all deliberations. They ultimately decided to divide the conquered nation into four occupation zones, each governed by one of the Allied nations. But the Allies could not agree on long-term plans. Having borne the brunt of German aggression, France and the USSR both opposed reunification. The latter, in addition, demanded heavy reparations along with a limit on postwar reindustrialization. Although Roosevelt appeared to agree with the Soviets, Truman shared Winston Churchill's hope of rebuilding Germany into

MAP EXPLORATION

To explore an interactive version of this map, go to **www.prenhall.com/faragher5/map26.1**

MAP 26.1 Divided Europe During the cold war, Europe was divided into opposing military alliances, the North American Treaty Organization (NATO) and the Warsaw Pact (Communist bloc).

a powerful counterforce against the Soviet Union and a strong market for U.S. and British goods.

After the war, continuing disagreements about the future Germany darkened hopes for cooperation between the Soviet Union and the United States. By July 1946, Americans had begun to withhold reparations from their zone and to institute a program of amnesty for former Nazis. Then, in December, the American and British merged their zones and extended

an invitation to France and the USSR to join. Although France accepted the offer, the Soviets, fearing a resurgence of united Germany, held out.

The United States and the Soviet Union were now at loggerheads. Twice in the twentieth century, Germany had invaded Russia, and the USSR now interpreted these moves toward German reunification an act of supreme hostility. For its part, the United States envisioned a united Germany as a bulwark against Soviet expansion.

The United Nations and Hopes for Collective Security

The dream of postwar international cooperation had been seeded earlier by President Roosevelt. In late summer and fall 1944 at the Dumbarton Oaks Conference in Washington DC, and again in April 1945 in San Francisco, the Allies worked to shape the United Nations as a world organization that would arbitrate disputes among members as well as impede aggressors, by military force if necessary.

The terms of membership, however, limited the UN's ability to mediate disputes. Although all of the fifty nations that signed the UN charter enjoyed representation in the General Assembly, only five members (the United States, Great Britain, the Soviet Union, France, and Nationalist China) served permanently on on the Security Council, which had the "primary responsibility for the maintenance of international peace and security," and each enjoyed absolute veto power over the decisions of the other members. By this arrangement, the Security Council could censure one of its members only if that nation made the unlikely decision of abstaining from voting.

The UN achieved its greatest success with its humanitarian programs. Its relief agency provided the war-torn countries of Europe and Asia with billions of dollars for medical supplies, food, and clothing. The UN also dedicated itself to protecting human rights, and its high standards of human dignity owed much to the lobbying of Eleanor Roosevelt, one of the first delegates from the United States.

On other issues, however, the UN operated strictly along lines dictated by the cold war. The Western nations allied with the United States held the balance of power and maintained their position by controlling the admission of new member nations. They successfully excluded Communist China, for example. Moreover, the polarization between East and West made negotiated settlements virtually impossible.

THE POLICY OF CONTAINMENT

With the world seemingly dividing into two hostile camps, the dream of a community of nations dissolved. But perhaps it had never been more than a fantasy contrived to maintain a fragile alliance amid the urgency of World War II. In March 1946, in a speech delivered in Fulton, Missouri, Winston Churchill spoke to the new reality. With President Harry Truman at his side, the former British prime minister declared that "an iron curtain has descended across the [European] continent." He called directly upon the United States, standing "at this time at the pinnacle of world power," to recognize its "awe-inspiring accountability to the future" and, in alliance with Great Britain, act aggressively to turn back Soviet expansion.

Although Truman at first responded cautiously to Churchill's pronouncement, within a short time he committed the United States to leadership in a world-wide struggle against the spread of communism. As a doctrine uniting military, economic, and diplomatic strategies, the "containment" of communism also fostered an ideological opposition, an "us"-versus-"them" theme that divided the world into "freedom" and "slav-

Appointed to the UN delegation by President Harry Truman in 1946, Eleanor Roosevelt (1884–1962) pressured the organization to adopt the Declaration of Human Rights in 1948. In this photograph, taken in 1946, the former First Lady is exchanging ideas with Warren Austin, also a delegate to the United Nations.

SOURCE: UPI Corbis/Bettmann.

ery," "democracy" and "autocracy," and "tolerance" and "coercive force." The Truman Doctrine laid down the first plank in a global campaign against communism.

The Truman Doctrine

Many Americans believed that Franklin D. Roosevelt, had he lived, would have been able to stem the tide of tensions between the Soviet Union and the United States. His successor sorely lacked FDR's talent for diplomacy. More comfortable with machine politicians than with polished New Dealers, the new president liked to talk tough and act defiantly. "I do not think we should play compromise any longer," Truman decided, "I'm tired of babying the Soviets."

A perceived crisis in the Mediterranean prompted President Truman to show his colors. On February 21, 1947, amid a civil war in Greece, Great Britain informed the U.S. State Department that it could no longer afford to prop up the anti-Communist government there and announced its intention to withdraw all aid. Without U.S. intervention, Truman concluded, Greece, Turkey, and perhaps the entire oil-rich Middle East would fall under Soviet control.

OVERVIEW

MAJOR COLD WAR POLICIES

Policy	Date	Provisions
Truman Doctrine	*1947*	Pledged the United States to the containment of communism in Europe and elsewhere. The doctrine was the foundation of Truman's foreign policy. It impelled the United States to support any nation whose stability was threatened by communism or the Soviet Union.
Federal Employees Loyalty and Security Program	*1947*	Established by Executive Order 9835, this barred Communists and fascists from federal employment and outlined procedures for investigating current and prospective federal employees.
Marshall Plan	*1947*	U.S. program to aid war-torn Europe, also known as the European Recovery Program. The Marshall Plan was a cornerstone in the U.S. use of economic policy to contain communism.
National Security Act	*1947*	Established Department of Defense (to coordinate the three armed services), the National Security Council (to advise the president on security issues), and the Central Intelligence Agency (to gather and evaluate intelligence data).
Smith-Mundt Act	*1948*	Launched an overseas campaign of anti-Communist propaganda.
North Atlantic Treaty Organization (NATO)	*1948*	A military alliance of twelve nations formed to deter possible aggression of the Soviet Union against Western Europe.
NSC-68	*1950*	National Security Council Paper calling for an expanded and aggressive U.S. defense policy, including greater military spending and higher taxes.
Internal Security Act (also known as the McCarran Act and the Subversive Activities Control Act)	*1950*	Legislation providing for the registration of all Communist and totalitarian groups and authorizing the arrest of suspect persons during a national emergency.
Psychological Strategy Board created	*1951*	Created to coordinate anti–Communist propaganda campaigns
Immigration and Nationality Act (also known as McCarran Walter Immigration Act)	*1952*	Reaffirmed the national origins quota system but tightened immigration controls, barring homosexuals and people considered subversive from entering the United States.

On March 12, 1947, the president made his argument before Congress: "At the present moment in world history, nearly every nation must choose between alternative ways of life. . . . One way of life is based upon the will of the majority, and is distinguished by free institutions . . . and freedom from political oppression. The second way of life is based upon the will of a minority forcibly imposed on the majority . . . and the suppression of personal freedoms." Never mentioning the Soviet Union by name, he appealed for all-out resistance to a "certain ideology" wherever it appeared in the world.

Congress approved a $400 million appropriation in aid for Greece and Turkey, which helped the monarchy and right-wing military crush the rebel movement. Truman's victory buoyed his popularity for the upcoming 1948 election. It also helped to generate popular support for his campaign to "contain" communism, both at home and abroad.

The significance of what became known as the Truman Doctrine far outlasted the events in the Mediterranean: the United States had declared its right to intervene to save other nations from communism. As early as February 1946, foreign-policy adviser George F. Kennan had sent an 8,000-word "long telegram" to the State Department insisting that Soviet fanaticism made cooperation impossible. The USSR intended to extend its realm not by military means alone, he explained, but by "subversion" within "free" nations. It was now the responsibility of the United States, Truman and his advisors insisted, to safeguard the "Free World" by diplomatic, economic, and, if necessary, military means. They had, in sum, fused anticommunism and internationalism into an aggressive foreign policy.

The Marshall Plan

The Truman Doctrine complemented the European Recovery Program, commonly known as the Marshall Plan. Introduced in a commencement speech at Harvard University on June 5, 1947, by secretary of state and former army chief of staff George C. Marshall, the plan sought to reduce "hunger, poverty, desperation, and chaos" and to restore "the confidence of the European people in the economic future of their own countries and of Europe as a whole." Indirectly, the Marshall Plan aimed to turn back both socialist and Communist electoral bids for power in northern and western Europe.

Considered by many historians the most successful postwar U.S. diplomatic venture, the Marshall Plan improved the climate for a viable capitalist economy in western Europe and, in effect, brought recipients of aid into a bilateral agreement with the United States. In addition, the western European nations, seventeen in all, ratified the General Agreement on Tariffs and Trade (GATT), which reduced commercial barriers among member nations and opened all to U.S. trade and investment. The plan was costly to Americans, in its initial year taking 12 percent of the federal budget, but effective. Industrial production in the European nations covered by the plan rose by 200 percent between 1947 and 1952. Although deflationary programs cut wages and increased unemployment, profits soared and the standard of living improved. The Marshall Plan also introduced many Europeans to American consumer goods and lifestyle.

The Marshall Plan drove a deeper wedge between the United States and the Soviet Union. Although invited to participate, Stalin denounced the plan for what it was, an American scheme to rebuild Germany and to incorporate it into an anti-Soviet bloc. The president readily acknowledged that the Marshall Plan and the Truman Doctrine were "two halves of the same walnut."

The Berlin Crisis and the Formation of NATO

As Stalin recognized, the Marshall Plan also sought to rebuild and integrate the western zones of Germany into a unified region compatible with U.S. political and economic interests. Within a year of its introduction, the United States and Britain moved closer to this goal by introducing a common currency in the western zones. Stalin reacted to this challenge on June 24, 1948, by halting all traffic to West Berlin, formally controlled by the Western allies but situated deep within the Soviet-occupied zone.

The Berlin blockade created both a crisis and an opportunity for the Truman administration to test its mettle. With help from the Royal Air Force, the United States began an around-the-clock airlift of historic proportions—Operation Vittles—that delivered nearly 2 million tons of supplies to West Berliners. The Soviet Union finally lifted the blockade in May 1949, clearing the way for the Western powers to merge their occupation zones into a single nation, the Federal Republic of West Germany. The USSR countered by establishing the German Democratic Republic in their sector.

The Berlin Crisis made a U.S.–led military alliance against the USSR attractive to western European nations. In April 1949 ten European nations, Canada, and the United States formed the North Atlantic Treaty Organization (NATO), a mutual defense pact in which "an armed attack against one or more of them . . . shall be considered an attack against them all." NATO complemented the Marshall Plan, strengthening economic ties among the member nations by, according to one analyst, keeping

Located deep within communist East Germany, West Berlin was suddenly cut off from the West when Josef Stalin blockaded all surface traffic in an attempt to take over the warn-torn city. Between June 1948 and May 1949, British and U.S. pilots made 272,000 flights, dropping food and fuel to civilians. The Berlin Airlift successfully foiled the blockade, and the Soviet Union reopened access on May 12, 1949.

SOURCE: Corbis/Bettmann.

"the Russians out, the Americans in, and the Germans down." It also deepened divisions between eastern and western Europe, making a permanent military mobilization on both sides almost inevitable.

Congress approved $1.3 billion in military aid, which involved the creation of U.S. Army bases and the deployment of American troops abroad. Critics, such as isolationist senator Robert A. Taft, warned that the United States could not afford to police all Europe without sidetracking domestic policies and undercutting the UN. But opinion polls revealed strong support for Truman's tough line against the Soviets.

Between 1947 and 1949, the Truman administration had defined the policies that would shape the cold war for decades to come. The Truman Doctrine explained the ideological basis of containment; the Marshall Plan put into place its economic underpinnings in western Europe; and NATO created the mechanisms for military enforcement. When NATO extended membership to a rearmed

West Germany in May 1955, the Soviet Union responded by creating a counterpart, the Warsaw Pact, including East Germany. The division of East and West was complete.

Atomic Diplomacy

The policy of containment depended on the ability of the United States to back up its commitments through military means, and Truman invested his faith in the U.S. monopoly of atomic weapons. The United States began to build atomic stockpiles and to conduct tests on the Bikini Islands in the Pacific. By 1950, as a scientific adviser subsequently observed, the United States "had a stockpile capable of somewhat more than reproducing World War II in a single day."

Despite warnings to the contrary by leading scientists, U.S. military analysts estimated it would take the Soviet Union three to ten years to produce an atomic bomb. In August 1949, the Soviet Union proved them wrong by testing its own atomic bomb. "There is only one thing worse than one nation having the atomic bomb," Nobel Prize-winning scientist Harold C. Urey said, "that's two nations having it."

Within a few years, both the United States and the Soviet Union had tested hydrogen bombs a thousand times more powerful than the weapons dropped on Hiroshima and Nagasaki in 1945. Both proceeded to stockpile bombs attached to missiles, inaugurating the fateful nuclear arms race that scientists had feared since 1945.

The United States and the Soviet Union were now firmly locked into the cold war. The nuclear arms race imperiled their futures, diverted their economies, and fostered fears of impending doom. Prospects for global peace had dissipated, and despite the Allied victory in World War II, the world had again divided into hostile camps.

COLD WAR LIBERALISM

Truman's aggressive, gutsy personality suited the confrontational mood of the cold war. He linked the Soviet threat in Europe to the need for a strong presidency. Pressed to establish his own political identity, "Give 'em Hell" Harry successfully portrayed himself as a fierce fighter against all challengers, yet loyal to Roosevelt's legacy.

Truman set out to enlarge the New Deal but settled on a a modest domestic agenda to promote social welfare and an antiisolationist, fiercely anti-Communist foreign policy. Fatefully, during the course of his administration, domestic and foreign policy became increasingly entangled to lay the basis of a distinctive brand of liberalism—cold war liberalism.

"To Err Is Truman"

Within a year of assuming office, Harry Truman rated lower in public approval than any twentieth-century president except Roosevelt's own predecessor, Herbert Hoover, who had been blamed for the Great Depression. The responsibilities of reestablishing peacetime conditions seemed to overwhelm the new president's administration. "To err is Truman," critics jeered.

In handling the enormous task of reconverting from a wartime to a peacetime economy, the president faced millions of restless would-be consumers tired of rationing and eager to spend their wartime savings on shiny cars, new furniture, choice cuts of meat, and colorful clothing. The demand for consumer items rapidly outran sup-

ply, fueling inflation and creating a huge black market. Truman asked Congress to extend wartime price controls, but the Republicans, backed by business leaders, refused and instead cut back the powers of the Office of Price Administration (OPA). Prices continued to skyrocket.

In 1945 and 1946, the country appeared ready to explode. While homemakers protested rising prices by boycotting neighborhood stores, industrial workers struck in unprecedented numbers. Employers, fearing a rapid decline to Depression-level profits, determined to slash wages or at least hold them steady; workers wanted a bigger cut of the huge war profits they had heard about. The spectacle of nearly 4.6 million workers on picket lines alarmed the new president. In May 1946, Truman proposed to draft striking railroad workers into the army. The usually conservative Senate killed this plan.

Congress defeated most of Truman's proposals to revive the New Deal. One week after Japan's surrender, the president introduced a twenty-one-point program that included greater unemployment compensation, higher minimum wages, and housing assistance. Later he added proposals for national health insurance and atomic energy legislation. Congress turned back the bulk of these bills, passing the Employment Act of 1946 only after substantial modification. The act created a new executive body, the Council of Economic Advisers, which would confer with the president and formulate policies for maintaining employment, production, and purchasing power. But the measure did not include funding mechanisms to guarantee full employment, thus falling far short of the bill's intent.

By 1946 Truman's popularity had dipped. Republicans, sensing victory in the upcoming off-year elections, asked the voters, "Had enough?" Apparently the voters had. They gave Republicans majorities in both houses of Congress and in the state capitols. And in a symbolic repudiation of Roosevelt, they passed an amendment to the Constitution establishing a two-term limit for the presidency.

The Republicans, dominant in Congress for the first time since 1931, prepared a counteroffensive against the New Deal, beginning with an attack on organized labor. Unions had by this time reached a peak in size and prestige, with membership topping 15 million and encompassing nearly 40 percent of all wage earners. Concluding that labor had gone too far, the Republican-dominated Eightieth Congress aimed to outlaw many practices approved by the Wagner Act of 1935 (see Chapter 24).

The Labor-Management Relations Act of 1947, better known as the Taft-Hartley Act, brought to an end the closed shop, the secondary boycott, and the use of union dues for political activities. It also mandated an eighty-day cooling-off period in the case of strikes affect-

Police and strikers confront each other in Los Angeles during one of many postwar strikes in 1946. Employers wanted to cut wages, and workers refused to give up the higher living standard achieved during the war.

SOURCE: AP/Wide World Photos.

ing national safety or health. Taft-Hartley furthermore required all union officials to swear under oath that they were not Communists—a cold war mandate that abridged freedoms ordinarily guaranteed by the First Amendment. Unions that refused to cooperate were denied the services of the National Labor Relations Board, which arbitrated strikes and issued credentials to unions.

Truman regained some support from organized labor when he vetoed the Taft-Hartley Act, saying it would "conflict with important principles of our democratic society." Congress, however, overrode his veto, and Truman himself went on to invoke the act against strikers.

The 1948 Election

Harry Truman had considered some of Roosevelt's advisers to be "crackpots and the lunatic fringe," and by 1946 had forced out most of the social planners who staffed the New Deal for over a decade. Truman also fired the secretary of commerce, Henry Wallace for advocating a more conciliatory policy toward the Soviet Union.

Wallace, however, refused to retreat and made plans to run against Truman for president. He pledged to expand New Deal programs by moving boldly to establish full employment, racial equality, and stronger labor unions. He also promised peace with the Soviet Union. As the 1948 election neared, Wallace appeared a viable candidate on the New Progressive party ticket until Truman accused him of being a tool of Communists.

In addition to Wallace, Truman had to contend with Democrats defecting from the Right. At the party convention, the Democrats endorsed a civil rights platform, proposed by liberal Minneapolis mayor Herbert Humphrey, that called on Congress to "wipe out discrimination." When the plank narrowly passed, the bulk of the conservative southern delegation bolted. Just days later, southern Democrats endorsed the States' Rights ("Dixiecrat") ticket, headed by Governor J. Strom Thurmond of South Carolina, known for his racist views. With the South as good as lost, and popular New York governor Thomas E. Dewey heading the Republican ticket, Truman appeared hopelessly far from victory.

Truman set out to reposition himself by discrediting congressional Republicans. He proposed bold programs calling for federal funds for education and new housing and a national program of medical insurance that he knew the Republicans would oppose. He also called a reluctant Congress back for a special session. On opening day, July 26, 1948, Truman signed two executive orders, one integrating the federal workforce, the other the U.S. armed forces. He then began to hammer away at the Republican controlled "do-nothing Congress."

As the election neared, "Give 'em Hell Harry" campaigned vigorously and garnered lots of grassroots support. Fear of the Republicans won back the bulk of organized labor, while the recognition of the new State of Israel in May 1948 helped prevent the defection of many liberal Jewish voters from Democratic ranks. The success of the Berlin airlift also buoyed the president's popularity. By election time, Truman had deprived Henry Wallace of nearly all his liberal support and gone far in reviving the New Deal coalition. Meanwhile, Dewey, who had run a hard-hitting campaign against Roosevelt in 1944, expected to coast to victory.

Truman won the popular vote by a margin of 5 percent and trounced Dewey 303 to 189 in the electoral college. Moreover, Democrats again had majorities in both houses of Congress. But, as it turned out, Truman had hit the highest point of his popularity and was about to begin a steady slide downhill (see Map 26.2).

The Fair Deal

"Every segment of our population and every individual has a right," Truman announced in January 1949, "to expect from our Government a fair deal." The return of Democratic congressional majorities, he hoped, would enable him to translate campaign promises into concrete legislative achievements and expand the New Deal. But a powerful bloc of conservative southern Democrats and midwestern Republicans turned back his domestic agenda (see Figure 26.1).

Truman broke no new ground. Congress passed a National Housing Act in 1949, promoting federally funded construction of low-income housing. It also raised the minimum wage from 40 to 75 cents per hour and expanded the Social Security program to cover an additional 10 million people. Otherwise, Truman made little headway. He and congressional liberals introduced a variety of bills to weaken southern segregationism: a federal antilynching law; outlawing the poll tax; prohibiting discrimination in interstate transportation. These measures were all defeated by southern-led filibusters. Proposals to create a national health insurance plan, provide federal aid for education, and repeal or modify Taft-Hartley remained bottled up in committees.

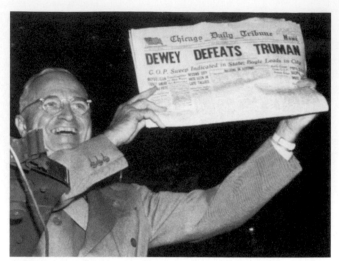

SOURCE: ©Bettmann/CORBIS.

MAP EXPLORATION

To explore an interactive version of this map, go to **www.prenhall.com/faragher5/map26.2**

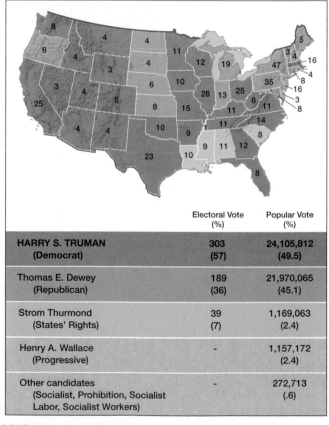

	Electoral Vote (%)	Popular Vote (%)
HARRY S. TRUMAN (Democrat)	303 (57)	24,105,812 (49.5)
Thomas E. Dewey (Republican)	189 (36)	21,970,065 (45.1)
Strom Thurmond (States' Rights)	39 (7)	1,169,063 (2.4)
Henry A. Wallace (Progressive)	–	1,157,172 (2.4)
Other candidates (Socialist, Prohibition, Socialist Labor, Socialist Workers)	–	272,713 (.6)

MAP 26.2 The Election of 1948 Harry Truman holds up a copy of the *Chicago Tribune* with headlines confidently and mistakenly predicting the victory of his opponent, Thomas E. Dewey. An initially unpopular candidate, Truman made a whistle-stop tour of the country by train to win 49.5 percent of the popular vote to Dewey's 45.1 percent.

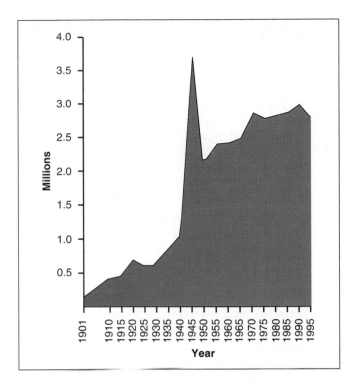

FIGURE 26.1 Number of Employees in Executive Branch, 1901–95 The federal bureaucracy, which reached a peak of nearly 4 million people during World War II, remained at unprecedentedly high levels during the cold war.

SOURCE: U.S. Bureau of the Census, *Historical Statistics of the United States, Colonial Times through 1970; Statistical Abstract of the United States, 1997.*

Truman managed best to lay out the basic principles of cold war liberalism. Toning down the rhetoric of economic equality espoused by the visionary wing of the Roosevelt coalition, his Fair Deal exalted economic growth—not the reapportionment of wealth or political power—as the proper mechanism for ensuring social harmony and national welfare. His administration insisted, therefore, on an ambitious program of expanded foreign trade, while relying on the federal government to encourage high levels of productivity at home. Equally important, Truman further reshaped liberalism by making anticommunism a key element in both foreign policy and the domestic agenda.

THE COLD WAR AT HOME

"Communists . . . are everywhere—in factories, offices, butcher shops, on street corners, in private businesses," Attorney General J. Howard McGrath warned in 1949: "At this very moment [they are] busy at work—undermining your government, plotting to destroy the liberties of every citizen, and feverishly trying in whatever way they can, to aid the Soviet Union." Republican

senator Joseph R. McCarthy even claimed to have in his personal possession a list of communists serving secretly in government agencies. By this time, the Communist Party, U.S.A., which had formed in 1919, was steadily losing ground.

Nevertheless, during the earliest days of the cold war, anticommunism already occupied center stage in domestic politics. Thus FBI director J. Edgar Hoover characteristically warned Americans not to be complacent in the face of low numbers of Communists because "for every party member there are ten others ready, willing, and able to do the Party's work" in infiltrating and corrupting "various spheres of American life." Hoover also helped to set the tone, using hyperbolic rhetoric to describe "the diabolic machinations of sinister figures engaged in un-American activities."

The federal government, with the help of the media, would lead the campaign, finding in the threat of communism a rationale for the massive reordering of its operation and the quieting of the voices of dissent. In this far-reaching quest for security, Americans moved toward a greater concentration of power in government, and, while promising to lead the "free world," allowed many of their own rights to be circumscribed.

The National Security Act of 1947

The imperative of national security destroyed old-fashioned isolation, forcing the United States into international alliances such as NATO and into the role of world leader. "If we falter in our leadership," Truman warned, "we may endanger the peace of the world—and we shall surely endanger the welfare of this nation." Such a responsibility required a massive amount of resources. Truman went on, therefore, to argue successfully that national security demanded a substantial increase in the size of the federal government, including both military forces and surveillance agencies. Security measures were required to keep the nation in a steady state of preparedness, readily justified during wartime, now extended into the very uneasy peacetime.

The National Security Act of 1947, passed by Congress in July, laid the foundation for this expansion. The act established the Department of Defense and the National Security Council (NSC) to administer and coordinate defense policies and to advise the president. The Department of Defense replaced the War Department and united the armed forces—the army, navy, and air force—under the jurisdiction of a single secretary with cabinet-level status. As result, with the distinction between citizen and soldier blurred, the ties between the armed forces and the State Department grew closer, as former military officers routinely began

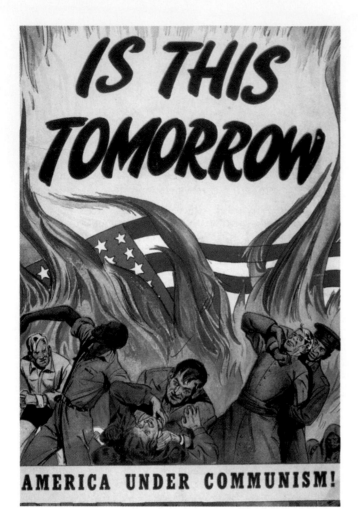

Published in 1947, this full-color comic book appeared as one of many sensationalistic illustrations of the threat of the "commie menace" to Americans at home. Approximately 4 million copies of *Is This Tomorrow?* were printed, the majority distributed to church groups or sold for ten cents a copy.

SOURCE: Michael Barson.

to fill positions in the State Department and diplomatic corps. The act also created the National Security Resources Board (NSRB) to coordinate plans throughout the government "in the event of war" and, for the first time in American history, to maintain a program of military preparedness in peacetime.

The Department of Defense, together with the NSRB, became the principal sponsor of scientific research during the first ten years of the cold war. It was commonly recognized at the time that World War II had been "a physicists' war," leading to the creation of the ultimate weapon, the atom bomb, but also to major advances in military technology in areas of systems of navigation and detection, strategic targeting, and communication. The National Science Foundation was created in 1950 for education and research, although the Office of Naval Research

conducted basic research and development on a much larger budget. Federal agencies tied to military projects meanwhile supplied well over 90 percent of funding for research in the physical sciences, a large part of the research being located in major universities.

The National Security Act added to this system of defense in 1947 by establishing the Central Intelligence Agency (CIA). With roots in the wartime Office of Strategic Services, the CIA now became a permanent operation devoted to collecting political, military, and economic information for security purposes throughout the world. Although information about the CIA was classified—that is, secret from both Congress and the public—historians have estimated that the agency soon dwarfed the State Department in number of employees and size of budget.

The national security state required a huge workforce. Before World War II, approximately 900,000 civilians worked for the federal government, with about 10 percent engaged in security work; by the beginning of the cold war, nearly 4 million people were on the government's payroll, with 75 percent working in national security agencies. The Pentagon, which had opened in 1943 as the largest office building in the world, now housed the Joint Chiefs of Staff and 35,000 military personnel.

National security took up increasingly large portions of the nation's resources. By the end of Truman's second term, defense allocations accounted for 10 percent of the gross national product, directly or indirectly employed hundreds of thousands of well-paid workers, and subsidized some of the nation's most profitable corporations. This vast financial outlay created the rationale for permanent, large-scale military spending as a basic stimulus to economic growth.

The Loyalty-Security Program

National security also required increased surveillance at home. Within two weeks of proclaiming the Truman Doctrine, the president signed Executive Order 9835 on March 21, 1947, and thereby established a loyalty program for all federal employees. The new Federal Employees Loyalty and Security Program, directed at members of the Communist Party—as well as fascists and anyone guilty of "sympathetic association" with either—in effect established a political test for federal employment. It also outlined procedures for investigating current and prospective federal employees. The loyalty review boards often asked employees about their opinions on the Soviet Union, the Marshall Plan, or NATO, or if they would report fellow workers if they found out they were Communists. Any employee could be dismissed merely on "reasonable grounds" rather than on proof of disloyalty. Later amendments added "homosexuals" as potential security risks on the grounds that they might succumb to blackmail by enemy agents.

Many state and municipal governments enacted loyalty programs and required public employees, including teachers at all levels, to sign loyalty oaths. In all, some 6.6 million people underwent loyalty and security checks. An estimated 500 government workers were fired and perhaps as many as 6,000 more chose to resign. Numerous private employers and labor unions also instituted loyalty programs.

Attorney General Clark aided this effort by publishing a list of hundreds of potentially subversive organizations selected by criteria so vague that any views "hostile or inimical to the American form of government" (as Clark's assistants noted in a memo) could make an organization liable for investigation and prosecution. There was, moreover, no right of appeal. Although designed primarily to screen federal employees, the attorney general's list effectively outlawed many political and social organizations, indirectly stigmatizing hundreds of thousands of individuals who had done nothing illegal. Church associations, civil rights organizations, musical groups, and even summer camps appeared on the list. Fraternal and social institutions, especially popular among aging European immigrants of various nationalities, were among the largest organizations destroyed. The state of New York, for example, legally dismantled the International Workers' Order, which had provided insurance to nearly 200,000 immigrants and their families. Only a handful of organizations had the funds to challenge the listing legally; most simply closed their doors.

In 1950 Congress overrode the president's veto to pass a bill that Truman called "the greatest danger to freedom of press, speech, and assembly since the Sedition Act of 1798." The Internal Security (McCarran) Act required Communist organizations to register with the Subversive Activities Control Board and authorized the arrest of suspect persons during a national emergency. The Immigration and Nationality Act, also sponsored by Republican senator Pat McCarran of Nevada and adopted in 1952, again over Truman's veto, barred people deemed "subversive" or "homosexual" from becoming citizens or even from visiting the United States. It also empowered the attorney general to deport immigrants who were members of Communist organizations, even if they had become citizens. Challenged repeatedly on constitutional grounds, the Subversive Activities Control Board remained in place until 1973, when it was terminated.

The Red Scare in Hollywood

Anti-Communist Democratic representative Martin Dies of Texas, who had chaired a congressional committee on "un-American activities" since 1938, told reporters at a press conference in Hollywood in 1944:

Hollywood is the greatest source of revenue in this nation for the Communists and other subversive groups. . . . Two elements stand out in . . . the making of pictures which extoll foreign ideology—propaganda for a cause which seeks to spread its ideas to our people[,] and the "leftist" or radical screenwriters. . . . In my opinion, [motion picture executives] will do well to halt the propaganda pictures and eliminate every writer who has un-American ideas.

A few years later, Dies's successor, J. Parnell Thomas of New Jersey directed the committee to investigate supposed Communist infiltration of the movie industry.

Renamed and made a permanent standing committee in 1945, the House Un-American Activities Committee (HUAC) had the power to subpoena witnesses and to compel them to answer all questions or face contempt of Congress charges. In well-publicized hearings held in Hollywood in October 1947, the mother of actress Ginger Rogers defended her daughter by saying that she had been duped into appearing in the pro-Soviet wartime film *Tender Comrade* (1943) and "had been forced" to read the subversive line "Share and share alike, that's democracy." HUAC encouraged such testimony by "friendly witnesses," including Ronald Reagan and Gary Cooper. The committee intimidated many others into naming former friends and co-workers.

A small but prominent minority refused to cooperate with HUAC. Known as "unfriendly witnesses," they declined to testify by claiming the freedoms of speech and association guaranteed by the First and Sixth Amendments. Several received prison sentences for contempt of Congress. A stars' delegation to "Defend the First Amendment," led by Humphrey Bogart, appeared before Congress but generated only headlines.

Hollywood studios refused to employ any writer, director, or actor who refused to cooperate with HUAC. The resulting blacklist remained in effect until the 1960s and limited the production of films dealing directly with social or political issues.

Spy Cases

In August 1948, Whittaker Chambers, a *Time* magazine editor, appeared before HUAC to name Alger Hiss as a fellow Communist in the Washington underground during the 1930s. Hiss, then president of the prestigious Carnegie Endowment for International Peace and former member of FDR's State Department, denied the charges and sued his accuser for slander. Chambers then revealed his trump card, a cache of films of secret documents—hidden in and then retrieved from a hollowed-out pumpkin on his farm in Maryland—that he claimed Hiss had passed to him for transmission to the USSR. Republican representative Richard Nixon of California described the so-called "Pumpkin Papers" as proof of "the most serious series of treasonable activities . . . in the history of America." The statute of limitations for espionage having run out, a federal grand jury in January 1950 convicted Hiss of perjury (for denying he knew Chambers), and he received a five-year prison term. Hiss was released two years later, still proclaiming his innocence.

Many Democrats, including Truman himself, at first dismissed the allegations against Hiss—conveniently publicized at the start of the 1948 election campaign—as a red herring, a Republican maneuver to gain votes. Indeed, Nixon himself circulated a pamphlet entitled *The Hiss Case* to promote his own candidacy for vice president. Nevertheless, the highly publicized allegations against Hiss proved detrimental to Democrats, suggesting that both FDR and Truman had allowed Communists to infiltrate the federal government.

The most dramatic spy case of the era involved Julius Rosenberg, former government engineer, and his wife, Ethel, who were accused of stealing and plotting to convey atomic secrets to Soviet agents during World War II. The government had only a weak case against Ethel Rosenberg, hoping that her conviction would force her husband to "break." The case against Julius Rosenberg depended on documents too highly classified to present as evidence at a public trial and therefore rested on the testimony of his supposed accomplices, some of them secretly coached by the FBI. Although the Rosenbergs maintained their innocence to the end, in March 1951 a jury found them guilty of conspiring to commit espionage. The American press showed them no sympathy, but their convictions were protested in large demonstrations in the United States and abroad. Scientist Albert Einstein, the pope, and the president of France, among many prominent figures, all pleaded for clemency. Julius and Ethel Rosenberg died in the electric chair on June 19, 1953.

McCarthyism

In a sensational Lincoln Day speech to the Republican Women's Club of Wheeling, West Virginia, on February 9, 1950, Republican senator Joseph R. McCarthy of Wisconsin announced that the United States had been sold out by the "traitorous actions" of men holding important positions in the federal government. These "bright young men who have been born with silver spoons in their mouths"—such as Secretary of State Dean Acheson, whom McCarthy called a "pompous diplomat in striped pants, with a phony English accent"—were part of a conspiracy, he charged, of 205 card-carrying Communists working in the State Department.

McCarthy refused to reveal names, however, and a few days later, after a drinking bout, he told persistent reporters: "I'm not going to tell you anything. I just want you to know I've got a pailful [of dirt] . . . and I'm going to use it where it does the most good." Although investigations uncovered not a single Communist in the State Department, McCarthy succeeded in launching a flamboyant offensive against New Deal Democrats and the Truman administration for failing to defend the nation's security. His name provided the label for the entire campaign to silence critics of the cold war: McCarthyism.

Behind the blitz of publicity, the previously obscure junior senator from Wisconsin had struck a chord. Communism seemed to many Americans to be much more than a military threat—indeed, nothing less than a demonic force capable of undermining basic values. It compelled patriots to proclaim themselves ready for atomic warfare: "Better Dead Than Red." McCarthy also had help from organizations such as the American Legion and the Chamber of Commerce, and prominent religious leaders and union leaders.

Civil rights organizations faced the severest persecution since the 1920s. The Civil Rights Congress and the Negro Youth Council, for instance, were destroyed after frequent charges of Communist influence. W. E. B. Du Bois, the renowned African American historian, and famed concert singer (and former All-American football hero) Paul Robeson had public appearances canceled and their right to travel abroad abridged.

In attacks on women's organizations and homosexual groups, meanwhile, anti-Communist rhetoric cloaked deep fears about changing sexual mores. Deputy undersecretary John Peurifoy, in defending the State Department against McCarthy's charges of Communist infiltration, boasted that its screening system was so effective that a large number of employees had already been dismissed as security risks, including more than ninety homosexuals. A short time later, a high-ranking officer in the Washington DC vice squad testified that more than 5,000 homosexuals were living in the nation's capital, three-quarters of them employees of the federal government. Some in the news media and politics responded to these revelations with alarm and called for a "purge of the perverts." A senate committee investigated homosexuality in the federal government and concluded that "sex perverts" represented a risk to national security because they were vulnerable to blackmail. Aided by the FBI, the federal government proceeded to fire up to sixty homosexuals per month in the early 1950s. Dishonorable discharges from the U.S. armed forces for homosexuality, an administrative procedure without appeal, also increased dramatically, to 2,000 per year.

Much of McCarthy's rhetoric was merely opportunistic, his campaign a ruthless attempt to gain power and fame by exploiting cold war fears. He succeeded

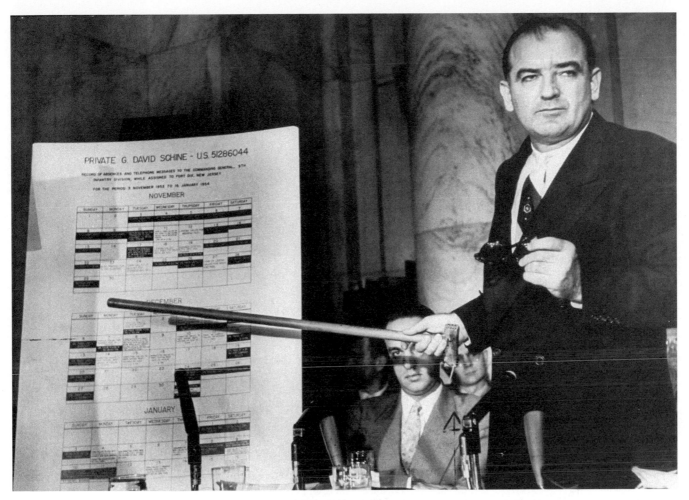

The tables turned on Senator Joseph McCarthy (1908–57) after he instigated an investigation of the U.S. Army for harboring communists. A special congressional committee then investigated McCarthy for attempting to make the Army grant special privileges to his staff aide, Private David Schine. During the televised hearings, Senator McCarthy discredited himself. In December 1954, the Senate voted to censure him, thus robbing him of his power. He died three years later.

SOURCE: Getty Images/Time Life Pictures.

partly because he brilliantly used the media to his own advantage. McCarthy also perfected the inquisitorial technique, asking directly, "Are you now, or have you ever been, a member of the Communist Party?"

Joseph McCarthy eventually brought on his own demise. In 1954 he accused several high-ranking officers in the Army of plotting subversion. During televised congressional hearings, not only did McCarthy fail to prove his wild charges, but in the glare of the television cameras he appeared deranged. Cowed for years, the Senate finally censured him for "conduct unbecoming a member." The news media quickly lost interest in him, and McCarthy succumbed to alcoholism. He died just three years later.

COLD WAR CULTURE

As the Truman Doctrine clearly specified, the cold war did not necessarily depend on military confrontation; nor was it defined exclusively by a quest for economic supremacy. The cold war embodied the struggle of one "way of life" against another. It was, in short, a contest of values. The president therefore pledged the United States to "contain" communism from spreading beyond the parameters of the Soviet Union and its client states and simultaneously called for fortifications at home. The cold war therefore required a total mobilization covering all aspects of American life, not just its formal political institutions. And to prepare Americans for this

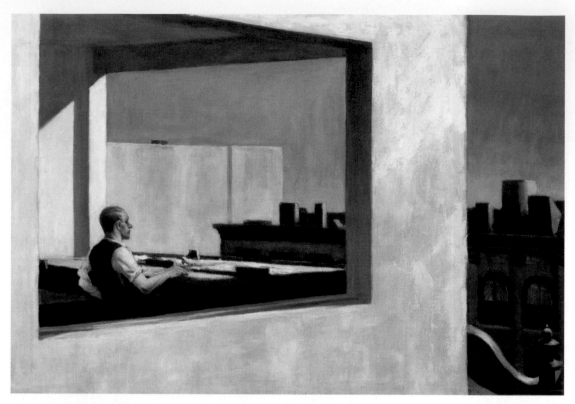

Edward Hopper (1882–1967) was the most well-known realist painter in the United States at mid-century. Many of his paintings portray the starkness and often the loneliness of American life, his cityscapes depicting empty streets or all-night restaurants where the few patrons sat at a distance from each other. This painting, owned by the Metropolitan Museum of Art in New York, expresses the mood of alienation associated with cold war culture.

SOURCE: Edward Hopper (1882-1967), *Office in a Small City*, 1953. Oil on canvas, H. 28 in. W. 40 in. Signed (lower left) Edward Hopper. The Metropolitan Museum of Art, George A. Hearn Fund, 1953. (53.183).

challenge, it might be necessary first—as Republican senator Arthur Vandenberg advised Truman—to "scare hell out of the country."

An Anxious Mood

"We have about 50 percent of the world's wealth," George Kennan noted in 1948, "but only 3.6 percent of its population." However, prosperity did not dispel an anxious mood, fueled in part by the reality and the rhetoric of the cold war. Many Americans also feared an economic backslide. If war production had ended the hardships of the Great Depression, how would the economy fare in peacetime? No one could say. Above all, peace itself seemed precarious. President Truman himself suggested that World War III appeared inevitable, and his secretary of state, Dean Acheson, warned the nation to keep "on permanent alert."

Anxieties intensified by the cold war surfaced as major themes in popular culture. One of the most acclaimed Hollywood films of the era, the winner of nine Academy Awards, *The Best Years of Our Lives* (1946), followed the stories of three returning veterans as they tried

to readjust to civilian life. The former soldiers found that the dreams of reunion with family and loved ones that had sustained them through years of fighting now seemed hollow. In some cases, their wives and children had become so self-reliant that the men had no clear function to perform in the household; in other cases, the prospect for employment appeared dim. The feeling of community shared with wartime buddies dissipated, leaving only a profound sense of loneliness.

The genre of *film noir* (French for "black") deepened this mood into an aesthetic. Movies like *Out of the Past, Detour*, and *They Live by Night* featured stories of ruthless fate and betrayal. Their protagonists were usually strangers or loners falsely accused of crimes or trapped into committing them. The high-contrast lighting of these black and white films accentuated the difficulty of distinguishing friend from foe. Feelings of frustration and loss of control came alive in tough, cynical characters played by actors such as Robert Mitchum and Robert Ryan.

Plays and novels also described alienation and anxiety in vivid terms. Playwright Arthur Miller in *Death of a Salesman* (1949) sketched an exacting portrait of self-destructive individualism. Willy Loman, the play's hero, is obsessively devoted to his career in sales but is nevertheless a miserable failure. Worse, he has trained his sons to excel in personal presentation and style—the very methods prescribed by standard American success manuals—making them both shallow and materialistic. J. D. Salinger's widely praised novel *Catcher in the Rye* (1951) explored the mental anguish of a teenage boy estranged from the crass materialism of his parents.

Cold war anxiety manifested itself in a flurry of unidentified flying object (UFO) sightings. Thousands of Americans imagined that a Communist-like invasion from outer space was already under way, or they hoped that superior creatures might arrive to show the way to world peace. The U.S. Air Force discounted the sightings of flying saucers, but dozens of private researchers and faddists claimed to have been contacted by aliens.

Hollywood films fed these beliefs. In *The Invasion of the Body Snatchers* (1956), for example, a small town is captured by aliens who take over the minds of its inhabitants when they fall asleep, a subtle warning against apathy toward the threat of communist "subversion." (See out of Many Voices: Building Bomb Shelters.)

The Family as Bulwark

Postwar prosperity helped to strengthen the ideal of domesticity, although many Americans interpreted their rush toward marriage and parenthood, as one writer put it, as a "defense—an impregnable bulwark" against the anxieties of the era (see Figure 26.2).

The ultimate symbol of postwar prosperity, the new home in the suburbs, reflected more than simple self-confidence. In 1950 the *New York Times* ran advertisements that captured a chilling quality of the boom in real estate: country properties for the Atomic Age located

OUT OF MANY VOICES

BUILDING BOMB SHELTERS

During the Cold War, many Americans built bomb shelters in their backyards while city and state government planned programs of civil defense. In a letter to The New York Times, a local resident, Wynant D. Hubbard, responded to some proposals for New York City.

AS AN AMERICAN I REFUSE TO BE EITHER intimidated by or to become hysterical about the possibility of an atomic bombing by the Russians or anyone else.

While I am 100 per cent in favor of the full development of all possible defensive improvement by this country, I think that the talk of making underground bomb shelters under our parks, etc., has become a means of getting through certain political plums, or contractual plums, on the theory that if the populace is sufficiently scared it will agree to anything.

Let us be factual. Suppose that Russia or some other country were to drop atomic bombs on this country. They would be dropped on our major ports and our greater industrial centers. Portions of these cities would be knocked out. Perhaps. Would the remainder of the country collapse? Are we so decadent that we would not rally together and fight back?

Would we be expected to surrender just because these cities had been severely injured? How would the Russians or any other country follow up such an atomic attack on the United States? Does any country have the ships to bring attacking forces to our shores? Can any country in the world bring sufficient troops to the United States, by air or otherwise, to take over this country as a result of its collapse or surrender because of an atomic bombing? I doubt this very much. . . .

Let's not have quite so many unconvincing declarations as to the necessity of underground bomb shelters. . . . Let's have the truth. Are there any real reasons to believe that New York or any other American city is to be bombed? Why? Does the State Department or the Defense Department have any concrete, solid reasons to believe that we shall be attacked? They may not be able to give us the exact reasons, but couldn't we have something more convincing than the general statements which have come out so far?

If the necessity is truly genuine, why not, as an example, turn the Wollman ice-skating rink, which is being built in Central Park, into a bomb shelter? Saving lives would be more of a memorial than having skeletons glide over nonexistent ice. ■

SOURCE: "Letters to the Times," September 27, 1950. *ProQuest Historical Newspapers: The New York Times* (1851–2001), p. 29.

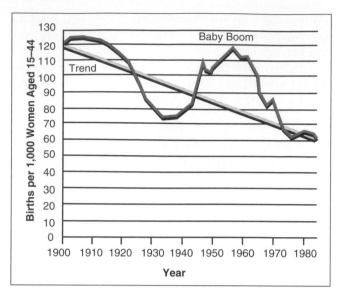

FIGURE 26.2   U.S. Birth Rate, 1930–80 The bulge of the "baby boom," a leading demographic factor in the postwar economy, stands out for this fifty-year period.

SOURCE: National Archives and Records Administration.

at least fifty miles outside major cities—the most likely targets, it was believed, of a Soviet nuclear attack. Not a few suburbanites built underground bomb shelters made of steel-reinforced concrete and outfitted with provisions to maintain a family for several weeks after an atomic explosion.

Young couples were marrying younger and producing more children than at any time in the past century. The U.S. Census Bureau predicted that the "baby boom" would be temporary. To everyone's surprise, the birthrate continued to grow at a record pace, peaking at over 118 per 1,000 women in 1957.

The new families who enjoyed postwar prosperity inaugurated a spending spree of trailblazing proportions. "The year 1946," *Life* magazine proclaimed, "finds the U.S. on the threshold of marvels, ranging from runless stockings and shineless serge suits to jet-propelled airplanes that will flash across the country in just a little less than the speed of sound." The conversion from wartime to peacetime production took longer than many eager shoppers had hoped, but by 1950 the majority of Americans could own consumer durables, such as automatic washers, and small appliances, from do-it-yourself power tools to cameras. By the time Harry Truman left office two-thirds of all American households claimed at least one television set.

These two trends—the baby boom and high rates of consumer spending—encouraged a major change in the middle-class family. Having worked during World War II, often in occupations traditionally closed to them,

many women wished to continue in full-time employment. Reconversion to peacetime production forced the majority from their factory positions, but most women quickly returned, taking jobs at a faster rate than men and providing half the total growth of the labor force. By 1952, 2 million more wives worked than during the war. Gone, however, were the high-paying unionized jobs in manufacturing. Instead, most women found minimum-wage jobs in the expanding service sector: clerical work, health care and education, and restaurant, hotel, and retail services. Older women whose children were grown might work because they had come to value a job for its own sake. Younger women often worked for reasons of "economic necessity"—that is, to maintain a middle-class standard of living that now required more than one income. Indeed, mothers of young children were the most likely to be employed.

Even though most women sought employment primarily to support their families, they ran up against

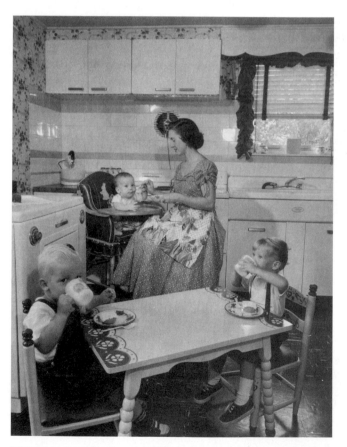

This photograph, taken in 1955, presents an ideal image of domestic life for American women during the cold war. This young mother sits with her three small children in a well-equipped kitchen that depicts the high standard of living that symbolized the "America way of life."

SOURCE: Harold M. Lambert. Getty Images Inc. Hulton Archive Photos.

popular opinion and expert advice urging them to return to their homes. Public opinion registered resounding disapproval—by 86 percent of those surveyed—of a married woman's working if jobs were scarce and her husband could support her. Noting that most Soviet women worked outside the home, many commentators appealed for a return to an imaginary "traditional" family where men alone were breadwinners and American women were exclusively homemakers.

This campaign began on a shrill note. Ferdinand Lundberg and Marynia Farnham, in their best-selling *Modern Woman: The Lost Sex* (1947), attributed the "super-jittery age in which we live" to women's abandonment of the home to pursue careers. To counter this trend, they proposed federally funded psychotherapy to readjust women to their housewifely roles and cash subsidies to encourage them to bear more children.

Articles in popular magazines, television shows, and high-profile experts chimed in with similar messages. Talcott Parsons, the distinguished Harvard sociologist, delineated the parameters of the "democratic" family: husbands served as breadwinners while wives—"the emotional hub of the family"—stayed home to care for their families. In the first edition of *Baby and Child Care* (1946), the child-rearing advice manual that soon outsold the Bible, Benjamin Spock similarly advised women to devote themselves full time, if financially possible, to their maternal responsibilities.

Patterns of women's higher education reflected this conservative trend. Having made slight gains during World War II when college-age men were serving in the armed forces or working in war industries, women lost ground after the G.I. Bill created a huge upsurge in male enrollment. Women represented 40 percent of all college graduates in 1940 but only 25 percent a decade later.

With a growing number of middle-class women working to help support their families, these cold war policies and prescriptions worked at cross-purposes. As early as 1947, *Life* magazine registered concern in a thirteen-page feature, "American Woman's Dilemma." How could women comfortably take part in a world beyond the home and at the same time heed the advice of FBI director J. Edgar Hoover, who exhorted the nation's women to fight "the twin enemies of freedom—crime and communism" by fulfilling their singular role as "homemakers and mothers"?

Military-Industrial Communities in the West

All regions of the United States felt the impact of the cold war but perhaps none so directly as the Trans–Mississippi West. Defense spending during World War II had stimulated the western economy and encouraged a mass migration of people eager to find employment in wartime industry. Following the war, many cities successfully converted to peacetime production; Los Angeles, for example, attracted one-eighth of all new business in the nation during the late 1940s. However, the cold war, by reviving defense funding, provided the most important boost to the western economy. The Department of Defense and private corporations and subcontractors generated billions of dollars for research and development of military equipment of various kinds.

The federal government poured so much defense money—nearly 10 percent of the entire military

TABLE 26.1	DISTRIBUTION OF TOTAL PERSONAL INCOME AMONG VARIOUS SEGMENTS OF THE POPULATION, 1947–70 (IN PERCENTAGES)*					
Year	Poorest Fifth	Second Poorest Fifth	Middle Fifth	Second Wealthiest Fifth	Wealthiest Fifth	Wealthiest 5 Percent
1947	3.5	10.6	16.7	23.6	45.6	18.7
1950	3.1	10.5	17.3	24.1	45.0	18.2
1960	3.2	10.6	17.6	24.7	44.0	17.0
1970	3.6	10.3	17.2	24.7	44.1	16.9

Despite the general prosperity of the postwar era, the distribution of income remained essentially unchanged.
* Monetary income only.

SOURCE: Adapted from U.S. Bureau of the Census, *Historical Statistics of the United States, Colonial Times to 1970*, Bicentennial ed. (Washington DC: U.S. Government Printing Office, 1975), p. 292.

budget—into California that the state's rate of economic growth between 1949 and 1952 outpaced that of the nation as a whole, with nearly 40 percent coming from the manufacture of aircraft alone. Ten years later, it was estimated that one-third of all workers in Los Angeles were employed by defense industries, particularly aerospace, and that their absolute number was far greater than during the peak of production in World War II. The concentration of defense workers was even greater in the suburbs of Los Angeles. Orange County, for example, grew quickly during the cold war to become a major producer of communication equipment. The San Francisco Bay Area also benefited economically from defense spending, and cities such as Sunnyvale, Mountain View, and San Jose began their ascendance as home to the nation's budding high-technology industry.

The cold war also pumped new life into communities that had grown up during World War II. Hanford, Washington, and Los Alamos, New Mexico, both centers of the Manhattan Project, employed a greater number of people in the construction of the cold war nuclear arsenal than in the development of the atom bomb that brought an end to World War II. Los Alamos grew from its rural origins at such a fast pace that thirty years later its population density was one of the highest in the state, second only to the metropolitan region of Albuquerque. The community lost little of its secretive quality, with entry restricted to mainly well-paid workers and residents who could neither own land nor homes within its boundary. Meanwhile, the federal government continued to place its distinctive stamp on the architecture, with institutional and purely functional aesthetics governing the design of concrete structures with hospital-green interiors.

Other parts of New Mexico were virtually transformed by cold war exigencies. Three hundred miles southeast of Los Alamos, Espanola Valley, home to a population nearly 90 percent Hispanic and Native American, saw its economy grow as it became the location of Waste Isolation Pilot Project, the dump site of the laboratory's waste projects. Alamogordo, New Mexico, experienced more than a 200 percent increase in population during the first decade of the cold war because of its location next to White Sands Missile Range and Holloman Air Force Base.

New communities accompanied the growth of the U.S. military bases and training camps in the Western states. Many of these installations, as well as hospitals and supply depots, not only survived but expanded during the transition from the actual warfare of World War II to the virtual warfare of the cold war. Between 1950 and 1953 approximately twenty western bases were reopened. California became at least a temporary home to more military personnel than any other state, but Texas was not far behind. The availability of public lands with areas of sparse population made western states especially attractive to military planners commissioned to design dangerous and secretive installations such as the White Sands Missile Range in the New Mexican desert.

Local politicians, real estate agents, and merchants usually welcomed these developments as sources of revenue and employment for the residents of their communities. There were, however, heavy costs for speedy and unplanned federally induced growth. To accommodate the new populations, the government poured money into new highway systems and did little to bolster or build public transportion. Uncontrolled sprawl, traffic congestion, air pollution, and strains on limited water and energy resources all grew with the military-industrial communities in the West. For those populations living near nuclear weapons testing grounds, environmental degradation complemented the ultimate threat to their own physical well-being, as cancer rates soared over the next forty years.

Zeal for Democracy

World War II revitalized patriotism by rallying Americans to define themselves and their institutions against Nazi and fascist forces abroad. Pledging allegiance to the flag, for example, gained new symbolic meaning as school children were directed to avoid saluting, a gesture now perceived as disturbingly similar to the militaristic Nazi hand-raising, and were instead told to hold their right hand steadily over their heart. By 1941, the celebration of Flag Day moved even President Roosevelt, who previously showed no interest in the event, to implore Americans to show their colors "when the principles of unity and freedom symbolized by Old Glory are under attack."

Following the massive V-J Day celebrations that marked the end of World War II, Americans began to retreat from public displays of patriotism but were soon chastized for their "national apathy" by organizations like the Freedoms Foundation of Valley Forge, which aimed to mobilize a "vast articulate, creative army of ministers, teachers, professional people, students, men and women from the farm and factory" to defend "the American Way." Soon, other new groups, such as the American Heritage Foundation, founded in 1947, joined such stalwarts as the American Legion, the Chamber of Commerce, and local business and veterans groups in this endeavor.

During the tense election year of 1948, for example, the Junior Chamber of Commerce of Kansas City,

Missouri, sponsored "Democracy Beats Communism" Week and prepared a small army of speakers to explain the virtues of American democracy over Soviet slavery, focusing to a large extent on superiority of free enterprise over a state-controlled economy. Students in the city's high schools thus learned that whereas one in every five Americans had a phone, only one in 188 Russians did. The week climaxed in a "Torch of Freedom" parade, a caravan of automobiles, trucks, and marching bands carrying the message to all parts of the city.

The American Legion of Mosinee, Wisconsin, utilized political theatre to inculcate the virtues of the American way, orchestrating an imaginary Communist coup of the small community. In 1950 on May Day, the traditional Communist holiday, "Communist agents," followed by more than sixty reporters, forced the mayor from his home and announced that the Council of People's Commissars had taken over the local government. The chief of police met with a similar fate, and roadblocks were put up to prevent any of the residents from escaping to "free" territory. The restaurants served only Soviet fare: black bread, potato soup, and coffee. The local newspaper, the *Mosinee Times*, printed a special edition on pink stock under its new masthead, "Red Star." The citizens of Mosinee discovered that all private property had been confiscated by the state and that all rights guaranteed by the Constitution had been anulled. Moreover, every adult was required "to contribute to the State four extra hours of labor without compensation." That evening, after a full day of Communist indoctrination, the local residents rallied in "Red Square" where they declared an end to the Communist rule of their community. Mosinee's defenders of freedom raised the American flag and headed home to the refrain of "God Bless America." The national media, including *Life* magazine and all the radio networks, covered Mosinee's "Day Under Communism."

Meanwhile, Attorney General Tom Clark, with the support of President Truman, funding from private donors, and planning by the American Heritage Foundation, had been putting on track the "Freedom Train." Carrying copies of the Bill of Rights and the Constitution, the Freedom Train traveled to various cities across the United States where local citizens got aboard to view various patriotic displays at the average rate of 8,500 people per day. The popular songwriter Irving Berlin memorialized the Freedom Train, lyrically assuring the expectant viewers who endured long lines that inside "you'll find a precious freight."

Patriotic messages also permeated public education. According to guidelines set down by the Truman administration, teachers were to "strengthen national security through education," specifically designing their lesson plans to illustrate the superiority of the American democratic system over Soviet communism. In 1947 the federal Office of Education launched the "Zeal for Democracy" program for implementation by school boards nationwide. The program veered toward propaganda, announcing its intention to "promote and strengthen democratic thinking and practice, just as the schools of totalitarian states have so effectively promoted the ideals of their respective cultures." Meanwhile, as part of a separate program in civil defense, schoolchildren were taught to "duck" under their desks and "cover" their heads to protect themselves in the event of a surprise nuclear attack by the Soviets.

There were voices of protest to these cold war programs. The black poet Langston Hughes, for example, expressed his skepticism in verse, writing that he hoped the Freedom Train would carry no Jim Crow car. A fearless minority of scholars protested infringements on their academic freedom by refusing to sign loyalty oaths and by writing books pointing out the potential dangers of aggressively nationalistic foreign and domestic policies. But the chilling atmosphere, such as the political climate pervading the campus of the University of Washington, made many individuals reluctant to express contrary opinions or ideas.

STALEMATE FOR THE DEMOCRATS

With cold war tensions festering in Europe, neither the United States nor the Soviet Union would have predicted that events in Asia would bring them to the brink of a war that threatened to destroy the world. Yet, in 1949, Communists in China seized power in the most populous nation in the world. Then, a few months later, in June 1950, Communists threatened to take over all of Korea.

Truman asked Americans to sanction a "police action" in Korea, and within a few years more than 1.8 million Americans had been sent to fight a war with no victory in sight. For Truman, the "loss" of China to communism and the stalemate in Korea proved political suicide, bringing to an end the twenty-year Democratic lock on the presidency and the greatest era of reform in U.S. history.

The "Loss" of China

At the close of World War II, the United States acted deliberately to secure Japan as a stabilizing force in Asia, particularly in relation to China. General Douglas MacArthur directed an interim government in a modest reconstruction program that included land reform, the creation of independent trade unions, the abolition of contract marriages, the granting of woman suffrage, sweeping demilitarization, and, eventually, a constitutional democracy that barred Communists from all posts. American leaders worked to rebuild the nation's economy along capitalist lines and integrate Japan, like West Germany, into an anti-Soviet bloc. Japan also housed huge U.S. military bases, thus placing U.S. troops and weapons strategically close to the Soviet Union's Asian rim.

The situation in China could not be handled so easily. After years of civil war, the pro-Western Nationalist government of Jiang Jeishi (Chiang Kai-shek) collapsed. Since World War II, the United States had been sending aid to the unpopular government while warning Jiang that without major reforms the Nationalists were heading for defeat. Moreover, they tried to convince him to accept a coalition government. After refusing to intervene on their behalf, the United States watched as Jiang's troops were finally forced to surrender to the Communists, led by Mao Zedong, who enjoyed the support of the Chinese countryside, where 85 percent of the population lived. Surrendering to Mao the entire China mainland, the defeated Nationalist government withdrew to the island of Formosa (Taiwan). On October 1, 1949, the People's Republic of China (PRC) was formally established.

The news of China's "fall" to communism created an uproar in the United States. The Asia First wing of the Republican Party, which envisioned the Far East rather than Europe as the prime site of U.S. trade and investment, blamed the Truman administration for the "loss" of China. For Truman, the situation worsened when, in February 1950, the USSR and the PRC joined in a formal alliance. The president's adversaries, capitalizing on the growing threat of "international" communism, called the Democrats the "party of treason."

The Korean War

At the end of World War II, the Allies had divided the small peninsula of Korea, ceded by Japan, at the 38th parallel. Although all parties hoped to reunite the nation under its own government, the line between North and South instead hardened. The United States backed the unpopular government of Syngman Rhee (the Republic of Korea), and the Soviet Union sponsored a rival government in North Korea under Kim Il Sung (see Map 26.3).

On June 25, 1950, the U.S. State Department received a cablegram reporting a military attack on South Korea by the Communist-controlled North. "If we are tough enough now," President Truman pledged, "if we stand up to them like we did in Greece three years ago, they won't take any next steps." The Soviet Union, on the other hand, regarded the invasion as Kim Il Sung's affair. Despite Soviet disclaimers, Truman sought approval from the UN Security Council to send in troops to South Korea. Because of the absence of the Soviet delegate, who could have vetoed the decision, the Security Council agreed. Two-thirds of Americans polled approved the president's decision to send troops under the command of General Douglas MacArthur.

Military events seemed at first to justify the president's decision. Seoul, the capital of South Korea, had

By midcentury, General Douglas MacArthur (1880–1964) had earned a reputation as one of the most flamboyant and controversial Americans. This photograph, taken in September 1950, shows him during his finest hour as commander of the UN troops during the Korean war. He is observing the shelling of enemy forces shortly before he led a brilliant and successful amphibious landing at the Inchon peninsula. Nearly 1.8 million Americans served in Korea.

SOURCE: CORBIS- NY.

fallen to North Korean troops within weeks of the invasion, and Communist forces continued to push south until they had taken most of the peninsula. The situation appeared grim until Truman authorized MacArthur to carry out an amphibious landing at Inchon, which he did on September 15, 1950. With tactical brilliance and

good fortune, the general orchestrated a military campaign that halted the Communist drive. By October, UN troops had retaken South Korea.

Basking in victory, the Truman administration could not resist the temptation to expand its war aims. Hoping to prove that Democrats were not "soft" on communism,

MAP EXPLORATION

To explore an interactive version of this map, go to **www.prenhall.com/faragher5/map26.3**

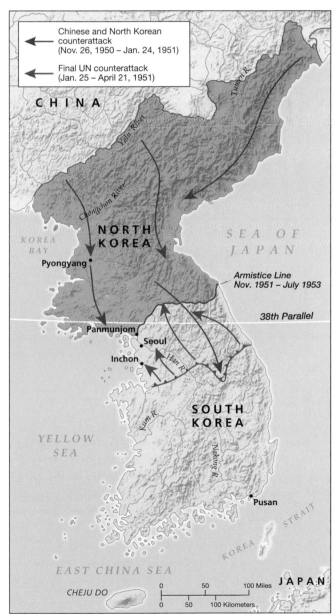

MAP 26.3 The Korean War The intensity of battles underscored the strategic importance of Korea in the cold war.

the president and his advisers decided to roll back the Communists beyond the 38th parallel and ultimately to reunite Korea as a showcase for democracy. Until this point, China had not been actively involved in the war. But it now warned that any attempt to cross the dividing line would be interpreted as a threat to its own national security. Truman flew to Wake Island in the Pacific on October 15 for a conference with MacArthur, who assured the president of a speedy victory.

MacArthur had sorely miscalculated. Chinese troops massed just above the UN offensive line, at the Yalu River. Suddenly, and without any air support, the Chinese attacked in human waves. MacArthur's force was all but crushed. The Chinese drove the UN troops back into South Korea, where they regrouped along the 38th parallel. By summer 1951 a stalemate had been reached very near the old border. Negotiations for a settlement went on for the next eighteen months amid heavy fighting. (See Out of Many Voices: Fighting the Chinese in Korea.)

"There is no substitute for victory," MacArthur insisted as he tried without success to convince Truman to prepare for a new invasion of Communist territory. Encouraged by strong support at home, he continued to provoke the president by speaking out against official policy, calling for bombing of supply lines in China and a naval blockade of the Chinese coast—actions certain to lead to a Chinese-American war. Finally, on April 10, 1951, Truman dismissed MacArthur for insubordination and other unauthorized activities.

The Price of National Security

The Korean War had profound implications for the use of executive power. By instituting a peacetime draft in 1948 and then ordering American troops into Korea, Truman had bypassed congressional authority. Republican Senator Robert Taft called the president's actions "a complete usurpation" of democratic checks and balances and charged Truman with transforming his office into an "imperial presidency." For awhile, Truman sidestepped such criticisms and their constitutional implications by declaring a national emergency and by carefully referring to the military deployment not as a U.S. war but as a UN-sanctioned "police action."

OUT OF MANY VOICES

FIGHTING THE CHINESE IN KOREA

In the fall of 1950, as U.S.–led troops moved farther north, Chinese troops rushed into North Korea and by October waged a massive offensive against American soldiers. In late November, Fred Lawson, a Marine rifleman, was recovering from wounds suffered a few weeks earlier and rejoining his company. Interviewed many years later, he recalled the scene near Yudam.

THAT NIGHT THE CHINESE REALLY HIT US. WE knew they were out there somewhere, because we'd already had a fight with them at Sudong a couple weeks before, but nobody thought there'd be so many. We had no idea what was happening over on the other side of the mountains, that the army was getting the shit kicked out of them over there by hordes of Chinese. We had absolutely no idea what we were doing. As far as we knew we were still headed for the Yalu River, and if we got there quick enough we'd be home for Christmas.

It wasn't too long after dark, eight, nine o'clock, when we heard the bugles. At the same time we started taking mortar and artillery fire. Then lights came on. The Chinese lit up the whole side of the hill with searchlights, and then charged into the light, and Jesus, what a sight. They looked like a bunch of sheep swarming up the hill.

None of us had ever seen anything like it. They didn't seem to have any training at all. They just came straight at us, like a mob. You couldn't help but hit them. And we were really stacking them up. But there were so goddamn many. And they just kept coming.

Pretty soon we were in it hand to hand. Gun butts. Knives, Fists. After I ran out of ammo I conked a couple with a helmet, swinging it by the strap. A lot of the positions got overrun, but nobody retreated. . . .

There were Chinese bodies still lying around. Hundred of them, as stiff as boards. We suffered a lot from the cold, but those poor suckers were *really* in bad shape. They were wearing tennis shoes, and you could tell when they were attacking that some could hardly walk. Some didn't even have weapons. I don't see how in the world their officers ever got them to go up that hill. I really felt sorry for some of those Chinese. ■

SOURCE: Rudy Tomedi, *No Bugles, No Drums: An Oral History of the Korean War* (New York: John Wiley & Sons, 1993), pp. 86–88.

The president derived his authority from NSC-68, a paper released to him by the National Security Council in April 1950 that reinterpreted both the basic policy of containment and decision making at the highest levels of government. Demonizing communism as "a new fanatic faith" that "seeks to impose its absolute authority over the rest of the world," NSC-68 pledged the United States not only to "contain" communism but to take a further step to drive back Communist influence wherever it appeared and to "foster the seeds of destruction within the Soviet Union." Moreover, the document designated the struggle between the United States and Soviet Union as "permanent," the era one of "total war." It specified that American citizens must be willing to make sacrifices—"to give up some of the benefits which they have come to associate with their freedom"—to defend their way of life. NSC-68 articulated the intellectual and psychological rationale behind U.S. national security policies for the next forty years.

Initially reluctant, Truman fulfilled the prescriptions of NSC-68 after the outbreak of the Korean War and agreed to its mandate for a rapid and permanent military buildup. By the time the conflict subsided, the defense budget had quadrupled, from $13.5 billion to more than $52 billion in 1953. The U.S. Army had grown to 3.6 million, or six times its size at the beginning of the conflict. At the same time, the federal government accelerated the development of both conventional and nonconventional weapons. In the first instance, it began to stockpile nuclear bombs and weapons, including the first hydrogen, or H-bomb, which was tested in November 1952. NCS-68 also proposed expensive "large-scale covert operations" for the "liberation" of Communist countries, particularly in Eastern Europe.

The Korean War also provided the rationale for the expansion of anti-Communist propaganda. At the end of World War II President Truman had taken steps to transform the Office of War Information into a peacetime program that operated on a much smaller budget. But by 1948 Congress was ready to pass with bipartisan support the Smith-Mundt Act, designed "to promote the better understanding of the United States among the peoples of the world and to strengthen cooperative international relations." Within a year, Congress doubled the budget for such programming, granting $3 million to revive the Voice of America, the short-wave international radio program that had been established in 1942. The new legislation also funded the development of film, print media, cultural exchange programs, and exhibitions, and it created a foundation to promote anti-Communist propaganda throughout the world. By mid-1950, the immediate

goal was the "reorientation" of North Korea toward the Free World.

The government's vast "information programs" were designed less to "contain" communism than to "liberate" those countries already under Communist rule by causing disaffection among the people. By 1951 a massive "Campaign of Truth" was reaching 93 nations, and the Voice of America was broadcasting anti-Communist programming in 45 languages. Project Troy, which was initially designed by professors from Harvard and the Massachusetts Institute of Technology, aimed to penetrate the Iron Curtain, for example, by using air balloons to distribute leaflets and cheap American goods, such as playing cards and plastic chess sets. Army pilots joined the effort, dropping leaflets on North Korean troops reading "ENJOY LIFE and plenty of cigarettes away from the war by coming over to the UN side. Escape. Save your life." On April 4, 1951, President Truman signed the order that created the Psychological Strategy Board to coordinate various operations aimed to rollback Soviet power. In his annual message to Congress that year, he had requested $115 million to fund these programs but, as the Korean War bogged down, he managed to get only $85 million.

By the time it ended, the Korean War had cost the United States approximately $100 billion and inaugurated an era of huge deficits in the federal budget and massive national debt but did nothing to improve the case for rolling back communism. Negotiations and fighting proceeded in tandem until the summer of 1953, when a settlement was reached in which both North Korea and South Korea occupied almost the same territory as when the war began. Approximately 54,000 Americans died in Korea; the North Koreans and Chinese lost well over 2 million people. The UN troops had employed both "carpet bombing" (an intense, destructive attack on a given area) and napalm (jellied gasoline bombs), destroying most of the housing and food supplies in both Koreas. True to the pattern of modern warfare, which emerged during World War II, the majority of civilians killed were women and children. Nearly 1 million Koreans were left homeless.

For the United States, the Korean War enlarged the geographical range of the cold war to include East Asia. The war also lined up the People's Republic of China and the United States as unwavering enemies for the next twenty years and heightened the U.S. commitment to Southeast Asia. Now, as one historian commented, the "frontiers on every continent were going to remain frontiers in the traditional American meaning of a frontier—a region to penetrate and control and police and civilize."

The Korean War, moreover, did much to establish an ominous tradition of "unwinnable" conflicts that left many Americans skeptical of official policy. Truman had initially rallied popular support for U.S. intervention by contrasting the Communist North with the "democratic" South, thus casting the conflict in the ideological terms of the cold war. MacArthur's early victories had promised the liberation of North Korea and even the eventual disintegration of the Soviet and Chinese regimes. But with the tactical stalemate came mass disillusionment.

In retrospect many Americans recognized that Truman, in fighting communism in Korea, had pledged the United States to defend a corrupt government and a brutal dictator. Decades later the Korean War inspired the dark comedy *M*A*S*H*, adapted for television from the film written by Hollywood screenwriter Ring Lardner Jr., an "unfriendly witness" before HUAC, who was jailed during the Korean War for contempt of Congress. As late as 1990, members of Congress were still debating the terms of a Korean War memorial. "It ended on a sad note for Americans," one historian has concluded, "and the war and its memories drifted off into a void."

"I like Ike": The Election of 1952

There was only one burning issue during the election campaign of 1952: the Korean War. Truman's popularity had wavered continually since he took office in 1945, but it sank to an all-time low in the early 1950s shortly after he dismissed MacArthur as commander of the UN troops in Korea. Congress received thousands of letters and telegrams calling for Truman's impeachment. "Oust President Truman" bumper stickers could be seen. MacArthur, meanwhile, returned home a hero, welcomed by more than 7 million fans in New York City alone.

Popular dissatisfaction with Truman increased. The Asia First lobby argued that if the president had acted more aggressively to turn back communism in China, the "limited war" in Korea would not have been necessary. Following these charges were accusations of large-scale corruption in his administration. Newspapers reported that several agencies had been dealing in 5 percent kickbacks for government contracts. Business and organized labor complained about the price and wage freezes imposed during the Korean War. A late-1951 Gallup poll showed the president's approval rating at 23 percent. In March 1952, Truman announced he would not run for reelection, a decision rare for a president eligible for another term.

In accepting political defeat and disgrace, Truman turned to the popular but uncharismatic governor of Illinois, Adlai E. Stevenson Jr. Admired for his honesty and intelligence, Stevenson offered no solutions to the conflict in Korea, the accelerating arms race, or the cold war generally. Accepting the Democratic nomination, he candidly admitted that "the ordeal of the twentieth century is far from over," a prospect displeasing to voters aching for peace.

The Republicans made the most of the Democrats' dilemma. Without proposing any sweeping answers of their own, they pointed to all the obvious shortcomings of their opponents. Their campaign strategy, known as "K_1C_2"—Korea, Communism, and Corruption—took steady aim at the Truman administration, and when opinion polls showed that Dwight Eisenhower possessed an "unprecedented" 64 percent approval rating, they found in "Ike" the perfect candidate to head the ticket.

Eisenhower styled himself the representative of "modern Republicanism." He wisely avoided the negative impressions made by the unsuccessful 1948 Republican candidate, Thomas Dewey, who had seemed as aggressive as Truman on foreign policy and simultaneously eager to overturn the New Deal domestic legislation. Eisenhower knew better: voters wanted peace and a limited welfare state. He referred to New Deal reforms as "a solid floor that keeps all of us from falling into the pit of disaster." And athough he did not go into specifics, he promised to end the Korean War with "an early and honorable" peace. Whenever he was tempted to address questions of finance or the economy, his advisers warned him: "The chief reason that people want to vote for you is because they think you have more ability to keep us out of another war."

Meanwhile, Eisenhower's vice presidential candidate, Richard Nixon, waged a relentless and defamatory attack on Stevenson, calling him "Adlai the Appeaser." Senator Joseph McCarthy chimed in, proclaiming that with club in hand he might be able to make "a good American" of Stevenson. A month before the election, McCarthy went on network television with his requisite "exhibits" and "documents," this time purportedly showing that the Democratic presidential candidate had promoted communism at home and abroad. These outrageous charges kept the Stevenson campaign off balance.

The Republican campaign was itself not entirely free of scandal: Nixon had been caught accepting personal gifts from wealthy benefactors. Pleading his case on national television, he described his wife Pat's "good Republican cloth coat" and their modest style of living. He then contritely admitted that he had indeed accepted one gift, a puppy named Checkers that his daughters loved and that he refused to give back. "The Poor Richard Show," as critics called the event, defused the scandal without answering the most important charges.

Unaffected by the scandal, Eisenhower continued to enchant the voters as a peace candidate. Ten days before the election he dramatically announced, "I shall go to Korea" to settle the war. Eisenhower received 55 percent of the vote and carried thirty-nine states, in part because he brought out an unusually large number of voters in normally Democratic areas. He won the popular vote in much of the South and in the

C H R O N O L O G Y

1941	Henry Luce forecasts the dawn of "the American Century"
1944	G.I. Bill of Rights benefits World War II veterans International Monetary Fund and World Bank founded
1945	Franklin D. Roosevelt dies in office; Harry S. Truman becomes president United Nations charter signed World War II ends Strike wave begins Truman proposes program of economic reforms
1946	Employment Act creates Council of Economic Advisers Churchill's Iron Curtain speech Atomic Energy Act establishes Atomic Energy Commission Republicans win control of Congress Benjamin Spock publishes *Baby and Child Care*
1947	Truman Doctrine announced; Congress appropriates $400 million in aid for Greece and Turkey Federal Employees Loyalty and Security Program established and attorney general's list of subversive organizations authorized Marshall Plan announced Taft-Hartley Act restricts union activities National Security Act establishes Department of Defense, the National Security Council, and the Central Intelligence Agency House Un-American Activities Committee hearings in Hollywood
1948	Smith-Mundt Act passed by Congress Ferdinand Lundberg and Marynia Farnham publish *Modern Woman: The Lost Sex* State of Israel founded Berlin blockade begins Henry Wallace nominated for president on Progressive Party ticket

	Truman announces peacetime draft and desegregates U.S. armed forces and civil service Truman wins election; Democrats sweep both houses of Congress
1949	Truman announces Fair Deal North Atlantic Treaty Organization (NATO) created Communists, led by Mao Zedong, take power in China Berlin blockade ends Soviet Union explodes atomic bomb
1950	Alger Hiss convicted of perjury Senator Joseph McCarthy begins anti-Communist crusade Soviet Union and the People's Republic of China sign an alliance Adoption of NSC-68 consolidates presidential war powers Korean War begins Internal Security (McCarran) Act requires registration of Communist organizations and arrest of Communists during national emergencies
1951	Truman dismisses General Douglas MacArthur Psychological Strategy Board created Armistice talks begin in Korea
1952	Immigration and Nationality Act retains quota system, lifts ban on immigration of Asian and Pacific peoples, but bans "subversives" and homosexuals United States explodes first hydrogen bomb Dwight D. Eisenhower wins presidency; Richard Nixon becomes vice president
1953	Julius and Ethel Rosenberg executed for atomic espionage Armistice ends fighting in Korea
1954	Army-McCarthy hearings end
1955	Warsaw Pact created

Richard Nixon used the new medium of television to convince American voters that he had not established an illegal slush fund in his campaign for the vice presidency in 1952. Viewers responded enthusiastically to his melodramatic delivery and swamped the Republican campaign headquarters with telegrams endorsing his candidacy.

SOURCE: AP/Wide World Photos.

northern cities of New York, Chicago, Boston, and Cleveland. Riding his coattails, the Republicans regained narrow control of Congress. The New Deal coalition of ethnic and black voters, labor, northern liberals, and southern conservatives no longer commanded a majority.

CONCLUSION

In his farewell address, in January 1953, Harry Truman reflected: "I suppose that history will remember my term in office as the years when the 'cold war' began to overshadow our lives. I have hardly had a day in office that has not been dominated by this all-embracing struggle."

The election of Dwight Eisenhower helped to diminish the intensity of this dour mood without actually bringing a halt to the conflict. The new president pledged himself to liberate the world from communism by peaceful means rather than force. "Our aim is more subtle," he announced during his campaign, "more pervasive, more complete. We are trying to get the world, by peaceful means, to believe the truth. . . ." Increasing the budget of the CIA, Eisenhower took the cold war out of the public eye by relying to a far greater extent than Truman on psychological warfare and covert operations.

"The Eisenhower Movement," wrote journalist Walter Lippmann, was a "mission in American politics" to restore a sense of community among the American people. In a larger sense, many of the issues of the immediate post–World War II years seemed to have been settled, or put off for a distant future. The international boundaries of communism were frozen with the Chinese Revolution, the Berlin Crisis, and now the Korean War. Meanwhile, at home cold war defense spending had become a permanent part of the national budget, an undeniable drain on tax revenues but an important element in the government contribution to economic prosperity. If the nuclear arms race remained a cause for anxiety, joined by more personal worries about the changing patterns of family life, a sense of relative security nevertheless spread. Prospects for world peace had dimmed, but the worst nightmares of the 1940s had eased as well.

REVIEW QUESTIONS

1. Discuss the origins of the cold war and the sources of growing tensions between the United States and the Soviet Union at the close of World War II.
2. Describe the basic elements of President Harry Truman's policy of containment. How did the threat of atomic warfare affect this policy?
3. Compare the presidencies of Franklin D. Roosevelt and Harry S. Truman, both Democrats.
4. Describe the impact of McCarthyism on American political life. How did the anti-

Communist campaigns affect the media? What were the sources of Senator Joseph McCarthy's popularity? What brought about his downfall?
5. How did the cold war affect American culture?
6. Discuss the role of the United States in Korea in the decade after World War II. How did the Korean War affect the 1952 presidential election?
7. Why did Dwight D. Eisenhower win the 1952 presidential election?

RECOMMENDED READING

Mark S. Byrnes, *The Truman Years, 1945–1953* (2000). A concise history of the Truman administration and its role at the moment when the United States became the dominant economic power in the world. Byrnes covers this transformation with particular attention to the way the president helped to shape a view of the world that presented the United States and the Soviet Union as permanent enemies in a struggle for domination. Includes a set of twenty-one key documents and a detailed chronology of events.

Kevin J. Fernlund, ed., *The Cold War American West, 1945–1989* (1998). Ten essays illustrating the impact of the cold war on the region of the United States that housed the bulk of military bases, airfields, nuclear testing grounds, and toxic waste dumps. Presenting a variety of interpretations, the contributors ask a common question: Was the West transformed or deformed by the policies of the growing national security state?

John Fousek, *To Lead the Free World: American Nationalism and the Cultural Roots of the Cold War* (2000). Examines the "public culture" of the cold war through an innovative study of various responses to the official doctrines and declarations of the Truman administration. Fousek pays special attention to the publications of major civil rights organizations and the two largest labor unions of the period and argues that "a broad public consensus" supported Truman's nationalistic foreign policy.

Richard M. Fried, *The Russians Are Coming! The Russians Are Coming!: Pageantry and Patriotism in Cold-War America* (1998). Examines, through vivid example, the creation of the fear of communism and its translation into patriotic zeal. Fried takes as his thesis that rallying the public to "fight" the cold war required as much organization and energy as mobilizing Americans to defend the home front during World War II.

Margot A. Henriksen, *Dr. Strangelove's America: Society and Culture in the Atomic Age* (1997). Argues in a lively fashion that the atomic bomb played the "central, defining role" in American culture and society from 1945 into the early 1980s. Henriksen culls evidence from a wide range of sources, including novels, movies, TV programs, and rock 'n' roll songs.

David K. Johnson, *The Lavender Scare: The Cold War Persecution of Gays and Lesbians in the Federal Government* (2004). Goes beyond McCarthy and the persecution of Communists to examine the role of the national security state in purging homosexuals from positions in federal government. Johnson also covers the gay subculture of Washington DC that grew with the expansion of government during the New Deal and World War II.

Elaine Tyler May, *Homeward Bound: American Families in the Cold War Era* (1988). A lively account of the effects on family life and women's roles of the national mood of "containment." May argues that government policy became part of a popular culture that solidified the cold war era's "feminine mystique."

Robert J. McMahon, *The Cold War: A Very Short Introduction* (2003). A compact history of the Cold War that emphasizes its global dimensions. McMahon traces its origins to the devastation of World War II and ends with the unification of Germany in 1990.

Ellen Schrecker, *The Age of McCarthyism: A Brief History with Documents*, 2d ed (2002). A useful collection of primary sources on internal security and anticommunism by one of the foremost scholars of the field.

Stanley Weintraub, *MacArthur's War: Korea and the Undoing of an American Hero* (2000). Tells the story of the downfall of the commander of U.S. forces in the Far East, who was "senior to everyone but God" in the military services. The author additionally offers a detailed description of the horror and ruin accompanying the brutal ground war in Korea.

 For additional study resources for this chapter, go to the *Companion Website,* http://www.prenhall.com/faragher.

America
at Midcentury

1952–1963

Popular Music in Memphis

The nineteen-year-old Elvis Presley peered nervously out over the large crowd at Overton Park, Memphis's outdoor amphitheater. He knew that people had come that hot, sticky July day in 1954 to hear the headliner, country music star Slim Whitman. Sun Records, a local Memphis label, had just released Elvis's first record, and it had begun to receive some airplay on local radio. The singer and his two bandmates had never played in a setting even remotely as large as this one. And their music defied categories: it wasn't black and it wasn't white; it wasn't pop and it wasn't country. But when Elvis launched into his version of a black blues song called "That's All Right," the crowd went wild. "I came offstage," he later recalled, "and my manager told me that they was hollering because I was wiggling my legs. I went back out for an encore, and I did a little more, and the more I did, the wilder they went." Elvis Presley had arrived.

Elvis combined a hard-driving, rhythmic approach to blues and country music with a riveting performance style, inventing the new music known as rock 'n' roll. An unprecedented cultural phenomenon, rock 'n' roll was made largely for and by teenagers. In communi-

Memphis

ties all over America, rock 'n' roll brought teens together around jukeboxes, at sock hops, in cars, and at private parties. It also demonstrated the enormous consumer power of an emerging youth culture. Postwar teenagers would constitute the most affluent generation of young people in American history. Their ability and eagerness to buy records, phonograph players, transistor radios, clothing, makeup, and even cars forced business and advertisers to recognize a new teen market. Their buying power helped define the affluent society of the postwar era.

Located halfway between St. Louis and New Orleans on the Mississippi River, Memphis enjoyed healthy growth during World War II, with lumber mills, furniture factories, and chemical manufacturing supplementing the cotton market as sources of jobs and prosperity. Memphis also boasted a remarkable diversity of popular theater and music, including a large opera house, numerous brass bands, vaudeville and burlesque, minstrel shows, jug bands, and blues clubs. And like the rest of the South, Memphis was a legally segregated city; whites and blacks lived, went to school, and worked apart. Class differences among whites were important as well. Like thousands of other poor rural whites in these years, Elvis Presley had moved from Mississippi to Memphis in 1949, where his father found work in a munitions plant. The Presleys were poor enough to qualify for an apartment in Lauderdale Courts, a Memphis public housing project. To James Conaway, who grew up in an all-white, middle-class East Memphis neighborhood, people like the Presleys were "white trash." Negroes, he recalled, were "not necessarily below the rank of a country boy like Elvis, but of another universe, and yet there was more affection for them than for some whites."

Gloria Wade-Gayles, who lived in the all-black Foote Homes housing project in Memphis, vividly remembered that her family and neighbors "had no illusion about their lack of power, but they believed in their strength." For them, strength grew from total immersion in a black community that included ministers, teachers, insurance men, morticians, barbers, and entertainers. "Surviving meant being black, and being black meant believing in our humanity, and retaining it, in a world that denied we had it in the first place."

Yet in the cultural realm, class and racial barriers could be challenged. Elvis Presley grew up a dreamy, shy boy, who turned to music for emotional release and spiritual expression. He soaked up the wide range of music styles available in Memphis. The Assembly of God Church his family attended featured a renowned hundred-voice choir. Elvis and his friends went to marathon all-night "gospel singings" at Ellis Auditorium, where they enjoyed the tight harmonies and emotional style of white gospel quartets.

Elvis also drew from the sounds he heard on Beale Street, the main black thoroughfare of Memphis and one of the nation's most influential centers of African American music. In the postwar years, local black rhythm and blues artists like B. B. King, Junior Parker, and Muddy Waters attracted legions of black and white fans with their emotional power and exciting showmanship. Elvis himself performed along with black contestants in amateur shows at Beale Street's Palace Theater. Nat D. Williams, a prominent black Memphis disc jockey and music promoter, recalled how black audiences responded to Elvis's unique style. "He had a way of singing the blues that was distinctive. He could sing 'em not necessarily like a Negro, but he didn't sing 'em altogether like a typical white musician. . . . Always he had that certain humanness about him that Negroes like to put in their songs." Elvis himself understood his debt to black music and black performers. "The colored folks," he told an interviewer in 1956, "been singing and playing it just like I'm doing now, man, for more years than I know. They played it like that in the shanties and in their juke joints and nobody paid it no mind until I goosed it up. I got it from them."

Dissatisfied with the cloying pop music of the day, white teenagers across the nation were increasingly turning to the rhythmic drive and emotional intensity of black rhythm and blues. They quickly adopted rock 'n' roll (the term had long been an African American slang expression for dancing and sexual intercourse) as their music. But it was more than just music: it was also an attitude, a celebration of being young, and a sense of having something that adult authority could not understand or control. For millions of young people, rock 'n' roll was an expression of revolt against the conformity and blandness found in so many new postwar suburbs.

When Sun Records sold Presley's contract to RCA Records in 1956, Elvis became an international star. Records like "Heartbreak Hotel," "Don't Be Cruel," and "Jailhouse Rock" shot to the top of the charts and blurred the old boundaries between pop, country, and rhythm and blues. His appearances on network television shows contributed to his enormous popularity and demonstrated the extraordinary power of this new medium of communication. Television helped Elvis attract legions of new fans despite—and partly because of—the uproar over his overtly sexual performance style.

By helping to accustom white teenagers to the style and sound of black artists, Elvis helped establish rock 'n' roll as an interracial phenomenon. Institutional racism would continue to plague the music business—many black artists were routinely cheated out of royalties and severely underpaid—but the music of postwar Memphis at least pointed the way toward the exciting cultural possibilities that could emerge from breaking down the barriers of race. It also gave postwar American teenagers a newfound sense of community. In a broader sense, rock 'n' roll heralded a generational shift in american society. In 1960 the nation elected John F. Kennedy, the youngest president in its history, and a leader who came to symbolize youthful idealism. His assassination cut short the promise of the new frontier, but not before young people had established a crucial new presence in the nation's economy, culture, and political life.

KEY TOPICS

- Post–World War II prosperity
- Suburban life: ideal and reality
- The emergence of youth culture
- Television, mass culture, and their critics
- Foreign policy in the Eisenhower years
- John F. Kennedy and the promise of a New Frontier

AMERICAN SOCIETY AT MIDCENTURY

With the title of his influential work, *The Affluent Society* (1958), economist John Kenneth Galbraith gave a label to postwar America. Galbraith observed that American capitalism had worked "quite brilliantly" in the years since World War II. But Americans, he argued, needed to spend less on personal consumption and devote more public funds to schools, medical care, cultural activities, and social services. For most Americans, however, strong economic growth was the defining fact of the postwar period. A fierce desire for consumer goods and the "good life" imbued American culture, and the deeply held popular belief in a continuously expanding economy and a steadily increasing standard of living—together with the tensions of the cold war—shaped American social and political life.

The Eisenhower Presidency

Dwight D. Eisenhower's landslide election victory in 1952 set the stage for the first full two-term Republican presidency since that of Ulysses S. Grant. At the core of Eisenhower's political philosophy lay a conservative vision of community. He saw America as a corporate commonwealth, similar to the "associative state" envisioned by Herbert Hoover a generation earlier (see Chapter 23). Eisenhower believed the industrial strife, high inflation, and fierce partisan politics of the Truman years could be corrected only through cooperation, self-restraint, and disinterested public service. As president, Eisenhower emphasized limiting the New Deal trends that had expanded federal power, and he encouraged a voluntary, as opposed to regulatory, relationship between government and business. Social harmony and "the good life" at home were

closely linked, in his view, to maintaining a stable and American-led international order abroad.

Consciously, Eisenhower adopted an evasive style in public, and he was fond of the phrase "middle of the road." He told a news conference, "I feel pretty good when I'm attacked from both sides. It makes me more certain I'm on the right track." Intellectuals and liberals found it easy to satirize Eisenhower for his blandness, his frequent verbal gaffes, his vagueness, and his often contradictory pronouncements. The majority of the American public, however, evidently agreed with Eisenhower's easygoing approach to his office. He kept the conservative and liberal wings of his party united and appealed to many Democrats and independent voters.

Eisenhower wanted to run government in a businesslike manner while letting the states and corporate interests guide domestic policy and the economy. He appointed nine businessmen to his first cabinet, including three with ties to General Motors. Former GM chief Charles Wilson served as Secretary of Defense and epitomized the administration's economic views with his famous aphorism "What was good for our country was good for General Motors, and vice versa." In his appointments to the Federal Trade Commission, the Federal Communications Commission, and the Federal Power Commission, Eisenhower favored men congenial to the corporate interests they were charged with regulating. Eisenhower also secured passage of the Submerged Lands Act in 1953, which transferred $40 billion worth of disputed offshore oil lands from the federal government to the Gulf states. This transfer ensured a greater role for the states and private companies in the oil business—and cost the Treasury billions in lost revenues.

At the same time, Eisenhower accepted the New Deal legacy of greater federal responsibility for social welfare. He rejected calls from conservative Republicans, for example, to dismantle the Social Security system. His administration agreed to a modest expansion

Subsidizing Prosperity

During the Eisenhower years the federal government played a crucial role in subsidizing programs that helped millions of Americans achieve middle-class status. Federal aid helped people to buy homes, attend college and technical schools, and live in newly built suburbs. Much of this assistance expanded on programs begun during the New Deal and World War II. The Federal Housing Administration (FHA), established in 1934, extended the government's role in subsidizing the housing industry. The FHA insured long-term mortgage loans made by private lenders for home building. By putting the full faith and credit of the federal government behind residential mortgages, the FHA attracted new private capital into home building and revolutionized the industry. A typical FHA mortgage required less than 10 percent for a down payment and spread low-interest monthly payments over thirty years.

Yet FHA policies also had long-range drawbacks. FHA insurance went overwhelmingly to new residential developments, usually on the fringes of urban areas, hastening the decline of older, inner-city neighborhoods. A bias toward suburban, middle-class communities manifested itself in several ways: it was FHA policy to favor the construction of single-family projects while discouraging multi-unit housing, to refuse loans for the repair of older structures and rental units, and to require for any loan guarantee an "unbiased professional estimate" rating the property, the prospective borrower, and the neighborhood. In practice, these estimates resulted in blatant discrimination against communities that were racially mixed. The FHA's Underwriting Manual bluntly warned: "If a neighborhood is to retain stability, it is necessary that properties shall continue to be occupied by the same social and racial classes." FHA policies in effect inscribed the racial and income segregation of suburbia in public policy.

The majority of suburbs were built as planned communities. One of the first was Levittown, which opened in Hempstead, Long Island, in 1947, on 1,500 acres of former potato fields. Developer William Levitt, who described his firm as "the General Motors of the housing industry," was the first entrepreneur to bring mass-production techniques to home building. All building materials were precut and prefabricated at a central factory, then assembled on-site into

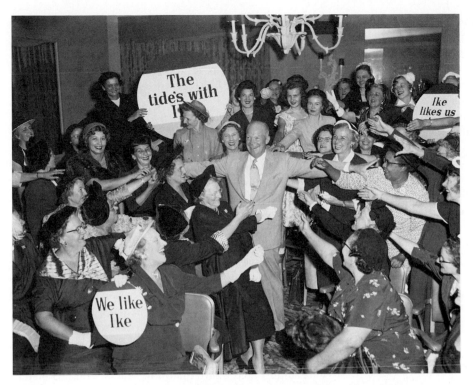

Presidential contender Dwight D. Eisenhower hosts a group of Republican National Committee women at his campaign headquarters in 1952. Ike's status as America's biggest war hero, along with his genial public persona, made him an extremely popular candidate with voters across party lines.

SOURCE: © Bettmann/CORBIS.

of Social Security and unemployment insurance and small increases in the minimum wage. Ike also created the Department of Health, Education and Welfare, appointing Oveta Culp Hobby as its secretary, making her the second woman to hold a cabinet post. In agriculture, Eisenhower continued the policy of parity payments designed to sustain farm prices. Between 1952 and 1960, federal spending on agriculture jumped from about $1 billion to $7 billion.

Eisenhower proved hesitant to use fiscal policy to pump up the economy, which went into recession after the Korean War ended in 1953 and again in 1958, when the unemployment rate reached 7.5 percent. The administration refused to cut taxes or increase spending to stimulate growth. Eisenhower feared starting an inflationary spiral more than he worried about unemployment or poverty. By the time he left office, he could proudly point out that real wages for an average family had risen 20 percent during his term. With low inflation and steady, if modest, growth, the Eisenhower years brought greater prosperity to most Americans. Long after he retired from public life, Ike liked to remember his major achievement as having created "an atmosphere of greater serenity and mutual confidence."

houses by largely unskilled, nonunion labor. In this way Levitt put up hundreds of identical houses each week. Eventually, Levittown encompassed more than 17,000 houses and 82,000 people. Yet in 1960 not one of Levittown's residents was African American, and owners who rented out their homes were told to specify that their houses would not be "used or occupied by any person other than members of the Caucasian race." Levitt himself angrily rejected any criticism of his racial policies: "As a company our position is simply this: we can solve a housing problem, or we can try to solve a racial problem, but we cannot combine the two."

The revolution in American life wrought by the 1944 Servicemen's Readjustment Act, known as the GI Bill of Rights, extended beyond its impact on higher education (see Chapter 26). In addition to educational grants, the act provided returning veterans with low-interest mortgages and business loans, thus subsidizing the growth of the suburbs as well as the postwar expansion of higher education. Through 1956, nearly 10 million veterans received tuition and training benefits under the act. Veteran's Administration–insured loans totaled more than $50 billion by 1962, providing assistance to millions of former GIs who started businesses.

The Federal Highway Act of 1956 gave another key boost to postwar growth, especially in the suburbs. It originally authorized $32 billion for the construction of a national interstate highway system. Financing was to come from new taxes on gasoline, as well as on oil, tires, buses, and trucks. Key to this ambitious program's success was that these revenues were held separately from general taxes in a Highway Trust Fund. By 1972 the program had become the single largest public works program in American history; 41,000 miles of highway were built at a cost of $76 billion. Federal subsidy of the interstate highway system stimulated both the automobile industry and suburb building. But it also accelerated the decline of American mass transit and older cities. By 1970, the nation possessed the world's best roads and one of its worst public transportation systems.

The shadow of the cold war prompted the federal government to take new initiatives in aid for education. After the Soviet Union launched its first Sputnik satellite in the fall of 1957, American officials worried that the country might be lagging behind the Soviets in training scientists and engineers. The Eisenhower administration, with the bipartisan support of Congress, pledged to strengthen support for educating American students in mathematics, science, and technology. The National Defense Education Act (NDEA) of 1958 allocated $280 million in grants—tied to matching grants from the states—for state universities to upgrade their science facilities. The NDEA also created $300 million in low-interest loans for college students, who had to repay only half the amount if they went on to teach in elementary or secondary school after graduation. In addition, the NDEA provided fellowship support for graduate students planning to go into college and university teaching. The NDEA represented a new consensus on the importance of high-quality education to the national interest.

Suburban Life

The suburban boom strengthened the domestic ideal of the nuclear family as the model for American life. In particular, the picture of the perfect suburban wife—efficient, patient, always charming—became a dominant image in television, movies, and magazines. Suburban domesticity was usually presented as women's only path to happiness and fulfillment. This cultural image often masked a stifling existence defined by housework, child care, and boredom. In the late 1950s, Betty Friedan, a wife, mother, and journalist, began a systematic sur-

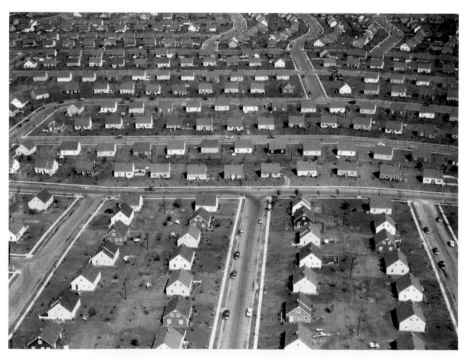

An aerial view of 1950s tract houses in the suburban development of Levittown, New York. Mass production techniques were key to providing affordable housing in the new postwar suburbs—but they required a "cookie cutter" approach to architecture, with little or no variation among the houses.

SOURCE: Getty Images, Inc. Hulton Archive Photos.

vey of her Smith College classmates. She found "a strange discrepancy between the reality of our lives as women and the image to which we were trying to conform." Friedan expanded her research and in 1963 published *The Feminine Mystique*, a landmark book that articulated the frustrations of suburban women and helped to launch a revived feminist movement. (See Out of Many Voices: "The Problem That Has No Name".)

For millions of suburban families the middle-class life could be achieved only with two incomes. The expansion of the female labor force, growing from 17 million in 1946 to 22 million in 1958, was a central economic fact of the post World War II years, By 1960, 40 percent of women were employed full-time or part-time, and 30 percent of all married women worked outside of the home. Taking jobs largely in clerical, white collar, and other service fields, married women looked to sup-

plement income and ensure a solidly middle-class standard of living for their families. The opportunity to move to a more fashionable neighborhood, to purchase a second car, or take a family vacation often depended upon a wife's second income (see Figure 27.1).

The postwar rebirth of religious life was strongly associated with suburban living. In 1940 less than half the American population belonged to institutionalized churches; by the mid-1950s nearly three-quarters identified themselves as church members. A church-building boom was centered in the expanding suburbs. Best-selling religious authors such as Norman Vincent Peale and Bishop Fulton J. Sheen offered a shallow blend of reassurance and "the power of positive thinking." They stressed individual solutions to problems, opposing social or political activism. Their emphasis on the importance of belonging, of fitting in,

OUT OF MANY VOICES

"THE PROBLEM THAT HAS NO NAME," TWO SUBURBAN HOUSEWIVES IN THE 1950S

Journalist Betty Friedan combined questionnaires, interviews, and research into the lives of postwar American women and published The Feminine Mystique *in 1963. The book's pathbreaking analysis of the unhappiness felt by many middle-class suburban housewives helped spark the modern feminist movement. Here are excerpts from two interviews.*

I ASK MYSELF WHY I'M SO DISSATISFIED. I'VE GOT my health, fine children, a lovely new home, enough money. My husband has a real future as an electronics engineer. He doesn't have any of these feelings. He says maybe I need a vacation, let's go to New York for a weekend. But that isn't it. I always had this idea we should do everything together. I can't sit down and read a book alone. If the children are napping and I have one hour to myself I just walk through the house waiting for them to wake up. I don't make a move until I know where the rest of the crowd is going. It's as if ever since you were a little girl, there's always been somebody or something that will take care of your life: your parents, or college, or falling in love, or having a child, or moving to a new house. Then you wake up one morning and there's nothing to look forward to.

A film made of any typical morning in my house would look like an old Marx Brothers' comedy. I wash the dishes, rush the older children off to school, dash out in the yard to cultivate the chrysanthemums, run back in to make a phone call about a committee meeting, help the youngest child build a blockhouse, spend fifteen minutes skimming the newspapers so I can be well-informed, then scamper down to the washing machines where my thrice-weekly laundry includes enough clothes to keep a primitive village going for an entire year. By noon I'm ready for a padded cell. Very little of what I've done has been really necessary or important. Outside pressures lash me through the day. Yet I look upon myself as one of the more relaxed housewives in the neighborhood. Many of my friends are even more frantic. In the past sixty years we have come full circle and the American housewife is once again trapped in a squirrel cage. If the cage is now a modern plateglass-and-broadloom ranch house or a convenient modern apartment, the situation is no less painful than when her grandmother sat over an embroidery hoop in her gilt-and-plush parlor and muttered angrily about women's rights. ■

SOURCE: http://www.h-net.org/~hst203/documents/friedan1.html
[Betty Friedan, *The Feminine Mystique* (W.W. Norton, 1963)]

meshed well with suburban social life and the ideal of family-centered domesticity.

California came to embody postwar suburban life. At the center of this lifestyle was the automobile. Cars were a necessity for commuting to work. California also led the nation in the development of drive-in facilities: motels, movies, shopping malls, fast-food restaurants, and banks. More than 500 miles of highways would be constructed around Los Angeles alone. In Orange County, southeast of Los Angeles, the "centerless city" emerged as the dominant form of community. The experience of one woman resident was typical: "I live in Garden Grove, work in Irvine, shop in Santa Ana, go to the dentist in Anaheim, my husband works in Long Beach, and I used to be the president of the League of Women Voters in Fullerton" (see Figure 27.2).

Contemporary journalists, novelists, and social scientists contributed to the popular image of suburban life as essentially dull, conformist, and peopled exclusively by the educated middle class. John Cheever, for example, won the National Book Award for *The Wapshot Chronicle* (1957),

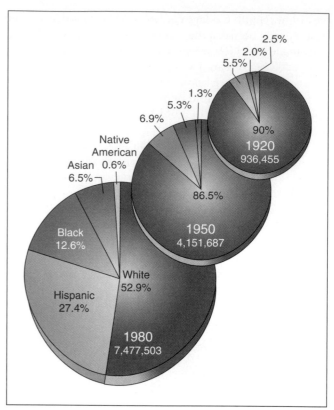

FIGURE 27.2   L.A. County Population 1920–80

a novel set in fictional Remsen Park, "a community of four thousand identical homes." Yet these writers tended to obscure the real class and ethnic differences found among and between suburban communities. Many new suburbs had a distinctively blue-collar cast. Milpitas, California, for example, grew up around a Ford auto plant about fifty miles outside San Jose. Its residents were blue-collar assembly-line workers and their families, rather than salaried, college-educated, white-collar employees. Self-segregation and zoning ordinances gave some new suburbs distinctively Italian, Jewish, or Irish ethnic identities, similar to older urban neighborhoods. For millions of new suburbanites, architectural and psychological conformity was an acceptable price to pay for the comforts of home ownership, a small plot of land, and a sense of security and status.

Organized Labor and the AFL-CIO

By the mid-1950s American trade unions reached an historic high-point in their penetration of the labor market, reflecting the enormous gains made during the organizing drives in core mass-production industries during the New Deal and World War II. Whereas only one in eight nonagricultural workers were union members on the eve of the Great Depression, twenty-five years later the figure stood at one in three. Union influence in political life, especially

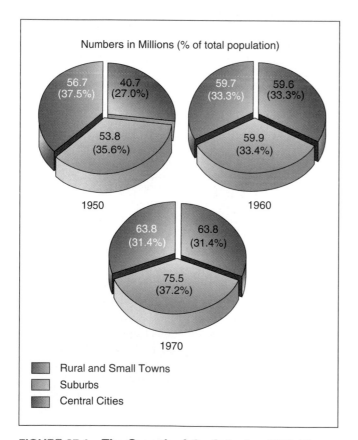

FIGURE 27.1   The Growth of the Suburbs, 1950–70

Suburban growth, at the expense of older inner cities, was one of the key social trends in the twenty-five years following World War II. By 1970, more Americans lived in suburbs than in either inner cities or rural areas.

SOURCE: Adapted from U.S. Bureau of the Census, *Current Censuses, 1930–1970* (Washington DC: U.S. Government Printing Office, 1975).

within the Democratic Party, had also increased. Yet the Republican sweep to power in 1952 meant that for the first time in a generation organized labor was without an ally in the White House. New leaders in the nation's two major labor organizations, the American Federation of Labor (dominated by old-line construction and craft unions) and the Congress of Industrial Organizations (centered around unions in mass-production industry), now pushed for a merger of the two rival groups as the way to protect and build on the movement's recent gains.

George Meany, the brusque, cigar-chomping head of the AFL, seemed the epitome of the modern labor boss. Originally a plumber, he had worked his way through the AFL bureaucracy and had played a leading role on National War Labor Board during World War II. An outspoken anti-Communist, Meany had pushed the AFL closer to the Democratic Party, and he took pride in never having been on a strike or a picket line. Unions, he believed, must focus on improving the economic well-being of their members. Meany's counterpart in the CIO was Walter Reuther, originally a tool-and-die maker in the auto shops of Detroit. Reuther had come to prominence as a leader of the United Automobile Workers during the tumultuous organizing drives of the 1930s and 1940s. Although he had moved away from his early socialist leanings, Reuther believed strongly that American unions ought to stand for something beyond the bread-and-butter needs of their members. His support of a broader social vision, including racial equality, aggressive union organizing, and expansion of the welfare state, reflected the more militant tradition of CIO unions. Despite their differences, both Meany and Reuther believed a merger of their two organizations offered the best strategy for the labor movement. In 1955 the newly combined AFL-CIO brought some 12.5 million union members under one banner, with Meany as president and Reuther as director of the Industrial Union Department.

The merger marked the apex of trade union membership, and after 1955 its share of the labor market began a slow and steady decline. To be sure, union membership helped bring the trappings of middle-class prosperity to millions of workers and their families: home ownership, higher education for children, travel, and comfortable retirement. But the AFL-CIO showed little commitment to bringing unorganized workers into the fold. Scandals involving union corruption and racketeering hurt the labor movement's public image. In 1957 the AFL-CIO expelled its largest single affiliate, the International Brotherhood of Teamsters, because of its close ties to organized crime. In 1959, after highly publicized hearings into union corruption, Congress passed the Landrum-Griffin Act, which widened government control over union affairs and further restricted union use of picketing and secondary boycotts during strikes. While union membership as a percentage of the total workforce declined, important growth did take place in new areas, reflecting a broader shift in the American workplace from manufacturing to service jobs. During the 1950s and 1960s union membership among public sector employees, especially at the state and local level, increased dramatically. Only 400,000 government workers belonged to unions in 1955. By the early 1970s the figure reached 4 million, as civil servants, postal employees, teachers, police, and firefighters joined unions for the first time.

Lonely Crowds and Organization Men

Perhaps the most ambitious and controversial critique of postwar suburban America was sociologist David Riesman's *The Lonely Crowd* (1950). Riesman argued that modern America had given birth to a new kind of character type, the "other-directed" man. Previously the nation had cultivated "inner-directed" people—self-reliant individualists who early on in life had internalized self-discipline and moral standards. By contrast, the "other-directed" person typical of the modern era was peer-oriented. Morality and ideals came from the overarching desire to conform. Americans, Riesman thought, were now less likely to take risks or act independently. Their thinking and habits had come to be determined by cues they received from the mass media.

Similarly, William H. Whyte's *Organization Man* (1956), a study of the Chicago suburb of Park Forest, offered a picture of people obsessed with fitting into their communities and jobs. In place of the old Protestant ethic of hard work, thrift, and competitive struggle, Whyte believed, middle-class suburbanites now strove mainly for a comfortable, secure niche in the system. They held to a new social ethic, he argued: "a belief in the group as the source of creativity; a belief in 'belongingness' as the ultimate need of the individual."

The most radical critic of postwar society, and the one with the most enduring influence, was Texas-reared sociologist C. Wright Mills. In *White Collar* (1951), Mills analyzed the job culture that typified life for middle-class salaried employees, office workers, and bureaucrats. "When white collar people get jobs," he wrote, "they sell not only their time and energy, but their personalities as well. They sell by the week or month their smiles and their kindly gestures, and they must practice the prompt repression of resentment and aggression." In *The Power Elite* (1956), Mills argued that a small, interconnected group of corporate executives, military men, and political leaders had come to dominate American society. The arms race in particular, carried out in the name of cold war policies, had given an unprecedented degree of power to what President Eisenhower later termed the military-industrial complex.

The Expansion of Higher Education

American higher education experienced rapid growth after the war. This expansion both reflected and reinforced other trends in postwar society. The number of

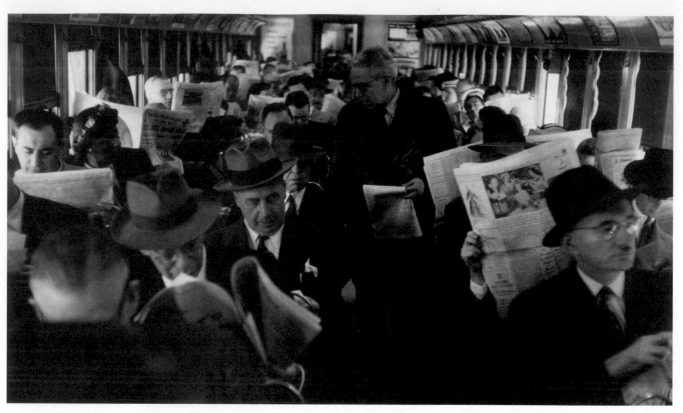

A crowded commuter train in Philadelphia, ca. 1955. The rapid growth of suburbs in the postwar era made commuting to work, either by mass transit or auto, a routine part of life for millions of Americans.

SOURCE: Getty Images Inc.

students enrolled in colleges and universities climbed from 2.6 million in 1950 to 3.2 million in 1960. It then more than doubled—to 7.5 million—by 1970, as the baby boom generation came of age. Most of these new students attended greatly enlarged state university systems. Several factors contributed to this explosion. A variety of new federal programs, including the GI Bill and the National Defense Education Act, helped subsidize college education for millions of new students. Government spending on research and development in universities, especially for defense-related projects, promoted a postwar shift to graduate education and faculty research and away from traditional undergraduate teaching.

Colleges and universities by and large accepted the values of postwar corporate culture. By the mid-1950s, 20 percent of all college graduates majored in business or other commercial fields. The college degree was a gateway to the middle class. It became a requirement for a whole range of expanding white-collar occupations in banking, insurance, real estate, advertising and marketing, and other corporate enterprises. Most administrators accommodated large business interests, which were well represented on university boards of trustees. Universities themselves were increasingly run like businesses, with administrators adopting the language of input-output, cost effectiveness, and quality control.

Health and Medicine

Dramatic improvements in medical care allowed many Americans to enjoy longer and healthier lives. New antibiotics such as penicillin were manufactured and distributed on a mass basis, and after the war they became widely available to the general population. Federal support for research continued after the war with the reorganization of the National Institutes of Health in 1948.

By 1960 many dreaded epidemic diseases, such as tuberculosis, diphtheria, whooping cough, and measles, had virtually disappeared from American life. Perhaps the most celebrated achievement of postwar medicine was the victory over poliomyelitis. Between 1947 and 1951 this disease, which usually crippled those it did not kill, struck an annual average of 39,000 Americans. In 1952, 58,000 cases, most of them children, were reported. Frightened parents warned children to stay away from crowded swimming pools and other gathering places. In 1955 Jonas Salk pioneered the first effective vaccine against the disease, using a preparation of killed virus. A nationwide program of polio vaccination, later supplemented by the oral Sabin vaccine, virtually eliminated polio by the 1960s.

Yet the benefits of "wonder drugs" and advanced medical techniques were not shared equally by all Americans. More sophisticated treatments and expensive new hospital facilities sharply increased the costs of health care. The very poor and many elderly Americans found themselves unable to afford modern medicine. Thousands of communities, especially in rural areas and small towns, lacked doctors or decent hospital facilities. Critics of the medical establishment charged that the proliferation of medical specialists and large hospital complexes had increased the number of unnecessary surgical operations, especially for women and children. The decline of the general practitioner—the family doctor—meant fewer physicians made house calls; more and more people went to hospital emergency rooms or outpatient clinics for treatment.

The American Medical Association (AMA), which certified medical schools, did nothing to increase the flow of new doctors. The number of physicians per 100,000 people actually declined between 1950 and 1960; the shortage was made up by doctors trained in other countries. The AMA also lobbied hard against efforts to expand government responsibility for the public's health. President Harry Truman had advanced a plan for national health insurance, to be run along the lines of Social Security. President Dwight Eisenhower had proposed a program that would offer government assistance to private health insurance companies. The AMA denounced both proposals as "socialized medicine." It helped block direct federal involvement in health care until the creation of Medicare (for the elderly) and Medicaid (for the poor) in 1965.

YOUTH CULTURE

The term "teenager," describing someone between thirteen and nineteen, entered standard usage only at the end of World War II. According to the *Dictionary of American Slang*, the United States is the only country with a word for this age group and the only country to consider it "a separate entity whose influence, fads, and fashions are worthy of discussion apart from the adult world." The fifteen years following World War II saw unprecedented attention to America's adolescents. Deep fears were expressed about everything from teenage sexuality and juvenile delinquency to young people's driving habits, hairstyles, and choice of clothing. At the same time, advertisers and businesses pursued the disposable income of America's affluent youth with a vengeance. Teenagers often found themselves caught between their desire to carve out their own separate sphere and the pressure to become an adult as quickly as possible.

The Youth Market

Birthrates had accelerated gradually during the late 1930s and more rapidly during the war years. The children born in those years had by the late 1950s grown into the original teenagers, the older siblings of the celebrated baby boomers of 1946–64. They came of age in a society that, compared with that of their parents and the rest of the world, was uniquely affluent. Together, the demographic growth of teens and the postwar economic expansion created a burgeoning youth market. Manufacturers and advertisers rushed to cash in on the special needs and desires of young consumers: cosmetics, clothing, radios and phonographs, and cars.

In 1959, *Life* summarized the new power of the youth market. "Counting only what is spent to satisfy their special teenage demands," the magazine reported, "the youngsters and their parents will shell out about $10 billion this year, a billion more than the total sales of GM." In addition, advertisers and market researchers found that teenagers often played a critical, if hard-to-measure, role as "secret persuaders" in a family's large purchase decisions. Specialized market research organizations, such as Eugene Gilbert & Company and Teen-Age Survey Incorporated, sprang up to serve business clients eager to attract teen consumers and instill brand loyalty. Through the 1950s and into the 1960s, teenagers had a major, sometimes dominant, voice in determining America's cultural fads.

To many parents, the emerging youth culture was a dangerous threat to their authority. One mother summarized this fear in a revealing, if slightly hysterical, letter to *Modern Teen*:

> Don't you realize what you are doing? You are encouraging teenagers to write to each other, which keeps them from doing their school work and other chores. You are encouraging them to kiss and have physical contact before they're even engaged, which is morally wrong and you know it. You are encouraging them to have faith in the depraved individuals who make rock and roll records when it's common knowledge that ninety percent of these rock and roll singers are people with no morals or sense of values.

The increasing uniformity of public school education also contributed to the public recognition of the special status of teenagers. In 1900, about one of every eight teenagers was in school; by the 1950s, the figure was six out of eight. Psychologists wrote guidebooks for parents, two prominent examples being Dorothy Baruch's *How to Live with Your Teenager* (1953) and Paul Landis's *Understanding Teenagers* (1955). Social scientists stressed the importance of peer pressure for understanding teen behavior. "Traditional sources of adult authority and socialization—the marketplace, schools, child-rearing manuals, the mass media—all reinforced the notion of teenagers as a special community, united by age, rank, and status".

"Hail! Hail! Rock 'n' Roll!"

The demands of the new teen market, combined with structural changes in the postwar American mass media, reshaped the nation's popular music. As television broadcasting rapidly replaced radio as the center of family entertainment, people began using radios in new ways. The production of portable transistor radios and car radios grew rapidly in the 1950s as listeners increasingly tuned them in for diversion from or an accompaniment to other activities. By 1956, some 2,700 AM radio stations were on the air across the United States, with about 70 percent of their broadcast time given to record shows. Most of these concentrated on popular music for the traditional white adult market: pop ballads, novelty songs, and show tunes.

In the recording industry, meanwhile, a change was in the air. Small independent record labels led the way in aggressively recording African American rhythm and blues artists. Atlantic Records, in New York, developed the most influential galaxy of artists, including Ray Charles, Ruth Brown, the Drifters, Joe Turner, LaVerne Baker, and the Clovers. Chess, in Chicago, had the blues-based, singer-songwriter-guitarists Chuck Berry and Bo Diddley, and the "doo-wop" group the Moonglows. In New Orleans, Imperial had the veteran pianist-singer

Fats Domino, while Specialty unleashed the outrageous Little Richard on the world. On radio, over jukeboxes, and in record stores, all of these African American artists "crossed over," adding millions of white teenagers to their solid base of black fans. In 1954 the music trade magazine *Billboard* noted this trend among white teenagers: "The present generation has not known the rhythmically exciting dance bands of the swing era. It therefore satisfies its hunger for 'music with a beat' in modern r&b (rhythm and blues) groups."

The older, more established record companies, such as RCA, Decca, M-G-M, and Capitol, had largely ignored black music. Their response to the new trend was to offer slick, toned-down "cover" versions by white pop singers of rhythm and blues originals. Cover versions were invariably pallid imitations, artistically inferior to the originals. One has only to compare, say, Pat Boone's covers of Fats Domino's "Ain't That a Shame" or Little Richard's "Tutti Frutti" with the originals to hear how much was lost. While African American artists began to enjoy newfound mass acceptance, there were limits to how closely white kids could identify with black performers. Racism, especially in so sexually charged an arena as musical performance, was still a powerful force in American life. Because of the superior promotional power of the major companies and the institutional racism in the music business, white cover versions almost always outsold the black originals. But some disc jockeys refused to play cover versions and attracted enthusiastic audiences of both black and white young people. Alan Freed, a white Cleveland disc jockey, popularized the term "rock 'n' roll" to describe the black rhythm and blues that he played on the air and promoted in live concerts before enthusiastic and racially mixed audiences of teenagers. (See Out of Many Voices: Alan Freed Defends 'The Big Beat," 1955.)

The stage was thus set for the arrival of white rock 'n' roll artists who could exploit the new sounds and styles. As a rock 'n' roll performer and recording artist, Elvis Presley reinvented American popular music. His success challenged the old lines separating black music from white, and pop from rhythm and blues or country. As a symbol of rebellious youth and as the embodiment of youthful sexuality, Elvis revitalized American popular culture. In his wake came a host of white rock 'n' rollers, many of them white South-

This photo of Elvis Presley singing at a 1956 state fair in Memphis captured his dramatic stage presence. Performing with only a trio, his sound was spare but hard driving. Both the music and Presley's stage moves owed a great deal to African American rhythm and blues artists.

SOURCE: Getty Images, Inc.

OUT OF MANY VOICES

ALAN FREED DEFENDS "THE BIG BEAT," 1955

As a radio disk jockey and concert promoter, Alan Freed championed the music of African American rhythm and blues artists. He popularized the term "rock 'n' roll" to describe the music that attracted millions of young white fans in the 1950s. Here Freed defends the music against its detractors in a piece published, significantly, in the Pittsburgh Courier, *a leading black newspaper.*

"THE BIG BEAT IN AMERICAN MUSIC," WHICH HAS surely become the great new "swing" and dance era for today's teenage generation, as well as for their parents, has finally burst loose on the popular music horizon. Just as has always happened with the emergence of any other great era in music, literature and the arts through the ages of history it has not been spared the caustic criticism and "whispering campaigns" of those who don't like it, don't understand it, and who do not appreciate it.

To me, this campaign against "Rock 'n' Roll" smells of discrimination of the worst kind against the great and accomplished Negro song writers, musicians and singers who are responsible for this outstanding contribution to American music. It is Amer-

ican! And people throughout our nation can look forward to the day when they will be able to see on their TV screens, and eventually in person, the famous Negro artists who have brought us the "off spring" of the only basic American musical heritage we can call our own. It has been nurtured and has grown through oppressions, prejudices, narrow minded bigotry, and through such critic inflicted terminologies as "Race Music" and "Honky Tonk Rhythm and Blues."

Even its most caustic critics must soon learn that the young people of America, as well as their parents, want "music with a beat" that will set their feet tapping. Those "prophets of doom" who are constantly harping about juvenile delinquency, yet have never been known to do anything to materially assist young people, should do themselves a favor by awakening to the realization that the wholesome kids of America are not interested in "dirty leerics." They want to dance. They want to "let off steam" in a happy American way at well supervised events! I am proud to have helped expose the Big Beat, instead of suppressing it! So, let's "Rock 'n' Roll"! ■

SOURCE: *Pittsburgh Courier*, 1955, from http://www.alanfreed.com.

erners like Elvis: Jerry Lee Lewis, Buddy Holly, the Everly Brothers, Roy Orbison. But the greatest songwriter and the most influential guitarist to emerge from this first "golden age of rock 'n' roll" was Chuck Berry, an African American from St. Louis who worked part-time as a beautician and house painter. Berry proved especially adept at capturing the teen spirit with humor, irony, and passion. He composed hits around the trials and tribulations of school ("School Days"), young love ("Memphis"), cars ("Maybellene"), and making it as a rock 'n' roller ("Johnny B. Goode"). As much as anyone, Berry created music that defined what it meant to be young in postwar America.

Almost Grown

Teenage consumers remade the landscape of popular music into their own turf. The dollar value of annual record sales nearly tripled between 1954 and 1959, from $213 million to $603 million. New magazines aimed

exclusively at teens flourished in the postwar years. *Modern Teen*, *Teen Digest*, and *Dig* were just a few. Most teen magazines, like rock 'n' roll music, focused on the rituals, pleasures, and sorrows surrounding teenage courtship. Paradoxically, behavior patterns among white middle-class teenagers in the 1950s and early 1960s exhibited a new kind of youth orientation and at the same time a more pronounced identification with adults.

While many parents worried about the separate world inhabited by their teenage children, many teens seemed determined to become adults as quickly as possible. Postwar affluence multiplied the number of two-car families, making it easier for sixteen-year-olds to win driving privileges formerly reserved for eighteen-year-olds. Girls began dating, wearing brassieres and nylon stockings, and using cosmetics at an earlier age than before—twelve or thirteen rather than fifteen or sixteen. Several factors contributed to this trend, including a continuing decline in the age of menarche (first menstruation), the sharp drop in the age of marriage after World War II, and the precocious social climate of junior high schools (institutions that became widespread only after 1945). The practice of going steady, derived from the college custom of fraternity and sorority pinning, became commonplace among high schoolers. By the late 1950s, eighteen had become the most common age at which American females married.

Teenagers often felt torn between their identification with youth culture and pressures to assume adult responsibilities. Many young people juggled part-time jobs with school and very active social lives. Teen-oriented magazines, music, and movies routinely dispensed advice and sympathy regarding this dilemma. Rock 'n' roll songs offered the most sympathetic treatments of the conflicts teens experienced over work ("Summertime Blues"), parental authority ("Yakety Yak"), and the desire to look adult ("Sweet Little Sixteen"). By 1960, sociologist James S. Coleman reflected a growing consensus when he noted that postwar society had given adolescents "many of the instruments which can make them a functioning community: cars, freedom in dating, continual contact with the opposite sex, money, and entertainment, like popular music and movies, designed especially for them."

Deviance and Delinquency

Many adults held rock 'n' roll responsible for the apparent decline in parental control over teens. Much of the opposition to rock 'n' roll, particularly in the South, played on long-standing racist fears that white females might be attracted to black music and black performers. The undercurrent beneath all this opposition was a deep anxiety over the more open expression of sexual feelings by both performers and audiences.

Paralleling the rise of rock 'n' roll was a growing concern with an alleged increase in juvenile delinquency. An endless stream of magazine articles, books, and newspaper stories asserted that criminal behavior among the nation's young was chronic. Gang fights, drug and alcohol abuse, car theft, and sexual offenses received the most attention. The U.S. Senate established a special subcommittee on juvenile delinquency. Highly publicized hearings in 1955 and 1956 convinced much of the public that youthful criminals were terrorizing the country. Although crime statistics do suggest an increase in juvenile crime during the 1950s, particularly in the suburbs, the public perception of the severity of the problem was surely exaggerated.

In retrospect, the juvenile delinquency controversy tells us more about anxieties over family life and the erosion of adult authority than about crime patterns. Teenagers seemed more defined by and loyal to their peer culture than to their parents. A great deal of their music, speech, dress, and style was alien and threatening. The growing importance of the mass media in defining youth culture brought efforts to regulate or censor media forms believed to cause juvenile delinquency. In 1954, for example, psychiatrist Fredric Wertham published *Seduction of the Innocent*, arguing that crime comic books incited youngsters to criminal acts. Mass culture, he believed, could overwhelm the traditonal influences of family, school, and religion. He led a highly publicized crusade that forced the comic book industry to adopt a code strictly limiting the portrayal of violence and crime.

As reactions to two of the most influential "problem youth" movies of the postwar era indicate, teens and their parents frequently interpreted depictions of youthful deviance in the mass media in very different ways. In *The Wild One* (1954), Marlon Brando played the crude, moody leader of a vicious motorcycle gang. Most adults thought of the film as a critique of mindless gang violence, but many teenagers identified with the Brando character, who, when asked, "What are you rebelling against?" coolly replied, "Whattaya got?" In *Rebel Without a Cause* (1955), James Dean, Natalie Wood, and Sal Mineo played emotionally troubled youths in an affluent California suburb. The movie suggests that parents can cause delinquency when they fail to conform to conventional roles—Dean's father wears an apron and his mother is domineering.

Brando and Dean, along with Elvis, were probably the most popular and widely imitated teen idols of the era. For most parents, they were vaguely threatening figures whose sexual energy and lack of discipline placed them outside the bounds of middle-class respectability. For teens, however, they offered an irresistible combination of rough exterior and sensitive core. They embodied, as well, the contradiction of individual rebellion versus the attractions of a community defined by youth.

MASS CULTURE AND ITS DISCONTENTS

No mass medium ever achieved such power and popularity as rapidly as television. The basic technology for broadcasting visual images with sound had been developed by the late 1930s but World War II and corporate competition postponed television's introduction to the public until 1946. By 1960, nearly nine in ten American families owned at least one set, which was turned on an average of more than five hours a day. Television reshaped leisure time and political life. It also helped create a new kind of national community defined by the buying and selling of consumer goods (see Figure 27.3).

Important voices challenged the economic trends and cultural conformity of the postwar years. Academics, journalists, novelists, and poets offered a variety of works criticizing the overall direction of American life. These critics of what was dubbed "mass society"

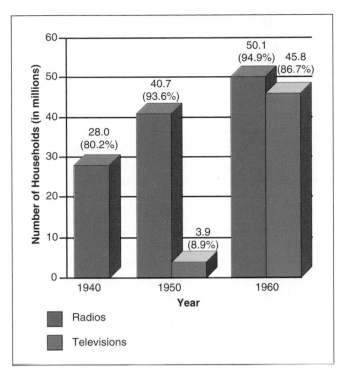

were troubled by the premium American culture put on conformity, status, and material consumption. Although a distinct minority, these critics were persistent. Many of their ideas and prescriptions would reverberate through the political and cultural upheavals of the 1960s and 1970s.

Television: Tube of Plenty

Television constituted a radical change from radio, and its development as a mass medium was quicker and less chaotic. The three main television networks—NBC, CBS, ABC—grew directly from radio organizations. The networks led the industry from the start, rather than following individual stations, as radio had done. Nearly all TV stations were affiliated with one or more of the networks; only a handful of independent stations could be found around the country.

Television not only depended on advertising, it also transformed the advertising industry. The television business, like radio, was based on the selling of time to advertisers who wanted to reach the mass audiences tuning into shows. Radio had offered entire shows produced by and for single sponsors, usually advertisers who wanted a close identification between their product and a star. But the higher costs of television production forced key changes. Sponsors left the production of programs to the networks, independent producers, and Hollywood studios.

Sponsors now bought scattered time slots for spot advertisements rather than bankrolling an entire show. Ad agencies switched their creative energy to producing slick thirty-second commercials rather than entertainment programs. A shift from broadcasting live shows to filming them opened up lucrative opportunities for reruns and foreign export. The total net revenue of the TV networks and their affiliated stations in 1947 was about $2 million; by 1957 it was nearly $1 billion. Advertisers spent $58 million on TV shows in 1949; ten years later the figure was almost $1.5 billion.

The staple of network radio, the comedy-variety show, was now produced with pictures. The first great national TV hit, *The Milton Berle Show*, followed this format when it premiered in 1948. Radio

FIGURE 27.3 Radio and Television Ownership, 1940–60 By 1960 nearly 90 percent of American households owned at least one television set, as TV replaced radio as the nation's dominant mass medium of entertainment. Radio ownership rose as well, but Americans increasingly listened to radio as an accompaniment to other activities, such as driving.

A 1950s family watching "I Love Lucy," one of the most popular situation comedies in the early days of television. Manufacturers designed and marketed TV sets as living room furniture and emphasized their role in fostering family togetherness.

SOURCE: PPP/Popperfoto. H. Armstrong Roberts.

Fess Parker, the actor who starred as Davy Crockett in Walt Disney's popular television series, greets young fans at New York's Idlewild Airport in 1955. The series generated enormous sales of coonskin caps and other Crockett inspired merchandise, demonstrating the extraordinary selling power of the new medium of television.

SOURCE: Bettmann. Corbis/Bettmann.

stars such as Jack Benny, Edgar Bergen, George Burns and Gracie Allen, and Eddie Cantor switched successfully to television. Boxing, wrestling, the roller derby, and other sporting events were also quite popular. For a brief time, original live drama flourished on writer-oriented shows such as *Goodyear Television Playhouse* and *Studio One*. In addition, early television featured an array of situation comedies with deep roots in radio and vaudeville.

Set largely among urban ethnic families, early shows like *I Remember Mama, The Goldbergs, The Life of Riley, Life with Luigi,* and *The Honeymooners* often featured working-class families struggling with the dilemmas posed by consumer society. Most plots turned around comic tensions created and resolved by consumption: contemplating home ownership, going out on the town, moving to the suburbs, buying on credit, purchasing a new car. Generational discord and the loss of ethnic identity were also common themes. To some degree, these early shows mirrored and spoke to the real dilemmas facing families that had survived the Great Depression and the Second World War and were now finding their place in a prosperous consumer culture.

By the late 1950s all the urban ethnic comedy shows were off the air. A new breed of situation comedies presented nonethnic white, affluent, and insular suburban middle-class families. Shows like *Father Knows Best, Leave It to Beaver, The Adventures of Ozzie and Harriet,* and *The Donna Reed Show* epitomized the ideal suburban American family of the day. Their plots focused on genial crises, usually brought on by children's mischief and resolved by kindly fathers. In retrospect, what is most striking about these shows is what is absent—politics, social issues, cities, white ethnic groups, African Americans, and Latinos were virtually unrepresented.

Television also demonstrated a unique ability to create overnight fads and crazes across the nation. Elvis Presley's 1956 appearances on several network television variety shows, including those hosted by Milton Berle and Ed Sullivan, catapulted him from regional success to international stardom. Successful television advertising campaigns made household names out of previously obscure products. A memorable example of TV's influence came in 1955 when Walt Disney produced a series of three one-hour shows on the life of frontier legend Davy Crockett. The tremendous success of the series instantly created a $300 million industry of Davy Crockett shirts, dolls, toys, and coonskin caps.

Television and Politics

Prime-time entertainment shows carefully avoided any references to the political issues of the day. Network executives bowed to the conformist climate created by the domestic cold war. Any hint of political controversy could scare off sponsors, who were extremely sensitive to public protest. Anti-Communist crusaders set themselves up as private watchdogs, warning of alleged subversive influence in the broadcasting industry. Television executives responded by effectively blacklisting many talented individuals.

As in Hollywood, the cold war chill severely restricted the range of political discussion on television. Any honest treatment of the conflicts in American society threatened the consensus mentality at the heart of the television business. Even public affairs and documentary programs were largely devoid of substantial political debate. An important exception was Edward R. Murrow's *See It Now* on CBS—but that show was off the air by 1955. Television news did not come into its own until 1963, with the beginning of half-hour nightly network newscasts. Only then did television's extraordinary power to rivet the nation's attention during a crisis become clear.

Still, some of the ways that TV would alter the nation's political life emerged in the 1950s. Television made Democratic senator Estes Kefauver of Tennessee a national political figure through live coverage of his 1951 Senate investigation into organized crime. It also contributed to the political downfall of Senator Joseph McCarthy in 1954 by showing his cruel bullying tactics during Senate hearings into alleged subversive Communist influence in the army. In 1952, Republican vice presidential candidate Richard M. Nixon effectively used an emotional, direct television appeal to voters—the "Checkers" speech—to counter charges of corruption (see Chapter 26).

The 1952 election also brought the first use of TV political advertising for presidential candidates. The Republican Party hired a high-powered ad agency, Batten, Barton, Durstine & Osborn (BBD&O), to create a series of short, sophisticated advertisements touting Dwight D. Eisenhower. The BBD&O campaign saturated TV with twenty-second Eisenhower spots for two weeks before election day. Ever since then, television image-making has been the single most important element in American electoral politics.

Culture Critics

The urge to denounce the mass media for degrading the quality of American life tended to unite radical and conservative critics. Thus Marxist writer Dwight Macdonald sounded an old conservative warning when he described mass culture as "a parasite, a cancerous growth on High Culture." Society's most urgent problem, Macdonald claimed, was "a tepid, flaccid Middlebrow Culture that threatens to engulf everything in its spreading ooze."

Critics of mass culture argued that the audiences for the mass media were atomized, anonymous, and detached. The media themselves had become omnipotent, capable of manipulating the attitudes and behavior of the isolated individuals in the mass. Many of these critics achieved great popularity themselves, suggesting that the public was deeply ambivalent about mass culture. One of the best-selling authors of the day was Vance Packard, whose 1957 exposé *The Hidden Persuaders* showed how advertisers exploited motivational research into the irrational side of human behavior. These critics undoubtedly overestimated the power of the media. They ignored the preponderance of research suggesting that most people watched and responded to mass media in family, peer group, and other social settings. The critics also missed the genuine vitality and creative brilliance to be found within mass culture: African American music; the films of Nicholas Ray, Elia Kazan, and Howard Hawks; the experimental television of Ernie Kovacs; the satire of *Mad* magazine.

Some of the sharpest dissents from the cultural conformity of the day came from a group of writers known collectively as the Beats. Led by the novelist Jack Kerouac and the poet Allen Ginsberg, the Beats shared a distrust

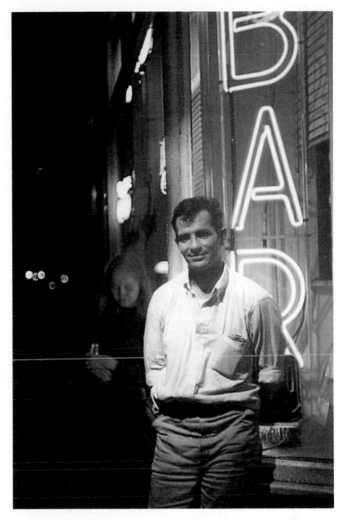

Jack Kerouac, founding voice of the Beat literary movement, in front of a neon lit bar, ca. 1950. Kerouac's public readings, often to the accompaniment of live jazz music, created a performance atmosphere underlining the connections between his writing style and the rhythms and sensibility of contemporary jazz musicians.

SOURCE: Globe Photos, Inc.

of the American virtues of progress, power, and material gain. The Beat sensibility celebrated spontaneity, friendship, jazz, open sexuality, drug use, and the outcasts of American society. Kerouac, born and raised in a working-class French Canadian family in Lowell, Massachusetts, coined the term "beat" in 1948. It meant for him a "weariness with all the forms of the modern industrial state"— conformity, militarism, blind faith in technological progress. Kerouac's 1957 novel *On the Road*, chronicling the tumultuous adventures of Kerouac's circle of friends as they traveled by car back and forth across America, became the Beat manifesto. Allen Ginsberg had grown up in New Jersey in an immigrant Jewish family. His father was a poet and teacher, and his mother had a history of mental problems. After being expelled from Columbia University, Ginsberg grew close to Kerouac and another writer, William Burroughs. At a 1955 poetry reading in San Francisco, Ginsberg introduced his epic poem *Howl* to a wildly enthusiastic audience:

> I saw the best minds of my generation destroyed
> by madness, starving hysterical naked,
> dragging themselves through the negro streets at dawn
> looking for an angry fix,
> angelheaded hipsters burning for the ancient heavenly connection
> to the starry dynamo in the machinery of night.

Howl became one of the best-selling poetry books in the history of publishing, and it established Ginsberg as an important new voice in American literature.

Beat writers received a largely antagonistic, even virulent reception from the literary establishment. But millions of young Americans read their work and became intrigued by their alternative visions. The mass media soon managed to trivialize the Beats. A San Francisco journalist coined the term "beatnik," and by the late 1950s it had become associated with affected men and women dressed in black, wearing sunglasses and berets, and acting rebellious and alienated. But Beat writers like Kerouac, Ginsberg, Burroughs, Diane DiPrima, Gary Snyder, LeRoi Jones, and others continued to produce serious work that challenged America's official culture. They foreshadowed the mass youth rebellion and counterculture to come in the 1960s.

THE COLD WAR CONTINUED

Dwight Eisenhower's experience in foreign affairs had been one of his most attractive assets as a presidential candidate. His success as supreme commander of the Allied forces in World War II owed as much to diplomatic skill as to military prowess. As president, Eisenhower sustained the anti-Communist rhetoric of cold war diplomacy, and his administration persuaded Americans to accept the cold war stalemate as a more or less permanent fact. Eisenhower developed new strategies for containment and for the support of United States power abroad, including a greater reliance on nuclear weapons and the aggressive use of the Central Intelligence Agency (CIA) for covert action. Yet Eisenhower also resolved to do everything he could to forestall an all-out nuclear conflict. He recognized the limits of raw military power. He accepted a less than victorious end to the Korean War, and he avoided a full military involvement in Indochina. Ironically, Eisenhower's promotion of high-tech strategic weaponry fostered development of a military-industrial complex. By the time he left office in 1961, he felt compelled to warn the nation of the growing dangers posed by burgeoning military spending.

The "New Look" in Foreign Affairs

Although Eisenhower recognized that the United States was engaged in a long-term struggle with the Soviet Union, he feared that permanent mobilization for the cold war might overburden the American economy and result in a "garrison state." He therefore pursued a high-tech, capital-intensive defense policy that emphasized America's qualitative advantage in strategic weaponry.

The emphasis on massive retaliation, the administration claimed, would also make possible cuts in the military budget. As Secretary of Defense Charles Wilson said, the goal was to "get more bang for the buck." Eisenhower largely succeeded in stabilizing the defense budget. Between 1954 and 1961 absolute spending rose only $800 million, from $46.6 billion to $47.4 billion. Military spending as an overall percentage of the federal budget fell from 66 percent to 49 percent during his two terms. Much of this saving was gained through the increased reliance on nuclear weapons and long-range delivery systems, which were relatively less expensive than conventional forces.

Secretary of State John Foster Dulles gave shape to the "new look" in American foreign policy in the 1950s. Raised a devout Presbyterian and trained as a lawyer, Dulles had been involved in diplomatic affairs since World War I. He brought a strong sense of righteousness to his job, an almost missionary belief in America's responsibility to preserve the "free world" from godless, immoral communism. Dulles articulated a more assertive policy toward the Communist threat by calling not simply for containment but for a "rollback." The key would be greater reliance on America's nuclear superiority. This policy appealed to Republicans, who had been frustrated by the restriction of United Nations forces to conventional arms during the Korean War. But the limits of a policy based on nuclear strategy became painfully clear when American leaders faced tense situations that offered no clear way to intervene without provoking full-scale war.

When East Berliners rebelled against the Soviets in 1953, cold war hard-liners thought they saw the long awaited opportunity for rollback. But precisely how could the United States respond? Public bitterness over the Korean conflict merged with Eisenhower's sense of restraint and in the end, apart from angry denunciations, the United States did nothing to prevent the Soviets from crushing the rebellion. U.S. leaders faced the same dilemma on a grander scale when Hungarians revolted against their Soviet-dominated Communist rulers in 1956, staging a general strike and taking over the streets and factories in Budapest and other cities. The United States opened its gates to thousands of Hungarian refugees, but despite urgent requests, it refused to intervene when Soviet tanks and troops crushed the revolt.

Eisenhower recognized that the Soviets would defend their own borders, and all of Eastern Europe as well, by all-out military force if necessary.

The death of Josef Stalin in 1953 and the worldwide condemnation of his crimes, revealed by his successor, Nikita Khrushchev, in 1956, gave Eisenhower fresh hope for a new spirit of peaceful coexistence between the two superpowers. Khrushchev, in a gesture of goodwill, withdrew Soviet troops from Austria. The first real rollback had been achieved by negotiations and a spirit of common hope, not threats or force. In 1958 Khrushchev, probing American intentions and hoping to redirect the Soviet economy toward the production of more consumer goods, unilaterally suspended nuclear testing. Khrushchev made a twelve-day trip to America in 1959 during which he visited an Iowa farm, went sightseeing in Hollywood, and spent time with Eisenhower at Camp David, the presidential retreat in Maryland.

The two leaders achieved nothing concrete, but with summit diplomacy seeming to offer at least a psychological thaw in the cold war. In early 1960 Khrushchev called for

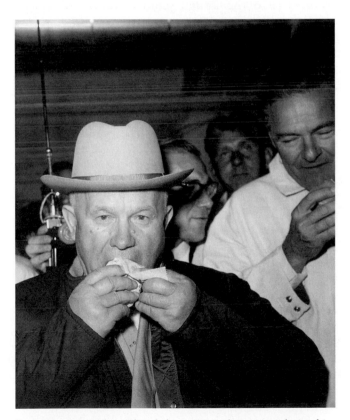

Soviet Premier Nikita Khrushchev enjoys a bite to eat during his tour of an Iowa farm in 1959. A colorful, earthy, and erratic man, Khrushchev loomed as the most visible human symbol of the USSR for Americans. On this trip he called for Soviet-American friendship, yet also boasted "We will bury you."
SOURCE: © Bettmann/CORBIS.

another summit in Paris, to discuss German reunification and nuclear disarmament. Eisenhower, meanwhile, planned his own friendship tour of the Soviet Union. But in May 1960 the Soviets shot down an American U-2 spy plane gathering intelligence on Soviet military installations. A deeply embarrassed Eisenhower at first denied the existence of U-2 flights, but the Soviets produced the pilot, Francis Gary Powers, who readily confessed. The summit collapsed when Eisenhower refused Khrushchev's demands for an apology and an end to the spy flights. The U-2 incident demonstrated the limits of personal diplomacy in resolving the deep structural rivalry between the superpowers.

Eisenhower often provided a moderate voice on issues of defense spending and missile development. The Soviet Union's dramatic launch of Sputnik, the first space-orbiting satellite, in October 1957 upset many Americans' precarious sense of security. In particular, this demonstration of Soviet technological prowess raised fears about Russian ability to deploy intercontinental ballistic missiles (ICBMs) against American cities. Critics attacked the Eisenhower administration for failure to keep up with the enemy. Senator Stuart Symington (D-MO) bluntly warned that, "Unless our defense policies are promptly changed, the Soviets will move from superiority to supremacy." In addition to huge increases in defense spending, some urged a massive program to build "fallout shelters" for the entire population in case of nuclear attack. But Eisenhower rejected these more radical responses. He knew from evidence provided by U-2 spy planes that the Soviet Union in fact trailed far behind the United States in ICBM development, but he kept this knowledge secret. Instead of panicking before Sputnik, he held to a doctrine of "sufficiency": maintaining enough military strength to survive any foreign attack and enough nuclear capability to deliver a massive counterattack. In 1958 Eisenhower did support creation of the National Aeronautics and Space Agency (NASA), to coordinate space exploration and missile development. And he also backed the National Defense Education Act that year, which funneled more federal aid into science and foreign language education. Yet, in Congress a bipartisan majority voted to increase the military budget by another $8 billion in 1958, thereby accelerating the arms race and expanding the defense sector of the economy.

Covert Action

Eisenhower combined the overt threat of massive retaliation in his "new look" approach to foreign affairs with a heavy reliance on covert interventions by the Central Intelligence Agency (CIA). He had been an enthusiastic supporter of covert operations during World War II, and during his presidency CIA-sponsored covert paramilitary operations became a key facet of American foreign policy. With the American public wary of direct U.S. military interventions, the CIA promised a cheap, quick, and quiet way to depose hostile or unstable regimes, or prop up more conservative governments under siege by indigenous revolutionaries.

For CIA director, Eisenhower named Allen Dulles, brother of the secretary of state and a former leader in the CIA's World War II precursor, the Office of Strategic Services. The CIA's mandate was to collect and analyze information, but it did much more under Dulles's command. Thousands of covert agents stationed all over the world carried out a wide range of political activities. Some agents arranged large, secret financial payments to friendly political parties, such as the conservative Christian Democrats in Italy and in Latin America, or foreign trade unions opposed to socialist policies.

The Soviet Union tried to win influence in Africa, Asia, and Latin America by appealing to a shared "antiimperialism" and by offering modest amounts of foreign aid. In most cases, Communists played only small roles in third world independence movements. But the issue of race and the popular desire to recover national resources from foreign investors inflamed already widespread anti-European and anti-American feelings. When new nations or familiar allies threatened to interfere with U.S. regional security arrangements, or to expropriate the property of American businesses, the Eisenhower administration turned to covert action and military intervention.

Intervening Around the World

The Central Intelligence Agency produced a swift, major victory in Iran in 1953. The country's popular prime minister, Mohammed Mossadegh, had nationalized Britain's Anglo-Iranian Oil Company, and the State Department worried that this might set a precedent throughout the oil-rich Middle East. Kermit Roosevelt, CIA chief in Iran, organized and financed an opposition to Mossadegh within the Iranian army and on the streets of Teheran. This CIA-led movement forced Mossadegh out of office and replaced him with Riza Shah Pahlavi. The shah proved his loyalty to his American sponsors by renegotiating oil contracts so as to assure American companies 40 percent of Iran's oil concessions (see Map 27.1).

The rivalry between Israel and its Arab neighbors complicated U.S. policy in the rest of the Middle East. The Arab countries launched an all-out attack on Israel in 1948 immediately after the United States and the Soviet Union had recognized its independence. Israel repulsed the attack, drove thousands of Palestinians from their homes, occupied territory that hundreds of thousands of others had fearfully fled, and seized lands far in excess of the terms of a United Nations–sponsored armistice of 1949. The Arab states refused to recognize Israel's right to exist and subjected it to a damaging economic boycott. Meanwhile, hundreds of thousands of Palestinians languished in refugee camps. Eisenhower believed that Truman had perhaps been too hasty in encouraging the Israelis. Yet most Americans supported the new Jewish state as a refuge for a people who had suffered so much persecution, especially during the Holocaust.

Israel stood as a reliable U.S. ally in an unstable region. Arab nationalism continued to vex American policymakers, culminating in the Suez crisis of 1956. Egyptian president Gamal Abdel Nasser, a leading voice of Arab nationalism, looked for American and British economic aid. He had long dreamed of building the Aswan High Dam on the Nile to create more arable land and provide cheap electric power. When negotiations broke down, Nasser announced he would nationalize the strategically sensitive Suez Canal, and he turned to the Soviet Union for aid. Eisenhower refused European appeals for U.S. help in seizing the Suez Canal and returning it to the British. When British, French, and Israeli forces attacked Egypt in October 1956, the United States sponsored a UN resolution calling for a cease-fire and a withdrawal of foreign forces. Yielding to this pressure and to Soviet threats of intervention, the British and French withdrew, and eventually so did the Israelis. Eisenhower had won a major diplomatic battle through patience and pressure, but he did not succeed in bringing lasting peace to the troubled region.

The most publicized CIA intervention of the Eisenhower years took place in Guatemala, where a fragile democracy had taken root in 1944. President Jácobo Arbenz Guzmán, elected in 1950, aggressively pursued land reform and encouraged the formation of trade unions. At the time, 2 percent of the Guatemalan population owned 72 percent of all farmland. Arbenz also challenged the long-standing dominance of the American-based United Fruit Company by threatening to expropriate hundreds of thousands of acres that United Fruit was not cultivating. The company had powerful friends in the administration (CIA director Dulles had sat on its board of trustees), and it began intensive lobbying for U.S. intervention. United Fruit linked the land-reform program to the evils of international communism, and the CIA spent $7 million training antigovernment dissidents based in Honduras.

The American navy stopped ships bound for Guatemala and seized their cargoes, and on June 14, 1954, a U.S.–sponsored military invasion began. Guatemalan citizens resisted by seizing United Fruit buildings, but U.S. Air Force bombing saved the

MAP EXPLORATION

To explore an interactive version of this map, go to **www.prenhall.com/faragher5/map27.1**

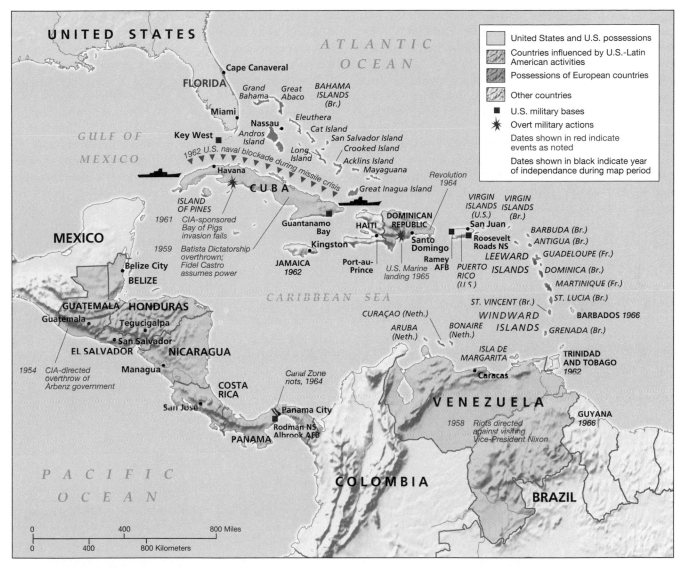

MAP 27.1 The U.S. in the Caribbean, 1948–66 U.S. military intervention and economic presence grew steadily in the Caribbean following World War II. After 1960, opposition to the Cuban Revolution dominated U.S. Caribbean policies.

invasion effort. Guatemalans appealed in vain to the United Nations for help. Meanwhile, President Eisenhower publicly denied any knowledge of CIA activities. The newly appointed military leader, Carlos Castillo Armas, flew to the Guatemalan capital in a U.S. embassy plane. Widespread terror followed, unions were outlawed, and thousands arrested. United

Fruit circulated photos of Guatemalans murdered by the invaders, labeling them "victims of communism." In 1957 Castillo Armas was assassinated, and a decades-long civil war ensued between military factions and peasant guerrillas.

American intervention in Guatemala increased suspicion of and resentment against American foreign policy throughout Central and Latin America. Vice President Nixon declared that the new Guatemalan government had earned "the overwhelming support of the Guatemalan people." But in 1958, while making a "goodwill" tour of Latin America, Nixon was stoned by angry mobs in Caracas, Venezuela, suggesting that U.S. actions in the region had triggered an anti-American backlash.

In Indochina, the United States provided France with massive military aid and CIA cooperation in its desperate struggle to maintain its colonial empire. From 1950 to 1954 the United States poured $2.6 billion (about three-quarters of the total French costs) into the fight against the nationalist Vietminh movement, led by Communist Ho Chi Minh. When Vietminh forces surrounded 25,000 French troops at Dien Bien Phu in March 1954, France pleaded with the United States to intervene directly. Secretary of State Dulles and Vice President Nixon, among others, recommended the use of tactical nuclear weapons and a commitment of ground

troops. But Eisenhower, recalling the difficulties of the Korean conflict, rejected this call. "I can conceive of no greater tragedy," he said, "than for the United States to become engaged in all-out war in Indochina."

At the same time, Eisenhower feared that the loss of one country to communism would inevitably lead to the loss of others. As he put it, "You have a row of dominoes set up, and you knock over the first one and what will happen to the last one is the certainty that it will go over quickly." According to this so-called domino theory, the "loss" of Vietnam would threaten other Southeast Asian nations, such as Laos, Thailand, the Philippines, and perhaps even India and Australia. After the French surrender at Dien Bin Phu, a conference in Geneva established a cease-fire and a temporary division of Vietnam along the 17th parallel into northern and southern sectors. The Geneva accord called for reunification and national elections in 1956. But the United States, although it had attended the conference along with the Soviet Union and China, refused to sign

Venezuelan soldiers (right) tried to disperse rioters who attacked Vice President Richard M. Nixon's car in Caracas during his 1958 "goodwill tour." Demonstrations such as these revealed a reservoir of resentment in Latin America against the interventionist policies of the United States in the region.

SOURCE: AP/Wide World Photos.

the accord. In response to the Vietnam situation the Eisenhower administration created the Southeast Asia Treaty Organization (SEATO) in 1954. This NATO-like security pact included the United States, Great Britain, France, Australia, New Zealand, Thailand, the Philippines, and Pakistan, and was dominated by the United States.

South Vietnamese leader Ngo Dinh Diem, a former Japanese collaborator and a Catholic in a country that was 90 percent Buddhist, quickly alienated many peasants with his corruption and repressive policies. American economic and military aid, along with continuing covert CIA activity, was crucial in keeping the increasingly isolated Diem in power. Both Diem and Eisenhower refused to permit the 1956 elections stipulated in Geneva because they knew popular hero Ho Chi Minh would easily win. By 1959 Diem's harsh and unpopular government in Saigon faced a civil war; thousands of peasants had joined guerrilla forces determined to drive him out. Eisenhower's commitment of military advisers and economic aid to South Vietnam, based on cold war assumptions, laid the foundation for the Vietnam War of the 1960s.

Ike's Warning: The Military-Industrial Complex

Throughout the 1950s small numbers of peace advocates in the United States had pointed to the ultimate illogic of the "new look" in foreign policy. The increasing reliance on nuclear weapons, they argued, did not strengthen national security but rather threatened the entire planet with extinction. They demonstrated at military camps, atomic-test sites, and missile-launching ranges, often getting arrested to make their point. Reports of radioactive fallout around the world rallied a larger group of scientists and prominent intellectuals against further nuclear testing. In Europe, a Ban the Bomb movement gained a wide following; an American counterpart, the National Committee for a Sane Nuclear Policy (SANE), claimed 25,000 members by 1958. Small but well-publicized actions against civil defense drills took place in several big cities: protesters marched on the streets rather than entering bomb shelters.

As he neared retirement, President Eisenhower came to share some of the protesters' anxiety and doubts about the arms race. Ironically, Eisenhower found it difficult to restrain the system he helped create. He chose to devote his Farewell Address, delivered in January 1961, to warning the nation about the dangers of what he termed the "military-industrial complex." Its total influence, he cautioned, "economic, political, even spiritual—is felt in every city, every statehouse, every office of the federal government." The conjunction of a large military estab-

lishment and a large arms industry, Eisenhower noted, was new in American history. "The potential for the disastrous rise of misplaced power exists and will persist. We must never let the weight of this combination endanger our liberties or democratic processes."

The old soldier understood perhaps better than most the dangers of raw military force. Eisenhower's public posture of restraint and caution in foreign affairs accompanied an enormous expansion of American economic, diplomatic, and military strength. Yet the Eisenhower years also demonstrated the limits of power and intervention in a world that did not always conform to the simple dualistic assumptions of cold war ideology.

JOHN F. KENNEDY AND THE NEW FRONTIER

No one could have resembled Dwight Eisenhower less in personality, temperament, and public image than John Fitzgerald Kennedy. The handsome son of a prominent, wealthy Irish American diplomat, husband of a fashionable, trend-setting heiress, forty-two-year-old JFK embodied youth, excitement, and sophistication. As only the second Catholic candidate for president—the first was Al Smith in 1928—Kennedy ran under the banner of the New Frontier. His liberalism inspired idealism and hope in millions of young people at home and abroad. In foreign affairs, Kennedy generally followed, and in some respects deepened, the cold war precepts that dominated postwar policymaking. But by the time of his assassination in 1963, he may have been veering away from the hard-line anti-Communist ideology he had earlier embraced. What a second term might have brought remains debatable, but his death ended a unique moment in American public life.

The Election of 1960

John F. Kennedy's political career began in Massachusetts, which elected him to the House in 1946 and then the Senate in 1952. Kennedy won the Democratic nomination after a bruising series of primaries in which he defeated party stalwarts Hubert Humphrey of Minnesota and Lyndon B. Johnson of Texas. Vice President Richard M. Nixon, the Republican nominee, had faithfully served the Eisenhower administration for eight years, and was far better known than his younger opponent. The Kennedy campaign stressed its candidate's youth and his image as a war hero. During his World War II tour of duty in the Pacific, Kennedy had bravely rescued one of his crew after

Presidential candidates John F. Kennedy and Richard M. Nixon during the second of three televised debates held during the 1960 election. Moderator Frank McGee sits at a desk upstage, facing a panel of newsmen. Eighty-five million viewers watched at least one of the first-ever televised debates, which both reflected and increased the power of television in the electoral process.

SOURCE: Bettmann. Corbis/Bettmann.

their PT boat had been sunk. Kennedy's supporters also pointed to his intellectual ability. JFK had won the Pulitzer Prize in 1957 for his book *Profiles in Courage*, which in fact had been written largely by his aides (see Map 27.2).

The election featured the first televised presidential debates. Political analysts have long argued over the impact of these four encounters, but agree that they moved television to the center of presidential politics, making image and appearance more critical than ever. Nixon appeared nervous and the camera made him look unshaven. Kennedy, in contrast, benefited from a confident manner and telegenic good looks. Both candidates emphasized foreign policy. Nixon defended the Republican record and stressed his own maturity and experience. Kennedy hammered away at the alleged "missile gap" with the Soviet Union and promised more vigorous executive leadership. He also countered the anti-Catholic prejudice of evangelical Protestants with a promise to keep church and state separate.

Kennedy squeaked to victory in the closest election since 1884. He won by a little more than 100,000 votes out of nearly 69 million cast. He ran poorly in the South, but won the Catholic vote so overwhelmingly that he carried most of the Northeast and Midwest. Though the margin of victory was tiny, Kennedy was a glorious win-

ner. Surrounding himself with prestigious Ivy League academics, Hollywood movie stars, and talented artists and writers, he imbued the presidency with an aura of celebrity. The inauguration brought out a bevy of poets, musicians, and fashionably dressed politicians from around the world. The new administration promised to be exciting and stylish, a modern-day Camelot peopled by heroic young men and beautiful women. The new president's ringing inaugural address ("Ask not what your country can do for you—ask what you can do for your country") had special resonance for a whole generation of young Americans.

New Frontier Liberalism

Kennedy promised to revive the long-stalled liberal domestic agenda. His New Frontier advocated such liberal programs as a higher minimum wage, greater federal aid for education, increased Social Security benefits, medical care for the elderly, support for public housing, and various antipoverty measures. Yet the thin margin of his victory and the stubborn opposition of conservative southern Democrats in Congress made it difficult to achieve these goals. Congress refused, for example, to enact the administration's attempt to extend Social Security and unemployment benefits to millions of uncovered workers.

MAP EXPLORATION

To explore an interactive version of this map,
go to **www.prenhall.com/faragher5/map27.2**

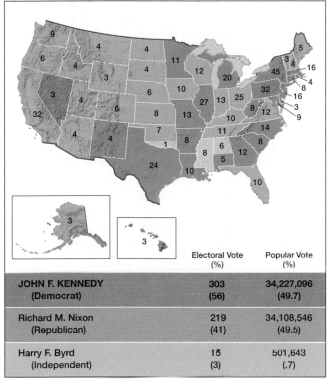

	Electoral Vote (%)	Popular Vote (%)
JOHN F. KENNEDY (Democrat)	303 (56)	34,227,096 (49.7)
Richard M. Nixon (Republican)	219 (41)	34,108,546 (49.5)
Harry F. Byrd (Independent)	15 (3)	501,643 (.7)

MAP 27.2 The Election of 1960 Kennedy's popular vote margin over Nixon was only a little over 100,000, making this one of the closest elections in American history.

Congress also failed to enact administration proposals for aid to public schools, mass-transit subsidies, and medical insurance for retired workers over sixty-five.

There were a few New Frontier victories. Congress did approve a modest increase in the minimum wage (to $1.25 per hour), agreed to a less ambitious improvement in Social Security, and appropriated $5 billion for public housing. It also passed the Manpower Retraining Act, appropriating $435 million to train the unemployed. The Area Redevelopment Act provided federal funds for rural, depressed Appalachia. The Higher Education Act of 1963 offered aid to colleges for constructing buildings and upgrading libraries. One of the best-publicized New Frontier programs was the Peace Corps, in which thousands of mostly young men and women traveled overseas for two-year stints in underdeveloped countries. There they provided technical and educational assistance in setting up health-care programs and improving agricultural efficiency. As a force for change, the Peace Corps produced modest results, but it epitomized Kennedy's promise to provide opportunities for service for a new generation of idealistic young people.

Kennedy helped revive the issue of women's rights with his Presidential Commission on the Status of Women, led by Eleanor Roosevelt. The commission's 1963 report was the most comprehensive study of women's lives ever produced by the federal government. It documented the ongoing discrimination faced by American women in the workplace and in the legal system, as well as the inadequacy of social services such as day care. It called for federally supported day-care programs, continuing education programs for women, and an end to sex bias in Social Security and unemployment benefits. The commission also insisted that more women be appointed to policy-making positions in government. President Kennedy also directed executive agencies to prohibit sex discrimination in hiring and promotion. The work of the commission contributed to a new generation of women's rights activism.

Kennedy took a more aggressive stance on stimulating economic growth and creating new jobs than had Eisenhower. The administration pushed lower business taxes through Congress, even at the cost of a higher federal deficit. The Revenue Act of 1962 encouraged new investment and plant renovation by easing tax depreciation schedules for business. Kennedy also gained approval for lower U.S. tariffs as a way to increase foreign trade. To help keep inflation down, he intervened in the steel industry in 1961 and 1962, pressuring labor to keep its wage demands low and management to curb price increases.

Kennedy also increased the federal commitment to a wholly new realm of government spending: the space program. The National Aeronautics and Space Administration (NASA) had been established under Eisenhower in response to the Soviet success with Sputnik. In 1961, driven by the cold war motivation of beating the Soviets to the moon and avoiding "another Sputnik," Kennedy won approval for a greatly expanded space program. He announced the goal of landing an American on the moon by the end of the decade. NASA eventually spent $33 billion before reaching this objective in 1969. This program of manned space flight—the Apollo missions—appealed to the public, acquiring a science fiction aura. In space, if not on earth, the New Frontier might actually be reached.

Overall, Kennedy's most long-lasting achievement as president may have been his strengthening of the executive branch itself. He insisted on direct presidential control of details that Eisenhower had left to advisers and appointees. Moreover, under Kennedy the White House staff assumed many of the decision-making and advisory functions previously held by cabinet members. This arrangement increased Kennedy's authority, since these appointees, unlike cabinet secretaries, escaped congressional oversight and confirmation proceedings. White House aides also lacked an independent constituency; their power and authority derived solely from their ties to the president. Kennedy's aides, "the best and the brightest," as he called them, dominated policymaking. Kennedy intensified a pattern whereby American presidents increasingly operated through small groups of fiercely loyal aides, often acting in secret.

Kennedy and the Cold War

During Kennedy's three years in office his approach to foreign policy shifted from aggressive containment to efforts at easing U.S.–Soviet tensions. Certainly when he first entered office, Kennedy and his chief aides considered it their main task to confront the Communist threat. In his first State of the Union Address, in January 1961, Kennedy told Congress that America must seize the initiative in the cold war. The nation must "move outside the home fortress, and . . . challenge the enemy in fields of our own choosing." To head the State Department Kennedy chose Dean Rusk, a conservative former assistant to Truman's secretary of state, Dean Acheson. Secretary of Defense Robert McNamara, a Republican and Ford Motor Company executive, was determined to streamline military procedures and weapons buying. McNamara typified the technical, cost-efficient, superrational approach to policymaking. Allen Dulles, Eisenhower's CIA director, remained at his post. These and other officials believed with Kennedy that Eisenhower had timidly accepted stalemate when the cold war could have been won.

Between 1960 and 1962 defense appropriations increased by nearly a third, from $43 billion to $56 billion. JFK expanded Eisenhower's policy of covert operations, deploying the army's elite Special Forces as a supplement to CIA covert operations in counterinsurgency battles against third world guerrillas. These soldiers, fighting under the direct orders of the president, could provide "rapid response" to "brush-fire" conflicts where Soviet influence threatened American interests. The Special Forces, authorized by Kennedy to wear the green berets that gave them their unofficial name, reflected the president's desire as president to acquire greater flexibility, secrecy, and independence in the conduct of foreign policy.

The limits on the ability of covert action and the Green Berets to further American interests became apparent in Southeast Asia. In Laos, where the United States had ignored the 1954 Geneva agreement and installed a friendly military regime, the CIA-backed government could not defeat Soviet-backed Pathet Lao guerrillas. The president had to arrange with the Soviets to neutralize Laos. In neighboring Vietnam, the situation proved more difficult. When Communist Vietcong guerrillas launched a civil war in South Vietnam against the U.S.–supported government in Saigon, Kennedy began sending hundreds of Green Berets and other military advisers to support the rule of Ngo Dinh Diem. In May 1961, in response to North Vietnamese aid to the Vietcong, Kennedy ordered a covert action against Ho Chi Minh's government that included sabotage and intelligence gathering.

Kennedy's approach to Vietnam reflected an analysis of the situation in that country by two aides, General Maxwell Taylor and Walt Rostow, who saw it through purely cold war eyes. "The Communists are pursuing a clear and systematic strategy in Southeast Asia," Taylor and Rostow concluded, ignoring the inefficiency, corruption, and unpopularity of the Diem government. By 1963, with Diem's army unable to contain the Vietcong rebellion, Kennedy had sent nearly 16,000 support and combat troops to South Vietnam. By then, a wide spectrum of South Vietnamese society had joined the revolt against the hated Diem, including highly respected Buddhist monks and their students. Americans watched in horror as television news reports showed footage of Buddhists burning themselves to death on the streets of Saigon—the ultimate protest against Diem's repressive rule. American press and television also reported the mounting casualty lists of U.S. forces in Vietnam. The South Vietnamese army, bloated by U.S. aid and weakened by corruption, continued to disintegrate. In the fall of 1963, American military officers and CIA operatives stood aside with approval as a group of Vietnamese generals removed President Diem, killing him and his top advisers. It was the first of many coups that racked the South Vietnamese government over the next few years.

In Latin America, Kennedy looked for ways to forestall various revolutionary movements that were gaining ground. Millions of impoverished peasants were forced to relocate to already overcrowded cities. In 1961 Kennedy unveiled the Alliance for Progress, a ten-year, $100 billion plan to spur economic development in Latin America. The United States committed $20 billion to the project, with the Latin nations responsible for the rest. The main goals included greater industrial growth and agricultural productivity, more equitable distribution of income, and improved health and housing.

Kennedy intended the Alliance for Progress as a kind of Marshall Plan that would benefit the poor and middle classes of the continent. The alliance did help raise growth rates in Latin American economies. But the expansion in export crops and in consumption by the tiny upper class did little to aid the poor or encourage democracy. The United States hesitated to challenge the power of dictators and extreme conservatives who were staunch anti-Communist allies. Thus the alliance soon degenerated into just another foreign aid program, incapable of generating genuine social change.

The Cuban Revolution and the Bay of Pigs

The direct impetus for the Alliance for Progress was the Cuban Revolution of 1959, which loomed over Latin America. The U.S. economic domination of Cuba that began with the Spanish-American War (see Chapter 20) had continued through the 1950s. American-owned businesses controlled all of Cuba's oil production, 90 percent of its mines, and roughly half of its railroads and sugar and cattle industries. Havana, the island's capital, was an attractive tourist center for Americans, and U.S. crime syndicates shared control of the island's lucrative gambling, prostitution, and drug trade with dictator Fulgencio Batista As a response to this, in the early 1950s, a peasant-based revolutionary movement, led by Fidel Castro, began gaining strength in the rural districts and mountains outside Havana.

On New Year's Day 1959, after years of guerrilla war, the rebels entered Havana and seized power amid great public rejoicing. For a brief time, Castro seemed a hero to many North Americans as well. *The New York Times* had conducted sympathetic interviews with Castro in 1958, while he was still fighting in Cuba's mountains. The CIA and President Eisenhower, however, shared none of this exuberance. Castro's land-reform program, involving the seizure of acreage from the tiny minority that controlled much of the fertile land, threatened to set an example for other Latin American countries. Although Castro had not joined the Cuban Communist Party, he turned to the Soviet Union after the United States withdrew economic aid. He began to sell sugar to the Soviets and soon nationalized American-owned oil companies and other enterprises. Eisenhower established an economic boycott of Cuba in 1960, then severed diplomatic relations.

Kennedy inherited from Eisenhower plans for a U.S. invasion of Cuba, including the secret arming and training of Cuban exiles. The CIA drafted the invasion plan, which was based on the assumption that a U.S.-led invasion would trigger a popular uprising of the Cuban people and bring down Castro. Kennedy went along with the plan, but at the last moment decided not to supply an Air Force cover for the operation. On April 17, 1961, a ragtag army of 1,400 counterrevolutionaries led by CIA operatives landed at the Bay of Pigs, on Cuba's south coast. Castro's efficient and loyal army easily subdued them.

The debacle revealed that the CIA, blinded by cold war assumptions, had failed to understand the Cuban Revolution. There was no popular uprising against Castro. Instead, the invasion strengthened Castro's standing among the urban poor and peasants, already attracted by his programs of universal literacy and medical care. As Castro stifled internal opposition, many Cuban intellectuals and professionals fled to the United States. An embarrassed Kennedy reluctantly took the blame for the abortive invasion, and his administration was censured time and again by third world delegates to the United Nations. American liberals criticized Kennedy for plotting Castro's overthrow, while conservatives blamed him for not supporting the invasion. Despite the failure, Kennedy remained committed to getting rid of Castro and keeping up the economic boycott. The CIA continued to support anti-Castro operations and launched at least eight attempts to assassinate the Cuban leader.

The Missile Crisis

The aftermath of the Bay of Pigs led to the most serious confrontation of the cold war: the Cuban missile crisis of October 1962. Frightened by U.S. belligerency, Castro asked Soviet premier Khrushchev for military help. Khrushchev responded in the summer of 1962 by shipping to Cuba a large amount of sophisticated weaponry, including intermediate-range nuclear missiles. In early October, U.S. reconnaissance planes found camouflaged missile silos dotting the island. Several Kennedy aides demanded an immediate bombing of Cuban bases, arguing that the missiles had decisively eroded the strategic global advantage the United States had previously enjoyed. The president and his advisers pondered their options in a series of tense meetings. Kennedy's aggressive attempts to exploit Cuba in the 1960 election now came back to haunt him, as he worried that his critics would accuse him of weakness in failing to stand up to the Soviets. The disastrous Bay of Pigs affair still rankled. Even some prominent Democrats, including Senator J. William Fulbright, chair of the Senate Foreign Relations Committee, called for an invasion of Cuba.

Kennedy went on national television on October 22. He announced the discovery of the missile sites, demanded the removal of all missiles, and ordered a strict naval blockade of all offensive military equipment shipped to Cuba. He also requested an emergency meeting of the UN Security Council and promised that any missiles launched from Cuba would bring "a full retaliatory response upon the Soviet Union." For a tense week, the American public wondered if nuclear Armageddon was imminent. Eyeball to eyeball, the two superpowers waited for each other to blink. On October 26 and 27 Khrushchev yielded, ordering twenty-five Soviet ships off their course to Cuba, thus avoiding a challenge to the American blockade.

Khrushchev offered to remove all the missiles in return for a pledge from the United States not to invade Cuba. Khrushchev later added a demand for removal of American weapons from Turkey, as close to the Soviet Union as Cuba is to the United States. Kennedy secretly assured Khrushchev that the United States would dismantle the obsolete Jupiter missiles in Turkey. On November 20, after weeks of delicate negotiations, Kennedy publicly announced the withdrawal of Soviet missiles and bombers from Cuba. He

also pledged to respect Cuban sovereignty, and promised that U.S. forces would not invade the island.

The crisis had passed. The Soviets, determined not to be intimidated again, began the largest weapons buildup in their history. For his part Kennedy, perhaps chastened by this flirtation with nuclear disaster, made important gestures toward peaceful coexistence with the Soviets. In a June 1963 address at American University, Kennedy called for a rethinking of cold war diplomacy. Both sides, he said, had been "caught up in a vicious and dangerous cycle in which suspicion on one side breeds suspicion on the other, and new weapons beget counterweapons."

Shortly after, Washington and Moscow set up a "hot line"—a direct phone connection to permit instant communication during times of crisis. More substantial was the Limited Nuclear Test-Ban Treaty, signed in August 1963 by the United States, the Soviet Union, and Great Britain. The treaty prohibited above-ground, outer space, and underwater nuclear weapons tests. It eased international anxieties over radioactive fallout. But underground testing continued to accelerate for years. The limited

C H R O N O L O G Y

1950	David Riesman publishes *The Lonely Crowd*		Jack Kerouac publishes *On the Road*
1952	Dwight D. Eisenhower is elected president	*1958*	National Defense Education Act authorizes grants and loans to college students
1953	CIA installs Riza Shah Pahlavi as leader of Iran	*1959*	Nikita Khrushchev visits the United States
1954	Vietminh force French surrender at Dien Bien Phu	*1960*	Soviets shoot down U-2 spy plane
	CIA overthrows government of Jácobo Arbenz Guzmán in Guatemala		John F. Kennedy is elected president
	United States explodes first hydrogen bomb		Almost 90 percent of American homes have television
1955	Jonas Salk pioneers vaccine for polio	*1961*	President Kennedy creates "Green Berets"
	James Dean stars in the movie *Rebel Without a Cause*		Bay of Pigs invasion of Cuba fails
1956	Federal Highway Act authorizes Interstate Highway System	*1962*	Cuban missile crisis brings the world to the brink of a superpower confrontation
	Elvis Presley signs with RCA	*1963*	Report by the Presidential Commission on the Status of Women documents ongoing discrimination
	Eisenhower is reelected		Betty Friedan publishes *The Feminine Mystique*
	Allen Ginsberg publishes *Howl*		Limited Nuclear Test-Ban Treaty is signed
1957	Soviet Union launches Sputnik, first space-orbiting satellite		President Kennedy is assassinated

Vice President Lyndon B. Johnson took the oath of office as president aboard *Air Force One* after the assassination of John F. Kennedy, November 22, 1963. Onlookers included the grief-stricken Jacqueline Kennedy (right) and Lady Bird Johnson (left). This haunting photo captured both the shock of Kennedy's assassination and the orderly succession of power that followed.

SOURCE: AP/Wide World Photos.

test ban was perhaps more symbolic than substantive, a psychological breakthrough in East-West relations after a particularly tense three years.

The Assassination of President Kennedy

The assassination of John F. Kennedy in Dallas on November 22, 1963, sent the entire nation into shock and mourning. Just forty-six years old and president for only three years, Kennedy quickly ascended to martyrdom in the nation's consciousness. Millions had identified his strengths—intelligence, optimism, wit, charm, coolness under fire—as those of American society. In life, Kennedy had helped place television at the center of American political life. Now in the aftermath of his death, television riveted a badly shocked nation. One day after the assassination, the president's accused killer, an obscure political misfit named Lee Harvey Oswald, was himself gunned down before television cameras covering his arraignment in Dallas. Two days later tens of millions watched the televised spectacle of Kennedy's funeral, trying to make sense of the brutal murder. Although a special commission headed by Chief Justice Earl Warren found the killing to be the work of Oswald acting alone, many Americans doubted this conclusion. Kennedy's death gave rise to a host of conspiracy theories, none of which seems provable.

We will never know, of course, what Kennedy might have achieved in a second term. But in his 1,000 days as president, he demonstrated a capacity to change and grow in office. Having gone to the brink during the missile crisis, he managed to launch new initiatives toward peaceful coexistence. At the time of his death, relations between the United States and the Soviet Union were more amicable than at any time since the end of World War II. Much of the domestic liberal agenda of the New Frontier would be finally implemented by Kennedy's successor, Lyndon B. Johnson, who dreamed of creating a Great Society.

CONCLUSION

America in 1963 still enjoyed the full flush of its postwar economic boom. To be sure, millions of Americans, particularly African Americans and Latinos, did not share in the good times. But millions of others had managed to achieve middle-class status since the early 1950s. An expanding economy, cheap energy, government subsidies, and a dominant position in the world marketplace had made the hallmarks of "the good life" available to more Americans than ever. The postwar "American dream" promised home ownership, college education, secure employment at decent wages, affordable appliances, and the ability to travel—for one's children if not for one's self. The nation's public culture—its schools, mass media, politics, advertising—presented a powerful consensus based on the idea that the American dream was available to all who would work for it.

The presidential transition from the grandfatherly Dwight Eisenhower to the charismatic John F. Kennedy symbolized for many a generational shift as well. By 1963 young people had more influence than ever before in shaping the nation's political life, its media images, and its burgeoning consumer culture. Kennedy himself inspired millions of young Americans to pursue public service and to express their political idealism. But even by the time of Kennedy's death, the postwar consensus and the conditions that nurtured it were beginning to unravel.

REVIEW QUESTIONS

1. How did postwar economic prosperity change the lives of ordinary Americans? Which groups benefited most and which were largely excluded from "the affluent society"?

2. What role did federal programs play in expanding economic opportunities?

3. Analyze the origins of postwar youth culture. How was teenage life different in these years from previous eras? How did popular culture both reflect and distort the lives of American youth?

4. How did mass culture become even more central to American everyday life in the two decades fol-lowing World War II? What problems did various cultural critics identify with this trend?

5. How did cold war politics and assumptions shape American foreign policy in these years? What were the key interventions the United States made in Europe and the third world?

6. Evaluate the domestic and international policies associated with John F. Kennedy and the New Frontier. What continuities with Eisenhower-era politics do you find in the Kennedy administration? How did JFK break with past practices?

RECOMMENDED READING

Glenn C. Altschuler, *All Shook Up: How Rock 'n' Roll Changed America* (2003). The best new social history of rock 'n' roll, with excellent coverage of the generational and racial controversies surrounding the new music.

Lizabeth Cohen, *A Consumers' Republic: The Politics of Mass Consumption in Postwar America* (2003). An ambitious, deeply researched overview of how postwar Americans negotiated the tensions between expanding opportunities for consumption and traditional ideals of citizenship and political activism.

Lawrence Freedman, *Kennedy's Wars: Berlin, Cuba, Laos, and Vietnam* (2000). A new analysis of JFK's foreign policy, emphasizing the context of cold war liberalism.

Kenneth T. Jackson, *Crabgrass Frontier* (1985). The most comprehensive overview of the history of American suburbs. Jackson provides a broad historical context for understanding postwar suburbanization, and offers an excellent analysis of the impact of government agencies such as the Federal Housing Administration.

David E. Kaiser, *American Tragedy: Kennedy, Johnson, and the Origins of the Vietnam War* (2000). The most detailed account yet of how the contradictions of cold war thinking pushed policymakers in three administrations toward an unnecessary and unwinnable war.

Elaine Tyler May, *Homeward Bound: American Families in the Cold War* (1988). A thoughtful social history linking family life of the 1950s with the political shadow of the cold war.

Grace Palladino, *Teenagers: An American History* (1996). A lively and witty narrative account of the emergence of teenagers as a new social class.

James T. Patterson, *Grand Expectations: Postwar America, 1945–1974* (1996). A comprehensive overview of postwar life that centers on the "grand expectations" evoked by unprecedented prosperity.

Mark J. White, ed., *Kennedy: The New Frontier Revisited* (1998). Wide-ranging collection of recent essays that together offer a balanced view of Kennedy's presidency.

 For additional study resources for this chapter, go to the *Companion Website*, http://www.prenhall.com/faragher.

WHOSE HISTORY IS IT?

ANY OLD WAY YOU CHOOSE IT:
ROCK AND ROLL AS HISTORY, MYTH, AND COMMERCE

In 1983 several music business executives gathered in New York City to celebrate the creative achievements and artistic legacies of rock and roll. Their central premise was that rock and roll began as a liberating force, both reflecting and pushing fundamental social and cultural changes in American life. They created the non-profit Rock and Roll Hall of Fame Foundation, which, in 1986, began naming members annually from rock pioneers who had released their first records at least 25 years earlier. The careers of the two driving forces behind the Hall embodied rock and roll's steady evolution from a scruffy, rebellious, thoroughly populist music to a multi-billion dollar, corporate global industry.

In 1995, the Rock and Roll Hall of Fame and Museum opened in Cleveland, the city where legendary radio disc jockey Alan Freed had first popularized the term "rock and roll" among millions of young white fans. More importantly, Cleveland had aggressively pursued the project as a tourist attraction, providing half the construction cost through tax-exempt bonds, state funds, and corporate donations. The $92 million building was designed by noted architect I.M. Pei.

The Hall has stimulated fierce and continuing debates over its mission, its inclusiveness, and its vision of rock and roll history. The annual induction ceremonies, honoring new Hall members, take place in New York City. Hall membership and the permanent exhibitions privilege mass commercial success above everything, especially 1960s and 70s rock bands led by white singers and songwriters. The exhibit, "Rock Style," showcased stage outfits worn by performers. Glass cases display objects as if they were religious relics: Jim Morrison's Boy Scout patch, the remains of the plane in which Otis Redding was killed,

Buddy Holly's high school diploma, John Lennon's grade school report card. To acknowledge the often forgotten contributions of blues, jazz, and country music artists, the Hall recognized as "Early Influences" such musical giants as Robert Johnson, Bessie Smith, Hank Williams, Howlin' Wolf, Louis Armstrong, and Charlie Christian. But only a small handful of women have made it in. Joni Mitchell, one of the most influential singer songwriters of the 1960s and 70s had to wait until 1997 for induction; by contrast, Ricky Nelson, a smooth, white "teen idol" who rose to fame singing songs on the 1950s TV show "Ozzie and Harriet," won election in 1987. And what of the studio musicians, who often created the actual music on hit records but received no credit? Responding to criticism the Hall created a new category of "Sidemen" in 2000, allowing it to admit artists like saxophonist King Curtis, drummer Earl Palmer, and bassist James Jamerson who had done as much as anyone to create the sound of rock and roll.

The Rock and Roll Hall of Fame will continue to stir controversy not only over who belongs in it but over the broader tensions within the music. Many younger music fans find themselves bemused by the enshrinement of rock and roll's past. A 21-year-old college student noted at the Hall's opening: "Their parents didn't like the music they listened to, and now they've built a monument to it. Now our parents hate our music. Is that really going to change?"

Big Joe Turner, a dynamic and influential Kansas City rhythm and blues singer, was elected to the Hall in 1987. Many of his records, such as "Shake, Rattle, and Roll," were "covered" by white bands like Bill Haley and the Comets, who had enormous popular success with toned down versions of his style.

Michael Ochs Archives.com.

Rock pioneer Chuck Berry and one of his many younger disciples, Bruce Springsteen, played together at the grand opening of the Hall in September 1995. Berry was among the inaugural class of inductees in 1986.

Terry Knerem/Corbis/Sygma.

This view of the pyramid side of the Rock and Roll Hall of Fame and Museum in Cleveland, Ohio.

Brownie Harris, CORBIS-NY.

The 1950s "rockabilly" sound from Sun Records in Memphis epitomized the cultural melding of African American blues and white country music that was the foundation for rock and roll. Sun producer Sam Phillips and singer Elvis Presley were key figures in creating these breakthrough recordings.

Brooks Kraft, CORBIS-NY.

Earl Palmer, the New Orleans studio drummer, helped invent the rock and roll beat by propelling scores of Top Ten hits made by Little Richard, Fats Domino, Ricky Nelson, Sam Cooke, and many others. But like most session musicians, he was unknown to the public.

Michael Ochs Archives.com.

CHAPTER 28

The Civil Rights Movement

1945–1966

CHAPTER OUTLINE

The Montgomery Bus Boycott:
An African American Community Challenges Segregation

On December 1, 1955, Rosa Parks, a seamstress and well-known activist in Montgomery, Alabama's African American community, had been taken from a bus, arrested, and put in jail for refusing to give up her seat to a white passenger. Composing roughly half the city's 100,000 people, Montgomery's black community had long endured the humiliation of a strictly segregated bus system. Drivers could order a whole row of black passengers to vacate their seats for one white person. And black people had to pay their fares at the front of the bus and then step back outside and reenter through the rear door.

In protest of Mrs. Parks's arrest, more than 30,000 African Americans had answered a hastily organized call to boycott the city's buses. On the day of the boycott, a steady stream of cars and pedestrians jammed the streets around the Holt Street Baptist Church in Montgomery, Alabama. By early evening a patient, orderly, and determined crowd of more than 5,000 African Americans had packed the church and spilled over onto the sidewalks. Loudspeakers had to be set up for the thousands who could not squeeze inside. After a brief prayer and a reading from Scripture, all attention focused on the twenty-six-year-old minister, The Reverend Martin Luther King Jr., who was to address the gathering. "We are here this evening," he began slowly, "for serious business. We are here in a general sense because first and foremost we are American citizens, and we are deter-

Montgomery

mined to apply our citizenship to the fullness of its means."

Sensing the expectant mood of the crowd, Dr. King got down to specifics and described Mrs. Parks's arrest. As he quickened his cadence and drew shouts of encouragement, he seemed to gather strength and confidence from the crowd. "You know, my friends, there comes a time when people get tired of being trampled over by the iron feet of oppression. There comes a time, my friends, when people get tired of being flung across the abyss of humiliation, when they experience the bleakness of nagging despair."

Even before Dr. King concluded his speech, it was clear to all present that the bus boycott would continue for more than just a day. The minister laid out the key principles that would guide the boycott—nonviolence, Christian love, unity. In his brief but stirring address the minister created a powerful sense of communion. "If we are wrong, justice is a lie," he told the clapping and shouting throng. "And we are determined here in Montgomery to work and fight until justice runs down like water and righteousness like a mighty stream." Dr. King made his way out of the church amid waves of applause and rows of hands reaching out to touch him.

Dr. King's prophetic speech catapulted him into leadership of the Montgomery bus boycott—but he had not started the movement. When Rosa Parks was arrested, local activists with deep roots in the black protest tradition galvanized the community with the idea of a boycott. Mrs. Parks herself had served for twelve years as secretary of the local NAACP chapter. She was a committed opponent of segregation and was thoroughly respected in the city's African American community. E. D. Nixon, president of the Alabama NAACP and head of the local Brotherhood of Sleeping Car Porters union, saw Mrs. Parks's arrest as the right case on which to make a stand. It was Nixon who brought Montgomery's black ministers together on December 5 to coordinate an extended boycott of city buses. They formed the Montgomery Improvement Association (MIA) and chose Dr. King as their leader. Significantly, Mrs. Parks's lawyer was Clifford Durr, a white liberal with a history of representing black clients. His politically active wife Virginia, for whom Mrs. Parks worked as a seamstress, had been a longtime crusader against the poll tax which prevented many blacks from voting. And two white ministers, Rev. Robert Graetz and Rev. Glenn Smiley, would offer important support to the MIA.

While Nixon organized black ministers, Jo Ann Robinson, an English teacher at Alabama State College, spread the word to the larger black community. Robinson led the Women's Political Council (WPC), an organization of black professional women founded in 1949. With her WPC allies, Robinson wrote, mimeographed, and distributed 50,000 copies of a leaflet telling the story of Mrs. Parks's arrest and urging all African Americans to stay off city buses on December 5. They did. Now the MIA faced the more difficult task of keeping the boycott going. Success depended on providing alternate transportation for the 30,000 to 40,000 maids, cooks, janitors, and other black working people who needed to get to work.

The MIA coordinated an elaborate system of car pools, using hundreds of private cars and volunteer drivers to provide as many as 20,000 rides each day. Many people walked. Local authorities, although shocked by the discipline and sense of purpose shown by Montgomery's African American community, refused to engage in serious negotiations. With the aid of the NAACP, the MIA brought suit in federal court against bus segregation in Montgomery. Police harassed boycotters with traffic tickets and arrests. White racists exploded bombs in the homes of Dr. King and E. D. Nixon. The days turned into weeks, then months, but still the boycott continued. All along, mass meetings in Montgomery's African American churches helped boost morale with singing, praying, and stories of individual sacrifice. One elderly woman, refusing all suggestions that she drop out of the boycott on account of her age, made a spontaneous remark that became a classic refrain of the movement: "My feets is tired, but my soul is rested."

The boycott reduced the bus company's revenues by two-thirds. In February 1956, city officials obtained indictments against King, Nixon, and 113 other boycotters under an old law forbidding hindrance to business without "just cause or legal excuse." A month later King went on trial. A growing contingent of newspaper reporters and TV crews from around the country watched as the judge found King guilty, fined him $1,000, and released him on bond pending appeal. But on June 4, a panel of three federal judges struck down Montgomery's bus segregation ordinances as unconstitutional. On November 13 the Supreme Court affirmed the district court ruling. After eleven hard months and against all odds, the boycotters had won.

Their victory would inspire a new mass movement to ensure civil rights for African Americans. A series of local struggles to dismantle segregation—in the schools of Little Rock, in the department stores of Atlanta, in the lunch counters of Greensboro, in the streets of Birmingham— would coalesce into a broad-based national movement at the center of American politics. By 1963, the massive March on Washington would win the endorsement of President John F. Kennedy, and his successor, Lyndon B. Johnson, would push through the landmark Civil Rights Act and Voting Rights Act.

The struggle to end legal segregation took root in scores of southern cities and towns. African American communities led these fights, developing a variety of tactics, leaders, and ideologies. With white allies, they engaged in direct-action protests such as boycotts, sit-ins, and mass civil disobedience as well as strategic legal battles in state and federal courts. The movement was not without its inner conflicts. Tensions between local movements and national civil rights organizations flared up regularly. Within African American communities, long-simmering distrust between the working classes and rural folk on the one hand and middle-class ministers, teachers, and business people on the other sometimes threatened to destroy political unity. There were generational conflicts between African American student activists and their elders. But overall, the civil rights movement created new social identities for African Americans and profoundly changed American society.

KEY TOPICS

- Legal and political origins of the African American civil rights struggle

- Martin Luther King's rise to leadership

- Student protesters and direct action in the South

- Civil rights and national politics

- Civil Rights Act of 1964 and Voting Rights Act of 1965

- America's other minorities

ORIGINS OF THE MOVEMENT

The experiences of African Americans during World War II and immediately after laid the foundation for the civil rights struggle of the 1950s and 1960s. Nearly 1 million black men and women had served in the armed forces. The discrepancy between fighting totalitarianism abroad while enduring segregation and other racist practices in the military embittered many combat veterans and their families. Between 1939 and 1945 nearly 2 million African Americans found work in defense plants, and another 200,000 entered the federal civil service. Black union membership doubled, reaching more than 1.2 million. But the wartime stress on national unity and consensus largely muted political protests. With the war's end, African Americans and their white allies determined to push ahead for full political and social equality.

Civil Rights After World War II

The boom in wartime production spurred a mass migration of nearly a million black Southerners to northern cities. Forty-three northern and western cities saw their black population double during the 1940s. Although racial discrimination in housing and employment was by no means absent in northern cities, greater economic opportunities and political freedom continued to attract rural African Americans after the war. With the growth of African American communities in northern cities, black people gained significant influence in local political machines in such cities as New York, Chicago, and Detroit. Within industrial unions such as the United Automobile Workers and the United Steel Workers, white and black workers learned the power of biracial unity in fighting for better wages and working conditions. Harlem congressman Adam Clayton Powell Jr. captured the new

mood of 1945 when he wrote that black people were eager "to make the dream of America become flesh and blood, bread and butter, freedom and equality."

After the war, civil rights issues returned to the national political stage for the first time since Reconstruction. Black voters had already begun to switch their allegiance from the Republicans to the Democrats during the New Deal. A series of symbolic and substantial acts by the Truman administration solidified that shift. In 1946 Truman created a President's Committee on Civil Rights. Its report, *To Secure These Rights* (1947), set out an ambitious program to end racial inequality. Recommendations included a permanent civil rights division in the Justice Department, voting rights protection, antilynching legislation, and a legal attack on segregated housing. Yet, although he publicly endorsed nearly all the proposals of the new committee, Truman introduced no legislation to make them law.

Truman and his advisers walked a political tightrope on civil rights. They understood that black voters in several key northern states would be pivotal in the 1948 election. At the same time, they worried about the loyalty of white southern Democrats adamantly opposed to changing the racial status quo. In July 1948, the president made his boldest move on behalf of civil rights, issuing an executive order barring segregation in the armed forces. When liberals forced the Democratic National Convention to adopt a strong civil rights plank that summer, a group of outraged Southerners walked out and nominated Governor Strom Thurmond of South Carolina for president on a States' Rights ticket. Thurmond carried four southern states in the election. But with the help of over 70 percent of the northern black vote, Truman barely managed to defeat Republican Thomas E. Dewey in November. The deep split over race issues would continue to rack the national Democratic Party for a generation.

Electoral politics was not the only arena for civil rights work. During the war, membership in the National Association for the Advancement of Colored People had mushroomed from 50,000 to 500,000. Working- and middle-class urban black people provided the backbone of this new membership. The NAACP conducted voter registration drives and lobbied against discrimination in housing and employment. Its Legal Defense and Education Fund, vigorously led by special counsel Thurgood Marshall, mounted several significant legal challenges to segregation laws. In *Morgan* v. *Virginia* (1946), the Supreme Court declared that segregation on interstate buses was an undue burden on interstate commerce. Other Supreme Court decisions struck down all-white election primaries, racially restrictive housing covenants, and the exclusion of blacks from law and graduate schools.

The NAACP's legal work demonstrated the potential for using federal courts in attacking segregation. Courts were one place where black people, using the constitutional language of rights, could make forceful arguments that could not be voiced in Congress or at political conventions. But federal enforcement of court decisions was often lacking. In 1947 a group of black and white activists tested compliance with the *Morgan* decision by traveling on a bus through the Upper South. This "Freedom Ride" was cosponsored by the Christian pacifist Fellowship of Reconciliation (FOR) and its recent offshoot, the Congress

of Racial Equality (CORE), which was devoted to interracial, nonviolent direct action. In North Carolina, several riders were arrested and sentenced to thirty days on a chain gang for refusing to leave the bus.

Two symbolic "firsts" raised black expectations and inspired pride. In 1947 Jackie Robinson broke the color barrier in major league baseball, winning rookie-of-the-year honors with the Brooklyn Dodgers. Robinson's courage in the face of racial epithets from fans and players paved the way for the black ballplayers who soon followed him to the big leagues. In 1950 United Nations diplomat Ralph Bunche won the Nobel Peace Prize for arranging the 1948 Arab-Israeli truce. Bunche, however, later declined an appointment as undersecretary of state because he did not want to subject his family to the humiliating segregation laws of Washington DC.

Cultural change could have political implications as well. In the 1940s, African American musicians created a new form of jazz that revolutionized American music and asserted a militant black consciousness. Although black musicians had pioneered the development of swing and, earlier, jazz, white bandleaders and musicians had reaped most of the recognition and money from the public. Artists such as Charlie Parker, Dizzy Gillespie, Thelonius Monk, Bud Powell, and Miles Davis revolted

Charlie Parker (alto sax) and Miles Davis (trumpet) with their group in 1947, at the Three Deuces Club in New York City. Parker and Davis were two creative leaders of the "bebop" movement of the 1940s. Working in northern cities, boppers reshaped jazz music and created a distinct language and style that was widely imitated by young people. They challenged older stereotypes of African American musicians by insisting that they be treated as serious artists.

SOURCE: Frank Driggs Collection.

against the standard big-band format of swing, preferring small groups and competitive jam sessions to express their musical visions. The new music, dubbed "bebop" by critics and fans, demanded a much more sophisticated knowledge of harmony and melody and featured more complex rhythms and extended improvisation than previous jazz styles. In urban black communities the "boppers" consciously created a music that, unlike swing, white popularizers found difficult to copy or sweeten. These black artists insisted on independence from the white-defined norms of show business. Serious about both their music and the way it was presented, they refused to cater to white expectations of grinning, easygoing black performers.

The Segregated South

In the postwar South, still home to over half the nation's 15 million African Americans, the racial situation had changed little since the Supreme Court had sanctioned "separate but equal" segregation in *Plessy* v. *Ferguson* (dis-

cussed in Chapter 20). In practice, segregation meant separate but unequal. A tight web of state and local ordinances enforced strict separation of the races in schools, restaurants, hotels, movie theaters, libraries, restrooms, hospitals, even cemeteries, and the facilities for black people were consistently inferior to those for whites. There were no black policemen in the Deep South and only a handful of black lawyers.

In the late 1940s only about 10 percent of eligible southern black people voted, most of these in urban areas. A combination of legal and extralegal measures kept all but the most determined black people disfranchised. Poll taxes, all-white primaries, and discriminatory registration procedures reinforced the belief that voting was "the white man's business." African Americans who insisted on exercising their right to vote, especially in remote rural areas, faced physical violence—beatings, shootings, lynchings. A former president of the Alabama Bar Association expressed a commonly held view when he declared, "No Negro is good enough and no Negro will ever be good enough to participate in

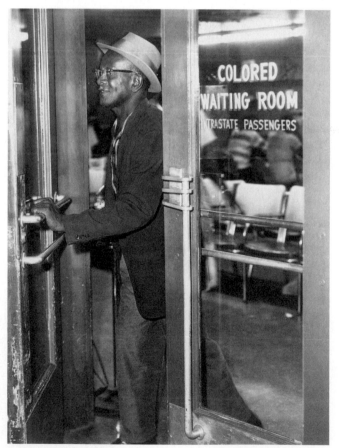

Signs designating "White" and "Colored" rest rooms, waiting rooms, entrances, benches, and even water fountains were a common sight in the segregated South. They were a constant reminder that legal separation of the races in public spaces was the law of the land.

SOURCE: (left) Photo by Dan McCoy. Black Star; (right) Segregation Trailways. Corbis/Bettmann.

making the law under which the white people of Alabama have to live."

Outsiders often noted that despite Jim Crow laws (see Chapter 20) contact between blacks and whites was ironically close. The mass of black Southerners worked on white-owned plantations and in white households. One black preacher neatly summarized the nation's regional differences this way: "In the South, they don't care how close you get as long as you don't get too big; in the North, they don't care how big you get as long as you don't get too close." The South's racial code forced African Americans to accept, at least outwardly, social conventions that reinforced their low standing with whites. A black person did not shake hands with a white person, or enter a white home through the front door, or address a white person except formally.

In these circumstances, survival and self-respect depended to a great degree on patience and stoicism. Black people learned to endure humiliation by keeping their thoughts and feelings hidden from white people. Paul Laurence Dunbar, an African American poet, captured this bitter truth in his turn-of-the-century poem "We Wear the Mask."

> We wear the mask that grins and lies,
> It hides our cheeks and shades our eyes,
> This debt we pay to human guile;
> With torn and bleeding hearts we smile,
> And mouth with myriad subtleties.
> Why should the world be over-wise,
> In counting all our tears and sighs?
> Nay, let them only see us, while
> We wear the mask.

Brown v. Board of Education

Since the late 1930s, the NAACP had chipped away at the legal foundations of segregation. Rather than making a frontal assault on the *Plessy* separate-but-equal rule, civil rights attorneys launched a series of suits seeking complete equality in segregated facilities. The aim of this strategy was to make segregation so prohibitively expensive that the South would be forced to dismantle it. In the 1939 case *Missouri v. ex.rel. Gaines,* the Supreme Court ruled that the University of Missouri law school must either admit African Americans or build another, fully equal law school for them. NAACP lawyers pushed their arguments further, asserting that equality could not be measured simply by money or physical plant. In *McLaurin v. Oklahoma State Regents* (1950), the Court agreed with Thurgood Marshall's argument that regulations forcing a black law student to sit, eat, and study in areas apart from white students inevitably created a "badge of inferiority."

By 1951, Marshall had begun coordinating the NAACP's legal resources for a direct attack on the separate-but-equal doctrine. The goal was to overturn *Plessy* and the constitutionality of segregation itself. For a test case, Marshall combined five lawsuits challenging segregation in public schools. One of these suits argued the case of Oliver Brown of Topeka, Kansas, who sought to overturn a state law permitting cities to maintain segregated schools. The law forced Brown's eight-year-old daughter Linda to travel by bus to a black school even though she lived only three blocks from an all-white elementary school. The Supreme Court heard initial arguments on the cases, grouped together as *Brown v. Board of Education,* in December 1952.

In his argument before the Court, Thurgood Marshall tried to establish that separate facilities, by definition, denied black people their full rights as American citizens. Marshall used sociological and psychological evidence that went beyond standard legal arguments. For example, he cited the research of African American psychologist Kenneth B. Clark, who had studied the self-esteem of black children in New York City and in segregated schools in the South. Using black and white dolls and asking the children which they preferred, Clark illustrated how black children educated in segregated schools developed a negative self-image. When Chief Justice Fred Vinson died suddenly in 1953, President Dwight Eisenhower appointed California Governor Earl Warren to fill the post. After hearing further arguments, the Court remained divided on the issue of overturning *Plessy.* Warren, eager for a unanimous decision, patiently worked at convincing two holdouts. Using his political skills to persuade and achieve compromise, Warren urged his colleagues to affirm a simple principle as the basis for the decision.

On May 17, 1954, Warren read the Court's unanimous decision aloud. "Does segregation of children in public schools solely on the basis of race . . . deprive the children of the minority group of equal educational opportunities?" The chief justice paused. "We believe that it does." Warren made a point of citing several of the psychological studies of segregation's effects. He ended by directly addressing the constitutional issue. Segregation deprived the plaintiffs of the equal protection of the laws guaranteed by the Fourteenth Amendment. "We conclude that in the field of public education the doctrine of 'separate but equal' has no place. Separate educational facilities are inherently unequal." "Any language in *Plessy v. Ferguson* contrary to this finding is rejected."

African Americans and their liberal allies around the country hailed the decision and the legal genius of Thurgood Marshall. Marshall himself predicted that all segregated schools would be abolished within five years. Black newspapers were full of stories on the imminent dismantling of segregation. The *Chicago Defender* called the decision "a second emancipation proclamation." But the issue of enforcement soon dampened this enthusiasm. To gain a unanimous decision, Warren had had to agree to let the Court delay for one year its ruling on how to implement desegregation. This second *Brown* ruling, handed down in May 1955, assigned responsibility for desegregation plans to local school boards. The Court left it to federal district judges to monitor compliance, requiring only that desegregation proceed "with all deliberate speed." Thus, although the Court had made a momentous and clear constitutional ruling, the need for compromise dictated gradual enforcement by unspecified means.

Crisis in Little Rock

Resistance to *Brown* took many forms. Most affected states passed laws transferring authority for pupil assignment to local school boards. This prevented the NAACP

from bringing statewide suits against segregated school systems. Counties and towns created layers of administrative delays designed to stop implementation of *Brown*. Some school boards transferred public school property to new, all-white private "academies." State legislatures in Virginia, Alabama, Mississippi, and Georgia, resurrecting pre–Civil War doctrines, passed resolutions declaring their right to "interpose" themselves between the people and the federal government and to "nullify" federal laws. In 1956, 101 congressmen from the former Confederate states signed the Southern Manifesto, urging their states to refuse compliance with desegregation. President Dwight Eisenhower declined to publicly endorse *Brown*, contributing to the spirit of southern resistance. "I don't believe you can change the hearts of men with laws or decisions," he said (see Map 28.1).

In Little Rock, Arkansas, the tense controversy over school integration became a test case of state versus fed-

MAP EXPLORATION

To explore an interactive version of this map, go to **www.prenhall.com/faragher5/map28.1**

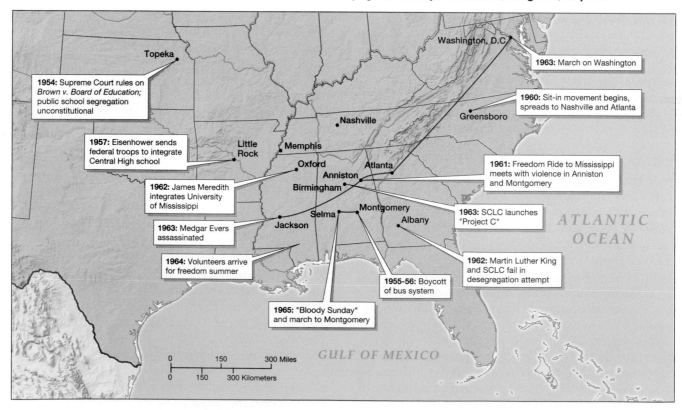

MAP 28.1 The Civil Rights Movement Key battlegrounds in the struggle for racial justice in communities across the South.

eral power. A federal court ordered public schools to begin desegregation in September 1957, and the local school board made plans to comply. But Governor Orval Faubus, facing a tough reelection fight, decided to make a campaign issue out of defying the court order. He dispatched Arkansas National Guard troops to Central High School to prevent nine black students from entering. For three weeks, armed troops stood guard at the school. Screaming crowds, encouraged by Faubus, menaced the black students, beat up two black reporters, and chanted "Two, four, six, eight, we ain't going to integrate." Moderate whites, such as *Arkansas Gazette* editor Harry Ashmore, opposed Faubus, fearing that his controversial tactics would make it harder to attract new businesses and investment capital to the city.

At first, President Eisenhower tried to intervene quietly, gaining Faubus's assurance that he would protect the nine black children. But when Faubus suddenly withdrew his troops, leaving the black students at the mercy of the white mob, Eisenhower had to move. On September 24 he placed the Arkansas National Guard under federal control and ordered a thousand paratroopers of the 101st Airborne Division to Little Rock. The nine black students arrived in a U.S. Army car. With fixed bayonets, the soldiers protected the students as they finally integrated Central High School in Little Rock. Eisenhower, the veteran military commander, justified his actions on the basis of upholding federal authority and enforcing the law. He also defended his intervention as crucial to national prestige abroad, noting the propaganda victory Faubus had handed to the Soviet bloc. "Our enemies," the President argued, "are gloating over this incident and using it everywhere to misrepresent our whole nation." But he made no endorsement of desegregation. But as the first president since Reconstruction to use armed federal troops in support of black rights, Eisenhower demonstrated that the federal government could, indeed, protect civil rights. Unfazed, Governor Faubus kept Little Rock high schools closed during the 1958–59 academic year to prevent what he called "violence and disorder."

NO EASY ROAD TO FREEDOM, 1957–62

The legal breakthrough represented by the *Brown* decision heartened opponents of segregation everywhere. Most important, *Brown* demonstrated the potential for using the federal court system as a weapon against discrimination and as a means of protecting the full rights of citizenship. Yet the wide-spread opposition to *Brown* and its implications showed the limits of a strictly legal strategy. In Little Rock, the ugly face of white racism received wide coverage in the mass media and quickly sobered the more optimistic champions of integration. However welcome Eisenhower's intervention, his reluctance to endorse desegregation suggested that civil rights activists could still not rely on federal help. As the Montgomery bus boycott had proved, black communities would have to help themselves first.

Martin Luther King Jr. and the SCLC

When it ended with the Supreme Court decision in November 1956, the 381-day Montgomery bus boycott had made Martin Luther King Jr. a prominent national figure. In January 1957 *Time* magazine put King on its cover. *The New York Times Magazine* published a detailed history of the bus boycott, focusing on King's role. NBC's *Meet the Press* invited him to become only the second African American ever to appear on that program. Speaking invitations poured in from universities and organizations around the country. King himself was an extraordinary and complex man. Born in 1929 in Atlanta, he enjoyed a middle-class upbringing as the son of a prominent Baptist minister. After graduating from prestigious Morehouse College, an all-black school, King earned a divinity degree at Crozer Theological Seminary in Pennsylvania and a Ph.D. in theology from Boston University.

In graduate school King was drawn to the social Christianity of American theologian Walter Rauschenbusch, who insisted on connecting religious faith with struggles for social justice. Above all, King admired Mohandas Gandhi, a lawyer turned ascetic who had led a successful nonviolent resistance movement against British colonial rule in India. Gandhi taught his followers to confront authorities with a readiness to suffer, in order to expose injustice and force those in power to end it. This tactic of nonviolent civil disobedience required discipline and sacrifice from its followers, who were sometimes called upon to lay their lives on the line against armed police and military forces. Crucially, King believed Gandhian nonviolence to be not merely a moral imperative but a potent political strategy that had "muzzled the guns of the British empire in India and freed more than three hundred and fifty million people from colonialism." A unique blend of traditional African American folk preacher and erudite intellectual, King used his passion and intelligence to help transform a community's pain into a powerful moral force for change.

In a December 1956 address celebrating the Montgomery bus boycott victory, King laid out six key lessons from the year-long struggle: "(1) We have discovered that we can stick together for a common cause; (2) our leaders do not have to sell out; (3) threats and violence do not necessarily intimidate those who are sufficiently aroused and nonviolent; (4) our church is becoming militant, stressing a social gospel as well as a gospel of personal salvation; (5) we have gained a new sense of dignity and destiny; (6) we have discovered a new and powerful weapon—nonviolent resistance." The influence of two visiting northern pacifists, Bayard Rustin of the War Resisters' League and Glenn Smiley of the Fellowship of Reconciliation, had helped deepen King's own commitment to the Gandhian philosophy.

King recognized the need to exploit the momentum of the Montgomery movement. In early 1957, with the help of Rustin and other aides, he brought together nearly 100 black ministers to found the Southern Christian Leadership Conference (SCLC). The clergymen elected King president and his close

friend, the Reverend Ralph Abernathy, treasurer. The SCLC called upon black people "to understand that nonviolence is not a symbol of weakness or cowardice, but as Jesus demonstrated, nonviolent resistance transforms weakness into strength and breeds courage in the face of danger."

But King and other black leaders also understood that the white South was no monolith. They believed white Southerners could be divided roughly into three groups: a tiny minority—often with legal training, social connections, and money—that might be counted on to help overthrow segregation; extreme segregationists who were willing and able to use violence and terror in defense of white supremacy; and a broad middle group who favored and benefited from segregation, but who were unwilling to take personal risks to prevent its destruction. In the battles to come, civil rights leaders made this nuanced view of the white South a central part of their larger political strategy. Extreme segrega-

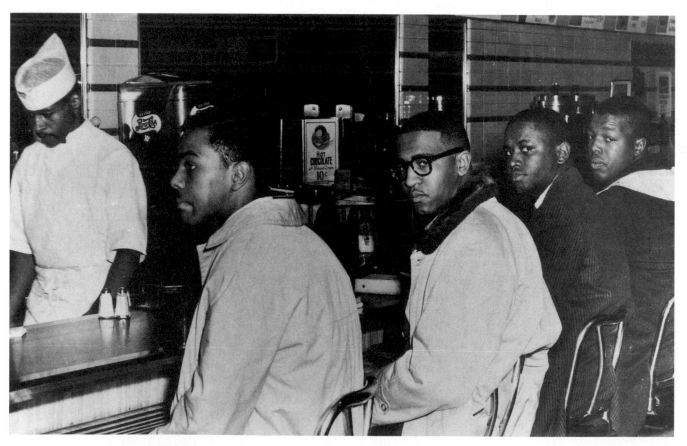

The second day of the sit-in at the Greensboro, North Carolina, Woolworth lunch counter, February 2, 1960. From left: Joseph McNeil, Franklin McCain, Billy Smith, and Clarence Henderson. The Greensboro protest sparked a wave of sit-ins across the South, mostly by college students, demanding an end to segregation in restaurants and other public places.

SOURCE: News & Record Library/John G. Moebes.

tionists could be counted on to overreact, often violently, to civil rights campaigns, and thereby help to win sympathy and support for the cause. White moderates, especially in the business community, might be reluctant to initiate change, but they would try to distance themselves from the desperate violence of extremists and present themselves as pragmatic supporters of order and peace.

The SCLC gained support among black ministers, and King vigorously spread his message in speeches and writings. But the organization failed to generate the kind of mass, direct-action movement that had made history in Montgomery. Instead, the next great spark to light the fire of protest came from what seemed at the time a most unlikely source: black college students.

Sit-Ins: Greensboro, Nashville, Atlanta

On Monday, February 1, 1960, four black freshmen from North Carolina Agricultural and Technical College in Greensboro sat down at the whites-only lunch counter in Woolworth's. They politely ordered coffee and doughnuts. As the students had anticipated while planning the action in their dorm rooms, they were refused service. Although they could buy pencils or toothpaste, black people were not allowed to eat in Woolworth's. But the four students stayed at the counter until closing time. Word of their actions spread quickly, and the next day they returned with over two dozen supporters. On the third day, students occupied sixty-three of the sixty-six lunch counter seats. By Thursday they had been joined by three white students from the Women's College of the University of North Carolina in Greensboro. Scores of sympathizers overflowed Woolworth's and started a sit-in down the street in S. H. Kress. On Friday hundreds of black students and a few whites jammed the lunch counters.

The week's events made Greensboro national news. City officials, looking to end the protest, offered to negotiate in exchange for an end to demonstrations. But white business leaders and politicians proved unwilling to change the racial status quo, and the sit-ins resumed on April 1. In response to the April 21 arrest of forty-five students for trespassing, an outraged African American community organized an economic boycott of targeted stores. With the boycott cutting deeply into merchants' profits, Greensboro's leaders reluctantly gave in. On July 25, 1960, the first African American ate a meal at Woolworth's.

The Greensboro sit-in sent a shock wave throughout the South. During the next eighteen months 70,000 people—most of them black students, a few of them white allies—participated in sit-ins against segregation in dozens of communities. More than 3,000 were arrested. African Americans had discovered a new form of direct-action protest, dignified and powerful, which white people could not ignore. The sit-in movement also transformed participants' self-image, empowering them psychologically and emotionally. Franklin McCain, one of the original four Greensboro students, later recalled a great feeling of soul cleansing: "I probably felt better on that day than I've ever felt in my life. Seems like a lot of feelings of guilt or what-have-you suddenly left me, and I felt as though I had gained my manhood, so to speak, and not only gained it, but had developed quite a lot of respect for it."

In Nashville, Reverend James Lawson, a northern-born black minister, had led workshops in nonviolent resistance since 1958. Lawson had served a jail term as a conscientious objector during the Korean War and had become active in the Fellowship of Reconciliation. He had also spent three years as a missionary in India, where he had learned close-up the Gandhian methods of promoting social change. Lawson gathered around him a group of deeply committed black students from Fisk, Vanderbilt, and other Nashville colleges. Young activists there talked not only of ending segregation but also of creating a "Beloved Community" based on Christian idealism and Gandhian principles.

In the spring of 1960 more than 150 Nashville students were arrested in disciplined sit-ins aimed at desegregating downtown lunch counters. Lawson, who preached the need for sacrifice in the cause of justice, found himself expelled from the divinity school at Vanderbilt. Lawson and other veterans of the Nashville sit-ins, such as John Lewis, Diane Nash, and Marion Barry, would go on to play influential roles in the national civil rights movement. The Nashville group developed rules of conduct that became a model for protesters elsewhere: "Don't strike back or curse if abused. . . . Show yourself courteous and friendly at all times. . . . Report all serious incidents to your leader in a polite manner. Remember love and nonviolence."

The most ambitious sit-in campaign developed in Atlanta, the South's largest and richest city, home to the region's most powerful and prestigious black community. Students from Morehouse, Spelman, and the other all-black schools that made up Atlanta University took the lead. On March 15, 1960, 200 young black people staged a well-coordinated sit-in at restaurants in City Hall, the State Capitol, and other government offices. Police arrested and jailed seventy-six demonstrators that day, but the experience only strengthened the activists' resolve. Led by Julian Bond and Lonnie King, two Morehouse undergraduates, the students formed the Committee on an Appeal for

Human Rights. We will "use every legal and nonviolent means at our disposal to secure full citizenship rights as members of this great democracy of ours," the students promised. Over the summer they planned a fall campaign of large-scale sit-ins at major Atlanta department stores and a boycott of downtown merchants. In October 1960 Martin Luther King Jr. and thirty-six students were arrested when they sat down in the all-white Magnolia Room restaurant in Rich's Department Store. As in Greensboro and Montgomery, the larger African American community in Atlanta supported the continuing sit-ins, picketing, and boycotts. The campaign stretched on for months, and hundreds of protesters went to jail. The city's business leaders finally relented in September 1961, and desegregation came to Atlanta.

SNCC and the "Beloved Community"

The sit-in movement pumped new energy into the civil rights cause, creating a new generation of activists and leaders. Mass arrests, beatings, and vilification in the southern white press only strengthened the resolve of those in the movement. Students also had to deal with the fears of their families, many of whom had made great sacrifices to send them off to college. John Lewis, a seminary student in Nashville, remembered his mother in rural Alabama pleading with him to "get out of that mess, before you get hurt." Lewis wrote to his parents that he acted out of his Christian conscience: "My soul will not be satisfied until freedom, justice, and fair play become a reality for all people."

The new student militancy also caused discord within black communities. The authority of local African American elites had traditionally depended on their influence and cooperation with the white establishment. Black lawyers, schoolteachers, principals, and businessmen had to maintain regular and cordial relations with white judges, school boards, and politicians. Student calls for freedom disturbed many community leaders worried about upsetting traditional patronage networks. Some black college presidents, pressured by trustees and state legislators, sought to moderate or stop the movement altogether. The president of Southern University in Baton Rouge, the largest black college in the nation, suspended eighteen sit-in leaders in 1960 and forced the entire student body of 5,000 to reapply to the college so that agitators could be screened out.

An April 1960 conference of 120 black student activists in Raleigh, North Carolina, underlined the generational and radical aspects of the new movement. The meeting had been called by Ella Baker, executive director of the SCLC, to help the students assess their experiences and plan future actions. Fifty-five at the time, Baker had for years played an important behind-the-scenes role in the civil rights cause, serving as a community organizer and field secretary for the NAACP before heading the staff of the SCLC. She understood the psychological importance of the students' remaining independent of adult control. She counseled them to resist affiliating with any of the national civil rights organizations. Baker also encouraged the trend toward group-centered leadership among the students. She later commented that social movements needed "the development of people who are interested not in being leaders as much as in developing leadership among other people."

With Baker's encouragement, the conference voted to establish a new group, the Student Nonviolent Coordinating Committee (SNCC). The strong influence of the Nashville students, led by James Lawson, could be found in the SNCC statement of purpose:

> We affirm the philosophical or religious ideal of nonviolence as the foundation of our purpose, the presupposition of our faith, and the manner of our action. Nonviolence as it grows from Judaic-Christian tradition seeks a social order of justice permeated by love. Integration of human endeavor represents the crucial first step towards such a society.

In the fall of 1960 SNCC established an organizational structure, a set of principles, and a new style of civil rights protest. The emphasis was on fighting segregation through direct confrontation, mass action, and civil disobedience. SNCC fieldworkers initiated and supported local, community-based activity. Three-quarters of the first fieldworkers were less than twenty-two years old. Leadership was vested in a nonhierarchical Coordinating Committee, but local groups were free to determine their own direction. SNCC people distrusted bureaucracy and structure; they stressed spontaneity and improvisation. A small but dedicated group of young white southerners, inspired by SNCC's idealism and activism, joined the cause. Groups such as the Southern Student Organizing Committee, led by Sam Shirah and Sue Thrasher, as well as SNCC activists like Bob Zellner, looked for ways to extend SNCC's radicalism to white communities. Over the next few years SNCC was at the forefront of nearly every major civil rights battle.(See Out of Many Voices: "Fanny Lou Hamer Tries to Register to Vote".)

The Election of 1960 and Civil Rights

The issue of race relations was kept from center stage during the very close presidential campaign of 1960. As vice president, Richard Nixon had been a leading

OUT OF MANY VOICES

FANNY LOU HAMER TRIES TO REGISTER TO VOTE, INDIANOLA, MISSISSIPPI, 1962

Born in 1918, Fanny Lou Hamer grew up in an impoverished family in the Mississippi Delta region, and worked as a sharecropper alongside her husband. When the civil rights movement came to Mississippi, Mrs. Hamer joined the Student Nonviolent Coordinating Committee (SNCC) as a field worker in voter registration drives. She later became a prominent leader in the Mississippi Freedom Democratic Party. Here she recounts her first attempt to register to vote.

I WENT TO INDIANOLA ON THE THIRTY-FIRST OF August in 1962; that was to try to register. When we got there—there was eighteen of us went that day—so when we got there, there were people there with guns and just a lot of strange-looking people to us. We went on in the circuit clerk's office, and he asked us what did we want; and we told him what we wanted. We wanted to try to register. He told us that all of us would have to get out of there except two. So I was one of the two persons that remained inside, to try to register, [with] another young man named Mr. Ernest Davis. We stayed in to take the literacy test. So the registrar gave me the sixteenth section of the Constitution of Mississippi. He pointed it out in the book and told me to look at it and then copy it down just like I saw it in the book: Put a period where a period was supposed to be, a comma and all of that. After I copied it down he told me right below that to give a real reasonable interpretation then, interpret what I had read. That was impossible. I had tried to give it, but I didn't even know what it meant, much less to interpret it.

Well, when we got back I went on out to where I had been staying for eighteen years, and the landowner had talked to my husband and told him I had to leave the place. My little girl, the child that I raised, met me and told me that the landowner was mad and I might have to leave. So during the time that my husband was talking about it, I was back in the house. The landowner drove up and asked him had I made it back. He [my husband] told him I had. I got up and walked out on the porch, and he [told] me did Pap tell me what he said. I told him, "He did." He said, "Well, I mean that, you'll have to go down and withdraw your registration, or you'll have to leave this place." I didn't call myself saying nothing smart, but I couldn't understand it. I answered the only way I could and told him that I didn't go down there to register for him; I went down there to register for myself. This seemed like it made him madder when I told him that. ■

SOURCE: *Civil Rights in Mississippi Digital Archive*
http://www.lib.usm.edu/~spcol/crda/index.html/ Created and maintained by the Special Collections Digital Lab, a division of University of Southern Mississippi Libraries, Hattiesburg, MS.

Republican voice for stronger civil rights legislation. In contrast, Democratic nominee Senator John F. Kennedy had played virtually no role in the congressional battles over civil rights during the 1950s. But during the campaign, their roles reversed. Kennedy praised the sit-in movement as part of a revival of national reform spirit. He declared, "It is in the American tradition to stand up for one's rights—even if the new way is to sit down." While the Republican platform contained a strong civil rights plank, Nixon, eager to court white southern voters, minimized his own identification with the movement. In October, when

Martin Luther King Jr. was jailed after leading a demonstration in Atlanta, Kennedy telephoned King's wife, Coretta Scott King, to reassure her and express his personal support. Kennedy's brother Robert telephoned the judge in the case and angrily warned him that he had violated King's civil rights and endangered the national Democratic ticket. The judge released King soon afterward.

News of this intervention did not gain wide attention in the white South, much to the relief of the Kennedys. The race was tight, and they knew they could not afford to alienate traditional white southern

Democrats. But the campaign effectively played up the story among black voters all over the country. Kennedy won 70 percent of the black vote, which helped put him over the top in such critical states as Illinois, Texas, Michigan, and Pennsylvania and secure his narrow victory over Nixon. Many civil rights activists optimistically looked forward to a new president who would have to acknowledge his political debt to the black vote.

But the very closeness of his victory constrained Kennedy on the race question. Democrats had lost ground in the House and Senate, and Kennedy had to worry about alienating conservative southern Democrats who chaired key congressional committees. Passage of major civil rights legislation would be virtually impossible. The new president told leaders such as Roy Wilkins of the NAACP that a strategy of "minimum legislation, maximum executive action" offered the best road to change. The president did appoint some forty African Americans to high federal positions, including Thurgood Marshall to the federal appellate court. He established a Committee on Equal Employment Opportunity, chaired by Vice President Lyndon B. Johnson, to fight discrimination in the federal civil service and in corporations that received government contracts.

Most significantly, the Kennedy administration sought to invigorate the Civil Rights Division of the Justice Department. That division had been created by the Civil Rights Act of 1957, which authorized the attorney general to seek court injunctions to protect people denied their right to vote. But the Eisenhower administration had made little use of this new power. Robert Kennedy, the new attorney general, began assembling a staff of brilliant and committed attorneys, headed by Washington lawyer Burke Marshall. Kennedy encouraged them to get out of Washington and get into the field wherever racial troubles arose. In early 1961, when Louisiana school officials balked at a school desegregation order, Robert Kennedy warned them that he would ask the federal court to hold them in contempt. When Burke Marshall started court proceedings, the state officials gave in. But the new, more aggressive mood at Justice could not solve the central political dilemma: how to move forward on civil rights without alienating southern Democrats. Pressure from the newly energized southern civil rights movement soon revealed the true difficulty of that problem. The movement would also provoke murderous outrage from white extremists determined to maintain the racial status quo.

Freedom Rides

In the spring of 1961 James Farmer, national director of CORE, announced plans for an interracial Freedom Ride through the South. The goal was to test compliance with court orders banning segregation in interstate travel and terminal accommodations. CORE had just recently made Farmer its leader in an effort to revitalize the organization. One of the founders of CORE in 1942, Farmer had worked for various pacifist and socialist groups and served as program director for the

A Freedom Riders' bus burns after being firebombed in Anniston, Alabama, May 14, 1961. After setting the bus afire, whites attacked the passengers fleeing the smoke and flames. Violent scenes like this one received extensive publicity in the mass media and helped compel the Justice Department to enforce court rulings banning segregation on interstate bus lines.

SOURCE: UPI/CORBIS.

NAACP. He designed the Freedom Ride to induce a crisis, in the spirit of the sit-ins. "Our intention," Farmer declared, "was to provoke the southern authorities into arresting us and thereby prod the Justice Department into enforcing the law of the land." CORE received financial and tactical support from the SCLC and several NAACP branches. It also informed the Justice Department and the Federal Bureau of Investigation of its plans, but received no reply.

On May 4 seven blacks and six whites split into two interracial groups and left Washington on public buses bound for Alabama and Mississippi. At first the two buses encountered only isolated harassment and violence as they headed south. But when one bus entered Anniston, Alabama, on May 14, an angry mob surrounded it, smashing windows and slashing tires. Six miles out of town, the tires went flat. A firebomb tossed through a window forced the passengers out. The mob then beat the Freedom Riders with black-jacks, iron bars, and clubs, and the bus burst into flames. A caravan of cars organized by the Birmingham office of the SCLC rescued the wounded. Another mob attacked the second bus in Anniston, leaving one Freedom Rider close to death and permanently brain-damaged.

The violence escalated. In Birmingham, a mob of forty whites waited on the loading platform and attacked the bus that managed to get out of Anniston. Although police had been warned to expect trouble, they did nothing to stop the mob from beating the Freedom Riders with pipes and fists, nor did they make any arrests. FBI agents observed and took notes but did nothing. The remaining Freedom Riders decided to travel as a single group on the next lap, from Birmingham to Montgomery, but no bus would take them. Stranded and frightened, they reluctantly boarded a special flight to New Orleans arranged by the Justice Department. On May 17 the CORE-sponsored Freedom Ride disbanded.

But that was not the end of the Freedom Rides. SNCC leaders in Atlanta and Nashville assembled a fresh group of volunteers to continue the trip. On May 20, twenty-one Freedom Riders left Birmingham for Montgomery. The bus station in the Alabama capital was eerily quiet and deserted as they pulled in. But when the passengers left the bus a mob of several hundred whites rushed them, yelling "Get those niggers!" and clubbing people to the ground. James Zwerg, a white Freedom Rider from the University of Wisconsin, had his spinal cord severed. John Lewis, veteran of the Nashville sit-in movement, suffered a brain concussion. As he lay in a pool of blood, a policeman handed him a state court injunction forbidding inter-racial travel in Alabama. The mob indiscriminately beat

journalists and clubbed John Siegenthaler, a Justice Department attorney sent to observe the scene. It took police more than an hour to halt the rioting. Montgomery's police commissioner later said, "We have no intention of standing guard for a bunch of trouble-makers coming into our city."

The mob violence and the indifference of Alabama officials made the Freedom Ride page-one news around the country and throughout the world. Newspapers in Europe, Africa, and Asia denounced the hypocrisy of the federal government. The Kennedy administration, preparing for the president's first summit meeting with Soviet premier Nikita Khrushchev, saw the situation as a threat to its international prestige. On May 21, an angry mob threatened to invade a support rally at Montgomery's First Baptist Church. A hastily assembled group of 400 U.S. marshals, sent by Robert Kennedy, barely managed to keep the peace. The attorney general called for a cooling-off period, but Martin Luther King Jr., James Farmer, and the SNCC leaders announced that the Freedom Ride would continue. A bandaged but spirited group of twenty-seven Freedom Riders prepared to leave Montgomery for Jackson, Mississippi, on May 24. To avoid further violence Robert Kennedy arranged a compromise through Mississippi senator James Eastland. In exchange for a guarantee of safe passage through Mississippi, the federal government promised not to interfere with the arrest of the Freedom Riders in Jackson. This Freedom Ride and several that followed thus escaped violence. But more than 300 people were arrested that summer in Jackson on charges of traveling "for the avowed purpose of inflaming public opinion." Sticking to a policy of "jail, no bail," Freedom Riders clogged the prison, where they endured beatings and intimidation by prison guards that went largely unreported in the press. Their jail experiences turned most of them into committed core leaders of the student movement.

The Justice Department eventually petitioned the Interstate Commerce Commission to issue clear rules prohibiting segregation on interstate carriers. At the end of 1962, CORE proclaimed victory in the battle against Jim Crow interstate travel. By creating a crisis, the Freedom Rides had forced the Kennedy administration to act. But they also revealed the unwillingness of the federal government to fully enforce the law of the land. The Freedom Rides exposed the ugly face of southern racism to the world. At the same time, they reinforced white resistance to desegregation. The jailings and brutality experienced by Freedom Riders made clear to the civil rights community the limits of moral suasion alone for effecting change.

The Albany Movement: The Limits of Protest

Where the federal government chose not to enforce the constitutional rights of black people, segregationist forces tenaciously held their ground, especially in the more remote areas of the Deep South. In Albany, a small city in southwest Georgia, activists from SNCC, the NAACP, and other local groups formed a coalition known as the Albany movement. Starting in October 1961 and continuing for more than a year, thousands of Albany's black citizens marched, sat in, and boycotted as part of a citywide campaign to integrate public facilities and win voting rights. More than a thousand people spent time in jail. In December, the arrival of Martin Luther King Jr. and the SCLC transformed Albany into a national symbol of the struggle.

But the gains at Albany proved minimal. Infighting among the various civil rights organizations hurt the cause. Local SNCC workers opposed the more cautious approach of NAACP officials, even though the more established organization paid many of the campaign's expenses. The arrival of King guaranteed national news coverage, but local activists worried that his presence might undermine the community focus and their own influence. Most important, Albany police chief Laurie Pritchett shrewdly deprived the movement of the kind of national sympathy won by the Freedom Riders. Pritchett filled the jails with black demonstrators, kept their mistreatment to a minimum, and prevented white mobs from running wild. King himself was twice arrested in the summer of 1962, but Albany officials quickly freed him to avoid negative publicity. The Kennedy administration kept clear of the developments in Albany, hoping to help the gubernatorial campaign of "moderate" Democrat Carl Sanders. By late 1962 the Albany movement had collapsed, and Pritchett proudly declared the city "as segregated as ever." One activist summed up the losing campaign: "We were naive enough to think we could fill up the jails. Pritchett was hep to the fact that we couldn't. We ran out of people before he ran out of jails." Albany showed that mass protest without violent white reaction and direct federal intervention could not end Jim Crow.

The successful battle to integrate the University of Mississippi in 1962 contrasted with the failure at Albany and reinforced the importance of federal intervention for guaranteeing civil rights to African Americans. In the fall of 1962 James Meredith, an air force veteran and a student at all-black Jackson State College, tried to register as the first black student at the university. Governor Ross Barnett defied a federal court order and personally blocked Meredith's path at the admissions office. When Barnett refused to assure

Robert Kennedy that Meredith would be protected, the attorney general dispatched 500 federal marshals to the campus. Over the radio, Barnett encouraged resistance to the "oppressive power of the United States," and an angry mob of several thousand whites, many of them armed, laid siege to the campus on September 30. A night of violence left 2 people dead and 160 marshals wounded, 28 from gunfire. President Kennedy ordered 5,000 army troops onto the campus to stop the riot. A federal guard remained to protect Meredith, who graduated the following summer.

THE MOVEMENT AT HIGH TIDE, 1963-65

The tumultuous events of 1960-62 convinced civil rights strategists that segregation could not be dismantled merely through orderly protest and moral persuasion. Only comprehensive civil rights legislation, backed by the power of the federal government, could guarantee full citizenship rights for African Americans. To build the national consensus needed for new laws, civil rights activists looked for ways to gain broader support for their cause. By 1963, their sense of urgency had led them to plan dramatic confrontations that would expose the violence and terror routinely faced by southern blacks. With the whole country—indeed, the whole world—watching, the movement reached the peak of its political and moral power.

Birmingham

At the end of 1962, Martin Luther King Jr. and his SCLC allies decided to launch a new campaign against segregation in Birmingham, Alabama. After the failure in Albany, King and his aides looked for a way to shore up his leadership and inject new momentum into the freedom struggle. They needed a major victory. Birmingham was the most segregated big city in America, and it had a deep history of racial violence. African Americans endured total segregation in schools, restaurants, city parks, and department store dressing rooms. Although black people constituted more than 40 percent of the city's population, fewer than 10,000 of Birmingham's 80,000 registered voters were black. The city's prosperous steel industry relegated black workers to menial jobs.

Working closely with local civil rights groups led by the longtime Birmingham activist Reverend Fred Shuttlesworth, the SCLC carefully planned its campaign. The strategy was to fill the city jails with protesters, boycott downtown department stores, and enrage Public Safety Commissioner Eugene "Bull" Connor. In April, King arrived with a manifesto demanding an end to racist hiring practices and segregated public accommodations and the creation of a biracial committee to oversee desegregation. "Here in Birmingham," King told reporters, "we have reached the point of no return." Connor's police began jailing hundreds of demonstrators, including King himself, who defied a state court injunction against further protests.

Held in solitary confinement for several days, King managed to write a response to a group of Birmingham clergy who had deplored the protests. King's *Letter from Birmingham Jail* was soon widely reprinted and circulated as a pamphlet. It set out the key moral issues at stake, and scoffed at those who claimed the campaign was illegal and ill timed. King wrote:

We know through painful experience that freedom is never voluntarily given by the oppressor; it must be demanded by the oppressed. Frankly, I have never yet engaged in a direct-action campaign that was "well timed" in the view of those who have not suffered unduly from the disease of segregation. For years now I have heard the word "Wait!" It rings in the ear of every Negro with a piercing familiarity. This "Wait" has almost always meant "Never." We must come to see, with one of our distinguished jurists, that "justice too long delayed is justice denied."

After King's release on bail, the campaign intensified. The SCLC kept up the pressure by recruiting thousands

Police dogs attacked a seventeen-year-old civil rights demonstrator for defying an antiparade ordinance in Birmingham, Alabama, May 3, 1963. He was part of the "children's crusade" organized by SCLC in its campaign to fill the city jails with protesters. More than 900 Birmingham schoolchildren went to jail that day.

SOURCE: Photo by Bill Hudson. AP/Wide World Photos.

of Birmingham's young students for a "children's cru-sade." In early May, Bull Connor's forces began using high-powered water cannons, billy clubs, and snarling police dogs to break up demonstrations. Millions of Americans reacted with horror to the violent scenes from Birmingham shown on national television. Many younger black people, especially from the city's poor and working-class districts, began to fight back, hurl-ing bottles and bricks at police. On May 10, mediators from the Justice Department negotiated an uneasy truce. The SCLC agreed to an immediate end to the protests. In exchange, businesses would desegregate and begin hiring African Americans over the next three months, and a biracial city committee would oversee desegrega-tion of public facilities.

King claimed the events in Birmingham represented "the most magnificent victory for justice we've ever seen in the Deep South." But whites such as Bull Connor and Governor George Wallace denounced the agreement. A few days after the announcement, more than a thousand robed Ku Klux Klansmen burned a cross in a park on the outskirts of Birmingham. When bombs rocked SCLC headquarters and the home of King's brother, a Birm-ingham minister, enraged blacks took to the streets and pelted police and firefighters with stones and bottles. President Kennedy ordered 3,000 army troops into the city and prepared to nationalize the Alabama National Guard. The violence receded, and white business people and politicians began to carry out the agreed-upon pact. But in September a bomb killed four black girls in a Birm-ingham Baptist church, reminding the city and the world that racial harmony was still a long way off.

The Birmingham campaign and the other protests it sparked over the next seven months engaged more

As the Civil Rights movement received greater coverage in the international press, editorial cartoonists in America expressed fears that white resistance to integration provided an effective propaganda weapon to the Soviet Union and its allies. This *Oakland Tribune* cartoon appeared on September 11, 1957, in the midst of the crisis in Little Rock.

SOURCE: The Oakland Tribune.

than 100,000 people and led to nearly 15,000 arrests. The civil rights community now drew support from millions of Americans, black and white, who were inspired by the protesters and repelled by the face of southern bigotry. At the same time, Birmingham changed the nature of black protest. The black unemployed and working poor who joined in the struggle brought a different perspective from that of the students, professionals, and members of the religious middle class who had dominated the movement before Birmingham. They cared less about the philosophy of nonviolence and more about immediate gains in employment and housing and an end to police brutality.

JFK and the March on Washington

The growth of black activism and white support convinced President Kennedy the moment had come to press for sweeping civil rights legislation. Continuing white resistance in the South also made clearer than ever the need for federal action. In June 1963, Alabama governor George Wallace threatened to personally block the admission of two black students to the state university. Only the deployment of National Guard troops, placed under federal control by the president, ensured the students' safety and their peaceful admission into the University of Alabama.

It was a defining moment for Kennedy. Even more than for Eisenhower at Little Rock, the realities of international cold war politics pushed Kennedy toward support for civil rights. On June 11 the president went on national television and offered his personal endorsement of the civil rights activism: "Today we are committed to a worldwide struggle to promote and protect the rights of all who wish to be free. And when Americans are sent to Vietnam or West Berlin, we do not ask for whites only. . . . Are we to say to the rest of the world, and much more importantly, to each other, that this is a land of the free except for Negroes?" Reviewing the racial situation, Kennedy told his audience that "We face . . . a moral crisis as a country and a people. It cannot be met by repressive police action. It cannot be left to increased demonstrations in the streets. It cannot be quieted by token moves or talk. It is a time to act in the Congress, in your state and local legislative body, and, above all, in all our daily lives." The next week Kennedy asked Congress for a broad law that would ensure voting rights, outlaw segregation in public facilities, and bolster federal authority to deny funds for discriminatory programs. Knowing they would face a stiff fight from congressional conservatives, administration officials began an intense lobbying effort in support of the law. After three years of fence

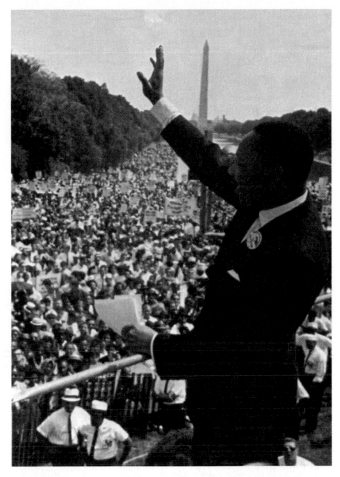

Reverend Dr. Martin Luther King Jr. acknowledging the huge throng at the historic March on Washington for "jobs and freedom," August 28, 1963. The size of the crowd, the stirring oratory and song, and the live network television coverage produced one of the most memorable political events in the nation's history.

SOURCE: AP Wide World Photos.

sitting, Kennedy finally committed his office and his political future to the civil rights cause.

Movement leaders lauded the president's initiative. Yet they understood that racial hatred still haunted the nation. Only a few hours after Kennedy's television speech, a gunman murdered Medgar Evers, leader of the Mississippi NAACP, outside his home in Jackson, Mississippi. To pressure Congress and demonstrate the urgency of their cause, a broad coalition of civil rights groups planned a massive, nonviolent March on Washington. The idea had deep roots in black protest. A. Philip Randolph, head of the Brotherhood of Sleeping Car Porters, had originally proposed such a march in 1941 to protest discrimination against blacks in the wartime defense industries. Now, more than twenty years later, Randolph, along with his aide Bayard Rustin, revived the concept and convinced leaders of the major civil rights groups to support it.

The Kennedy administration originally opposed the march, fearing it would jeopardize support for the president's civil rights bill in Congress. But as plans for the rally solidified, Kennedy reluctantly gave his approval. Leaders from the SCLC, the NAACP, SNCC, the Urban League, and CORE—the leading organizations in the civil rights community—put aside their tactical differences to forge a broad consensus for the event.

John Lewis, the young head of SNCC, who had endured numerous brutal assaults, planned a speech that denounced the Kennedys as hypocrites. Lewis's speech enraged Walter Reuther, the white liberal leader of the United Auto Workers union, which had helped finance the march. Reuther threatened to turn off the loudspeakers he was paying for, believing Lewis's speech would embarrass the Kennedys. Randolph, the acknowledged elder statesman of the movement, convinced Lewis at the last moment to tone down his remarks. "We've come this far," he implored. "For the sake of unity, change it."

OVERVIEW

LANDMARK CIVIL RIGHTS LEGISLATION, SUPREME COURT DECISIONS, AND EXECUTIVE ORDERS

Year	Decision, law, or executive order	Significance
1939	*Missouri v. ex.rel.Gaines*	Required University of Missouri Law School either to admit African Americans or build another fully equal law school
1941	**Executive Order 8802 (by President Roosevelt)**	Banned racial discrimination in defense industry and government offices; established Fair Employment Practices Committee to investigate violations
1946	*Morgan v. Virginia*	Ruled that segregation on interstate buses violated federal law and created an "undue burden" on interstate commerce
1948	**Executive Order 9981 (by President Truman)**	Desegregated the U.S. armed forces
1950	*McLaurin v. Oklahoma State Regents*	Ruled that forcing an African American student to sit, eat, and study in segregated facilities was unconstitutional because it inevitably created a "badge of inferiority"
1950	*Sweatt v. Painter*	Ruled that an inferior law school created by the University of Texas to serve African Americans violated their right to equal protection and ordered Herman Sweatt to be admitted to University of Texas Law School
1954	*Brown v. Board of Education of Topeka I*	Declared "separate educational facilities are inherently unequal," thus overturning *Plessy v. Ferguson* (1896) and the "separate but equal" doctrine as it applied to public schools
1955	*Brown v. Board of Education of Topeka II*	Ordered school desegregation to begin with "all deliberate speed," but offered no timetable
1957	**Civil Rights Act**	Created Civil Rights Division within the Justice Department
1964	**Civil Rights Act**	Prohibited discrimination in employment and most places of public accommodation on basis of race, color, religion, sex, or national origin; outlawed bias in federally assisted programs; created Equal Employment Opportunity Commission
1965	**Voting Rights Act**	Authorized federal supervision of voter registration in states and counties where fewer than half of voting age residents were registered; outlawed literacy and other discriminatory tests in voter registration

On August 28, 1963, more than a quarter of a million people, including 50,000 whites, gathered at the Lincoln Memorial to rally for "jobs and freedom." Union members, students, teachers, clergy, professionals, musicians, actors—Americans from all walks of life joined the largest political assembly in the nation's history until then. The sight of all those people holding hands and singing "We Shall Overcome," led by the white folk singer Joan Baez, would not be easily forgotten. At the end of a long, exhilarating day of speeches and freedom songs, Martin Luther King Jr. provided an emotional climax. Combining the democratic promise of the Declaration of Independence with the religious fervor of his Baptist heritage, King stirred the crowd with his dream for America:

> I have a dream today that one day this nation will rise up and live out the true meaning of its creed: "We hold these truths to be self-evident—that all men are created equal." . . . When we allow freedom to ring, when we let it ring from every village and every hamlet, from every state and every city, we will be able to speed up that day when all of God's children—black men and white men, Jews and Gentiles, Protestants and Catholics—will be able to join hands and sing in the words of the old Negro spiritual, "Free at last! Free at last! Thank God Almighty, we are free at last!"

LBJ and the Civil Rights Act of 1964

An extraordinary demonstration of interracial unity, the March on Washington stood as the high-water mark in the struggle for civil rights. It buoyed the spirits of movement leaders as well as the liberals pushing the new civil rights bill through Congress. But the assassination of John F. Kennedy on November 22, 1963, in Dallas threw an ominous cloud over the whole nation and the civil rights movement in particular. In the Deep South, many ardent segregationists welcomed the president's death because of his support for civil rights. Most African Americans probably shared the feelings of Coretta Scott King, who recalled her family's vigil: "We felt that President Kennedy had been a friend of the Cause and that with him as President we could continue to move forward. We watched and prayed for him."

Lyndon Baines Johnson, Kennedy's successor, had never been much of a friend to civil rights. As a senator from Texas (1948–60, including six years as majority leader), Johnson had been one of the shrewdest and most powerful Democrats in Congress. Throughout the 1950s he had worked to obstruct the passage and enforcement of civil rights laws—though as vice president he had ably chaired Kennedy's working group on equal employment. Johnson reassured a grieving nation that "the ideas and the ideals which [Kennedy] so nobly represented must and will be translated into effective action." Even so, civil rights activists looked upon Johnson warily as he took over the Oval Office.

As president, Johnson realized that he faced a new political reality, one created by the civil rights movement. Eager to unite the Democratic Party and prove himself as a national leader, he seized on civil rights as a golden political opportunity. Throughout the early months of 1964, the new president let it be known publicly and privately that he would brook no compromise on civil rights. Johnson exploited all his skills as a political insider. He cajoled, flattered, and threatened key members of the House and Senate. Working with the president, the fifteen-year-old Leadership Conference on Civil Rights coordinated a sophisticated lobbying effort in Congress. Groups such as the NAACP, the AFL-CIO, the National Council of Churches, and the American Jewish Congress made the case for a strong civil rights bill. The House passed the bill in February by a 290–130 vote. The more difficult fight would be in the Senate, where a southern filibuster promised to block the bill or weaken it. But by June, Johnson's persistence had paid off and the southern filibuster had collapsed.

On July 2, 1964, Johnson signed the Civil Rights Act of 1964. Every major provision had survived intact. This landmark law represented the most significant civil rights legislation since Reconstruction. It prohibited discrimination in most places of public accommodation; outlawed discrimination in employment on the basis of race, color, religion, sex, or national origin; outlawed bias in federally assisted programs; authorized the Justice Department to institute suits to desegregate public schools and other facilities; created the Equal Employment Opportunity Commission; and provided technical and financial aid to communities desegregating their schools.

Mississippi Freedom Summer

While President Johnson and his liberal allies won the congressional battle for the new civil rights bill, activists in Mississippi mounted a far more radical and dangerous campaign than any yet attempted in the South. In the spring of 1964, a coalition of workers led by SNCC launched the Freedom Summer project, an ambitious effort to register black voters and directly challenge the iron rule of segregation. Mississippi stood as the toughest test for the civil rights movement, racially and economically. It was the poorest, most backward state in the nation, and had remained

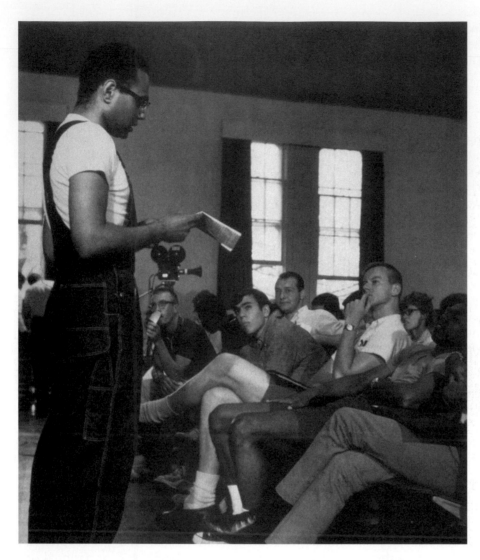

Bob Moses of the Student Nonviolent Coordinating Committee was one of the driving forces behind the 1964 Freedom Summer Project. Here he instructs student volunteers gathered in Oxford, Ohio, before they leave for voter registration and other community organizing work in Mississippi. Moses, who had been working for voting rights in Mississippi since 1961, played a key role in persuading SNCC to accept white volunteers from the North.

SOURCE: Photo by Steve Shapiro. Black Star.

largely untouched by the freedom struggle. African Americans constituted 42 percent of the state's population, but fewer than 5 percent could register to vote. Median black family income was under $1,500 a year, roughly one-third that of white families. A small white planter elite controlled most of the state's wealth, and a long tradition of terror against black people had maintained the racial caste system.

Bob Moses of SNCC and Dave Dennis of CORE planned Freedom Summer as a way of opening up this closed society to the glare of national publicity. The project recruited over 900 volunteers, mostly white college students, to aid in voter registration, teach in "freedom schools," and help build a "freedom party" as an alternative to Mississippi's all-white Democratic Party. Organizers expected violence, which was precisely why they wanted white volunteers. Dave Dennis later explained their reasoning: "The death of a

white college student would bring on more attention to what was going on than for a black college student getting it. That's cold, but that was also in another sense speaking the language of this country." Mississippi authorities prepared for the civil rights workers as if expecting a foreign army, beefing up state highway patrols and local police forces.

On June 21, while most project volunteers were still undergoing training in Ohio, three activists disappeared in Neshoba County, Mississippi, when they went to investigate the burning of a black church that was supposed to serve as a freedom school. Six weeks later, after a massive search belatedly ordered by President Johnson, FBI agents discovered the bodies of the three—white activists Michael Schwerner and Andrew Goodman, and a local black activist, James Chaney—buried in an earthen dam. Goodman and Schwerner had been shot once; Chaney had been severely beaten

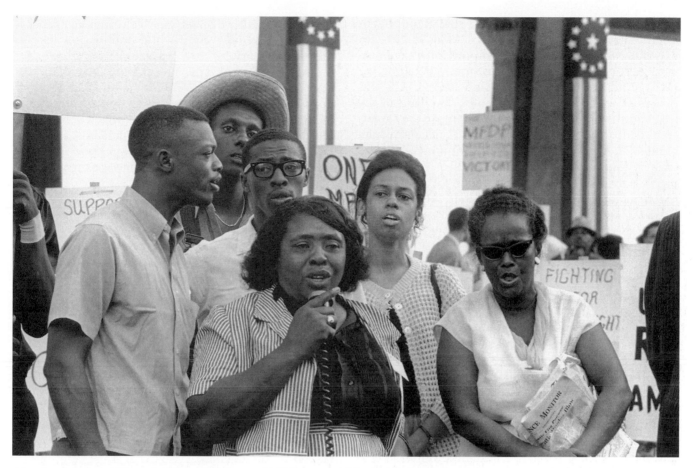

After they were barred from the floor of the August 1964 Democratic National Convention, members of the Mississippi Freedom Democratic Party were led by Fanny Lou Hamer in a song-filled protest outside the hotel. Women from left to right: Fannie Lou Hamer, Eleanor Holmes Norton, and Ella Baker.

SOURCE: Photo by George Ballis. Take Stock–Images of Change.

before being shot three times. Over the summer, at least three other civil rights workers died violently. Project workers suffered 1,000 arrests, 80 beatings, 35 shooting incidents, and 30 bombings in homes, churches, and schools.

Within the project, simmering problems tested the ideal of the Beloved Community. Black veterans of SNCC resented the affluent white volunteers, many of whom had not come to terms with their own racial prejudices. White volunteers, staying only a short time in the state, often found it difficult to communicate in the southern communities with local African Americans, who were wary of breaking old codes of deference. Sexual tensions between black male and white female volunteers also strained relations. A number of both black and white women, led by Ruby Doris Robinson, Mary King, and Casey Hayden, began to raise the issue of women's equality as a companion goal to racial equality. The day-to-day reality of violent reprisals,

police harassment, and constant fear took a hard toll on everyone.

The project did manage to rivet national attention on Mississippi racism, and it won enormous sympathy from northern liberals. Among their concrete accomplishments, the volunteers could point with pride to more than forty freedom schools that brought classes in reading, arithmetic, politics, and African American history to thousands of black children. Some 60,000 black voters signed up to join the Mississippi Freedom Democratic Party (MFDP). In August 1964 the MFDP sent a slate of delegates to the Democratic National Convention looking to challenge the credentials of the all-white regular state delegation.

In Atlantic City, the idealism of Freedom Summer ran into the more cynical needs of the national Democratic Party. Lyndon Johnson opposed the seating of the MFDP because he wanted to avoid a divisive floor fight. He was already concerned that Republicans might carry a number of southern states in November. But MFDP leaders and sympathizers gave dramatic testimony before the convention, detailing the racism and brutality in Mississippi politics. "Is this America," asked Fannie Lou Hamer, "the land of the free and the home of the brave, where we are threatened daily because we want to live as decent human beings?" Led by vice presidential nominee Senator Hubert Humphrey, Johnson's forces offered a compromise that would have given the MFDP a token two seats on the floor. Bitter over what they saw as a betrayal, the MFDP delegates turned the offer down. Within SNCC, the defeat of the MFDP intensified African American disillusionment with the Democratic Party and the liberal establishment.

Malcolm X and Black Consciousness

Frustrated with the limits of nonviolent protest and electoral politics, younger activists within SNCC found themselves increasingly drawn to the militant rhetoric and vision of Malcolm X, who since 1950 had been the preeminent spokesman for the black nationalist religious sect, the Nation of Islam (NOI). Founded in Depression-era Detroit by Elijah Muhammad, the NOI, like the followers of black nationalist leader Marcus Garvey in the 1920s (see Chapter 23) aspired to create a self-reliant, highly disciplined, and proud community—a separate "nation" for black people. Elijah Muhammad preached a message of racial solidarity and self-help, criticized crime and drug use, and castigated whites as "blue-eyed devils" responsible for the world's evil. During the 1950s the NOI (also called Black Muslims) successfully organized in northern black communities, appealing especially to criminals, drug addicts, and others living on the margins of urban life. It operated restaurants, retail stores, and schools as models for black economic self-sufficiency.

The man known as Malcolm X had been born Malcolm Little in 1925 and raised in Lansing, Michigan. His father, a preacher and a follower of Marcus Garvey, was killed in a racist attack by local whites. In his youth, Malcolm led a life of petty crime, eventually serving a seven-year prison term for burglary. While in jail he educated himself and converted to the Nation of Islam. He took the surname "X" to symbolize his original African family name, lost through slavery. Emerging from jail in 1952, he became a dynamic organizer, editor, and speaker for the Nation of Islam. He spoke frequently on college campuses as well on the street corners of black neighborhoods like New York's Harlem. He encouraged his audiences to take pride in their African heritage and to consider armed

self-defense rather than relying solely on nonviolence—in short, to break free of white domination "by any means necessary."

Malcolm ridiculed the integrationist goals of the civil rights movement. Black Muslims, he told audiences, do not want "to integrate into this corrupt society, but to separate from it, to a land of our own, where we can reform ourselves, lift up our moral standards, and try to be godly." In his best-selling *Autobiography of Malcolm X* (1965), he admitted that his position was extremist. "The black race here in North America is in extremely bad condition. You show me a black man who isn't an extremist," he argued, "and I'll show you one who needs psychiatric attention."

In 1964, troubled by Elijah Muhammad's personal scandals (he faced paternity suits brought by two

Born Malcolm Little, Malcolm X (1925–65) took the name "X" as a symbol of the stolen identity of African slaves. He emerged in the early 1960s as the foremost advocate of racial unity and black nationalism. The Black Power movement, initiated in 1966 by SNCC members, was strongly influenced by Malcolm X.

SOURCE: *Malcolm X in Egypt, 1964*. Photo by John Launois. Black Star.

young female employees) and eager to find a more politically effective approach to improving conditions for blacks, Malcolm X broke with the Nation of Islam. He made a pilgrimage to Mecca, the Muslim holy city, where he met Islamic peoples of all colors and underwent a "radical alteration in my whole outlook about 'white' men." He returned to the United States as El-Hajj Malik El-Shabazz, abandoned his black separatist views, and founded the Organization of Afro-American Unity. Malcolm now looked for common ground with the civil rights movement, addressing a Mississippi Freedom Democrats rally in Harlem and meeting with SNCC activists. He stressed the international links between the civil rights struggle in America and the problems facing emerging African nations. On February 21, 1965, Malcolm X was assassinated during a speech at Harlem's Audubon Ballroom. His assailants were members of a New Jersey branch of the NOI, possibly infiltrated by the FBI.

SNCC leader John Lewis thought Malcolm had been the most effective voice "to articulate the aspirations, bitterness, and frustrations of the Negro people," forming "a living link between Africa and the civil rights movement in this country." In his death he became a martyr for the idea that soon became known as Black Power. As much as anyone, Malcolm X pointed the way to a new black consciousness that celebrated black history, black culture, the African heritage, and black self-sufficiency.

Selma and the Voting Rights Act of 1965

Lyndon Johnson won reelection in 1964 by a landslide, capturing 61 percent of the popular vote. Of the 6 million black people who voted in the election, 2 million more than in 1960, an overwhelming 94 percent cast their ballots for Johnson. Republican candidate Senator Barry Goldwater managed to carry only his home state of Arizona and five Deep South states, where fewer than 45 percent of eligible black people could vote. With Democrats in firm control of both the Senate and the House, civil rights leaders believed the time was ripe for further legislative gains. Johnson and his staff began drafting a tough voting rights bill in late 1964, partly with an eye toward countering Republican gains in the Deep South with newly registered black and Democratic voters (see Map 28.2).

Once again, movement leaders plotted to create a crisis that would arouse national indignation, pressure Congress, and force federal action. Martin Luther King Jr. and his aides chose Selma, Alabama, as the target of their campaign. Selma, a city of 27,000 some fifty miles west of Montgomery, had a notorious record of preventing black voting. Of the

15,000 eligible black voters in Selma's Dallas County, registered voters numbered only in the hundreds. In 1963, local activists Amelia Boynton and Reverend Fred Reese had invited SNCC workers to aid voter registration efforts in the community. But they had met a violent reception from county sheriff Jim Clark. Sensing that Clark might be another Bull Connor, King arrived in Selma in January 1965, just after accepting the Nobel Peace Prize in Oslo. "We are not asking, we are demanding the ballot," he declared. King, the SCLC staff, and SNCC workers led daily marches on the Dallas County Courthouse, where hundreds of black citizens tried to get their names added to voter lists. By early February, Clark had imprisoned more than 3,000 protesters.

Voting rights demonstrators on the historic four-day, fifty-four mile trek from Selma to Montgomery Alabama, March 1965. Intensive media coverage helped swell the original 3,000 marchers to over 30,000 supporters at a climactic rally in front of the Alabama state capitol in Montgomery.

SOURCE: Bob Adelman. Magnum Photos, Inc.

MAP EXPLORATION

To explore an interactive version of this map, go to **www.prenhall.com/faragher5/map28.2**

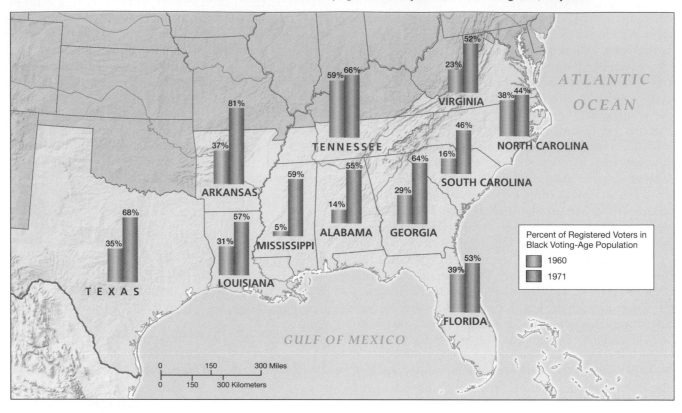

MAP 28.2 Impact of the Voting Rights Act of 1965 Voter registration among African Americans in the South increased significantly between 1960 and 1971.

Despite the brutal beating of Reverend James Bevel, a key SCLC strategist, and the killing of Jimmy Lee Jackson, a young black demonstrator in nearby Marion, the SCLC failed to arouse the level of national indignation it sought. Consequently, in early March SCLC staffers called on black activists to march from Selma to Montgomery, where they planned to deliver a list of grievances to Governor Wallace. On Sunday, March 7, while King preached to his church in Atlanta, a group of 600 marchers crossed the Pettus Bridge on the Alabama River, on their way to Montgomery. A group of mounted, heavily armed county and state lawmen blocked their path and ordered them to turn back. When the marchers did not move, the lawmen attacked with billy clubs and tear gas, driving the protesters back over the bridge in a bloody rout. More than fifty marchers had to be treated in local hospitals.

The dramatic "Bloody Sunday" attack received extensive coverage on network television, prompting a national uproar. Demands for federal intervention poured into the White House from all over the country. King issued a public call for civil rights supporters to come to Selma for a second march on Montgomery. But a federal court temporarily enjoined the SCLC from proceeding with the march. King found himself trapped. He reluctantly accepted a face-saving compromise: in return for a promise from Alabama authorities not to harm marchers, King would lead his followers across the Pettus Bridge, stop, pray briefly, and then turn back. This plan outraged the more militant SNCC activists and sharpened their distrust of King and the SCLC.

But just when it seemed the Selma movement might die, white racist violence revived it. A gang of white toughs attacked four white Unitarian ministers who had come to Selma to participate in the march. One of them,

Reverend James J. Reeb of Boston, died of multiple skull fractures. His death brought new calls for federal action. On March 15, President Johnson delivered a televised address to a joint session of Congress to request passage of a voting rights bill. In a stirring speech, the president fused the political power of his office with the moral power of the movement. "Their cause must be our cause, too. Because it is not just Negroes, but really all of us who must overcome the crippling legacy of bigotry and injustice. And," he concluded firmly, invoking the movement's slogan, "we shall overcome." Johnson also prevailed upon federal judge Frank Johnson to issue a ruling allowing the march to proceed, and he warned Governor Wallace not to interfere.

On March 21 Martin Luther King Jr. led a group of more than 3,000 black and white marchers out of Selma on the road to Montgomery, where the bus boycott that marked the beginning of his involvement had occurred nine years before. Four days later they arrived at the Alabama statehouse. Their ranks had been swelled by more than 30,000 supporters, including hundreds of prominent politicians, entertainers, and black leaders. "I know some of you are asking today," King told the crowd, "'How long will it take?'" He went on in a rousing, rhythmic cadence:

> How long? Not long, because the arc of the moral universe is long but it bends toward justice. How long? Not long, because mine eyes have seen the glory of the coming of the Lord!

In August 1965 President Johnson signed the Voting Rights Act into law. It authorized federal supervision of registration in states and counties where fewer than half of voting-age residents were registered. It also outlawed literacy and other discriminatory tests that had been used to prevent blacks from registering to vote. Between 1964 and 1968, black registrants in Mississippi leaped from 7 percent to 59 percent of the statewide black population; in Alabama, from 24 percent to 57 percent. In those years the number of southern black voters grew from 1 million to 3.1 million. For the first time in their lives, black Southerners in hundreds of small towns and rural communities could enjoy full participation in American politics. Ten years after the Montgomery bus boycott, the civil rights movement had reached a peak of national influence and interracial unity.

CIVIL RIGHTS BEYOND BLACK AND WHITE

The civil rights movement revolved around the aspirations and community strength of African Americans. The historic injustices of slavery, racism, and segregation gave a moral and political urgency to the black struggle for full citizenship rights. Yet other minorities as well had long been denied their civil rights. After World War II, Latinos, Indian peoples, and Asian Americans began making their own halting efforts to improve their political, legal, and economic status. They faced strong opposition from institutional racism and various economic interests that benefited from keeping these groups in a subordinate position. At the same time, the civil rights struggle helped spur a movement to reform immigration policies. The largely unintended consequences of the 1965 Immigration and Nationality Act would radically increase and reshape the flow of new immigrants into the United States.

Mexican Americans and Mexican Immigrants

The Mexican American community in the West and Southwest included both longtime U.S. citizens—who found white authorities nonetheless unwilling to recognize their rights—and noncitizen immigrants from Mexico. After World War II, several Mexican American political organizations sought to secure equal rights and equal opportunity for their community by stressing its American identity. The most important of these groups were the League of United Latin American Citizens (LULAC), founded in Texas in 1928, and the GI Forum, founded in Texas in 1948 by Mexican American veterans of World War II. Both emphasized the learning of English, assimilation into American society, improved education, and the promotion of political power through voting. LULAC successfully pursued two important legal cases that anticipated *Brown* v. *Board of Education*. In *Mendez* v. *Westminster*, a 1947 California case, and in the 1948 *Delgado* case in Texas, the Supreme Court upheld lower-court rulings that declared segregation of Mexican Americans unconstitutional. Like *Brown*, these two decisions did not immediately end segregation, but they offered pathbreaking legal and psychological victories to Mexican American activists. LULAC won another significant legal battle in the 1954 *Hernandez* decision, in which the Supreme Court ended the exclusion of Mexican Americans from Texas jury lists. (See Out of Many Voices: "The American GI Forum Desegregates a Texas School".)

Mexican migration to the United States increased dramatically during and after World War II. The *bracero* program, a cooperative effort between the U.S. and Mexican governments, brought some 300,000 Mexicans to the United States during the war as temporary agricultural and railroad workers.

Delegates to the 1948 National Convention of the League of United Latin American Citizens met in Kingsville, Texas. After World War II, LULAC grew to about 15,000 memebers active in 200 local councils, mostly in Texas and California.

SOURCE: Benson Latin American Collection.

American agribusiness came to depend on Mexicans as a key source of cheap farm labor, and the program continued after the war. Most *braceros* endured harsh work, poor food, and substandard housing in the camps in which they lived. Some migrated into the newly emerging barrio neighborhoods in cities such as San Antonio, Los Angeles, El Paso, and Denver. Many *braceros* and their children became American citizens, but most returned to Mexico. Another group of postwar Mexican immigrants were the *mojados*, or "wetbacks," so called because many swam across the Rio Grande River to enter the United States illegally.

This continued flow of immigrant workers into the Southwest heightened tensions within the Mexican American community. Both LULAC and the GI Forum contended that Mexican American civil rights activists needed to focus their efforts on American citizens of Mexican descent. Thus, they lobbied to end the *bracero* program and for stricter limits on immigration from Mexico to help maintain strict boundaries between Mexican American citizens and Mexican immigrants. Yet within Mexican American communities, where citizens and noncitizens shared language and work experience, and made families together, this

distinction had always been blurry. "I've been following the crops in California for about twelve years," one Mexican American farm worker noted in 1955, "and still don't know if I'm for or against the *braceros*. I guess that's because I first came to this country as a *bracero* myself in 1944, and know something about their problems."

In 1954, in an effort to curb the flow of undocumented immigrants from Mexico, the Eisenhower administration launched the massive "Operation Wetback." Over the next three years Immigration and Naturalization Service (INS) agents rounded up some 3.7 million allegedly illegal migrants and sent them back over the border. INS agents made little effort to distinguish the so-called illegals from *braceros* and Mexican American citizens. Many families were broken up, and thousands who had lived in the United States for a decade or more found themselves deported. Many deportees were denied basic civil liberties, such as due process, and suffered physical abuse and intimidation. The break-up of families caused enormous resentment and anger, as did the contradictory policies of the federal government. As Ernesto Galarza, a leader of the National Agricultural Workers Union put it, "while one agency

OUT OF MANY VOICES

THE AMERICAN GI FORUM DESEGREGATES A TEXAS SCHOOL, 1954

Founded in 1948, the American GI Forum, along with other Mexican American civil rights groups, fought against discrimination in employment, housing, schools, and the judicial system. It joined in lawsuits challenging the segregation of Mexican American school children, but sometimes it succeeded without a court ruling. GI Forum organizer Ed Idar recounts one such grassroots campaign in Kyle, Texas, just south of Austin.

IT WAS TWO OR THREE ROOMS. AND THAT WAS THE Mexican school. They had the first three grades there. And then they had another campus over here in the main part of the city, good buildings, brick buildings and everything. Where they had the first three grades for the Anglos and the rest of the elementary and high school. So, when I talked to local people, we organized a G.I. Forum in Kyle, we had two, three meetings, and then the local establishment got a little concerned. We had proposed to them that we would be happy to raise the money with which to move that frame building from where it was over to the other campus, providing that once that was done, the classes in the first three grades would be integrated. And we agreed to have a meeting of the community—and see we had been working with a small group; we decided, alright let's call the whole community and see if they'll go for this.

So we called the meeting of the whole community—two, three hundred people. To lay the proposition before them. And the sheriff and two, three deputies were there—there was a little tension for a while. And this guy who was our friend, allegedly, this professor at the school turned on us. He started making accusations of outside agitators coming into Kyle, agitating the people. He came pretty close to using the word Communist, and accused us of that. And when my turn came I told the crowd, with the sheriff being there, I told them: I'm aware of the McCarran-[Wood] Act. The Congress had just enacted an act a year or two earlier providing for anybody that was a Communist had to register with the Department of Justice. So I told them: I want everybody here to know that I am aware of this act and I don't intend to register under it, and neither does anybody in my organization. Because we are not Communists. All we are seeking here is equal opportunity and so forth.

The people voted to go ahead and move that building and pay the expense, raise the money to pay for it. The school board never did like the idea but within a few months they put out a bond issue and they raised enough money to enlarge the downtown campus. They built a nice building there and they did away with the frame building, and they integrated the school. And we didn't have to go to court for that one. It was just public pressure organizing the people to get them to do something—that's what happened. ■

SOURCE: Oral History courtesy of *U.S. Latinos & Latinas and World War II Oral History Project*, University of Texas, Austin. Interview with Ed Idar, organizer/volunteer for the American G.I. Forum and the Mexican American Legal Defense and Educational Fund, December 2, 2000, in San Antonio, Texas, by Maggie Rivas-Rodriguez.

of the United States government rounded up the illegal aliens and deported them to Mexico . . . another government agency was busily engaged in recruiting workers in Mexico to return them to U.S. farms."

The government campaign against aliens pushed LULAC, the GI Forum, and other activist groups to change their strategy in a critical way. The campaign to win full civil rights for American citizens of Mexican descent would increasingly be linked to improv-

ing the lives—and asserting the rights—of all Mexican immigrants, both legal and illegal. If the government and the broader American public refused to distinguish between a Mexican national, a resident alien of the United States, a naturalized American citizen, or a native born American, why should Mexican Americans cling to these distinctions? By the 1960s a new civil rights movement emerged, *la raza*, based on the shared ethnicity and historical experiences of the broader Mexican American community.

Puerto Ricans

The United States took possession of the island of Puerto Rico in 1898, during the final stages of the Spanish-American War. The Jones Act of 1917 made the island an unincorporated territory of the United States and granted U.S. citizenship to all Puerto Ricans. Over the next several decades, Puerto Rico's economic base shifted from a diversified, subsistence-oriented agriculture to a single export crop—sugar. U.S. absentee owners dominated the sugar industry, claiming most of the island's arable land, previously tilled by small farmers growing crops for local consumption. Puerto Rico's sugar industry grew enormously profitable, but few island residents benefited from this expansion. By the 1930s, unemployment and poverty were widespread and the island was forced to import its foodstuffs.

Small communities of Puerto Rican migrants had begun to form in New York City during the 1920s. The largest was on the Upper East Side of Manhattan—*el barrio* in East Harlem. During World War II, labor shortages led the federal government to sponsor the recruitment of Puerto Rican workers for industrial jobs in New Jersey, Philadelphia, and Chicago. But the "great migration" took place from 1945 to 1964. During these two decades the number of Puerto Ricans living on the mainland jumped from less than 100,000 to roughly 1 million. Economic opportunity was the chief impetus for this migration, for the island suffered from high unemployment rates and low wages.

The advent of direct air service between Puerto Rico and New York in 1945 made the city easily accessible. The Puerto Rican community in East (or Spanish) Harlem mushroomed, and new communities in the South Bronx and Brooklyn began to emerge. By 1970 there were about 800,000 Puerto Ricans in New York—more than 10 percent of the city's population. New Puerto Rican communities also took root in Connecticut, Massachusetts, New Jersey, and the Midwest. Puerto Ricans frequently circulated between the island and the mainland, often returning home when economic conditions on the mainland were less favorable.

The experience of Puerto Rican migrants both resembled and differed from that of other immigrant groups in significant ways. Like Mexican immigrants, Puerto Ricans were foreign in language, culture, and experience, yet unlike them they entered the United States as citizens. Many Puerto Ricans were also African Americans. Racial and ethnic discrimination came as a double shock, since Puerto Ricans, as citizens, entered the United States with a sense of entitlement. In New York, Puerto Ricans found themselves barred from most craft unions, excluded from certain neighborhoods, and forced to take jobs largely in the low-paying garment industry and service trades. Puerto Rican children were not well served by a public school system insensitive to language differences and too willing to track Spanish-speaking students into obsolete vocational programs.

By the early 1970s, Puerto Rican families were substantially poorer on average than the total population of the country, and they had the lowest median income of any Latino groups. The steep decline in manufacturing jobs and in the garment industry in New York during the 1960s and 1970s hit the Puerto Rican community especially hard. So did the city's fiscal crisis, which brought sharp cuts in funding for schools, health care, libraries, government jobs, and other public services traditionally available to immigrant groups. The structural shift in the U.S. economy away from manufacturing and toward service and high-technology jobs reinforced the Puerto Rican community's goal of improving educational opportunities for its members. The struggle to establish and improve bilingual education in schools became an important part of this effort. Most Puerto Ricans, especially those who had succeeded in school and achieved middle-class status, continued to identify strongly with their Puerto Rican heritage and the Spanish language.

Japanese Americans

The harsh relocation program of World War II devastated the Japanese American community on the west coast (see Chapter 25). But the war against Nazism also helped weaken older notions of white superiority and racism. During the war the state of California had aggressively enforced an alien land law by confiscating property declared illegally held by Japanese. In November 1946 a proposition supporting the law appeared on the state ballot. But, thanks in part to a campaign by the Japanese American Citizens League (JACL) reminding voters of the wartime contributions of Nisei (second-generation Japanese Americans) soldiers, voters overwhelmingly rejected the referendum. One JACL leader hailed the vote as proof that "the people of California will not approve discriminatory and prejudiced treatment of persons of Japanese ancestry." Two years later the Supreme Court declared the law unconstitutional, calling it "nothing more than outright racial discrimination."

The 1952 Immigration and Nationality Act (see Chapter 26) removed the old ban against Japanese immigration, and also made Issei (first-generation Japanese Americans) eligible for naturalized citizenship. Japanese Americans, who lobbied hard for the new law, greeted it with elation. "It gave the Japanese equality with all other immigrants," said JACL leader Harry Takagi, "and that was the principle we had been struggling for from the very beginning." By 1965 some 46,000 immigrant Japanese, most of them elderly Issei, had taken their citizenship oaths. One of these wrote a poem to celebrate the achievement:

> Going steadily to study English,
> Even through the rain at night,
> I thus attain,
> Late in life,
> American citizenship.

Indian Peoples

The postwar years also brought significant changes in the status and lives of Indian peoples. Congress reversed the policies pursued under the New Deal, which had stressed Indian sovereignty and cultural independence. Responding to a variety of pressure groups, including mining and other economic interests wishing to exploit the resources on Indian reservations, Congress adopted a policy known as "termination," designed to cancel Indian treaties and terminate sovereignty rights. In 1953, Congress passed House Concurrent Resolution 108, which allowed Congress to terminate a tribe as a political entity by passing legislation specific to that tribe. The leader of the termination forces, Senator Arthur Watkins of Utah, declared the new law meant that "the concept that the Indian people exist within the United States as independent nations has been rejected." Supporters of termination had varied motives, but the policy added up to the return of enforced assimilation for solving the "Indian problem."

Between 1954 and 1962, Congress passed twelve termination bills covering more than sixty tribes, nearly all in the West. Even when tribes consented to their own termination, they discovered that dissolution brought unforeseen problems. For example, members of the Klamaths of Oregon and the Paiutes of Utah received large cash payments from the division of tribal assets. But after these one-time payments were spent, members had to take poorly paid, unskilled jobs to survive. Many Indian peoples became dependent on state social services and slipped into poverty and alcoholism.

Along with termination, the federal government gave greater emphasis to a relocation program aimed at speeding up assimilation. The Bureau of Indian Affairs encouraged reservation Indians to relocate to cities, where they were provided housing and jobs. For some, relocation meant assimilation, intermarriage with whites, and the loss of tribal identity. Others, homesick and unable to adjust to an alien culture and place, either returned to reservations or wound up on the margins of city life. Still others regularly traveled back and forth. In some respects, this urban migration paralleled the larger postwar shift of rural peoples to cities and suburbs.

Indians increasingly came to see termination as a policy geared mainly to exploiting resources on Indian lands. By the early 1960s, a new movement was emerging to defend Indian sovereignty. The National Congress of American Indians (NCAI) condemned termination, calling for a review of federal policies and a return to self-determination. The NCAI led a political and educational campaign that challenged the goal of assimilation and created a new awareness among white people that Indians had the right to remain Indians. When the termination policy ended in the early 1960s, it had affected only about 3 percent of federally recognized Indian peoples.

Taking their cue from the civil rights movement, Indian activists used the court system to reassert sovereign rights. Indian and white liberal lawyers, many with experience in civil rights cases, worked through the Native American Rights Fund, which became a powerful force in western politics. A series of Supreme Court decisions, culminating in *United States* v. *Wheeler* (1978), reasserted the principle of "unique and limited" sovereignty. The Court recognized tribal independence except where limited by treaty or Congress.

The Indian population had been growing since the early years of the century, but most reservations had trouble making room for a new generation. Indians suffered increased rates of poverty, chronic unemployment, alcoholism, and poor health. The average Indian family in the early 1960s earned only one-third of the average family income in the United States. Those who remained in the cities usually became "ethnic Indians," identifying themselves more as Indians than as members of specific tribes. By the late 1960s, ethnic Indians had begun emphasizing civil rights over tribal rights, making common cause with African Americans and other minorities. The National Indian Youth Council (NIYC), founded in 1960, tried to unite the two causes of equality for individual Indians and special status for tribes. But the organization faced difficult contradictions between a common Indian identity, emphasizing Indians as a single ethnic group, and tribal identity, stressing the citizenship of Indians in separate nations.

Remaking The Golden Door: The Immigration and Nationality Act of 1965

The egalitarian political climate created by the civil rights movement nurtured efforts to modernize and reform the country's immigration policies. "Everywhere else in our national life, we have eliminated discrimination based on national origins," Attorney General Robert Kennedy told Congress in 1964. "Yet, this system is still the foundation of our immigration law." In 1965 Congress passed a new Immigration and Nationality Act, abolishing the national origins quotas that had been in place since the 1920s, and substituting overall hemispheric limits: 120,000 visas annually for immigrants from the Western Hemisphere, and 170,000 for those from the Eastern Hemisphere (with a 20,000 limit from any single country). The act was intended to redress the grievances of Eastern and Southern European ethnic groups who had been largely shut out since 1924. President Lyndon B. Johnson played down its importance. "It does not affect the lives of millions," he said when he signed the bill into law. "It will not reshape the structure of our daily lives, or really add importantly to our wealth or our power."

But the new law included several provisions that proved LBJ's prediction wrong. Exempted from numerical quotas were immigrants seeking family reunification with American citizens or resident aliens. In addition, preferences to those with specialized job skills and training, in fields like medicine and engineering, were extended to people from the nations of the Eastern Hemisphere. The high priority given family reunification created an unprecedented cycle of *chain immigration and sponsorship* of people seeking to join relatives already in the United States. As initial immigrants attained permanent resident or citizenship status, they would sponsor family members and relatives to come over. Once these family members and relatives arrived in the U.S., and became resident aliens or citizens, they in turn could sponsor their family members, and so on.

The consequences for Asian American communities in particular were profound. The number of Asian Americans soared from about 1 million in 1965 to 11 million by the end of the century. Immigrants from India and the Philippines included a high percentage of health-care professionals, while many Chinese and Korean immigrants found work in professional and managerial occupations as well as their own small businesses. At the same time, low-skilled and impoverished Asians poured into the "Chinatowns" and "Koreatowns" of cities like New York and Los Angeles, taking jobs in restaurants, hotels, and garment manufacturing. Four times as many Asians settled in the United States in this period as in the entire previous history of the nation. This new wave also brought a strikingly different group of Asian immigrants to America. In 1960 the Asian American population was 52 percent Japanese, 27 percent Chinese, and 20 percent Filipino. In 1985, the composition was 21 percent Chinese, 21 percent Filipino, 15 percent Japanese, 12 percent Vietnamese, 11 percent Korean, 10 percent Asian Indian, 4 percent Laotian, and 3 percent Cambodian.

The 1965 act also created conditions that increased undocumented immigration from Latin America. The new limits on Western Hemisphere

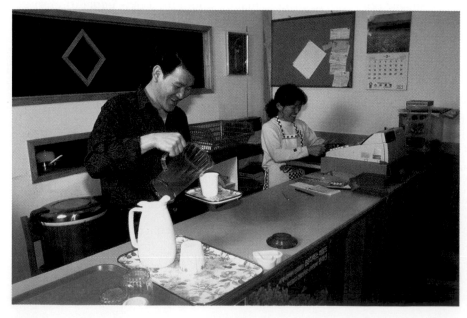

A Korean couple working behind the counter of their newly opened restaurant in Los Angeles, ca. 2000. In the thirty-five years after the Immigration and Nationality Act of 1965, the city's Asian American population had grown to over 1.2 million, including the largest Korean community outside of Korea.

SOURCE: Michael Newman/PhotoEdit.

C H R O N O L O G Y

1941	Executive Order 8802 forbids racial discrimination in defense industries and government
1946	In *Morgan* v. *Virginia*, U.S. Supreme Court rules that segregation on interstate buses is unconstitutional
	President Harry Truman creates the Committee on Civil Rights
1947	Jackie Robinson becomes the first African American on a major league baseball team
1948	President Truman issues executive order desegregating the armed forces
1954	In *Brown* v. *Board of Education*, Supreme Court rules segregated schools inherently unequal
1955	Supreme Court rules that school desegregation must proceed "with all deliberate speed"
	Montgomery bus boycott begins
1956	Montgomery bus boycott ends in victory as the Supreme Court affirms a district court ruling that segregation on buses is unconstitutional
1957	Southern Christian Leadership Conference (SCLC) is founded
	President Dwight Eisenhower sends in federal troops to protect African American students integrating Little Rock, Arkansas high school
1960	Sit-in movement begins as four colege students sit at a lunch counter in Greensboro, North Carolina, and ask to be served
	Student Nonviolent Coordinating Committee (SNCC) founded

	Board of Indian Commissioners is created
1961	Freedom Rides begin
1962	James Meredith integrates the University of Mississippi
	The Albany movement fails to end segregation in Albany, Georgia
1963	SCLC initiates campaign to desegregate Birmingham, Alabama
	Medgar Evers, leader of the Mississippi NAACP, is assassinated
	March on Washington; Martin Luther King Jr. delivers his historic "I Have a Dream" speech
1964	Mississippi Freedom Summer project brings students to Mississippi to teach and register voters
	President Johnson signs the Civil Rights Act of 1964
	Civil rights workers Michael Schwerner, James Chaney, and Andrew Goodman are found buried in Philadelphia, Mississippi
	Mississippi Freedom Democratic Party (MFDP) is denied seats at the 1964 Democratic Presidential Convention
1965	SCLC and SNCC begin voter registration campaign in Selma, Alabama
	Malcolm X is assassinated
	Civil rights marchers walk from Selma to Montgomery
	Voting Rights Act of 1965 is signed into law
	Immigration and Nationality Act

migration, along with simultaneous ending of the *bracero* program, tempted many thousands to enter the United States illegally. The Immigration and Naturalization Service arrested and deported 500,000 illegal aliens each year in the decade following the act, most all of them from Mexico, central America, and the Caribbean. By the 1980s, more than 80 percent of all legal immigrants to the United States came from either Asia or Latin America; if one included illegal immigrants, the figure would surpass 90 percent.

CONCLUSION

The mass movement for civil rights was arguably the most important domestic event of the twentieth century. The struggle that began in Montgomery, Alabama, in December 1955 ultimately transformed race relations in thousands of American communities. By the early 1960s this community-based movement had placed civil rights at the very center of national political life. It achieved its greatest successes by invoking the law of the land to destroy legal segregation and win individual freedom for African Americans. The Civil Rights Act of 1964 and the Voting Rights Act 1965 testified to the power of an African American and white liberal coalition. Yet the persistence of racism, poverty, and ghetto slums challenged a central assumption of liberalism: that equal protection of constitutional rights would give all Americans equal opportunities in life. By the mid-1960s, many black people had begun to question the core values of liberalism, the benefits of alliance with whites, and the philosophy of nonviolence. At the same time, a conservative white backlash against the gains made by African Americans further weakened the liberal political consensus.

In challenging the persistence of widespread poverty and institutional racism, the civil rights movement called for deep structural changes in American life. By 1967, Martin Luther King Jr. was articulating a broad and radical vision linking the struggle against racial injustice to other defects in American society. "The black revolution," he argued, "is much more than a struggle for the rights of Negroes. It is forcing America to face all its interrelated flaws—racism, poverty, militarism, and materialism. It is exposing evils that are deeply rooted in the whole structure of our society." Curing these ills would prove far more difficult than ending legal segregation.

REVIEW QUESTIONS

1. What were the key legal and political antecedents to the civil rights struggle in the 1940s and early 1950s? What organizations played the most central role? Which tactics continued to be used, and which were abandoned?

2. How did African American communities challenge legal segregation in the South? Compare the strategies of key organizations, such as the NAACP, SNCC, SCLC, and CORE.

3. Discuss the varieties of white resistance to the civil rights movement. Which were most effective in slowing the drive for equality?

4. Analyze the civil rights movement's complex relationship with the national Democratic Party between 1948 and 1964. How was the party transformed by its association with the movement? What political gains and losses did that association entail?

5. What legal and institutional impact did the movement have on American life? How did it change American culture and politics? Where did it fail?

6. What relationship did the African Americans who struggled for civil rights have with other American minorities? How—if at all—did these minorities benefit? Did they build their own versions of the movement?

RECOMMENDED READING

Thomas Borstelmann, *The Cold War and the Color Line: American Race Relations in the Global Arena* (2001). Analyzes how presidents from Harry S Truman to George H.W. Bush have responded to the civil rights movement in the context of Cold War politics and the fight against colonialism and white supremacy in Africa.

Taylor Branch, *Parting the Waters: America in the King Years, 1954–1963* (1988); *Pillar of Fire: America in the King Years, 1963–1965* (1998). A deeply researched and monumental narrative history of the southern civil rights movement organized around the life and influence of Reverend Martin Luther King Jr.

Clayborne Carson, et al., eds., *Reporting Civil Rights* (2003). A wide-ranging compilation of contemporary reportage on the movement and resistance to it.

David Chappell, *Inside Agitators: White Southerners in the Civil Rights Movement* (1994). A thoughtful and sophisticated analysis of the varying roles played by whites in the movement.

Roger Daniels, *Guarding the Golden Door: American Immigration Policy and Immigrants Since 1882* (2004). A comprehensive history, including excellent coverage of the legislative and political battles behind post–World War II changes in immigration laws.

Mary L. Dudziak, *Cold War Civil Rights: Race and the Image of American Democracy* (2000). Excellent analysis of the connections between the struggle for racial equality in America and the nation's contest with communism abroad.

Aldon D. Morris, *The Origins of the Civil Rights Movement: Black Communities Organizing for Change* (1984). An important study combining history and social theory. Morris emphasizes the key role of ordinary black people, acting through their churches and other community organizations before 1960.

Howell Raines, *My Soul Is Rested: Movement Days in the Deep South Remembered* (1977). The best oral history of the civil rights movement, drawing from a wide range of participants and points of view. It is brilliantly edited by Raines, who covered the events as a journalist.

J. Mills Thornton, *Dividing Lines: Municipal Politics and the Struggle for Civil Rights in Montgomery, Birmingham, and Selma* (2002). A sophisticated analysis of these three key civil rights battlegrounds, highlighting the gaps between their symbolic importance for the movement and local realities. Excellent treatment as well of the range of responses within white communities.

 For additional study resources for this chapter, go to the *Companion Website,* http://www.prenhall.com/faragher.

CHAPTER 29

War Abroad,
War at Home

1965–1974

CHAPTER OUTLINE

Uptown, Chicago, Illinois

During freedom summer of 1964, while teams of northern college students traveled south to join voter registration campaigns among African Americans, a small group moved to Chicago to help the city's poor people take control of their communities. They targeted a neighborhood known as Uptown, a one-mile-square section five miles north of the Loop, the city center. The residents, many transplanted from the poverty of the Appalachian South, lived in crowded tenements or in once-elegant mansions now subdivided into tiny, run-down apartments. Four thousand people lived on just one street running four blocks, 20 percent of them on welfare. The student organizers intended to mobilize the community "so as to demand an end to poverty and the construction of a decent social order."

With the assistance of the Packinghouse Workers union, the students formed Jobs or Income Now (JOIN), opened a storefront office, and invited local residents to work with them to demand jobs and better living conditions. They spent hours listening to people, drawing out their ideas and helping them develop scores of programs. They campaigned against Mayor Richard Daley's policy of "police omnipresence" that had a fleet of squad cars and paddy wagons continually patrolling the neighborhood. They

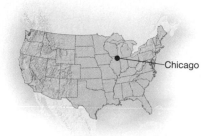
Chicago

also helped establish new social clubs, a food-buying cooperative, a community theater, and a health clinic. Within a few years, Uptown street kids had formed the Young Patriots organization, put out a community newspaper, *Rising Up Angry,* and staffed free breakfast programs.

Chicago JOIN was one of ten similar projects sponsored by Students for a Democratic Society (SDS). Impatient with the nation's chronic poverty and cold war politics, twenty-nine students from nine universities had met in June 1960 to form a new kind of campus-based political organization. SDS soon caught the attention of liberal students, encouraging them, as part of the nation's largest college population to date, to make their voices heard. By its peak in 1968, SDS had 350 chapters and between 60,000 and 100,000 members. Its principle of participatory democracy—with its promise to give people control over the decisions affecting their lives—appealed to a wider following of more than a million students.

In June 1962, in Port Huron, Michigan, SDS issued a declaration of principles, drafted mainly by graduate student Tom Hayden. "We are people ... bred in at least modest comfort, housed now in universities," *The Port Huron Statement* opened, "looking uncomfortably to the world we inherit." The dire effects of poverty and social injustice, it continued, were not the only problems. A deeper ailment plagued American society. Everyone, including middle-class students with few material wants, suffered from a sense of "loneliness, estrangement, and alienation." *The Port Huron Statement* defined SDS as a new kind of political movement that would bring people "out of isolation and into community" so that not just the poor but all Americans could overcome their feelings of "powerlessness [and hence] resignation before the enormity of events."

SDS began with a campaign to reform the university, especially to disentangle the financial ties between campus-based research programs and the military-industrial complex. In expanding to include the nation's cities, SDS sent small groups of students to live and organize in the poor communities of Boston, Louisville, Cleveland, and Newark as well as Chicago. Ultimately, none of these projects managed to recruit large numbers of people. Protests against local government did little to combat unemployment, and campaigns for better garbage collection or more playgrounds rarely evolved into lasting movements. Nevertheless, organizers did succeed, to some degree, in realizing the goal specified in its slogan: "Let the People Decide." By late 1967, SDS prepared to leave JOIN in the hands of the people it had organized, which was its intention from the beginning.

Initially, even Lyndon Baines Johnson promoted the ideal of civic participation. The Great Society, as the president called his domestic program, promised more than the abolition of poverty and racial inequality. In May 1964, at the University of Michigan, the president described his goal as a society "where every child can find knowledge to enrich his mind and to enlarge his talents," where "the city of man serves not only the needs of the body and the demands of commerce but the desire for beauty and the hunger for community."

By 1967 the Vietnam War had pushed aside such ambitions. If SDSers had once believed they could work with liberal Democrats like Johnson, they now interpreted social injustice at home as the inevitable consequence of the president's dangerous and destructive foreign policies. SDS threw its energies into building a movement against the war in Vietnam. President Johnson, meanwhile, pursued a foreign policy that would swallow up the funding for his own plans for a war on poverty and would precipitate a very different war at home, Americans against Americans. As hawks and doves lined up on opposite sides, the Vietnam War created a huge and enduring rift. SDS member Richard Flacks had warned that the nation had to "choose between devoting its resources and energies to maintaining military superiority and international hegemony or rechanneling those resources and energies to meeting the desperate needs of its people." Ultimately, even President Johnson himself understood that the "bitch of a war" in Asia ruined "the woman I really loved—the Great Society."

The dream of community did not vanish, but consensus became increasingly remote by the late 1960s. By this time, parents and children were at odds over values and aspirations, urban riots were rocking the nation, and political leaders were being struck down by assassins' bullets. New protest groups—Black Power, Women's Liberation, Gay Liberation, as well as Chicano, Native American, and Asian—were staking out a highly charged "politics of identity." Political conservatives managed to triumph in the election of Richard Nixon, who went on to disgrace the office. Meanwhile, the United States continued to fight—and eventually lost—the longest war in its history.

KEY TOPICS

- Widening U.S. involvement in the war in Vietnam
- "The sixties generation" and the antiwar movement
- Poverty and urban crisis
- The election of 1968
- The rise of "liberation" movements
- The Nixon presidency and the Watergate conspiracy

VIETNAM: AMERICA'S LONGEST WAR

The Vietnam War had its roots in the Truman Doctrine and its goal of containing communism (see Chapter 26). After the defeat of the French by the Communist forces of Ho Chi Minh in 1954, Vietnam emerged as a major zone of cold war contention. President John Kennedy called it "the cornerstone of the Free World in Southeast Asia, the keystone in the arch, the finger in the dike," a barrier to the spread of communism throughout the region and perhaps the world. President Lyndon Johnson sounded the same note at the beginning of his presidency. With American security at stake, he insisted, Americans had little choice but to fight for "the principle for which our ancestors fought in the valleys of Pennsylvania."

Vietnam was not Valley Forge, however, and the United States ultimately paid a huge price for its determination to turn back communism in Indochina. More than 50,000 Americans died in an unwinnable overseas war that only deepened divisions at home.

Johnson's War

Although President Kennedy had greatly increased the number of military advisors in South Vietnam (see Chapter 27), it was his successor, Lyndon B. Johnson, who made the decision to engage the United States in a major war there. At first, Johnson simply hoped to stay the course. Facing a presidential election in November 1964, he knew that a major military setback would cripple his election campaign. But he was equally determined to avoid the fate of President Truman, who had bogged down politically after "losing" China to communism and producing a stalemate in Korea.

Throughout the winter and spring of 1964, as conditions grew steadily worse in South Vietnam, Johnson and his advisors quietly laid the groundwork for a sustained bombing campaign against North Vietnam. In early August, they found a pretext to set this plan in motion. After two U.S. destroyers in the Gulf of Tonkin, off the coast of North Vietnam, reported attacks by North Vietnamese patrol boats, Johnson ordered retaliatory air strikes against bases in North Vietnam.

Johnson now appealed to Congress to pass a resolution giving him the authority "to take all necessary measures" and "all necessary steps" to defend U.S. armed forces and to protect Southeast Asia "against aggression or subversion." This Tonkin Gulf resolution, secretly drafted six weeks before the incident for which it was named, passed the Senate on August 7 with only two dissenting votes and moved unanimously through the House. It served, in Undersecre-

tary of State Nicholas Katzenbach's words, as the "functional equivalent" of a declaration of war.

Ironically, Johnson campaigned for the presidency in 1964 with a call for restraint in Vietnam. He assured voters that "we are not about to send American boys nine or ten thousand miles away from home to do what Asian boys ought to be doing for themselves." This strategy helped him win a landslide victory over conservative Republican Barry Goldwater of Arizona, who had proposed the deployment of nuclear weapons in Vietnam.

With the election behind him, Johnson now faced a hard decision. The limited bombing raids against North Vietnam had failed to slow the movement of the Communist Vietcong forces across the border into the South. Meanwhile, the government in Saigon, the capital city of South Vietnam, appeared near collapse. Faced with the prospect of a Communist victory, the president chose to escalate U.S. involvement in Vietnam massively.

Deeper into the Quagmire

In early February 1965, Johnson found a rationale to justify massive bombing of the North. The Vietcong had fired at the barracks of the U.S. Marine base at Pleiku in the central highlands of Vietnam, killing nine and wounding more than 100 Americans. Waving the list of casualties, the president rushed into an emergency meeting of the National Security Council to announce that the time had passed for keeping "our guns over the mantel and our shells in the cupboard." He ordered immediate reprisal bombing and one week later, on February 13, authorized Operation Rolling Thunder, a campaign of gradually intensifying air attacks against North Vietnam.

Johnson and his advisers hoped that the air strikes against North Vietnam would demonstrate U.S. resolve "both to Hanoi and to the world" and make the deployment of ground forces unnecessary. Intelligence reports, however, suggested that the bombing had little impact and noted, moreover, that North Vietnam was now sending troops into South Vietnam. With retreat his only alternative, Johnson decided to introduce ground troops for offensive operations.

Once Rolling Thunder had begun, President Johnson found it increasingly difficult to speak frankly with the American public about his policies. Initially, he announced that only two battalions of marines were being assigned to Danang to defend the airfields where bombing runs began. But six weeks later, 50,000 U.S. troops were in Vietnam. By November 1965 the total topped 165,000, and more troops were on the way. But even after Johnson authorized a buildup to 431,000 troops in mid-1966, victory was still nowhere in sight.

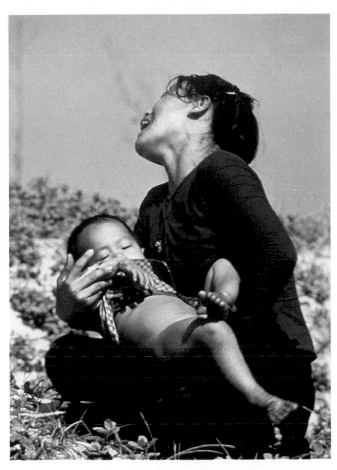

The massive bombing and ground combat created huge numbers of civilian casualties in Vietnam. The majority killed were women and children.

SOURCE: Jim Pickerell/BlackStar.

The strategy pursued by the Johnson administration and implemented by General William Westmoreland—a war of attrition—was based on the premise that continued bombing would eventually exhaust North Vietnam's resources. Meanwhile, U.S. ground forces would defeat the Vietcong in South Vietnam and thereby restore political stability to South Vietnam's pro-Western government. As Johnson once boasted, the strongest military power in the world surely could crush a Communist rebellion in a "pissant" country of peasants.

In practice, the United States wreaked havoc in South Vietnam, tearing apart its society and bringing ecological devastation to its land. Intending to locate and eradicate the support network of the Vietcong, U.S. ground troops conducted search-and-destroy missions throughout the countryside. They attacked villagers and their homes. Seeking to ferret out Vietcong sympathizers, U.S. troops turned at any one time as

many as 4 million people—approximately one-quarter of the population of South Vietnam—into refugees. By late 1968, the United States had dropped more than 3 million tons of bombs on Vietnam, and eventually delivered more than three times the tonnage dropped by the Allies on all fronts during World War II. Using herbicides such as Agent Orange to defoliate forest, the United States also conducted the most destructive chemical warfare in history.

Several advisers urged the president to inform the American people about his decisions in Vietnam, even to declare a state of national emergency. But Johnson feared he would lose momentum on domestic reform, including his antipoverty programs, if he drew attention to foreign policy. Seeking to avoid "undue excitement in the Congress and in domestic public opinion," he held to a course of intentional deceit.

The Credibility Gap

Johnson's popularity had surged at the time of the Tonkin Gulf resolution, skyrocketing in one day from 42 to 72 percent, according to a Louis Harris poll. But afterward it waned rapidly. Every night network television news reported the soaring American body count, from 26 per week in 1965 to 180 in 1967. No president had worked so hard to control the news media, but by 1967 Johnson found himself badgered at press conferences by reporters who accused the president of creating a credibility gap.

Scenes of human suffering and devastation recorded by television cameras increasingly undermined the administration's moral justification of the war as a defense of freedom and democracy in South Vietnam. During the early 1960s, network news had either ignored Vietnam or had been patriotically supportive of U.S. policy. Beginning with a report on a ground operation against the South Vietnamese village of Cam Ne by Morley Safer for CBS News in August 1965, however, the tenor of news reporting changed. Although government officials described the operation as a strategic destruction of "fortified Vietcong bunkers," the *CBS Evening News* showed pictures of Marines setting fire to the thatched homes of civilians. After CBS aired Safer's report, President Johnson complained bitterly to the news director. But more critical commentary soon followed. By 1967, according to a noted media observer, "every subject tended to become Vietnam." Televised news reports now told of new varieties of American cluster bombs, which released up to 180,000 fiberglass shards, and showed the nightmarish effects of the defoliants used on forests in South Vietnam to uncover enemy strongholds.

Coverage of the war in the print media also became more skeptical of Johnson's policies. By 1967 independent news teams were probing the government's official claims. Harrison Salisbury, Pulitzer Prize–winning *New York Times* reporter, questioned the administration's claims that its bombing of the North precisely targeted military objectives, charging that U.S. planes had bombed the population center of Hanoi, capital of North Vietnam, and intentionally ravaged villages in the South. As American military deaths climbed at the rate of more than 800 per month during the first half of 1967, newspaper coverage of the war focused yet more intently on such disturbing events.

The most vocal congressional critic of Johnson's war policy was Democratic senator J. William Fulbright of Arkansas, who chaired the Senate Foreign Relations Committee and who had personally speeded the passage of the Tonkin Gulf resolution. A strong supporter of the cold war, Fulbright had decided that the war in Vietnam was unwinnable and destructive to domestic reform. In *Arrogance of Power*, which became a national bestseller in 1967, he proposed a negotiated withdrawal from a neutralized Southeast Asia. Fulbright persuaded prominent Democrats in Congress to put aside their personal loyalty to Johnson and oppose his conduct of the war. In 1967 the Congress passed a nonbinding resolution appealing to the United Nations to help negotiate an end to hostilities. Meanwhile, some of the nation's most trusted European allies called for restraint in Vietnam.

The impact of the war, which cost Americans $21 billion per year, was also felt at home. Johnson convinced Congress to levy a 10 percent surcharge on individual and corporate taxes. Later adjustments in the national budget tapped the Social Security fund, heretofore safe from interference. Inflation raced upward, fed by spending on the war. Johnson replaced advisers who questioned his policy, but as casualties multiplied, more and more Americans began to question his handling of the war.

A GENERATION IN CONFLICT

As the war in Vietnam escalated, Americans from all walks of life demanded an end to U.S. involvement. But between 1965 and 1971, its years of peak activity, it had a distinctly generational character. At the forefront were the baby boomers who were just coming of age.

This so-called sixties generation, the largest generation in American history, was also the best educated. By the late 1960s, nearly half of all young adults between the ages of 18 and 21 were enrolled in college. In 1965 there were 5 million college students; in 1973 the number had doubled to 10 million. Public universities made

the largest gains; by 1970 eight had more than 30,000 students apiece.

Although a small minority among their peers, groups of students began to combine protest against the war in Vietnam with a broader, penetrating critique of American society. Through music, dress, and even hairstyle, they expressed a deep estrangement from the values and aspirations of their parents' generation. In 1967, when opposition to the war swelled, "flower children" put daisies in the rifle barrels of troops stationed to quash campus protests, providing a seemingly innocent counterpoint to the grim news of slaughter abroad. Meanwhile, campus organizations such as SDS encouraged college students to take a militant stand against the war, calling for an immediate and unconditional withdrawal of U.S. troops from Vietnam.

"The Times They Are A-Changin'"

The first sign of a new kind of protest was the free speech movement at the University of California at Berkeley in 1964. That fall, civil rights activists returned to the 27,000-student campus from Freedom Summer in Mississippi. They soon began to picket Bay Area stores that practiced discrimination in hiring and to recruit other students to join them. When the university administration moved to prevent them from setting up information booths on campus, eighteen groups protested, including the archconservative Students for Goldwater, claiming that their right to free speech had been abridged. The administration responded by sending police to break up the protest rally and arrest participants. University president Clark Kerr met with students, agreed not to press charges, and seemed set to grant them a small space on campus for political activity. Then, under pressure from conservative regents, Kerr reversed himself and announced in November that the university planned to press new charges against the free speech movement's leaders. On December 2 a crowd of 7,000 gathered to protest this decision. Joining folk singer Joan Baez in singing "We Shall Overcome," a group of 1,000 people marched toward the university's administration building, where they planned to stage a sit-in until Kerr rescinded his order. The police arrested nearly 800 protestors in the largest mass arrest in California history.

Mario Savio, a Freedom Summer volunteer and philosophy student, explained that the free speech movement wanted more than just the right to conduct political activity on campus. He spoke for many students when he complained that the university had become a faceless bureaucratic machine rather than a community of learning. Regulating the activities of students while preparing them for colorless lives as corporation clerks, the university made them "so sick at heart" that they had decided to put their "bodies upon the gears" to make it stop.

Across the country college students began to demand a say in the structuring of their education. Brown University students, for example, demanded a revamp of the curriculum that would eliminate all required courses and make grades optional. Students also protested campus rules that treated students as children instead of as adults. After a string of campus protests, most large universities, including the University of California, relinquished *in loco parentis* (in the place of parents) policies and allowed students to live off-campus and to set their own hours.

Across the bay in San Francisco, other young adults staked out a new form of community—a counterculture. In 1967, the "Summer of Love," the population of the Haight-Ashbury district swelled by 75,000 as youthful adventurers gathered for the most celebrated "be-in" of the era. Although the *San Francisco Chronicle* featured a headline reading "Mayor Warns Hippies to Stay Out of Town," masses of long-haired young men and women dressed in bell-bottoms and tie-dyed T-shirts congregated in "the Haight" to listen to music, take drugs, and "be" with each other. "If you're going to San Francisco," a popular rock group sang, "be sure to wear some flowers in your hair . . . you're going to meet some gentle people there." In the fall, the majority returned to their own communities, often bringing with them a new lifestyle. *Time* magazine announced the appearance of new "hippie enclaves" in every major U.S. city from Boston to Seattle, from Detroit to New Orleans."

The generational rebellion took many forms, including a revolution in sexual behavior that triggered countless quarrels between parents and their maturing sons and daughters. During the 1960s more teenagers experienced premarital sex—by the decade's end three-quarters of all college seniors had engaged in sexual intercourse—and far more talked about it openly than in previous eras. With birth control widely available, including the newly developed "pill," many young women were no longer deterred from sex by fear of pregnancy. "We've discarded the idea that the loss of virginity is related to degeneracy," one college student explained. "Premarital sex doesn't mean the downfall of society, at least not the kind of society that we're going to build." Many heterosexual couples chose to live together outside marriage, a practice few parents condoned. A much smaller but significant number formed communes—approximately 4,000 by 1970—where members could share housekeeping and child care as well as sexual partners.

Mood-altering drugs played a large part in this counterculture. In the 1950s, doctors had begun to freely prescribe tranquilizers and antidepressants, and alcohol and tobacco were popular stimulants. The drug subculture that emerged in the 1960s, however, was associated primarily with illicit psychoactive substances and hallucinogenic drugs. Harvard professor Timothy Leary urged young people to "turn on, tune in, drop out" and also advocated the mass production and distribution of LSD (lysergic acid diethylamide), which was not criminalized until 1968. Marijuana, illegal yet readily available, was often paired with rock music in a collective ritual of love and laughter. Singer Bob Dylan taunted adults with the lyrics of his hit single, "Everybody must get stoned."

Music played a large part in defining the counterculture. With the emergence of rock 'n' roll in the 1950s, popular music had begun to express a deliberate generational identity (see Chapter 27), a trend that gained momentum with the emergence of the British rock group

The Woodstock Festival, promoted as "3 Days of Peace and Music," attracted more than 450,000 people to the rain-soaked pasture of Max Yasgur's New York farm. The huge rock concert, staged in August 1969, became a landmark of the counterculture.

SOURCE: John Dominis/The Image Works.

The Beatles in 1964. Folk music, which had gained popularity on campuses in the early 1960s with the successful recordings of Peter, Paul, and Mary, Phil Ochs, and Judy Collins, as well as Joan Baez, continued to serve the voice of protest. Shortly after Freedom Summer, folk singer Bob Dylan issued a warning to parents:

> Your sons and your daughters
> are beyond your command
> Your old road is
> rapidly agin'.
> Please get out of the new one
> If you can't lend your hand
> For the times they are a-changin'.

By 1965 Dylan himself had turned to the electric guitar and rock, which triumphed as the musical emblem of a generation.

At a farm near Woodstock, New York, more than 400,000 people gathered in August 1969 for a three-day rock concert and to give witness to the ideals of the counterculture. Richie Havens opened with "Freedom," and performers including Joan Baez, Janis Joplin, Santana, and The Grateful Dead among others entertained the crowd. Thousands took drugs while security officials and local police stood by, some stripped off their clothes to dance or swim, and a few even made love in the grass. "We were exhilarated," one reveler recalled. "We felt as though we were in liberated territory."

The Woodstock Nation, as the counterculture was mythologized, did not actually represent the sentiments of most young Americans. But its attitudes and styles, especially its efforts to create a new community, did speak for the large minority seeking a peaceful alternative to the intensifying climate of war. "We used to think of ourselves as little clumps of weirdos," rock star Janis Joplin explained. "But now we're a whole new minority group." The slogan "Make Love, Not War" linked generational rebellion and opposition to the U.S. invasion of Vietnam.

From Campus Protest to Mass Mobilization

Three weeks after the announcement of Operation Rolling Thunder in 1965, peace activists called for a day-long boycott of classes so that students and faculty might meet to discuss the war. At the University of Michigan in Ann Arbor, more than 3,000 students turned out for sessions held through the night because university administrators had bowed to the pressure of state legislators and had refused to cancel classes. During the following weeks, "teach-ins" spread across the United States and to Europe and Japan as well.

Students also began to protest against war-related research on their campuses. The expansion of higher education in the 1960s had depended largely on federally funded programs, including military research on counterinsurgency tactics and new chemical weapons. Student protesters demanded an end to these programs and, receiving no response from university administrators, turned to civil disobedience. In October 1967, the Dow Chemical Company, manufacturers of napalm, a form of jellied gasoline often used against civilians in Vietnam, sent job recruiters to the University of Wisconsin at Madison despite warnings that a group of students would try to prevent them from conducting interviews. A few hundred students staged a sit-in at the building where the recruitment interviews were scheduled, and 2,000 onlookers gathered outside. Ordered by university administrators to disperse the crowd, the city's police broke glass doors, dragged students through the debris, and clubbed those who refused to move. Suddenly the campus erupted. Students chanted *Sieg Heil* at the police, who attempted to disperse them with tear gas and Mace. Undergraduate students and their teaching assistants boycotted classes for a week. During the next three years, the momentum grew, and demonstrations took place on campuses in every region of the country.

Many student strikes and demonstrations merged opposition to the war with other campus and community issues. At Columbia University, students struck in 1968 against the administration's plans to build a new gymnasium in a city park used by residents of neighboring Harlem. In the Southwest, Mexican American students demonstrated against the use of funds for military projects that might otherwise be allocated to antipoverty and educational programs.

By the late 1960s, the peace movement had spread well beyond the campus. In April 1967, a day-long antiwar rally at the Sheep Meadow in Manhattan's Central Park drew more than 300,000 people. Meanwhile, 60,000 protesters turned out in San Francisco. By summer, Vietnam Veterans Against the War had begun to organize returning soldiers and sailors, encouraging them to cast off the medals and ribbons they had won in battle.

The steadily increasing size of antiwar demonstrations provoked conservatives and prowar Democrats to take a stronger stand in support of the war. Several newspaper and magazine editorialists called for the arrest of antiwar leaders on charges of treason. Secretary of State Dean Rusk, appearing on NBC's *Meet the Press*, expressed his concern that "authorities in Hanoi" might conclude, incorrectly, that the major-

On May 8, 1970 New York construction workers surged into Wall Street in Lower Manhattan, violently disrupting an antiwar rally and attacking the protesters with lead pipes and crowbars. Known as the "hard hat riots," the well-publicized event was followed later in the month by a march, 100,000 strong, of hard-hat workers unfurling American flags and chanting "All the way U.S.A."

SOURCE: AP Wide World Photos.

ity of Americans did not back their president and that "the net effect of these demonstrations will be to prolong the war, not to shorten it."

Many demonstrators themselves concluded that mass mobilizations alone had little impact on U.S. policy. Making popular the slogan "From Protest to Resistance," some sought to serve as moral witnesses. Despite a congressional act of 1965 providing for a five-year jail term and a $10,000 fine for destroying a draft card, nearly 200 young men destroyed their draft cards at the April Sheep Meadow demonstration and encouraged approximately a half-million more to resist the draft or refuse induction. Two Jesuit priests, Daniel and Philip Berrigan, raided the offices of the draft board in Catonsville, Maryland, in May 1968 and poured homemade napalm over records. Other activists determined to "bring the war home." An estimated 40,000 bombing incidents or bomb threats took place from January 1969 to April 1970; more than $21 million of property was damaged, and forty-three peo-

ple were killed. Most of the perpetrators were never identified.

Observers at the time noted a similarity between the violence in Vietnam and the violence in the United States. Parallel wars were now being fought, one between two systems of government in Vietnam, another between the American government and masses of its citizens. Those Americans sent to Vietnam were caught in between.

Teenage Soldiers

Whereas the average age of the World War II soldier was twenty-six, the age of those who fought in Vietnam hovered around nineteen. Until late 1969 the Selective Service System—the draft—gave deferments to college students and to workers in selected occupations while recruiting hard in poor communities by advertising the armed forces as a provider of vocational training and social mobility. Working-class young men, disproportionately African American and Latino, signed up in large numbers under these inducements. They also bore the brunt of combat. Whereas college graduates constituted only 12 percent of the 2.5 million men who served in Vietnam and 9 percent of those who were killed in combat, high school dropouts were the most likely to serve in Vietnam and by far the most likely to die there. The casualty rate for African Americans was approximately 30 percent higher than the overall death rate for U.S. forces in Southeast Asia. These disparities created a rupture that would last well past the end of the war.

Yet the soldiers were not entirely isolated from the changes affecting their generation. G.I.s in significant numbers smoked marijuana, listed to rock music, hung psychedelic posters in their barracks, and participated in the sexual revolution. In 1968 more than 200 soldiers from Fort Hood, Texas, attended a "be-in." But most condemned antiwar protest as the expressions of their privileged peers who did not have to fight.

As the war dragged on, some soldiers began to show their frustration. By 1971 many G.I.s were putting peace symbols on their combat helmets, joining antiwar demonstrations, and staging their own events such as "Armed Farces Day." Sometimes entire companies refused to carry out duty assignments or even to enter battle. A smaller number took revenge by "fragging" reckless commanding officers with grenades meant for the enemy. Meanwhile African American soldiers closed ranks and often flaunted their racial solidarity by weaving their bootlaces into "slave bracelets" and carrying Black Power canes, which were topped with a clenched fist. Some openly complained about being asked to fight "a white man's war" and emblazoned their helmets with slogans like "No Gook Ever Called Me Nigger." By 1971, at least fourteen organizations claimed affiliation with RITA, an acronym for "Resistance in the Army." The largest was

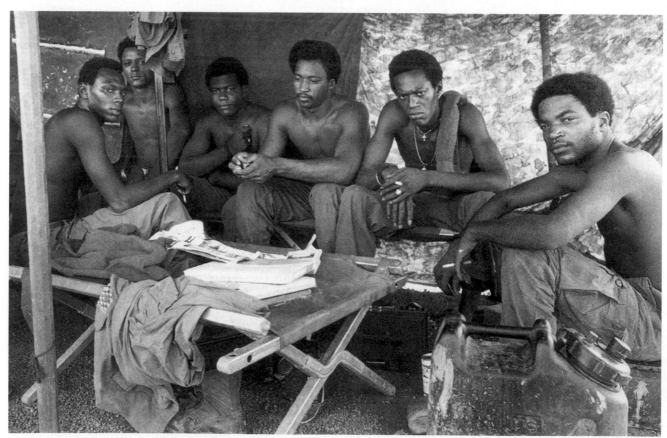

African American Troops in Vietnam, 1970. Serving on the front lines in disproportionate numbers, many black soldiers echoed the growing racial militancy in the United States and increasingly chose to spend their off-duty time apart from white soldiers.

SOURCE: Mark Jury, *The Vietnam Photo Book.*

the American Servicemen's Union, which claimed more than 10,000 members.

The nature of the war fed feelings of disaffection in the armed forces. U.S. troops entering South Vietnam expected a warm welcome from the people whose homeland they had been sent to defend. Instead, they encountered anti-American demonstrations and placards with slogans like "End Foreign Dominance of Our Country." Hostile Vietnamese civilians viewed the Americans as invaders. The enemy avoided open engagements in which the Americans could benefit from their superior arms and air power. Soldiers found themselves instead stumbling into booby traps as they chased an elusive guerrilla foe through deep, leech-infested swamps and dense jungles swarming with fire ants. They could never be sure who was friend and who was foe. Patently false U.S. government press releases that heralded glorious victories and extolled the gratitude of Vietnamese civilians deepened bitterness on the front lines.

Approximately 8.6 million men and women served in the armed forces, and many returned to civilian life quietly and without fanfare, denied the glory earned by the combat veterans of previous wars. They reentered a society divided over the cause for which they had risked their lives. Tens of thousands suffered debilitating physical injuries. As many as 40 percent of them came back with drug dependencies or symptoms of post-traumatic stress disorder, haunted and depressed by troubling memories of atrocities. Moreover, finding and keeping a job proved to be particularly hard in the shrinking economy of the 1970s. (See Out of Many Voices: A Soldier's Letter from Vietnam.)

OUT OF MANY VOICES

A SOLDIER'S LETTER FROM VIETNAM

As the war in Vietnam dragged on, soldiers commonly expressed their frustration with official policy. Written on September 10, 1967 by Rodney R. Chastant of Mobile, Alabama, this letter to his brother targets President Lyndon Johnson. The next month, the writer celebrated his promotion to captain in the United States Marine Corps; one year later he extended his tour of duty in Vietnam. Captain Chastant, age twenty-five, was killed on October 22, 1968.

DAVID, . . . HERE IN VIETNAM THE WAR GOES ON. Morale is very high in spite of the fact that most men think the war is being run incorrectly. One of the staggering facts is that most men here believe we will *not* win the war. And yet they stick their necks out every day and carry on with their assigned tasks as if they were fighting for the continental security of the United States. Hard to believe but true.

The Marines are taking a fierce beating over here. They don't have enough men. We must have more men, at least twice as many, or we are going to get the piss kicked out of us this winter when the rains come. The Marines have been assigned a task too big for so few. We are fighting for our very lives in the north. In the last 15 weeks we've lost 47 percent of all helicopters in Vietnam. One of the basic problems is that [President] Johnson is trying to fight this war the way he fights his domestic wars—he chooses an almost unattainable goal with a scope so large it is virtually undefinable, and he attacks his goal with poorly allocated funds, minimum manpower, limited time, and few new ideas. The magnitude of what he is trying to accomplish here can only be realized when you firmly establish in your own mind that Johnson is trying to take 5,000 villages living on a rice economy with a 2,000-year-old Asian tradition of chieftain rule warped by 100 years of ugly colonialism and build a nation with an industrial base and a democratic tradition in the midst of a 20-year-old war.

We should have never committed ourselves to this goal, but now that we have, what shall we do? We must destroy the will of Hanoi quickly and stop doling out American lives in that penny-ante effort. Then reallocate our resources of money and material and, with two or three times the present manpower, crush the guerrillas. ■

SOURCE: Bernard Edelman, ed., for the New York Vietnam Veterans Memorial Commission, *Dear America: Letters Home from Vietnam* (New York: W.W. Norton, 1985), pp. 209–10.

WARS ON POVERTY

During the early 1960s, the civil rights movement spurred a new awareness of and concern with poverty. What good was winning the right to sit at a lunch counter if one could not afford to buy a hamburger?

One of the most influential books of the times, Michael Harrington's *The Other America* (1962), argued that one-fifth of the nation—as many as 40 to 50 million people—suffered from bad housing, malnutrition, poor medical care, and other deprivations of poverty. Harrington documented the miseries of the "invisible land of the other Americans," the rejects of society who simply did not exist for affluent suburbanites or the mass media. The other America, Harrington wrote, "is populated by failures, by those driven from the land and bewildered by the city, by old people suddenly confronted with the torments of loneliness and poverty, and by minorities facing a wall of prejudice."

These arguments motivated President Johnson to expand the antipoverty program that he had inherited from the Kennedy administration. Ironically, it was another kind of war that ultimately undercut his aspiration to wage "an unconditional war on poverty" (see Figures 29.1 and 29.2).

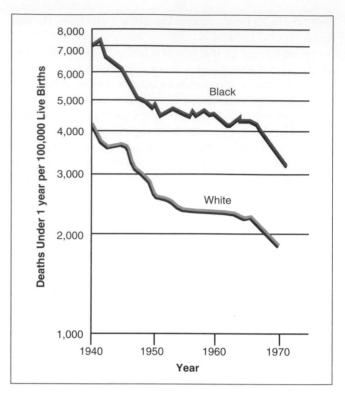

FIGURE 29.2   Comparative Figures on Infant Mortality by Race, 1940–70 The causes of infant mortality such as inadequate maternal diets, prenatal care, and medical services were all rooted in poverty, both rural and urban. Despite generally falling rates of infant mortality, nonwhite people continued to suffer the effects more than white people.

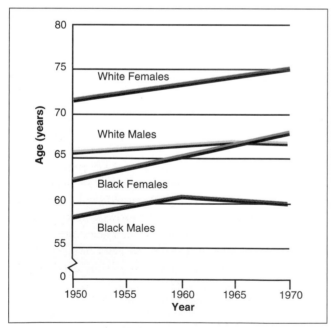

FIGURE 29.1   Comparative Figures on Life Expectancy at Birth by Race and Sex, 1950–70 Shifting mortality statistics suggested that the increased longevity of females increasingly cut across race lines, but did not diminish the difference between white people and black people as a whole.

The Great Society

In his State of the Union message in 1964, Johnson announced his plans to build a Great Society. Over the next two years, he used the political momentum of the civil rights movement and the overwhelming Democratic majorities in the House and Senate to push through the most ambitious reform program since the New Deal. In August 1964 the Economic Opportunity Act launched the War on Poverty.

The Office of Economic Opportunity (OEO) coordinated a network of federal programs designed to increase opportunities in employment and education and achieved mixed results. The Job Corps provided vocational training mostly for urban black youth considered unemployable. Housed in dreary barrackslike camps far from home, trainees often found themselves learning factory skills that were already obsolete. The Neighborhood Youth Corps managed to provide work for about 2 million young people aged sixteen to twenty-one, but nearly all the jobs were low paying and dead-end. Educational programs proved more successful. VISTA (Volunteers in Service to America) was a kind of domestic Peace Corps that brought several thousand idealistic volunteers into poor communities for social service work.

The most innovative and controversial element of the OEO was the Community Action Program (CAP). The program invited local communities to establish community action agencies (CAAs), to be funded through the OEO. The Economic Opportunity Act included language requiring these agencies to be "developed, conducted, and administered with the maximum feasible participation of residents of the areas and members of the groups served." In theory, as the SDS organizers had also believed, community action would empower the poor by giving them a direct say in mobilizing resources. By 1966 the OEO was funding more than 1,000 CAAs, mostly in black neighborhoods of big cities.

The traditional powers in cities—mayors, business elites, and political machines—who generally resisted institutional change, looked at CAAs as merely another way to dispense services and patronage, with the federal government picking up the tab. A continual tug-of-war over who should control funding and decision making plagued the CAP, sparking intense power struggles that helped to cripple the antipoverty effort. Such was the case in Chicago, where Mayor Richard Daley demanded absolute control over the allocation of federal funds.

The most successful and popular offshoots of the CAAs were the so-called national-emphasis programs, designed in Washington and administered according to federal guidelines. The Legal Services Program, staffed by attorneys, helped millions of poor people in legal battles with housing authorities, welfare departments, police, and slumlords. Head Start and Follow Through reached more than 2 million poor children and significantly improved the long-range educational achievement of participants. Comprehensive Community Health Centers provided basic medical services to poor patients who could not afford to see doctors. Upward Bound helped low-income teenagers develop the skills and confidence needed for college. Birth control programs dispensed contraceptive supplies and information to hundreds of thousands of poor women (see Figure 29.3).

But the root cause of poverty lay in unequal income distribution. The Johnson administration never committed itself to the redistribution of income or wealth. Spending on social welfare jumped from 7.7 percent of the gross national product in 1960 to 16 percent in 1974. But roughly three-quarters of social

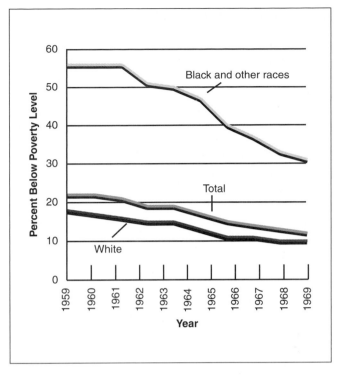

FIGURE 29.3 Percent of Population Below Poverty Level, by Race, 1959–69 Note: The poverty threshold for a nonfarm family of four was $3,743 in 1969 and $2,973 in 1959.

SOURCE: *Congressional Quarterly, Civil Rights: A Progress Report,* 1971, p. 46.

welfare payments went to the nonpoor. The largest sums went to Medicare, established by Congress in 1965 to provide basic health care for the aged, and to expanded Social Security payments and unemployment compensation.

The War on Poverty, like the Great Society itself, became a forgotten dream. "More than five years after the passage of the Economic Opportunity Act," a 1970 study concluded, "the war on poverty has barely scratched the surface. Most poor people have had no contact with it, except perhaps to hear the promises of a better life to come." The OEO finally expired in 1974. Having made the largest commitment to federal spending on social welfare since the New Deal, Johnson could take pride in the gains scored in the War on Poverty. At the same time, he had raised expectations higher than could be reached without a more drastic redistribution of economic and political power. Even in the short run, the president could not sustain the welfare programs and simultaneously fight a lengthy and expensive war abroad.

Crisis in the Cities

With funds for new construction limited during the Great Depression and World War II, and the postwar boom taking place in the suburbs, the housing stock in the nation's cities deteriorated. The Federal Housing Administration had encouraged this trend by insuring loans to support the building of new homes in suburban areas (see Chapter 27). The federal government also encouraged "redlining," which left people in poor neighborhoods without access to building loans. In these areas, the supply of adequate housing declined sharply. Slumlords took advantage of this situation, collecting high rents while allowing their properties to deteriorate. City officials meanwhile appealed for federal funds under Title I of the 1949 Housing Act to upgrade housing. Designed as a program of civic revitalization, these urban renewal projects more often than not sliced apart poor neighborhoods with new highways, demolished them in favor of new office complexes, or, as in Chicago's Uptown, favored new developments for the middle class rather than the poor. In 1968 a federal survey showed that 80 percent of those residents who had been displaced under this program were nonwhite.

Urban employment opportunities declined along with the urban housing stock. The industries and corporations that had lured working men and women to the cities a century earlier either automated their plants, thus scaling back their workforces, or relocated to the suburbs or other regions, such as the South and Southwest, that promised lower corporate taxes and nonunion labor. Nationwide, military spending prompted by the escalation of the Vietnam War brought the unemployment rate down from 6 percent, where it was in 1960, to 4 percent in 1966, where it remained until the end of the decade. Black unemployment, however, was nearly twice that of white unemployment. In northern cities, the proportion of the workforce employed in the higher-paying manufacturing jobs declined precipitously while the proportion working in minimum-wage service industries rose at a fast rate. In short, African Americans were losing good jobs and steadily falling further behind whites.

Pollution, which had long plagued traffic-congested cities like Los Angeles and industrial cities like steel-producing Pittsburgh, became an increasingly pervasive urban problem. Cities like Phoenix that once had clean air began to issue smog alerts. Pointing to high levels of lead in the blood of urban children, scientists warned of the long-term threat of pollution to public health.

Despite deteriorating conditions, millions of Americans continued to move to the cities, mainly African Americans from the Deep South, white people from the Appalachian Mountains, and Latinos from Puerto Rico. By the mid-1960s, African Americans had become near majorities in the nation's decaying inner cities. Many had fled rural poverty only to find themselves earning minimum wages at best and living in miserable, racially segregated neighborhoods.

Urban Uprisings

These deteriorating conditions brought urban pressures to the boiling point in the mid-1960s. In the "long, hot summers" of 1964 to 1968 the nation was rocked by more than 100 urban uprisings. As poet Imamu Amiri Baraka (formerly LeRoi Jones) noted, these incidents were spontaneous rebellions against authority. Unlike the race riots of the 1920s and 1940s, when angry whites assaulted blacks, masses of African Americans now took revenge for the white domination of their communities and specifically for police abuse (see Map 29.1).

The first major uprising erupted in August 1965 in the Watts section of Los Angeles. Here, the male unemployment rate hovered around 30 percent. Watts lacked health-care facilities—the nearest hospital was twelve miles away—and in a city with little public transportation, fewer than one-fifth of its residents owned cars. It took only a minor arrest to set off the uprising, which quickly spread outward for fifty miles. Throwing rocks and bottles through store windows, participants reportedly shouted, "This is for Selma! This is for Birmingham!" and "Burn, baby, burn!" Nearly 50,000 people turned out, and 20,000 National Guard troops were sent in. After six days, 34 people lay dead, 900 were injured, and 4,000 more had been arrested. Los Angeles chief of police William H. Parker blamed civil rights workers, the mayor accused Communists, and both feigned ignorance when the media reported that white police assigned to "charcoal alley," their name for the Watts district, had for years referred to their nightsticks as "nigger knockers."

The following summer, large-scale uprisings occurred in San Francisco, Milwaukee, Dayton, and Cleveland. On July 12, 1967, in Newark, New Jersey, a city with severe housing shortages and the nation's highest black unemployment rate, the beating and arrest of a black taxi driver by a white police officer provoked a widespread protest. Five days of looting and burning of white-owned buildings ended with twenty-five people dead. One week later the Detroit "Great Rebellion" began. This time a vice squad of the Detroit police had raided a bar and arrested the after-hours patrons. Army tanks and paratroopers were brought in to quell the massive distur-

MAP EXPLORATION

To explore an interactive version of this map, go to **www.prenhall.com/faragher5/map29.1**

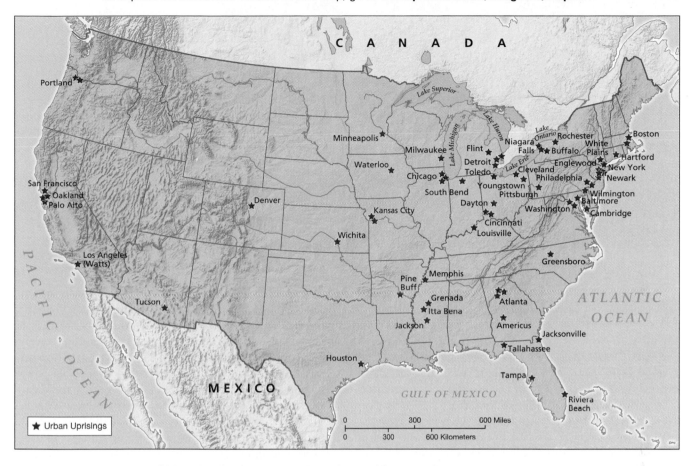

MAP 29.1 Urban Uprisings, 1965–1968 After World War II urban uprisings precipitated by racial conflict increased in African American communities. In Watts in 1965 and in Detroit and Newark in 1967, rioters struck out at symbols of white control of their communities, such as white-owned businesses and residential properties.

bance, which lasted a week and left 34 people dead and 7,000 under arrest.

The uprisings seemed at first to prompt badly needed reforms. After Watts, President Johnson set up a task force headed by Deputy Attorney General Ramsey Clark and allocated funds for a range of antipoverty programs. Several years later the Kerner Commission, headed by Governor Otto Kerner of Illinois, studied the riots and found that the participants in the uprisings were not the poorest or least-educated members of their communities. They suffered instead from heightened expectations sparked by the civil rights movement and Johnson's promise of a Great

Society, expectations that were not to be realized. The Kerner Commission concluded its report by indicting "white racism" for creating an "explosive mixture" of poverty and police brutality.

But Congress ignored the commission's warning that "our nation is moving toward two societies, one black, one white—separate and unequal." Moreover, the costs of the Vietnam War left little federal money for antipoverty programs. Senator William Fulbright noted, "Each war feeds on the other, and, although the President assures us that we have the resources to win both wars, in fact we are not winning either of them."

Between 1965 and 1968, racial tensions exploded into violence in more than seventy-five cities. Unlike earlier episodes of racial violence, which often took the form of clashes between black and white residents over contested neighborhoods, the riots of the 1960s were more often attacks by residents against retail establishments and property owned primarily by whites. Most deaths and injuries resulted from confrontations between police and rioters, not from fighting between black and white residents. This photograph, taken in 1967, shows police officers arresting suspected looters in Newark, New Jersey, where twenty-three people were killed in the course of the uprising.

SOURCE: CORBIS- NY

1968

The urban uprisings of the summer of 1967 marked the most drawn-out violence in the United States since the Civil War. But, rather than offering a respite, 1968 proved to be even more turbulent. The bloodiest and most destructive fighting of the Vietnam War resulted in a hopeless stalemate that soured most Americans on the conflict and undermined their faith in U.S. invincibility in world affairs. Disillusionment deepened in the spring when two of the most revered political leaders were struck down by assassins' bullets. Once again protesters and police clashed on the nation's campuses and city streets, and millions of Americans asked what was wrong with their country. Why was it so violent?

The Tet Offensive

On January 30, 1968, the North Vietnamese and their Vietcong allies launched the Tet Offensive (named for the Vietnamese lunar new year holiday), stunning the U.S. military command in South Vietnam. The Vietcong managed to push into the major cities and provincial capitals of the South, as far as the courtyard of the U.S. embassy in Saigon. U.S. troops ultimately halted the offensive, suffering comparatively modest casualties of 1,600 dead and 8,000 wounded. The North Vietnamese and Vietcong suffered more than 40,000 deaths, about one-fifth of their total forces. Civilian casualties ran to the hundreds of thousands. As many as 1 million South Vietnamese became refugees, their villages totally ruined (see Map 29.2).

The Tet Offensive, despite the U.S. success in stopping it, shattered the credibility of American officials who had repeatedly claimed the enemy to be virtually beaten. Television and press coverage—including scenes of U.S. personnel shooting from the embassy windows in Saigon—dismayed the public. Americans saw the beautiful, ancient city of Hue devastated almost beyond recognition and heard a U.S. officer casually remark about a village in the Mekong Delta, "We had to destroy it, in order to save it." Television newscasters began to warn parents: "The following scenes might not be suitable viewing for children."

The United States had chalked up a major military victory during the Tet Offensive but lost the war at home. For the first time, polls showed strong opposition to the war, 49 percent concluding that the entire operation in Vietnam was a mistake. The majority believed that the stalemate was hopeless. Meanwhile, in Rome, Berlin, Paris, and London, students and others turned out in huge demonstrations to protest U.S. involvement in Vietnam. At home, sectors of the antiwar movement began to shift from resistance to open rebellion.

The Tet Offensive also opened a year of political drama at home. Congress resoundingly turned down a request for a general increase in troops issued by General Westmoreland. President Johnson, facing the 1968 election campaign, knew the odds were now against him. He watched as opinion polls showed his popularity plummet to an all-time low. After he squeaked to a narrow victory in the New Hampshire primary, Johnson decided to step down. On March 31 he announced he would not seek the Democratic Party's nomination. He also declared a bombing halt over North Vietnam and called Hanoi to peace talks, which began in Paris in May. Like Truman almost thirty years earlier, and despite his determination not to repeat that bit of history, Johnson had lost his presidency in Asia.

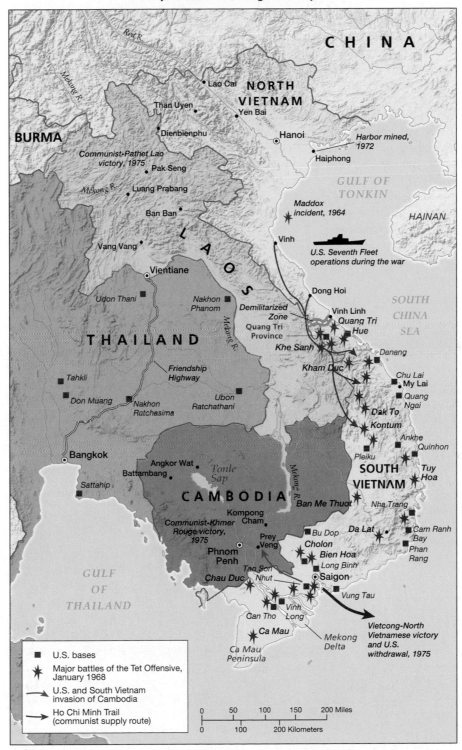

MAP 29.2 The Southeast Asian War The Indo-Chinese subcontinent, home to long-standing regional conflict, became the center of a prolonged war with the United States.

King, the War, and the Assassination

By 1968 the civil rights leadership stood firmly in opposition to the war, and Martin Luther King Jr. had reached a turning point in his life. The Federal Bureau of Investigation had been harassing King, tapping his telephones and spreading malicious rumors about him. Despite the threat from the FBI (Bureau Chief J. Edgar Hoover had sworn to "destroy the burrhead"), King abandoned his customary caution in criticizing U.S. policy in Vietnam. In the fall of 1965, he began to connect domestic unrest with the war abroad, calling the U.S. government the "greatest purveyor of violence in the world today." As he became more militant in opposing the war, King lost the support of liberal Democrats who remained loyal to Johnson. King refused to compromise.

In the spring of 1968 King chose Memphis, Tennessee, home of striking sanitation workers, as the place to inaugurate a Poor People's Campaign for peace and justice. There he delivered, in what was to be his final speech, a message of hope. "I have a dream this afternoon that the brotherhood of man will become a reality," King told the crowd. "With this faith, I will go out and carve a tunnel of hope from a mountain of despair." The next evening, April 4, 1968, as he stepped out on the balcony of his motel, King was shot and killed by a lone assassin, James Earl Ray.

Throughout the world crowds turned out to mourn King's death. Student Nonviolent Coordinating Committee leader Stokely Carmichael stormed, "When white America killed Dr. King, she declared war on us." Riots broke out in more than 100 cities. Chicago Mayor Richard Daley ordered his police to shoot to kill. In Washington DC, U.S. Army units set up machine guns outside the Capitol and the White House. By week's end, nearly 27,000 African Americans had been jailed. The physical scars of these riots remained for years, as

"Martin Luther King," Robert Kennedy said when he heard the news of the assassination of the civil rights leader, "dedicated his life to love and to justice for his fellow human beings, and he died because of that effort." The funeral service for King was held in the Ebenezer Baptist Church in Atlanta on April 7, 1968.

SOURCE: © James L. Amos/CORBIS.

banks redlined black neighborhoods and refused funds for rebuilding. The psychic scars survived even longer. With King's death, his vision of humanity as a "Beloved Community" faded.

The Democratic Campaign

The dramatic events of the first part of the year had a direct impact on the presidential campaign. For those liberals dissatisfied with Johnson's conduct of the war, and especially for African Americans suffering the loss of their greatest national leader, New York senator Robert F. Kennedy emerged as the candidate of choice. Kennedy enjoyed a strong record on civil rights, and, like King, he had begun to interpret the war as a mirror of injustice at home. Kennedy insisted during the Tet Offensive that "our nation must be told the truth about this war, in all its terrible reality." On this promise he began to build a campaign for the Democratic nomination.

Ironically, Kennedy faced an opponent who agreed with him, Minnesota senator Eugene McCarthy. The race for the Democratic nomination positioned McCarthy, the witty philosopher, against Kennedy, the charismatic campaigner. McCarthy garnered support from liberal Democrats and white suburbanites. On college campuses his popularity with antiwar students was so great that his campaign became known as the "children's crusade." Kennedy reached out successfully to African Americans and Latinos and won all but the Oregon primary.

Kennedy appeared to be the Democratic Party's strongest candidate as June 4, the day of the California primary, dawned. But as the final tabulation of his victory came in just past midnight, Robert Kennedy was struck down by an assassin's bullet.

Vice President Hubert H. Humphrey, a longtime presidential hopeful, was now the sole Democrat with the credentials to succeed Johnson. But his reputation as a cold war Democrat had become a liability. In the 1950s Humphrey had delivered stirring addresses for civil rights and antipoverty legislation; yet he also sponsored repressive cold war measures and supported huge defense appropriations that diverted needed funds from domestic programs. He fully supported the Vietnam War and had publicly scorned peace activists as cowardly and un-American. Incongruously calling his campaign the "Politics of Joy," Humphrey simultaneously courted Democrats who grimly supported the war and the King-Kennedy wing, which was sickened by it.

Humphrey skillfully cultivated the Democratic power brokers. Without entering a single state primary, he lined up delegates loyal to city bosses, labor leaders, and conservative southern Democrats. As the candidate least likely to rock the boat, he had secured his party's nomination well before delegates met in convention.

"The Whole World Is Watching!"

The events surrounding the Democratic convention in Chicago, August 21–26, demonstrated how deep the divisions within the United States had become. Antiwar activists had called for a massive demonstration at the delegates' hotel and at the convention center. The media focused, however, on the plans announced by the "Yippies," or Youth International Party, a largely imaginary organization of politicized hippies led by jokester and counterculture guru Abbie Hoffman. Yippies called for a Festival of Life, including a "nude-in" on Lake Michigan beaches and the release of a greased pig—Pigasus, the Yippie candidate for president. Still reeling from the riots following King's assassination, Chicago's Mayor Richard Daley refused to issue parade permits. According to later accounts, he sent hundreds of undercover police into the crowds to encourage rock throwing and generally to incite violence so that retaliation would appear necessary and reasonable.

Daley's strategy boomeranged when his officers staged what a presidential commission later termed a "police riot," randomly assaulting demonstrators, casual passersby, and television crews filming the events. For one of the few times in American history, the media appeared to join a protest against civil authorities. Angered by the embarrassing publicity, Daley sent his agents to raid McCarthy's campaign headquarters, where Democrats opposed to the war had gathered.

Inside the convention hall, a raging debate over a peace resolution underscored the depth of the division within the party over the war. Representative Wayne Hays of Ohio lashed out at those who substituted "beards for brains . . . [and] pot [for] patriotism." When the resolution failed, McCarthy delegates put on black armbands and followed folk singer Theodore Bikel in singing "We Shall Overcome." Later, as tear gas used against the demonstrators outside turned the amphitheater air acrid, delegates heard the beaming Humphrey praise Mayor Daley and Johnson's conduct of the Vietnam War. When Senator Abraham Ribicoff of Connecticut addressed the convention and protested the "Gestapo tactics" of the police, television cameras focused on Mayor Daley saying, "You Jew son of a bitch . . ., go home!" The crowd outside chanted, "The whole world is watching! The whole world is watching!" Indeed, through satellite transmission, it was.

Protest spread worldwide. Across the United States the antiwar movement picked up steam. In Paris, students took over campuses and workers occupied factories. Young people scrawled on the walls such humorous and half-serious slogans as "Be Realistic, Demand the Impossible!" Similar protests against authority occurred in eastern Europe. In Prague, Czechoslovakia, students wearing blue jeans and singing Beatles songs threw rocks at Soviet tanks. Meanwhile, demonstrations in Japan, Italy, Ireland, Germany,

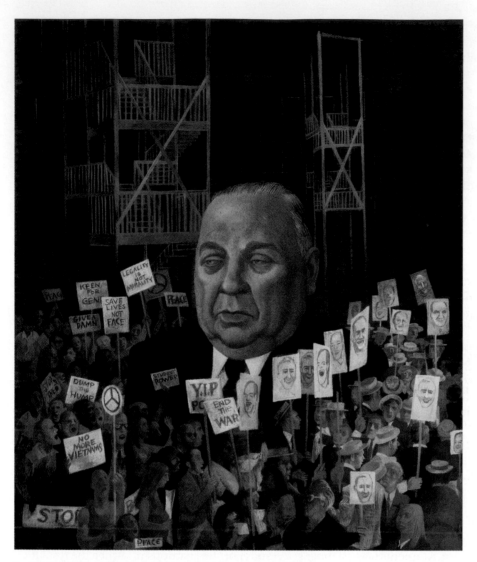

In 1968, Richard J. Daley had been elected mayor of Chicago four times and held power as a traditional city boss. In December of that year, the National Commission on Violence released a report that concluded that Chicago police, acting under Mayor Daley's orders had been "unrestrained and indiscriminate" in their attacks on demonstrators at the National Democratic Convention held the previous August. In response, Mayor Daley brazenly announced a 22 percent salary increase for members of the city's police and fire personnel.

SOURCE: Library of Congress.

and England all brought young people into the streets to demand democratic reforms in their own countries and an end to the war in Vietnam.

THE POLITICS OF IDENTITY

The tragic events of 1968 brought whole sectors of the counterculture into political activism. With great media fanfare, gay liberation and women's liberation movements emerged in the late 1960s. By the early 1970s, young Latinos, Asian Americans, and Indian peoples had pressed their own claims. In different ways, these groups drew their own lessons from the nationalist movement that formed in the wake of Malcolm X's death—Black Power. Soon, "Brown Power," "Yellow Power," and "Red Power" became the slogans of movements constituted distinctly as new communities of protest.

Black Power

Impatient with the strategies of social change based on voting rights and integration, many young activists spurned the tactics of civil disobedience of King's generation for direct action and militant self-defense. In 1966, Stokely Carmichael, who had helped turn SNCC into an all-black organization, began to advocate Black Power as a means for African Americans to take control of their own communities.

Derived from a century-long tradition of black nationalism, the key tenets of Black Power were self-determination and self-sufficiency. National conferences of activists, held annually beginning in 1966, adopted separatist resolutions, including a plan to partition the United States into black and white nations. Black Power also promoted self-esteem by affirming the unique history and heritage of African peoples.

The movement's boldest expression was the Black Panther Party for Self-Defense, founded in Oakland, California, in 1966 by Huey P. Newton and Bobby Seale. "We want freedom," Newton demanded. "We want power. . . . We want full employment. . . . We want all black men to be exempt from military service. We want . . . an end to POLICE BRUTALITY. . . . We want land, bread, housing, education, clothing, and justice." Armed self-defense was the Panthers' strategy, and they adopted a paramilitary style—black leather jackets, shoes, black berets, and firearms—that infuriated local authorities. Monitoring local police, a practice Panthers termed "patrolling the pigs," was their major activity. In several communities, Panthers also ran free breakfast programs for schoolchildren, established medical clinics, and conducted educational classes. For a time the Panthers became folk heroes. Persecuted by local police and the FBI—there were more than thirty raids on Panther offices in eleven states during 1968 and 1969—the Panthers were arrested, prosecuted, and sentenced to long terms in jail that effectively destroyed the organization.

Black Power nevertheless continued to grow during the late 1960s and became a multifaceted movement. The Reverend Jesse Jackson, for example, rallied African Americans in Chicago to boycott the A&P supermarket chain until the firm hired 700 black workers. A dynamic speaker and skillful organizer, Jackson encouraged African Americans to support their own businesses and services. His program, Operation Breadbasket, strengthened community control. By 1970 it had spread beyond Chicago to fifteen other cities.

Cultural nationalism became the most enduring component of Black Power. In their popular book *Black Power* (1967), Stokely Carmichael and Charles V. Hamilton urged African Americans "to assert their own definitions, to reclaim their history, their culture; to create their own sense of community and togetherness." Thousands of college students responded by calling for more scholarships and for more classes on African American history and culture. At San Francisco State University, students, with help from the Black Panthers, demanded the creation of a black studies department. After a series of failed negotiations with the administration, the black students called for a campus-wide strike and in December 1968 shut down the university. In the end, 134 school days later, the administration agreed to fund a black studies department but also fired about twenty-five faculty members and refused to drop charges against 700 arrested campus activists. Strikes for "third world studies" soon broke out on other campuses, including the University of Wisconsin at Madison, where the national guard was brought in to quell the protest.

Meanwhile, trendsetters put aside Western dress for African-style dashikis and hairdos, and black parents gave their children African names. Many well-known African Americans such as Imamu Amiri Baraka (formerly LeRoi Jones), Muhammad Ali (formerly Cassius Clay), and Kwame Touré (formerly Stokely Carmichael) rejected their "slave names." The new African American holiday Kwanzaa began to replace Christmas as a seasonal family celebration. This deepening sense of racial pride and solidarity was summed up in the popular slogan "Black Is Beautiful."

Sisterhood Is Powerful

Betty Friedan's best-selling *Feminine Mystique* (1963) had swelled feelings of discontent among many middle-class white women who had come of age in the 1950s (see Chapter 27) and sparked the formation of the National Organization for Women (NOW) in 1966. NOW pledged

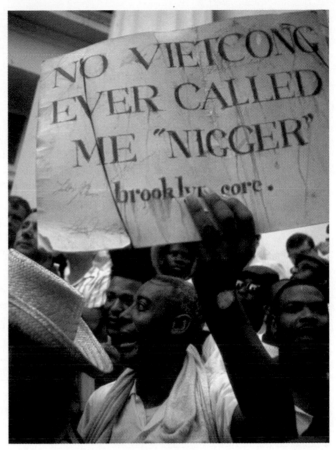

The war in Vietnam contributed to the growing racial militancy in the United States. African Americans served on the front lines in Vietnam in disproportionate numbers, and many came to view the conflict as a "white man's war."

SOURCE: © 2001 Matt Herron c/o Mira.com.

itself "to take action to bring women into full participation in the mainstream of American society now." Members spearheaded campaigns for the enforcement of laws banning sex discrimination in work and in education, for maternity leaves for working mothers, and for government funding of day-care centers. NOW also came out for the Equal Rights Amendment, first introduced in Congress in 1923, and demanded the repeal of legislation that prohibited abortion or restricted birth control.

The second half of the decade produced a different kind of movement: women's liberation. Like Black Power, the women's liberation movement attracted young women who had been active in civil rights, SDS, and campus antiwar movements. Angered by the sexism of SNCC and SDS yet impatient with the legislative reforms promoted by NOW, these women took a militant stance, proclaiming "Sisterhood Is Powerful." "Women are an oppressed class. Our oppression is total, affecting every facet of our lives,"

OVERVIEW

PROTEST MOVEMENTS OF THE 1960s

Year	Organization/Movement	Description
1962	*Students for a Democratic Society (SDS)*	Organization of college students that became the largest national organization of left-wing white students. Calling for "participatory democracy," SDS involved students in community-based campaigns against poverty and for citizens' control of neighborhoods. SDS played a prominent role in the campaign to end the war in Vietnam.
1964	*Free Speech Movement*	Formed at the University of California at Berkeley to protest the banning of on-campus political fund-raising. Decried the bureaucratic character of the "multi-university" and advocated an expansion of student rights.
1965	*Anti-Vietnam War Movement*	Advocated grass-roots opposition to U.S. involvement in Southeast Asia. By 1970 a national mobilization committee organized a demonstration of a half-million protesters in Washington DC.
1965	La raza	A movement of Chicano youth to advance the cultural and political self-determination of Mexican Americans. *La raza* included the Brown Berets, which addressed community issues, and regional civil rights groups such as the Crusade for Social Justice, formed in 1965.
1966	*Black Power*	Militant movement that emerged from the civil rights campaigns to advocate independent institutions for African Americans and pride in black culture and African heritage. The idea of Black Power, a term coined by Stokely Carmichael, inspired the formation of the paramilitary Black Panthers.
1968	*American Indian Movement (AIM)*	Organization formed to advance the self-determination of Indian peoples and challenge the authority of the Bureau of Indian Affairs. Its most effective tactic was occupation. In February, 1973, AIM insurgents protesting land and treaty violations occupied Wounded Knee, South Dakota, the location of an 1890 massacre, until the FBI and BIA agents drove them out.
1968	*Women's Liberation*	Movement of mainly young women that took shape following a protest at the Miss America Beauty Pageant. Impatient with the legislative reforms promoted by the National Organization for Women, founded in 1966, activists developed their own agenda shaped by the slogan "The Personal Is Political." Activities included the formation of "consciousness-raising" groups and the establishment of women's studies programs.
1968	*Asian American Political Alliance (AAPA)*	Formed at the University of California at Berkeley, the AAPA was one of the first pan–Asian political organizations to struggle against racial oppression. The AAPA encouraged Asian Americans to claim their own cultural identity and to protest the war against Asian peoples in Vietnam.
1969	*Gay Liberation*	Movement to protest discrimination against homosexuals and lesbians that emerged after the Stonewall Riots in New York City. Unlike earlier organizations such as the Mattachine Society, which focused on civil rights, Gay Liberationists sought to radically change American society and government, which they believed were corrupt.

read the Redstocking Manifesto of 1969. "We are exploited as sex objects, breeders, domestic servants, and cheap labor."

The women's liberation movement developed a scathing critique of patriarchy—that is, the power of men to dominate all institutions, from the family to business to the military to the protest movements themselves. Patriarchy, they argued, was the prime cause of exploitation, racism, and war. Outraged and sometimes outrageous, radical feminists, as they called themselves, conducted "street theater" at the 1968 Miss America Beauty Pageant in Atlantic City, crowning a live sheep as queen and "throwing implements of female torture" (bras, girdles, curlers, and copies of the *Ladies' Home Journal*) into a "freedom trash can." A few months later, the Women's International Terrorist Conspiracy from Hell (WITCH) struck in Lower Manhattan, putting a hex on the male-dominated New York Stock Exchange.

The media focused on the audacious acts and brazen pronouncements of radical feminists, but the majority involved in the women's liberation movement were less flamboyant women who were simply trying to rise above the limitations imposed on them because of their gender. Most of their activism took place outside the limelight in consciousness-raising (CR) groups. CR groups, which multiplied by the thousands in the late 1960s and early 1970s, brought women together to discuss the relationship between public events and private lives, particularly between politics and sexuality. Here women shared their most intimate feelings toward men or other women and established the constituency for the movement's most important belief, expressed in the aphorism "The personal is political." Believing that no aspect of life lacked a political dimension, women in these groups explored the power dynamics of the institutions of family and marriage as well as the workforce and government.

Participants in the women's liberation movement engaged in a wide range of activities. Some staged sit-ins at *Newsweek* to protest demeaning media depictions of women. Others established health clinics, day-care centers, rape crisis centers, and shelters for women fleeing abusive husbands or lovers. The women's liberation movement also had a significant educational impact. Feminist bookstores and publishing companies, such as the Feminist Press, reached out to eager readers. Scholarly books such as Kate Millett's *Sexual Politics* (1970) found a wide popular audience. By the early 1970s, campus activists were demanding women's studies programs and women's centers. Like black studies, women's studies programs included traditional academic goals, such as the generation of new scholarship, but also encouraged personal change and self-esteem. Between 1970 and 1975, as many as 150 women's stud-

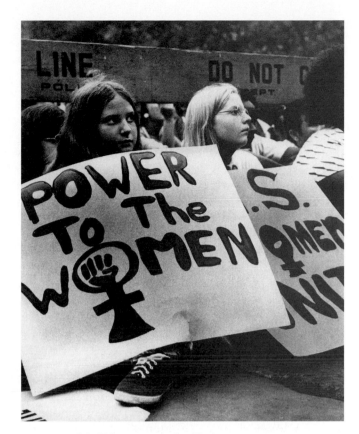

On August 26, 1970, to mark the fiftieh anniversary of the passage of the Nineteenth Amendment, women nationwide staged demonstrations for women's rights. The young women in this photograph gathered in Central Park, New York, in the largest demonstration ever held for women's rights. Proposed by Representative Bella Abzug and designated by Congress in 1971, Women's Equality Day is celebrated every year on August 26.

SOURCE: Jesse-Steve Rose/The Image Works.

ies programs had been established. The movement continued to grow; by 1980 nearly 30,000 women's studies courses were offered at colleges and universities throughout the United States.

The women's liberation movement remained, however, a bastion of white middle-class women. The appeal to sisterhood did not unite women across race or class or even sexual orientation. Lesbians, who charged the early leaders of NOW with homophobia, found large pockets of "heterosexism" in the women's liberation movement and broke off to form their own organizations. Although some African American women were outraged at the posturing of Black Power leaders like Stokely Carmichael, who joked that "the only position for women in SNCC is prone," the majority remained wary of white women's appeals to sisterhood. African American women formed their own "womanist" movement to address their distinct cultural and political concerns. Similarly, by 1970 a Latina feminist movement had begun to address issues uniquely relevant to women of color in an Anglo-dominated society.

Gay Liberation

The gay community had been generations in the making but only gained visibility during World War II (see Chapter 25). By the mid-1950s, two pioneering homophile organizations, the Mattachine Society and the Daughters of Bilitis, were campaigning to reduce discrimination against homosexuals in employment, the armed forces, and all areas of social and cultural life. Other groups, such as the Society for Individual Rights, rooted themselves in New York's Greenwich Village, San Francisco's North Beach, and other centers of gay night life. But it was during the tumultuous 1960s that gay and lesbian movements encouraged many men and women to proclaim publicly their sexual identity: "Say It Loud, Gay Is Proud."

The major event prompting gays to organize grew out of repeated police raids of gay bars and the harassment of their patrons. In February 1966 New York City's popular liberal mayor John Lindsay announced a crackdown against "promenading perverts" and assigned police to patrol the bars between Times Square and Washington Square. The American Civil Liberties Union responded by pointing out that the mayor was "confusing deviant social behavior with criminal activity." Lindsay's police commissioner soon announced the end of the entrapment policy by which undercover police had been luring homosexuals into breaking the law, but various forms of individual harassment continued. Finally, on Friday, June 27, 1969, New York police raided the Stonewall Inn, a well-known gay bar in Greenwich Village, and provoked an uprising of angry homosexuals that lasted the entire night. The next day, "Gay Power" graffiti appeared on buildings and sidewalks throughout the neighborhood.

The Stonewall Riot, as it was called, sparked a new sense of collective identity among many gays and lesbians and touched off a new movement for both civil rights and liberation. Gay men and women in New York City formed the Gay Liberation Front (GLF), announcing themselves as "a revolutionary homosexual group of men and women formed with the realization that complete sexual liberation for all people cannot come about unless existing social institutions are abolished. We reject society's attempt to impose sexual roles and definitions of our nature. We are stepping outside these roles and simplistic myths. We are going to be who we are." The GLF also took a stand against the war in Vietnam and supported the Black Panthers. It quickly adopted the forms of public protest, such as street demonstrations and sit-ins, developed by the civil rights movement and given new direction by antiwar protesters.

Changes in public opinion and policies followed. As early as 1967 a group of Episcopal priests had urged church leaders to avoid taking a moral position against same-sex relationships. The San Francisco–based Council on Religion and Homosexuality established a network for clergy sympathetic to gay and lesbian parishioners. In 1973 the American Psychiatric Association, which since World War II had viewed homosexuality as a treatable mental illness, reclassified it as a normal sexual orientation. Meanwhile, there began a slow process of decriminalization of homosexual acts between consenting adults. In 1975 the U.S. Civil Service Commission ended its ban on the employment of homosexuals.

The founders of gay liberation encouraged not only legal changes and the establishment of supporting institutions but self-pride. "Gay Is Good" (like "Black Is Beautiful" and "Sisterhood Is Powerful") expressed the aspiration of a large hidden minority to "come out" and demand public acceptance of their sexual identity. By the mid-1970s Gay Pride marches held simultaneously in several cities were drawing nearly 500,000 participants.

The Chicano Rebellion

By the mid-1960s young Mexican Americans adopted the slang term *Chicano*, in preference to Mexican American, to express a militant ethnic nationalism. Chicano militants demanded not only equality with white people but recognition of their distinctive culture and history. Tracing their roots to the heroic Aztecs, they identified *la raza* (the race or people) as the source of a common language, religion, and heritage.

Students played a large role in shaping the Chicano movement. In East Los Angeles, high school students staged "blowouts" or strikes to demand educational reform and a curricular emphasis on the history, literature, art, and language of Mexican Americans. Fifteen thousand students from five Los Angeles schools went on strike against poor educational facilities. The police conducted a mass arrest of protesters, and within a short time students in San Antonio and Denver were conducting their own blowouts, holding placards reading "Teachers, Sí, Bigots, No!" By 1969, on September 16, Mexican Independence Day, high school students throughout the Southwest skipped classes in the First National Chicano Boycott. Meanwhile, students organized to demand Mexican American studies on their campuses. In 1969, a group staged a sit-in at the administrative offices of the Uni-

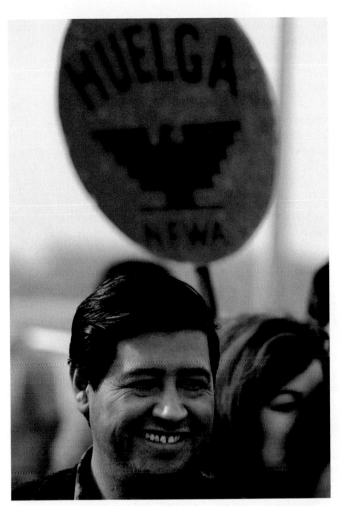

Labor activist Cesar Chavez spearheaded the organization of Chicano agricultural workers into the United Farm Workers (UFW), the first successful union of migrant workers. In 1965, a strike of grape pickers in the fields around Delano, California, and a nationwide boycott of table grapes brought Chavez and the UFW into the media spotlight. Like Martin Luther King Jr., he advocated nonviolent methods for achieving justice and equality.

SOURCE: Paul Fusco/Magnum Photos, Inc.

versity of California at Berkeley, which one commentator called "the first important public appearance of something called Brown Power."

In 1967 David Sanchez of East Los Angeles formed the Brown Berets, modeled on the Black Panthers, to address such community issues as housing and employment and generally to encourage teenagers to express *Chicanismo*, or pride in their Mexican American identity and heritage. By 1972, when the organization disbanded, the Brown Berets had organized twenty chapters, published a newspaper, *La Causa*, and run a successful health clinic. From college campuses spread

a wider cultural movement that spawned literary journals in "Spanglish" (a mixture of English and Spanish), theatrical companies and music groups, and murals illustrating ethnic themes on buildings in Los Angeles and elsewhere.

Chicano nationalism inspired a variety of regional political movements in the late 1960s. One of these, Rodolfo "Corky" Gonzales's Crusade for Justice, formed in 1965 to protest the failure of the Great Society's antipoverty programs. A former boxer and popular poet, Gonzales was especially well liked by barrio youth and college students. He led important campaigns for greater job opportunities and land reform throughout the Southwest well into the 1970s. In Colorado and New Mexico, the *Alianza Federal de Mercedes*, formed in 1963 by Reies López Tijerina, fought to reclaim land fraudulently appropriated by white settlers. The Texas-based *La Raza Unida Party* (LRUP), meanwhile, increased Mexican American representation in local government and established social and cultural programs. The student-led Mexican American Youth Organization (MAYO) worked closely with the LRUP to help Mexican Americans take political power in Crystal City, Texas. The two organizations registered voters, ran candidates for office, and staged a massive boycott of Anglo-owned businesses.

Mexican American activists, even those who won local office, soon discovered that economic power remained out of community hands. Stifled by poverty, ordinary Mexican Americans had less confidence in the political process, and many fell back into apathy after early hopes of great, sudden change. Despite these setbacks, a sense of collective identity had been forged among many Mexican Americans.

The Chicano movement found vivid expression in the performing and visual arts and in literature. *Teatro*, comprising film and drama, drew creatively on Mexican and Anglo cultural forms to explore the political dimensions of Mexican American society. *La Carpa de los Rasquachis (The Tent of the Underdogs)*, appeared in 1974 as the first full-length Chicano play and was subsequently staged in many communities. One of the most popular and visible media was the mural, often based on the works of Mexican masters such as Diego Rivera. Chicano muralists painted an estimated 1,500 murals on public buildings throughout their communities, from the exteriors of retail shops to freeway overpasses, even to large drainage pipes. Artistic expression found its way into music and dance. The rock group *Los Lobos*, for example, dedicated their first recorded album to the United Farm Workers. One of the most important writers to capture the excitement of the Chicano movement was Oscar Zeta Acosta, whose *Revolt of the Cockroach*, published in 1973, renders into fiction some of the major events of the era.

Red Power

The phrase "Red Power," attributed to Vine Deloria Jr., commonly expressed a growing sense of pan-Indian identity. At the forefront of this movement was the American Indian Movement (AIM), which was founded in 1968. Its members represented mainly urban Indian communities, and its leaders were young and militant. Like the Black Panthers and Brown Berets, AIM was initially organized to monitor law enforcement practices such as police harassment and brutality. It soon played a major role in building a network of urban Indian centers, churches, and philanthropic organizations and in establishing the "powwow circuit" that publicized news of protest activities across the coun-

try. Skillful in attracting attention from the news media, AIM quickly inspired a plethora of new publications and local chapters. Many young Indians turned to their elders to learn tribal ways, including traditional dress and spiritual practices (see Map 29.3).

The major catalyst of Red Power was the occupation of the deserted federal prison on Alcatraz Island in San Francisco Bay on November 20, 1969. A group of eighty-nine Indians, identifying themselves as "Indians of All Tribes," claimed the island according to the terms of an 1868 Sioux treaty that gave Indians rights to unused federal property on Indian land. The group demanded federal funds for a multifaceted cultural and educational center. For the next year and a half, an occupation force averaging

MAP EXPLORATION

To explore an interactive version of this map, go to **www.prenhall.com/faragher5/map29.3**

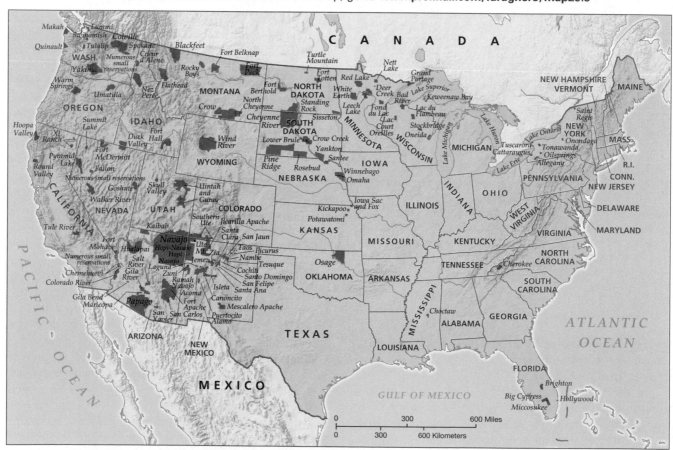

MAP 29.3 Major Indian Reservations, 1976 Although sizable areas, designated Indian reservations represented only a small portion of territory occupied in earlier times.

around 100 and a stream of visitors from a large number of tribes celebrated the occupation. Although the protestors ultimately failed to achieve their specific goals, they had an enormous impact on the Indian community. With the occupation at Alcatraz, a participant testified, "we got back our worth, our pride, our dignity, our humanity."

The most dramatic series of events of the Red Power movement began in 1972, when Indian activists left the cities to return to their rural roots. In November, AIM staged an event known as the "Trail of Broken Treaties" that culminated in a week-long occupation of the Bureau of Indian Affairs in Washington DC. Emphasizing treaty violation rather than civil rights, AIM insurgents then moved to the Pine Ridge Reservation, the site of the 1890 massacre at Wounded Knee, South Dakota, where in the spring of 1973 they began a siege that lasted ten weeks. AIM activists demanded the removal of the leader of the Oglala Lakota, whom they believed to be a corrupt puppet of the Bureau of Indian Affairs, and the restoration of treaty rights. Dozens of FBI agents then invaded under shoot-to-kill orders, leaving two Indians dead and an unknown number of casualties on both sides.

The Red Power movement culminated in the "Longest Walk," a five-month protest march that began in San Francisco and ended in Washington DC, in July 1978. The event emphasized the history of the forced removal of Indians from their homelands and protested the U.S. government's repeated violation of treaty rights. By this time, several tribes had won in court, by legislation or by administrative fiat, small parts of what had earlier been taken from them. The sacred Blue Lake was returned to Pueblo Indians in Taos, New Mexico, and Alaskan natives were granted legal title to 40 million acres (and compensation of almost $1 billion). The Native American Rights Fund (NARF), established in 1971, gained additional thousands of acres in Atlantic coast states. But despite these victories, many tribal lands continued to suffer from industrial and government waste dumping and other commercial uses. On reservations and in urban areas with heavy Indian concentrations, alcohol abuse and ill health remained serious problems.

The 1960s also marked the beginning of an "Indian Renaissance" in literature. New books like Vine Deloria Jr.'s *Custer Died for Your Sins* (1969) and the classic *Black Elk Speaks* (1961), reprinted from the 1930s, reached millions of readers inside and outside Indian communities. A wide variety of Indian novelists, historians, and essayists, such as Pulitzer Prize–winning N. Scott Momaday and Leslie Silko, followed up these successes, and fiction and nonfiction works about Indian life and lore continued to attract a large audience.

The Asian American Movement

In 1968 students at the University of California at Berkeley founded the Asian American Political Alliance (AAPA), one of the first pan-Asian political organizations bringing together Chinese, Japanese, and Filipino American activists. Similar organizations soon appeared on campuses throughout California and spread quickly to the East Coast and Midwest.

These groups took a strong stand against the war in Vietnam, condemning it as a violation of the national sovereignty of the small Asian country. They also protested the racism directed against the peoples of Southeast Asia, particularly the practice common among American soldiers of referring to the enemy as "Gooks." This racist epithet, first used to denigrate Filipinos during the Spanish-American War, implied that Asians were something less than human and therefore proper targets for slaughter. In response, Asian American activists rallied behind the people of Vietnam and proclaimed racial solidarity with their "Asian brothers and sisters."

In 1968 and 1969 students at San Francisco State College and the University of California at Berkeley, for example, rallied behind the slogan "Shut It Down!" and waged prolonged campus strikes to demand the establishment of ethnic studies programs. These students sought alternatives to the goal of assimilation into mainstream society, promoting instead a unique sense of ethnic identity, a pan-Asian counterculture. Berkeley students, for example, sponsored the "Asian American Experience in America–Yellow Power" conference, inviting their peers to learn about "Asian American history and destiny, and the need to express Asian American solidarity in a predominantly white society."

Between 1968 and 1973, major universities across the country introduced courses on Asian American studies, and a few set up interdisciplinary departments. Meanwhile, artists, writers, documentary filmmakers, oral historians, and anthropologists worked to recover the Asian American past. Maxine Hong Kingston's *Woman Warrior: A Memoir of a Girlhood among Ghosts* (1976) became a major bestseller.

Looking to the example of the Black Panthers, young Asian Americans also took their struggle into the community. In 1968, activists presented the San Francisco municipal government with a list of grievances about conditions in Chinatown, particularly the poor housing and medical facilities, and organized a protest march down the neighborhood's main street. They led a community-wide struggle to save San Francisco's International Hotel, a low-income residential facility mainly for Filipino and Chinese men, which was ultimately leveled for a new parking lot.

Community activists ranging from college students to neighborhood artists worked in a variety of campaigns to heighten public awareness. The Redress and Reparations Movement, initiated by Sansei (third-generation Japanese Americans), for example, encouraged students to ask their parents about their wartime experiences and prompted older civil rights organizations, such as the Japanese American Citizens League, to bring forward the issue of internment. At the same time, trade union organizers renewed labor organizing among new Asian workers, mainly in service industries, such as hotel and restaurant work, and in clothing manufacturing. Other campaigns reflected the growing diversity of the Asian population. Filipinos, the fastest-growing group, organized to protest the destructive role of U.S.–backed Philippine dictator Ferdinand Marcos. Students from South Korea similarly denounced the repressive government in their homeland. Samoans sought to publicize the damage caused by nuclear testing in the Pacific Islands. Ultimately, however, in blurring intergroup differences, the Asian American movement failed to reach the growing populations of new immigrants, especially the numerous Southeast Asians fleeing their devastated homeland.

Despite its shortcomings, the politics of identity would continue to grow through the next two decades of mainly conservative rule, broadening the content of literature, film, television, popular music, and even the curricula of the nation's schools. Collectively, the various movements for social change pushed issues of race, gender, and sexual orientation to the forefront of American politics and simultaneously spotlighted the nation's cultural diversity as a major resource.

THE NIXON PRESIDENCY

The sharp divisions among Americans in 1968, mainly due to President Johnson's policies in Vietnam, paved the way for the election of Richard Milhous Nixon. The new Republican president inherited not only an increasingly unpopular war but a nation riven by internal discord. Without specifying his plans, he promised a "just and honorable peace" in Southeast Asia and the restoration of law and order at home. Yet, once in office, Nixon puzzled both friends and foes. He ordered unprecedented illegal government action against private citizens while agreeing with Congress to enhance several welfare programs and improve environmental protection. He widened and intensified the war in Vietnam, yet made stunning moves toward détente with the People's Republic of China. An architect of the cold war in the 1950s, Nixon became the first president to foresee its end. Nixon worked hard in the White House, centralizing authority and reigning defiantly as an "Imperial President"—until he brought himself down.

The Southern Strategy

In 1968, Republican presidential contender Richard Nixon deftly built on voter hostility toward youthful protesters and the counterculture. He represented, he said, the "silent majority"—those Americans who worked, paid taxes, and did not demonstrate, picket, or protest loudly, "people who are not haters, people who love their country." Recovering from defeats in elections for the presidency in 1960 and the governorship of California in 1962, Nixon declared himself the one candidate who could restore law and order to the nation (see Map 29.4).

After signing the landmark Civil Rights Act of 1964, President Johnson said privately, "I think we just delivered the South to the Republicans for a long time to come." Republican strategists moved quickly to make this prediction come true. They also recognized the growing electoral importance of the Sunbelt, where populations grew with the rise of high-tech industries and retirement communities. A powerful conservatism dominated this region, home to many military bases, defense plants, and an increasingly influential Protestant evangelism. Nixon appealed directly to these voters by promising to appoint to federal courts judges who would undercut liberal interpretations of civil rights and be tough on crime.

Nixon selected as his running mate Maryland governor Spiro T. Agnew, known for his vitriolic oratory. Agnew treated dissent as near treason. He courted the silent majority by attacking all critics of the war as "an effete corps of impudent snobs" and blasted liberal newscasters as "nattering nabobs of negativism."

The 1968 campaign underscored the antiliberal sentiment of the voting public. The most dramatic example was the relative success of Alabama governor George Wallace's third-party bid for the presidency. Wallace took state office in 1963 promising white Alabamans "Segregation now! Segregation tomorrow! Segregation forever!" In 1968 he waged a national campaign around a conservative hate list that included school busing, antiwar demonstrations, and urban uprisings. Winning only five southern states, Wallace nevertheless captured 13.5 percent of the popular vote.

The Nixon-Agnew team squeaked to victory, capturing the popular vote by the slim margin of 43.6 percent to Democrat Hubert Humphrey and Maine senator Edmund Muskie's 42.7 percent but taking nearly all the West's electoral votes. Bitterly divided by the campaign, the Democrats would remain out of presidential contention for over two decades, except when the Republicans suffered scandal and disgrace. The Republicans in 1968 had paved the way for the conservative ascendancy.

MAP EXPLORATION

To explore an interactive version of this map, go to **www.prenhall.com/faragher5/map29.4**

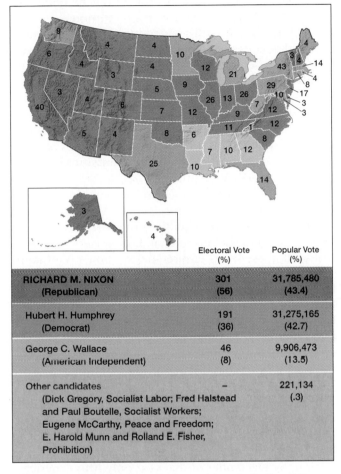

	Electoral Vote (%)	Popular Vote (%)
RICHARD M. NIXON (Republican)	301 (56)	31,785,480 (43.4)
Hubert H. Humphrey (Democrat)	191 (36)	31,275,165 (42.7)
George C. Wallace (American Independent)	46 (8)	9,906,473 (13.5)
Other candidates (Dick Gregory, Socialist Labor; Fred Halstead and Paul Boutelle, Socialist Workers; Eugene McCarthy, Peace and Freedom; E. Harold Munn and Rolland E. Fisher, Prohibition)	–	221,134 (.3)

MAP 29.4 The Election of 1968 Although the Republican Nixon-Agnew team won the popular vote by only a small margin, the Democrats lost in most of the northern states that had voted Democratic since the days of FDR. Segregationist Governor George Wallace of Alabama polled more than 9 million votes.

Nixon's War

Nixon promised to bring "peace with honor." Yet, despite this pledge, the Vietnam War raged for four more years before a peace settlement was reached (see Figure 29.4).

Much of the responsibility for the prolonged conflict rested with Henry A. Kissinger. A dominating personality on the National Security Council, Kissinger insisted that the United States could not retain its global leadership by appearing weak to either allies or enemies. Brilliant and ruthless, Kissinger helped Nixon centralize foreign policymaking in the White House. Together, they overpowered those members of the State Department who had concluded that the majority of Americans no longer supported the war (see Figure 29.5).

In public Nixon followed a policy of "Vietnamization." On May 14, 1969, he announced that the time was approaching "when the South Vietnamese . . . will be able to take over some of the fighting." During the next several months, he ordered the withdrawal of 60,000 U.S. troops. Hoping to placate public opinion, Nixon also intended to "demonstrate to Hanoi that we were serious in seeking a diplomatic settlement." In private, with Kissinger's guidance, Nixon mulled over the option of a "knockout blow" to the North Vietnamese.

On April 30, 1970, Nixon made one of the most controversial decisions of his presidency. Without seeking congressional approval, he ordered U.S. troops to invade the tiny nation of Cambodia. Nixon had hoped in this way to end North Vietnamese infiltration into the South, but he had also decided to live up to what he privately called his "wild man" or "mad bomber" reputation. The enemy would be unable to anticipate the location or severity of the next U.S. strike, Nixon reasoned, and would thus feel compelled to negotiate.

Nixon could not have predicted the outpouring of protest that followed the invasion of Cambodia. The largest series of demonstrations and police-student confrontations in the nation's history took place on campuses and in city streets. At Kent State University in Ohio, twenty-eight National Guardsmen apparently panicked, shooting into an unarmed crowd of about 200 students, killing four and wounding nine. Ten days later, on May 14, at Jackson State University,

---

In view of the developments since we entered the fighting in Vietnam, do you think the United States made a mistake sending troops to fight in Vietnam?

Yes	52%
No	39
No opinion	9

Interviewing Date 1/22–28/1969, Survey #774-K, Question #6/Index #45

FIGURE 29.4 Public Opinion on the War in Vietnam By 1969 Americans were sharply divided in their assessments of the progress of the war and peace negotiations. The American Institute of Public Opinion, founded in 1935 by George Gallup, charted a growing dissatisfaction with the war in Vietnam.

SOURCE: *The Gallup Poll: Public Opinion, 1935–74* (New York: Random House, 1974), p. 2189.

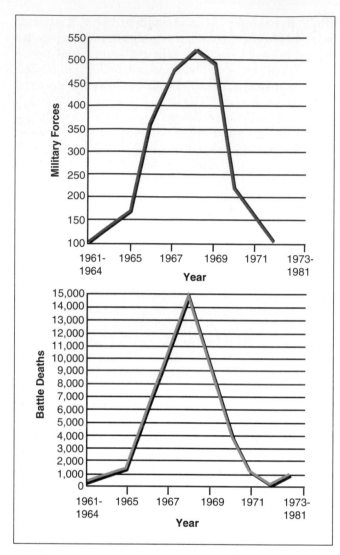

FIGURE 29.5 **U.S. Military Forces in Vietnam and Casualties, 1961–81** The United States government estimated battle deaths between 1969 and 1973 for South Vietnamese troops at 107,504 and North Vietnamese and Vietcong at more than a half-million. Although the United States suffered fewer deaths, the cost was enormous.

SOURCE: U.S. Department of Defense, *Selected Manpower Statistics*, annual and unpublished data; beginning 1981, National Archives and Records Service, "Combat Area Casualty File" (3-330-80-3).

a black school in Mississippi, state troopers entered a campus dormitory and began shooting wildly, killing two students and wounding twelve others. Demonstrations broke out on fifty campuses. (See Out of Many Voices: Tragedy on the Campus at Kent State University. on page 912.)

The nation was shocked. Thirty-seven college and university presidents signed a letter calling on the president to end the war. A few weeks later the Senate adopted a bipartisan resolution outlawing the use of funds for U.S. military operations in Cambodia, starting July 1, 1970. Although the House rejected the resolution, Nixon saw the writing on the wall. He had planned to negotiate a simultaneous withdrawal of North Vietnamese and U.S. troops, but he could no longer afford to hold out for this condition.

The president, still goaded by Kissinger, did not accept defeat easily. In February 1971 Nixon directed the South Vietnamese army to invade Laos and cut supply lines, but the demoralized invading force suffered a quick and humiliating defeat. Faced with enemy occupation of more and more territory during a major offensive in April 1972, Nixon ordered the mining of North Vietnamese harbors and directed B-52s to conduct massively destructive bombing missions in Cambodia and North Vietnam.

Nixon also sent Kissinger to Paris for secret negotiations with delegates from North Vietnam. They agreed to a cease-fire specifying the withdrawal of all U.S. troops and the return of all U.S. prisoners of war. Knowing these terms ensured defeat, South Vietnam's president refused to sign the agreement. On Christmas Day 1972, hoping for a better negotiating position, Nixon ordered one final wave of bomb attacks on North Vietnam's cities. To secure a halt to the bombing, the North Vietnamese offered to resume negotiations. But the terms of the Paris Peace Agreement, signed by North Vietnam and the United States in January 1973, differed little from the settlement Nixon could have procured in 1969, costing hundreds of thousands of deaths that might have been prevented. Beginning in March 1973, the withdrawal of U.S. troops left the outcome of the war a foregone conclusion. By December of that year only fifty American military personnel remained, and the government of South Vietnam had no future.

In April 1975 North Vietnamese troops took over Saigon, and the Communist-led Democratic Republic of Vietnam soon united the small nation. The war was finally over. It had cost the United States 58,000 lives and $150 billion. The country had not only failed to achieve its stated war goal but had lost an important post in Southeast Asia. Equally important, the policy of containment introduced by President Truman had proved impossible to sustain.

While Nixon was maneuvering to bring about "peace with honor," the chilling crimes of war had already begun to haunt Americans. In 1971 the army court-martialed a young lieutenant, William L. Calley Jr. for the murder of "at least" twenty-two Vietnamese civilians during a 1968 search-and-destroy mission subsequently known as the My Lai Massacre. Calley's platoon had destroyed a village and slaughtered more than 350 unarmed South Vietnamese, raping and beating many of the women before killing them. "My Lai was

On Monday, May 4, 1970, after a weekend of antiwar demonstrations against the invasion of Cambodia, Ohio National Guardsmen fired 67 bullets into a crowd of students, killing four and wounding nine others on the campus of Kent State University. As news of the killings spread, students at hundreds of colleges and universities turned out in mass demonstrations to protest widening the war in Southeast Asia and the increasing violence on campus. Approximately 5 million students joined the national student strike, boycotting classes for the remainder of the week. As news of the Kent State "massacre" spread to Vietnam, some U.S. troops refused orders to invade Cambodia; others wore black armbands to demonstrate their solidarity with students at home.

SOURCE: Getty Images Inc./Hulton Archive Photos.

not an isolated incident," one veteran attested, but "only a minor step beyond the standard official United States policy in Indochina." Commander of the platoon at My Lai, Calley was first sentenced to life imprisonment before being given a reduced term of ten years. The secretary of the army paroled Calley after he served three years under house arrest in his apartment.

"The China Card"

Apart from Vietnam, Nixon's foreign policy defied the expectations of liberals and conservatives alike. Actually, he followed traditions of previous Republican moderates such as Herbert Hoover and Dwight Eisenhower, who had so effectively "proved" their anticommunism that they could conciliate international foes without undermining their popularity at home. Nixon added a new page, however—a policy of détente that replaced U.S.–Soviet bipolarity with multilateral relations. Nixon could cultivate relations with the People's Republic of China, a rising world power more rigidly Communist than the Soviet Union, to form an alliance against the Soviet Union. And he could easily persuade the Soviet Union to cooperate on trade agreements, thus limiting the two nations' ruthless competition to control governments in Asia, the Middle East, and Africa. Opponents of the Vietnam War accused Nixon of double dealing, while conservatives howled at any compromise with Communist governments. But Nixon persisted in his plans, anticipating an end to the cold war on American terms.

Playing the "China card" was the most dramatic of the president's moves. Early in his political career Nixon had avidly supported the archconservative China lobby. But as president he considered the People's Republic of China too important to be isolated by the West and too obviously hostile to the Soviet Union to be discounted as a potential ally.

"Ping-pong diplomacy" began in April 1971, when the Chinese hosted a table tennis team from the United States. Henry Kissinger embarked on a secret mission a few months later. Finally, in February 1972, Richard and Pat Nixon flew to Beijing, where they were greeted by foreign minister Zhou Enlai and a band playing "The Star-Spangled Banner."

It was a momentous and surprising event, one that marked a new era in East-West diplomacy. Nixon claimed that he had succeeded in bridging "16,000 miles and twenty-two years of hostility." The president's move successfully increased diplomatic pressure on the Soviet Union but simultaneously weakened the Nationalist Chinese government in Taiwan, which now slipped into virtual diplomatic obscurity.

Next the president went to Moscow to negotiate with Soviet leader Leonid Brezhnev, who was anxious about U.S. involvement with China and eager for economic assistance. Declaring, "There must be room in this world for two great nations with different systems to live together and work together," Nixon offered to sell $1 billion of grain to the Soviets. Winning the favor of American wheat farmers, this deal simultaneously relieved

OUT OF MANY VOICES

TRAGEDY ON THE CAMPUS AT KENT STATE UNIVERSITY

Leone Keegan was an undergraduate student at Kent State University in Ohio, and in 1970 she witnessed some of the most dramatic events of campus protest against the war in Vietnam, which included the killing of four students by armed National Guard. In an interview taped in the 1980s, she recalled the day of the shooting.

SUNDAY NIGHT I WENT BACK TO KENT STATE, AND when I got there, it was just unbelievable. There was so much tension. There was the National Guard, and there were helicopters flying at low altitudes with spotlights all night long. It was like a war situation. You could see that all the stores were busted out, windows broken. It was just chaos, chaos. . . .

Going onto the campus, I saw all these young men in uniforms standing on the street corners with their rifles, and I was thinking, What is this? When I got to the building where the class was held and went in, I was told, "There's no class this morning. It's been canceled." I said, "Why?" "Because there's been a bomb threat in this building."

So I went back to my apartment that morning. . . .

A couple of hours later I woke up to the sound of gunfire. It sounded like—you know, when you sit in your backyard and fireworks are going off on the Fourth of July? . . . A few minutes later, my roommates came back in, and they were bawling their eyes out. They were very upset, and I said, "What happened?" They said, "There was a shooting on the commons, people were killed." All they knew was what had happened as they were running off. They didn't know any of the details. They were scared, and they were crying.

A few minutes later we heard the police coming through with their megaphones, saying, "You must leave the campus immediately. Leave within an hour. Don't take anything. Just get out of here." It was like a police state. . . .

Of course, we couldn't finish the year after we were ordered home. We had to finish our courses at home. . . . I was remembering my father's words to me when he drove me to college the first time the fall before. He said, "Remember, Leone, that everything you learn isn't out of books. It's life experience, too." Well, he was certainly right. I learned a lot that year, and most of it wasn't from books. ■

Source: Joan Morrison and Robert K. Morrison, *From Camelot to Kent State: The Sixties Experience in the Words of Those Who Lived It* (New York: Times Books, 1987), pp. 336–37.

U.S. trade deficits and crop surpluses. Afterward, the Soviet leader became visibly more cautious about supporting revolutions in the third world. Nixon also completed negotiations of the Strategic Arms Limitation Treaty (SALT, known later as SALT I). A limited measure, SALT I represented the first success at strategic arms control since the opening of the cold war and a major public relations victory for the leaders of the two superpowers.

Nixon's last major diplomatic foray proved far less effective. The president sent Kissinger on a two-year mission of "shuttle diplomacy" to mediate Israeli-Arab disputes, to ensure the continued flow of oil, and to increase lucrative U.S. arms sales to Arab countries. The Egyptians and Israelis agreed to a cease-fire in their October 1973 Yom Kippur War, but little progress toward peace in the area was achieved.

Domestic Policy

Nixon deeply desired to restore order in American society. "We live in a deeply troubled and profoundly unsettled time," he noted. "Drugs, crime, campus revolts, racial discord, draft resistance—on every hand we find old standards violated, old values discarded." Despite his hostility to liberalism, however, Nixon had some surprises for conservatives. Determined to win reelection in 1972, he supported new Social Security benefits and subsidized housing for the poor and oversaw the creation of the Environmental Protection Agency and the Occupational Safety and Health Administration. Most notable was his support, under the guidance of Democratic adviser Daniel P. Moynihan, for the Family Assistance Plan, which proposed a minimal income for the poor in place of welfare benefits. Conservatives judged the plan too generous while liberals found it inadequate. Moreover, the plan was expensive. Bipartisan opposition ultimately killed the bill.

Nixon also embraced a policy of fiscal liberalism. Early in 1971 he accepted the idea of deficit spending. Later that year he ordered a first: he took the nation off the gold standard. Subsequently, the dollar's value would float on the world market rather than being tied to the value of gold. His ninety-day freeze on wages, rents, and prices, designed to halt the inflation caused by the massive spending on the Vietnam War, also closely resembled Democratic policies. Finally, Nixon's support of "black capitalism"—adjustments or quotas favoring minority contractors in construction projects—created an explosive precedent for "set-aside" programs later blamed on liberals.

Nixon lined up with conservatives, however, on most civil rights issues and thus enlarged southern Republican constituencies. He accepted the principle of school integration but rejected the busing programs required to implement racial balance. His nominees to the Supreme Court were far more conservative than those appointed by Eisenhower. Warren E. Burger, who replaced Chief Justice Earl Warren, steered the Court away from the liberal direction it had taken since the 1950s.

One of the most newsworthy events of Nixon's administration was a distant result of President Kennedy's determination to outshine the Soviets in outer space (see Chapter 27). On July 21, 1969, the lunar module of Apollo 11 descended to the moon's Sea of Tranquility. As millions watched on television, astronauts Neil Armstrong and Buzz Aldrin stepped out to plant an American flag and to bear the message, "We came in peace for all mankind."

WATERGATE

At times Richard Nixon expressed his yearning for approval in strange ways. A few days after the bombing of Cambodia in May 1970, he wandered out of the White House alone at 5:00 in the morning to talk to antiwar demonstrators. He tried to engage them in small talk about football and pleaded, "I know that probably most of you think I'm an SOB, but I want you to know I understand just how you feel." According to H. R. Haldeman, one of Nixon's closest advisers, the student killings at Kent State deeply troubled the president.

Yet only a few months later Nixon ordered illegal wiretaps of news professionals. He also reaffirmed his support of Central Intelligence Agency (CIA) surveillance of U.S. citizens and organizations—a policy specifically forbidden by the CIA charter—and encouraged members of his administration to spy on Democrats planning for the 1972 election campaign. When news of these illegal activities

surfaced, one of the most canny politicians in American history found himself the first president since Andrew Johnson to face the likelihood of impeachment proceedings.

Foreign Policy as Conspiracy

Nixon's conduct of foreign policy offered early clues into his political character. Although he had welcomed the publicity surrounding his historic moves toward détente with the Soviet Union and normalized relations with China, Nixon generally handled the nation's foreign affairs in surreptitious fashion. But as opposition to the Vietnam War mounted in Congress, he began to face hard questions about this practice. As early as 1970, Republicans as well as Democrats had condemned covert operations in foreign countries. In response, the president, the Department of State, and the CIA developed plans to tighten security even further. Nixon issued a tough mandate against all leaks of information by government personnel, news specialists, or politicians.

At the time, apart from the highly publicized tour to China, Nixon revealed little about his policy for other parts of the globe. Unknown to most Americans, he accelerated the delivery of arms supplies to foreign dictators, including the shah of Iran, Ferdinand Marcos of the Philippines, and the regime of Pieter William Botha in South Africa. His CIA assistants trained and aided SAVAK, the Iranian secret police force notorious for torturing political dissidents. They also stood behind the South African government in its effort to curtail the activities of the antiapartheid African National Congress. In Latin America, Nixon provided financial assistance and military aid to repressive regimes such as that of Anastasio Somoza of Nicaragua, notorious for its blatant corruption and repeated violations of human rights.

Still more controversial was Nixon's plan to overthrow the legally elected socialist government of Salvador Allende in Chile. With the assistance of nongovernment agencies, such as the AFL-CIO's American Institute for Free Labor Development, the CIA destabilized the regime by funding right-wing parties, launching demonstrations, and preparing the Chilean army for a coup. In September 1973, a military junta killed President Allende and captured, tortured, or murdered thousands of his supporters. Nixon and Kissinger warmly welcomed the new ruler, Augusto Pinochet, granting him financial assistance to restabilize the country.

Toward the end of Nixon's term, members of Congress who had been briefed on these policies began to break silence, and reports of clandestine operations flooded the media. Several former CIA agents issued anguished confessions of their activities in other countries. More troubling to Nixon, in spite of all his efforts the United States continued to lose ground as a superpower.

The Age of Dirty Tricks

As Nixon approached the 1972 reelection campaign, he tightened his inner circle of White House staff who assisted him in withholding information from the public, discrediting critics, and engaging in assorted "dirty tricks." Circle members solicited illegal contributions for the campaign and laundered the money through Mexican bank accounts. They also formed a secret squad, "the plumbers," to halt the troublesome leaks of information. This team, headed by former CIA agent E. Howard Hunt and former FBI agent G. Gordon Liddy, assisted in conspiracy at the highest levels of government.

The first person on the squad's "hit list" was Daniel Ellsberg, a former researcher with the Department of Defense, who in 1971 had turned over to the press secret documents outlining the military history of American involvement in Vietnam. The so-called Pentagon Papers exposed the role of presidents and military leaders in deceiving the public and Congress about the conduct of the United States in Southeast Asia. Nixon sought to bar publication by *The New York Times*, but the Supreme Court ruled in favor of the newspaper on the basis of the First Amendment. Within weeks, a complete version of the Pentagon Papers became a best-selling book, and in 1972 *The New York Times* won a Pulitzer Prize for the series of articles. Frustrated in his attempt to suppress the report, Nixon directed the Department of Justice to prosecute Ellsberg on charges of conspiracy, espionage, and theft. Meanwhile, Hunt and Liddy, seeking to discredit Ellsberg, broke into the office of his former psychiatrist. They found nothing that would make their target less heroic in the eyes of an increasingly skeptical public, and by 1973 the charges against Ellsberg were dropped after the Nixon administration itself stood guilty of misconduct.

At the same time, Nixon ran a skillful negative campaign charging George McGovern, the liberal Democrat who had won his party's nomination on the first ballot, with supporting "abortion, acid [LSD], and amnesty" for those who had resisted the draft or deserted the armed forces. The Republicans also informed the news media that McGovern's running mate, Senator Thomas Eagleton, had once undergone electric shock therapy for depression, thus forcing his resignation from the Democratic team. Voter turnout fell to an all-time low, and McGovern lost every state but Massachusetts. (Later, when Nixon faced disgrace, bumper stickers appeared reading, "Don't Blame Me, I'm from Massachusetts.")

The Committee to Re-Elect the President (CREEP) enjoyed a huge war chest and spent a good portion on dirty tricks designed to divide the Democrats and discredit them in the eyes of the voting public. The most ambitious plan—wiretapping the Democratic National Committee headquarters—backfired.

On June 17, 1972, a security team had tripped up a group of intruders hired by CREEP to install listening devices in the Washington DC, Watergate apartment and office complex where the Democrats were headquartered. The police arrested five men, who were later found guilty of conspiracy and burglary. Although Nixon disclaimed any knowledge of the plan, two *Washington Post* reporters, Bob Woodward and Carl Bernstein, followed a trail of evidence back to the nation's highest office.

Televised Senate hearings opened to public view more than a pattern of presidential wrongdoing: they showed an attempt to impede investigations of the Watergate case. Testifying before the committee, a former Nixon aide revealed the existence of secret tape recordings of conversations held in the Oval Office. After special prosecutor Archibald Cox refused to allow Nixon to claim executive privilege and withhold the tapes, the president ordered Cox fired. This "Saturday Night Massacre," as it came to be called, further tarnished Nixon's reputation and swelled curiosity about the tapes. On June 24, 1974, the Supreme Court voted unanimously that Nixon had to release the tapes to a new special prosecutor, Leon Jaworski.

The Fall of the Executive

Although incomplete, the Watergate tapes proved damning. They documented Nixon's ravings against his enemies, including anti-Semitic slurs, and his conniving efforts to harass private citizens through federal agencies. The tapes also proved that Nixon had not only known about plans to cover up the Watergate break-in but had ordered it. The news media enjoyed a field day with the revelations. In July 1974, the House Judiciary Committee adopted three articles of impeachment, charging Nixon with obstructing justice.

Charges of executive criminality had clouded the Nixon administration since his vice president had resigned in disgrace. In 1972 Spiro Agnew had admitted accepting large kickbacks while serving as governor of Maryland. Pleading no contest to this and to charges of federal income tax evasion, Agnew had resigned from office in October 1973. Gerald Ford, a moderate Republican representative from Michigan, had replaced him and now stood in the wings while the president's drama unfolded.

Facing certain impeachment by the House of Representatives, Richard Nixon became, on August 9, 1974, the first U.S. president to resign from office.

CONCLUSION

The resignations of Richard Nixon and Spiro Agnew brought little to relieve the feeling of national exhaustion that attended the Vietnam War. U.S. troops had pulled out of Vietnam in 1973 and the war officially ended in

CHRONOLOGY

1964 President Lyndon Johnson calls for "an unconditional war on poverty" in his state of the union address

Tonkin Gulf resolution

The Economic Opportunity Act establishes the Office of Economic Opportunity

Free speech movement gets under way at University of California at Berkeley

Johnson defeats conservative Barry Goldwater for president

1965 President Johnson authorizes Operation Rolling Thunder, the bombing of North Vietnam

Teach-ins begin on college campuses

First major march on Washington for peace is organized

Watts uprising begins a wave of rebellions in black communities

1966 J. William Fulbright publishes *The Arrogance of Power*

Black Panther Party is formed

National Organization for Women (NOW) is formed

1967 Antiwar rally in New York City draws 300,000

Vietnam Veterans against the War is formed

Uprisings in Newark, Detroit, and other cities

Hippie "Summer of Love"

1968 U.S. ground troop levels in Vietnam number 500,000

Tet Offensive in Vietnam, followed by international protests against U.S. policies

Martin Luther King Jr. is assassinated; riots break out in more than 100 cities

Vietnam peace talks begin in Paris

Robert Kennedy is assassinated

Democratic National Convention, held in Chicago, nominates Hubert Humphrey; "police riot" against protesters

Richard Nixon elected president

American Indian Movement (AIM) founded

1969 Woodstock music festival marks the high tide of the counterculture

Stonewall Riot in Greenwich Village sparks the gay liberation movement

Apollo 11 lands on the moon

1970 U.S. incursion into Cambodia sparks campus demonstrations; students killed at Kent State and Jackson State universities

Women's Strike for Equality marks the fiftieth anniversary of the woman suffrage amendment

1971 Lieutenant William Calley Jr. court-martialed for My Lai Massacre

The New York Times starts publishing the Pentagon Papers

1972 Nixon visits China and Soviet Union

SALT I limits offensive intercontinental ballistic missiles

Intruders attempting to "bug" Democratic headquarters in the Watergate complex are arrested

Nixon is reelected in a landslide

Nixon orders Christmas Day bombing of North Vietnam

1973 Paris Peace Agreement ends war in Vietnam

FBI seizes Indian occupants of Wounded Knee, South Dakota

Watergate burglars tried; congressional hearings on Watergate

CIA destabilizes elected Chilean government, which is overthrown

Vice President Spiro T. Agnew resigns

1974 House Judiciary Committee adopts articles of impeachment against Nixon

Nixon resigns the presidency

1975, but bitterness lingered over the unprecedented—and, for many, humiliating—defeat. Moreover, confidence in the government's highest office was severely shaken. The passage of the War Powers Act in 1973, written to compel any future president to seek congressional approval for armed intervention abroad, dramatized both the widespread suspicion of presidential intentions and a yearning for peace. But the positive dream of community that had inspired Johnson, King, and a generaton of student activists could not be revived. No other vision took its place.

Richard Nixon bid a final farewell to his White House staff as he left Washington DC on August 9, 1974. The first president to resign from office, Nixon had become so entangled in the Watergate scandal that his impeachment appeared certain. He was succeeded by Vice-President Gerald Ford. After taking the oath of office later that day, President Ford remarked that the wounds of Watergate were "more painful and more poisonous than those of foreign wars."

SOURCE: CORBIS- NY.

In 1968 seven prominent antiwar protesters had been brought to trial for allegedly conspiring to disrupt the Democratic National Convention in Chicago. Just a few years later, the majority of Americans had concluded that presidents Johnson and Nixon had conspired to do far worse. They had intentionally deceived the public about the nature and fortunes of the war. This moral failure signaled a collapse at the center of the American political system. Since Dwight Eisenhower left office warning of the potential danger embedded in the "military-industrial complex," no president had survived the presidency with his honor intact. Watergate, then, appeared to cap the politics of the cold war, its revelations only reinforcing futility and cynicism. The United States was left psychologically at war with itself.

REVIEW QUESTIONS

1. Discuss the events that led up to and contributed to U.S. involvement in Vietnam. How did U.S. involvement in the war affect domestic programs?
2. Discuss the reasons the protest movement against the Vietnam War started on college campuses. Describe how these movements were organized and how the opponents of the war differed from the supporters.
3. Discuss the programs sponsored by Johnson's plan for a Great Society. What was their impact on urban poverty in the late 1960s?
4. What was the impact of the assassinations of Martin Luther King Jr. and Robert Kennedy on the election of 1968? How were various communities affected?

5. How were the "politics of identity" movements different from earlier civil rights organizations? In what ways did the various movements resemble one another?

6. Why did Richard Nixon enjoy such a huge electoral victory in 1972? Discuss his foreign and domestic policies. What led to his sudden downfall?

RECOMMENDED READING

John A. Andrew III, *Lyndon Johnson and the Great Society* (1998). An assessment of the Great Society, with special emphasis on the two major issues of civil rights and poverty. Andrew discusses Johnson's aspirations and the obstacles that kept them out of reach.

Keith Beattie, *The Scar That Binds: American Culture and the Vietnam War* (1998). Examines memoirs, war novels and films, and the Vietnam Veterans Memorial in Washington DC, to discuss the cultural legacy of the war.

Alexander Bloom, ed., *Long Time Gone: Sixties America Then and Now* (2001). Ten essays covering various aspects of the social and political movements of the 1960s. The authors draw out the meaning of the "sixties" for today and dispel commonplace myths by providing accurate information and a sound context for interpretation.

Robert Dallek, *Lyndon B. Johnson* (2005). A condensation of a two-volume study, Dallek's biography presents rich details of Johnson's life from his origins in Texas to his troubled years in the White House. The author does little to soften the image of Johnson and instead portrays him as both complex and flamboyant.

Jane F. Gerhard, *Desiring Revolution: Second-Wave Feminism and the Rewriting of American Sexual Thought, 1920–1982* (2001). Discusses the background of the feminist side of the sexual revolution with special attention to popular versions of Freud's theories. Gerhard discusses disagreements among feminists on the meaning and experience of sexual liberation.

Michael H. Hunt, *Lyndon Johnson's War: America's Cold War Crusade in Vietnam, 1945–1968* (1996). Tracks Johnson's decisions to wage all-out war in Vietnam. Hunt interprets Johnson's actions as consistent with the cold war foreign policy that had prevailed since the Truman administration and its pledge to "contain" communism.

Rebecca E. Klatch, *A Generation Divided: The New Left, the New Right, and the 1960s* (1999). Compares and contrasts the respective roles of Students for a Democratic Society and the conservative Young Americans for Freedom on college campuses. Klatch, a sociologist, presents lengthy oral interviews with former student activists in both camps.

Joan Morrison and Robert K. Morrison, eds., *From Camelot to Kent State: the Sixties Experience in the Words of Those Who Lived It* (2001). A collection of 59 oral histories with a range of people who lived through the 1960s. The volume includes stories of better-known activists, such as Eldridge Cleaver and Abbie Hoffman, as well as those who were soldiers in Vietnam or student activists. This edition also contains many photographs.

Joseph Tilden Rhea, *Race Pride and the American Identity* (1997). Examines American Indians, Asian Americans, Latinos, and African Americans in their search for recognition. Rhea emphasizes the importance of political struggles and their impact on historical consciousness, including the establishment of historical sites and museums.

Ruth Rosen, *The World Split Open: How the Modern Women's Movement Changed America* (2000). Discusses the impact of women's liberation on American politics, business, and family life. Through extensive archival research and interviews, Rosen provides compelling evidence for the magnitude of change accompanying second-wave feminism.

Melvin Small, *AntiWarriors: The Vietnam War and the Battle for America's Hearts and Minds* (2002). A readable, succinct study of the groundswell of opposition to the war in Vietnam. Small covers many facets of the antiwar movement, ranging from hippies to Vietnam Veterans Against the War.

Anthony Summers, *The Arrogance of Power: The Secret World of Richard Nixon* (2000). A popular biography of Nixon's life from his early political career in California through his presidency. Summers drew on more than a thousand interviews, including those with Nixon's psychotherapist, to portray the former president's erratic behavior and mental instability during as well as before the disastrous Watergate affair.

 For additional study resources for this chapter, go to the *Companion Website*, **http://www.prenhall.com/faragher.**

WHOSE HISTORY IS IT?
THE VIETNAM VETERANS MEMORIAL

In 1979, former infantryman Jan C. Scruggs decided to raise money for a memorial dedicated to those who served with him in Vietnam. Joined by volunteers, many of them wives and mothers of soldiers killed in Southeast Asia, he established the Vietnam Veterans Memorial Fund. The fund announced a national competition specifying that the winning design must include the names of all Americans who died in Vietnam, were missing in action, or were still held as prisoners of war; that it be contemplative rather than flamboyant; and that it harmonize with the other monuments in the Washington Mall, where it would be located. The purpose of the memorial, Scruggs explained, was to "begin a healing process, a reconciliation of the grievous divisions wrought by the war."

In 1971 a group of angry veterans create the first memorial to the war, throwing their Purple Hearts and Bronze Stars into a heap before the U.S. Capitol and adding their discharge papers to the pile. AP Wide World Photos.

A jury of eight prominent architects and sculptors surveyed more than 1,400 entries and chose the design of Maya Ying Lin, a twenty-one year old undergraduate architecture student at Yale University. Lin presented her winning design, a set of soft pastel drawings of a black, V-shaped wall merging into the surrounding green space, saying that it carried no particular political message.

Unlike most other war memorials, the Vietnam Veterans Memorial does not celebrate victory, display heroism, or underscore the morality of an event that necessarily brought death and destruction. Lin explained that the design was meant simply to evoke "feelings, thoughts, and emotions."

Even before it was built, the memorial proved extremely controversial. The New York Times approved the design's "extreme dignity and restraint," adding that the memorial "seems to capture all the feelings of ambiguity and anguish that the Vietnam War evoked [and] conveys the only point about the war on which people may agree: that those who died should be remembered." But to many critics, the design appeared anti-patriotic. The Chicago Tribune called it "a monumental insult to veterans." Another critic described the memorial as "a wailing wall for future anti-draft demonstrators." An angry veteran called the wall "a black gash of shame and sorrow."

As the debate heated up, Interior Secretary James Watt held up construction. Ultimately two changes in the original design allowed the project to go forward. A flagpole was inserted near the entryway, and a representational bronze sculpture of three male soldiers dressed in fatigues and carrying guns was positioned nearby. Scruggs accepted these compromises, although he stood by the integrity of Lin's original design. Some veterans, he noted, "wanted the Memorial to make Vietnam what it had never been in reality: a good, clean glorious war seen as necessary and supported by a united country."

The Vietnam Veterans Memorial carries the 58,132 names of men and women who were killed in Vietnam carved into the highly polished, reflective black granite in the order in which they were killed. The entire installation is below ground-level and not visible from most parts of the Mall. A replica, the "Moving Wall," travels to various cities and towns throughout the country.

Joyce Naltchayan/Agence France Presse/Getty Images.

"The Three Fightingmen," by sculptor Frederick Hart portrays strong, highly masculine soldiers returning from patrol. Positioned facing the wall, the soldiers appear to be gazing at the names on the wall. The sculture was added in 1984 in response to critics who complained that the wall was insufficiently patriotic and too unlike conventional war monuments, which usually depicts heroic images of military men.

Getty Images, Inc.

Editors of the conservative National Review have complained that the memorial focuses on individuals not the war, making "death in war a private matter rather than a sacrifice for collective cause." In this photograph, a sister touches the name of her brother. The objects left at the wall are carefully preserved in a warehouse in suburban Maryland.

Getty Images, Inc.

The Vietnam Women's Memorial, designed by Glenna Goodacre and dedicated in 1993, is the first national memorial to female veterans. The bronze sculpture, which stands about 300 feet from the wall, honors the ten thousand women, military and civilian, who served with the U.S. armed forces in Vietnam.

Sonda Dawes/The Image Works.

The Conservative Ascendancy

1974–1991

GAS SHORTAGE! Sales Limited to 10 GALS. OF GAS. PER CUSTOMER

Grass Roots Conservatism in Orange County, California

In 1962 Bee Gathright, a Brownie leader and mother of three young girls, opened her suburban Garden Grove home to bring together neighbors to hear a talk about politics by a man from the nearby Knott's Berry Farm Freedom Center. "This is when I discovered that I was a conservative," she later recalled. She soon arranged for the speaker to address a larger audience at the local public school. Gathright began to read widely in books and newspapers "because I began to hear that the Communists were going to bury us, were going to take over the world . . . I was afraid." She convinced her skeptical husband Neil, an aerospace engineer, to share her newfound activism. They soon joined the California Republican Assembly, a volunteer organization dedicated to electing conservatives to office. In 1964 the Gathrights' home served as a local headquarters for the presidential campaign of conservative Arizona Senator Barry Goldwater.

Orange County in the 1960s and 1970s had thousands of "kitchen table" activists like the Gathrights, and they began a transformation of American conservatism and American politics that would culminate in the election of Ronald Reagan as president in 1980. Most of them were middle-class men and women, including large numbers of professionals and owners of small businesses. Many, like the Gathrights, had moved to California, attracted by job opportunities in aerospace. Orange

Orange County

County's 800 square miles lie at the geographic center of the Southern California basin, and large lemon and orange groves dominated the economy until the 1940s. World War II and Cold War defense-related spending accelerated the county's growth as companies like Hughes Aircraft, Autonetics, and Beckman Instruments created thousands of new manufacturing jobs. A strong demand for housing spurred a construction boom and a roaring real estate market. By 1960, more than 700,000 people lived in Orange County, an increase of nearly 400 percent since 1940, and the population doubled again to almost 1.5 million by 1970.

While Barry Goldwater's 1964 campaign had ignited great enthusiasm in Orange County, his national defeat forced conservatives to consider ways to shed the "extremism" label and put more emphasis on winning office. In 1966 they succeeded in electing Ronald Reagan as governor. A former Hollywood actor and New Deal liberal, Reagan had evolved in the 1950s into a prominent conservative and Republican Party activist. His gubernatorial campaign stressed limiting state support for welfare and other social services, while expanding state power to enforce law and order.

Reagan's success in California, as well as Richard Nixon's election as president in 1968, signaled an important new turn for American conservatives. They still championed anticommunism, but no longer engaged in the kind of loose talk about using nuclear weapons that had hurt Goldwater. They attacked the growth of "big government," but no longer spoke openly about repealing popular New Deal programs like Social Security. Instead, they responded to the concerns over "social issues" that increasingly troubled and mobilized Orange County's grass-roots activists. These issues were largely defined by a "backlash" against the antiwar movement, counterculture, feminist activism, and urban uprisings, and an emphasis on so-called family issues, in which opposition to sex education, obscenity, abortion rights, and gay liberation and the equal rights amendment were all linked together. On the economic side, conservatives began to tap a deep well of resentment over rising property taxes and high inflation.

Two of the central themes of this new conservatism found powerful expression in Orange County and resonated with millions of Americans well beyond it. One was the so-called tax revolt led by Howard Jarvis, a flamboyant campaigner in Southern California conservative circles. Jarvis told his supporters, "Lower taxes and less government became my holy grail." Jarvis relied on local networks to gather 1.3 million signatures to get his Proposition 13 on the ballot—a constitutional amendment that slashed the property tax rate and strictly limited future tax increases. After its passage in 1978, the "tax revolt" soon spread to other states and attracted millions to the conservative message of limiting government and lowering taxes.

Orange County was a center of the second new force reshaping conservatism, the spectacular growth of "born again" evangelical Christianity. Fundamentalist sects had long been associated with the rural poor of the South. But Orange County's religious revival featured educated professionals and middle-class suburbanites who turned to Christianity for spirituality and meaning and as a way to assert order amidst rapid cultural and social change. "Born again" Christians found community not only in Sunday services but in a wide range of tightly organized activities: Bible study groups, summer retreats, "singles' fellowships," prayer breakfasts, and "Christian" consumer culture, which allowed people to simultaneously embrace faith, modern business techniques, and worldly goods. The political implications of the new evangelicalism soon became clear. Most fundamentalist preachers tied their sermons and prophesies to conservative political themes, especially fears about the decline of morality and of American power in the world.

President Jimmy Carter, who took office in 1976, was a "born-again" Christian, and his successor, Ronald Reagan, raced to victory in 1980 with the strong backing of newly politicized Christian voters. For Bee Gathright, Reagan's victory vindicated her years of grass-roots activism and set the nation on a conservative course that affected national politics into the twenty-first century.

As president, Reagan introduced a new economic program—"Reaganomics"—that reduced income taxes for wealthy Americans and at the same time increased federal spending for the largest military buildup in American history. Abolishing the Great Society antipoverty programs, he fostered the growth of a two-tiered society characterized by a disproportionate number of women and children filling the ranks of the nation's poor. Meanwhile, the increases in military spending complemented Reagan's foreign policy, which included a revival of cold war patriotism, interventions in the Caribbean and Central America, and a reference to the Soviet Union as "an Evil Empire." However, Reagan's term in office expired before one of the most dramatic events of the final years of the twentieth century: the dissolution of the Soviet Union.

KEY TOPICS

- Structural shifts in the economy
- The Ford and Carter presidencies
- Crisis in the cities and environment
- Community politics and the rise of the New Right
- Iran hostage crisis
- The Reagan Republican presidential victory
- Reagan's domestic and foreign policies
- The growth of inequality

THE OVEREXTENDED SOCIETY

In the 1970s Americans faced an unfamiliar combination of skyrocketing prices, rising unemployment, and low economic growth. Economists termed this novel condition "stagflation." The annual rate of economic growth slowed by almost one-quarter from its robust 3.2 percent average of the 1950s. By 1975, the unemployment rate had reached nearly 9 percent, its highest level since the Great Depression, and it remained close to 7 percent for most of the rest of the decade. Inflation, meanwhile, reached double-digits.

The United States had come to a turning point in its economic history. Emerging from World War II as the most prosperous nation in the world and retaining this status through the 1960s, the country suddenly found itself falling behind western Europe and Japan. Polls conducted at the end of the 1970s revealed that a majority of Americans believed that conditions would worsen.

The gloomy economy shadowed the nation's political leaders. Republican Gerald Ford and Democrat Jimmy Carter promised little and, as far as many voters were concerned, delivered less. Neither managed to secure a second term in the White House.

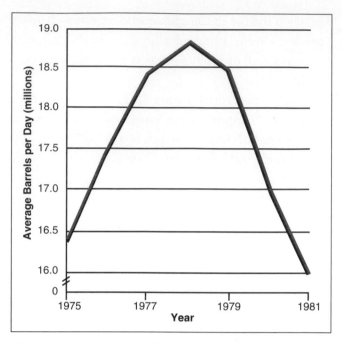

FIGURE 30.1 Decline of U.S. Oil Consumption, 1975–81

SOURCE: Department of Energy, *Monthly Energy Review*, June 1982.

A Troubled Economy

In October 1973 gasoline prices nearly doubled, jumping from 40 to nearly 70 cents per gallon. Several states responded to the shortage by introducing rationing programs. Gas lines grew up to four miles long, and fistfights broke out among frustrated motorists (see Figure 30.1).

The oil crisis began suddenly, although it had been decades in the making. The United States, which used about 70 percent of all oil produced in the world, had found the domestic supply sufficient until the mid-1950s. But rising demand had outstripped national reserves, and by 1973 the nation was importing one-third of its crude oil, mainly from the Middle East. In that year, following the Arab-Israeli War, oil prices skyrocketed. On October 17, the Organization of Petroleum Exporting Countries (OPEC), a cartel of mainly Arab oil producers, announced an embargo on oil shipments to Israel's allies, including the United States (see Map 30.1).

Caught off guard, President Nixon responded to the embargo by creating an "energy czar" and paving the way for the creation of the Department of Energy in 1977. He ordered a 10 percent reduction in air travel and appealed to Congress to lower speed limits on interstate highways to 55 miles per hour (incidentally reducing highway deaths in the process), and to extend daylight-saving time into the winter months. Many state governments introduced their own programs, turning down the thermostats in public buildings to a chilly 68 degrees, reducing nonessential lighting, and restricting hours of service.

With the cost of gasoline, oil, and electricity up, many other prices also rose, from apartment rents and telephone bills to restaurant checks. As oil prices continued to rise through the 1970s, many Americans also began to look suspiciously at the pricing practices of U.S. oil companies. Whatever the causes, the oil crisis played a major role in the economic downturn, the worst since the Great Depression.

The economic downturn, according to many experts, had deeper roots in the failure of the United States to keep up with the rising industrial efficiency of other nations. Manufacturers from Asia, Latin America, and Europe now offered consumers cheaper and better products, including automobiles, long considered the monopoly of Detroit. U.S. automakers, determined to reduce costs, turned to "outsourcing"—that is, making cars and trucks from parts cheaply produced abroad and imported into the United States as semifinished materials (which were subject to a lower tariff than finished goods.) In high-tech electronics, the United States scarcely competed against Japanese-produced televisions, radios, tape players, cameras, and computers.

An AFL-CIO leader complained that the United States was becoming "a nation of hamburger stands . . . a country stripped of industrial capacity and meaningful work." There was truth in this observation. At the close

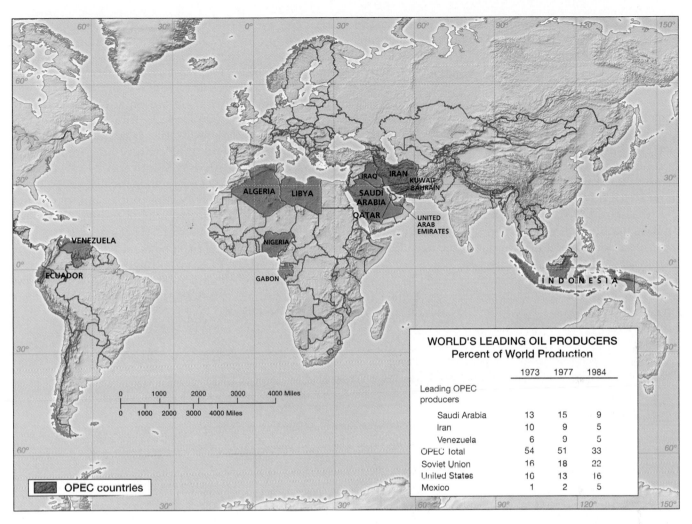

WORLD'S LEADING OIL PRODUCERS Percent of World Production			
	1973	1977	1984
Leading OPEC producers			
Saudi Arabia	13	15	9
Iran	10	9	5
Venezuela	6	9	5
OPEC Total	54	51	33
Soviet Union	16	18	22
United States	10	13	16
Mexico	1	2	5

MAP 30.1 World Leading Oil Producers

of World War II, industry accounted for 30 percent of the GNP; by 1980, industry's share dropped to 24 percent. At the same time, the lower-paying, hard-to-organize service trades grew from 33 percent of the total economy in 1946 to over 45 percent in 1980. Enduring a shift of this magnitude, the trade union movement lost steam.

In past decades labor unions had typically responded to inflation by negotiating new contracts or, if necessary, striking for higher pay. But while factories closed, the National Labor Relations Board increasingly ruled in favor of management, making the organization of new union locals far more difficult. Between 1970 and 1982 the AFL-CIO lost nearly 30 percent of its membership. The only real growth took place among public employees, including teachers, civil service workers, and health professionals—all of them dependent on sagging public budgets. Union-backed measures now routinely failed in Congress, despite the Democratic majority.

Typical of hard times, women sought jobs to support their families. By 1980 more than half of all married women with children at home were in the labor force. Yet despite their growing numbers, women lost ground relative to men. In 1955 women earned 64 percent of the average wages paid to men; in 1980 they earned only 59 percent. The reason for this dip was that women were clustered in the clerical and service trades where the lowest wages prevailed.

African American women made some gains. Through Title VII of the Civil Rights Act, which outlawed workplace discrimination by sex or race, and the establishment of the Equal Employment Opportunity Commission to enforce it, they managed to climb the lower levels of the job ladder. By 1980, northern black women's median earnings were about 95 percent of white women's earnings.

In contrast, Hispanic women, whose labor force participation leaped by 80 percent during the decade, were restricted to a very few poorly paid occupations. Puerto Ricans found jobs in the garment industry of the Northeast; Mexican Americans more typically worked as domestics or agricultural laborers in the

Southwest. Neither group earned much more than the minimum wage. (See Out of Many Voices: Confessions of a "Panic" Buyer.)

Sunbelt/Snowbelt Communities

By the 1970s the Sunbelt offered a rare showplace of American prosperity. It boasted a gross product greater than many nations and more cars, television sets, houses, and even miles of paved roads than the rest of the United States. Large influxes of immigrants from Latin America, the Caribbean, and Asia combined with the shift of Americans from the depressed Northeast to boost the region's population. From 56 million people in 1940, the Sunbelt's population more than doubled to 118 million just four decades later (see Map 30.2).

This increase had been made possible by a huge outlay of federal funds, including defense spending and the allocation of Social Security funds. The number of residents over the age of sixty-five increased by 30 percent during the 1970s, reaching 26 million by 1980. Armed with retirement packages won decades earlier, huge "golden age" migrations created new communities in Florida, Arizona, and southern California.

The South witnessed a dramatic turnaround in demographic and economic trends. While manufacturing and highly subsidized agribusiness flourished, southern cities reversed the century-long trend of out-migration among African Americans. The Southwest and West changed yet more dramatically. Aided by air conditioning, water diversions, public improvements, and large-scale development, California became the nation's most populous state; Texas moved to third, behind New York. Former farms and deserts were turned almost overnight into huge metropolitan areas by the automobile and suburbs. Phoenix grew from 664,000 in 1960 to 1,509,000 in 1980, Las Vegas from 127,000 to 463,000.

OUT OF MANY VOICES

CONFESSIONS OF A "PANIC" BUYER

In 1974, with gasoline in short supply, Ezra Herman of New York wrote this letter to The New York Times *describing his feelings as he approached the gas pumps. Like many other drivers, he suspected that the Arab oil boycott was only partly to blame for the short supply of fuel.*

THE FUEL CRISIS HAS STIRRED UP ENOUGH concern and aggravation for car owners, especially those of us whose cars are essential to our livelihood. . . .

It has been my habit, for years, to run my tank down to about one-fourth full and then stop in at my regular station to fill up on my way home or perhaps on my way out in the morning. But can I do that now? Do I have any choice? I'm not using any more gas than before. My tank doesn't hold any more than it did.

If I don't "panic" and run my tank down to the one-fourth mark are these "federal energy officials" who are so quick to denounce me going to guarantee that I will find a station open at the end of my workday? Will they guarantee that I won't burn up the remainder of my gas while standing on line? And when I get to the pump, will they guarantee that I won't be limited to a $3 ration?

Of course I am "obsessed with keeping my tank full." So is my doctor, and so is the suburban housewife whose car is essential to living, if not necessarily to her livelihood.

My gut feeling is that this is a carefully nurtured rip-off triggered by the leaky Arab boycott, which if absolute would reduce our crude oil supply by not more than 6 per cent.

Rather than spend their time castigating the car owner and the gas station operator, the Federal officials might turn their attention to getting the oil companies to use some of their skyrocketing windfalls to build more refineries, the real bottleneck. During World War II, refineries were built on a crash program basis in one and a half years instead of the usual three.

I drive today with one eye on the road, one eye on my gas gauge and one eye looking for an open gas station. I will because I must continue to "top off" my tank at every opportunity. I wager that I have company in the millions. ■

SOURCE: "Letters to the Editor," February 11, 1974. *Proquest Historical Newspapers: The New York Times (1851–2001)*, p. 34

MAP EXPLORATION

To explore an interactive version of this map,
go to **www.prenhall.com/faragher5/map30.2**

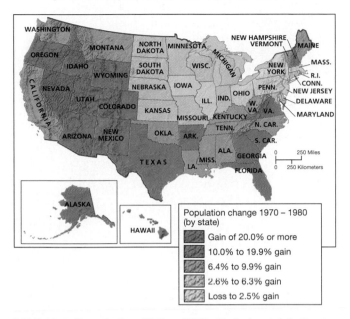

Population change 1970 – 1980
(by state)

- Gain of 20.0% or more
- 10.0% to 19.9% gain
- 6.4% to 9.9% gain
- 2.6% to 6.3% gain
- Loss to 2.5% gain

MAP 30.2 Population Shifts, 1970–80 Industrial decline in the Northeast coincided with an economic boom in the Sunbelt, encouraging millions of Americans to head for warmer climates and better jobs.

Much of the Sunbelt wealth tended to be temporary or sharply cyclical, producing a boom-and-bust economy of sudden expansion and disordered sprawl. Corporate office buildings in cities such as Houston emptied almost as fast as they filled. Income was also distributed very unevenly. Older Hispanic populations made only modest gains, while recent Mexican immigrants and Indian peoples suffered from a combination of low wages and poor public services. The Sunbelt states concentrated their tax and federal dollars on strengthening police forces, building roads or sanitation systems for the expanding suburbs, and creating budget surpluses, in contrast to eastern and midwestern states that continued to spend significantly on public housing, education, and mass transit.

The "Snowbelt" (or "Rustbelt") states meanwhile suffered severe population losses accompanying the sharp decline of industry. Of the nineteen metropolitan areas that lost population during the 1970s, all were old manufacturing centers, topped by New York, Cleveland, Pittsburgh, Boston, Philadelphia, and Buffalo.

A feeling of defeat intensified in the aging industrial cities of the Monogahela River valley in western Pennsylvania. Since the late nineteenth century, "Mon Valley" had proudly stood as the steelmaking center of the nation and much of the world. With the decline of steel production, however, major firms such as U.S. Steel increased investments in overseas mining and mineral processing companies, some of which worked closely with foreign steelmakers. This policy of "disinvestment" had a devastating impact on the people and communities who for generations had helped build the nation's basic industries. During the 1980s the Mon Valley lost 30,000 people, or 10 percent of its population.

New York City offered a still more spectacular example. A fiscal crisis in 1975 forced liberal mayor Abraham Beame to choose between wage freezes for public employees and devastating cuts and layoffs. Eventually, with the municipal government teetering on the brink of bankruptcy, he chose both. In response to cutbacks in mass transit and the deterioration of municipal services, a large sector of the middle class fled. At the same time, the proportion of poor people rose from 15 percent in 1969 to nearly 25 percent fourteen years later.

"Lean Years Presidents": Ford and Carter

Gerald R. Ford and Jimmy Carter presided over not only a depressed economy but a nation of disillusioned citizens. The revelations of the Watergate break-in and Nixon's subsequent resignation as president cast a pall over politics. Replacing Nixon in August 1974, Gerald Ford reassured the public that "our long national nightmare is over"—then quickly pardoned Nixon for all the federal crimes he may have committed. The pardon reinforced public cynicism toward government and Ford in particular. Elections later that year added fifty-two Democrats to the House and four to the Senate (see Map 30.3).

Ford, who issued more vetoes of major bills than any other president in the twentieth century but saw Congress override most of them, struck most Americans as a pleasant person of modest ability. His WIN plan (Whip Inflation Now), which encouraged the public to conserve energy, had little impact on the nation's economy. First Lady Betty Ford was the shining star of the White House. She broke ranks with other Republicans to champion the Equal Rights Amendment. She also won praise for her courage in discussing her mastectomy for breast cancer and her voluntary entry into a substance abuse clinic for a drinking problem.

These newly built houses in Phoenix, Arizona, a popular retirement community as well as the state capital, helped accommodate a 55 percent rise in the city's population between 1970 and 1980. Like other burgeoning cities of the Mountain West, Phoenix experienced many urban tensions during this decade, including racial conflict, antagonism between affluent suburbs and the decaying downtown, air pollution, traffic congestion, and strained water supplies.

SOURCE: Guido Alberto Rossi./TIPS North America.

Ford banked on his incumbency for the 1976 election and welcomed Senator Robert Dole of Kansas as his running mate. Democrats chose Jimmy Carter, a former navy officer and governor of Georgia, who presented himself as a political outsider. When Carter told his mother he was running for president, she reportedly asked, "President of what?"

A "born again" Christian, Carter declined to call himself a liberal, offering instead personal integrity as his chief qualification for the nation's highest office. On domestic issues, he campaigned as a moderate. Counting on support from both conservative and southern voters who would ordinarily vote Republican, he defended existing entitlement programs while opposing Senator Edward Kennedy's call for comprehensive health coverage. He capitalized on Ford's unpopular Nixon pardon and, with his running mate Senator

Walter Mondale of Minnesota, won with just over 50 percent of the popular vote and a 297-to-240 margin in the Electoral College. Carter won more than 90 percent of the black vote, which provided his margin of victory in Pennsylvania, Ohio, and seven southern states. But apathy proved the next most important factor. A record 46.7 percent of eligible voters did not bother to cast ballots.

In office, Carter seemed to many observers enigmatic, even uninterested in the presidency. His most successful innovation, deregulation of the airlines, brought lower fares for millions of passengers. But by freeing banks from congressional control, he inadvertently encouraged bad investments, outright fraud, and a round of disastrous bank failures. Inflation proved to be his worst enemy. As older Americans could recognize, half of all the inflation since 1940 had occurred in

MAP EXPLORATION

To explore an interactive version of this map,
go to **www.prenhall.com/faragher5/map30.3**

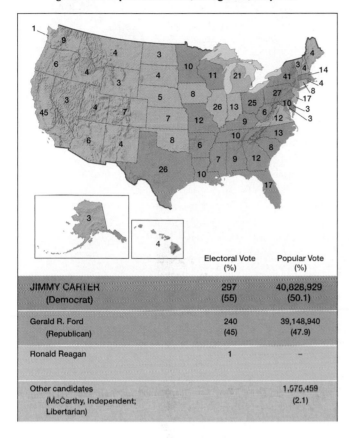

	Electoral Vote (%)	Popular Vote (%)
JIMMY CARTER (Democrat)	297 (55)	40,828,929 (50.1)
Gerald R. Ford (Republican)	240 (45)	39,148,940 (47.9)
Ronald Reagan	1	–
Other candidates (McCarthy, Independent; Libertarian)		1,575,459 (2.1)

MAP 30.3 The Election of 1976 Incumbent Gerald Ford could not prevail over the disgrace brought to the Republican Party by Richard Nixon. The lingering pall of the Watergate scandal, especially Ford's pardon of Nixon, worked to the advantage of Jimmy Carter, who campaigned as an outsider to national politics. Although Carter and his running mate Walter Mondale won by only a narrow margin, the Democrats gained control of both the White House and Congress.

just ten years. Interest rates rose, driving mortgages out of reach for many would-be home buyers. Rents in many locations doubled, sales of automobiles and other consumer products slumped, and many small businesses went under. Tuition costs skyrocketed along with unemployment, and many young men and women who could neither afford to go to college nor find a job moved back home. A fiscal conservative, Carter could not deliver on his promise to turn the economy around. By the time he left office in 1980, a majority of those polled agreed that "the people running the country don't really care what happens to you."

The New Urban Politics

The mass demonstrations of the 1960s gave way in the 1970s to a style of political mobilization centered squarely in communities. Unlike national elections, which after 1968 registered increasing voter apathy, local campaigns brought a great many people to the voting booth.

In many cities, new groups came into political power. In several college towns, such as Berkeley, California, and Eugene, Oregon, both of which had been centers of political activism during the 1960s, student coalitions were formed to secure seats for their candidates on city councils. In 1973 labor unions, college students, and community groups in Madison, Wisconsin, elected a former student activist to the first of three terms as mayor.

African American candidates scored impressive victories during the 1970s. The newly elected African American mayor of Atlanta, Maynard Jackson, concluded that "politics is the civil rights movement of the 1970s." By 1978, 2,733 African Americans held elected offices in the South, ten times the number a decade earlier. Mississippi, a state where the civil rights movement had encountered violent opposition, had more African American elected officials by 1980 than any other state in the union. Most of these elected officials served on city councils, county commissions, school boards, and law enforcement agencies. But voters elected African American mayors in New Orleans and Atlanta. In other parts of the country, black mayors, such as Coleman Young in Detroit, Richard Hatcher in Gary, and Tom Bradley in Los Angeles, held power along with many minor black officials.

Other racial or ethnic groups advanced more slowly, rarely in proportion to their actual numbers in the population. Mexican Americans had already won offices in Crystal City, Texas, and in 1978 took control of a major city council, in San Antonio, for the first time. They also scored electoral victories in other parts of Texas and in New Mexico and developed strong neighborhood or ward organizations in southern California. Puerto Ricans elected a handful of local officials in New York, mostly in the Bronx. Asian Americans advanced in similar fashion in parts of Hawai'i.

The fiscal crises of the 1970s nevertheless undercut the efforts to reform municipal government. Most new officials found themselves unable to make the sweeping changes they had promised during their campaigns. Community-based job programs could not counteract the effects of factory shutdowns and the disappearance of industrial jobs. Affirmative action programs aroused cries of "reverse discrimination" from angered whites who felt that minorities' progress had been registered at their expense. Conservatives put forward their own candidates,

Geronimo, 1981, by Victor Orozco Ochoa. During the 1970s public murals appeared in many cities, often giving distinctive expression to a community's racial or ethnic identity. The murals painted in the mid-1970s on the outside of the Centro Cultural de la Raza, in San Diego, were among the most striking. After vandals ruined one section, Ochoa, whose grandmother was Yaqui, replaced it with this enormous representation of Geronimo, surrounded by figures of contemporary Chicano cultural life.

SOURCE: *Untitled,* Geronimo mural. Victor Orozco Ochoa.

charging that government at all levels favored minorities, the jobless, and criminals over the law-abiding, hard-working, tax-paying majority.

The Endangered Environment

On March 28, 1979, a series of mechanical problems and judgment errors at the nuclear generating facility at Three Mile Island (TMI), near Harrisburg, Pennsylvania, led to the breakdown of the plant cooling system, causing the formation of a dangerously explosive hydrogen bubble and posing the danger of a catastrophic core meltdown. After the news broke, nearly 150,000 residents fled their homes. President Carter and First Lady Rosalynn Carter tried to reassure the stricken community by visiting the site. Ten days later, the Nuclear Regulatory Commission announced that any danger of explosion had passed, but what had seemed an isolated event in one community had already grown into a regional phenomenon with national repercussions. Elevated levels of radioactivity were found in milk supplies several hundred miles away. Massive demonstrations against nuclear power followed the accident, concluding in a rally of more than 200,000 people in New York City. Groups organized in many communites to defeat referendums to fund new nuclear power facilities or rallied around candidates who promised to shut down existing ones. Of the ninety-six under construction and the thirty more planned at the time of the TMI crisis, only a handful were completed.

Earlier in the 1970s, the discovery of high rates of cancer and birth defects in Love Canal, near Buffalo, New York, had offered compelling evidence of a growing danger to many American communities. Here toxic wastes dumped by the Hooker Chemical Laboratory had oozed into basements and backyards, and homemaker Lois Gibbs organized a vigorous publicity campaign to draw attention to the grim situation. Meanwhile, outraged Florida residents realized that the damming of the Everglades for sugar production and housing developments, undertaken by the Army Corps of Engineers decades earlier, had degraded thousands of acres of wilderness, eliminating natural filtration systems and killing millions of birds and other species.

The roots of the modern environmentalist movement can be traced to the publication of the works of marine biologist Rachel Carson. In 1962 she published *Silent Spring,* which detailed the devastating effects of DDT and other

This infrared photograph of Love Canal, a residential neighborhood east of Niagara Falls, New York, shows toxic chemicals bubbling up in lawns and yards. The media attention given to the Love Canal residents, who reported high incidents of birth defects and rates of cancer, led to the passage of a new federal law in 1980 regulating toxic waste disposal.

SOURCE: New York State Department of Environmental Conservation.

Cutting across nearly all population groups and regions, environmentalists reached such traditionally conservative areas as the Deep South with warnings of the dangers of toxic wastes, the destruction of wetlands, and the ruin of fishing industries. Sometimes campaigns succeeded in blocking massive construction projects, such as nuclear energy plants; more often they halted small-scale destruction of a natural habitat or historic urban district. These campaigns made the public more aware of the consequences of private and government decisions about the environment.

Responding to organized pressure groups, Congress passed scores of bills designed to protect endangered species, reduce pollution caused by automobile emissions, limit and ban the use of some pesticides, and control strip-mining practices. The Environmental Protection Agency (EPA), established in 1970, grew to become the federal government's largest regulatory agency, employing more than 10,000 people by the end of the decade.

Environmentalists enjoyed only limited success in bringing about large-scale changes in policy. Cities often avoided congressional mandates for reduction in air pollution by requesting lengthy extensions of deadlines for compliance. Despite the introduction of lead-free gasoline, the air in major metropolitan areas grew no better in the long run because automobile traffic increased at a fast pace. Environmentalists lost an important campaign with the approval of the Alaskan Pipeline, 800 miles of pipe connecting oil fields with refining facilities.

pesticides. By 1970, opinion polls showed the state of the environment outranking all other domestic issues. Senator Gaylord Nelson of Wisconsin and Representative Paul "Pete" McCloskey of California invited Americans to devote an entire day—April 22, Earth Day—to discuss the environment. The response was overwhelming; nearly 20 million Americans gathered in local parks, high schools, and colleges, and at the nation's capital.

Even before the energy crisis, many Americans had begun to make changes in their own ways of living. Many families began to save glass bottles and newspapers for reuse. Some began to reduce or eliminate their consumption of beef, since beef is far more costly and uses more resources to produce than grain. Backyard vegetable gardens became popular, as did grocers who stocked organic foods.

The environmentalist movement grew stronger in long-standing organizations, such as the Audubon Society and the Wilderness Society. The Sierra Club, formed in 1892 as a small society of western mountain hikers, grew from 15 million members in 1960 and to 136 million in 1972. New groups, such as the Environmental Defense Fund and Friends of the Earth, sprang up, most advocating the development of renewable energy sources such as solar power.

THE NEW CONSERVATISM

Sizable numbers of taxpayers resented the tax hikes required to fund government programs that benefited minorities, provided expanded social services for the poor, or protected the environment at the expense of economic development. In 1978 California voters staged a "taxpayers' revolt," approving Proposition 13, which cut property taxes and government revenues for social programs and education. In other economically hard-pressed urban areas, white voters who resented the gains made by African Americans and Latinos formed a powerful backlash movement. By the end of the decade, the only substantial increase in voter participation was among conservatives.

The New Right

By the end of the 1970s, evangelical Christians had become the backbone of the New Right and chief fundraisers for key organizations such as the National Conservative Political Action Committee and, most especially, the Moral Majority. They united behind major conservative and political leaders not merely to promote

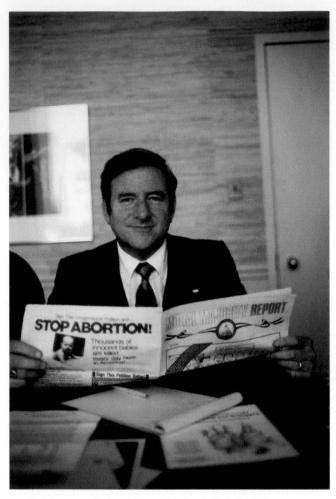

In the aftermath of the *Roe* v. *Wade* decision in 1973,
the televangelist Jerry Falwell became increasingly political in his
sermons on the *Old-Time Gospel Hour.* He declared a "war against
sin" by opposing abortion, homosexual rights, pornography,
and crime, and by appealing for financial contributions
he generated an annual income of more than $100 million.
The Reverend Falwell reached his peak in the early 1980s
and was, at that time, the most visible fundamentalist preacher
in the United States.

SOURCE: Eve Arnold/Magnum Photos, Inc.

an ideology but to target specific issues that they
believed further undermined what they termed "traditional family values."

Although conservative political organizations were
among the first to employ direct mail campaigns, tele-
vangelists met with even greater success. By the late
1960s, the TV ministries of Pat Robertson and Jim Bakker
frequently mixed conservative political messages with
appeals to prayer. Jerry Falwell's *Old-Time Gospel Hour* was
broadcast over 200 television stations and 300 radio stations each week. Christian broadcasters generally
endorsed Falwell's faith that "the free-enterprise system

is clearly outlined in the Book of Proverbs of the Bible."
By the end of the 1970s more than 1,400 radio stations
and thirty TV stations specialized in religious broadcasts
that reached an audience of perhaps 20 million weekly.

The Reverend Jerry Falwell formed the Moral Majority as a political lobbying group to advocate tough laws
against homosexuality and pornography, to promote a
reduction of government services (especially welfare
payments to poor families), and to increase spending
for a stronger national defense. He also waged well-publicized campaigns against abortion, the ERA, and the
busing of schoolchildren.

Jesse Helms was the first major politician to appeal
directly to the New Right and to build his own impressive fundraising empire with its help. A North Carolina
journalist who had fought the integration of public schools
and defended the Ku Klux Klan, he had often attacked
Martin Luther King Jr. as a Communist-influenced dem-
agogue. Helms entered national politics as a Goldwater
supporter in 1964 and ran for the Senate in 1972. Carried
to victory with Nixon's success in North Carolina, Helms
immediately promoted a host of conservative bills as well
as federal support for regional tobacco interests. He introduced legislation to allow automobile owners or dealers
to disconnect mandatory antipollution devices. He also
defended the Watergate break-ins as necessary to offset
the "traitorous conduct" of antiwar activists. By 1978 he
had raised $8.1 million, the largest amount ever, for his
successful reelection campaign. Helms built a powerful,
loyal, and wealthy following.

The political surge rightward gained intellectual
respectability from neoconservatives, former liberals
who blamed the social movements of the 1960s for the
demoralization of the nation. The American Enterprise
Institute and the Heritage Foundation, heavily supported
by major corporations, established research centers for
conservative scholars. These and other foundations also
funded campus publications attacking welfare programs,
affirmative action, and environmentalism

Anti-ERA, Antiabortion

The New Right rallied grass-roots support for a balanced
budget amendment to the Constitution, sought unsuc-
cessfully to return prayer to the public schools, and
endorsed the Supreme Court's approval of the death
penalty in 1977. The New Right also waged a counterattack against programs and policies that they believed
endangered the "traditional" family, such as government-
sponosred day care centers, legislative reforms to establish
educational equity, and social services for battered women
and single mothers (see Figures 30.2 and 30.3).

The defeat of the Equal Rights Amendment (ERA)
stood at the top of the New Right agenda. Approved
by Congress in March 1972, nearly fifty years after its

the ERA died in congress in 1982, with 85 percent of the Democrats and only 30 percent of the Republicans voting in favor of the amendment.

The New Right also waged a steady campaign against abortion, which the women's liberation movement had defined as a woman's right rather than a mere medical issue. In 1973 the Supreme Court had ruled in *Roe* v. *Wade* that state laws decreeing abortion a crime during the first two trimesters of pregnancy constituted a violation of a woman's right to privacy. Opponents of *Roe* rallied for a constitutional amendment defining conception as the beginning of life and arguing that the "rights of the unborn" supersede a woman's right to control her own body. The Roman Catholic Church organized the first antiabortion demonstrations after the Supreme Court's decision and sponsored the formation of the National Right to Life Committee, which claimed 11 million members by 1980.

Antiabortion groups also rallied against sex education programs in public schools. They picketed Planned Parenthood counseling centers, intimidating

---

Asked of those who said they had heard of or read about the Equal Rights Amendment: Do you favor or oppose this amendment?

Favor	58%
Oppose	24%
No opinion	18%

By Sex

Male

Favor	63%
Oppose	22%
No opinion	15%

Female

Favor	54%
Oppose	25%
No opinion	21%

Interviewing Date 3/7–10/1975, Survey #925-K

FIGURE 30.2 Gallup Poll on the Equal Rights Amendment, 1975 By 1973 thirty of the thirty-eight states required to ratify the ERA had done so. Although the amendment ultimately failed to achieve ratification and died in June 1982, public support was strong. In the 1976 presidential campaign, the platforms of both Democrats and Republicans included planks favoring its passage.

SOURCE: *The Gallup Poll: Public Opinion, 1935–1974* (New York: Random House, 1974).

introduction (see Chapter 22), the ERA stated: "Equality of rights under the law shall not be denied or abridged by the United States or by any State on account of sex." Endorsed by both the Democratic and Republican Parties, the amendment appeared likely to be ratified by the individual states. Nearly all mainstream women's organizations, including the Girl Scouts of America, endorsed the ERA. Even the AFL-CIO retracted its long-standing opposition and endorsed the amendment.

Cued by this groundswell of support in favor of the ERA, the New Right swung into action. Phyllis Schlafly, a self-described suburban housewife and popular conservative lecturer, headed the STOP ERA campaign, describing the amendment's supporters as "a bunch of bitter women seeking a constitutional cure for their personal problems." The New Right mounted large, expensive campaigns in each swing state and overwhelmed pro-ERA resources. Although thirty-five states had ratified the ERA by 1979, the amendment remained three votes short of passage. Despite a three-year extension,

---

Would you favor or oppose a law that would permit a woman to go to a doctor to end pregnancy at any time during the first three months?

Favor	40%
Oppose	50%
No opinion	10%

Interviewing Date 11/12–17/1969, Survey #793-K, Question #4, Index #54

The United States Supreme Court has ruled that a woman may go to a doctor to end pregnancy at any time during the first three months of pregnancy. Do you favor or oppose this ruling?

Favor	47%
Oppose	44%
No opinion	9%

Interviewing Date 3/8–11; 3/15–18/1974, Survey #894-K; 895-K

FIGURE 30.3 Gallup Polls on Abortion, 1969, 1974 During the 1960s, numerous American women began to demand control over their own reproductive processes and the repeal of legislation in place in all fifty states rendering abortion illegal. The American Institute of Public Opinion surveyed Americans in 1969, when abortion was still illegal, and again in 1974, one year after *Roe* v. *Wade*, the Supreme Court ruling that struck down state laws prohibiting abortion during the first three months of pregnancy.

SOURCE: *The Gallup Poll: Public Opinion, 1935–1974* (New York: Random House, 1974).

potential clients. A small minority turned to more extreme actions and bombed dozens of abortion clinics. (See Out of Many Voices: Opposition to the Equal Rights Amendment.)

"The Me Decade"

The shift in the political winds of the 1970s registered not only the rise of the New Right but also the disengagement of a sizable number of Americans from politics altogether. In 1976 novelist Tom Wolfe coined the phrase the "Me Decade" to describe an era obsessed with personal well-being and emotional security. Health foods and diet crazes, a mania for physical fitness, and a quest for happiness through therapy involved millions of middle-class Americans. Historian Christopher Lasch provided his own label for this enterprise in the title of his best-selling book *The Culture of Narcissism: American Life in an Age of Diminishing Expectations* (1978). "After the political tur-

moil of the sixties," he observed, "Americans have returned to purely personal preoccupations."

The rise of the "human potential movement" provided a vivid example of this trend. The most successful was Erhard Seminars Training (EST), a self-help program blending insights from psychology and mysticism. Founded by Werner Erhard (a former door-to-door seller of encyclopedias), the institute taught individuals to form images of themselves as successful and satisfied. Through sixty hours of intensive training involving play-acting and humiliation, participants learned one major lesson: "You are the one and only source of your experience. You created it." Priced at $400 for a series of two weekend sessions, EST peaked at 6,000 participants per month, grossing $25 million in revenue in 1980.

Transcendental meditation (TM) promised a shortcut to mental tranquility and found numerous advocates among Wall Street brokers, Pentagon officials, and star athletes. Techniques of TM were taught in more than

OUT OF MANY VOICES

OPPOSITION TO THE EQUAL RIGHTS AMENDMENT

In August 1978, the Senate Committee on the Judiciary held hearings on a resolution to extend the deadline for the ratification of the Equal Rights Amendment. Dr. Charles F. Stanley, pastor of the First Baptist Church of Atlanta, presented this series of arguments against extension.

WHILE THE EQUAL RIGHTS AMENDMENT AND THE extension is a political issue, I believe that there is a moral and spiritual issue here. Therefore, any discussion that leaves God out and ignores the unchanging principles of the word of God is inadequate. As every citizen is subject to the laws of the land, so is every man subject to the laws of God. This is whether he believes in God or the Bible, it really does not alter that fact.

I would like to very briefly state the four reasons I am opposed to the equal rights amendment time extension bill. . . .

First of all, it is designed to extend the time for the passage of the amendment that I believe is in violation of the principles of scripture. It violates God's plan for leadership in the home. It is important here that we understand the real issues involved. Our Nation is not embroiled primarily in the battle of the sexes, but

rather it is a battle of philosophies between those who hold pro-family biblical viewpoints upon which our Nation was founded and those who embrace the humanistic philosophy which leaves God out entirely. God established the home and in His divine wisdom He gave the husband the awesome responsibility of being the leader in the home to provide, protect, and care for his family. . . .

I have been a counselor for over 20 years. The membership of my congregation is over 7,000. I spend a lot of my time listening to people's problems. When women become independent, the men give up on the marriage and sometimes leave and finally there is a broken home. . . .

The passage of the amendment will contribute further to this growing problem. Instead of solving the problem, women will become more and more independent, and more and more embittered as they face life alone in the battle for survival. Economic independence, I believe, destroys the woman's ability to need and to love her husband. ■

SOURCE: *Hearings Before the Subcommittee on the Constitution of the Committee on the Judiciary, United States Senate, 95th Congress, Second Session, on S.J. Res. 134* (Washington: U.S. Government Printing Office, 1979), pp. 369–70.

200 special teaching centers and practiced by a reputed 350,000 devotees.

Religious cults also formed in large numbers during the 1970s. The Unification Church, founded by the Korean Reverend Sun Myung Moon, extracted intense personal loyalty from its youthful disciples, dubbed by the media as "Moonies." Moon's financial empire, which included hundreds of retail businesses and the conservative *Washington Star*, proved highly lucrative and kept his church solvent despite numerous lawsuits. By contrast, Jim Jones's People's Temple, an interracial movement organized in the California Bay Area, ended in a mass murder and suicide when Jones induced more than 900 of his followers to drink cyanide-laced Kool-Aid in a remote retreat in Guyana in 1978.

Popular music expressed and reinforced many of these trends. The songs of community and hope common in the late 1960s gave way to songs of search for more meaningful personal relationships, and to songs of nostalgia, despair, or nihilism. Bruce Springsteen, whose lyrics lamented the disappearance of the white working class, became the decade's most popular new rock artist. At the same time, heavy metal bands such as KISS, as well as punk and new wave artists underscored themes of decadence and futility. Meanwhile country and western music hit its peak with crossover hits and numerous new all-C&W radio stations. Charismatic stars like Willie Nelson sang melodic refrains reeking of loneliness and nostalgia and appealing to older, white, working-class Americans.

ADJUSTING TO A NEW WORLD

In April 1975 the North Vietnamese struck Saigon and easily captured the city as the South Vietnamese army, now without U.S. assistance, fell apart. All fighting stopped within a few weeks, and Saigon was renamed Ho Chi Minh City. Vietnam was reunited under a government dominated by Communists. For many Americans, this outcome underscored the futility of U.S. involvement in the Vietnam War.

By the mid-1970s a new realism seemed to prevail in U.S. diplomacy. Presidents Ford and Carter, as well as their chief advisers, acknowledged that the cost of fighting the Vietnam War had been too high, speeding the decline of the United States as the world's reigning superpower. The realists shared with dissatisfied nationalists a single goal: "No More Vietnams."

A Thaw in the Cold War

The military defeat in Vietnam forced the makers of U.S. foreign policy to reassess priorities. The United States must continue to defend its "vital interests," declared Ford's secretary of state Henry Kissinger, but must also recognize that "Soviet-American relations are not designed for tests of manhood." Both nations had experienced a decline of power in world affairs. And both were suffering from the already enormous and relentlessly escalating costs of sustaining a prolonged cold war.

At the close of World War II, the United States could afford to allocate huge portions of its ample economic resources to maintaining and enlarging its global interests. Soon, however, military and defense expenses began to grow at a much faster rate than the economy itself. Whereas the Korean War had cost around $69.5 billion, the Vietnam War cost $172.2 billion. Clandestine operations, alliance building, and weapons production accounted for trillions of dollars more.

Military spending at this level eventually took its toll on the American economy, especially as the federal government increasingly relied on deficit spending in an attempt to cover the bill. The federal debt, which stood at $257 billion in 1950, had jumped to $908 billion by 1980, and an increasingly large part of the federal budget went to paying just the interest on this debt. At the same time, military spending diverted funds from programs that could have strengthened the economy. The results were disastrous. While the United States endured falling productivity levels and rates of personal savings, and a disappearing skilled workforce, other nations rushed ahead.

Western European nations acted to nudge U.S. foreign policy away from its cold war premises. In 1975, in Helsinki, Finland, representatives of thirty-five nations approved the national boundaries drawn in eastern and western Europe after World War II, and in return the Soviet Union agreed to enact a more liberal human rights policy, including the loosening of restrictions on the emigration of Soviet Jews. Recognizing that the Soviet Union no longer posed a military threat to their national sovereignty—if indeed it ever had—Western leaders also sought to strengthen economic relations between the two major blocs.

The Soviet Union, whose economy suffered even greater setbacks from defense spending, joined the United States in moving toward détente. The signing of SALT I, the first Strategic Arms Limitation Treaty, during Nixon's administration, followed by the U.S. withdrawal from Vietnam, encouraged new efforts to negotiate on strategic arms control. In November 1974, Ford and Soviet leader Leonid Brezhnev met in Vladivostok to set the terms of SALT II, and President Carter secured the final agreement in 1979. However, the Senate refused to ratify the treaty when the Soviet Union invaded Afghanistan in December 1979.

Although repeated conflicts in the third world continued to slow the pace toward détente, leaders in both the United States and the Soviet Union usually recognized that their economic well-being depended on a reduction in defense spending. However haltingly, steps toward reconciliation had to be taken.

Foreign Policy and "Moral Principles"

When he took office, President Carter presented his lack of experience in foreign affairs as an asset. "We've seen a loss of morality," he noted, "and we're ashamed." The "soul" of his policy would be an "absolute" commitment to human rights.

Carter condemned policies that allowed the United States to support "right-wing monarchs and military dictators" in the name of anticommunism. In 1976 a powerful human rights lobby pressured Congress to pass a bill that required the secretary of state to report annually on the status of human rights in all countries receiving aid from the United States and to cut off assistance to any country with a record of "gross violations." Carter's secretary of state, Cyrus R. Vance, and the assistant secretary for human rights

and humanitarian affairs, Pat Derrian, worked to punish or at least to censure repressive military regimes in Brazil, Argentina, and Chile. For the first time, leading U.S. diplomats spoke out against the South African apartheid regime.

In line with this policy, Carter attempted to institute reforms at the Central Intelligence Agency (CIA), particularly to halt the blatant intervention in the affairs of foreign governments. He appointed Admiral Stansfield Turner, a Rhodes scholar, as director and ordered a purge of the "rogue elephants" who had pursued covert operations in Southeast Asia during the Vietnam War. "The CIA must operate within the law," Carter insisted. Under Turner, however, these reforms remained incomplete; they later proved temporary.

Carter nearly triumphed in the Middle East. Early in his administration, Carter met privately with Israeli prime

President Carter signs the Middle East Peace Treaty with Egyptian President Anwar Sadat and Israeli Prime Minister Menachem Begin, in Washington DC, March 1979. President Carter had invited both leaders to Camp David, the presidential retreat in Maryland, where for two weeks he mediated between them on territorial rights to the West Bank and Gaza Strip. Considered Carter's greatest achievement in foreign policy, the negotiations, known as the Camp David Peace Accords, resulted in not only the historic peace treaty but the Nobel Peace Prize for Begin and Sadat.

SOURCE: Corbis/Bettmann.

minister Menachem Begin to encourage conciliation with Egypt. When negotiations between the two countries stalled in 1978, Carter brought Begin together with Egyptian president Anwar el-Sadat for a thirteen-day retreat at Camp David, Maryland.

The Camp David Accords, signed in September 1978, set the formal terms for peace in the region. Egypt became the first Arab country to recognize Israel's right to exist, as the two nations established mutual diplomatic relations for the first time since the founding of Israel in 1948. In return, Egypt regained control of the Sinai Peninsula, including important oil fields and airfields. In 1979 Begin and Sadat shared the Nobel Prize for Peace.

But disappointment lay ahead. Carter staked his hopes for regional peace on the final achievement of statehood, or at least political autonomy, for Palestinians in a portion of their former lands now occupied by the Israelis. The accords specified that Israel would eventually return to its approximate borders of 1967. However, although Begin agreed to dismantle some Israeli settlements in the Sinai, the Israeli government continued to sponsor more and more Jewish settlements, expropriating Palestinian holdings. The final status of the Palestinians remained in limbo, as did that of Jerusalem, which many Christians and Muslims felt should be an autonomous holy city. Meanwhile Sadat grew increasingly isolated within the Arab world. In 1981 he was asassinated by Islamic fundamentalists.

Carter scored his biggest moral victory in foreign affairs by paving the way for Panama to assume the ownership, operation, and defense of the Panama Canal Zone. Negotiations with Panama had begun during Johnson's administration, following riots by Panamanians against U.S. territorial rule in their country. Carter pressured the Senate to ratify new treaties in 1978 (by a vote of 68 to 32) that would turn the Panama Canal over to Panama by the year 2000.

But when it came to nations considered vital to U.S. interests, such as South Korea, the Philippines, and El Salvador, Carter put aside his principles to stabilize repressive regimes and dictatorships. In restoring diplomatic relations with the People's Republic of China in January 1979, Carter likewise overlooked the regular imprisonment of dissidents. "The real problem," a U.S. diplomat observed, was that human rights was "not a policy but an attitude."

(Mis)Handling the Unexpected

Mired in problems inherited from his predecessors, Carter often found himself disoriented by contradictory advice. Carter's secretary of state Cyrus Vance recommended well-planned negotiations to soothe Soviet–U.S. relations and resolve disagreements with third world nations. But national security adviser Zbigniew Brzezinski, a bitterly anti-

Communist Polish exile, adhered to cold war policies and interpreted events in even remote sections of Africa or South America as plays in a zero-sum game: wherever the United States lost influence, the Soviet Union gained, and vice versa. Despite Carter's commitment to human rights, he allowed U.S. policy to resume cold war postures.

In 1979 the overthrow of the brutal Nicaraguan dictatorship of Anastasio Somoza, long-time ally of the United States, left Carter without a succcessor to support. When the new Sandinista revolutionary government pleaded for help, Congress turned down Carter's request for $75 million in aid to Nicaragua. Meanwhile, in El Salvador, the Carter administration continued to back a repressive government even after the assassination of Oscar Romero, a Catholic archbishop and opposition leader. Following the rape and murder of four U.S. Catholic Church women, apparently by the ultraright Salvadoran armed forces trained in the United States, peace activists and other Americans pleaded with Carter to withhold further military aid. Conservatives meanwhile demanded yet more funds to bolster the repressive anti-Communist regime.

African nations vacillated between allying with the United States and courting the Soviet Union. In this tricky political territory, UN ambassador (and former civil rights leader) Andrew Young, the first major African American diplomat assigned to Africa, could not persuade Carter to recognize the antiapartheid government of Angola, which had invited 20,000 Cuban troops to help in its fight against South African–backed rebels. Nor did Carter's and Young's verbal criticisms of the South African regime, unaccompanied by economic sanctions, satisfy black Africans. After Carter fired Young for having met secretly with officials of the Palestine Liberation Organization (PLO), the president proved even less effective in negotiating with antiapartheid leaders.

The Soviet invasion of Afghanistan produced a major stalemate. In December 1979, 30,000 Soviet troops invaded their neighbor to put down a revolt by Islamic fundamentalists against the weakening Soviet-backed government. The invasion succeeded mainly in heating up the civil war, which the American press quickly labeled the "Russian Vietnam." As the war bogged down, Americans heard familiar stories, this time of Soviet soldiers using drugs and expressing disillusionment with their government.

President Carter responded to these events with his own corollary to the Monroe Doctrine. The so-called Carter Doctrine asserted the determination of the United States to protect its interests in yet another area of the world, the Persian Gulf. Carter acted on the advice of Brzezinski, who believed that the Soviet Union would soon try to secure for itself a warm-water port on the gulf, an area rich in oil and now vital to U.S. interests. The president backed up his increasingly hard-line policies by halting exports of grain and high technology to the Soviet Union, supporting Afghani resistance against the Russians, and by cancelling American participation in the 1980 Moscow Olympics.

By the end of Carter's term, conservatives had swamped liberals within the Democratic Party. With the economy still hurting from the effects of cold war spending, Carter called for ever-larger increases in the military budget. He also signed Presidential Directive 59, guaranteeing the production of weapons alleged necessary to win a prolonged nuclear war. The prospect of peace and détente dried up.

The Iran Hostage Crisis

On November 4, 1979, Iranian fundamentalists seized the U.S. embassy in Tehran and held fifty-two American employees hostage for 444 days. This event made President Carter's previous problems seem small by comparison.

For decades, U.S. foreign policy in the Middle East had depended on a friendly government in Iran. After the CIA had helped to overthrow the reformist, constitutional government and installed the Pahlavi royal family and the shah of Iran in 1953, millions of U.S. dollars had poured into the Iranian economy and the shah's armed forces. President Carter had toasted the shah for his "great leadership" and overlooked the rampant corruption in government and a well-organized opposition. But, by early 1979, a revolution led by Islamic fundamentalist Ayatollah Ruhollah Khomeini had overthrown the shah.

After Carter had allowed the deposed Reza Shah Pahlavi to enter the United States for medical treatment, a group of Khomeini's followers retaliated, storming the U.S. embassy and taking the American staff as hostages.

Cyrus Vance assured Carter that only negotiations could free the Americans. Caught up in a reelection campaign and lobbied by Brzezinski for decisive action, Carter ordered U.S. military forces to stage a nighttime helicopter rescue mission. But a sandstorm caused some of the aircraft to crash and burn, leaving eight Americans dead, their burned corpses displayed by the enraged Iranians. Short of an all-out attack, which surely would have resulted in the hostages' death, Carter had used up his options.

The political and economic fallout was heavy. Cyrus Vance resigned, the first secretary of state in sixty-five years to leave office over a political difference with the president. The price of oil rose by 60 percent. Carter had failed in the one area he had proclaimed central to the future of the United States: energy. He had also violated his own human rights policy, which was intended to be his distinctive mark on American foreign affairs.

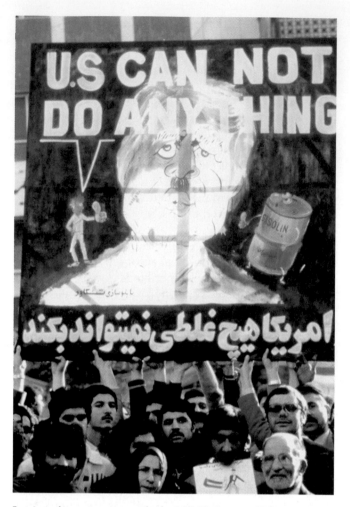

Iranians demonstrate outside the U.S. Embassy in Tehran, raising a poster with a caricature of President Carter. The Iran hostage crisis, which began November 8, 1979, when a mob of Iranians seized the U.S. embassy in Tehran, contributed to Carter's defeat at the polls the following year. Fifty-two embassy employees were held hostage for 444 days.

SOURCE: AP WideWorld Photos.

The 1980 Election

By 1979 inflation once again soared, and it was clear that Carter's program for economic recovery had failed. In July, with Vice President Walter Mondale increasingly opposed to his policies and toying with the idea of resigning from office, Carter withdrew with his staff to Camp David to reassess priorities. In his first public speech after the retreat, the president announced that the nation was experiencing a "crisis of confidence," and he called upon the people to change their attitude, to stop wallowing in personal problems, and to show more faith in their leaders.

Carter's "malaise speech," as it was called—although Carter never actually used the term "malaise"—backfired.

Many Americans resented the president for heaping blame on the public instead of taking responsibility for his own failures. News analysts now attacked Carter with zeal, breaking stories of minor scandals in his administration and ridiculing the president in various ways. His prospects for reelection therefore appeared to rest on his conduct of international affairs. If he only could put his human rights policy on a firm ground, move toward lasting peace in the Middle East, or strike a bargain with the Soviets on arms limitation, he might restore voter confidence. If not, his presidency would end after a single term.

Ultimately, Carter's bid for renomination depended more on his incumbency than on his popularity. Delegates at the Democratic National Convention unenthusiastically endorsed Carter along with Mondale. On the Republican side, former California governor Ronald Reagan had been building his campaign since his near nomination in 1976. Former CIA director and Texas oil executive George H. W. Bush, more moderate than Reagan, became the Republican candidate for vice president. The Moral Majority placed itself squarely in Reagan's camp, and Senator Jesse Helms's Congressional Club contributed $4.6 million to the campaign.

Reagan repeatedly asked voters, "Are you better off now than you were four years ago?" Although critics questioned Reagan's competence, the attractive, soft-spoken actor shrugged off criticisms while spotlighting the many problems besetting the country.

The Republican ticket cruised to victory. Carter won only 41.2 percent of the popular vote to Reagan's 50.9 percent, 49 votes in the Electoral College to Reagan's 489. The Republicans won control of the Senate for the first time since 1952 and with the largest majority since 1928. Still, barely half of the eligible voters turned out in the 1980 election, bringing Ronald Reagan into office with a mandate of a thin 25 percent.

REAGAN REVOLUTION

No other twentieth-century president except Franklin D. Roosevelt left as deep a personal imprint on American politics as Ronald Reagan. Ironically, Reagan himself began his political life as an ardent New Deal Democrat who admired Roosevelt as an inspirational leader. But by the time he entered the White House in 1981, shortly before his seventieth birthday, Reagan had rejected the activist welfare state legacy of the New Deal era. Following his overwhelming electoral victories in 1980 and 1984, Reagan and his allies tried to reshape the political and social landscape of the nation along conservative lines and rolled back the federal government's support of women's rights and civil rights (see Map 30.4).

MAP EXPLORATION

To explore an interactive version of this map, go to **www.prenhall.com/faragher5/map30.4**

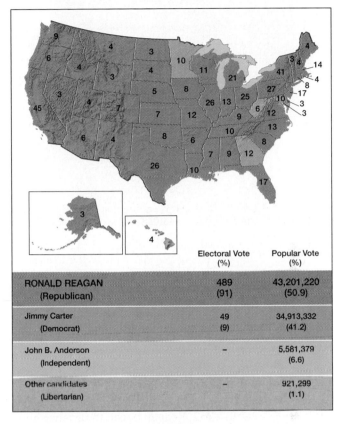

	Electoral Vote (%)	Popular Vote (%)
RONALD REAGAN (Republican)	489 (91)	43,201,220 (50.9)
Jimmy Carter (Democrat)	49 (9)	34,913,332 (41.2)
John B. Anderson (Independent)	–	5,581,379 (6.6)
Other candidates (Libertarian)	–	921,299 (1.1)

MAP 30.4 The Election of 1980 Ronald Reagan won a landslide victory over incumbent Jimmy Carter, who managed to carry only six states and the District of Columbia. Reagan attracted millions of traditionally Democratic voters to the Republican camp.

The Great Communicator

Ronald Reagan was born in 1911 and raised in the small town of Dixon, Illinois. His father, who worked in sales, was an alcoholic who had a tough time holding a job. His mother was a fundamentalist Christian who kept the family together despite frequent moves and encouraged her son to act in church plays and, later, in college productions.

In 1937 Reagan embarked on a Hollywood acting career that would last for a quarter-century. Although never a big star, on screen he appeared tall, handsome, and affable. In later years, he credited his political success to his acting experience. He told one interviewer: "An actor knows two important things—to be honest

Ronald Reagan, the fortieth president of the United States, was known for his ability to articulate broad principles of government in a clear fashion. The most popular president since Dwight Eisenhower, he built a strong coalition of supporters from long-term Republicans, disillusioned Democrats, and evangelical Protestants.

SOURCE: Wally McNamee/CORBIS-NY.

in what he's doing and to be in touch with the audience. That's not bad advice for a politician either."

While serving as president of the Screen Actors Guild from 1947 to 1952, Reagan began to distance himself from New Deal liberalism by becoming a leader of the anti-Communist forces in Hollywood. In 1954 he became the host of a new national television program, General Electric Theater, and began a long stint as a national promoter for GE. In this role he made numerous speeches celebrating the achievements of corporate America and emphasizing the dangers of excessive liberalism and radical trade unions.

Reagan switched his party affiliation to the Republicans and became a successful fund-raiser and popular speaker for the California GOP. After playing a leading role in Republican Barry Goldwater's 1964 presidential campaign, and with the financial backing of a group of wealthy conservatives, he entered the race for governor of California. In 1966 he defeated Democratic governor Edmund G. Brown and won reelection in 1970. As governor, Reagan cut the state welfare rolls, placed limits on the number of state employees, and funneled a large share of state tax revenues back to local governments. He vigorously attacked student protesters and black militants, thereby tapping into the conservative backlash against the activism of the 1960s.

When Reagan entered the White House in January 1981, his supporters confidently predicted that the "Rea-

gan revolution" would usher in a new age in American political life. Despite his narrow margin of victory, they interpreted his election as a popular mandate for the conservatism that had been growing since Nixon took office.

Reaganomics

"The Republican program for solving economic problems," Reagan announced, "is based on growth and productivity." During his presidency, he sought to revitalize the American economy by a strategy, dubbed Reaganomics, that was based on supply-side economic theory. In lashing out at a growing bureaucracy in government and simultaneously celebrating the achievement of entrepreneurs unfettered by government regulation or aid, his administration broke sharply with the Keynesian policies that had been dominant since the New Deal era (see Chapter 24).

Keynesians traditionally favored moderate tax cuts and increases in government spending to stimulate the economy and reduce unemployment during recessions. By putting more money in people's pockets, they argued, greater consumer demand would lead to economic expansion. By contrast, supply-siders emphasized productivity and sought plans to raise it. They also abhorred big government, calling for simultaneous tax cuts and reductions in public spending. This combination—which Reagan himself described as simple "common sense"—would give private entrepreneurs and investors greater incentives to start businesses, take risks, invest capital, and thereby create new wealth and jobs. Whatever revenues were lost in lower tax rates would be offset by revenue from new economic growth. At the same time, spending cuts would keep the federal deficit under control and thereby keep interest rates down.

George Gilder, conservative author of the best-selling *Wealth and Poverty* (1981), summarized the supply-side view: "A successful economy depends on the proliferation of the rich." On the political level, supply-siders looked to reward the most loyal Republican constituencies: the affluent and the business community. At the same time, they hoped to reduce the flow of federal dollars received by two core Democratic constituencies: the recipients and professional providers of health and welfare programs.

Reagan quickly won bipartisan approval for two key pieces of legislation that culminated in the largest tax cut in the nation's history. The Economic Recovery Tax

Act of 1981 lowered income and corporate taxes by $747 billion over five years. For individuals, the act cut taxes across the board. It also reduced the maximum tax on all income from 70 percent to 50 percent, lowered the maximum capital gains tax—the tax paid on profitable investments—from 28 percent to 20 percent, and eliminated the distinction between earned and unearned income. This last measure proved a boon to the small, richest fraction of the population that derives most of its income from rent, dividends, and interest instead of from wages.

With the help of conservative southern and western Democrats in the House, the administration also pushed through a comprehensive program of spending cuts, awkwardly known as the Omnibus Reconciliation Act of 1981. This bill mandated cuts of $136 billion in federal spending for the period 1982–1984, affecting more than 200 social and cultural programs. The hardest-hit areas included federal appropriations for education, the environment, health, housing, urban aid, food stamps, research on synthetic fuels, and the arts. The conservative coalition in the House allowed only one vote on the entire package of spending cuts, a strategy that allowed conservatives to slash appropriations for a wide variety of domestic programs in one fell swoop.

While reducing spending on domestic programs, the Reagan administration greatly increased the defense budget. During the 1980 election campaign, Reagan's calls to "restore America's defenses" helped reinforce the public perception that President Carter had dealt ineffectively with the Iran hostage crisis. Once in office he greatly accelerated a trend already under way during the last two years of the Carter presidency. a sharp increase in defense spending. Overall, the Reagan budgets for the military buildup totaled nearly $2 trillion and indicated a significant shift in federal budget priorities under his administration.

Meanwhile, the Reagan administration created a chilly atmosphere for organized labor. In the summer of 1981, some 13,000 federal employees, all members of the Professional Air Traffic Controllers Organization (PATCO), went on strike. The president retaliated against the strikers by firing them, and the Federal Aviation Administration started a crash program to replace them. Conservative appointees to the National Labor Relations Board and the federal courts toughened its antiunion position. The militantly antilabor mood in Washington, combined with the continuing decline of the nation's manufacturing infrastructure, kept trade unions on the defensive. By 1990 fewer than 15 percent of American workers belonged to a labor union, the lowest proportion since before World War II.

Reagan appointed conservatives to head the Environmental Protection Agency, the Occupational Safety and Health Administration, and the Consumer Product Safety Commission. These individuals abolished or weakened hundreds of rules governing environmental protection, workplace safety, and consumer protection, all in the interest of increasing the efficiency and productivity of business. The deregulatory fever dominated cabinet departments as well. Secretary of the Interior James Watt opened up formerly protected wilderness areas and wetlands to private developers. Secretary of Transportation Andrew L. "Drew" Lewis Jr. eliminated regulations passed in the 1970s aimed at reducing air pollution and improving fuel efficiency in cars and trucks.

Following the tenets of supply-side economics, the Reagan administration weakened the Antitrust Division of the Justice Department, the Securities and Exchange Commission, and the Federal Home Loan Bank Board. Large corporations, Wall Street stock brokerages, investment banking houses, and the savings and loan industry were all allowed to operate with a much freer hand than ever before. The appointment of Alan Greenspan in 1983, to succeed Carter appointee Paul Volker, greatly encouraged trends toward the dominance of speculation in market trading. By the late 1980s, the unfortunate consequences of this freedom would become apparent in a series of unprecedented scandals in the nation's financial and banking industries.

The Election of 1984

As the 1984 election approached, many Americans expressed doubts about the Reagan administration's defense initiatives. Polls showed that more than 70 percent of Americans favored a nuclear freeze with the Soviet Union. In June 1982, three-quarters of a million people—the largest political rally in American history—demonstrated in New York City for a halt to spending on and deployment of nuclear weapons. Many observers noted that Reagan also appeared politically vulnerable for his economic policies and cutbacks in social programs.

Hoping to win back disgruntled voters, Democrats chose Carter's vice president, Walter Mondale, as their nominee. As a former senator from Minnesota, Mondale had close ties with the party's liberal establishment and also the support of its more military-minded wing. At the Democratic National Convention, Mondale named Representative Geraldine Ferraro of New York as his running mate, a first for women in American politics. Charismatic speakers such as the Reverend Jesse Jackson, a dynamic disciple of Martin Luther King Jr., and Governor Mario Cuomo of New York stirred the delegates and many television viewers with their appeals to compassion, fairness, and brotherhood.

Opinion polls showed Mondale running even with Reagan. But the president's enormous personal popularity, along with the booming economy, overwhelmed the Democratic ticket. While Mondale emphasized the growing deficit and called attention to Americans who were left out of prosperity, Reagan cruised above it all.

It was "morning again in America," his campaign ads claimed. He offered the voters a choice between a Democratic "government of pessimism, fear, and limits" or his own, based on "hope, confidence, and growth." In one of the biggest landslides in American history, Reagan won 59 percent of the popular vote and carried every state but Minnesota and the District of Columbia. A majority of blue-collar voters cast their ballots for the president, as did 54 percent of women, despite Ferraro's presence on the Democratic ticket.

Recession, Recovery, Fiscal Crisis

Over the course of his two terms in office, Reagan's economic policies had mixed results. In 1982 a severe recession, the worst since the 1930s, gripped the nation. The official unemployment rate reached nearly 11 percent, or more than 11.5 million people. Another 3 million had been out of work so long they no longer actively looked for jobs and therefore were not counted in official statistics. But by the middle of 1983 the economy had begun to recover, and unemployment dropped to about 8 percent while inflation fell below 5 percent. The stock market boomed, pushing the Dow Jones industrial average from 776 in August 1982 to an all-time high of 2,722 in August 1987. The administration took credit for the turnaround, hailing the supply-side fiscal policies that had drastically cut taxes and domestic spending. But critics pointed to other factors: the Federal Reserve Board's tight-money policies, an energy resource glut and a consequent sharp drop in energy prices, and the billions of dollars pumped into the economy for defense spending.

Few doubted, however, that the supply-side formula intensified an ominous fiscal crisis. Although President Reagan had promised to balance the federal budget, his policies had the opposite effect. The national debt tripled, growing from $914 billion in 1980 to over $2.7 trillion in 1989, more than the federal government had accumulated in its entire previous history. Expenditures for paying just the interest on the national debt reached 14 percent of the annual budget in 1988, double the percentage set aside for that purpose in 1974.

In the Reagan years the fiscal crisis became a structural problem with newly disturbing and perhaps permanent implications for the American economy. Big deficits kept interest rates high, as the government drove up the cost of borrowing the money it needed to pay its own bills. Foreign investors, attracted by high interest rates on government securities, pushed up the value of the dollar in relation to foreign currencies. The overvalued dollar made it difficult for foreigners to buy American products, while making overseas goods cheaper to American consumers. Basic American industries—steel, autos, textiles—thus found it difficult to compete abroad and at home. In 1980, the United States still enjoyed a trade surplus of $166 billion. By 1987 the nation had an indebtedness to foreigners of $340 billion. Since World War I, the United States had been the world's leading creditor; in the mid-1980s it became its biggest debtor. New York senator Daniel Patrick Moynihan referred to the deficit as "the first fact of national government."

After the Dow Jones reached an all-time high at the end of August, stocks began to slide and then crashed. On October 19, 1987—"Black Monday"—traders at the New York Stock Exchange panicked, selling off stocks at such a rate that the market lost almost twenty-three percent of its value, marking the end of a five-year "bull" market. The market soon bounced back, and by September 1989 the Dow Jones had made up all its losses.

SOURCE: AP Wide World Photos.

Reaganomics also provided the backdrop for one of the biggest stock scandals in history. In late 1986, under investigation by the Securities and Exchange Commission (SEC), Ivan Boesky, one of the nation's leading stock speculators, admitted to using confidential information about upcoming corporate takeovers to trade stocks illegally. Just two years earlier the dapper Boesky had made more than $100 million on just two deals. "Greed is all right," he told a cheering University of California Business School audience in 1985. "Everybody should be a little bit greedy. . . . You shouldn't feel guilty." Once indicted, Boesky agreed to cooperate with SEC investigators and turned state's evidence to inform on several other operators.

The biggest fish caught in their net was Michael Milken. An investment banker for Drexel Burnham Lambert, Milken perfected the art of corporate raiding through creative manipulation of debt. He showed how enormous profits could be earned from weak firms that were tempting targets for takeovers and mergers. Their debt could be used as tax write-offs; less efficient units could be sold off piecemeal; and more profitable units could be retained, merged, or sold again to form new entities. Instead of borrowing from banks, Milken financed his deals by underwriting high-yield, risky "junk bonds" for companies rated below investment grade. Investors in turn reaped huge profits by selling these junk bonds to hostile-takeover dealers.

Milken and other corporate raiders reshaped the financial world, setting off the greatest wave of buying and selling in American business history. Milken himself made a staggering $550 million in one year alone. Just before filing for bankruptcy in 1990, Drexel Burnham Lambert paid its executives $350 million in bonuses— almost as much as it owed its creditors. Milken was eventually convicted of insider trading and stock fraud and sentenced to ten years in prison. Critics pointed out that too frequently profits now depended more on debt manipulation and corporate restructuring rather than investment in research and development or the creation of new products. In 1987, the Hollywood film *Wall Street* dramatized this world of ruthless profiteering.

On Wall Street, the bull market of the 1980s ended abruptly in the fall of 1987. After reaching its new high of 2,722 at the end of August, the Dow Jones average of thirty leading industrial stocks began to slide downward and then crashed. On October 19, the Dow lost almost 23 percent of its value. The panic on the trading floors recalled the pandemonium set off by the stock market crash of 1929. Millions of Americans now feared that the 1987 crash would signal the onset of a great recession or even a depression.

BEST OF TIMES, WORST OF TIMES

The celebration of wealth, moneymaking, and entrepreneurship dominated much of popular culture, politics, and intellectual life in the 1980s. But grimmer realities lay under the surface. A variety of measures strongly suggested that the nation had moved toward greater inequality, that the middle class was shrinking, and that poverty was on the rise. Analysts disagreed over the causes of these trends. No doubt some reflected

structural changes in the American economy and a rapidly changing global marketplace. After eight years of tax cuts, defense buildup, growing budget deficits, and record trade imbalances, the economic future looked uncertain at best. Two of the most cherished basic assumptions about America—that life would improve for most people and their children, and that membership in the comfortable middle class was available to all who worked for it—looked shaky by the end of the decade.

The Celebration of Wealth

The very wealthy did extremely well during the 1980s. In 1989, the richest 1 percent of American households accounted for 37 percent of the nation's private wealth—up from 31 percent in 1983, a jump of almost 20 percent. This top 1 percent, consisting of 834,000 households with about $5.7 trillion of net worth, owned more than the bottom 90 percent of Americans, the remaining 84 million households, whose total net worth was about $4.8 trillion.

Other affluent Americans also made huge gains. In 1980 the top 5 percent of families earned 15.3 percent of the nation's total income. By 1992 their share had grown to 17.6 percent, an increase of 15 percent; their average income was $156,000 a year. In 1980 the top 20 percent of families earned 41.6 percent of the nation's total. By 1992 their share had grown to 44.6 percent, an increase of about 7 percent, with an average income of $99,000 a year. In contrast, the bottom 40 percent of families had 16.7 percent of aggregate income in 1980. By 1992 their share had declined to 14.9 percent, a drop of nearly 2 percent, with an average income of about $16,500 a year.

The theme of money, status, and power —the values embraced by the Reagan administration—dominated popular culture. The newly elected president himself set the tone when he responded to a reporter's question asking him what was best about America. "What I want to see above all," Reagan replied, "is that this remains a country where someone can always get rich." Many thousands of Americans made fortunes in the expansive and lucrative sectors of the economy: stock trading, real estate, business services, defense contracting, and high-tech industries. A step below the new rich were the "yuppies," who were defined by their upscale consumer behavior. Yuppies ate gourmet foods, wore designer clothes, drove expensive automobiles, and lived in "gentrified" neighborhoods.

Popular culture reflected and reinforced an obsession with getting rich and living well. Once again, novelist Tom Wolfe gave a name to the cultural phenomenon—"plutography," which represented "graphic depictions of the acts of the rich." Hit TV series like *Dallas* and *Dynasty* (and their imitators) focused on the family wars and business intrigues of oil tycoons and fashion queens. Shows such as *Lifestyles of the Rich and Famous* and *Entertainment Tonight* offered vicarious pleasures by taking viewers into the homes and on the shopping sprees of wealthy celebrities.

Tie-ins proliferated among films, television shows, advertising, newspapers and magazines, popular music, and politicians. A growing concentration of ownership among television networks, movie studios, publishers, and cable companies accelerated this trend. New media forms—the newspaper *USA Today*, the news channel Cable News Network (CNN), the weekly magazine *People*—intensified the national culture of celebrity. Demographic analysis created the most important "communities" in American life—communities of consumers, so that advertisers could define and target them to sell a product or provide a service (see Tables 30.1, 30.2, and 30.3).

A Two-Tiered Society

During the 1960s, despite the diversion of federal funds to military spending during the Vietnam War, President Johnson's Great Society had brought a higher standard of living to many Americans. By the time Carter took office in 1977, the sinking economy was undercutting these gains. Reagan's supply-side policies enlivened the economy but at the same time widened the gap between rich and poor.

The number and percentage of Americans in poverty grew at an alarming rate. Since the mid-1970s, most of the new jobs clustered in low-paying service and manufacturing sectors and less than half of them paid more than the $11,611 poverty-level income for a family of four. In 1979 the government classified about 26.1 million people as poor, 11.7 percent of the total population; by 1992 the number of poor had reached 36.9 million, or 14.5 percent of the population, and nearly 22 percent of all American children under eighteen lived in poverty.

The widening gap between rich and poor was sharply defined by race. By 1992, 33 percent of all African Americans lived in poverty, as did 29 percent of Hispanics (the rate was especially high among Puerto Ricans, yet low among Cuban Americans). The gains achieved by the civil rights movement were steadily eroding. In 1954, the year of the *Brown* v. *Board of Education* decision, black families earned about 53 percent of the income of white families. This figure rose to 60 percent in 1969 and peaked at 62 percent in 1975. By 1979, black family income had fallen back to 57 percent and continued to slide during the next decade. Similarly, the number of African Americans attending college peaked in 1976 at 9.3 percent of the black population, a 500 percent increase over the 1960 average.

The majority of African Americans, six out of ten, lived in central cities with high unemployment rates, and the bleak prospects took a toll especially on the young. A black child was twice as likely as a white child to die before reaching the first birthday and four times more likely to be killed between the ages of one and four. Among black teenagers, the unemployment rate topped 40 percent; the few jobs available to them were among the lowest-paid in the economy. Meanwhile, the high school dropout rate skyrocketed, and the number of serious crimes, such as burglary, car theft, and murder, perpetrated by children between the ages of ten and seventeen increased at an alarming rate.

TABLE 30.1 PERCENTAGE SHARE OF AGGREGATE FAMILY INCOME, 1980–92

	1980	1992
Top 5 Percent	15.3%	17.6%
Highest Fifth	41.6	44.6
Fourth Fifth	24.3	24.0
Third Fifth	17.5	16.5
Second Fifth	11.6	10.5
First Fifth	5.1	4.4

SOURCE: U.S. Bureau of the Census, *Current Population Reports: Consumer Incomes*, Series P-60, Nos. 167 and 184, 1990, 1993. U.S. federal data compiled by Ed Royce, Rollins College.

TABLE 30.2 SHARE OF TOTAL NET WORTH OF AMERICAN FAMILIES

	1983	1989
Richest 1 percent of families	31%	37%
Next richest 9 percent	35	31
Remaining 90 percent	33	32

SOURCE: *The New York Times*, April 21, 1992, from Federal Reserve Survey of Consumer Finances.

TABLE 30.3 MEASURES OF AVERAGE EARNINGS, 1980–92 (IN 1990 DOLLARS)

Year	Average Weekly Earnings	Average Hourly Earnings
1980	$373.81	$10.59
1985	363.30	10.41
1992	339.37	9.87

SOURCE: U.S. House of Representatives, Committee on Ways and Means, *Overview of Entitlement Programs* (Washington DC: GPO, 1993), table 35, p. 557. U.S. federal data compiled by Ed Royce, Rollins College.

TABLE 30.4	NUMBER OF POOR, RATE OF POVERTY, AND POVERTY LINE, 1979–92	
	1979	1992
Millions of poor	26.1	36.9
Rate of poverty	11.7%	14.5%
Poverty line (family of four)	$7,412	$14,335

SOURCE: U.S. Bureau of the Census, *Current Population Reports: Consumer Income*, Series P-60, Nos. 161 and 185, 1988, 1993. U.S. federal data compiled by Ed Royce, Rollins College.

The gap between rich and poor also increased within the African American community. While the poor stayed behind in increasingly segregated urban neighborhoods, nearly 45 percent of black families managed to achieve middle-class status by the mid-1970s. This trend dramatically affected the black community. Until the 1970s the majority of African Americans had held to common residential neighborhoods, institutions, and political outlooks. By the end of the decade, growing income and residential disparity, which widened faster among black people than among white people, produced sharp differences among African Americans on social, economic, and political issues.

Moreover, opportunities for advancement into the middle class were dwindling. By 1980 fewer black students attended integrated schools than in 1954, except in the South, where about half the black students did. The turnabout resulted in part from increasing opposition by white parents to court-ordered school busing, which had served since *Brown* v. *Board of Education* as the principal means of achieving racial balance in urban school systems. In 1975 a major clash between local white residents and black parents and their children occurred in Boston when a federally mandated busing

plan was put into operation. During the 1980s the busing controversy nearly disappeared because federal judges hesitated to mandate such programs. But more important was the change in the racial composition of American cities. As a consequence of "white flight" to the suburbs, big-city school systems were serving mainly African American and Latino children, making the issue of integration moot. By this time, the dropout rate of black teenagers had reached 50 percent in inner-city schools (see Tables 30.4, 30.5 and 30.6).

New legal rulings closed off important routes to employment in the professions. A 1978 U.S. Supreme Court decision dealt a sharp blow to affirmative action. To ensure acceptance of a minimum number of minority students, the University of California at Davis Medical School had established a quota system under affirmative action guidelines. In 1973 and 1974 the school denied admission to Allan Bakke, a white student. Bakke sued the university for "reverse discrimination," claiming his academic record was better than that of the sixteen minority students who were admitted. The U.S. Supreme Court handed down a five-to-four decision on June 18, 1978, stating that the use of an "explicit racial classification" in situations where no earlier discrimination had been demonstrated violated the equal protection clause of the Fourteenth Amendment. The Court ordered the University of California to admit Bakke to its medical school. During the 1980s, therefore, affirmative action programs could operate only when "a legacy of unequal treatment" could be proved.

The Feminization of Poverty

Despite a growing rate of labor force participation, the majority of women gainfully employed earned less than a living wage. Even if employed, women usually lost ground following a divorce, especially as new no-fault divorce laws lowered or eradicated alimony. Moreover, the majority of men defaulted on child-support payments within one year after separation. Whereas

TABLE 30.5	NET NEW JOB CREATION BY WAGE LEVEL, 1979–87	
	Number of Net New Jobs Created	Percentage of Net New Jobs Created
Low-wage Jobs (less than $11,611)	5,955,000	50.4%
Middle-wage Jobs ($11.612 to $46,444)	4,448,000	31.7%
High-wage Jobs ($46,445 and above)	1,405,000	11.9%

SOURCE: U.S. Senate, Committee on the Budget, *Wages of American Workers in the 1980s* (Washington DC: GPO, 1988). U.S. federal data compiled by Ed Royce, Rollins College.

TABLE 30.6	MEDIAN FAMILY INCOME AND RATIO TO WHITE, BY RACE AND HISPANIC ORIGIN, 1980–92 (IN 1992 DOLLARS)			
Year	All Races	White	Black	Hispanic
1980	$35,839	$37,341	$21,606 (58%)	$25,087 (67%)
1985	36,164	38,011	21,887 (58%)	25,596 (67%)
1992	36,812	38,909	21,161 (54%)	23,901 (61%)

SOURCE: U.S. Bureau of the Census, *Current Population Reports*, Series P-60, No. 184, 1993. U.S. federal data compiled by Ed Royce, Rollins College.

divorced men enjoyed a sizable increase in their standard of living, divorced women suffered a formidable decline. During the 1970s alone, the number of poor families headed by women increased nearly 70 percent.

A sharp rise in teenage pregnancy reinforced this pattern. Many of these mothers were too young to have gained either the education or skills to secure jobs that would pay enough to support themselves and their children. Even with Aid to Families with Dependent Children (AFDC) payments and food stamps, it was impossible for these single mothers to keep their families above the poverty line. By 1992, female-headed households, comprising 13.7 million people, accounted for 37 percent of the poor. African American and Latino women and their children had by far the highest poverty rates.

Moreover, political mobilization for protecting the rights of poor women was at a low ebb. Since its founding in 1967, the National Welfare Rights Organization (NWRO), led by African American women, had spearheaded a campaign to enable welfare recipients to have a voice in policy decisions. They demanded adequate day-care facilities and job-training programs and insisted on the legitimacy of female-headed households. NWRO activists occasionally staged sit-ins at welfare agencies to secure benefits for their members. More often, they informed poor women of their existing rights and encouraged them to apply for benefits. In 1975, NWRO, exhausted from fighting cutbacks in the federal welfare system, filed for bankruptcy.

Epidemics: Drugs, AIDS, Homelessness

Drug addiction and drug trafficking took on frightening new dimensions in the early 1980s. The arrival of "crack," a cheap, smokable, and highly addictive form of cocaine, made that drug affordable to the urban poor. As crack addiction spread, the drug trade assumed alarming new proportions both domestically and internationally. Crack ruined hundreds of thousands of lives and led to a dramatic increase in crime rates. Studies showed that over half the men arrested in the nation's largest cities tested positive for cocaine. The crack trade spawned a new generation of young drug dealers who were willing to risk jail and death for enormous profits. In city after city, drug wars over turf took the lives of dealers and innocents, both caught in the escalating violence.

By the end of the 1980s, opinion polls revealed that Americans identified drugs as the nation's number one problem. The Reagan administration declared a highly publicized "war on drugs," a multibillion-dollar campaign to bring the traffic under control. Critics charged that the war on drugs focused on supply from abroad when it needed to look at demand here at home. They urged more federal money for drug education, treatment, and rehabilitation. Drug addiction and drug use, they argued, were primarily health problems, not law enforcement issues.

In 1981 doctors in Los Angeles, San Francisco, and New York began encountering a puzzling new medical phenomenon. Young homosexual men were dying suddenly from rare types of pneumonia and cancer. The underlying cause was found to be a mysterious new viral disease that destroyed the body's natural defenses against illness, making its victims susceptible to a host of opportunistic infections. Researchers at the Centers for Disease Control (CDC) in Atlanta called the new disease Acquired Immune Deficiency Syndrome (AIDS). The virus that causes AIDS is transmitted primarily in semen and blood. Full-blown AIDS might not appear for years after initial exposure to the virus. Thus one could infect others without knowing one had the disease. Although tests emerged to determine whether one carried HIV, there was no cure. The majority of early AIDS victims were homosexual men who had been infected through sexual contact. Many Americans thus perceived AIDS as a disease of homosexuals. But other victims became infected through intravenous drug use, blood transfusions, heterosexual transmission, or birth to AIDS-carrying mothers. By 1990 nearly 160,000 Americans had contracted the disease, and nearly 100,000 had died from it.

AIDS provoked fear, anguish, and anger. It also brought an upsurge of organization and political involvement. In city after city, the gay community

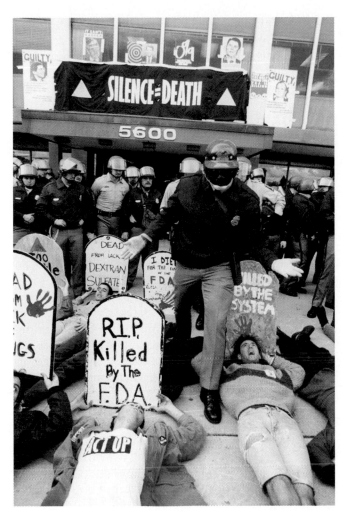

In May 1987, members of the Lesbian and Gay Community Services in downtown Manhattan organized ACT-UP. Protesting what they perceived to be the Reagan administration's mismanagement of the AIDs crisis, they used nonviolent direct action, which often took the form of dramatic acts of civil disobedience. ACT-UP grew to more than 70 chapters in the United States and the world.

SOURCE: Scott Applewhite/AP Wide World Photos.

responded to the AIDS crisis with energy and determination. Most gay men changed their sexual habits, practicing "safe sex" to lessen the chances of infection. The Reagan administration, playing to antihomosexual prejudices, largely ignored the epidemic. One important exception was Surgeon General C. Everett Koop, who urged a comprehensive sex education program in the nation's schools.

Homelessness emerged as a chronic social problem during the 1980s. Often disoriented, shoeless, and forlorn, growing numbers of street people slept over heating grates, on subways, and in parks. Homeless people

wandered city sidewalks panhandling and struggling to find scraps of food. Winters proved especially difficult. In the early 1980s, the Department of Housing and Urban Development placed the number of the nation's homeless at between 250,000 and 350,000. But advocates for the homeless estimated that the number was as high as 3 million.

Who were the homeless? Analysts agreed that at least a third were mental patients who had been discharged from psychiatric hospitals amid the deinstitutionalization trend of the the 1970s. Many more were alcoholics and drug addicts unable to hold jobs. But the ranks of the homeless also included female-headed families, battered women, Vietnam veterans, AIDS victims, and elderly people with no place to go. Some critics pointed to the decline in decent housing for poor people and the deterioration of the nation's healthcare system as a cause of homelessness. Some communities made strong efforts to place their homeless residents in city-run shelters, but violence and theft in the shelters scared away many people. No matter how large and what its components, the permanent class of American homeless reflected the desperate situation of America's poor.

REAGAN'S FOREIGN POLICY

Throughout his presidency, Reagan campaigned to restore American leadership in world affairs. He revived cold war patriotism and championed American interventionism in the third world, especially in the Caribbean and Central America. His infusion of funds into national security programs would have enormous consequences for the domestic economy as well as for America's international stance. Yet along with its hard-line exhortations against the Soviet Union and international terrorism, the Reagan administraton also pursued a less ideological, more pragmatic approach in key foreign policy decisions. Most important, sweeping and unanticipated internal changes within the Soviet Union made the entire cold war framework of American foreign policy largely irrelevant by the late 1980s.

The Evil Empire

In the early 1980s, the Reagan administration made vigorous anti-Communist rhetoric the centerpiece of its foreign policy. In a sharp turn from President Nixon's pursuit of détente and President Carter's focus on human rights, Reagan described the Soviet Union as "an evil empire . . . the focus of evil in the modern world."

Administration officials argued that during the 1970s the nation's military strength had fallen dangerously behind that of the Soviet Union. Critics disputed this assertion, pointing out that the Soviet advantage in intercontinental ballistic missiles (ICBMs) was offset by American superiority in submarine-based forces and strategic aircraft. Nonetheless, the administration proceeded with plans to enlarge America's nuclear strike force.

In 1983 President Reagan introduced an unsettling new element into superpower relations when he presented his Strategic Defense Initiative (SDI), the plan for a space-based ballistic-missile defense system that journalists dubbed "Star Wars," after the popular Hollywood film series. This proposal for a five-year $26 billion program promised to give the United States the capacity to shoot down incoming missiles with laser beams and homing rockets. To critics, the plan seemed unworkable, impossibly expensive, and likely to destabilize existing arms treaties. The Reagan administration pressed ahead, spending $17 billion in research before the president left office—without achieving any convincing results. Nevertheless, the Soviets viewed the SDI as an offensive strategy to ensure a first-strike advantage to the United States. The prospect of meaningful arms control dimmed in this atmosphere, and U.S.–Soviet relations deteriorated.

The Reagan Doctrine and Central America

Declaring the "Vietnam syndrome" over, the president confidently reasserted America's right to intervene anywhere in the world to fight Communist insurgency. The Reagan Doctrine, as this declaration was later called, assumed that all political instability in the third world resulted not from indigenous factors such as poverty or corruption but from the pernicious influence of the Soviet Union. It found its most important expression in Central America, where the United States hoped to reestablish its historical control over the Caribbean basin (see Map 30.5).

The Reagan administration believed that all problems throughout Central America stemmed from "Fidel Castro's Soviet directed, armed, and financed marauders" and required a military solution. Between 1980 and 1983 the United States poured more military aid into Central America than it had during the previous thirty years. In October 1983, the administration directed American marines to invade Grenada, claiming that the tiny island had become a base for the Cuban military and therefore posed a dangerous threat to the hemisphere. The easy triumph proved popular with most Grenadans and Americans. In the larger and more complicated nations of El Salvador and Nicaragua, this sort of unilateral military action proved politically and strategically more difficult to carry out.

In El Salvador, the Reagan administration continued to support the repressive regime. Military aid jumped from $6 million in 1980 to $82 million in 1982, and El Salvador received more U.S. economic assistance than any other Latin American country. By 1983 right-wing death squads, encouraged by military elements within the regime, had tortured and assassinated thousands of opposition leaders. The election in 1984 of centrist president José Napoleón Duarte failed to end the bloody civil war. Some 53,000 Salvadorans, more than one out of every hundred, lost their lives in the conflict.

In Nicaragua, the Reagan administration claimed that the revolutionary Sandinista government posed "an unusual and extraordinary threat to the national security." U.S. officials accused the Sandinistas of shipping arms to antigovernment rebels in El Salvador. In December 1981, Reagan approved a $19 million CIA plan arming and organizing Nicaraguan exiles, known as Contras, to fight against the Sandinista government. As Reagan escalated this undeclared war, the aim became not merely the cutting of Nicaraguan aid to Salvadoran rebels but the overthrow of the Sandinista regime itself.

In 1984 the CIA secretly mined Nicaraguan harbors. When Nicaragua won a judgment against the United States in the World Court over this violation of its sovereignty, the Reagan administration refused to recognize the court's jurisdiction in the case and ignored the verdict. Predictably, the U.S. covert war pushed the Sandinistas closer to Cuba and the Soviet bloc. Meanwhile, U.S. grassroots opposition to Contra aid grew more vocal and widespread. A number of U.S. communities set up sister-city projects offering humanitarian and technical assistance to Nicaraguan communities. Scores of U.S. churches offered sanctuary to political refugees from Central America.

In 1984 Congress reined in the covert war by passing the Boland Amendment, introduced by Democratic Representative Edward Boland of Massachusetts. It forbid government agencies from supporting "directly or indirectly military or paramilitary operations" in Nicaragua. Denied funding by Congress, President Reagan turned to the National Security Council to find a way to keep the Contra war going. Between 1984 and 1986, the NSC staff secretly assisted the Contras, raising $37 million in aid from foreign countries and private contributors, creating the largest mercenary army in hemispheric history. In 1987 the revelation of this unconstitutional scheme exploded before the public as part of the Iran-Contra affair, the most damaging political scandal of the Reagan years.

MAP EXPLORATION

To explore an interactive version of this map, go to **www.prenhall.com/faragher5/map30.5**

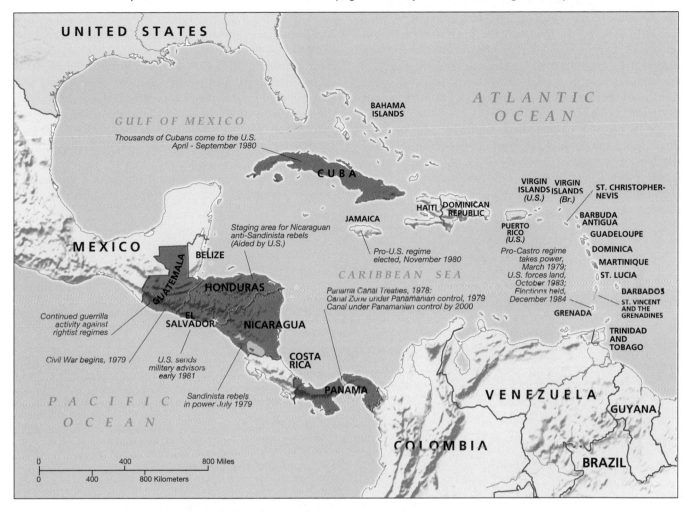

MAP 30.5 The United States in Central America, 1978–90 U.S. intervention in Central America reached a new level of intensity with the so-called Reagan Doctrine. The bulk of U.S. aid came in the form of military support for the government of El Salvador and the Contra rebels in Nicaragua.

The Iran-Contra Scandal

In 1987 the revelations of the Iran-Contra affair laid bare the continuing contradictions and difficulties attending America's role in world affairs. The affair also demonstrated how overzealous and secretive government officials subverted the Constitution and compromised presidential authority under the guise of patriotism (see Map 30.6).

The Middle East presented the Reagan administration with its most frustrating foreign policy dilem-

mas. Terrorist acts, including the seizing of Western hostages and the bombing of commercial airplanes and cruise ships, redefined the politics of the region. These were desperate attempts by small sects, many of them splinter groups associated with the Palestinian cause or Islamic fundamentalism, to inhibit U.S. support of Israel. However, the Reagan administration insisted that behind international terrorism lay the sinister influence and money of the Soviet bloc, the Ayatollah Khomeini of Iran, and Libyan leader Muammar el-Qaddafi. In the spring of 1986 the president, eager to demonstrate his antiterrorist resolve, ordered the bombing of Tripoli in a failed effort to kill Qaddafi.

As a fierce war between Iran and Iraq escalated, the administration tilted publicly toward Iraq to please the Arab states around the Persian Gulf. But in 1986 Reagan's advisors began secret negotiations with the revolutionary Iranian government. They eventually offered to supply Iran with sophisticated weapons for use against Iraq in exchange for help in securing the release of Americans held hostage by radical Islamic groups in Lebanon.

Subsequent disclosures elevated the arms-for-hostages deal into a major scandal. Some of the money from the arms deal had been secretly diverted into covert aid for the Nicaraguan Contras. The American public soon learned the sordid details from investigative journal-

ists and through televised congressional hearings held during the summer of 1987. In order to escape congressional oversight of the CIA, Reagan and CIA director William Casey had essentially turned the National Security Council, previously a policy-coordinating body, into an operational agency. Under the direction of National Security Advisers Robert McFarlane and later Admiral John Poindexter, the NSC had sold weapons and missiles to the Iranians, using Israel as a go-between. Millions of dollars from these sales were then given to the Contras in blatant and illegal disregard of the Boland Amendment.

In the televised congressional hearings, NSC staffer and marine lieutenant colonel Oliver North emerged as the figure running what he euphemistically referred to as "the Enterprise." North defiantly

MAP EXPLORATION

To explore an interactive version of this map, go to **www.prenhall.com/faragher5/map30.6**

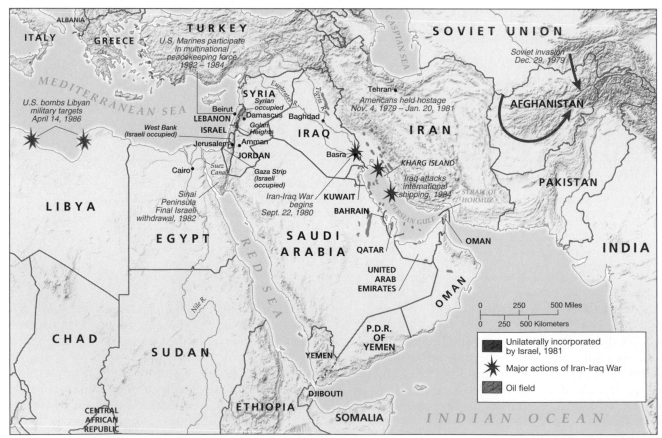

MAP 30.6 The United States in the Middle East in the 1980s The volatile combination of ancient religious and ethnic rivalries, oil, and emerging Islamic fundamentalism made peace and stability elusive in the Middle East.

defended his actions in the name of patriotism. Some Americans saw the handsome and dashing North as a hero; most were appalled by his and Poindexter's blithe admissions that they had lied to Congress, shredded evidence, and refused to inform the president of details in order to guarantee his "plausible deniability." A blue-ribbon commission concluded that Reagan himself "did not seem to be aware" of the policy or its consequences. But the report offered a stunning portrait of a president who was at best confused and far removed from critical policy-making responsibilities. Ultimately, the Iran-Contra investigation raised more questions than it answered. The full role of CIA director Casey, who died in 1987, particularly his relationships with North and the president, remained murky. The role of Vice President George H. W. Bush remained mysterious as well, and it would return as an issue in the 1992 presidential election. Both North and Poindexter were convicted of felonies, but their convictions were overturned by higher courts on technical

grounds. Reagan held fast to his plea of ignorance. When pressed on what had happened, he repeatedly claimed, "I'm still trying to find out."

In December 1992, following his reelection defeat and six years after the scandal broke, President George H. W. Bush granted pardons to six key players in the Iran-Contra affair. The Bush pardons made it unlikely that the full truth about the arms-for-hostages affair would ever be known.

The Collapse of Communism

Meanwhile, momentous political changes within the Soviet Union led ultimately to the end of the cold war itself. Soviet premier Leonid Brezhnev, in power since 1964, died toward the end of 1982. His successors, Yuri Andropov and Konstantin Chernenko, both died after brief terms in office. But in 1985 a new, reform-minded leader, Mikhail Gorbachev, won election as general secretary of the Soviet Communist Party.

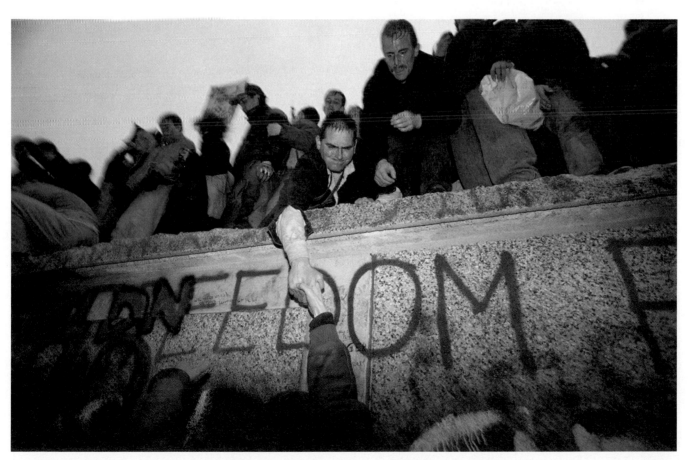

In August 1961, the border between East and West Berlin was closed, and the Berlin Wall was built to divide the city into two sections. After twenty-eight years, on November 9, 1989, the government in East Germany lifted travel restrictions. This photograph shows demonstrators defiantly tearing down the Berlin Wall, which for three decades had embodied the political divisions of the cold war.

SOURCE: Robert Maass/CORBIS-NY.

Although a lifelong Communist, Gorbachev represented a new generation of disenchanted party members. He initiated a radical new program of economic and political reform under the rubrics of *glasnost* (openness) and *perestroika* (restructuring).

Gorbachev and his advisers opened up political discussion and encouraged criticism of the Soviet economy and political culture. The government released longtime dissidents like Andrei Sakharov from prison and took the first halting steps toward profit-based, private initiatives in the economy. This "new thinking" inspired an unprecedented wave of diverse, often critical perspectives in Soviet art, literature, journalism, and scholarship.

In Gorbachev's view, improving the economic performance of the Soviet system depended first on halting the arms race. Over 10 percent of the Soviet GNP (gross national product) went to defense spending, while the majority of its citizens still struggled to find even the most basic consumer items in shops. Gorbachev thus took the lead to end the arms race with the United States. The historical ironies were stunning. Reagan had made militant anticommunism the centerpiece of his administration, but between 1985 and 1988 he had four separate summit meetings with the new Soviet leader. Although negotiations stalled over the Star Wars initiative, the two sides eventually agreed to a modest treaty that called for comprehen-

CHRONOLOGY

1973	*Roe* v. *Wade* legalizes abortion
	Arab embargo sparks oil crisis in the United States
1974	Richard Nixon resigns presidency; Gerald Ford takes office
	President Ford pardons Nixon and introduces antiinflation program
1975	Unemployment rate reaches nearly 9 percent
	South Vietnamese government falls to communists
	Antibusing protests break out in Boston
1976	Percentage of African Americans attending college peaks at 9.3 percent and begins a decline
	Jimmy Carter is elected president
1977	President Carter announces human rights as major tenet in foreign policy
1978	*Bakke* v. *University of California* decision places new limits on affirmative action programs
	Camp David meeting sets terms for Middle East peace
	California passes Proposition 13, cutting taxes and government social programs
1979	Three Mile Island nuclear accident threatens a meltdown

	Nicaraguan Revolution overthrows Anastasio Somoza
	Iranian fundamentalists seize the U.S. embassy in Tehran and hold U.S. citizens hostage for 444 days
	Soviets invade Afghanistan
1980	Inflation reaches 13.5 percent
	Ronald Reagan is elected president
1981	Reagan administration initiates major cuts in taxes and domestic spending.
	Military buildup accelerates
	AIDS is recognized and named
1982	Economic recession grips the nation
1983	Reagan announces the Strategic Defense Initiative, labeled "Star Wars" by critics.
	241 marines killed in Beirut terrorist bombing
1985	Mikhail Gorbachev initates reforms—*glasnost* and *perestroika*—in the Soviet Union
1986	Iran-Contra hearings before Congress reveal arms-for-hostages deal and funds secretly and illegally diverted to Nicaraguan rebels
1989	Communist authority collapses in Eastern Europe
1991	Soviet Union dissolves into Commonwealth of Independent States

sive, mutual, on-site inspections. The meetings provided an important psychological breakthrough. At one of the summits a Soviet leader humorously announced, "We are going to do something terrible to you Americans—we are going to deprive you of an enemy."

Indeed, the reforms initiated by Gorbachev—and, more immediately, the failed Soviet war in Afghanistan—led to the dissolution of the Soviet Union and to the end of Communist rule throughout Eastern Europe. Beginning in June 1989, when Poland held its first free elections since the close of World War II in 1945, prodemocracy demonstrations forced out long-time Communist leaders in Hungary, Czechoslovakia, Bulgaria, and Romania. Most dramatic of all were the events in East Germany. The Berlin Wall, which for thirty years had loomed as the ultimate symbol of cold war division, came down on November 9, 1989. Hundreds of thousands of East Germans immediately rushed into West Berlin. Popular protest intensified, paving the way for German reunification the following year.

Political changes in the Soviet Union came more slowly, accompanied by such drastically reduced living standards that successful transition to a liberal market economy and democratic political system was uncertain. In March 1989 the Soviet Union held its first open elections since 1917, and a new Congress of People's Deputies replaced the old Communist Party dominated Supreme Soviet. In the next elections the following year, hundreds of party officials went down in defeat in key Russian cities. In August 1991 party hard-liners made a final attempt to hold on to the old order and staged a coup, placing President Gorbachev under house arrest. Although the coup quickly failed, most of the fifteen republics had meanwhile announced their withdrawal from the Soviet Union. Gorbachev found he could no longer control the government. On Christmas Day 1991 the weary and bitter president of the USSR resigned and recognized the new Commonwealth of Independent States.

The Soviet Union had dissolved, marking the end of the great superpower rivalry that had shaped American foreign policy and domestic politics for nearly a half-century. Reagan's successor, President George Bush proclaimed the end of the cold war as an event of "biblical proportions."

CONCLUSION

The success of conservatives to halt and in some cases actually reverse key trends in American politics, from Franklin Roosevelt's New Deal to Lyndon Johnson's Great Society, was made possible by the legacy of the cold war and the trauma of defeat in Vietnam. But it also owed a great deal to a deepening anxiety of the public about cultural changes and a growing pessimism about the ability of politicians to offer solutions, especially at the national level. Those community activists struggling to extend the protest movements of the 1960s into an updated, comprehensive reformism encompassing such issues as feminism, ecology, and affirmative action readily recognized that the liberal era had ended.

President Ronald Reagan, a charismatic figure who sometimes invented his own past and seemed to believe in it, offered remedies for a weary and nostalgic nation. By insisting that the rebellious 1960s had been a terrible mistake, lowering national self-confidence along with public morals and faith in the power of economic individualism, he successfully wedded the conservatism of Christian fundamentalists, many suburbanites, and Sunbelt voters with the more traditional conservatism of corporate leaders. In many respects, the Reagan administration actually continued and added ideological fervor to the downscaling of government services and upscaling of military spending already evident under President Jimmy Carter, while offering supporters the hope of a sweeping conservative revolution.

In the end, critics suggested, supporters of Ronald Reagan and Reaganism could not go back to the 1950s—just as the erstwhile rebels of the 1960s could not go back to their favorite era. Economically, conservatives achieved many of their goals, including widespread acceptance of sharper economic divisions within society and fewer restraints on corporations and investments. But socially and culturally, their grasp was much less secure.

REVIEW QUESTIONS

1. Evaluate the significance of the major population shifts in the United States from the 1940s through the 1970s. What was their impact on local and national politics?
2. Discuss the connections between the energy crisis and the rise of the environmental movement.
3. Why was the 1970s dubbed the "Me Decade"? Interpret the decline of liberalism and the rise of conservative political groups. How did these changes affect the outcome of presidential elections?
4. Was the Iran hostage crisis a turning point in American politics or only a thorn in Carter's reelection campaign? How did Iran-Contra affect the Republicans?
5. Describe the central philosophical assumptions behind Reaganomics. What were the key policies by which it was implemented? To what extent were these policies a break with previous economic approaches?
6. Evaluate Reagan's foreign policy. How did it differ from Carter's approach to foreign affairs?
7. Analyze the key structure factors underlying recent changes in American economic and cultural life. Do you see any political solutions for the growth of poverty and inequality?

RECOMMENDED READING

Lee Edwards, *The Conservative Revolution: The Movement That Remade America* (1999). Traces the rise of modern political conservatism from its origins in cold war anticommunism. A longtime conservative activist and writer, Edwards credits much of Reagan's success in office to the presence of a strong, vital, and grassroots conservative movement.

David Farber, *Taken Hostage: The Iran Hostage Crisis and America's First Encounter with Radical Islam* (2004). Examines the events of November 1979, emphasizing the larger context of a decade of uncertainty and anxiety. Farber also considers the meaning of Carter's hostage crisis for the larger war on terrorism at the turn of the century.

Frances FitzGerald, *Way Out There in the Blue: Reagan, Star Wars, and the End of the Cold War* (2000). A well-documented study of the conservative mood that made Star Wars both credible and popular among conservatives. FitzGerald provides a sweeping historical context for Star Wars with special attention given to the impact of the cold war on traditional isolationism.

John Karaagac, *Between Promise and Policy: Ronald Reagan and Conservative Reformism* (2000). Assesses Reagan's major polities, such as increased funding for federal government and regulatory reform, in light of his professed conservative ideals. Karaagac argues that Reagan wielded ideology as a political weapon to gain support for his programs while acting pragmatically and with a good deal of flexibility on particular issues.

Michael B. Katz, *Improving Poor People: The Welfare State, the "Underclass," and Urban Schools as History* (1995). Provides a broad overview of the history of urban poverty, welfare policy, and public education. Katz examines the "underclass" debates of the 1970s as a function of the interaction between politics and economics within the postindustrial inner city.

Melani McAlister, *Epic Encounters: Culture, Media, and U.S. Interests in the Middle East, 1945–2000* (2001). A close reading of American popular culture, including films, television news broadcasts, museum exhibits, and fiction, representing relationships between the Middle East and the United States. McAlister considers the importance of the abundance of oil and the Islamic religion of the Middle East as factors shaping U.S. foreign policy.

Lisa McGirr, *Suburban Warriors: The Origins of the New American Right* (2001). Traces the resurgence of American conservatism by analyzing issues that galvanized grassroots middle-class activism in 1960s and 1970s Southern California.

Bruce J. Schulman, *The Seventies: The Great Shift in American Culture, Society, and Politics* (2001). Examines the move away from the public-spirited universalism that characterized the New Deal and civil rights movement toward the sovereignty of the free market and celebration of private life. With a geopolitical twist that emphasizes the increasing importance of the Sunbelt, Schulman argues that the conservative 1980s actually began a decade earlier.

Judith Stein, *Running Steel, Running America: Race, Economic Policy, and the Decline of Liberalism* (1998). Discusses the impact of the decline of the U.S. steel industry on its large African American labor force. Stein analyzes trade policy, especially under Carter, that benefited foreign steel producers and led to the closing of American plants.

Robert A. Strong, *Working in the World: Jimmy Carter and the Making of American Foreign Policy* (2000). A collection of nine case studies of international affairs covering Carter's presidency. Strong's goal is not to provide new insight into the central crises of the era but to open a window to the range of presidential responsibilities in the diplomatic arena.

Andrew Szasz, *EcoPopulism: Toxic Waste and the Movement for Environmental Justice* (1994). A careful analysis of a turning point in federal regulation of toxic waste. Szasz shows how the prevention of pollution, previously considered a local issue, through strengthened state and federal regulations became a national issue and a springboard for the environmental movement.

J. Samuel Walker, *Three Mile Island: A Nuclear Crisis in Historical Perspective* (2004). Sponsored by the United States Nuclear Regulatory Commission, this book provides a detailed description of the "accident" at Three Mile Island and a broad historical context, including the growth of commercial nuclear power and the emergence of forces in opposition to this source of energy.

Winifred D. Wandersee, *On the Move: American Women in the 1970s* (1988). A highly readable overview of the changes that brought American women into political life but also kept them at the margins of power. This study includes a close description of the National Organization for Women as well as media personalities, such as Jane Fonda, who gave feminism a public face.

 For additional study resources for this chapter, go to the *Companion Website*, http://www.prenhall.com/faragher.

Toward a Transnational America

since 1988

957

The World Trade Center, New York, as a Transnational Community

Telmo Alvear had quit his job as a busboy in August 2001 to become a waiter at Windows on the World, a restaurant on the 106th and 107th floors of the north tower of the World Trade Center (WTC) that was once described by *New York* magazine as "the most spectacular restaurant in the world." The posh restaurant was huge and elegant, accommodating as many as 1,000 people. In the decade after it opened in 1976, Windows was one of the most successful restaurants in the world, earning revenues that topped $20 million a year. In the early 1990s, the reputation of Windows began to slip, and following a terrorist attack on the WTC in February 1993, the restaurant closed. But by the time Alvear found a job there, Windows on the World was once again thriving. With views on a clear day extending for forty-five miles, and with a wine cellar and liquor stock that was modestly named "The Greatest Bar on Earth," Windows had become a prime tourist attraction and a popular dining spot for some of the most powerful international traders and merchants in the world. "It's more than a restaurant," one reviewer enthused. "It's a New York experience."

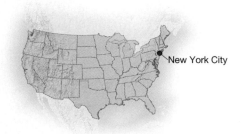

New York City

And so it was. Not just Windows on the World but the entire World Trade Center had come to represent both the best and worst of New York City, the commercial capital of the world. The twin skyscrapers, which were designed to be the tallest in the world, were audacious. Completed in 1973 at a cost of $400 million, they rose 110 stories above ground and occupied a thirteen-square-block site in Lower Manhattan, conveniently close to Wall Street and the New York Stock Exchange. When the WTC was first built, many New Yorkers, including distinguished architects, complained that the mammoth, boxy structures destroyed the city's unrivaled skyline. They stood too self-assuredly, critics charged, as tasteless monuments to commerce, wealth, and ambition. But over the years, the WTC became a preeminent symbol of the glory of New York and, by extension, the United States.

The WTC provided office space to hundreds of businesses and government agencies and served as a workplace for more than 50,000 people. The people who worked in the twin towers constituted a remarkable transnational community. Although many were native New Yorkers, a large number were relative newcomers. Alvear himself was one in a huge wave of Hispanic immigration that had been transforming New York City since 1990. Immigrating from Ecuador as a teenager, he represented what census takers term "other Hispanics"—immigrants from South and Central America, and the Caribbean who had replaced the Puerto Ricans and Cubans as the city's Hispanic majority. Alvear lived with his wife Blanca and their one-year-old son in the borough of Queens, one of the the most ethnically diverse areas of the country. Alvear and the other workers at Windows on the World proudly described themselves as a "little United Nations" because they represented just about every nation of the world and spoke nearly as many languages.

The WTC rented space primarily to tenants engaged in international commerce: importers, exporters, freight handlers, steamship lines, oil traders, and insurance organizations as well as multinational banks, and financial and commercial firms. Many of these firms chose the WTC not because their businesses benefited directly from physical proximity to other international traders, but because an address at New York's most imposing landmark offered visibility and prestige to firms seeking a high profile in the world of commerce.

On the morning of September 11, 2001 at 8:45 AM, a commercial passenger jet, American Airlines Flight 11 from Boston, hijacked by terrorists, crashed into the north tower of the World Trade Center, tearing a gaping hole in the building and setting it on fire. A second hijacked airliner, Flight 175 from Boston, crashed into the south tower at 9:03 AM. The city and the nation watched the horrific scenes on their television: burning towers and soot-filled office workers fleeing the area. Within an hour and a half these symbols of American wealth and power had collapsed: at 10:05 the south tower fell in a massive cloud of dust and debris, and at 10:28 the north tower collapsed from the top down as if it were being peeled apart, releasing a tremendous cloud of debris and smoke.

Telmo Alvear, who usually worked the night shift, had been covering for a friend that morning. At age twenty-five he perished, along with nearly eighty members of the Hotel and Restaurant Workers Union who, like Alvear, were serving a special breakfast meeting. Nearly 3,000 people—citizens of the United States and eighty other nations—died at the World Trade Center that day. Uncounted were an unknown number of homeless New Yorkers who had sought what they believed to be a safe haven in the cavernous underground spaces of the WTC.

After the towers were hit, airports, bridges, and tunnels into the New York area were quickly closed and the Federal Aviation Administration halted all air traffic nationwide, for the first time in U.S. history. The terrorists, many Saudi nationals and members of Osama bin Laden's Al Qaeda organization, had hijacked four planes. At 9:43 AM, the third plane crashed into the Pentagon, killing 184 people. The White House and later all federal buildings were evacuated. Heroic passengers on the fourth plane fought the hijackers and the plane crashed into rural Pennsylvania and did not reach its target.

The WTC symbolized, if any building could, the confidence of American leadership in an era when national borders seemed to melt away. It also symbolized the transnationalism that many believed laid the foundation for a new world order based on the democratic liberalism that Americans treasured. The attacks underscored the global reach of terrorism, and America's vulnerability to surprise attack suggested the fragile nature of the swiftly changing world.

Above all, the 9/11 attacks placed the issue of security at the very center of American political and cultural life, and forced a reassessment of the nation's foreign policy. While most Americans agreed that the terrorist threat was real, the complicated question of how to respond to and ultimately eliminate it provoked some of the deepest political divisions in recent history. George W. Bush made reshaping U.S. foreign policy the centerpiece of his presidency, and his administration sought radical changes in domestic policy as well, often justifying these in the name of national security. The nation—indeed the world—had come together to condemn the 9/11 attacks and show support for its victims. But the divisive war in Iraq and the bitterly fought presidential election of 2004 revealed how fleeting that consensus had been.

KEY TOPICS

- American foreign policy after the cold war
- The impact of the New Economy and the boom of the 1990s
- Revelations of the 2000 Census
- The Clinton presidency and centrist politics
- Globalization
- International Terrorism
- The Bush presidency and resurgent conservatism
- New Directions in U.S. foreign policy
- War in Iraq

"A KINDER, GENTLER NATION"

During his 1988 presidential campaign, George Herbert Walker Bush hoped to ride on Reagan's coattails and presented himself to the voters as his true successor. Winning the general election handily over Massachusetts governor George Dukakis with forty out of fifty states and 56 percent of the popular vote, he decided he could count on widespread support for his own agenda. In his inaugural address, President Bush began to distance himself from Reagan, promising to deliver a "kinder, gentler nation."

In international affairs, President Bush had prepared well to provide leadership in a dramatically changing world. Before serving as vice president, he had held several major appointive offices that had involved him directly in foreign policy—UN ambassador, envoy to China, and director of the CIA. However, as president, he soon found himself facing a host of problems complicated rather than resolved by the end of the cold war. Somewhat belatedly, President Bush announced that it was "time to move beyond containment to a new policy for the 1990s" without specifying what that new policy would be.

Reagan's Successor: George H. W. Bush

Born in 1924, George Herbert Walker Bush grew up among the New England patrician elite, attended Yale University, and went on to establish a career in the Texas oil industry. Although active in Republican politics since the early 1960s and a two-term vice-president, he assumed the presidency without a clear legislative agenda. He also faced a congress with a Democratic majority.

President Bush carried over several policies from the Reagan administration, such as the war on illegal drugs. He appointed William Bennet as the new "drug czar" and outlined a plan to increase funding for more police and for the construction of more prisons. He also fortified the border patrols in an attempt to stem the flow of drugs from Latin America. In December 1989, President Bush sent U.S. troops to Panama on a mission to capture General Manuel Noriega, an international drug-dealer who at one time had been on the CIA payroll. Thousands of Panamanians died before Noriega was taken into custody and brought to the United States to stand trial on drug-trafficking and racketeering charges. During the Bush presidency, the federal budget for drug-control tripled.

As a self-proclaimed "compassionate" Republican, President Bush gave his support to the Americans With Disabilities Act, which had been introduced during the Reagan administration and now passed through congress. The act penalized employers who discriminated against disabled workers who were qualified for the job and required businesses and local governments to provide access to their facilities. Against the oposition of many business leaders, President Bush signed the bill in July 1990. Showing less compassion, he vetoed a family-leave bill that would have provided up to six-months of unpaid leave to workers with new children or with family emergencies.

The Persian Gulf War

President Bush soon saw that the end of the cold war did not bring world peace but instead let loose a multitude of furies in the form of renewed nationalism, ethnic and religious conflict, and widening divisions between the world's rich and poor. Just as dramatically, as the old geopolitical order disappeared, ideological rivalry shifted to the Middle East and other areas in the world where Islamic militants had forcefully turned against the West.

On August 2, 1990, Iraqi troops swept into neighboring Kuwait and quickly seized control of its rich oil fields. The motives of Saddam Hussein, Iraq's military dictator, were mixed. Like most Iraqis, Hussein believed that oil-rich Kuwait was actually an ancient province of Iraq that had been illegally carved away by British imperial agents in the 1920s as part of the dismemberment of the Ottoman Empire. Control of Kuwait would give Saddam Hussein control of its huge oil reserves, as well as Persian Gulf ports for his landlocked country. Just emerging from an exhausting and inconclusive eight-year war with Iran, Iraqis also bitterly resented Kuwait's production of oil beyond OPEC quotas, which had helped send the world price of oil plummeting from the highs of the 1970s and early 1980s.

The United States responded swiftly to news of the invasion. Its first concern was that Saddam Hussein might also attack Saudi Arabia, which the United States had defined as vital to its interests as far back as 1943. On August 15, President Bush ordered U.S. forces to Saudi Arabia and the Persian Gulf, calling the action Operation Desert Shield. The United States also led a broad coalition in the United Nations, including the Soviet Union, that condemned the Iraqi invasion of Kuwait and declared strict economic sanctions against Iraq if it did not withdraw.

U.S. Marines swept into Kuwait City, March 1991. After six weeks of intensive bombing and less than five days after the start of a massive ground offensive, U.S. and allied forces overwhelmed the Iraqi army and ended Saddam Hussein's occupation of Kuwait.

SOURCE: © *Los Angeles Times*. Photo by Patrick Downs. Reprint by permission.

In early November, President Bush announced a change in policy to what he called "an offensive military option." Administration officials now demonized Saddam Hussein as another Adolf Hitler. The UN sanctions failed to budge Hussein from Kuwait, and the drift to war now looked inevitable. In January 1991, Congress narrowly passed a joint resolution authorizing the president to use military force.

After a last-minute UN peace mission failed to break the deadlock, President Bush announced, on January 16, 1991, the start of Operation Desert Storm. U.S.–led air strikes began forty-two days of massive bombing of Iraqi positions in Kuwait, as well as Baghdad and other Iraqi cities. The ground war, which began on February 24, took only 100 hours to force Saddam Hussein's troops out of Kuwait. Hussein's vaunted military machine—the fourth largest army in the world—turned out to be surprisingly weak. U.S. forces lost only 184 dead, compared to nearly 100,000 Iraqi deaths, mostly from the bombing. Victory in the Gulf War rekindled national pride in many Americans. But for the 18 million people of Iraq, it produced the worst possible outcome. The ecological damage in the Gulf region was extensive and long-lasting. Oil fires burned out of control. Human rights groups reported an appalling death toll among civilians.

The limits of military power to solve complex political and economic disputes became clear in the aftermath of victory. The Persian Gulf war failed to dislodge Saddam Hussein, who remained in power despite CIA attempts to overthrow him and repeated bombings of Iraqi military positions. Iraqi Kurds, who had supported the U.S. invasion in hopes it would topple Saddam, faced violent reprisals, including gassing and chemical weapons, from the Iraqi army. Trade sanctions did little to weaken his rule, although the economic boycott, which brought increasing hardship to the civilian population, eventually divided the Western powers, leaving the United States and Great Britain isolated in their sanctions against Iraq.

The repercussions of the Gulf War were long-lasting. The leading U.S. ally in the region, the oil-rich kingdom of Saudi Arabia, had served as the launching-pad for the invasion of Iraq, and following the war the Saudis had allowed the continuing presence of U.S. troops and weapons. This occupation of Saudi territory, which included Islamic holy sites, intensified the hatred of Americans among many Muslims and prompted appeals for revenge. Between 1980 and the turn of the twenty-first century, they bitterly observed, the United States had waged seventeen distinct military operations in the Middle East, all against Muslims.

Among those actively opposed to the U.S. role in the region was Saudi millionaire Osama bin Laden, just a few years earlier a close ally of the United States during the Russian invasion of Afghanistan. He now turned squarely against his former arms suppliers and CIA contacts. Using his own funds and a tribal network, bin Laden built his shadowy Al Qaeda organization, training small groups in terror tactics to be used against Western interests, particularly to force American troops out of the Middle East.

The Economy and The Election of 1992

Politically, the Persian Gulf War marked the high point of Bush's popularity. His approval rating with the public reached nearly 90 percent, higher than President Franklin Roosevelt's during World War II. Basking in his success, Bush proclaimed the responsibility of the United States to lead in the creation of a "new world order" that would be "freer from the threat of terror, stronger in the pursuit of justice, and more secure in the quest for peace, an era in which the nations of the world, East and West, North and South, can prosper and live in harmony."

However, it was the economy rather than foreign affairs that fueled the 1992 presidential election cam-paign. Republicans took credit for forcing the fall of communism and reviving America's military strength. But they had also promised to cut government spending and balance the budget. In 1985, the Republican Congress had enacted, amid great fanfare, the Balanced Budget and Emergency Deficit Reduction Act, more popularly known as Gramm-Rudman after its principal authors, senators Phil Gramm and Warren Rudman. The act mandated automatic spending cuts if the government failed to meet fixed deficit reduction goals leading to a balanced budget by 1991. But just as Bush was about to take office in 1989, many of the nation's savings and loan institutions, which had been deregulated by Reagan, collapsed. Then, on Friday, October 13, 1989, the stock market took its worst nosedive since 1987, signaling the beginning of a major recession. With the national debt reaching an astronomical $4 trillion, the paradoxes of the Reagan-Bush years had become readily apparent.

Republican President George Bush, Democrat Bill Clinton, and independent H. Ross Perot debated the issues on television three times during the 1992 presidential campaign. Bush emphasized the "character" issue by hammering away at Clinton's failure to serve during the Vietnam War. Clinton focused on the plight of the "forgotten middle class," many of whom had deserted the Democratic party. Perot appealed to voter frustration with the two major parties.

SOURCE: Corbis/Sygma.

American consumers had been spending extravagantly, many falling deep into debt, and now, with the prospect of a recession, they pulled back. Real estate prices plummeted, unemployment hovered at 7 percent, and many businesses filed for bankruptcy. Meanwhile, the Bush administration did little but offer assurances that the recession would be short-lived and promise not to raise taxes. By the end of 1991, the president's performance rating had dropped to just 51 percent.

As the 1992 campaign heated up, President Bush found himself facing a formidable opponent, William Jefferson Clinton. Unlike Bush, the last of the World War II veterans to enter the White House, the youthful Arkansas governor belonged to the Vietnam War generation and had opposed U.S. military intervention in Southeast Asia. Personable, articulate, and highly intelligent, Bill Clinton won the Democratic nomination on the first ballot and chose Tennessee senator Albert Gore as his running mate.

In the Democrats' campaign headquarters a sign humorously reminded the staff: "It's the economy, stupid." Candidate Bill Clinton promised economic leadership, including deficit reduction and a tax cut for the middle class. He also effectively adopted many of the conservative themes that proved so advantageous to Republicans over the past twelve years. He called for "responsibility" on the part of recipients of social programs and spoke of the importance of stable families, promised to be tough on crime and to reduce the bureaucracy, and stressed the need for encouraging private investment to create new jobs. Economic issues also fueled the independent campaign of Texas billionaire H. Ross Perot, who with his folksy East Texas twang argued that a successful businessman such as himself was better qualified to solve the nation's economic woes than Washington insiders.

At the polls in November, Clinton won 43 percent of the popular vote and 32 states. Although failing to carry a single state, Perot scored 19 percent of the popular vote (see Map 31.1). The newly elected Clinton interpreted Perot's relative success at the polls as a mandate to focus, as he put it, "like a laser beam on the economy."

THE CLINTON PRESIDENCY

President Clinton brought a new kind of Democratic leadership to the presidency. Since 1985, he had been active in the Democratic Leadership Council (DLC), a group of Democrats serving in Congress or as governors who became especially concerned about the fate of their party when the Reagan Republicans won forty-nine of fifty states during the 1984 election. Responding to the conservative challenge, they sought to shift the Democratic party away from the liberal tradition established by Franklin D. Roosevelt

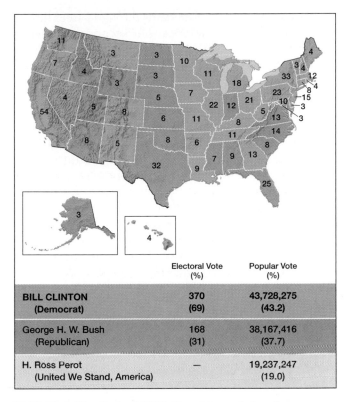

	Electoral Vote (%)	Popular Vote (%)
BILL CLINTON (Democrat)	370 (69)	43,728,275 (43.2)
George H. W. Bush (Republican)	168 (31)	38,167,416 (37.7)
H. Ross Perot (United We Stand, America)	—	19,237,247 (19.0)

MAP 31.1 Election of 1992 Promising to bring about deficit reduction, Ross Perot won the largest percentage of the popular vote of any third-party candidate in U.S. history in the presidential election of 1992.

and revived by Lyndon Johnson in the 1960s. Hoping to recapture suburban and white Southern voters in particular, the DLC set itself to rebuild the party "by redefining and reclaiming the political center." Clinton carried this mission to the White House, presenting an agenda that included balancing the federal budget, reforming welfare, reducing crime, promoting economic growth, and ensuring a strong national defense. Reducing the size of the federal government and promoting free markets worldwide became hallmarks of his administration.

A "New Democrat" in the White House

During his first term, President Clinton pushed two major trade agreements through Congress that built on efforts by the Reagan and Bush administrations to expand markets and encourage "free trade." Approved in November 1993, the North American Free Trade Agreement (NAFTA) eased the international flow of goods, services, and investments among the United States, Mexico, and Canada by eliminating tariffs and other trade barriers. The stated goal of NAFTA was to improve productivity and living standards through a freer flow of commerce in North America. The second trade agreement, the General Agreement on Tariffs and Trade (GATT), slashed tariffs on thousands of goods throughout the world and phased out import quotas imposed by the United States and other industrialized nations. It also established the World Trade Organization (WTO) to mediate commercial disputes among 117 nations.

Critics and supporters of NAFTA and GATT argued over whether the agreements would encourage global competition, thereby boosting American export industries and creating new high-wage jobs for American workers, or simply erode the American industrial base and accelerate environmental degradation. Cities on the U.S.–Mexican border, such as Tijuana and San Diego were clear beneficiaries, but the downside was considerable. New *maquiladora* (factories and assembly plants) lacked pollution controls and spewed tons of toxic wastes into the air and groundwater. Despite the boost from NAFTA, the Mexican peso collapsed, and only a $20 billion bailout of the Mexican economy directed by executive order from the White House on January 31, 1995, prevented a serious depression there.

President Clinton could take credit for several modest successes on the domestic front. He fulfilled one campaign promise by signing the 1993 Family and Medical Leave Act which President Bush had earlier vetoed—requiring large employers to allow workers to take unpaid leave for family or medical emergency. He expanded the Earned Income Tax Credit program (begun in 1975), a refundable tax credit that increases the income of low- and moderate-income working families, especially those with children, by providing tax reductions and cash supplements. A new tax bill reversed some of the inequities of the 1980s by increasing taxes on the top 1.2 percent of households. Clinton championed creation of the AmeriCorps volunteer program, which recruited college graduates for teaching and other service and invoked the idealism associated with John F. Kennedy's Peace Corps of the early 1960s. And Clinton also signed the Brady Bill, a pioneering federal effort to regulate the sale and ownership of handguns.

Clinton's biggest setback during this first term was in the area of health-care reform. Nearly 40 million Americans had no health insurance at all. Many simply could not afford it, and others were denied coverage by private insurers because of preexisting conditions such as AIDS and heart disease. For millions of others, health insurance was tied to the workplace; and a loss or change of jobs threatened their coverage. National spending on health care had skyrocketed from roughly $200 billion in 1980 to more than $800 billion in 1992, constituting about one-seventh of the entire domestic economy.

Shortly after taking office, in a controversial move, President Clinton appointed Hillary Rodham Clinton to head a task force charged with preparing a sweeping legislative overhaul of health care. An accomplished attorney and outspoken feminist, Hillary Clinton, quickly became a target for conservative forces who claimed it was inappropriate for a First Lady to have such a prominent policy-making role. The task force sought a political middle ground between conservative approaches, which stressed fine tuning the system by making private insurance available to all, and more liberal approaches, which would have the federal government guarantee health care as a right. Powerful forces such as the Chamber of Commerce, the National Association of Manufacturers, and most Republicans immediately attacked the proposal. The Health Insurance Association of America spent millions of dollars on negative advertisements. In August, as the 1994 midterm election campaign moved into its final phase, Clinton conceded that his proposal had died in Congress. The complicated Clinton health plan pleased few Americans and was difficult to sell politically—or even explain.

Clinton's defeat on health-care reform helped the Republicans gain control of both the House and Senate for the first time in forty years—a disaster of historic proportions for Clinton and the Democratic Party. Congress was now dominated by a new breed of younger, ideologically more conservative Republicans led by the new House Speaker, Newt Gingrich of Georgia. With his scathing denunciations of big government and celebration of entrepreneurship, the formidable polemicist Gingrich challenged Clinton as the key figure setting the nation's political agenda. His priorities were expressed in a set of proposals labeled the "Contract with America." The House did indeed pass much of the "Contract," including a large tax cut, an increase in military spending, cutbacks in federal regulatory power in the environment and at the workplace, a tough anticrime bill, and a sharp reduction in federal welfare programs.

Differences with the Senate, however, and the threat of presidential veto ultimately thwarted Gingrich's plans and created conditions that allowed President Clinton to make a political comeback. In December of 1995 the Republican-controlled Congress forced a shutdown of the federal government rather than accede to President Clinton's demand for changes in their proposed budget. The result was a public relations disaster for the Republicans. Gingrich's reputation plummeted.

Meanwhile, Clinton undercut the Republicans by adapting many of their positions to his own. He endorsed the goal of a balanced federal budget and declared, in his January 1996 State of the Union message, that "the era of big government is over." For example, despite his attacks on the Republicans as radicals, Clinton opposed his own party's efforts to block a Republican plan to dismantle the federal welfare system in place since the New Deal. The new legislation—the Welfare Reform Act—abolished the sixty-year-old Aid to Families with Dependent Children program (AFDC). Poor mothers with dependent children would now have access to aid for only a limited period and only if they were preparing for or seeking work. When Congress passed the act in August of 1996, Clinton held a public signing ceremony and declared "an end to welfare as we know it."

With such deft maneuvers, Clinton set the theme for his 1996 reelection campaign. The Republican contender, Robert Dole of Kansas, majority leader of the Senate and one of the World War II generation of politicians, waged an inept, unfocused campaign, in part because his party was undergoing an internal struggle between moderate, probusines Republicans, more radical proponents of free markets, and religious conservatives who wanted to make morality and so-called "social issues" the main focus. Staking out the political center, Clinton and his staff crafted a brilliant and well-funded campaign. The president won a resounding reelection victory in November of 1996, confounding the predictions of the political pundits who had pronounced his political death. He won 49 percent of the popular vote compared to Dole's 41 percent, and carried thirty-three states (winning 70 percent of the electoral vote). But it was a victory without coattails: the Republicans retained control of both houses of Congress.

In his State of the Union address in 1997, Clinton backed yet further away from liberalism, promising a "new kind of government—not to solve all of our problems for us, but to give all our people the tools to make the most of their own lives." The era of big government may have ended, as the president proclaimed, but the era of divided government would continue.

Clinton's Internationalism

Like his Democratic predecessor, Jimmy Carter, President Clinton insisted that U.S. foreign policy reflect "the moral principles most Americans share." Now that the cold war had ended, he explained, the United States could replace the strategy of containment with humanitarian goals. However, as president, Clinton also sought to enlarge "the world's free community of market democracies" under the leadership of the United States.

These principles drove Clinton's policy toward the People's Republic of China (PRC). During the spring of 1989, Chinese government forces had brutally attacked prodemocracy demonstrators in Beijing's Tiananmen Square, resulting in the killing of some 3,000 protestors and the wounding of 10,000 more. Scenes of the massacre were broadcast live on television and provoked outrage around the world. President Bush, who had only recently extended Most Favored Nation (MFN) economic and trading status toward the PRC, hoped to maintain ties but was soon pressured by Congress to impose trade sanctions.

During his election campaign, Clinton had criticized Bush for continuing "to coddle" China in light of such gross human rights violations. Then, after taking office, he modified his position and, looking for "hopeful seeds of change," recommended restoring MFN status with the PRC. He acknowledged that serious human rights abuses continued, such as China's religious and cultural persecution in Tibet, but he pointed out that China, the world's most populous nation, had the world's fastest growing economy—as well as a nuclear arsenal and veto in the National Security Council of the UN. He defeated congressional opposition to detach human rights from MFN status and instead promoted free enterprise as a principal means to advance democracy in not only the PRC but in other nations, such as Turkey, Saudi Arabia, and Indonesia.

In seeking to prevent North Korea from acquiring nuclear weapons, Clinton pursued a "carrot and stick" approach that succeeded at first, only to unravel after he left office. North Korea agreed to abandon its goal of creating a nuclear arsenal, in exchange for assistance with its energy needs. However, by 2005, North Korea announced that it did in fact possess nuclear weapons, a development that portended new instability in East Asia.

However reluctantly, in 1995, Clinton committed U.S. troops to a multinational effort in Bosnia where, following the collapse of communism, ethnic and religious rivalry among Serbs, Croats, and Muslims had erupted into a violent civil war. President Bush and his foreign policy advisers, seeing no threat to American interests, opposed U.S. military intervention. But as reports of "ethnic cleansing"—forced removal and murder of Croats and Muslims by Bosnian Serbs—increased, and as the numbers of refugees grew, Clinton, with congressional support, joined NATO in bombing Serbian strongholds in Bosnia. After negotiating with Yugoslavian president Slobodan Milosevic, on November 27 Clinton announced a peace accord that called for a federated, multiethnic state of Bosnia. An International Protection Force, one-third of whom were U.S. troops, was then installed as peacekeepers. One year later, the date Clinton had marked for withdrawal of American troops, Bosnia was still deeply divided, and American troops had settled in for a long haul.

The worst foreign crisis of Clinton's presidency erupted in this region, in the province of Kosovo, where clashes between Serbs and Albanians intensified and spread to neighboring Macedonia and to Albania itself. President Clinton once again attempted to negotiate, but he failed to resolve the problems through diplomacy. After NATO authorized air strikes, he addressed Americans in March 1999, stating that U.S. armed forces had that day joined their allies to attack Serbian forces in Kosovo. On June 10, after a little more than two months of intensive bombing, he reported that the Serbian army was withdrawing from Kosovo, to be replaced by a NATO peacekeeping force.

Presiding over the Boom

By any number of measures, Bill Clinton presided over one of the strongest and longest economic booms in American history. While economists, political analysts, and journalists argued over who deserved the credit, most Americans were content to enjoy the benefits apparent all around them. Between 1992 and 2000 the economy produced over 20 million new jobs and by 2000 the unemployment rate fell below 4 percent, the lowest in over thirty years. Despite fears of new inflation, prices remained low. A world glut of oil production kept energy prices down, while American corporations and workers found it difficult to raise prices or win wage increases in the face of stiffer global competition. With government spending down and economic growth increasing tax revenues, the largest federal budget deficit in American history (a quarter trillion dollars) became a surplus nearly as large by the time Clinton left office.

Perhaps the greatest boost to Clinton's second term as president came from the soaring stock market of the 1990s, with "tech stocks" leading the way. The record highs of the Bush years, when the Dow Jones index of thirty industrials approached 4,000, paled by comparison to the leap in 1999 when the Dow hit 10,000 in March and then peaked above 11,000 in May. The fastest growing sector of the market was NASDAQ, the acronym for National Association of Securities Dealers Automated Quotations, which was created in 1971 to report on the trading of domestic securities. NASDAQ grew to become the largest securities market in the United States and the prime-trading venue for technology stocks. Throughout the decade, the market remained volatile, but profits were extraordinarily high. Annual returns on investments, generally under 6 percent during the 1970s, had risen to more than 18 percent.

Equally remarkable was the involvement "in the market" of ordinary citizens. By the end of the century, Americans had 60 percent of their investments and savings in stocks, more than double the proportion in 1982. An estimated 78.7 million people held stocks, often through mutual funds or in retirement fund portfolios managed by their employers or unions. Thousands of white-collar employees working for fast-rising firms like

Microsoft also acquired stock options that made them "instant millionaires" at the stocks' peak value.

The downside of the economic boom was nearly invisible. Productivity had risen sharply since the 1970s while labor costs had actually declined, hoisting profits to new levels. But critics observed that while a corporate official had earned around twenty or thirty times the pay of a blue-collar worker at the same company a few decades earlier, corporate executive income was more than two hundred times greater than that of a blue-collar employee. Moreover, "downsizing" remained a common strategy for increasing profit levels or defeating negative trends. In the blue-collar sector, industrial jobs continued to disappear as factories closed or companies moved production of textiles, auto parts, and even electronics across borders or overseas. By the end of Clinton's second term, during the second half of 1999, the "dot-com" internet-related stocks began to tumble, and economic analysts began to wonder if the business cycle had indeed been rendered obsolete.

CHANGING AMERICAN COMMUNITIES

The dark side of the post–cold war era seemed to be offset during the 1990s by the unprecedented surge of the U.S. economy and the inclusion of millions of new immigrants, who easily found places for themselves within the rapidly expanding service sector. The patterns of growth indicated a dynamic shift toward a "new economy," a phrase coined by economists in the 1970s to characterize the increasing importance of the service sector, corporate restructuring, and globalization. In turn, the new economy depended on high technology, wherein today's worker with a large degree of skill and entrepreneurial initiative might be tomorrow's millionaire. After the recession bottomed out in 1994, Americans settled in to enjoy record profits, low unemployment rates, and unsurpassed prosperity. By the 1990s, United States economy revolved around services. The service sector included all those workers not directly involved in producing or processing a physical product: from highly paid lawyers, financial analysts, and software designers to poorly paid fast food employees. In 1965 an estimated 50 percent of all jobs were in the service sector; by 2000, the figure had grown to about 70 percent.

Silicon Valley

The real and symbolic capital of the new economy was a thirty-by-ten-mile strip of Santa Clara County, California. As late as 1960 this region was the major processor of fruits and vegetables in the world; forty years later one-third of the valley's workforce were employed by the high-tech companies of microelectronics.

Dubbed "Silicon Valley" in 1971 after the semiconductor chip, which is made of silicon, and which became the basic building block of modern microelectronics, the region flourished thanks to its unique combination of research facilities, investment capital, attractive environment, and a large pool of highly educated people. At first, military contracts predominated, but the consumer electronics revolution of the 1970s fueled an explosive new wave of growth. Silicon Valley firms gave birth to pocket calculators, video games, home computers, cordless telephones, digital watches, and almost every other new development in electronics. It became home to more than 1,700 high-tech firms that specialized in gathering, processing, or distributing information or in manufacturing information technology. Companies like Hewlett-Packard, Apple, and Intel achieved enormous success and became household names. Silicon Valley boasted the greatest concentration of new wealth in the United States.

By the end of the century, Silicon Valley had become a continuous sprawl of two dozen cities between San Francisco and San Jose and the home and workplace of a diverse population. The managers and engineers, nearly all of whom were white males, had settled in affluent communities such as Palo Alto, Mountain View, and Sunnyvale. Manual workers on assembly lines and in low-paying service jobs clustered in San Jose and Gilroy. Most of these were Latino, African American, Vietnamese, Cambodian, and Filipino men and women who constituted a cheap, nonunionized labor pool with an extremely high turnover rate.

The prime example of the new economy, Silicon Valley was also part of a global enterprise. Its firms were closely linked to the microelectronic industry of the greater Pacific Rim. The end of the cold war and the accompanying decline in military spending in the United States forced high-tech firms in California into greater competition on the world market and especially against similar companies in Japan, Korea, China, and Malaysia. But many American companies protected themselves against such competition by owning and managing a large share of the plants in these countries.

By the end of the century, the rate of growth showed signs of slowing, as did the infusion of new venture capital into high-tech industries. Young entrepreneurs throughout the Pacific Rim found it more difficult to start successful new companies and to make the leap from a small, start-up company to a large corporation. By this time, scarcity in housing, traffic jams, and an inflated cost of living were already leading many companies and individuals to move out of the area.

An Electronic Culture

The technological developments produced in Silicon Valley helped reconfigure cultural life in the United States and the world. Revolutions in computers and telecommunications merged telephones, televisions, computers, cable, and satellites into a global system of information exchange. The new technologies changed the way people worked and played. They made the nation's cultural life more homogeneous and played a greater role than ever in shaping politics.

The twin arrivals of cable and the videocassette recorder (VCR) expanded and redefined the power of television. By the end of the 1980s pay cable services and VCRs had penetrated roughly two-thirds of American homes. Cable and satellite in the 1990s offered television viewers scores of new programming choices, especially sports events and movies. The VCR revolutionized the way people used their sets, allowing them to organize program-watching around their own schedules. Hollywood studios began releasing movies on videotape, and the rental and sale of movies for home viewing quickly outstripped ticket sales at theaters as the main profit source for filmmakers.

In 1981, a new cable channel called MTV (for Music Television) began airing videos of popular music stars performing their work. The intent was to boost sales of the stars' audio recordings, but the music video soon became a new art form in itself. Artists who best exploited music video, such as Madonna and Michael Jackson, achieved international superstar status. MTV also helped transform smaller, cult musical forms, such as rap and heavy metal, into giant mass-market phenomena. MTV pioneered an imaginative visual style, featuring rapid cutting, animation, and the sophisticated fusion of sound and image. More than ever, television drove the key strategies and tactics defining American political life. Politicians and their advisers focused intently on a candidate's television image. Issues, positions, and debate all paled alongside the key question: How did it look on television? Fewer citizens voted or took an active role in campaigns, and most relied on television coverage to make their choices. Thus, creating an effective television "character" emerged as perhaps the most crucial form of political discourse.

New digital technologies continued to reshape American culture through the 1990s and early 2000s. Compact Discs (CDs) and Digital Video Discs (DVDs) emerged as the dominant media for popular music and movies, replacing tape-based technologies. Millions of Americans now used digital cameras to document their vacations and everyday lives. Digital telephones—"cell phones"—became a ubiquitous presence in the streets, malls, campuses, cars, and workplaces of American communities.

Perhaps no aspect of the electronic culture was more revolutionary than the creation of cyberspace, the conceptual region occupied by people linked through computers and communications networks. It began with ARPANET, the first computer network, which was created by the Department of Defense in

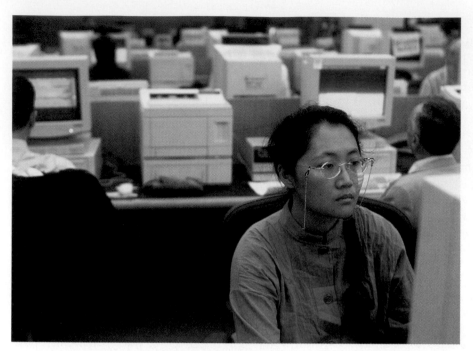

Yi Li, a graduate student from Taiwan, uses a computer terminal at the New York Public Library to gain access to the Internet. By the 1990s banks of personal computers had become a familiar sight in American offices, businesses, schools, and libraries. Millions of Americans made connecting with the new world of "cyberspace" a part of their daily routines.

SOURCE: MarkLennihan/AP Wide World Photos.

the early 1970s. Computer enthusiasts known as "hackers" created unexpected grassroots spinoffs from ARPANET, including electronic mail, computer conferencing, and computer bulletin board systems. In the mid-1980s the boom in cheap personal computers capable of linking to the worldwide telecommunications network began a population explosion in cyberspace. By then, tens of thousands of researchers and scholars at universities and in private industry were linked to the Internet—the U.S. government-sponsored successor to ARPANET—through their institutions' computer centers. The establishment of the World Wide Web and easy-to-use browser software such as Netscape, introduced in 1994, made the "information highway" accessible to millions of Americans with few computer skills and created a popular communications medium with global dimensions.

By the beginning of the new century, the U. S. Census Bureau estimated that more than half of all households had at least one computer and more than 40 percent were connected to the Internet. Nearly 85 percent of classrooms in public schools were online. At work, Americans spent an average of 21 hours per week online. At home, they spent an average of 9.5 hours per week online, gaining access to the Web from independent service providers such as America Online and Earthlink. For a flat monthly fee users could play games, send electronic mail, discuss issues in public forums, and purchase a huge array of goods and services, ranging from books and airline tickets to automobiles and psychotherapy sessions.

These new information technologies gave birth to a media community that transcended national boundaries. During the 1980s, exports from Hollywood to the rest of the world doubled in value. The number of hours of television watched throughout the world nearly tripled: MTV was broadcast to an estimated 250 million households. By the mid-1990s there were more television sets in China than in the United States. The growth of cable was phenomenal; in the Netherlands, for example, 98 percent of households received programming by cable. Americans, however, owned a disproportionate share of the largest media corporations in the world, with Microsoft, Disney, and Time Warner in the lead. More than 40 percent of television programs in the world originated in the United States, and in Latin America the percentage of U.S.–produced programs reached 75 percent.

The New Immigrants and Their Communities

The 2000 census showed that the nation's population during the 1990s grew by 32.7 million, a number greater than that of any other decade in U.S. history. Even the 1950s, which witnessed the post–World War II baby boom, could not compete against a decade marked by a huge number of immigrants and a birthrate that surpassed the death rate. At the beginning of the new millennium, Americans numbered 281.4 million.

The 2000 census confirmed what many Americans had observed over the previous decade in their communities and workplaces. The face of the nation was perceptibly changing and changing on a scale that compared to the first decades of the twentieth century, when immigration from Europe peaked. At the turn of the twenty-first century, more than a third of the nation's population growth came from the influx of new immigrants (see Figure 31.1). Although three-quarters of the newcomers joined many other Americans in flocking to the Sunbelt states, headed by California, Texas, and Florida, they not only helped to reverse population loss in such major urban centers as New York and Chicago and slow the decline in Rustbelt cities like Cleveland, Detroit, and Milwaukee, but also for the first time in any census, they played a major role in the population increase in all fifty states. Nationally, the percentage of Americans born outside the United States was 11.2 percent, its highest point since 1930; in California the percentage of foreign born approached 26 percent.

The Immigration Act of 1965, passed almost unnoticed in the context of the egalitarian political climate created by the civil rights movement, had revolutionary consequences, some of them unintended. The act abolished the discriminatory national origins quotas that had been in place since the 1920s. It also limited immigration from the Western Hemisphere for the first time, while giving preferences to people from the nations of the Eastern Hemisphere who had specialized job skills and training. This provision created the conditions for Asian immigrants to become the fastest-growing ethnic group in the United States. But in setting limits on Western Hemisphere immigration, the 1965 act tempted many thousands of people from Latin American to enter the United States illegally. By the mid-1980s, growing concern over "illegal aliens" had become a hotly debated political issue, particularly in the Southwest. The Immigration Reform and Control Act of 1986 marked a break with the past attempts to address this problem. Instead of mass deportation programs, the law offered an amnesty to all undocumented workers who had entered the country since 1982. Four years later, additional revisions of this act enlarged the quota of immigrants, once again giving priority to skilled and professional workers. Hispanics and Asians benefited from these changes in immigration law. Within the twenty fastest-growing cities, the number of Hispanics and Asians increased by approximately 70 percent.

Demographers predicted that Hispanics, who had grown from 22.4 million in 1990 to 35.3 million in 2000, according to census data, would replace African Americans as the largest minority group in the nation by the middle of the twenty-first century. By 1990 Hispanics had already formed over a third of the population of New Mexico, a quarter of the population of Texas, and over 10 percent of the populations of California, Ari-

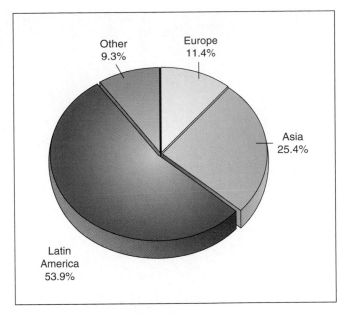

FIGURE 31.1 Continent of Birth for Immigrants, 1990–2000 By 2000, the number of foreign-born residents and their children—56 million according to the Census Bureau—had reached the highest level in U.S. history.

zona, and Colorado. Nearly a million Mexican Americans lived in Los Angeles alone.

The 2000 census showed that Mexicans were the largest Hispanic group in the United States at 20.6 million, representing nearly 60 percent of the total Hispanic population. The boom of the U.S. economy in the 1990s, with service, agricultural, and even factory jobs readily available, had provided a significant "pull" for these newcomers. But other factors encouraged many immigrants to make an often difficult and dangerous sojourn. First, a drop in worldwide oil prices followed by the deflation of the Mexican national currency dramatically lowered living standards in Mexico in the mid-1990s. NAFTA and the greater integration of the U.S. and Mexican economies brought new jobs but often with increasingly expensive living conditions. Tens and perhaps hundreds of thousands of Mexicans worked in the United States temporarily while planning a permanent move north, with or without legal documentation.

After settling across the border, most new Mexican Americans struggled in low-wage and often dangerous jobs such as meatpacking or construction, and they were more likely to die from workplace injuries than other workers. Through education and success in business, a significant number achieved middle-class status and wealth. But almost 20 percent of Mexican Americans lived below the poverty line. They tended to live

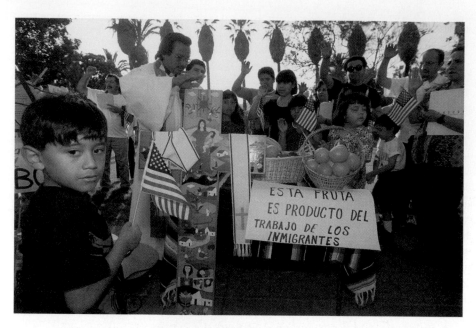

The sign at this 1996 vigil in Echo Park, Los Angeles reads, "This fruit is the product of immigrants' labor." Members of the city's Latino community bless fruit baskets as they protest a state crack down on illegal immigration and the increase of border patrol guards.

SOURCE: AP Wide World Photos.

in segregated neighborhoods and were less likely than non-Hispanic whites to have health insurance or to own their own homes.

In New York, the Puerto Rican–born population jumped from 100,000 in 1945 to roughly 1 million twenty years later. However, during the 1990s, this trend had begun to reverse, their numbers falling by 12 percent. The smaller but highly influential Cuban population declined even more, by 27 percent. Meanwhile, other Latin populations grew at an extraordinary rate of 50 percent. The Mexican-born population more than doubled, and Filipinos, who often speak Spanish as a first language, increased by 27 percent. Immigrants from the Dominican Republic, now second in population size only to Puerto Ricans, dominated sizable sections of Washington Heights and Brooklyn, while immigrants from various countries in Central and South America created new communities throughout the greater metropolitan region (see Map 31.2).

The cultural implications for all Americans, not just new New Yorkers, were far-reaching. Children born to the new immigrants of the 1980s and 1990s, despite increasing neighborhood segregation by race, played on the streets together, attended the same schools and often married outside their racial group. In the 2000 census, 6.8 million Americans nationwide listed themselves as multiracial. Identities blurred as popular entertainment created new mixes of traditions and styles. "World beat" music (heavily influenced by "Afro-Pop"), *Alternalatino* (alternative Latin music—a mixture of salsa and merengue), Tjano, Reggae, and other music in fusion mixtures became as common to Manhattan or Los Angeles as to Mexico City or Rio. By the 1990s, the West Indian carnival held annually in Brooklyn at the end of summer had become the most popular ethnic festival in Greater New York City.

Although smaller in number than Hispanics, Asians were the fastest-growing racial group in the United States. The number of Asian Americans soared from 7.3 million in 1990 to approximately 10.2 million in 2000. With a steady flow of professionals and workers skilled in technology into their communities, Chinese Americans maintained their status as the largest Asian ethnicity in the United States. However, other groups grew at faster rates, particularly Indo Americans (from the subcontinent of India), whose numbers doubled during the 1990s to 1.68 million to become the third-largest Asian group. Meanwhile Japanese Americans, once the largest and most influential members of the pan-Asian community, declined. Immigration from Japan had virtually ceased during the decade, while many young Japanese Americans married someone of a different race.

Like earlier immigrant groups, new Americans from Korea, Vietnam, and the Philippines tended to cluster in their own communities and maintain a durable group identity. As a whole, Asian Americans made mobility through education a priority, along with pooling family capital and labor to support small businesses.

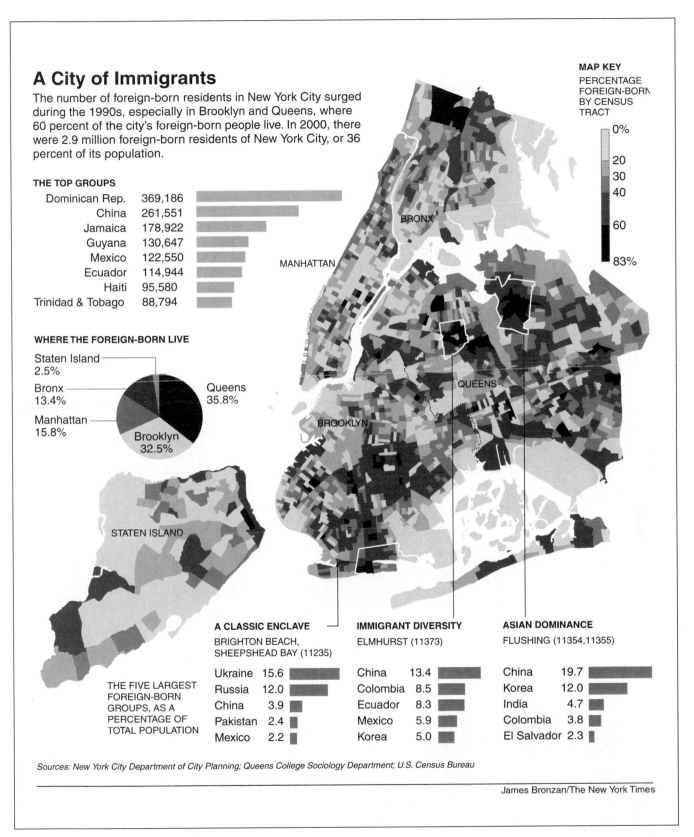

A City of Immigrants

The number of foreign-born residents in New York City surged during the 1990s, especially in Brooklyn and Queens, where 60 percent of the city's foreign-born people live. In 2000, there were 2.9 million foreign-born residents of New York City, or 36 percent of its population.

THE TOP GROUPS

Dominican Rep.	369,186
China	261,551
Jamaica	178,922
Guyana	130,647
Mexico	122,550
Ecuador	114,944
Haiti	95,580
Trinidad & Tobago	88,794

WHERE THE FOREIGN-BORN LIVE

Staten Island 2.5%
Bronx 13.4%
Manhattan 15.8%
Brooklyn 32.5%
Queens 35.8%

MAP KEY
PERCENTAGE FOREIGN-BORN BY CENSUS TRACT

0%
20
30
40
60
83%

BRONX
MANHATTAN
QUEENS
BROOKLYN
STATEN ISLAND

A CLASSIC ENCLAVE
BRIGHTON BEACH, SHEEPSHEAD BAY (11235)

THE FIVE LARGEST FOREIGN-BORN GROUPS, AS A PERCENTAGE OF TOTAL POPULATION

Ukraine	15.6
Russia	12.0
China	3.9
Pakistan	2.4
Mexico	2.2

IMMIGRANT DIVERSITY
ELMHURST (11373)

China	13.4
Colombia	8.5
Ecuador	8.3
Mexico	5.9
Korea	5.0

ASIAN DOMINANCE
FLUSHING (11354,11355)

China	19.7
Korea	12.0
India	4.7
Colombia	3.8
El Salvador	2.3

Sources: New York City Department of City Planning; Queens College Sociology Department; U.S. Census Bureau

James Bronzan/The New York Times

MAP 31.2 Ethnic Neighborhoods New York City

SOURCE: *New Ethnic Neighborhoods*, "A City of Immigrants", *The New York Times*, 1/30/05.

Newcomers selected communities with job opportunities or where family members and friends had settled previously. This "chain migration" is illustrated by the large numbers of Hmongs, a tribal group from Laos, living in Minneapolis and St. Paul. The stream of Hmongs began with church-sponsored refugee programs, then gained momentum as more and more family members followed. As one of the nation's leading states in the resettlement of refugees, Minnesota saw its total Asian population triple, increasing during the 1980s from 26,000 to 78,000, and then nearly doubling in the next decade. (See Out of Many Voices: "A Cambodian Woman In Chicago.")

The 2000 census also revealed sharp divisions among Americans. Although the poverty rate had dropped to 11.3 percent of the population, near the lowest level ever recorded, more than 31 million people still lived in poverty. Moreover, the new economy had done little to close the gap between the highest and lowest income earners. Women as a group made few gains, earning 73 cents to each dollar earned by men. And with African Americans and Latinos continuing to earn, on average, far less than non-Hispanic whites, race relations benefited little from the economic boom of the 1990s.

A NEW AGE OF ANXIETY

Despite the prosperity of the 1990s, many Americans experienced an uneasiness that resembled the anxiety of mid-twentieth century, when the world seemed on the brink of nuclear destruction. The threat of communism had expired along with the cold war, but doubts and fears about the fate of their own society had multiplied. So many changes had occurred in just the last three decades of the century that a sense of permanence had disappeared. The new economy had transformed the way Americans worked and played. The new wave of immigration had dramatically altered the demographic landscape. Even the way the nation's leaders conducted themselves appeared not only new but potentially

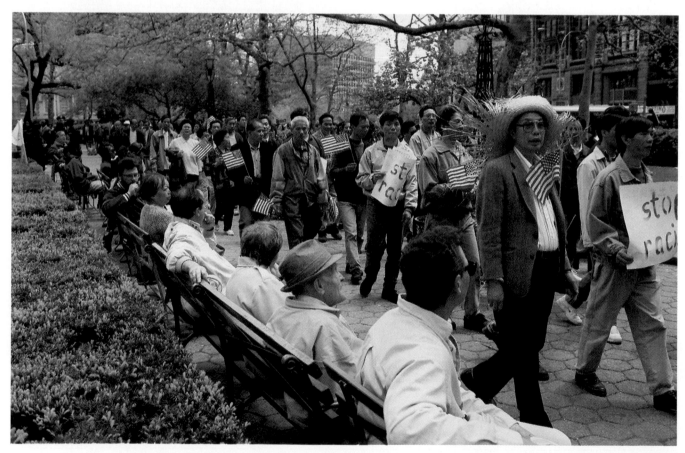

Demonstrators file past New York's City Hall, protesting proposed antiimmigrant legislation, May 2, 1996. Organized by the Asian American Alliance, actions like this reflected the growing political mobilization of Asian Americans, especially around immigration related issues.

SOURCE: AP Wide World Photos.

hazardous to the moral order. In addition, many Americans had begun to fear for their personal safety, even within their own communities.

The Racial Divide

More than a quarter-century after the uprising in Watts, the situation in South Central Los Angeles in 1992 seemed more desperate than ever to most African Americans. The poverty rate was 30.3 percent, more than twice the national average. The unemployment rate for adult black males hovered around 40 percent, and a quarter of the population was on welfare. The passage of a statewide tax cut in 1978 had led to a sharp reduction in public investment in the inner-city educational system. Drug dealing and gang warfare had escalated, reflecting the sense of despair among young people.

In the spring of 1992 an upheaval in Los Angeles offered the starkest evidence that racial tensions had not eased. The spark that ignited the worst riot of the century was outrage over police brutality. A year earlier, Rodney King, a black motorist, had been pulled from his vehicle and severely beaten by four white police officers. When, despite the graphic evidence of an amateur videotape of the incident, a jury acquitted the officers of all but one of eleven counts of assault, several minority communities erupted in anger, looting and burning businesses in South Central Los Angeles and Koreatown. Fifty-one people were killed, and 500 buildings were destroyed before L.A. police and National Guard troops restored order.

The events in Los Angeles exposed the deep animosity among various groups—so much so that the observers referred to the event as a "multicultural riot."

OUT OF MANY VOICES

A Cambodian Woman In Chicago

"My," a rice farmer born in 1940, fled Cambodia with her family in 1979 to escape the fierce fighting between the Khmer Rouge and the Vietnamese. After a stay in the Philipines, the family made it to Chicago in 1988. Her struggle to hold her family together and to learn English, as well as the hopes invested in her children, reflected the mixed experiences of many Asian immigrants in the 1980s.

SEVEN FAMILIES IN EVANSTON SPONSORED OUR family and we've lived in Chicago ever since. When I first got here, my blood nearly froze. It was really cold. My husband was very reluctant to come because he didn't want to leave his mother. He was so distant from us when we arrived here. He asked to enter the monastery, then he became a monk in Ohio. I've lost all ties with him. I hear he has a new family out in California, but I don't care much. I think only of my children now.

I always say that I'm going to learn English, but it's so hard to learn. I was at a workshop one time and it was time for everyone to leave, but my son was late in coming to pick me up. The case worker was in a rush and he was very rude to me. He kept on asking me for my address and asked if I knew my phone number. All I knew was "no." So all I said was, "no." So he grabbed my folder and wrote some profanity on it and left. I didn't know it was bad, except for his facial expressions. I was really shook up. I was so humiliated from it that I had learned that I need to force myself to learn English. Now I take English lessons from a tutor who comes to my house once a week. I can't remember, just a little here and a little there. I never went to school when I was young. I don't really remember the letters, I just remember things orally.

But education is the most important thing. I would do anything for my kids. I'll be their mother and their father, if they keep on studying like they do. I'm an old ox and I can't be forced to learn new things. I try to obey the commandments of Buddhism. My children are very bright; they've made my life easier. A few years ago, I didn't want to live. I wanted to be hit by a car. But I've changed my mind recently for the sake of my younger children. They are good children, but they remain in ignorance about the world. I always encourage them to tell me about their sorrows and their concerns. I want them to fit in this society. ■

SOURCE: Collected and translated by Elizabeth Chey, 1995. Mekong Network http://www.mekong.net/cambodia/3women2.htm.

Almost 2,000 Korean businesses were destroyed, and Koreans angrily accused the police of making no effort to defend their stores. The division was sharpest, though, between whites and the minority populations. "We are all quite isolated in our own communities," a resident of Westwood, a mostly white middle-class neighborhood, explained. "We don't know and don't care about the problems in the inner cities. Driving to work every day most of us don't even know where South Central is—except many of us saw the fires from that direction when we were stuck in traffic."

The situation in Los Angeles was not unique. The 2000 census showed that segregation was on the rise, and not only in cities but in their surrounding suburbs. For example, in the Atlanta region, which claimed the largest share of black suburbanites in the nation (26 percent), the percent living separately from whites had increased from 52 percent in 1990 to nearly 60 percent by 2000. Similarly, in the nation's schools, the gains from the civil rights era were diminishing and, in some communities, disappearing altogether. A report released in 2001 showed that, despite the increasing racial and ethnic diversity of the nation's youth, segregation was becoming more pronounced in grades K–12.

The publicity generated by the arrest of Rodney King fed several major controversies concerning the U.S. criminal justice system. In 1999 the Bureau of Justice reported that 6.3 million people were on probation, in jail or prison, or on parole, representing 3.1 percent of all adult residents. Incarceration rates, highest in the southern states of Louisiana, Texas, and Mississippi, showed a slight decline in early 2000 but nevertheless had more than tripled since 1980. Racial disparities were pronounced, with ethnic and racial minorities accounting for approximately two-thirds of state prison inmates. Based on these figures, the Bureau of Justice estimated that 28 percent of African American men would enter a state or federal prison during their lifetimes.

Various civil liberties groups reviewed these statistics and concluded that African Americans were not necessarily more prone to criminal activity but were far more likely to be stopped, searched, arrested, convicted, and given harsher penalties than white Americans. Critics singled out the practice of "racial profiling" whereby police disproportionately stopped African Americans and Latinos as the most likely offenders. By the end of the decade, in a review of various data nationwide, the National Institute of Drug Abuse estimated that although 12 percent of illegal drug users were black, they now made up 50 percent of all drug possession arrestees. By this time, "driving while black" had become a news item in all the major media, leading to the introduction of a bill into the U.S. Senate in 1999 to collect statistics on traffic stops.

The Forces of Fear

During the 1990s and first years of the new century, anxiety about terrorism and random violence escalated. Within their own borders, Americans were actually far safer from terrorist attacks than the citizens of many other countries. Nevertheless, two events—the attack on the World Trade Center in 1993 and the destruction of the federal building in Oklahoma City in 1995—alerted Americans to danger at home and to U.S. interests abroad.

On February 26, 1993, a small group associated with Osama bin Laden bombed the World Trade Center in New York City. The terrorists used a rented van to deliver explosives that demolished an underground parking lot, killed six people, and injured more than a thousand others. Taken in retaliation for U.S. policies in the Middle East, the attack was the most destructive act of terrorism committed within the United States to that time. It spurred the Antiterrorism and Effective Death Penalty Act of 1996, which greatly expanded the budget and powers of federal authorities to monitor likely terrorists. Despite increased surveillance of terrorist groups, bin Laden's organization struck another lethal blow. On August 7, 1998, car bombings of U.S. embassies in Kenya and Tanzania injured more than 5,500 people and killed 225.

The bombing of the Alfred P. Murrah Federal Building in Oklahoma City raised an entirely different specter: terrorism by self-described patriotic Americans. The perpetrators represented the extremist wing of the New Right, the superpatriot movement, which included groups of people who set up "survivalist" encampments in rural areas and organized themselves into armed militias. Inspired by author William Pierce's *Turner Diaries* (1978), which predicted a revolt of "Aryans" against people of color and the federal government, the patriots found their martyrs in the Branch Davidians and their revenge in Oklahoma.

Two years earlier, on February 28, 1993, agents of the FBI and the Federal Bureau of Alcohol, Tobacco, and Firearms (ATF) had conducted a "search and arrest" operation against the Branch Davidians that turned deadly. Their object was David Koresh, the leader of the obscure religious sect who was suspected of stockpiling illegal firearms and ammunition. After a round of shots, which took the lives of four ATF agents and six Branch Davidians, Koresh's heavily armed followers barricaded themselves in their compound in Waco, Texas. Fifty-one days later, on April 19, government agents brought their siege to a fiery end. Nine Davidians managed to escape the flames engulfing their buildings, while seventy-six others, including twenty-one children, perished.

On April 19, 1995, Timothy McVeigh and his accomplices took revenge for the tragedy in Waco. Shortly after 9:00 AM, a bomb went off in the federal office building in Oklahoma City, killing 168 people, including 19 children, and injuring more than 500 others. They had chosen April 19, the anniversary of the federal raid at Waco, as their "Date of Doom." Arrested within hours of the bombing on a misdemeanor traffic violation, McVeigh was charged in connection with the crime just three days later. After a trial in federal court and demonstrations both for and against the death penalty, he was executed in June 2001.

Immediately after the Oklahoma City bombing, President Clinton declared a national day of mourning for the victims and their families. He addressed the nation, saying "Let us let our own children know that we will stand against the forces of fear. When there is talk of hatred, let us stand up and talk against it. When there is talk of violence, let us stand up and talk against it."

But terrorism continued, with many of the attacks politically or ideologically motivated. For example, medical clinics that provided abortion services to women became a prime target. Although the ratio of abortions to live pregnancies had been declining since 1979, groups opposed to abortion became more belligerent. Operation Rescue launched a well-publicized and illegal blockade of three abortion clinics in Wichita, Kansas in September 1991. Although the "war in Wichita" ended peacefully after forty-six days,

antiabortion protests became increasingly violent in its wake. Several medical providers were murdered outside their clinics. In 1994, with the support of President Clinton, Congress enacted the Freedom of Access to Clinic Entrance Act, which provides protection to any abortion clinic requesting it. Although the number of violent incidents declined since the peak of nineteen bombings in 1992 and forty-two murders in 1994, the attacks did not stop.

The Culture Wars

In the 1980s and 1990s, moral and social issues, many observers noted, were replacing long-standing political markers such as religion, ethnicity, and socioeconomic class. Whereas the "New Democrats" of Clinton's administration and conservative Republicans differed little on their perception of the appropriate size and power of the federal government, they were at loggerheads over what constituted American values. Thus what one scholar described as "the struggle to define America" became hotly contested in the 1990s, with politics increasingly centered in discussions about reproductive rights and reproductive technology, homosexuality and gay rights, the curriculum in public schools, codes of speech and standards in the arts, gun control, and scientific developments such as cloning, genetic alteration, and fetal tissue research, and even the validity of Darwin's theory of evolution.

Rescue workers carried an injured man from the ruble of the U.S. Embassy in Nairobi, Kenya. A terrorist bomb killed more than 100 people and injured more than 1,600 on August 8, 1998.

SOURCE: Agence France Presse/Getty Images.

The increasing racial and ethnic diversity of American society, as well as the expansion of rights for groups such as women and gays, had become the impetus for a broad and controversial movement known as "multiculturalism." Unlike earlier conceptions of America as a "melting pot," new metaphors such as "salad bowl" or "mosaic" became popular expressions that emphasized the unique attributes and achievements of formerly marginal groups and recent immigrants. This celebration of diversity played a big part in the campaign strategy of Bill Clinton, and he won a large share of votes by tailoring his appeals to specific groups. Like other Democrats, he received upward of 80 percent of black votes, but he won more votes from Latinos and Asian Americans than any other candidate in American history. On college campuses, multiculturalism marked the high point of the curricular reform that had been ongoing since the late 1960s and early 1970s, when specialized programs in women's studies and African American studies were launched (see Chapter 29). The increased visibility of career women in the professions, business, and government—embodied by the outspoken and influential First Lady, Hillary Rodham Clinton—offered one important measure of the long-range impact of 1960s–70s feminism.

Both multiculturalism and the steady advances made by professional women fueled a conservative backlash. For many conservatives, multiculturalism had replaced communism as the nation's most dangerous enemy, and they rallied to reinstate what they called universal truths and traditional moral values. University of Chicago professor Allan Bloom's bestselling *The Closing of the American Mind* (1987), for example, argued that the new lesson plans failed to prepare Americans for the responsibility of preserving their democratic legacy.

The culture wars were not restricted to the academic world. Americans divided sharply over many issues, including immigration policy. In 1994, a referendum on California's ballot, Proposition 187, called for making all undocumented aliens ineligible for any welfare services, schooling, and nonemergency medical care, and it required teachers and clinic doctors to report illegal immigrants to the police. Proposition 187 passed by a three-to-two margin, but it was immediately challenged in the streets and in the courts. In 1998, after several years of legal wrangling, a Los Angeles federal district court judge ruled that Proposition 187 unconstitutionally usurped federal authority over immigration policy. In June 2001, the U.S. Supreme Court ruled that immigrants are entitled to the same protection by the Constitution as that afforded to citizens.

But the national debate over immigration policy, in which economic issues and racial fears were deeply entangled, continued unabated in California and elsewhere. As one Stanford law professor who had worked to overturn Proposition 187 put it: "Some people genuinely worry about the problem of too many immigrants in a stagnant economy. But for most, economics is a diversion. Underneath it is race." California voters also upheld legislation enacted in 1996 that banned the consideration of race, ethnicity, and gender in college admissions and public employment, and thereby abolished the affirmative action programs established thirty years earlier.

A similar backlash gathered steam against gays. A major controversy erupted around a push for the legal recognition of marriage for same-sex couples. Although the first law suits dated to the early 1970s, in May 1993 the Supreme Court of Hawai'i ruled that the laws barring same-sex couples from getting a marriage license were discriminatory and therefore in violation of the state constitution. This highly controversial decision prompted conservative state legislators to propose an amendment to the state constitution barring same-sex marriages, which the Hawai'ian voters overwhelmingly approved in 1998. Meanwhile, several Republicans in the U.S. Congress, fearing that if any state recognized same-sex marriages all other states would be forced to recognize these marriages as legal, sponsored legislation to deny recognition to these unions. In 1996, President Clinton signed the Defense of Marriage Act, which specified that gay couples would be ineligible for spousal benefits provided by federal law.

The issue of gay marriage continued to evolve on the state level. In 2000, Vermont became the first state to recognize civil unions, allowing same-sex couples to receive many, although not all, of the legal benefits of marriage. Several other states passed versions of civil union or domestic partner laws. In 2004, Massachusetts became the first state in America to legally permit gay marriage. The law allowing same-sex marriage was the outcome of a landmark ruling by the state's Supreme Judicial Court that declared the prohibition of gay marriage to be a violation of the state's constitution. But seventeen states passed constitutional provisions defining marriage as a union of one man and one woman, while twenty-five others enacted legislative statutes with similar definitions. The gay marriage issue would continue hovering as a powerful symbolic issue in the 2004 presidential election.

At the end of the century, the antiabortion movement took a new turn by opposing government financing of an area of scientific research that had

After the University of California regents voted to end the affirmative action policy governing admissions to the statewide system, students at the University of California–Irvine protested outside the campus administration building in October, 1995.

SOURCE: AP Wide World Photos.

been growing in importance since the birth of the first test-tube baby in 1981—embryonic stem cell research. Because these microscopic clusters of cells have the potential to grow into any tissue in the body, embryonic stem cells hold promise, scientists believe, for refurbishing or replacing damaged tissues or organs and therefore might prove useful in treating or perhaps even curing diseases such as diabetes, Parkinson's, and Alzheimer's. Conservatives opposed this research because it involves the destruction of human embryos, usually derived from the excess products of *in vitro* fertilization processes and scheduled for disposal by fertility clinics. In 1995, in response to pressure from conservative groups such as the National Right to Life Committee, Congress enacted legislation banning the use of federal funds for research that involves the destruction of human embryos. However, in his last year in office, Clinton loosened the ban and thereby generated another round of controversy. Most conservative groups remained firm in their opposition, agreeing with the United States Conference of Catholic Bishops, which insisted "that the government must not treat any living human being as research material, as a mere means for benefit to others."

High Crimes and Misdemeanors

As lightning rods in the ongoing culture wars, Bill and Hillary Clinton found themselves the object of relentless attacks by conservative moralists. Questions of private and public morality dogged Bill

Clinton's political career. During the 1992 election campaign, while intending to focus on the economy, he found himself offering explanations for past behavior, such as avoiding the draft during the Vietnam War and smoking—but "not inhaling," he claimed—marijuana during his college years. However, once in office, he acted boldly on reproductive rights and put forward a controversial "don't ask, don't tell" policy for gays in the armed forces. Conservatives, including such religious groups as the Christian Coalition, the American Family Association, and the Traditional Values Coalition, as well as many Republicans, struck back.

During his second term as president, Clinton had to answer many questions about his moral conduct. Real estate deals involving both him and Hillary Rodham Clinton blew up into a scandal known as Whitewater. More predictive of troubles ahead, a former Arkansas state employee, Paula Jones, charged Clinton with sexual assault during his gubernatorial term. Attorney General Janet Reno, under extreme pressure from conservatives, appointed an independent counsel, former judge Kenneth Starr, to investigate allegations. But in the summer of 1998, Starr delivered to the House Judiciary Committee a report focusing on an extramarital affair that the president conducted with a young White House intern, Monica Lewinsky. Starr's report outlined several potential impeachable offenses, including false testimony under oath, witness tampering, and obstruction of justice, all allegedly committed by the president to keep his relationship with Lewinsky secret.

After agreeing to testify before a grand jury empaneled by Starr—a first for an American president—Clinton made an extraordinary television address to the nation. He defended his legal position and attacked the Starr inquiry as politically motivated. The Congress and the American people at large fiercely debated the nature of the charges against the president: Were they truly impeachable—"high crimes and misdemeanors" as the Constitution put it—or merely part of a partisan political effort to overturn the election of 1996? For only the third time in history, in October 1998, the House of Representatives voted to open an inquiry into possible grounds for the impeachment.

Republicans hoping to reap a wholesale victory from the scandal in the midterm elections were bitterly disappointed. Contrary to predictions and traditions in off-term elections, the president's party added seats, trimming the Republican majority in the 105th Congress. Voters evidently had more on their minds than President Clinton's sex life. Democratic candidates benefited from continued strength in the economy, and they made effective appeals on a range of issues, from preserving Social Security and Medicare to protecting a woman's right to choose an abortion. Higher than expected turnout from such core constituencies as union members and African Americans (especially in the South) also contributed to the unexpectedly strong Democratic showing. The election also brought a shakeup in the Republican leadership. Newt Gingrich, under pressure from Republican colleagues angry about a campaign strategy that had narrowly focused on Clinton's impeachment problem, announced his resignation as Speaker of the House and from his seat in Congress. Ironically Gingrich, who had led the Republican resurgence in the 1990s, now appeared to be the first political victim of the Lewinsky scandal.

In the aftermath of the 1998 election, most politicians and analysts, and indeed most Americans, believed the impeachment inquiry to be at a dead end. But the House Judiciary Committee, after raucous televised debate, voted to bring four articles of impeachment—charging President Clinton with perjury, obstruction of justice, witness tampering, and abuse of power—to the full House. But unlike the bipartisan case the Judiciary Committee brought against Richard Nixon in 1974 (see Chapter 29), this time the votes were all along strictly party lines. Neither the 1998 election results, nor polls showing a large majority of Americans opposed to removing the president, curbed the Republican determination to push impeachment through the House and then on to the Senate for trial. On February 12, 1999, the Senate trial concluded with the president's acquittal.

THE NEW MILLENNIUM

At the beginning of the twenty-first century, citizens, politicians, and business and religious leaders had to rethink their basic assumptions about the American way of life. American society had become more stratified along lines of race and income. New immigrant groups, especially from Asia and Latin America, had changed the face of the nation's communities, schools, and workplaces. New media technologies had made cultural life more homogenized and caused the manipulation of image to become more crucial than ever to both politics and entertainment. The New Economy, service-oriented and high-tech, had fundamentally altered the way many Americans did business and earned a livelihood, and it depended not only on American consumers heavily burdened with debt but also on an expanding global market.

The end of the cold war had reconfigured global politics, ending the bilateralism that had dominated international affairs since the end of World War II. The United States alone held fast to its superpower status, but this achievement did not necessarily make Americans more secure or safe. The old enemy, Soviet communism, was succeeded by more fanatic, less predictable foes. It was clear that international terrorism was emerging as a

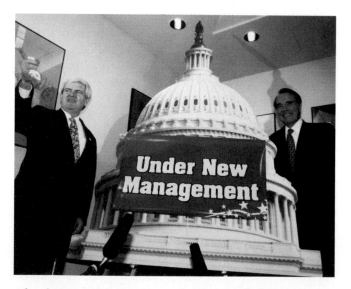

After the 1994 midterm election gave Republicans control of the House of Representatives for the first time in forty years, the new speaker, Newt Gingrich of Georgia, presented a list of legislative initiatives to be completed within the first one hundred days of the new session. On April 7, 1995, he appeared at a rally on Capitol Hill to celebrate the success of the Republicans' "Contract with America."

SOURCE: John Duricka. Wide World Photos.

persistent threat, as witnessed by yet another terrorist attack, the October 12, 2000, bombing of the USS *Cole* in Aden, Yemen, which cost the lives of seventeen American sailors. In this world of growing uncertainties, no one knew how a new Republican administration would respond to the enormous challenges accompanying the new millennium.

The Election of 2000

After a relatively dull campaign season, the 2000 election played out as high drama. Voters went to the polls as usual on election day, watched as late-night television newscasters projected a victory for the Democratic candidate, Clinton's vice president Al Gore, and then woke up the next morning to learn that perhaps the winner was not the vice president but his Republican opponent, Governor George W. Bush of Texas, son of former president George H. W. Bush. It was clear that Gore and his running mate, Connecticut Senator Joseph Lieberman, had won the popular vote, although by the closest margin since John F. Kennedy defeated Richard Nixon in 1961. In doubt was the number of votes in the Electoral College. At 2:15 A.M., the pollsters who had projected Gore as the winner changed their minds. The cliffhanger in Florida had finally ended with the state's decisive twenty-five electoral votes earmarked for the Republicans. By morning Gore had called Bush to concede. *The New York Times,* however, ran a guarded headline "Bush Appears to Defeat Gore." Only a few hundred votes in Florida gave Bush the edge, and in cases where the margin is so narrow Florida law mandates a machine recount in all sixty-seven counties. Gore soon retracted his concession, putting voters into suspense until the middle of December, when the vice president finally ended his campaign (see Map 31.3).

Such a spectacular ending to the 2000 campaign could not have been foreseen from the primaries. As the son of a former president, George W. Bush had run a low-key campaign, calling himself a "compassionate conservative" who cared about the underdog and the nation's educational system. He nevertheless did not swerve from the Republican agenda that President Reagan had shaped: tax cuts, strong military defense, and the overhaul of Social Security and Medicare. He also promised relief from environmental regulations, new judicial appointments that would eventually limit reproductive rights, and the restoration of morality to public life. Albert Gore Jr., also the son of a prominent politician, carried the burden of association with Bill Clinton and waged an uphill battle. More notable was his running mate, Lieberman, the first Jewish candidate for vice president. Dick Cheney, who had

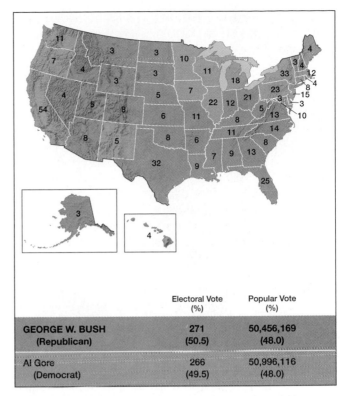

	Electoral Vote (%)	Popular Vote (%)
GEORGE W. BUSH (Republican)	271 (50.5)	50,456,169 (48.0)
Al Gore (Democrat)	266 (49.5)	50,996,116 (48.0)

MAP 31.3 Election of 2000 The 2000 presidential election was the closest one in U.S. history and the first one to be decided by a decision of the Supreme Court.

served prominently in the senior Bush's administration, balanced the younger Bush's relative lack of experience in federal government. The emergence of consumer advocate Ralph Nader as Green Party candidate added spice to an often dull campaign.

The 2000 campaign played out as the first disputed presidential election since 1876, when Democrat Samuel J. Tilden, who won the popular vote, charged his Republican opponent, Rutherford B. Hayes, with fraudulent vote counting. A similar question of legitimacy hung over the 2000 election. After Florida completed its machine recount of votes, the Democrats requested a hand tally in selected counties where the ballots were in dispute. The Republicans responded by suing in the Miami district court to prohibit the manual recounting. Meanwhile Florida election officials, mainly Republicans, set November 14 as the date to certify the election results, thereby disallowing the returns on overseas ballots which might favor Al Gore. In turn, Democrats sued to extend the deadline. Eventually, appeals by both parties reached the Florida Supreme Court and finally the U.S. Supreme Court, which voted five to four along partisan lines to halt the counting. Time had run out, and

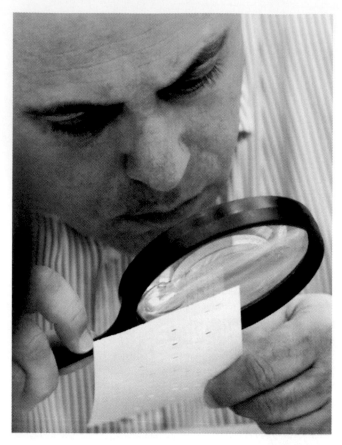

An election official examined a disputed punch-card ballot in the Presidential election in Florida in November 2001. He tried to figure out whether the "chad" had been dislodged or merely "dimpled."

SOURCE: © Reuters NewMedia Inc./CORBIS.

on December 12 Gore conceded defeat. With less fanfare than usual, George W. Bush took the oath of office in January 2001.

Global Warming

On policies concerning the environment, Bush acted quickly and aggressively to defer or to overturn several key programs established under Clinton. In July 2001, the Environmental Protection Agency announced a delay in asking states to draft plans to protect some 21,000 waterways severely impaired by agricultural runoff. Meanwhile, Bush's advisers reconsidered proposals that would have prohibited the development of nearly one-third of the national forests.

No issue was so important or so controversial as climate change, a challenge that most scientists and world leaders agreed required international solutions. During the late 1970s, scientists presented data indi-cating that the earth was warming, causing polar ice-caps to melt, oceans to rise, and ultimately marine life to die, and they pointed to the emission of "greenhouse gases," the by-products of the fossil fuels burned to run factories and automobiles, as the main cause. To curb this dangerous trend, the United States, the European Economic Community, and twenty-eight other countries had ratified the Montreal Protocol on Substances that Deplete the Ozone Layer of 1987, which established a timetable for phasing out the production of greenhouse gases by the end of the century. However, a few years later, in June 1992, at the first Earth Summit sponsored by the United Nations, the U.S. delegates took a more cautious approach, demanding that limits on greenhouse gas emissions be voluntary rather than mandatory. Although responsible for the production of more greenhouse gases than any other nation, nearly 25 percent of the total worldwide, the United States now refused to make a firm commitment.

The controversy came to a head four years later at the world summit on global warming held in Kyoto, Japan. In advance of the meetings, the major U.S. automakers advised President Clinton against signing any treaty. Meanwhile Senate Republicans secured a nonbinding resolution that specified that the terms of any treaty require developing nations, including China, India, and Mexico, to control their emissions as well. Clinton sent Gore to Kyoto to find a middle ground. In the end, the Kyoto Protocol outlined targets and timetables for the reduction of greenhouse gases and required the richer, industrialized countries to take the lead, specifying an average 5.2 percent reduction from 1990s levels by 2012. Although the fifteen-member nations of the European Union endorsed the terms of the treaty, both Japan and the United States held out.

Shortly after taking office, President George W. Bush announced his opposition to the terms of the Kyoto Protocol, leaving 178 other countries to agree to mandatory reductions in greenhouse gases without the participation of the United States. Bush instead created a task force to conduct additional studies on the impact of human activity on climate change. Meanwhile, the U.S. Energy Information Administration released new data showing that carbon dioxide emissions had risen 3 percent in the United States during the previous year alone, one of the largest increases in recent times. In July 2001, 1,500 scientists affiliated with the UN Intergovernmental Panel on Climate Change, the leading authority on global warming, met in Amsterdam and confirmed, as a key member said, that "the problem of global change is real, and it is more serious than is currently perceived politically." The Kyoto treaty took effect in early 2005; but with the United States on the sidelines, its greatest value may prove mostly symbolic.

A Global Community?

The changing climate was only one issue tied to globalization, a term used to characterize the belief that worldwide processes were causing national economies, cultures, and borders to melt away. Beginning in the 1970s, social scientists began to study and debate the degree to which people throughout the world were affected by events happening far from their homelands. The big questions concerning globalization centered on political economy. Now that communism has collapsed, they asked, would a steady expansion of free trade among nations create the basis for a global community?

There were many answers to this question. Some observers argued that the interpenetration of markets and cultural patterns—the enormous sales of Hollywood movies in China, for example—set the stage for other exchanges. Others argued that the global economy depended less on "interpenetration" than "domination" of the marketplace by the industrialized nations. Whereas physical occupation of territory defined the form of colonialism that prevailed before World War II, a new "colonialism" had come into existence since the 1960s that relied on a few multinational corporations controlling distant economies throughout the world. To back up this argument, they referred to a UN report that estimated that about 90 percent of the multinational corporations that did business worldwide were headquartered in the industrialized nations of North America, Europe, and Japan. Known collectively as the Triad, the consortium of these nations, home to only 15 percent of the world's population, produced nearly 75 percent of the world's goods by the late 1990s.

What made the current trend toward "globalization" distinctive was, therefore, not the rate of growth but the absolute volume and character of the exchange. Revenues from multinational corporations grew phenomenally at the end of the twentieth century. Because the member nations of the Triad were homes to the world's largest multinational corporations, they also reaped the largest share of the wealth. A UN annual human development report stated that "global inequalities in income and living standards have reached grotesque proportions." The report offered statistics showing that the gap in wealth between the upper 20 percent and the world's poorest people was at the end of the nineteenth century 30 to 1; by 1990 it reached 60 to 1; and by the end of the twentieth century it had widened to 74 to 1.

While many political observers and scholars predicted that globalization would bring both free markets and democracy to more and more of the world's people, others became increasingly skeptical. At the turn of the twenty-first century, an international protest movement emerged that targeted the most powerful organization in the global economy, the World Trade Organization (WTO) and the International Monetary Fund (IMF), or World Bank. In November 1999, thousands of protestors converged in Seattle, Washington, site of the annual meeting of the WTO, only to be pushed back by local police. In response, the WTO formulated new procedures for its meetings, secreting delegates behind walls and banning demonstrations from the area near future sites. Nevertheless, confrontations continued, the most dramatic occurring at a meeting of delegates from the eight leading industrial nations in Genoa, Italy, in 2001, which resulted in the death of one protestor.

Experts on globalization could not agree if the trend toward a single international market challenged traditional notions of national sovereignty and laid the foundation for global democracy or if the post–cold war world order was increasingly challenged by civil wars, ethnic and religious clashes, and the breakup of nation-states.

WAR ON TERROR

Terrorist Attack on America

On September 11, 2001, hijackers, armed only with knives and box cutters, crashed two jetliners into New York's World Trade Center towers, while a third jetliner slammed into the Pentagon in Virginia. A fourth plane, diverted from its terrorist mission by courageous passengers, hurtled to the ground near Pittsburgh. In all, 246 people perished in the four planes. At the sites of the attack, the damage was devastating. At the Pentagon, which had been built to withstand terrorist attacks, a huge explosion followed by fierce fires destroyed a large section of the defense complex. The death toll soon reached 184, including 59 people who had been on board the hijacked airliner. In New York City, the collapse of the twin towers, most likely caused by the intense fires propelled by the planes' jet fuel, brought death to 2,752 people including hundreds of police and rescue workers who had dashed into the buildings to help. At the end of the day, the New York City Fire Department had lost 350 firefighters, nearly thirty times the number ever lost by the department in a single incident. The stark images of the second plane hitting the WTC, the dramatic collapse of the buildings, and the fear on the faces of thousands fleeing the sites were replayed over and over again on televisions throughout the world.

More than 5,000 activists gathered in Seattle in November 1999 to demonstrate against the meeting of the World Trade Organization. The event, which was marked by a violent clash with police and the arrest of dozens of protestors, marked the beginning of a movement for global economic justice.

SOURCE: Agence France Presse/Getty Images.

While the media recalled Pearl Harbor, President Bush declared the deadly attacks an act of war and vowed to hunt down those responsible for the "evil, despicable acts of terror." Congress, with only one dissenting vote, granted him power to take whatever steps necessary. The Department of Justice began what it described as the largest and most intensive investigation ever conducted, and the president issued a blanket warning to all nations who harbor terrorists. Secretary of State Colin Powell stated clearly, "You're either with us or against us." For the first time ever, NATO invoked the mutual defense clause in its founding treaty, which in effect supported any U.S. military response.

Observers described Bush's response as the defining moment of his presidency, as it was for the lives of many Americans. Millions of Americans rushed to donate blood, and thousands traveled to New York to assist rescue efforts. Prayer vigils were held in churches, synagogues, mosques, public buildings, and parks, and flags were displayed on homes and cars. Millions of dollars were soon raised for the relief effort and to assist the families of those who perished.

Many businesses, especially those in the travel, entertainment, or hazardous materials industries, were closed in the days following the attack. The stock market, after a three-day pause, reopened to the worst week in the history of Wall Street since the Great Depression. Financial analysts declared that the already faltering economy had now certainly entered a recession.

Perhaps most dramatic was the unprecedented shutdown of all airports in the United States, stranding thousands around the world. Service returned several days later at greatly reduced levels and with enhanced security. But fear had chilled most Americans' spirit. In the face of a $15 billion bailout of the airline industry quickly passed by the Senate, they cancelled vacations and applied for refunds for airline tickets already purchased. Two-thirds of those polled believed the worst might still come.

The day following the highly coordinated terrorist attack, President Bush identified the Saudi Arabian Osama bin Laden as the prime suspect. Administration officials linked the airline hijackers, all presumed to be Islamic fundamentalists, to his Al Qaeda network, which apparently had dispatched them to train at American flight schools. Bin Laden and Al Qaeda had based their operations in Afghanistan, where they enjoyed the protection of a government run by the Taliban, a radical Islamist group. The Taliban said their aim was to set up the world's most pure Islamic state, banning what they viewed as the corrupt influences of Western culture, such as movies, television, and the education of women. Although a communique from bin Laden denied involvement, U.S. intelligence sources insisted that only bin Laden had the resources to carry out such a sophisticated operation and sufficient motivation. In 1998, bin Laden had issued a decree that granted religious legitimacy to all efforts to expel the United States from the lands of Islam in the Middle East. His network of terrorist cells, which reportedly operated in sixty countries, had directed rage at what they believe to be the global arrogance of the United States—its accumulation of unprecedented wealth when poverty and hopelessness extended across the Middle East.

Reshaping U.S. Foreign Policy

The September 11 terrorist attacks transformed the presidency of George W. Bush and prompted dramatic changes in the conduct and goals of American foreign policy. At a memorial service for victims Bush issued an ominous warning: "Our responsibility to history is already clear: to answer these attacks and rid the world of evil." And he outlined a new vision that would guide his policies. "From this day forward," the president announced, "any nation that continues to harbor or support terrorists will be regarded by the United States as a hostile regime." The first theater of the campaign against terror would be Afghanistan. With the support of a United Nations Security Council resolution, the United States delivered an ultimatum to the Taliban-dominated government of Afghanistan: hand over Osama bin Laden and other Al Qaeda leaders presumed to be responsible, and close all terrorist training camps immediately and unconditionally.

On October 7, after the Taliban had refused to comply, President Bush announced the beginning of Operation Enduring Freedom, a joint American–British military campaign aimed at capturing bin Laden and overthrowing the Taliban regime that had sheltered him. An aerial bombing campaign targeted Taliban and Al Qaeda forces, many of whom were Arab fighters from abroad. U.S. Special Forces launched a raid deep into the Taliban stronghold of Kandahar, in southeastern Afghanistan. A prerecorded video tape of Osama bin Laden, broadcast on Al-Jazeera, an Arabic satellite news channel, boasted that the United States would fail in Afghanistan just as the Soviet Union had twenty years earlier. Bin Laden called for a *Jihad*, or holy war, of Muslims against the entire non-Muslim world. By mid-November American and British forces, joined by a loose coalition of anti-Taliban Afhgans known as the Northern Alliance, captured the capital city of Kabul. Fierce fighting continued through December as U.S.-led coalition troops grew to a force of over 10,000. Intensive bombing routed the last remnants of Taliban and Al Qaeda forces from the mountain cave complex of Tora Bora. But bin Laden and much of the Al Qaeda leadership escaped into the tribal areas of Pakistan to the south and east. Despite a massive manhunt and the aid of Pakistan's government, American forces proved unable to capture bin Laden as of early 2005.

A grand council, or *loya jirga*, of Afghan factions and tribal leaders established an interim Afghan government in Kabul under the leadership of Hamid Karzai. In the fall of 2004 Karzai became the first democratically elected president of Afghanistan. But his power was limited largely to Kabul and old problems stubbornly persisted. Warlords dominated much of the countryside, the Taliban remained a force in much of the

The United States conducted air strikes on the village of Rahesh, near the capital city Kabul, in November 2001 in a military campaign to drive the Taliban from power in Afghanistan.

SOURCE: AP Wide World Photos.

countryside, and the illegal opium trade flourished. A Pentagon report examining the invasion of Afghanistan concluded that the Taliban's removal had given "warlordism, banditry, and opium production a new lease on life."

In his January 2002 State of the Union address President Bush expanded on his vision of a global war on terror. He argued that America now faced a grave and unprecedented danger not merely from Al Qaeda terrorists but from nation states seeking chemical, biological, or nuclear weapons of mass destruction (WMD). He denounced the regimes of North Korea, Iran, and Iraq as an "axis of evil, arming to threaten the peace of the world." America, the President promised, "will not permit the world's most dangerous regimes to threaten us with the world's most destructive weapons." The new focus on the threat of WMD formed a central part of a sweeping reformulation of American foreign policy. In the fall of 2002 the Bush Administration released a new National Security Strategy Report that offered the most radical revision of American foreign policy since the Truman Administration in the early days of the Cold War (see Chapter 26). It argued that "the struggle against global terrorism is different from any other war in our history," requiring the United States to "deter and defend against the threat before it is unleashed," acting pre-emptively and alone if necessary.

The war on terror had a domestic front as well. The partisan bitterness of the 2000 election largely dissolved amid post–9/11 calls for national unity, making it easier for the Bush Administration to push new legislation through Congress. Signed into law in the fall of 2001, the USA Patriot Act gave federal officials greater author-ity to track and intercept communications for law-enforcement and intelligence-gathering purposes, new powers to curb foreign money laundering, and broader discretion in tightening borders against suspected foreign terrorists. It created new crimes and penalties against suspected domestic and international terrorists. In the months after the 9/11 attacks, over one thousand Mus-lims, some of them U.S. citizens, were arrested and detained, the largest such round-up since the Palmer Raids following World War I (see Chapter 22). Only a handful of these suspects were actually charged with crimes related to terrorism. Although there were scat-tered legal and political protests against these secret detentions, Congress passed the USA Patriot Act II in 2003, further expanding the ability of law-enforcement and intelligence-gathering authorities to perform sur-veillance and authorize secret arrests.

The Bush Administration also created a new Cabinet level Department of Homeland Security (DHS), consol-idating twenty-two different domestic agencies to coor-dinate the nation's defense against military threats. Charged with guarding borders and airports, protecting critical infrastructure, and coordinating responses to future emergencies, the DHS represented the most ambitious reorganization of the federal government since the National Security Act of 1947. Its components included the Immigration and Naturalization Service, the U.S. Cus-toms Service, the Secret Service, the Coast Guard, and the Federal Emergency Management Agency. Not surpris-ingly, combining so many huge federal bureaucracies into one effective whole proved quite difficult. Critics of the new department worried especially about the continued vulnerability of the nation's ports, rail system, chemical facilities, and nuclear plants to terrorist attacks.

Many questions remained unanswered about the events and circumstances surrounding the 9/11 attacks, particularly the multiple failures within the U.S. intelli-gence community. The Bush Administration at first resis-ted efforts to mount a full scale inquiry. But pressure from the families of 9/11 victims, as well as widespread calls for a bipartisan investigation, forced the adminis-tration to reverse its opposition, and in November 2002 Congress established the National Commission on Ter-rorist Attacks Upon the United States. The panel of five Republicans and five Democrats worked for twenty months, interviewing more than 1,000 people, includ-ing members of the Clinton and Bush administrations,

New York City emergency workers, and victims' fami-lies, in an effort to paint the most complete picture of what happened and why. In July 2004 it issued its final report—which became an instant best seller—concluding that the government "failed to protect the American people" because it did not understand the "gravity of the threat." The report was especially damning on the bureaucratic rivalry between the CIA and FBI, which made it difficult to act despite clear evidence that "Islamist terrorists mean to kill Americans in high num-bers." It noted that as late as August 2001 National Secu-rity Adviser Condoleeza Rice had ignored urgent warnings of impending Al Qaeda attacks brought directly to her by Richard Clarke, the president's counter-terrorism chief. The report's recommendations included creation of a new post of National Intelligence Director, who could lead counterterrorism efforts and coordinate the disparate intelligence operations of the CIA, FBI, Homeland Security, and the Pentagon. In early 2005 President Bush appointed John Negroponte, former Ambassador to Iraq, as the first person to hold this office.

Invasion of Iraq

The new pledge to confront threats to security before they reached American shores became known as the Bush Doctrine and its first major test was Iraq. Planning for a U.S.–led invasion and the overthrow of Sadaam Hussein had actually begun in the first weeks after the Septem-ber 11 attacks. The President himself had come to believe that "regime change" was necessary, and several major figures in his administration focused their attention on making the case to the nation and the world. Vice Pres-ident Dick Cheney, Secretary of Defense Donald Rums-feld, and his deputy secretary, Paul Wolfowitz, had all worked for Bush's father, President George H.W. Bush, and they viewed removal of Sadaam as the unfinished business of the Persian Gulf War of 1991. Along with National Security Adviser Condoleeza Rice and a more reluctant Secretary of State Colin Powell, these aides began to plan for war in early 2002.

Proponents of war made three central claims which they repeated in various public speeches, testimony before Congress, and finally at the United Nations. First, Sadaam Hussein must be removed by force because he possessed biological and chemical weapons that posed an imminent threat, and he was making serious efforts to develop nuclear weapons. A National Intelligence Estimate circulated in October 2002 seemed to provide evidence for this view. And advocates for war charged that UN weapons inspectors, active in Iraq throughout the 1990s, had failed to uncover large caches of WMD. Second, they argued that Sadaam's intelligence services had direct connections to the September 11 hijackers and had broader linkages with Al Qaeda operatives around the world. Third, toppling Sadaam would make possible a democratic Iraq that could then stand as a beacon of political change throughout the Middle East and Muslim world. The majority of the Iraqi people, they asserted, would welcome and support an American campaign to oust the brutal dictator, ensuring a swift and fairly painless victory.

Throughout late 2002 and early 2003, as American military planners prepared for battle, significant opposition to war emerged at home and abroad. In the United States, many intelligence analysts and veteran diplomats expressed serious doubts about Bush Administration claims regarding Sadaam's weapons capabilities. They charged that Vice President Cheney and Secretary Rumsfeld had manipulated Pentagon intelligence estimates, selectively emphasizing data based on ideology rather than dispassionate analysis. Others doubted Sadaam's links to Al Qaeda and argued that war with Iraq was a distraction from the hunt for bin Laden. Brent Scowcroft, former national security adviser for Bush's father, warned that an invasion of Iraq "could turn the whole region into a cauldron, and thus destroy the war on terrorism." A growing number of Americans questioned the assumption that removing Sadaam would make America safer, and many worried that an invasion would likely boost the recruitment efforts of Al Qaeda and other terrorist organizations. Antiwar groups pointed to the large amounts of WMD that had already been identified and destroyed by UN inspectors before they had left Iraq in 1998. Why not let these inspections resume as an alternative to invasion? Millions of citizens began organizing against the push for war via Internet organizations such as MoveOn.org and in vigils and gatherings in their local communities. (See Out of Many Voices: Waiting to Be "Called Up".)

Growing opposition to war helped impel the Bush Administration to seek international support. In November 2002 the UN Security Council unanimously passed Resolution 1441 calling upon Iraq to fully disarm, provide a detailed account of its WMD programs, and to accept the return of UN weapons inspectors. The U.S. Senate

OUT OF MANY VOICES

WAITING TO BE "CALLED UP"

Many reservists were called to fight in the second U.S.-led war in Iraq. Thirty-seven-year-old Marchelle Watson, of North Portland, Oregon, a chemical operations specialist with the 104th Division Army Reserve, remembers the day the war began, on March 22, 2003, and wondering if she would be called up for active duty.

I'M VERY NERVOUS ABOUT A LOT OF THINGS. FOR one, I know a lot of young people that are over in the Middle East. And I also think about myself because I'm in the military. I'm in the Army Reserves and I've been in the Army Reserves for about 16 years and I worry that maybe I might get called up. The time is getting shorter on the call-up notices. First it was 30 days and then it was a week, and then I had a friend who—she only had three days. She had two small children and she was on her way to Texas. Most of the deployments are for a year, some say a year to two years, and that's a lot of uncertainty to families who really, I don't think, were prepared for that.

I have two small children myself, so I worry about that, and my husband worries about that. I try to, when I talk with them about the possibility of Mom having to go off to war, I just want them to think about Mommy's going away to do a good thing for the Army because she's dedicated to our country. And I have a lot of doubts right now. Sometimes I really can't even let myself give in to some of my thoughts and my doubts because I have to be focused on my responsibility as a mother and my responsibility as a soldier. And those are two huge responsibilities. And sometimes they tug at me in opposite ways. And I just have to stay focused and maintain a balance and do the best I can for both, because I love them both. I love my family and I love the military too.

I find it difficult when people approach me and they say, "What are you going to do if you get called up and you have to go to war?" And I say, "Then I'll just have to go." And they say, "Well, how can you leave your family?" And I say, "Well, I don't think about it like that. I have a duty and that's just what I have to do. . . ."

It's a very hard choice. And I don't know that fathers feel that. I think mothers feel so responsible for both it's difficult. And my girlfriends that are in the military, they feel just as torn as I do. ■

SOURCE: NPR: *War Diaries*: "Marchelle Watson (2003)"
http://npr.org/news/specials/war diaries/mwatson.

and House of Representatives both voted to authorize the use of military action against Iraq should Sadaam Hussein refuse to comply with UN resolutions. But although Iraq released voluminous records about its weapons programs as UN inspectors resumed their work, the United States concluded in December that the documents were inadequate and that Iraq was in "material breach" of Resolution 1441. In February 2003 Secretary of State Powell made a detailed argument for war before the Security Council. Meanwhile, the antiwar movement went global on February 15 as millions of demonstrators turned out in the streets of over 300 cities, including 500,000 in New York, 2 million in London, and 1 million in Rome. This was the single largest expression of antiwar sentiment in history. At the UN, facing staunch opposition to war from France, Russia, and Germany, who argued for giving the UN inspection process more time, the United States withdrew its proposed resolution authorizing the use of force in Iraq (see Map 31.4).

Lacking UN approval, the Bush Administration would invade Iraq with what it called a "coalition of the willing," with Great Britain as its major partner. On March 19 President Bush announced the beginning of war, claiming the United States "has the sovereign authority to use force in assuring its own national security." He also told Iraqis "the tyrant will soon be gone; the day of your liberation is near." Some 150,000 American troops based in Kuwait, along with a smaller British force, began a thrust toward Baghdad; and a "shock and awe" campaign of massive aerial bombing began on several major Iraqi cities. The American and British forces overwhelmed the regular Iraqi army fairly easily, suffering relatively light casualties. By early April they had secured Baghdad, Mosul, Basra, Kirkuk, and other major cities. Hundreds of journalists "embedded" with American combat units provided live television coverage of various battles. On May 1, 2003, on the flight deck of the USS *Abraham Lincoln*, anchored off the San Diego coast, President Bush made a dramatic appearance before a cheering throng of American sailors and a live television audience. Standing beneath a large banner reading "Mission Accomplished," Bush announced the official end of combat operations. "In the battle of Iraq," the president declared, "the United States and our allies have prevailed."

But the purely military act of removing Sadaam's regime from power proved far simpler than bringing peace and stability to Iraq. And rather than weaken terrorists, it instead strengthened a new generation of terror networks now drawn to do battle with American forces there. As the invasion turned into an occupation, the plight of ordinary Iraqis and American soldiers worsened quickly. In the summer of 2003 the Coalition Provisional Authority (CPA), led by Ambassador Paul Bremer, created the Governing Council to serve as an interim government for the new Iraq. But many parts of the country plunged into chaos amidst widespread looting, killing, and near anarchy. Several decisions made by the CPA, including the disbanding of the Iraqi Army, contributed to the lawless climate.

MAP 31.4 Invasion in Iraq On March 20, 2003 American and British troops poured into Iraq from bases in Kuwait, crossing the Iraqi border to the east near Safwan. The American Third Infantry Division used armored bulldozers to create wide gaps in the Iraqi defensive line.

President George W. Bush announces the end of major combat operations in Iraq, May 1, 2003, speaking on the deck of the aircraft carrier USS Abraham Lincoln, anchored near San Diego. A banner proclaimed "Mission Accomplished," but American troops would continue to face stiff opposition and endure thousands of casualties battling Iraqi insurgents.

SOURCE: AP Wide World Photos.

Millions of Iraqis found their electricity, water, and basic food supplies disrupted or unavailable. As UN relief workers, journalists, and private American contractors poured into the country to help with reconstruction efforts, a violent campaign of suicide bombings, shootings, roadside ambushes, and kidnappings spread across Iraq. Insurgents began releasing videos of gruesome executions—often by beheading—of captured prisoners. In December 2003 the capture of Sadaam Hussein, who had gone into hiding, proved a symbolic victory at best.

A coordinated, heavily armed, and well-financed resistance to the American occupation gained strength in early 2004. It included elements of Sadaam's Baath party, foreign Islamist fighters, disaffected Sunni Muslims, and criminal gangs. Desperate poverty, widespread unemployment, deep anger toward the American occupiers, and hundreds of thousands of alienated former soldiers provided a continual supply of fresh recruits. The CPA was both unprepared and overwhelmed as it tried to wrestle with problems no one had even thought about, much less planned for. Tensions between major religious groups fueled the insurgency, as Sunni Muslims feared the loss of their traditional power to the majority Shiites. Badly stretched American forces, which included a high percentage of National Guard and Army Reserve units, were forced back into combat. In cities like Falluja and Najaf, a year after President Bush had confidently declared the fighting over, American troops engaged in the toughest fighting since the Vietnam War.

Troubling new questions about the decision to invade and the conduct of the war emerged. In early 2004 David Kay, the Bush Administration's former chief weapons inspector, told Congress that any stockpiles of chemical or biological weapons Saddam might have possessed in the early 1990s had been destroyed by UN inspections and Iraq's own actions. Nor was there any nuclear weapons program. "It turns out," Kay testified, "we were all wrong, probably, in my judgment. And that is most disturbing."

In the spring of 2004, graphic images and descriptions of Iraqi detainees abused and tortured by American guards in the Abu Ghraib prison were broadcast around the world, inciting international outrage and protest. In public President Bush expressed "a deep disgust that those prisoners were treated the way they were treated." But White House memos revealed that the President's legal counsel Alberto Gonzales had urged Bush to declare the war on terror and the treatment of Al Qaeda and Taliban prisoners exempt from the provisions of the Geneva Convention. This would reduce the threat of American officials being prosecuted for committing war crimes. In an angry open letter to President Bush a distinguished group of 130 American jurists, including twelve former federal judges, a former director of the FBI, and the heads of several human rights organizations, denounced these memos for seeking to "circumvent long established and universally acknowledged principles of law and common decency."

With American forces bogged down in the occupation and the resistance to it widening, American military commanders found themselves strapped for replacement troops. Tens of thousands of National Guard and Army Reserve soldiers were forced to stay in Iraq beyond their regular tour of duty, subject in effect to a "backdoor draft." By early 2005 over 1500 Americans had been killed in Iraq and nearly 12,000 wounded, many of them severely. Estimates of Iraqi civilian casualties ranged as high as 100,000.

In July 2004 the Coalition Provisional Authority dissolved itself and formally transferred sovereignty to the interim Iraqi government. In January 2005 Iraq conducted its first national elections for an assembly charged with writing a new constitution by 2006. Amidst enormous media coverage, the Bush Administration hailed the elections as a historic step toward

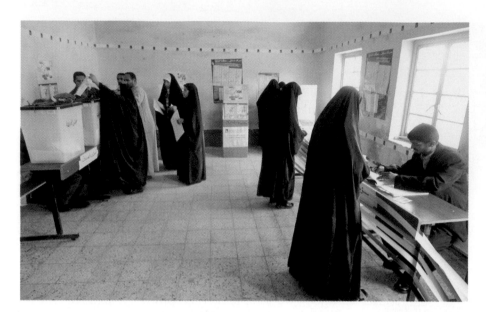

Iraqi election officials (right) check ID cards against voter rolls as an Iraqi woman (left) casts her ballot at a school polling station in the town of Abu Al-Kahasib, Iraq, January 30, 2005. Despite insurgent threats and a string of deadly mortar attacks and suicide bombings, millions of Iraqi voters participated in the nation's first election in a half century.

SOURCE: AP Wide World Photos.

democracy. Shiite Muslims, representing roughly sixty percent of the population, stood ready to replace the minority Sunni Muslims as the dominant political force. The Shiites themselves were divided into factions, including those with close ties to the Shiite rulers of neighboring Iran. The ongoing insurgency, meanwhile, showed little sign of abating.

The Election of 2004

President Bush launched his reelection bid determined to make national security and the war on terror the centerpieces of his campaign. With Iraq dominating the news, Bush described himself as a "wartime president" and appealed to patriotism and national unity. This strategy allowed him to largely ignore domestic issues, where his political strength was less certain. Bush promoted a sweeping tax cut in 2001 as the best way to jump-start the economy and create new jobs. The Economic Growth and Tax Relief Reconciliation Act squeaked through Congress with bipartisan support. It lowered tax rates and included a popular provision resulting in most Americans receiving a check in the mail from the IRS as "reconciliation" for paying too much in taxes. Yet a small percentage of wealthy Americans benefited disproportionately from the cuts, which also expanded budget deficits as the government took in less money. While many Americans did see a decline in their income tax payments, many found that increases in local property taxes, school tuitions, and other fees continued to climb. Although by 2002 the

economy was technically in recovery from the recession of 2000, economic growth and job creation were weak across most of the nation. And the historically unprecedented combination of fighting an expensive war abroad while lowering income and corporate taxes at home brought spiraling budget deficits that wiped out the surpluses of the Clinton years.

As the American dollar weakened against foreign currencies like the Euro and the Chinese *yuan*, a growing chorus of economists warned that high levels of American consumption and the superheated real estate markets in many U.S. cities made the economy increasingly vulnerable to the whims of foreign investors. If budget deficits continued to grow, foreign buyers of U.S. government securities might look elsewhere, with potentially devasting effects on the American economy.

Democrats, still smarting from the disputed 2000 election in which their nominee Al Gore had won the popular vote by over half a million, believed their chances for retaking the White House were strong. But the political aftermath of the September 11 attacks, the new focus on strengthening national security, and the invasion of Iraq forced attention away from the economic issues that had traditionally been their greatest source of voter appeal. In the early months of campaigning for the nomination, former Vermont Governor Howard Dean emerged as a surprising front-runner. Dean, looking to distinguish himself from more conservative Democrats, strongly opposed the invasion of Iraq and touted himself as representing "the Democratic wing of the Democratic Party." He energized antiwar sentiment and attracted large sums of money from Democrats through innovative use of the Internet. But once Democrats in primary states like Iowa and New Hampshire actually started voting Dean stumbled badly and his campaign fizzled.

After winning in Iowa and New Hampshire, Senator John Kerry of Massachusetts quickly assumed the mantle

of front-runner and he captured the Democratic nomination. Kerry's life story helped him appeal to a broad cross-section of the party. He had volunteered for Naval combat duty in Vietnam, where he was wounded and highly decorated. When he returned home he became a leader in the Vietnam Veterans Against the War (VVAW)

CHRONOLOGY

1981	MTV and CNN start broadcasting as cable channels		Congress passes "Defense of Marriage" Act
			California voters approve Proposition 187
1986	Immigration Reform and Control Act addresses concerns about illegal aliens	**1995**	Bombing of Alfred P. Murrah Federal Building in Oklahoma City kills 168 people
1987	Allan Bloom publishes *The Closing of the American Mind*	**1996**	Congress passes Welfare Reform Act
			Congress enacts the Antiterrorism and Effective Death Penalty Act
1988	George H. W. Bush is elected president		President Bill Clinton is reelected
1989	Tiananmen Square demonstration in China	**1997**	Kyoto Protocol endorsed by European Union but not United States
1990	Iraqi invasion of Kuwait leads to massive U.S. military presence in the Persian Gulf	**1998**	U.S. embassies in Kenya and Tanzania bombed by terrorists
1991	Operation Desert Storm forces Iraq out of Kuwait		House of Representatives votes to impeach President Clinton, but vote fails in Senate
	Operation Rescue launched in Wichita, Kansas	**1999**	U.S. joins NATO forces in Kosovo
1992	Rodney King verdict sparks rioting in Los Angeles		Protesters disrupt meetings of the World Trade Organization in Seattle
	Bill Clinton is elected president	**2000**	USS *Cole* bombed by terrorists
1993	Terrorist bombing of World Trade Center kills six people	**2001**	George W. Bush becomes president after contested election
	Federal agents conduct seige of Branch Davidian compound in Waco, Texas		Terrorists attack World Trade Center and Pentagon
	Clinton administration introduces comprehensive health-care reform, but it fails to win passage in Congress		U.S. begins military campaign in Afghanistan
			Homeland Security Department Established
	Congress approves the North American Free Trade Agreement (NAFTA)		USA Patriot Act passed
1994	Republicans win control of Senate and House for first time in forty years	**2003**	Invasion of Iraq and occupation
			USA Patriot Act II passed
	Congress approves the General Agreement on Tariffs and Trade (GATT)	**2004**	Release of *The 9/11 Commission Report*
			Reelection of George. W. Bush
	Congress passes the Comprehensive AIDS Revenue Emergency Act	**2005**	Elections in Iraq

and in 1971 had made a memorable televised appearance before Congress criticizing U.S. policy. He had gone into state politics and won election to the Senate in 1984. His biography suggested he could bridge some of the deep Vietnam-era differences that still divided Americans. And his status as an authentic war hero would bolster Democrats' chances of appealing to voters' concerns about national security.

But after capturing the nomination Kerry's campaign faltered. Republicans and their allies attacked his war record, claiming that his Purple Hearts and other medals had been undeserved. His patrician background, distant personality, and cool manner made it difficult for many voters to warm up to him. He could not articulate a clear vision or theme for his candidacy and the Republican campaign succeeded in painting him as a "flip flopper" who constantly changed his position on issues. Perhaps most damningly, Kerry was unable to communicate a clear position on the Iraq war. Along with many other Democrats he had voted to authorize the use of force, but he criticized President Bush's conduct of the war. Yet even when asked, in the late summer of 2004, whether he would have voted differently if he knew that there was no Iraqi WMD threat and no Iraqi link with the September 11 attacks, he refused to change his view.

President George W. Bush won reelection with 51 percent of the popular vote to Kerry's 48 percent, a three-million-vote margin. He garnered 279 electoral votes to Kerry's 252, as Ohio, with twenty electoral votes, proved the key state. The results could be interpreted in a variety of ways. Bush polled the first popular vote majority in twenty years and the overall turnout of 60 percent was the highest since 1968. Republicans fielded a formidable grassroots get-out-the-vote operation, especially in small town and rural America, where they appealed effectively to many voters on so-called "moral values" issues: opposition to gay marriage and abortion rights. Republicans also increased their majorities in both the House and the Senate. But Bush's victory margin was also the smallest for reelection in a century.

President Bush claimed his victory represented a victory for his Iraq war policy and promised to spend his hard-won "political capital" on the domestic front as well. In his State of the Union Address delivered in February 2005, Bush defined his second term agenda around two issues. On the foreign policy front, he hailed the recent Iraqi elections and promised to keep American forces there until Iraqis could provide their own security. Domestically, the President challenged Congress to "reinvent Social Security," as he called for a major overhaul of the New Deal era social insurance program by emphasizing private investment accounts. Though not as close as the 2000 election, and without the disconnect between popular and electoral vote, few would dispute that the 2004 election revealed a nation that was as politically divided as any time since the Civil War.

REVIEW QUESTIONS

1. How is the "new economy" different from the old economy? How has it reshaped American business and financial practices? Explain the relationship between the new economy and electronic media, such as the Internet and cable television.

2. Evaluate the presidency of Bill Clinton. Compare his domestic and foreign policies to those of the Republican presidents who preceded and followed him in office. What was the impact of the scandals that plagued his presidency?

3. Describe the major demographic trends revealed by the 2000 census. Identify the racial and ethnic groups with the greatest gains in population. How have various legislation acts since 1965 affected immigration to the United States? How have communities changed as a result of the influx of new immigrants?

4. The concept of globalization is highly controversial. Are borders between nations "melting away" as some scholars contend? How does this concept square with the description of the United States as the single superpower in the world? Does this concept apply primarily to economics, or is it useful for discussing issues related to culture, media, the environment, and population trends?

5. How has the "war on terror" differed from other wars in this century? How and why did the 9/11 attacks lead to fundamental changes in the conduct of U.S. foreign policy? What arguments for the American invasion of Iraq in 2003 do you find most and least persuasive?

RECOMMENDED READING

William C. Berman, *From the Center to the Edge: The Politics and Policies of the Clinton Presidency* (2001). A highly readable assessment of Clinton's accomplishments as president. Although focusing on domestic issues, including the impact of Clinton's impeachment, Berman also considers major foreign policy developments in the context of globalization.

Richard Clarke, *Against All Enemies: Inside America's War on Terror* (2004). A critical look at the war on terror from a veteran diplomat and counterterrorism expert who argues that the invasion of Iraq will serve to strengthen Al Qaeda and allied groups.

Stephen Coll, *Ghost Wars: The Secret History of the CIA, Afghanistan, and Bin Laden from the Soviet Invasion to September 10, 2001* (2004). Deeply researched examination of the CIA's influence in Afghanistan and its support for Islamic fundamentalists resisting Soviet occupation.

Thomas Frank, *What's the Matter With Kansas? How Conservatives Won the Heart of America* (2004). A provocative look at how political conservatives have successfully recast themselves as the voice of populism and ordinary Americans over the last thirty years.

James Glanz and Eric Lipton, *City in the Sky: The Rise and Fall of the World Trade Center* (2003). A thorough investigation of the planning that gave birth to the two iconic towers in New York City and their destruction on September 11, 2001. Written by two journalists, this clear, detailed, and well-illustrated study poses hard questions about the collapse and recovery efforts.

Neil Howe, *Millennials Rising: The Next Generation* (2000). An optimistic assessment of the generation of Americans who were born on or after 1982 and projections for their future. Howe surveys statistics as well as cultural trends and concludes that the rising generation shows a return to conservative family values and a respect for rules.

National Commission on Terrorist Attacks Upon the United States, *The 9/11 Commission Report* (2004). The best-selling final report of the independent bipartisan inquiry into the events surrounding the 9/11 attacks, including recommendations for reorganizing American intelligence to more effectively meet terrorist threats.

Todd S. Purdum, *A Time of Our Choosing: America's War in Iraq* (2004). An excellent narrative account of how the Bush Administration made the decision to invade Iraq.

Micah L. Sifry and Christopher Cerf, eds., *The Iraq War Reader* (2003). A collection of historical essays, government documents, and political addresses providing a fine overview of the debates over war with Iraq.

Sam Roberts, *Who We Are Now: The Changing Face of America in the Twenty-First Century* (2004). Using the 2000 Census, Roberts focuses on the changes in American society that occurred between 1990 and 2000. He discusses population growth, the largest decadal increase in American history, as well as shifts in ethnic composition, family structure, and inequality.

Janet Thomas, *The Battle in Seattle: The Story Behind and Beyond the WTO* (2000). An impassioned, eyewitness account by a participant in the 1999 demonstrations against the World Trade Organization, which the author describes as a "global tailspin at the end of the century."

 For additional study resources for this chapter, go to the *Companion Website*, **http://www.prenhall.com/faragher**.

APPENDIX

THE DECLARATION OF INDEPENDENCE

When in the course of human events it becomes necessary for one people to dissolve the political bands which have connected them with another and to assume, among the powers of the earth, the separate and equal station to which the laws of nature and of nature's God entitle them, a decent respect to the opinions of mankind requires that they should declare the causes which impel them to the separation.

We hold these truths to be self-evident, that all men are created equal; that they are endowed by their Creator with certain unalienable rights; that among these are life, liberty, and the pursuit of happiness. That, to secure these rights, governments are instituted among men, deriving their just powers from the consent of the governed; that, whenever any form of government becomes destructive of these ends, it is the right of the people to alter or to abolish it, and to institute a new government, laying its foundation on such principles, and organizing its powers in such form, as to them shall seem most likely to effect their safety and happiness. Prudence, indeed, will dictate that governments long established should not be changed for light and transient causes; and, accordingly, all experience hath shown that mankind are more disposed to suffer, while evils are sufferable, than to right themselves by abolishing the forms to which they are accustomed. But when a long train of abuses and usurpations, pursuing invariably the same object, evinces a design to reduce them under absolute despotism, it is their right, it is their duty, to throw off such government and to provide new guards for their future security. Such has been the patient sufferance of these colonies, and such is now the necessity which constrains them to alter their former systems of government. The history of the present King of Great Britain is a history of repeated injuries and usurpations, all having, in direct object, the establishment of an absolute tyranny over these States. To prove this, let facts be submitted to a candid world:

He has refused his assent to laws the most wholesome and necessary for the public good.

He has forbidden his governors to pass laws of immediate and pressing importance, unless suspended in their operation till his assent should be obtained; and, when so suspended, he has utterly neglected to attend to them.

He has refused to pass other laws for the accommodation of large districts of people, unless those people would relinquish the right of representation in the legislature, a right inestimable to them and formidable to tyrants only.

He has called together legislative bodies at places unusual, uncomfortable, and distant from the depository of their public records, for the sole purpose of fatiguing them into compliance with his measures.

He has dissolved representative houses, repeatedly for opposing, with manly firmness, his invasions on the rights of the people.

He has refused, for a long time after such dissolutions, to cause others to be elected; whereby the legislative powers, incapable of annihilation, have returned to the people at large for their exercise; the state remaining, in the meantime, exposed to all the danger of invasion from without and convulsions within.

He has endeavored to prevent the population of these States; for that purpose, obstructing the laws for naturalization of foreigners, refusing to pass others to encourage their migration hither, and raising the conditions of new appropriations of lands.

He has obstructed the administration of justice by refusing his assent to laws for establishing judiciary powers.

He has made judges dependent on his will alone for the tenure of their offices and the amount and payment of their salaries.

He has erected a multitude of new offices and sent hither swarms of officers to harass our people and eat out their substance.

He has kept among us, in time of peace, standing armies, without the consent of our legislatures.

He has affected to render the military independent of, and superior to, the civil power.

He has combined with others to subject us to a jurisdiction foreign to our Constitution and unacknowledged by our laws, giving his assent to their acts of pretended legislation—

For quartering large bodies of armed troops among us;

For protecting them by mock trial, from punishment for any murders which they should commit on the inhabitants of these States;

For cutting off our trade with all parts of the world;

For imposing taxes on us without our consent;

For depriving us, in many cases, of the benefit of trial by jury;

For transporting us beyond seas to be tried for pretended offences;

For abolishing the free system of English laws in a neighboring province, establishing therein an arbitrary government, and enlarging its boundaries, so as to render it at once an example and fit instrument for introducing the same absolute rule into these colonies;

For taking away our charters, abolishing our most valuable laws, and altering, fundamentally, the powers of our governments.

For suspending our own legislatures and declaring themselves invested with power to legislate for us in all cases whatsoever.

He has abdicated government here by declaring us out of his protection and waging war against us.

He has plundered our seas, ravaged our coasts, burnt our towns, and destroyed the lives of our people.

He is, at this time, transporting large armies of foreign mercenaries to complete the works of death, desolation, and tyranny already begun with circumstances of cruelty and perfidy scarcely paralleled in the most barbarous ages, and totally unworthy the head of a civilized nation.

He has constrained our fellow citizens, taken captive on the high seas, to bear arms against their country, to become the executioners of their friends and brethren, or to fall themselves by their hands.

He has excited domestic insurrections amongst us and has endeavored to bring on the inhabitants of our frontiers, the merciless Indian savages, whose known rule of warfare is an undistinguished destruction of all ages, sexes, and conditions.

In every stage of these oppressions, we have petitioned for redress in the most humble terms; our repeated petitions have been answered only by repeated injury. A prince whose character is thus marked by every act which may define a tyrant is unfit to be the ruler of a free people.

Nor have we been wanting in attention to our British brethren. We have warned them, from time to time, of attempts made by their legislature to extend an unwarrantable jurisdiction over us. We have reminded them of the circumstances of our emigration and settlement here. We have appealed to their native justice and magnanimity, and we have conjured them, by the ties of our common kindred, to disavow these usurpations, which would inevitably interrupt our connections and correspondence. They, too, have been deaf to the voice of justice and consanguinity. We must, therefore, acquiesce in the necessity which denounces our separation, and hold them, as we hold the rest of mankind, enemies in war, in peace, friends.

We, therefore, the representatives of the United States of America, in general Congress assembled, appealing to the Supreme Judge of the world for the rectitude of our intentions, do, in the name and by the authority of the good people of these colonies, solemnly publish and declare, that these united colonies are, and of right ought to be, free and independent states: that they are absolved from all allegiance to the British Crown, and that all political connection between them and the state of Great Britain is, and ought to be, totally dissolved; and that, as free and independent states, they have full power to levy war, conclude peace, contract alliances, establish commerce, and to do all other acts and things which independent states may of right do. And, for the support of this declaration, with a firm reliance on the protection of Divine Providence, we mutually pledge to each other our lives, our fortunes, and our sacred honor.

THE CONSTITUTION OF THE UNITED STATES OF AMERICA

We the people of the United States, in order to form a more perfect union, establish justice, insure domestic tranquillity, provide for the common defense, promote the general welfare, and secure the blessings of liberty to ourselves and our posterity, do ordain and establish this Constitution for the United States of America.

Article I

Section 1. All legislative powers herein granted shall be vested in a Congress of the United States, which shall consist of a Senate and House of Representatives.

Section 2. 1. The House of Representatives shall be composed of members chosen every second year by the people of the several States, and the electors in each State shall have the qualifications requisite for electors of the most numerous branch of the State legislature.

2. No person shall be a representative who shall not have attained to the age of twenty-five years, and been seven years a citizen of the United States, and who shall not, when elected, be an inhabitant of that State in which he shall be chosen.

3. Representatives and direct taxes[1] shall be apportioned among the several States which may be included within this Union, according to their respective numbers, which shall be determined by adding to the whole number of free persons, including those bound to service for a term of years, and excluding Indians not taxed, three fifths of all other persons.[2] The actual enumeration shall be made within three years after the first meeting of the Congress of the United States, and within every subsequent term of ten years, in such manner as they shall by law direct. The number of representatives shall not exceed one for every thirty thousand, but each State shall have at least one representative; and until such enumeration shall be made, the State of New Hampshire shall be entitled to choose three, Massachusetts eight, Rhode Island and Providence Plantations one, Connecticut five, New York six, New Jersey four, Pennsylvania eight, Delaware one, Maryland six, Virginia ten, North Carolina five, South Carolina five, and Georgia three.

4. When vacancies happen in the representation from any State, the executive authority thereof shall issue writs of election to fill such vacancies.

5. The House of Representatives shall choose their speaker and other officers; and shall have the sole power of impeachment.

Section 3. 1. The Senate of the United States shall be composed of two senators from each State, chosen by the legislature thereof,[3] for six years; and each senator shall have one vote.

2. Immediately after they shall be assembled in consequence of the first election, they shall be divided as equally as may be into three classes. The seats of the senators of the first class shall be vacated at the expiration of the second year, of the second class at the expiration of the fourth year, and of the third class at the expiration of the sixth year, so that one third may be chosen every second year; and if vacancies happen by resignation, or otherwise, during the recess of the legislature of any State, the executive thereof may make temporary appointments until the next meeting of the legislature, which shall then fill such vacancies.[4]

3. No person shall be a senator who shall not have attained to the age of thirty years, and been nine years a citizen of the United States, and who shall not, when elected, be an inhabitant of that State for which he shall be chosen.

4. The Vice President of the United States shall be President of the Senate, but shall have no vote, unless they be equally divided.

5. The Senate shall choose their other officers, and also a president pro tempore, in the absence of the Vice President, or when he shall exercise the office of the President of the United States.

6. The Senate shall have the sole power to try all impeachments. When sitting for that purpose, they shall be on oath or affirmation. When the President of the United States is tried, the chief justice shall preside: and no person shall be convicted without the concurrence of two thirds of the members present.

7. Judgment in cases of impeachment shall not extend further than to removal from office, and disqualification to hold and enjoy any office of honor, trust or profit under the United States: but the party convicted shall nevertheless be liable and subject to indictment, trial, judgment and punishment, according to law.

Section 4. 1. The times, places, and manner of holding elections for senators and representatives, shall be prescribed in each State by the legislature thereof; but the Congress may at any time by law make or alter such regulations, except as to the places of choosing senators.

2. The Congress shall assemble at least once in every year, and such meeting shall be on the first Monday in December, unless they shall by law appoint a different day.

Section 5. 1. Each House shall be the judge of the elections, returns and qualifications of its own members, and a majority of each shall constitute a quorum to do business; but a smaller number may adjourn from day to day, and may be authorized to compel the attendance of absent members, in such manner, and under such penalties as each House may provide.

2. Each House may determine the rules of its proceedings, punish its members for disorderly behavior, and, with the concurrence of two thirds, expel a member.

3. Each House shall keep a journal of its proceedings, and from time to time publish the same, excepting such parts as may in their judgment require secrecy; and the yeas and nays of the members of either House on any question

---

[1] See the Sixteenth Amendment.
[2] See the Fourteenth Amendment.
[3] See the Seventeenth Amendment.

[4] See the Seventeenth Amendment.

shall, at the desire of one fifth of those present, be entered on the journal.

4. Neither House, during the session of Congress, shall, without the consent of the other, adjourn for more than three days, nor to any other place than that in which the two Houses shall be sitting.

Section 6. 1. The senators and representatives shall receive a compensation for their services, to be ascertained by law, and paid out of the Treasury of the United States. They shall in all cases, except treason, felony, and breach of the peace, be privileged from arrest during their attendance at the session of their respective Houses, and in going to and returning from the same; and for any speech or debate in either House, they shall not be questioned in any other place.

2. No senator or representative shall, during the time for which he was elected, be appointed to any civil office under the authority of the United States, which shall have been created, or the emoluments whereof shall have been increased, during such time; and no person holding any office under the United States shall be a member of either House during his continuance in office.

Section 7. 1. All bills for raising revenue shall originate in the House of Representatives; but the Senate may propose or concur with amendments as on other bills.

2. Every bill which shall have passed the House of Representatives and the Senate, shall, before it become a law, be presented to the President of the United States; If he approves he shall sign it, but if not he shall return it, with his objections, to that House in which it shall have originated, who shall enter the objections at large on their journal, and proceed to reconsider it. If after such reconsideration two thirds of that House shall agree to pass the bill, it shall be sent, together with the objections, to the other House, by which it shall likewise be reconsidered, and if approved by two thirds of that House, it shall become a law. But in all such cases the votes of both Houses shall be determined by yeas and nays, and the names of the persons voting for and against the bill shall be entered on the journal of each House respectively. If any bill shall not be returned by the President within ten days (Sundays excepted) after it shall have been presented to him, the same shall be a law, in like manner as if he had signed it, unless the Congress by their adjournment prevent its return, in which case it shall not be a law.

3. Every order, resolution, or vote to which the concurrence of the Senate and the House of Representatives may be necessary (except on a question of adjournment) shall be presented to the President of the United States; and before the same shall take effect, shall be approved by him, or being disapproved by him, shall be repassed by two thirds of the Senate and House of Representatives, according to the rules and limitations prescribed in the case of a bill.

Section 8. 1. The Congress shall have the power

1. To lay and collect taxes, duties, imposts, and excises, to pay the debts and provide for the common defense and general welfare of the United States; but all duties, imposts, and excises shall be uniform throughout the United States.

2. To borrow money on the credit of the United States;

3. To regulate commerce with foreign nations, and among the several States, and with the Indian tribes;

4. To establish a uniform rule of naturalization, and uniform laws on the subject of bankruptcies throughout the United States;

5. To coin money, regulate the value thereof, and of foreign coin, and fix the standard of weights and measures;

6. To provide for the punishment of counterfeiting the securities and current coin of the United States;

7. To establish post offices and post roads;

8. To promote the progress of science and useful arts, by securing for limited times to authors and inventors the exclusive right to their respective writings and discoveries;

9. To constitute tribunals inferior to the Supreme Court;

10. To define and punish piracies and felonies committed on the high seas, and offenses against the law of nations;

11. To declare war, grant letters of marque and reprisal, and make rules concerning captures on land and water;

12. To raise and support armies, but no appropriation of money to that use shall be for a longer term than two years;

13. To provide and maintain a navy;

14. To make rules for the government and regulation of the land and naval forces;

15. To provide for calling forth the militia to execute the laws of the Union, suppress insurrections and repel invasions;

16. To provide for organizing, arming, and disciplining the militia, and for governing such part of them as may be employed in the service of the United States, reserving to the States respectively, the appointment of the officers, and the authority of training the militia according to the discipline prescribed by Congress;

17. To exercise exclusive legislation in all cases whatsoever, over such district (not exceeding ten miles square) as may, by cession of particular States, and the acceptance of Congress, become the seat of the government of the United States, and to exercise like authority over all places purchased by the consent of the legislature of the State in which the same shall be, for the erection of forts, magazines, arsenals, dockyards, and other needful buildings; and

18. To make all laws which shall be necessary and proper for carrying into execution the foregoing powers, and all other powers vested by this Constitution in the government of the United States, or any department or officer thereof.

Section 9. 1. The migration or importation of such persons as any of the States now existing shall think proper to admit, shall not be prohibited by the Congress prior to the year one thousand eight hundred and eight, but a tax or duty may be imposed on such importation, not exceeding ten dollars for each person.

2. The privilege of the writ of habeas corpus shall not be suspended, unless when in cases of rebellion or invasion the public safety may require it.

3. No bill of attainder or ex post facto law shall be passed.

4. No capitation, or other direct, tax shall be laid, unless in proportion to the census or enumeration hereinbefore directed to be taken.[5]

5. No tax or duty shall be laid on articles exported from any State.

6. No preference shall be given by any regulation of commerce or revenue to the ports of one State over those of another: nor shall vessels bound to, or from, one State be obliged to enter, clear, or pay duties in another.

7. No money shall be drawn from the treasury, but in consequence of appropriations made by law; and a regular statement and account of the receipts and expenditures of all public money shall be published from time to time.

8. No title of nobility shall be granted by the United States: and no person holding any office of profit or trust under them, shall, without the consent of the Congress, accept of any present, emolument, office, or title, of any kind whatever, from any king, prince, or foreign State.

Section 10. 1. No State shall enter into any treaty, alliance, or confederation; grant letters of marque and reprisal; coin money; emit bills of credit; make any thing but gold and silver coin a tender in payment of debts; pass any bill of attainder, ex post facto law, or law impairing the obligation of contracts, or grant, any title of nobility.

2. No State shall, without the consent of the Congress, lay any imposts or duties on imports or exports, except what may be absolutely necessary for executing its inspection laws: and the net produce of all duties and imposts laid by any State on imports or exports, shall be for the use of the treasury of the United States; and all such laws shall be subject to the revision and control of the Congress.

3. No State shall, without the consent of the Congress, lay any duty of tonnage, keep troops, or ships of war in time of peace, enter into any agreement or compact with another State, or with a foreign power, or engage in war, unless actually invaded, or in such imminent danger as will not admit of delay.

Article II

Section 1. 1. The executive power shall be vested in a President of the United States of America. He shall hold his office during the term of four years, and, together with the Vice President, chosen for the same term, be elected, as follows:

2. Each State shall appoint, in such manner as the legislature thereof may direct, a number of electors, equal to the whole number of senators and representatives to which the State may be entitled in the Congress: but no senator or representative, or person holding any office of trust or profit under the United States, shall be appointed an elector.

The electors shall meet in their respective States, and vote by ballot for two persons, of whom one at least shall not be an inhabitant of the same State with themselves. And they shall make a list of all the persons voted for, and of the number of votes for each; which list they shall sign and certify, and transmit sealed to the seat of the government of the United States, directed to the president of the Senate. The president of the Senate shall, in the presence of the Senate and House of Representatives, open all the certificates, and the votes shall then be counted. The person having the greatest number of votes shall be the President, if such number be a majority of the whole number of electors appointed; and if there be more than one who have such majority, and have an equal number of votes, then the House of Representatives shall immediately choose by ballot one of them for President; and if no person have a majority, then from the five highest on the list the said House shall in like manner choose the President. But in choosing the President, the votes shall be taken by States, the representation from each State having one vote; a quorum for this purpose shall consist of a member or members from two thirds of the States, and a majority of all the States shall be necessary to a choice. In every case after the choice of the President, the person having the greatest number of votes of the electors shall be the Vice President. But if there should remain two or more who have equal votes, the Senate shall choose from them by ballot the Vice President.[6]

3. The Congress may determine the time of choosing the electors, and the day on which they shall give their votes; which day shall be the same throughout the United States.

4. No person except a natural born citizen, or a citizen of the United States, at the time of the adoption of this Constitution, shall be eligible to the office of President; neither shall any person be eligible to the office who shall not have attained to the age of thirty-five years, and been fourteen years a resident within the United States.

5. In case of the removal of the President from office, or of his death, resignation, or inability to discharge the powers and duties of the said office, the same shall devolve on the Vice President, and the congress may by law provide for the case of removal, death, resignation or inability, both of the President and Vice President, declaring what officer shall then act as President, and such officer shall act accordingly until the disability be removed, or a President shall be elected.

6. The President shall, at stated times, receive for his services a compensation which shall neither be increased nor diminished during the period for which he shall have been elected, and he shall not receive within that period any other emolument from the United States, or any of them.

7. Before he enter on the execution of his office, he shall take the following oath or affirmation:—"I do solemnly swear (or affirm) that I will faithfully execute the

---

[5]See the Sixteenth Amendment.

[6]Superseded by the Twelfth Amendment.

office of President of the United States, and will to the best of my ability, preserve, protect and defend the Constitution of the United States."

Section 2. 1. The President shall be commander in chief of the army and navy of the United States, and of the militia of the several States, when called into the actual service of the United States; he may require the opinion in writing, of the principal officer in each of the executive departments, upon any subject relating to the duties of their respective offices, and he shall have power to grant reprieves and pardons for offenses against the United States, except in cases of impeachment.

2. He shall have power, by and with the advice and consent of the Senate, to make treaties, provided two thirds of the senators present concur; and he shall nominate, and by and with the advice and consent of the Senate, shall appoint ambassadors, other public ministers and consuls, judges of the Supreme Court, and all other officers of the United States, whose appointments are not herein otherwise provided for, and which shall be established by law; but the Congress may by law vest the appointment of such inferior officers, as they think proper, in the President alone, in the courts of laws, or in the heads of departments.

3. The President shall have power to fill up all vacancies that may happen during the recess of the Senate, by granting commissions which shall expire at the end of their next session.

Section 3. He shall from time to time give to the Congress information of the state of the Union, and recommend to their consideration such measures as he shall judge necessary and expedient; he may, on extraordinary occasions, convene both Houses, or either of them, and in case of disagreement between them with respect to the time of adjournment, he may adjourn them to such time as he shall think proper; he shall receive ambassadors and other public ministers; he shall take care that the laws be faithfully executed, and shall commission all the officers of the United States.

Section 4. The President, Vice President, and all civil officers of the United States, shall be removed from office on impeachment for, and conviction of, treason, bribery, or other high crimes and misdemeanors.

Article III

Section 1. The judicial power of the United States shall be vested in one Supreme Court, and in such inferior courts as the Congress may from time to time ordain and establish. The judges, both of the Supreme and inferior courts, shall hold their offices during good behavior, and shall, at stated times, receive for their services, a compensation, which shall not be diminished during their continuance in office.

Section 2. 1. The judicial power shall extend to all cases, in law and equity, arising under this Constitution, the laws of the United States, and treaties made, or which shall be made, under their authority;—to all cases of admiralty and maritime jurisdiction;—to controversies to which the United States shall be a party;[7]—

to controversies between two or more States;—between a State and citizens of another State;—between citizens of different States;—between citizens of the same State claiming lands under grants of different States, and between a State, or the citizens thereof, and foreign States, citizens or subjects.

2. In all cases affecting ambassadors, other public ministers and consuls, and those in which a State shall be party, the Supreme Court shall have original jurisdiction. In all the other cases before mentioned, the Supreme Court shall have appellate jurisdiction, both as to law and fact, with such exceptions, and under such regulations as the Congress shall make.

3. The trial of all crimes, except in cases of impeachment, shall be by jury; and such trial shall be held in the State where the said crimes shall have been committed; but when not committed within any State, the trial shall be such place or places as the congress may by law have directed.

Section 3. 1. Treason against the United States shall consist only in levying war against them, or in adhering to their enemies, giving them aid and comfort. No person shall be convicted of treason unless on the testimony of two witnesses to the same overt act, or on confession in open court.

2. The Congress shall have power to declare the punishment of treason, but no attainder of treason shall work corruption of blood, or forfeiture except during the life of the person attained.

Article IV

Section 1. Full faith and credit shall be given in each State to the public acts, records, and judicial proceedings of every other State. And the Congress may by general laws prescribe the manner in which such acts, records and proceedings shall be proved, and the effect thereof.

Section 2. 1. The citizens of each State shall be entitled to all privileges and immunities of citizens in the several States.[8]

2. A person charged in any State with treason, felony, or other crime, who shall flee from justice, and be found in another State, shall on demand of the executive authority of the State from which he fled, be delivered up to be removed to the State having jurisdiction of the crime.

3. No person held to service or labor in one State under the laws thereof, escaping into another, shall, in consequence of any law or regulation therein, be discharged from such service or labor, but shall be delivered up on claim of the party to whom such service or labor may be due.[9]

Section 3. 1. New States may be admitted by the Congress into this Union; but no new State shall be formed or erected within the jurisdiction of any other State, nor any State be formed by the junction of two or more States, or parts of States, without the consent of the legislatures of the States concerned as well as of the Congress.

[7]See the Eleventh Amendment.

[8]See the Fourteenth Amendment, Sec. 1.
[9]See the Thirteenth Amendment.

2. The Congress shall have power to dispose of and make all needful rules and regulations respecting the territory or other property belonging to the United States; and nothing in this Constitution shall be so construed as to prejudice any claims of the United States, or of any particular State.

Section 4. The United States shall guarantee to every State in this Union a republican form of government, and shall protect each of them against invasion; and on application of the legislature, or of the executive (when the legislature cannot be convened) against domestic violence.

Article V

The Congress, whenever two thirds of both Houses shall deem it necessary, shall propose amendments to this Constitution, or, on the application of the legislatures of two thirds of the several States, shall call a convention for proposing amendments, which in either case shall be valid to all intents and purposes, as part of this Constitution, when ratified by the legislatures of three fourths of the several States, or by conventions in three fourths thereof, as the one or the other mode of ratification may be proposed by the Congress; Provided that no amendment which may be made prior to the year one thousand eight hundred and eight shall in any manner affect the first and fourth clauses in the ninth section of the first article; and that no State, without its consent, shall be deprived of its equal suffrage in the Senate.

Article VI

1. All debts contracted and engagements entered into, before the adoption of this Constitution, shall be as valid against the United States under this Constitution, as under the Confederation.[10]

2. This Constitution, and the laws of the United States which shall be made in pursuance thereof; and all treaties made, or which shall be made, under the authority of the United States, shall be the supreme law of the land; and the judges in every State shall be bound thereby, any thing in the Constitution or laws of any State to the contrary notwithstanding.

3. The senators and representatives before mentioned, and the members of the several State legislatures, and all executive and judicial officers, both of the United States and of the several States, shall be bound by oath or affirmation to support this Constitution; but no religious test shall ever be required as a qualification to any office or public trust under the United States.

Article VII

The ratification of the conventions of nine States shall be sufficient for the establishment of this Constitution between the States so ratifying the same.

Done in Convention by the unanimous consent of the States present the seventeenth day of September in the year of our Lord one thousand seven hundred and eighty-seven, and of the independence of the United States of America the twelfth. In witness whereof we have hereunto subscribed our names.

[Signatories' names omitted]

* * *

Articles in addition to, and amendment of, the Constitution of the United States of America, proposed by Congress, and ratified by the legislatures of the several States, pursuant to the fifth article of the original Constitution.

Amendment I
[First ten amendments ratified December 15, 1791]

Congress shall make no law respecting an establishment of religion, or prohibiting the free exercise thereof; or abridging the freedom of speech, or of the press; or the right of the people peaceably to assemble, and to petition the government for a redress of grievances.

Amendment II

A well regulated militia, being necessary to the security of a free State, the right of the people to keep and bear arms, shall not be infringed.

Amendment III

No soldier shall, in time of peace be quartered in any house, without the consent of the owner, nor in time of war, but in a manner to be prescribed by law.

Amendment IV

The right of the people to be secure in their persons, houses, papers, and effects, against unreasonable searches and seizures, shall not be violated, and no warrants shall issue, but upon probable cause, supported by oath or affirmation, and particularly describing the place to be searched, and the persons or things to be seized.

Amendment V

No person shall be held to answer for a capital or otherwise infamous crime, unless on a presentment or indictment of a grand jury, except in cases arising in the land or naval forces, or in the militia, when in actual service in time of war or public danger; nor shall any person be subject for the same offense to be twice put in jeopardy of life or limb; nor shall be compelled in any criminal case to be a witness against himself, nor be deprived of life, liberty, or property, without due process of law; nor shall private property be taken for public use, without just compensation.

Amendment VI

In all criminal prosecutions, the accused shall enjoy the right to a speedy and public trial, by an impartial jury of the State and district wherein the crime shall have been committed, which district shall have been previously ascertained by law, and to be informed of the nature and cause of the accusation; to be confronted with the witnesses against him; to have compulsory process for obtaining witnesses in his favor, and to have the assistance of counsel for his defense.

---

[10]See the Fourteenth Amendment, Sec. 4.

Amendment VII

In suits at common law, where the value in controversy shall exceed twenty dollars, the right of trial by jury shall be preserved, and no fact tried by a jury shall be otherwise reexamined in any court of the United States, than according to the rules of the common law.

Amendment VIII

Excessive bail shall not be required, nor excessive fines imposed, nor cruel and unusual punishments inflicted.

Amendment IX

The enumeration in the Constitution of certain rights shall not be construed to deny or disparage others retained by the people.

Amendment X

The powers not delegated to the United States by the Constitution, nor prohibited by it to the States, are reserved to the States respectively, or to the people.

Amendment XI [January 8, 1798]

The judicial power of the United States shall not be construed to extend to any suit in law or equity, commended or prosecuted against one of the United States by citizens of another State, or by citizens or subjects of any foreign State.

Amendment XII [September 25, 1804]

The electors shall meet in their respective States, and vote by ballot for President and Vice President, one of whom, at least, shall not be an inhabitant of the same State with themselves; they shall name in their ballots the person voted for as President, and in distinct ballots the person voted for as Vice President, and they shall make distinct lists of all persons voted for as President and of all persons voted for as Vice President, and of the number of votes for each, which lists they shall sign and certify, and transmit sealed to the seat of the government of the United States, directed to the President of the Senate;—The President of the Senate shall, in the presence of the Senate and House of Representatives, open all the certificates and the votes shall then be counted;—The person having the greatest number of votes for President, shall be the President, if such number be a majority of the whole number of electors appointed; and if no person have such majority, then from the persons having the highest numbers not exceeding three on the list of those voted for as President, the House of Representatives shall choose immediately, by ballot, the President. But in choosing the President, the votes shall be taken by States, the representation from each State having one vote; a quorum for this purpose shall consist of a member or members from two thirds of the States, and a majority of all the States shall be necessary to a choice. And if the House of Representatives shall not choose a President whenever the right of choice shall devolve upon them, before the fourth day of March next following, then the Vice President shall act as President,

as in the case of the death or other constitutional disability of the President. The person having the greatest number of votes as Vice President shall be the Vice President, if such number be a majority of the whole number of electors appointed, and if no person have a majority, then from the two highest numbers on the list, the Senate shall choose the Vice President; a quorum for the purpose shall consist of two thirds of the whole number of Senators, and a majority of the whole number shall be necessary to a choice. But no person constitutionally ineligible to the office of President shall be eligible to that of Vice President of the United States.

Amendment XIII [December 18, 1865]

Section 1.   Neither slavery nor involuntary servitude, except as a punishment for crime whereof the party shall have been duly convicted, shall exist within the United States, or any place subject to their jurisdiction.

Section 2.   Congress shall have power to enforce this article by appropriate legislation.

Amendment XIV [July 28, 1868]

Section 1.   All persons born or naturalized in the United States, and subject to the jurisdiction thereof, are citizens of the United States and of the State wherein they reside. No State shall make or enforce any law which shall abridge the privileges or immunities of citizens of the United States; nor shall any State deprive any person of life, liberty, or property, without due process of law; nor deny to any person within its jurisdiction the equal protection of the laws.

Section 2.   Representatives shall be apportioned among the several States according to their respective numbers, counting the whole number of persons in each State, excluding Indians not taxed. But when the right to vote at any election for the choice of electors for President and Vice President of the United States, representatives in Congress, the executive and judicial officers of a State, or the members of the legislature thereof, is denied to any of the male inhabitants of such State, being twenty-one years of age, and citizens of the United States, or in any way abridged, except for participating in rebellion, or other crime, the basis of representation there shall be reduced in the proportion which the number of such male citizens shall bear to the whole number of male citizens twenty-one years of age in such State.

Section 3.   No person shall be a senator or representative in Congress, or elector of President and Vice President, or hold any office, civil or military, under the United States, or under any State, who having previously taken an oath, as a member of Congress, or as an officer of the United States, or as a member of any State legislature, or as an executive or judicial officer of any State, to support the Constitution of the United States, shall have engaged in insurrection or rebellion against the same, or given aid or comfort to the enemies thereof. But Congress may by a vote of two thirds of each House, remove such disability.

Section 4.   The validity of the public debt of the United States, authorized by law, including debts incurred for payment of pensions and bounties for services in suppressing insurrection or rebellion; shall not be questioned. But neither the United States nor any State shall assume or pay any debt or obligation incurred in aid of insurrection or rebellion against the United States, or any claim for the loss or emancipation of any slave; but all such debts, obligations, and claims shall be held illegal and void.

Section 5. The Congress shall have the power to enforce, by appropriate legislation, the provisions of this article.

Amendment XV [March 30, 1870]

Section 1. The right of citizens of the United States to vote shall not be denied or abridged by the United States or by any State on account of race, color, or previous condition of servitude.

Section 2. The Congress shall have power to enforce this article by appropriate legislation.

Amendment XVI [February 25, 1913]

The Congress shall have power to lay and collect taxes on incomes, from whatever source derived, without apportionment among the several States, and without regard to any census or enumeration.

Amendment XVII [May 31, 1913]

The Senate of the United States shall be composed of two senators from each State, elected by the people thereof, for six years; and each senator shall have one vote. The electors in each State shall have the qualifications requisite for electors of the most numerous branch of the State legislature.

When vacancies happen in the representation of any State in the Senate, the executive authority of such State shall issue writs of election to fill such vacancies: Provided, That the legislature of any State may empower the executive thereof to make temporary appointments until the people fill the vacancies by election as the legislature may direct.

This amendment shall not be so construed as to affect the election or term of any senator chosen before it becomes valid as part of the Constitution.

Amendment XVIII[11] [January 29, 1919]

After one year from the ratification of this article, the manufacture, sale, or transportation of intoxicating liquors within, the importation thereof into, or the exportation thereof from the United States and all territory subject to the jurisdiction thereof for beverage purposes is thereby prohibited.

The Congress and the several States shall have concurrent power to enforce this article by appropriate legislation.

This article shall be inoperative unless it shall have been ratified as an amendment to the Constitution by the legislatures of the several States, as provided in the constitution, within seven years from the date of the submission hereof to the States by Congress.

---

[11]Repealed by the Twenty-first Amendment.

Amendment XIX [August 26, 1920]

The right of citizens of the United States to vote shall not be denied or abridged by the United States or by any State on account of sex.

Congress shall have the power to enforce this article by appropriate legislation.

Amendment XX [January 23, 1933]

Section 1. The terms of the President and Vice President shall end at noon on the 20th day of January and the terms of Senators and Representatives at noon on the 3d day of January, of the years in which such terms would have ended if this article had not been ratified; and the terms of their successors shall then begin.

Section 2. The Congress shall assemble at least once in every year, and such meeting shall begin at noon on the 3d day of January, unless they shall by law appoint a different day.

Section 3. If, at the time fixed for the beginning of the term of President, the President-elect shall have died, the Vice President-elect shall become President. If a President shall not have been chosen before the time fixed for the beginning of his term, or if the President-elect shall have failed to qualify, then the Vice President-elect shall act as President until a President shall have qualified; and the Congress may by law provide for the case wherein neither a President-elect nor a Vice President-elect shall have qualified, declaring who shall then act as President, or the manner in which one who is to act shall be selected, and such person shall act accordingly until a President or Vice President shall have qualified.

Section 4. The Congress may by law provide for the case of the death of any of the persons from whom, the House of Representatives may choose a President whenever the right of choice shall have devolved upon them, and for the case of the death of any of the persons from whom the Senate may choose a Vice President whenever the right of choice shall have devolved upon them.

Section 5. Sections 1 and 2 shall take effect on the 15th day of October following the ratification of this article.

Section 6. This article shall be inoperative unless it shall have been ratified as an amendment to the Constitution by the legislatures of three-fourths of the several States within seven years from the date of its submission.

Amendment XXI [December 5, 1933]

Section 1. The Eighteenth Article of amendment to the Constitution of the United States is hereby repealed.

Section 2. The transportation or importation into any State, Territory, or possession of the United States for delivery or use therein of intoxicating liquors in violation of the laws thereof, is hereby prohibited.

Section 3. This article shall be inoperative unless it shall have been ratified as an amendment to the Constitution by conventions in the several States, as provided in the Constitution, within seven years from the date of the submission thereof to the States by the Congress.

Amendment XXII [March 1, 1951]

No person shall be elected to the office of the President more than twice, and no person who has held the office of President, or acted as President, for more than two years of a term to which some other person was elected President shall be elected to the office of the President more than once.

But this article shall not apply to any person holding the office of President when this article was proposed by the Congress, and shall not prevent any person who may be holding the office of President, or acting as President, during the term within which this article becomes operative from holding the office of President or acting as President during the remainder of such term.

This article shall be inoperative unless it shall have been ratified as an amendment to the Constitution by the legislatures of three-fourths of the several States within seven years from the date of its submission to the States by the Congress.

Amendment XXIII [March 29, 1961]

Section 1.   The District constituting the seat of Government of the United States shall appoint in such manner as the Congress may direct.

A number of electors of President and Vice President equal to the whole number of Senators and Representatives in Congress to which the District would be entitled if it were a State, but in no event more than the least populous State; they shall be in addition to those appointed by the States, but they shall be considered, for the purposes of the election of President and Vice President, to be electors appointed by a State; and they shall meet in the District and perform such duties as provided by the twelfth article of amendment.

Section 2.   The Congress shall have power to enforce this article by appropriate legislation.

Amendment XXIV [January 23, 1964]

Section 1.   The right of citizens of the United States to vote in any primary or other election for President or Vice President, for electors for President or Vice President, or for Senator or Representative in Congress, shall not be denied or abridged by the United States or any State by reason of failure to pay any poll tax or other tax.

Section 2.   The Congress shall have power to enforce this article by appropriate legislation.

Amendment XXV [February 10, 1967]

Section 1.   In case of the removal of the President from office or of his death or resignation, the Vice President shall become President.

Section 2.   Whenever there is a vacancy in the office of the Vice President, the President shall nominate a Vice President who shall take office upon confirmation by a majority of both Houses of Congress.

Section 3.   Whenever the President transmits to the President pro tempore of the Senate and the Speaker of the House of Representatives his written declaration that he is unable to discharge the powers and duties of his office, and until he transmits to them a written declaration to the contrary, such powers and duties shall be discharged by the Vice President as Acting President.

Section 4.   Whenever the Vice President and a majority of either the principal officers of the executive departments or of such other body as Congress may by law provide, transmit to the President pro tempore of the Senate and the Speaker of the House of Representatives their written declaration that the President is unable to discharge the powers and duties of his office, the Vice President shall immediately assume the powers and duties of the office as Acting President.

Thereafter, when the President transmits to the President pro tempore of the Senate and the Speaker of the House of Representatives his written declaration that no inability exists, he shall resume the powers and duties of his office unless the Vice President and a majority of either the principal officers of the executive departments or of such other body as Congress may by law provide, transmit within four days to the President pro tempore of the Senate and the Speaker of the House of Representatives their written declaration that the President is unable to discharge the powers and duties of his office. Thereupon Congress shall decide the issue, assembling within forty-eight hours for that purpose if not in session. If the Congress, within twenty-one days after receipt of the latter written declaration, or, if Congress is not in session, within twenty-one days after Congress is required to assemble, determines by two-thirds vote of both Houses that the President is unable to discharge the powers and duties of his office, the Vice President shall continue to discharge the same as Acting President; otherwise, the President shall resume the powers and duties of his office.

Amendment XXVI [June 30, 1971]

Section 1.   The right of citizens of the United States who are eighteen years of age or older to vote shall not be denied or abridged by the United States or by any State on account of age.

Section 2.   The Congress shall have power to enforce this article by appropriate legislation.

Amendment XXVII[12] [May 7, 1992]

No law, varying the compensation for services of the Senators and Representatives, shall take effect until an election of Representatives shall have intervened.

---

[12]James Madison proposed this amendment in 1789 together with the ten amendments that were adopted as the Bill of Rights, but it failed to win ratification at the time. Congress, however, had set no deadline for its ratification, and over the years—particularly in the 1980s and 1990s—many states voted to add it to the Constitution. With the ratification of Michigan in 1992 it passed the threshold of 3/4ths of the states required for adoption, but because the process took more than 200 years, its validity remains in doubt.

PRESIDENTS AND VICE PRESIDENTS

1. George Washington (1789)
John Adams (1789)

2. John Adams (1797)
Thomas Jefferson (1797)

3. Thomas Jefferson (1801)
Aaron Burr (1801)
George Clinton (1805)

4. James Madison (1809)
George Clinton (1809)
Elbridge Gerry (1813)

5. James Monroe (1817)
Daniel D. Thompkins (1817)

6. John Quincy Adams (1825)
John C. Calhoun (1825)

7. Andrew Jackson (1829)
John C. Calhoun (1829)
Martin Van Buren (1833)

8. Martin Van Buren (1837)
Richard M. Johnson (1837)

9. William H. Harrison (1841)
John Tyler (1841)

10. John Tyler (1841)

11. James K. Polk (1845)
George M. Dallas (1845)

12. Zachary Taylor (1849)
Millard Fillmore (1849)

13. Millard Fillmore (1850)

14. Franklin Pierce (1853)
William R. King (1853)

15. James Buchanan (1857)
John C. Breckinridge (1857)

16. Abraham Lincoln (1861)
Hannibal Hamlin (1861)
Andrew Johnson (1865)

17. Andrew Johnson (1865)

18. Ulysses S. Grant (1869)
Schuyler Colfax (1869)
Henry Wilson (1873)

19. Rutherford B. Hayes (1877)
William A. Wheeler (1877)

20. James A. Garfield (1881)
Chester A. Arthur (1881)

21. Chester A. Arthur (1881)

22. Grover Cleveland (1885)
T. A. Hendricks (1885)

23. Benjamin Harrison (1889)
Levi P. Morgan (1889)

24. Grover Cleveland (1893)
Adlai E. Stevenson (1893)

25. William McKinley (1897)
Garret A. Hobart (1897)
Theodore Roosevelt (1901)

26. Theodore Roosevelt (1901)
Charles Fairbanks (1905)

27. William H. Taft (1909)
James S. Sherman (1909)

28. Woodrow Wilson (1913)
Thomas R. Marshall (1913)

29. Warren G. Harding (1921)
Calvin Coolidge (1921)

30. Calvin Coolidge (1923)
Charles G. Dawes (1925)

31. Herbert C. Hoover (1929)
Charles Curtis (1929)

32. Franklin D. Roosevelt (1933)
John Nance Garner (1933)
Henry A. Wallace (1941)
Harry S Truman (1945)

33. Harry S Truman (1945)
Alben W. Barkley (1949)

34. Dwight D. Eisenhower (1953)
Richard M. Nixon (1953)

35. John F. Kennedy (1961)
Lyndon B. Johnson (1961)

36. Lyndon B. Johnson (1963)
Hubert H. Humphrey (1965)

37. Richard M. Nixon (1969)
Spiro T. Agnew (1969)
Gerald R. Ford (1973)

38. Gerald R. Ford (1974)
Nelson A. Rockefeller (1974)

39. James E. Carter Jr. (1977)
Walter F. Mondale (1977)

40. Ronald W. Reagan (1981)
George H. W. Bush (1981)

41. George H. W. Bush (1989)
James D. Quayle III (1989)

42. William J. Clinton (1993)
Albert Gore (1993)

43. George W. Bush (2001)
Richard Cheney (2001)

PRESIDENTIAL ELECTIONS

Year	Number of States	Candidates	Party	Popular Vote	Electoral Vote[†]	Percentage of Popular Vote[*]
1789	11	GEORGE WASHINGTON	No party designations		69	
		John Adams			34	
		Other Candidates			35	
1792	15	GEORGE WASHINGTON	No party designations		132	
		John Adams			77	
		George Clinton			50	
		Other Candidates			5	
1796	16	JOHN ADAMS	Federalist		71	
		Thomas Jefferson	Democratic-Republican		68	
		Thomas Pinckney	Federalist		59	
		Aaron Burr	Democratic-Republican		30	
		Other Candidates			48	
1800	16	THOMAS JEFFERSON	Democratic-Republican		73	
		Aaron Burr	Democratic-Republican		73	
		John Adams	Federalist		65	
		Charles C. Pinckney	Federalist		64	
		John Jay	Federalist		1	
1804	17	THOMAS JEFFERSON	Democratic-Republican		162	
		Charles C. Pinckney	Federalist		14	
1808	17	JAMES MADISON	Democratic-Republican		122	
		Charles C. Pinckney	Federalist		47	
		George Clinton	Democratic-Republican		6	
1812	18	JAMES MADISON	Democratic-Republican		128	
		DeWitt Clinton	Federalist		89	
1816	19	JAMES MONROE	Democratic-Republican		183	
		Rufus King	Federalist		34	
1820	24	JAMES MONROE	Democratic-Republican		231	
		John Quincy Adams	Independent-Republican		1	
1824	24	JOHN QUINCY ADAMS	Democratic-Republican	108,740	84	30.5
		Andrew Jackson	Democratic-Republican	153,544	99	43.1
		William H. Crawford	Democratic-Republican	46,618	41	13.1
		Henry Clay	Democratic-Republican	47,136	37	13.2
1828	24	ANDREW JACKSON	Democrat	647,286	178	56.0
		John Quincy Adams	National-Republican	508,064	83	44.0
1832	24	ANDREW JACKSON	Democrat	687,502	219	55.0
		Henry Clay	National-Republican	530,189	49	42.4
		William Wirt	Anti-Masonic	33,108	7	2.6
		John Floyd	National-Republican		11	

*Percentage of popular vote given for any election year may not total 100 percent because candidates receiving less than 1 percent of the popular vote have been omitted.

†Prior to the passage of the Twelfth Amendment in 1904, the electoral college voted for two presidential candidates; the runner-up became Vice-President. Data from *Historical Statistics of the United States, Colonial Times to 1957* (1961), pp. 682–683, and *The World Almanac.*

PRESIDENTIAL ELECTIONS (continued)

Year	Number of States	Candidates	Party	Popular Vote	Electoral Vote	Percentage of Popular Vote
1836	26	MARTIN VAN BUREN	Democrat	765,483	170	50.9
		William H. Harrison	Whig		73	
		Hugh L. White	Whig	739,795	26	49.1
		Daniel Webster	Whig		14	
		W. P. Mangum	Whig		11	
1840	26	WILLIAM H. HARRISON	Whig	1,274,624	234	53.1
		Martin Van Buren	Democrat	1,127,781	60	46.9
1844	26	JAMES K. POLK	Democrat	1,338,464	170	49.6
		Henry Clay	Whig	1,300,097	105	48.1
		James G. Birney	Liberty	62,300		2.3
1848	30	ZACHARY TAYLOR	Whig	1,360,967	163	47.4
		Lewis Cass	Democrat	1,222,342	127	42.5
		Martin Van Buren	Free-Soil	291,263		10.1
1852	31	FRANKLIN PIERCE	Democrat	1,601,117	254	50.9
		Winfield Scott	Whig	1,385,453	42	44.1
		John P. Hale	Free-Soil	155,825		5.0
1856	31	JAMES BUCHANAN	Democrat	1,832,955	174	45.3
		John C. Frémont	Republican	1,339,932	114	33.1
		Millard Fillmore	American ("Know Nothing")	871,731	8	21.6
1860	33	ABRAHAM LINCOLN	Republican	1,865,593	180	39.8
		Stephen A. Douglas	Democrat	1,382,713	12	29.5
		John C. Breckinridge	Democrat	848,356	72	18.1
		John Bell	Constitutional Union	592,906	39	12.6
1864	36	ABRAHAM LINCOLN	Republican	2,206,938	212	55.0
		George B. McClellan	Democrat	1,803,787	21	45.0
1868	37	ULYSSES S. GRANT	Republican	3,013,421	214	52.7
		Horatio Seymour	Democrat	2,706,829	80	47.3
1872	37	ULYSSES S. GRANT	Republican	3,596,745	286	55.6
		Horace Greeley	Democrat	2,843,446	*	43.9
1876	38	RUTHERFORD B. HAYES	Republican	4,036,572	185	48.0
		Samuel J. Tilden	Democrat	4,284,020	184	51.0
1880	38	JAMES A. GARFIELD	Republican	4,453,295	214	48.5
		Winfield S. Hancock	Democrat	4,414,082	155	48.1
		James B. Weaver	Greenback-Labor	308,578		3.4
1884	38	GROVER CLEVELAND	Democrat	4,879,507	219	48.5
		James G. Blaine	Republican	4,850,293	182	48.2
		Benjamin F. Butler	Greenback-Labor	175,370		1.8
		John P. St. John	Prohibition	150,369		1.5
1888	38	BENJAMIN HARRISON	Republican	5,447,129	233	47.9
		Grover Cleveland	Democrat	5,537,857	168	48.6
		Clinton B. Fisk	Prohibition	249,506		2.2
		Anson J. Streeter	Union Labor	146,935		1.3

*Because of the death of Greeley, Democratic electors scattered their votes.

PRESIDENTIAL ELECTIONS (continued)

Year	Number of States	Candidates	Party	Popular Vote	Electoral Vote	Percent- age of Popular Vote
1892	44	GROVER CLEVELAND	Democrat	5,555,426	277	46.1
		Benjamin Harrison	Republican	5,182,690	145	43.0
		James B. Weaver	People's	1,029,846	22	8.5
		John Bidwell	Prohibition	264,133		2.2
1896	45	WILLIAM MCKINLEY	Republican	7,102,246	271	51.1
		William J. Bryan	Democrat	6,492,559	176	47.7
1900	45	WILLIAM MCKINLEY	Republican	7,218,491	292	51.7
		William J. Bryan	Democrat; Populist	6,356,734	155	45.5
		John C. Woolley	Prohibition	208,914		1.5
1904	45	THEODORE ROOSEVELT	Republican	7,628,461	336	57.4
		Alton B. Parker	Democrat	5,084,223	140	37.6
		Eugene V. Debs	Socialist	402,283		3.0
		Silas C. Swallow	Prohibition	258,536		1.9
1908	46	WILLIAM H. TAFT	Republican	7,675,320	321	51.6
		William J. Bryan	Democrat	6,412,294	162	43.1
		Eugene V. Debs	Socialist	420,793		2.8
		Eugene W. Chafin	Prohibition	253,840		1.7
1912	48	WOODROW WILSON	Democrat	6,296,547	435	41.9
		Theodore Roosevelt	Progressive	4,118,571	88	27.4
		William H. Taft	Republican	3,486,720	8	23.2
		Eugene V. Debs	Socialist	900,672		6.0
		Eugene W. Chafin	Prohibition	206,275		1.4
1916	48	WOODROW WILSON	Democrat	9,127,695	277	49.4
		Charles E. Hughes	Republican	8,533,507	254	46.2
		A. L. Benson	Socialist	585,113		3.2
		J. Frank Hanly	Prohibition	220,506		1.2
1920	48	WARREN G. HARDING	Republican	16,143,407	404	60.4
		James M. Cox	Democrat	9,130,328	127	34.2
		Eugene V. Debs	Socialist	919,799		3.4
		P. P. Christensen	Farmer-Labor	265,411		1.0
1924	48	CALVIN COOLIDGE	Republican	15,718,211	382	54.0
		John W. Davis	Democrat	8,385,283	136	28.8
		Robert M. La Follette	Progressive	4,831,289	13	16.6
1928	48	HERBERT C. HOOVER	Republican	21,391,993	444	58.2
		Alfred E. Smith	Democrat	15,016,169	87	40.9
1932	48	FRANKLIN D. ROOSEVELT	Democrat	22,809,638	472	57.4
		Herbert C. Hoover	Republican	15,758,901	59	39.7
		Norman Thomas	Socialist	881,951		2.2
1936	48	FRANKLIN D. ROOSEVELT	Democrat	27,752,869	523	60.8
		Alfred M. Landon	Republican	16,674,665	8	36.5
		William Lemke	Union	882,479		1.9
1940	48	FRANKLIN D. ROOSEVELT	Democrat	27,307,819	449	54.8
		Wendell L. Willkie	Republican	22,321,018	82	44.8
1944	48	FRANKLIN D. ROOSEVELT	Democrat	25,606,585	432	53.5
		Thomas E. Dewey	Republican	22,014,745	99	46.0

PRESIDENTIAL ELECTIONS (continued)

Year	Number of States	Candidates	Party	Popular Vote	Electoral Vote	Percentage of Popular Vote
1948	48	HARRY S TRUMAN	Democrat	24,105,812	303	49.5
		Thomas E. Dewey	Republican	21,970,065	189	45.1
		J. Strom Thurmond	States' Rights	1,169,063	39	2.4
		Henry A. Wallace	Progressive	1,157,172		2.4
1952	48	DWIGHT D. EISENHOWER	Republican	33,936,234	442	55.1
		Adlai E. Stevenson	Democrat	27,314,992	89	44.4
1956	48	DWIGHT D. EISENHOWER	Republican	35,590,472	457[*]	57.6
		Adlai E. Stevenson	Democrat	26,022,752	73	42.1
1960	50	JOHN F. KENNEDY	Democrat	34,227,096	303[†]	49.9
		Richard M. Nixon	Republican	34,108,546	219	49.6
1964	50	LYNDON B. JOHNSON	Democrat	42,676,220	486	61.3
		Barry M. Goldwater	Republican	26,860,314	52	38.5
1968	50	RICHARD M. NIXON	Republican	31,785,480	301	43.4
		Hubert H. Humphrey	Democrat	31,275,165	191	42.7
		George C. Wallace	American Independent	9,906,473	46	13.5
1972	50	RICHARD M. NIXON[‡]	Republican	47,165,234	520	60.6
		George S. McGovern	Democrat	29,168,110	17	37.5
1976	50	JAMES E. CARTER JR.	Democrat	40,828,929	297	50.1
		Gerald R. Ford	Republican	39,148,940	240	47.9
		Eugene McCarthy	Independent	739,256		
1980	50	RONALD W. REAGAN	Republican	43,201,220	489	50.9
		James E. Carter Jr.	Democrat	34,913,332	49	41.2
		John B. Anderson	Independent	5,581,379		
1984	50	RONALD W. REAGAN	Republican	53,428,357	525	59.0
		Walter F. Mondale	Democrat	36,930,923	13	41.0
1988	50	GEORGE H. W. BUSH	Republican	48,901,046	426	53.4
		Michael Dukakis	Democrat	41,809,030	111	45.6
1992	50	WILLIAM J. CLINTON	Democrat	43,728,275	370	43.2
		George H. W. Bush	Republican	38,167,416	168	37.7
		H. Ross Perot	United We Stand, America	19,237,247		19.0
1996	50	WILLIAM J. CLINTON	Democrat	45,590,703	379	49.0
		Robert Dole	Republican	37,816,307	159	41.0
		H. Ross Perot	Reform	7,874,283		8.0
2000	50	GEORGE W. BUSH	Republican	50,459,624	271	47.9
		Albert Gore	Democrat	51,003,328	266	49.4
		Ralph Nader	Green	2,882,985	0	2.7
2004	50	GEORGE W. BUSH	Republican	59,117,523	286	51.1
		John Kerry	Democrat	55,557,584	252	48.0
		Ralph Nader	Green	405,623	0	0.3

[*]Walter B. Jones received 1 electoral vote.

[†]Harry F. Byrd received 15 electoral votes.

[‡]Resigned August 9, 1974: Vice President Gerald R. Ford became President.

ADMISSION OF STATES INTO THE UNION

	State	Date of Admission		State	Date of Admission
1.	Delaware	December 7, 1787	26.	Michigan	January 26, 1837
2.	Pennsylvania	December 12, 1787	27.	Florida	March 3, 1845
3.	New Jersey	December 18, 1787	28.	Texas	December 29, 1845
4.	Georgia	January 2, 1788	29.	Iowa	December 28, 1846
5.	Connecticut	January 9, 1788	30.	Wisconsin	May 29, 1848
6.	Massachusetts	February 6, 1788	31.	California	September 9, 1850
7.	Maryland	April 28, 1788	32.	Minnesota	May 11, 1858
8.	South Carolina	May 23, 1788	33.	Oregon	February 14, 1859
9.	New Hampshire	June 21, 1788	34.	Kansas	January 29, 1861
10.	Virginia	June 25, 1788	35.	West Virginia	June 20, 1863
11.	New York	July 26, 1788	36.	Nevada	October 31, 1864
12.	North Carolina	November 21, 1789	37.	Nebraska	March 1, 1867
13	Rhode Island	May 29, 1790	38.	Colorado	August 1, 1876
14.	Vermont	March 4, 1791	39.	North Dakota	November 2, 1889
15.	Kentucky	June 1, 1792	40.	South Dakota	November 2, 1889
16.	Tennessee	June 1, 1796	41.	Montana	November 8, 1889
17.	Ohio	March 1, 1803	42.	Washington	November 11, 1889
18.	Louisiana	April 30, 1812	43.	Idaho	July 3, 1890
19.	Indiana	December 11, 1816	44.	Wyoming	July 10, 1890
20.	Mississippi	December 10, 1817	45.	Utah	January 4, 1896
21.	Illinois	December 3, 1818	46.	Oklahoma	November 16, 1907
22.	Alabama	December 14, 1819	47.	New Mexico	January 6, 1912
23.	Maine	March 15, 1820	48.	Arizona	February 14, 1912
24.	Missouri	August 10, 1821	49.	Alaska	January 3, 1959
25.	Arkansas	June 15, 1836	50.	Hawaii	August 21, 1959

DEMOGRAPHICS OF THE UNITED STATES

POPULATION GROWTH

Year	Population	Percent Increase
1630	4,600	
1640	26,600	478.3
1650	50,400	90.8
1660	75,100	49.0
1670	111,900	49.0
1680	151,500	35.4
1690	210,400	38.9
1700	250,900	19.2
1710	331,700	32.2
1720	466,200	40.5
1730	629,400	35.0
1740	905,600	43.9
1750	1,170,800	29.3
1760	1,593,600	36.1
1770	2,148,100	34.8
1780	2,780,400	29.4
1790	3,929,214	41.3
1800	5,308,483	35.1
1810	7,239,881	36.4
1820	9,638,453	33.1
1830	12,866,020	33.5
1840	17,069,453	32.7
1850	23,191,876	35.9
1860	31,443,321	35.6
1870	39,818,449	26.6
1880	50,155,783	26.0
1890	62,947,714	25.5
1900	75,994,575	20.7
1910	91,972,266	21.0
1920	105,710,620	14.9
1930	122,775,046	16.1
1940	131,669,275	7.2
1950	150,697,361	14.5
1960	179,323,175	18.5
1970	203,302,031	13.4
1980	226,542,199	11.4
1990	248,718,301	9.8
2000	281,421,906	13.1

Source: *Historical Statistics of the United States* (1975); *Statistical Abstract of the United States* (2001).

Note: Figures for 1630–1780 include British colonies within limits of present United States only; Native American population included only in 1930 and thereafter.

WORKFORCE

Year	Total Number Workers (1000s)	Farmers as % of Total	Women as % of Total	% Workers in Unions
1810	2,330	84	(NA)	(NA)
1840	5,660	75	(NA)	(NA)
1860	11,110	53	(NA)	(NA)
1870	12,506	53	15	(NA)
1880	17,392	52	15	(NA)
1890	23,318	43	17	(NA)
1900	29,073	40	18	3
1910	38,167	31	21	6
1920	41,614	26	21	12
1930	48,830	22	22	7
1940	53,011	17	24	27
1950	59,643	12	28	25
1960	69,877	8	32	26
1970	82,049	4	37	25
1980	106,940	3	43	23
1990	125,840	3	45	16
2000	140,863	2	47	12

Source: *Historical Statistics of the United States* (1975); *Statistical Abstract of the United States* (2001).

VITAL STATISTICS
(in thousands)

Year	Births	Deaths	Marriages	Divorces
1800	55	(NA)	(NA)	(NA)
1810	54.3	(NA)	(NA)	(NA)
1820	55.2	(NA)	(NA)	(NA)
1830	51.4	(NA)	(NA)	(NA)
1840	51.8	(NA)	(NA)	(NA)
1850	43.3	(NA)	(NA)	(NA)
1860	44.3	(NA)	(NA)	(NA)
1870	38.3	(NA)	9.6 (1867)	0.3 (1867)
1880	39.8	(NA)	9.1 (1875)	0.3 (1875)
1890	31.5	(NA)	9.0	0.5
1900	32.3	17.2	9.3	0.7
1910	30.1	14.7	10.3	0.9
1920	27.7	13.0	12.0	1.6
1930	21.3	11.3	9.2	1.6
1940	19.4	10.8	12.1	2.0
1950	24.1	9.6	11.1	2.6
1960	23.7	9.5	8.5	2.2
1970	18.4	9.5	10.6	3.5
1980	15.9	8.8	10.6	5.2
1990	16.7	8.6	9.8	4.7
1997	14.6	8.6	8.9	4.3

Source: *Historical Statistics of the United States* (1975); *Statistical Abstract of the United States* (1999). Population Estimates Program, Population Division, U.S. Census Bureau, January 2001.

RACIAL COMPOSITION OF THE POPULATION
(in thousands)

Year	White	Black	Indian	Hispanic	Asian
1790	3,172	757	(NA)	(NA)	(NA)
1800	4,306	1,002	(NA)	(NA)	(NA)
1820	7,867	1,772	(NA)	(NA)	(NA)
1840	14,196	2,874	(NA)	(NA)	(NA)
1860	26,923	4,442	(NA)	(NA)	(NA)
1880	43,403	6,581	(NA)	(NA)	(NA)
1900	66,809	8,834	(NA)	(NA)	(NA)
1910	81,732	9,828	(NA)	(NA)	(NA)
1920	94,821	10,463	(NA)	(NA)	(NA)
1930	110,287	11,891	(NA)	(NA)	(NA)
1940	118,215	12,866	(NA)	(NA)	(NA)
1950	134,942	15,042	(NA)	(NA)	(NA)
1960	158,832	18,872	(NA)	(NA)	(NA)
1970	178,098	22,581	(NA)	(NA)	(NA)
1980	194,713	26,683	1,420	14,609	3,729
1990	208,727	30,511	2,065	22,372	2,462
2000	211,461	34,658	2,476	35,306	10,642

Source: U.S. Bureau of the Census, *U.S. Census of Population: 1940*, vol. II, part 1, and vol. IV, part 1; *1950*, vol. II, part 1; *1960*, vol. I, part 1; *1970*, vol. I, part B; and *Current Population Reports*, P25-1095 and P25-1104; *Statistical Abstract of the United States* (2001).

IMMIGRATION, BY ORIGIN
(in thousands)

Period	Europe	Americas	Asia
1820–30	106	12	—
1831–40	496	33	—
1841–50	1,597	62	—
1851–60	2,453	75	42
1861–70	2,065	167	65
1871–80	2,272	404	70
1881–90	4,735	427	70
1891–1900	3,555	39	75
1901–10	8,065	362	324
1911–20	4,322	1,144	247
1921–30	2,463	1,517	112
1931–40	348	160	16
1941–50	621	355	32
1951–60	1,326	997	150
1961–70	1,123	1,716	590
1971–80	800	1,983	1,588
1981–90	762	3,616	2,738
1991–2000	1,100	3,800	2,200

Source: *Historical Statistics of the United States* (1975); *Statistical Abstract of the United States* (1991); Population Estimates Program, Population Division, U.S. Census Bureau, April 2001.

BIBLIOGRAPHY

CHAPTER 1

Settling the Continent

Larry D. Agenbroad, et al., eds., *Megafauna and Man* (1990)

John Bierhorst, ed., *The Red Swan: Myths and Tales of the American Indians* (1976)

Robson Bonnichsen and Karen L. Turnmire, *Ice Age People of North America: Environments, Origins, and Adaptations* (1999)

Michael H. Crawford, *The Origins of Native Americans: Evidence from Anthropological Genetics* (1998)

Tom D. Dillehay, *The Settling of the Americas: A New Prehistory* (2000)

E. James Dixon, *Bones, Boats, and Bison: Archaeology and the First Colonization of Western North America* (2000)

Richard Erdoes and Alfonso Ortiz, eds., *American Indian Myths and Legends* (1984)

Guy Gibbon, *Archaeology of Prehistoric Native America: An Encyclopedia* (1998)

Lee Eldridge Huddleston, *Origins of the American Indians: European Concepts, 1492–1729* (1967)

George Kubler, *Esthetic Recognition of Ancient Amerindian Art* (1991)

Hanns J. Prem, *The Ancient Americas: A Brief History and Guide to Research* (1997)

Heather Anne Pringle, *In Search of Ancient North America: An Archaeological Journey to Forgotten Cultures* (1996)

Richard F. Townsend, ed., *The Ancient Americas: Art from Sacred Landscapes* (1992)

Frederick Hadleigh West, ed., *American Beginnings: The Prehistory and Palaeoecology of Beringia* (1996)

New Ways of Living on the Land

Kenneth M. Ames and Herbert D. G. Mascher, *Peoples of the Northwest Coast: Their Archaeology and Prehistory* (2000)

Leonard W. Blake and Hugh C. Cutler, *Plants from the Past* (2001)

David S. Brose, et al., *Ancient Art of the American Woodland Indians* (1985)

Thomas E. Emerson, et al., eds. *Late Woodland Societies: Tradition and Transformation Across the Midcontinent* (2000)

Richard I. Ford, ed., *Prehistoric Food Production in North America* (1985)

Sarah W. Neusius, *Foraging, Collecting, and Harvesting: Archaic Period Subsistence and Settlement in the Eastern Woodlands* (1986)

James L. Phillips and James A. Brown, eds., *Archaic Hunters and Gatherers in the American Midwest* (1983)

Richard H. Steckel and Jerome C. Rose, *The Backbone of History: Health and Nutrition in the Western Hemisphere* (2002)

The Development of Farming

Frances R. Berdan, *The Aztecs of Central Mexico* (1982)

David S. Brose and N'omi Greber, eds., *Hopewell Archaeology* (1979)

David Carrasco, et al., eds., *Mesoamerica's Classic Heritage: From Teotihuacan to the Aztecs* (2000)

William S. Dancey and Paul J Pacheco, eds., *Ohio Hopewell Community Organization* (1997)

Emil W. Haury, *The Hohokam* (1976)

Ted Hirschfield, *Middle Mississippians: Encounters with the Prehistoric Amerindians* (1996)

Rosemary Joyce, *Gender and Power in Prehispanic Mesoamerica* (2000)

William F. Keegan, ed., *Emergent Horticultural Economies of the Eastern Woodlands* (1987)

R. Barry Lewis and Charles Stout, eds., *Mississippian Towns and Sacred Spaces* (1998)

George R. Milner, *The Cahokia Chiefdom: The Archaeology of a Mississippian Society* (1998)

Warren King Moorehead, *The Cahokia Mounds* (2000)

Barker H. Morrow and V. B. Price, eds., *Anasazi Architecture and American Design* (1997)

Timothy R. Pauketat and Thomas E. Emerson, eds., *Cahokia: Domination and Ideology in the Mississippian World* (1997)

Stephen Plog, *Ancient Peoples of the American Southwest* (1998)

Paul F. Reed, ed., *Foundations of Anasazi Culture: The Basketmaker-Pueblo Transition* (2000)

Bruce D. Smith, *The Mississippian Emergence* (1990)

David E. Stuart, *Anasazi America: Seventeen Centuries on the Road from Center Place* (2000)

Christy G. Turner, *Man Corn: Cannibalism and Violence in the Prehistoric American Southwest* (2000)

W. H. Wills, *Early Prehistoric Agriculture* (1988)

Biloine W. Young and Melvin L. Fowler, *Cahokia, The Great Native American Metropolis* (2000)

Cultural Regions of North America on the Eve of Colonization

Michael A. Adler, ed., *The Prehistoric Pueblo World, A.D. 1150–1350* (1996)

Kenneth M. Ames and Herbert D. G. Mascher, *Peoples of the Northwest Coast: Their Archaeology and Prehistory* (2000)

Elizabeth M. Brunfiel and John W. Fox, *Factional Competition and Political Development in the New World* (1993)

Catherine M. Cameron, *Hopi Dwellings: Architecture at Oryi* (1999)

Lyle Campbell and Marianne Mithun, eds., *The Languages of Native America* (1979)

Paul H. Carlson, *The Plains Indians* (1999)

James Taylor Carson, *Searching for the Bright Path: The Mississippi Choctaws from Prehistory to Removal* (1999)

May Castleberry, *The New World's Old World: Photographic Views of Ancient America* (2003)

Cheryl Claassen and Rosemary A. Joyce, eds., *Women in Prehistory: North America and Mesoamerica* (1997)

Olive P. Dickason, *Canada's First Nations: A History of Founding Peoples* (1992)

Michelle Hegmon, ed., *The Archaeology of Regional Interaction: Religion, Warfare, and Exchange Across the American Southwest* (1999)

June Helm, *The People of Denendah: Ethnohistory of the Indians of Canada's Northwest Territories* (2000)

David LaVere, *The Caddo Chiefdoms: Caddo Economics and Politics, 700–1835* (1998)

Steven A. LeBlanc, *Prehistoric Warfare in the American Southwest* (1999)

Stephen H. Lekson, *The Chaco Meridian: Centers of Political Power in the Ancient Southwest* (1999)

Jill E. Neitzel, ed., *Great Towns and Regional Politics: In the Prehistoric American Southwest and Southeast* (1999)

Mallory McCane O'Connor, *Lost Cities of the Ancient Southeast* (1995)

Alfonso Ortiz, ed., *New Perspectives on the Pueblos* (1972)

Howard S. Russell, *Indian New England Before the* Mayflower (1980)

Frank G. Speck, *Penobscot Man* (1940)

Bruce Trigger, *The Children of Aataentsic: A History of the Huron People to 1660* (1976)

CHAPTER 2

The Expansion of Europe

James M. Blaut, *1492: The Debate on Colonialism, Eurocentrism, and History* (1992)

Fernand Braudel, *The Mediterranean and the Mediterranean World in the Age of Philip II* (1972)

Carol Cipolla, *Before the Industrial Revolution: European Society and Economy, 1100–1700* (1976)

Patrick Collinson, *The Religion of Protestants: The Church in English Society, 1559–1625* (1982)

Andre Gunder Frank, *World Accumulation, 1492–1789* (1978)

Giancarlo Masini and Iacopo Gari, *How Florence Invented America: Vespucci, Verranzano, and Mazzei and Their Contribution to the Conception of the New World* (1998)

Douglass North, *The Rise of the Western World: A New Economic History* (1973)

José Casas Pardo, ed., *Economic Effects of the European Expansion, 1492–1824* (1992)

J. H. Parry, *The Age of Reconnaissance* (1963)

———, *Europe and a Wider World: The Establishment of the European Hegemony: Trade and Expansion in the Age of the Renaissance* (1966)

Geoffrey Vaughn Scannell, *The First Imperial Age: European Overseas Expansion c. 1400–1715* (1989)

The Spanish in the Americas

Fredi Chiapelli, ed., *First Images of America: The Impact of the New World on the Old* (1976)

Kathleen Deagan and José María Cruxent, *Columbus's Outpost among the Taínos: Spain and America at La Isabela, 1493–1498* (2002)

Henry F. Dobyns, *Their Number Become Thinned: Native American Population Dynamics in Eastern North America* (1983)

J. H. Elliott, *The Old World and the New, 1492–1650* (1970)

Anthony Grafton, *New Worlds, Ancient Texts: The Power of Tradition and the Shock of Discovery* (1992)

John H. Hann, *A History of the Timucua Indians and Missions* (1996)

Hugh Honour, *New Golden Land: European Images of America from the Discoveries to the Present Time* (1975)

Charles Hudson and Carmen Chaves Tesser, eds., *The Forgotten Centuries: Indians and Europeans in the American South, 1521–1704* (1994)

René Jara and Nicholas Spadaccini, eds., *Amerindian Images and the Legacy of Columbus* (1992)

Elizabeth A. H. John, *Storms Brewed in Other Men's Worlds: The Confrontation of Indians, Spanish, and French in the Southwest, 1540–1795* (1975)

James Lang, *Conquest and Commerce: Spain and England in the Americas* (1975)

James Lockhart and Stuart B. Schwartz, *Early Latin America: A History of Colonial Spanish America and Brazil* (1983)

Albert Manucy, *Sixteenth-Century St. Augustine: The People and Their Homes* (1997)

Jerald T. Milanich, *Laboring in the Fields of the Lord: Spanish Missions and Southeastern Indians* (1999)

Jerald T. Milanich and Charles Hudson, *Hernando de Soto and the Indians of Florida* (1993)

James Howlett O'Donnell III, *Southeastern Frontiers: Europeans, Africans, and American Indians, 1513–1840: A Critical Bibliography* (1982)

Edmundo O'Gorman, *The Invention of America: An Inquiry into the Historical Nature of the New World and the Meaning of its History* (1961)

Stuart B. Schwartz, *Victors and Vanquished: Spanish and Nahua Views of the Conquest of Mexico* (2000)

David M. Traboulay, *Columbus and Las Casas: The Conquest and Christianization of America, 1492–1566* (1994)

Northern Explorations and Encounters

Alfred Goldsworthy Bailey, *The Conflict of European and Eastern Algonkian Cultures, 1504–1700* (1969)

Peter T. Bradley, *British Maritime Enterprise in the New World: From the Late Fifteenth to the Mid-Eighteenth Century* (1999)

Carl Bridenbaugh, *Vexed and Troubled Englishmen, 1590–1642* (1968)

Susan Danforth, *Encountering the New World, 1493–1800* (1991)

Philip J. Deloria and Neal Salisbury, eds., *A Companion to American Indian History* (2002)

G. R. Elton, *England under the Tudors* (1974)

C. H. George and Katherine George, *The Protestant Mind of the English Reformation* (1961)

John Guy, *Tudor England* (1988)

R. J. Knecht, *The French Civil Wars, 1562–1598* (2000)

Karen Ordahl Kupperman, *Indians and English: Facing Off in Early America* (2000)

Peter Laslett, *The World We Have Lost* (1965)

Anthony McFarlane, *The British in the Americas, 1480–1815* (1994)

Lee Miller, *Roanoke: Solving the Mystery of England's Lost Colony* (2000)

James S. Pritchard, *In Search of Empire: The French in the Americas, 1670–1730* (2004)

David B. Quinn, *North America from Earliest Discovery to First Settlements* (1977)

———, *The Roanoke Voyages, 1584–1590*, 2 vols. (1955)

Bernard W. Sheehan, *Savagism and Civility: Indians and Englishmen in Colonial Virginia* (1980)

Russell Thornton, *American Indian Holocaust and Survival* (1987)

Margo Todd, ed., *Reformation to Revolution: Politics and Religion in Early Modern England* (1995)

Marcel Trudel, *The Beginnings of New France, 1524–1663* (1973)

Keith Wrightson, *English Society, 1580–1680* (1982)

Biography

Miles H. Davidson, *Columbus Then and Now: A Life Reexamined* (1997)

David A. Howard, *Conquistador in Chains: Cabeza de Vaca and the Indians of the Americas* (1997)

Harry Kelsey, *Sir Francis Drake: The Queen's Pirate* (1998)

Carole Levin, *The Heart and Stomach of a King: Elizabeth I and the Politics of Sex and Power* (1994)

Richard Lee Marks, *Cortés: The Great Adventurer and the Fate of Aztec Mexico* (1993)

James McDermott, *Martin Frobisher: Elizabethan Privateer* (2001)

P. E. Russell, *Prince Henry the Navigator: A Life* (2000)

David Starkey, *Elizabeth: The Struggle for the Throne* (2000)

Henry Raup Wagner, *The Life and Writings of Bartolomé de las Casas* (1967)

CHAPTER 3

Spain and Its Competitors in North America

Gary Clayton Anderson, *The Indian Southwest, 1580–1830: Ethnogenesis and Reinvention* (1999)

James Axtell, *The Invasion Within: The Contest of Culture in Colonial North America* (1985)

Denys Delâge, *Bitter Feast: Amerindians and Europeans in Northeastern North America, 1600–64* (1993)

W. J. Eccles, *The Canadian Frontier, 1534–1760* (1983)

Carl J. Ekberg, *French Roots in the Illinois Country: The Mississippi Frontier in Colonial Times* (1998)

Eric Hinderaker and Peter C. Mancall, *At the Edge of Empire: The Backcountry in British North America* (2003)

J. R. Jones, *The Anglo–Dutch Wars of the Seventeenth Century* (1996)

Cathy D. Matson, *Merchants and Empire: Trading in Colonial New York* (1998)

Peter Moogk, *La Nouvelle France: The Making of French Canada, a Cultural History* (2000)

Daniel Paul, *We Were Not the Savages: A Mi'kmaq Perspective on the Collision Between European and Native American Civilizations* (2000)

Oliver Rink, *Holland on the Hudson: An Economic and Social History of Dutch New York* (1986)

Sylvia Van Kirk, *Many Tender Ties: Women in Fur-Trade Society in Western Canada, 1670–1870* (1999)

England in the Chesapeake

Edward L. Bond, *Damned Souls in a Tobacco Colony: Religion in Seventeenth-Century Virginia* (2000)

Kathleen M. Brown, *Good Wives, Nasty Wenches, and Anxious Patriarchs: Gender, Race, and Power in Colonial Virginia* (1996)

Wesley F. Craven, *White, Red, and Black: The Seventeenth Century Virginian* (1971)

April Lee Hatfield, *Atlantic Virginia: Intercolonial Relations in the Seventeenth Century* (2004)

Ronald Hoffman, *Princes of Ireland, Planters of Maryland: A Carroll Saga, 1500–1782* (2000)

Karen Ordahl Kupperman, *Settling with the Indians: The Meeting of English and Indian Cultures in America, 1580–1640* (1980)

Gloria L. Main, *Tobacco Colony: Life in Early Maryland, 1650–1720* (1982)

Michael Leroy Oberg, *Dominion and Civility: English Imperialism and Native America, 1585–1685* (1999)

The New England Colonies

David Grayson Allen, *In English Ways: The Movement of Societies and the Transferal of English Local Law and Custom* (1981)

Bernard Bailyn, *The New England Merchants in the Seventeenth Century* (1955)

Carl Bridenbaugh, *Fat Mutton and Liberty of Conscience: Society in Rhode Island, 1636–1690* (1974)

Joyce E. Chaplin, *Subject Matter: Technology, the Body, and Science on the Anglo–American Frontier, 1500–1676* (2001)

David Cressy, *Coming Over: Migration and Communication between England and New England in the Seventeenth Century* (1987)

William Cronon, *Changes in the Land: Indians, Colonists, and the Ecology of New England* (1983)

John Demos, *A Little Commonwealth: Family Life in Plymouth Colony* (1970)

David D. Hall, ed., *Puritans in the New World: A Critical Anthology* (2004)

Timothy Hall, *Separating Church and State: Roger Williams and Religious Liberty* (1998)

Francis Jennings, *The Invasion of America: Indians, Colonialism, and the Cant of Conquest* (1975)

Benjamin W. Labaree, *America and the Sea: A Maritime History* (1998)

Amy Scrager Lang, *Prophetic Women: Anne Hutchinson and the Problem of Dissent in the Literature of New England* (1987)

Elizabeth Reis, *Damned Women: Sinners and Witches in Puritan New England* (1997)

The Restoration Colonies

Wesley F. Craven, *The Southern Colonies in the Seventeenth Century, 1607–1689* (1949)

Michael Kammen, *Colonial New York: A History* (1975)

Sung Bok Kim, *Landlord and Tenant in Colonial New York: Manorial Society, 1664–1775* (1978)

H. T. Merrens, *Colonial North Carolina* (1964)

Donna Merwick, *Death of a Notary: Conquest and Change in Colonial New York* (1999)

Gary B. Nash, *Quakers and Politics: Pennsylvania, 1681–1726* (1968)

M. Eugene Sirmans, *Colonial South Carolina: A Political History, 1663–1763* (1966)

Jack M. Sosin, *English America and the Restoration Monarchy of Charles II: Transatlantic Politics, Commerce, and Kinship* (1980)

Conflict and War

Thomas J. Archdeacon, *New York City, 1664–1710* (1976)

Paul Boyer and Stephen Nissenbaum, *Salem Possessed* (1974)

Colin G. Calloway, ed., *After King Philip's War: Presence and Persistence in Indian New England* (1997)

Guy Chet, *Conquering the American Wilderness: The Triumph of European Warfare in the Colonial Northeast* (2003)

Eveline Cruickshanks, *The Glorious Revolution* (2000)

James D. Drake, *King Philip's War: Civil War in New England, 1675–1676* (1999)

Ramón A. Gutiérrez, *When Jesus Came, the Corn Mothers Went Away: Marriage, Sexuality, and Power in New Mexico, 1500–1846* (1991)

Richard R. Johnson, *Adjustment to Empire: The New England Colonies, 1675–1715* (1981)

D. W. Jordan, *Maryland's Revolution of Government, 1689–1692* (1974)

Carol F. Karlsen, *The Devil in the Shape of a Woman: Witchcraft in Colonial New England* (1987)

Karen Ordahl Kupperman, *Indians and English: Facing Off in Early America* (2000)

Almon Wheeler Lauber, *Indian Slavery in Colonial Times within the Present Limits of the United States* (1913)

Jill Lepore, *The Name of War: King Philip's War and the Origins of American Identity* (1998)

David S. Lovejoy, *The Glorious Revolution in America* (1972)

Nancy Shoemaker, *A Strange Likeness: Becoming Red and White in Eighteenth-Century North America* (2004)

Wilcomb E. Washburn, *The Governor and the Rebel: A History of Bacon's Rebellion in Virginia* (1957)

Stephen S. Webb, *1676: The End of American Independence* (1980)

Biography

Mary K. Geiter, *Willlam Penn* (2000)

J. A. Leo Lemay, *The American Dream of Captain John Smith* (1991)

Edmund S. Morgan, *Puritan Dilemma: The Story of John Winthrop* (1958)

Ann Sanford, *Anne Bradstreet, the Worldly Puritan* (1974)

Marc Simmons, *The Last Conquistador: Juan de Oñate and the Settling of the Far Southwest* (1991)

Robert S. Tilton, *Pocahontas: The Evolution of an American Narrative* (1994)

Alvin Gardner Weeks, *Massasoit of the Pokanokets* (1919)

Selma R. Williams, *Divine Rebel: The Life of Anne Marbury Hutchinson* (1981)

CHAPTER 4

The African Slave Trade

Jay Coughtry, *The Notorious Triangle: Rhode Island and the African Slave Trade, 1799–1807* (1981)

Philip D. Curtin, *Economic Change in Precolonial Africa: Senegambia in the Era of the Slave Trade* (1975)

Basil Davidson, *The African Slave Trade* (1980)

Benedict G. Der, *The Slave Trade in Northern Ghana* (1998)

Elizabeth Donnan, ed., *Documents Illustrative of the History of the Slave Trade to America*, 4 vols. (1930–35)

David Eltis, et al., eds., *Slavery in the Development of the Americas* (2004)

Eli Faber, *Jews, Slaves, and the Slave Trade: Setting the Record Straight* (1998)

Philip Gould, *Barbaric Traffic: Commerce and Antislavery in the Eighteenth-Century Atlantic World* (2003)

Robert W. Harms, *The Diligent: A Voyage through the Worlds of the Slave Trade* (2001)

J. E. Inikori, *Forced Migration: The Impact of the Export Slave Trade on African Societies* (1982)

Robert W. July, *A History of the African People* (1992)

Herbert S. Klein, *The Middle Passage: Comparative Studies in the Atlantic Slave Trade* (1978)

Robin Law, *The Slave Coast of West Africa, 1550–1750: The Impact of the Atlantic Slave Trade on an African Society* (1991)

Paul E. Lovejoy, ed., *Africans in Bondage: Studies in Slavery and the Slave Trade* (1986)

Daniel P. Mannix and Malcolm Crowley, *Black Cargoes: A History of the Atlantic Slave Trade* (1962)

David Northrup, ed., *The Atlantic Slave Trade* (1994)

J. A. Rawley, *The Transatlantic Slave Trade* (1981)

Edward Reynolds, *Stand the Storm: A History of the Atlantic Slave Trade* (1985)

A. C. de C. M. Saunders, *A Social History of Black Slaves and Freemen in Portugal, 1441–1555* (1982)

Randy J. Sparks, *Two Princes of Calabar: An Eighteenth-Century Atlantic Odyssey* (2004)

Jon Vogt, *Portuguese Rule on the Gold Coast, 1469–1682* (1979)

James Walvin, *Making the Black Atlantic: Britain and the African Diaspora* (2000)

The Development of North American Slave Societies

L. R. Bailey, *Indian Slave Trade in the Southwest: A Study of Slave-Taking and the Traffic in Indian Captives* (1966)

Ira Berlin, *Generations of Captivity: A History of African-American Slaves* (2003)

T. H. Breen and Stephen Innes, *"Myne Owne Ground": Race and Freedom on Virginia's Eastern Shore* (1980)

Verner W. Crane, *The Southern Frontier, 1670–1732* (1929)

Richard S. Dunn, *Sugar and Slaves: The Rise of the Planter Class in the English West Indies, 1624–1713* (1972)

David Eltis, *The Rise of African Slavery in the Americas* (2000)

Sharla M. Fett, *Working Cures: Healing, Health, and Power on Southern Slave Plantations* (2002)

Laura Foner and Eugene D. Genovese, eds., *Slavery in the New World: A Reader in Comparative History* (1969)

Allan Gallay, *The Indian Slave Trade: The Rise of the English Empire in the American South, 1670–1717* (2002)

Graham Russell Hodges, *Root and Branch: African Americans in New York and East Jersey, 1613–1863* (1999)

Thomas N. Ingersoll, *Mammon and Manon in Early New Orleans: The First Slave Society in the Deep South, 1718–1819* (1999)

Charles Joyner, *Down by the Riverside: A South Carolina Slave Community* (1984)

Alan Kulikoff, *Tobacco and Slaves: The Development of Southern Cultures in the Chesapeake, 1680–1800* (1986)

Jane Landers, *Black Society in Spanish Florida* (1999)

Daniel Littlefield, *Rice and Slaves: Ethnicity and the Slave Trade in Colonial South Carolina* (1981)

Paul E. Lovejoy, *Transformations in Slavery: A History of Slavery in Africa* (1983)

Edgar J. McManus, *Black Bondage in the North* (1973)

Gary B. Nash, *Red, White, and Black: The Peoples of Early North America* (1992)

Julia Floyd Smith, *Slavery and Rice Culture in Low Country Georgia, 1750–1860* (1985)

Peter H. Wood, *Black Majority: Negroes in Colonial South Carolina from 1670 through the Stono Rebellion* (1974)

African to African American
John B. Boles, *Black Southerners, 1619–1869* (1984)

Alex Bontemps, *The Punished Self: Surviving Slavery in the Colonial South* (2001)

Sylviane A. Diouf, *Servants of Allah: African Muslims Enslaved in the Americas* (1998)

John Hope Franklin and Loren Schweniger, *Runaway Slaves: Rebels in the Plantation* (1999)

Michael Gomez, *Exchanging Our Country Marks: The Transformation of African Identities in the Colonial and Antebellum South* (1998)

Annette Gordon-Reed, *Thomas Jefferson and Sally Hemings: An American Controversy* (1997)

Herbert G. Gutman, *The Black Family in Slavery and Freedom, 1750–1925* (1976).

Joseph E. Harris, ed., *Global Dimensions of the African Diaspora* (1982)

Gerald W. Mullin, *Flight and Rebellion: Slave Resistance in Eighteenth-Century Virginia* (1972)

Orlando Patterson, *Slavery and Social Death: A Comparative Study* (1982)

Mark M. Smith, *Mastered by the Clock: Time, Slavery, and Freedom in the American South* (1997)

Sterling Stuckey, *Slave Culture: Nationalist Theory and the Foundations of Black America* (1987).

V. B. Thompson, *The Making of the African Diaspora in the Americas, 1441–1900* (1984)

Slavery and Empire
Joyce O. Appleby, *Economic Thought and Ideology in Seventeenth-Century England* (1978)

Heather Cateau and S. H. H. Carrington, eds., *Capitalism and Slavery Fifty Years Later: Eric Eustace Williams—A Reassessment of the Man and His Work* (2000)

Eugene Genovese and Elizabeth Fox-Genovese, *Fruits of Merchant Capital: Slavery and Bourgeois Property in the Rise and Expansion of Capitalism* (1983)

E. J. Hobsbawn, *Industry and Empire: The Making of Modern English Society, 1750 to the Present Day* (1968)

Michael Kammen, *Empire and Interest: The American Colonies and the Politics of Mercantilism* (1970)

John J. McCusker and Russell R. Menard, *The Economy of British America, 1607–1787* (1985)

Barbara L. Solow, ed., *Slavery and the Rise of the Atlantic System* (1991)

Eric Williams, *Capitalism and Slavery* (1944)

Slavery and Freedom
David Brion Davis, *The Problem of Slavery in Western Culture* (1966)

Carl N. Degler, *Neither Black nor White: Slavery and Race Relations in Brazil and the United States* (1971)

Edmund S. Morgan, *American Slavery, American Freedom: The Ordeal of Colonial Virginia* (1975)

Joel Williamson, *New People: Miscegenation and Mulattoes in the United States* (1980)

Biography
Philip D. Curtin, ed., *Africa Remembered: Narratives of West Africans from the Era of the Slave Trade* (1967)

Paul Edwards, ed., *The Interesting Narrative of the Life of Olaudah Equiano, or Gustavus Vassa, the African, written by himself* (1987)

James B. Hedges, *The Browns of Providence Plantation* (1952)

Kenneth A. Lockridge, *The Diary and Life of William Byrd II of Virginia, 1674–1744* (1987)

Phinizy Spalding, *Oglethorpe in America* (1977)

CHAPTER 5

North American Regions
Patricia Albers and Beatrice Medicine, eds., *The Hidden Half: Studies of Plains Indian Women* (1983)

Carole Blackburn, *Harvest of Souls: The Jesuit Missions and Colonialism in North America, 1632–1650* (2000)

Richard L. Bushman, *From Puritan to Yankee: Character and the Social Order in Connecticut, 1690–1765* (1967)

David Bussiert and Steven G. Reinhardt, eds., *Creolization in the Americas* (2000)

Edward D. Castillo, ed., *Native American Perspectives on the Hispanic Colonization of Alta California* (1992)

Andrew R. L. Cayton and Frederika J. Teute, eds., *Contact Points: American Frontiers from the Mohawk Valley to the Mississippi, 1750–1830* (1998)

Cornelia Hughes Dayton, *Women before the Bar: Gender, Law, and Society in Connecticut, 1639–1789* (1995)

Brian Leigh Dunnigan, *Frontier Metropolis: Picturing Early Detroit, 1701–1838* (2001)

John C. Ewers, *The Horse in Blackfoot Indian Culture* (1955)

David Hackett Fischer and James C. Kelly, *Bound Away: Virginia and the Westward Movement* (2000)

Joseph W. Glass, *The Pennsylvania Culture Region: A View from the Barn* (1986)

Robert F. Heizer, *The Destruction of California Indians* (1974)

Donald A. Hutslar, *The Architecture of Migration: Log Construction in the Ohio Country, 1750–1850* (1986)

Christine Leigh Hyrman, *Commerce and Culture: The Maritime Communities of Colonial Massachusetts* (1984)

Rhys Isaac, *Worlds of Experience: Communities in Colonial Virginia* (1987)

Robert H. Jackson, *Indian Population Decline: The Missions of Northwestern New Spain, 1687–1840* (1994)

———, *From Savages to Subjects: Missions in the History of the American Southwest* (2000)

Francis Jennings, *The Ambiguous Iroquois Empire* (1984)

Terry G. Jordan and Matti Kaups, *The American Backwoods Frontier: An Ethnic and Ecological Interpretation* (1988)

Lyle Kohler, *A Search for Power: "The Weaker Sex" in Seventeenth-Century New England, 1650–1750* (1982)

James T. Lemon, *The Best Poor Man's Country: A Geographical Study of Early Southeastern Pennsylvania* (1972)

Kenneth Lockridge, *Literacy in Colonial New England* (1974)

James H. Merrell, *The Indians' New World: Catawbas and Their Neighbors from European Contact through the Era of Removal* (1989)

———, *Into the American Woods: Negotiators on the Pennsylvania Frontier* (1999)

Jane T. Merritt, *At the Crossroads: Indians and Empires on a Mid-Atlantic Frontier, 1700–1763* (2003)

Gary B. Nash, *The Urban Crucible* (1979)

Jacqueline Peterson and Jennifer S. H. Brown, eds., *The New Peoples: Being and Becoming Métis in North America* (1985)

Daniel K. Richter, *The Ordeal of the Longhouse: The Peoples of the Iroquois League in the Era of European Colonization* (1992)

Darrett B. Rutman and Anita H. Rutman, *A Place in Time: Middlesex County, Virginia, 1650–1750* (1984)

Marylynn Salmon, *Women and the Law of Property in Early America* (1986)

Sally Schwartz, *A Mixed Multitude: The Struggle for Toleration in Colonial Pennsylvania* (1987)

William S. Simmons, *Spirit of the New England Tribes: Indian History and Folklore, 1620–1984* (1986)

Daniel Blake Smith, *Inside the Great House: Planter Family Life in Eighteenth-Century Chesapeake Society* (1980)

Laurel T. Ulrich, *Good Wives: Image and Reality in the Lives of Women in Northern New England, 1650–1750* (1982)

Daniel H. Usner Jr., *Indians, Settlers, and Slaves in a Frontier Exchange Economy: The Lower Mississippi Valley before 1783* (1992)

Diverging Social and Political Patterns

James E. Block, *Nation of Agents: The American Path to a Modern Self and Society* (2002)

Bernard Bailyn, *The Peopling of British North America: An Introduction* (1986)

Bruce C. Daniels, ed., *Power and Status: Essays on Officeholding in Colonial America* (1986)

Robert J. Dinkin, *Voting in Provincial America: A Study of Elections in the Thirteen Colonies, 1680–1776* (1977)

A. Roger Ekirch, *Bound for America: The Transportation of British Convicts to the Colonies, 1718–1775* (1987)

Carla Gardina Pestana and Sharon V. Salinger, eds., *Inequality in Early America* (1999)

Thomas L. Purvis, *Proprietors, Patronage, and Paper Money: Legislative Politics in New Jersey, 1703–1776* (1986)

Sharon V. Salinger, *"To Serve Well and Faithfully": Labor and Indentured Servants in Pennsylvania, 1682–1800* (1987)

The Cultural Transformation of British North America

Linda Baumgarten, *What Clothes Reveal: The Language of Clothing in Colonial and Federal America: The Colonial Williamsburg Collection* (2002)

Patricia U. Bonomi, *Under the Cope of Heaven: Religion, Society, and Politics in Colonial America* (1986)

Henry Steele Commager, *The Empire of Reason: How Europe Imagined and America Realized the Enlightenment* (1977)

Patricia Crain, *The Story of A: The Alphabetization of America from "The New England Primer" to "The Scarlet Letter"* (2000)

John Demos, *Circles and Lines: The Shape of Life in Early America* (2004)

Nancy Isenberg and Andrew Burstein, eds., *Mortal Remains: Death in Early America* (2003)

Ned C. Landsman, *From Colonials to Provincials: American Thought and Culture, 1680–1760* (1997)

Jackson Turner Main, *The Social Structure of Revolutionary America* (1965)

Barbara B. Oberg and Harry S. Stout, eds., *Benjamin Franklin, Jonathan Edwards, and the Representation of American Culture* (1993)

Mark A. Peterson, *The Price of Redemption: The Spiritual Economy of Puritan New England* (1997)

Nina Reid-Mahoney, *Philadelphia's Enlightenment, 1740–1800: Kingdom of Christ, Empire of Reason* (2001)

Frank Shuffelton, ed., *The American Enlightenment* (1993)

Biography

Verner W. Crane, *Benjamin Franklin and a Rising People* (1952)

Harry Kelsey, *Juan Rodriguez Cabrillo* (1986)

Gerald R. McDermott, *Jonathan Edwards Confronts the Gods* (2000)

Robert Middlekauff, *The Mathers: Three Generations of Puritan Intellectuals, 1596–1728* (1999)

Martin J. Morgado, *Junípero Serra's Legacy* (1987)

Harry S. Stout, *The Divine Dramatist: George Whitefield and the Rise of Modern Evangelicalism* (1991)

Laurel Ulrich, *A Midwife's Tale: The Life of Martha Ballard, Based on Her Diary, 1785–1812* (1990)

CHAPTER 6

The Seven Years' War in America

Fred Anderson, *A People's Army: Massachusetts Soldiers and Society in the Seven Years' War* (1984)

Frank W. Brecher, *Losing a Continent: France's North American Policy, 1753–1763* (1998)

Gregory Evans Dowd, *War Under Heaven: Pontiac, the Indian Nations, and the British Empire* (2002)

Sylvia R. Frey, *The British Soldier in America: A Social History of Military Life in the Colonial Period* (1981)

Douglas E. Leach, *Roots of Conflict: British Armed Forces and Colonial Americans, 1677–1763* (1986)

Richard Middleton, *The Bells of Victory: The Pitt–Newcastle Ministry and the Conduct of the Seven Years' War, 1757–1762* (1985)

Robert C. Newbold, *The Albany Congress and Plan of Union of 1754* (1955)

William Pencak, *War, Politics, and Revolution in Provincial Massachusetts* (1981)

Tom Pocock, *Battle for Empire: The Very First World War, 1756–63* (1998)

Alan Rogers, *Empire and Liberty* (1974)

David Curtis Skaggs and Larry L. Nelson, eds., *The Sixty Years' War for the Great Lakes, 1754–1814* (2001)

Noel T. St. John Williams, *Redcoats along the Hudson* (1997)

Richard White, *The Middle Ground: Indians, Empires, and Republics in the Great Lakes Region, 1650–1815* (1991)

Imperial Crisis in British North America

Stuart Andrews, *The Rediscovery of America: Transatlantic Crosscurrents in an Age of Revolution* (1998)

Thomas C. Barrow, *Trade and Empire: The British Customs Service in Colonial America* (1967)

Don Cook, *The Long Fuse: How England Lost the American Colonies, 1760–1785* (1995)

Theodore Draper, *A Struggle for Power: The American Revolution* (1996)

Marc Egnal, *A Mighty Empire: The Origins of the American Revolution* (1988)

Eliga H. Gould, *The Persistence of Empire: British Political Culture in the Age of the American Revolution* (2000)

Woody Holton, *Forced Founders: Indians, Debtors, Slaves, and the Making of the American Revolution in Virginia* (1999)

Alice Hanson Jones, *The Wealth of a Nation to Be* (1980)

John J. McCusker, *Rum and the American Revolution* (1989)

Philip James McFarland, *The Brave Bostonians: Hutchinson, Quincy, Franklin, and the Coming of the American Revolution* (1998)

J. G. A. Pocock, *The Machiavellian Moment: Florentine Political Thought and the Atlantic Republican Tradition* (1975)

William Lowell Putnam, *John Peter Zenger and the Fundamental Freedom* (1997)

Caroline Robbins, *The Eighteenth-Century Commonwealthman* (1959)

Arthur M. Schlesinger, *The Colonial Merchants and the American Revolution* (1917)

John W. Tyler, *Smugglers and Patriots: Boston Merchants and the Advent of the American Revolution* (1986)

Carl Ubbelohde, *The Vice-Admiralty Courts and the American Revolution* (1960)

Kathleen Wilson, *Island Race: Englishness, Empire, and Gender in the Eighteenth Century* (2003)

From Resistance to Rebellion

David Ammerman, *In the Common Cause: American Response to the Coercive Acts of 1774* (1974)

T. H. Breen, *Tobacco Culture: The Mentality of the Great Tidewater Planters on the Eve of Revolution* (1985)

Richard D. Brown, *Revolutionary Politics in Massachusetts: The Boston Committee of Correspondence and the Towns, 1772–1774* (1970)

Richard L. Bushman, *King and People in Provincial Massachusetts* (1985)

H. Trevor Colbourn, *The Lamp of Experience: Whig History and the Intellectual Origins of the American Revolution* (1965)

Light Townsend Cummins, *Spanish Observers and the American Revolution, 1775–1783* (1991)

Derek Davis, *Religion and the Continental Congress, 1774–1789: Contributions to Original Intent* (2000)

Bernard Donoughue, *British Politics and the American Revolution: The Path to War, 1773–1775* (1964)

Gregory T. Edgar, *Reluctant Break with Britain: From Stamp Act to Bunker Hill* (1997)

Jack P. Greene, *Understanding the American Revolution: Issues and Actors* (1995)

Benjamin W. Labaree, *The Boston Tea Party* (1974)

Pauline Maier, *From Resistance to Rebellion* (1972)

Edmund S. Morgan, *The Birth of the Republic, 1763–1789* (1956)

Ray Raphael, *First American Revolution: Before Lexington and Concord* (2002)

Jackson O'Shaughnessy, *An Empire Divided: The American Revolution and the British Caribbean* (2000)

John Shy, *Toward Lexington: The Role of the British Army in the Coming of the American Revolution* (1965)

Peter David Garner Thomas, *Tea Party to Independence: The Third Phase of the American Revolution, 1773–1776* (1991)

Morton White, *The Philosophy of the American Revolution* (1978)

Gary Wills, *Inventing America* (1978)

Biography

Bernard Bailyn, *The Ordeal of Thomas Hutchinson* (1974)

Della Gray Barthelmas, *The Signers of the Declaration of Independence* (1997)

Richard R. Beeman, *Patrick Henry: A Biography* (1974)

Jeremy Black, *Pitt the Elder* (1992)

John Brooke, *King George III* (1974)

John E. Ferling, *The Loyalist Mind: Joseph Galloway and the American Revolution* (1977)

———, *Setting the World Ablaze: Washington, Adams, and Jefferson and the American Revolution* (2000)

William M. Fowler, Jr., *The Baron of Beacon Hill: A Biography of John Hancock* (1979)

———, *Samuel Adams: Radical Puritan* (1997)

Rhys Isaac, *Landon Carter's Uneasy Kingdom: Revolution and Rebellion on a Virginia Plantation* (2004)

David A. McCants, *Patrick Henry, the Orator* (1990)

Colin Nicolson, "Infamas Govener" Francis Bernard and the Origins of the American Revolution (2001)

Peter Shaw, The Character of John Adams (1976)

Peter D. G. Thomas, Lord North (1974)

Andrew S. Walmsley, Thomas Hutchinson and the Origins of the American Revolution (1999)

Gordon S. Wood, Americanization of Benjamin Franklin (2004)

CHAPTER 7

The War for Independence

Ian Barnes, The Historical Atlas of the American Revolution (2000)

Ira Berlin and Ronald Hoffman, eds., Slavery and Freedom in the Age of the American Revolution (1983)

Wayne Bodle, Valley Forge Winter: Civilians and Soldiers in War (2002)

T.H. Breen, Marketplace of Revolution: How Consumer Politics Shaped American Independence (2004)

Charles E. Claghorn, Women Patriots of the American Revolution (1991)

Stephen Conway, British Isles and the War of American Independence (2000)

Lawrence D. Cress, Citizens in Arms: The Army and the Militia in American Society to the War of 1812 (1982)

Paul Finkleman, ed., Slavery, Revolutionary America, and the New Nation (1989)

William M. Fowler Jr., Rebels Under Sail: The American Navy During the Revolution (1976)

Francis Fox, Sweet Land of Liberty: The Ordeal of the American Revolution in Northampton County, Pennsylvania (2000)

Barbara Graymont, The Iroquois in the American Revolution (1972)

Leslie Hall, Land and Allegiance in Revolutionary Georgia (2001)

David C. Hendrickson, Peace Pact: The Lost World of the American Founding (2003)

Ronald Hoffman and Peter J. Albert, eds., Arms and Independence: The Military Character of the American Revolution (1984)

———— eds., Women in the Age of the American Revolution (1989)

Ronald Hoffman and Thad W. Tate, eds., An Uncivil War: The Southern Backcountry during the American Revolution (1985)

Francis Jennings, The Creation of America: Through Revolution to Empire (2000)

Mark E. Kann, A Republic of Men: The American Founders, Gendered Language, and Patriarchial Politics (1998)

Cynthia A. Kierner, Southern Women in Revolution, 1776–1800 (1998)

Arthur S. Lefkowitz, The Long Retreat: The Calamitous American Defense of New Jersey, 1776 (1999)

Paul C. Nagel, The Adams Women: Abigail and Louise Adams, Their Sisters and Daughters (1987)

Gary B. Nash, Race and Revolution (1990)

Mary Beth Norton, The British Americans: The Loyalist Exiles in England, 1774–1789 (1972)

James O'Donnell, Southern Indians in the American Revolution (1973)

Andrew Jackson O'Shaughnessy, An Empire Divided: The American Revolution and the British Caribbean (2000)

Howard W. Peckham, The Toll of Independence: Engagements and Battle Casualties of the American Revolution (1974)

Elizabeth Perkins, Border Life: Experience and Memory in the Revolutionary Ohio Valley (1998)

Benjamin Quarles, The Negro in the American Revolution, rev. ed. (1996)

David Lee Russell, The American Revolution in the Southern Colonies (2000)

James W. St. G. Walker, The Black Loyalists (1976)

Anthony F. C. Wallace, The Death and Rebirth of the Seneca (1970)

Alfred F. Young, ed., The American Revolution: Explorations in American Radicalism (1976).

The United States in Congress Assembled

Joyce Appleby, Inheriting the Revolution: The First Generation of Americans (2000)

Richard Beeman, et al., eds., Beyond Confederation: Origins of the Constitution and American National Identity (1987)

E. Wayne Carp, To Starve the Army at Pleasure: Continental Army Administration and American Political Culture, 1774–1783 (1984)

E. J. Ferguson, The Power of the Purse: A History of American Public Finance, 1776–1790 (1960)

Calvin C. Jillson, Congressional Dynamics: Structure, Coordination, and Choice in the First American Congress, 1774–1789 (1994)

Jackson Turner Main, Political Parties before the Constitution (1973)

Jack N. Rakove, The Beginnings of National Politics: An Interpretive History of the Continental Congress (1979)

Gerald Sourzh, Benjamin Franklin and American Foreign Policy (1969)

Gordon S. Wood, The Creation of the American Republic, 1776–1787 (1969)

Revolutionary Politics in the States

Willi Paul Adams, The First American Constitutions: Republican Ideology and the Making of the State Constitutions (1980)

Roger H. Brown, Redeeming the Republic: Federalists, Taxation, and the Origins of the Constitution (1993)

Donald S. Lutz, Popular Consent and Popular Control: Whig Political Theory in the Early State Constitutions (1980)

Jackson Turner Main, The Sovereign States, 1775–1789 (1973)

Biography

William Howard Adams, Gouverneur Morris: An Independent Life (2003)

Silvio A. Bedini, The Life of Benjamin Banneker (1972)

Patricia Cleary, Elizabeth Murray: A Woman's Pursuit of Independence in Eighteenth-Century America (2000)

John Mack Faragher, Daniel Boone: The Life and Legend of an American Pioneer (1992)

Douglas Southall Freeman, George Washington, 7 vols. (1948–57)

Lowell Hayes Harrison, George Rogers Clark and the War in the West (1976)

John W. Hartmann, The American Partisan: Henry Lee and the Struggle for Independence, 1776–1780 (2000)

Isabel Thompson Kelsay, *Joseph Brant, 1743–1807: Man of Two Worlds* (1984)

James Kirby Martin, *Benedict Arnold, Revolutionary Hero* (1997)

Gregory D. Massey, *John Laurens and the American Revolution* (2000)

William Henry Robinson, *Phillis Wheatley and Her Writings* (1984)

Susan Burgess Shenstone, *So Obstinately Loyal: James Moody, 1744–1809* (2000)

Henry Wiencek, *Imperfect God: George Washington, His Slaves, and the Creation of America* (2003)

Alfred F. Young, *Masquerade: The Life and Times of Deborah Sampson, Continental Soldier* (2004)

Rosemarie Zagarri, *A Woman's Dilemma: Mercy Otis Warren and the American Revolution* (1995)

CHAPTER 8

The Crisis of the 1780s

Roger H. Brown, *Redeeming the Republic: Federalists, Taxation, and the Origin of the Constitution* (1993)

Keith L. Dougherty, *Collective Action Under the Articles of Confederation* (2001)

Ronald Hoffman and Peter J. Albert, eds., *Soverign States in an Age of Uncertainty* (1982)

Robert A. Gross, eds., *In Debt to Shays: The Bicentennial of an Agrarian Rebellion* (1993)

Merrill Jensen, *The New Nation: A History of the United States during the Confederation, 1781–1789* (1950)

Leonard L. Richards, *Shay's Rebellion: The American Revolution's Final Battle* (2002)

David Szatmary, *Shay's Rebellion: The Making of an Agrarian Insurrection* (1980)

The New Constitution

Douglass Adair, *Fame and the Founding Fathers*, ed. Trevor Colbourn (1974)

Bernard Bailyn, *To Begin the World Anew: The Genius and Ambiguities of the American Founders* (2003)

Charles A. Beard, *An Economic Interpretation of the Constitution of the United States* (1913)

Saul Cornell, *The Other Founders: Anti-Federalism and the Dissenting Tradition in America, 1788–1828* (1999)

Robert A. Dahl, *How Democratic Is the American Constitution?* (2003)

Max Farrand, ed., *Records of the Federal Convention of 1787*, 4 vols. (1911–37)

Paul Finkelman, *Slavery and the Founders: Race and Liberty in the Age of Jefferson* (2001)

John P. Kaminski and Gaspare J. Saladino, eds., *The Documentary History of the Ratification of the Constitution* (1982)

Mark E. Kann, *A Republic of Men: The American Founders, Gendered Language, and Patriarchal Politics* (1998)

Leonard W. Levy, *Origins of the Bill of Rights* (1999)

James H. Read, *Power Versus Liberty: Madison, Hamilton, Wilson, and Jefferson* (2000)

Gary Rosen, *American Compact: James Madison and the Problem of Founding* (1999)

Herbert J. Storing, ed., *The Complete Anti-Federalist*, 7 vols. (1981)

The New Nation

Kenneth R. Bowling and Donald R. Kennon, eds., *Neither Separate Nor Equal: Congress in the 1790s* (2000)

Collin G. Calloway, *Crown and Calumet: British-Indian Relations, 1783–1815* (1987)

Noble E. Cunningham, *Jefferson vs. Hamilton: Confrontations That Shaped a Nation* (2000)

Wilbur Edel, *Kekionga! The Worst Defeat in the History of the U.S. Army* (1997)

James Horn et al., eds., *Revolution of 1800: Democracy, Race, and the New Republic* (2002)

Edward S. Kaplan, *The Bank of the United States and the American Economy* (1999)

Peter McNamara, *Political Economy and Statesmanship: Smith, Hamilton, and the Foundation of the Commercial Republic* (1998)

Mark J. Rozell, et al., eds., *George Washington and the Origins of the American Presidency* (2000)

Garrett Ward Sheldon, *The Political Philosophy of James Madison* (2001)

Wiley Sword, *President Washington's Indian War: The Struggle for the Old Northwest, 1790–1795* (1985)

Garry Wills, *Negro President: Jefferson and the Slave Power* (2003)

Federalists and Jeffersonian Republicans

Doron Ben-Atar and Barbara B. Oberg, eds., *Federalists Reconsidered* (1998)

Alexander De Conde, *The Quasi-War: Politics and Diplomacy of the Undeclared War with France, 1797–1801* (1966)

Andrew Lenner, *The Federal Principle in American Politics, 1790–1833* (2001)

Forrest McDonald, *States' Rights and the Union: Imperium in Imperio, 1776–1876* (2000)

Michael A. Palmer, *Stoddert's War: Naval Operations During the Quasi-War with France, 1798–1801* (2000)

Andrew W. Robertson, *The Language of Democracy: Political Rhetoric in the United States and Britain, 1790–1900* (1995)

James Roger Sharp, *American Politics in the Early Republic: The New Nation in Crisis* (1993)

David Waldsteicher, *In the Midst of Perpetual Fetes: The Making of American Nationalism, 1776–1820* (1997)

"The Rising Glory of America"

R. A. Burchell, ed., *The End of Anglo–America: Historical Essays in the Study of Cultural Divergence* (1991)

Andrew Burstein, *Sentimental Democracy: The Evolution of America's Romantic Self-Image* (1999)

Ellen Fernandez-Sacco, *Spectacular Masculinities: The Museums of Peale, Baker, and Bowen in the Early Republic* (1998)

Linda Kerber, *Women of the Republic: Intellect and Ideology in Revolutionary America* (1980)

Biography

Gay Wilson Allen, *St. John de Crèvecoeur: The Life of an American Farmer* (1987)

Aleine Austin, *Matthew Lyon, "New Man" of the Democratic Revolution, 1749–1822* (1981)

Lance Banning, *The Sacred Fire of Liberty: James Madison and the Founding of the Federal Republic* (1995)

R. B. Bernstein, *Thomas Jefferson* (2003)

Richard Brookhiser, *Alexander Hamilton, American* (1999)

Harvey Lewis Carter, *The Life and Times of Little Turtle: First Sagamore of the Wabash* (1987)

Helen A. Cooper, *John Trumbull: The Hand and Spirit of a Painter* (1982)

John Patrick Diggins, *John Adams* (2003)

Dorinda Evans, *The Genius of Gilbert Stuart* (1999)

Roger G. Kennedy, *Burr, Hamilton, and Jefferson: A Study in Character* (2000)

David McCullough, *John Adams* (2001)

David Micklethwait, *Noah Webster and the American Dictionary* (2000)

Jules David Prown, *John Singleton Copley* (1966)

William M. S. Rasmussen and Robert S. Tilton, *George Washington: The Man Behind the Myths* (1999)

Sheila L. Skemp, *Judith Sargent Murray: A Brief Biography with Documents* (1998)

K. Alan Synder, *Defining Noah Webster: Mind and Morals in the Early Republic* (1990)

Harlow G. Unger, *Noah Webster: The Life and Times of an American Patriot* (1998)

Mason Locke Weems, *The Life of Washington*, ed. Marcus Cunliffe (1962)

CHAPTER 9

North American Communities from Coast to Coast
James Gibson, *Imperial Russia in Frontier America* (1976)

Marcel Giraud, *A History of French Louisiana, 1698–1715* (1974)

Barbara Sweetland Smith and Redmond Barnett, eds., *Russian America* (1990)

David Weber, *The Spanish Frontier in North America* (1993)

The National Economy
W. Eliot Brownlee, *Dynamics of Ascent: A History of the American Economy* (1979)

Stuart Bruchey, *The Roots of American Economic Growth, 1607–1861* (1965)

Curtis P. Nettels, *The Emergence of a National Economy, 1775–1815* (1962)

Douglass C. North, *The Economic Growth of the United States, 1790–1860* (1966)

The Jefferson Presidency
Henry Adams, *The United States in 1800* (1955)

Robert Lowry Clinton, *Marbury v. Madison and Judicial Review* (1989)

Noble E. Cunningham, *The Jeffersonian Republicans and Power: Party Operations, 1801–1809* (1963)

George Drago, *Jefferson's Louisiana: Politics and the Clash of Legal Traditions* (1975)

Burton Spivak, *Jefferson's English Crisis: Commerce, Embargo, and the Republican Revolution* (1979)

Robert W. Tucker and David Hendrickson, *Empire of Liberty: The Statecraft of Thomas Jefferson* (1990)

G. Edward White, *The Marshall Court and Cultural Change, 1815–1835*, abridged ed. (1991)

James S. Young, *The Washington Community, 1800–1828* (1966)

Renewed Imperial Rivalry in North America
Henry Warner Bowden, *American Indians and Christian Missions: Studies in Cultural Conflict* (1981)

Gregory Evans Dowd, *A Spirited Resistance: The North American Indian Struggle for Unity, 1745–1815*

Reginald Horsman, *Expansion and American Indian Policy, 1783–1812* (1967)

Drew R. McCoy, *The Last of the Fathers: James Madison and the Republican Legacy* (1989)

Francis Paul Prucha, *The Great Father: The United States Government and the American Indians*, 2 vols. (1984)

Defining the Boundaries
John Boles, *Religion in Antebellum Kentucky* (1976)

Andrew Cayton, *The Frontier Republic: Ideology and Politics in the Ohio Country, 1789–1812* (1986)

———, *Frontier Indiana* (1996)

George Dangerfield, *The Era of Good Feelings* (1952)

Anita Shafer Goodstein, *Nashville, 1780–1860: From Frontier to City* (1989)

Christine Leigh Heyrman, *Southern Cross: The Beginnings of the Bible Belt* (1997)

Walter LaFeber, ed., *John Quincy Adams and the American Continental Empire* (1965)

Malcolm J. Rohrbough, *The Land Office Business* (1968)

———, *The Trans-Appalachian Frontier: Peoples, Societies, and Institutions, 1775–1850* (1978)

Richard Slotkin, *Regeneration through Violence: The Mythology of the American Frontier* (1973)

Richard C. Wade, *The Urban Frontier: The Rise of Western Cities, 1790–1850* (1973)

CHAPTER 10

King Cotton and Southern Expansion
Bruce Levine, *Half Slave and Half Free: The Roots of Civil War* (1992).

Daniel S. Dupre, *Transforming the Cotton Frontier, Madison County, Alabama, 1800–1840* (1997)

Robert W. Fogel and Stanley Engerman, *Time on the Cross: The Economics of American Negro Slavery* (1974)

Joseph P. Reidy, *From Slavery to Agrarian Capitalism in the Cotton Plantation South: Central Georgia, 1800–1880* (1992)

Gavin Wright, *The Political Economy of the Cotton South: Households, Markets, and Wealth in the Nineteenth Century* (1978)

Slavery and African American Communities

Ira Berlin and Philip D. Morgan, eds., *Cultivation and Culture: Labor and the Shaping of Slave Life in the Americas* (1993)

John Blassingame, *The Slave Community*, rev. ed. (1979)

Randolph B. Campbell, *An Empire for Slavery: The Peculiar Institution in Texas, 1821–1865* (1989)

Charles B. Dew, *Bond of Iron: Master and Slave at Buffalo Forge* (1994)

Douglas Egerton, *Gabriel's Rebellion: The Virginia Slave Conspiracies of 1800 and 1802* (1993)

Barbara Field, *Slavery on the Middle Ground: Maryland during the Nineteenth Century* (1985)

Eugene D. Genovese, *From Rebellion to Revolution: Afro-American Slave Revolts in the Making of the Modern World* (1979)

Charles Joyner, *Down by the Riverside: A South Carolina Slave Community* (1984)

Lawrence W. Levine, *Black Culture and Black Consciousness: Afro-American Folk Thought from Slavery to Freedom* (1977)

Ann Patton Malone, *Sweet Chariot: Slave Family and Household Structure in Nineteenth-Century Louisiana* (1992)

Albert Raboteau, *Slave Religion: The "Invisible Institution" in the Antebellum South* (1978)

Kenneth Stampp, *The Peculiar Institution* (1956)

Sterling Stuckey, *Slave Culture: Nationalist Theory and the Foundation of Black America* (1987)

Richard C. Wade, *Slavery in the Cities: The South 1820–1860* (1964)

Deborah Gray White, *Arn't I a Woman?* (1985)

Yeomen, Planters, and the Defense of Slavery

David T. Bailey, *Shadow on the Church: Southwestern Evangelical Religion and the Issue of Slavery, 1783–1860* (1985)

F. N. Boney, *Southerners All* (1990)

Joan Cashin, *A Family Venture: Men and Women on the Southern Frontier* (1991)

Bill Cecil-Fronsman, *Common White: Class and Culture in Antebellum North Carolina* (1992)

William J. Cooper, *The South and the Politics of Slavery, 1829–1856* (1978)

Clement Eaton, *The Freedom of Thought Struggle in the Old South* (1964)

Drew Gilpin Faust, ed., *The Ideology of Slavery: Proslavery Thought in the Antebellum South, 1830–1860* (1981)

Elizabeth Fox-Genovese, *Within the Plantation Household* (1988)

Jean Friedman, *The Enclosed Garden: Women and Community in the Evangelical South, 1830–1900* (1985)

J. William Harris, *Plain Folk and Gentry in a Slave Society: White Liberty and Black Slavery in Augusta's Hinterlands* (1985)

Christopher Morris, *Becoming Southern: The Evolution of a Way of Life, Warren County and Vicksburg, Mississippi, 1770–1860* (1995)

Michael Wayne, *Death of an Overseer* (2001)

Bertram Wyatt-Brown, *Southern Honor: Ethics and Behavior in the Old South* (1982)

CHAPTER 11

The New Democratic Politics and Jackson Presidency

Glenn C. Altschuler and Stuart M. Blumin, *Rude Republic: Americans and Their Politics in the Nineteenth Century* (2000)

William L. Anderson, *Cherokee Removal: Before and After* (1991)

Steven C. Bullock, *Revolutionary Brotherhood: Freemasonry and the Transformation of the American Social Order, 1730–1840* (1996)

John Ehle, *Trail of Tears* (1988)

Lucy Maddox, *Removals: Nineteenth-Century American Literature and the Politics of Indian Affairs* (1991)

Reeve Huston, *Land and Freedom: Rural Society, Popular Protest, and Party Politics in Antebellum New York* (2000).

Arthur M. Schlesinger Jr., *The Age of Jackson* (1945)

John Ward, *Andrew Jackson: Symbol for an Age* (1955)

Chilton Williamson, *American Suffrage: From Property to Democracy, 1760–1860* (1960)

The Rise of the Whigs and the Second American Party System

Daniel W. Howe, *The Political Culture of the American Whigs* (1980)

Lawrence F. Kohl, *The Politics of Individualism: Parties and the American Character in the Jacksonian Era* (1989)

Richard P. McCormick, *The Second American Party System: Party Formation in the Jacksonian Era* (1966)

Joel H. Sibley, *The Partisan Imperative: The Dynamics of American Politics before the Civil War* (1985)

American Arts and Letters

Richard D. Brown, *Knowledge Is Power: The Diffusion of Information in Early America, 1700–1865* (1989)

Cathy N. Davidson, *Revolution and the Word: The Rise of the Novel in America* (1986)

Nathan O. Hatch, *The Democratization of American Christianity* (1989)

Barbara Novak, *Nature and Culture: American Landscape Painting 1825–1875* (1982)

Gwendolyn Wright, *Building the Dream: A Social History of Housing in America* (1981)

CHAPTER 12

The Transportation Revolution

Clarence Danhof, *Changes in Agriculture: The Northern United States, 1820–1870* (1969)

E. M. Dodd, *American Business Corporations until 1860* (1954)

Albert Fishlow, *American Railroads and the Transformation of the Ante-Bellum Economy* (1965)

John Denis Haeger, *The Investment Frontier: New York Businessmen and the Economic Development of the Old Northwest* (1981)

Thomas Dublin, *Women at Work: The Transformation of Work and Community in Lowell, Massachusetts, 1826–1860* (1979).

Oscar Handlin and Mary Handlin, *Commonwealth: A Study of the Role of Government in the American Economy: Massachusetts, 1774–1861* (1947)

Morton J. Horwitz, *The Transformation of American Law, 1780–1860* (1977)

Karl Raitz, ed., *The National Road* (1995)

Ronald E. Shaw, *Canals for a Nation: The Canal Era in the United States, 1790–1860* (1990)

Peter Way, *Common Labour: Workers and the Digging of North American Canals, 1780–1860* (1993)

The Market Revolution

Thomas C. Cochran, *Frontiers of Change: Early Industrialism in America* (1981)

Robert F. Dalzell Jr., *Enterprising Elite: The Boston Associates and the World They Made* (1987)

David J. Jeremy, *Transatlantic Industrial Revolution: The Diffusion of Textile Technology between Britain and America* (1981)

Paul Johnson, *A Shopkeeper's Millennium: Society and Revivals in Rochester, New York, 1815–1837* (1978)

Bruce Laurie, *Artisans into Workers: Labor in Nineteenth-Century America* (1989)

Walter Licht, *Industrializing America: The Nineteenth Century* (1995)

Merritt R. Smith, *Harpers Ferry Armory and the New Technology* (1977)

Melvyn Stokes and Stephen Conway, eds., *The Market Revolution in America: Social, Political and Religious Expressions 1800–1880* (1996)

Barbara Tucker, *Samuel Slater and the Origins of the American Textile Industry, 1790–1860* (1984)

From Artisan to Worker

Mary H. Blewett, *Men, Women, and Work: Class, Gender, and Protest in the New England Shoe Industry, 1780–1910* (1988)

Paul G. Faler, *Mechanics and Manufacturers in the Early Industrial Revolution: Lynn, Massachusetts* (1981)

Michael H. Glickstein, *Concepts of Free Labor in Antebellum America* (1991)

Joan M. Jensen, *Loosening the Bonds: Mid-Atlantic Farm Women, 1750–1850* (1986)

Bruce Laurie, *Working People of Philadelphia, 1800–1850* (1980)

W. J. Rorabaugh, *The Craft Apprentice: From Franklin to the Machine Age in America* (1986)

A New Social Order

Stuart M. Blumin, *The Emergence of the Middle Class: Social Experience in the American City* (1989)

Jeanne Boydston, *Home and Work* (1990)

Janet Farrell Brodie, *Contraception and Abortion in Nineteenth-Century America* (1994)

Nancy E. Cott, *The Bonds of Womanhood: "Woman's Sphere" in New England, 1780–1835* (1977)

Anthony F. C. Wallace, *Rockdale: The Growth of an American Village in the Early Industrial Revolution* (1977)

Middle-Class Culture

Barbara A. Bardes and Suzanne Gossett, *Declarations of Independence: Women and Political Power in Nineteenth-Century American Fiction* (1990)

John F. Kasson, *Rudeness and Civility: Manners in Nineteenth-Century America* (1990)

Walter Benn Michaels and Donald E. Pease, eds., *The American Renaissance Reconsidered* (1985)

Lewis Perry, *Intellectual Life in America* (1984)

Ann Rose, *Transcendentalism as a Social Movement* (1981)

Richard Teichgraeber III, *Sublime Thoughts/Penny Wisdom: Situating Emerson and Thoreau in the American Market* (1995)

Jane Tompkins, *Sensational Designs: The Cultural World of American Fiction, 1790–1860* (1986)

Steven J. Ross, *Workers on the Edge: Work, Leisure and Politics in Industrializing Cincinnati, 1788–1890* (1985). Studies the growth of wage labor in a major western city.

CHAPTER 13

Immigration and Ethnicity

Oscar Handlin, *The Uprooted* (1951; 2nd ed. 1973)

Noel Ignatiev, *How the Irish Became White* (1995)

Kerby A. Miller, *Emigrants and Exiles: Ireland and the Irish Exodus to North America* (1985)

Stanley Nadel, *Little Germany: Ethnicity, Religion, and Class in New York City, 1845–1880* (1990)

Dennis P. Ryan, *Beyond the Ballot Box: A Social History of the Boston Irish, 1845–1917* (1989)

Urban America

Oliver E. Allen, *The Tiger: The Rise and Fall of Tammany Hall* (1995)

John Duffy, *The Sanitarians* (1990)

Paul A. Gilje, *The Road to Mobocracy: Popular Disorder in New York City, 1763–1834* (1987)

Herbert G. Gutman, *Work, Culture, and Society in Industrializing America: Essays in American Working-Class History* (1976)

James Oliver Horton, *Free People of Color: Inside the African American Community* (1993)

Gary B. Nash, *Forging Freedom: Philadelphia's Black Community, 1720–1840* (1988)

Charles E. Rosenberg, *The Cholera Years* (1962)

Dennis C. Rousey, *Policing the Southern City, New Orleans 1805–1889* (1997)

Sam Bass Warner, *The Private City: Philadelphia in Three Periods of Its Growth* (1968)

Religion, Reform, and Utopianism

Lawrence Cremin, *American Education: The National Experience, 1783–1861* (1981)

Whitney R. Cross, *The Burned-Over District: The Social and Intellectual History of Enthusiastic Religion in Western New York, 1800–1850* (1950)

Barbara Epstein, *The Politics of Domesticity: Women, Evangelism, and Temperance in Nineteenth Century America* (1981)

Lori D. Ginzberg, *Women and the Work of Benevolence: Morality, Politics, and Class in the Nineteenth-Century United States* (1990)

Carl F. Kaestle, *Pillars of the Republic: Common Schools and American Society, 1780–1860* (1983)

W. J. Rorabaugh, *The Alcoholic Republic: An American Tradition* (1979)

Abolitionism

David Brion Davis, *The Problem of Slavery in the Age of Revolution, 1770–1823* (1975)

Frederick Douglass, *The Narrative of the Life of Frederick Douglass, An American Slave* (1845)

Peter P. Hinks, *To Awaken My Afflicted Brethren: David Walker and the Problem of Antebellum Slave Resistance* (1997)

Howard Jones, *Mutiny on the Amistad* (1987)

Jean Fagan Yellin, *Women and Sisters: The Antislavery Feminists in American Culture* (1989)

Women's Rights

Ellen C. DuBois, *Feminism and Suffrage: The Emergence of an Independent Women's Movement in America, 1848–1869* (1978)

Gerda Lerner, *The Grimké Sisters from South Carolina: Pioneers for Women's Rights and Abolition* (1967)

Sandra S. Weber, *Special History Study, Women's Rights National Historical Park, Seneca Falls, New York* (1985)

CHAPTER 14

Exploration and Expansion

Jennifer S. H. Brown, *Strangers in Blood: Fur Trade Company Families in Indian Country* (1980)

William H. Goetzmann, *Army Exploration in the American West, 1803–1863* (1959)

William H. Goetzmann and William N. Goetzmann, *The West of the Imagination* (1986)

Norman A. Graebner, *Empire on the Pacific: A Study in American Continental Expansion* (1955)

LeRoy R. Hafen, ed., *The Mountain Men and the Fur Trade of the Far West*, 10 vols. (1968–72)

Sam W. Haynes, *James Polk and the Expansionist Impulse,* (1997)

Thomas R. Hietala, *Manifest Design: Anxious Aggrandizement in Late Jacksonian America* (1985)

Reginald Horsman, *Race and Manifest Destiny* (1981)

Theodore J. Karaminski, *Fur Trade and Exploration: Opening of the Far Northwest, 1821–1852* (1983)

Patricia Nelson Limerick, *The Legacy of Conquest: The Unbroken Past of the Unbroken West* (1987)

Frederick Merk, *Manifest Destiny and Mission in American History: A Reinterpretation* (1963)

———, *History of the Westward Movement* (1978)

Dale Morgan, *Jedediah Smith and the Opening of the West* (1982)

Peter Nabakov, ed., *Native American Testimony: An Anthology of Indian and White Relations* (1978)

James P. Ronda, *Astoria and Empire* (1990)

Charles G. Sellers, *James K. Polk: Jacksonian, 1795–1843* (1957)

———, *James K. Polk: Continentalist, 1843–1846* (1966)

Henry Nash Smith, *Virgin Land: The American West as Symbol and Myth* (1950)

Edward H. Spicer, *Cycles of Conquest: The Impact of Spain, Mexico, and the United States on the Indians of the Southwest, 1533–1960* (1981)

Robert A. Trennert, *Alternative to Extinction: Federal Indian Policy and the Beginnings of the Reservation System, 1846–1851* (1975)

Sylvia Van Kirk, *"Many Tender Ties": Women in Fur Trade Society in Western Canada, 1670–1870* (1980)

Albert K. Weinberg, *Manifest Destiny: A Study of Nationalist Expansionism in American History* (1957)

Peter Booth Wiley with Korogi Ichiro, *Yankees in the Land of the Gods: Commodore Perry and the Opening of Japan* (1990)

David J. Wishart, *The Fur Trade of the American West, 1807–1840: A Geographic Synthesis* (1979)

California and Oregon

John W. Caughey, *The California Gold Rush* (1975)

Malcolm Clark Jr., *Eden Seekers: The Settlement of Oregon, 1818–1862* (1981)

Douglas H. Daniels, *Pioneer Urbanites: A Social and Cultural History of Black San Francisco* (1980)

James R. Gibson, *Farming the Frontier: The Agricultural Opening of Oregon Country, 1786–1846* (1985)

Ramon Gutierrez and Richard J. Orsi, *Contested Eden: California Before the Gold Rush* (1998)

Albert L. Hurtado, *Indian Survival on the California Frontier* (1988)

Julie Roy Jeffrey, *Frontier Women: Civilizing The West? 1840–1860* (1998)

Marquis James, *The Raven: The Story of Sam Houston* (1929)

David Johnson, *Founding the Far West: California, Oregon, and Nevada, 1840–1890* (1992)

Alvin Josephy, *The Nez Percé and the Opening of the Northwest* (1965)

Rodman W. Paul, *California Gold: The Beginning of Mining in the Far West* (1974)

Leonard Pitt, *The Decline of the Californios: A Social History of the Spanish-Speaking Californians, 1846–1890* (1966)

James J. Rawls, *Indians of California: The Changing Image* (1984)

Brian Roberts, *American Alchemy: The California Gold Rush and Middle-Class Culture* (2000)

Kevin Starr, *Americans and the California Dream, 1850–1915* (1973)

John I. Unruh Jr., *The Plains Across: Overland Emigrants and the Trans-Mississippi West, 1840–1860* (1979)

Texas and the Mexican–American War

K. Jack Bauer, *The Mexican War, 1846–1848* (1974)

William C. Binkley, *The Texas Revolution* (1952)

Gene M. Brack, *Mexico Views Manifest Destiny* (1976)

Holly Beachley Brear, *Inherit the Alamo: Myth and Ritual at an American Shrine* (1995)

Donald E. Chipman, *Spanish Texas, 1519–1821* (1992)

Seymour Conner and Odie Faulk, *North America Divided: The Mexican War, 1846–1848* (1971)

Arnoldo De León, *They Called Them Greasers: Anglo Attitudes toward Mexicans in Texas, 1821–1900* (1983)

John S. D. Eisenhower, *So Far from God: The U.S. War with Mexico 1846–1848* (1989)

Neil Harlow, *California Conquered: War and Peace on the Pacific, 1846–1850* (1982)

Ernest McPherson Lander Jr., *Reluctant Imperialist: Calhoun, South Carolina, and the Mexican War* (1980)

Timothy Matovina, *Tejano Religion and Ethnicity: San Antonio, 1921–1860* (1995)

Frederick Merk, *Slavery and the Annexation of Texas* (1972)

David Montejano, *Anglos and Mexicans in the Making of Texas, 1836–1986* (1987)

Stanley Noyes, *Los Comanches: The Horse People, 1751–1845* (1994)

David Pletcher, *The Diplomacy of Annexation: Texas, Oregon, and the Mexican War* (1973)

Andreas V. Reichstein, *Rise of the Lone Star: The Making of Texas* (1989)

Susan Scholwer, *Alamo Images: Changing Perceptions of a Texas Experience* (1985)

John H. Schroeder, *Mr. Polk's War: American Opposition and Dissent, 1846–1848* (1971)

Otis A. Singletary, *The Mexican War* (1960)

Jésus F. de la Teja, *San Antonio de Béxar: A Community on New Spain's Northern Frontier* (1995)

The Politics of Manifest Destiny

Chaplain W. Morrison, *Democratic Politics and Sectionalism: The Wilmot Proviso Controversy* (1967)

Michael Morrison, *Slavery and the American West: The Eclipse of Manifest Destiny and the Coming of the Civil War* (1997).

Joseph G. Raybeck, *Free Soil: The Election of 1848* (1970)

Joel H. Sibley, *The Shrine of Party: Congressional Voting Behavior, 1841–1852* (1967)

CHAPTER 15

The Crisis over Slavery

Richard H. Abbott, *Cotton and Capital: Boston Businessmen and Antislavery Reform, 1854–1868* (1991)

Gary Collison, *Shadrach Minkins: From Fugitive Slave to Citizen* (1997)

W. Ehrlich, *They Have No Rights: Dred Scott's Struggle for Freedom* (1979)

C. C. Goen, *Broken Churches, Broken Nation* (1985)

Thomas F. Grossett, *Uncle Tom's Cabin and American Culture* (1985)

William Lee Miller, *Arguing About Slavery: The Great Battle in the United States Congress* (1996)

H. Craig Miner and William E. Unrau, *The End of Indian Kansas* (1978)

Stephen Oates, *To Purge This Land with Blood: A Biography of John Brown* (1970)

J. Rossbach, *Ambivalent Conspirators: John Brown, the Secret Six and a Theory of Black Political Violence* (1982)

Thomas P. Slaughter, *Bloody Dawn: The Christiana Riots and Racial Violence in the Antebellum North* (1991)

Gerald W. Wolff, *The Kansas-Nebraska Bill: Party, Section, and the Coming of the Civil War* (1977)

Bertram Wyatt-Brown, *Yankee Saints and Southern Sinners* (1985)

The Crisis of the National Party System

Tyler Anbinder, *Nativism and Slavery: The Northern Know-Nothings and the Politics of the 1850s* (1992)

J. H. Baker, *Affairs of Party: The Political Culture of Northern Democrats in the Mid-Nineteenth Century* (1983)

Ronald Formisano, *The Birth of Mass Political Parties: Michigan, 1827–1861* (1971)

William E. Gienapp, *The Origins of the Republican Party, 1852–1856* (1987)

Michael Holt, *The Political Crisis of the 1850s* (1978)

Robert W. Johannsen, *The Lincoln-Douglas Debates* (1965)

John Mayfield, *Rehearsal for Republicanism: Free Soil and the Politics of Antislavery* (1980)

The South Secedes

William. L. Barney, *The Road to Secession* (1972)

Charles H. Brown, *Agents of Manifest Destiny: The Lives and Times of the Filibusters* (1980)

Steven A. Channing, *Crisis of Fear: Secession in South Carolina* (1970)

William J. Cooper, *The South and the Politics of Slavery* (1978)

Avery O. Craven, *The Growth of Southern Nationalism 1848–1861* (1953)

William W. Freehling, *The Road to Disunion*, Vol. I: *Secessionists at Bay, 1776–1854* (1991)

Michael P. Johnson, *Secession and Conservatism in the Lower South: The Social and Ideological Bases of Secession in Georgia, 1860–1861* (1983)

Robert E. May, *The Southern Dream of a Caribbean Empire, 1854–1861* (1973)

John McCardell, *The Idea of a Southern Nation: Southern Nationalists and Southern Nationalism, 1830–1861* (1979)

K. M. Stampp, *And the War Came: The North and the Secession Crisis 1860–1861* (1950)

Joe A. Stout, *The Liberators: Filibustering Expeditions into Mexico, 1848–1862, and the Last Thrust of Manifest Destiny* (1973)

Ronald L. Takaki, *A Proslavery Crusade: The Agitation to Reopen the African Slave Trade* (1971)

J. Mills Thornton, *Politics and Power in a Slavery Society* (1978)

Eric H. Walter, *The Fire-Eaters* (1992)

CHAPTER 16

The Lincoln Presidency and the Northern Home Front

Jeanie Attie, *Patriotic Toil: Northern Women and the American Civil War* (1998)

Richard Franklin Bensel, *Yankee Leviathan: The Origins of Central State Authority in America, 1859–1877* (1991)

George M. Frederickson, *The Inner Civil War: Northern Intellectuals and the Crisis of the Union* (1965)

J. Matthew Gallman, *The North Fights the Civil War: The Home Front* (1994)

Ernest A. McKay, *The Civil War and New York City* (1990)

James M. McPherson, *Abraham Lincoln and the Second American Revolution* (1990)

Mark E. Neely, *The Fate of Liberty: Abraham Lincoln and Civil Liberties* (1991)

Thomas H. O'Connor, *Civil War Boston: Homefront and Battlefield* (1997)

Phillip Shaw Paludan, *The Presidency of Abraham Lincoln* (1994)

Heather Cox Richardson, *The Greatest Nation of the Earth: Republican Economic Policies during the Civil War* (1997)

Anne C. Rose, *Victorian America and the Civil War* (1992)

Joel Sibley, *A Respectable Minority: The Democratic Party in the Civil War Era, 1860–1868* (1977)

Lyde Cullen Sizer, *The Political Work of Northern Women Writers and the Civil War* (2000)

Bell I. Wiley, *The Life of Johnny Reb* (1943)

———, *The Life of Billy Yank* (1952)

The Death of Slavery

Ira Berlin et al. eds., *Freedom, A Documentary History of Emancipation, 1861–1867*, Series 1, Volume I: *The Destruction of Slavery* (1985)

———, eds., *Freedom, A Documentary History of Emancipation, 1861–1867*, Series 1, Volume II: *The Wartime Genesis of Free Labor: The Upper South* (1993)

———, eds. *Freedom, A Documentary History of Emancipation, 1861–1867*, Series 1, Volume III: *The Wartime Genesis of Free Labor: The Lower South* (1990)

———, eds. *Freedom, A Documentary History of Emancipation, 1861–1867*, Series 2: *The Black Military Experience* (1988)

John Hope Franklin, *The Emancipation Proclamation* (1963)

Willie Lee Rose, *Rehearsal for Reconstruction: The Port Royal Experiment* (1964)

The Confederacy and the Southern Home Front

Steven V. Ash, *When the Yankees Came: Conflict and Chaos in the Occupied South 1861–1865* (1995)

William Blair, *Virginia's Private War: Feeding Body and Soul in the Confederacy, 1861–1865* (1998)

Daniel W. Crofts, *Reluctant Confederates: Upper South Unionists in the Secession Crisis* (1989)

William C. Davis, *"A Government of Our Own": The Making of the Confederacy* (1994)

Wayne K. Durrill, *War of Another Kind: A Southern Community in the Great Rebellion* (1990)

Drew Gilpin Faust, *The Creation of Confederate Nationalism* (1988)

———, *The Confederate Republic: A Revolution against Politics* (1994)

William W. Freehling, *The South vs. The South: How Anti-Confederate Southerners Shaped the Course of the Civil War*

James L. Roark, *Masters without Slaves: Southern Planters in the Civil War and Reconstruction* (1978)

William Rogers, *Confederate Home Front: Montgomery During the Civil War* (1999)

Daniel E. Sutherland, *Seasons of War: The Ordeal of a Confederate Community 1861–1865* (1995)

LeeAnn Whites, *The Civil War as a Crisis in Gender: Augusta, Georgia, 1860–1890* (1995)

The Fighting

Michael Barton, *Good Men: The Character of Civil War Soldiers* (1981)

Ken Burns, *The Civil War* (1990)

Bruce Catton, *A Stillness at Appomattox* (1953)

David Eocher, *The Longest Night* (2001)

Shelby Foote, *The Civil War: A Narrative*, 3 vols. (1958–1974)

Joseph T. Glatthaar, *Forged in Battle: The Civil War Alliance of Black Soldiers and White Officers* (1990)

———, *The March to the Sea and Beyond: Sherman's Troops in the Savannah and Carolinas Campaign* (1985)

Mark Grimsley, *The Hard Hand of War: Union Policy toward Southern Civilians, 1861–1865* (1995)

Edward Hagerman, *The American Civil War and the Origins of Modern Warfare* (1988)

Alvin Josephy, *The Civil War in the West* (1992)

Gerald F. Linderman, *Embattled Courage: The Experience of Combat in the American Civil War* (1987)

Edwin S. Redkey, ed., *A Grand Army of Black Men: Letters from African-American Soldiers in the Union Army, 1861–1865* (1992)

Charles Royster, *The Destructive War: William Tecumseh Sherman, Stonewall Jackson, and the Americans* (1991)

CHAPTER 17

The Politics of Reconstruction

Richard H. Abbott, *The Republican Party and the South, 1855–1877* (1986)

Herman Belz, *Emancipation and Equal Rights* (1978)

Michael Les Benedict, *A Compromise of Principle: Congressional Republicans and Reconstruction* (1974)

———, *The Impeachment and Trial of Andrew Johnson* (1973)

Michael Kent Curtis, *No State Shall Abridge: The Fourteenth Amendment and the Bill of Rights* (1990)

Ellen Carol DuBois, *Feminism and Suffrage* (1978)

Eric Foner, *Politics and Ideology in the Age of the Civil War* (1980)

William C. Harris, *With Charity for All: Lincoln and the Restoration of the Union* (1997)

Robert Kaczorowski, *The Politics of Judicial Interpretation: The Federal Courts, Department of Justice, and Civil Rights, 1866–1876* (1985)

James McPherson, *Ordeal by Fire: The Civil War and Reconstruction* (1982)

Michael Perman, *Emancipation and Reconstruction, 1862–1879* (1987)

Brooks D. Simpson, *The Reconstruction Presidents* (1998)

Kenneth M. Stampp, *The Era of Reconstruction, 1865–1877* (1965)

The Meaning of Freedom

Ira Berlin et al., eds., *Freedom: A Documentary History*, 3 vols. (1985–91)

W. E. B. DuBois, *Black Reconstruction* (1935)

Barbara J. Fields, *Slavery and Freedom on the Middle Ground* (1985)

Eric Foner, *Freedom's Lawmakers: A Directory of Black Officeholders during Reconstruction* (1996)

Noralee Frankel, *Freedom's Women: Black Women and Families in Civil War Era Mississippi* (1999)

Herbert G. Gutman, *The Black Family in Slavery and Freedom* (1976)

Sharon Ann Holt, *Making Freedom Pay: North Carolina Freedpeople Working For Themselves, 1865–1900* (2000)

Thomas Holt, *Black over White: Negro Political Leadership in South Carolina during Reconstruction* (1977)

Lynda J. Morgan, *Emancipation in Virginia's Tobacco Belt* (1992)

Nell Irvin Painter, *Exodusters* (1977)

Howard N. Rabinowitz, *Race Relations in the Urban South,
1865–1890* (1978)

Roger L. Ransom and Richard Sutch, *One Kind of Freedom: The
Economic Consequences of Emancipation* (1977)

Edward Royce, *The Origins of Southern Sharecropping* (1993).

Leslie A. Schwalm, *A Hard Fight for We: Women's Transition from
Slavery to Freedom in South Carolina* (1997)

Southern Politics and Society

James A. Baggett, *The Scalawags: Southern Dissenters in the Civil
War and Reconstruction* (2003)

Pamela Brandwein, *Reconstructing Reconstruction: The Supreme
Court and the Production of Historical Truth* (1999)

Dan T. Carter, *When the War Was Over: The Failure of Self
Reconstruction in the South, 1865–1877* (1985)

Richard N. Current, *Those Terrible Carpetbaggers* (1988)

Stephen Hahn, *The Roots of Southern Populism* (1983)

Sally McMillen, *To Raise Up the South: Sunday Schools in Black and
White Churches, 1865–1915* (2001)

Scott Reynolds Nelson, *Iron Confederacies: Southern Railroads,
Klan Violence, and Reconstruction* (1999)

Michael S. Perman, *The Road to Redemption: Southern Politics,
1868–1979* (1984)

Daniel W. Stowell, *Rebuilding Zion: The Religious Reconstruction of
the South, 1863–1877* (1998)

Allen W. Trelease, *White Terror: The Ku Klux Klan Conspiracy and
Southern Reconstruction* (1971)

Jonathan M. Wiener, *Social Origins of the New South* (1978)

Reconstructing the North

Stephen Buechler, *The Transformation of the Woman Suffrage
Movement* (1986)

Morton Keller, *Affairs of State* (1977)

David Montgomery, *Beyond Equality: Labor and the Radical
Republicans, 1862–1872* (1967)

Keith I. Polakoff, *The Politics of Inertia: The Election of 1876 and the
End of Reconstruction* (1973)

Heather Cox Richardson, The Death of Reconstruction:
Race, Labor, and Politics in the Post Civil War North,
1865–1901 (2001)

Amy Dru Stanley, *From Bondage to Contract: Wage Labor, Marriage,
and the Market in the Age of Slave Emancipation* (1998)

Mark W. Summers, *Railroads, Reconstruction, and the Gospel of
Prosperity* (1984)

———, *The Era of Good Stealings* (1993)

Xi Wang, *The Trial of Democracy: Black Suffrage and Northern
Republicans, 1860–1910* (1997)

C. Vann Woodward, *Reunion and Reaction: The Compromise of
1877 and the End of Reconstruction* (1956)

Biography

David Donald, *Charles Sumner and the Rights of Man* (1970)

Russell Duncan, *Freedom's Shore: Tunis Campbell and the Georgia
Freedmen* (1986)

William S. McFeely, *Frederick Douglass* (1989)

———, *Grant: A Biography* (1981)

———, *Yankee Stepfather: General O. O. Howard and the Freedmen*
(1968)

Hans L. Trefousse, *Andrew Johnson* (1989)

———, *Thaddeus Stevens: Nineteenth Century Egalitarian* (1997)

CHAPTER 18

Indian Peoples and Indian–White Relations

David Wallace Adams, *Education for Extinction: American Indians
and the Boarding School Experience, 1875–1928* (1995)

Morris W. Foster, *Being Comanche: A Social History of an American
Indian Community* (1991)

Lisbeth Haas, *Conquests and Historical Identities in California,
1769–1936* (1995)

Shelley Bowen Hatfield, *Chasing Shadows: Indians Along the
United States–Mexico Border, 1876–1911* (1998)

Frederick E. Hoxie, *A Final Promise: The Campaign to Assimilate the
Indians, 1880–1920* (1984, 2001)

Albert L. Hurtado, *Indian Survival on the California Frontier* (1988)

Patricia Nelson Limerick, *The Legacy of Conquest: The Unbroken
Past of the American West* (1987)

John D. McDermott, *A Guide to the Indian Wars of the West* (1998)

Devon Abbott Mihesuah, *Cultivating the Rosebuds: The Education
of Women at the Cherokee Female Seminary, 1851–1909* (1993)

Theda Perdue, ed., *Sifters: Native American Women's Lives* (2001)

Catherine Price, *The Oglala People, 1841–1879* (1996)

Glenda Riley, *Women and Indians on the Frontier, 1825–1915* (1984)

Elliott West, *The Way to the West: Essays on the Central Plains*
(1995)

Richard White, *The Roots of Dependency: Subsistence, Environment,
and Social Change among the Choctaws, Pawnees, and Navajos*
(1983)

Murray R. Wickett, *Contested Territory: Whites, Native Americans,
and African Americans in Oklahoma, 1865–1907* (2000)

Internal Empire

Armando C. Alonzo, *Tejano Legacy: Rancheros and Settlers in South
Texas, 1734–1900* (1998)

Susan Armitage and Elizabeth Jameson, eds., *The Women's West*
(1987)

Susan Armitage, Ruth B. Moynihan, and Christiane Fischer
Dichamp, eds., *So Much to Be Done: Women Settlers on the
Mining and Ranching Frontier* (1990)

Arnoldo De Leon, *Racial Frontiers: Africans, Chinese, and Mexicans
in Western America, 1848–1890* (2002)

Sarah Deutsch, *No Separate Refuge: Culture, Class and Gender on an
Anglo-Hispanic Frontier in the American Southwest, 1880–1940*
(1987)

David M. Emmons, *The Butte Irish: Class and Ethnicity in an
American Mining Town, 1875–1925* (1989)

Sarah Barringer Gordon, *The Mormon Question: Polygamy and
Constitutional Conflict in Nineteenth-Century America* (2002)

Douglas Monroy, *Thrown among Strangers: The Making of Mexican
Culture in Frontier California* (1990)

Katherine G. Morrissey, *Mental Territories: Mapping the Inland
Empire* (1997)

Gunter Peck, *Reinventing Free Labor: Padrones and Immigrant Workers in the North American West, 1880–1930* (2000)

William G. Robbins, *Colony and Empire: The Capitalist Transformation of the American West* (1994)

Quintard Taylor, *In Search of the Racial Frontier: African Americans in the American West, 1528–1990* (1998)

Sally Zanjani, *A Mine of Her Own: Women Prospectors in the American West, 1850–1950* (1997)

Ranching and Farming

Allan G. Bogue, *From Prairie to Corn Belt: Farming on the Illinois and Iowa Prairies in the Nineteenth Century* (1963)

Sucheng Chan, *This Bitter-Sweet Soil: The Chinese in California Agriculture, 1860–1910* (1986)

Philip Durham and Everett L. Jones, *The Negro Cowboys* (1965)

Mark Fiege, *Irrigated Eden: the Making of an Agricultural Landscape in the American West* (1999)

Dee Garceau, *The Important Things of Life: Women, Work, and Family in Sweetwater County, Wyoming, 1880–1929* (1997)

C. Robert Haywood, *Victorian West: Class and Culture in Kansas Cattle Towns* (1991)

Stan Hoig, *The Oklahoma Land Rush of 1889* (1984)

Lawrence Jelinek, *Harvest Empire: A History of California Agriculture*, 2d ed. (1982)

Frederick C. Luebke, ed., *European Immigrants in the American West: Community Histories* (1998)

David Vaught, *Cultivating California: Growers, Specialty Crops, and Labor, 1875–1920* (1999)

Paul I. Wellman, *The Trampling Herd: The Story of the Cattle Range in America* (1988)

The Western Landscape

Alfred L. Bush and Lee Clark Mitchell, *The Photograph and the American Indian* (1994)

William Cronon, George Miles, and Jay Gitlin, eds., *Under an Open Sky: Rethinking America's Western Past* (1992).

Mick Gidley, *Edward S. Curtis and the North American Indian, Incorporated* (1998)

William H. Goetzmann and William N. Goetzmann, *The West of the Imagination* (1986)

Joy S. Kasson, *Buffalo Bill's Wild West: Celebrity, Memory, and Popular History* (2000)

Chris J. Magoc, *Yellowstone: The Creation and Selling of an American Landscape, 1870–1903* (1999)

Walter Nugent and Martin Ridge, eds., *The American West: The Reader* (1999)

Paul Reddin, *Wild West Shows* (1999)

Richard Slotkin, *Gunfighter Nation: The Myth of the Frontier in 20th-Century America* (1992)

Mark David Spence, *Dispossessing the Wilderness: Indian Removal and the Making of the National Parks* (1999)

Richard White, *"It's Your Misfortune and None of My Own": A History of the American West* (1991)

Richard White and Patricia Nelson Limerick, *The Frontier in American Culture* (1994)

Donald Worster, *An Unsettled Country: Changing Landscapes of the American West* (1994)

David M. Wrobel, *Promised Lands: Promotion, Memory, and the Creation of the American West* (2002)

Biography

Matthew Baigell, *Albert Bierstadt* (1981)

Louise Barnett, *Touched by Fire: The Life, Death, and Mythic Afterlife of George Armstrong Custer* (1996)

Robert W. Larson, *Red Cloud: Warrior-Statesman of the Lakota Sioux* (1997)

Joan T. Mark, *A Stranger in Her Native Land: Alice Fletcher and the American Indians* (1988)

Sara R. Massey, ed., *Black Cowboys of Texas* (2000)

Valerie Mathes, *Helen Hunt Jackson and Her Indian Reform Legacy* (1990)

Elinore Pruitt Stewart, *Letters of a Woman Homesteader* (1914, 1989)

Edwin R. Sweeney, *Cochise, Chiricahua Apache Chief* (1991)

Jerry D. Thompson, ed., *Juan Cortina and the Texas-Mexico Frontier, 1859–1877* (1994)

Benson Tong, *Susan La Flesche Picotte, M.D.: Omaha Indian Leader and Reformer* (1999)

Robert M. Utley, *The Lance and the Shield: The Life and Times of Sitting Bull* (1993)

Donald Worster, *A River Running West: The Life of John Wesley Powell* (2001)

Sally Zanjani, *Sarah Winnemucca* (2001)

CHAPTER 19

Science, Technology, and Industry

Alfred D. Chandler Jr., *The Visible Hand: The Managerial Revolution in American Business* (1977)

David A. Hounshell, *From the American System to Mass Production, 1800–1932* (1984)

Walter Licht, *Industrializing America: The Nineteenth Century* (1995)

A. J. Millard, *Edison and the Business of Innovation* (1990)

William S. Pretzer, ed., *Working at Inventing: Thomas A. Edison and the Menlo Park Experience* (2001)

Leonard S. Reich, *The Making of American Industrial Research: Science and Business at G. E. and Bell, 1876–1926* (1985)

Business and the Economy

Wendy Gamber, *The Female Economy: The Millinery and Dressmaking Trades, 1860–1930* (1997)

Pamela Walker Laird, *Advertising Progress: American Business and the Rise of Consumer Marketing* (1998)

Naomi R. Lamoreaux, *The Great Merger Movement in American Business, 1895–1904* (1985)

Daniel Nelson, *Managers and Workers: Origins of the Factory System in the United States, 1880–1920* (1975)

Sarah Lyons Watts, *Order against Chaos: Business Culture and Labor Ideology in America, 1800–1915* (1991)

Olivier Zunz, *Making America Corporate, 1870–1920* (1990)

Working Class and Labor

Eric Arnesen, *Waterfront Workers of New Orleans: Race, Class, and Politics, 1863–1923* (1991)

John Bodnar, *Immigration and Industrialization: Ethnicity in an American Mill Town* (1977)

Lisa M. Fine, *The Souls of the Skyscraper: Female Clerical Workers in Chicago, 1870–1930* (1990)

Herbert G. Gutman, *Work, Culture and Society in Industrializing America: Essays in American Working-Class and Social History* (1977)

David M. Katzman, *Seven Days a Week: Women and Domestic Service in Industrializing America* (1978)

Joanne Meyerowitz, *Women Adrift: Industrial Wage Earners in Chicago, 1880–1930* (1988)

David Montgomery, *The Fall of the House of Labor: The Workplace, the State, and American Labor Activism, 1865–1925* (1987)

Daniel T. Rodgers, *The Work Ethic in Industrial America, 1850–1920* (1978)

Roy Rosenzweig, *Eight Hours for What We Will: Workers and Leisure in an Industrial City, 1870–1920* (1983)

Robert E. Weir, *Beyond Labor's Veil: The Culture of the Knights of Labor* (1996)

The Industrial City

John S. Garner, ed., *The Midwest in American Architecture* (1991)

Dolores Hayden, *The Grand Domestic Revolution: A History of Feminist Designs for American Homes, Neighborhoods, and Cities* (1981)

Scott Molloy, *Trolley Wars: Streetcar Workers on the Line* (1996)

Mark H. Rose, *Cities of Light and Heat: Domesticating Gas and Electricity in Urban America* (1995)

Carl Smith, *Urban Disorder and the Shape of Belief: The Great Chicago Fire, the Haymarket Bomb, and the Model Town of Pullman* (1995)

John R. Stilgoe, *Borderland: Origins of the American Suburb, 1820–1939* (1988)

The New South

Edward L. Ayers, *The Promise of the New South* (1992)

Don Doyle, *New Men, New Cities, New South* (1990)

Jacquelyn Dowd Hall, et al., *Like a Family: The Making of a Southern Cotton Mill World* (1987, 2000)

Gerald D. Jaynes, *Branches without Roots: Genesis of the Black Working Class in the American South, 1862–1882* (1986)

Lawrence H. Larsen, *The Rise of the Urban South* (1985)

Cathy McHugh, *Mill Family: The Labor System in the Southern Textile Industry, 1880–1915* (1988)

Karin A. Shapiro, *A New South Rebellion: The Battle Against Convict Labor in the Tennessee Coalfields, 1871–1896* (1998)

Rise of Consumer Society

Elaine S. Abelson, *When Ladies Go A-Thieving* (1989)

Stuart Blumin, *The Emergence of the Middle Class* (1989)

Sarah Burns, *Inventing the Modern Artist: Art and Culture in Gilded Age America* (1996)

Yong Chen, *Chinese San Francisco, 1850–1943* (2000)

Priscilla Ferguson Clement, *Growing Pains: Children in the Industrial Age, 1850–1890* (1997)

Steven Conn, *Museums and American Intellectual Life, 1876–1926* (1998)

Perry Duis, *Challenging Chicago: Coping with Everyday Life, 1837–1920* (1998)

Warren Goldstein, *Playing for Keeps: A History of Early Baseball* (1989)

Katherine C. Grier, *Culture and Comfort: Parlor Making and Middle-Class Identity, 1850–1930* (1988, 1997)

Judy Hilkey, *Character Is Capital: Success Manuals and Manhood in Gilded Age America* (1997)

John F. Kasson, *Amusing the Millions: Coney Island at the Turn of the Century* (1978)

Lawrence W. Levine, *Highbrow/Lowbrow: The Emergence of Cultural Hierarchy in America* (1988)

Patricia Marks, *Bicycles, Bangs, and Bloomers: The New Woman in the Popular Press* (1990)

Madelon Powers, *Faces along the Bar: Lore and Order in the Working-Man's Saloon, 1870–1920* (1998)

Steven A. Riess, *City Games: The Evolution of American Urban Society and the Rise of Sports* (1989)

Leigh Eric Schmidt, *Consumer Rites: The Buying and Selling of American Holidays* (1995)

Biography

Ron Chernow, *Titan: The Life of John D. Rockefeller, Sr.* (1998)

Helen Lefkowitz Horowitz, *The Power and Passion of M. Carey Thomas* (1994)

Paul Israel, *Edison: A Life of Invention* (1998)

Harold Livesay, *Andrew Carnegie and the Rise of Big Business*, 2d ed. (2000)

Craig Phelan, *Grand Master Workman: Terence Powderly and the Knights of Labor* (2000)

Jean Strouse, *Morgan: American Financier* (1999)

Robert C. Twombly, *Louis Sullivan* (1986)

Michael Zuckerman, *Almost Chosen People: Oblique Biographies in the American Grain* (1993)

CHAPTER 20

The Nation and Politics

Paula C. Baker, *The Moral Frameworks of Public Life: Gender, Politics and the State in Rural New York, 1870–1930* (1991)

Michael Lewis Goldberg, *An Army of Women: Gender and Politics in Gilded Age Kansas* (1997)

J. William Harris, *Deep Souths: Delta, Piedmont, and Sea Island Society in the Age of Segregation* (2001)

Erika Lee, *At America's Gates: Chinese Immigration during the Exclusion Era, 1882–1943* (2003)

Gwendolyn Mink, *Old Labor and New Immigrants in American Political Development* (1986)

Nell Irvin Painter, *Standing at Armageddon: The United States, 1877–1919* (1987)

Douglas Steeples and David O. Whitten, *Democracy in Desperation: The Depression of 1893* (1998)

Brook Thomas, Plessy v. Ferguson: A Brief History with Documents (1997)

David Traxel, 1898: The Birth of the American Century (1998)

C. Vann Woodward, The Strange Career of Jim Crow, 3rd rev. ed. (1974)

Populism

Peter Argersinger, The Limits of Agrarian Radicalism: Western Populism and American Politics (1995)

Lawrence Goodwyn, Democratic Promise: The Populist Moment in America (1976)

Steven Hahn, The Roots of Southern Populism (1983)

Robert C. McMath, American Populism: A Social History (1993)

Scott G. McNall, The Road to Rebellion: Class Formation and Kansas Populism 1865–1900 (1988)

Norman Pollack, The Humane Economy: Populism, Capitalism and Democracy (1990)

Protest and Reform Movements

Ruth Bordin, Woman and Temperance: The Quest for Power and Liberty, 1873–1900 (1981)

Susan Curtis, A Consuming Faith: The Social Gospel and Modern American Culture (1991)

Barbara Leslie Epstein, The Politics of Domesticity: Women, Evangelism, and Temperance in Nineteenth-Century America (1981)

Paul Krause, The Battle for Homestead, 1880–1892 (1992)

Ralph E. Luker, The Social Gospel in Black and White (1991)

Alison M. Parker, Purifying America: Women, Cultural Reform, and Pro-Censorship Activism, 1873–1933 (1997)

Gretchen Ritter, Goldbugs and Greenbacks: The Antimonopoly Tradition and the Politics of Finance in America, 1865–1896 (1997)

Richard Schneirov, Shelton Stromquist, and Nick Salvatore, eds., The Pullman Strike and the Crisis of the 1890s: Essays on Labor and Politics (1999)

Carlos A. Schwantes, Coxey's Army (1985)

Gary Scott Smith, The Search for Social Salvation: Social Christianity and America, 1880–1925 (2000)

Imperialism and Empire

Tunde Adeleke, Unafrican Americans: Nineteenth-Century Black Nationalists and the Civilizing Mission (1998)

Nupur Chaudhuri and Margaret Strobel, eds., Western Women and Imperialism (1992)

Willard B. Gatewood, Jr., Black Americans and the White Man's Burden (1975)

Patricia Hill, The World Their Household: The American Women's Foreign Mission Movement and Cultural Transformation, 1870–1920 (1985)

Amy Kaplan and Donald E. Pease, eds., Cultures of United States Imperialism (1993)

Emily S. Rosenberg, Spreading the American Dream: American Economic and Cultural Expansion, 1890–1945 (1982)

Robert W. Rydell, All the World's a Fair: Vision of Empire at the American International Expositions, 1876–1916 (1984)

Anders Stephanson, Manifest Destiny: American Expansion and the Empire of Right (1995)

Spanish–American War and the Philippines

Virginia M. Bouvier, ed., Whose America? The War of 1898 and the Battles to Define the Nation (2001)

H. W. Brands, Bound to Empire: The United States and the Philippines (1992)

Kristin L. Hoganson, Fighting for American Manhood: How Gender Politics Provoked the Spanish–American and Philippine–American Wars (1998)

Brian McAllister Linn, The Philippine War, 1899–1902 (2000)

Stuart Creighton Miller, "Benevolent Assimilation": The American Conquest of the Philippines, 1899–1903 (1982)

Ivan Musicant, Empire By Default: The Spanish-American War and the Dawn of the American Century (1998)

Louis A. Perez, Jr., The War of 1898: The United States and Cuba in History and Historiography (1998)

Harvey Rosenfeld, Diary of a Dirty Little War: The Spanish–American War of 1898 (2000)

Angel Smith and Emma Davila-Cox, eds., The Crisis of 1898: Colonial Redistribution and Nationalist Mobilization (1999)

Biography

Ruth Bordin, Frances Willard: A Biography (1986)

Mari Jo Buhle, Paul Buhle, and Harvey J. Kaye, eds., The American Radical (1995)

Edward P. Crapol, James G. Blaine: Architect of Empire (2000)

Bruce J. Evensen, God's Man for the Gilded Age: D.L. Moody and the Rise of Modern Mass Evangelism (2003)

Jane Taylor Nelsen, A Prairie Populist: The Memoirs of Luna Kellie (1992)

Allan Peskin, Garfield: A Biography (1978)

Ben Procter, William Randolph Hearst: The Early Years, 1863–1910 (1998)

Nick Salvatore, Eugene V. Debs (1982)

Peggy Samuels and Harold Samuels, Teddy Roosevelt at San Juan: The Making of a President (1997)

Patricia A. Schechter, Ida B. Wells-Barnett and American Reform, 1880–1930 (2001)

C. Van Woodward, Tom Watson (1963)

CHAPTER 21

The Currents of Progressivism

Walter M. Brasch, Forerunners of Revolution: Muckrakers and the American Social Conscience (1990)

John D. Buenker, Urban Liberalism and Progressive Reform (1973)

Mina Carson, Settlement Folk: Social Thought and the American Settlement Movement, 1885–1930 (1990)

Nancy Cohen, Reconstruction of American Liberalism, 1865–1914 (2002)

Leon Fink, Progressive Intellectuals and the Dilemmas of Democratic Commitment (1997)

Richard Hofstadter, The Age of Reform: From Bryan to FDR (1955)

Robert D. Johnston, The Radical Middle Class: Populist Democracy and the Question of Capitalism in Progressive Era Portland, Oregon (2003)

James T. Kloppenberg, *Uncertain Victory: Social Democracy and Progressivism in European and American Thought, 1870–1920* (1986)

William A. Link, *The Paradox of Southern Progressivism, 1880–1930* (1992)

Richard McCormick, *The Party Period and Public Policy* (1986)

Robert Wiebe, *The Search for Order, 1877–1920* (1967)

Social Control and Its Limits

Paul M. Boyer, *Urban Masses and Moral Order in America, 1820–1920* (1978)

Eldon J. Eisenach, *The Lost Promise of Progressivism* (1994)

Randy D. McBee, *Dance Hall Days: Intimacy and Leisure Among Working-Class Immigrants in the United States* (2000)

Ruth Rosen, *The Lost Sisterhood: Prostitutes in America, 1900–1918* (1982)

Andrea Tone, *The Business of Benevolence: Industrial Paternalism in Progressive America* (1997)

Working-Class Communities and Protest

John Bodnar, *The Transplanted* (1985)

Susan A. Glenn, *Daughters of the Shtetl: Life and Labor in the Immigrant Generation* (1990).

James R. Green, *The World of the Worker: Labor in Twentieth-Century America* (1980)

Alice Kessler-Harris, *Out to Work: A History of Wage-Earning Women in the United States* (1982)

David Montgomery, *The Fall of the House of Labor* (1987)

Kathy Peiss, *Cheap Amusements: Working Women and Leisure in Turn-of-the-Century New York* (1986)

Roy Rosenzweig, *Eight Hours for What We Will* (1983)

Ronald Takaki, *Strangers from a Different Shore: A History of Asian Americans* (1989)

Women's Movements and Black Awakening

Paula Baker, *The Moral Frameworks of Public Life* (1991)

Mari Jo Buhle, *Women and American Socialism* (1983)

Rebecca Edwards, *Angels in the Machinery: Gender in American Party Politics from the Civil War to the Progressive Era* (1997)

Linda Gordon, *Woman's Body, Woman's Right: A Social History of Birth Control* (1976)

Molly Ladd-Taylor, *Mother Work: Women, Child Welfare, and the State, 1890–1930* (1994)

National Progressivism

Kendrick A. Clements, *The Presidency of Woodrow Wilson* (1992)

John M. Cooper Jr., *The Warrior and the Priest: Theodore Roosevelt and Woodrow Wilson* (1983)

Lewis L. Gould, *The Presidency of Theodore Roosevelt* (1991)

Biography

Ellen Chesler, *Woman of Valor: Margaret Sanger and the Birth Control Movement in America* (1992)

Louis R. Harlan, *Booker T. Washington: Wizard of Tuskegee, 1901–1915* (1983)

J. Joseph Huthmacher, *Senator Robert F. Wagner and the Rise of Urban Liberalism* (1971)

Stephen Kantrowitz, *Ben Tillman and the Reconstruction of White Supremacy* (2000)

David Levering Lewis, *W.E.B. Du Bois: Biography of a Race, 1868–1919* (1993)

Nick Salvatore, *Eugene V. Debs: Citizen and Socialist* (1982)

Patricia A. Schechter, *Ida B. Wells-Barnett and American Reform, 1880–1930* (2001)

Kathryn Kish Sklar, *Florence Kelley and the Nation's Work* (1995)

Bernard A. Weisberger, *The LaFollettes of Wisconsin* (1994)

Robert Westbrook, *John Dewey and American Democracy* (1991)

CHAPTER 22

Becoming a World Power

Richard H. Collin, *Theodore Roosevelt's Caribbean* (1990)

John M. Hart, *Empire and Revolution: The Americans in Mexico Since the Civil War* (2002).

Walter LaFeber, *The Panama Canal* (1978)

Lester E. Langley, *The Banana Wars: An Inner History of American Empire, 1900–1934* (1983)

Mary A. Renda, *Taking Haiti: Military Occupation and the Culture of U.S. Imperialism, 1915–1940* (2001)

The Great War

Lloyd E. Ambrosius, *Woodrow Wilson and the American Diplomatic Tradition* (1987)

Paul Fussell, *The Great War and Modern Memory* (1973)

Martin Gilbert, *The First World War: A Complete History* (1994)

James Joll, *The Origins of the First World War* (1984)

American Mobilization

A. E. Barbeau and Florette Henri, *The Unknown Soldiers: Black American Troops in World War I* (1974)

John W. Chambers, *To Raise an Army: The Draft in Modern America* (1987)

Nancy Gentile Ford, *Americans All! Foreign Born Soldiers in World War I* (2001).

Stephen Vaughn, *Holding Fast the Inner Lines: Democracy, Nationalism, and the Committee on Public Information* (1980)

Over Here

Allen J. Brandt, *No Magic Bullet: A Social History of Venereal Disease in the United States since 1880* (1985)

Leslie M. DeBauche, *Reel Patriotism: The Movies and World War I* (1997)

Frances R. Early, *A World Without War: How U.S. Feminists and Pacifists Resisted World War I* (1997)

Margaret Mary Finnegan, *Selling Suffrage: Consumer Culture and Votes for Women* (1999)

Maureen Greenwald, *Women, War, and Work* (1980)

Ellis W. Hawley, *The Great War and the Search for Modern Order*, 2d ed. (1992)

Jeffrey Haydu, *Making American Industries Safe for Democracy* (1997)

David M. Kennedy, *Over Here* (1980)

Barbara Steinson, *American Women's Activism in World War I* (1982)

Neil A. Wynn, *From Progressivism to Prosperity: World War I and American Society* (1986)

Repression and Reaction

James P. Grossman, *Land of Hope: Chicago, Black Southerners, and the Great Migration* (1989)

Frederick C. Luebke, *Bonds of Loyalty: German Americans and World War I* (1974)

Regin Schmidt, *Red Scare: The FBI and the Origins of Anticommunism in the United States, 1919–1943* (2000)

Mark Robert Schneider, *"We Return Fighting": The Civil Rights Movement in the Jazz Age* (2002).

An Uneasy Peace

Dana Frank, *Purchasing Power: Consumer Organizing, Gender, and the Seattle Labor Movement, 1919–1929* (1994)

Lloyd Gardner, *Safe for Democracy: The Anglo-American Response to Revolution, 1913–1923* (1984)

Robert D. Johnson, *The Peace Progressives and American Foreign Relations* (1995)

Carol Wilcox Melton, *Between War and Peace: Woodrow Wilson and the American Expeditionary Force in Siberia, 1918–1921* (2002).

Richard Polenberg, *Fighting Faiths: The Abrams Case, the Supreme Court, and Free Speech* (1987)

Daniel D. Stid, *The President As Statesman: Woodrow Wilson and the Constitution* (1998)

Biography

Kendrick Clements, *Woodrow Wilson: World Statesman* (1987)

Ellen Carol DuBois, *Harriot Stanton Blatch and the Winning of Woman Suffrage* (1997)

Frank E. Vandiver, *Black Jack: The Life and Times of John J. Pershing* (1977)

Jacqueline van Voris, *Carrie Chapman Catt* (1987)

Warren Zimmerman, *First Great Triumph: How Five Americans Made Their Country A World Power* (2002).

CHAPTER 23

Postwar Prosperity and Its Price

David Brody, *Workers in Industrial America* (1980)

Gilbert C. Fite, *Cotton Fields No More: Southern Agriculture, 1865–1980* (1984)

Ellis W. Hawley, *The Great War and the Search for Modern Order* (1979).

Kenneth T. Jackson, *Crabgrass Frontier* (1985)

William Leuchtenberg, *The Perils of Prosperity, 1914–1932* (1958)

Clay McShane, *Down the Asphalt Path* (1994)

Gwendolyn Wright, *Building the American Dream* (1981)

Gerald Zahavi, *Workers, Managers, and Welfare Capitalism* (1988)

The New Mass Culture

Beth A. Bailey, *From Front Porch to Back Seat: Courtship in Twentieth-Century America* (1988)

Douglas B. Craig, *Fireside Politics: Radio and Political Culture in the United States, 1920–1940* (2000)

Daniel J. Czitrom, *Media and the American Mind* (1982)

John D'Emilio and Estelle B. Freedman, *Intimate Matters: A History of Sexuality in America* (1988)

Susan J. Douglas, *Listening In: Radio and the American Imagination* (1999)

Pamela Walker Laird, *Advertising Progress: American Business and the Rise of Consumer Marketing* (1998)

Jackson Lears, *Fables of Abundance: A Cultural History of Advertising in America* (1994)

Roland Marchand, *Advertising the American Dream: Making Way for Modernity, 1920–1940* (1985).

Steven J. Ross, *Working Class Hollywood: Silent Film and the Shaping of Class in America* (1998)

Robert Sklar, *Movie Made America*, rev. ed. (1995)

Resistance to Modernity

Katherine M. Blee, *Women and the Klan: Racism and Gender in the 1920s* (1991)

John Higham, *Strangers in the Land: Patterns of American Nativism, 1860–1925* (1955)

Edward J. Larson, *Summer of the Gods: The Scopes Trial and America's Continuing Debate Over Science* (1997)

Mae M. Ngai, *Impossible Subjects: Illegal Aliens and the Making of Modern America* (2004)

Thomas R. Pegram, *Battling Demon Rum: The Struggle for a Dry America, 1800–1933* (1998)

Daniel J. Tichenor, *Dividing Lines: Immigration Control in America* (2002)

The State, the Economy, and Business

Kendrick A. Clements, *Hoover, Conservation, and Consumerism: Engineering the Good Life* (2000)

Warren I. Cohen, *Empire without Tears* (1987)

Louis Galambos and Joseph Pratt, *The Rise of the Corporate Commonwealth* (1988)

John Earl Haynes, ed., *Calvin Coolidge and the Coolidge Era* (1998)

Roland Marchand, *Creating the Corporate Soul: The Rise of Public Relations and Corporate Imagery in American Big Business* (1998)

Charles L. Mee, *The Ohio Gang: The World of Warren G. Harding* (1981)

Emily S. Rosenberg, *Spreading the American Dream* (1982)

Promises Postponed

Nancy F. Cott, *The Grounding of American Feminism* (1987)

Ann Douglas, *Terrible Honesty: Mongrel Manhattan in the 1920s* (1995)

Nathan I. Huggins, *Harlem Renaissance* (1971)

Cary D. Mintz, *Black Culture and the Harlem Renaissance* (1988)

Kathy H. Ogren, *The Jazz Revolution: Twenties America and the Meaning of Jazz* (1989)

George J. Sanchez, *Becoming Mexican American* (1993)

Mark Robert Schneider, *"We Return Fighting": The Civil Rights Movement in the Jazz Age* (2002)

Judith Stein, *The World of Marcus Garvey* (1985)

Biography

Edith L. Blumhofer, *Aimee Semple McPherson* (1993)

David Burner, *Herbert Hoover: The Public Life* (1979)

Robert Creamer, *Babe: The Legend Comes to Life* (1975)

Neal Gabler, *Winchell: Gossip, Power, and the Culture of Celebrity* (1994)

Fred Hobson, *Mencken: A Life* (1994)

David Levering Lewis, *W. E. B. DuBois: The Fight for Equality and the American Century, 1919–1963* (2000)

David Nasaw, *The Chief: The Life of William Randolph Hearst* (2000)

Arnold Rampersad, *The Life of Langston Hughes*, 2 vols. (1986–88)

Robert A. Slayton, *Empire Statesman: The Rise and Redemption of Al Smith* (2001)

CHAPTER 24

Hard Times

Michael A. Bernstein, *The Great Depression* (1987)

Michael D. Bordo, et al., eds., *The Defining Moment: The Great Depression and the American Economy in the Twentieth Century* (1998)

John A. Garraty, *The Great Depression* (1986)

Robert S. McElvaine, ed., *Down and Out in the Great Depression* (1983)

Janet Poppendieck, *Breadlines Knee-Deep in Wheat* (1986)

Jeff Singleton, *The American Dole: Unemployment Relief and the Welfare State in the Great Depression* (2000)

Studs Terkel, *Hard Times* (1970)

T.H. Watkins, *The Hungry Years: A Narrative History of the Great Depression in America* (1999)

Elmos Wicker, *The Banking Panics of the Great Depression* (1996)

FDR and the First New Deal

Paul K. Conkin, *The New Deal*, 2d ed. (1975)

Steve Fraser and Gary Gerstle, eds., *The Rise and Fall of the New Deal Order* (1988)

Ellis Hawley, *The New Deal and the Problem of Monopoly* (1966)

William Leuchtenberg, *The FDR Years* (1995)

George McJimsey, *The Presidency of Franklin Delano Roosevelt* (2000)

James S. Olson, *Saving Capitalism* (1988)

Albert U. Romasco, *The Politics of Recovery: Roosevelt's New Deal* (1983)

Theodore M. Saloutos, *The American Farmer and the New Deal* (1982)

Left Turn and the Second New Deal

Kristi Andersen, *The Creation of a Democratic Majority, 1928–1936* (1979)

Irving Bernstein, *The Turbulent Years: A History of the American Worker, 1933–1941* (1970)

John Braeman et al., eds., *The New Deal: The State and Local Levels* (1975).

Alan Brinkley, *Voices of Protest: Huey Long, Father Coughlin, and the New Deal* (1982)

Peter Friedlander, *The Emergence of a UAW Local* (1975)

Gary Gerstle, *Working Class Americanism* (1989)

Kenneth J. Heineman, *A Catholic New Deal: Religion and Reform in Depression Pittsburgh* (1999)

Robin D. G. Kelley, *Hammer and Hoe: Alabama Communists during the Great Depression* (1990)

Joseph P. Lash, *Dealers and Dreamers* (1988)

Roy Lubove, *The Struggle for Social Security* (1968)

Robert H. Zieger, *The CIO, 1935–1955* (1995)

The New Deal and the West

James M. Gregory, *American Exodus: The Dust Bowl Migration and Okie Culture in California* (1989)

Norris Hundley Jr., *The Great Thirst: California and Water, 1770s–1990s* (1992)

Laurence Kelly, *The Assault on Assimilation: John Collier and the Origins of Indian Policy Reform, 1920–1954* (1983)

Vicki Ruiz, *Cannery Women/Cannery Lives: Mexican Women, Unionization, and the California Food Processing Industry, 1930–1950* (1987)

Charles J. Shindo, *Dust Bowl Migrants in the American Imagination* (1997)

Kevin Starr, *Endangered Dreams: The Great Depression in California* (1996)

Graham D. Taylor, *The New Deal and American Indian Tribalism* (1980)

Donald Worster, *Dust Bowl* (1979)

Depression-Era Culture

Thomas P. Doherty, *Pre-Code Hollywood: Sex, Immorality, and Insurrection in American Cinema, 1930–1934* (1999)

Lewis A. Erenberg, *Swingin' the Dream: Big Band Jazz and the Rebirth of American Culture* (1998)

Vivian Gornick, *The Romance of American Communism* (1976)

Harvey Klehr, *The Heyday of American Communism* (1984)

Anthony W. Lee, *Painting on the Left* (1999)

J. Fred MacDonald, *Don't Touch That Dial* (1979)

Richard McKinzie, *The New Deal for Artists* (1973)

Barbara Melosh, *Engendering Culture: Manhood and Womanhood in New Deal Public Art and Theater* (1991)

David P. Peeler, *Hope among Us Yet* (1987)

Richard H. Pells, *Radical Visions and American Dreams: Culture and Social Thought in the Depression Years* (1973)

Thomas Schatz, *The Genius of the System: Hollywood Filmmaking in the Studio Era* (1988)

William Stott, *Documentary Expression and Thirties America* (1973).

The Limits of Reform

Francisco E. Balderrama, *Decade of Betrayal: Mexican Repatriation in the 1930s* (1995)

Suzanne Mettler, *Dividing Citizens: Gender and Federalism in New Deal Public Works* (1998)

Mark Naison, *Communists in Harlem during the Depression* (1983)

James T. Patterson, *Congressional Conservatism and the New Deal* (1967)

Landon R.Y. Storrs, *Civilizing Capitalism: The National Consumers' League, Women's Activism, and Labor Standards in the New Deal Era* (2000)

Patricia Sullivan, *Days of Hope: Race and Democracy in the New Deal Era* (1996)

Susan Ware, *Beyond Suffrage: Women in the New Deal* (1981)

———, *Partner and I: Molly Dewson, Feminism, and New Deal Politics* (1987)

Nancy J. Weiss, *Farewell to the Party of Lincoln: Black Politics in the Age of FDR* (1983)

G. Edward White, *The Constitution and the New Deal* (2000)

Robert L. Zangrando, *The NAACP Crusade against Lynching* (1980)

Biography

David Burner, *Herbert Hoover* (1978)

Blanche W. Cook, *Eleanor Roosevelt: A Life* (1992)

Kenneth S. Davis, *FDR*, 4 vols. (1972, 1975, 1986, 1992)

Steven Fraser, *Labor Will Rule: Sidney Hillman and the Rise of American Labor* (1991)

Dorothy Healey and Maurice Isserman, *California Red: A Life in the American Communist Party* (1990)

June Hopkins, *Harry Hopkins: Sudden Hero, Brash Reformer* (1999)

J. Joseph Huthmacher, *Robert F. Wagner and the Rise of Urban Liberalism* (1968)

Nelson Lichtenstein, *The Most Dangerous Man in Detroit: Walter Reuther and the Fate of American Labor* (1995)

Karen Becker Ohrn, *Dorothea Lange and the Documentary Tradition* (1980)

Naomi E. Pasachoff, *Frances Perkins: Champion of the New Deal* (1999)

Lois Scharf, *Eleanor Roosevelt* (1987)

Robert Zieger, *John L. Lewis* (1988)

CHAPTER 25

Coming of World War II

Justus D. Doenecke, *Storm on the Horizon: The Challenge to American Intervention, 1939–1941* (2000)

Akira Iriye, *The Origins of the Second World War in Asia and the Pacific* (1987)

Deborah Lipstadt, *Beyond Belief: The American Press and the Coming of the Holocaust, 1933–1945* (1986)

Ernest Mandel, *The Meaning of the Second World War* (1986)

Geoffrey S. Smith, *To Save a Nation* (1992)

Robert B. Stinnett, *Day of Deceit: The Truth about FDR and Pearl Harbor* (2000)

Arsenal of Democracy and the Home Front

Karen Anderson, *Wartime Women* (1981)

Amy Bentley, *Eating for Victory: Food Rationing and the Politics of Domesticity* (1998)

Alison R. Bernstein, *American Indians and World War II* (1991)

Dominic J. Capeci and Martha Wilkerson, *Layered Violence: The Detroit Rioters of 1943* (1991)

Paul D. Casdorph, *Let the Good Times Roll: Life at Home in America During World War II* (1989)

Charles D. Chamberlain, *Victory at Home: Manpower and Race in the American South during World War II* (2003)

Roger Daniels, *Concentration Camps USA: Japanese Americans and World War II* (1971)

Thomas Doherty, *Projections of War: Hollywood, American Culture and World War II* (1993)

Lewis A. Erenberg and Susan E. Hirsch, eds., *The War in American Culture: Society and Consciousness During World War II* (1996)

Sherna Berger Gluck, *Rosie the Riveter Revisited: Women, the War, and Social Change* (1987).

Rachel Waltner Goosen, *Women Against the Good War: Conscientious Objection and Gender on the American Home Front, 1941–1947* (1997)

Maureen Honey, *Bitter Fruit: African American Women in World War II* (1999)

Daniel Kryder, *Divided Arsenal: Race and the American State during World War II* (2000)

Roger W. Lotchin, *The Bad City in the Good War: San Francisco, Los Angeles, Oakland, and San Diego* (2003)

Gary Y. Okihiro, *Whispered Silences: Japanese Americans and World War II* (1996)

Greg Robinson, *By Order of the President: FDR and the Internment of Japanese Americans* (2001)

George H. Roeder, *The Censored War: American Visual Experience during World War II* (1993)

Lawrence R. Samuel, *Pledging Allegiance: American Identity and the Bond Drive of World War II* (1997)

Bartholomew H. Sparrow, *From the Outside In: World War II and the American State* (1996)

Kevin Starr, *Embattled Dreams: California in War and Peace, 1940–1950* (2002)

William M. Tuttle Jr., *"Daddy's Gone to War": The Second World War in the Lives of America's Children* (1993)

World at War

William H. Bartsch, *December 8, 1941: MacArthur's Pearl Harbor* (2003)

Alison Bernstein, *American Indians and World War II* (1991)

Conrad C. Crane, *Bombs, Cities, and Civilians* (1993)

John W. Dower, *War without Mercy* (1986)

Akira Iriye, *Power and Culture: The Japanese-American War, 1941–1945* (1981)

Lee Kennett, *G.I.: The American Soldier in World War II* (1987)

Eric Markusen and David Kopf, *The Holocaust and Strategic Bombing: Genocide and Total War in the Twentieth Century* (1995)

Peter Maslowski, *Armed with Cameras: The American Military Photographers of World War II* (1993)

Brenda L. Moore, *Serving Our Country: Japanese American Women in the Military during World War II* (2003)

Williamson Murray and Allan R. Millett, *A War to be Won: Fighting the Second World War* (2000)

Barbara Brooks Tomblin, *G.I. Nightingales: The Army Nurse Corps in World War II* (1996)

David S. Wyman, *The Abandonment of the Jews: America and the Holocaust, 1941–1945* (1984)

Last Stages of War

John D. Chappell, *Before the Bomb: How America Approached the End of the Pacific War* (1997)

David P. Colley, *Blood for Dignity: The Story of the First Integrated Combat Unit in the U.S. Army* (2003)

Paul Fussell, *The Boy's Crusade: The American Infantry in Northwestern Europe, 1944–1945* (2003)

Lloyd C. Gardner, *Spheres of Influence: The Great Powers Partition Europe, from Munich to Yalta* (1993)

Peter Schrijvers, *The Crash of Ruin: American Combat Soldiers in Europe during World War II* (1998)

Michael S. Sherry, *The Rise of American Air Power* (1987)

Atomic Bomb

Gar Alperovitz, *The Decision to Use the Atomic Bomb and the Architecture of an American Myth* (1995)

Paul Boyer, *By the Bomb's Early Light: American Thought and Culture at the Dawn of the Atomic Age* (1985)

Peter Bacon Hales, *Atomic Spaces: Living on the Manhattan Project* (1997)

Ruth H. Howes, *Their Day in the Sun: Women of the Manhattan Project* (1999)

J. Samuel Walker, *Prompt and Utter Destruction: Truman and the Use of Atomic Bombs against Japan* (1997)

Eileen Welsome, *The Plutonium Files: America's Secret Medical Experiments in the Cold War* (1999)

Biography/Memoir

Mark M. Anderson, ed., *Hitler's Exiles: Personal Stories of the Flight from Nazi Germany to America* (1998)

Jeremy Bernstein, *Oppenheimer: Portrait of an Enigma* (2004)

Carlo D'Este, *Patton: A Genius for War* (1995)

Preston John Hubbard, *Apocalypse Undone: My Survival of Japanese Imprisonment during World War II* (1990)

Paula F. Pfeffer, *A. Philip Randolph* (1990)

Robert Underhill, *FDR and Harry: Unparalleled Lives* (1996)

CHAPTER 26

Global Insecurities and the Policy of Containment

Christian G. Appy, ed., *Cold War Constructions: The Political Culture of United States Imperialism, 1945–1966* (2000)

H. W. Brands Jr., *The Devil We Knew: Americans and the Cold War* (1993)

Warren I. Cohen, *America in the Age of Soviet Power, 1945–1991* (1993)

John Gaddis, *We Now Know: Rethinking Cold War History* (1997)

Walter Hixson, *Parting the Curtain: Propaganda, Culture, and the Cold War, 1945–1961* (1997)

Townsend Hoopes and Douglas Brinkley, *FDR and the Creation of the U.N.* (1997)

Walter LaFeber, *America, Russia, and the Cold War, 1945–1992*, 7th ed. (1993)

Arnold A. Offner, *Another Such Victory: President Truman and the Cold War* (2002)

Arch Puddington, *Broadcasting Freedom: The Cold War Triumph of Radio Free Europe and Radio Liberty* (2000)

Richard Rhodes, *Dark Sun: The Making of the Hydrogen Bomb* (1995)

David F. Rudgers, *Creating the Secret State: The Origins of the Central Intelligence Angency, 1943–1947* (2000)

Michael Schaller, *American Occupation of Japan: The Origins of the Cold War in Asia* (1985)

The Truman Presidency

Gary A. Donaldson, *Truman Defeats Dewey* (1999)

Michael R. Gardner, *Harry Truman and Civil Rights* (2002)

Zachary Karabell, *The Last Campaign: How Harry Truman Won the 1948 Election* (2000)

Melvyn P. Leffler, *A Preponderance of Power: National Security, the Truman Administration, and the Cold War* (1992)

Steve Neal, ed., *HST: Memories of the Truman Years* (2003)

Sean J. Savage, *Truman and the Democratic Party* (1997)

The Cold War at Home

Larry Ceplair and Steven Englund, *The Inquisition in Hollywood: Politics in the Film Community, 1930–1960* (1980)

Noam Chomsky, ed., *The Cold War and the University: Toward an Intellectual History of the Postwar Years* (1997)

Sigmund Diamond, *Compromised Campus: The Collaboration of Universities with the Intelligence Community, 1945–1995* (1992)

Andrew D. Grossman, *Neither Dead Nor Red: Civilian Defense and American Political Development During the Early Cold War* (2001)

Michael J. Hogan, *A Cross of Iron: Harry S Truman and the Origins of the National Security State, 1945–1954* (1998)

Scott Lucas, *Freedom's War: The American Crusade Against the Soviet Union* (1999)

Patrick McGilligan and Paul Buhle, *Tender Comrades: A Backstory of the Hollywood Blacklist* (1997).

Lisle A. Rose, *The Cold War Comes to Main Street: America in 1950* (1999)

Ellen Schrecker, *Many Are the Crimes: McCarthyism in America* (1998)

Ellen W. Schrecker, *No Ivory Tower: McCarthyism and the Universities* (1986)

Cold War Culture

Michael Barson, *"Better Dead Than Red!" A Nostalgic Look at the Golden Years of Russiaphobia, Red-Baiting, and Other Commie Madness* (1992)

Paul Buhle and Dave Wagner, *Radical Hollywood* (2002)

George Lipsitz, *A Rainbow at Midnight: Labor and Culture in the 1940s* (1994).

Lary May, ed., *Recasting America: Culture and Politics in the Age of the Cold War* (1989)

Elaine McClarnand and Steve Goodson, eds., *The Impact of the Cold War on American Popular Culture* (1999)

John L. Rudolph, *Scientists in the Classroom: the Cold War Reconstruction of American Science Education* (2002)

David Seed, *American Science Fiction and the Cold War* (1999)

Joanne P. Sharp, *Condensing the Cold War: Reader's Digest and American Identity* (2000)

Jessica Wang, *American Science in an Age of Anxiety: Scientists, Anticommunism, and the Cold War* (1999)

Korean War

Bevin Alexander, *Korea: The First War We Lost*, rev. ed., 2000

William T. Bowers, William M. Hammond, George L. MacGarrigle, *Black Solider, White Army: The 24th Infantry Regiment in Korea* (1996)

Albert E. Cowdrey, *The Medics' War* (1987)

Stephen Endicott and Edward Hagerman, *The United States and Biological Warfare: Secrets from the Early Cold War and Korea* (1998)

Paul G. Pierpaoli Jr., *Truman and Korea: The Political Culture of the Early Cold War* (1999)

Ron Robin, *The Making of the Cold War Enemy* (2001)

Stanley Sandler, *The Korean War: No Victors, No Vanquished* (1999)

Biography

Allida M. Black, *Casting Her Own Shadow: Eleanor Roosevelt and the Shaping of Postwar Liberalism* (1996)

John C. Culver, *American Dreamer: The Life and Times of Henry A. Wallace* (2000)

Martin Bauml Duberman, *Paul Robeson* (1988)

Curt Gentry, *J. Edgar Hoover: The Man and the Secrets* (1991)

Alonzo L. Hamby, *Man of the People: A Life of Harry S Truman* (1995)

Arthur Herman, *Joseph McCarthy: Reexamining the Life and Legacy of America's Most Hated Senator* (1999)

Robert M. Lichtman, *Deadly Farce: Harvey Matusow and the Informer System in the McCarthy Era* (2004)

David G. McCullough, *Truman* (1992)

Wilson D. Miscamble, *George F Kennan and the Making of American Foreign Policy, 1947–1950* (1992)

Geoffrey Perret, *Old Soldiers Never Die: The Life of Douglas MacArthur* (1996)

CHAPTER 27

American Society at Midcentury

Roslayn Fraad Baxandall and Elizabeth Ewen, *Picture Windows: How the Suburbs Happened* (2000)

Stephanie Coontz, *The Way We Never Were* (1992)

John P. Diggins, *The Proud Decades: America in War and Peace, 1941–1960* (1988)

Benita Eisler, *Private Lives: Men and Women of the Fifties* (1986)

Adam Ward Rome, *The Bulldozer in the Countryside: Suburban Sprawl and the Rise of American Environmentalism* (2001)

Jessica Weiss, *To Have and to Hold: Marriage, the Baby Boom and Social Change* (2000)

Youth Culture

Wini Breines, *Young, White, and Miserable: Growing Up Female in the Fifties* (1992)

Thomas Doherty, *Teen Pics* (1994)

Nelson George, *The Death of Rhythm and Blues* (1988)

James B. Gilbert, *A Cycle of Outrage: America's Reaction to the Juvenile Delinquent in the 1950s* (1986)

Kirse Granat May, *Golden State, Golden Youth: The California Image in Popular Culture* (2002)

Jim Miller, *Flowers in the Dustbin: The Rise of Rock and Roll, 1947–1977* (1999)

Mass Culture and Its Discontents

Erik Barnouw, *Tube of Plenty* (1982)

Nancy E. Bernhard, *U.S. Television News and Cold War Propaganda, 1947–1960* (1999)

Joel Foreman, ed., *The Other Fifties: Interrogating Midcentury American Icons* (1997)

George Lipsitz, *Time Passages* (1990).

J. Fred MacDonald, *Television and the Red Menace* (1985)

David Marc, *Demographic Vistas: Television and American Culture* (1984)

Lynn Spigel, *Make Room for TV* (1992)

Stephen J. Whitfield, *The Culture of the Cold War* (1991)

The Cold War Continued

James G. Blight and Peter Kornbluh, eds., *Politics of Illusion: The Bay of Pigs Invasion Reexamined* (1999)

Robert R. Bowie, *Waging Peace: How Eisenhower Shaped an Enduring Cold War Strategy* (1998)

Nick Cullather, *Secret History: The CIA's Classified Account of its Operations in Guatemala, 1952–1954* (1999)

Paul Dickson, *Sputnik: The Shock of the Century* (2001)

Piero Gleijeses, *Shattered Hope: The Guatemalan Revolution and the United States, 1944–1954* (1991)

Zachary Karabell, *Architects of Intervention: The United States, the Third World, and the Cold War, 1946–1962* (1999)

Richard A. Melanson and David A. Mayers, eds., *Reevaluating Eisenhower* (1986)

John F. Kennedy and the New Frontier

Trumbull Higgins, *The Perfect Failure: Kennedy, Eisenhower, and the CIA at the Bay of Pigs* (1988)

Walter LaFeber, *Inevitable Revolutions* (1983)

Thomas G. Paterson, ed., *Kennedy's Quest for Victory* (1989)

Gerald L. Posner, *Case Closed: Lee Harvey Oswald and the Assassination of JFK* (1993)

Sheldon M. Stern, *Averting 'The Final Failure': John F. Kennedy and the Secret Cuban Missile Crisis Meetings* (2003)

Richard E. Welch Jr., *Response to Revolution: The United States and Cuba, 1959–1961* (1985)

Garry Wills, *The Kennedy Imprisonment* (1983)

Biography

Chuck Berry, *Chuck Berry: The Autobiography* (1987)

Robert Dallek, *An Unfinished Life: John F. Kennedy, 1917–1963* (2003)

Carol George, *God's Salesman: Norman Vincent Peale and the Power of Positive Thinking* (1993)

Peter Guralnick, *Last Train to Memphis: The Rise of Elvis Presley* (1994)

Daniel Horowitz, *Betty Friedan and the Making of the Feminine Mystique* (1998)

Barry Miles, *Allen Ginsberg* (1989)

Gerald Nicosia, *Memory Babe: A Critical Biography of Jack Kerouac* (1983)

Geoffrey Perret, *Eisenhower* (1999)

CHAPTER 28

Origins of the Movements

Michael R. Belknap, *Federal Law and Southern Order* (1987)

Scott DeVeaux, *The Birth of BeBop* (1998)

Grace Elizabeth Hale, *Making Whiteness: The Culture of Segregation in the South, 1890–1940* (1998)

Charles P. Henry, *Ralph Bunche: Model Negro or American Other* (1999)

Grace Williams O'Brien, *The Color of the Law: Race, Violence, and Justice in the Post–World War II South* (1999)

James T. Patterson, Brown v. Board of Education: *A Civil Rights Milestone and Its Troubled Legacy* (2001)

Bernard Schwartz, *The NAACP's Legal Strategy against Segregated Education* (1987)

Mark Tushnet, *Making Civil Rights Law: Thurgood Marshall and the Supreme Court, 1936–1961* (1994)

No Easy Road to Freedom, 1957–62

Clayborne Carson, *In Struggle: SNCC and the Black Awakening of the 1960s* (1981)

William Chafe, *Civilities and Civil Rights: Greensboro, North Carolina, and the Black Struggle for Equality* (1980)

Constance Curry, et al., *Deep In Our Hearts: Nine White Women in the Freedom Movement* (2000)

John Dittmer, *Local People: The Struggle for Civil Rights in Mississippi* (1994)

James Farmer, *Lay Bare the Heart* (1985)

David J. Garrow, *The FBI and Martin Luther King, Jr.* (1983)

Cheryl L. Greenberg, ed., *A Circle of Trust: Remembering SNCC* (1998)

Charles M. Payne, *I've Got the Light of Freedom: The Organizing Tradition and the Mississippi Freedom Struggle* (1995)

Miles Wolff, *Lunch at the 5&10* (1990)

The Movement at High Tide, 1963–65

Seth Cagin and Philip Dray, *We Are Not Afraid* (1988)

Sara Evans, *Personal Politics: The Roots of Women's Liberation in the Civil Rights Movement and the New Left* (1979)

Henry Hampton and Steve Fayer, *Voices of Freedom: An Oral History of the Civil Rights Movement* (1990)

Doug McAdam, *Freedom Summer* (1988)

Diane McWhorter, *Carry Me Home: Birmingham, Alabama: The Climax of the Civil Rights Revolution* (2001)

Belinda Robnett, *How Long? How Long? African American Women in the Struggle for Civil Rights* (1997)

Clive Webb, *Fight Against Fear: Southern Jews and Black Civil Rights* (2001)

Robert Weisbrot, *Freedom Bound: A History of America's Civil Rights Movement* (1990).

Civil Rights Beyond Black and White

Thomas W. Conger, *The National Congress of American Indians* (1999)

Donald Fixico, *Termination and Relocation: Federal Indian Policy, 1945–1960* (1986)

Manuel G. Gonzalez, *Mexicanos: A History of Mexicans in the United States* (1999)

David G. Gutierrez, *Walls and Mirrors: Mexican Americans, Mexican Immigrants, and the Politics of Ethnicity* (1998)

Gabriel Haslip-Viera, et al., eds, *Boricuans in Gotham : Puerto Ricans and the Making of New York City* (2004)

Mae M. Ngai, *Impossible Subjects: Illegal Aliens and the Making of Modern America* (2004)

David Palumbo-Liu, *Asian Americans: Historical Crossings of a Racial Frontier* (1999)

Maria E. Perez y Gonzalez, *Puerto Ricans in the United States* (2000)

Kenneth R. Philip, *Termination Revisited: American Indians on the Trail to Self Determination, 1933–1953* (1999)

Carmen Theresa Whalen, *From Puerto Rico to Philadelphia: Puerto Rican Workers and Postwar Economies* (2001)

Biography

Robert Dallek, *Flawed Giant: Lyndon B. Johnson and His Times, 1961–1973* (1998)

John D'Emilio, *Lost Prophet: The Life and Times of Bayard Rustin* (2003)

Michael Eric Dyson, *I May Not Get There With You: The True Martin Luther King, Jr.* (2000)

James Forman, *The Making of Black Revolutionaries* (1985)

David J. Garrow, *Bearing the Cross: Martin Luther King, Jr., and the Southern Christian Leadership Conference* (1986)

Chana Kai Lee, *For Freedom's Sake: The Life of Fannie Lou Hamer* (1999)

John Lewis, *Walking With the Wind: A Memoir of the Movement* (1998)

Barbara Ramsey, *Ella Baker and the Black Freedom Movement* (2003)

Jo Ann Gibson Robinson, *The Montgomery Bus Boycott and the Women Who Started It* (1987)

Malcolm X, with Alex Haley, *The Autobiography of Malcolm X* (1965)

CHAPTER 29

Vietnam: America's Longest War

David L. Anderson, *The Columbia Guide to the Vietnam War* (2002)

Christian G. Appy, *Working-Class War: American Combat Soldiers in Vietnam* (1993)

Larry Berman, *No Peace, No Honor: Nixon, Kissinger, and Betrayal in Vietnam* (2001)

Robert Buzzanco, *Vietnam and the Transformation of American Life* (1999)

Kenton J. Clymer, *The Vietnam War: Its History, Literature and Music* (1998)

Gerald J. DeGroot, *A Noble Cause? America and the Vietnam War* (1999)

Michael S. Foley, *Confronting the War Machine: Draft Resistance during the Vietnam War* (2003)

Herman Graham III, *The Brothers' War: Black Power, Manhood, and the Military Experience* (2003)

William M Hammond, *Reporting Vietnam: Media and Military at War* (1998)

George C. Herring, *America's Longest War: The United States and Vietnam, 1950–1975*, 3rd ed. (1996)

————, ed., *The Pentagon Papers*, abridged ed. (1993)

Andrew E. Hunt, *The Turning: A History of Vietnam Veterans Against the War* (1999)

David Kaiser, *American Tragedy: Kennedy, Johnson, and the Origins of the Vietnam War* (2000)

Jeffrey Kimball, *Nixon's Vietnam War* (1998)

Fredrik Logevall, *Choosing War: The Lost Chance for Peace and the Escalation of War in Vietnam* (1999)

Robert Mann, *A Grand Illusion: America's Descent into Vietnam* (2001)

James S. Olson and Randy Roberts, *My Lai: A Brief History with Documents* (1998)

Randy Shilts, *Conduct Unbecoming: Lesbians and Gays in the U.S. Military, Vietnam to the Persian Gulf* (1993)

Fred Turner, *Echoes of Combat: The Vietnam War in American Memory* (1996)

James E. Westheider, *Fighting on Two Fronts: African Americans and the Vietnam War* (1997)

Marilyn B. Young, *The Vietnam Wars, 1945–1990* (1991)

A Generation in Conflict

David Allyn, *Make Love, Not War: The Sexual Revolution, Unfettered History* (2000)

Beth Bailey, *Sex in the Heartland* (1999)

Alexander Bloom and Wini Breines, eds., *Takin' It to the Streets: A Sixties Reader* (1995)

Aniko Bodroghkozy, *Groove Tube: Sixties Television and the Youth Rebellion* (2001)

Peter Braunstein and Michael William Doyle, eds., *Imagine Nation: The American Counterculture of the 1960s and '70s* (2002)

Howard Brick, *Age of Contradiction: American Thought and Culture in the 1960s* (1998)

Paul Buhle and John McMillian, eds., *The New Left Revisited* (2003)

David Farber, *The Age of Great Dreams: America in the 1960s* (1994)

James J. Farrell, *The Spirit of the Sixties: The Making of Postwar Radicalism* (1997)

Jennifer Frost, *"An Interracial Movement of the Poor": Community Organizing and the New Left in the 1960s* (2001)

Maurice Isserman and Michael Kazin, *America Divided: The Civil War of the 1960s* (2000)

Paul Lyons, *New Left, New Right, and the Legacy of the Sixties* (1996)

John C. McWilliams, *The 1960s Cultural Revolution* (2000)

Timothy Miller, *The 60s Communes: Hippies and Beyond* (1999)

Mark Oppenheimer, *Knocking on Heaven's Door: American Religion in the Age of Counterculture* (2003)

George Rising, *Clean for Gene: Eugene McCarthy's 1968 Presidential Campaign* (1997)

William L. Van Deburg, *New Day in Babylon: The Black Power Movement and American Culture, 1965–1975* (1992)

Mary Ann Wynkoop, *Dissent in the Heartland: The Sixties at Indiana University* (2002)

The Politics of Identity

Kathleen C. Berkeley, *The Women's Liberation Movement in America* (1999)

Dudley Clendinen and Adam Nagourney, *Out for Good: The Struggle to Build a Gay Rights Movement in America* (1999)

Rachel Blau De Plessis and Ann Snitow, *The Feminist Memoir Project: Voices from Women's Liberation* (1998)

Susan J. Douglas, *Where the Girls Are: Growing Up Female with the Mass Media* (1994)

Martin Duberman, *Stonewall* (1993)

Gerald Horne, *Fire This Time: The Watts Uprising and the 1960s* (1995)

Blance Linden-Ward and Carol Hurd Green, *American Women in the 1960s* (1993)

Marguerite V. Marin, *Social Protest in an Urban Barrio: A Study of the Chicano Movement, 1966–1974* (1991)

Peter Matthiessen, *In the Spirit of Crazy Horse* (1992)

Joane Nagel, *American Indian Ethnic Renewal: Red Power and the Resurgence of Identity and Culture* (1996)

Armando Navarro, *Mexican American Youth Organization: Avant-Garde of the Chicano Movement in Texas* (1995)

Joy Ann Williamson, *Black Power on Campus* (2003)

The Nixon Presidency and Watergate

Mary C. Brennan, *Turning Right in the Sixties: The Conservative Capture of the GOP* (1995)

J. Brooks Flippen, *Nixon and the Environment* (2000)

Leonard Garment, *In Search of Deep Throat: The Greatest Political Mystery of Our Time* (2000)

Lewis L. Gould, *1968: The Election That Changed America* (1993)

Dean J. Kotlowski, *Nixon's Civil Rights: Politics, Principle, and Policy* (2001)

Allen J. Matusow, *Nixon's Economy: Booms, Busts, Dollars and Votes* (1998)

Keith W. Olson, *Watergate: The Presidential Scandal that Shook America* (2003)

Richard Reeves, *President Nixon: Alone in the White House* (2001)

Biography

David L. Anderson, ed., *The Human Tradition in the Vietnam Era* (2000)

Elaine Brown, *A Taste of Power: A Black Woman's Story* (1992)

Jody Carlson, *George C. Wallace and the Politics of Powerlessness* (1981)

Robert Dallek, *Flawed Giant: Lyndon Johnson and His Times, 1961–1973* (1998)

Adam Fortunate Eagle, *Heart of the Rock: The Indian Invasion of Alcatraz* (2002)

Robert Alan Goldberg, *Barry Goldwater* (1995)

Elliot Gorn, ed., *Muhammed Ali: The People's Champ* (1996)

Joan Hoff, *Nixon Reconsidered* (1994)

Daniel Horowitz, *Betty Friedan and the Making of the Feminine Mystique: The American Left, the Cold War, and Modern Feminism* (1998)

Maurice Isserman, *The Other American: The Life of Michael Harrington* (2000)

Joseph A. Palermo, *In His Own Right: The Political Odyssey of Senator Robert F. Kennedy* (2001)

Jonah Raskin, *For the Hell of It: The Life and Times of Abbie Hoffman* (1996)

Kenneth S. Stern, *Loud Hawk: The United States versus the American Indian Movement* (1994)

Evan Thomas, *Robert Kennedy: His Life* (2000)

Jack Todd, *Desertion: In the Time of Vietnam* (2001)

Irwin Unger and Debi Unger, *LBJ: A Life* (1999)

CHAPTER 30

The Overextended Society

Michael A. Bernstein and David E. Adler, eds., *Understanding American Economic Decline* (1994)

W. Carl Biven, *Jimmy Carter's Economy: Policy in an Age of Limits* (2002)

Gordon L. Clark, *Unions and Communities Under Siege* (1989)

Claudia Goldin, *Understanding the Gender Gap: An Economic History of American Women* (1990)

Burton I. Kaufman, *The Arab Middle East and the United States: Inter-Arab Rivalry and Superpower Diplomacy* (1996)

Paul Krugman, *Peddling Prosperity: Economic Sense and Nonsense in the Age of Diminished Expectations* (1994)

Bruce J. Schulman, *From Cotton Belt to Sunbelt* (1991)

Jon Teaford, *Cities of the Heartland: The Rise and Fall of the Industrial Midwest* (1993)

Daniel Yergin, *The Prize: The Epic Quest for Oil, Money, and Power* (1990)

"Lean Year" Presidents

George C. Edwards III, *At the Margins: Presidential Leadership of Congress* (1989)

Gary M. Fink and Hugh Davis Graham, eds., *The Carter Presidency: Policy Choices in the Post–New Deal Era* (1998)

John Robert Greene, *The Presidency of Gerald R. Ford* (1995)

Gary Sick, *October Surprise: America's Hostages in Iran and the Election of Ronald Reagan* (1991)

The New Conservatism

William C. Berman, *America's Right Turn: From Nixon to Clinton* (1998)

Joel A. Carpenter, *Revive Us Again: The Reawakening of American Fundamentalism* (1997)

Dan T. Carter, *From George Wallace to Newt Gingrich: Race in the Conservative Counterrevolution, 1963–1994* (1996)

Betty A. Dobratz and Stephanie L. Shanks-Meile, *"White Power, White Pride!" The White Separatist Movement in the United States* (1997)

Susan Faludi, *Backlash: The Undeclared War Against American Women* (1991)

Angela Howard and Sasha Ranae Adams Tarrant, eds., *Reaction to the Modern Women's Movement, 1963 to the present* (1997)

William Martin, *With God on Our Side: The Rise of the Religious Right in America* (1996)

Grass-Roots Politics

Henry F. Bedford, *Seabrook Station: Citizen Politics and Nuclear Power* (1990)

Nicholas Dagen Bloom, *Suburban Alchemy: 1960s New Towns and the Transformation of the American Dream* (2001)

Craig Cox, *Storefront Revolution: Food Co-ops and the Counterculture* (1994)

David Frum, *How We Got Here: The 70s, The Decade That Brought You Modern Life (For Better or Worse)* (2000)

Lois Gibbs, *Love Canal: The Story Continues* (1998)

Gerald Markowitz and David Rosner, *Deceit and Denial: The Deadly Politics of Industrial Pollution* (2002)

Donald G. Mathews and Jane S. De Hart, *Sex, Gender, and the Politics of ERA* (1990)

Stephen Paul Miller, *The Seventies Now: Culture as Surveillance* (1999)

Gordana Rabrenovic, *Community Builders: A Tale of Neighborhood Mobilization in Two Cities* (1996)

David Brian Robertson, ed., *Loss of Confidence: Politics and Policy in the 1970s* (1998)

Suzanne Staggenborg, *The Pro-Choice Movement: Organization and Activism in the Abortion Conflict* (1991)

Foreign Policy

William J. Broad, *Teller's War: The Top-Secret Story Behind the Star Wars Deception* (1992)

Beth A. Fischer, *The Reagan Reversal: Foreign Policy and the End of the Cold War* (1997)

Mark Gasiorowski, *U.S. Foreign Policy and the Shah* (1991)

Christopher Hemmer, *Which Lessons Matter? American Foreign Policy Decision Making in the Middle East, 1979–1987* (2000)

William M. LeoGrande, *Our Own Backyard: The United States in Central America, 1977–1992* (1998)

Timothy P. Maga, *The World of Jimmy Carter: U.S. Foreign Policy, 1977–1981* (1994)

Jack F. Matlock Jr., *Reagan and Gorbachev: How the Cold War Ended* (2004)

Morris H. Morley, *Washington, Somoza, and the Sandinistas: State and Regime in U.S. Policy Toward Nicaragua, 1969–1981* (1994)

Bob Woodward, *Veil: The Secret Wars of the CIA* (1987)

The Reagan Revolution

Robert M. Collins, *More: The Politics of Economic Growth in Postwar America* (2000)

Matthew Dallek, *The Right Moment: Ronald Reagan's First Victory and the Decisive Turning Point in American Politics* (2000, 2004)

Nicholas Laham, *Ronald Reagan and the Politics of Immigration Reform* (2000)

Michael Schaller, *Reckoning with Reagan* (1992)

John W. Sloan, *The Reagan Effect: Economics and Presidential Leadership* (1999)

Best of Times, Worst of Times

James D. Cockcroft, *Outlaws in the Promised Land: Mexican Immigrant Workers and America's Future* (1986)

Barbara Ehrenreich, *Fear of Falling: The Inner Life of the Middle Class* (1989)

Elizabeth Fee and Daniel M. Fox, eds., *AIDS: The Making of a Chronic Disease* (1992)

Jacqueline Jones, *The Dispossessed: America's Underclasses from the Civil War to the Present* (1992)

Michael B. Katz, ed., *The "Underclass" Debate* (1993)

Hilda Scott, *Working Your Way to the Bottom: The Feminization of Poverty* (1985)

Randy Shilts, *And the Band Played On: Politics, People, and the AIDS Epidemic* (1987)

Ruth Sidel, *Women and Children Last: The Plight of Poor Women in Affluent America* (1986)

Lenore J. Weitzman, *The Divorce Revolution: The Unexpected Social and Economic Consequences for Women and Children in America* (1985)

Richard White, *Rude Awakenings: What the Homeless Crisis Tells Us* (1992)

Biography

Peter G. Bourne, *Jimmy Carter: A Comprehensive Biography From Plains to Postpresidency* (1997)

Jimmy Carter, *Keeping Faith: Memoirs of a President* (1982, 1995)

Rosalynn Carter, *First Lady from Plains* (1984)

Adam Clymer, *Edward M. Kennedy: A Biography* (1999)

Jim Cullen, *Born in the U.S.A.: Bruce Springsteen and the American Tradition* (1997, 2005)

Betty Ford, with Chris Chase, *Betty, A Glad Awakening* (1987)

Marshall Frady, *Jesse: The Life and Pilgrimage of Jesse Jackson* (1996)

Ernest B. Furgurson, *The Hard Right: The Rise of Jesse Helms* (1986)

Steven M. Gillon, *The Democrats' Dilemma: Walter F. Mondale and the Legacy of Liberalism* (1992)

Kitty Kelley, *Nancy Reagan* (1991)

Linda J. Lear, *Rachel Carson* (1997)

Peter Meyer, *Defiant Patriot: The Life and Exploits of Lt. Colonel Oliver L. North* (1987)

Edmund Morris, *Dutch: A Memoir of Ronald Reagan* (1999)

William E. Pemberton, *Exit with Honor: The Life and Presidency of Ronald Reagan* (1997)

Wilbur C. Rich, *Coleman Young and Detroit Politics* (1989)

CHAPTER 31

"A Kinder, Gentler Nation"

Meena Bose and Rosanna Perotti, eds., *From Cold War to New World Order: The Foreign Policy of George H.W. Bush* (2002)

Stephen F. Cohen, *Failed Crusade: America and the Tragedy of Post-Communist Russia* (2000)

John L. Gaddis, *The United States and the End of the Cold War* (1992)

David Halberstam, *War in a Time of Peace: Bush, Clinton, and the Generals* (2001)

William G. Hyland, *Clinton's World: Remaking American Foreign Policy* (1999)

Robert D. Kaplan, *The Coming Anarchy: Shattering the Dreams of the Post–Cold War* (2000)

Tomas W. Lippman, *Madeleine Albright and the New American Diplomacy* (2000)

Robert Litwak, *Rogue States and U.S. Foreign Policy: Containment After the Cold War* (2000)

David Mosler and Bob Catley, *Global America: Imposing Liberalism on a Recalcitrant World* (2000)

Micah L. Sifry and Christopher Cerf, eds., *The Gulf War Reader* (1991)

Jeff Wheelwright, *The Irritable Heart: The Medical Mystery of the Gulf War* (2001)

The Clinton Presidency

Lauren Berlant and Lisa Duggan, eds., *Our Monica, Ourselves: The Clinton Affair and the National Interest* (2001)

Sidney Blumenthal, *The Clinton Wars* (2003)

James Carville, *Stickin': The Case for Loyalty* (2000)

Joe Conason and Gene Lyons, *The Hunting of the President: The Ten-Year Campaign to Destroy Bill and Hillary Clinton* (2000)

Richard A. Posner, *An Affair of State: The Investigation, Impeachment, and Trial of President Clinton* (1999)

Alvin Z. Rubinstein, Albina Shayevich, and Boris Zlotnikov, eds., *The Clinton Foreign Policy Reader: Presidential Speeches with Commentary* (2000)

Steven E. Schier, ed., *The Postmodern Presidency: Bill Clinton's Legacy in U.S. Politics* (2000)

Susan Schmidt and Michael Weisskopf, *Truth at Any Cost: Ken Starr and the Unmaking of Bill Clinton* (2000)

Hanes Walton Jr., *Reelection: William Jefferson Clinton as a Native-Son Presidential Candidate* (2000)

Alex Waddan, *Clinton's Legacy: A New Democrat in Governance* (2001)

Changing American Communities

David Brooks, *Bobos in Paradise: The New Upper Class and How They Got There* (2000)

Sara M. Evans, *Tidal Wave: How Women Changed America at Century's End* (2003).

Helen Hayes, *U.S. Immigration and the Undocumented: Ambivalent Lives, Furtive Lives* (2001)

Denis Lynn Daly Heyck, ed., *Barrios and Borderlands: Cultures of Latinos and Latinas in the United States* (1994)

Bill Ong Hing, *Making and Remaking Asian America through Immigration Policy, 1850–1990* (1993)

Godfrey Hodgson, *More Equal Than Others: America from Nixon to the New Century* (2004).

Ted G. Lewis, *Microsoft Rising: . . . and Other Tales of Silicon Valley* (1999)

New York Times, *The Downsizing of America* (1996)

J. Eric Oliver, *Democracy in Suburbia* (2001)

Howard Rheingold, *The Virtual Community* (1994).

Adam Ward Rome, *The Bulldozer in the Countryside: Suburban Sprawl and the Rise of American Environmentalism* (2001)

Reed Ueda, *Postwar Immigrant America* (1994)

A New Age of Anxiety

Jewelle Taylor Gibbs, *Race and Justice: Rodney King and O. J. Simpson in a House Divided* (1996)

Mark S. Hamm, *Apocalypse in Oklahoma: Waco and Ruby Ridge Revenged* (1997)

Chester Hartman, ed., *Double Exposure: Poverty and Race in America* (1997)

Randall Kennedy, *Race, Crime, and the Law* (1997)

Lawrence Levine, *The Opening of the American Mind: Canons, Culture, and History* (1996)

Joanne Meyerowitz, ed. *History and September 11th* (2003)

Christian Parenti, *Lockdown America: Police and Prisons in the Age of Crisis* (1999)

David M. Reimers, *Unwelcome Strangers: American Identity and the Turn Against Immigration* (1998)

Roger Simon, *Divided We Stand: How Al Gore Beat George Bush and Lost the Presidency* (2001)

Robert C. Smith, *Racism in the Post–Civil Rights Era* (1995)

James D. Tabor and Eugene V. Gallagher, *Why Waco? Cults and the Battle for Religious Freedom in America* (1995)

The New Millennium

Walden Bello, *The Future in the Balance* (2001)

Jeremy Brecher, Tim Costello, and Brendan Smith, *Globalization From Below* (2000)

Alexander Cockburn, Jeffrey St. Clair, and Alan Sekula, *Five Days That Shook the World: Seattle and Beyond* (2000)

Anthony Giddens, *Runaway World* (1999)

Michael Hardt and Antonio Negri, *Empire* (2000)

David Held, ed., *A Globalizing World? Culture, Economics, Politics* (2000).

Edward S. Herman and Robert W. McChesney, *The Global Media: The New Missionaries of Corporate Capitalism* (1997)

Joshua Karliner, *The Corporate Planet: Ecology and Politics in the Age of Globalization* (1997)

Margaret Keck and Kathryn Sikkink, *Activists Beyond Borders: Advocacy Networks in International Politics* (1998)

Michael T. Klare, Blood and Oil: *The Dangers and Consequences of America's Growing Dependency* (2004)

Amory Starr, *Naming the Enemy: Anti-Corporate Movements Confront Globalization* (2000)

John D. Wirth, *Smelter Smoke in North America: The Politics of Transborder Pollution* (2000)

Biography

Barbara Bush, *Reflections: Life After the White House* (2003)

Bill Clinton, *My Life* (2004)

Karlene Faith, *Madonna, Brawdy & Soul* (1997)

John Robert Greene, *The Presidency of George Bush* (2000)

Nigel Hamilton, *Bill Clinton: An American Journey* (2003)

Molly Ivins and Lou Dubose Shrub: *The Short But Happy Political Life of George W. Bush* (2000)

Joyce Milton, *The First Partner: Hillary Rodham Clinton* (1999)

Kevin Phillips, *American Dynasty* (2004)

Gerald L. Posner, *Citizen Perot: His Life and Times* (1996)

Richard A. Serrano, *One of Ours: Timothy McVeigh and the Oklahoma City Bombing* (1998)

Mel Steely, *The Gentleman from Georgia: The Biography of Newt Gingrich* (2000)

Tom Wicker, *George Herbert Walker Bush* (2004)

Text Credits

Chapter 1: **Page 9** Emergence Song, William Brandon, The Magic World: American Indian Songs and Poems, 1971. **Page 12** Winnebago Song: This Newly Created World, from the Winnebago Medicine Rite as Recoded in Raul Radin, The Road to Life and Death: A Ritual Drama of the American Indians, Princeton University Press © 1945.

Chapter 2: **Figure 2.2** The African, Indian and European Population of the Americas, from Colin McEvedy and Richard Jones Atlas of World Population History, Allen Lane © 1978. Curtis Brown.

Chapter 4: **Figure 4.1** Reproduced from *The American Colonies: From Settlement to Independence* Copyright © R.C. Simmons 1976 by permission of PFD (www.pfd.co.uk) on behalf of Professor Richard Simmons. **Figure 4.2** Africans as a Percentage of Total Population of the British Colonies, 1650–1977, from Robert W. Fogel and Stanley L. Engerman, *Time on the Cross: The Economics of American Negro Slavery*, 1974, p.21. **Page 90** Courtesy of The Historical Society of Pennsylvania.

Chapter 5: **Figure 5.1** Sobel, Mechal. *The World They Made Together*, © 1987 Princeton University Press, 1989 paperback edition. Reprinted by permission of Princeton University Press. **Table 5.2** Main Jackson, Turner. *Social Structure of Revolutionary America* © 1965 Princeton University Press, 1993 renewed PUP. Reprinted by permission of Princeton University Press.

Chapter 7: **Page 203** "A Former Slave Appeals to Remain Free Philip S. Fonre, *A Plea Against Reenslavement*, Pennsylvania History, 39 (1972), pp. 239–41".

Chapter 8: **Figure 8.1** Postwar Inflation 1777–1780 The Depreciation of Continental Currency from John McCusker, *How Much is That in Real Money?*, Proceedings of the American Antiquarian Society, NS 102 © 1992 Courstesy, American Antiquarian Society.

Chapter 9: **Figure 9.1** American Export Trade 1790–1815, Douglas C. North, The Economic Growth of the United States 1790–1860, Norton, 1966, p. 26. **Figure 9.2** Western Land Sales, Robert Riegel & Robert Athearn, American Moves West, © 1964.

Chapter 11: **Figure 11.1** Race Exclusion for Suffrage, 1790–1855, Alexander Keysiar, The Right to Vote, Basic Books, 2000, p. 45 Perseus Books. **Page 314** Our Hearts are Sickened: Letter from Cherokee Chief John Ross to the Senate and House of Representatives, Sept. 28, 1836, Papers of Chief John Ross, University of Oklahoma Press, 1985.

Chapter 12: **Figure 12.1** Occupation of Women Wage Earners in Massachusetts, 1837, based on Thomas Dublin, Transforming Women's Work, © 1994 T1.1, p. 20.

Chapter 13: **Figure 13.1** Participation of Irish and German Immigrants in the New York City Work Force for Selected Occupations in 1855, Robert Ernst, *Immigrant Life in New York City 1825–1863* © 1994. Reprinted by permission of the estate of Robert Ernst. **Figure 13.2** From *The Alcoholic Republic: An American Tradition* by W.J. Rarabaugh, Copyright © 1979 by Oxford Univerisity Press, Inc. Used by permission of Oxford University Press, Inc. **Map 13.2** Reprinted from Whitney R. Cross, *The Burned-Over District: The Social and Intellectual History of Enthusiastic Religion in Western New York 1800–1850*. Copyright © 1950 by Cornell University. Used with permission of the publisher, Cornell University Press.

Chapter 14: **Figure 14.1** From *The Plains Across: The Overland Emigrants and the Trans-Mississippi West, 1840–60*. Copyright 1979 by the Board of Trustees of the University of Illinois. Used with permission of the University of Illinois Press. **Map 14.7** From *Historical Atlas of California*, by Warren A. Beck and Ynez D. Haase. Copyright © 1974 by The University of Oklahoma Press, Norman. Reprinted by permission of the publisher. All rights reserved.

Chapter 16: **Page 475** Lunt, Dolly Summer. *A Woman's Wartime Journal: An Account of Passage over Georgia's Plantation of Sherman's Army on the March of the Sea, Documenting the American South*. University Library, The University of North Carolina at Chapel Hill, 1996 http://docsouth.unc. edu/burge/lunt.html

Chapter 17: **Page 496** Freedmen's Bureau Records: Contract Between D. Kunkle and Reuben Gouldin, January 1, 1867

Chapter 18: **Map 18.1** From *Historical Atlas of Oklahoma*, 3rd edition, by John W. Morris, Charles R. Goins and Edwin C. McReynolds. Copyright © 1965, 1976, 1986 by the University of Oklahoma Press, Norman. Reprinted by permission of the publisher. All rights reserved. **Map 18.4** Mormon Cultural Diffusion, ca. 1883, Donald W. Meinig, *The Geography of the American West, 1847–1964* from *The Annals of the Association of American Geographers* 55, no. 2, June 1965. **Page. 533** "Memories of Calvary Life Mrs. Orsemus Boyd, Calvary Life in the Tent and Field, (New York: J. Selwin Tait & Son) 1894 as reprinted in Christiane Fischer, ed. *Let Them Speak for Themselves: Women in the America West, 1849–1900*, EJP Dutton, 1978, pp. 11–12, 116."

Chapter 19: **Map 19.2** Population of Foreign Birth by Region, 1880, Clifford L. Lord and Elizabeth H. Lord, ed., Lord & Lord Historical Atlas of the United States, 1953.

Chapter 20: **Map 20.1** Strikes by State, 1880, Carville Earle, Geography Inquiry and American Historical Problems, Copyright © 1992 Stanford University Press.

Chapter 22: **Map 22.3** Women Suffrage by State, 1869–1914, Barbara C. Shortridge, *Atlas of American Women*, Macmillan 1987. **Page 665** Letters From the Great Migration, 1917 *Journal of Negro History*, Vol. IV, 1919, pp. 317.

Chapter 23: **Page 689** "To Bob or Not to Bob: Changing Fashion and The New Woman of the 1920s." Mary Garden Pictorial Review, April 1927, 8FF. Hearst.

Chapter 24: **Page 723** "I Was Able to Make My Voice Really Ring Out" http:www.historicalvoices.org/flint. Oral history courtesy of Sherna Gluck, Feminist History Project.

Chapter 25: **Figure 25.1** From The Gallup Poll, 1835–1971 by George Gallup, Copyright © 1972 by the American Institute of Public Opinion. Used by permission of Random House. **Page 758** From *The Collected Poems of Langston Hughes* by Langston Hughes, Copyright © 1994 by The Estate of Langston Hughes. Used by permission of Alfred A. Knopf, a division of Random House, Inc.

U.S. HISTORY DOCUMENTS CD-ROM

Over 300 Primary Source Documents

INDEX

U